The Modern Law of Evidence

Thirteenth Edition

ADRIAN KEANE LL.B
of the Inner Temple, Barrister,
Emeritus Professor of Law, The City Law School,
City, University of London,
Former Dean of the Inns of Court School of Law

PAUL MCKEOWN LL.B, LL.M
of Lincoln's Inn, Barrister,
Associate Professor of Law, The City Law School,
City, University of London

OXFORD
UNIVERSITY PRESS

OXFORD

UNIVERSITY PRESS

Great Clarendon Street, Oxford, OX2 6DP,
United Kingdom

Oxford University Press is a department of the University of Oxford.
It furthers the University's objective of excellence in research, scholarship,
and education by publishing worldwide. Oxford is a registered trade mark of
Oxford University Press in the UK and in certain other countries

Tenth edition 2014
Eleventh edition 2016
Twelfth Edition 2018

Impression: 1

Published in the United States of America by Oxford University Press
198 Madison Avenue, New York, NY 10016, United States of America

British Library Cataloguing in Publication Data
Data available

Library of Congress Control Number: 2019957897

ISBN 978–0–19–884848–6

Printed in Great Britain by
Bell & Bain Ltd., Glasgow

PREFACE TO THE THIRTEENTH EDITION

The twin aims of this work are, as always, to explore the theory of the law of evidence as well as its practical application taking into account the different needs of our readers, and to state the law both accurately and clearly, sometimes a challenging combination. It is gratifying that our readers continue to include judges, practitioners, academics, educators, and undergraduate and post graduate students. It is also gratifying that our readership continues to be international.

Since the last edition of this text, there have been many significant developments in the law of evidence. As ever, a wide range of issues have produced a large volume of case law. New principles have been laid down and existing principles have been extended, limited, or otherwise refined. New legislation has also come into force, for example, concerning intercept evidence. There have been many revisions to the Criminal Procedure Rules and Criminal Practice Directions, for example, revisions placing new duties of disclosure on parties seeking to admit expert evidence aimed at improving the reliability, credibility, and impartiality of such evidence. There have also been, since the last edition, no fewer than three amended versions of the Crown Court Compendium, the most recent being in July 2019.

We have also drawn on the wealth of critical thinking and commentary from the peer-reviewed journals which is reflected in the text and the end of chapter 'Additional Reading' summaries.

This edition covers all the significant developments including:

- The Investigatory Powers Act 2016 on the exclusion of evidence of intercepted communications.

- The Court of Appeal decision in *R v Syed* concerning the similarities, in relation to entrapment, between the Strasbourg and English jurisprudence.

- The Court of Appeal decision in *R v Hampson* on best practice when a court has made a special measures order for video-recorded cross-examination.

- The Court of Appeal decision in *R v Inns* on judicial interventions during examination-in-chief and jurors' written requests for clarification.

- The Court of Appeal decision in *R v M* on the identification of limitations on the cross-examination of vulnerable witnesses.

- The Court of Appeal decisions in *R v Steltner* and *R v Aidarus* on the cross-examination of complainants in sexual cases about sexual experiences.

- The Court of Appeal decision in *R v Daley*, concerning the direction to be given to the jury in respect of hearsay evidence.

- The Court of Appeal decision in *R v Mader* concerning the admissibility of evidence of the good character of prosecution witnesses.

- The decision in *R v Hajdarmataj* on the admissibility of evidence of an accused's misconduct from an earlier trial at which he was acquitted.

- *R v Omotoso* on the admissibility of evidence of the accused's bad character evidence on the grounds that he has created a false impression or attacked the character of another.

- *R v Green* on the meaning of being questioned under caution for the purposes of s 34 CJPOA 1994 (adverse inferences from failure to mention facts).

- *R (Haralambous) v St Albans Crown Court* on the exceptional circumstances in which a 'closed material procedure' (CMP) may be used in the criminal context.

- The Court of Appeal decision in *Competition and Markets Authority v Concordia International RX (UK)* which establishes an exception to the general ban on the use of the CMP in civil litigation.

- *R (River East Supplies Ltd) v Crown Court at Nottingham* on the privilege against self-incrimination in relation to 'independent material'.

- The Court of Appeal decision in *Director of the Serious Fraud Office v Eurasian Natural Resources Corporation Ltd* concerning legal advice privilege.

- The Court of Appeal decision in *W H Holdings Ltd v E20 Stadium LLP* on the scope of litigation privilege.

There are bound to be further developments during the production stage of this text. Any developments which occur during this period will be covered in updates. These will be available on the date of publication and readers will be able to access them from online resources which accompany the text.

In this edition, we have sought to make the text easier to navigate through the increased use of sub-headings (to break up some of the lengthier sections of text) and through more cross-referencing within and between chapters (and including, for the first time, cross-references to specific pages). We have also given attention to the order of chapters. Readers who have used the text before will see that the chapters titled 'Proof of facts without evidence' and 'Evidence obtained by illegal or unfair means' have been repositioned and renumbered. 'Proof of facts without evidence' now comes immediately after the chapter titled 'The burden and standard of proof'; considering the subject matter of these two chapters, it seemed logical to have one following on immediately from the other.

We hope all of this will make the text more accessible and user-friendly, albeit that the law of evidence will always remain a complex and difficult subject for any reader. There are also some new problem questions. Note form answers to these and all other end-of-chapter questions may be accessed from online resources.

We are very grateful to all our readers and reviewers here and around the world for using this book and for their constructive feedback. We are grateful to one reviewer in particular who provided an in-depth chapter-by-chapter review of the previous edition and offered many valuable suggestions and reflections. That in-depth review was commissioned by our new editor Jessica Lehman. Our thanks to her for doing this and for all her support so far. In respect of my work on this edition, my thanks go to Emeritus Professor Keane for his guidance and for the very many important suggestions he made. Thanks also to Michael McKeown and Andrew McFeeters for coming up with the design for the cover of this edition.

We have attempted to state the law accurately as at 1 September 2019.

Paul McKeown
Bangor, County Down
September 2019

OUTLINE CONTENTS

1 Introduction   1

2 Preliminaries   8

3 The burden and standard of proof   57

4 Proof of facts without evidence   98

5 Witnesses   126

6 Examination-in-chief   179

7 Cross-examination and re-examination   214

8 Corroboration and care warnings   252

9 Visual and voice identification   276

10 Documentary and real evidence   301

11 Evidence obtained by illegal or unfair means   320

12 Hearsay in criminal cases   349

13 Hearsay admissible by statute in civil proceedings   412

14 Hearsay admissible at common law   433

15 Confessions   453

16 Adverse inferences from an accused's silence or conduct   497

17 Evidence of character: evidence of character in civil cases   533

18 Evidence of character: evidence of the good character of the accused   538

19 Evidence of character: evidence of bad character in criminal cases   553

20 Experts and opinion evidence   633

21 Public policy   675

22 Privilege   711

23 Judgments as evidence of the facts upon which they were based   757

INDEX   775

DETAILED CONTENTS

TABLE OF STATUTES   xvi

TABLE OF STATUTORY INSTRUMENTS   xxvii

TABLE OF CODES, CODES OF PRACTICE AND PRACTICE DIRECTIONS   xxx

TABLE OF CASES   xxxii

1 Introduction   1

Key issues	1
Truth and the fact-finding process	2
The development of the law	3
Additional reading	6

2 Preliminaries   8

Key issues	8
Facts open to proof or disproof	9
The varieties of evidence	11
Relevance and admissibility	22
Weight	33
The functions of the judge and jury	34
Judicial discretion	47
Proof of birth, death, age, convictions, and acquittals	53
Additional reading	55

3 The burden and standard of proof   57

Key issues	57
The burden of proof	58
The incidence of the legal burden	61
The incidence of the evidential burden	80
The standard of proof	84
The burden and standard of proof in a trial within a trial	94
Additional reading	96

4 Proof of facts without evidence   98

Key issues	98
Presumptions	99

Judicial notice   117

Formal admissions   124

Additional reading   125

5 Witnesses   126

Key issues   126

Competence and compellability   127

Live links   144

The time at which evidence should be adduced   146

Witnesses in civil cases   149

Witnesses in criminal cases   152

Witness training and witness familiarization   175

Additional reading   177

6 Examination-in-chief   179

Key issues   179

Young and vulnerable witnesses   180

Leading questions   181

Judicial interventions   182

Jury notes   183

Refreshing the memory   183

Previous consistent or self-serving statements   193

Unfavourable and hostile witnesses   206

Additional reading   212

7 Cross-examination and re-examination   214

Key issues   214

Cross-examination   215

Re-examination   249

Additional reading   249

8 Corroboration and care warnings   252

Key issues   252

General rule and exceptions   253

The meaning of corroboration   254

Corroboration required by statute   255

Care warnings   257

Cases where special need for caution   269

Additional reading   275

9 Visual and voice identification   **276**

Key issues   276

The risk of mistake   277

Visual identification   278

Visual identification by the jury   288

Evidence of analysis of films, photographs, and images   289

Pre-trial procedure   290

Voice identification   295

Additional reading   299

10 Documentary and real evidence   **301**

Key issues   301

Documentary evidence   302

Real evidence   314

Additional reading   319

11 Evidence obtained by illegal or unfair means   **320**

Key issues   320

Principles for exclusion   321

Law   322

Discretion   325

Additional reading   347

12 Hearsay in criminal cases   **349**

Key issues   349

Background and rationale   350

Admissibility of hearsay under the Criminal Justice Act 2003   352

The statutory scheme and Art 6 of the European Convention
on Human Rights   353

The meaning of hearsay in the Criminal Justice Act 2003   360

Cases where a witness is unavailable   373

Business and other documents   382

Admissibility in the interests of justice   386

Previous inconsistent statements of witnesses   391

Other previous statements of witnesses   392

Multiple hearsay   396

Other safeguards   398

Questions of proof   405

Evidence by video recording   407

Expert evidence   407

Written statements under s 9 of the Criminal Justice Act 1967   409

Depositions of vulnerable children and young persons under s 43
of the Children and Young Persons Act 1933   410

Additional reading   410

13 Hearsay admissible by statute in civil proceedings   **412**

Key issues   412

The background   413

Admissibility of hearsay under the Civil Evidence Act 1995   415

Safeguards   420

Proof of statements contained in documents   426

Evidence formerly admissible at common law   429

Ogden tables   432

Additional reading   432

14 Hearsay admissible at common law   **433**

Key issues   433

Statements in public documents   434

Works of reference   438

Evidence of age   439

Evidence of reputation   439

Statements forming part of the *res gestae*   442

Additional reading   452

15 Confessions 453

Key issues	453
Admissibility	454
The discretion to exclude	468
The *voir dire*	481
The trial	485
Facts discovered in consequence of inadmissible confessions	494
Additional reading	496

16 Adverse inferences from an accused's silence or conduct 497

Key issues	497
Inferences from silence	498
Inferences from refusal to consent to the taking of samples	525
Inferences from failure to provide advance disclosure of the defence case	526
Additional reading	531

17 Evidence of character: evidence of character in civil cases 533

Key issues	533
Character in issue or relevant to a fact in issue	534
Evidence of the disposition of the parties towards good conduct	534
Evidence of the disposition of the parties towards bad conduct	535
Character relevant to credit	537
Additional reading	537

18 Evidence of character: evidence of the good character of the accused 538

Key issues	538
Introduction	539
The evidence admissible	539
The direction to the jury	540
The meaning of 'good character' and the entitlement to the direction	543
Other issues relating to good character directions	550
Additional reading	552

19 Evidence of character: evidence of bad character in criminal cases   553

Key issues	553
Introduction	554
Evidence of the bad character of a person other than the defendant	562
Evidence of the bad character of the defendant	570
General	621
Other provisions governing the admissibility of evidence of bad character	628
Additional reading	630

20 Experts and opinion evidence   633

Key issues	633
The general rule and the two exceptions	634
Expert evidence	635
Non-expert opinion evidence	672
Additional reading	673

21 Public policy   675

Key issues	675
The development of the modern law	676
The scope of exclusion on grounds of public policy	680
Procedural issues	697
Additional reading	710

22 Privilege   711

Key issues	711
The nature of privilege	712
The privilege against self-incrimination	713
Legal professional privilege	725
Without prejudice negotiations	749
Additional reading	755

23 Judgments as evidence of the facts upon which they were based   **757**

Key issues   757

Introduction   758

The principle of *Hollington v Hewthorn & Co Ltd*   758

Civil proceedings   759

Criminal proceedings   765

Additional reading   773

INDEX   775

TABLE OF STATUTES

Page references in bold indicate that the text is reproduced in full.

United Kingdom

Abortion Act 1968. . . 690

Administration of Justice Act 1920

s 15. . . 36

Administration of Justice Act 1985

s 33. . . 726

Adoption and Children Act 2002

s 77(4). . . 308

Affiliation Proceedings Act 1957

s 4. . . 269

Anti-social Behaviour, Crime and Policing Act 2014

s 1(1). . . 86

s 1(2). . . 86

s 1(3). . . 86

s 22(3). . . 85

s 30(1). . . 71

Arbitration Act 1996

s 41(3). . . 78

Bankers' Books Evidence Act 1879. . . 304, 309, 310, 418

s 3. . . **309**, 310, 311

s 4. . . 310

s 5. . . 310

s 6. . . **142**

s 7. . . 310, 311

s 9(1). . . 309

s 9(1A)–(1C). . . 309

s 9(2). . . 309

Banking Act 1987. . . 470

Bankruptcy Act 1986

s 352. . . 74

s 353(1). . . 74

s 357. . . 74

Bills of Exchange Act 1882

s 30(2). . . 80

Births and Deaths Registration Act 1953

s 34. . . 53, 308, 417, 435, 439

British Law Ascertainment Act 1859. . . 637

Child Abduction Act 1984

s 1. . . 216

s 2. . . 216

Child Support Act 1991. . . 418

Children Act 1989. . . 738, 741, 742, 755, 763

s 8(2). . . 418

s 92(2). . . 418

s 96. . . **140**, 418

s 96(1). . . **140**

s 96(2). . . **140**

s 96(2)(a). . . **140**, 419

s 96(2)(b). . . **140**, 419

s 96(7). . . 418

s 98. . . 721, 722

s 98(1). . . 721

s 98(2). . . 721, 722

s 105. . . 140

Children and Young Persons Act 1933. . . 410

s 1. . . 216

s 38(1). . . 254, 267, 268

s 42. . . 410

s 43. . . 352, 410

s 50. . . 101

s 99. . . 54

Civil Evidence Act 1968. . . 413, 414, 415, 416, 420, 425, 427, 758, 760, 761

s 2(2). . . 420

s 3(2). . . 190

s 6(1). . . 407, 426

s 7(5). . . 425

s 9. . . 429

s 9(1). . . 429

s 9(2)(a). . . 429

ss 11–13. . . 759

s 11. . . 99, 759, 761, 762, 763, 765

s 11(1). . . **759**

s 11(2). . . **759**, 761

s 11(2)(a). . . **759**, 760

s 11(2)(b). . . 761

s 11(3). . . 759

s 11(4). . . 761

s 11(5). . . 760

s 12. . . 99, 761, 762, 763, 764

s 12(1). . . **762–3**

s 12(2). . . **763**

s 12(3). . . **763**

s 12(4). . . 761

s 12(5). . . 763

s 13. . . 22, 534, 759, 761, 762, 764

s 13(1). . . 33, 101, **762**

s 13(2). . . **762**

s 13(2A). . . **762**

s 13(3). . . **762**

s 13(4). . . 761

s 14(1). . . 175

s 14(1)(a). . . 715

s 14(1)(b). . . 717

s 16(1)(a). . . 714

s 18(1). . . 750

Civil Evidence Act 1972. . . 415, 416, 666

s 3. . . 673

s 3(1). . . 657

s 3(2). . . **673**

s 3(3). . . 657, 673

s 4. . . 637

s 4(1). . . **645**

s 4(2)(a). . . 637

s 4(2)(b). . . 637, 638

s 4(5). . . 637

Civil Evidence Act 1995. . . 54, 302, 303, 306, 317, 414, 415, 416, 417, 418, 420, 426, 429, 430, 431, 434, 440, 443, 655, 661, 761

s 1. . . 190, 198, 210, 224, **415**, **417**, 419, 429

s 1(1). . . **415**, 429

s 1(2). . . **415**, 416

s 1(2)(a). . . **415**, 416

s 1(2)(b). . . **415**, 430

s 1(3). . . **417**

s 1(4). . . **417**

s 2. . . **421**, 440

s 2(1). . . **421**, 422

s 2(1)(a). . . **421**, 422

s 2(2). . . **421**

s 2(3). . . **421**

s 2(4). . . **422**

s 2(4)(a). . . **422**

s 2(4)(b). . . **422**

s 3. . . **423**, 424, 425, 429

s 4. . . 33, 422, **424**, 430, 440

s 4(1). . . **424**

s 4(2). . . **424**

s 4(2)(a). . . **424**

s 4(2)(b). . . **424**

s 4(2)(c). . . **424**

s 4(2)(d). . . **424**

s 4(2)(e). . . **424**, 425

s 4(2)(f). . . **424**

s 5(1). . . **418**, 419

s 5(2). . . **425**, 426

s 5(2)(a). . . **425**

s 5(2)(b). . . **425**

s 6. . . **419**, 420

s 6(1). . . **419**

s 6(2). . . 195, **419**, 424

s 6(2)(a). . . 184, 205, 209, **419**

s 6(2)(b). . . **198**, **419**, 420

s 6(3). . . 209, 419, 425

s 6(3)(a). . . **210**

s 6(3)(b). . . **224**

s 6(3)(c). . . **224**

s 6(4). . . **190**, 419, 420

s 6(5). . . **190**, **198**, 209, **210**, **224**, 425

s 7. . . 434

s 7(1). . . 305, 429

s 7(2). . . 429, 434

s 7(2)(a). . . **438**

s 7(2)(b). . . **434**, 435

s 7(2)(c). . . **434**, 435

s 7(3). . . 434, 440

s 7(3)(a). . . **439**, 440

s 7(3)(b). . . **439**, 440

s 7(3)(b)(i). . . **439**

s 7(4). . . 434

s 8. . . 303, 304, 306, 407, **426**

s 8(1). . . **426**, 427

s 8(2). . . **426**, 427

s 9. . . 303, 304, 306, **427**

s 9(1). . . 303, **427**, 428

s 9(2). . . 303, **427**

s 9(3). . . 303, **428**

s 9(4). . . 427, 428

s 9(5). . . **428**

s 10. . . **432**

s 11. . . 415, 418

s 11(2)(b). . . 761

s 13. . . 302, 317, 415, 416, 424, 426, 431

s 14. . . 304

s 14(1). . . **415**

s 14(2). . . 304

s 14(3). . . 304

Civil Evidence (Scotland) Act 1988. . . 422

Civil Partnership Act 2004

s 84(5). . . 439

Civil Procedure Act 1997. . . 5

s 1(3). . . 5

Sch 1, para 4. . . 5

Colonial Laws Validity Act 1865

s 6. . . 637

Common Law Procedure (Amendment) Act 1856

s 22. . . 209

Companies Act 1948. . . 435, 437

Companies Act 1967. . . 765

Companies Act 1985

Pt XIV. . . 722, 765

s 434. . . 722

s 434(5A). . . 722

s 434(5B). . . 722

s 436. . . 461

Companies Act 2006. . . 435

Company Directors Disqualification Act 1986. . . 764

s 7(3). . . 735

Competition Act 1998

s 28. . . 703

s 28A. . . 703

Consular Relations Act 1968. . . 142

Consumer Credit Act 1974

s 137. . . 79

s 138. . . 79

s 171(7). . . 79

Contempt of Court Act 1981

s 8. . . 46

s 10. . . **692**, 693, 694, 695

Copyright Act 1956

s 21. . . 716

Copyright, Designs and Patents Act 1988

s 280. . . 726

Coroners and Justice Act 2009. . . 156, 166, 171, 173, 175, 268

s 54. . . 640

s 54(5). . . 80, 81

s 54(6). . . 81

s 55(1). . . 81

s 55(3). . . 81

s 55(4). . . 81

s 55(5). . . 81

s 55(6). . . 81

ss 74–85. . . 171

s 86. . . 171

s 87(1)–(3). . . 172

s 87(1). . . 171

s 87(2). . . 171

s 87(3). . . 172

s 87(6). . . 172

s 87(7). . . 172

s 88. . . 172, 173

s 89. . . 173

s 89(2). . . 172, 173, 175

s 89(2)(a). . . 174

s 89(2)(b). . . 174

s 89(2)(c). . . 174

s 89(2)(d). . . 174

s 89(2)(e). . . 174

s 89(2)(f). . . 174

s 90. . . 172, 173, 268

s 91. . . 172

s 97. . . 171

s 104. . . 169

s 112. . . 393

Explanatory Notes. . . 268

Explanatory Notes, para 340. . . 82

Corporate Manslaughter and Corporate Homicide Act 2007

s 2(5). . . 34

Counter-Terrorism Act 2008. . . 703

s 22. . . 507

County Courts Act 1984

s 63. . . 635

s 68. . . 36

Crime and Disorder Act 1998

s 2. . . 535

s 2(1)(a). . . 87

s 34. . . 620

s 51. . . 507

Sch 3, para 2. . . 507, 522, 525

Crime (International Cooperation) Act 2003. . . 144

s 7. . . 383

Criminal Appeal Act 1968

s 2(1). . . 142, 279

s 13(1). . . 142

s 16(1). . . 142

Criminal Appeal Act 1995
  s 9. . . 144, 145
  s 11. . . 144, 145
Criminal Attempts Act
  1981. . . 254
  s 1. . . 257
  s 2(1). . . **254**
  s 2(2)(g). . . **254**, 257
  s 4(3). . . 35
Criminal Damage Act 1971
  s 2(a). . . 132
  s 9. . . 722
Criminal Evidence Act 1898. . . 4,
  134, 557, 559, 576
  s 1. . . 18, 129, 134, 498,
    539, 555
  s 1(b). . . 506
  s 1(c). . . 134
  s 1(f). . . 573
  s 1(1). . . **128**, 130
  s 1(2). . . 129, 130, 714
  s 1(3). . . 554
  s 1(3)(ii). . . 50, 610, 611,
    612, 618
  s 1(4). . . 129, 130
Criminal Evidence Act
  1965. . . 350, 427
  s 1. . . 384
Criminal Evidence Act
  1988. . . 384
Criminal Evidence (Witness
  Anonymity) Act 2008. . . 171,
  173, 268
Criminal Justice Act 1948
  s 80(3). . . 54
Criminal Justice Act 1967
  s 3(1). . . 80
  s 8. . . 102
  s 9. . . 84, 352, 407, 409, 410
  s 9(2). . . 409
  s 9(4). . . 409
  s 9(5). . . 409
  s 9(6). . . 409
  s 10. . . 10, 55, 84, 125, 313, 637
  s 10(1). . . 33, 125
  s 10(2)(b). . . 125
  s 10(2)(c)–(e). . . 125
  s 10(3). . . 125
  s 10(4). . . 125
Criminal Justice Act 1987. . . 469,
  473, 498
  s 2. . . 722

s 2(8). . . 473, 722
s 2(8AA). . . 722
s 2(13). . . 473
s 7. . . 498
s 9. . . 498
s 10. . . 498
Criminal Justice Act 1988. . . 708
  ss 23–28. . . 350
  s 23. . . 94, 375, 405
  s 23(2)(a). . . 376
  s 23(2)(b). . . 376
  s 23(2)(c). . . 376
  s 24. . . 382, 405, 406
  s 24(1). . . 406
  s 25. . . 382
  s 25(2)(d). . . 381
  s 30. . . 364
  s 30(1). . . 408, 409
  s 30(2). . . 408
  s 30(3). . . 409
  s 30(4). . . 408
  s 30(5). . . 408
  s 32. . . 144, 376
  s 32A. . . 142, 159
  s 34(2). . . 267
  s 122. . . 37
  s 134. . . 324, 460
  s 139. . . 71
  s 139(4). . . 71
  s 139(5). . . 71
  Sch 13, para 6. . . 383
Criminal Justice Act 1991
  s 101(2). . . 267
  Sch 13. . . 267
Criminal Justice Act 2003. . . 5,
  29, 54, 205, 211, 220, 244, 302,
  303, 306, 317, 351, 352, 353,
  354, 355, 357, 358, 360, 363,
  364, 367, 370, 371, 373, 375,
  376, 378, 385, 386, 391, 392,
  405, 417, 442, 536, 543, 545,
  548, 554, 555, 557, 562, 573,
  574, 577, 581, 587, 589, 594,
  596, 602, 603, 605, 607, 608,
  610, 616, 619, 628, 630, 767
  Pt 8. . . 144
  Pt 11, Chap 1 (ss
    98–113). . . 554
  Pt 11, Chap 2. . . 350, 351, 352,
    355, 385, 434, 577
  s 48(3). . . 34
  s 48(5). . . 34
  ss 51–66. . . 144

s 51(1)–(3). . . 145
s 51(2). . . 145
s 51(4)(a). . . 145
s 51(6). . . 145
s 51(7). . . **145**
s 52(2). . . 145
s 52(5). . . 145
s 52(6). . . 145
s 54. . . 145
s 55. . . 145
s 56(2). . . 145
s 56(3). . . 145
s 56(4). . . 145
s 56(5)(a). . . 145
s 56(5)(b). . . 145
s 80. . . 145
ss 98–113. . . 29, 554
s 98. . . 220, 233, 245, 543,
  555, **556**, 560, 587, 596
s 98(a). . . **556**, 560, 561, 562,
  580, 581, 584, 595, 772
s 98(b). . . **556**, 560, 567, 628
s 99. . . 50, 220, 245, **555**, 556
s 99(1). . . 554, **555**, 560,
  563, 767
s 99(2). . . **555**
ss 100–106. . . 536
s 100. . . 173, 220, 244, 245, 399,
  400, 559, 562-3, 564, 569,
  570, 576, 600, 615, 621, 624
s 100(1). . . 233, **563**
s 100(1)(a). . . 569
s 100(1)(b). . . 245, 555, 564,
  565, 569, 583
s 100(1)(c). . . 568, 569
s 100(2). . . **564**, 569
s 100(2)(a). . . **564**, 579
s 100(3). . . **565**, 569
s 100(3)(a). . . 566
s 100(3)(b). . . 566, 567
s 100(3)(c). . . 567, 621
s 100(3)(d). . . 567, 621
s 100(4). . . 568, **569**, 575
s 101. . . 25, 129, 130, 220,
  244, 500, 544, 547, 548,
  551, 559, 570, 571, 574,
  576, 577, 590, 591, 600,
  612, 621, 624, 772
s 101(1). . . 549, **571–2**, 578
ss 101(1)(a)–(g). . . 555, **571–2**
s 101(1)(a). . . 572, 576, 577
s 101(1)(b). . . 547, 548, **571**,
  574, 576, 578

ss 101(1)(c)–(g). . . 574, 575, 622

s 101(1)(c). . . 330, 561, **572**, 576, 578–82, 584

s 101(1)(d). . . 536, 555, 561, 565, 567, **572**, 573, 575, 576, 580, 581, 582–6, 587, 589, 593, 594, 597, 598, 599, 600, 602, 612, 621, 624

s 101(1)(e). . . 555, 565, 566, **572**, 573, 576, 583, 598, 600, 601, 602, 603, 604, 605, 606, 607, 608, 621

s 101(1)(f). . . 330, **572**, 576, 596, 608–9, 610, 612, 613, 621

s 101(1)(g). . . 50, 245, 555, **572**, 573, 576, 577, 578, 599, 608, 612, 613, 614, 615, 616, 617, 618, 619, 620, 624

s 101(2). . . **572**

s 101(3). . . 52, 55, 330, 535, 561, **572**, 575, 576, 577, 582, 584, 585, 586, 588, 591, 600, 604, 609, 617, 618, 624

s 101(4). . . **572**, 575, 586

s 102. . . **578**, 579

s 102(b). . . **578**, 579

s 103. . . 577, 584, 585, 586, 587, 590

s 103(1). . . 564, **584**, 585

s 103(1)(a). . . 573, 585, 587, 596, 598, 600

s 103(1)(b). . . 573, 575, **597**, 598, 599, 600, 606

s 103(2). . . **584–5**, 586, 587, 590, 596

s 103(2)(a). . . 586

s 103(2)(b). . . 586

s 103(3). . . **585**, 586

s 103(4). . . **585**

s 103(4)(a). . . 586

s 103(4)(b). . . 586

ss 103(5). . . **585**, 586

s 103(6). . . 583, **585**

s 103(7)–(11). . . 587

s 104. . . 606

s 104(1). . . **606**, 607, 608

s 104(2). . . **603**

s 104(2)(b). . . 572

s 105. . . 608, **609**, 611, 614, 616

s 105(1). . . **609**

s 105(1)(a). . . 609

s 105(1)(b). . . 611

s 105(2). . . **609**

s 105(2)(c). . . 612

s 105(2)(b). . . 612

s 105(2)(d). . . 611

s 105(3). . . **609**, 612, 614

s 105(4). . . **609**, 610

s 105(5). . . **609**, 610

s 105(6). . . **609**, 611

s 105(7). . . **609**

s 106. . . **613–14**, 615, 616

s 106(1). . . **613–14**

s 106(1)(a). . . 614

s 106(1)(c). . . 614. 620

s 106(2). . . **614**, 615, 616, 620

s 106(2)(a). . . 615

s 106(2)(b). . . 615

s 106(3). . . **614**

s 107. . . 555, 622, 623, 624

s 107(1). . . **622**, 623

s 107(1)(b). . . 624

s 107(1)(b)(ii). . . 623

s 107(2). . . **623**

s 107(3). . . 623

s 107(4). . . **623**

s 107(5). . . **623**

s 107(5)(a). . . **623**

s 107(5)(b). . . **623**

s 108. . . 220, 244

s 108(2). . . **620**

s 108(2A). . . 620

s 108(2B). . . 620

s 108(3). . . **620**

s 109. . . 621, 622

s 109(1). . . **621**

s 109(2). . . **621**, 622

s 110. . . 624, 625

s 110(1). . . **624**

s 110(2). . . **624**

s 110(2)(b). . . 625

s 111(1). . . 625

s 111(2). . . **625**

s 111(2)(b). . . 572

s 112. . . 587, 605

s 112(1). . . 555, 556, 571, 572, 583, 585, 596, 597, 601

s 112(2). . . **591**

s 112(3). . . 628

s 114. . . 365, 366, 367, 374, 384, 385

s 114(1). . . 352, 353, 360, **363**, 365

s 114(1)(a). . . **352**

s 114(1)(b). . . **352**

s 114(1)(c). . . 195, 353

s 114(1)(d). . . 134, 175, 184, 195, 210, 353, 354, 359, 364, 373, 377, 379, 386, 387, 388, 389, 390, 391, 397, 398, 402, 418, 457

s 114(2). . . 133, 386, **388**, 389, 390, 397, 398

s 114(2)(a)–(g). . . **388**

s 114(2)(a)–(i). . . **388**, 402

s 114(2)(a). . . **388**

s 114(2)(c). . . 388

s 114(2)(d). . . 389

s 114(2)(e). . . 389

s 114(2)(f). . . 389

s 114(2)(g). . . **388**

s 114(2)(h). . . **388**, 389

s 114(3). . . **353**, 364

s 115(2). . . 303, 364, 369, 370, 371

s 115(3). . . **365**, 366, 367, 368, 369, 370, 417

s 115(3)(a). . . 364, **365**

s 115(3)(b). . . **365**

s 116. . . 94, 173, 175, 352, 354, 373, 374, 375, 385, 387, 396, 398, 405, 418, 434

s 116(1). . . **374**

s 116(1)(a). . . 375, 384

s 116(1)(b). . . 375

s 116(1)(c). . . 375

s 116(2). . . **374**, 375, 383, 405

s 116(2)(a)–(e). . . 376, 385

s 116(2)(a). . . 354, **374**, 375

s 116(2)(b). . . **374**, 376, 405

s 116(2)(c). . . **374**, 376

s 116(2)(d). . . **374**, 375, 377, 379, 387, 402, 405

s 116(2)(e). . . 354, 358, **374**, 378, 379, 405

s 116(3). . . **374**, 378

s 116(4). . . 379, 402

s 116(4)(a)–(c). . . 402

s 116(4)(a). . . **379**

s 116(4)(b). . . **379**

s 116(4)(c). . . 379, 382

s 116(4)(d). . . 379, 380, 382

s 116(5). . . **374**, 375

s 117. . . 40, 184, 187, 352, 370, 382, **383**, 384, 396, 397, 398, 399, 434

s 117(1). . . **383**, 384, 385

s 117(1)(a). . . **383**, 384

s 117(2). . . **383**, 385

s 117(2)(a). . . **383**, 384, 406

s 117(2)(b). . . **383**, 384, 406

s 117(2)(c). . . **383**, 384, 385

s 117(3). . . **383**, 384

s 117(4). . . **383**, 385

s 117(5). . . **383**, 385

s 117(5)(a). . . 405

s 117(5)(b). . . **383**, 385

s 117(6). . . **383**, 385

s 117(7). . . **383–4**, 385

s 118. . . 202, 352, 367, 406,
    408, 434, 491

s 118(1). . . 434, 451, 490,
    540, 555

s 118(1)1(a). . . 438

s 118(1)1(b). . . 434

s 118(1)1(c). . . 434

s 118(1)1(d). . . **439**

s 118(1)2. . . 352, 440, 556

s 118(1)3. . . 440

s 118(1)4. . . 94, 205

s 118(1)4(a). . . 387, **442**

s 118(1)4(b). . . **448**

s 118(1)4(c). . . **449**

s 118(1)(5). . . 202

s 118(1)6(a). . . **450**

s 118(1)8. . . 657

s 119. . . 187, 205, 206, 207,
    210, 211, 212, 225, 354,
    364, 396, 397, 398

s 119(1). . . **206**, **225**, 391, **392**

s 119(1)(a). . . **206**, 207, 210, 211

s 119(1)(b). . . 211, 397

s 119(2). . . 400

s 120. . . 186, 190, 352, **393**,
    394, 396, 397, 398

s 120(1). . . **186**, **190**, **199**, **202**,
    354, **393**

s 120(2). . . **199**, **393**

s 120(3). . . 190, **393**, 394

s 120(3)(a). . . **190**

s 120(4). . . 186, 190, 202, **393**,
    394, 396, 397

s 120(4)(b). . . 395

s 120(5). . . 202, **393**, 394

s 120(6). . . **186**, 190, **393**, 394,
    395, 397

s 120(7). . . 195, 196, 262, **393**,
    395, 396

s 120(7)(e). . . 395

s 120(7)(f). . . 395

s 120(8). . . **393**, 395

s 121. . . **396**

s 121(1). . . **396**

s 121(1)(a). . . **396**, 397

s 121(1)(b). . . **396**, 397

s 121(1)(c). . . **396**, 397, 398, 402

s 121(2). . . **396**

s 122. . . 191, 212

s 123. . . 353, 382

s 123(1). . . 376, 398

s 123(2). . . 398

s 123(3). . . 398

s 123(4). . . 398

s 124. . . 353, 355, 382, 398

s 124(1). . . **399**

s 124(2). . . **399**, 400

s 124(2)(a). . . **399**, 400, 565

s 124(2)(b). . . **399**, 400

s 124(2)(c). . . 382, **399**, 400

s 124(3). . . **399**, 400

s 124(4). . . **399**

s 125. . . 41, 211, 225, 254,
    355, 392, **401**

s 125(1). . . **401**

s 125(2). . . **401**

s 125(3). . . **401**

s 125(4). . . **401**

s 126. . . 52, 352, 353, **401**, 403

s 126(1). . . **401–2**, 403

s 126(1)(b). . . **402**, 403, 570

s 126(2). . . **402**, 403, 577

s 126(2)(b). . . 51

s 127. . . 352, 353, **407–8**, 654

s 127(1). . . **407**

s 127(2). . . **408**

s 127(3). . . **408**

s 127(4). . . **408**

s 127(5). . . **408**

s 127(6). . . **408**

s 128(1). . . 352

s 128(2). . . 352

s 129. . . **371**

s 129(1). . . **371**

s 129(2). . . **371**

s 131(1)(a)–(c). . . 387

s 132. . . 404

s 132(3). . . 404

s 132(4). . . 404

s 132(5). . . 404

s 132(7). . . 404

s 133. . . 302, **303**, 306, **406**, 407

s 134(1). . . 302, 317, 352, 363,
    384, 406

s 136. . . 350

s 137. . . 155, 184, 407

s 137(2). . . 155

s 139. . . 184, 185, 188, 192

s 139(1). . . **184**, 185, 187,
    188, 303

s 139(2). . . **184**, 185

s 140. . . 187

s 331. . . 554

Sch 36, para 79. . . 554

Sch 36, para 80(b). . . 554

Explanatory Notes. . . 366, 370,
    371, 564, 599, 623

Explanatory Notes, para
    374. . . 599

Explanatory Notes, para
    375. . . 599, 603

Explanatory Notes, para
    384. . . 623

Explanatory Notes, para
    385. . . 623

Criminal Justice and Immigration
    Act 2008

s 76(3). . . 81

s 76(5A). . . 81

s 76(6). . . 81

s 76(7). . . 81

Criminal Justice and Police
    Act 2001

s 59. . . 708

Criminal Justice and Public Order
    Act 1994. . . 257, 498, 506, 508

s 3. . . 75

s 32. . . 258, 259, 260, 266

s 32(1). . . **259**, 260

s 32(2). . . **259**, 267

ss 34–37. . . 262, 485, 521

ss 34–38. . . 498

s 34. . . 21, 70, 491, 492, 494,
    499, **507**, 508, 510, 511,
    512, 516, 517, 518, 519,
    520, 523, 524, 525

s 34(1). . . **507**, 508, 524

s 34(1)(a). . . **507**, 508, 509, 510

s 34(1)(b). . . **507**, 508, 509

s 34(2). . . **507**, 508, 521, 530

s 34(2)(b). . . 521

s 34(2)(c). . . 511

s 34(2A). . . **508**

s 34(3). . . **513**

s 34(4). . . 508

s 34(5). . . **521**
s 35. . . 286, 485, 498, **499,**
  502, 519, 520, 525, 529
s 35(1). . . **499,** 501, 503
s 35(1)(b). . . 500, 501
s 35(2). . . 55, 95, **499,** 501, 502
s 35(3). . . **499,** 500, 502, 521
s 35(4). . . **499,** 502
s 35(5). . . **499**
s 36. . . 491, 492, 494, 499,
  522, 523, 524, 525
s 36(1). . . **522**
s 36(1)(a)(iv). . . **522,** 524
s 36(1)(b). . . 523
s 36(2). . . 521, **522,** 523,
  524, 530
s 36(2)(b). . . 521
s 36(3). . . **522**
s 36(4). . . **522,** 523
s 36(4A). . . **522**
s 36(5). . . **522,** 523
s 36(6). . . **522**
s 37. . . 491, 492, 494, 499,
  522, **523,** 524, 525
s 37(1). . . **523**
s 37(1)(b). . . 522
s 37(2). . . 521, **523,**
  524, 530
s 37(2)(b). . . 521
s 37(3). . . **523**
s 37(3A). . . **523**
s 37(4). . . **523**
s 37(5). . . **523**
s 38. . . 491
s 38(1). . . 522
s 38(2). . . 499, 507, 522
s 38(2A). . . 508
s 38(3). . . **500,** 502, 503, **521,**
  524
s 38(4). . . **521**
s 38(6). . . **525**
s 51. . . 74
s 51(1). . . **74**
s 51(1)(a). . . **74**
s 51(1)(b). . . **74**
s 51(1)(c). . . **74**
s 51(7). . . **74**
Criminal Law Act 1977
s 2(2). . . 132
s 54. . . 216
Criminal Procedure Act
  1865. . . 95, 223

s 3. . . 133, 206, **209,** 210, 225,
  391, 392, 397, 419, 554, 628
s 4. . . 206, 209, 210, 219,
  222, 223, 224, 225, 391,
  392, 419
s 5. . . 206, 210, 222, **223,** 224,
  225, 391, 392, 419
s 6. . . **244,** 399, 554, 766
s 7. . . 312
s 8. . . **95, 311–12,** 637
Criminal Procedure and
  Investigations Act 1996
Pt 1. . . 680, 735
ss 1–21. . . 735
s 3. . . 526
s 5. . . 528
s 5(5). . . 526
s 5C. . . 526
s 6. . . 531
s 6A. . . **526–7,** 528
s 6A(1). . . **526–7**
s 6A(2). . . **527**
s 6A(2)(a). . . 527
s 6A(3). . . **527**
s 6C. . . 528, 529
s 6C(1). . . **528**
s 6E(5)(b). . . 529
s 11. . . 499, **528,** 530
s 11(1). . . **528**
s 11(2). . . **528,** 529
s 11(2)(f)(i). . . 529
s 11(3). . . **528,** 531
s 11(4). . . **529**
s 11(5). . . 528, **529,** 531
s 11(5)(b). . . **529,** 530
s 11(6). . . **529**
s 11(7). . . **529**
s 11(8). . . **529**
s 11(8)(a). . . 530
s 11(9). . . **529**
s 11(10). . . **529,** 530, 531
s 11(12)(e). . . 529
s 12. . . 526
s 14. . . 679, 710
s 15. . . 679
s 21(2). . . 680
Criminal Procedure (Attendance
  of Witnesses) Act 1965
s 2. . . 127, 153, 154
Criminal Procedure (Insanity) Act
  1964. . . 401
s 4. . . 63

s 4A. . . 352, 555
s 4A(2). . . 623
s 6. . . 63
Criminal Procedure (Insanity and
  Unfitness to Plead) Act 1991
s 1(1). . . 253, 640, 643, 672
s 4(6). . . 253
Crown Proceedings Act 1947
s 28. . . 697
Customs and Excise Management
  Act 1979
s 86. . . 35
Data Protection Act 1998
s 55(1). . . 72
s 55(2). . . 72
Diplomatic Privileges Act
  1964. . . 142
Divorce Reform Act 1969. . . 91
Documentary Evidence Act 1868
s 2. . . 304
Documentary Evidence Act 1882
s 2. . . 118, 304, 309
Domestic Violence, Crime and
  Victims Act 2004
s 5. . . 62
s 6. . . 62, 502
s 6A. . . 502
Drugs Trafficking Act 1994
Pt I. . . 68
Employment Rights Act 1996
s 98. . . 79
Enterprise and Regulatory Reform
  Act 2013
s 14. . . 749
Environmental Protection Act 1990
s 33(1)(a). . . 65
s 71. . . 721
European Communities Act
  1972. . . 715
s 3(2). . . 118
Evidence Act 1845
s 1. . . 308
s 2. . . 118
s 3. . . 118, 309
Evidence Act 1851
s 7. . . 308, 767
s 14. . . 308
Evidence Act 1938
s 3. . . 312
s 4. . . 313
Evidence (Colonial Statutes) Act
  1907. . . 637

s 1. . . 304, 637

Evidence (Foreign, Dominion
  and Colonial Documents) Act
  1933. . . 435
  s 1. . . 54, 304, 429

Factories Act 1961
  s 29(1). . . 65
  s 155(1). . . 65

Family Law Reform Act
  1969. . . 17
  s 20. . . 17, 269
  s 23(1). . . 18
  s 26. . . 91, 92, 100, 105, 109

Family Law Reform Act 1987
  s 17. . . 269

Fatal Accidents Act 1846. . . 62

Financial Services and Markets
  Act 2000
  Pt 4. . . 309

Firearms Act 1968
  s 21. . . 628
  s 5(1)(b). . . 36
  s 51(A). . . 85

Football Spectators Act 1989
  s 14B. . . 87

Forestry Act 1967
  s 17. . . 77

Fraud Act 2006. . . 723
  s 13. . . 723

Health and Safety at Work Act
  1974. . . 76
  s 40. . . 76

Health and Safety (Offences) Act
  2008
  s 1(1). . . 76
  s 1(2). . . 76
  Sch 1. . . 76

Highways Act 1959
  s 140(1). . . 65

Highways Act 1980
  s 32. . . 441

Homicide Act 1957
  s 2. . . 658, 659
  s 2(1)(a). . . 640
  s 2(1)(b). . . 35
  s 2(2). . . 63
  s 4. . . 74
  s 4(1). . . 74
  s 4(2). . . 74

Human Rights Act 1998. . . 4, 63,
  64, 68, 69, 341, 418
  s 2. . . 353

s 3. . . 68, 69, 71, 77, 172, 238,
  353, 577

Hunting Act 2004
  s 1. . . 73
  s 2. . . 73
  Sch 1. . . 73

Immigration Act 1971
  s 25. . . 637
  s 25(3). . . 637

Immigration and Asylum Act 1999
  s 31(1). . . 73

Indecency with Children Act
  1960. . . 216
  s 1. . . 216

Inheritance (Family Provision) Act
  1938. . . 106

Insolvency Act 1986. . . 720
  s 208(4)(a). . . 74
  s 235. . . 721
  s 311(1). . . 738
  s 354. . . 721
  s 354(3). . . 721

Interception of Communications
  Act 1985. . . 325

International Organisations Act
  1968. . . 142

Interpretation Act 1978
  s 3. . . 118, **309**
  s 22(1). . . 118
  Sch 2, para 2. . . 118

Investigatory Powers Act
  2016. . . 339
  Pt 2, Chap 1. . . 325
  s 3(1). . . 325
  s 9. . . 325
  s 10. . . 325
  s 20. . . 692
  s 28. . . 692
  s 56(1). . . **325**
  s 56(2)(a)–(e). . . 325
  s 56(4). . . 325
  Sch 3, para 5. . . 325
  Sch 3, para 7. . . 325

Juries Act 1974
  s 20A. . . 122

Justice and Security Act
  2013. . . 703
  Pt 2. . . 704
  s 6. . . 705, 706
  s 6(1). . . **704**, 705
  s 6(2). . . **704**
  s 6(3)–(6). . . 705

s 6(3). . . **705**, 706
  s 6(4). . . **705**
  s 6(5). . . **705**
  s 6(6). . . **705**
  s 6(7). . . **706**
  s 6(8). . . 704
  s 6(11). . . 704, 705
  s 7. . . 706
  s 8(1). . . 705
  s 8(1)(a). . . 705
  s 9(1). . . 705
  s 9(2). . . 705
  s 9(3). . . 705
  s 9(4). . . 705
  s 14(2)(c). . . 704

Landlord and Tenant Act
  1954. . . 655

Larceny Act 1916
  s 43(1). . . 51, 629

Law of Property Act 1925
  s 184. . . **112**

Legal Services Act 2007
  s 190. . . 726

Licensing Act 1964
  s 160(1)(a). . . 66

Limitation Act 1980
  s 33. . . 742

Local Government Act 1972
  s 238. . . 308

Local Government (Miscellaneous
  Provisions) Act 1976. . . 415
  s 75. . . 64

Local Government (Miscellaneous
  Provisions) Act 1982
  Sch 3, para 6. . . 65
  Sch 3, para 20(1)(a). . . 65

Magistrates' Courts Act 1952
  s 81. . . 63, 64, 65

Magistrates' Courts Act 1980
  s 97. . . 127
  s 101. . . 63, **64**, 65, 66, 67
  s 161. . . 65

Maintenance Orders Act 1950
  s 22(2). . . 119

Marriage Act 1949
  s 65(3). . . 418, 435

Matrimonial and Family
  Proceedings Act 1984
  s 31G(6). . . 216

Matrimonial Causes Act
  1973. . . 91
  s 48(1). . . 107

Mental Capacity Act 2005
 s 1(2). . . 114
Mental Health Act 1959
 s 128. . . 216
Mental Health Act 1983. . . 168
 s 72. . . 93
 s 73. . . 93
Misuse of Drugs Act 1971. . . 83
 s 5. . . 66, 71
 s 5(3). . . 36, 69
 s 28. . . 69, 70, 71
 s 28(2). . . 71
 s 28(3). . . 71
Modern Slavery Act 2015. . . 67
 s 2. . . 133, 216
 s 3(3). . . 133
 s 45. . . 67
Northern Ireland (Emergency
 Provisions) Act 1978. . . 484
 s 8(2). . . 460
Oaths Act 1978
 s 1(1). . . 142
 s 1(2). . . 143
 s 1(3). . . 143
 s 3. . . 143
 s 4(2). . . 143
 s 5(1). . . 143
 s 5(2). . . 143
 s 5(3). . . 143
 s 5(4). . . 143
Oaths and Evidence (Overseas
 Authorities and Countries) Act
 1963
 s 5. . . 429
Obscene Publications Act
 1959. . . 639
 s 4. . . 637
Offences Against the Person Act
 1861. . . 410
 s 16. . . 65
 s 18. . . 588
 s 57. . . **113**
Offences Against the State Act
 1939
 s 21. . . 719
 s 52. . . 718, 719
Official Secrets Act 1911
 s 1(1). . . 630
 s 1(2). . . 628, **630**, 772
Official Secrets Act 1989
 s 2. . . 77
 s 2(3). . . 77

s 3. . . 77
s 3(4). . . 77
Partnership Act 1890
 s 15. . . 431
Perjury Act 1911. . . 256
 s 1. . . 143, 144
 s 1(1). . . 37, 256
 s 1(6). . . 37
 s 2. . . 722
 s 5. . . 722
 s 13. . . **256**
 s 32(3). . . 144
Police Act 1964
 s 64. . . 271
Police and Criminal Evidence Act
 1984 (PACE). . . 131, 134, 330,
 331, 336, 346, 357, 454, 455,
 458, 459, 460, 466, 468, 469,
 473, 476, 479, 482, 484, 485,
 509, 525, 758
 s 2A. . . 270
 s 8. . . 737
 s 9. . . 737
 s 9(1). . . 717
 s 10. . . 725, 728, 737
 s 10(1). . . **725**, 741
 s 10(1)(c). . . 735, 737
 s 10(2). . . **725**, 737, 741
 s 11. . . 737
 s 14(2). . . 737
 s 37. . . 478
 s 37(7). . . 509
 s 56. . . 473, 474
 s 56(1). . . **473**, 474
 s 56(2)(b). . . 474
 s 56(3). . . 474
 s 56(4). . . 474
 s 56(5). . . 474, 475
 s 56(5A). . . 475
 s 56(6). . . 475
 s 56(7). . . 475
 s 56(8). . . 473
 s 58. . . 200, 333, 334, 466,
  473, 474, 476, 478, 506
 s 58(1). . . **473**, 474
 s 58(2). . . **473**
 s 58(3). . . **473**
 s 58(4). . . 467, **473**
 s 58(5). . . 474
 s 58(6)(b). . . 474
 s 58(7). . . 474
 s 58(8). . . 474, 475, 476

s 58(8)(a)–(c). . . 475
s 58(8A). . . 475
s 58(9). . . 475
s 58(10). . . 475
s 58(11). . . 475
s 61. . . 16, 526
ss 62–63. . . 499
s 62. . . 18, 525
s 62(1)(b). . . 525
s 62(1A)(b). . . 525
s 62(2A)(c). . . 525
s 62(4). . . 525
s 62(10). . . 18, 262, 333,
 525, 526
s 63. . . 526
s 64. . . 333
s 65. . . 16, 525, 526
s 66. . . 202, 203
s 67(9). . . 331, 470, 508
s 67(11). . . 459, 486
ss 68–72. . . 350
s 68. . . 385, 427
s 68(2). . . 377
s 68(2)(a)(ii). . . 376
s 71. . . 303, 306
ss 73–82. . . 468
s 73. . . 54, 629, 772
s 73(1). . . **54**, 55
s 73(4). . . 54
s 74. . . 28, 53, 99, 364, 488,
 586, 765, 766, 767, 768,
 769, 770, 771
s 74(1). . . 364, **766**, 767, 768
s 74(2). . . 364, **766**, 767,
 771, 772
s 74(3). . . 586, 626, **766**,
 771, 772
s 74(4)(a). . . 766
s 74(4)(b). . . 766
s 75. . . 586, 769
s 75(1). . . **766**
s 75(2). . . 766
s 75(3). . . 767
s 75(4). . . 767
s 76. . . 270, 272, 352, 456,
 458, 459, 467, 482, 486, 490
s 76(1). . . 454, 455, **456**,
 468, 484
s 76(2). . . 37, 39, 40, 94, 324,
 331, 458, 464, 468, 481,
 482, 484, 486, 487, 490
s 76(2)(a). . . **456**, 459, 486

s 76(2)(b). . . 270, **456**, 460, 461, 462, 463, 464, 465, 466, 467, 469, 486

s 76(3). . . **456**, 458, 482

s 76(4). . . **494, 496**

s 76(5). . . **495**

s 76(6). . . **495**

s 76(8). . . 324, 459, 460

s 76A. . . 352, 389, 456, 457, 458, 483, 490

s 76A(1). . . 454, **456**

s 76A(2). . . **457**, 458, 459, 490

s 76A(2)(b). . . 462

s 76A(3). . . **457**, 458

s 76A(4). . . **494, 496**

s 76A(5). . . **495**

s 76A(6). . . **495**

s 76A(7). . . 459

s 77. . . 267, 270. 271, 272, 458, 466, 469, 485

s 77(1). . . **270**, 271

s 77(1)(a). . . **270**, 271

s 77(1)(b). . . **270**, 271, 272

s 77(2). . . **270**

s 77(3). . . 271

s 78. . . 39, 40, 52, 53, 55, 137, 186, 233, 272, 293, 297, 327, 329, 330, 331, 332, 333, 334, 337, 338, 339, 342, 343, 344, 345, 346, 374, 377, 388, 402, 403, 404, 447, 451, 452, 455, 458, 461, 466, 468, 472, 476, 477, 479, 480, 481, 482, 484, 485, 486, 525, 535, 570, 576, 577, 582, 596, 604, 609, 708, 718, 744, 751, 768, 769, 770, 771, 772

s 78(1). . . **52**, 53, 133, 270, **329**, 330, 331, 332, 343, 344, 468, 469, **476**, 494

s 78(2). . . **329**

s 78(3). . . 331

s 79. . . **155**

s 80. . . 131, 132, 133, 390

s 80(1). . . 131

s 80(2). . . **134**

s 80(2A). . . **131**, 132, 133, 135

s 80(2A)(a). . . 135

s 80(2A)(b). . . 133

s 80(3). . . **132**, 133, 135

s 80(3)(b). . . 133

s 80(4). . . **132**, 134, 135

s 80(4A). . . **132**

s 80(5). . . **135**, 136

s 80(5A). . . **135**

s 80(6). . . 132

s 80(7). . . 133

s 80A. . . 18

s 82(1). . . **454**, 455, 456, 457, 484, 490, 766, 767

s 82(3). . . 53, 270, 272, **468–9**, 486, 490

s 89. . . 708

s 107(1). . . 474

s 118. . . 16

Postal Services Act 2000

s 85(4). . . 35

Presumption of Death Act 2013. . . 111, 308

s 1(1). . . 111

s 1(2). . . 111

s 1(3). . . 111

s 1(4). . . 111

s 1(5). . . 112

s 2. . . **112**

s 2(1)(a). . . **112**

s 2(1)(b). . . **112**

s 3(1). . . 112

s 3(2). . . 112

s 3(3). . . 112

s 3(4). . . 112

s 5. . . 112

Sch 1, para 3 (Register of Presumed Deaths). . . 53, 308

Sch 1, para 4 (Register of Presumed Deaths). . . 53, 308

Prevention of Corruption Act 1906. . . 696

Prevention of Terrorism Act 2005. . . 703

Proceeds of Crime Act 2002. . . 386, 415

Pt V. . . 93

s 241(3). . . 93

s 328(1). . . 723

Prosecution of Offences Act 1985

s 19. . . 652

Protection from Eviction Act 1977

s 1(2). . . 74 90

Protection from Harassment Act 1997. . . 71

s 1(1)(A). . . 90

Protection of Children Act 1978. . . 133, 216, 410

Public Bodies Corrupt Practices Act 1889. . . 696

Public Order Act 1936

s 5. . . 35

Public Order Act 1986

s 5. . . 639

Public Records Act 1958

s 9. . . 308

Regulation of Investigatory Powers Act 2000. . . 325, 338, 341, 739

s 71. . . 341

Rehabilitation of Offenders Act 1974. . . 244, 630

s 4(1). . . 244

s 4(1)(a). . . 630

s 5(1). . . 630

s 5(2). Table A. . . 630

s 5(2), Table B. . . 630

s 6. . . 244, 245

s 7(2)(a). . . 630

s 7(3). . . 244, 630

Road Traffic Act 1988. . . 471

s 5(2). . . 75

s 7. . . 473

s 7(6). . . 61

s 37(3). . . 73

s 87(1). . . 64

s 103. . . 628

s 143. . . 64

s 172. . . 718

s 172(2)(a). . . 718

s 172(3). . . 718

Road Traffic Acts. . . 114

Road Traffic Offenders Act 1988

s 15. . . 71

s 16(1)(a). . . 373

Road Traffic Regulation Act 1984

s 89(2). . . 256, 672

Senior Courts Act 1981

s 33. . . 712

s 33(2). . . 743

s 34. . . 712

s 69(5). . . 36

s 70. . . 635

s 72. . . 714, 723, 724

s 72(3). . . 724

s 72(5). . . 723

Serious Crime Act 2007

Pt 2. . . 132

s 63(1). . . 132

Sch 6, para 9. . . 132

Serious Organized Crime and Police Act 2005. . . 641

s 73. . . 266–7

Sexual Offences Act 1956
  ss 1–32. . . 216
  ss 2–12. . . 216
  ss 14–17. . . 216
  ss 33–36. . . 216

Sexual Offences Act 1967. . . 216

Sexual Offences Act 1985
  s 1(1). . . 123

Sexual Offences Act 2003. . . 59, 87, 410
  Pt 1. . . 133, 158, 163, 216
  s 1(1)(c). . . 235
  s 62. . . 216
  ss 75–77. . . 235
  s 75. . . 62, 80
  s 76. . . 62, 101
  s 104. . . 87
  s 123(3). . . 87
  s 123(4). . . 87

Sexual Offences (Amendment) Act 1976. . . 231, 236
  s 2. . . 230, 236

Solicitors Act 1974
  s 18. . . 418

Stamp Act 1891
  s 14. . . 313

State Immunity Act 1978. . . 142
  Pt I. . . 22
  s 21a. . . 22

Supreme Court of Judicature Act 1875. . . 5

Taxes Management Act 1970
  s 20. . . 719
  s 98(1). . . 179
  s 105. . . 467–8
  s 105(1). . . **468**
  s 105(2). . . 468

Terrorism Act 2000. . . 720
  s 11(1). . . 75
  s 11(2). . . 75
  s 41. . . 334
  s 118(2). . . 80
  Sch 7, para 2. . . 718
  Sch 8. . . 335, 478

Terrorism Act 2003
  Sch 8(4)(a)–(g). . . 335

Theft Act 1968. . . 51, 722, 723
  s 22(1). . . 35, 102
  s 27(3). . . 51, **628–9**
  s 27(3)(a). . . **629**
  s 27(3)(b). . . **629**, 772

s 31. . . 722, 723
s 31(1). . . 722, 723

Torts (Interference with Goods) Act 1977
  s 3. . . 693

Trade Marks Act 1994
  s 87. . . 726
  s 92(5). . . 72, 73

Treason Act 1795
  s 1. . . 256

Video Recordings Act 1984
  s 11(1). . . 344

Wills Act 1837
  s 21. . . 313

Wireless Telegraphy Act 1949. . . 90

Youth Justice and Criminal Evidence Act 1999. . . 5, 132, 144, 156, 168, 173, 230, 232, 386, 394
  ss 16–33. . . 155
  s 16. . . 163, 164, 167
  s 16(1). . . **162**
  s 16(1)(a). . . **162**, 163, 164, 167
  s 16(1)(b). . . 167
  s 16(2). . . 162, **163**
  s 16(3). . . 163
  s 16(4). . . 163
  s 16(5). . . 163, 217
  s 17. . . 164, 167
  s 17(1). . . 163
  s 17(2). . . 163
  s 17(3). . . 163
  s 17(4). . . 163
  s 19. . . 137, 165, 379, 382
  s 19(1). . . 163
  s 19(2). . . 163, **164**, 165, 167
  s 19(3). . . 164
  s 19(6). . . 170
  s 20(1). . . 164
  s 20(2). . . 164
  s 20(5). . . 164
  s 21. . . 164, 166
  s 21(1)(a). . . **164**
  s 21(1)(c). . . **164**
  s 21(2)–(4). . . 166
  s 21(2). . . **165**
  s 21(3). . . **165**
  s 21(3)(a). . . **165**, 166
  s 21(4)(b). . . **165**
  s 21(4)(ba). . . **165**
  s 21(4)(c). . . **165**

s 21(4A). . . **165**
s 21(4B). . . **165**
s 21(4C). . . **165–6**
s 21(8). . . 166
s 21(9). . . 166
s 22. . . 166
s 22A. . . 166
s 22A(1). . . **166**
s 22A(2). . . **166**
s 22A(3). . . **167**
s 22A(4). . . **167**
s 22A(5). . . **167**
s 22A(6). . . **167**
s 22A(7). . . **167**
s 22A(8). . . **167**
s 22A(9). . . **167**
s 22A(10). . . **167**
s 23. . . 157, 165
s 23(1). . . 157
s 23(2). . . 157
s 24. . . 144, 157, 164, 165
s 24(1A). . . 157
s 24(3). . . 157
s 25. . . 157, 180
s 25(3). . . 157
s 25(4). . . 158
s 26. . . 158
s 27. . . 142, 149, 158, 159, 161, 162, 164, 165, 166, 167, 207, 217
s 27(1). . . **158**
s 27(2). . . **158**, 159, 165, 167
s 27(3). . . **158**
s 27(4). . . 159
s 27(5). . . 158
s 27(6). . . 158, 159
s 27(7). . . 159
s 27(9). . . 159
s 27(9A). . . 159
s 27(11). . . 159
s 28. . . 138, 156, 158, 160, 161, 166, 227
s 28(1). . . 160, 161
s 28(2). . . 161
s 28(4). . . 161
s 28(5). . . 161
s 28(6). . . 161
s 28(7). . . 161
s 29. . . 162
s 29(2). . . 162, 169
s 29(3). . . 162
s 29(6). . . 162

s 30. . . 162
s 31(1). . . **167**
s 31(2). . . **167**
s 31(3). . . **167**
s 31(4). . . **167**
s 31(8). . . 167
s 32. . . 161, 162, 168, 268
s 33A. . . 168
s 33A(2). . . 168
s 33A(4). . . 168, 169
s 33A(5). . . 168, 169
s 33BA. . . 169
s 33BA(2). . . 169
s 33BA(4). . . 169
s 33BA(5). . . 169
s 33BA(6). . . 169
s 33BA(7). . . 169
ss 34–39. . . 216
s 34. . . 216, 217
s 35. . . 216, 217
s 35(2). . . 217
s 35(3)(a). . . 216, 217
s 35(3)(b). . . 216, 217
s 35(3)(c). . . 216, 217
s 35(3)(d). . . 216, 217
s 35(5). . . 217
s 36. . . 217
s 36(2). . . 217
s 36(2)(a). . . 217
s 36(3). . . 217
s 36(4)(a). . . 217
s 36(4)(b). . . 217
s 38(1)–(5). . . 217
s 38(4). . . 216
s 39. . . 217
ss 41–43. . . 230
s 41. . . 220, 231, 232, 233,
    235, 236, 238, 239, 240,
    242, 563, 569, 628
s 41(1). . . **231**, 232, 233
s 41(2). . . 233, **234**, 240
s 41(2)(b). . . **234**, 235
s 41(3). . . 233, **234**, 241
s 41(3)(a). . . **234**, 235
s 41(3)(b). . . 236, 237
s 41(3)(c). . . 236, 237, 238,
    239, 240
s 41(3)(c)(i). . . 231, **234**
s 41(4). . . **234**, 240, 241
s 41(5). . . 233, **234**, 241, 242

s 41(5)(a). . . 231, **234**
s 41(6). . . **234**, 242
s 41(7). . . **234–5**
s 41(8). . . **235**
s 42(1). . . 237
s 42(1)(a). . . 233
s 42(1)(b). . . 233, 237
s 42(1)(c). . . **231**, 236,
    241, 569
s 42(1)(d). . . 231
s 42(2). . . 231
s 42(3). . . 231
s 43(1). . . 242
s 43(2). . . 242
s 53. . . **128**, 136, 137, 398, 498
s 53(1). . . 127, **128**, 129, 130,
    131, 134, 135, **136**, 539
s 53(2). . . **136**
s 53(3). . . 131, **136**, 137
s 53(3)(a). . . **136**
s 53(4). . . 131, 136
s 53(5). . . **128**, 131
s 54. . . 137
s 54(1). . . 137
s 54(2). . . 94, 137
s 54(3). . . 137, 159
s 54(4). . . 137
s 54(5). . . 137
s 54(6). . . 137, 138
s 55(1). . . **138**
s 55(2). . . **138**, 142
s 55(2)(b). . . **138**, 139
s 55(3). . . **139**
s 55(4). . . **139**
s 55(5). . . **139**
s 55(6). . . **139**
s 55(7). . . **139**
s 55(8). . . **139**
s 56(1). . . **139**
s 56(2). . . **139**
s 56(3). . . **139**
s 56(4). . . **139**
s 56(5). . . 142
s 57. . . 139
s 62. . . 158, 163

International Instruments

European Convention on Human
    Rights (ECHR). . . 4, 69, 173,
    324, 330, 344, 355, 506, 577

Art 2. . . 173
Art 3. . . 93, 173, 459
Art 5. . . 704
Art 6. . . 63, 64, 71, 73, 74, 77,
    144, 168, 173, 182, 233,
    238, 324, 326, 334, 335,
    338, 339, 343, 346, 349,
    353, 354, 355, 356, 358,
    359, 374, 378, 380, 387,
    397, 455, 494, 504, 514,
    519, 536, 576, 604, 626,
    679, 707, 709, 717, 718,
    719, 720, 721
Art 6(1). . . 204, 226, 334, 335,
    339, 340, 353, **354**, 356,
    380, 391, 403, 418, 474,
    708, 719
Art 6(2). . . 63, 68, 69, 70,
    72, 93
Art 6(3). . . 172, 592
Art 6(3)(c). . . 334, 335, 474
Art 6(3)(d). . . 144, 171, 226,
    353, **354**, 355, 356, 357,
    380, 391, 403
Art 8. . . 132, 173, 326, 338,
    339, 536, 738
Art 8(2). . . 132
Art 10. . . 692, 695
Art 10(1). . . **692**
Art 10(2). . . **692**
United Nations Convention
    Against Torture and Other
    Cruel, Inhuman or Degrading
    Treatment or Punishment 1987
Art 1 (Draft
    Convention). . . 460
Art 15. . . 324

Ireland (Republic of)

Criminal Justice Act 1984
    s 18. . . 522
    s 19. . . 522

New Zealand

Evidence Act 2006
    s 54(3). . . 751

United States

Federal Rules. . . 40
    r 104(a). . . 40
    r 104(c). . . 38
    r 702. . . 638

TABLE OF STATUTORY INSTRUMENTS

Page references in bold indicate that the text is reproduced in full

Accreditation of Forensic Science
  Providers Regulations 2018, SI
  2018/1276. . . 652
  reg 3. . . 652
  reg 4. . . 652
  Explanatory Note to reg
    4. . . 652
Children (Admissibility of
  Hearsay Evidence) Order 1993,
  SI 1993/621. . . 418
Civil Partnership (Registration
  Provisions) Regulations 2005,
  SI 2005/3176
  reg 13(4). . . 308
  reg 14(4). . . 308
Civil Procedure Rules 1998, SI
  1998/3132 (CPR). . . 5, 47, 149,
  307, 325, 662, 666, 699
  Pt 1. . . 665
  r 1.1. . . 48, 218
  r 1.1(1). . . 48
  r 1.1(2). . . **48**, 49
  r 1.2. . . 48, 536
  r 1.4. . . 536
  r 3.4. . . 151
  Pt 14. . . 124
  r 14.1(1). . . **124**
  r 14.1(2). . . **124**
  r 14.1(3). . . 124
  r 14.1(5). . . **124**
  r 14.1A(1). . . **124**
  r 14.1A(2)–(5). . . 124
  rr 14. 4–14.7. . . 124
  PD 14, para 7.2. . . 124
  r 16.4(1). . . 9
  r 16.4(1)(a). . . **9**
  r 16.5(1). . . **9**
  r 16.5(1)(c). . . 124
  r 16.5(3). . . 9
  r 16.5(4). . . 9
  r 16.5(5). . . 9, 124
  PD 16, para 8.1. . . 761, 763
  r 18.1. . . 124, 712
  PD 18. . . 124
  Pt 19. . . 764
  Pt 20. . . 764
  r 22.1(6). . . 151

r 22.3. . . 151
r 26.5(3). . . 124
r 27.2. . . 421
r 27.2(1). . . 48, 150
r 27.2(4). . . 150
r 27.8(3). . . 2
r 27.8(4). . . 142
PD 27. . . 150
r 27.2(1)e. . . 660
r 28.2. . . 150, 667
r 28.3. . . 150, 667
PD 28. . . 150
PD 28 paras 3.5–3.9. . . 667
PD 28, para 3.9. . . 150
PD 28, para 5.1. . . 151
r 29.2. . . 150, 667
r 29.4. . . 667
PD 29. . . 150
PD 29 paras 4.6–4.13. . . 667
PD 29, para 4.10. . . 150
PD 29, para 7.1. . . 151
Pt 31. . . 313, 676
r 31. . . 317
r 31.4. . . 302, 317
r 31.6. . . 699
r 31.12. . . 699
r 31.17. . . 309
r 31.19. . . 697
r 31.19(6). . . 697
r 31.22. . . 750
Pt 32. . . 150, 151
r 32. . . 244, 735
r 32.1. . . 48, 150, 180,
  423, 536
r 32.1(1). . . **48**, 150
r 32.1(2). . . 48, 49, 150, 325
r 32.1(3). . . 49, 218
r 32.2. . . 180
r 32.3. . . 11, 144
r 32.4. . . 152
r 32.4(1). . . 150
r 32.4(2). . . 150
r 32.4(3). . . 150
r 32.5. . . **151**, 184
r 32.5(1). . . **151**
r 32.5(2). . . **151**, 419

r 32.5(3). . . **151, 152**
r 32.5(3)(a). . . 152
r 32.5(4). . . **151**, 152
r 32.5(5). . . **151**
r 32.5(5)(b). . . 423
r 32.8. . . 151, 152
r 32.9. . . **152**, 207
r 32.9(1). . . **152**
r 32.9(2). . . **152**
r 32.9(3). . . **152**
r 32.9(4). . . **152**
r 32.9(5). . . **152**
r 32.10. . . 152
r 32.11. . . 222
r 32.14. . . 151
r 32.18. . . 124
r 32.19(1). . . 313, 317
PD 32. . . 151
PD 32, para 17.2. . . 151
PD 32, para 18.1. . . 151
PD 32, para 18.2. . . 151
PD 32, para 20.1. . . 151
PD 32, para 25.1. . . 151
PD 32, Annex 3,
  Videoconferencing
  Guidance. . . 144
r 33. . . 421
r 33.2. . . **421–2**, 434
r 33.2(1). . . **421**
r 33.2(2). . . **421**
r 33.2(3). . . 421, **422**
r 33.2(4). . . **422**
r 33.3. . . **422**, 434
r 33.4. . . **423**
r 33.4(1). . . **423**
r 33.4(2). . . **423**
r 33.5. . . 426
r 33.6(2). . . 428
r 33.6(3). . . 428
r 33.6(4). . . 428
r 33.6(8). . . 428
r 34.2–34.6. . . 127
r 34.2. . . 307, 309
r 34.13. . . 310
Pt 35. . . 660, 661
r 35.1. . . 660, **661**

r 35.2. . . 667
r 35.2(1). . . 661
r 35.3. . . 652, 660
r 35.4. . . **661**, 662
r 35.4(1). . . **661**, 667
r 35.4(2). . . **661**
r 35.4(3). . . **661**
r 35.4(3A). . . **661**
r 35.4(3B). . . **661**
r 35.4(4). . . **661**
r 35.5(1). . . **662**
r 35.5(2). . . **662**
r 35.6. . . **664**
r 35.6(1). . . **664**
r 35.6(2). . . **664**
r 35.6(2)(c). . . **664**
r 35.6(3). . . **664**
r 35.6(4). . . **664**
r 35.7. . . 660, **662**, 663, 664
r 35.7(1). . . **662**
r 35.7(2). . . **662**
r 35.8. . . 660, **663**
r 35.8(1). . . **663**
r 35.8(2). . . **663**
r 35.8(3). . . **663**
r 35.8(4). . . **663**
r 35.8(5). . . **663**
r 35.9. . . 663
r 35.10(1). . . 665
r 35.10(2). . . 665
r 35.10(3). . . **665**
r 35.10(4). . . **665**, 667
r 35.10(4)(b). . . 665
r 35.11. . . **666**, 667
r 35.12. . . 653, 666
r 35.13. . . 416, **666**, 667
r 35.14. . . 667
r 35.15. . . 635
PD 35. . . 660, 665, 668
PD 35, para 3.2. . . 665
PD 35, para 3.3. . . 665
PD 35, para 4. . . 663
PD 35, para 5. . . 665
Pt 36. . . 754
r 36.3(g). . . 754
r 36.5(1)(c). . . 754
r 36.5(3). . . 754
r 36.6(1). . . 754
r 36.7. . . 754
r 36.16(2). . . 754
r 36.17(3). . . 754

r 36.18. . . 754
Practice Directions. . . 5
Court of Protection (Amendment)
    Rules 2015, SI 2015/548. . . 419
Court of Protection Rules 2007, SI
    2007/1744
    r 95(d). . . 419
    r 95(e). . . 419
Criminal Evidence (NI) Order
    1988, SI 1988/1987 (NI
    120). . . 506
art 3. . . 511
art 4. . . 500, 504, 505
Criminal Procedure and
    Investigations Act 1996
    (Defence Disclosure Time
    Limits) Regulations 2011, SI
    2011/209
    reg 2. . . 526
Criminal Justice Act 2003
    (Categories of Offences) Order
    2004, SI 2004/3346. . . 586
Criminal Procedure Rules 2005, SI
    2005/384. . . 5
    r 1.1. . . 5
    r 3.2. . . 5, 6
    r 3.3. . . 6
Criminal Procedure Rules 2015, SI
    2015/1490. . . 5, 44, 162, 169,
    434, 451, 498, 670, 671
    r 1.1. . . 626
    r 1.1(2)(e). . . 218
    r 3.2(2)(e). . . 218
    r 3.2(3). . . 218
    r 3.3. . . 152, 153
    r 3.9(7)(a). . . 180
    r 3.10. . . 153
    r 3.11. . . 153
    r 3.11(a). . . 451
    r 3.21(4). . . 591
Pt 6.6. . . 625
r 10. . . 242
Pt 15. . . 707
r 15.4(1). . . 558
rr 18.18–18.22. . . 171
r 19. . . 669
r 19.2. . . 652, 668
r 19.3. . . 409, 498
r 19.3(1). . . 125, **669**
r 19.3(2). . . 125, **669–70**
r 19.3(3). . . **670**
r 19.3(3)(c). . . **670**
r 19.3(4). . . **670**

r 19.4. . . 668
r 19.4(e). . . 668
r 19.4(h). . . 647, 668
r 19.4(k). . . 668
r 19.5. . . 668
r 19.6. . . 653, 669, 671
r 19.6(3). . . 669
r 19.7. . . 669
r 19.8(1). . . 669
r 19.8(2). . . 669
r 19.8(3). . . 669
r 19.9(1). . . 669
Pt 20. . . 404
r 20.2. . . 452
r 20.2(1). . . 434
r 20.5(1)(c). . . 452
r 21. . . 625, 626
r 21.2. . . 572
r 21.4. . . 572, 625
r 21.4(8). . . 550
r 21.6. . . 625
r 22.3(1). . . 242
r 22.7(3). . . 242
r 24.3(3)(d). . . 42
r 24.5. . . 409
r 24(6). . . 125
r 24.13(2). . . 451
r 24.15(2). . . 34
r 25.11(3). . . 142
r 25.11(4)(c)(i). . . 215
r 25.11(6)(b). . . 216
r 25.13. . . 125
r 25.14. . . 550
r 25.14(2). . . 44
r 25.14(4). . . 44
r 26(3). . . 122
r 33.39. . . 421
Sch. . . 242
Employment Tribunals
    (Constitution and Rules of
    Procedure) Regulations 2013, SI
    2013/1237
    r 41. . . 2
    Sch 1. . . 2
Environmental Permitting
    (England and Wales)
    Regulations 2007, SI 2007/3538
    reg 12. . . 65
    reg 38. . . 65
Family Procedure (Amendment
    No 3) Rules 2017, SI
    2017/1033. . . 156

Pt 3A 1–12. . . 156

PD 5.2–5.7. . . 156

Family Procedure Rules 2010, SI
2010/2955. . . 5

Merchant Shipping (Returns of
Births and Deaths) Regulations
1979, SI 1979/1577. . . 54

Misuse of Drugs Regulations 1973,
SI 1973/797. . . 66, 67

Motor Vehicles (Compulsory
Insurance) Regulations 2000, SI
2000/726

reg 2(2)(a). . . 64

Rules of the Supreme
Court. . . 699

Ord 24, r 8. . . 690

Ord 24, r 10. . . 307

Ord 38, r 2A. . . 735

Youth Justice and Criminal
Evidence Act 1999
(Commencement No 13)
Order, SI 2013/3236. . . 160

Youth Justice and Criminal
Evidence Act 1999
(Commencement No 15)
Order, SI 2016/1201. . . 160

TABLE OF CODES, CODES OF PRACTICE AND PRACTICE DIRECTIONS

Page references in bold indicate that the text is reproduced in full

Bar Standards Handbook, Code of Conduct for Barristers
r C7.1. . . 218
r C7.2. . . 221
r C15.1. . . **228**
r C21.8. . . **230**
City Code on Takeovers and Mergers. . . 35
Code of Practice for Arranging and Conducting Interviews of Witnesses notified by the Accused. . . 528
Code of Practice on Audio Recording of Interviews with Suspects, Code E. . . 95
Code of Practice on the proper conduct of formal identification procedures. . . 202
Code D, para 3.3. . . 203
Code D, para 3.12(ii). . . 204
Code D, para 3.28. . . 203
Code D, Annex E. . . 203
Covert Human Intelligence Sources Code of Practice. . . 341
Criminal Practice Directions. . . 451
Criminal Practice Direction I
para 3D.2. . . 218
para 3D.7. . . 181
para 3E.1. . . **225**
para 3E.2. . . 180
para 3E.4. . . 180, 225, **226**, 227
para 3E.5. . . 225, **227**
para 3E.6. . . 181
para 3F.1. . . 180
para 3F.12. . . 169
para 3F.13. . . 169
para 3F.15. . . 170
para 3F.27. . . 180
Criminal Practice Directions V
Pt 16A. . . 410
Pt 16A, para 16A.4(b). . . 490
Pt 16C. . . 95, 303, 316, 470

Pt 17A. . . 128
para 18C.1. . . 191, 193
para 18C.4. . . **193**
para 18C.5. . . **193**
Pt 18D. . . 171
Pt 19A. . . 409
Pt 19A, paras 19A.4–19A.6. . . 647
Pt 19A, para 19A.4. . . **647**, 648, 649
Pt 19A, para 19A.5. . . **647–8**
Pt 19A, para 19A.6. . . **648**
Pt 19A, para 19A.7. . . 670
Pt 19A, para 19A.8. . . 670
Pt 19A, para 19A.9. . . 670
Pt 21A. . . 628, 630
Pt 21A, para 21A.2. . . 244, 630, 647
Pt 22A.3. . . 242
para 22A.4. . . 242
Criminal Practice Directions VI
Pt 24A. . . 34
para 24B.4. . . 451
para 26J.1. . . 318
para 26K.8. . . 44
para 26K.11. . . 44
para 26K.12. . . 44
para 26L, 2. . . 160
Pt 26M. . . 686
para 26P.2–26P.5. . . 501
para 26P.2. . . **501**
para 26P.3. . . **501**
para 26P.4. . . **501**
para 26P.5. . . **502**
Criminal Practice Directions 2015 (Amendment No 6)
para 6. . . 216
para 23A.1. . . 216
Criminal Procedure and Investigations Act 1996, Code of Practice on Disclosure
para 3.4. . . 2

Police and Criminal Evidence Act 1984 (PACE) Codes of Practice (Codes A–H). . . 330, 331, 333, 337, 343, 346, 458, 459, 466, 467, 469, 470, 473, 476, 479, 481, 486, 509, 525, 620
Code A (Stop and Search). . . 330, 469
Code B (Search of Premises and the Seizure of Property). . . 330, 335, 469
Code C (Detention, Treatment, and Questioning). . . 272, 330, 331, 334, 335, 337, 345, 467, 468, 469, 470, 472, 473, 478, 479, 480–1, 725
Code C, para 1.7(b). . . 272
Code C, para 3.1. . . 478, 479
Code C, para 3.2. . . 478, 479
Code C, para 3.5. . . 478
Code C, para 5. . . 473
Code C, para 6. . . 473
Code C, para 6.6. . . 478
Code C, para 6.12. . . 474
Code C, para 6.12A. . . 474
Code C, para 6.13. . . 474
Code C, para 10. . . 467, 471
Code C, paras 10.1–10.9. . . 335
Code C, para 10.1. . . **471**, 472, 479
Code C, para 10.2. . . 479
Code C, para 10.4. . . **471**
Code C, para 10.5. . . 471, **508**
Code C, para 10.7. . . 471, **508**
Code C, para 10.8. . . **471**, 479
Code C, para 10.10. . . 523
Code C, para 10.11. . . 523
Code C, para 11.1. . . 479
Code C, para 11.1A. . . 473, 479
Code C, para 11.2. . . 479
Code C, para 11.4. . . 508
Code C, para 11.5. . . 480
Code C, para 11.6. . . 509
Code C, para 11.7. . . 467, 479

Code C, para 11.9. . . 480

Code C, para 11.10. . . 480

Code C, para 11.11. . . 467, 479

Code C, para 11.13. . . 337,
471, 479

Code C, para 11.15. . . 272,
336, 467, 477, 479

Code C, para
11.17–11.20. . . 477

Code C, para 11.18. . . 272

Code C, para 13.4. . . 479

Code C, para 13.5. . . 476

Code C, para 16. . . 471

Code C, para 16.1. . . **471**, 509

Code C, para 16.2. . . **472**,
473, **509**

Code C, para 16.5. . . 467, 473

Code C, Annex B, para
A1. . . 474

Code C, Annex B, para
A4. . . 475

Code C, Annex C. . . 472

Code C, Annex D,
para 2. . . 472

Code C, Annex E. . . 272

Code C, Note 1B. . . 467

Code C, Note 10D. . . 508

Code C, Note 16B. . . 472

Code D (Identification). . . 278,
282, 284, 290, 291, 293,
294, 297, 298, 330, 337, 469

Code D, para 1.2. . . 290, 297

Code D, para 3. . . 290

Code D, para 3, Pt A. . . 290

Code D, para 3, Pt B. . . 290, 291

Code D, para 3, Pt C. . . 290, 292

Code D, para 3.1. . . 282, 290

Code D, para 3.1(b). . . 293

Code D, para 3.2 (a). . . 291

Code D, para 3.2 (b). . . 291

Code D, para 3.2 (c). . . 291

Code D, para 3.2 (d)–(e). . . 291

Code D, paras 3.9–3.10. . . 293

Code D, para 3.11. . . 293

Code D, para 3.12. . . 290,
291, 293

Code D, paras 3.14–3.16. . . 291

Code D, paras 3.17–3.20. . . 291

Code D, para 3.17. . . 293

Code D, paras 3.34–3.37. . . 291

Code D, para 3.35. . . 293

Code D, para 3.36. . . 291, 293,
294

Code D, paras 3.38–3.41. . . 292

Code D, para 6.3. . . 526

Code D, Annex 3. . . 293

Code D, Note 6D. . . 526

Code E (Audio Recording
Interviews with Suspects). . .
303, 316, 331, 470

Code F (Visual Recording with
Sound of Interviews with
Suspects). . . 316, 470

Code G (Statutory Powers
of Arrest by Police
Officers). . . 470

Code G, section 3. . . 471

Code H (Questioning of
Suspects under the Terrorism
Act 2000). . . 470

Practice Direction (Criminal
Proceedings: Consolidation)
[2002] 1 WLR 2870. . . 43

Practice Direction (Submission
of No Case) [1962] 1 WLR
227. . . 43

Undercover Operations Code of
Practice. . . 341

TABLE OF CASES

United Kingdom

A v H [2016] EWHC 762 (Fam). . . 112

A v Secretary of State for the Home Department (No 2) [2005] 3 WLR 1249, HL. . . 324

AAZ v BBZ [2016] EWHC 3349 (Fam). . . 731, 740

A (Care Proceedings: Burden of Proof) [2018] Re 4 WLR 117, CA. . . 88

A (a Child) (Abduction: Contempt), Re [2009] 1 FLR 1, CA. . . 87

A (a child) (disclosure), Re [2012] UKSC 60. . . 703

AB (Child Abuse: Expert Witnesses), Re [1995] 1 FLR 181. . . 653

AB v Crown Prosecution Service [2017] EWHC 2963. . . 102, 505, 512

Abbas v CPS [2015] EWHC 579. . . 217

Ablitt v Mills & Reeve (1995) The Times, 25 Oct, Ch D. . . 745

Aegis Blaze, The [1986] 1 Lloyd's Rep 203, CA. . . 742

Agassiz v London Tramway Co (1872) 21 WR 199. . . 28

Ahmed v Brumfitt (1967) 112 Sol Jo 32, CA. . . 194

Ainsworth v Wilding [1900] 2 Ch 315. . . 729

Air Canada v Secretary of State for Trade (No 2) [1983] 2 AC 394, HL. . . 678, 687, 699, 700, 701, 702

Aird v Prime Meridian Ltd [2007] BLR 105, CA. . . 666

Ajami v Comptroller of Customs [1954] 1 WLR 1405, PC. . . 645

Ajodha v The State [1981] 2 All ER 193, PC. . . 95, 481, 482, 487

Ajum Goolam Hossen & Co v Union Marine Insurance Co [1901] AC 362, PC. . . 103

Al Fayed v Metropolitan Police Commissioner [2002] EWCA Civ 780. . . 746

Al Rawi v Security Service [2011] UKSC 34. . . 702, 704

Al-Saedy v Musawi [2010] EWHC 3293 (Fam). . . 107

Alagaratnam v R [2011] Crim LR 232, CA. . . 482

Aldersey, Gibson v Hall, Re [1905] 2 Ch 181. . . 111

Alderson v Clay (1816) 1 Stark 405. . . 305, 430

Alexander v Arts Council of Wales [2001] 4 All ER 205, CA. . . 43

Alexander v Rayson [1936] 1 KB 169, CA. . . 43

Alfred Crompton Amusement Machines Ltd v Customs and Excise Comrs (No 2) [1974] AC 405, HL. . . 688, 689, 698, 700, 725

Ali v Secretary of State for the Home Department [1988] Imm AR 274, CA. . . 90

Alivon v Furnival (1834) 1 Cr M&R 277. . . 308

Alli v Alli [1965] 3 All ER 480. . . 269

Alves v DPP [1992] 4 All ER 787, HL. . . 211

Ambrose v Harris [2011] 1 WLR 2435, SC. . . 474

Amore v R (1994) 99 Cr App R 279, PC. . . 281

Anderson v Bank of British Columbia (1876) 2 Ch D 644. . . 732

Anderson v Morice (1875) LR 10 CP 609. . . 103

Anderson v R [1972] AC 100, PC. . . 314

Anderson v Weston (1840) 6 Bing NC 296. . . 313

Anderson v Whalley (1852) 3 Car&Kir 54. . . 187

Anthony v Anthony (1919) 35 TLR 559. . . 686

Aquarius Financial Enterprises Inc v Certain Underwriters at Lloyd's (2001) NLJ 694, QBD. . . 151

Arab Monetary Fund v Hashim [1989] 1 WLR 565, Ch D. . . 715

Arab Monetary Fund v Hashim (No 2) [1990] 1 All ER 673, Ch D. . . 715, 760

Arbrath v North Eastern Rly Co (1883) 11 QBD 440, CA, aff'd on appeal (1886) 11 App Cas 247, HL. . . 78

Armia Ltd v Daejan Developments Ltd [1979] SC 56. . . 746

Armory v Delamirie (1722) 1 Stra 505. . . 314

Armstrong v First York Ltd [2005] EWCA Civ 277. . . 658

Arthurton v R [2005] 1 WLR 949 PC. . . 540

Ashworth Hospital Authority v MGN Ltd [2002] 1 WLR 2033, HL, [2001] 1 WLR 515, CA. . . 692, 695

Asiatic Petroleum Co Ltd v Anglo-Persian Oil Co Ltd [1916] 1 KB 822, CA. . . 681

Assets Recovery Agency v Virtosu see Director of the Assets Recovery Agency v Virtosu

Associated Provincial Picture Houses Ltd v Wednesbury Corpn [1948] 1 KB 223, CA. . . 49, 261, 331, 501, 600

AT & T Istel Ltd v Tully [1993] AC 45, HL. . . 713, 720, 724

Attorney-General v Bowman (1791) 2 Bos&P 532n. . . 535

Attorney-General v Good (1825) M'Cle&Yo 286. . . 361

Attorney-General v Hitchcock (1847) 1 Exch 91. . . 28, 243, 245, 246

Attorney-General v Lundin (1982) 75 Cr App R 90, DC. . . 691

Attorney-General v Mulholland [1963] 2 QB 477. . . 691

Attorney-General v Radloff (1854) 10 Exch 84. . . 535

Attorney-General v Theakston (1820) 8 Price 89. . . 435

Attorney-General of Hong Kong v Yip Kai-foon [1988] 1 All ER 153, PC. . . 102

Attorney-General's Reference (No 3 of 1979) (1979) 69 Cr App R 411. . . 188

Attorney-General's Reference (No 3 of 1999) [2001] 1 All ER 577, HL. . . 332

Attorney-General's Reference (No 2 of 2000) [2001] 1 Cr App R 503 (36). . . 42

Attorney-General's Reference (No 3 of 2000) see R v Looseley; Attorney General's Reference (No 3 of 2000)

Attorney-General's Reference (No 7 of 2000) [2001] 1 WLR 1879, CA. . . 720

Attorney-General's Reference (No 2 of 2002) [2003] 1 Cr App R 321 (21), CA. . . 289, 317

Attorney-General's Reference (No 4 of 2002) [2003] 3 WLR 1153, [2005] 1 AC 264, HL. . . 75

Attorney-General's Reference (No 1 of 2003) [2003] 2 Cr App R 453 (29), CA. . . 446

Attorney-General's Reference (No 1 of 2004) [2004] 1 WLR 2111, CA. . . 74–5

Augustien v Challis (1847) 1 Exch 279. . . 305

Aveson v Lord Kinnaird (1805) 6 East 188. . . 449

Aviva v Kovacic [2017] EWHC 2772 (QB). . . 87

Avonwick Holdings Ltd v Willmont and Sayers [2016] EWCA Civ 1138. . . 738

B (a minor), Re [2000] 1 WLR 790, CA. . . 658

B (Children) (Care Proceedings: Standard of Proof), Re [2009] 1 AC 11, HL. . . 88, 90

B (Children) (Sexual Abuse), Re [2009] 1 AC 11, HL. . . 84

B (Children) (Sexual Abuse: Standard of Proof), Re [2009] 1 AC 61, HL. . . 90, 92, 93

B v Auckland District Law Society [2003] 2 AC 736, PC. . . 738, 747

B v Chief Constable of Avon and Somerset Constabulary [2001] 1 WLR 340, DC. . . 87

Baigent v Random House Group Ltd [2006] EWHC 719 (Ch). . . 17

Bains v DPP [1992] Crim LR 795, DC. . . 140

Baker v Rabetts (1954) 118 JPN 303. . . 140

Balabel v Air-India [1988] Ch 317, CA. . . 730, 731

Baldwin and Francis Ltd v Patents Appeal Tribunal [1959] AC 663. . . 119

Balfour v Foreign and Commonwealth Office [1994] 1 WLR 681, CA. . . 681, 701

Banbury Peerage Case (1811) 1 Sim&St 153. . . 107

Bank of England v Vagliano Bros [1891] AC 107, HL. . . 460

Bankers' Books Evidence Act 1879, R v Bono, Re (1913) 29 TLR 635. . . 311

Banque Keyser Ullmann SA v Skandia (UK) Insurance Co Ltd [1986] 1 Lloyd's Rep 336, CA. . . 740–1

Barclays Bank plc v Eustice [1995] 1 WLR 1238, CA. . . 740

Barford v Barford and McLeod [1918] P 140. . . 644

Barings plc, Re [1998] Ch 356, Ch D. . . 734, 735

Barings plc v Coopers and Lybrand [2001] EWCA Civ 1163; [2001] CPLR 451. . . 23

Barker v Wilson [1980] 1 WLR 884, DC. . . 310

Barkway v South Wales Transport Co Ltd [1948] 2 All ER 460, CA. . . 116

Barlow Clowes Gilt Managers Ltd, Re [1992] Ch 208, Ch D. . . 690

Barnaby v DPP [2015] 2 Cr App R 53 (4), DC. . . 387, 434, 446

Barnes v Chief Constable of Durham [1997] 2 Cr App R 505, DC. . . 205

Barnetson v Framlington Group Ltd [2007] 1 WLR 2443, CA. . . 750

Baron de Bode's Case (1845) 8 QB 208. . . 644

Baronetcy of Pringle of Stichill, Re [2016] UKPC 16. . . 107, 108

Barrett v Long (1851) 3 HL Cas 395. . . 535

Bastable v Bastable and Sanders [1968] 1 WLR 1684, CA. . . 91, 105

Bastin v Carew (1824) Ry&M 127. . . 210

Bater v Bater [1951] P 35, CA. . . 88, 89, 91

Battie-Wrightson, Cecil v Battie-Wrightson, Re [1920] 2 Ch 330. . . 304

Bayer v Clarkson Puckle Overseas Ltd [1989] NLJR 256, QBD. . . 149, 655

BBGP Managing General Partner Ltd v Babcock & Brown Global Partners [2011] Ch 296, Ch D. . . 739

Beare v Garrod (1915) 85 LJKB 717, CA. . . 218

Beck v Ministry of Defence [2005] 1 WLR 2206, CA. . . 667

Beckford v R (1993) 97 Cr App R 409, PC. . . 283, 284

Beckwith v Sydebotham (1807) 1 Camp 116. . . 654

Beech v Jones (1848) 5 CB 696. . . 188

Beer v W H Clench (1930) Ltd [1936] 1 All ER 449, DC. . . 431

Beeres v CPS West Midlands [2014] EWHC 283 (Admin). . . 458

Beghal v DPP [2015] UKSC 49. . . 52, 718

Belhaj v Director of Public Prosecutions [2018] 3 WLR 435, SC. . . 704

Benedetto v R [2003] 1 WLR 1545, PC. . . 265

Benham Ltd v Kythira Investments Ltd [2003] EWCA Civ 1794. . . 43

Bennett v Metropolitan Police Comr [1995] 2 All ER 1, Ch D. . . 698

Beresford v St Albans Justices (1905) 22 TLR 1. . . 17

Berezovsky v Abramovich [2011] EWHC 1143 (Comm). . . 747

Berger v Raymond & Son Ltd [1984] 1 WLR 625. . . 536

Berkeley Peerage Case (1811) 4 Camp 401, HL. . . 440, 441, 442

Berry Trade Ltd v Moussavi [2003] EWCA Civ 715. . . 753

Bessela v Stern (1877) 2 CPD 265, CA. . . 430

Bhimji v Chatwani (No 2) [1992] 1 WLR 1158, Ch D. . . 715

BHP Billiton Petroleum Ltd v Dalmine SpA [2003] BLR 271, CA. . . 78

Bilta (UK) Ltd (in liquidation) v Royal Bank of Scotland plc [2017] EWHC 3535 (Ch). . . 733

Bird v Keep [1918] 2 KB 692, CA. . . 437

Bishopsgate Investment Management Ltd (in provisional liquidation) v Maxwell [1992] 2 All ER 856, CA. . . 715

Black v Pastouna [2005] EWCA Civ 1389. . . 144

Black & Decker Inc v Flymo Ltd [1991] 1 WLR 753, Ch D. . . 735

Blake v DPP (1992) 97 Cr App R 169, DC. . . 684

Blunt v Park Lane Hotel [1942] 2 KB 253, CA. . . 714

Blyth v Blyth [1966] AC 643. . . 91, 105

BNP Paribas v Mezzotero [2004] IRLR 508, EAT. . . 751, 754

Bolkiah v KPMG [1999] 2 AC 222. . . 127

Bowen v Norman [1938] 1 KB 689. . . 108

Bowker v Williamson (1889) 5 TLR 382. . . 313

Bowman v Hodgson (1867) LR 1 P&D 362. . . 312

Boyle v Wiseman (1855) 11 Exch 360. . . 305

Bradford & Bingley plc v Rashid [2006] 1 WLR 2066, HL. . . 750, 751

Bradley v Ricardo (1831) 8 Bing 57. . . 207

Bradshaw v Bradshaw [1956] P 274n. . . 110

Bradshaw, Blandy v Willis, Re [1938] 4 All ER 143. . . 107

Brady (Inspector of Taxes) v Group Lotus Car Companies plc [1987] 3 All ER 1050, CA. . . 59

Braganza v BP Shipping [2015] 1 WLR 1661, SC. . . 90, 93

Brailey v Rhodesia Consolidated Ltd [1910] 2 Ch 95. . . 644

Bramblevale Ltd, Re [1970] Ch 128, CA. . . 87

Brandao v Barnett (1846) 12 Cl&Fin 787, HL. . . 121

Bratty v A-G for Northern Ireland [1963] AC 386, HL. . . 81, 83, 94, 103

Breadalbane Case, Campbell v Campbell (1867) LR 1 Sc&Div 182. . . 107

Brenan and Galen's Case (1847) 10 QB 492. . . 119

Brewster v Sewell (1820) 3 B&Ald 296. . . 11, 37, 307

Briamore Manufacturing Ltd, Re [1986] 1 WLR 1429, Ch D. . . 744

Brierley v Brierley and Williams [1918] P 257, P, D and Admlty. . . 437

Brighty v Pearson [1938] 4 All ER 127. . . 257

Brinks Ltd v Abu-Saleh [1995] 1 WLR 1478. . . 761

Briscoe v Briscoe [1966] 1 All ER 465. . . 149

Bristol Corpn v Cox (1884) 26 Ch D 678. . . 728

Bristow v Sequeville (1850) 5 Exch 275. . . 645

British Coal Corpn v Dennis Rye Ltd (No 2) 1 WLR 1113, CA. . . 747

British Steel Corpn v Granada Television Ltd [1981] AC 1096, HL. . . 691, 716, 717

British Thomson-Houston Co Ltd v British Insulated and Helsby Cables Ltd [1924] 2 Ch 160, CA. . . 432

Brizzalari v R [2004] EWCA Crim 310. . . 517

Brodie v Nicola Ward (t/a First Steps Nursery) [2008] All ER (D) 115 (Feb), EAT. . . 754

Broome v Broome [1955] P 190. . . 767

Brown v Rice [2007] EWHC 625, Ch. . . 753

Brown v Stott [2001] 2 WLR 817, PC. . . 718

Browne v Dunn (1893) 6 R 67, HL. . . 221

Bruce v Garden (1869) 18 WR 384. . . 430

Brunel University v Vaseghi [2007] IRLR 592, CA. . . 754

Brutus v Cozens [1973] AC 854. . . 35, 36

Bryce v Bryce [1933] P 83. . . 448

Buckingham v Daily News Ltd [1956] 2 QB 534, CA. . . 32, 318

Buckley v Law Society (No 2) [1984] 1 WLR 1101, Ch D. . . 680

Bullard v R [1957] AC 635, PC. . . 58, 80

Bulley's Settlement, Re [1886] WN 80, Ch D. . . 439

Bullivant v A-G for Victoria [1901] AC 196, HL. . . 726

Bullock v Bullock [1960] 1 WLR 975, DC. . . 110

Bumper Development Corpn Ltd v Metropolitan Police Comr [1991] 4 All ER 638, CA. . . 637

Burmah Oil Co Ltd v Bank of England [1980] AC 1090, HL. . . 678, 687, 697, 699, 700, 701

Burr v Ware RDC [1939] 2 All ER 688, CA. . . 431

Burrough v Martin (1809) 2 Camp 112. . . 187

Burton v Gilbert [1984] RTR 162, DC. . . 257

Butler v Board of Trade [1971] Ch 680. . . 739, 746

Butler v Mountgarret (1859) 7 HL Cas 633. . . 441

Buttes Gas and Oil Co v Hammer (No 3) [1981] QB 223, CA. . . 682, 729, 734

Byrne v Boadle (1863) 2 H&C 722. . . 114

C v C [1972] 3 All ER 577. . . 315

C v DPP [1995] 2 All ER 43, HL. . . 5

C plc v P [2007] 3 All ER 1034, CA. . . 720

C (a minor) (care proceedings: disclosure), In Re [1997] 2 WLR 322, CA. . . 721

C (a minor) v The Director of Public Prosecutions [1996] AC 1, HL. . . 620

Calcraft v Guest [1898] 1 QB 759, CA. . . 323, 742, 743, 746

Calenti v North Middlesex NHS Trust (2001) LTL 10 Apr 2001, QBD. . . 661

Callis v Gunn [1964] 1 QB 495, DC. . . 327, 454

Camelot Group v Centaur Communications Ltd [1999] QB 124, CA. . . 695

Campbell v DPP [2003] Crim LR 118, DC. . . 334

Campbell v Tameside Metropolitan Borough Council [1982] QB 1065, CA. . . 678, 698

Campbell v Wallsend Slipway & Engineering Co Ltd [1978] ICR 1015, DC. . . 114

Capron v R [2006] UKPC 34. . . 283, 284

Carl Zeiss Stiftung v Rayner & Keeler Ltd (No 2) [1967] 1 AC 853, HL. . . 121

Carlson v Townsend [2001] 3 All ER 663, CA. . . 664

Casey v Cartwright [2007] 2 All ER 78, CA. . . 662

CAS (Nominees) Ltd v Nottingham Forest plc [2001] 1 All ER 954, Ch D. . . 730

Castle v Cross [1984] 1 WLR 1372; [1985] 1 All ER 87, DC. . . 104, 372

Catherina Maria, The (1866) LR 1 A&E 53. . . 436

CF v The Security Service [2013] EWHC 3402 (QB). . . 706

CH Beazer (Commercial and Industrial) Ltd v R M Smith Ltd (1984) 3 Const LJ 196. . . 744

Chambers v DPP [1995] Crim LR 896, DC. . . 35

Chan Kau v R [1955] AC 206, PC. . . 81

Chan Wai-Keung v R [1995] 2 All ER 438, PC. . . 266

Chan Wei Keung v R [1967] 2 AC 160, PC. . . 486

Chandler v Church [1987] NLJ Rep 451, Ch D. . . 740

Chandrasekera v R [1937] AC 220, PC. . . 365, 366

Chapman v Kirke [1948] 2 KB 450. . . 118

Chapman v Walton (1833) 10 Bing 57. . . 22

Chappell v DPP (1988) 89 Cr App R 82. . . 16

Chapronière v Mason (1905) 21 TLR 633, CA. . . 114

Chard v Chard [1956] P 259. . . 99, 103, 109, 110

Chatterton v Secretary of State for India in Council [1895] 2 QB 189, CA. . . 681, 697

Cheddar Valley Engineering Ltd v Chaddlewood Homes Ltd [1992] 1 WLR 820. . . 752

Chenie v Watson (1797) Peake Add Cas. . . 123 31

Chief Constable of Avon and Somerset Constabulary v Jest [1986] RTR 372, DC... 42

Chief Constable of Greater Manchester Police v McNally [2002] 2 Cr App R 617 (37), CA. . . 685

Chipchase v Chipchase [1939] P 391. . . 110, 111

Chocoladefabriken Lindt & Sprüngli AG v Nestlé Co Ltd [1978] RPC 287. . . 752

Christopher Brown Ltd v Genossenschaft Oesterreichischer [1954] 1 QB 8. . . 113

Clarke v Clarke (1879) 5 LR Ir 47. . . 312

Clarke v Saffery (1824) Ry&M 126. . . 210

Cleveland County Council v F 1995] 1 WLR 785, Fam Div. . . 722

Clifford v Clifford [1961] 1 WLR 1274 P, D and Admlty. . . 244

Clifford v Timms [1908] AC 12. . . 765

Clingham v Kensington and Chelsea London Borough Council (2001) 165 JP 322, DC. . . 418

Closmadeuc v Carrel (1856) 18 CB 36. . . 314

Cobra Golf Ltd v Rata [1998] Ch 109, Ch D. . . 715

Coldman v Hill [1919] 1 KB 443, CA. . . 79

Collier v Nokes (1849) 2 Car&Kir 1012. . . 120

Collier v Simpson (1831) 5 C&P 73. . . 655

Collins v Carnegie (1834) 1 Ad&El 695. . . 436

Collins v Secretary of State for Justice [2016] 2 WLR 1303, DC. . . 81

Collinson v Mabbott (1984) The Times, 10 Oct, DC. . . 257

Colvilles Ltd v Devine [1969] 1 WLR 475, HL. . . 116

Comfort Hotels Ltd v Wembley Stadium Ltd [1988] 1 WLR 872, Ch D. . . 735

Commissioner of Police of the Metropolis v Ebanks (2012) 176 JP 751, DC. . . 87

Competition and Markets Authority v Concordia International RX (UK) [2018] EWCA Civ 1881. . . 703

Comptroller of Customs v Western Electric Co Ltd [1966] AC 367. . . 431

Conerney v Jacklin [1985] Crim LR 234, CA. . . 689

Conlon v Conlons Ltd [1952] 2 All ER 462, CA. . . 742

Conlon v Simms [2007] 3 All ER 802, CA. . . 765

Connell v The Crown Prosecution Service (2011) 175 JP 151, DC. . . 257

Constandas v Lysandrou [2018] 2 FLR 983, CA. . . 59

Conway v Hotten [1976] 2 All ER 213, DC. . . 473

Conway v Rimmer [1968] AC 910. . . 676, 677, 678, 680, 686, 687, 700, 701, 702

Cook v DPP [2001] Crim LR 321, DC. . . 148

Cooke v Tanswell (1818) 8 Taunt 450. . . 313

Cooper v Rowlands [1972] Crim LR 53. . . 114

Cope v Cope (1833) 1 Mood&R 269. . . 108

Copeland v Commissioner of Police of the Metropolis [2015] 3 All ER 391, CA 59

Corfield v Hodgson [1966] 2 All ER 205. . . 261

Corke v Corke and Cook [1958] P 93. . . 194, 195

Cornwell v Myskow [1987] 2 All ER 504, CA. . . 534

Cosgrave v Pattison [2001] CPLR 177, Ch D. . . 663

Coulson v Disborough [1894] 2 QB 316, CA. . . 216

Council for the Regulation of Healthcare Professionals v General Medical Council [2007] 1 WLR 3094, (Admin). . . 323, 340

Council of Civil Service Unions v Minister for the Civil Service [1985] AC 374, HL. . . 682

Countess of Shelburne v Earl of Inchiquin (1784) 1
    Bro CC 338. . . 92

Coventry Newspapers Ltd ex p [1993] QB 278,
    CA. . . 689

Crease v Barrett (1835) 1 Cr M&R 919. . . 441

Credland v Knowler (1951) 35 Cr App R 48,
    DC. . . 261

Crescent Farm (Sidcup) Sports Ltd v Sterling Offices
    Ltd [1972] Ch 553. . . 739, 742

Crest Homes plc v Marks [1987] AC 529, HL. . . 715

Crosdale v R [1995] 2 All ER 500, PC. . . 41

Crossland v DPP [1988] 3 All ER 712. . . 257

Cummings v CPS [2016] EWHC 3624
    (Admin). . . 187, 188

Cummins, Re [1972] Ch 62, CA. . . 269

Curtis v Curtis (1905) 21 TLR 676. . . 269

CXX v DXX [2012] EWHC 1535 (QB). . . 760, 761

D v NSPCC [1978] AC 171, HL. . . 47, 680–1, 685,
    688, 690, 746, 754

D (a child), Re [2011] 4 All ER 434, CA. . . 747

D (a minor), Re [1986] 2 FLR 189, Fam D. . . 375, 428

D (Children), Re [2009] 2 FLR 668, CA. . . 90

D (Infants), Re [1970] 1 WLR 599, CA. . . 680

D (minors), Re [1993] Fam 231, CA. . . 755

D B Deniz Nakliyati TAS v Yugopetrol [1992] 1 All ER
    205, CA. . . 310

Daintrey ex p Holt, Re [1893] 2 QB 116. . . 753

Daley v R [1993] 4 All ER 86; [1994] 1 AC 117,
    PC. . . 41, 285, 401

Daniel v Wilkin (1852) 7 Exch 429. . . 436

Daniel Alfredo Condori Vilca v Xstrata Limited,
    Compania Minera Antapaccay SA [2017] EWHC
    1582 (QB). . . 667

Daniels v Walker [2001] 1 WLR 1382, CA. . . 663

Davarifar v R [2009] EWCA Crim 2294. . . 232, 233

Davey v Harrow Corpn [1958] 1 QB 60, CA. . . 121

Davie v Edinburgh Magistrates 1953 SC 34 (Court of
    Session). . . 655, 658

Davies v DPP [1954] AC 378, HL. . . 258

Davies v Fortior Ltd [1952] 1 All ER 1359,
    QBD. . . 443

Davies v Lowndes (1843) 6 Man&G 471. . . 441

Dawson v McKenzie (1908) 45 SLR 473. . . 262

Day v Grant [1987] 3 All ER 678 CA. . . 688

de Beéche v South American Stores [1935] AC 148,
    HL. . . 645

De Thoren v A-G (1876) 1 App Cas 686, HL. . . 104

Dean v Dean [1987] 1 FLR 517, CA. . . 87

Dechert LLP v Eurasian Natural Resources
    Corporation Limited [2016] EWCA Civ 375. . . 747

Dellow's Will Trusts, Re [1964] 1 WLR 451, Ch
    D. . . 88, 90

Den Norske Bank ASA v Antonatos [1999] QB 271,
    CA. . . 716

Dennis v White [1916] 2 KB 1. . . 118

Deokinanan v R [1969] 1 AC 20, PC. . . 455

Dera Commercial Estate v Derya Inc, 'The Sur' [2018]
    EWHC 1673 (Comm). . . 61, 78

Derby & Co Ltd v Weldon (No 7) [1990] 1 WLR
    1156, Ch D. . . 739

Derby & Co Ltd v Weldon (No 8) [1991] 1 WLR 73,
    CA. . . 745

Derby & Co Ltd v Weldon (No 10) [1991] 1 WLR
    660, Ch D. . . 747, 748

Desmond v Bower [2010] EMLR 5, CA. . . 535

Devala Provident Gold Mining Co, Re (1883) 22 Ch
    D 593. . . 431

Deybel's Case (1821) 4 B&Ald 243. . . 120

Dickinson v Rushmer (2002) 152 NLJ 58. . . 727

Dillon v R [1982] AC 484, PC. . . 114

Dingwall v J Wharton (Shipping) Ltd [1961] 2 Lloyd's
    Rep 213, HL. . . 85

Director of the Assets Recovery Agency v Virtosu
    [2009] 1 WLR 2808, [2008] EWHC 149 (QB). . .
    93, 760

Director of the Serious Fraud Office v Eurasian
    Natural Resources Corporation Ltd [2018] EWCA
    Civ 2006, [2019] 1 All ER 1026, CA; [2017] EWHC
    1017 (QB). . . 727, 728, 729, 730, 732

Dixons Stores Group Ltd v Thames Television plc
    [1993] 1 All ER 349. . . 752

Doe d Banning v Griffin (1812) 15 East 293. . . 441

Doe d Bowley v Barnes (1846) 8 QB 1037. . . 113

Doe d Church and Phillips v Perkins (1790) 3 Term
    Rep 749. . . 188

Doe d France v Andrews (1850) 15 QB 756. . .
    110, 436

Doe d Gilbert v Ross (1840) 7 M&W 102. . . 306

Doe d Jenkins v Davies (1847) 10 QB 314. . . 38, 441

Doe d Lord Arundel v Fowler (1850) 14 QB
    700. . . 313

Doe d Mudd v Suckermore (1837) 5 Ad&El 703. . .
    311, 636, 672

Doe d Strode v Seaton (1834) 2 Ad&El 171. . . 436

Doe d Tatum v Catomore (1851) 16 QB 745. . . 313

Doe d Tilman v Tarver (1824) Ry&M 141. . . 441

Doe d Warren v Bray (1828) 8 B&C 813. . . 438

Doe d West v Davis (1806) 7 East 363. . . 304

Dost Aly Khan's Goods (1880) 6 PD 6. . . 644

Douglas v Hello! Ltd [2003] CP Rep 42, CA. . . 423

Dowling v Dowling (1860) 10 ICLR 236. . . 31

DPP v A & B C Chewing Gum Ltd [1968] 1 QB
    159. . . 639

DPP v Agyemayang (2009) 173 JP 487, DC. . . 562

DPP v Barker [2004] EWHC 2502 (Admin). . . 73

DPP v Berry [2019] EWHC 825 (Admin). . . 42

DPP v Billington [1988] 1 All ER 435, DC. . . 473

DPP v Blake [1989] 1 WLR 432, (1989) 89 Cr App R 179, DC. . . 467

DPP v Boardman [1975] AC 421, HL. . . 237, 621

DPP v Chard [2007] EWHC 90 (DC). . . 571

DPP v Christof [2016] 2 Cr App R 56 (6), DC. . . 35, 118

DPP v D; DPP v Rous (1992) 94 Cr App R 185, DC. . . 473

DPP v Evans [2003] Crim LR 338, DC. . . 334

DPP v Goodwin [1991] RTR 303. . . 334

DPP v Hester [1973] AC 296, HL. . . 253, 255

DPP v Hynde [1998] 1 All ER 649, [1998] 1 Cr App R 288, DC. . . 118

DPP v Jobling, 26 May 2016, DC, unreported. . . 285

DPP v Jordan [1977] AC 699, HL. . . 639

DPP v Kearley [1992] 2 AC 28. . . 367

DPP v Kilbourne [1973] AC 729, HL. . . 14, 24, 255

DPP v Lawrence [2008] 1 Cr App R 147 (10), CA. . . 39

DPP v Leigh [2010] EWHC 3450 (DC). . . 370

DPP v Marshall [1988] 3 All ER 683, DC. . . 344

DPP v Morgan [1976] AC 182, HL. . . 58

DPP v Ping Lin [1976] AC 574, HL. . . 454, 464

DPP v R [2007] All ER 176; [2007] EWHC 1842 (DC). . . 136, 376, 386, 394

DPP v Smith [1961] AC 290. . . 102

DPP v Stonehouse [1978] AC 55, HL. . . 35, 45, 46

DPP v Sugden [2018] 2 Cr App R 101 (8), (Admin), [2018] Crim LR 752. . . 185, 188, 303, 305, 306

DPP v Whittaker [2016] 1 WLR 1035, DC. . . 64

DPP v Wright [2010] QB 224, DC. . . 73

DPP v Wynne [2001] EWHC 21 (Admin). . . 658

DPP (Jamaica) v Bailey [1995] 1 Cr App R 257, PC. . . 80

Drinkwater v Porter (1835) 7 C&P 181. . . 441

Dubai Aluminium Co Ltd v Al Alawi [1999] 1 WLR 1964, QBD. . . 739, 740

Dubai Bank Ltd v Galadari [1990] Ch 98, CA. . . 733

Duchess Di Sora v Phillipps (1863) 10 HL Cas 624. . . 637

Duff Development Co v Government of Kelantan [1924] AC 797. . . 119, 121

Duke of Beaufort v John Aird & Co (1904) 20 TLR 602. . . 436

Duke of Beaufort v Smith (1849) 4 Exch 450. . . 436

Duke of Wellington, Glentanar v Wellington, Re [1947] Ch 506. . . 36, 644

Duncan, Re [1968] P 306. . . 725

Duncan v Cammell Laird & Co Ltd [1942] AC 624, HL. . . 676, 677, 681, 697, 699, 700

Dunlop Slazenger International Ltd v Joe Bloggs Sports Ltd [2003] EWCA Civ 901. . . 747

Dunn v Snowden (1862) 32 LJ Ch 104. . . 110

Duporte v The Queen [2015] UKPC 18. . . 283

Dwyer v Collins (1852) 21 LJ Ex 225, 7 Exch 639. . . 307, 736

E (a child) (Family Proceedings: Evidence), Re [2016] 4 WLR 105, CA. . . 68, 92, 141, 326

Ealing London Borough v Woolworths plc [1995] Crim LR 58, DC. . . 344

Earl v Hector Whaling Ltd [1961] 1 Lloyd's Rep 459, CA. . . 92

Earl of Dunraven v Llewellyn (1850) 15 QB 791. . . 441

Easson v London & North Eastern Rly Co [1944] KB 421. . . 115

East London Rly Co v Thames Conservators (1904) 90 LT 347, Ch D. . . 439

East Riding of Yorkshire Council v Dearlove [2012] EWHC 278 [2012] RTR 29 (DC). . . 340

Edward C Behague v The Commissioners for Her Majesty's Revenue & Customs [2013] UKFTT 596 (TC). . . 728

Edwards v Brookes (Milk) Ltd [1963] 1 WLR 795, QBD. . . 431

Edwards and Osakwe v DPP [1992] Crim LR 576, DC. . . 446

Edwards-Tubb v JD Wetherspoon plc [2011] EWCA Civ 136, [2011] 1 WLR 1373. . . 664, 667

EG Music v SF (Film) Distributors [1978] FSR 121. . . 536

Eli Lilley v Genetech, Inc [2018] EWHC 3522 (Pat). . . 661

Ellis v Allen [1914] 1 Ch 904. . . 124

Ellis v Home Office [1953] 2 QB 135, CA. . . 676

Ellor v Selfridge & Co Ltd (1930) 46 TLR 236. . . 114

Enfield London Borough Council v SA [2010] 1 FLR 1836, COP. . . 415, 419

Engelke v Mussmann [1928] AC 433, HL. . . 121

English and American Insurance Co Ltd v Herbert Smith & Co [1988] FSR 232, Ch D. . . 745

English Exporters (London) Ltd v Eldonwall Ltd [1973] Ch 415. . . 11, 655

Enoch and Zaretzky, Bock & Co's Arbitration, Re [1910] 1 KB 327, CA. . . 150

Environment Agency v ME Foley Contractors Ltd [2002] 1 WLR 1754, DC. . . 65

Esso Petroleum Co Ltd v Southport Corpn [1956] AC 218, HL. . . 9

Ettenfield v Ettenfield [1940] P 96, CA. . . 108

Evans v Chief Constable of Surrey [1988] QB 588, QBD. . . 687, 699

Evans v Getting (1834) 6 C&P 586. . . 121, 438

Everingham v Roundell (1838) 2 Mood&R 138. . . 306

Ewer v Ambrose (1825) 3 B&C 746. . . 207, 209

F v Child Support Agency [1999] 2 FLR 244, QBD. . . 108

F v CPS [2015] EWHC 2527 (DC). . . 331

F v F [1968] P 506. . . 91

F (an infant) v Chief Constable of Kent [1982] Crim LR 682, DC. . . 39

Fagernes, The [1927] P 311. . . 121

Fairfield-Mabey Ltd v Shell UK Ltd [1989] 1 All ER 576, QBD. . . 222, 748

Fairman v Fairman [1949] P 341. . . 269

Fallon v Calvert [1960] 2 QB 201, CA. . . 150

Family Housing Association (Manchester) Ltd v Michael Hyde & Partners (a firm) [1993] 1 WLR 354, CA. . . 750

Farm Assist Ltd v Secretary of State for the Environment, Food and Rural Affairs (No 2) [2009] EWHC 1102 (TCC). . . 752

Farm Assist Ltd (in liquidation) v Secretary of State for Environment, Food and Rural Affairs [2008] EWHC 3079 (TCC). . . 749

Farrell v Secretary of State for Defence [1980] 1 WLR 172, HL. . . 9

Faulder v Silk (1811) 3 Camp 126. . . 436, 765

Fayed v Al-Tajir [1988] QB 712, CA. . . 682

Fazil-Alizadeh v Nikbin (1993) The Times, 19 Mar, CA. . . 753

Fennell v Jerome Property Maintenance Ltd (1986) The Times, 26 Nov, QBD. . . 194

Ferguson v R [1979] 1 WLR 94, PC. . . 85

Ferster v Ferster [2016] EWCA Civ 717. . . 753

Field v Leeds City Council [2001] CPLR 129. . . 645

Financial Reporting Council Ltd v Sports Direct International plc [2019] 2 All ER 974, Ch D. . . 737, 739, 747

Fitzwalter Peerage Claim (1844) 10 Cl&Fin 193, HL. . . 312

Flack v Baldry [1988] 1 All ER 673, HL. . . 36

Fleet v Murton (1871) LR 7 QB 126. . . 22

Fletcher, Reading v Fletcher, Re [1917] 1 Ch 339, CA. . . 450

Folkes v Chadd (1782) 3 Doug KB 157. . . 28, 644

Forbes v Samuel [1913] 3 KB 706. . . 304

Forster v Friedland [1992] CA Transcript 1052. . . 753

Fowke v Berington [1914] 2 Ch 308, Ch D. . . 438

Fox v General Medical Council [1960] 1 WLR 1017, PC. . . 197

France v The Queen [2012] UKPC 28. . . 281

Frank Truman Export Ltd v Metropolitan Police Comr [1977] QB 952. . . 736

Fred Chappell Ltd v National Car Parks Ltd (1987) The Times, 22 May, QBD. . . 79

Freemantle v R [1994] 3 All ER 225, PC. . . 279

Fryer v Gathercole (1849) 13 Jur 542. . . 672

Fryer v Pearson & Anor (2000) The Times, 4 Apr, CA. . . 115

Fuld's Estate (No 3), Re, Hartley v Fuld [1968] P 675. . . 92, 637

Fulham Leisure Holdings Ltd v Nicholson Graham and Jones (a firm) [2006] 2 All ER 599, Ch D. . . 748

Fuller v Strum [2002] 1 WLR 525. . . 658

G (A) v G (T) [1970] 2 QB 643, CA. . . 431, 432

G (a Child) (Non-accidental Injury: Standard of Proof), Re [2001] 1 FCR 97, CA. . . 92

G (a minor), Re [1996] 1 WLR 1407, CA. . . 721

Gale v Serious Organised Crime Agency [2011] 1 WLR 2760, SC. . . 93

Galler v Galler [1954] P 252, CA. . . 91, 269

Galliford Try Construction Ltd v Mott MacDonald [2008] EWHC 603 (TCC). . . 749

Gamlen Chemical Co (UK) Ltd v Rochem Ltd [1980] 1 All ER 1049. . . 740

Garner v DPP (1990) 90 Cr App R 178, DC. . . 373

Garton v Hunter [1969] 2 QB 37, CA. . . 32

Garvin v Domus Publishing Ltd [1989] 3 WLR 344, Ch D. . . 715

Gaskin v Liverpool City Council [1980] 1 WLR 1549, CA. . . 680

Gatland v Metropolitan Police Comr [1968] 2 QB 279. . . 65

Gatty and Gatty v A-G [1951] P 444. . . 106

Geest plc v Lansiquot [2002] 1 WLR 3111, PC. . . 78

General Accident Fire and Life Assurance Co Ltd v Tanter [1984] 1 WLR 100. . . 748

George v Davies [1911] 2 KB 445. . . 121

George v Eagle Air Services Ltd [2009] UKPC 21. . . 116

George Doland Ltd v Blackburn, Robson, Coates & Co [1972] 1 WLR 1338, QBD. . . 747, 748

Gestmin SGPS SA v Credit Suisse (UK) Limited [2013] EWHC 3560 (Comm). . . 3

Gibbins v Skinner [1951] 2 KB 379. . . 114

Gilbey v Great Western Rly Co (1910) 102 LT 202, CA. . . 449

Ginesi v Ginesi [1948] P 179, CA. . . 91

Glendarroch, The [1894] P 226, CA. . . 80

Glinski v McIver [1962] AC 726, HL. . . 373

Gnitrow Ltd v Cape plc [2000] 1 WLR 2327, CA. . . 751

Goddard v Nationwide Building Society [1987] QB 670, CA. . . 744, 745, 746

Goldman v Hesper [1988] 1 WLR 1238, CA. . . 747

Goldsmith v DPP (2010) 174 JP 84, DC. . . 71

Gollins v Gollins [1964] AC 644, HL. . . 102

Goodridge v Chief Constable of Hampshire Constabulary [1999] 1 WLR 1558, QBD. . . 701, 725

Goodright d Stevens v Moss (1777) 2 Cowp 591. . . 440

Goody v Odhams Press Ltd [1967] 1 QB 333. . . 762

Goold v Evans & Co [1951] 2 TLR 1189, CA. . . 318

Gordon v Gordon [1903] P 141. . . 108

Gorjat v Gorjat [2010] EWHC 1537 (Ch D). . . 61

Gough v Chief Constable of the Derbyshire Constabulary [2002] QB 1213, CA. . . 87

Gough v DPP [2013] EWHC 3267 (Admin). . . 639

Graham v Chorley Borough Council [2006] EWCA Civ 92. . . 43

Grant v Southwestern and County Properties Ltd [1975] Ch 185, Ch D. . . 729

Grant v The State [2006] 2 WLR 835, PC. . . 50, 405

Great Atlantic Insurance Co v Home Insurance Co [1981] 1 WLR 529, CA. . . 747

Great Future International Ltd v Sealand Housing Corporation (2002) LTL 25 July. . . 48

Great Future International Ltd v Sealand Housing Corporation [2004] EWHC 124 (Ch). . . 714

Greaves v Greenwood (1877) 2 Ex D 289, CA. . . 110

Greenough v Eccles (1859) 5 CBNS 786. . . 209

Greenough v Gaskell (1833) 1 My&K 98. . . 727

Gregory v Tavernor (1833) 6 C&P 280. . . 189

Griffiths v CPS [2018] EWHC 3062 (Admin). . . 206, 210

Grinsted v Hadrill [1953] 1 WLR 696, CA. . . 43

Grobbelaar v Sun Newspapers Ltd (1999) The Times, 12 Aug, CA. . . 48

Guinness Peat Properties Ltd v Fitzroy Robinson Partnership (a firm) [1987] 1 WLR 1027, [1987] 2 All ER 716, CA. . . 729, 734, 735, 744

Gumbley v Cunningham [1989] 1 All ER 5, HL. . . 635

GUR Corpn v Trust Bank of Africa Ltd [1987] QC 599, [1986] 3 All ER 449, CA. . . 121

H v L and R, Re [2007] 2 FLR 162, Fam D. . . 216

H v Schering Chemicals Ltd [1983] 1 WLR 143, QBD. . . 427, 655

H (minors) (sexual abuse: standard of proof), Re [1996] AC 563, HL. . . 89, 92

Haines v Guthrie (1884) 13 QBD 818, CA. . . 441

Halawa v Federation Against Copyright Theft [1995] 1 Cr App R 21, DC. . . 39, 40

Hales v Kerr [1908] 2 KB 601, DC. . . 24, 535

Hall v R [1971] 1 WLR 298, PC. . . 492, 493

Hamilton v Naviede [1995] 2 AC 75, HL. . . 687

Hammond v Wilkinson [2001] Crim LR 323. . . 147

Handmade Films (Productions) Ltd v Express Newspapers [1986] FSR 463, Ch D. . . 692, 693, 694

Harley v Smith [2010] EWCA Civ 78. . . 637

Harmony Shipping Co SA v Saudi Europe Line Ltd [1979] 1 WLR 1380, CA. . . 127

Harrison v Turner (1847) 10 QB 482. . . 430

Hart v Lancashire & Yorkshire Rly Co (1869) 21 LT 261. . . 25

Harvey v R [1901] AC 601, PC. . . 436, 765

Hatton v Cooper [2001] RTR 544, CA. . . 535

Haw Tua Tau v Public Prosecutor [1982] AC 136. . . 505

Hawick Jersey International Ltd v Caplan (1988) The Times, 11 Mar, QBD. . . 753

Haynes v Doman [1899] 2 Ch 13, CA. . . 657

Heath v Deane [1905] 2 Ch 86, Ch D. . . 436

Heath, Re; Stacey v Bird [1945] Ch 417. . . 108

Heather v PE Consulting Group [1973] Ch 189. . . 121

Hehir v Metropolitan Police Comr [1982] 1 WLR 715. . . 698

Hellard v Irwin Mitchell [2012] EWHC 2656, Ch. . . 747

Helliwell v Piggott-Sims [1980] FSR 582. . . 325

Henderson v Henry E Jenkins & Sons and Evans [1970] AC 282, HL. . . 115, 116

Hennessy v Wright (1888) 21 QBD 509. . . 681

Her Majesty's Advocate v P (Scotland) [2011] UKSC 44. . . 494

Herniman v Smith [1938] AC 305, HL. . . 37

Hetherington v Hetherington (1887) 12 PD 112. . . 109

Hickman v Berens [1895] 2 Ch 638, CA. . . 142

Hickman v Peacey [1945] AC 304, HL. . . 112

Highgrade Traders Ltd, Re [1984] BCLC 151, CA. . . 680–1, 734, 735

Hill v Clifford [1907] 2 Ch 236, CA. . . 436, 765

Hill v Hill [1959] 1 WLR 127, [1959] 1 All ER 281, PC. . . 104

Hill v Manchester and Salford Waterworks Co (1833) 5 B&Ad 866. . . 436

Hinds v London Transport Executive [1979] RTR 103, CA. . . 644

Hinds v Sparks [1964] Crim LR 717. . . 762

Hitchins v Eardley (1871) LR 2 P&D 248. . . 38

HIV Haemophiliac Litigation, Re [1996] PIQR P220. . . 678

Hobbs v Tinling [1929] 2 KB 1, CA. . . 220, 563

Hocking v Ahlquist Bros Ltd [1944] KB 120. . . 31, 314

Hodgson, Beckett v Ramsdale, Re (1885) 31 Ch D 177, CA. . . 269

Holcombe v Hewson (1810) 2 Camp 391, KB. . . 24

Holland v Her Majesty's Advocate [2005] HRLR 25, PC. . . 203, 204

Hollingham v Head (1858) 27 LJCP 241. . . 24, 28

Hollington v Hewthorn & Co Ltd [1943] KB 587, CA. . . 634, 758–9, 760, 762, 763, 764, 765, 767

Homes v Newman [1931] 2 Ch 112, Ch D. . . 442, 448

Hornal v Neuberger Products Ltd [1957] 1 QB 247, CA. . . 88, 89, 90, 91, 103

Hoskyn v Metropolitan Police Comr [1979] AC 474, HL. . . 131

Howe v Malkin (1878) 40 LT 196, DC. . . 448

Howglen Ltd, Re [2001] 1 All ER 376, Ch. . . 309

Hui Chi-ming v R [1991] 3 All ER 897, PC. . . 25, 773

Hunter v Chief Constable of West Midlands [1982] AC 529, HL. . . 760, 761, 764

Hurst v Evans [1917] 1 KB 352, KBD. . . 79, 89

Huth v Huth [1915] 3 KB 32, CA. . . 118

Iaciofano v DPP [2011] RTR 15, DC. . . 257

IBM Corpn v Phoenix International (Computers) Ltd [1995] 1 All ER 413, Ch D. . . 746

IBM United Kingdom Ltd v Prima Data International Ltd [1994] 4 All ER 748, Ch D. . . 715

Ibrahim v CPS [2016] EWHC 1750 (DC). . . 446

Ibrahim v R [1914] AC 599, PC. . . 454

Imerman v Tchenguiz [2011] Fam 116, CA. . . 326

Ingram v Percival [1969] 1 QB 548. . . 123

Inquiry under the Company Securities (Insider Dealing) Act 1985, Re an [1988] AC 660, HL. . . 693, 696

Interflora Inc v Marks and Spencer plc [2013] EWHC 936 (Ch). . . 661

Irish Society v Bishop of Derry (1846) 12 Cl&Fin 641, HL. . . 435, 438

Issais v Marine Insurance Co Ltd (1923) 15 Ll L Rep 186, CA. . . 89

ISTIL Group Inc v Zahoor [2003] EWHC 165 (Ch). . . 744

ITC Film Distributors v Video Exchange Ltd [1982] Ch 431. . . 323, 746

J v Oyston [1994] 1 WLR 694. . . 761

Jackson v Marley Davenport Ltd [2004] 1 WLR 2926, CA. . . 667

Jackson, Re; Jackson v Ward [1907] 2 Ch 354. . . 110

Jaggers v Binnings (1815) 1 Stark 64. . . 431

James v R (1970) 55 Cr App R 299, PC. . . 263

James v South Glamorgan County Council (1994) 99 Cr App R 321, DC. . . 147

Jamieson v Jamieson [1952] AC 525, HL. . . 102

Jankowski v District Court Wroclaw (Poland) [2016] EWHC 747 (Admin). . . 120

Jasiewicz v Jasiewicz [1962] 1 WLR 1426. . . 637

Jayasena v R [1970] AC 618, PC. . . 58, 60, 94

JC v CC [2001] EWCA Civ 1625. . . 419

Jefferies Group & Kvaerner International, 19 January 2007, unreported. . . 753

Jeffrey v Black [1978] QB 490, DC. . . 323, 327

Jenion, Re; Jenion v Wynne [1952] Ch 454, CA. . . 108

JN Dairies Ltd v Johal Dairies Ltd [2010] EWCA Civ 348. . . 152

John v Humphreys [1955] 1 WLR 325, DC. . . 64, 66

Johnson v Lindsay (1889) 53 JP 599, DC. . . 431

Johnston v Lawson (1824) 2 Bing 86. . . 440, 441

Joint Stock Co 'Aeroflot-Russian Airlines' v Leeds [2017] 1 WLR 4537 (Ch). . . 637

Jolly v DPP [2000] Crim LR 471, DC. . . 147

Jones v DPP [1962] AC 635, HL. . . 714

Jones v GD Searle & Co Ltd [1979] 1 WLR 101, CA. . . 742

Jones v Godrich (1845) 5 Moo PCC 16. . . 736

Jones v Great Central Rly Co [1910] AC 4, HL. . . 734

Jones v Great Western Rly Co (1930) 144 LT 194, HL. . . 62

Jones v Greater Manchester Police Authority [2002] ACD 4, DC. . . 535

Jones v Owens (1870) 34 JP 759. . . 323

Jones v University of Warwick [2003] 1 WLR 954, CA. . . 326

Joseph v Joseph [1915] P 122. . . 269

Joseph Constantine Steamship Line Ltd v Imperial Smelting Corpn Ltd [1942] AC 154, HL. . . 79

Joseph Hargreaves, Re [1900] 1 Ch 347. . . 686

Joseph Hill & Co, In re [2013] 2 Cr App R 218, CA. . . 527

Joy v Federation against Copyright Theft Ltd [1993] Crim LR 588, DC. . . 470

Joy v Phillips, Mills & Co Ltd [1916] 1 KB 849. . . 535

JSC BTA Bank v Ablyazov [2010] 1 Cr App R 131, CA. . . 723

JSC BTA Bank v Solodchenko [2010] EWHC 2843 (Ch), [2013] Ch 1, Ch D. . . 87, 727

Judd v Minister of Pensions and National Insurance [1966] 2 QB 580. . . 87

K (minors), Re [1988] 1 All ER 214, Fam D. . . 128

K (minors), Re [1994] 3 All ER 230, Fam Div. . . 722

K and H, Re [2015] EWCA Civ 543. . . 217

Kajala v Noble (1982) 75 Cr App R 149, CA. . . 32, 302, 316

Kanapathipillai v Parpathy [1956] AC 580. . . 108

Karamat v R [1956] AC 256, PC. . . 319

Karia v DPP (2002) 166 JP 753, QBD. . . 205

Karis v Lewis [2005] EWCA Civ 1637. . . 17

Karsten v Wood Green Crown Court [2014] EWHC 2900 (DC). . . 296

Kaslefsky v Kaslefsky [1951] P 38, CA. . . 102

Keane v Mount Vernon Colliery Co Ltd [1933] AC 309. . . 123

Keefe v Isle of Man Steam Packet Co Ltd [2010] EWCA Civ 683. . . 17

Kelly v Purvis [1983] QB 663, DC. . . 362

Kelly Communications Ltd v DPP [2003] Crim LR 479, DC. . . 104

Kennedy v Cordia (Services) LLP [2016] UKSC 6. . . 634, 638, 643, 645, 646, 652, 656, 658

Kennedy v DPP [2003] Crim LR 120, DC. . . 334

Kennedy v HM Advocate 1944 JC 171. . . 81

Kensington International Ltd v Republic of Congo [2007] EWCA Civ 1128. . . 723

Khaled v The Security Service [2016] EWHC 1727 (QB). . . 705

Khan v Khan [1982] 1 WLR 513, CA. . . 716, 723

Khawaja v Secretary of State for the Home Department [1983] 1 All ER 765. . . 88, 90

Kicks v Leigh [2014] EWHC 3926 (Ch). . . 61

Kilgour v Owen (1889) 88 LT Jo 7. . . 307

King v R [1969] 1 AC 304, PC. . . 327, 494

Kingley Developments v Brudenell & Ors [2016] EWCA Civ 980. . . 658

Kirby v Hickson (1850) 14 Jur 625. . . 120

Kirkup v DPP [2004] Crim LR 230, DC. . . 334

Kite, The [1933] P 154. . . 115

Knight v David [1971] 1 WLR 1671, Ch D. . . 427

Knowles v Knowles [1962] P 161. . . 108

Koscot Interplanetary (UK) Ltd, Re; Re Koscot AG [1972] 3 All ER 829. . . 428

Krajewski v Circuit Law Court, Swidnica, Poland [2016] EWHC 3241 (Admin). . . 120

Krishna v Trinidad & Tobago [2011] UKPC 18, PC. . . 266

Kuruma, Son of Kaniu v R [1955] AC 197, PC. . . 323, 327, 494

Kuwait Airways Corporation v Iraqi Airways Co [2005] 1 WLR 2734, CA. . . 740

L, Re [1997] 1 AC 16, HL. . . 732, 742

L v DPP [2003] QB 137, DC. . . 58, 60, 71

La Roche v Armstrong [1922] 1 KB 485. . . 749

Lafone v Griffin (1909) 25 TLR 308. . . 306

Lal Chand Marwari v Mahant Ramrup Gir (1925) 42 TLR 159. . . 111

Lam Chi-ming v R [1991] 3 All ER 172, PC. . . 495

Land Securities plc v Westminster City Council [1993] 1 WLR 286. . . 765

Lang v Lang [1955] AC 402, PC. . . 102

Langham v Wellingborough School Governors and Fryer (1932) 101 LJKB 513. . . 115

Lask v Gloucester Health Authority (1985) 2 PN 96, CA. . . 733

Lauderdale Peerage Case (1885) 10 App Cas 692, HL. . . 104

Lawrence v R [2014] UKPC 2. . . 204

Lazard Brothers & Co v Midland Bank [1933] AC 289. . . 120

Lee v South West Thames Regional Health Authority [1985] 1 WLR 845, CA. . . 743

Leeds City Council v Azam (1988) 153 JP 157, DC. . . 64

Leeds City Council v Hussain [2003] RTR 13, DC. . . 415

Legge v Edmonds (1855) 25 LJ Ch 125. . . 108

Lego Systems A/S v Lego M Lemelstrich Ltd [1983] FSR 155. . . 636

Lemos, Re [2018] 1 All ER 313, Ch D. . . 742

Leigh Ravenscroft v Canal & River Trust [2016] EWHC 2282 (Ch). . . 750

Levene v Roxhan [1970] 1 WLR 1322, CA. . . 762

Levison v Patent Steam Carpet Cleaning Ltd [1978] QB 69, CA. . . 79

Levy v Assicurazioni Generali [1940] AC 791, PC. . . 79

Li Shu-ling v R [1988] 3 All ER 138, PC. . . 32, 455

Lidderdale, Re (1912) 57 Sol Jo 3. . . 110

Lilley v Pettit [1946] KB 401, DC. . . 438

Lillicrap v Nalder & Son (a firm) [1993] 1 WLR 94, CA. . . 749

Line v Taylor (1862) 3 F&F 731. . . 315

Lively Ltd v City of Munich [1976] 1 WLR 1004, QBD. . . 127

Lloyd v Mostyn (1842) 10 M&W 478. . . 323

Lobban v R [1995] 1 WLR 877, [1995] 2 All ER 602, PC. . . 51, 487, 576

Lockheed-Arabia Corpn v Owen [1993] 3 All ER 641, CA. . . 311

London and County Securities v Nicholson [1980] 1 WLR 948. . . 688

London Borough of Newham v Osmar [2015] EWHC 3800 (DC). . . 410

London General Omnibus Co Ltd v Lavell [1901] 1 Ch 135, CA. . . 317

Lonrho Ltd v Shell Petroleum [1980] 1 WLR 627, HL. . . 687, 690

Lonrho plc v Fayed (No 4) [1994] QB 755, CA. . . 687, 690

Lonsdale v Heaton (1830) 1 You 58. . . 441

Lord Ashburton v Pape [1913] 2 Ch 469, CA. . . 744, 746

Lord Talbot de Malahide v Cusack (1864) 17 ICLR 213. . . 185

Loughans v Odhams Press [1963] 1 QB 299, CA. . . 762, 764

Lowery v R [1974] AC 85, PC. . . 605, 642

Lucas v Barking, Havering and Redbridge Hospitals NHS Trust [2004] 1 WLR 220, CA. . . 665

Lucas v Williams & Sons [1892] 2 QB 113. . . 672

Lui-Mei Lin v R [1989] AC 288, PC. . . 219

LW (Children) (Enforcement and Committal: Contact), Re [2011] 1 FCR 78, CA. . . 87

Lyell v Kennedy (1889) 14 App Cas 437, HL. . . 435

Lyell v Kennedy (No 3) (1884) 27 Ch D 1. . . 733, 736

M v DPP [2009] EWHC 752 (Admin). . . 318

M and R (minors), Re [1996] 4 All ER 239, CA. . . 641, 657

M (Children), Re [2008] EWCA Civ 1216. . . 92

M Isaacs & Sons Ltd v Cook [1925] 2 KB 391. . . 681

MA (Somalia) v Secretary of State for the Home Department [2011] 2 All ER 65, SC. . . 19

McCarthy v The Melita (Owners) (1923) 16 BWCC 222, CA. . . 439

McDarmaid v A-G [1950] P 218. . . 103

MacDonnell v Evans (1852) 11 CB 930. . . 305

McGartland v Secretary of State for the Home Department [2015] EWCA Civ 686. . . 704

McGrath v Field [1987] RTR 349, DC. . . 330

McGreevy v DPP [1973] 1 WLR 276, HL. . . 14

McIlkenny v Chief Constable of West Midlands Police Force [1980] QB 283, CA. . . 760, 764

McKeon v DPP [2008] RTR 14, DC. . . 61

MacKinnon v Donaldson Lufkin and Jenrette Securities Corpn [1986] 1 All ER 653, Ch D. . . 310

McPhee v The Queen [2016] 4 WLR 166, PC. . . 467

McPhilemy v Times Newspapers Ltd [1999] 3 All ER 775, CA. . . 49

McQuaker v Goddard [1940] 1 KB 687, CA. . . 120

McTaggart v McTaggart [1949] P 94, CA. . . 754

McVeigh v Beattie [1988] 2 All ER 500. . . 18

Mahadervan v Mahadervan [1964] P 233. . . 92, 104, 105

Maher v DPP (2006) 170 JP 441, DC. . . 389, 397

Mahon v Osborne [1939] 2 KB 14, CA. . . 99

Makanjuola v Metropolitan Police Comr [1992] 3 All ER 617, CA. . . 697, 698

Malcolm v DPP [2007] 1 WLR 1230, DC. . . 148

Manchester Brewery Co Ltd v Coombs (1901) 82 LT 347, Ch D. . . 366, 370, 417

Mancini v DPP [1942] AC 1, HL. . . 81, 85

Marchioness of Blandford v Dowager Duchess of Marlborough (1743) 2 Atk 542. . . 439

Marcq v Christie Manson and Woods Ltd [2002] 4 All ER 1005, QBD. . . 79

Marine Fisheries Agency v Inter Fish Limited [2009] EWHC 753 (DC). . . 404

Marks v Beyfus (1890) 25 QBD 494, CA. . . 683

Marsh v DPP [2007] Crim LR 163. . . 293

Matthews v Morris [1981] Crim LR 495. . . 147

Matthews ex p Powell, Re (1875) 1 Ch D 501. . . 121

Matto v Crown Court at Wolverhampton [1987] RTR 337, DC. . . 53, 331, 332, 476, 477

Mattouk v Massad [1943] AC 588. . . 257

Maturin v A-G [1938] 2 All ER 214. . . 108

Maugham v Hubbard (1828) 8 B&C 14. . . 185

Mawaz Khan v R [1967] 1 AC 454. . . 361

Mawdesley v Chief Constable of the Cheshire Constabulary [2004] 1 WLR 1035 (Admin Court). . . 456, 718

Maxwell v DPP [1935] AC 309, HL. . . 557, 612

Maxwell v Pressdram Ltd [1987] 1 WLR 298, CA. . . 694

M'Cormick v Garnett (1854) 23 LJ Ch 777. . . 637

Mears v R (1993) 97 Cr App R 239, PC. . . 45

Meat Corporation of Namibia Ltd v Dawn Meats (UK) Ltd [2011] EWHC 474 (Ch). . . 127, 645

Meath (Bishop) v Marquis of Winchester (1836) 3 Bing NC 183, HL. . . 313

Mechanical & General Inventions Co Ltd v Austin [1935] AC 346, HL. . . 49, 218

Medway v Doublelock Ltd [1978] 1 WLR 710. . . 680

Memory Corpn plc v Sidhu [2000] Ch 645, Ch D. . . 714

Mercer v Chief Constable of the Lancashire Constabulary [1991] 2 All ER 504, CA. . . 152

Mercer v Denne [1905] 2 Ch 538, CA. . . 438, 442

Mercer v Whall (1845) 14 LJ QB 267. . . 84

Metropolitan Asylum District Managers v Hill (1882) 47 LT 29, HL. . . 28

Metropolitan Police Comr v Caldwell [1982] AC 341, HL. . . 36

Metropolitan Police Comr v Locker [1993] 3 All ER 584, EAT. . . 689

Metropolitan Rly Co v Wright (1886) 11 App Cas 152, HL. . . 253

Michel v R [2010] 1 Cr App R 359, PC. . . 45

Middleton v Rowlett [1954] 1 WLR 831. . . 147

Mighell v Sultan of Johore [1894] 1 QB 149, CA. . . 121

Miller v Cawley [2002] EWCA Civ 1100. . . 43, 87

Miller v Minister of Pensions [1947] 2 All ER 372. . . 87, 109

Mills v Oddy (1834) 6 C&P 728. . . 307

Mills v R [1995] 3 All ER 865, PC. . . 281

Milton v R [2015] UKPC 42. . . 137

Minet v Morgan (1873) 8 Ch App 361. . . 742

Minter v Priest [1930] AC 558. . . 727

Misick v The Queen [2015] 1 WLR 3215, PC. . . 62, 330, 386

Mitchell v R [1998] 2 Cr App R 35, PC. . . 483

M'Naghten's Case (1843) 10 Cl & Fin 200, HL. . . 63, 103

Moat Housing Group South Ltd v Harris [2006] QB 606, CA. . . 424

Mole v Mole [1951] P 21, CA. . . 754, 755

Monckton v Tarr (1930) 23 BWCC 504, CA. . . 106, 116

Mood Music Publishing Co Ltd v De Wolfe Publishing Ltd [1976] Ch 119. . . 536

Moor v Moor [1954] 1 WLR 927, CA. . . 181

Moorhouse v Lord (1863) 10 HL Cas 272. . . 92

Morgan v DPP [2016] EWHC 3414 (DC). . . 445

Moriarty v London, Chatham and Dover Rly Co (1870) LR 5 QB 314. . . 430

Morris v Beardmore [1981] AC 446, HL. . . 49, 328

Morris v Davies (1837) 5 Cl&Fin 163. . . 10, 108, 109

Morris v Davies [2011] EWHC 1773 (Ch). . . 94

Morris v Miller (1767) 4 Burr 2057. . . 107

Morris v Stratford-on-Avon RDC [1973] 1 WLR 1059, CA. . . 420

Morrow v DPP [1994] Crim LR 58, DC. . . 690

Mortimer v M'Callan (1840) 6 M&W 58. . . 308

Morton v Morton, Daly and McNaught [1937] P 151, P, D and Admlty. . . 432

Moseley v Davies (1822) 11 Price 162. . . 442

Mullan v Birmingham City Council (1999) The Times, 29 July, QBD. . . 43

Mullen v Hackney London Borough Council [1997] 1 WLR 1103, CA. . . 120, 123

Muller v Linsley & Mortimer (a firm) [1996] PNLR 74, CA. . . 750

Multi Guarantee Co Ltd v Cavalier Insurance Co Ltd (1986) The Times, 24 June, Ch D. . . 688, 698–9

Munro, Brice & Co v War Risks Association [1918] 2 KB 78. . . 79

Murdoch v Taylor [1965] AC 574, HL. . . 607

Murray v DPP [1994] 1 WLR 1, (1994) 99 Cr App R 396, HL. . . 504, 505, 506

Mutch v Allen [2001] CPLR 200, CA. . . 664

Myatt v Myatt and Parker [1962] 1 WLR 570, P, D and Admlty. . . 432

Myers v DPP [1965] AC 1001, HL. . . 47, 390

Myers v DPP see Myers v The Queen

Myers v R see Myers v The Queen

Myers v The Queen [2016] AC 314, PC. . . 15, 408, 579, 581, 582, 634, 636, 644, 654, 655, 656

N (a child) (residence order) Re [2006] EWHC 1189 (Fam). . . 635

National Justice Cia Naviera SA v Prudential Assurance Co Ltd, The Ikarian Reefer [1993] 2 Lloyd's Rep 68. . . 645, 653

Nederlandse Reassurantie Groep Holding NV v Bacon & Woodrow (a firm) [1995] 1 All ER 976, [1995] 2 Lloyd's Rep 77, QBD. . . 730, 749

Neill v North Antrim Magistrates' Court [1992] 1 WLR 1220; [1992] 4 All ER 846, HL. . . 40, 406, 450

Neilly v R [2012] 2 Cr App R 248 (20), PC. . . 204

Neilson v Harford (1841) 8 M&W 806. . . 36

Neilson v Laugharne [1981] QB 736, CA. . . 698, 700, 733

Nelson (Earl) v Lord Bridport (1845) 8 Beav 527. . . 637

Nesbitt, Re (1844) 14 LJMC 30. . . 119

Nevill v Fine Arts & General Insurance Co Ltd [1897] AC 68, HL. . . 34

Ng Chun Pui v Lee Chuen Tat [1988] RTR 298, PC. . . 115

Nicholas v Penny [1950] 2 KB 466. . . 104, 257

Nicholls v Parker (1805) 14 East 331. . . 441

Nimmo v Alexander Cowan & Sons Ltd [1968] AC 107, HL. . . 65, 67

Noble v Kennoway (1780) 2 Doug KB 510. . . 22

North Yorkshire Trading Standards Dept v Williams (1994) 159 JP 383, DC. . . 205

Norwich Pharmacal Co v Commissioners of Customs & Excise [1974] AC 133, HL. . . 688, 691, 693, 694, 712, 723

Nottingham City Council v Amin [2000] 1 WLR 1071, DC. . . 340, 341

O, Re [1991] 2 WLR 475, CA. . . 724

Oakes v Uzzell [1932] P 19. . . 312

O'Brien v Chief Constable of South Wales Police [2005] 2 AC 534, HL. . . 536

Oceanbulk Shipping and Trading SA v TMT Asia Ltd [2011] 1 AC 662, SC. . . 753

O'Connell v Adams [1973] Crim LR 313, DC. . . 221

Official Solicitor to the Supreme Court v K [1965] AC 201, HL. . . 415

Ofulue v Bossert [2009] UKHL 16. . . 750, 751, 753

Omychund v Barker (1745) 1 Atk 21. . . 31

O'Rourke v Darbishire [1920] AC 581. . . 739

Osborne v Chocqueel [1896] 2 QB 109. . . 535

Oven's Goods, Re (1892) 29 LR Ir 451. . . 312

Overbury, Sheppard v Matthews, Re [1955] Ch 122, Ch D. . . 108

Overseas Programming Co Ltd v Cinematographische Commerz-Anstalt and Iduna Film GmbH (1984) The Times, 16 May, QBD. . . 715

Owen v Chesters [1985] RTR 191, DC. . . 373

Owen v Edwards (1983) 77 Cr App R 191, DC. . . 191, 192

Owner v Bee Hive Spinning Co Ltd [1914] 1 KB 105, DC. . . 308

Oxfordshire County Council v M [1994] 2 WLR 393, CA. . . 741, 742

Oxfordshire County Council v P [1995] 2 WLR 543, Fam Div. . . 722

Oxley v Penwarden [2001] Lloyds Rep Med 347, CA. . . 662

P, Re [1989] Crim LR 897, CA. . . 218

Packer v Clayton (1932) 97 JP 14, DC. . . 763

Palastanga v Solman [1962] Crim LR 334. . . 147

Palermo, The (1883) 9 PD 6, CA. . . 733

Palmer v R [1971] AC 814, PC. . . 80

Parkes v R [1976] 1 WLR 1251, PC. . . 262, 492

Parkin v Moon (1836) 7 C&P 408. . . 182, 217

Parks v Clout [2003] EWCA Civ 893. . . 90

Parry v Boyle (1986) 83 Cr App R 310, DC. . . 318

Parry v News Group Newspapers Ltd [1990] NLJR 1719, CA. . . 729

Parry's Estate, Parry v Fraser, Re [1977] 1 All ER 309. . . 84

Patel v Comptroller of Customs [1966] AC 356, PC. . . 364

Paterson v DPP [1990] Crim LR 651, DC. . . 409

Pattison v DPP [2006] 2 All ER 317, QBD. . . 54–5

Paul v DPP (1989) 90 Cr App R 173, DC. . . 123

Payne v Harrison [1961] 2 QB 403, CA. . . 43

Peach v Metropolitan Police Comr [1986] QB 1064, CA. . . 689

Pearce v Foster (1885) 15 QBD 114, CA. . . 742

Peet v Mid Kent Healthcare Trust [2002] 1 WLR 210, CA. . . 662, 663, 664

Peete, Re; Peete v Crompton [1952] 2 All ER 599, Ch D. . . 103, 106, 107

Percy v DPP [1995] 3 All ER 124, DC. . . 87

Perkins v Vaughan (1842) 4 Man&G 988. . . 417

Perry v Gibson (1834) 1 Ad&El 48. . . 142

Persad v State of Trinidad and Tobago [2008] 1 Cr App R 140 (9), PC. . . 488

Phené's Trusts, Re (1870) 5 Ch App 139, CA. . . 111

Phillip v The Director of Public Prosecutions (St Christopher and Nevis) [2017] UKPC 14, PC. . . 579, 581

Phillips v News Group Newspapers Ltd [2013] 1 AC 1, SC. . . 723

Phillips v Symes (No 2) [2005] 1 WLR 2043, Ch D. . . 666

Phipps v DPP [2012] UKPC 24. . . 296

Phoenix Marine Inc v China Ocean Shipping Co [1999] 1 All ER 138. . . 638, 761

Pickup v Thames & Mersey Marine Insurance Co Ltd (1878) 3 QBD 594, CA. . . 103

Piermay Shipping Co SA and Brandt's Ltd v Chester, The Michael [1979] 1 Lloyd's Rep 55. . . 90

Piers v Piers (1849) 2 HL Cas 331. . . 92, 104, 105

Piggott v Sims [1973] RTR 15. . . 147

Pim v Curell (1840) 6 M&W 234. . . 441

Pinkus v Direct Line [2018] EWHC 1671 (QB), [2018] PIQR 20, QB. . . 87, 665, 668, 672

Pizzey v Ford Motor Co Ltd [1994] PIQR P15, CA. . . 746

Plant v Taylor (1861) 7 H&N 211. . . 441

Polanski v Condé Nast Publications Ltd [2004] 1 WLR 387, CA. . . 423

Polanski v Condé Nast Publications Ltd [2005] 1 All ER 945, HL. . . 144

Pontifex v Jolly (1839) 9 C&P 202. . . 84

Popek v National Westminster Bank plc [2002] EWCA Civ 42. . . 664

Pora v R [2015] UKPC 9. . . 657, 658

Post Office v Estuary Radio Ltd [1967] 1 WLR 1396, CA. . . 90

Post Office Counters Ltd v Mahida [2003] EWCA Civ 1583; (2003) The Times, 31 Oct. . . 32, 306

Poulett Peerage Case [1903] AC 395, HL. . . 108

Pozzi v Eli Lilly & Co (1986) The Times, 3 Dec, QBD. . . 747

Prest v Petrodel Resources Ltd [2013] UKSC 34. . . 17

Preston-Jones v Preston-Jones [1951] AC 391, HL. . . 91, 118

Price v Humphries [1958] 2 All ER 725, DC. . . 147

Price v Manning (1889) 42 Ch D 372, CA. . . 208

Prince v Samo (1838) 7 Ad&El 627. . . 249

Pringle v R [2003] UKPC 9. . . 265

Proulx, Re [2001] 1 All ER 57, DC. . . 343, 463

Prudential Assurance Co v Edmonds (1877) 2 App Cas 487. . . 109, 110

Prudential Assurance Co Ltd v Prudential Insurance Co of America [2002] EWHC 2809, Ch D. . . 751, 752

Public Prosecution Service of Northern Ireland v Elliott [2013] 1 WLR 1611, [2013] 2 Cr App R 180, SC. . . 114

Queen Caroline's Case (1820) 2 Brod&Bing 284. . . 249

R, Re; Re G (minors) [1990] 2 All ER 633, Fam D. . . 128

R (minors), Re [1991] 2 All ER 193, CA. . . 128

R v A [1997] Crim LR 883, CA. . . 500

R v A [2009] EWCA Crim 513. . . 590

R v A [2012] EWCA Crim 1273, (2011) 175 JP 437, CA,. . . 232, 394

R v A Ltd [2016] 4 WLR 176, CA. . . 361, 489

R v A (No 2) [2002] 1 AC 45, HL. . . 230, 235, 237, 238, 239, 240

R v AA [2007] EWCA Crim 1779. . . 394, 395

R v A(B) [2012] 2 Cr App R 467, CA. . . 132, 133

R v Abadom [1983] 1 WLR 126; [1983] 1 All ER 364, CA. . . 408, 656

R v Abbott [1955] 2 QB 497. . . 41

R v Abdullah [2010] EWCA Crim 3078. . . 768, 770

R v Abdullah [2019] EWCA Crim 1137. . . 204, 573

R v Abraham (1848) 3 Cox CC 430. . . 202

R v Absolam (1988) 88 Cr App R 332, CA. . . 337

R v Acton Justices ex p McMullen; R v Tower Bridge Magistrates' Court ex p Lawlor (1990) 92 Cr App R 98, DC. . . 378

R v Adair [1990] Crim LR 571, CA. . . 607

R v Adams [1980] QB 575, CA. . . 328

R v Adams [1993] Crim LR 525, CA. . . 35

R v Adams [1996] 2 Cr App R 467, CA. . . 636

R v Adams [1997] Crim LR 292, CA. . . 679

R v Adams [2008] 1 Cr App R 430 (35), CA. . . 377, 391

R v Adenusi [2006] Crim LR 929, CA. . . 590

R v AG [2018] 1 WLR 5876. . . 625

R v Agar [1990] 2 All ER 442, CA. . . 684

R v Agricultural Land Tribunal, ex p Benney [1955] 2 QB 140, CA. . . 439

R v Ahmed (1984) 6 Cr App R (S) 391. . . 85

R v Ahmed [2011] EWCA Crim 184. . . 324, 636, 655

R v Ahmed [2015] 1 Cr App R 275 (21), CA. . . 541, 547

R v Ahmed [2019] EWCA Crim 1085. . . 512

R v Aidarus [2018] EWCA Crim 2073. . . 237, 241

R v Ainscough [2006] Crim LR 635, CA. . . 384, 586

R v Aitken (1991) 94 Cr App R 85, CA. . . 148

R v AJC [2006] EWCA Crim 284. . . 559

R v Akaidere [1990] Crim LR 808, CA. . . 41, 286

R v Akram [1995] Crim LR 50, CA. . . 26

R v Alexander [2013] 1 Cr App R 334 (26), CA. . . 281, 292

R v Alexander [2018] EWCA Crim 239. . . 565, 566, 568, 592

R v Ali [2004] 1 Cr App R 501 (39), CA. . . 194

R v Ali [2006] EWCA Crim 1976. . . 551, 552

R v Ali [2008] EWCA Crim 146. . . 708

R v Ali [2008] EWCA Crim 1522, [2009] Crim LR 40, CA. . . 283, 284, 286, 287, 289

R v All Saints, Worcester (1817) 6 M&S 194. . . 717

R v All-Hilly [2014] 2 Cr App R 530 (33). . . 232, 569

R v Allad [2014] EWCA Crim 421. . . 634

R v Alladice (1988) 87 Cr App R 380, CA. . . 333, 334, 466, 474, 475, 476, 477, 478, 506

R v Allan [2005] Crim LR 716, CA. . . 347

R v Allen [1995] Crim LR 643, CA. . . 282

R v Allen [1996] Crim LR 426, CA. . . 203

R v Allen [2009] EWCA Crim 2881. . . 559

R v Allen (No 2) [2002] 1 AC 509, HL. . . 719

R v Alves (1997) 1 Cr App R 78, CA. . . 182

R v Amado-Taylor [2001] EWCA Crim 1898. . . 27, 551, 552

R v Ameer and Lucas [1977] Crim LR 104, CA. . . 327

R v Amin [2014] EWCA Crim 1924. . . 389

R v Amjad [2017] 1 Cr App R 331 (22), CA. . . 363

R v Ananthanarayanan [1994] 1 WLR 788, CA. . . 621

R v Anderson (1930) 21 Cr App R 178, CCA. . . 224

R v Anderson [1972] 1 QB 304. . . 639

R v Anderson [1988] QB 678, CA. . . 555, 714

R v Anderson [1991] Crim LR 361, CA. . . 83

R v Anderson [1993] Crim LR 447, CA. . . 329, 478

R v Anderson [2012] EWCA Crim 1785. . . 638

R v Andover Justices, ex p Rhodes [1980] Crim LR 644, DC. . . 310

R v Andrade [2015] EWCA Crim 1722. . . 242, 403

R v Andrews [1987] AC 281, HL. . . 443, 444–5, 446, 447

R v Andrews [1993] Crim LR 590, CA. . . 280

R v Angeli [1979] 1 WLR 26, CA. . . 95

R v Anjum [2003] EWCA Crim 493. . . 21

R v Antill [2002] EWCA Crim 2114. . . 29

R v Antrim Justices [1895] 2 IR 603. . . 122

R v Anwoir [2008] 4 All ER 582, CA. . . 500

R v Apabhai [2011] EWCA Crim 917. . . 601

R v Apicella (1985) 82 Cr App R 295, CA. . . 328

R v Argent [1997] 2 Cr App R 27, CA. . . 512, 515, 518, 520

R v Arif (1993) The Times, 17 June, CA. . . 189

R v Armstrong [1995] Crim LR 831, CA. . . 154

R v Arnold [2004] EWCA Crim 1293. . . 378

R v Arshad [2012] EWCA Crim 18. . . 660

R v Asghar [1995] 1 Cr App R 223, CA. . . 266

R v Ashworth [2012] EWCA Crim 1064. . . 27

R v Askew [1981] Crim LR 398, CA. . . 224

R v Asmeron [2013] 1 WLR 3457, CA. . . 46

R v Aspinall [1999] Crim LR 741, CA. . . 336

R v Assani [2008] EWCA Crim 2563; [2009] Crim LR 514, CA. . . 604, 608

R v Ataou [1988] QB 798, CA. . . 738

R v Athwal [2009] 1 WLR 2430, CA. . . 198, 199

R v Atkins [2010] 1 Cr App R 117 (8), CA. . . 635, 643, 649

R v Atta-Dankwa [2018] 2 Cr App R 248 (16), CA. . . 6, 44

R v Attfield (1961) 45 Cr App R 309. . . 44

R v Aubrey (1916) 11 Cr App R 182. . . 102

R v Audley [1907] 1 KB 383. . . 67

R v Austin [2013] EWCA Crim 1028. . . 709

R v Aves [1950] 2 All ER 330, CCA. . . 102

R v Awoyemi [2017] Crim LR 131, [2017] 2 Cr App R 303 (22), CA. . . 574, 581

R v Aziz [1995] AC 41, [1995] 3 All ER 149, HL. . . 200, 201, 455, 541, 542, 543–4, 545, 546, 547, 548

R v Aziz [2018] EWCA Crim 2412. . . 173

R v B [1996] Crim LR 499, CA. . . 149

R v B [1997] Crim LR 220, CA. . . 196

R v B [2003] 1 WLR 2809, CA. . . 220

R v B [2006] Crim LR 54, CA. . . 218

R v B [2007] Crim LR 910, CA. . . 231

R v B [2008] All ER 108; [2008] EWCA Crim 365. . . 390

R v B [2008] EWCA Crim 1850. . . 577

R v B [2010] EWCA Crim 4, CA. . . 268

R v B [2010] EWCA Crim 1251. . . 561

R v B [2011] EWCA Crim 1403. . . 589

R v B [2011] EWCA Crim 1630. . . 590

R v B, 25 February 2016, CA. . . 579

R v B (E) [2017] 1 Cr App R 457 (31), CA. . . 583

R v B (MT) [2000] Crim LR 181, CA. . . 261, 510

R v B (T) [2006] 2 Cr App R 22, CA. . . 668

R v BA [2013] Crim LR 170. . . 133

R v Badjan (1966) 50 Cr App R 141. . . 44

R v Bagot [2010] EWCA Crim 1983. . . 587, 588

R v Bagshaw [1984] 1 WLR 477, CA. . . 267

R v Bailey [1993] 3 All ER 513, CA. . . 338, 473

R v Bailey [1995] 2 Cr App R 262, CA, [1995] Crim LR 723, CA. . . 267, 270, 271

R v Bailey [2001] EWCA Crim 733. . . 187

R v Bailey [2017] EWCA Crim 35. . . 543

R v Bala [2016] EWCA Crim 560. . . 132

R v Baldwin (1925) 18 Cr App R 175, CCA. . . 218

R v Baldwin [1986] Crim LR 681, CA. . . 209

R v Ball [1911] AC 47, HL. . . 15, 620

R v Balmforth [1992] Crim LR 825, CA. . . 154

R v Bansal [1999] Crim LR 484, CA. . . 520

R v Barbery (1975) 62 Cr App R 248, CA. . . 200

R v Barham [1997] 2 Cr App R 119, CA. . . 489

R v Barker (1916) 11 Cr App R 191, CCA. . . 458

R v Barker [2010] EWCA Crim 4. . . 136, 138, 226

R v Barking and Dagenham Justices, ex p DPP (1995) 159 JP 373, DC. . . 43

R v Barkshire [2011] EWCA Crim 1885. . . 341

R v Barnes [1994] Crim LR 691, CA. . . 231

R v Barnes [1995] 2 Cr App R 491, CA. . . 282, 595

R v Barnett [2002] Cr App R 168, CA. . . 21

R v Barratt and Sheehan [1996] Crim LR 495, CA. . . 137, 141

R v Barry (1992) 95 Cr App R 384, CA. . . 463, 467

R v Barry [2011] 1 Cr App R 466, CA. . . 500

R v Barsoum [1994] Crim LR 194, CA. . . 19

R v Barton [1973] 1 WLR 115, CC. . . 738

R v Barton (1986) 85 Cr App R 5, CA. . . 236

R v Bashir and Manzur [1969] 1 WLR 1303, Assizes. . . 223

R v Baskerville [1916] 2 KB 658. . . 254

R v Bass [1953] 1 QB 680, CCA. . . 188

R v Batchelor [2013] EWCA Crim 2638. . . 81

R v Bath [1990] Crim LR 716, CA. . . 280

R v Bathurst [1968] 2 QB 99, CA. . . 498, 505

R v Batt [1994] Crim LR 592, CA. . . 29

R v Batt and Batt [1995] Crim LR 240, CA. . . 380

R v Bayliss (1994) 98 Cr App R 235, CA. . . 470

R v Beale [2019] 2 Cr App R 194 (19), CA. . . 263

R v Beales [1991] Crim LR 118, CC. . . 461

R v Bean [1991] Crim LR 843, CA. . . 686

R v Beard [1998] Crim LR 585, CA. . . 248

R v Beattie (1989) 89 Cr App R 302, CA. . . 194, 224

R v Beck [1982] 1 WLR 461, CA. . . 266

R v Beckett (1913) 8 Cr App R 204, CCA. . . 672, 673

R v Beckford (1991) 94 Cr App R 43, CA. . . 219

R v Beckford [1996] 1 Cr App R 94, CA. . . 322

R v Beckford; R v Daley [1991] Crim LR 833, CA. . . 456

R v Beckles [2005] 1 All ER 705, CA. . . 516, 519

R v Beckles and Montague [1999] Crim LR 148, CA. . . 284

R v Beckwith [1981] Crim LR 646. . . 41

R v Becouarn [2005] 1 WLR 2589, HL. . . 503

R v Bedford (1990) 93 Cr App R 113, CA. . . 591, 594, 621

R v Bedingfield (1879) 14 Cox CC 341 (Assizes). . . 443

R v Beezley (1830) 4 C&P 220. . . 249

R v Bellamy (1985) 82 Cr App R 222, CA. . . 141, 143

R v Bellis (1911) 6 Cr App R 283, CCA. . . 439

R v Belmarsh Magistrates' Court, ex p Gilligan [1998] 1 Cr App R 14, DC. . . 40, 406

R v Belogun [2008] EWCA Crim 2006. . . 598

R v Ben-Rejab [2012] 1 Cr App R 35, CA. . . 231

R v Benjamin (1913) 8 Cr App R 146, CCA. . . 197

R v Benjamin (2015, 21 July, unreported), CA. . . 546

R v Bennett (1978) 68 Cr App R 168, CA. . . 83

R v Bennett [1988] Crim LR 686, CA. . . 769

R v Bennett [1995] Crim LR 877, CA. . . 45

R v Bennett [2008] EWCA Crim 248. . . 206, 211, 225

R v Bentley (1991) 99 Cr App R 342, CA. . . 283

R v Bentley (Deceased) [2001] 1 Cr App R 307, CA. . . 44

R v Bentum (1989) 153 JP 538, CA. . . 658

R v Berberi [2015] 2 Cr App R 11 (2). . . 654

R v Berry (1986) 83 Cr App R 7. . . 15

R v Berry [1998] Crim LR 487, CA. . . 41

R v Betterley [1994] Crim LR 764, CA. . . 769

R v Betts [2001] 2 Cr App R 257 (16), CA. . . 511, 515, 516, 518

R v Bevan (1993) 98 Cr App R 354, CA. . . 130

R v Beveridge [1987] Crim LR 401, CA. . . 285, 329

R v Beverley [2006] Crim LR 1064, CA. . . 593

R v Beycan [1990] Crim LR 185, CA. . . 478

R v Bhagchandka [2016] EWCA Crim 700. . . 20

R v Biddle [2019] 2 Cr App R 209 (20), CA. . . 170, 500, 501

R v Billingham [2009] 2 Cr App R 341 (20), CA. . . 211, 225, 392

R v Bina [2014] 2 Cr App R 496 (30). . . 637

R v Binham [1991] Crim LR 774, CA. . . 362

R v Birchall [1999] Crim LR 311, CA. . . 504

R v Bircham [1972] Crim LR 430, CA. . . 221

R v Birks [2003] 2 Cr App R 122 (7), CA. . . 197

R v Birtles (1911) 6 Cr App R 177. . . 107

R v Black (1922) 16 Cr App R 118, CCA. . . 449, 491

R v Blackburn [2005] 2 Cr App R 440 (30), CA. . . 643

R v Blackburn [2008] 2 Cr App R (S) 16 (5). . . 266

R v Blackford [2009] EWCA Crim 1684. . . 86

R v Blake [1991] Crim LR 119, CC. . . 465, 480

R v Blake [1993] Crim LR 133, CA. . . 487

R v Blake [2006] EWCA Crim 871. . . 287

R v Blake and Tye (1844) 6 QB 126. . . 488–9

R v Bland (1987) 151 JP 857, CA. . . 41

R v Blastland [1986] AC 41, HL. . . 26, 350, 361, 390, 406, 450

R v Blenkinsop [1995] 1 Cr App R 7, CA. . . 288, 289

R v Bliss (1837) 7 Ad&El 550. . . 441, 442

R v Boal [1965] 1 QB 402. . . 130

R v Boetang [2011] EWCA Crim 861. . . 85

R v Bond [1906] 2 KB 389. . . 581

R v Bone [1968] 1 WLR 983, CA. . . 81

R v Bonnick (1977) 66 Cr App R 266, CA. . . 80

R v Booth (1981) 74 Cr App R 123. . . 209

R v Boothman [2011] EWCA Crim 1143. . . 368

R v Botmeh [2002] 1 WLR 531, CA. . . 707

R v Bottrill, ex p Kuechenmeister[1947] KB 41. . . 120

R v Bournemouth Justices, ex p Grey [1987] 1 FLR 36, DC. . . 681

R v Bovell [2005] 2 Cr App R 401 (27), CA. . . 557, 618

R v Bowden [1993] Crim LR 379, CA. . . 283

R v Bowden [1999] 4 All ER 43, CA. . . 515

R v Bowditch [1991] Crim LR 831, CA. . . 44

R v Bower [1994] Crim LR 281, CA. . . 679

R v Bowers [1998] Crim LR 817, CA. . . 511, 520

R v Bowles [1992] Crim LR 726, CA. . . 148

R v Bowman [2014] EWCA Crim 716. . . 588

R v Boyes (1861) 1 B&S 311, QB. . . 716

R v Boyson [1991] Crim LR 274, CA. . . 542, 767, 769

R v Bracewell (1978) 68 Cr App R 44, CA. . . 605, 642

R v Brackenbury [1965] 1 WLR 1475n. . . 473

R v Bradley (1979) 70 Cr App R 200, CA. . . 629

R v Bradshaw (1985) 82 Cr App R 79, CA. . . 654

R v Brady [2004] 3 All ER 520, CA. . . 721

R v Brain (1919) 13 Cr App R 197. . . 102

R v Braithwaite [2010] 2 Cr App R 149 (20), CA. . . 565

R v Brasier (1779) 1 Leach 199. . . 140

R v Bray (1988) 88 Cr App R 354. . . 376

R v Brennan [2014] EWCA Crim 2387, [2015] 1 WLR 2060, CA. . . 658, 659

R v Bresa [2006] Crim LR 179, CA. . . 519

R v Breslin (1984) 80 Cr App R 226, CA. . . 285

R v Brewster [2011] 1 WLR 601, CA. . . 566

R v Briggs-Price [2009] 1 AC 1026, HL. . . 68

R v Briley [1991] Crim LR 444, CA. . . 44

R v Brima [2007] 1 Cr App R 316 (24), CA. . . 592, 593

R v Brine [1992] Crim LR 122, CA. . . 53

R v Britton [1987] 1 WLR 539, CA. . . 185, 189

R v Britzman; R v Hall [1983] 1 WLR 350, CA. . . 52, 607, 616, 617

R v Bromley Magistrates' Court, ex p Smith [1995] 4 All ER 146. . . 710

R v Broome [2012] EWCA Crim 2879. . . 581

R v Brophy [1982] AC 476, HL. . . 483, 484–7

R v Broughton [2010] EWCA Crim 549, CA. . . 636

R v Brower [1995] Crim LR 746, CA. . . 44

R v Brown [1991] Crim LR 368, CA. . . 286

R v Brown [1991] Crim LR 835, CA. . . 364

R v Brown [1998] 2 Cr App R 364, CA. . . 216

R v Brown [2002] 1 Cr App R 46, CA. . . 42

R v Brown [2004] Crim LR 1034, CA. . . 168

R v Brown [2015] EWCA Crim 1328. . . 738

R v Brown [2019] EWCA Crim 1143. . . 175, 387, 391

R v Brown (Winston) [1994] 1 WLR 1599, CA. . . 679

R v Brown and Brown [1997] 1 Cr App R 112, CA. . . 153

R v Brown, R v Daley (1987) 87 Cr App R 52, CA. . . 685

R v Browning (1991) 94 Cr App R 109, CA. . . 280

R v Browning [1995] Crim LR 227, CA. . . 638

R v Bruce [1975] 1 WLR 1252, CA. . . 607, 608

R v Bryce [1992] 4 All ER 567, CA. . . 343, 346, 479

R v Buckingham (1994) 99 Cr App R 303, CA. . . 768

R v Buckley (1873) 13 Cox CC 293 (Assizes). . . 16, 450

R v Bullen [2008] 2 Cr App R 364 (25), CA. . . 593, 603, 625

R v Bunch [2013] EWCA Crim 2498. . . 640

R v Burchell [2016] EWCA Crim 1559. . . 565

R v Burge [1996] 1 Cr App R 163, CA. . . 19, 20, 21, 22

R v Burgess (1956) 40 Cr App R 144, CCA. . . 258

R v Burgess [1968] 2 QB 112, CA. . . 485

R v Burgess (1991) 93 Cr App R 41, CA. . . 83

R v Burgess and McLean [1995] Crim LR 425, CA. . . 80

R v Burke (1858) 8 Cox CC 44. . . 243, 400

R v Burke (1985) 82 Cr App R 156, CA. . . 618

R v Burke and Kelly (1847) 2 Cox CC 295. . . 202

R v Burnett [2016] EWCA Crim 1941. . . 500, 501

R v Burnett and Lee [1973] Crim LR 748. . . 327

R v Burns (1973) 58 Cr App R 364. . . 83

R v Burns [2006] 1 WLR 1273, CA. . . 54

R v Burrows [2000] Crim LR 48, CA. . . 264

R v Burton [2011] EWCA Crim 1990; (2011) 175 JP 385, CA. . . 387, 389

R v Busby (1981) 75 Cr App R, CA. . . 246

R v Butler [1999] Crim LR 835, CA. . . 581

R v Button [2005] Crim LR 571. . . 338

R v Buzalek [1991] Crim LR 116, CA. . . 544

R v Byrne [2002] 2 Cr App R 311. . . 25

R v Byrne [2016] EWCA Crim 2124. . . 291, 294

R v Byrne and Trump [1987] Crim LR 689, CA. . . 203

R v C [2006] 1 WLR 2994, CA. . . 376, 403

R v C [2006] Crim LR 1058, CA. . . 623, 624

R v C [2010] Crim LR 858, CA. . . 387

R v C [2011] 1 WLR 1942, CA. . . 626, 772, 773

R v C [2011] 3 All ER 509, CA. . . 636

R v C [2011] EWCA Crim 939. . . 613

R v C [2012] EWCA Crim 1478. . . 641

R v C [2016] EWCA Crim 1631. . . 239

R v C [2019] EWCA Crim 88 (11). . . 627

R v C [2019] Cr App R 88 (10), CA. . . 375, 388

R v Cadette [1995] Crim LR 229, CA. . . 345, 346

R v Cadman [2008] EWCA Crim 1418. . . 148

R v Cain [1994] 2 All ER 398, CA. . . 542

R v Cairns [2003] 1 WLR 796, CA. . . 154, 526

R v Caldwell (1993) 99 Cr App R 73, CA. . . 284, 287

R v Caley-Knowles [2007] 1 Cr App R 197, CA. . . 46

R v Callan (1994) 98 Cr App R 467, CA. . . 389

R v Callender [1998] Crim LR 337, CA. . . 442, 450

R v Cambridge [1994] 2 All ER 760, CA. . . 81

R v Camelleri [1922] 2 KB 122, CCA. . . 196

R v Cameron [1973] Crim LR 520, CA. . . 80

R v Campbell (1986) 84 Cr App R 255, CA. . . 63

R v Campbell [1995] 1 Cr App R 522, CA. . . 271

R v Campbell [2007] 1 WLR 2798, CA. . . 567, 573, 574, 597, 598

R v Campbell [2009] EWCA Crim 1076. . . 18

R v Canale [1990] 2 All ER 187, CA. . . 333, 337, 480

R v Cannan [1998] Crim LR 284, CA. . . 221

R v Cannings [2004] 1 WLR 2607, CA. . . 273, 274, 634, 636, 651, 652

R v Canny (1945) 30 Cr App R 143. . . 33

R v Carnall [1995] Crim LR 944, CA. . . 445, 448

R v Carr-Briant [1943] KB 607, CCA. . . 84, 86, 94, 771

R v Carrington (1993) 99 Cr App R 376, CA. . . 385

R v Carroll (1993) 99 Cr App R 381, CA. . . 256

R v Cartwright (1914) 10 Cr App R 219, CCA. . . 203

R v Cascoe [1970] 2 All ER 83, CA. . . 80, 81

R v Case [1991] Crim LR 192, CA. . . 377, 406

R v Cash [1985] QB 801, CA. . . 102

R v Castillo [1996] 1 Cr App R 438, CA. . . 377, 406

R v Castle [1989] Crim LR 567, CA. . . 286, 768

R v Castleton (1909) 3 Cr App R 74. . . 16

R v Causley [1999] Crim LR 572, CA. . . 267

R v Central Criminal Court, ex p Francis and Francis [1989] AC 346, HL. . . 725, 740, 741

R v Chaaban [2003] Crim LR 658, CA. . . 218

R v Chal [2008] 1 Cr App R 247 (18), CA. . . 352

R v Chalkley and Jeffries [1998] QB 848, CA. . . 52, 331, 333, 342

R v Challen [2019] EWCA Crim 916. . . 636, 640

R v Challenger [1994] Crim LR 202, CA. . . 550, 551

R v Chan-Fook [1994] 2 All ER 552, CA. . . 640

R v Chance [1988] 3 All ER 225, CA. . . 258, 264

R v Chandler [1976] 1 WLR 585, CA. . . 6, 262, 493

R v Chapman (1838) 8 C&P 558. . . 153

R v Chapman [1989] Crim LR 60, CA. . . 540

R v Chapman [1991] Crim LR 44, CA. . . 770, 771

R v Chard (1971) 56 Cr App R 268, CA. . . 640

R v Chargot Ltd (trading as Contract Services) and others [2009] 1 WLR 1, HL. . . 76

R v Charles (1976) 68 Cr App R 334n, HL. . . 36, 255

R v Charles [2010] WLR 644, CA. . . 71

R v Chauhan (1981) 73 Cr App R 232, CA. . . 262

R v Chauhan [2019] EWCA Crim 1111. . . 41

R v Cheema [1994] 1 All ER 639, CA. . . 264

R v Cheltenham Justices, ex p (Secretary of State for Trade) [1977] 1 WLR 95. . . 688

R v Cheng (1976) 63 Cr App R 20. . . 188

R v Chenia [2004] 1 All ER 543, CA. . . 295, 515, 518, 519, 520

R v Chief Constable of South Wales, ex p Merrick [1994] Crim LR 852, DC. . . 474

R v Chief Constable of the West Midlands Police, ex p Wiley [1995] 1 AC 274, HL. . . 689, 698, 700, 702

R v Childs [2014] EWCA Crim 1884. . . 643

R v Chinn [2012] 2 Cr App R 39; [2012] 1 WLR 3401, CA. . . 186, 190, 206, 394

R v Chisholm [2010] EWCA Crim 258. . . 710

R v Chisnell [1992] Crim LR 507, CA. . . 188

R v Chivers [2011] EWCA Crim 1212. . . 520

R v Chopra [2007] 1 Cr App R 225 (16), CA. . . 583, 587, 591, 592, 593, 594, 603

R v Christie [1914] AC 545, HL. . . 31, 49, 51, 203, 442, 449, 491, 493

R v Christou [1992] QB 979, CA. . . 331, 333, 343, 345, 472

R v Chrysostomou [2010] EWCA Crim 1403; [2010] Crim LR 942, CA. . . 363, 561, 577, 617

R v Chung (1990) 92 Cr App R 314, CA. . . 467

R v Churchill [1993] Crim LR 285, CA. . . 405

R v Clancy [1997] Crim LR 290, CA. . . 244

R v Clapham (1829) 4 C&P 29. . . 437

R v Clare and Peach [1995] 2 Cr App R 333, CA. . . 317, 639

R v Clark [1955] 2 QB 469. . . 616

R v Clark [2003] EWCA Crim 1020. . . 671

R v Clark [2006] EWCA Crim 231. . . 639, 641

R v Clarke [1969] 2 QB 91. . . 309

R v Clarke [1989] Crim LR 892, CA. . . 476

R v Clarke [1995] 2 Cr App R 425, CA. . . 315, 317, 636

R v Clarke [2008] EWCA Crim 893. . . 73

R v Clarke [2013] EWCA Crim 162. . . 644

R v Cleal [1942] 1 All ER 203, CCA. . . 267

R v Cleghorn [1967] 2 QB 584, CA. . . 153

R v Cliburn (1898) 62 JP 232, CCC. . . 216

R v Clift 2013] 1 WLR 2093, CA. . . 772

R v Clifton [1986] Crim LR 399, CA. . . 279

R v Clipston [2011] 2 Cr App R (S) 569 (101),
CA. . . 386, 415

R v Clowes [1992] 3 All ER 440, CA. . . 690, 702

R v Coates [2008] 1 Cr App R 52 (3), CA. . . 211, 225

R v Cochrane [1993] Crim LR 48, CA. . . 371, 373

R v Coelho [2008] EWCA Crim 627. . . 479

R v Cole (1941) 165 LT 125. . . 482

R v Cole [1990] 1 WLR 866, CA. . . 379, 380, 381

R v Cole [2008] 1 Cr App R 81(5), CA. . . 402

R v Cole [2013] EWCA Crim 1149. . . 281, 282, 293

R v Coleman (1987) The Times, 21 Nov, CA. . . 153

R v Coles [1995] 1 Cr App R 157, CA. . . 640

R v Coll (1889) 25 LR Ir 522. . . 194

R v Coll [2005] EWCA Crim 3675. . . 493

R v Colliard [2008] EWCA Crim 1175. . . 583

R v Collier; R v Stenning [1965] 1 WLR 1470,
CCA. . . 473

R v Collins (1960) 44 Cr App R 170. . . 306

R v Collins [2004] 1 WLR 1705, CA. . . 492

R v Colman [2005] QB 996. . . 773

R v Compton [2002] EWCA Crim 2835. . . 515, 523

R v Conde (1867) 10 Cox CC 547. . . 449

R v Condron and Condron [1997] 1 WLR 827,
CA. . . 513, 514, 525

R v Conibeer [2002] EWCA Crim 2059. . . 280

R v Connolly and McCartney (1992) Belfast CC, 5
June. . . 515

R v Constantinou (1989) 91 Cr App R 74, CA. . . 280,
317, 365

R v Conti (1973) 58 Cr App R 387, CA. . . 130

R v Conway [1994] Crim LR 838, CA. . . 481

R v Cook [1959] 2 QB 340. . . 613

R v Cook [1987] QB 417, CA. . . 317, 365

R v Cook [2005] EWCA Crim 2011. . . 148

R v Cooke (1986) 84 Cr App R 286, CA. . . 25

R v Cooke [1995] 1 Cr App R 318, CA. . . 332

R v Cooper [1969] 1 QB 267, CA. . . 253, 389

R v Cooper (1985) 82 Cr App R 74, CA. . . 219

R v Cooper [2010] 1 WLR 2390, CA. . . 256

R v Cooper [2018] EWCA Crim 1454. . . 590

R v Cooper [2017] EWCA Crim 43. . . 591

R v Cooper and Schaub [1994] Crim LR 531, CA. . . 157

R v Cordingley [2007] EWCA Crim 2174. . . 183

R v Corelli [2001] Crim LR 913, CA. . . 219

R v Cornwell [2013] EWCA Crim 2414. . . 589

R v Corrie (1904) 20 TLR 365. . . 505

R v Cottrill [1997] Crim LR 56, CA. . . 744

R v Coughlan and R v Young (1976) 63 Cr App R 33,
CA. . . 627

R v Coulson [1997] Crim LR 886, CA. . . 125

R v Court (1960) 44 Cr App R 242, CCA. . . 16

R v Courtnell [1990] Crim LR 115, CA. . . 283, 284

R v Courtnell; R v Cape [1996] 1 Cr App R 191,
CA. . . 284

R v Courtney [1995] Crim LR 63, CA. . .
479, 607, 616

R v Cousins [1982] QB 526, CA. . . 65, 67

R v Couzens [1992] Crim LR 822, CA. . . 18

R v Cowan [1996] QB 373, [1996] 1 Cr App R 1,
CA. . . 501, 502–6

R v Cowell [1940] 2 KB 49. . . 129

R v Cox [1898] 1 QB 179. . . 672

R v Cox [1991] Crim LR 276, CA. . . 270, 463

R v Cox (1993) 96 Cr App R 464, CA. . . 479

R v Cox [2012] 2 Cr App R 63 (6), CA. . . 170

R v Cox [2014] EWCA Crim 804. . . 613

R v Cox and Railton (1884) 14 QBD 153,
CCR. . . 739, 741

R v Crabtree [1992] Crim LR 65, CA. . . 203, 284

R v Cramp (1880) 14 Cox CC 390. . . 262

R v Crampton (1991) 92 Cr App R 369, CA. . . 462,
463, 464, 465

R v Crawford [1998] 1 Cr App R 338, CA. . . 607, 608

R v Creed [2011] EWCA Crim 144. . . 555, 608

R v Crees [1996] Crim LR 830, CA. . . 148

R v Cresswell (1876) 1 QBD 446, CCR. . . 113

R v Cross (1990) 91 Cr App R 115, CA. . . 219

R v Crossland [2013] EWCA Crim 2313. . . 242

R v Crowley. . . 74

R v Crown Court at Inner London Sessions, ex p
Baines and Baines [1988] QB 579, DC. . . 730

R v Crown Court at Manchester, ex p Rogers [1999] 1
WLR 832, DC. . . 728

R v Crown Court at Northampton, ex p DPP (1991)
93 Cr App R 376, DC. . . 741

R v Crown Court at Snaresbrook, ex p DPP [1988] QB
532. . . 740

R v Crown Court at Southampton, ex p J and P
[1993] Crim LR 962, DC. . . 737

R v Crush [1978] Crim LR 357. . . 120

R v Cruttenden [1991] 3 All ER 242, CA. . . 135

R v CT (2011) 175 JP 462, CA. . . 377, 379, 387,
388, 389

R v Cullinane [1984] Crim LR 420, CA. . . 255

R v Cummings [1948] 1 All ER 551, CA CCA. . . 197

R v Cundell [2009] EWCA Crim 2072. . . 265

R v Cunningham [1989] Crim LR 435, CA. . . 385

R v Curgerwen (1865) LR 1 CCR 1. . . 67, 113

R v Curley [2004] EWCA Crim 2395. . . 202

R v Curry [1983] Crim LR 737. . . 283

R v Curry [1988] Crim LR 527, CA. . . 770

R v Curtin [1996] Crim LR 831, CA. . . 44

R v D (1995) The Times, 15 Nov, CA. . . 137

R v D [2003] QB 90, CA. . . 402

R v D [2008] EWCA Crim 2557. . . 219, 263

R v D [2009] 2 Cr App R 306 (17), CA. . . 577, 579, 580

R v D [2009] EWCA Crim 2137, CA. . . 232

R v D [2012] EWCA Crim 2163. . . 612

R v D (2013) 177 JP 158, CA. . . 294

R v D(M) [2015] EWCA Crim 818. . . 588

R v D(N) [2013] 1 WLR 676. . . 590

R v Da Silva [1990] 1 WLR 31, CA. . . 191, 192

R v Dadson (1983) 77 Cr App R 91, CA. . . 310

R v Daley [2017] EWCA Crim 1971. . . 404, 405

R v Dallagher [2003] 1 Cr App R 195 (12), CA. . . 636, 649

R v Dalloz (1908) 1 Cr App R 258. . . 17

R v Daly [2002] 2 Cr App R 201 (14), CA. . . 518

R v Daniel (1998) 2 Cr App R 373, CA. . . 518

R v Daniels [2011] 1 Cr App R 228 (18), CA. . . 267

R v Darby [1989] Crim LR 817, CA. . . 208

R v Darnley [2012] EWCA Crim 1148. . . 42

R v Dat [1998] Crim LR 488, CA. . . 207

R v David R [1999] Crim LR 909, CA. . . 243

R v Davies [1962] 1 WLR 1111, C-MAC. . . 672, 673

R v Davies (2002) 166 JP 243, CA. . . 127

R v Davies [2003] ICR 586, CA. . . 76

R v Davies [2007] 2 All ER 1070, CA. . . 405

R v Davies [2008] 1 AC 1128, HL. . . 387

R v Davies [2011] EWCA Crim 1177. . . 164

R v Davis (1975) 62 Cr App R 194; [1975] 1 WLR 345, CA. . . 148

R v Davis [1979] Crim LR 167, CC. . . 469

R v Davis [1990] Crim LR 860, CA. . . 482, 484

R v Davis [1993] 1 WLR 613, CA. . . 707

R v Davis [1998] Crim LR 659, CA. . . 361

R v Davis [2006] 1 WLR 3130, CA. . . 268

R v Davis [2008] 1 AC 1128; [2008] 3 All ER 461, HL. . . 170, 171, 268

R v Davison-Jenkins [1997] Crim LR 816, CA. . . 619

R v Dawes [2014] 1 WLR 947, CA. . . 82

R v Day (1940) 27 Cr App R 168. . . 147

R v Daye [1908] 2 KB 333. . . 302

R v De Oliveira [1997] Crim LR 600, CA. . . 216

R v De Silva [2003] 2 Cr App R 74 (5), CA. . . 480

R v Deakin [1994] 4 All ER 769, CA. . . 38

R v Deakin [2012] EWCA Crim 2637. . . 293

R v Deboussi [2007] EWCA Crim 684. . . 25–6, 773

R v Deenik [1992] Crim LR 578, CA. . . 330, 345, 672

R v Delaney (1989) 88 Cr App R 338, CA. . . 333, 467

R v Del-Valle [2004] EWCA Crim 1013. . . 539, 540

R v Denham [2017] 1 Cr App R 64 (7) CA. . . 768, 770

R v Denton [2007] All ER (D) 492 (Apr); [2007] EWCA Crim 1111. . . 74, 215

R v Derby Magistrates' Court, ex p B [1996] AC 487, HL. . . 222, 673, 684–5, 726, 737, 738, 739

R v Derodra [2000] 1 Cr App R 41, CA. . . 385

R v Dervish [2002] 2 Cr App R 105 (6), CA. . . 509

R v Devani [2008] 1 Cr App R 65. . . 336

R v Devonport [1996] 1 Cr App R 221, CA. . . 489

R v DGF [2008] EWCA Crim 2859. . . 235

R v Dhillon [1997] 2 Cr App R 104, CA. . . 80

R v Dhorajiwala [2010] 2 Cr App R 161(21), CA. . . 458

R v Diane [2010] 2 Cr App R 1 (1), CA. . . 144

R v Dickman (1910) 5 Cr App R 135. . . 18

R v Dillon (1983) 85 Cr App R 29, CA. . . 189

R v Dillon [2013] EWCA Crim 122. . . 542

R v Dinc [2017] EWCA Crim 1206. . . 227, 569

R v Director of Serious Fraud Office, ex p Smith [1992] 3 All ER 456, HL. . . 469

R v Dixon [2014] 1 WLR 525, CA. . . 500, 501

R v Dizaei [2013] EWCA Crim 88, [2013] 1 Cr App R 411 (31), CA. . . 565, 568, 621

R v DJ [2010] 2 Cr App R 8 (2), CA. . . 353, 577

R v Dlugosz [2013] EWCA Crim 2, [2013] 1 Cr App R 425 (32), CA. . . 647, 649

R v Docherty [1999] 1 Cr App R 274, CA. . . 627

R v Dodson; R v Williams [1984] 1 WLR 971, (1984) 79 Cr App R 220, CA. . . 288, 289, 316, 365

R v Doheny and Adams [1997] 1 Cr App R 369, CA. . . 636

R v Dolan [2003] 1 Cr App R 281 (18). . . 582

R v Doldur [2000] Crim LR 178, CA. . . 282, 519

R v Donaldson (1977) 64 Cr App R 59, CA. . . 200

R v Donat (1985) 82 Cr App R 173, CA. . . 489

R v Doncaster (2008) JP 202, CA. . . 544, 548, 551

R v Donoghue (1987) 86 Cr App R 267, CA. . . 44

R v Donovan [1934] 2 KB 498. . . 62

R v Doolan [1988] Crim LR 747, CA. . . 463, 467

R v Doolin (1882) 1 Jebb CC 123, IR. . . 215

R v Doran (1972) 56 Cr App R 429, CA. . . 146

R v Dossett [2013] EWCA Crim 710. . . 595

R v Dossi (1918) 13 Cr App R 158, CCA. . . 261

R v Douglass (1989) 89 Cr App R 264, CA. . . 605

R v Dowley [1983] Crim LR 168, CA. . . 262

R v Downer [2009] 2 Cr App R 452, CA. . . 769

R v Downey [1995] 1 Cr App R 547, CA. . . 288, 289

R v Doyle [2018] EWCA Crim 2198. . . 368, 405

R v DPP, ex p Kebilene [1999] Crim LR 994. . . 77

R v DPP, ex p Warby [1994] Crim LR 281, DC. . . 710

R v Dragic [1996] 2 Cr App R 232, CA. . . 381

R v Drake [1996] Crim LR 109, CA. . . 21

R v Drinkwater [2016] 4 WLR 42, CA. . . 403

R v Drummond [2002] 2 CR App 352 (25), CA. . . 72

R v DS [2010] EWCA Crim 1016. . . 588

R v DT [2009] EWCA Crim 1213. . . 377

R v Duarte [2019] EWCA Crim 1466. . . 527, 529, 530

R v Dudley [2004] EWCA Crim 3336. . . 635

R v Duffy [1999] QB 919, CA. . . 382

R v Duncan (1981) 73 Cr App R 359. . . 70, 200, 201, 542

R v Duncan (1992) The Times, 24 July, CA. . . 288

R v Dunford (1990) 91 Cr App R 150, CA. . . 334, 477, 478

R v Dunkley [1927] 1 KB 323, CCA. . . 616

R v Dunn (1990) 91 Cr App R 237, CA. . . 480

R v Dunphy (1994) 98 Cr App R 393, CA. . . 159, 331, 470

R v Durbin [1995] 2 Cr App R 84, CA. . . 544, 545

R v Dures [1997] 2 Cr App R 247, CA. . . 331

R v Dwyer; R v Ferguson [1925] 2 KB 799, CCA. . . 203

R v E [2005] Crim LR 227, CA. . . 231

R v E [2009] EWCA Crim 2668. . . 232

R v E [2011] EWCA Crim 3028. . . 226

R v Eades [1972] Crim LR 99, Assizes. . . 246

R v Early [2003] 1 Cr App R 288, CA. . . 707

R v Eastlake (2007) 151 SJLB 258, CA. . . 584, 595

R v ED [2010] EWCA Crim 1213. . . 387, 389

R v Eden [2011] EWCA Crim 1690. . . 248

R v Edgington [2013] EWCA Crim 2185. . . 25

R v Edwards [1975] QB 27, CA. . . 64, 66, 67, 113

R v Edwards (1983) 77 Cr App R 5. . . 44

R v Edwards [1991] 1 WLR 207; [1991] 2 All ER 266, CA. . . 25, 244, 246, 563

R v Edwards [1997] Crim LR 348, CA. . . 346

R v Edwards [1998] Crim LR 207, CA. . . 30

R v Edwards [2001] EWCA Crim 2185. . . 644, 656

R v Edwards [2004] EWCA Crim 2102. . . 42

R v Edwards [2006] 1 WLR 1524, CA. . . 556, 560, 561, 573, 574, 575, 576, 579, 599, 600, 604, 608

R v El-Hannachi [1998] 2 Cr App R 226, CA. . . 504

R v Eleftheriou [1993] Crim LR 947, CA. . . 187

R v Elleray [2003] 2 Cr App R 165 (11), CA. . . 327, 481

R v Elliot [2010] EWCA Crim 2378. . . 584

R v Elliot (2011) 175 JP 39, CA. . . 368

R v Ellis (1826) 6 B&C 145. . . 580

R v Ellis [2010] EWCA Crim 163. . . 600

R v Ellis [2010] EWCA Crim 1893. . . 571

R v Elworthy (1867) LR 1 CCR 103. . . 305

R v Ely Justices, ex p Burgess [1992] Crim LR 888, DC. . . 319

R v EM [2014] EWCA Crim 1523. . . 576

R v Emmerson (1991) 92 Cr App R 284, CA. . . 95, 149, 316, 461

R v Ensor [1989] 1 WLR 497, CA. . . 263

R v Ensor [2010] 1 Cr App R 255 (18), CA. . . 500, 501, 671

R v Epping and Ongar Justices, ex p Manby [1986] Crim LR 555, DC. . . 39

R v Evans [1965] 2 QB 295. . . 266

R v Evans [2005] 1 WLR 1435, CA. . . 71

R v Evans [2009] 1 WLR 1999, CA. . . 34

R v Evans [2016] EWCA Crim 452. . . 234, 239

R v Evans-Jones; R v Jenkins (1923) 87 JP 115. . . 84

R v Everett [1988] Crim LR 826, CA. . . 465

R v Everett [1995] Crim LR 76, CA. . . 45

R v Ewens [1967] 1 QB 322, CCA. . . 66

R v Ewing [1983] 3 WLR 1; [1983] 2 All ER 645, CA. . . 94, 95, 312

R v Exall (1866) 4 F&F 922. . . 14

R v Eyidah [2010] EWCA Crim 987. . . 571

R v F [2005] 1 WLR 2848, CA. . . 235, 236, 240

R v F [2008] EWCA Crim 2859. . . 241

R v F (JR) [2013] 1 WLR 2143, CA. . . 137, 138

R v F (S) [2011] 2 Cr App R 393, CA. . . 42

R v Fairfax [1995] Crim LR 949, CA. . . 378, 380, 406

R v Fallis [2004] EWCA Crim 923. . . 260

R v Fallon [1993] Crim LR 591, CA. . . 255

R v Farnham Justices, ex p Gibson [1991] Crim LR 642, DC. . . 130

R v Farr [1999] Crim LR 506, CA. . . 45

R v Fedrick [1990] Crim LR 403, CA. . . 769

R v Fender [2018] EWCA Crim 2829. . . 611, 644

R v Fenlon (1980) 71 Cr App R 307, CA. . . 188, 189, 221

R v Ferdinand [2014] EWCA Crim 1243. . . 376, 402, 636, 650

R v Fergus [1992] Crim LR 363, CA. . . 204

R v Fergus (1994) 98 Cr App R 313, CA. . . 83, 282, 285

R v Field (Justices), ex p White (1895) 64 LJMC 158. . . 122

R v Finch [2007] 1 WLR 1645, CA. . . 288, 390, 457

R v Findlay; R v Francis [1992] Crim LR 372, CA. . . 478, 480

R v Finley [1993] Crim LR 50, CA. . . 293

R v Fitton [2001] EWCA Crim 215, CA. . . 542

R v Fitzpatrick [1999] Crim LR 832, CA. . . 658

R v Flemming (1987) 86 Cr App R 32, CA. . . 285, 329, 481

R v Flynn (1957) 42 Cr App R 15. . . 148

R v Flynn [2008] 2 Cr App R 266 (20), CA. . . 278, 295, 298, 650, 672

R v FNC [2016] 1 Cr App R 176 (12). . . 41

R v Foote [1964] Crim LR 405. . . 81

R v Forbes [1992] Crim LR 593, CA. . . 286

R v Forbes [2001] 1 AC 473, HL. . . 182, 291

R v Ford [2010] EWCA Crim 2250, [2011] Crim LR 475. . . 387

R v Forsyth [1997] 2 Cr App R 299, CA. . . 144

R v Foster (1834) 6 C&P 325 (Central Criminal Court). . . 443

R v Foster [1974] Crim LR 544, CA. . . 498

R v Foster [1984] 2 All ER 679, CA. . . 760, 767

R v Foster [1987] Crim LR 821, CC. . . 479

R v Foster [1995] Crim LR 333, CA. . . 157

R v Foster [2009] EWCA Crim 353. . . 599

R v Fotheringham [1975] Crim LR 710, CA. . . 188

R v Foulder, Foulkes and Johns [1973] Crim LR 45. . . 327

R v Foulger [2012] EWCA Crim 1516. . . 643

R v Fowden and White [1982] Crim LR 588, CA. . . 284, 317

R v Fowkes (1856) The Times, 8 Mar, Assizes. . . 205, 443

R v Fowler (1987) 86 Cr App R 219, CA. . . 629

R v Fox [1986] AC 281, HL. . . 328

R v Fox [2009] EWCA Crim 653. . . 558, 577

R v Fox [2010] EWCA Crim 1280. . . 387

R v Foxley [1995] 2 Cr App R 523, CA. . . 384, 406

R v Foxley; R v Ilyas and Knight [1996] Crim LR 810, CA. . . 406, 489

R v Foye (2013) 177 JP 449, CA. . . 63

R v France [2012] UKPC 28. . . 204

R v Francis (1874) LR 2 CCR 128. . . 31, 32, 314

R v Francis [1991] 1 All ER 225, CA. . . 147

R v Francis [2013] EWCA Crim 123. . . 643, 644

R v Franklin [1989] Crim LR 499, CA. . . 263

R v Fraser; R v Warren (1956) 40 Cr App R 160, CCA. . . 208

R v Freeman [2009] 1 Cr App R 137 (11), CA. . . 591

R v Freeman [2010] EWCA Crim 1997. . . 359, 379, 386, 388, 389, 391

R v French (1993) 97 Cr App R 421, CA. . . 377, 380

R v Friel [2012] EWCA Crim 2871. . . 357, 397

R v Friend [1997] 1 WLR 1433, CA. . . 501

R v Friend (No 2) [2004] EWCA Crim 2661. . . 500

R v Frost (1839) 4 State Tr NS 85. . . 146

R v Fulling [1987] 2 All ER 65, CA. . . 460, 461, 462, 467

R v Funderburk [1990] 1 WLR 587, CA. . . 219, 223, 240, 243, 244, 246

R v G [2004] 2 Cr App R 638 (38), CA. . . 643

R v G [2016] EWCA Crim 1633. . . 239

R v G (T) [2018] 1 Cr App R 405 (30), CA. . . 248

R v Gadsby [2006] Crim LR 631, CA. . . 26

R v Gai [2012] EWCA Crim 2033. . . 545

R v Galbraith [1981] 1 WLR 1039, CA. . . 41, 43, 269, 400, 401, 597, 659

R v Gale [1994] Crim LR 208, CA. . . 45

R v Gall (1989) 90 Cr App R 64, CA. . . 293

R v Gallagher [1974] 1 WLR 1204, CA. . . 18, 45

R v Gandfield (1846) 2 Cox CC 43. . . 450

R v Garaxo [2005] Crim LR 883, CA. . . 232

R v Gardener [2004] EWCA Crim 1693. . . 290

R v Garnham [2008] EWCA Crim 266. . . 566, 599

R v Garratty [2010] EWCA Crim 1156. . . 563

R v Garrod [1997] Crim LR 445, CA. . . 201

R v Garth [1949] 1 All ER 773, CCA. . . 102

R v Gayle [1994] Crim LR 679, CA. . . 327

R v Gayle [1999] Crim LR 502, CA. . . 509

R v Gbajabiamila [2011] EWCA Crim 734. . . 542

R v Gent [1990] 1 All ER 364, CA. . . 46

R v Genus [1996] Crim LR 502, CA. . . 21

R v George [2003] Crim LR 282, CA. . . 280

R v George [2015] 1 Cr App R 183 (15). . . 636

R v George (Barry) [2007] EWCA Crim 2722. . . 636

R v Gian [2009] EWCA Crim 2553, CA. . . 646

R v Gibbons [2009] Crim LR 197, CA. . . 210

R v Gibson (1887) LR 18 QBD 537, CCR. . . 364, 449

R v Gibson (1991) 93 Cr App R 9, CA. . . 541

R v Gibson [1993] Crim LR 453, CA. . . 223

R v Giga [2007] Crim LR 571, CA. . . 283, 284

R v Gilbert (1977) 66 Cr App R 237, CA. . . 498

R v Gilder [1997] Crim LR 668, CA. . . 148

R v Gilfoyle [1996] 3 All ER 883, CA. . . 361

R v Gilfoyle [2001] 2 Cr App R 57 (5), CA. . . 646

R v Gill [1963] 1 WLR 841, CCA. . . 81

R v Gill [2001] 1 Cr App R 160 (11), CA. . . 518

R v Gill [2004] 1 WLR 49, CA. . . 336, 468, 470

R v Gillard and Barrett (1990) 92 Cr App R 61, CA. . . 480

R v Gillespie and R v Simpson (1967) 51 Cr App R 172, CA. . . 219

R v GJB [2011] EWCA Crim 867. . . 219, 551

R v Gjoni [2014] EWCA Crim 457. . . 236

R v Glaves [1993] Crim LR 685, CA. . . 481

R v Gloster (1888) 16 Cox CC 471 (Central Criminal Court). . . 449

R v Glover [1991] Crim LR 48, CA. . . 447

R v Gojra [2010] EWCA Crim 1939. . . 294

R v Gokal [1997] 2 Cr App R 266, CA. . . 381

R v Goldenberg (1988) 88 Cr App R 285, CA. . . 463, 464

R v Golder [1960] 1 WLR 1169, CCA. . . 211

R v Goldie [2013] EWCA Crim 1472. . . 635

R v Golds [2016] UKSC 61. . . 35, 659

R v Golizadeh [1995] Crim LR 232, CA. . . 655

R v Gonzales de Arango (1991) 96 Cr App R 399, CA. . . 377

R v Goodsir [2006] EWCA Crim 852. . . 509

R v Goodway [1993] 4 All ER 894, CA. . . 19, 211, 530

R v Goodwin [2018] 4 WLR 165, CA. . . 81, 82

R v Gordon (1789) 1 Leach 515. . . 113

R v Gordon (1987) 92 Cr App R 50n, CA. . . 46

R v Gordon [1995] 1 Cr App R 290, CA. . . 636

R v Gordon [1995] 2 Cr App R 61, CA. . . 29

R v Gordon [2002] EWCA Crim 412. . . 192

R v Goring [2011] EWCA Crim 2. . . 42

R v Goss [2005] Crim LR 61, CA. . . 543

R v Gough [2002] Cr App R 121 (8), CA. . . 501

R v Governor of Brixton Prison, ex p Levin [1997] AC 741, HL. . . 372

R v Governor of Brixton Prison, ex p Osman [1991] 1 WLR 281, QBD. . . 679, 683, 699, 702

R v Governor of Pentonville Prison, ex p Chinoy [1992] 1 All ER 317, DC. . . 344

R v Governor of Pentonville Prison, ex p Osman [1990] 1 WLR 277, QBD. . . 489, 739, 743

R v Governor of Pentonville Prison, ex p Voets [1986] 1 WLR 470, QBD. . . 203

R v Gowan [1982] Crim LR 821, CA. . . 466

R v Gowland-Wynn [2002] 1 Cr App R 569 (41), CA. . . 518

R v Grafton (1993) 96 Cr App R 156, CA. . . 153

R v Graham [1973] Crim LR 628, CA. . . 188

R v Graham [1994] Crim LR 212, CA. . . 282

R v Graham [2007] EWCA Crim 1499. . . 29

R v Grannell (1989) 90 Cr App R 149, CA. . . 293, 331

R v Grant (1865) 4 F&F 322. . . 15

R v Grant [1960] Crim LR 424. . . 63

R v Grant [1996] 1 Cr App R 73, CA. . . 29

R v Grant [1996] 2 Cr App R 272. . . 595

R v Grant [2008] EWCA Crim 1890. . . 41

R v Grant-Murray [2017] EWCA Crim 1228. . . 180, 226, 227, 228, 230

R v Gray [1995] 2 Cr App R 100, CA. . . 488, 489

R v Gray [1998] Crim LR 570, CA. . . 218

R v Gray [2004] 2 Cr App R 498 (30), CA. . . 542, 545, 548

R v Gray [2007] EWCA Crim 2658. . . 384

R v Green [2009] EWCA Crim 1688. . . 29

R v Green [2018] 4 WLR 39, CA. . . 28, 539, 552

R v Green [2019] EWCA Crim 411. . . 509, 518, 519, 520

R v Greene (2009) The Times, 28 Oct. . . 212

R v Greenwood [2005] Crim LR 59, CA. . . 26

R v Greer [1994] Crim LR 745, CA. . . 25

R v Greer [1998] Crim LR 572, CA. . . 40, 380

R v Gregory [1993] Crim LR 623, CA. . . 44

R v Gregory and Mott [1995] Crim LR 507, CA. . . 381

R v Gregson [2003] 2 Cr App R 521 (34), CA. . . 361

R v Griffiths [1998] Crim LR 567, CA. . . 30

R v Grimer [1982] Crim LR 674, CA. . . 317

R v Grimes [1994] Crim LR 213, CA. . . 685

R v Grimes [2017] NICA 19. . . 539, 540

R v Groark [1999] Crim LR 669, CA. . . 80, 81

R v Grossman (1981) 73 Cr App R 302, CA. . . 310

R v Guildhall Magistrates' Court, ex p Primlaks Holdings Co (1989) 89 Cr App R 215, DC. . . 737

R v Gultutan [2006] EWCA Crim 207. . . 21

R v Gumbrell [2009] EWCA Crim 550. . . 600

R v Gummerson and Steadman [1999] Crim LR 680, CA. . . 297, 768

R v Gunewardene [1951] 2 KB 600, CCA. . . 31, 487

R v Guney [1998] 2 Cr App R 242. . . 30

R v Gunning (1994) 98 Cr App R 303, CA. . . 182

R v Guppy [1995] 16 Cr App R (S) 25. . . 85

R v Gurney [1976] Crim LR 567, CA. . . 319

R v Gurpinar [2015] 1 WLR 3442, CA. . . 81, 82

R v Gyima [2007] EWCA Crim 429, [2007] Crim LR 890, CA. . . 588

R v H (1989) 90 Cr App R 440, CA. . . 25

R v H [1992] Crim LR 516, CA. . . 192, 470

R v H [1995] 2 AC 596, HL. . . 621, 622, 623

R v H [2001] Crim LR 815, CA. . . 378

R v H [2003] EWCA Crim 1208. . . 169

R v H [2004] 2 AC 134, HL. . . 679, 703, 708, 709, 710

R v H [2010] EWCA Crim 312. . . 620

R v H [2014] EWCA Crim 1555. . . 246, 639, 641, 648, 649

R v H [2018] EWCA Crim 2868. . . 561

R v H [2019] 1 Cr App R 331 (25). . . 690

R v H (JR) (1990) 90 Cr App R 440, CA. . . 557

R v H (JR) (childhood amnesia) [2006] 1 Cr App R 195 (10), CA. . . 638

R v Hacker [1995] 1 All ER 45, HL. . . 629

R v Hackett [2011] 2 Cr App R 35 (3), CA. . . 21, 516, 517

R v Haddock [2011] EWCA Crim 303. . . 28

R v Hagan (1873) 12 Cox CC 357. . . 450

R v Hagan [1997] 1 Cr App R 464, CA. . . 149

R v Hajdarmayaj [2019] EWCA Crim 303. . . 25, 557

R v Halford (1978) 67 Cr App R 318, CA. . . 146

R v Hall (1987) 86 Cr App R 159, CA. . . 641

R v Hall [1993] Crim LR 527, CA. . . 769

R v Hall [2015] EWCA Crim 581. . . 748

R v Hall-Chung (2007) 151 SJLB 1020. . . 559

R v Hallam [2007] EWCA Crim 1495. . . 148

R v Hallett [1986] Crim LR 462, CA. . . 683

R v Halpin [1975] QB 907, CA. . . 435, 437, 438

R v Halpin [1996] Crim LR 112, CA. . . 30

R v Hamadi [2008] Crim LR 635, CA. . . 241

R v Hamand (1985) 82 Cr App R 65, CA. . . 200

R v Hamer [2011] 1 WLR 528, CA. . . 543

R v Hamid (1979) 69 Cr App R 324, CA. . . 254, 256

R v Hamidi [2010] EWCA Crim 66, CA. . . 501

R v Hamilton [1969] Crim LR 486, CA. . . 182

R v Hammer [1923] 2 KB 786 CCA. . . 36

R v Hammond [1941] 3 All ER 318, CCA. . . 38, 482

R v Hammond [2013] EWCA Crim 2709. . . 81

R v Hampshire [1995] 2 All ER 1019, CA. . . 138, 159

R v Hampson [2012] EWCA Crim 1807. . . 144

R v Hampson [2019] 1 WLR 3243. . . 161

R v Handbridge [1993] Crim LR 287, CA. . . 542

R v Hanson [2005] 1 WLR 3169, [2005] 2 Cr App R 299 (21), CA. . . 571, 587, 592, 599, 606, 616

R v Hanton (1985) The Times, 14 Feb, CA. . . 266

R v Harborne Inhabitants (1835) 2 Ad&El 540. . . 103

R v Harden [1963] 1 QB 8, CCA. . . 312, 637

R v Hardwicke [2001] Crim LR 220. . . 323

R v Hardy (1794) 24 State Tr 199. . . 683

R v Haringey Justices, ex p DPP [1996] 2 Cr App R 119, DC. . . 153

R v Harman (1984) 148 JP 289, CA. . . 185

R v Harper [2019] EWCA 343. . . 337

R v Harris (1986) 84 Cr App R 75, CA. . . 35

R v Harris [1986] Crim LR 123, CA. . . 45

R v Harris [2001] Crim LR 227, CA. . . 771

R v Harris [2006] 1 Cr App R 55 (5), CA. . . 653, 654, 660

R v Harris [2010] Crim LR 54, CA. . . 238

R v Harris [2016] 1 Cr App R 69 (4), CA. . . 517

R v Harron [1996] 2 Cr App R 457, CA. . . 20, 21

R v Hart (1932) 23 Cr App R 202, CCA. . . 221

R v Hart (1957) 42 Cr App R 47, CCA. . . 223

R v Hartley [2003] EWCA Crim 3027. . . 196

R v Harvey [1988] Crim LR 241, CC. . . 462, 466

R v Harvey [2014] EWCA Crim 54. . . 357, 378, 399, 400, 565

R v Harwood [1989] Crim LR 285, CA. . . 329

R v Hasan [2005] 2 AC 467, HL. . . 52, 455

R v Haslam (1925) 19 Cr App R 59, CCA. . . 203

R v Hassan [1970] 1 QB 423, CA. . . 758, 765

R v Hassan [1995] Crim LR 404, CA. . . 486

R v Hatton (1976) 64 Cr App R 88, CA. . . 608

R v Hay (1983) 77 Cr App R 70, CA. . . 25, 773

R v Hay [2018] Crim LR 400, CA. . . 583

R v Hayes [1977] 1 WLR 234. . . 140, 141

R v Hayes [2005] 1 Cr App R 557, CA. . . 749

R v Hayes [2018] 1 Cr App R 134 (10), CA. . . 375, 384, 641

R v Hayter [2005] 1 WLR 605, HL. . . 488

R v Hearne, 4 May 2000, unreported, CA. . . 518

R v Heaton [1993] Crim LR 593, CA. . . 461

R v Hedges (1910) 3 Cr App R 262, CCA. . . 197

R v Hegarty [1994] Crim LR 353, CA. . . 640

R v Helliwell [1995] Crim LR 79, CA. . . 83

R v Hemberger [2017] EWCA Crim 273. . . 375

R v Henderson [2010] 2 Cr App R 185 (24), CA. . . 636, 659, 660, 671

R v Hendley. . . 74

R v Hendrick [1992] Crim LR 427, CA. . . 768

R v Hendry (1988) 153 JP 166, CA. . . 482

R v Hengari-Ajufo [2016] EWCA Crim 1913. . . 209, 388, 391

R v Hennessey (1978) 68 Cr App R 419, CA. . . 683

R v Henney [2016] EWCA Crim 1853. . . 41

R v Henry [1990] Crim LR 574. . . 498

R v Henry [2006] 1 Cr App R 118 (6), CA. . . 641

R v Hepworth and Fearnley [1955] 2 QB 600, CCA. . . 102

R v Herron [1967] 1 QB 107, CCA. . . 51, 629

R v Hersey [1998] Crim LR 281, CA. . . 295, 297

R v Hertfordshire County Council, ex p Green Environmental Industries Ltd [2000] 2 AC 412, HL. . . 721

R v Hetherington [1972] Crim LR 703, CA. . . 455

R v Hewitt; R v Davis (1991) 95 Cr App R 81, CA. . . 685

R v Hewlett [2008] EWCA Crim 270. . . 588

R v Hickin [1996] Crim LR 584, CA. . . 293

R v Higgins [2017] EWCA Crim 224. . . 470

R v Highton [2005] 1 WLR 3472, CA. . . 52, 570, 573, 577, 593, 618

R v Hill (1851) 2 Den CC 254. . . 137, 141

R v Hill (1992) 96 Cr App R 456, CA. . . 672

R v Hill [1996] Crim LR 419, CA. . . 20

R v Hillier (1992) 97 Cr App R 349, CA. . . 44, 768

R v Hills (1987) 86 Cr App R 26, CA. . . 263

R v Hilton [1972] 1 QB 421, CA. . . 129, 215

R v Hinds [1979] Crim LR 111 (Crown Court). . . 231

R v Hinds [2017] EWCA Crim 464, CA. . . 386, 390

R v Hoare [2005] 1 WLR 1804, CA. . . 507, 516

R v Hobson [1998] 1 Cr App R 31, CA. . . 635

R v Hodges [2003] 2 Cr App R 247 (15), CA. . . 644, 655, 656, 658

R v Hoey [2007] NICC 49. . . 636, 648

R v Hogan [1997] Crim LR 349, CA. . . 385

R v Holden (1838) 8 C&P 606. . . 153

R v Holdsworth [2009] Crim LR 195, CA. . . 651

R v Holmes [1953] 1 WLR 686, CA. . . 657

R v Holmes [2014] EWCA Crim 420. . . 287, 595

R v Holt (1793) 5 Term Rep 436. . . 435

R v Holy Trinity, Hull (Inhabitants) (1827) 7 B&C 611. . . 305

R v Honeyghon and Sayles [1999] Crim LR 221, CA. . . 207

R v Hookway [1999] Crim LR 750, CA. . . 657

R v Hookway [2011] EWCA Crim 1989. . . 646, 652

R v Hopes [2011] EWCA Crim 1869. . . 208

R v Hopper [1915] 2 KB 431. . . 80

R v Horley [1999] Crim LR 488, CA. . . 149

R v Horn (1912) 7 Cr App R 200. . . 62

R v Horncastle [2009] 2 Cr App R 230 (15), CA. . . 354, 355, 378, 379, 401

R v Horncastle [2010] 2 AC 373, [2010] 2 WLR 47, SC. . . 174, 354, 355, 357, 358, 359, 387, 404

R v Horne [1990] Crim LR 188, CA. . . 493

R v Horne [1992] Crim LR 304, CA. . . 363

R v Horne [1994] Crim LR 584, CA. . . 640

R v Horseferry Road Magistrates' Court, ex p Bennett [1993] 3 All ER 138; [1994] 1 AC 42. . . 322

R v Horseferry Road Magistrates, ex p Bennett (No 2) [1994] 1 All ER 289, DC. . . 680, 687

R v Horsnell [2012] EWCA Crim 227. . . 134, 357, 364, 366, 390

R v Horwood [1970] 1 QB 133, CA. . . 597

R v Houlden (1993) 99 Cr App R 244, CA. . . 541

R v Howden-Simpson [1991] Crim LR 49, CA. . . 480

R v Howe [1987] 1 All ER 771, HL. . . 83

R v Howe [2017] EWCA Crim 2400. . . 280, 287, 589

R v Howell [2005] 1 Cr App R 1 (1), CA. . . 512, 515

R v Hoyte [1994] Crim LR 215, CA. . . 336, 472

R v Huckerby [2004] EWCA Crim 3251. . . 641

R v Hudson [1994] Crim LR 920, CA. . . 25

R v Hulme [2007] 1 Cr App R 334, CA. . . 212

R v Humphreys and Tully [1993] Crim LR 288, CA. . . 771

R v Humphris (2005) 169 JP 718, CA. . . 384, 586

R v Hundal [2004] 2 Cr App R 307 (19), CA. . . 720

R v Hunjan (1978) 68 Cr App R 99, CA. . . 279

R v Hunt (1820) 3 B&Ald 566. . . 308

R v Hunt [1987] AC 352, HL. . . 64, 66, 68

R v Hunt [1992] Crim LR 582, CA. . . 472

R v Hunt [1994] Crim LR 747, CA. . . 770

R v Hunter [1969] Crim LR 262, CA. . . 18

R v Hunter [1985] 2 All ER 173, CA. . . 319

R v Hunter [2015] 1 WLR 5367, [2015] 2 Cr App R116 (9), CA. . . 544, 545, 547, 548, 549, 550, 551

R v Hurst [1995] 1 Cr App R 82, CA. . . 377, 640

R v Hussain [2004] EWCA Crim 1064. . . 286

R v Hussain [2008] EWCA Crim 1117. . . 557, 577

R v Hussain [2010] EWCA Crim 1327, CA. . . 297

R v Hussain [2015] EWCA Crim 383. . . 565

R v Hutchinson (1985) 82 Cr App R 51, CA. . . 147

R v Hutton (1988) The Times, 27 Oct, CA. . . 200

R v I [2007] 2 Cr App R 316 (24), CA. . . 282

R v I [2012] EWCA Crim 1288. . . 646

R v IA [2013] EWCA Crim 1308. . . 136

R v Ibrahim [2009] 1 WLR 578, CA. . . 390, 457

R v Ibrahim [2012] 2 Cr App R 420 (32), CA. . . 53, 357, 358, 402

R v Ibrahima [2005] Crim LR 887, CA. . . 644, 656

R v IJ [2011] EWCA Crim 2734. . . 559, 596

R v Ikram [2009] 1 WLR 1419, CA. . . 148

R v IL [2011] EWCA Crim 2734. . . 596

R v Ilyas and Knight see R v Foxley; R v Ilyas and Knight

R v Imran [1997] Crim LR 754, CA. . . 149

R v Inch (1989) 91 Cr App R 51, C-MAC. . . 644

R v Inns [2019] 1 Cr App R 61(5), CA. . . 182, 183

R v Ioannou [1999] Crim LR 586, CA. . . 509

R v IRC, ex parte TC Coombs & Co [1991] 2 AC 283. . . 17

R v Irish [1995] Crim LR 145, CA. . . 244

R v Iroegbu (1988) The Times, 2 Aug, CA. . . 45

R v Isequilla [1975] 1 WLR 716, CA. . . 469

R v Islam [1999] 1 Cr App R 22, CA. . . 196

R v Ismail [1990] Cr App R 109, CA. . . 461, 465

R v J [2011] EWCA Crim 3021. . . 357

R v Jabber [2006] EWCA Crim 2694. . . 42

R v Jackson [1996] 2 Cr App R 420, CA. . . 147, 655

R v Jackson [2000] Crim LR 377, CA. . . 707

R v Jackson-Mason [2014] EWCA Crim 1993. . . 640

R v James [1996] Crim LR 650, CA. . . 472

R v Jarvis [2008] EWCA Crim 488; [2008] Crim LR 632, CA. . . 598, 604, 606, 626

R v Jefferson [1994] 1 All ER 270, CA. . . 467

R v Jelen; R v Katz (1989) 90 Cr App R 456, CA. . . 346

R v Jenkins (1869) LR 1 CCR 187. . . 94

R v Jenkins (1945) 31 Cr App R 1, CA. . . 50, 613

R v Jenkins [2003] Crim LR 107, CA. . . 488

R v Jennings [1995] Crim LR 810, CA. . . 40, 405

R v Jewell [2014] EWCA Crim 414. . . 82

R v JG [2018] EWCA Crim 1318 (4). . . 242

R v Jiminez-Paez (1994) 98 Cr App R 239, CA. . . 376

R v JL [2018] Crim LR 184. . . 86

R v John [1973] Crim LR 113, CA. . . 204

R v Johnson (1847) 2 Car&Kir 354. . . 449

R v Johnson [1961] 3 All ER 969, CCA. . . 83

R v Johnson [1988] 1 WLR 1377, CA. . . 684, 685

R v Johnson [1989] 2 All ER 839, CA. . . 80

R v Johnson [1994] Crim LR 376, CA. . . 45

R v Johnson [1995] Crim LR 242, CA. . . 83

R v Johnson [1996] Crim LR 504, CA. . . 293

R v Johnson [2005] EWCA Crim 971. . . 508

R v Johnson [2007] EWCA Crim 1651. . . 454

R v Johnson [2009] 2 Cr App R 101 (7), CA. . . 587

R v Johnson [2017] EWCA Crim 191. . . 510

R v Johnstone [2003] 1 WLR 1736, HL. . . 72, 75

R v Jonas [2015] EWCA Crim 562. . . 227

R v Jones (1883) 11 QBD 118. . . 113

R v Jones (1909) 3 Cr App R 67, CCA. . . 607

R v Jones (1923) 17 Cr App R 117, CCA. . . 616

R v Jones (1968) 54 Cr App R 63, CA. . . 118

R v Jones [1970] 1 WLR 16, CA. . . 122

R v Jones [1987] 2 All ER 692, CA. . . 35

R v Jones [1997] 2 Cr App R 119, CA. . . 489

R v Jones [1998] Crim LR 579, CA. . . 208

R v Jones [2004] 1 Cr App R 60, CA. . . 264, 265

R v Jones [2010] 2 Cr App R 69 (10). . . 341

R v Jones [2015] 1 Cr App R 50 (5). . . 559

R v Jones [2015] EWCA Crim 1317. . . 355

R v Jones [2018] EWCA Crim 2816. . . 226

R v Jones (Terence) [1992] Crim LR 365, CA. . . 286,
293

R v Jones; R v Sullivan [1978] 1 WLR 195, CA. . . 427

R v Jordan [2009] EWCA Crim 953. . . 583

R v Joseph [1993] Crim LR 206, CA. . . 479

R v Joseph [2010] EWCA Crim 2580. . . 636

R v Jovan [2017] EWCA Crim 1359. . . 81

R v Joyce [2005] EWCA Crim 1785. . . 206, 210, 211,
225, 392

R v Joyce [2005] NTS 21. . . 641

R v JP [1999] Crim LR 401, CA. . . 375

R v Juett [1981] Crim LR 113, CA. . . 41

R v Jukes [2018] 2 Crim App R 114 (9), CA. . . 566,
600, 732

R v Justice of the Peace for Peterborough, ex p Hicks
[1977] 1 WLR 1371, DC. . . 736

R v JVG [2015] EWCA Crim 1630. . . 541

R v K (1993) 97 Cr App R 342, CA. . . 690

R v K [2006] 2 Cr App R 175 (10), CA. . . 159

R v K (2008) 172 JP 538, CA. . . 366

R v K [2008] EWCA Crim 3177. . . 624

R v K(A) [2010] QB 343, [2010] 1 Cr App R 44,
CA. . . 719, 750, 751

R v K(M) [2019] QB 86, CA. . . 67

R v K(P) [2008] EWCA Crim 434. . . 231

R v Kabariti (1990) 92 Cr App R 362, CA. . . 544

R v Kachikwu (1968) 52 Cr App R 538, CA. . . 80

R v Kai-Whitewind [2005] 2 Cr App R 457 (31),
CA. . . 274, 651

R v Kalia [1975] Crim LR 181, CA. . . 218

R v Kalu [2007] EWCA Crim 22. . . 561, 577

R v Kane (1977) 65 Cr App R 270, CA. . . 146, 279

R v Kay (1887) 16 Cox CC 292. . . 100, 105

R v Keane [1994] 1 WLR 746, CA. . . 679, 683, 707

R v Kearley [1992] 2 AC 228, HL. . . 26, 350, 362,
366, 367, 370

R v Kearns [2003] 1 Cr App R 111 (7), CA. . . 719,
720, 721

R v Keast [1998] Crim LR 748, CA. . . 27

R v Keenan [1990] 2 QB 54, CA. . . 329, 331, 333,
334, 337, 477, 479

R v Kelleher [2003] EWCA Crim 3525. . . 46

R v Kelly (1985) The Times, 27 July, CA. . . 127

R v Kelly [2015] EWCA Crim 817. . . 14, 564

R v Kelsey (1982) 74 Cr App R 213. . . 187

R v Kemble [1990] 3 All ER 116, CA. . . 143

R v Kempster (1989) 90 Cr App R 14, CA. . . 767,
768, 771

R v Kempster (No 2) [2008] 2 Cr App R 256 (19),
CA. . . 636, 649

R v Kennedy [1992] Crim LR 37, CA. . . 605

R v Kennedy [1994] Crim LR 50, CA. . . 381

R v Kenny [1992] Crim LR 800, CA. . . 486

R v Kenny [1994] Crim LR 284, CA. . . 463

R v Keogh [2007] 1 WLR 1500, CA. . . 77

R v Kerawalla [1991] Crim LR 451, CA. . . 474

R v Khan (1981) 73 Cr App R 190, CA. . . 140

R v Khan (1987) 84 Cr App R 44, CA. . . 132

R v Khan [1993] Crim LR 54, CA. . . 335

R v Khan [1995] Crim LR 78, CA. . . 80

R v Khan [1997] Crim LR 508, CA. . . 331, 335

R v Khan [1997] Crim LR 584, CA. . . 293

R v Khan [2001] Crim LR 673, CA. . . 18

R v Khan [2003] Crim LR 428, CA. . . 208

R v Khan [2008] EWCA Crim 1112. . . 148

R v Khan [2009] EWCA Crim 86. . . 389

R v Khan [2013] EWCA Crim 2230. . . 338

R v Khan [2015] EWCA Crim 1755. . . 593

R v Khan (Sultan) [1997] AC 558, HL. . . 323,
328, 338

R v King (1914) 10 Cr App R 117, CCA. . . 258, 266

R v King [1983] 1 WLR 411, CA. . . 736

R v King [2012] EWCA Crim 805. . . 338, 489

R v King [2014] EWCA Crim 2465. . . 14

R v King [2015] EWCA Crim 1631. . . 565, 568

R v Kinghorn [1908] 2 KB 949. . . 310

R v Kinglake (1870) 22 LT 335. . . 712

R v King's Lynn Magistrates' Court and Walker, ex p
Moore [1988] Fam Law 393, QBD. . . 108

R v Kinsella (1993) Belfast CC, Dec. . . 515

R v Kirk [1999] 4 All ER 698, CA. . . 478

R v Kirk [2006] Crim LR 850, CA. . . 35

R v Kirkpatrick [1998] Crim LR 63, CA. . . 608

R v Kiziltan [2018] 4 WLR 43, CA. . . 377, 402, 403, 404, 405

R v Knight [1966] 1 WLR 230. . . 262

R v Knight [2004] 1 WLR 340, CA. . . 510, 515

R v Knight; R v Thompson (1946) 31 Cr App R 52. . . 490

R v Knott [1973] Crim LR 36, CA. . . 629

R v Knowlden (1983) 77 Cr App R 94, CA. . . 264

R v Konscol [1993] Crim LR 950. . . 336

R v Koon Cheung Tang [1995] Crim LR 813, CA. . . 309

R v Kordasinski [2007] 1 Cr App R 238, CA. . . 767

R v Krezolek [2014] EWCA Crim 2782. . . 165

R v Kwaik [2013] EWCA Crim 2397. . . 646

R v L [1994] Crim LR 839, CA. . . 461

R v L [1999] Crim LR 489, CA. . . 268

R v L [2009] 1 WLR 626, CA. . . 133, 134, 354, 379, 390

R v L (2012) 176 JP 231, CA. . . 579, 580

R v L [2015] EWCA Crim 741. . . 235

R v L [2018] EWCA Crim 1821. . . 323, 341

R v L (R) [2008] 2 Cr App R 243 (18), CA. . . 133

R v La Rose [2003] EWCA Crim 1471. . . 520

R v Ladds [2009] EWCA Crim 1249. . . 557, 580

R v Lafayette [2008] EWCA Crim 3238. . . 592

R v Lake (1976) 64 Cr App R 172. . . 487

R v Lamaletie [2008] EWCA Crim 314, (2008) 172 JP 249, CA. . . 613, 620

R v Lamb [2007] EWCA Crim 1766. . . 594, 624

R v Lambert [2002] 2 AC 545, HL. . . 68, 71, 73, 75, 76, 77

R v Lamont [1989] Crim LR 813, CA. . . 271, 272

R v Land [1998] 1 Cr App R 301, CA. . . 639

R v Landon [1995] Crim LR 338, CA. . . 21

R v Lang [2002] 2 Cr App R (S) 44 (15), CA. . . 81

R v Lang-Hall (1989) The Times, 24 Mar, CA. . . 44

R v Langiert [1991] Crim LR 777, CA. . . 337

R v Langley [2001] Crim LR 651, CA. . . 482

R v Langton (1876) 2 QBD 296, CCR. . . 113, 187

R v Lariba [2015] EWCA Crim 478. . . 291, 293, 294, 316

R v Lashari [2011] 1 Cr App R (S) 72, CA. . . 85

R v Latif [1996] 1 WLR 104, HL. . . 341, 344

R v Latif; R v Shahzad [1996] 1 All ER 353; [1996] 1 WLR 104. . . 322

R v Law (1996) The Times, 15 Aug. . . 679

R v Law-Thompson [1997] Crim LR 674, CA. . . 336

R v Lawal [1994] Crim LR 746, CA. . . 362

R v Lawless (1993) 98 Cr App R 342, CA. . . 215

R v Lawrence [2002] Crim LR 584, CA. . . 707

R v Lawrence [2014] 1 Cr App R 33 (5), CA. . . 357, 387

R v Lawson [2007] Crim LR 232, CA. . . 598

R v Lawson [2007] 1 WLR 1191, CA, [2007] Crim LR 232, CA. . . 593, 598, 600, 606, 626

R v Lawson [2007] 1 Cr App R 277 (20), CA. . . 627

R v Leatham (1861) 8 Cox CC 498. . . 323

R v Leathem [2017] EWCA Crim 42. . . 582

R v Leckey [1944] KB 80. . . 498

R v Lee (1953) 104 CCC 400. . . 94

R v Lee [1996] Crim LR 825, CA. . . 771

R v Leeds Magistrates' Court, ex p Dumbleton [1993] Crim LR 866, DC. . . 737, 741

R v Leonard (2009) 173 JP 366, CA. . . 561

R v Lesley [1996] 1 Cr App R(S) 39, CA. . . 21

R v Levy (1966) 50 Cr App R 198. . . 147

R v Levy (1966) 50 Cr App R 238, CA. . . 616

R v Lewendon [2006] 2 Cr App R 294, CA. . . 54

R v Lewes Justices, ex p Home Secretary [1973] AC 388, HL. . . 680, 687, 697, 699

R v Lewis (1973) 57 Cr App R 860, CA. . . 498

R v Lewis [1989] Crim LR 61, CA. . . 125

R v Lewis [1996] Crim LR 260, CA. . . 272

R v Lewis [2014] EWCA Crim 48. . . 559, 575, 584

R v Lewis [2018] EWCA Crim 1101. . . 41, 510

R v Ley [2007] 1 Cr App R 325, (25), CA. . . 287

R v LH [2017] NICA 67. . . 598, 599

R v Lillyman [1896] 2 QB 167, CCR. . . 196

R v Lin [1995] Crim LR 817, CA. . . 346

R v List [1965] 3 All ER 710, [1966] 1 WLR 9 (Assizes). . . 50, 51, 629

R v Liverpool Juvenile Court, ex p R [1987] 2 All ER 668, DC. . . 39, 481, 482, 486

R v Llanfaethly (Inhabitants) (1853) 2 E&B 940. . . 307

R v Lloyd [2000] 2 Cr App R 355. . . 542

R v Lobell [1957] 1 QB 547, CCA. . . 81

R v Lockley [1995] 2 Cr App R 554, CA. . . 382, 385

R v Lodge [2013] EWCA Crim 987. . . 28, 551, 552

R v Loizou [2006] EWCA Crim 1719. . . 515

R v Looseley; Attorney-General's Reference (No 3 of 2000) [2001] 1 WLR 2060, HL. . . 327, 332, 339

R v Lovell [1990] Crim LR 111, CA. . . 266

R v Lovell [2018] 1 Cr App R (S) 364 (48), CA. . . 581

R v Lovelock [1997] Crim LR 821, CA. . . 221

R v Loveridge [2001] 2 Cr App R 591 (29), CA. . . 339

R v LT [2019] 4 WLR 51, CA. . . 291, 292

R v Lubemba [2014] EWCA Crim 2064, [2015] 1 WLR 1579. . . 180, 181, 226, 227, 229

R v Lucas [1981] QB 720, CA. . . 19, 20, 21, 261, 262, 510, 517

R v Lucas [1991] Crim LR 844, CA. . . 686

R v Lucas [1995] Crim LR 400, CA. . . 30

R v Luffe (1807) 8 East 193. . . 118

R v Lumley (1869) LR 1 CCR 196. . . 103, 113

R v Lunkulu [2015] EWCA Crim 1350. . . 125, 560, 561, 581, 773

R v Lunnon [1988] Crim LR 456, CA. . . 770

R v Luttrell [2004] 2 Cr App R 520 (41), CA. . . 272, 315, 636, 649

R v Lydon (1987) 85 Cr App R 221, CA. . . 362

R v Lynch [2008] 1 Cr App R 338, CA. . . 449

R v Lyons [2010] EWCA Crim 2029. . . 379, 405

R v M [1996] 2 Cr App R 56, CA. . . 149

R v M [2006] EWCA Crim 3408, [2007] Crim LR 637, CA. . . 589

R v M [2009] 2 Cr App R 54 (3), CA. . . 541, 547

R v M [2009] EWCA Crim 618. . . 232

R v M [2010] EWCA Crim 1578. . . 588

R v M [2011] EWCA Crim 648. . . 342

R v M [2012] EWCA Crim 1588. . . 627

R v M [2014] Crim LR 300. . . 387

R v M [2014] Crim LR 823, CA. . . 377, 566

R v M [2014] EWCA Crim 1457. . . 357, 559, 568

R v M [2019] 2 Cr App R 39 (5), CA. . . 226, 227, 230

R v M (A) [2013] 1 Cr App R 245 (17), CA. . . 158

R v M (E) [2014] 2 Cr App R 484 (29), CA. . . 586, 618

R v M (KJ) [2003] 2 Cr App R 322, CA. . . 380

R v M, R v G [2017] 1 Cr App R 413 (27), CA. . . 589

R v McAfee [2006] EWCA Crim 2914. . . 185

R v McAllister (2009) 1 Cr App R 129 (10), CA. . . 586, 592

R v McBride (1961) 45 Cr App R 262. . . 27

R v McCarthy [1996] Crim LR 818, CA. . . 335

R v McCay [1990] 1 WLR 645, CA. . . 448, 449

R v McCleary [1994] Crim LR 121, CA. . . 201

R v McCullough [2011] EWCA Crim 1413. . . 291, 292

R v McDonald [1991] Crim LR 122, CA. . . 327, 481

R v McDowell [1984] Crim LR 486, CA. . . 153

R v McE [2009] AC 908, HL. . . 739

R v McEvilly; R v Lee (1973) 60 Cr App R 150, CA. . . 327

R v McEvoy [1997] Crim LR 887, CA. . . 293

R v McEwan [2011] EWCA Crim 1026. . . 128

R v McGarry [1999] 1 Cr App R 377, CA. . . 520

R v McGeough [2015] UKSC 62. . . 713

R v McGillivray (1992) 97 Cr App R 232, CA. . . 375

R v McGovern (1990) 92 Cr App R 228, CA. . . 465

R v McGranaghan [1995] 1 Cr App R 559, CA. . . 596

R v McGrath and Casey (1983) 5 Cr App R (S) 460. . . 85

R v McGuinness [1999] Crim LR 318, CA. . . 20, 509

R v Machado (2006) 170 JP 400. . . 560

R v McInnes (1989) 90 Cr App R 99, CA. . . 255, 286

R v McIntosh [1992] Crim LR 651, CA. . . 363

R v McIvor [1987] Crim LR 409, CC. . . 475

R v McKenna (1956) 40 Cr App R 65. . . 147, 148

R v MacKenney [2004] 2 Cr App R 32 (5), CA. . . 247, 642

R v MacKenzie [1993] 1 WLR 453, CA. . . 269

R v McKenzie [2008] RTR 277, CA. . . 586, 589, 590

R v Maclean [1993] Crim LR 687, CA. . . 345

R v McLean [2007] EWCA Crim 219. . . 457

R v McLean [2008] 1 Cr App R 156. . . 390

R v McLeod [1994] 1 WLR 1500, CA. . . 608, 619

R v McLernon [1992] NIJB 41, CA, (1990) Belfast CC, 20 Dec. . . 504, 511

R v McManus [2001] EWCA Crim 2455. . . 504

R v McNab [2002] Crim LR 129, CA. . . 336

R v McNamara [1996] Crim LR 750, CA. . . 289

R v McNamara [1998] Crim LR 278, CA. . . 41

R v McPhee [2016] 1 WLR 166, PC. . . 467, 473

R v MacPherson [2006] 1 Cr App R 459 (30), CA. . . 136, 137, 138

R v McQuiston [1998] 1 Cr App R 139, CA. . . 149

R v McVey [1988] Crim LR 127. . . 44

R v Madden [1986] Crim LR 804, CA. . . 361

R v Mader [2018] EWCA Crim 2454. . . 27, 248, 539, 551

R v Maggs (1990) 91 Cr App R 243, CA. . . 149

R v Maginnis [1987] AC 303, HL. . . 36

R v Maguire [1992] 2 All ER 433, CA. . . 671

R v Maguire [2008] EWCA Crim 1028. . . 517

R v Mahil [2013] EWCA Crim 673. . . 559, 626

R v Mahmood and Manzur [1997] 1 Cr App R 414, CA. . . 769

R v Majid [2009] EWCA Crim 2563, CA. . . 85, 86, 143

R v Makanjuola [1995] 1 WLR 1348, CA. . . 260, 261, 263, 264, 267, 268

R v Makuwa [2006] 1 WLR 2755, CA. . . 73

R v Malcolm [2011] EWCA Crim 2069. . . 153

R v Malicki [2009] EWCA Crim 365. . . 138

R v Malik [2000] Crim LR 197, CA. . . 29

R v Mallinson [1977] Crim LR 161, CA. . . 458

R v Malloy [1997] 2 Cr App R 283, CA. . . 726

R v Malone [2006] All ER 32, CA. . . 571, 575

R v Maloney [1994] Crim LR 525, CA. . . 376

R v Mangena [2009] EWCA Crim 2535. . . 185

R v Manji [1990] Crim LR 512, CA. . . 329

R v Mann (1972) 56 Cr App R 750, CA. . . 207

R v Mann [1995] Crim LR 647, CA. . . 345

R v Mansfield Inhabitants (1841) 1 QB 444. . . 108

R v Maqsud Ali [1966] 1 QB 688, CCA. . . 316

R v Marchant [2019] 1 WLR 20, CA. . . 182

R v Marcus [2005] Crim LR 384, CA. . . 293

R v Marlborough Street Magistrates' Court, ex p Simpson (1980) 70 Cr App R 291, DC. . . 310

R v Marlow [1997] Crim LR 457, CA. . . 769

R v Marquis and Graham. . . 354

R v Marriner [2002] EWCA Crim 2855. . . 323, 339

R v Marsh [1994] Crim LR 52, CA. . . 611, 612

R v Marsh [2008] All ER (D) 338 (Jul); [2008] EWCA Crim 1816. . . 386, 387, 389, 390

R v Martin (1872) LR 1 CCR 378. . . 319

R v Martin [1996] Crim LR 589, CA. . . 378

R v Martin [1998] 2 Cr App R 385, CA. . . 724

R v Martin [2004] 2 Cr App R 354 (22), CA. . . 240

R v Martin [2017] EWCA Crim 1359. . . 82, 83

R v Martin and Nicholls [1994] Crim LR 218, CA. . . 293, 329

R v Martinez-Tobon [1994] 2 All ER 90, CA. . . 505

R v Masih [1986] Crim LR 395, CA. . . 640

R v Mason (1911) 7 Cr App R 67, CCA. . . 654, 657

R v Mason [1987] 3 All ER 481; [1988] 1 WLR 139, CA. . . 330, 333, 345, 476

R v Mason [2002] 2 Cr App R 628 (38), CA. . . 338

R v Mateza [2011] EWCA Crim 2587. . . 369

R v Matheson [1958] 1 WLR 474, CCA. . . 61

R v Mathews [2004] QB 690, CA. . . 71

R v Mathias [1989] Crim LR 64, CC. . . 135, 487

R v Mattey; R v Queeley [1995] 2 Cr App R 409, CA. . . 94, 406

R v Matthews [2004] QB 690, CA. . . 71

R v Matthews, R v Dennison, and R v Voss (1989) 91 Cr App R 43, CA. . . 480

R v Mattison [1990] Crim LR 117, CA. . . 769

R v Mauricia [2002] 2 Cr App R 377 (27), CA. . . 308

R v Maw [1994] Crim LR 841, CA. . . 208, 210, 211

R v Maxwell [2011] 1 WLR 1837, SC. . . 322

R v May [2005] 1 WLR 2902, CA. . . 708

R v Mayers [2009] 1 WLR 1915, CA. . . 173, 387

R v Mazekelua [2011] EWCA Crim 1458. . . 207

R v MD [2016] 2 Cr App R 289 (20), CA. . . 620

R v Meachen [2009] EWCA Crim 1701. . . 659

R v Mealey; R v Sheridan (1974) 60 Cr App R 59, CA. . . 327

R v Meany (1867) 10 Cox CC 506. . . 488

R v Mehmedov [2014] EWCA Crim 1523. . . 55

R v Mehrban [2002] 1 Cr App R 561 (40), CA. . . 143

R v Mellars [2019] EWCA Crim 42. . . 557

R v Menard [1995] 1 Cr App R 306, CA. . . 479

R v Mendy (1976) 64 Cr App R 4, CA. . . 11, 245

R v Menga [1998] Crim LR 58, CA. . . 707

R v Menza and Marshalleck [1998] Crim LR 58, CA. . . 684

R v Merchant [2018] 1 Cr App R 165 (11). . . 771

R v Meredith (1943) 29 Cr App R 40. . . 129

R v Metcalfe [2016] 2 Cr App R 297 (21). . . 32, 655

R v MH [2012] EWCA Crim 2725. . . 138, 198

R v M(I) [2012] 1 Cr App R 26 (3), CA. . . 513

R v Miah [1997] 2 Cr App R 12, CA. . . 541

R v Miah [2011] Crim LR 662, CA. . . 606, 607

R v Miah [2014] EWCA Crim 938. . . 263

R v Miah [2018] EWCA Crim 563. . . 86

R v Middleton [2001] Crim LR 251. . . 20

R v Midmore [2017] EWCA Crim 533. . . 369

R v Mihal [2013] EWCA Crim 673. . . 627

R v Milford [2001] Crim LR 330, CA. . . 518, 519

R v Miller [1952] 2 All ER 667 (Winchester Assizes) [1952] Cr App R 169. . . 604, 605

R v Miller [1986] 3 All ER 119, CA. . . 461, 469

R v Miller [1998] Crim LR 209, CA. . . 332

R v Miller [2009] EWCA Crim 2890. . . 287

R v Miller [2010] 2 Cr App R 138 (19). . . 564

R v Miller [2010] EWCA Crim 1578. . . 119, 219

R v Milliken (1969) 53 Cr App R 330, CA. . . 147

R v Mills [1962] 1 WLR 1152, CCA. . . 187, 188

R v Minchin [2013] EWCA Crim 2412. . . 384, 740

R v Minnott [2016] EWCA Crim 2215. . . 149

R v Minors; R v Harper [1989] 1 WLR 441, CA. . . 405

R v Mir [1989] Crim LR 894, CA. . . 607

R v Mirza [2004] 1 AC 118. . . 686

R v Mitchell (1892) 17 Cox CC 503. . . 262, 493

R v Mitchell [2005] EWCA Crim 731. . . 636

R v Mitchell [2017] AC 571, [2017] 3 WLR 1405, [2017] 1 Cr App R 92 (9), SC. . . 587, 592, 594

R v Mittal [2016] 4 WLR 91, CA. . . 547, 548, 625

R v M (KJ) [2003] Cr App R 322. . . 380

R v MM [2011] EWCA Crim 1291. . . 238

R v Moghal (1977) 65 Cr App R 56, CA. . . 450

R v Mokrecovas [2002] 1 Cr App R 226 (20), CA. . . 236

R v Moloney [1985] AC 905, [1985] 1 All ER 1025, HL. . . 102

R v Momodou [2005] 1 WLR 3442, [2005] 2 All ER 571, CA. . . 175, 176, 189

R v Moody [2019] EWCA Crim 1222. . . 236, 566

R v Moon [2004] All ER (D) 167 (Nov), CA. . . 340

R v Moore [1992] Crim LR 882, CA. . . 381

R v Moore [2013] EWCA Crim 85. . . 341, 342

R v Moore [2017] EWCA Crim 1304. . . 318, 319, 655

R v Morley [1994] Crim LR 919, CA. . . 344

R v Morris [1994] Crim LR 596, CA. . . 35

R v Morris [1995] 2 Cr App R 69, CA. . . 29

R v Morris [1998] 1 Cr App R 386, CA. . . 640

R v Morris [1998] Crim LR 416, CA. . . 149, 160

R v Morris [2019] EWCA Crim 147. . . 560

R v Morrison (1911) 6 Cr App R 159. . . 154

R v Morse [1991] Crim LR 195. . . 467

R v Moshaid [1998] Crim LR 420, CA. . . 511

R v Moss (1990) 91 Cr App R 371, CA. . . 270, 272, 467

R v Moss [2011] EWCA Crim 252. . . 294

R v Moulding [1996] Crim LR 440. . . 102

R v Mountford [1999] Crim LR 575, CA. . . 517–18

R v Moustakim [2008] EWCA Crim 3096. . . 541, 542

R v Muhadeen [2016] EWCA Crim 1. . . 565

R v Muir (1983) 79 Cr App R 153, CA. . . 373

R v Mukadi [2004] Crim LR 373, CA. . . 237

R v Mulindwa [2017] 2 Cr App R 94 (10). . .
155, 248, 641

R v Mullen [1992] Crim LR 735, CA. . . 595, 596

R v Mullings [2011] 2 Cr App R 21 (2), CA. . . 560

R v Mullins (1848) 3 Cox CC 526. . . 258

R v Muncaster [1999] Crim LR 409, CA. . . 264

R v Munnery (1990) 94 Cr App R 164, CA. . . 147

R v Murphy [1965] NI 138, C-MAC. . . 327

R v Murphy [1980] QB 434, CA. . . 644

R v Murray (1950) 34 Cr App R 203. . . 486

R v Murray [1994] Crim LR 927, CA. . . 539

R v Murray [1997] 2 Cr App R 136, CA. . . 489

R v Murray [2016] 4 WLR 142. . . 20, 21

R v Muscot (1713) 10 Mod Rep 192. . . 255

R v Mushtaq [2005] 1 WLR 1513, HL. . . 486

R v Musone [2007] 1 WLR 2467, CA. . . 388, 389,
397, 404, 576, 604, 626

R v Mussell [1995] Crim LR 887, CA. . . 83, 282

R v Mutch [1973] 1 All ER 178, CA. . . 505

R v MW [2008] EWCA Crim 3091. . . 542

R v Myers [1998] AC 124, HL. . . 219

R v Myers [2019] Crim LR 181. . . 183

R v Myers and others [2009] 1 WLR 1519, 1 Cr App R
30, CA. . . 268

R v N (1992) 95 Cr App R 256, CA. . . 139

R v N (2007) 171 JPN 382, CA. . . 364, 366

R v N [2011] EWCA Crim 730. . . 594

R v N [2014] EWCA Crim 419. . . 598, 599, 600

R v N [2014] EWCA Crim 506. . . 287

R v N [2015] Crim LR 439, CA. . . 584

R v N Ltd [2009] 1 Cr App R 56, CA. . . 42

R v Nagah (1990) 92 Cr App R 344, CA. . . 330

R v Nagrecha [1997] 2 Cr App R 401, CA. . . 223, 243

R v Nagy [1990] Crim LR 187, CA. . . 286

R v Najjar [2014] EWCA Crim 1309. . . 288, 289

R v Napper [1996] Crim LR 591, CA. . . 503

R v Nash [2005] Crim LR 232, CA. . . 281

R v Nathaniel [1995] 2 Cr App R 565, CA. . . 333

R v Naudeer [1984] 3 All ER 1036, CA. . . 18

R v Naylor [2010] EWCA Crim 1188. . . 125

R v Nazeer [1998] Crim LR 750, CA. . . 303

R v Neale [1998] Crim LR 737, CA. . . 223, 243

R v Neil [1994] Crim LR 441, CA. . . 480

R v Nelson [2006] EWCA Crim 3412. . . 614, 617

R v Nelson [2009] EWCA Crim 1600. . . 378

R v Nelson and Rose [1998] 2 Cr App R 399,
CA. . . 335, 472, 480

R v Nethercott [2002] 2 Cr App R 117 (7), CA. . . 23

R v Newell [1989] Crim LR 906. . . 81

R v Newell [2012] 1 WLR 3142, CA. . . 451

R v Newport [1998] Crim LR 581, CA. . . 443

R v Newsome (1980) 71 Cr App R 325, CA. . . 200

R v Newton (1912) 7 Cr App R 214. . . 686

R v Ngando [2014] EWCA Crim 506. . . 595

R v Ngyuen (2008) 2 Cr App 99 (9), CA. . . 576, 592

R v Nicholas [1995] Crim LR 942, CA. . . 29

R v Nickolson [1999] Crim LR 61, CA. . . 510

R v Nix 15 March 2016, CA. . . 590

R v NK [1999] Crim LR 980, CA. . . 196

R v Noble [2016] EWCA Crim 2219, [2017] Crim LR
473. . . 368, 562, 615

R v Norris [2013] EWCA Crim 712. . . 590

R v Northam (1967) 52 Cr App R 97. . . 462

R v Norton [1910] 2 KB 496, CCA. . . 491, 492

R v Nottingham City Justices, ex p Lynn [1984] Crim
LR 554. . . 311

R v Nowaz [1976] 3 All ER 5, CA. . . 307

R v Nugent [1977] 3 All ER 662. . . 154

R v Nyanteh [2005] Crim LR 651, CA. . . 20

R v Nye, R v Loan (1977) 66 Cr App R 252,
CA.. . 444

R v O [2006] 2 Cr App R 405 (27), CA. . . 395

R v Oakley (1979) 70 Cr App R 7, CA. . . 644

R v Oakwell (1978) 66 Cr App R 174, CA. . . 279, 283

R v O'Boyle (1990) 92 Cr App R 202, CA. . . 219

R v O'Brien [2000] Crim LR 676, CA. . . 643

R v O'Brien [2016] EWCA Crim 698. . . 768, 769

R v O'Connor (1986) 85 Cr App R 298, CA. . . 53,
769, 771

R v O'Connor [2010] EWCA Crim 2287. . . 40, 384

R v Odeyemi [1999] Crim LR 828, CA. . . 509

R v O'Doherty [2003] 1 Cr App R 77 (5), CA
(NI). . . 295, 650

R v O'Donnell (1917) 12 Cr App R 219. . . 33

R v O'Dowd [2009] 2 Cr App R 280 (16), CA. . . 570,
577, 586, 592

R v Ofori (No 2) (1993) 99 Cr App R 223, CA. . .
119, 637

R v Ogden [2013] EWCA Crim 1294. . . 41

R v O'Hadhmaill [1996] Crim LR 509, CA. . . 146

R v O'Hare [2006] EWCA Crim 2512. . . 387

R v Okafor [1994] 3 All ER 741, CA. . . 479

R v Okokono [2014] EWCA Crim 2521. . . 561, 579, 581, 582, 772

R v Okusanya [1995] Crim LR 941, CA. . . 29

R v O'Leary (1988) 87 Cr App R 387, CA. . . 53, 331, 476

R v O'Leary [2002] EWCA Crim 2055, CA. . . 280

R v O'Leary [2013] EWCA Crim 1371. . . 591

R v Oliphant [1992] Crim LR 40, CA. . . 478

R v Olisa [1990] Crim LR 721, CA. . . 427

R v Oliva [1965] 1 WLR 1028, CCA. . . 153, 154, 211

R v Oliver [1944] KB 68. . . 66

R v Oliver [2016] EWCA Crim 1053. . . 653

R v O'Loughlin [1988] 3 All ER 431, CCC. . . 330

R v Olu [2010] EWCA Crim 2975; [2011] 1 Cr App R 404 (33), CA. . . 543, 551, 626, 767

R v Olumegbon [2004] EWCA Crim 2337. . . 208

R v Omotoso [2018] EWCA Crim 1394, [2019] Crim LR 156, CA. . . 609, 610, 611, 614, 615, 617

R v O'Neill [1969] Crim LR 260, CA. . . 223

R v Oni [1992] Crim LR 183, CA. . . 472

R v Orton (1873) and R v Jameson (1896) Stephen's Digest of the Law of Evidence (10th edn) 48. . . 439

R v Osborne [1905] 1 KB 551, CCR. . . 196, 197

R v Osborne [2010] EWCA Crim 1981. . . 207

R v Osborne [2007] Crim LR 712, CA. . . 558

R v Osbourne; R v Virtue [1973] QB 678, CA. . . 202, 373

R v Oscar [1991] Crim LR 778, CA. . . 293

R v O'Sullivan [1969] 1 WLR 497, CA. . . 312

R v Ovba [2015] EWCA Crim 725. . . 610

R v Owen (1952) 36 Cr App R 16. . . 148

R v Owen (1985) 83 Cr App R 100, CA. . . 617

R v Oxfordshire County Council [1992] 3 WLR 88, Fam D. . . 418

R v Oyesiku (1971) 56 Cr App R 240, CA. . . 197, 249

R v P [1991] 2 AC 447, HL. . . 536, 594, 595

R v P [2002] 1 AC 46, HL. . . 339

R v P [2008] 2 Cr App R 68, CA. . . 42

R v P (31 May 2012, unreported), CA. . . 559

R v P (GR) [1998] Crim LR 663, CA. . . 194, 222

R v P (R) [2014] 1 WLR 3058, CA. . . 231

R v Pabon [2018] EWCA Crim 420. . . 643

R v Pall (1991) 156 JP 424, CA. . . 335, 472

R v Palmer (1914) 10 Cr App R 77, CCA. . . 203

R v Palmer [2014] EWCA Crim 1681. . . 340

R v Papworth [2008] 1 Cr App R 439 (36), CA. . . 201

R v Paris (1992) 97 Cr App R 99, CA. . . 461

R v Park (1993) 99 Cr App R 270, CA. . . 470

R v Parker [1995] Crim LR 233, CA. . . 459, 460, 461

R v Parris (1989) 89 Cr App R 68, CA. . . 331, 334, 476, 478

R v Parvez [2010] EWCA Crim 3229. . . 211

R v Pashmfouroush [2006] EWCA Crim 2330. . . 190

R v Patel [1951] 2 All ER 29. . . 28

R v Patel [1981] 3 All ER 94. . . 370

R v Patel (1981) 73 Cr App R 117, CA. . . 428

R v Patel (1992) 97 Cr App R 294, CA. . . 379, 380

R v Patel [1992] Crim LR 739, CA. . . 146

R v Patel [2001] EWCA Crim 2505. . . 682

R v Patel [2010] EWCA Crim 976. . . 542

R v Pattemore [1994] Crim LR 836, CA. . . 344

R v Pattinson (1973) 58 Cr App R 417, CA. . . 458

R v Pattinson [1996] 1 Cr App R 51, CA. . . 282

R v Paul [1920] 2 KB 183. . . 129

R v Payne [1963] 1 WLR 637, CCA. . . 327, 328, 345

R v Payton [2006] EWCA Crim 1226. . . 545

R v PB [2016] EWCA Crim 1462. . . 625

R v PD [2012] 1 Cr App R 448 (33), CA. . . 545

R v Peach [1990] 2 All ER 966, CA. . . 256

R v Peacock [1998] Crim LR 681, CA. . . 21

R v Pearce (1979) 69 Cr App R 365, CA. . . 199, 200, 490

R v Pearce [2002] 1 WLR 1553, CA. . . 132

R v Pedersen [2013] EWCA Crim 464. . . 402

R v Pemberton (1993) 99 Cr App R 228, CA. . . 288

R v Penny (1991) 94 Cr App R 345, CA. . . 286

R v Percy Smith [1976] Crim LR 511, CA. . . 365

R v Perman [1995] Crim LR 736, CA. . . 264

R v Perry [1984] Crim LR 680, CA. . . 629

R v Pestano [1981] Crim LR 397, CA. . . 211

R v Petcherini (1855) 7 Cox CC 79. . . 450

R v Petkar [2004] 1 Cr App R 270 (22), CA. . . 265, 518, 519

R v Pettman, 2 May 1985, unreported, CA. . . 564, 579, 581, 582

R v PF [2017] EWCA Crim 983. . . 621

R v Pham [2008] EWCA Crim 3182. . . 486

R v Phillips (1936) 26 Cr App R 17, CCA. . . 243, 246

R v Phillips [2003] 2 Cr App R 528 (35), CA. . . 15, 581

R v Phillips [2012] 1 Cr App R 332 (25), CA. . . 565, 601, 602, 603 604

R v Phillips [2015] EWCA Crim 836. . . 503

R v Phillipson (1989) 91 Cr App R 226, CA. . . 146

R v Pieterson [1995] 2 Cr App R 11, CA. . . 16

R v Pigram [1995] Crim LR 808, CA. . . 767

R v Pilcher (1974) 60 Cr App R 1, CA. . . 146

R v Pipe (1966) 51 Cr App R 17, CA. . . 128

R v Pipe [2014] EWCA Crim 2570. . . 215

R v Pitt [1983] QB 25, [1982] 3 All ER 63, CA. . . 134, 717

R v Pittard [2006] EWCA Crim 2028. . . 125

R v Pitts (1912) 8 Cr App R 126. . . 258

R v Platt [2016] 4 WLR 51, CA. . . 555, 602, 604, 605

R v Platten [2006] EWCA Crim 140. . . 489

R v Pleydell [2006] 1 Cr App R 212 (12), CA. . . 27

R v Plunkett [2013]1 WLR 3212, CA. . . 338

R v Podola [1960] 1 QB 325, CCA. . . 63

R v Pointer [1997] Crim LR 676, CA. . . 509

R v Polin [1991] Crim LR 293, CA. . . 201

R v Pommell [1995] 2 Cr App R 607, CA. . . 60

R v Ponting [1985] Crim LR 318. . . 46

R v Pook (1871) 13 Cox CC 172. . . 450

R v Popescu [2010] EWCA Crim 1230. . . 160

R v Porritt (1961) 45 Cr App R 348. . . 45

R v Pouladian-Kari [2013] EWCA Crim 158. . . 35

R v Pountney [1989] Crim LR 216, CA. . . 263

R v Powar [2009] EWCA Crim 594. . . 175

R v Powell [1985] Crim LR 592, CA. . . 208

R v Powell [1986] 1 All ER 193, CA. . . 52, 619

R v Powell [2006] 1 Cr App R 468 (31), CA. . . 137, 138

R v Power [1919] 1 KB 572. . . 41

R v Prager [1972] 1 WLR 260, CA. . . 454, 459, 469

R v Prater [1960] 2 QB 464, CCA. . . 264

R v Preddie [2011] EWCA Crim 312. . . 293, 294

R v Preko [2015] EWCA Crim 242. . . 25, 557

R v Price [1991] Crim LR 707, CA. . . 381

R v Priestley (1965) 51 Cr App R 1n. . . 459

R v Pryce [1991] Crim LR 379, CA. . . 268

R v Puaca [2005] EWCA Crim 3001. . . 654

R v Pullen [1991] Crim LR 457, CA. . . 81

R v Purcell [1992] Crim LR 806, CA. . . 472

R v Putland [2010] EWCA Crim 459. . . 296

R v Putland and Sorrell [1946] 1 All ER 85,
CCA. . . 67

R v Q [2011] All ER (D) 210 (Jun). . . 28

R v Qadir [1998] Crim LR 828, CA. . . 282

R v Qayyum [2007] Crim LR 160, CA. . . 272

R v Quinn [1990] Crim LR 581, CA. . . 53, 293, 336

R v Quinn [1995] 1 Cr App R 480, CA. . . 294

R v Quinn; R v Bloom [1962] 2 QB 245. . . 32

R v R [1994] 1 WLR 758, [1994] 4 All ER 260,
CA. . . 127, 725, 736

R v R [1996] Crim LR 815, CA. . . 260, 261

R v R [2003] EWCA Crim 2754. . . 239

R v R [2010] EWCA Crim 2469. . . 138

R v R [2017] EWCA Crim 1487. . . 160

R v Rabheru [2013] EWCA Crim 137. . . 627

R v Radak [1999] 1 Cr App R 187, CA. . . 376, 381

R v Rahman [2015] 1 Cr App R 457 (30). . . 168

R v Rajakuruna [1991] Crim LR 458, CA. . . 337

R v Ramirez [2009] EWCA Crim 1721. . . 571, 626

R v Rampling [1987] Crim LR 823, CA. . . 95, 316

R v Ramsden [1991] Crim LR 295, CA. . . 282

R v Rana [2007] EWCA Crim 2261, CA. . . 21, 517

R v Rance and Herron (1975) 62 Cr App R 118,
CA. . . 592

R v Randall [2004] 1 WLR 56, HL. . . 24, 602, 642

R v Randall [2006] EWCA Crim 1413. . . 287

R v Randall [2018] EWHC 1048 (Admin). . . 391

R v Rankine [1986] 2 All ER 566, CA. . . 683, 684, 685

R v Raphaie [1996] Crim LR 812, CA. . . 329, 335

R v Rashid [2017] EWCA Crim 2, [2017] 1 WLR
2449. . . 170

R v Rasini (1986) The Times, 20 Mar, CA. . . 629

R v Ratten [1986] AC 41. . . 361

R v Raviraj (1986) 85 Cr App R 93, CA. . . 498

R v Rawlings [1995] 1 All ER 580, CA. . . 149

R v Rearden (1864) 4 F&F 76. . . 580

R v Redgrave (1981) 74 Cr App R 10. . . 539

R v Redpath (1962) 46 Cr App R 319, CCA. . . 262

R v Reed [2010] 1 Cr App R 310 (23), CA. . . 635,
636, 649

R v Reeves (1979) 68 Cr App R 331, CA. . . 36

R v Regan (1887) 16 Cox CC 203. . . 304

R v Rehman [2007] Crim LR 101, CA. . . 336

R v Reid [1989] Crim LR 719, CA. . . 608

R v Reilly [1994] Crim LR 279, CA. . . 684

R v Renda [2006] 1 WLR 2948, CA. . . 330, 549, 557,
558, 562, 566, 567, 609, 612, 614, 620

R v Rennie [1982] 1 WLR 64, CA. . . 464, 465

R v Reszpondek [2010] EWCA Crim 2358. . . 20

R v Reynolds [1950] 1 KB 606. . . 38

R v Reynolds [1989] Crim LR 220, CA. . . 640

R v RG [2002] EWCA Crim 1056. . . 27, 551

R v Riat [2013] 1 WLR 2592, CA. . . 357, 379, 387,
388, 399, 401, 402, 403

R v Riaz (1991) 94 Cr App R 339, CA. . . 95, 149

R v Rice [1963] 1 QB 857, CCA (1963) 47 Cr App R
79, CCA. . . 146, 219, 315, 362, 363, 364

R v Richards [1997] Crim LR 499, CA. . . 30

R v Richardson (1967) 51 Cr App R 381. . . 130

R v Richardson [1971] 2 QB 484. . . 188, 191

R v Richardson (1993) 98 Cr App R 174, CA. . . 153

R v Richardson [2014] EWCA Crim 1785. . . 287, 584

R v Rider (1986) 83 Cr App R 207, CA. . . 256

R v Riley (1866) 4 F&F 964. . . 224

R v Riley (1887) 18 QBD 481, CCR. . . 236

R v Rimmer [1972] 1 WLR 268, CA. . . 454

R v Rimmer and Beech [1983] Crim LR 250,
CA. . . 642

R v Rizwan Mawji [2003] EWCA Crim 3067. . . 360

R v RJ [2017] EWCA Crim 1943. . . 562, 573

R v RK [2018] EWCA Crim 603. . . 227, 228

R v Roads [1967] 2 QB 108. . . 686

R v Robb (1991) 93 Cr App R 161, CA. . . 636, 650, 658, 672

R v Roberts (1878) 14 Cox CC 101 (CCR). . . 113

R v Roberts [1942] 1 All ER 187, CCA. . . 193, 194

R v Roberts [1998] Crim LR 682, CA. . . 365

R v Roberts [2000] Crim LR 183, CA. . . 278, 295, 299

R v Roberts [2011] EWCA Crim 2974. . . 463

R v Robertson [1968] 1 WLR 1767, CA. . . 63

R v Robertson; R v Golder [1987] QB 920, [1987] 3 All ER 231, CA. . . 28, 767, 768, 771

R v Robinson [1994] 3 All ER 346, CA. . . 248, 641, 642

R v Robinson [1996] Crim LR 417, CA. . . 22

R v Robinson [2001] Crim LR 478, CA. . . 610

R v Roble [1997] Crim LR 449, CA. . . 514, 515

R v Robson; R v Harris [1972] 1 WLR 651, CA. . . 38, 95, 316

R v Rochford [2011] 1 WLR 534, CA. . . 527

R v Rogers [1993] Crim LR 386, CA. . . 293

R v Rogers and Tarran [1971] Crim LR 413. . . 487

R v Romeo [2004] 1 Cr App R 418 (30), CA. . . 263

R v Roncoli [1998] Crim LR 584, CA. . . 215

R v Rosenberg [2006] Crim LR 540, CA. . . 339

R v Ross [2008] Crim LR 306, CA. . . 206

R v Ross [2009] EWCA Crim 1165. . . 567

R v Rossiter [1994] 2 All ER 752, CA. . . 81

R v Rothwell (1994) 99 Cr App R 388, CA. . . 350, 364

R v Rowley [2013] 1 WLR 89, CA. . . 375

R v Rowson [1986] QB 174, [1985] 2 All ER 539, CA. . . 219, 483

R v Rowton (1865) Le&Ca 520, CCR. . . 539, 540

R v Royce-Bentley [1974] 1 WLR 535, CA. . . 258

R v Royston Jackson [2011] EWCA Crim 1870. . . 588

R v Rubin [1995] Crim LR 332, CA. . . 596

R v Rudd (1948) 32 Cr App R 138. . . 129, 487

R v Russell-Jones [1995] 3 All ER 239, CA. . . 153

R v Rutherford [1998] Crim LR 490, CA. . . 406

R v Ryan [1992] Crim LR 187, CA. . . 293

R v Ryder [1994] 2 All ER 859, CA. . . 283, 284

R v S [1992] Crim LR 307, CA. . . 243

R v S [1993] Crim LR 293, CA. . . 596

R v S [2003] 1 Cr App R 602 (35), CA. . . 72, 76, 77

R v S [2004] 1 WLR 2940, CA. . . 196

R v S [2006] 2 Cr App R 437 (31). . . 565, 566

R v S [2006] EWCA Crim 2389. . . 248, 641

R v S [2009] 1 All ER 716, CA. . . 720

R v S [2009] EWCA Crim 2457. . . 569

R v S [2010] EWCA Crim 1579. . . 239

R v S [2012] EWCA Crim 1433. . . 636

R v S; R v W [2007] 2 All ER 974, CA. . . 638

R v Sadiq (2009) 173 JP 471, CA. . . 387, 390

R v Saint [2010] EWCA Crim 1924. . . 580

R v St Louis and Fitzroy Case (1984) 79 Cr App R 53, CA. . . 616

R v Sakyi [2014] EWCA Crim 1784. . . 515

R v Saleem (Zafan Akhtar) [2007] EWCA Crim 1923. . . 558, 603

R v Samms [1991] Crim LR 197, CC. . . 293

R v Sampson [2014] EWCA Crim 1968. . . 41, 636

R v Samuel (1956) 40 Cr App R 8, CCA. . . 610, 612

R v Samuel [1988] QB 615 [1988] 2 All ER 135, CA. . . 53, 332, 334, 473, 474, 475, 478

R v Samuel [1992] Crim LR 189, CA. . . 381

R v Sanders (1920) 14 Cr App R 11. . . 102

R v Sanders (1991) 93 Cr App R 245, CA. . . 659

R v Sanderson (1953) 37 Cr App R 32. . . 148

R v Sandhu [1997] Crim LR 288, CA. . . 25

R v Sandhu, R v Byrne [2002] 2 Cr App R 311 (21). . . 25

R v Sang [1980] AC 402, HL. . . 49–50, 323, 326, 327, 328, 330, 468

R v Sanghera [2001] 1 Cr App R 299, CA. . . 335

R v Sansom [1991] 2 QB 130, CA. . . 146

R v Sanusi [1992] Crim LR 43, CA. . . 470, 478

R v Sardar [2012] EWCA Crim 134. . . 160

R v Sardar [2017] 1 WLR 917, CA. . . 42, 172, 387, 391

R v Sargeant [2019] EWCA Crim 1088. . . 659

R v Sargent [1993] Crim LR 713, CA. . . 44, 264

R v Sargent [2003] 1 AC 347, HL. . . 339

R v Sartori [1961] Crim LR 397. . . 94

R v Sat-Bhambra (1988) 88 Cr App R 55, CA. . . 53, 455, 466, 482, 486

R v Saunders [1899] 1 QB 490, CCR. . . 373

R v Saunders [1995] 2 Cr App R 313, CA. . . 149

R v Saunders [1996] 1 Cr App R 463, CA. . . 19

R v Saunders [2012] EWCA Crim 1185. . . 444

R v Scarrott [1978] QB 1016, CA. . . 254

R v Schama and Abramovitch (1914) 11 Cr App R 45. . . 102

R v Schofield (1917) 12 Cr App R 191, CCA. . . 458

R v Schreiber and Schreiber [1988] Crim LR 112, CA. . . 384

R v Scott (1984) 79 Cr App R 49, CA. . . 146

R v Scott [1991] Crim LR 56, CA. . . 480

R v Scott [1994] Crim LR 947, CA. . . 25

R v Scott [1996] Crim LR 652, CA. . . 30

R v Scranage [2001] EWCA Crim 1171. . . 542

R v Sealby [1965] 1 All ER 701 (Crown Court). . . 364, 436, 437, 438

R v Sed [2004] 1 WLR 3218, [2005] 1 Cr App R 55, CA. . . 137

R v Seelig [1991] 4 All ER 429, CA. . . 461, 470, 508

R v Sekhon (1986) 85 Cr App R 19, CA. . . 185, 187, 189

R v Sellick [2005] 1 WLR 3257, CA. . . 380

R v Sellu [2016] EWCA Crim 1716. . . 658

R v Selwyn [2012] EWCA Crim 2968. . . 294

R v Senat; R v Sin (1968) 52 Cr App R 282, CA. . . 316

R v Senior [2004] 3 All ER 9, CA. . . 336

R v Seton [2010] EWCA Crim 450, (2010) 174 JP 241, CA. . . 359, 379, 387, 388, 390, 391

R v Setz-Dempsey (1994) 98 Cr App R 23, CA. . . 376, 381

R v SG [2017] EWCA Crim 617. . . 229

R v Shabir, 11 May 2016, CA. . . 569

R v Shah [1994] Crim LR 125, CA. . . 472

R v Shaid [2019] EWCA Crim 142. . . 570

R v Shanmugarajah [2015] 2 Cr App R 215 (14), CA. . . 288, 289

R v Shannon [2001] 1 WLR 51, CA. . . 323, 342, 343

R v Sharp [1988] 1 All ER 65, [1988] 1 WLR 7, HL. . . 200, 350, 455, 542

R v Sharp [1994] QB 261, CA. . . 215

R v Shaw (1888) 16 Cox CC 503, Assizes. . . 245

R v Shaw [2002] EWCA Crim 3004. . . 191

R v Sheikh [2013] EWCA Crim 907. . . 579

R v Shellard (1840) 9 C&P 277. . . 488

R v Shephard (1991) 93 Cr App R 139, CA. . . 372

R v Shepherd [1995] Crim LR 153, CA. . . 550

R v Sherif [2008] EWCA Crim 2653. . . 463

R v Shervington [2008] EWCA Crim 658, [2008] Crim LR 581, CA. . . 281

R v Shirley [2013] EWCA Crim 1990. . . 201

R v Shirt [2019] 1 Cr App R 199 (15). . . 770, 771

R v Shone (1983) 76 Cr App R 72, CA. . . 370, 428

R v Silcott [1987] Crim LR 765, CC. . . 487, 641

R v Silverlock [1894] 2 QB 766, CCR. . . 312, 644

R v Simmonds [1969] 1 QB 685, CA. . . 185, 188

R v Simmonds [1996] Crim LR 816, CA. . . 142

R v Simmons [1987] Crim LR 630, CA. . . 258

R v Simms [1995] Crim LR 304, CA. . . 30

R v Simons (1834) 6 C&P 540. . . 429

R v Simpson [1983] 1 WLR 1494, CA. . . 35, 118

R v Sims [1946] KB 531, CCA. . . 10, 594

R v Singh [2006] 1 WLR 146, PC. . . 549

R v Singh [2006] 1 WLR 1564, CA. . . 352, 366, 367

R v Singh [2007] EWCA Crim 2140, CA. . . 613, 616, 618

R v Singh [2013] EWCA Crim 669. . . 294

R v Singleton [1995] 1 Cr App R 431. . . 737

R v Skinner (1993) 99 Cr App R 212, CA. . . 189, 191

R v Skinner [1995] Crim LR 805, CA. . . 768

R v Skirving; R v Grossman [1985] 2 All ER 705. . . 539

R v Slater [1995] 1 Cr App R 584, CA. . . 280

R v Sliogeris [2015] EWCA Crim 22; (2015) 179 JP 156, CA. . . 389, 457, 458

R v Slowcombe [1991] Crim LR 198, CA. . . 684

R v Smith (1968) 52 Cr App R 224. . . 154

R v Smith [1979] 1 WLR 1445, CA. . . 640, 657

R v Smith [1994] 1 WLR 1396, CA. . . 331, 470

R v Smith [1998] 2 Cr App R 1, CA. . . 707

R v Smith [2001] 1 WLR 1031. . . 708

R v Smith [2003] EWCA Crim 927. . . 643

R v Smith [2007] EWCA Crim 215. . . 768

R v Smith [2009] 1 Cr App R 521 (36), CA. . . 291, 559

R v Smith [2011] 2 Cr App R 174 (16), CA. . . 636, 645

R v Smith [2019] EWCA Crim 1151. . . 154, 155, 207

R v Smith (Brian) [1995] Crim LR 658, CA. . . 345

R v Smith (Eric) [1987] Crim LR 579, CC. . . 475

R v Smith (Ivor) [1995] Crim LR 940, CA. . . 29

R v Smith (Robert William) (1985) 81 Cr App R 286, CA. . . 262

R v Smith and Doe (1986) 85 Cr App R 197, CA. . . 41, 286

R v Smith and Mercieca [2005] 2 All ER 29. . . 686

R v Smurthwaite and Gill [1994] 1 All ER 898, CA. . . 343, 345

R v Somers [1963] 1 WLR 1306, CCA. . . 644

R v Soroya [2007] Crim LR 181, CA. . . 233

R v Sothilingham [2019] 4 WLR 17, CA. . . 160

R v South [2011] EWCA Crim 754. . . 567

R v South Ribble Magistrates' Court, ex p Cochrane [1996] 2 Cr App R 544, DC. . . 192

R v South Worcestershire Magistrates, ex p Lilley [1995] 1 WLR 1595, DC. . . 710

R v Sparks [1991] Crim LR 128, CA. . . 337, 479

R v Spartley [2007] EWCA Crim 1789, [2007] All ER 233, 151 Sol Jo LB 670, CA. . . 571, 575, 611

R v Speed [2013] EWCA Crim 1650. . . 578

R v Spencer; R v Smails [1986] 2 All ER 928, HL. . . 267

R v Spens [1991] 4 All ER 421, CA. . . 35

R v Spiby (1990) 91 Cr App R 186, CA. . . 372

R v Spinks [1982] 1 All ER 587, CA. . . 758, 765

R v Spittle [2009] RTR 14, CA. . . 584

R v Spottiswood [2019] EWCA Crim 949. . . 517, 583, 589

R v Stamford [1972] 2 QB 391, CA. . . 639

R v Stannard [1964] 1 All ER 34. . . 264

R v Stanton [2004] EWCA Crim 490. . . 279

R v Stark [2015] EWCA Crim 1513. . . 560

R v Steane [1947] KB 997. . . 102

R v Steen [2008] 2 Cr App R 380 (26), CA. . . 391

R v Steltner [2018] EWCA Crim 1479. . . 235, 241, 589

R v Stephens [2002] EWCA Crim 1529. . . 85, 86

R v Stephenson [2006] EWCA Crim 2325. . . 566

R v Stevenson [1971] 1 WLR 1. . . 38, 95, 316

R v Stewart (1972) 56 Cr App R 272, CCC. . . 469

R v Stewart (1986) 83 Cr App R 327, CA. . . 258

R v Stewart [1995] 1 Cr App R 441, CA. . . 770

R v Stewart [1995] Crim LR 500, CA. . . 335

R v Stewart [1999] Crim LR 746, CA. . . 769

R v Stewart [2016] EWCA Crim 447. . . 561, 581, 584

R v Stewart, R v Sappleton (1989) 89 Cr App R 273, CA. . . 149

R v Stipendiary Magistrate for Norfolk, ex p Taylor [1998] Crim LR 276, DC. . . 710

R v Stockwell (1993) 97 Cr App R 260, CA. . . 636, 658

R v Stokes [2015] EWCA Crim 1911. . . 610

R v Stone [2005] Crim LR 569, CA. . . 265

R v Storey (1968) 52 Cr App R 334. . . 199

R v Stoutt [2014] UKPC 14. . . 282, 405

R v Stretton; R v McCallion (1986) 86 Cr App R 7, CA. . . 215

R v Stripp (1978) 69 Cr App R 318, CA. . . 81

R v Strudwick (1993) 99 Cr App R 326, CA. . . 19, 640

R v Stubbs [2006] EWCA Crim 2312, CA. . . 645

R v Styles [2015] EWCA Crim 1619. . . 548

R v Sule [2012] EWCA Crim 1130, [2013] 1 Cr App R 42 (3). . . 561, 581

R v Suleman [2012] 2 Cr App R 30, CA. . . 591

R v Sullivan (1887) 16 Cox CC 347. . . 458

R v Sullivan [1923] 1 KB 47. . . 148

R v Sullivan [2015] EWCA Crim 1565. . . 561

R v Sunny Islam [2012] EWCA Crim 3106. . . 240

R v Surgenor (1940) 27 Cr App R 175. . . 140

R v Surgue [2017] EWCA Crim 1840. . . 562

R v Suski [2016] 2 Cr App R 32 (3). . . 132

R v Sutton (1816) 4 M&S 532. . . 435

R v Sutton (1969) 53 Cr App R 504, CA. . . 627

R v Sutton (1991) 94 Cr App R 70, CA. . . 185

R v Suurmeijer [1991] Crim LR 773, CA. . . 41

R v Sweet-Escott (1971) 55 Cr App R 316, Assizes. . . 220, 221, 223, 244

R v Sweeting and Thomas [1999] Crim LR 75, CA. . . 382

R v Swellings [2009] EWCA Crim 3249, [2009] 2 Cr App R (S) 30, CA. . . 593

R v Syed [2019] 1 Cr App R 267 (21), CA. . . 345

R v Sykes [1997] Crim LR 752, CA. . . 16

R v Symonds (1924) 18 Cr App R 100. . . 130

R v T [2002] 1 WLR 632, CA. . . 232, 233

R v T [2004] 2 Cr App R 32, CA. . . 238

R v T [2008] EWCA Crim 484. . . 199, 395

R v T [2011] 1 Cr App R 85 (9), CA. . . 650, 668

R v T [2012] EWCA Crim 2358. . . 235, 236

R v T (AB) [2007] 1 Cr App R 43 (4), CA. . . 26

R v T (D) (2009) 173 JP 425, CA. . . 387, 405

R v Tabbakh [2009] EWCA Crim 464. . . 500, 501

R v Tagg [2002] 1 Cr App R 22 (2), CA. . . 672

R v Tahery [2013] EWCA Crim 1053. . . 357, 358, 382, 402

R v Tattenhove [1996] 1 Cr App R 408, CA. . . 707

R v Taylor 1961 (3) SA 614. . . 447

R v Taylor [1993] Crim LR 223, CA. . . 498

R v Taylor [1994] Crim LR 680, CA. . . 19

R v Taylor [1998] Crim LR 822, CA. . . 20

R v Taylor [1999] Crim LR 77, CA. . . 503, 514

R v Taylor [2006] 2 Cr App R 222 (14), CA. . . 389

R v Taylor, Weaver and Donovan (1928) 21 Cr App R 20, CA. . . 14

R v Teasdale [1994] 99 Cr App R 80. . . 550, 551

R v Tedjame-Mortty [2011] EWCA Crim 950. . . 183

R v Tee [2011] EWCA Crim 462. . . 770

R v Terry [2005] QB 996, [2005] 2 Cr App R 118, CA. . . 23, 25, 773

R v Thakrar [2010] EWCA Crim 1505. . . 397

R v Thomas (1985) 81 Cr App R 331, CA. . . 255

R v Thomas [1986] Crim LR 682. . . 32, 316

R v Thomas [1994] Crim LR 128, CA. . . 204

R v Thomas (Sharon) [1995] Crim LR 314, CA. . . 81

R v Thompson [1893] 2 QB 12, CCR. . . 454, 458

R v Thompson [1962] 1 All ER 65. . . 686

R v Thompson (1976) 64 Cr App R 96, CA. . . 208, 209, 210

R v Thompson [1984] 3 All ER 565, CA. . . 46

R v Thompson [1995] 2 Cr App R 589, CA. . . 52

R v Thompson [1999] Crim LR 747, CA. . . 379

R v Thompson [2018] EWCA Crim 2082. . . 330

R v Thomson [1912] 3 KB 19, CCA. . . 218, 350, 450

R v Thornton [1995] 1 Cr App R 578, CA. . . 280

R v Thorpe [1972] 1 WLR 342. . . 27

R v Threlfall (1914) 10 Cr App R 112. . . 256

R v Tibbs [2000] 2 Cr App R 309, CA. . . 530

R v Tilley [1961] 1 WLR 1309, CCA. . . 312, 314

R v Tillman [1962] Crim LR 261. . . 44

R v Tiplady [1995] Crim LR 651, CA. . . 293

R v Tirado (1974) 59 Cr App R 80, CA. . . 427

R v Tirnaveanu [2007] 1 WLR 3049, [2007] 2 Cr App R 295 (2) CA. . . 561, 570, 577, 581

R v Tobin [2003] Crim LR 408, CA. . . 248

R v Tollady [2010] EWCA Crim 2614. . . 578

R v Tolson (1864) 4 F&F 103. . . 672

R v Tomlinson and Kelly EWCA Crim 1143. . . 368

R v Tompkins (1977) 67 Cr App R 181, CA. . . 323, 743, 744

R v Toner (1991) 93 Cr App R 382, CA. . . 641

R v Toner [2019] EWCA Crim 447. . . 591

R v Tonge [1993] Crim LR 876, CA. . . 95, 149

R v Tooke (1794) 25 State Tr 344. . . 450

R v Tooke (1989) 90 Cr App R 417, CA. . . 199

R v Townsend [2003] EWCA Crim 3173. . . 27

R v Tragen [1956] Crim LR 332. . . 36, 255

R v Treacy [1944] 2 All ER 229, CCA. . . 218, 483

R v Tregear [1967] 2 QB 574, CA. . . 153, 216

R v Trew [1996] Crim LR 441, CA. . . 280

R v Trump (1979) 70 Cr App R 300, CA. . . 328

R v Tsekiri [2017] 1 Cr App R 479 (32), CA. . . 41

R v Tucker [1994] Crim LR 683, CA. . . 19

R v Turay [2007] EWCA Crim 2821. . . 319

R v Turnbull [1977] QB 224, CA. . . 41, 263, 278, 279,
    280, 281, 283, 284, 285, 286, 288, 294, 295, 296,
    297, 372

R v Turnbull (1984) 80 Cr App R 104, CA. . . 444

R v Turner (1816) 5 M&S 206. . . 66

R v Turner (1832) 1 Mood CC 347. . . 765

R v Turner [1910] 1 KB 346, CCA. . . 431

R v Turner (1975) 61 Cr App R 67, CA. . . 26, 128,
    389, 451

R v Turner [1975] QB 834, CA. . . 297, 373, 638, 642,
    654, 655

R v Turner [1991] Crim LR 57, CA. . . 769

R v Turner [1995] 1 WLR 264, CA. . . 683, 707

R v Turner [2004] 1 All ER 1025, CA. . . 510

R v Turner [2010] EWCA Crim 2300. . . 588

R v Turner [2011] EWCA Crim 450. . . 600

R v Turner [2013] EWCA Crim 642; [2013] 1 Cr App
    R 327 (25), CA. . . 323, 515

R v Turpin [1990] Crim LR 514, CA. . . 769

R v Twaites; R v Brown (1990) 92 Cr App R 106,
    CA. . . 470

R v Twist [2011] 1 WLR 1564, [2011] 2 Cr App R 189
    (17), CA. . . 367, 368, 369, 387, 417

R v Tyagi (1986) The Times, 21 July, CA. . . 185

R v Tyler [1993] Crim LR 60, CA. . . 281, 282

R v Tyndale [1999] Crim LR 320, CA. . . 197

R v Tyrer (1988) The Times, 13 Oct, CA. . . 627

R v Tyrer (1990) 90 Cr App R 446, CA. . . 464, 483

R v Tyson [1985] Crim LR 48, CA. . . 279

R v Udenze [2001] EWCA Crim 1381. . . 658

R v Ukpabio [2008] 1 Cr App R 101, CA. . . 168

R v Ul-Haq [2010] EWCA Crim 1683. . . 566, 567

R v Ullah [2007] EWCA Crim798. . . 501

R v Umoh (1986) 84 Cr App R 138, CA. . . 690

R v Usayi [2017] EWCA Crim 1394. . . 227, 396

R v Uxbridge Justices, ex p Sofaer (1986) 85 Cr App
    R 367. . . 314

R v V [2006] EWCA Crim 1901. . . 232, 233, 559

R v Vaid [2015] EWCA Crim 298. . . 42

R v Vaillencourt [1993] Crim LR 311, CA. . . 684

R v Valentine [1996] 2 Cr App R 213, CA. . . 197

R v Van Verden (1973) 57 Cr App R 818, CA. . . 366

R v Varley (1914) 10 Cr App R 125, CCA. . . 203

R v Varley [1982] 75 Cr App R 242, CA. . . 608

R v Venn [2003] All ER (D) 207 (Feb) [2003] EWCA
    Crim 236. . . 27, 594

R v Verelst (1813) 3 Camp 432. . . 113

R v Vernon [1962] Crim LR 35. . . 258

R v Vibert (21 Oct 1974 unreported), CA. . . 207

R v Vickers [1972] Crim LR 101, CA. . . 619

R v Vincent, Frost and Edwards (1840) 9 C&P
    275. . . 450

R v Viola [1982] 1 WLR 1138, CA. . . 231

R v Virgo (1978) 67 Cr App R 323, CA. . . 185

R v Voisin [1918] 1 KB 531, CCA. . . 16, 495

R v Vye [1993] 1 WLR 471 CA. . . 540–4, 545,
    546, 550, 551

R v W [1994] 1 WLR 800, CA. . . 621

R v W [2005] Crim LR 965, CA. . . 233

R v W [2010] EWCA Crim 126. . . 226

R v W [2011] EWCA Crim 1142. . . 149

R v W (John) [1998] 2 Cr App R 289, CA. . . 595

R v Wahab [2003] 1 Cr App R 232 (15), CA. . .
    463, 465

R v Wainwright (1875) 13 Cox CC 171 (Central
    Criminal Court). . . 16, 450

R v Wainwright (1925) 19 Cr App R 52, CCA. . . 203

R v Walker [1996] Crim LR 742, CA. . . 260

R v Walker [1998] Crim LR 211, CA. . . 466, 642

R v Walker [2003] All ER (D) 64 (Jun). . . 640

R v Walker [2007] EWCA Crim 1698. . . 398

R v Walker [2014] PTSR 929, CA. . . 65

R v Wallace [2008] 1 WLR 572, CA. . . 556, 591,
    594, 595

R v Waller [1910] 1 KB 364, CCA. . . 147

R v Wallett [1968] 2 QB 367, CA. . . 102

R v Walls [2011] 2 Cr App R 61 (6), CA. . . 659

R v Wallwork (1958) 42 Cr App R 153, CCA. . . 197

R v Walsh (1990) 91 Cr App R 161, CA. . . 334,
    477, 478

R v Walters [2013] EWCA Crim 1361. . . 284, 288

R v Walters; R v Tovey (1979) 69 Cr App R
    115. . . 488

R v Wang [2005] 1 WLR 661, HL. . . 46

R v Wannell (1924) 17 Cr App R 53, CCA. . . 196

R v Ward [1993] 1 WLR 619, [1993] 2 All ER 577,
    CA. . . 642, 671, 679, 680

R v Ward (1994) 98 Cr App R 337, CA. . . 331, 479

R v Ward [2001] Crim LR 316, CA. . . 456

R v Warickshall (1783) 1 Leach 263. . . 494

R v Warner (1992) 96 Cr App R 324, CA. . . 771

R v Warnick [2013] EWCA Crim 2320. . . 387

R v Warren [2010] EWCA Crim 3267. . . 565

R v Waters [1989] Crim LR 62, CA. . . 467

R v Waters [1997] Crim LR 823, CA. . . 406

R v Watford Magistrates' Court, ex p Lenman [1993] Crim LR 388, DC. . . 157

R v Watson (1834) 6 C&P 653. . . 148

R v Watts (1983) 77 Cr App R 126. . . 620

R v Watts [2010] EWCA Crim 1824. . . 162

R v Wayte (1982) 76 Cr App R 110, CA. . . 306, 307

R v Weaver (1873) LR 2 CCR 85. . . 439

R v Weaver [1968] 1 QB 353, CA. . . 490, 627

R v Webber [1987] Crim LR 412, CA. . . 255

R v Webber [2004] 1 WLR 404, HL. . . 511, 512, 516, 518, 520

R v Weeder (1980) 71 Cr App R 228, CA. . . 285, 286

R v Weekes [1988] Crim LR 244, CA. . . 194

R v Weekes (1993) 97 Cr App R 222, CA. . . 479

R v Weeks [1995] Crim LR 52, CA. . . 464

R v Weerdesteyn [1995] 1 Cr App R 405, CA. . . 479

R v Weightman (1990) 92 Cr App R 291, CA. . . 643

R v Weir [2006] 1 WLR 1885, CA. . . 557, 559, 565, 570, 576, 577, 583, 590, 591, 596, 610

R v Welcher [2007] Crim LR 804, CA. . . 470

R v Welland [2018] EWCA Crim 2036. . . 129

R v Weller [1994] Crim LR 856, CA. . . 18

R v Wellingborough Magistrates' Court, ex p François (1994) 158 JP 813. . . 153

R v Wellington [1991] Crim LR 543, CA. . . 636

R v Wells [2015] EWCA Crim 2. . . 555, 589

R v Welstead [1996] 1 Cr App R 59, CA. . . 160

R v West [2005] EWCA Crim 3034. . . 288

R v Westwell [1976] 2 All ER 812. . . 192

R v Wheeler [1917] 1 KB 283. . . 129

R v Wheeler [1995] Crim LR 312, CA. . . 619

R v Wheeler [2001] Crim LR 745, CA. . . 527

R v Whitaker (1976) 63 Cr App R 193, CA. . . 264

R v White 2011 SCC 13. . . 19

R v White [1991] Crim LR 779, CA. . . 480

R v White [2004] EWCA Crim 946. . . 239, 242

R v Whitehead (1848) 3 Car&Kir 202. . . 25

R v Whitehead [1929] 1 KB 99, CCA. . . 255, 262

R v Whitnell [2014] 1 Cr App R 109 (9), CA. . . 607

R v Whitton [1998] Crim LR 492, CA. . . 18

R v Wilbourne (1917) 12 Cr App R 280, CCA. . . 197

R v Wilcocks [2017] Cr App R 338 (23), CA. . . 63, 86

R v Wilkins [1975] 2 All ER 734, CA. . . 629

R v Willett [2011] EWCA Crim 2710. . . 172

R v Williams (1986) 84 Cr App R 299, CA. . . 15

R v Williams [1990] Crim LR 409, CA. . . 28

R v Williams (1994) 99 Cr App R 163, CA. . . 45

R v Williams [1998] Crim LR 494, CA. . . 26

R v Williams [2002] EWCA Crim 2208. . . 489

R v Williams [2012] EWCA Crim 264. . . 337

R v Williams [2012] EWCA Crim 2516. . . 20

R v Williams [2013] 1 WLR 1200, CA. . . 73

R v Williams [2014] EWCA Crim 1862. . . 391, 398

R v Williams; R v Davis (1992) 95 Cr App R 1, CA. . . 487

R v Williamson (1978) 67 Cr App R 35, CA. . . 35

R v Willis [1960] 1 WLR 55, CCA. . . 361

R v Willis [2004] EWCA Crim 3472. . . 744

R v Willoughby (1988) 88 Cr App R 91, CA. . . 286

R v Wills [2012] 1 Cr App R 16 (2). . . 226, 229

R v Willshire (1881) 6 QBD 366, CCR. . . 100, 117

R v Wilmot (1988) 89 Cr App R 341, CA. . . 18

R v Wilson [1991] Crim LR 838, CA. . . 218

R v Wilson [2008] 2 Cr App R 39 (3), CA. . . 627

R v Wilson [2009] Crim LR 193, CA. . . 16

R v Windass (1988) 89 Cr App R 258, CA. . . 218

R v Winn-Pope [1996] Crim LR 521, CA. . . 45

R v Winter [2008] Crim LR 971, CA. . . 233, 236, 241

R v Withecombe [1969] 1 WLR 84. . . 114

R v Witts and Witts [1991] Crim LR 562, CA. . . 154, 266

R v Witty [2014] EWCA Crim 2333. . . 575

R v Wong [1986] Crim LR 683 (Crown Court). . . 208, 249

R v Wood (1983) 76 Cr App R 23, CA. . . 316, 371, 372

R v Wood [1987] 1 WLR 779, CA. . . 629

R v Wood [1990] Crim LR 264, CA. . . 640

R v Wood [1994] Crim LR 222, CA. . . 270, 481

R v Wood [1995] Crim LR,154, CA. . . 19

R v Wood and Fitzsimmons [1998] Crim LR 213, CA. . . 40, 405, 406

R v Woodcock [1963] Crim LR 273, CCA. . . 188

R v Wright (1866) 4 F&F 967. . . 224

R v Wright (1910) 5 Cr App R 131, CCA. . . 616

R v Wright (1934) 25 Cr App R 35, CCA. . . 669

R v Wright [1993] Crim LR 607, CA. . . 149

R v Wright [1994] Crim LR 55, CA. . . 29, 335

R v Wright [2000] Crim LR 851, CA. . . 559

R v Wright, R v Ormerod (1987) 90 Cr App R 91, CA. . . 197

R v Wyatt [1990] Crim LR 343, CA. . . 215

R v Wynes [2014] EWCA Crim 2585. . . 589

R v X, Y and Z (1989) 91 Cr App R 36, CA. . . 157

R v Xhabri [2006] 1 Cr App R 413 (26), CA. . . 354, 355, 396

R v Y [2008] EWCA Crim 10, [2008] 1 WLR 1683, CA. . . 359, 386, 387, 389, 390

R v Yacoob (1981) 72 Cr App R 313, CA. . . 132

R v Yap Chuan Ching (1976) 63 Cr App R 7, CA. . . 85, 118

R v Yousry (1914) 11 Cr App R 13, CCA. . . 219

R v Yu [2006] Crim LR 643, CA. . . 377

R v Yusuf [2003] 2 Cr App R 488 (32), CA. . . 127

R v Z [2002] 2 AC 483, HL. . . 557, 591

R v Z [2003] 1 WLR 1489, CA. . . 491

R v Z [2009] 1 Cr App R 500 (34), CA. . . 387, 388, 390

R v Zala [2014] EWCA Crim 2181. . . 27, 263

R v Zaman [2017] EWCA Crim 1783. . . 21

R v Zarezadeh [2011] EWCA Crim 271. . . 215

R v Zaveckas (1970) 54 Cr App R 202, CA. . . 462

R v Zawadzka [2016] EWCA Crim 1712. . . 562

R v Zoppola-Barraza [1994] Crim LR 833, CA. . . 544

R (AL) v Serious Fraud Office [2018] EWHC 856 (Admin). . . 732

R (Arthur) v Crown Court at Blackfriars [2017] EWHC 3416 (Admin). . . 542

R (AS) v Great Yarmouth Youth Court [2011] EWHC 2059 (Admin). . . 169

R (B) v DPP [2009] EWHC 106 (Admin). . . 137

R (B) v Westminster Magistrates' Court [2014] UKSC 59. . . 171

R (Bonhoeffer) v General Medical Council [2011] EWHC 1585 (DC). . . 418

R (Bright) v Central Criminal Court [2001] 1 WLR 662. . . 717

R (British Sky Broadcasting Ltd) v Commissioner of Police of the Metropolis [2014] UKSC 17. . . 704, 737

R (C) v Sevenoaks Youth Court [2010] 1 All ER 375. . . 169

R (Chief Constable of Cleveland Police) v H (2010) 174 JP 132, DC. . . 87

R (Cleary) v Highbury Corner Magistrates' Court [2007] 1 WLR 1272, DC. . . 424

R (Crown Prosecution Service) v Bolton Magistrates' Court [2004] 1 WLR 835, DC. . . 716

R (Crown Prosecution Service Harrow) v Brentford Youth Court [2004] Crim LR 159 (DC). . . 158

R (Cuns) v Hammersmith Magistrates' Court [2016] EWHC 748 (DC). . . 60

R (D) v Camberwell Green Youth Court [2005] 1 All ER 999, HL. . . 166, 169

R (D) v Life Sentence Review Commissioners (Northern Ireland) [2008] 1 WLR 1499, HL. . . 88

R (DPP) v Acton Youth Court [2001] 1 WLR 1828. . . 710

R (DPP) v Aylesbury Crown Court [2018] 4 WLR 30. . . 652

R (DPP) v Kavanagh [2006] Crim LR 370, DC. . . 501

R (DPP) v Leicester Magistrates' Court [2016] 1 Cr App R 74 (5), DC. . . 716

R(DPP) v Stratford Magistrates' Court [2018] 4 WLR 47 (Admin). . . 634, 657, 668

R (Factortame Ltd) v Secretary of State for Transport, Local Government and the Regions [2002] EWCA Civ 932. . . 645

R (Faisaltex Ltd) v Preston Crown Court [2009] 1 WLR 1687, DC. . . 728

R (Firth) v Epping Magistrates' Court [2011] 1 WLR 1818, DC. . . 451

R (Ford) v Financial Services Authority [2012] 1 All ER 1238, QBD. . . 730

R (Griffin) v Richmond Magistrates' Court [2008] 1 WLR 1525 DC. . . 74

R (Grundy & Co Excavations Ltd) v Halton Division Magistrates' Court (2003) 167 JP 387, DC. . . 64, 77

R (Hallinan, Blackburn-Gitting and Nott (a Firm)) v Middlesex Guildhall Crown Court [2005] 1 WLR 766. . . 740

R (Haralambous v St Albans Crown Court [2018] 2 WLR 357, SC. . . 703, 708

R (Hassani) v West London Magistrates' Court [2017] EWHC 1270, (Admin). . . 451

R (Hicks) v Commissioner of Police of the Metropolis [2014] EWCA Civ 3. . . 353

R (Howe) v South Durham Magistrates' Court [2004] EWHC 362 (Admin). . . 736

R (HRH Sultan of Pahang) v Secretary of State for the Home Department [2011] EWCA Civ 616. . . 22

R (I) v Secretary of State for the Home Department [2005] EWHC 1025 (Admin). . . 635

R (Kelly) v Warley Magistrates' Court [2008] 1 Cr App R 195. . . 732

R (McCann) v Crown Court at Manchester [2003] 1 AC 787, HL. . . 418

R (Malik) v Crown Court at Manchester [2008] 4 All ER 403, DC. . . 717, 720

R (Meredith) v Harwich Magistrates' Court (2007) 171 JP 249, DC. . . 405

R (Mohamed) v Secretary of State for Foreign and Commonwealth Affairs [2009] EWHC 152. . . 679

R (Morgan Grenfell) v Special Commissioner of Income Tax [2003] 1 AC 563, HL. . . 738

R (N) v Dr M [2003] 1 WLR 562, CA. . . 93

R (N) v Mental Health Review Tribunal [2006] QB 468, CA. . . 88, 89, 93

R (OP) v Secretary of State for Justice [2014] EWHC 1944 (Admin). . . 170

R (O'Shea) v Coventry Magistrates' Court [2004] ACD 50, DC. . . 372

R (Prudential plc) v Special Commissioner of Income Tax [2013] 2 AC 185, SC. . . 726

R (River East Supplies Ltd) v Crown Court at Nottingham [2017] 2 Cr App R 384 (27). . . 717, 720

R (RJM) v SSWP [2009] 1 AC 311. . . 358

R (Robinson) v Sutton Coldfield Magistrates' Court [2006] 2 Cr App R 208 (13), DC. . . 626

R (S) v Waltham Forest Youth Court [2004] 2 Cr App R 335 (21), DC. . . 144, 167, 168, 217

R (Sarkandi) v Secretary of State for Foreign and Commonwealth Affairs [2015] EWCA Civ 687. . . 704, 705

R (Saunders) v Independent Police Complaints Commission [2009] 1 All ER 379, DC. . . 189

R (The Law Society) v Lord Chancellor [2018] EWHC 2094 (Admin). . . 634

R (Thompson) v Chief Constable of the Northumberland Constabulary [2001] 1 WLR 1342, CA. . . 474

R (Tinnion) v Reading Crown Court [2009] EWHC 2930 (Admin). . . 527

R (WV) v Crown Prosecution Service [2011] EWHC 2480 (Admin). . . 683

R (Y) v London Borough of Hillingdon [2011] EWHC 1477 (Admin). . . 439

Radcliffe v Marsden UDC (1908) 72 JP 475, Ch D. . . 441

Raja v Hoogstraten [2005] EWHC 2890 (Ch). . . 17

Raja v Van Hoogstraten [2005] EWHC 1642, Ch D. . . 760

Rall v Hume [2001] 3 All ER 248, CA. . . 49, 317

Ramanauskas v Lithuania [2008] Crim LR 639. . . 342

Rank Film Distributors Ltd v Video Information Centre [1982] AC 380, HL. . . 714, 715, 716, 720, 723, 724

Raphael, Re; Raphael v D'Antin [1973] 1 WLR 998. . . 760

Ras Behari Lal v R (1933) 102 LJPC 144. . . 686

Ratten v R [1972] AC 378, PC. . . 360, 443, 444, 447

Rawlinson v Miller (1875) 1 Ch D 52. . . 110

Rawlinson and Hunter Trustees SA v Akers [2014] EWCA Civ 136. . . 733

Rawson v Haigh (1824) 2 Bing 99. . . 448

RBS Rights Issue Litigation [2016] EWHC 3161 (Ch). . . 728

Read v Bishop of Lincoln [1892] AC 644, PC. . . 121, 438

Reckitt & Colman Products v Borden Inc (No 2) [1987] FSR 407. . . 636

Redpath v Redpath and Milligan [1950] 1 All ER 600, CA. . . 79

Rees and Roberts [2004] Crim LR 939. . . 272

Reid v R (1989) 90 Cr App R 121, PC. . . 279, 281, 282

Renworth Ltd v Stephansen [1996] 3 All ER 244, CA. . . 723

Republic of Djibouti v Boreh [2016] EWHC 405 (Comm). . . 176–7

Reynolds, ex p (1882) 20 Ch D 294. . . 717

Reynolds v Llanelly Associated Tinplate Co Ltd [1948] 1 All ER 140, CA. . . 123

Reynolds v Metropolitan Police Comr (1984) 80 Cr App R 125, CA. . . 37, 78

Rhodes, Re; Rhodes v Rhodes (1887) 36 Ch D 586. . . 111

Rice v Connolly [1966] 2 QB 414. . . 498

Rice v Howard (1886) 16 QBD 681. . . 208

Richards v Morgan (1863) 4 B&S 641. . . 432

Rickards and Rickards v Kerrier District Council (1987) 151 JP 625, DC. . . 61

Rio Tinto Zinc Corpn v Westinghouse Electric Corpn [1978] AC 547, HL. . . 715, 716, 717, 720

Rizan v Hayes [2016] EWCA Civ 481. . . 88, 90

Roberts v DPP [1994] Crim LR 926, DC. . . 363

Robson v Kemp (1802) 4 Esp 233. . . 450

Rochester Resources Limited v Lebedev [2014] EWHC 2185 (Comm). . . 752

Rogers v Hoyle [2013] EWHC 1409 (QB). . . 758

Rogers v Hoyle [2014] EWCA Civ 257. . . 661, 758

Rogers v Hoyle [2015] QB 265. . . 765

Rogers v Secretary of State for the Home Department [1973] AC 388, HL. . . 676, 677, 687

Rogers v Wood (1831) 2 B&Ad 245. . . 441

Roper v Taylor's Central Garages (Exeter) Ltd [1951] 2 TLR 284. . . 121

Rose v R [1995] Crim LR 939, PC. . . 281

Rosher, Re (1884) 26 Ch D 801. . . 121

Rouch v Great Western Rly Co (1841) 1 QB 51. . . 448

Rover International Ltd v Cannon Film Sales Ltd (No 2) [1987] 1 WLR 1597, Ch D. . . 416

Rowland v Bock [2002] 4 All ER 370, QBD. . . 144

Rowley v Dunlop [2014] EWHC 1995 (Ch). . . 645

Rowley v London and North Western Rly Co (1873) LR 8 Exch 221, Ex Ch. . . 439

Royal Brompton Hospital NHS Trust v Hammond [2001] BLR 297, CA. . . 86

Rumping v DPP [1964] AC 814, HL. . . 429, 743

Rush v Smith (1834) 1 Cr M&R 94. . . 215

Rush & Tompkins Ltd v Greater London Council [1989] AC 1280, HL. . . 751

Russell v A-G [1949] P 391. . . 104

Ryan and French v DPP [1994] Crim LR 457, CA. . . 102

S v DPP [2017] EWHC 1162 (DC). . . 86

S v S [1972] AC 24. . . 109

S (a child) (adoption: psychological evidence), Re [2004] EWCA Civ 1029. . . 641

S (children), Re [2016] EWCA Civ 83. . . 141

S County Council v B [2000] 2 FLR 161. . . 742

Sagheera, The [1997] 1 Lloyd's Rep 160, QBD. . . 731

Saifi, Re [2001] 4 All ER 168, DC. . . 329

Sak v CPS (2008) 172 JP 89. . . 386

Salsbury v Woodland [1970] 1 QB 324, CA. . . 318

Sandilands, Re (1871) LR 6 CP 411. . . 313

Sang Kook Suh v Mace (UK) Limited [2016] EWCA Civ 4. . . 750, 753

Sarah C Getty Trust, Re [1985] QB 956, QBD. . . 728

Sastry Velaider Aronegary v Sembecutty Vaigalie (1881) 6 App Cas 364, PC. . . 107

Sattin v National Union Bank (1978) 122 Sol Jo 367, CA. . . 535

Saunders v Punch Ltd [1998] 1 WLR 986, Ch D. . . 695

Savage v Chief Constable of Hampshire [1997] 1 WLR 1061, CA. . . 686

Savings and Investment Bank Ltd v Fincken [2004] 1 WLR 667, CA. . . 753

Savings and Investment Bank Ltd v Gasco Investments (Netherlands) BV [1984] 1 WLR 271, Ch D. . . 428, 765

Savings and Investment Bank Ltd v Gasco Investments (Netherlands) BV (No 2) [1988] 2 WLR 1212, CA. . . 415

Saxby v Fulton [1909] 2 KB 208, CA. . . 119

Scappaticci v A-G [1955] P 47, P, D and Admlty. . . 448

Schering Corpn v Cipla Ltd (2004) The Times, 10 Nov, Ch D. . . 752

Schneider v Leigh [1955] 2 QB 195, CA. . . 743

Science Research Council v Nassé [1980] AC 1028, HL. . . 676, 688, 690, 691, 698, 702

Scott v Baker [1969] 1 QB 659, DC. . . 114

Scott v London & St Katherine Docks Co (1865) 3 H&C 596. . . 115

Scott v Martin [1987] 2 All ER 813, CA. . . 58

Scott v R [1989] AC 1242, PC [1989] 2 All ER 305. . . 279, 280, 381

Secretary of State for Defence v Guardian Newspapers Ltd [1985] AC 339, HL. . . 120, 692, 694, 695, 696

Secretary of State for the Home Department v AF [2009] 2 WLR 423, CA (Civ). . . 357

Secretary of State for the Home Department v MB [2008] AC 440. . . 703

Secretary of State for the Home Department v Rehman [2003] 1 AC 153. . . 89

Secretary of State for Trade and Industry v Bairstow [2003] 3 WLR 841, CA. . . 764

Selvanayagam v University of the West Indies [1983] 1 WLR 585, PC. . . 78

Selvey v DPP [1970] AC 304, HL. . . 49, 50, 52, 613, 616, 618, 619

Senat v Senat [1965] P 172 P, D and Admlty. . . 189

Serio v Serio (1983) 13 Fam Law 255, CA. . . 91, 92

Settebello Ltd v Banco Totta and Acores [1985] 1 WLR 1050, CA. . . 682

Seyfang v GD Searle & Co [1973] QB 148. . . 127, 655

Shand v R [1996] 1 All ER 511, PC. . . 283, 284

Sharp v Loddington Ironstone Co Ltd (1924) 132 LT 229, CA. . . 218

Shedden v A-G (1860) 2 Sw&Tr 170. . . 441

Shephard, Re; George v Thyer [1904] 1 Ch 456. . . 104, 107

Shepherd v Information Commissioner [2019] 4 WLR 50. . . 70, 72, 77

Sherrard v Jacob [1965] NI 151, NICA. . . 673

Shrewsbury v Hart (1823) 1 C&P 113. . . 435

Shrewsbury Peerage Case (1858) 7 HL Cas 1. . . 441

Simaan General Contracting Co v Pilkington Glass Ltd [1987] 1 WLR 516, CA. . . 750

Simba-Tola v Elizabeth Fry Hospital [2001] EWCA Civ 1371. . . 691

Slatterie v Pooley (1840) 6 M&W 664. . . 305

Slingsby v A-G (1916) 33 TLR 120, HL. . . 315

Smith (deceased), Re [2014] EWHC 3926 (Ch). . . 114

Smith v Blandy (1825) Ry&M 257. . . 430

Smith v DPP [2008] EWHC 771 (Admin). . . 147

Smith v Smith (1836) 3 Bing NC 29. . . 431

Smithkline Beecham plc v Avery [2011] Bus LR D 40. . . 90

Smiths Group plc v Weiss [2002] EWHC 582, Ch D. . . 751

Sociedade Nacional de Combustiveis de Angola UEE v Lundqvist [1991] 2 QB 310, CA. . . 714, 716, 717, 722

Society of Lloyd's v Jaffray (2000) The Times, 3 Aug, QBD. . . 150

Sodastream Ltd v Thorn Cascade Co Ltd [1982] RPC 459. . . 636

Sodeman v R [1936] 2 All ER 1138, PC. . . 86

Solway, The (1885) 10 PD 137, P, D and Admlty. . . 431

Somatra Ltd v Sinclair Roche and Temperley [2000] 1 WLR 2453. . . 750

South Coast Shipping Co Ltd v Havant Borough Council [2003] 3 All ER 779, Ch D. . . 747

South Shropshire District Council v Amos [1986] 1 WLR 1271, CA. . . 752

South Staffordshire Tramways Co v Ebbsmith [1895] 2 QB 669, CA. . . 310

Southwark and Vauxhall Water Co v Quick (1878) 3 QBD 315, CA. . . 732

Southwark London Borough Council v Kofi-Adu [2006] HLR 33, CA. . . 215

Soward v Leggatt (1836) 7 C&P 613. . . 78

Sparks v R [1964] AC 964, PC. . . 47

Spencer v Anderson [2017] 2 All ER 846 (Fam Div). . . 17

Spivack v Spivack (1930) 46 TLR 243. . . 104

Springsteen v Flute International Ltd [2001] EMLR 654, CA. . . 32, 305

Stainer v Droitwich (Burgesses) (1695) 1 Salk 281. . . 438

Stallwood v David [2007] 1 All ER 206, QBD. . . 666

Statue of Liberty, The [1968] 1 WLR 739. . . 316, 317, 372

Stephens v Cannon [2005] CP Rep 31, CA. . . 59

Stevens v Gullis [2000] 1 All ER 527, CA. . . 666

Stevens v Simons [1988] CLY 1161, CA. . . 658

Stewart v The Queen [2011] UKPC 11. . . 549

Stirland v DPP [1944] AC 315, HL. . . 557

Stockdale v Hansard (1839) 9 Ad&El 1. . . 120

Stocznia Gdanska SA v Latvian Shipping Co (2000) LTL 19/10/2000, QBD. . . 146

Stollery, Re; Weir v Treasury Solicitor [1926] Ch 284, CA. . . 437

Stoney v Eastbourne RDC [1927] 1 Ch 367, CA. . . 441

Stowe v Querner (1870) LR 5 Exch 155. . . 38

Stroude v Beazer Homes Ltd [2005] EWCA Civ 265. . . 38

Stupple v Royal Insurance Co Ltd [1971] 1 QB 50. . . 760

Sturla v Freccia (1880) 5 App Cas 623, HL. . . 435, 436, 438

Subramaniam v Public Prosecutor [1956] 1 WLR 965, PC. . . 361

Sudgen v Lord St Leonards (1876) 1 PD 154, CA. . . 450

Sumitomo Corp v Credit Lyonnais Rouse Ltd [2002] 1 WLR 479, CA. . . 733

Summers v Moseley (1834) 2 Cr&M 477. . . 215

Sumner and Leivesley v John Brown & Co (1909) 25 TLR 745, Assizes. . . 207

Sutton v Sadler (1857) 3 CBNS 87. . . 61, 114

Sutton v Sutton [1970] 1 WLR 183, PD. . . 758, 763

T v DPP [2007] EWHC 1793 (Admin). . . 510, 512, 520

T (Children) (Abuse:Standard of Proof), Re [2004] 2 FLR 838. . . 88

T (HH) v T (E) [1971] 1 WLR 429. . . 109

Talbot v Von Boris [1911] 1 KB 854, CA. . . 80

Tameshwar v R [1957] AC 476, PC. . . 319

Taplin, Watson v Tate, Re [1937] 3 All ER 105, Ch D. . . 107

Tate & Lyle International Ltd v Government Trading Corpn [1984] LS Gaz R 3341, CA. . . 746

Tate Access Floors Inc v Boswell 1991] Ch 512, Ch D. . . 714, 715

Taylor, Re [1961] 1 WLR 9, CA. . . 105, 107

Taylor v Anderton (1986) The Times, 21 Oct, Ch D. . . 687

Taylor v Anderton [1995] 1 AC 274, HL, [1995] 2 All ER 420, CA. . . 689, 700

Taylor v Chief Constable of Cheshire [1986] 1 WLR 1479; [1987] 1 All ER 225, DC. . . 289, 316, 372

Taylor v Taylor [1965] 2 WLR 779, [1967] P 25. . . 106, 116

Taylor v Taylor [1970] 1 WLR 1148, CA. . . 427, 760

TC Coombs & Co (a firm) v IRC [1991] 3 All ER 623, HL. . . 113–14

Teeluck v The State [2005] 2 Cr App R 378, PC. . . 549

Teper v R [1952] AC 480, PC. . . 14, 366, 369

Theodoropoulas v Theodoropoulas [1964] P 311, CA. . . 754, 755

Thomas, Re [1992] 4 All ER 814, CA. . . 724

Thomas v Connell (1838) 4 M&W 267. . . 449

Thomas v David (1836) 7 C&P 350. . . 245

Thomas v Jenkins (1837) 6 Ad&El 525. . . 441

Thomas v Metropolitan Police Comr [1997] QB 813, CA. . . 244, 630

Thompson v The Queen [1998] AC 811. . . 549

Thompson v Trevanion (1693) Skin 402. . . 443

Thorpe v Chief Constable of Greater Manchester Police [1989] 2 All ER 827, CA. . . 760

Thrasyvoulos Ioannou v Papa Christoforos Demetriou [1952] AC 84, PC. . . 436, 438

Three Rivers District Council v Bank of England [2005] CP Rep 46, CA. . . 218

Three Rivers District Council v Bank of England (No 3) [2003] 2 AC 1, HL. . . 765

Three Rivers District Council v Governor and Company of the Bank of England (No 5) [2003] QB 1556, CA. . . 727, 728, 729

Three Rivers District Council v Governor and Company of the Bank of England (No 6) [2005] 1 AC 610, HL; [2004] QB 916, CA. . . 726–7, 731, 732

Tido v R [2012] 1 WLR 115, [2011] 2 Cr App R 336, PC. . . 204

Times Newspapers Ltd, Re; R v Abdulaziz [2016] 2 Cr App R 367 (28), CA. . . 625

Tingle Jacobs and Co v Kennedy [1964] 1 All ER 888n, CA. . . 104

Tobi v Nicholas [1987] Crim LR 774, DC. . . 125, 446

Tomlin v Standard Telephones and Cables Ltd [1969] 1 WLR 1378, CA. . . 753

Toohey v Metropolitan Police Comr [1965] AC 595, HL. . . 10, 246–7, 399, 642

Topham v McGregor (1844) 1 Car&Kir 320. . . 188

Toth v Jarman [2006] EWCA Civ 1028. . . 645

Trelawney v Coleman (1817) 1 B&Ald 90. . . 450

Triplex Safety Glass Co Ltd v Lancegaye Safety Glass (1934) Ltd [1939] 2 KB 395. . . 716

TSB Bank plc v Robert Irving & Burns (a firm) [2000] 2 All ER 826, CA. . . 729

TSB (Scotland) plc v James Mills (Montrose) Ltd (in receivership) 1992 SLT 519. . . 422

Tumahole Bereng v R [1949] AC 253. . . 262

Turner v Underwood [1948] 2 KB 284, DC. . . 490

Tweney v Tweney [1946] P 180. . . 105

Twyman v Knowles (1853) 13 CB 222. . . 305

U (a Child) (Serious Injury: Standard of Proof), Re [2005] Fam 134, CA. . . 92, 274

Ultraframe (UK) Ltd v Fielding [2005] EWHC 1638 (Ch). . . 176

Unilever plc v Procter & Gamble Co [2000] 1 WLR 2436, CA. . . 750, 752

Union Carbide Corpn v Naturin Ltd [1987] FSR 538, CA. . . 760

Universal City Studios v Hubbard [1984] Ch 225, CA. . . 723

Urquhart v Butterfield (1887) 37 Ch D 357, CA. . . 124

USA v Philip Morris [2003] EWHC 3028 (Comm). . . 732

Valiati v DPP, KM v DPP [2019] 1 WLR 1221. . . 434, 451

Vander Donckt v Thellusson (1849) 8 CB 812. . . 645

Vasiliou v Hajigeorgiou [2005] 1 WLR 2195, CA. . . 667

VB v Westminster Magistrates' Court [2014] UKSC 59. . . 704

Vel v Owen [1987] Crim LR 496, DC. . . 39

Ventouris v Mountain, The Italia Express [1991] 1 WLR 607, CA. . . 726, 732

Ventouris v Mountain (No 2) [1992] 1 WLR 887, CA. . . 407, 413, 426

Versailles Trade Finance Ltd v Clough [2001] All ER (D) 209; (2001) The Times, 1 Nov, CA. . . 714

Vowles v Young (1806) 13 Ves 140. . . 440

W, Re [2001] Ch 609, CA. . . 59

W, Re [2010] 1 WLR 701, SC. . . 68

W v K (1986) 151 JP 589. . . 109

W v K [1988] Fam Law 64. . . 92

W (a minor), Re (1992) The Times, 22 May, CA. . . 101

W (children) (care proceedings: disclosure), Re [2003] EWHC 1624 (Fam). . . 685

W (children) (Family Proceedings: Evidence), Re [2010] UKSC 12. . . 92, 141, 152

W H Holding Ltd v E20 Stadium LLP [2018] EWCA Civ 2652. . . 727, 732

Wagstaff v Wilson (1832) 4 B&Ad 339. . . 431

Wakeford v Bishop of Lincoln (1921) 90 LJPC 174. . . 312

Wakelin v London and South Western Rly Co (1886) 12 App Cas 41, HL. . . 61–2

Walker v Wilsher (1889) 23 QBD 335, CA. . . 749, 750, 753

Walsh v Holst & Co Ltd [1958] 1 WLR 800, CA. . . 116

Walters, Re [1987] Crim LR 577, DC. . . 476

Walters v Lewis (1836) 7 C&P 344. . . 448

Ward v Tesco Stores Ltd [1976] 1 WLR 810, CA. . . 114, 115

Warren v Attorney General for Jersey [2012] AC 22, PC. . . 322, 323

Warren v Warren [1997] QB 488, CA. . . 686

Waterhouse v Barker [1924] 2 KB 759, CA. . . 311

Watkins v Woolas [2010] EWHC 2702 (QB). . . 68, 87

Watson v Cammell Laird & Co Ltd [1959] 1 WLR 702, CA. . . 733

Watson v Chief Constable of Cleveland Police [2001] EWCA Civ 1547. . . 49, 244

Watson v DPP [2003] All ER (D) 132 (Jun), DC. . . 479

Watson v England (1844) 14 Sim 29. . . 110

Waugh v British Railways Board [1980] AC 521, HL. . . 726, 733, 743

Webster v James Chapman & Co [1989] 3 All ER 939, Ch D. . . 745

Wednesbury Corpn v Ministry of Housing and Local Government [1965] 1 WLR 261, CA. . . 571

Wentworth v Lloyd (1864) 10 HL Cas 589. . . 712

Wessely v White [2018] EWHC 1499 (Ch). . . 78

West Midlands Probation Board v French [2009] 1 WLR 1715, DC. . . 309, 360, 385, 436

Westbrook's Trusts, Re [1873] WN 167. . . 111

Western v DPP [1997] 1 Cr App R 474, DC. . . 201

Westminster City Council v Croyalgrange Ltd (1986) 83 Cr App R 155, HL. . . 65

Westminster City Council v Zestfair Ltd (1989) 88 LGR 288, DC. . . 415

Westminster International BV v Dornoch [2009] EWCA Civ 1323. . . 727

Wetherall v Harrison [1976] QB 773, DC. . . 122

Wheatley v Commissioner of Police of the British Virgin Islands [2006] 1 WLR 1683, PC. . . 311

White v R [1999] 1 Cr App R 153, PC. . . 196

White v Taylor [1969] 1 Ch 150, Ch D. . . 436, 437, 438, 441

Whitehead v Scott (1830) 1 Mood&R 2. . . 305

Whitley v DPP [2003] EWHC 2512 (Admin). . . 334

Wiedemann v Walpole [1891] 2 QB 534, CA. . . 430

Wilkinson v DPP [2003] EWHC 865 (Admin). . . 221

Williams v DPP [1993] 3 All ER 365, DC. . . 342, 344

Williams v East India Co (1802) 3 East 192. . . 31, 103

Williams v Home Office [1981] 1 All ER 1151, QBD. . . 678, 687

Williams v Innes (1808) 1 Camp 364, KB. . . 431

Williams v Summerfield [1972] 2 QB 512, DC. . . 311

Williams v Williams [1964] AC 698, HL. . . 102

Williams v Williams [1987] 3 All ER 257, CA. . . 309

Williams v Williams [2003] WTLR 1371. . . 61

Willis v Bernard (1832) 8 Bing 376. . . 31, 450

Wills v Crown Prosecution Service [2016] EWHC 3779 (DC). . . 446

Wills v DPP [2016] EWHC 3779 (DC). . . 446

Willyams v Scottish Widows' Fund Life Assurance Society (1888) 4 TLR 489. . . 110

Wilton & Co v Phillips (1903) 19 TLR 390 (KBD). . . 437, 439

Wisniewski v Central Manchester Health Authority [1998] PIQR 324. . . 17

Wong Kam-Ming v R [1980] AC 247. . . 483–4

Wood v Braddick (1808) 1 Taunt 104. . . 431

Wood v Mackinson (1840) 2 Mood&R 273. . . 216

Woodhouse v Hall (1981) 72 Cr App R 39, DC. . . 362

Woodhouse & Co (Ltd) v Woodhouse (1914) 30 TLR 559. . . 730

Woods v Duncan [1946] AC 401, HL. . . 115, 116

Woolf v Woolf [1931] P 134, CA. . . 16

Woolmington v DPP [1935] AC 462, HL. . . 62, 67, 85, 102, 103

Woolway v Rowe (1834) 1 Ad&El 114. . . 431

Worley v Bentley [1976] 2 All ER 449, DC. . . 192

Wright v Doe d Tatham (1837) 7 Ad&El 313, Ex Ch (1838) 4 Bing NC 489. . . 366, 417, 672

Wright v Sullivan [2006] 1 WLR 172, CA. . . 743

Wright v The Queen [2016] UKPC 181. . . 502

X (a child) (evidence), Re [2011] EWHC 3401 (Fam). . . 141

X v Y [1988] 2 All ER 648, QBD. . . 696

X v Y Ltd UKEAT/0261/17/JOJ. . . 740

X Ltd v Morgan-Grampian Ltd [1991] 1 AC 1, HL. . . 693, 695, 696

XX v Secretary of State for the Home Department [2012] 4 All ER 692, CA. . . 324

Y v DPP [1991] Crim LR 917, DC. . . 461, 481

Yianni v Yianni [1966] 1 WLR 120. . . 150

Young v HM Advocate 1932 JC 63. . . 129

Young v Rank [1950] 2 KB 510. . . 43

Young v Trinidad and Tobago [2008] UKPC 27. . . 204

Australia

Adelaide Chemical and Fertilizer Co Ltd v Carlyle (1940) 64 CLR 514, HCA. . . 442

Ahern v R [1988] ALR 162, HCA. . . 489

Axon v Axon (1937) 59 CLR 395, HCA. . . 105, 113

Briginshaw v Briginshaw (1938) 60 CLR 336. . . 91

Bunning v Cross (1978) 141 CLR 54. . . 347

Davidson v R [2009] NSWCCA 150. . . 15

Driscoll v R (1977) 137 CLR 517, HCA. . . 211

Gage v HM Advocate [2011] HCAJC 40. . . 638

Lustre Hosiery Ltd v York (1936) 54 CLR 134, HCA. . . 431

Nominal Defendant v Clement (1961) 104 CLR 476, HCA. . . 198

Peatling, Re [1969] VR 214 (Supreme Court of Victoria). . . 113, 117

R v Bonnor [1957] VLR 227. . . 113

R v Bonython (1984) 38 SASR 45. . . 646

R v Dania [2019] EWCA Crim 796. . . 153, 154

R v Donohoe [1963] SRNSW 38. . . 94

R v Fannon (1922) 22 SRNSW 427. . . 202

R v Forbes [2001] 1 AC 473, HL. . . 294

R v Forbes [2009] ACTSC 1. . . 639

R v Liristis [2004] NSWCCA 287. . . 221

R v Palmer (1998) 193 CLR 1, HCA. . . 220

R v Szach (1980) 23 SASR 504 (Supreme Court of South Australia). . . 26

R v Umanski [1961] VLR 242. . . 107

Railway Comr v Murphy (1967) 41 ALJR 77, HCA. . . 318

Ramsay v Watson (1961) 108 CLR 642. . . 655

Ridgeway v The Queen (1995) 184 CLR 19. . . 340

Sankey v Whitlam (1978) 21 ALR 505. . . 678

Schultz v R [1982] WAR 171 (Supreme Court of Western Australia). . . 641

Shepherd v R [1990] HCA 56. . . 15

Tripodi v R (1961) 104 CLR 1, HCA. . . 489

Watkinson, Re [1952] VLR 123. . . 112

Wendo v R (1963) 109 CLR 559. . . 94

Wright v Wright (1948) 77 CLR 191. . . 91

Canada

Greenwood v Fitts (1961) 29 DLR (2d) 260, BC CA. . . 753

Pearlman v National Life Assurance Co of Canada (1917) 39 OLR 141. . . 753

Piché v R (1970) 11 DLR (3d) 709 (Supreme Court of Canada). . . 455

R v Haas (1962) 35 DLR (2d) 172 (Court of Appeal of British Columbia). . . 16

R v Harrison [2009] 2 SCR 494. . . 347

R v Khela 2009 SCC 4. . . 259

R v Lupien (1970) 9 DLR (3d) 1 (Supreme Court of Canada). . . 641

R v MT [2004] OJ No 4366 (Ont. CA). . . 27

R v Omar 2007 ONCA 117. . . 683

R v Rojas [2008] SCC 56; [2009] Crim LR 130. . . 201

R v Seaboyer [1991] 2 SCR 577 (Supreme Court of Canada). . . 230

R v Wholesale Travel Group (1991) 3 SCR 154. . . 76, 77

Thompson Newspapers Ltd v Director of Investigation & Research (1990) 54 CCC 417, (Supreme Court of Canada). . . 720

Underwood v Cox (1912) 4 DLR 66. . . 753

Vetrovec v R (1982) 136 DLR (3d) 89. . . 259

Wildman v R [1984] 2 SCR 311 (Supreme Court of Canada). . . 26

Court of Justice of the European Union

Akzo Nobel Chemicals Ltd v European Commission (C–550/07) [2010] EU ECJ. . . 725

AM & S Europe Ltd v EC Commission [1983] QB 878, ECJ. . . 725

European Commission of Human Rights Greek Case (1969) 12 Yearbook 1, EComHR at 186. . . 460

European Court of Human Rights

Adetoro v UK [2010] ECHR 609. . . 519

Al-Khawaja and Tahery v UK (2009) 49 EHRR
1. . . 355, 356

Al-Khawaja and Tahery v UK (2012) 54 EHRR 23;
Crim LR [2012] 375. . . 356, 357, 358, 379, 380,
387, 403

Allan v United Kingdom (2002) 36 EHRR 143. . . 346

Allen v UK [2003] Crim LR 280. . . 719

Atlan v UK [2002] 34 EHRR 833. . . 707

Beckles v UK [2001] 31 EHRR 1. . . 518, 519

Brennan v UK (2002) 34 EHRR 18, ECHR. . . 334

Bueze v Belgium (2019) 69 EHRR 1, GC. . . 335

Bykof v Russia [2010] Crim LR 413, ECHR. . . 346

Campbell and Cosans v United Kingdom (1982) 4
EHRR 293. . . 460

CG v United Kingdom (2002) 34 EHRR 31. . . 182

Chalkley v United Kingdom [2003] Crim LR
51. . . 338

Condron v United Kingdom (2001) 31 EHRR
1. . . 500, 514, 518, 521, 524

Doorson v Netherlands (1996) 22 EHRR 330. . . 355

Dowsett v UK [2003] Crim LR 890. . . 679

Edwards v UK (2003) 15 BHRC 189. . . 708, 709

Foxley v UK (2000) 8 BHRC 571. . . 738

Gäfgen v Germany, Application No 22978/05, 30
June 2008; [2010] Crim LR 865, ECHR. . . 324, 719

Goodwin v UK (1996) 22 EHRR 123, ECHR. . .
692, 695

Halford v UK (1997) 24 EHRR 523. . . 326

Heaney and McGuinness v Ireland [2001] 33 ECHR
264, ECHR. . . 718, 721

Ibrahim v UK [2014] ECHR 1492. . . 336, 478

Ibrahim v UK [2016] ECHR 750, GC. . . 334, 335,
474, 478

Ireland v United Kingdom (1978) 2 EHRR 25. . . 460

Jalloh v Germany [2007] Crim LR 717; (2007) 44
EHRR 32, ECHR. . . 324, 719

Jasper v UK (2000) 30 EHRR 441. . . 707, 709

JB v Switzerland [2001] Crim LR 748, ECHR. . . 719

Khan v United Kingdom (2001) 31 EHRR
1016. . . 338, 346

Kostovski v Netherlands (1990) 12 EHRR 434. . .
166, 357

Luca v Italy (2003) 36 EHRR 807. . . 355

Lückhof and Spanner v Austria (2008) Application
Nos 58452/00 and 61920/00. . . 718

Murray v United Kingdom (1996) 22 EHRR 29,
ECHR. . . 506, 519

Niemietz v Germany (1992) 16 EHRR 97. . . 326

O'Donnell v UK [2015] ECHR 16667/10. . . 500, 504

O'Halloran and Francis v UK, 15809/02, [2007] Crim
LR 897, ECHR. . . 718

Perry v United Kingdom [2003] Crim LR 281. . . 339

PG and JH v United Kingdom [2002] Crim LR
308. . . 338

Price v UK [2016] ECHR 15602/07. . . 357, 358, 380

Price v UK [2016] ECHR 55287/10. . . 356

RE v United Kingdom [2015] ECHR 62498/11. . . 725

Rowe and Davis v UK (2000) 30 EHRR 1. . . 679, 707

Salabiaku v France (1988) 13 EHRR 379, ECHR. . . 69

Salduz v Turkey (2008) 49 EHRR 421, ECHR. . . 334

Salduz v Turkey (2009) 49 EHRR 19, GC. . . 334, 335

Salduz v Turkey [2010] Crim LR 419, ECHR. . . 478

Saunders v UK (1997) 23 EHRR 313; (1997) 2 BHRC
358. . . 455, 717, 719, 720

SC v UK (2004) 17 BHRC 607, ECHR. . . 168

Schatschaschwili v Germany [2015] ECHR
1113. . . 358, 359

Schatschaschwili v Germany (2016) 63 EHRR 14. . .
380, 387

Seton v UK [2016] ECHR 318, [2016] Crim LR 653,
ECHR. . . 359, 379, 380, 387, 391

Shannon v UK [2005] Crim LR 133, ECHR. . . 343

Stanford v UK [1994] ECHR 16757/90. . . 168

T v UK (1999) 7 BHRC 659. . . 168

Teixeira de Castro v Portugal (1998) 28 EHRR 101. . .
343

Van Der Heijden v The Netherlands [2012] ECHR
588. . . 132

Hong Kong

Hong Kong Special Administrative Region v Kissel
[2014] HKCFA 39. . . 655

L v L [2007] HKCA 210. . . 116

Lau Pak Ngam v R [1966] Crim LR 443 (Supreme
Court). . . 191

India

Himanshu @ Chintu v State of NCT of Delhi 2011
STPL (Web) 6 SC, 4 Jan 2011 Supreme Court of
India. . . 211

Ireland (Republic of)

A-G (Rudely) v James Kenny (1960) 94 ILTR
185. . . 673

Flanagan v Fahy [1918] 2 IR 361, Ir KBD. . . 197

New Zealand

Butler v Countrywide Finance Ltd (1992) 5 PRNZ
447. . . 753

Customglass Boats Ltd v Salthouse Bros Ltd [1976] 1
NZLR 36 (New Zealand Supreme Court). . . 450

Dushkar Kanchan Singh v The Queen [2010] NZSC
161. . . 714, 716

Environmental Defence Society Inc v South Pacific
    Aluminium Ltd (No 2) [1981] 1 NZLR 153. . . 678
Police v Anderson [1972] NZLR 233. . . 94
R v Dehar [1969] NZLR 763, NZCA. . . 19
R v Howe [1982] 1 NZLR 618. . . 639
R v McKay [1967] NZLR 139, NZCA. . . 194
R v T [1998] 2 NZLR 257, NZCA. . . 220
R v Uljee [1982] 1 NZLR 561, NZCA. . . 746

United States of America

Chambers v Mississippi, 410 US 295 (1973) (US
    Supreme Ct). . . 390

Daubert v Merrell Dow Pharmaceuticals, 509 US 579
    (1993). . . 648
Frye v United States, 293 F 1013 (DC Cir,
    1923). . . 648
Miranda v Arizona (1975) 384 US 436 (US Supreme
    Ct). . . 455
Mutual Life Insurance Co v Hillman, 145 US 285
    (1892) (US Supreme Ct). . . 450
Nixon v United States, 418 US 683 (1974). . . 678
Smith v Rapid Transport 58 N.E. 2d 754 (Mass.
    1945). . . 24
Upjohn Co v United States, 499 US 383, 101 SCt 677
    (1981). . . 728

Introduction

1

Key issues

- What is 'evidence' and 'the law of evidence'?

- Typically, the parties to litigation dispute the facts. What are the factors that operate to prevent the court from looking at *all* the evidence that could assist in discovering where the truth lies?

- What human factors can operate to prevent the court from discovering where the truth lies?

- Are there any good reasons to restrict the evidence taken into account to a greater extent when the tribunal of fact is a jury or lay justices rather than a professional judge?

- Should the law of evidence be codified or allowed to continue to evolve by way of common law development and piecemeal statutory reform?

Evidence is information by which facts tend to be proved. The law of evidence is that body of law and discretion regulating the means by which facts may be proved. It applies in both courts of law and tribunals and arbitrations in which the strict rules of evidence apply.[1] It is adjectival rather than substantive law and overlaps with procedural law.

At the risk of oversimplification, the broad governing principle underlying the English law of evidence can be stated in no more than nine words: all relevant evidence is admissible, subject to the exceptions.

Truth and the fact-finding process

In most litigation, facts are in dispute. In an ideal world, perhaps, the court inquiring into those facts would take account of all evidence which is relevant to the dispute, that is all evidence that logically goes to prove or disprove the existence of those facts, and would thereby get to the truth of the matter.[2] In the real world, however, a variety of factors operate to restrict the evidence taken into account. First, there are practical constraints inherent in the fact-finding process and common to all legal systems: considerations of time and cost and the need for finality to litigation.[3] Second, under the English adversarial system of trial, whatever its undoubted merits, the court itself cannot undertake a search for relevant evidence but must reach its decision solely on the basis of such evidence as is presented by the parties.[4] As Damaška memorably puts it, by way of metaphor, it is a car being driven at night and lighting the world by two narrow beams.[5] Third, under the adversarial system as it applies in criminal cases, there is inequality of arms at the investigative stage; and although, in conducting an investigation, the police should pursue all reasonable lines of inquiry, whether they point towards or away from the suspect,[6] it is doubtful whether this duty is fulfilled fully or consistently in practice.[7] Fourth, there is the law of evidence itself, much of which comprises rules which exclude relevant evidence for a variety of different reasons. For example, evidence may be insufficiently relevant or of only minimal probative force; it may give rise to a multiplicity of essentially subsidiary issues, which could distract the court from the main issue; it may be insufficiently reliable or unreliable; its potential for prejudice to the party against whom it is introduced may be out of all proportion to its probative value on behalf of the party introducing it; its disclosure may be injurious to the national interest; and so on. Thus the court may aspire to the ascertainment of the truth, but at the end of the day it must come to a decision and settle the dispute even if the evidence introduced is inadequate or inconclusive.

---

[1] The strict rules of evidence do not apply, eg, to civil claims which have been allocated to the small claims track (see CPR r 27.8(3)) or at hearings before employment tribunals (see r 41, Sch 1, Employment Tribunals (Constitution and Rules of Procedure) Regulations 2013, SI 2013/1237).

[2] In support of the view that trials should be a search for the truth, see the Government's White Paper, *Justice for All*, Cm 563 (2002) at 32 and Lord Justice Auld's *Review of the Criminal Courts of England and Wales*, HMSO, 2001, para 154, ch 10.

[3] See Morgan, *Introduction to the American Law Institute Model Code of Evidence* (Philadelphia, 1942) 3–4.

[4] However, in criminal cases, the judge does have the power, albeit a power to be exercised most sparingly, to call a witness not called by either side: see Ch 5, **Witnesses in criminal cases, The witnesses to be called**, p 153.

[5] Damaška, *Evidence Law Adrift* (New Haven, 1997) 92.

[6] Criminal Procedure and Investigations Act 1996, Code of Practice on Disclosure, para 3.4.

[7] See Field and Eady, 'Truth-finding and the Adversarial Tradition: The Experience of the Cardiff Law School Innocence Project' [2017] Crim LR 292, who also doubt whether defence difficulties in this respect are compensated for by the right of access to 'unused material' held by the police.

The risk that the court will not get to the truth of the matter is heightened by virtue of the fact that litigation is, of course, a human endeavour and therefore will provide scope for differences of opinion, error, deceit, and lies. Thus judges, who are called upon to decide what evidence is relevant and to be taken into account, may take different views about whether one fact is relevant to prove or disprove another. As to the parties to litigation, they are hardly impartial and may well be more concerned with winning their case than in assisting to get to the truth. As to the fact-finders, they are most likely to use inferential reasoning to supplement the evidence in the case and fill the gaps in it, which may involve the creation of non-existent facts.[8] Research also reveals lack of accuracy and consistency in their decision-making as to whether witnesses are lying or telling the truth.[9] There is also the risk that fact-finders will operate on the basis of stereotypes and unwarranted assumptions, for example in sexual cases assumptions about delay in making a complaint or the type of clothing worn by the complainant.[10] Finally, there are the witnesses who, if not telling the truth, will either be lying or mistaken. Concerning the latter, there is obvious scope for error, not only in their observation of events, but also in their memory of them and in their recounting of those events in court.[11] There is also the risk that witnesses may give truthful but unreliable evidence of facts which have been created by parties involved in the legal process, a classic example being evidence of a false confession produced during the interrogation of a suspect.[12]

The development of the law

The largely exclusionary ethos of the modern law of evidence reflects its common law history. Many of the rules evolved at a time when the tribunal of fact comprised either jurors or lay justices to whom the judges adopted a paternalistic and protective attitude, excluding relevant evidence such as hearsay evidence, evidence of character, and the opinion evidence of non-experts on the basis that lay persons might overvalue its weight and importance, or even treat it as conclusive. A typical example is evidence of the accused's previous convictions or of his disposition towards wrongdoing which, to an extent, remains inadmissible because of fears that it might influence jurors disproportionately against the accused and distract their attention from other evidence tending to prove his guilt or innocence. Distrust of the jury probably had little to do with the origin of the rule against hearsay evidence, but much to do with the delay in the growth of exceptions to that rule. Historically, the judges also suffered from an ingrained fear of the deliberate concoction or manufacture of evidence by the parties to litigation and their witnesses. This accounted

[8] See Pennington and Hastie, 'The story model for juror decision making' in Hastie (ed), *Inside the Juror* (Cambridge, 1993) and Ellison and Munro, '"Telling tales": exploring narratives of life and law within the (mock) jury room' (2015) 35(2) Legal Studies 201. For insights that cognitive psychology can offer in understanding how decision-makers think about the facts and may be prone to error, see Cunliffe, 'Judging, fast and slow: using decision-making theory to explore judicial fact-determination' (2014) E&P 139.

[9] See generally Virj, *Detecting Lies and Deceit: Pitfalls and Opportunities* (Chichester, 2008) and Green, 'Credibility contests: the elephant in the room' (2014) E&P 28 at 33: 'The ability of lay persons to discern lies and truth is widely reported in the literature to be at or around the level of chance'.

[10] For directions on the dangers of such assumptions, see the Crown Court Compendium (July 2019), Part 1, 20–1.

[11] See Keane, 'The Use at Trial of Scientific Findings relating to Human Memory' [2010] Crim LR 19. As to the distortive effect that preparing for trial may have on a witness' memory, see per Leggatt J in *Gestmin SGPS SA v Credit Suisse (UK) Limited* [2013] EWHC 3560 (Comm) and Maples and Lund, 'If I recall correctly ...' (2014) NLJ, 11 April 17.

[12] See McConville, Sanders, and Leng, *The Case for the Prosecution* (London, 1991).

for the general ban on statements made out of court by a witness and consistent with his present testimony (the rule against previous consistent or self-serving statements). In large measure, it also explained why an out-of-court statement, even if it could be shown to be of virtually indisputable reliability, was generally excluded as evidence of the truth of its contents under the rule against hearsay. The dread of manufactured evidence went much further than the exclusion of specific kinds of evidence: it also meant that whole classes of persons were treated as incompetent to give evidence at all. The incompetence of persons with a pecuniary or proprietary interest in the outcome of the proceedings, including the parties themselves in civil cases, was not fully abolished until the mid-nineteenth century; and it was not until the Criminal Evidence Act 1898 that the accused and his spouse were entitled, in all criminal cases, to give evidence on oath. Another factor which contributed to the largely exclusionary nature of the law of evidence in criminal proceedings stemmed from an understandable desire to offer some judicial protection for the accused against injustice at a time when the dice were unfairly loaded against the defence: trials were often conducted with indecent haste, accused persons enjoyed far less legal representation, and convictions could be questioned only on narrow legal grounds.[13]

In civil cases, nowadays, trial is usually by a judge sitting alone who is perfectly capable, by virtue of her training, qualifications, and experience, of attaching no more weight to an item of evidence than the circumstances properly allow. In criminal cases, the scales can no longer be said to be unfairly loaded against the accused, especially since the coming into force of the Human Rights Act 1998. No doubt, it remains necessary to prevent some material being placed before juries on the ground of irretrievable prejudice against the accused, but the quality of juries and lay magistrates has greatly improved and it is questionable whether they are incapable, given clear and proper judicial direction, of properly evaluating the weight and reliability of some relevant evidence which continues to be excluded, such as evidence of the previous consistent statements of witnesses.

Over the years, there has been much statutory reform, sometimes significant, including in particular the enactments designed to bring domestic law into line with the European Convention on Human Rights. Statutory reform has done much to reduce the number of restrictions on the admissibility of relevant evidence, to rationalize and clarify the law, to enhance the discretionary powers of the judge, and to remove some of the more anomalous and unnecessary discrepancies between the rules in civil and criminal cases. Reform, however, has been piecemeal, sporadic, slow, and usually limited to one specific area of the law, with little or no consideration of the impact of change on other related areas of the subject. The current law of evidence, therefore, may be likened to a machine which has been constructed on common law principles by judicial engineers, but which is subject to periodic alteration by parliamentary mechanics, who variously remove or redesign parts or bolt on new parts. The judges oil and maintain the machine, and continually seek to refine, modify, and develop it to meet the continually changing needs it is designed to serve. However, there are constraints and limitations. Developments can only occur in relation to the specific issues brought before the judges by litigants, some of which are slow to surface.[14] Moreover, in relation to the issues that do surface, the basic framework of the law may be so unprincipled or out of line with

---

[13] See Criminal Law Revision Committee, 11th Report, *Evidence (General)*, Cmnd 4991 (1972), paras 21 ff.

[14] For example, it was only in the early 1990s that the courts were first asked to give detailed consideration to the applicability, in criminal proceedings, of the general doctrine of public interest immunity.

contemporary needs or moral and social values that the judges, bound by *stare decisis* or saddled with antiquated legislation, can only act on a 'make do and mend' basis and put out a call for parliamentary assistance.[15] Whether the call is answered, however, is something of a lottery, with the odds improving if the proposals are based on, or supported by, the recommendations of a law reform agency. Some proposals, however, are simply unacceptable to the government of the day or too dull to win votes, being technical or relating to the quality rather than the content of the law.

Speaking generally, statutory reform has done much to improve the civil rules across a range of subjects. Additionally, and as a result of Lord Woolf's review of the procedural rules in the civil courts,[16] the Civil Procedure Act 1997 provided for the creation of the Civil Procedure Rules (CPR) (and supplementary Practice Directions). The Rules, which replaced the former Rules of the Supreme Court and County Court Rules, and which may modify the rules of evidence,[17] constituted the most radical reform of the ethos and procedure of civil litigation since the Supreme Court of Judicature Act 1875.[18] The jury is still out on whether they render the civil justice system as a whole more 'accessible, fair, and efficient',[19] but concerning the law of evidence, they have done much to simplify and rationalize the relevant procedural rules.[20]

Parliament has also sought to rationalize and improve many of the criminal rules. For example, the Youth Justice and Criminal Evidence Act 1999 introduced long overdue 'special measures' designed to minimize the ordeal and trauma experienced by children and other vulnerable witnesses when giving evidence in criminal cases; unfortunately, the relevant provisions are needlessly complex, in parts almost impenetrable. The most recent of the major reforms, the Criminal Justice Act 2003, brought about radical change in relation to hearsay evidence and evidence of bad character. Many of the provisions are complex and technical but premised on a welcome new confidence that fact-finders can be trusted to evaluate evidence correctly. Thus they reflect only in part the view in Auld LJ's *Review of the Criminal Courts of England and Wales* that 'the English law of criminal evidence should, in general, move away from technical rules of inadmissibility to trusting judicial and lay fact finders to give relevant evidence the weight it deserves'.[21] As to the procedural rules, the Criminal Procedure Rules 2005[22] represented the first steps towards the creation of a new consolidated and comprehensive criminal procedure code of the kind recommended by Auld LJ in his *Review*. Although, initially, the rules merely consolidated and adopted all the pre-existing rules of court, r 1.1 sets out a new overriding objective of the code that criminal cases be dealt with justly. Under r 3.2, the court must further the overriding objective by actively managing the case, which

---

[15] For example, there have been repeated judicial requests for reform of the privilege against self-incrimination. See also the comments in *C v DPP* [1995] 2 All ER 43, HL, concerning the presumption of *doli incapax*, subsequently abolished by statute.

[16] *Access to Justice, Final Report* (HMSO, 1996).

[17] See Civil Procedure Act 1997, Sch 1, para 4.

[18] See also the Family Procedure Rules 2010, SI 2010/2955, which provide a separate code of procedure, including evidence rules, for family proceedings.

[19] See Civil Procedure Act 1997, s 1(3).

[20] See generally Dwyer (ed), *The Civil Procedure Rules Ten Years On* (Oxford, 2009).

[21] Para 78. See also, generally, Coen, 'Hearsay, bad character and trust in the jury: Irish and English contrasts' (2013) 17 E&P 250.

[22] SI 2005/384. See now the Criminal Procedure Rules 2015, SI 2015/1490.

includes ensuring that evidence, whether disputed or not, is presented in the shortest and clearest way; and under r 3.3, each party must (a) actively assist the court in fulfilling its duty under r 3.2, without, or if necessary with, a direction; and (b) apply for a direction if needed to further the overriding objective.[23] Other specific and notable achievements of the rules include implementation of the reforms recommended by the Law Commission in relation to the reliability of expert evidence,[24] although these have attracted considerable critical commentary, and provisions for giving the jury written directions and a written 'route to verdict', a series of questions tailored to the law and the issues and evidence in the case.[25] There is some evidence, however, that the rules have given rise to a number of practical problems and that defence lawyers may have difficulties reconciling their ethical obligations to the accused with their enhanced duties to the court.[26]

'It would be unfortunate', it has been said, 'if the law of evidence was allowed to develop in a way which was not in accordance with the common sense of ordinary folk',[27] not least, one might add, because it has to be used and understood not only by professional judges, but also by part-time judges, lay magistrates, jurors, and, increasingly, the police. Some complexity, however, is unavoidable and can only be minimized by appropriate training for judges and practitioners. This applies to the comprehension and assessment of the reliability of highly technical expert evidence and electronic evidence, the latter often calling for knowledge of how computers work and how data are stored.[28]

Looking at the law of evidence overall, there are strong grounds for believing that fairness, coherence, clarity, and accessibility will only come, not from common law development coupled with piecemeal statutory intervention, but from codification.

ADDITIONAL READING

Brewin and Andrews, 'Memory Accused: Research on Memory Error and its Relevance for the Courtroom' [2019] Crim LR 748.
> The authors argue that psychological research into memory error has led to a neglect of the previous consensus about memory being essentially accurate. They discuss evidence for memory error versus accuracy and suggest that overemphasizing the fallibility of memory could have a number of adverse implications for criminal justice systems.

Coen, 'Hearsay, bad character and trust in the jury: Irish and English contrasts' (2013) 17 E&P 250.
> Consideration is given to the extent to which the exclusionary rules relating to hearsay and bad character have been informed by distrust of jury capabilities and have been reformed on the basis of increased faith in jury competence. The rules are analysed in the light of empirical studies examining jurors' competence to evaluate hearsay and bad character evidence.

---

[23] All participants in criminal cases must follow and apply the rules, which are not mere guidance. Compliance is compulsory and the word 'must' means must. See Leveson LJ, *Essential case management: applying the Criminal Procedure Rules* (2009) at https://www.judiciary.uk/wp-content/uploads/JCO/Documents/Protocols/applying-crim-procedure-rules-dec-2009.pdf.

[24] See Part 19 and Law Commission, *Expert Evidence in Criminal Proceedings in England & Wales* (2011) Law Com No 325.

[25] See r 25.14(4), Criminal Practice Direction VI, para 26K.11 and *R v Atta-Dankwa* [2018] 2 Cr App R 248 (16) at [27]–[32]. See also, generally, Thomas, 'The Criminal Procedure Rules: 10 Years On' [2015] Crim LR 395.

[26] Garland and McEwan, 'Embracing the overriding objective: difficulties and dilemmas in the new criminal climate' (2012) 16 E&P 233.

[27] Per Lawton LJ in *R v Chandler* [1976] 1 WLR 585, CA at 590.

[28] See Mason and Leng (eds), *Electronic Evidence* (London, 2017).

Garland and McEwan, 'Embracing the overriding objective: difficulties and dilemmas in the new criminal climate' (2012) 16 E&P 233.
The results of empirical research into the impact of the case management system enshrined in the Criminal Procedure Rules showing the practical problems confronting judges and practitioners and the possible difficulty for defence lawyers in reconciling ethical obligations to their clients with the enhanced duties to the court.

McConville et al, *The Case for the Prosecution* (London, 1991).
A detailed argument, based on findings of research into prosecution decision-making, that cases are not investigated neutrally but are built or constructed by the police and the Crown Prosecution Service with a view to increasing the chance of conviction.

Pennington and Hastie, 'The story model for juror decision making' in Hastie (ed), *Inside the Juror* (Cambridge, 1993).
An explanation of a cognitive theory of juror decision-making under which meaning is assigned to evidence by its incorporation into plausible stories about what happened in the events testified to. It forms part of a book on the psychology of juror decision-making from the perspective of not only cognitive psychology, but also behavioural decision theory and behavioural modelling.

Research Board of the British Psychological Society, *The Guidelines on Memory and the Law* (Leicester, 2008).
Guidelines derived from a review of the scientific study of human memory whose stated purpose is to provide for those involved in legal work an accessible and scientifically accurate basis from which to consider issues relating to human memory.

Twining, *Rethinking Evidence* (Oxford, 1990).
A collection of self-standing but linked essays that argue for a broad inter-disciplinary approach to evidence. They include 'Taking facts seriously', 'The Rationalist tradition of evidence scholarship', 'Legal reasoning and argumentation', and 'Narratives and generalizations in argumentation about questions of fact'.

Preliminaries

2

Key issues

- What are the only facts that should be open to proof (or disproof) in any given trial?

- What forms can evidence take in a trial?

- What is 'circumstantial evidence'?

- Should adverse inferences be drawn if a party to a trial (a) fails to give evidence or call witnesses; or (b) can be shown to have told lies about the facts in dispute?

- When is evidence 'relevant' to the facts in dispute?

- When and why should evidence be excluded notwithstanding that it is relevant to the facts in dispute?

- What is meant by the 'weight' of an item of evidence?

- In a jury trial, which evidential issues should be for the judge and which for the jury?

- When and why should a question about the admissibility of an item of evidence be decided in the absence of the jury?

- Should the admissibility of evidence be governed entirely by rules of law or should the judge have discretionary power (a) to admit evidence inadmissible in law; and/or (b) to exclude evidence admissible in law?

Facts open to proof or disproof

Only certain types of fact are open to proof or disproof in English courts of law. They are facts in issue, relevant facts, and collateral facts.

Facts in issue

A fact in issue is sometimes referred to as a 'principal fact' or '*factum probandum*'. The facts in issue in any given case are those facts which the claimant (or the prosecutor) must prove in order to succeed in his claim (prosecution) together with those facts which the defendant (or the accused) must prove in order to succeed in his defence. The nature and number of facts in issue in a case is determined not by the law of evidence, but partly by reference to the substantive law and partly by reference to what the parties allege, admit, and deny. For example, in an action for damages for breach of contract in which the defendant simply denies the facts on which the claimant relies for his claim, the facts in issue will be those facts which, if proved, will establish the formation of a binding contract between the parties, breach of contract by the defendant, and consequential loss and damage suffered by the claimant. However, if the defendant, in his defence, pleads discharge by agreement, admitting that the contract was made but denying the breach and loss alleged by the claimant, then the facts in issue will then be those which, if proved, will establish breach by the defendant and consequential loss and damage suffered by the claimant together with those facts which, if proved, will establish that the parties discharged the contract by agreement. Another possibility is that the defendant admits the contract and its breach and makes no counterclaim. The only facts in issue will then be those which, if proved, will establish consequential loss and damage and the amount of damages to which the claimant claims he is entitled. There are many other possibilities. In civil proceedings, the facts in issue are usually identifiable by reference to the statement of case, its very purpose being to set out the factual (and legal) issues on which the parties agree and disagree so that they and the court know in advance exactly what matters are left in dispute and what facts, therefore, have to be proved or disproved at the trial.[1] Under the Civil Procedure Rules (CPR) r 16.4(1):

Particulars of claim must include—

(a) a concise statement of the facts on which the claimant relies; . . .

Under r 16.5(1):

In his defence, the defendant must state—

(a) which of the allegations in the particulars of claim he denies;
(b) which allegations he is unable to admit or deny, but which he requires the claimant to prove; and
(c) which allegations he admits.

As a general rule, a defendant who fails to deal with an allegation shall be taken to admit it.[2]

---

[1] See *Esso Petroleum Co Ltd v Southport Corpn* [1956] AC 218 at 241, HL; *Farrell v Secretary of State for Defence* [1980] 1 WLR 172, HL.

[2] CPR r 16.5(5). Under r 16.5(3), a defendant who fails to deal with an allegation but sets out in his defence the nature of his case in relation to the issue to which that allegation is relevant, shall be taken to require that allegation to be proved. Under r 16.5(4), where the claim includes a money claim, a defendant shall be taken to require that any allegation relating to the amount of money claimed be proved unless he expressly admits the allegation.

In criminal cases in which the accused pleads not guilty, the facts in issue are all those facts which the prosecution must prove in order to succeed, including the identity of the accused, the commission by him of the *actus reus*, and the existence of any necessary knowledge or intent on his part,[3] together with any further facts that the accused must prove in order to establish any defence other than a simple denial of the prosecution case. However, under s 10 of the Criminal Justice Act 1967, any fact of which oral evidence may be given in any criminal proceedings may be admitted for the purpose of those proceedings by or on behalf of either the prosecution or defence and an admission made by any party of any such fact shall be 'conclusive' evidence of the fact admitted. In other words, a fact which is formally admitted under the section is not open to contradictory proof and in effect ceases to be a fact in issue: the court must find the fact to have been proved.[4]

Relevant facts

A relevant fact, sometimes called a 'fact relevant to the issue', an 'evidentiary fact', or *'factum probans'*, is a fact from which the existence or non-existence of a fact in issue may be inferred. If the only facts which were open to proof or disproof were facts in issue, many claims and defences would fail. If, for example, the fact in issue is whether a man shot his wife, obviously an eye-witness to the incident may be called to give evidence that he saw the shooting. However, in many cases a statement by a witness that he perceived a fact in issue with one of his senses, which is described as 'direct evidence', is quite simply unavailable. Very often the only available evidence is that which can establish some other fact or facts relevant to the fact in issue, for example the evidence of a gunsmith that on the day before the shooting the man bought a gun from him, the evidence of a policeman that after the shooting he found that gun buried in the garden of the man's house, and the evidence of a forensic expert that the gun bore the man's fingerprints. Evidence of relevant facts is described as 'circumstantial evidence', some further examples of which are given later in this chapter. Where a party to proceedings seeks to establish a relevant fact the existence of which is denied by his opponent, the relevant fact may also be said to be a 'fact in issue'.

Collateral facts

Collateral facts, sometimes referred to as 'subordinate facts', are of three kinds: (i) facts affecting the competence of a witness; (ii) facts affecting the credibility of a witness; and (iii) facts, sometimes called 'preliminary facts', which must be proved or disproved as a condition precedent to the admissibility of certain items of evidence tendered to prove a fact in issue or a relevant fact. As to the first, an example would be that a potential witness suffers from a disorder of the mind rendering him incompetent to testify. An example of a collateral fact of the second kind would be a fact that goes to show that a witness has lied or is mistaken about a fact in issue or a relevant fact. Thus if a witness testifies to the effect that he saw a certain event at a distance of 50 yards but suffers from an eye complaint which prevents him from seeing anything at a distance greater than 20 yards, he may be cross-examined about his eye complaint and, if he denies its existence, evidence in rebuttal may be given by an oculist.[5] Similarly, a witness may be cross-examined about his bias or partiality towards one of the

---

[3] Per Lord Goddard CJ in *R v Sims* [1946] KB 531 at 539.

[4] See further Ch 4, Formal admissions, Criminal cases, p 125.

[5] See per Lord Pearce in *Toohey v Metropolitan Police Comr* [1965] AC 595, HL at 608 (see Ch 7).

parties to the proceedings and again, if he denies it, evidence may be called to contradict his denial.[6] A collateral fact of the third kind may be illustrated by reference to an exception to the rule against hearsay: in criminal proceedings a statement made by a participant in or observer of an event is admissible as evidence of the truth of its contents, by way of exception to the rule against hearsay, *on proof that* it was made by a person so emotionally overpowered by the event that the possibility of concoction or distortion can be disregarded.[7] Another illustration is an exception to the general rule that a party seeking to rely upon the contents of a document must adduce the original: a copy is admissible as evidence of the contents *on proof that* the original has been destroyed or cannot be found after due search.[8]

Where a party to proceedings seeks to establish a collateral fact the existence of which is denied by his opponent, the collateral fact may also be said to be a 'fact in issue'. The existence or non-existence of a preliminary fact in issue is, as we shall see, decided by the judge, not the jury, as part of his general function to rule on all questions concerning the admissibility of evidence.

The varieties of evidence

The evidence by which facts may be proved or disproved in court is known as 'judicial evidence'. Judicial evidence takes only three *forms*, namely oral evidence, documentary evidence, and things. Judicial evidence, however, is open to classification not only in terms of the form in which it may be presented in court but also in terms of its substantive content, the purpose for which it is presented, and the rules by which its admissibility is determined. Thus, any given item of judicial evidence may attract more than one of the labels by which the varieties of evidence have been classified. The principal labels are 'testimony', 'hearsay evidence', 'documentary evidence', 'real evidence', 'circumstantial evidence', and 'conclusive evidence'.

Testimony

Testimony is the oral statement of a witness made on oath in open court[9] and offered as evidence of the truth of that which is asserted. 'Direct testimony' is a term used to describe a witness's statement that he perceived a fact in issue with one of his five senses. In other words, it is testimony relating to facts of which the witness has or claims to have personal or first-hand knowledge.[10] Direct testimony, or 'direct evidence' as it is sometimes called, is a term commonly used in contrast with 'hearsay evidence'. The term is also used in contrast with 'circumstantial evidence'.

---

[6] See per Geoffrey Lane LJ in *R v Mendy* (1976) 64 Cr App R 4, CA at 6 (see Ch 7).

[7] See Ch 14, Statements forming part of the *res gestae*, p 442.

[8] *Brewster v Sewell* (1820) 3 B&Ald 296 (see Ch 10).

[9] In criminal proceedings, some witnesses may give their evidence by live television link and video recordings of interviews of some witnesses may be admitted as their evidence-in-chief: see Ch 5. In civil proceedings, the court may allow a witness to give evidence through a video link or by other means (eg by telephone): see CPR r 32.3.

[10] An appropriately qualified expert may give oral evidence of opinion on a matter calling for the expertise which he possesses and may do so even though substantial contributions to the formation of his opinion have been made by matters of which he has no personal or first-hand knowledge: see per Megarry J in *English Exporters (London) Ltd v Eldonwall Ltd* [1973] Ch 415 at 423. A statement of opinion may also be made by a non-expert witness, but only as a way of conveying *facts* personally perceived: see generally Ch 20.

Hearsay evidence

In common parlance, hearsay is used to describe statements, often gossip, that one hears but does not know to be true. In the law of evidence, the word is used in a broader technical sense. The common law concept of hearsay may be defined as any statement, other than one made by a witness in the course of giving his evidence in the proceedings in question, by any person, whether it was made on oath or unsworn and whether it was made orally, in writing, or by signs and gestures, which is offered as evidence of the truth of its contents. If the statement is tendered for any purpose other than that of proving the truth of its contents, for example to prove simply that the statement was made or to prove the state of mind of the maker of the statement, it is not hearsay but 'original evidence'. Provided that it is relevant to a fact in issue, original evidence is admissible. At common law, hearsay could only be received in evidence exceptionally. Under the modern law, in civil cases the rule has been abrogated; in criminal cases, there are many statutory exceptions; and in both civil and criminal cases a number of common law exceptions have been preserved and given statutory force.

The meaning of 'hearsay' and 'original evidence' and the distinction between them is perhaps best understood by way of examples. Suppose a fact in issue in criminal proceedings is whether a man, H, shot his wife, W. X was an eye-witness to the shooting and later said to Y: 'H shot W'. Y repeated X's statement to Z. If X is called as a witness to the proceedings he may, of course, give direct testimony of the shooting. It is something of which he has personal or first-hand knowledge, something he perceived with his own eyes. However, X may not narrate to the court the statement that he made to Y in order to prove that H shot W unless his statement comes within one of the exceptions to the rule against hearsay. The statement was made other than in the course of giving evidence in the proceedings in question and would be tendered in order to prove that H shot W (the truth of its contents). For the same reasons neither Y nor Z, if called, could recount X's out-of-court statement to prove that H shot W—and this is so whether or not they disclose the source or their own lack of personal or first-hand knowledge—unless it comes within one of the exceptions to the rule against hearsay. Now suppose a fact in issue in criminal proceedings is whether D is physically capable of speech. D is charged with obtaining property by deception. The prosecution allege that he dishonestly obtained money from a charity by pretending that he was incapable of speech. D, leaving the offices of the charity, held a conversation with E. E, if called as a witness for the prosecution, may give evidence of what D said, not to prove the truth of anything that D said, but simply to prove that D's statements were made, that D could speak. D's out-of-court statements are received as original evidence.

These are deliberately simple examples of difficult concepts. The meaning of hearsay evidence and the distinction between hearsay and original evidence give rise to difficult legal problems which are explored fully in **Chapter 12**. The numerous common law and statutory exceptions to the rule against hearsay comprise one of the largest topics in this work. They are considered in **Chapters 12–15**.

Documentary evidence

Documentary evidence usually consists of a document or a copy of a document, produced for inspection by the court. However, in some cases the evidence may be presented electronically, by a simultaneous display to all parties via courtroom monitors, thereby ensuring that all involved are looking at the same item of evidence at the same time. Presentation of evidence in this way is encouraged in fraud and other complex criminal cases because of its potential for saving time.[11]

A document, for the purposes of the law of evidence, has no single definition. The meaning of the word varies according to the nature of the proceedings and the particular context in question. Suffice it to say, for present purposes, that in certain circumstances the word is defined to include not only documents in writing, but also maps, plans, graphs, drawings, photographs, discs, tapes, videotapes, films, and negatives.[12] Documents may be produced to show their contents, their existence, or their physical appearance. The contents of a document may be received as evidence of their truth, by way of exception to the hearsay rule, or for some other purpose, ie as original evidence, for example to show what its author thought or believed. It is convenient to regard the contents of documents as a separate category of judicial evidence because although, like oral statements, they are subject to the general rules of evidence on admissibility, their reception in evidence is also subject to two additional requirements. One of these relates to the proof of their contents.[13] The matter is explored fully in **Chapter 10**. It is mentioned here merely in order to explain the distinction, mainly of importance in connection with documents, between 'primary evidence', which may be regarded as the best available evidence, and 'secondary evidence', that is evidence which by its nature suggests that better evidence may be available. As a general rule, a party seeking to rely on the contents of a document must adduce primary evidence of those contents, which is usually the original of the document in question, as opposed to secondary evidence of those contents, for example a copy of the document, a copy of a copy of the document, or oral evidence of the contents.[14] Where a document is produced to show the bare fact of its existence or its physical appearance, for example the substance of which it is made or the condition which it is in, it constitutes a variety of 'real evidence'.

Real evidence

Real evidence usually takes the form of some material object produced for inspection in order that the court may draw an inference from its own observation as to the existence, condition, or value of the object in question. Although real evidence may be extremely valuable as a means of proof, no weight attaches to such evidence in the absence of some accompanying testimony identifying the object in question and explaining its connection with, or significance in relation to, the facts in issue or relevant to the issue. In addition to material objects, including documents, examples of real evidence include the physical appearance of persons and animals, the demeanour of witnesses, the intonation of voices on a tape recording, views, that is inspections out of court of the *locus in quo* or of some object which it is impossible or highly inconvenient to bring to court, and, possibly, out-of-court demonstrations or re-enactments of acts or events into which the court is enquiring. Real evidence is considered in greater detail in **Chapter 10**.

---

[11] See the Protocol for the control and management of heavy fraud and other complex criminal cases [2005] 2 All ER 429, para 6(vi).

[12] See further Ch 10.

[13] The other concerns proof of the fact that the document was properly executed. See further Ch 10.

[14] The distinction between primary and secondary evidence is also of importance in relation to the proof of facts contained in a document to which a privilege attaches: see Ch 22.

Circumstantial evidence

General

Circumstantial evidence has already been defined as evidence of relevant facts (facts from which the existence or non-existence of a fact in issue may be inferred) and contrasted with 'direct evidence', a term which is used to mean testimony relating to facts in issue of which a witness has or claims to have personal or first-hand knowledge. Circumstantial evidence may take the form of oral or documentary evidence (including admissible hearsay) or real evidence.

'It is no derogation of evidence to say that it is circumstantial.'[15] Circumstantial evidence is particularly powerful when it proves a variety of different facts all of which point to the same conclusion, for example in a murder case evidence of the accused's preparation, motive, and opportunity for commission of the offence, together with evidence of the discovery of a weapon capable of having caused the injuries sustained by the victim buried in the accused's back garden and bearing his fingerprints. Circumstantial evidence, it has been said, 'works by cumulatively, in geometrical progression, eliminating other possibilities'[16] and has been likened to a rope comprised of several cords:

> One strand of the cord might be insufficient to sustain the weight, but three stranded together may be quite of sufficient strength. Thus it may be in circumstantial evidence—there may be a combination of circumstances, no one of which would raise a reasonable conviction or more than a mere suspicion; but the three taken together may create a conclusion of guilt with as much certainty as human affairs can require or admit of.[17]

In criminal proceedings involving circumstantial evidence, trial judges often point out the difference between proof by direct evidence and proof by circumstances leading to an inference of guilt, but there is no rule of law requiring such an explanation.[18] Nor is there any legal requirement, in cases in which the Crown's case is based on circumstantial evidence, to direct the jury to acquit unless they are sure that the facts proved are not only consistent with guilt but also inconsistent with any other reasonable conclusion.[19] However, as Lord Normand observed in *Teper v R*:[20]

> Circumstantial evidence may sometimes be conclusive, but it must always be narrowly examined, if only because evidence of this kind may be fabricated to cast suspicion on another. Joseph commanded the steward of his house, 'put my cup, the silver cup in the sack's mouth of the youngest', and when the cup was found there Benjamin's brethren too hastily assumed that he must have stolen it.[21] It is also necessary before drawing the inference of the accused's guilt from circumstantial evidence to be sure that there are no other co-existing circumstances which would weaken or destroy the inference . . .

According to the Australian authorities, where a fact relied on as circumstantial evidence is an indispensable link in a chain of reasoning towards guilt, it may be appropriate to identify

---

[15] *R v Taylor, Weaver and Donovan* (1928) 21 Cr App R 20, CA.

[16] Per Lord Simon in *DPP v Kilbourne* [1973] AC 729, HL at 758.

[17] Per Pollock CB in *R v Exall* (1866) 4 F&F 922 at 929.

[18] *R v Kelly* [2015] EWCA Crim 817.

[19] *McGreevy v DPP* [1973] 1 WLR 276, HL. See also *R v King* [2014] EWCA Crim 2465.

[20] [1952] AC 480, PC at 489.

[21] See Genesis, 44: 2.

the fact and direct the jury that it must be established beyond reasonable doubt before the ultimate inference can be drawn,[22] but where the evidence consists of strands in a cable rather than links in a chain and no one strand is indispensable for a conviction, the jury should be directed not to consider any particular fact separately, but to consider the circumstantial evidence as a whole.[23]

Examples

The circumstances in which a fact may be said to be relevant to a fact in issue, in the sense that the existence of the former gives rise to an inference as to the existence or non-existence of the latter, are many and various. Certain types of circumstantial evidence arise so frequently that they have been referred to as 'presumptions of fact' or 'provisional presumptions' such as the presumptions of intention, guilty knowledge, continuance of life, and seaworthiness, all of which are more conveniently considered in **Chapter 4**. Another type of circumstantial evidence is evidence of facts which are so closely associated in time, place, and circumstances with some transaction which is in issue that they can be said to form a part of that transaction. Such facts, referred to as facts forming part of the *res gestae*, are more conveniently explored in **Chapter 14**. The *res gestae* doctrine is mainly concerned with the admissibility of statements of fact as evidence of the truth of their contents by way of common law exception to the hearsay rule and has been described, not unfairly, in terms of a 'collection of fact situations . . . so confusing in its scope as almost to demand that a reader cease thinking before he go mad'![24] The following examples of circumstantial evidence are commonplace and pose little danger to mental health.

Motive

Evidence of facts which supply a motive for a particular person to do a particular act is often received to show that it is more probable that he performed that act. Such evidence is admissible notwithstanding that the motive is irrational[25] or shared by others. Thus, as to the latter, in the case of a feud between neighbouring families, the motive of the accused may be shared by other members of his family, but it is still relevant to show that he had a reason to do what is alleged.[26]

> Surely in an ordinary prosecution for murder you can prove previous acts or words of the accused to show that he entertained feelings of enmity towards the deceased, and this is evidence not merely of the malicious mind with which he killed the deceased, but of the fact that he killed him . . . it is more probable that men are killed by those that have some motive for killing them than by those who have not.[27]

Conversely, evidence of absence of motive may be relevant to show the relative unlikelihood of a particular person having performed a particular act.[28]

---

[22] *Shepherd v R* [1990] HCA 56.

[23] *Davidson v R* [2009] NSWCCA 150.

[24] Wright, 20 Can BR 714 at 716.

[25] *R v Phillips* [2003] 2 Cr App R 528, CA at [30], disapproving *R v Berry* (1986) 83 Cr App R 7, insofar as it suggests otherwise.

[26] *Myers v DPP* [2016] 3 AC 314, PC at [45].

[27] Per Lord Atkinson in *R v Ball* [1911] AC 47, HL at 68; affirmed in *R v Williams* (1986) 84 Cr App R 299, CA. Any doubt that may have been cast upon this classic statement in *R v Berry* (1986) 83 Cr App R 7, should be disregarded: *R v Phillips* [2003] 2 Cr App R 528, CA at [26].

[28] See *R v Grant* (1865) 4 F&F 322.

Plans and preparatory acts

Facts which tend to suggest that a person made plans or other preparations for the performance of a particular act are relevant to the question of whether she subsequently performed that act. Thus evidence may be given of the purchase by an alleged murderer of poison or, as the case may be, of a gun or knife. On the question whether a person's declaration of intention to do a certain act is relevant to prove its performance by him, the authorities conflict.[29]

Capacity

Evidence of a person's mental or physical capacity or incapacity to do a particular act has an obvious relevance to the question of whether he in fact performed it.

Opportunity

Circumstantial evidence of opportunity is evidence of the fact that a person was present at the time and place of some act allegedly performed by him, for example evidence, to establish adultery in divorce proceedings, that a couple occupied the same hotel bedroom for two nights.[30] Conversely, evidence of lack of opportunity is evidence of the fact that a person was absent. In a criminal case, this may assist the accused, for example alibi evidence, or the prosecution, for example evidence that after his arrest the accused had no opportunity to commit further offences (coupled with evidence that no further offences similar to those with which he is charged were committed in the same area).[31]

Identity

Circumstantial evidence of identity often takes the form of expert testimony that the fingerprints of the accused[32] or samples taken from his body match those discovered on or taken from some material object at the scene of the crime or the victim of the offence.[33] It can also take the form of evidence that a tracking dog tracked the accused by scent from the scene of the crime.[34] Identity may also be established by evidence that both the accused and the criminal share the same name, the same physical idiosyncrasy, for example left-handedness, the same style of handwriting, or the same particular manner of expression in speech or writing.[35] In civil proceedings, evidence as to the parentage of a person may be

---

[29] See *R v Buckley* (1873) 13 Cox CC 293; *R v Wainwright* (1875) 13 Cox CC 171 etc (see **Ch 14**).

[30] *Woolf v Woolf* [1931] P 134, CA.

[31] *R v Wilson* [2009] Crim LR 193, CA.

[32] *R v Castleton* (1909) 3 Cr App R 74; cf *R v Court* (1960) 44 Cr App R 242, CCA.

[33] It is for the prosecution to prove formally that the *sample* fingerprints were taken from the accused and evidence, by him, that he cannot explain, or does not know, how 'his' fingerprints were found on the material object does not amount to an admission that the fingerprints were his: *Chappell v DPP* (1988) 89 Cr App R 82. The police have the power to take fingerprints, including palm prints, of a person without his consent. The circumstances in which this may be done include (i) where he is detained at a police station, if he is detained in consequence of his arrest for a recordable offence or he has been charged with, or informed that he will be reported for, such an offence; and (ii) where he has been convicted of a recordable offence or given a caution in respect of a recordable offence which he has admitted: Police and Criminal Evidence Act 1984, ss 61, 65, and 118.

[34] See *R v Haas* (1962) 35 DLR (2d) 172 (Court of Appeal of British Columbia). Evidence of tracking by a dog is admissible provided that (i) there is detailed evidence establishing the reliability of the dog by reason of its training and experience; and (ii) the jury are directed to consider the evidence carefully and with circumspection: *R v Pieterson* [1995] 2 Cr App R 11, CA. See also *R v Sykes* [1997] Crim LR 752, CA.

[35] See, eg, *R v Voisin* [1918] 1 KB 531: 'Bloody Belgian' written as 'Bladie Belgiam'.

given by expert medical evidence showing that a person is or is not excluded from being the father or mother of that person.[36]

Continuance

The fact that a certain act or event was taking place at one point in time may justify the inference that it was also taking place at some prior or subsequent point in time. Thus evidence of the speed at which someone was driving at a particular point in time may be given to show the speed at which he was likely to have been driving a few moments earlier[37] or later.[38]

Failure to give evidence or call witnesses

In *Prest v Petrodel Resources Ltd*,[39] the Supreme Court adopted, subject to one modification, the view of Lord Lowry in *R v IRC, ex parte TC Coombs & Co*[40] as to the effect, in civil cases, of a party's failure to give evidence or call witnesses.

> . . . generally the silence of one party in face of the other party's evidence may convert that evidence into proof in relation to matters which are, or are likely to be, within the knowledge of the silent party and about which that party could be expected to give evidence. Thus, depending on the circumstances, a prima facie case may become a strong or even an overwhelming case. But, if the silent party's failure to give evidence (or to give the necessary evidence) can be credibly explained, even if not entirely justified, the effect of his silence in favour of the other party may be either reduced or nullified.[41]

The modification related to claims for ancillary financial relief in matrimonial proceedings, where there is a public interest in spouses making proper provision for one another, especially when there are children. This means that the court's role is inquisitorial and the parties have a duty to each other and to the court to make full and frank disclosure of all the material facts. If they do not, the court, in deciding the facts, may draw such inferences as can properly be drawn from all the available material, judicial experience of what is likely to have been concealed, and the inherent probabilities.[42]

The inferences that may be drawn, in criminal cases, from the accused's election not to give evidence, call for a more detailed analysis. The subject is covered in **Chapter 16**. Concerning the accused's failure to call a witness (other than his or her spouse or civil partner), in appropriate cases the judge may comment adversely on the fact that the witness was not called, but

---

[36] Under s 20 of the Family Law Reform Act 1969, in any civil proceedings in which the parentage of any person falls to be determined, the court may give a direction (i) for the use of scientific tests to ascertain whether a party to the proceedings is or is not the father or mother of that person; and (ii) for the taking of bodily samples from all or any of the following, namely, that person, any party who is alleged to be the father or mother of that person, and any other party to the proceedings. The 1969 Act governs the taking of samples from living people, but the High Court has an inherent jurisdiction to direct tests to provide evidence of parentage in cases outside the scope of the Act: *Spencer v Anderson* [2017] 2 All ER 846 (Fam Div).

[37] *R v Dalloz* (1908) 1 Cr App R 258.

[38] *Beresford v St Albans Justices* (1905) 22 TLR 1. See also the presumption of continuance of life (see **Ch 4**).

[39] [2013] UKSC 34 at [44].

[40] [1991] 2 AC 283 at 300. See also, to similar effect, *Wisniewski v Central Manchester Health Authority* [1998] PIQR 324 at 340.

[41] See also *Karis v Lewis* [2005] EWCA Civ 1637, *Baigent v Random House Group Ltd* [2006] EWHC 719, Ch D at [213]–[215], and *Raja v Hoogstraten* [2005] EWHC 2890, Ch D. Similarly, adverse factual findings may be made against a defendant who, in breach of statutory duty, made it difficult or impossible for a claimant to adduce relevant evidence: see *Keefe v Isle of Man Steam Packet Co Ltd* [2010] EWCA Civ 683.

[42] *Prest v Petrodel Resources Ltd* [2013] UKSC 34 at [45] and [85].

should exercise the same degree of care as when commenting on the failure of the accused himself to give evidence and in particular should avoid the suggestion that the failure is something of importance when there may be a valid reason for not calling the witness.[43] Whether a comment is justified and, if so, the terms in which it should be cast, are matters dependent upon the facts of the particular case. In *R v Khan*[44] the Court of Appeal gave guidance which is almost entirely general and ambivalent; one commentator has described it, not altogether unfairly, as 'not helpful'.[45] However, the court was unequivocal on one matter: a judge who is proposing to make a comment should first invite submissions from the advocate for the accused in the absence of the jury.

Section 80A of the Police and Criminal Evidence Act 1984 provides that the failure of the wife or husband or civil partner of a person charged in any proceedings to give evidence in the proceedings shall not be made the subject of any comment by the prosecution. Under proviso (b) to s 1 of the Criminal Evidence Act 1898, the precursor to s 80A, it was held that where the advocate for the prosecution does make an adverse comment on the failure of the accused to call his spouse to give evidence on his behalf, it is the duty of the trial judge, depending upon the circumstances of each case, to remedy that breach in his summing-up, especially when the accused is a man of good character and this is central to his defence.[46]

Section 80A applies only to the prosecution. In appropriate circumstances, therefore, the *judge* may comment on the failure of the spouse or civil partner of the accused to testify. However, if the judge, in the exercise of his discretion, does decide to make a comment, he must, save in exceptional circumstances, do so with a great deal of circumspection.[47] The same degree of circumspection would also seem to be required in the case of comment on failure to call cohabitees, who are not covered by s 80A.[48]

A breach of s 80A is unlikely to result in a successful appeal if the judge, in summing up, makes appropriate and suitable comments on the failure of the spouse to testify: the error made by the advocate is subsumed in the summing-up.[49]

Failure to provide samples

Under s 23(1) of the Family Law Reform Act 1969, if, in any civil proceedings in which the parentage of any person falls to be determined, the court gives a direction under s 20 of the Act[50] and if any person fails to take any step required of him for the purpose of giving effect to that direction, for example refusing to supply a bodily sample, the court may draw such inferences, if any, as appear proper in the circumstances.[51] Similarly, under s 62(10) of the Police and Criminal Evidence Act 1984, where an accused has refused without good cause to the taking from him of an intimate body sample, such inferences as appear proper may be

[43] Per Megaw LJ in *R v Gallagher* [1974] 1 WLR 1204, CA. See also *R v Wilmot* (1988) 89 Cr App R 341, CA at 352 and *R v Couzens* [1992] Crim LR 822, CA; and cf *R v Weller* [1994] Crim LR 856.

[44] [2001] Crim LR 673, CA, applied in *R v Campbell* [2009] EWCA Crim 1076.

[45] Roberts [2009] Crim LR 826.

[46] *R v Naudeer* [1984] 3 All ER 1036, CA. See also *R v Dickman* (1910) 5 Cr App R 135 and *R v Hunter* [1969] Crim LR 262, CA.

[47] Per Purchas LJ in *R v Naudeer* [1984] 3 All ER 1036, CA at 1039.

[48] See *R v Weller* [1994] Crim LR 856, CA.

[49] See *R v Whitton* [1998] Crim LR 492, CA.

[50] Considered at n 36.

[51] See *McVeigh v Beattie* [1988] 2 All ER 500.

drawn from the refusal in determining various matters, including whether he is guilty of the offence charged. Section 62 is considered further in **Chapter 16**, together with the inferences that may be drawn, pursuant to statute, from an accused's silence or conduct.

Lies

After an offence, lies told by an accused, on their own, do not prove guilt.[52] However, they may indicate a consciousness of guilt[53] and therefore in appropriate circumstances may be relied upon by the prosecution as evidence supportive of guilt.[54] An example is *R v Goodway*[55] in which the accused's lies to the police as to his whereabouts at the time of the offence were used in support of the identification evidence adduced by the prosecution.[56] It was held that whenever a lie told by an accused is relied on by the Crown, or may be used by the jury to support evidence of guilt, as opposed merely to reflecting on his credibility (and not only when it is relied on as corroboration or as support for identification evidence), a direction—often referred to as a *Lucas* direction[57]—should be given to the jury.[58] Under a *Lucas* direction, the jury should be directed that: (1) the lie must be deliberate and must relate to a material issue; (2) they must be satisfied that there was no innocent motive for the lie, reminding them that people sometimes lie, for example, in an attempt to bolster up a just cause, or out of shame or a wish to conceal disgraceful behaviour; and, in cases where the lie is relied upon as corroboration,[59] (3) the lie must be established by evidence other than that of the witness who is to be corroborated.[60] However, it was also said that such a direction need not be given where it is otiose, as indicated in *R v Dehar*,[61] that is, where the rejection of the explanation by the accused almost necessarily leaves the jury with no choice but to convict as a matter of logic. An example is *R v Barsoum*,[62] where the lie related to the presence of another person, M, at the scene of the crime and if M was present, B was entitled to be acquitted, but if M was an invention it automatically followed that B must be guilty.[63] Where a direction is given, it should also make the point that the lie must be admitted or proved beyond reasonable doubt.[64] At a trial for murder in which the only issue is provocation (now loss of self-control),

---

[52] *R v Strudwick* (1993) 99 Cr App R 326, CA at 331.

[53] As to the relevance to *mens rea* of post-offence flight, or flight without hesitation, see *R v White* 2011 SCC 13, with commentary by Pattenden in (2011) 15 E&P 261.

[54] See the Crown Court Compendium (July 2019), Part 1, 16–3.

[55] [1993] 4 All ER 894, CA.

[56] Similarly, in civil proceedings a party's lies may make it harder for him to prove his case: see *MA (Somalia) v Secretary of State for the Home Department* [2011] 2 All ER 65, SC.

[57] See *R v Lucas* [1981] QB 720, CA.

[58] If a lie is relied on merely to attack credibility, a direction may be appropriate in exceptional circumstances, as when the lie figures largely in the case and the jury may think that the accused must be guilty because he lied: *R v Tucker* [1994] Crim LR 683, CA.

[59] See Ch 8.

[60] Applied in *R v Taylor* [1994] Crim LR 680, CA.

[61] [1969] NZLR 763, NZCA.

[62] [1994] Crim LR 194, CA.

[63] Cf *R v Wood* [1995] Crim LR, CA, where the accused may have been influenced by panic or confusion and therefore guilt was not the only possible explanation for the lies he told. But see also *R v Saunders* [1996] 1 Cr App R 463, CA at 518–19, where it was held that a direction was not required, the accused having explained his lies on the basis that he was confused and under pressure, and the judge having dealt with that explanation fairly in his summing-up.

[64] *R v Burge* [1996] 1 Cr App R 163, CA.

and the accused's lie is a statement that he never had any contact with the victim, the jury should be directed that the lie can support the case of murder if they are sure that it was told to conceal the fact of murder, rather than connection with the death, that is, to avoid responsibility for murder rather than a provoked killing.[65]

The topic has spawned much case law and in *R v Middleton*[66] it was held, *per curiam*, that when the question arises whether a direction should be given, it will usually be more useful to analyse the question in the context of the individual case by examining the principles to be derived from the authorities rather than by trawling through hosts of cases. The court emphasized that the point of the direction is to avoid the risk of the forbidden reasoning that lies necessarily demonstrate guilt: where there is no risk that the jury may follow this prohibited line of reasoning, a direction is unnecessary.[67] It was also said that, generally, a direction is unlikely to be appropriate in relation to lies told by an accused in evidence because that situation is covered by the general directions on burden and standard of proof. Furthermore, even where a specific direction could be given about a lie told in evidence, it is not required if it will do more harm than good.[68]

In *R v Burge*[69] it was held that a *Lucas* direction is usually required in only four situations, which may overlap:

1. Where the defence relies on an alibi.

2. Where the judge suggests that the jury should look for support or corroboration of one piece of evidence from other evidence in the case, and amongst that other evidence draws attention to lies told or allegedly told by the accused.

3. Where the prosecution seek to show that something said in or out of court in relation to a separate and distinct issue was a lie and to rely on that lie as evidence of guilt, that is, to use it, in effect, as an implied admission of guilt.

4. Where, although the prosecution have not adopted the approach described in (3), the judge reasonably envisages that there is a real danger that the jury may do so.[70]

The Court of Appeal stressed that the direction is not required in run-of-the-mill cases in which the defence case is contradicted by the evidence of the prosecution witnesses in such a way as to make it necessary for the prosecution to say that the accused's account is untrue. Similarly, in *R v Hill*[71] it was said that a direction is not required simply because the jury reject

---

[65] *R v Taylor* [1998] Crim LR 822, CA. See also *R v Reszpondek* [2010] EWCA Crim 2358 at [19].

[66] [2001] Crim LR 251.

[67] See, eg, *R v Williams* [2012] EWCA Crim 2516, where the prosecution did not rely on a lie told in interview, the accused in his evidence gave an explanation for the lie, and a *Lucas* direction might have advanced the case *against* the accused. See also *R v Murray* [2016] 4 WLR 142 at [23], [25], and [26], where a *Lucas* direction would have confused and complicated a simple issue.

[68] *R v Nyanteh* [2005] Crim LR 651, CA. See also *R v Bhagchandka* [2016] EWCA Crim 700: a *Lucas* direction is not required in every case where a lie, of whatever significance, can be extracted from the evidence.

[69] [1996] 1 Cr App R 163, CA.

[70] However, the Court of Appeal is unlikely to be persuaded that there was such a danger if the advocate for the defence did not ask the trial judge to consider giving an appropriate direction: *R v Burge* [1996] 1 Cr App R 163 at 174. The failure of the advocate for the defence to raise the matter at trial may also be taken into account in cases in which both the third and the fourth situations arise, and may lead the Court of Appeal to conclude that the absence of a direction did not make the conviction unsafe: *R v McGuinness* [1999] Crim LR 318, CA.

[71] [1996] Crim LR 419, CA. See also *R v Harron* [1996] 2 Cr App R 457, CA.

the evidence of an accused about a central issue in the case, since that situation is covered by the general direction that the judge will give on burden and standard of proof.[72] Nor is a direction likely to be called for in the many cases of handling in which the accused denies knowledge or belief that the goods were stolen, including those in which he gives different and inconsistent versions as to how he came by the goods and the prosecution assert that the evidence is a lie.[73] It is usually unhelpful to give both a *Lucas* direction and a direction, under s 34 of the Criminal Justice and Public Order Act 1994, on inferences from an accused's failure to mention facts when questioned or charged.[74] The judge should select and adapt the direction more appropriate to the facts and issues in the case. If the lie is said to be the explanation given by the accused for his failure to mention a fact, a s 34 direction, incorporating the explanation, should suffice; it would be unnecessary, confusing, and unduly favourable to the defence to set out the *Lucas* examples of innocent motives for lying.[75]

Concerning the first situation identified in *R v Burge*, the Judicial Studies Board specimen direction relating to evidence called in support of an alibi used to conclude with the warning:

> even if you conclude that the alibi is false, that does not itself entitle you to convict the defendant. The prosecution must still make you sure of his guilt. An alibi is sometimes invented to bolster a genuine defence.

In *R v Lesley*[76] it was held that this version of the *Lucas* direction should be given routinely, although whether a failure to do so renders a conviction unsafe depends on the facts of the case and the strength of the evidence. The accused in that case had served an alibi notice but did not call the person named in it and did not give evidence himself. The prosecution inferentially invited the jury to conclude that the alibi was false and therefore evidence of guilt. Having regard to some weaknesses in the evidence given by the chief prosecution witness, it was held that failure to give the standard direction rendered the verdict unsafe.[77] *R v Lesley* was distinguished in *R v Harron*,[78] in which it was held that the judge had not erred in failing to give the standard direction because the central issue in the case was whether the prosecution witnesses were lying (rather than mistaken) or the accused was; it would only have confused the jury to have directed them that, if they accepted the evidence of the prosecution witnesses as to the presence of the accused, and therefore rejected the accused's evidence to the contrary, his evidence might have been falsified to bolster a genuine defence.[79]

R v Genus[80] furnishes an example of the third situation identified in *R v Burge*. The accused claimed to have been acting under duress. The prosecution case was that the accused had told lies to the police, and in their evidence, on collateral issues, that is, issues not directly relevant to the question of duress, by reason of which the jury should disbelieve their evidence of duress. It was held that the case cried out for a *Lucas* direction.[81]

---

[72] See also, to similar effect, *R v Landon* [1995] Crim LR 338, CA.

[73] *R v Barnett* [2002] Cr App R 168, CA.

[74] See Ch 16.

[75] *R v Hackett* [2011] 2 Cr App R 35, CA, applying *R v Rana* [2007] EWCA Crim 2261.

[76] [1996] 1 Cr App R(S) 39, CA.

[77] Cf *R v Drake* [1996] Crim LR 109, CA, and see also *R v Peacock* [1998] Crim LR 681, CA.

[78] [1996] 2 Cr App R 457, CA.

[79] See also *R v Gultutan* [2006] EWCA Crim 207.

[80] [1996] Crim LR 502, CA.

[81] See also *R v Zaman* [2017] EWCA Crim 1783 and *R v Anjum* [2003] EWCA Crim 493 and cf *R v Murray* [2016] 4 WLR 142 at [23] and [24].

R v Robinson[82] is an example of the fourth situation identified in *R v Burge*. The accused was charged with possession of drugs with intent to supply. In his summing-up, the judge gave considerable prominence to the issue whether the accused, in his evidence, had lied about when he had first complained to the police that they had planted the drugs on him. It was held that the issue whether the allegation of planting was a late invention was a separate issue, not a central one, and fell clearly within the fourth situation identified in *R v Burge*. The jury should have been directed on the possibility that the accused had lied to bolster a potentially weak defence.

Standards of comparison

In cases where it is necessary to decide whether a person's conduct meets some objective standard of behaviour, evidence of what other persons would do in the same circumstances is admissible as a standard of comparison. Thus, in *Chapman v Walton*,[83] where it was alleged that a broker was negligent in failing to vary the terms upon which certain goods were insured on receiving ambiguous information concerning their destination, evidence from other brokers as to what they would have done in such circumstances was admitted for the purpose of deciding whether the broker had exercised a reasonable degree of care, skill, and judgement in the performance of his duties. Similarly, where the issue concerns the existence of a practice in a trade carried out in a particular location, evidence may be admissible of the existence or non-existence of that practice in a similar trade located elsewhere. In *Noble v Kennoway*,[84] for example, the issue being whether underwriters were entitled to repudiate liability on an insurance of a ship's cargo on the grounds that its discharge in Labrador had been unreasonably delayed, it was held that evidence of a practice of delaying the discharge of cargo in the Newfoundland trade was admissible to show the likely existence of a similar practice in the Labrador trade.

Conclusive evidence

Conclusive evidence operates to prove a matter and to bar any evidence that might go to disprove it. An example is s 21(a) of the State Immunity Act 1978, whereby a certificate issued by the Secretary of State for the Foreign and Commonwealth Office is conclusive evidence as to whether any country is a state for the purposes of Part I of that Act or as to the person or persons to be regarded for those purposes as the head or government of a state.[85]

Relevance and admissibility

Such evidence as a court will receive for the purpose of determining the existence or non-existence of facts in issue is referred to as admissible evidence. The admissibility of evidence is a matter of law for the judge. The most important feature of the English law of evidence is that all evidence which is sufficiently relevant to prove or disprove a fact in issue and which is not excluded by the judge, either by reason of an exclusionary rule of

---

[82] [1996] Crim LR 417, CA.

[83] (1833) 10 Bing 57.

[84] (1780) 2 Doug KB 510. See also *Fleet v Murton* (1871) LR 7 QB 126.

[85] For an example, see *R (HRH Sultan of Pahang) v Secretary of State for the Home Department* [2011] EWCA Civ 616. See also Civil Evidence Act 1968, s 13 (see Ch 23).

evidence or in the exercise of her discretion, is admissible.[86] In *R v Terry*[87] it was held that evidence will be admissible if it is relevant *and* such that a jury, properly warned about any defects it might have, could place some weight on it. This is probably best understood not as the introduction of some new two-limb test for admissibility, but as a recognition that a judge's determination as to whether evidence is sufficiently relevant to be admissible will depend, to some extent, on her assessment of its weight.[88]

Relevance

Definition of relevance

The classic definition of relevance is contained in Art 1 of Stephen's *A Digest of the Law of Evidence*,[89] according to which the word means that:

any two facts to which it is applied are so related to each other that according to the common course of events one either taken by itself or in connection with other facts proves or renders probable the past, present or future existence or non-existence of the other.

Stephen also suggested that relevance may be tested by the use of a syllogism,[90] a form of reasoning in which a conclusion is drawn from two given or assumed propositions, a major premise, a generalization, and a minor premise, which in the context under discussion is a proposition of fact the relevance of which is being tested. For example, to test the relevance of motive on a charge of murder, the major premise is the generalization that those who had a motive to kill a person are more likely to have done so than those who had no such motive; the minor premise is that the accused had a motive to kill the person; and the conclusion is that the accused is more likely to have killed the person than those without a motive for killing him. As Cross and Tapper point out, care may have to be taken in selecting the appropriate major premise.[91] Indeed, the validity of this form of reasoning depends entirely upon the validity of the major premise, which has to be formulated having regard to common sense and general experience. This accords with the requirement in Stephen's definition of relevance that it be determined 'according to the common course of events'.

As Stephen's definition also makes clear, a fact may be relevant to the past, present, or future existence of another fact. *R v Nethercott*[92] provides an example of relevance to both the future and the past existence of a fact. N's defence was that he had acted under duress as a result of threats by his co-accused G and gave evidence that he feared for his own safety having regard to the way in which G had acted on previous occasions. It was held that evidence of the fact that three months later G had stabbed N with a knife was also relevant because it made it more likely that N, at the time of the offence, had genuinely feared for his safety.

---

[86] However, there is no principle that a judge cannot read or hear material that is actually or potentially inadmissible, especially if he is judge of both law and fact: see *Barings plc v Coopers and Lybrand* [2001] EWCA Civ 1163, [2001] CPLR 451, where it was held that to read background documentation in preparation for a long and complex case involved no danger of the judge being so influenced by the material that he would not decide the case on the basis of the admissible evidence.

[87] [2005] 2 Cr App R 118, CA at [34].

[88] See further, in this chapter, under **Weight**, p 33.

[89] (12th edn, London, 1936).

[90] *A General View of the Criminal Law of England* (London, 1863) 236.

[91] *Cross and Tapper on Evidence* (9th edn, London, 1999) 56.

[92] [2002] 2 Cr App R 117 (7), CA.

As one commentator has pointed out,[93] Stephen's definition of relevance appears to set the standard too high in that it requires a relevant fact to *prove or render probable* the fact requiring proof. In contrast, under the simpler working definition of Lord Simon of Glaisdale in *DPP v Kilbourne*:[94]

> Evidence is relevant if it is logically probative or disprobative of some matter which requires proof. I do not pause to analyse what is involved in 'logical probativeness' except to note that the term does not of itself express the element of experience which is so significant of its operation in law, and possibly elsewhere. It is sufficient to say, even at the risk of etymological tautology, that relevant (i.e. logically probative or disprobative) evidence is evidence which makes the matter which requires proof more or less probable.[95]

In *R v Randall*[96] Lord Steyn cited and applied the statement appearing in the fifth edition of this book that 'relevance is a question of degree determined, for the most part, by common sense and experience'.

Irrelevance

Examples of relevant evidence have already been given under the rubric of circumstantial evidence which, it will be recalled, is a term used to refer to evidence of *relevant* facts. Consideration may now be given to some examples of evidence which has been excluded on the grounds of irrelevance. *Holcombe v Hewson*[97] concerned an alleged breach of covenant by the defendant, a publican, to buy his beer from the plaintiff, a brewer. The plaintiff, in order to rebut the defence that he had previously supplied bad beer, intended to call publicans to give evidence that he had supplied them with good beer. Excluding this evidence, Lord Ellenborough said:

> We cannot here enquire into the quality of different beer furnished to different persons. The plaintiff might deal well with one, and not with the others. Let him call some of those who frequented the defendant's house, and there drank the beer which he sent in . . .

In *Hollingham v Head*[98] the defendant, in order to defeat an action for the price of goods sold and delivered, sought to establish that the contract was made on certain special terms by evidence that the plaintiff had entered into contracts with other customers on similar terms. The evidence was held to be inadmissible on the grounds that it would have afforded no reasonable inference as to the terms of the contract in dispute.[99] On a charge of manslaughter against a doctor, expert evidence may be adduced as to the doctor's skill as shown by his treatment of the case under investigation, but evidence of his skilful treatment of other

---

[93] Dennis, *The Law of Evidence* (3rd edn, London, 2007) 64.

[94] [1973] AC 729 at 756, HL.

[95] Concerning the role of probability theory in legal proceedings, see Eggleston, *Evidence, Proof and Probability* (2nd edn, London, 1983). Liability cannot be established purely on the basis of probabilistic evidence, such as statistical evidence showing that a defendant was 80 per cent likely to be the tortfeasor (known as the Blue Bus problem, based on *Smith v Rapid Transport* 58 N.E. 2d 754 (Mass. 1945)), the exception being DNA evidence. See Cheng and Nunn, 'DNA, Blue Bus, and phase changes' (2016) 20 E&P 112.

[96] [2004] 1 WLR 56, HL at 62.

[97] (1810) 2 Camp 391, KB.

[98] (1858) 27 LJCP 241.

[99] Evidence of 'similar facts' is not invariably excluded, however: see, eg, *Hales v Kerr* [1908] 2 KB 601, DC and the other cases on the point in **Ch 17**.

patients on other occasions must be excluded.[100] Evidence that after an accident the defendants to a negligence action altered and improved their practice has no relevance to the question whether the accident was caused by their negligence: 'Because the world gets wiser as it gets older, it was not therefore foolish before.'[101]

Where two criminal trials arise out of the same transaction, evidence of the outcome of the first will generally be inadmissible, because irrelevant, at the second; some exceptional feature is needed before it is considered relevant.[102] This is the position, *a fortiori*, where the earlier trial related to a different event.[103] It has been said that the rationale for the 'rule' is that the evidence amounts to nothing more than evidence of the opinion of the first jury,[104] but taken alone that would be a reason for never admitting evidence of a previous verdict. The true rationale, in the case of an earlier acquittal, is that in most cases it is not possible to be certain why a jury acquitted.[105] The 'exception' to the rule is where there is a clear inference from the verdict that the jury rejected a witness's evidence, on the basis that they did not believe him, as opposed to thinking that he was mistaken, and the witness's credibility is directly in issue in the second trial.[106] An example is where an officer who has given evidence of an admission in a trial resulting in an acquittal by virtue of which his evidence can be shown to have been disbelieved, faces an allegation, in a subsequent trial, that he has fabricated an admission.[107] Another example is where the prosecution allege that as part of a joint enterprise, A and B, one after the other, raped C; A and B are tried separately; the prosecution case against each man depends almost entirely on the evidence of C and therefore the jury have to decide which side is lying; and A is tried first and acquitted.[108]

In criminal trials, evidence relating to likely sentence is of no relevance to the issue whether or not the offence has been committed.[109] In *R v Sandhu*[110] it was held that, insofar as an offence of strict liability involves no proof of *mens rea*, evidence of motive, intention, or knowledge on the part of the accused is inadmissible because irrelevant to the issue of his guilt and merely prejudicial to him.[111]

---

[100] *R v Whitehead* (1848) 3 Car&Kir 202.

[101] Per Bramwell B in *Hart v Lancashire & Yorkshire Rly Co* (1869) 21 LT 261.

[102] *Hui Chi-ming v R* [1991] 3 All ER 897, PC. See also, concerning the admissibility, at a retrial, of the first jury's acquittal on some counts and failure to agree on others, *R v H* (1989) 90 Cr App R 440, CA; *R v Greer* [1994] Crim LR 745, CA; *R v Scott* [1994] Crim LR 947, CA; and, generally, Choo, 'The Notion of Relevance' [1993] Crim LR 114.

[103] *R v Terry* [2005] QB 996, CA at [34].

[104] *Hui Chi-ming v R* [1991] 3 All ER 897, PC.

[105] *R v Deboussi* [2007] EWCA Crim 684 and *R v Preko* [2015] EWCA Crim 42. The rule also seems to apply in the case of an acquittal based on a judge's ruling that there is insufficient evidence for the case to go to the jury: *R v Hudson* [1994] Crim LR 920, CA. As to the relevance and admissibility of previous convictions as evidence of the facts on which they were based, see Ch 23.

[106] *R v Deboussi* [2007] EWCA Crim 684.

[107] *R v Edwards* [1991] 1 WLR 207, CA. See also *R v Hay* (1983) 77 Cr App R 70, CA and *R v Cooke* (1986) 84 Cr App R 286, CA.

[108] *R v Deboussi* [2007] EWCA Crim 684. Evidence of an accused's previous offending given by a complainant in a previous trial which resulted in an acquittal may be admissible in a subsequent trial as bad character evidence under the Criminal Justice Act 2003, s 101 (see Ch 19). Where the complainant's evidence was the essence of the former case and her accuracy or credibility was the critical question, in the subsequent trial it may be appropriate to adduce, in addition to the evidence of the complainant, evidence of the acquittal : see *R v Hajdarmayaj* [2019] EWCA Crim 303.

[109] *R v Edgington* [2013] EWCA Crim 2185.

[110] [1997] Crim LR 288, CA.

[111] See also, applying *R v Sandhu*, *R v Byrne* [2002] 2 Cr App R 311 (21).

Another, but controversial, example of irrelevance is to be found in the decision of the House of Lords in *R v Blastland*.[112] The appellant B was charged with the buggery and murder of a boy. At the trial B admitted that he had met the boy and engaged in homosexual activity with him but said that when he saw another man nearby, who might have witnessed what he had done, he panicked and ran away. B gave a description of the other man which corresponded closely to M and alleged that M must have committed the offences charged. At the trial there were formal admissions[113] by the prosecution. Some related to M's movements on the evening in question and others showed that M had been investigated by the police after the murder and had been known to engage in homosexual activities in the past with adults but not children. The defence sought leave to call a number of witnesses to elicit from them that, before the victim's body had been found, M had made statements to them that a boy had been murdered. The trial judge held this evidence to be inadmissible. B was convicted on both counts. Before the House of Lords, the appellant submitted that, although the statements made by M were inadmissible hearsay if tendered for the truth of any fact stated, they were admissible, as original evidence, if tendered to prove the state of mind of their maker, that is, to show M's knowledge of the murder before the body had been found.[114] Lord Bridge, giving the judgment of the House, held that original evidence of this kind is only admissible if the state of mind in question 'is either itself directly in issue at the trial or is of direct and immediate relevance to an issue which arises at the trial'. The issue at the trial was whether B had committed the crimes and what was relevant to that issue was not the fact of M's knowledge but how he had come by it; since he might have done so in a number of different ways, there was no rational basis on which the jury could be invited to draw an inference as to the source of that knowledge or conclude that he rather than B was the offender. The evidence, therefore, had been properly rejected. The flaw in this reasoning, it is submitted, is the unwarranted introduction of the requirement that the evidence be 'of direct and immediate' relevance. The evidence was no less relevant than the evidence relating to M's movements which was thought to have been properly admitted, albeit neither item, by itself, could show that M, rather than B, was the offender.[115]

It is submitted that an unnecessarily strict approach to relevance was also taken in *R v T (AB)*.[116] The complainant alleged that A, the appellant, B, and C had each sexually abused her. There was no suggestion that they had acted in concert or that any one of them was aware of the abuse of either of the others. B admitted the allegations against him, but died before his trial, and C pleaded guilty to counts of indecent assault. It was held that evidence of B's

---

[112] [1986] AC 41, HL, applied in *R v Williams* [1998] Crim LR 494, CA. See also *R v Kearley* [1992] 2 AC 228, HL (see Ch 12); and *R v Akram* [1995] Crim LR 50, CA.

[113] See, in this chapter, under Facts in issue, p 10. There were also a number of *informal* admissions, M having successively made and withdrawn admissions of his own guilt of the offences in question, but these were properly rejected by the trial judge as inadmissible hearsay: see *R v Turner* (1975) 61 Cr App R 67, CA.

[114] See, in this chapter, under Hearsay evidence, p 12.

[115] Contrast the approach taken in *Wildman v R* [1984] 2 SCR 311 (Supreme Court of Canada) and *R v Szach* (1980) 23 SASR 504 (Supreme Court of South Australia). See also *R v Gadsby* [2006] Crim LR 631, CA, where it was held, obiter, that evidence may be relevant if capable of increasing (or diminishing) the probability of facts indicating that some other person committed the crime, eg, evidence that a person with the opportunity of committing the crime had a propensity to do so; and *R v Greenwood* [2005] Crim LR 59, CA, where it was held that an accused charged with murder is entitled to seek to establish that a third party had a motive to murder the victim.

[116] [2007] 1 Cr App R 43 (4), CA.

admission and of C's guilty plea was inadmissible because irrelevant to the issues of whether A had abused the complainant and that while it was 'tempting' to say that it was relevant to the issue of her credibility, evidence is inadmissible simply to bolster credibility because this would be a form of 'oath helping' which has never been a permissible ground for admitting evidence.

Evidence of demeanour may be relevant, depending on the circumstances. For example, in the case of an accused charged with murder, the evidence of an experienced physician that the accused was calm and uninterested when the baby was found to be dead may be relevant, but not evidence of the fact that the accused did not appear emotional at the funeral, because 'outward appearances at a funeral home offer no reliable barometer of one's grief'.[117] The demeanour of the victim of a crime immediately after its commission may be relevant and admissible to support his or her account, by analogy with the principle of *res gestae*.[118] However, it is submitted that the *res gestae* conditions[119] do not have to be met: the evidence is not hearsay. The condition imposed in *R v Keast*[120] seems unduly restrictive. In that case, it was held that unless there is some concrete basis for regarding long-term demeanour and state of mind of an alleged victim of sexual abuse as confirming or disproving the occurrence of such abuse, it cannot assist a jury bringing their common sense to bear on who is telling the truth.[121]

On a charge of causing death by dangerous driving, evidence that the accused took cocaine shortly before the accident is relevant, even without evidence as to the amount taken,[122] but evidence that the accused took drink will not be relevant without evidence to show that the amount taken would adversely affect a driver.[123] The reasoning for the distinction appears to be based on the dubious generalization that a modest dose of cocaine has a greater capacity to impair driving ability than a modest intake of alcohol.[124] However, it is submitted that in the case of drugs as well as drink, the question of relevance should turn on both the amount taken and the time at which it was taken.

In criminal proceedings, evidence of good character of a prosecution witness is generally inadmissible to bolster the witness's credibility; however, evidence of a disposition will be admissible if relevant to an issue in the case; the category of issues to which the evidence may be relevant is not closed; and if evidence of disposition is admitted, the judge should direct the jury on the issue to which it is relevant and ensure that its admission does not dilute the burden of proof on the prosecution and any good character direction given for the accused.[125] Examples of such relevance include: in a sexual case, the defence being consent, evidence of the complainant's disposition to resist pre-marital sexual intimacy;[126] in a case of murder, the defence being self-defence, evidence of the deceased's non-violent disposition;[127]

---

[117] *R v MT* [2004] OJ No 4366 (Ont. CA).

[118] *R v Townsend* [2003] EWCA Crim 3173.

[119] See Ch 14.

[120] [1998] Crim LR 748, CA.

[121] See also, applying *R v Keast* [1998] Crim LR 748, CA, *R v Venn* [2003] EWCA Crim 236; and also *R v Zala* [2014] EWCA Crim 2181, considered in Ch 8, 'Supporting material', p 263.

[122] *R v Pleydell* [2006] 1 Cr App R 212 (12), CA, applied in *R v Ashworth* [2012] EWCA Crim 1064.

[123] *R v McBride* (1961) 45 Cr App R 262, followed in *R v Thorpe* [1972] 1 WLR 342.

[124] See *R v Pleydell* [2006] 1 Cr App R 212 (12), CA at [27] and [28].

[125] *R v Mader* [2018] EWCA Crim 2454.

[126] *R v Amado-Taylor* [2001] EWCA Crim 1898.

[127] *R v RG* [2002] EWCA Crim 1056. See also *R v Mader* [2018] EWCA Crim 2454.

and evidence of non-racist disposition in rebuttal of an allegation of racist abuse forming an integral part of a defence of self-defence.[128]

In *R v Green*[129] the accused was of good character and the trial judge had given an appropriate direction to the jury to the effect that his good character was relevant to his credibility and may have made it less likely that he had committed the offence.[130] The judge added that since there was no suggestion that the complainant was of bad character, there was 'a level playing field' between her and the accused. This was held to be a misdirection, in effect watering down the direction on the good character of the accused. The Court of Appeal said that unless a jury hears that a Crown witness is not of good character, they will assume that there is nothing to speak against the witness' credibility. However, it is submitted that the jury may well assume exactly the opposite, reasoning that if she were of good character, evidence to that effect would have been adduced just as it had been in the case of the accused.

Insufficient relevance

There are occasions when the effect of evidence, albeit technically admissible, is likely to be so slight that it is wiser not to adduce it, particularly if, in a criminal trial, there is any danger that its admission will have an adverse effect on the fairness of the proceedings.[131] Evidence of marginal relevance may also be excluded on the grounds that it would lead to a multiplicity of subsidiary issues which, in addition to distracting the court from the main issue,[132] might involve the court in a protracted investigation[133] or a difficult and doubtful controversy of precisely the same kind as that which the court has to determine.[134] Similarly, questioning of a witness may be disallowed if it is no more than a fishing expedition.[135] In *Agassiz v London Tramway Co*[136] the plaintiff, a passenger in an omnibus, claimed damages for serious personal injuries arising out of a collision allegedly caused by the driver's negligence. The action was dismissed for want of evidence as to how the accident had happened. After the accident, the conductor, in reply to the suggestion of another passenger that the driver's conduct should be reported, said: 'Sir, he has been reported, for he has been off the points five or six times today; he is a new driver.' Kelly CB held that this evidence was properly excluded, since it neither related to the conduct of the driver at the relevant time nor explained the actual cause of the collision, but merely gave rise to a multiplicity of side issues.

---

[128] *R v Lodge* [2013] EWCA Crim 987. See also *R v Q* [2011] All ER (D) 210 (Jun).

[129] [2018] 4 WLR 39, CA.

[130] See Ch 18.

[131] Per Lord Lane CJ in *R v Robertson; R v Golder* [1987] 3 All ER 231 at 237, CA in relation to the admissibility of evidence under the Police and Criminal Evidence Act 1984, s 74 (see Ch 23). See also *R v Williams* [1990] Crim LR 409, CA.

[132] See per Byrne J in *R v Patel* [1951] 2 All ER 29 at 30.

[133] See per Rolfe B in *A-G v Hitchcock* (1847) 1 Exch 91 at 105 and per Willes J in *Hollingham v Head* (1858) 27 LJCP 241 at 242: 'litigants are mortal . . .'.

[134] Per Lord Watson in *Metropolitan Asylum District Managers v Hill* (1882) 47 LT 29, HL, where a majority of the House was of the opinion, without deciding the point, that in considering the effect of a smallpox hospital on the health of local residents, evidence of the effect of similar hospitals in other localities on their residents would be admissible. See also *Folkes v Chadd* (1782) 3 Doug KB 157.

[135] *R v Haddock* [2011] EWCA Crim 303.

[136] (1872) 21 WR 199.

Relevance of possession of money or drugs paraphernalia in offences relating to drugs

On charges of possession of drugs with intent to supply, there is a difficult distinction to be drawn between evidence which is relevant to the intention to supply the drug found, and evidence which, although of some relevance to that issue, is unduly prejudicial because it relates to past dealing or dealing generally. It is submitted that on the question of admissibility, rather than relevance, some of the reported cases must now be read subject to ss 98–113 of the Criminal Justice Act 2003, which govern admissibility of evidence of the accused's bad character.[137] In *R v Batt*,[138] a charge of possession of cannabis resin with intent to supply, the Court of Appeal did not question the admissibility in evidence of B's possession of weights and scales (on which there were traces of cannabis resin), but held that evidence of the discovery of £150 in an ornamental kettle in her house was inadmissible because it had nothing to do with intent to supply in future the drugs found, but had a highly prejudicial effect as 'a hallmark of a propensity to supply generally, or a hallmark of the fact that there had been a past supply, or that the money will be used in future to obtain cannabis for future supply'.

However, it seems that *Batt* has not laid down any general principle that evidence of possession of money is never admissible on a charge of possession with intent to supply, and on one view the decision in that case turned upon the fact that the trial judge had failed to direct the jury as to how they could properly use the evidence of the possession of money.[139] In *R v Wright*[140] it was held that drug traders needed to keep by them large sums of cash and therefore evidence of the discovery of £16,000 could have given rise to an inference of dealing and tended to prove that the drugs found were for supply. This approach was followed in *R v Gordon*,[141] where it was held that although evidence as to past deposits in, and withdrawals from, savings accounts was irrelevant, because it could only found an inference of past drug dealing, evidence of the discovery of £4,200 in G's home was admissible ('cash for the acquisition of stock for present active drug dealing must be relevant to a count of possession with intent to supply'), subject to an appropriate direction on any possible innocent explanations for the presence of the cash.[142] The jury should be directed that they should regard the finding of the money as relevant only if they reject any innocent explanation for it put forward by the accused, but that if they conclude that the money indicates not merely past dealing, but an ongoing dealing in drugs, they may take into account the finding of it, together with the drugs, in considering whether intent to supply has been proved.[143] The jury should also be directed not to treat such

---

[137] See **Ch 19**. However, it has been said that if the evidence would have been admissible before the 2003 Act, it would be 'highly artificial' to require the prosecution to apply to admit it under the Act: *R v Graham* [2007] EWCA Crim 1499. See further, Ormerod [2010] Crim LR 307–9.

[138] [1994] Crim LR 592, CA.

[139] See *R v Morris* [1995] 2 Cr App R 69, CA and *R v Nicholas* [1995] Crim LR 942, CA. Alternatively, it should be regarded as a case confined to its own facts, remembering that £150 was too small, and its hiding place too unremarkable, to be the hallmark of present and active drug dealing: *R v Okusanya* [1995] Crim LR 941, CA.

[140] [1994] Crim LR 55, CA.

[141] [1995] 2 Cr App R 61, CA. See also *R v Morris* [1995] 2 Cr App R 69, CA.

[142] Concerning the accounts, cf *R v Okusanya* [1995] Crim LR 941, CA. But see also *R v Smith (Ivor)* [1995] Crim LR 940, CA: evidence that £9,000 had been deposited in S's account in recent months, of which £2,100 was unexplained by various legitimate transactions, was admissible (subject to an appropriate direction).

[143] *R v Grant* [1996] 1 Cr App R 73, CA; see also *R v Green* [2009] EWCA Crim 1688 (a case of conspiracy to supply drugs); and cf *R v Antill* [2002] EWCA Crim 2114. However, the judge is not tied to this or any other particular form of words: *R v Malik* [2000] Crim LR 197, CA.

evidence as evidence of propensity, that is, not to pursue the line of reasoning that, by reason of past dealing, the accused is likely to be guilty of the offence charged.[144]

At one stage, it was thought that where *possession* of drugs is in issue, evidence of possession of money or drugs paraphernalia can never be relevant to that issue.[145] However, in *R v Guney*[146] the Court of Appeal, declining to follow the earlier authorities, held that although evidence of possession of a large sum of cash or enjoyment of a wealthy lifestyle does not, on its own, prove possession, there are numerous sets of circumstances in which it may be relevant to that issue, not least to the issue of knowledge as an ingredient of possession. The issue in that case was whether the accused was knowingly in possession of some 5 kilos of heroin or whether it had been 'planted', and the defence conceded that if possession were to be proved, then it would be open to the jury to infer intent to supply. It was held that, in all the circumstances, evidence of the finding of nearly £25,000 in cash in the wardrobe of the accused's bedroom, in close proximity to the drugs, was relevant to the issue of possession.[147]

The exclusionary rules

Evidence must be sufficiently relevant to be admissible, but sufficiently relevant evidence is only admissible insofar as it is not excluded by any rule of the law of evidence or by the exercise of judicial discretion. The consequence, of course, is that some relevant evidence is excluded. Thus although statutes make provision for the admissibility of various categories of hearsay, not *all* relevant hearsay is admissible.[148] Relevant evidence, including highly relevant evidence, may also be withheld as a matter of public policy on the grounds that its production and disclosure would jeopardize national security or would be injurious to some other national interest.[149] The opinion evidence of a non-expert is generally regarded as being insufficiently relevant to a subject not calling for any particular expertise but, whatever its degree of relevance, is generally excluded on the basis that the tribunal of fact might be tempted simply to accept the opinion proffered rather than draw its own inferences from the facts of the case.[150] These and other exclusionary rules make up much of the law of evidence and are considered throughout this book.

Multiple admissibility

Where evidence is admissible for one purpose, but inadmissible for another, it remains admissible in law for the first purpose (although it may be excluded by the exercise of judicial discretion). For example, an out-of-court statement may be inadmissible for the purpose of proving the truth of its contents, being inadmissible hearsay, but admissible, as original evidence, for the purpose of proving that the statement was made. The principle has been described, somewhat misleadingly, as one of 'multiple admissibility';[151] 'limited admissibility' might be a better tag. Where it applies, the judge is often required to warn the jury of

---

[144] See *R v Simms* [1995] Crim LR 304, CA and *R v Lucas* [1995] Crim LR 400, CA.

[145] See *R v Halpin* [1996] Crim LR 112, CA and *R v Richards* [1997] Crim LR 499, CA.

[146] [1998] 2 Cr App R 242.

[147] Applied in *R v Griffiths* [1998] Crim LR 567, CA. See also *R v Edwards* [1998] Crim LR 207, CA and *R v Scott* [1996] Crim LR 652, CA.

[148] See generally Chs 12–15.

[149] See Ch 21.

[150] See Ch 20.

[151] Wigmore, *A Treatise on the Anglo-American System of Evidence* (3rd edn, Boston, 1940) I, para 13.

the limited purpose for which the evidence has been admitted.[152] The risk that the jury may misunderstand or ignore such a warning is felt to be more than outweighed by the greater mischief that would be occasioned if the evidence were to be excluded altogether.[153]

Conditional admissibility

An item of evidence, viewed in isolation, may appear to be irrelevant and therefore inadmissible. Taken together with, or seen in the light of, some other item of evidence, its relevance may become apparent. Evidence, however, can only be given at a trial in piecemeal fashion, and it may be difficult to adduce the second item of evidence before the first. In order to overcome this difficulty, the first item of evidence may be admitted conditionally or *de bene esse*. If, viewed in the light of evidence subsequently adduced, it becomes relevant, it may be taken into account. If, notwithstanding the evidence subsequently adduced, it remains irrelevant, it must be disregarded. The operation of the principle may be illustrated by reference to the admissibility of accusations made in the presence of the accused, the relevance of which may depend on evidence, subsequently adduced, of the accused's reaction to them. An accusation made in the presence of the accused upon an occasion on which he might reasonably be expected to make some observation, explanation, or denial is, in certain circumstances, admissible in evidence against him, provided that a foundation for its admission is laid by proof of facts from which, in the opinion of the judge, a jury might reasonably draw the inference that the accused, by his answer, whether given by word, conduct, or silence, acknowledged the truth of the accusation made. The accusation may be admitted in evidence, however, even where the evidential foundation has not been laid, provided that, if evidence is *not* subsequently adduced from which it can be inferred that the accused did acknowledge the truth of the accusation made, the judge directs the jury to disregard the accusation altogether.[154]

The best evidence rule

The so-called best evidence rule, at one time thought to be a fundamental principle of the law of evidence, is now applied so rarely as to be virtually extinct. The eighteenth-century case of *Omychund v Barker*,[155] suggests that it was an inclusionary rule, allowing for the admissibility of the best evidence available that a party to litigation could produce. The rule, however, was rarely used in this way, and as an inclusionary doctrine of general application certainly finds no place in the modern law of evidence. The authorities show that the rule was normally treated as being of an exclusionary nature, preventing the admissibility of evidence where better was available.[156] As an exclusionary principle,

---

[152] For example, where a confession, admissible as evidence of the truth of its contents by way of exception to the hearsay rule, implicates both its maker and a co-accused, but is inadmissible against the co-accused, the trial judge is duty bound to impress upon the jury that it can be used only against its maker and not against the co-accused: *R v Gunewardene* [1951] 2 KB 600, CCA (see Ch 15). See also the Crown Court Compendium (July 2019), 14–15, paras 7–11.

[153] See per Tindall CJ in *Willis v Bernard* (1832) 8 Bing 376 at 383.

[154] Per Lords Atkinson and Reading in *R v Christie* [1914] AC 545, HL at 554 and 565 respectively.

[155] (1745) 1 Atk 21 at 49.

[156] See, eg, *Chenie v Watson* (1797) Peake Add Cas 123, where oral evidence relating to the condition of a material object was excluded on the grounds that the object itself ought to have been produced for inspection by the court; and *Williams v East India Co* (1802) 3 East 192, where circumstantial evidence was excluded because direct evidence was available. Both cases have, on the point in question, been reversed: as to the former, see *R v Francis* (1874) LR 2 CCR 128 and *Hocking v Ahlquist Bros Ltd* [1944] KB 120 (which are considered in Ch 10); as to the latter, see *Dowling v Dowling* (1860) 10 ICLR 236.

however, the rule is now virtually defunct. The rule that a party seeking to rely upon the contents of a document must adduce primary evidence of the contents, secondary evidence being admissible only exceptionally,[157] is sometimes said to be the only remaining instance of the best evidence rule,[158] notwithstanding that it pre-dates the best evidence rule. In *Springsteen v Flute International Ltd*[159] it was held, in this context, that it could be said with confidence that the best evidence rule, long on its deathbed, had finally expired. Prior to that decision, the rule did make a rare appearance in *R v Quinn and R v Bloom*.[160] The accused, two club proprietors, were charged with keeping a disorderly house. The charge arose out of certain allegedly indecent striptease acts performed at their clubs. One of the accused sought to put in evidence a film made three months after the events complained of and showing what the performers actually did, together with evidence that the performances shown in the film were identical with those in question. The Court of Criminal Appeal held that this evidence had been properly excluded. Ashworth J, giving the judgment of the court, said:

> it was admitted that some of the movements in the film (for instance, that of a snake used in one scene) could not be said with any certainty to be the same movements as were made at the material time . . . this objection goes not only to weight, as was argued, but to admissibility: it is not the best evidence.[161]

Although out-of-court demonstrations and re-enactments are admissible as a variety of real evidence,[162] the court held that a reconstruction made privately for the purpose of constituting evidence at a trial is inadmissible.[163]

The best evidence rule is of no more than marginal contemporary significance, but where a party fails to make use of the best evidence available and relies upon inferior evidence, the absence of the best evidence or the party's failure to account for its absence may always be the subject of adverse judicial comment. The inferior evidence may be slighted or ignored on the grounds that it lacks weight.[164] For example, in *Post Office Counters Ltd v Mahida*,[165] a debt action, it was held that the claimant company, which relied upon secondary evidence of documents submitted to it by the defendant, having itself destroyed the originals, had failed to prove the debts in question.

---

[157] See Ch 10.

[158] See, eg, per Lord Denning MR in *Garton v Hunter* [1969] 2 QB 37, CA at 44 and per Ackner LJ in *Kajala v Noble* (1982) 75 Cr App R 149, CA at 152.

[159] [2001] EMLR 654, CA.

[160] [1962] 2 QB 245.

[161] Cf *R v Thomas* [1986] Crim LR 682, a case of reckless driving in which a video recording of the route taken by the accused was admitted to remove the need for maps and still photographs and to convey a more accurate picture of the roads in question. See also *R v Metcalfe* [2016] 2 Cr App R 297 (21) (animations merely illustrating the opinion of an expert on the way in which a deceased person had come to suffer injuries and to be where she was found).

[162] See, eg, *Buckingham v Daily News Ltd* [1956] 2 QB 534, CA: a demonstration of the way in which a worker cleaned the blades of a rotary press in a printing house.

[163] Cf *Li Shu-ling v R* [1988] 3 All ER 138, PC: a video recording of a re-enactment of the crime by the accused may be admitted in evidence as a confession (see Ch 15).

[164] See per Lord Coleridge CJ in *R v Francis* (1874) LR 2 CCR 128.

[165] [2003] EWCA Civ 1583.

Weight

The weight of evidence is its cogency or probative worth in relation to the facts in issue. The assessment of the weight of evidence is in large measure a matter of common sense and experience, dependent upon a wide variety of factors such as: (i) the extent to which it is supported or contradicted by other evidence adduced; (ii) in the case of direct testimony, the demeanour, plausibility, and credibility of the witness and all the circumstances in which she claims to have perceived a fact in issue; and (iii) in the case of hearsay, all the circumstances from which any inference can reasonably be drawn as to the accuracy or otherwise of the out-of-court statement including, for example, whether the statement was made contemporaneously with the occurrence or existence of the facts stated and whether its maker had any incentive to conceal or misrepresent the facts.[166] Weight, like relevance, is a question of degree: at one extreme, an item of evidence may be of minimal probative value in relation to the facts in issue; at the other extreme, it may be virtually conclusive of them. Where the evidence adduced by a party in relation to a fact in issue is, even if uncontradicted, so weak that it could not reasonably justify a finding in his favour, it is described as 'insufficient evidence'. Where the evidence adduced by a party is so weighty that it could reasonably justify a finding in his favour, it is described as 'prima facie evidence'. Somewhat confusingly, however, this term is also used to describe evidence adduced by a party which is, in the absence of contradictory evidence, so weighty that it does justify a finding in his favour. 'Conclusive evidence' might be thought to denote the weightiest possible evidence. In fact, the term refers to evidence which, irrespective of its weight, concludes the fact in issue: the fact ceases to be in issue and is not even open to contradictory proof because the court must find the fact to have been proved.[167]

The issue of the weight to be attached to an item of evidence is related to, but distinct from, the issue of its admissibility. The weight of evidence is a question of fact, its admissibility a question of law. Thus, in a jury trial, the judge decides whether an item of evidence is relevant and admissible and, if the evidence is admitted, the jury decides what weight, if any, to attach to it. It does not follow from this, however, that the weight of evidence is solely the concern of the tribunal of fact. For a variety of different purposes, the judge must also form a view as to the weight of evidence. In determining admissibility, he must consider whether evidence is sufficiently relevant and this will depend, to some extent, on his assessment of its weight. In examining the evidence adduced to establish preliminary facts, which, it will be recalled, must be proved as a condition precedent to the admissibility of certain items of evidence, the weight of the evidence should be taken into account. As we shall see, a judge should withdraw an issue from the tribunal of fact where a party has adduced 'insufficient evidence' in support of that issue.[168] As we shall also see, the judge has a discretion to exclude certain items of evidence and, for these purposes also, may have regard to, inter alia, the weight of the evidence in question.[169] Last, and by no means least, in his summing-up the judge is entitled to comment upon the cogency of the evidence admitted, provided that he does not usurp the jury's function as the tribunal of fact.[170]

---

[166] See Civil Evidence Act 1995, s 4 (see Ch 13).

[167] See, eg, Criminal Justice Act 1967, s 10(1) (see Ch 4) and Civil Evidence Act 1968, s 13(1) (see Ch 23).

[168] See, in this chapter, under **The sufficiency of evidence**, p 40.

[169] See, in this chapter, under **Exclusionary discretion**, p 47.

[170] *R v O'Donnell* (1917) 12 Cr App R 219; *R v Canny* (1945) 30 Cr App R 143.

The functions of the judge and jury

The division of functions between tribunal of law and tribunal of fact, which dates from a time when jury trial was the norm in both civil and criminal proceedings, has left a deep impression on the modern law of evidence, even as it now applies in cases tried without a jury.

Questions of law and fact

The resolution of disputes in courts of law gives rise to questions of fact, or questions of law, and often both. In jury trials, the general rule is that questions of law are decided by the judge and questions of fact by the jury. This is not as straightforward a division as it may appear at first blush, because some questions of 'fact' for the jury, for example the issue of recklessness, may be considered to be as much questions of law as of fact, and some questions of 'law' for the judge, for example the existence or non-existence of preliminary facts, are essentially questions of fact.[171]

Questions of law for the judge include those relating to the substantive law, the competence of a person to give evidence as a witness, the admissibility of evidence, the withdrawal of an issue from the jury, and the way in which he should direct the jury on both the substantive law and the evidence adduced.[172] Questions of fact for the jury include those relating to the credibility of the witnesses called, the weight to be attached to the evidence adduced, and ultimately, of course, the existence or non-existence of the facts in issue.

In trials on indictment without a jury, that is, complex fraud cases and trials where there is a real danger of jury tampering, the judge decides all questions of both law and fact and, if the accused is convicted, must give a judgment which states the reasons for the conviction.[173] In the case of a trial by lay justices, they decide all questions of both law and fact, but on questions of law, including the law of evidence, questions of mixed law and fact, and matters of practice and procedure, should give heed to the advice of the justice's legal adviser.[174] Theoretically in the same position, district judges (magistrates' courts) tend to decide questions of law as well as fact. In civil cases tried by a judge sitting alone, the judge decides all questions of both law and fact.

Although questions of fact are generally decided by the jury, the judicial function includes the investigation of preliminary facts (for the purpose of determining the admissibility of evidence), the assessment of the sufficiency of evidence (for the purpose of deciding whether to withdraw an issue from the jury), and the evaluation of evidence adduced (for the purpose of commenting upon the matter to the jury in summing up). Each of these matters is considered separately in this chapter. Additionally, there is a variety of special cases in which questions of fact are also capable of being questions of law or are treated as being questions of law or for some other reason fall to be decided, wholly or in part, by the judge. They include the following.[175]

---

[171] See generally Glanville Williams, 'Law and Fact' [1976] Crim LR 472 and Allen and Pardo, 'Facts in Law and Facts of Law' (2003) 7 E&P 153.

[172] See further, below, under **Jury directions and the summing-up, p 44**.

[173] Criminal Justice Act 2003, s 48(3) and (5).

[174] For the duties of the justice's legal adviser, see *Criminal Practice Directions* VI, Part 24A and r 24.15(2), Criminal Procedure Rules 2015, SI 2015/1490.

[175] Other examples relate to defamation, in respect of which the judge decides whether the writing in question is capable of the defamatory meaning alleged and, if so, the jury then decides whether it does constitute a libel (*Nevill v Fine Arts & General Insurance Co Ltd* [1897] AC 68, HL) and manslaughter by gross negligence, in respect of which the existence of a duty of care or a duty to act is a question of law, but the jury has to decide whether the facts establish the existence of the duty (*R v Evans* [2009] 1 WLR 1999, CA). Contrast s 2(5) of the Corporate Manslaughter and Corporate Homicide Act 2007: the judge must make any findings of fact necessary to decide the question of law as to whether a particular organization owes a duty of care to a particular individual.

The construction of ordinary words

The modern authorities are in a state of disarray on the important question whether, in criminal cases, the construction of an ordinary word in a statute is a question for the tribunal of fact. The leading authority on the point, *Brutus v Cozens*,[176] expressly supports an affirmative answer, except where the context shows that the word is used in an unusual sense. There is another exception: where a word can bear two different meanings.[177] In *Brutus v Cozens*, on the question whether behaviour was 'insulting' for the purposes of s 5 of the Public Order Act 1936, Lord Reid said:[178]

> The meaning of an ordinary word of the English language is not a question of law. The proper construction of a statute is a question of law.[179] If the context shows that a word is used in an unusual sense the court will determine in other words what that unusual sense is. But here there is in my opinion no question of the word 'insulting' being used in any unusual sense. It appears to me . . . to be intended to have its ordinary meaning. It is for the tribunal which decides the case to consider, not as law but as fact, whether in the whole circumstances the words of the statute do or do not as a matter of ordinary usage of the English language cover or apply to the facts which have been proved. If it is alleged that the tribunal has reached a wrong decision then there can be a question of law but only of a limited character. The question would normally be whether their decision was unreasonable in the sense that no tribunal acquainted with the ordinary use of language could reasonably reach that decision.[180]

Whether an article is an 'offensive weapon' is a question of fact for the jury.[181] However, in the case of an item that betrays the purpose for which it was made by its very design, judicial notice[182] may be taken of the fact and the jury directed that the article is an offensive weapon; examples include a flick-knife[183] and a knuckle-duster.[184]

In *DPP v Stonehouse*[185] the question whether acts are sufficiently proximate to the intended complete offence to rank as an attempt, was treated as a question of fact. This was justified by Lord Diplock on the grounds that the concept of proximity is a question of degree on which the opinion of reasonable men may differ and as to which the legal training and experience of a judge does not make his opinion more likely to be correct than that of a non-lawyer.[186]

---

[176] [1973] AC 854.

[177] See per Lord Hughes in *R v Golds* [2016] UKSC 61 at [27] and [38] in relation to the word 'substantially' in the Homicide Act 1957, s 2(1)(b).

[178] [1973] AC 854 at 861.

[179] See also *R v Spens* [1991] 4 All ER 421, CA: it is for the judge to construe binding agreements between parties, and all forms of parliamentary and local government legislation, including codes which sufficiently resemble legislation as to require such construction, eg the City Code on Takeovers and Mergers; and cf *R v Adams* [1993] Crim LR 525, CA, and *R v Morris* [1994] Crim LR 596, CA. However, if the legislation contains ordinary straightforward words, no judicial interpretation of them is required: *R v Pouladian-Kari* [2013] EWCA Crim 158.

[180] See also *R v Harris* (1986) 84 Cr App R 75, CA: the words 'knowledge or belief' are words of ordinary usage and therefore, in most cases of handling stolen goods contrary to the Theft Act 1968, s 22(1); all that need be said to a jury is to ask whether the prosecution has established receipt, knowing or believing that the goods were stolen; *R v Jones* [1987] 2 All ER 692, CA: whether a person is 'armed' while being concerned in the illegal importation of cannabis contrary to the Customs and Excise Management Act 1979, s 86; *Chambers v DPP* [1995] Crim LR 896, DC: 'disorderly behaviour' contrary to the Public Order Act 1986, s 5; and *R v Kirk* [2006] Crim LR 850, CA: 'indecent or obscene' under the Postal Services Act 2000, s 85(4).

[181] See per Lord Lane CJ in *R v Williamson* (1978) 67 Cr App R 35, CA at 38–9.

[182] See Ch 4.

[183] *R v Simpson* [1983] 1 WLR 1494, CA.

[184] *DPP v Christof* [2016] 2 Cr App R 56 (6), DC.

[185] [1978] AC 55, HL.

[186] [1978] AC 55 at 69. See now the Criminal Attempts Act 1981, s 4(3).

Lord Reid's dictum, however, although never expressly disowned, has largely been ignored. As one commentator has observed, the number of cases when *Cozens v Brutus* ought to have been cited but was not 'are as the sands of the sea'.[187] This disregard extends to the House of Lords itself. In *Metropolitan Police Comr v Caldwell*,[188] for example, 'recklessly' was held to be an ordinary word, but given a legal definition. A similar approach has been taken in relation to the word 'supply' in s 5(3) of the Misuse of Drugs Act 1971[189] and the word 'discharge' in s 5(1)(b) of the Firearms Act 1968.[190] The need for such legal definition of ordinary words stems from the potential diversity of interpretation by jurors, and indeed judges, and the concomitant risk of inconsistent verdicts, and for these reasons, it is submitted, Lord Reid's dictum should continue to be ignored until it is expressly repudiated.

In civil cases tried with a jury, there is old authority to support the view that the meaning of ordinary words is a question of construction for the judge.[191]

Corroboration

In the now rare cases in which a conviction cannot be based on uncorroborated evidence, it is for the judge to direct the jury as to what evidence is capable, in law, of amounting to corroboration and for the jury to decide whether that evidence does, in fact, constitute corroboration.[192]

Foreign law

In the courts of England and Wales, questions of foreign law, that is questions relating to the law of any jurisdiction other than England and Wales, are issues of fact to be decided, on the evidence adduced, by the judge. Section 15 of the Administration of Justice Act 1920 provides that:

> Where for the purposes of disposing of any action or other matter which is being tried by a judge with a jury in any court in England or Wales it is necessary to ascertain the law of any other country which is applicable to the facts of the case, any question as to the effect of the evidence given with respect to that law shall, instead of being submitted to the jury, be decided by the judge alone.

This provision applies to criminal proceedings only,[193] but has been re-enacted, in relation to High Court proceedings and County Court proceedings, by s 69(5) of the Senior Courts Act 1981 and s 68 of the County Courts Act 1984 respectively. Foreign law is usually proved by the evidence of an appropriately qualified expert, who may refer to foreign statutes and decisions, or by the production of a report of a previous decision by an English court of superior status on the point of foreign law in question.[194] Where necessary, the judge must determine the point by deciding between the conflicting opinion evidence of the expert witnesses.[195]

---

[187] Elliott, '*Brutus v Cozens*; Decline & Fall' [1989] Crim LR 323 at 324.

[188] [1982] AC 341, HL.

[189] *R v Maginnis* [1987] AC 303, HL.

[190] *Flack v Baldry* [1988] 1 All ER 673, HL.

[191] Per Parke B in *Neilson v Harford* (1841) 8 M&W 806 at 823.

[192] *R v Tragen* [1956] Crim LR 332; *R v Charles* (1976) 68 Cr App R 334n, HL; and *R v Reeves* (1979) 68 Cr App R 331, CA. See generally Ch 8.

[193] *R v Hammer* [1923] 2 KB 786, CCA.

[194] See Ch 20. For the circumstances in which judicial notice may be taken of points of foreign law, see **Ch 4**.

[195] See, eg, *Re Duke of Wellington, Glentanar v Wellington* [1947] Ch 506.

Questions of reasonableness

What is reasonable is a question of fact and therefore normally decided by the jury. In some civil cases, however, it must be decided by the judge on the basis of facts which, if not agreed, have been ascertained by the jury. In an action for malicious prosecution, for example, it is the function of the jury to ascertain the facts, if disputed, which operated on the mind of the prosecutor, and the function of the judge, on the basis of the facts thus ascertained, to decide whether the prosecutor did or did not have reasonable and probable cause for commencing the prosecution in question.[196]

Perjury

The offence of perjury is committed where a person lawfully sworn as a witness or interpreter in a judicial proceeding wilfully makes a statement *material* in that proceeding which he knows to be false or does not believe to be true.[197] Section 1(6) of the Perjury Act 1911 provides that 'the question whether a statement on which perjury is assigned was material is a question of law to be determined by the court of trial'.

Autrefois acquit and convict

An accused charged with an offence which is the same as an offence in respect of which he has previously been acquitted or convicted or an offence in respect of which he could on some previous indictment have been lawfully convicted, may tender a special plea in bar of *autrefois acquit* or *convict* in order to quash the indictment. Where such a plea is tendered, it is for the judge to decide the issue, without empanelling a jury.[198]

The *voir dire*, or trial within a trial

Preliminary facts, as we have seen, must be proved as a condition precedent to the admissibility of certain items of evidence. For example, where the prosecution propose to adduce evidence of a confession made by the accused and the defence object to its admissibility on the grounds that it was or may have been obtained by oppression of the accused, or in consequence of something said or done which was likely, in the circumstances, to render unreliable any confession which might be made by him in consequence thereof, the court shall not allow the confession to be admitted except insofar as the prosecution prove to the court that the confession was not obtained by such means.[199] Proof of due search for the original of a lost document, on the contents of which a party seeks to rely, is a condition precedent to the admissibility of a copy of that document.[200] Similarly, it may become necessary to show that a person is competent to give evidence as a witness or that a witness is privileged from answering a particular question. Questions of this kind are matters of law for the judge. The preliminary facts may be agreed or assumed, but where they are in dispute it is for the judge

---

[196] *Herniman v Smith* [1938] AC 305, HL, applied, in relation to the tort of procuring the grant of a search warrant falsely, maliciously, and *without reasonable and probable cause*, in *Reynolds v Metropolitan Police Comr* (1984) 80 Cr App R 125, CA.

[197] Perjury Act 1911, s 1(1).

[198] Criminal Justice Act 1988, s 122.

[199] Police and Criminal Evidence Act 1984, s 76(2) (see Ch 15).

[200] *Brewster v Sewell* (1820) 3 B&Ald 296 (see Ch 10).

to hear evidence and adjudicate upon them.[201] The witnesses give their evidence on a special form of oath known as a *voir dire*. The hearing before the judge is called a hearing on the *voir dire* or a 'trial within a trial'.

In general, disputes about the admissibility of evidence in civil proceedings are best resolved by the judge at trial rather than at a separate preliminary hearing, because at such a hearing the judge will usually be less well informed and such a hearing can cause unnecessary costs and delays.[202]

In the Crown Court

In the Crown Court, questions of admissibility, including those involving the hearing of evidence on the *voir dire*, are usually determined in the absence of the jury because of the impossibility of deciding such questions without some reference either to the disputed evidence, which in the event may be ruled inadmissible, or to other material prejudicial to the accused. Thus where the prosecution propose to adduce a certain item of evidence and the advocate for the defence intends to make a submission that it is inadmissible, that intention will be conveyed to the prosecution either at the Plea and Trial Preparation Hearing or immediately before the trial commences so that the evidence is not referred to in the presence of the jury, whether in the prosecution opening speech or otherwise. The prosecution will adduce their evidence in the normal way but at that point in time when the evidence would otherwise be admitted, it will be intimated to the judge that a point of law has arisen which falls to be decided in the absence of the jury and the jury will be told to retire.[203] Whether or not the jury, on returning to court, hear the disputed evidence, depends, of course, on the judge's ruling on its admissibility. In *R v Reynolds*[204] Lord Goddard CJ was of the opinion that the determination of preliminary facts in the absence of the jury is confined to exceptional cases, such as those relating to the admissibility of a confession, where it is almost impossible to prevent some reference to the terms of the confession.[205] However, the modern practice is to ask the jury to retire whenever there is a risk of them being exposed to material which might be ruled inadmissible or which, in any event, would be likely to prejudice the accused.[206] The modern position, therefore, is probably accurately reflected in r 104(c) of the United States Federal Rules, which provides that hearings on the admissibility of confessions shall always be conducted in the absence of the jury and that hearings on other matters shall be so conducted when the interests of justice require.

[201] However, where the preliminary facts are identical with the facts in issue, the condition precedent is held to be established if the judge is satisfied that there is *sufficient evidence* of it to go before the jury. For example, if a party seeks to adduce a tape recording in evidence, the question of whether it is genuine and original being ultimately for the determination of the jury, the judge need satisfy himself by no more than prima facie evidence that the tape is genuine and original and therefore competent to be considered by the jury: *R v Robson, R v Harris* [1972] 1 WLR 651; cf *R v Stevenson* [1971] 1 WLR (see Ch 3). See also *Stowe v Querner* (1870) LR 5 Exch 155 and per Lord Penzance in *Hitchins v Eardley* (1871) LR 2 P&D 248. However, it has also been said that the judge must reach a definite decision on the preliminary fact in question: see per Lord Denman CJ in *Doe d Jenkins v Davies* (1847) 10 QB 314.

[202] *Stroude v Beazer Homes Ltd* [2005] EWCA Civ 265.

[203] Occasionally it is necessary to determine admissibility immediately after the jury has been empanelled, eg, where the evidence of a confession is so crucial to the prosecution case that, without reference to it, their case cannot even be opened: see *R v Hammond* [1941] 3 All ER 318.

[204] [1950] 1 KB 606.

[205] See further Ch 15, The *voir dire*, p 481.

[206] See *R v Deakin* [1994] 4 All ER 769, CA.

In criminal proceedings in the magistrates' court

In *F (an infant) v Chief Constable of Kent*[207] Lord Lane CJ observed that since the function of the *voir dire* is to allow the arbiter of law to decide a legal point in the absence of the arbiter of fact, in proceedings before magistrates, where the justices are judges of both fact and law, there can be no question of a trial within a trial. In that case, it was held that once the question of the admissibility of a confession has been decided as a separate issue, the magistrates having heard evidence on the preliminary facts and having ruled in favour of admissibility, it is unnecessary for the evidence about the confession to be repeated later in the trial proper. Lord Lane CJ also held that it was impossible to lay down any general rule as to when a question of admissibility should be taken in a summary trial or as to when the magistrates should announce their decision on it, every case being different. This flexible approach was reiterated in *R v Epping and Ongar Justices, ex p Manby*,[208] where the accused contested the admissibility of certain documentary evidence tendered by the prosecution and sought leave to have the question resolved as a preliminary issue. The magistrates refused and admitted the evidence as providing a prima facie case for the accused to deal with later, if he saw fit. The Divisional Court held that the justices had not erred: within statutory constraints, they should determine their own procedure.

Section 78 of the 1984 Act, whereby a criminal court has a discretion to exclude evidence on which the prosecution propose to rely on the grounds that it would have an adverse effect on the fairness of the proceedings,[209] is not a statutory constraint for these purposes and accordingly does not entitle an accused to have an issue of admissibility settled as a preliminary issue in a trial within a trial.[210]

In *Halawa v Federation Against Copyright Theft*[211] it was held that the duty of a magistrate, on an application under s 78, is either to deal with it when it arises or to leave the decision until the end of the hearing, the objective being to secure that the trial is fair and just to both sides. Thus, in some cases there will be a trial within a trial in which the accused is given the opportunity to exclude the evidence before he is required to give evidence on the main issues (because, if denied that opportunity, his right to remain silent on the main issues is impaired); but in most cases the better course will be for the whole of the prosecution case to be heard, including the disputed evidence, before any trial within a trial is held. In order to decide, the court may ask the accused the extent of the issues to be addressed by his evidence in the trial within a trial—a trial within a trial might be appropriate if the issues are limited, but not if it is likely to be protracted, raising issues which will have to be re-examined in the trial proper.

Where justices resolve to exclude, under s 78, evidence of statements made by an accused, they should consider, after seeking the views of the parties, whether the substantive hearing—if there still is one—should be conducted by a differently constituted bench.[212]

Section 76(2) of the 1984 Act[213] is a statutory constraint and an exception to the generally flexible approach. In *R v Liverpool Juvenile Court, ex p R*[214] the Divisional Court held that if,

[207] [1982] Crim LR 682, DC.
[208] [1986] Crim LR 555, DC.
[209] See, in this chapter, under Exclusionary discretion, Criminal cases, p 52.
[210] *Vel v Owen* [1987] Crim LR 496, DC.
[211] [1995] 1 Cr App R 21, DC.
[212] *DPP v Lawrence* [2008] 1 Cr App R 147 (10), CA, *per curiam* at 153–4.
[213] See, in this chapter, under The *voir dire*, or trial within a trial, p 37.
[214] [1987] 2 All ER 668, DC.

in a summary trial, the accused, before the close of the prosecution case, represents to the court that a confession was or may have been obtained by the methods set out in s 76(2), the magistrates are required to hold a trial within a trial, in which the accused is entitled to give evidence relating to the issue of admissibility, and are also required to make their ruling on admissibility before or at the end of the prosecution case.[215] In such a case, an alternative contention based on s 78 would also be examined at the same trial within a trial, at the same time.[216]

Applicability of the rules of evidence

Somewhat surprisingly, given the importance of the matter, there is little authority on the question whether the tribunal of law, whether judge or magistrates, in deciding what evidence is admissible for the purpose of proving or disproving disputed preliminary facts, is bound by the rules of evidence which apply at the trial proper. In the case of statutory exceptions to the hearsay rule, it has been held that preliminary facts call for proof by admissible evidence.[217] Under the United States Federal Rules,[218] the judge is only bound by those rules of evidence which concern privilege.

The sufficiency of evidence

The obligation on a party to adduce sufficient evidence on a fact in issue to justify a finding on that fact in his favour is referred to as 'the evidential burden'.[219] A party discharges an evidential burden borne by him by adducing sufficient evidence for the issue in question to be submitted to the jury (tribunal of fact). Whether there is sufficient evidence is a question of law for the judge. If the party has adduced enough evidence to justify, *as a possibility*, a favourable finding by the jury, the judge leaves it to them to decide whether or not the issue has been proved; if the evidence is insufficient, the judge withdraws the issue from the jury, whatever their view of the matter, directing them either to return a finding on that issue in favour of the other party or, in appropriate circumstances, to return a verdict on the whole case in favour of the other party. For example, in criminal proceedings, the evidential burden in relation to most common law defences is borne by the accused. If the accused, on a charge of assault, fails to adduce sufficient evidence of, say, self-defence, the judge will withdraw that issue from the jury, directing them that it must be taken as proved against the accused.[220] The prosecution normally bear the evidential burden in relation to all those facts essential to

---

[215] A trial within a trial will only take place before the close of the prosecution case if a representation is made pursuant to s 76(2). If no such representation is made, the accused may raise the question of the admissibility or weight of the confession at any subsequent stage of the trial. However, at this later stage in the proceedings, although the court retains an inherent jurisdiction to exclude the confession, as well as the power to exclude by virtue of s 78, it is not required to embark on a trial within a trial: see per Russell LJ at 672–3.

[216] *Halawa v Federation Against Copyright Theft* [1995] 1 Cr App R 21, per Ralph Gibson LJ at 33.

[217] See per Lord Mustill, obiter, in *Neill v North Antrim Magistrates' Court* [1992] 4 All ER 846, HL, at 854, applied in *R v Belmarsh Magistrates' Court, ex p Gilligan* [1998] 1 Cr App R 14, DC and *R v Wood and Fitzsimmons* [1998] Crim LR 213, CA. However, in appropriate circumstances, the preliminary facts relating to the compilation of business or other documents in s 117 Criminal Justice Act 2003 may be inferred by the judge from the documents themselves: *R v O'Connor* [2010] EWCA Crim 2287. See also *R v Greer* [1998] Crim LR 572, CA (proof of preliminary facts by unsworn evidence) and contrast *R v Jennings* [1995] Crim LR 810, CA.

[218] Rule 104(a).

[219] The meaning of this term is considered fully in Ch 3.

[220] See Ch 3.

the Crown case. If the prosecution fail to adduce sufficient evidence in relation to an essential element of the offence, they fail not only on that issue, but also in the whole case and the judge will direct the jury to return a verdict of not guilty; there is no case to answer.

Submission of no case to answer in the Crown Court

On a successful submission of no case to answer, the judge will direct the jury to return a verdict of not guilty. In criminal cases tried with a jury, the defence may make a submission of no case to answer after the prosecution have adduced all their evidence and closed their case.[221] If there is no evidence that the alleged crime has been committed by the accused, no evidence of an essential ingredient of that offence, or no corroborative evidence where corroboration is required as a matter of law, the submission will be upheld. Likewise, if the judge comes to the conclusion that the Crown's evidence, taken at its highest, is such that a jury properly directed could not properly convict on it, it is his duty to stop the case.[222] However, where the Crown's evidence is such that its strength or weakness depends on the view to be taken of a witness's reliability, or other matters which are, generally speaking, within the jury's province, and where on one view of the facts there is evidence on which a jury could properly conclude that the accused is guilty, the submission will fail.[223] The mere fact that as a matter of scientific

[221] The submission should be made in the absence of the jury and, if the trial proceeds thereafter, should not be referred to by the judge in his summing-up: see *R v Smith and Doe* (1986) 85 Cr App R 197, CA, and, in the case of visual identification evidence, *R v Akaidere* [1990] Crim LR 808, CA (see Ch 9). See also *Crosdale v R* [1995] 2 All ER 500, PC: if the judge rejects the submission, the jury need know nothing about the decision—no explanation is required; and if the judge rules in favour of the submission on some charges but not on others, all the jury need be told is that the decision was taken for legal reasons—any further explanation will risk potential prejudice. Whether the judge upholds or rejects the submission, she should give reasons for her decision; and if the submission is rejected and the conduct of the defence may depend on the reasons, she should give them promptly: *R v Chauhan* [2019] EWCA Crim 1111.

[222] For example, a case of assisting a criminal may be stopped where the only evidence is having lived with the criminal at the time of the offence: see *R v Bland* (1987) 151 JP 857, CA. Cf *R v Suurmeijer* [1991] Crim LR 773, CA; *R v McNamara* [1998] Crim LR 278, CA; and *R v Berry* [1998] Crim LR 487, CA. Where DNA is directly deposited in the course of the commission of a crime, a very high DNA match with the accused is, by itself, sufficient to raise a case to answer: *R v Sampson* [2014] EWCA Crim 1968 (DNA on a firearm possessed unlawfully) and *R v FNC* [2016] 1 Cr App R 176 (12) (semen on the clothing of the victim of an indecent assault). The same principle applies in the case of an article left at the scene of the crime, depending on the facts; many factors may be relevant, including whether there is evidence of another explanation for the presence of the DNA and how readily moveable the article was: *R v Tsekiri* [2017] 1 Cr App R 479 (32), CA, questioning earlier authorities to the contrary. Cf *R v Lewis* [2018] EWCA Crim 1101 where DNA on moveable articles was not the *only* evidence—there was visual identification evidence and further DNA on a non-moveable article, a wall. See also *R v Henney* [2016] EWCA Crim 1853. A submission of no case will succeed where the only evidence against an accused is evidence of a DNA match on an item of clothing found at the scene of the crime: *R v Grant* [2008] EWCA Crim 1890, followed in *R v Ogden* [2013] EWCA Crim 1294.

[223] See generally per Lord Lane CJ in *R v Galbraith* [1981] 1 WLR 1039, CA; cf *R v Beckwith* [1981] Crim LR 646. The Royal Commission on Criminal Justice recommended replacement of the rule in *R v Galbraith* by a new power for the judge to withdraw from the jury an issue or the whole case if he considers the evidence too weak or demonstrably unsafe or unsatisfactory: see para 42, ch 4, *Report of the Royal Commission on Criminal Justice*, Cm 2263 (1993). For the correct approach in cases where the issue is mistaken identity, see *R v Turnbull* [1977] QB 224, CA and *Daley v R* [1993] 4 All ER 86, PC (see Ch 9). See also, where a case against an accused is based wholly or partly on an 'unconvincing' hearsay statement, the Criminal Justice Act 2003, s 125 (see Ch 12). Where a judge improperly rejects a defence submission of no case to answer, a conviction may be set aside on appeal on the grounds that he made a wrong decision on a question of law. As to the position on appeal in cases where, subsequent to the improper rejection of the submission, evidence was given entitling the jury to convict, see *R v Power* [1919] 1 KB 572; and contrast *R v Abbott* [1955] 2 QB 497 and *R v Juett* [1981] Crim LR 113, CA.

certainty it is not possible to rule out a proposition consistent with innocence does not justify withdrawing the case from the jury.[224] Cases in which the evidence is purely circumstantial are not in a special category; the judge should not withdraw the case from the jury because some inference other than guilt can reasonably be drawn from the facts proved,[225] but should ask the simple question, looking at all the evidence with appropriate care: is there a case on which a jury properly directed could convict?[226] Nor should the test be altered for offences— whether or not sexual offences—alleged to have been committed some years ago.[227]

The judge also has a power to withdraw a case from the jury at any time after the close of the prosecution case, even as late as the end of the defence case, and whether or not a submission of no case to answer has been made at the end of the prosecution case. This is a power to be very sparingly exercised and only if the judge is satisfied that no jury properly directed could safely convict.[228] However, it is not open to a judge to entertain a submission of no case before the close of the prosecution case, because it is only at that stage that it is known what the evidence actually is and until then the most that can be known is what it is expected to be.[229] A ruling may be made at an earlier stage, where it is admitted or agreed what the outstanding prosecution evidence will be, but any direction to return a not guilty verdict should normally await the end of the prosecution case unless, of course, the Crown bows to the ruling and offers no further evidence. Similarly, before the calling of any evidence, the parties may agree that it would be helpful for the judge to rule on the question whether, on agreed, admitted, or assumed facts, the offence charged will be made out, with a view either to the Crown offering no evidence or to the accused considering whether to plead guilty.[230]

Submission of no case to answer in criminal proceedings in the magistrates' court

Under rule 24.3(3)(d) of the Criminal Procedure Rules 2015,[231] in a magistrates' court, at the conclusion of the prosecution case, on the application of the accused or on its own initiative, the court may acquit on the ground that the prosecution evidence is insufficient for any reasonable court properly to convict, but must not do so unless the prosecutor has had an opportunity to make representations.[232] Under the test in r 24.3(3)(d), a submission of no case should be upheld when there has been no evidence to prove an essential ingredient of the offence alleged.[233] It is submitted that the test should also be satisfied when the evidence adduced by the prosecution has been so discredited as a result of cross-examination or is so

---

[224] *R v Vaid* [2015] EWCA Crim 298.

[225] *R v Edwards* [2004] EWCA Crim 2102 at [84] and *R v Jabber* [2006] EWCA Crim 2694 at [21].

[226] *R v P* [2008] 2 Cr App R 68, CA; *R v Darnley* [2012] EWCA Crim 1148; and *R v Sardar* [2017] 1 WLR 917, CA. Thus although account may be taken of the fact that a prosecution witness gave evidence in some respects inconsistent with the inferential case being advanced by the prosecution, that could not, by itself, be determinative of a submission of no case to answer: *R v Goring* [2011] EWCA Crim 2.

[227] *R v F(S)* [2011] 2 Cr App R 393, CA.

[228] *R v Brown* [2002] 1 Cr App R 46, CA.

[229] *R v N Ltd* [2009] 1 Cr App R 56 (3), CA. Nor does the judge have power to prevent the prosecution from calling evidence and to direct an acquittal on the basis that he thinks that a conviction is unlikely: *Attorney General's Reference (No 2 of 2000)* [2001] 1 Cr App R 503 (36).

[230] See *R v N Ltd* [2009] 1 Cr App R 56 (3), CA at 66.

[231] SI 2015/1490.

[232] If the prosecution are denied the opportunity to make representations and the submission of no case to answer succeeds, this may result in a successful appeal by way of case stated: see *DPP v Berry* [2019] EWHC 825 (Admin).

[233] See, eg, *Chief Constable of Avon and Somerset Constabulary v Jest* [1986] RTR 372, DC.

manifestly unreliable that no reasonable tribunal could safely convict on it,[234] on the basis that magistrates are the tribunal of fact as well as law. Thus although it has been said that questions of credibility, except in the clearest of cases, should not normally be taken into account by justices on a submission of no case,[235] if magistrates conclude that the prosecution evidence has been so discredited or is so manifestly unreliable that they cannot safely convict on it in any event, there can be no point in allowing the case to continue.

Submission of no case to answer in civil proceedings

In civil cases tried by a judge sitting alone, a defendant can submit that there is no case to answer at the close of the claimant's case, but in most cases the judge will only rule on the submission if the defendant elects not to call evidence.[236] In *Benham Ltd v Kythira Investments Ltd*[237] the Court of Appeal, after reviewing the authorities, held that there were two disadvantages of entertaining a submission of no case to answer without putting the defendant to his or her election. First, it interrupted the trial and required the judge to make up his mind as to the facts on the basis of one side's evidence only, applying the lower test of a prima facie case, with the result that, if he rejected the submission, he had to make up his mind afresh in the light of further evidence and on the application of a different test. Second, if the judge acceded to a submission of no case, his judgment might be reversed on appeal, with all the expense and inconvenience of resuming or retrying the action. The court concluded that rarely, if ever, should a judge trying a civil action without a jury entertain a submission of no case, although it conceded that 'conceivably', as Mance LJ had suggested in *Miller v Cawley*,[238] there may be some flaw of fact or law of such a nature as to make it entirely obvious that the claimant's case must fail, and the determination at that stage may save significant costs. The conclusion, it is submitted, is unnecessarily inflexible, especially in the light of the wide powers of case management under the Civil Procedure Rules, which should enable a court to consider a submission with or without putting the defendant to his election. In some cases, albeit rare, there will be grounds for contending that the claimant has no reasonable prospect of success whether or not the defendant gives evidence, as when the judge forms the view that the claimant is not a reliable witness of fact and that the position will not change even if the defendant calls evidence.[239]

In civil cases tried with a jury, the judge has a discretion whether to rule on a submission of no case to answer without requiring the defendant to elect to call no evidence[240] and a submission may also be made, after all the evidence has been adduced, that there is insufficient evidence to go before the jury.[241] The test would appear to be the same test as is used in criminal jury trials,[242] namely whether the evidence, taken at its highest, is such that a jury properly directed could not properly reach a necessary factual conclusion.[243]

[234] See *Practice Direction (Submission of No Case)* [1962] 1 WLR 227, revoked by *Practice Direction (Criminal Proceedings: Consolidation)* [2002] 1 WLR 2870, but not replaced.

[235] *R v Barking and Dagenham Justices, ex p DPP* (1995) 159 JP 373, DC.

[236] *Alexander v Rayson* [1936] 1 KB 169, CA at 178.

[237] [2003] EWCA Civ 1794, followed in *Graham v Chorley Borough Council* [2006] EWCA Civ 92.

[238] [2002] EWCA Civ 1100.

[239] See *Mullan v Birmingham City Council* (1999) The Times, 29 July, QBD.

[240] *Young v Rank* [1950] 2 KB 510.

[241] *Grinsted v Hadrill* [1953] 1 WLR 696, CA. In civil cases, with or without a jury, if the judge rejects a submission of no case to answer, albeit improperly, and the defendant subsequently adduces evidence and is found liable, the Court of Appeal may consider all of the evidence adduced, including that of the defendant: *Payne v Harrison* [1961] 2 QB 403, CA.

[242] See *R v Galbraith* [1981] 1 WLR 1039, CA (see n 223).

[243] See *Alexander v Arts Council of Wales* [2001] 4 All ER 205, CA per May LJ at [37].

Jury directions and the summing-up

At a trial on indictment, after the conclusion of all the evidence and closing speeches by the advocates, the judge must sum up the case to the jury. In addition to directing them on the substantive law and reminding them of the evidence that has been given, the judge must also explain a number of evidential points.[244] Many directions will reflect or be based upon the guidance given in the Crown Court Compendium. Some, sometimes many, of the directions will have been given to the jury earlier in the trial because the court is required to provide directions about the relevant law at any time that will assist the jury to evaluate the evidence, prior to any evidence being called, prior to the evidence to which it relates, or shortly thereafter.[245]

Most judges now routinely provide *written* directions. Although written directions are permitted but not mandatory under the Criminal Procedure Rules,[246] the Crown Court Compendium,[247] cites the relevant research[248] as showing that juror understanding and recollection increases significantly if they are given written directions alongside oral directions and concludes that the argument in favour of written directions is now overwhelming. In most cases the jury will also be provided with a written route to verdict. This poses a series of questions that lead the jury to the appropriate verdict, each question tailoring the law to the issues and evidence in the case.[249] A written route to verdict should be provided except where the case is so straightforward that it would be superfluous to do so,[250] something that one should never be too quick to assume.[251]

The judge should direct the jury as to which party bears the obligation to prove which facts and the standard of proof required to be met before they are entitled to conclude that those facts have been proved.[252] He should remind the jury of the evidence adduced by the prosecution and defence[253] and refer to any defence which that evidence discloses,[254] even

---

[244] It would be helpful if the prosecuting advocate made a checklist of the directions on the law which they considered the trial judge ought to give and drew the attention of the judge to any failure on his part to give an essential direction before the jury retired: per Watkins LJ in *R v Donoghue* (1987) 86 Cr App R 267, CA.

[245] Criminal Procedure Rules, r 25.14(2) and Criminal Practice Direction VI, para 26K.8.

[246] Rule 25.14(4).

[247] (July 2019) Part 1, 1–7.

[248] Thomas, 'Are Juries Fair?', Ministry of Justice research Series 01/10 (2010) and Thomas, 'Avoiding the Perfect Storm of Juror Contempt' [2013] Crim LR 483.

[249] Criminal Practice Direction VI, para 26K.11.

[250] Ibid, para 26K.12.

[251] *R v Atta-Dankwa* [2018] 2 Cr App R 248 (16), CA at [31].

[252] See *R v McVey* [1988] Crim LR 127. See also, as to burden of proof, *R v Donoghue* (1987) 86 Cr App R 267, and as to standard of proof, *R v Edwards* (1983) 77 Cr App R 5 and *R v Bentley (Deceased)* [2001] 1 Cr App R 307 (21), CA. Where the prosecution case depends solely on the identification of a single witness, it is particularly important to give a general clear and simple direction on burden and standard: *R v Lang-Hall* (1989) The Times, 24 Mar, CA. In cases involving injuries to a very small child, any temptation on the part of the jury to succumb to emotion should be countered by a very clear direction on the burden of proof: *R v Bowditch* [1991] Crim LR 831, CA.

[253] *R v Tillman* [1962] Crim LR 261. See also *R v Gregory* [1993] Crim LR 623, CA, and cf *R v Sargent* [1993] Crim LR 713, CA. It may be that, in a straightforward case, failure to sum up on the facts is not necessarily a fatal defect (*R v Attfield* (1961) 45 Cr App R 309), but in the majority of cases it is clearly desirable that the judge should do so (*R v Brower* [1995] Crim LR 746, CA).

[254] *R v Badjan* (1966) 50 Cr App R 141. The judge is under no duty to build up a defence for an accused who has elected not to testify, but need only remind the jury of any relevant matter contained in pre-trial statements and interviews with the police and the assistance, if any, provided by the Crown's witnesses: *R v Hillier* (1992) 97 Cr App R 349, CA. See also *R v Curtin* [1996] Crim LR 831, CA. If the accused has said nothing in police interviews and adduces no evidence to refute, qualify, or explain the case against him, the judge is under no duty to remind the jury of the defence case: *R v Briley* [1991] Crim LR 444, CA.

if it has not been relied upon by the advocate for the defence.[255] He should also explain, where necessary, that the onus of disproving certain defences, such as self-defence, rests on the prosecution. Depending on the nature of the case and the evidence called, it may be necessary: (i) to give a warning on, or to explain the requirement for, corroboration, indicating the meaning of that word and pointing out the evidence capable in law of amounting to corroboration; (ii) to direct on any relevant presumptions of law, making it clear, where necessary, that if the jury are satisfied that certain matters are proved, they *must* find that other matters are proved; (iii) to warn of the special need for caution, where the case against the accused depends wholly or substantially on the correctness of identification, before convicting in reliance on the correctness of the identification or identifications; and (iv) to explain that certain items of evidence can only be used for certain restricted purposes.[256]

The judge is entitled to comment on the plausibility and credibility of the witnesses and the weight of the evidence. He may do so in strong or emphatic terms provided that he also makes it clear that, apart from whatever he says about the law, the jury are in no way bound by any view of his own about the evidence which he may have appeared to express.[257] The specimen direction of the Judicial Studies Board, concerning comments by the judge on the evidence, used to include the following passage: 'If I mention or emphasize evidence that you regard as unimportant, disregard that evidence. If I do not mention evidence that you regard as important, follow your own view and take that evidence into account.' Such a direction is best given at the start of the summing-up, especially if the judge is minded to express strong views on the evidence.[258]

The judge should never give an express indication of his own disbelief in relation to the evidence of a witness, especially the evidence of an accused, even in a case in which the evidence warrants incredulity;[259] and on certain matters, such as the accused's failure to call a particular witness,[260] the judge is restricted in the comments that he may properly make.

If a judge is satisfied that there is no evidence before the jury which could justify them in convicting the accused and that it would be perverse for them to do so, it is his duty to direct them to acquit. Equally, a judge may withdraw a defence from the jury if there is no evidence whatever to support it. However, a majority of the House of Lords in *DPP v Stonehouse*,[261] held that if there is evidence before the jury to support a defence, albeit no

---

[255] *R v Porritt* (1961) 45 Cr App R 348. See also *R v Bennett* [1995] Crim LR 877, CA and *R v Williams* (1994) 99 Cr App R 163, CA. The duty only arises, however, if there is a reasonable possibility of the jury finding in favour of the defence, and not where the matter is merely fanciful and speculative: *R v Johnson* [1994] Crim LR 376, CA.

[256] See, in this chapter, under **Multiple admissibility**, p 30.

[257] It is undesirable for judges to make comments which place police witnesses in any special category or which may lead a jury to think that there will be adverse consequences for police officers if a verdict of not guilty is returned: *R v Harris* [1986] Crim LR 123, CA. Nor should the prosecution suggest that an acquittal will ruin a prosecution witness: *R v Gale* [1994] Crim LR 208, CA. If the witness refers in his evidence to the consequences of his evidence being disbelieved, the judge should direct the jury that their verdict should not be influenced by such a consideration: *R v Gale*. See also *Mears v R* (1993) 97 Cr App R 239, PC.

[258] See *R v Everett* [1995] Crim LR 76, CA.

[259] *R v Iroegbu* (1988) The Times, 2 Aug, CA. See also *R v Winn-Pope* [1996] Crim LR 521, CA; *R v Farr* [1999] Crim LR 506, CA; and *Michel v R* [2010] 1 WLR 879, PC.

[260] *R v Gallagher* [1974] 1 WLR 1204, CA. See, in this chapter, under **Failure to give evidence or call witnesses**, p 17.

[261] [1978] AC 55, HL.

reasonable jury, properly directed, could acquit, which would be a perverse verdict, the judge has no power to direct them to convict, because the jury alone have the right to decide that the accused is guilty.[262]

In exceptional cases, a court may rule that an explanation advanced by an accused is incapable in law of amounting to a defence of 'good reason' or 'reasonable excuse' if, on a proper construction of the Act in question, it would be inconsistent with the essential nature and purpose of the offence for the explanation to be capable of amounting to the defence.[263] However, in *R v Wang*,[264] the House of Lords confirmed that there are no circumstances in which a judge is entitled to direct a jury to convict and that no distinction is to be drawn between cases in which a burden lies on the defence and those in which the burden lies solely on the Crown, because that distinction is inconsistent with the rationale of the majority in *DPP v Stonehouse*, which is that no matter how inescapable a judge may consider a conclusion to be, in the sense that any other conclusion would be perverse, it remains his duty to leave the decision to the jury and not to dictate what the verdict should be. The jury therefore retain the power to return a perverse verdict, a power which has been memorably exercised from time to time.[265] This is viewed by some as a blatant affront to the legal process,[266] but by others as a means of controlling oppressive state prosecutions and ensuring that the law conforms to the layman's idea of justice.[267]

Where there has been a direction to convict and the decision as to guilt was not in reality made by the jury at all, a conviction will be quashed, but an appeal may be dismissed, notwithstanding a direction to convict, if the jury were left to make a decision and retired to do so and the evidence of guilt was overwhelming.[268]

Many of the rules governing the way in which a judge should sum up rest on largely uninvestigated assumptions about the way in which jurors analyse and evaluate evidence. Section 8 of the Contempt of Court Act 1981 operates to prevent research involving real juries and therefore research within the jurisdiction has been confined to simulated and shadow juries, who obviously do not meet real parties and are not responsible for making real decisions. However, the research, together with research projects undertaken elsewhere with real jurors, has shed much light on the extent to which jurors understand, recall, and apply directions on such matters as the standard of proof and the use to which character evidence may be put. It also indicates that 'jurors routinely fail to comprehend fully the directions they are supposed to apply'.[269]

---

[262] See also per Lloyd LJ in *R v Gent* [1990] 1 All ER 364, CA at 367 and cf per May LJ in *R v Thompson* [1984] 3 All ER 565, CA at 571, approved in *R v Gordon* (1987) 92 Cr App R 50n, CA.

[263] *R v Asmeron* [2013] 1 WLR 3457, CA at [22], citing *R v Kelleher* [2013] EWCA Crim 3525 by way of example.

[264] [2005] 1 WLR 661, HL.

[265] See, eg, *R v Ponting* [1985] Crim LR 318.

[266] See Auld LJ's *Review of the Criminal Courts of England and Wales: Report* (2001), paras 99–108.

[267] See Lord Devlin, 'The Conscience of the Jury' (1991) 107 LQR 398.

[268] See *R v Kelleher* [2003] EWCA Crim 3525, approved in *R v Caley-Knowles* [2007] 1 Cr App R 197, CA.

[269] Ellison and Munro, 'Getting to (not) guilty: examining jurors' deliberative processes in, and beyond, the context of a mock rape trial' (2010) 30(1) Legal Studies 74 at 95 and n 80 and Ellison and Munro, '"Telling tales": exploring narratives of life and law within the (mock) jury room' (2015) 35(2) Legal Studies 201.

Judicial discretion

If all evidence was either legally admissible or legally inadmissible, the law of evidence would be more certain. The price of such increased certainty, however, would be a rigidity that would do nothing to promote the integrity of the judicial process because it would sometimes occasion injustice by the exclusion of highly relevant evidence or the admission of evidence that would be unduly prejudicial or unfair to one of the parties. This can be avoided if the judge, over and above his general duty to rule on the admissibility of evidence as a matter of law, has a discretionary power to admit legally inadmissible evidence and to exclude legally admissible evidence. The former, inclusionary discretion, is virtually non-existent in English law. The latter, exclusionary discretion may be exercised in civil cases in favour of either party and in criminal cases in favour of the accused.

Inclusionary discretion

Despite the absence of express authority on the point, it seems clear that at common law, in both civil and criminal cases, a judge has no discretionary power to admit legally inadmissible evidence. In *Sparks v R*[270] the accused, a white man aged 27, was convicted of indecently assaulting a girl. At the trial, the judge held that evidence by the girl's mother to the effect that shortly after the assault her daughter had said 'it was a coloured boy' was inadmissible. The child gave no evidence at the trial. The Privy Council held that the evidence had been properly excluded as hearsay evidence which came within no recognized exception to the rule against hearsay in criminal cases.[271] It seems clear that Lord Morris, who delivered the opinion of the Privy Council, was operating on the assumption that where evidence is inadmissible as a matter of law, there is no inclusionary discretion.[272]

Exclusionary discretion

Civil cases

Prior to the introduction of the Civil Procedure Rules, a judge in a civil case had no discretionary power to exclude evidence that would otherwise be admissible as a matter of law. There was an exception, arguably, in the case of information given and received under the seal of confidence. On one view, the judge had a wide discretion to permit a witness, whether or not a party to the proceedings, to refuse to disclose information where disclosure would be a breach of some ethical or social value and non-disclosure would be unlikely to result in serious injustice in the case in which it was claimed.[273] In *D v National Society for the Prevention of Cruelty to Children*[274] Lords Hailsham and Kilbrandon were of the opinion that such a discretionary power did exist, but Lords Simon and Edmund-Davies disagreed. Lord Simon was of the view that although the judge could exercise a considerable 'moral authority' on the course of a trial, by which he could either seek to persuade an advocate not to ask the question or gently guide the witness to overcome his reluctance to answer it, when 'it comes to the forensic crunch . . . it must be law not discretion which is in command'.[275]

[270] [1964] AC 964, PC.

[271] The appeal was allowed on different grounds.

[272] [1964] AC 964 at 978. See also per Lord Reid in *Myers v DPP* [1965] AC 1001 at 1024.

[273] 16th Report of the Law Reform Committee, *Privilege in Civil Proceedings*, Cmnd 3472 (1967), para 1.

[274] [1978] AC 171.

[275] [1978] AC 171 at 239.

CPR r 32.1(2) has introduced a general exclusionary discretion in civil cases.[276] Rule 32.1 provides as follows:

(1) The court may control the evidence by giving directions as to—

   (a) the issues on which it requires evidence;

   (b) the nature of the evidence which it requires to decide those issues; and

   (c) the way in which the evidence is to be placed before the court.

(2) The court may use its power under this rule to exclude evidence that would otherwise be admissible.

(3) The court may limit cross-examination.

When the court decides to exercise its power to exclude evidence under r 32.1(2), it must seek to give effect to the 'overriding objective',[277] which is to enable the court 'to deal with cases justly'.[278] Rule 1.1(2) provides as follows:

(2) Dealing with a case justly includes, so far as is practicable—

   (a) ensuring that the parties are on an equal footing;

   (b) saving expense;

   (c) dealing with the case in ways which are proportionate—

      (i) to the amount of money involved;

      (ii) to the importance of the case;

      (iii) to the complexity of the issues; and

      (iv) to the financial position of each party;

   (d) ensuring that it is dealt with expeditiously and fairly;

   (e) allotting to it an appropriate share of the court's resources, while taking into account the need to allot resources to other cases; and

   (f) enforcing compliance with rules, practice directions and orders.

Rule 32.1(1) invests the court with extraordinarily wide powers, whereby it can override the views of the parties as to which issues call for evidence, the nature of the evidence appropriate to decide the issues, and the way in which the evidence should be given, for example in documentary form rather than orally.

Rule 32.1(2) also confers extremely wide powers: subject to r 1.1, there are no express limitations as to the extent of the power or the manner of its exercise.[279] As we have seen, civil courts already have the common law power to exclude evidence of marginal relevance.[280] In theory r 32.1(2) allows the court to exclude evidence even if plainly relevant, but it has been said that the more relevant the evidence is, the more reluctant the court is likely to be to exercise its discretion to exclude and that the power to exclude under r 32.1(2) should be exercised with great circumspection.[281] However, r 32.1(2) can be used to exclude peripheral material which is not essential to the just determination of the real issues between the

---

[276] Including claims allocated to the small claims track: CPR r 27.2(1).

[277] CPR r 1.2.

[278] CPR r 1.1(1).

[279] *Grobbelaar v Sun Newspapers Ltd* (1999) The Times, 12 Aug, CA.

[280] See, in this chapter, under **Insufficient relevance**, p 28.

[281] *Great Future International Ltd v Sealand Housing Corporation* (2002) LTL 25 July.

parties[282] and, in appropriate circumstances, evidence that has been obtained illegally or improperly.[283] It can also be used, it is submitted, to restrict the number of witnesses and exclude superfluous evidence.

At common law, the judge has a discretion to prevent any questions in cross-examination which in his opinion are unnecessary, improper, or oppressive. Cross-examination, it has been held, should be conducted with restraint and a measure of courtesy and consideration to the witness.[284] Rule 32.1(3) supplements the common law powers of the judge and may be used to impose limits on the time permitted for cross-examination.[285] It may also be used to limit cross-examination about a witness's previous convictions. Thus although a witness may be asked about his convictions even where the offence is not one of dishonesty, in order to attack his credit,[286] r 32.1(3) gives the judge a discretion as to which previous convictions can be put. However, where sitting with a jury, he should be more hesitant to exercise the discretion because it is for the jury to decide what weight to give to such matters in relation to a witness's credibility.[287]

Because circumstances vary infinitely, it is submitted that it would be undesirable for the courts to go beyond the wording of r 1.1(2) with a view to providing additional guidance as to the way in which the discretion under r 32.1(2) and (3) should be exercised. It is further submitted that exercise of the discretionary powers should only be impugned on appeal if perverse in the *Wednesbury* sense,[288] that is, where the court makes a decision which no reasonable tribunal could have reached.

Criminal cases

That a judge in a criminal trial has a discretion to exclude legally admissible evidence tendered by the prosecution has been accepted for some time[289] and was confirmed by the House of Lords in *R v Sang*.[290] The House was of the unanimous albeit obiter view[291] that the judge, as a part of his inherent power and overriding duty in every case to ensure that the accused receives a fair trial, always has a discretion to refuse to admit legally admissible evidence if, in his opinion, its prejudicial effect on the minds of the jury outweighs its true probative value.[292] Exercise of the discretion is a subjective matter,[293] and each case will turn on its own facts and circumstances.[294] The judge must balance on the one hand the prejudicial effect of

---

[282] See *McPhilemy v Times Newspapers Ltd* [1999] 3 All ER 775, CA.

[283] See Ch 11, Civil cases, p 325.

[284] See *Mechanical and General Inventions Co Ltd v Austin* [1935] AC 346 at 360 and Ch 7, The permitted form of questioning in cross-examination, p 218.

[285] *Rall v Hume* [2001] 3 All ER 248.

[286] See Ch 7, The permitted form of questioning in cross-examination, p 220.

[287] *Watson v Chief Constable of Cleveland Police* [2001] EWCA Civ 1547.

[288] *Associated Provincial Picture Houses Ltd v Wednesbury Corpn* [1948] 1 KB 223, CA.

[289] See, eg, *R v Christie* [1914] AC 545, HL.

[290] [1980] AC 402.

[291] A view affirmed by Lord Roskill in *Morris v Beardmore* [1981] AC 446, HL at 469.

[292] This 'fair trial' discretion may be exercised not only in the case of evidence the prejudicial effect of which outweighs its probative value, but also in the case of evidence obtained from the accused, after the commission of the offence charged, by improper or unfair means: see per Lords Diplock, Fraser, and Scarman at 436, 450, and 456 respectively. See Ch 11.

[293] Per Lord Fraser at 450. See also per Lord Guest in *Selvey v DPP* [1970] AC 304 at 352: 'If it is suggested that the exercise of this discretion may be whimsical and depend on the individual idiosyncrasies of the judge, this is inevitable where it is a question of discretion.'

[294] Per Lord Scarman at 456.

the evidence against the accused on the minds of the jury and on the other its weight and value having regard to the purpose for which it is adduced. Where the former is out of all proportion to the latter, the judge should exclude it. In one sense, of course, all relevant evidence adduced by the prosecution is prejudicial to the accused and the greater its probative value, the greater its prejudicial effect. In some cases, however, there will be a serious risk that the jury will attach undue weight to an item of evidence which is, in reality, of dubious reliability or of no more than trifling or minimal probative value, and in these circumstances the judge should exclude that evidence. In the words of Roskill J in *R v List*:[295]

> A trial judge always has an overriding duty in every case to secure a fair trial, and if in any particular case he comes to the conclusion that, even though certain evidence is strictly admissible, yet its prejudicial effect once admitted is such as to make it virtually impossible for a dispassionate view of the crucial facts of the case to be thereafter taken by the jury, then the trial judge, in my judgment, should exclude that evidence.

The case law on the basis of which the House of Lords in *R v Sang* came to its conclusion shows the discretion operating in a number of different sets of circumstances in relation to particular kinds of evidence. Their Lordships, however, were of the firm view that the cases were no more than examples of the exercise of a single discretion of general application and not of several specific or limited discretions.[296] The existing cases were not the only ones in which the discretion could be exercised. Lord Salmon said:[297]

> I recognize that there may have been no categories of cases, other than those to which I have referred, in which technically admissible evidence proffered by the Crown has been rejected by the court on the ground that it would make the trial unfair. I cannot, however, accept that a judge's undoubted duty to ensure that the accused has a fair trial is confined to such cases. In my opinion the category of such cases is not and never can be closed except by statute.

There has been much scope for exercise of the discretion in relation to otherwise admissible evidence of the accused's bad character. For example, where the accused became liable to cross-examination about his previous convictions and bad character under s 1(3)(ii) of the Criminal Evidence Act 1898, that is, where the nature or conduct of the defence was such as to involve imputations on the character of the prosecutor or witnesses for the prosecution (see now s 101(1)(g) of the Criminal Justice Act 2003), the judge could exercise his discretion to disallow it.

> He may feel that even though the position is established in law, still the putting of such questions as to the character of the accused person may be fraught with results which immeasurably outweigh the result of questions put by the defence and which make a fair trial of the accused person almost impossible.[298]

There is also scope for exercise of the discretion in relation to hearsay. In *Grant v The State*[299] it was said to be clear that the judge in a criminal trial has an overriding discretion to exclude

---

[295] [1966] 1 WLR 9 at 12.

[296] Per Lords Scarman and Fraser at 452 and 447 respectively.

[297] At 445. See also per Lord Dilhorne at 438.

[298] Per Singleton J in *R v Jenkins* (1945) 31 Cr App R 1 at 15, approved in *Selvey v DPP* [1970] AC 304, HL. It seems that the discretion can still be exercised to exclude evidence of the bad character of the accused, notwithstanding Criminal Justice Act 2003, s 99: see Ch 19, Abolition of the common law rules, p 555.

[299] [2006] 2 WLR 835, PC.

evidence judged to be unfair to the accused in the sense that it will put him at an unfair dis-advantage or deprive him unfairly of the ability to defend himself, and that conscientiously exercised it affords the accused an important safeguard where statute permits the admission of hearsay.[300]

A judge can also exercise his discretion to exclude evidence otherwise admissible under s 27(3) of the Theft Act 1968. Under s 27(3), where a person is charged with handling stolen goods and evidence is given of his possession of the goods, evidence that he has within the five years preceding the date of the offence charged been convicted of theft or handling stolen goods is admissible to prove that he knew or believed the goods to be stolen. The trial judge has a discretion to disallow the admission of such evidence, albeit strictly admissible, if, on the facts of the particular case, there is a risk of injustice. This may occur, for exam-ple, where possession is in issue in the case and it will be difficult, therefore, for the jury to appreciate that the evidence is relevant not to that issue but only to the issue of guilty knowledge.[301]

The discretion can also be used to exclude an out-of-court accusation directed at the accused which is admissible in evidence against him because by his conduct or demeanour it is possible to infer that he accepted, in whole or in part, the truth of the accusation made. Again, in these circumstances, the judge may exercise his discretion to exclude where the prejudicial effect of the evidence in the minds of the jury is out of all proportion to its true evidential value.[302]

It remains to note two matters of general importance relating to the exercise of the discre-tion now under discussion. First, the discretion may only be exercised to exclude evidence on which the prosecution, as opposed to any co-accused, proposes to rely. There is no discretion to exclude, at the request of one co-accused, evidence tendered by another. This principle, and the description of it appearing in the third edition of this work, were approved by the Privy Council in *Lobban v R*.[303] In that case L and R were charged with three murders. R, under caution, made a 'mixed' statement, that is, a statement which contained admissions as well as an exculpatory explanation. An integral part of the exculpatory explanation impli-cated L by name. The prosecution tendered R's statement for the truth of its contents against R—it was no evidence against L. The advocate for L submitted that the trial judge should have exercised his discretion to edit R's statement so as to exclude the parts which implicated L on the basis that the prejudice to L by allowing the whole statement to be admitted out-weighed the relevance of the disputed material to the defence of R. The Privy Council held that no such discretion existed—the advocate's submission, if accepted, would result in a serious derogation of an accused's liberty to defend himself by such legitimate means as he thinks it wise to employ. It was held that the discretionary power applies only to evidence on which the prosecution propose to rely. Although R's statement was *tendered* by the pros-ecution, the disputed material supported R's defence and the prosecution were not entitled

---

[300] The discretion in relation to hearsay has been preserved by statute: see Criminal Justice Act 2003, s 126(2)(b) in Ch 12.

[301] *R v List* [1966] 1 WLR 9, Assizes, a decision under the Larceny Act 1916, s 43(1), which was repealed by the Theft Act 1968 but re-enacted, with some modification, in s 27(3). The decision was approved in *R v Herron* [1967] 1 QB 107, CCA. See further Ch 19.

[302] See per Lord Moulton in *R v Christie* [1914] AC 545, HL at 559.

[303] [1995] 1 WLR 877, PC.

to rely on it as evidence against L. Thus, although a trial judge has a discretion to exclude or edit evidence tendered by the prosecution which is wholly inculpatory and probative of the case against one co-accused on the ground that it is unduly prejudicial against another co-accused, there is no discretion to exclude the exculpatory part of a 'mixed' statement on which one co-accused wishes to rely on the grounds that it implicates another. One remedy to the latter situation is to order separate trials, but if that is not done then the interests of the implicated co-accused must be protected by the most explicit direction by the judge to the effect that the statement of the one co-accused is not evidence against the other.[304]

The second matter of general importance is that, because exercise of the discretion is, as we have seen, a subjective matter and each case turns on its own peculiar facts, it is difficult to appeal successfully against a judge's decision not to exclude. Thus although an appellate court will interfere with exercise of the discretion if there is no material on which the trial judge could properly have arrived at his decision, or where he has erred in principle,[305] it is not enough that the appellate court thinks that it would have exercised the discretion differently. However, the appellate courts have from time to time set out guidelines for exercise of the discretion in relation to various types of evidence.[306] This assists judges. It also assists the advocate for the defence in advising and deciding tactics, to predict whether the discretion will be exercised.

The discretionary common law power to exclude evidence on the basis that its prejudicial effect outweighs its probative value has been supplemented by statutory provisions. The most important of these is s 78(1) of the Police and Criminal Evidence Act 1984, which provides that:

> the court may refuse to allow evidence on which the prosecution propose to rely to be given if it appears to the court that, having regard to all the circumstances, including the circumstances in which the evidence was obtained, the admission of the evidence would have such an adverse effect on the fairness of the proceedings that the court ought not to admit it.

Section 78(1) is of general application. Other statutory provisions empower a criminal court to exclude, in the exercise of its discretion, specific varieties of otherwise admissible evidence.[307]

Although s 78(1) is formally cast in the form of a discretion ('the court may'), the objective criterion whether 'admission . . . would have such an adverse effect on the fairness of the proceedings' in truth imports a judgement whether, in the light of the criterion of fairness, the court ought to admit the evidence.[308]

---

[304] But see also *R v Thompson* [1995] 2 Cr App R 589, CA: without a discretion to exclude evidence which is relevant and therefore admissible in relation to an accused but inadmissible and prejudicial in relation to a co-accused, the only safeguard is the cumbersome device of separate trials. The court observed that this seemed undesirable and that it might be preferable to allow a discretion where the prejudice is substantial and the evidence is of only limited benefit to the accused.

[305] See per Viscount Dilhorne in *Selvey v DPP* [1970] AC 304, HL at 342 and per Lord Lane CJ in *R v Powell* [1986] 1 All ER 193, CA at 197.

[306] See, eg, per Lawton LJ in *R v Britzman; R v Hall* [1983] 1 WLR 350, CA.

[307] See, in the case of hearsay, the Criminal Justice Act 2003, s 126 (see Ch 12), which expressly preserves the general power to exclude under s 78; and in the case of evidence of the bad character of the accused, the Criminal Justice Act 2003, s 101(3) (see Ch 19), which also, it seems, provides protection additional to s 78(1): see *R v Highton* [2005] 1 WLR 3472, CA.

[308] Per Lord Steyn in *R v Hasan* [2005] 2 AC 467, HL at [53]. See also per Auld LJ in *R v Chalkley and Jeffries* [1998] QB 848, CA at 874 and per Lord Hughes in *Beghal v DPP* [2015] UKSC 49 at [66].

A simple example of the application of s 78(1) is *R v O'Connor*.[309] B and C were jointly charged in one count with having conspired to obtain property by deception. B pleaded guilty and C not guilty. The evidence of B's conviction was then admitted at the trial of C under s 74 of the 1984 Act to prove that B had committed the offence charged. The Court of Appeal held that the conviction should have been excluded under s 78 because evidence of B's admission of the offence charged might have led the jury to infer that C in his turn must have conspired with B.[310] Another straightforward illustration is furnished by *R v Ibrahim*,[311] a rape case in which it was held that the hearsay statements of the complainant, who had died by the time of the trial, should have been excluded under s 78: the statements were central to the Crown's case, but could not be shown to be reliable, and the complainant, a heroin addict, was potentially a very unreliable witness.

Section 78(1) operates without prejudice to the discretionary common law power to exclude. Section 82(3) of the 1984 Act provides that 'Nothing in this Part of this Act shall prejudice any power of a court to exclude evidence (whether from preventing questions from being put or otherwise) at its discretion'. The terms of s 78(1) are clearly wide enough to apply to items of prosecution evidence already subject to the common law discretion[312]—and the weighing of probative value against prejudicial effect can be an important factor in exercising the discretion under s 78(1)[313]—but s 78(1) is not confined to such cases.

Section 78(1) directs the court, when considering exercise of the discretion, to have regard to all the circumstances, 'including the circumstances in which the evidence was obtained'. Thus, although it is clear that s 78(1) can be applied by a court in the absence of any illegality or impropriety,[314] the chief importance of the subsection lies in its potential for the exclusion of evidence illegally or improperly obtained. That topic is considered in **Chapter 11**.

Applications to exclude evidence in reliance on s 78(1) should be made before the evidence is adduced: the section applies to evidence on which the prosecution 'propose' to rely.[315]

Proof of birth, death, age, convictions, and acquittals

Birth and death

The normal and easiest way of proving a person's birth or death is by (a) producing to the court a certified copy of an entry in the register of births (deaths),[316] which is admissible under an exception to the hearsay rule[317] and admissible, therefore, as evidence of the truth of its contents; *and* (b) adducing some evidence to identify the person whose birth (death)

---

[309] (1986) 85 Cr App R 298, CA.

[310] See further **Ch 23**, where additional cases on the issue are considered.

[311] [2012] 2 Cr App R 420, CA.

[312] See *Matto v Crown Court at Wolverhampton* [1987] RTR 337, DC, per Woolf LJ at 346: '[s 78] certainly does not reduce the discretion of the court to exclude unfair evidence which existed at common law. Indeed, in my view in any case where the evidence could properly be excluded at common law, it can certainly be excluded under s 78.'

[313] Per Lord Lane CJ in *R v Quinn* [1990] Crim LR 581, CA.

[314] *R v Samuel* [1988] QB 615, CA; *R v O'Leary* (1988) 87 Cr App R 387, CA at 391; and *R v Brine* [1992] Crim LR 122, CA.

[315] *R v Sat-Bhambra* (1988) 88 Cr App R 55, CA.

[316] See the Births and Deaths Registration Act 1953, s 34; and, in the case of deaths in the Register of Presumed Deaths, the Presumption of Death Act 2013, Sch 1, paras 3 and 4.

[317] See generally **Chs 12–14**.

is in question with the person named in the birth (death) certificate.[318] Proof of birth or death may also be effected by the testimony of someone present at the time of birth (death), by hearsay statements admissible under either the Criminal Justice Act 2003 or the Civil Evidence Act 1995[319] or, in proceedings in which a question of pedigree is directly in issue, by a declaration as to pedigree made by a deceased blood relation or spouse of a blood relation.[320] A person's death may also be proved in reliance on the presumption of death, which is considered in **Chapter 4**, or by the testimony of someone who saw the corpse and was capable of identifying it as that of the person whose death is in question.

Age

The date of a person's birth being contained in his or her birth certificate, the normal way of proving a person's age is by (a) producing to the court a certified copy of an entry in the register of births, which, as we have seen, is admissible as evidence of the truth of its contents; *and* (b) adducing some evidence identifying the person whose age is in question with the person named in the birth certificate. A person's age may also be proved by the testimony of someone present at the time of his or her birth, by inference from his or her appearance,[321] by hearsay statements admissible by statute, and by declarations as to pedigree.

Convictions and acquittals

Section 73 of the Police and Criminal Evidence Act 1984, which superseded a variety of outdated statutory provisions, provides for the proof, in criminal proceedings, of convictions and acquittals by means of a certificate signed by an appropriate court officer together with evidence identifying the person whose conviction (acquittal) is in question with the person named in the certificate. Section 73(1) provides as follows:

(1) Where in any proceedings[322] the fact that a person has in the United Kingdom or any other member State[323] been convicted or acquitted of an offence otherwise than by a Service court is admissible in evidence, it may be proved by producing a certificate of conviction or, as the case may be, of acquittal relating to that offence, and proving that the person named in the certificate as having been convicted or acquitted of the offence is the person whose conviction or acquittal of the offence is to be proved.

The section contains a saving for 'any other authorised manner of proving a conviction or acquittal'.[324] The issue of identity in s 73(1) is a question of fact for the jury.[325] In *Pattison v*

---

[318] See also the Evidence (Foreign, Dominion and Colonial Documents) Act 1933, s 1, whereby an Order in Council may be made providing for the proof by authorized copy of extracts from properly kept public registers kept under the authority of the law of the country in question and recognized by the courts of that country as authentic records. Concerning births (deaths) on board ship, see the Merchant Shipping (Returns of Births and Deaths) Regulations 1979, SI 1979/1577.

[319] See **Chs 12 and 13** respectively.

[320] See **Ch 14**.

[321] See, eg, the Children and Young Persons Act 1933, s 99 and the Criminal Justice Act 1948, s 80(3).

[322] 'Proceedings' means criminal proceedings including proceedings before a court-martial or Courts-Martial Appeal Court.

[323] Ie any other EU member State.

[324] Section 73(4).

[325] *R v Burns* [2006] 1 WLR 1273, CA and *R v Lewendon* [2006] 2 Cr App R 294, CA.

DPP[326] the following general principles were said to apply when s 73(1) is relied on by the prosecution to prove the conviction of an accused.

(a) Identity must be proved to the criminal standard.

(b) This may be effected by a formal or informal admission,[327] by evidence of fingerprints, or by the evidence of someone present in court at the time.

(c) There is no prescribed means of proof: identity can be proved by any admissible evidence, for example a match between the personal details of the accused and those on the certificate.

(d) Even if the personal details, such as the name, are not uncommon, a match will be sufficient for a prima facie case.

(e) The failure of the accused to give any contradictory evidence can be taken into account and may give rise to an adverse inference under section 35(2) of the Criminal Justice and Public Order Act 1994.[328]

In the case of a conviction in another EU member State, there is no requirement that the conviction took place after the country in question became a member State. However, if there is evidence that such a conviction was the result of a trial which failed to reach appropriate standards of fairness, the court may exercise its discretion to exclude it, either under s 78 of the Police and Criminal Evidence Act or s 101(3) of the Criminal Justice Act 2003.[329]

ADDITIONAL READING

Aitken and Taroni, 'Fundamentals of Statistical Evidence—a Primer for Legal Professionals' (2008) 12 E&P 181.
A review of basic statistical terminology and its forensic applications that also explores options for presenting statistical information to fact-finders effectively.

Anderson, Schum, and Twining, *Analysis of Evidence* (Cambridge, 2005).
Covers the concepts and principles underlying the logic of proof, the uses and dangers of story-telling, probabilities and proof, and methods of analysing and ordering evidence.

Crinion, 'Adducing the Good Character of Prosecution Witnesses' [2010] Crim LR 570.
An argument that there should be more scope to admit evidence of the good character of a complainant. A two-stage test for admissibility is proposed: (i) the value of the evidence in relation to the issues in the case; and (ii) the interests of justice.

Eggleston, *Evidence, Proof and Probability* (2nd edn, London, 1983).
The leading text on the way in which probability theory can assist in achieving the purposes of the rules of evidence.

Ellison and Munro, '"Telling tales": exploring narratives of life and law within the (mock) jury room' (2015) 35(2) Legal Studies 201.
Based on empirical research, an exploration of the extent to which mock jurors were able and willing to understand and apply judicial directions and whether and how the provision of written directions affected their discussion.

---

[326] [2006] 2 All ER 317, QBD.

[327] As to the former, see Criminal Justice Act 1967, s 10 (see Ch 4); as to the latter, see Ch 15.

[328] See Ch 16.

[329] *R v Mehmedov* [2014] EWCA Crim 1523. As to s 78, see in this chapter, under Exclusionary discretion, Criminal cases, p 52. As to s 101(3), see Ch 19.

Grove, *The Juryman's Tale* (London, 1998).
A book that reveals the realities of serving as a juror on the basis of personal experience.

Heaton-Armstrong et al (eds), *Analysing Witness Testimony: Psychological, Investigative and Evidential Perspectives* (Oxford, 2006).
A wide-ranging consideration of witness testimony written by a variety of distinguished judges, practitioners, and forensic psychiatrists and psychologists—exploring such matters as witness memory, the effect of learning disability, false allegations, the impact of investigative and questioning technique, visual identification procedures, witness demeanour, the use of experts, and judicial training.

QUESTION

Francis, a man, is charged with unlawful sexual activity with Vic, a boy aged 12, on a school playing field on a Friday at 2pm. Vic contacted the police in a distressed state at 2.35pm. Francis denies the offence, his defence being mistaken identity. The prosecution wish to adduce the following items of evidence. Advise on the relevance of the items, referring to case law as appropriate.

(i)   Evidence from Gus, a teacher at the school, that Edward, another teacher at the school, who is openly gay, told him on the Friday in question that he had seen Vic crying on the playing field, shortly after 2pm, but decided not to intervene.

(ii)   Evidence from Vic that, when he was 11 years old, he had reported his step-father to his mother, and then to the police, for assaulting him, as a result of which his step-father was charged with, and pleaded guilty to, the assault.

(iii) Evidence that Francis is married to Sam (a man).

(iv)   Evidence that Francis has downloaded pornographic images of adults engaging in lawful sexual activity.

(v)   Evidence that Francis has downloaded pornographic images of adults engaging in unlawful sexual activity with boys.

 For a note-form answer see the online resources, accessible at
www.oup.com/he/keane-mckeown13e.

The burden and standard of proof

3

Key issues

- Where facts are in issue in either a civil or criminal trial, which party should have the obligation to prove those facts, and why?

- Where a party in a criminal trial has the obligation to prove facts, why should a judge, before leaving it to the jury to decide if those facts are proved, first require the party to adduce sufficient evidence to found a prima facie case?

- How persuasive must the evidence of facts adduced by a party be before those facts can be regarded as having been proved (a) where the party is prosecuting; (b) where the party is the accused; and (c) where the party is a party in a civil trial?

- Should an accused have an obligation to prove facts in his defence?

The burden of proof

Standing alone, the expression 'burden of proof' is self-explanatory: it is the obligation to prove. There are two principal kinds of burden, the legal burden and the evidential burden. The legal burden is a burden of proof. However, as we shall see, it is confusing and misleading to speak of the evidential burden as a burden of proof: first because when borne by a defendant it may be discharged by evidence other than the evidence adduced by the defence and therefore may not in substance be a burden at all,[1] and second because it can be discharged by the production of evidence that falls short of proof.[2]

The first half of this chapter is largely concerned with the rules governing which party bears the legal and evidential burdens on which facts in issue. The practical importance of these rules is fourfold. They can, of course, determine the eventual outcome of proceedings. Additionally they determine: which party has the right to begin adducing evidence in court; in what circumstances a defendant, at the end of the case for the prosecution or claimant, may make a successful submission of no case to answer; and how the trial judge should direct the jury. However, easy as it is to outline the nature and importance of this subject, detailed analysis is made difficult by problems of classification and terminology. It is convenient, then, to begin by defining and distinguishing the legal, evidential, and other burdens before considering in detail which burden is borne by each of the parties on the various facts in issue in any given case.

The legal burden

This burden has been referred to as 'the burden of proof' or 'probative burden'[3] and as 'the ultimate burden'. Another label, 'the burden of proof on the pleadings',[4] is used to show that in civil cases this burden is sometimes indicated by the statements of case. Two further phrases, 'the risk of non-persuasion'[5] and 'the persuasive burden', are used to show that a party bearing the burden on a particular fact in issue will lose on that issue if he fails to discharge the burden. Most of these labels are, to some extent, misleading, and in the ensuing text this burden will be referred to simply as 'the legal burden'.

The legal burden may be defined as the obligation imposed on a party by a rule of law to prove a fact in issue. Whether a party has discharged this burden and proved a fact in issue is decided by the tribunal of fact, only once, at the end of the case when both parties have called all their evidence. The standard of proof required to discharge the legal burden depends upon whether the proceedings are criminal or civil. In the former the standard required of the prosecution is proof which makes the tribunal of fact 'sure'; in the latter the standard required is proof 'on the balance of probabilities'. A party who fails to discharge a legal burden borne by him to the required standard of proof will lose on the issue in question.

The legal burden relates to particular facts in issue.[6] Most cases, of course, involve more than one issue and the legal burden of proof in relation to these issues may be distributed

---

[1] See *Bullard v R* [1957] AC 635, PC, at n 119, and per Pill LJ in *L v DPP* [2003] QB 137, DC at [23].

[2] Per Lord Devlin in *Jayasena v R* [1970] AC 618, PC at 624.

[3] See *DPP v Morgan* [1976] AC 182, HL.

[4] Phipson, *Law of Evidence* (18th edn, London, 2013) Ch 6 paras 6–06–6–08.

[5] Wigmore, *A Treatise on the Anglo-American System of Evidence* (3rd edn, Boston, 1940) Ch IX, paras 248–9.

[6] A question of construction is a question of *law* in respect of which no burden lies on either side; but if a party relies on surrounding circumstances as an aid to construction, then the onus is on him to prove them: see per Nourse LJ, construing a conveyance in *Scott v Martin* [1987] 2 All ER 813, CA at 817.

between the parties to the action. We shall see, for example, that in a criminal case where insanity is raised as a defence, the legal burden in relation to that issue is borne by the defendant, whereas the prosecution may well bear the legal burden on all the other facts in issue. In civil proceedings, an example would be a negligence action in which the defendant alleges contributory negligence: the claimant bears the legal burden on the issue of negligence, the defendant on contributory negligence. The obligation on a party to prove a fact in issue may oblige that party to negative or disprove a particular fact. In a criminal case of rape, for example, the prosecution bear the legal burden of proving lack of consent.[7] In a civil case of false imprisonment based on a police officer's false allegation of assault, the police bear the burden of proving that the allegation of assault was not a lie.[8]

In civil cases, a judge may find it impossible to make a finding one way or the other on a fact in issue, so that it will then fall to be decided by reference to which party bears the legal burden on the issue. The principles governing this situation were summarized in *Stephens v Cannon*:[9] the situation has to be exceptional; nevertheless it can arise in relation to any issue; the court is only entitled to have such resort to the legal burden if it cannot reasonably make a finding; in which case it should tell the parties that it has striven to make a finding and explain why it cannot do so, except in those few cases where such matters can readily be inferred from the circumstances.

Judges sometimes refer to the 'shifting' of a burden of proof from one party to his opponent. The phrase is apt to mislead. The only sense in which the legal burden may be said to shift is on the operation of a rebuttable presumption of law. Rebuttable presumptions of law are considered in detail in **Chapter 4**, but it is convenient, at this stage, briefly to consider their operation. Where such a presumption applies, once a primary fact is proved or admitted, in the absence of further evidence another fact must be presumed. The quantity and quality of evidence required to rebut the presumed fact is determined by the substantive law in relation to the presumption in question. The party relying on the presumption bears the burden of proving the primary fact. Once he has adduced sufficient evidence on that fact, in the case of a 'persuasive' presumption his adversary will bear the legal burden of disproving the presumed fact. The burden may be said to have shifted. However, when judges refer to a shifting of the burden in circumstances other than on the operation of rebuttable presumptions of law, they mean that the burden may, at any given moment in the course of the trial, *appear* to have been satisfied by the party on whom it lies by virtue of the evidence adduced by that party. Insofar as this places a burden on that party's opponent, the opponent bears a 'tactical' burden. The legal burden has not shifted because, as has been noted, whether the legal burden has been discharged by a party is only determined once and that is at the end of the trial when *all* the evidence has been adduced.[10] The tactical burden is discussed more fully in contrast with the evidential burden.

---

[7] Under the Sexual Offences Act 2003, proof of certain circumstances or acts may give rise to a presumption of lack of consent. Presumptions are considered in Ch 4.

[8] *Copeland v Commissioner of Police of the Metropolis* [2015] 3 All ER 391, CA at [18]–[22].

[9] [2005] CP Rep 31, CA at [46]. See also *Constandas v Lysandrou* [2018] 2 FLR 983, CA.

[10] See per Sir Christopher Staughton in *Re W* [2001] Ch 609, CA at 616. See also per Mustill LJ in *Brady (Inspector of Taxes) v Group Lotus Car Companies plc* [1987] 3 All ER 1050, CA at 1059.

The evidential burden

This burden is also referred to as 'the burden of adducing evidence' and 'the duty of passing the judge'. It may be defined as the obligation on a party to adduce sufficient evidence of a fact to justify a finding on that fact in favour of the party so obliged. In other words, it obliges a party to adduce sufficient evidence for the issue to go before the tribunal of fact. It is confusing and misleading, therefore, to call the evidential burden a burden of *proof*: it can be discharged by the production of evidence that falls short of proof.[11] Whether a party has discharged the burden is decided only once in the course of a trial, and by the judge as opposed to the tribunal of fact. The burden is discharged when there is sufficient evidence to justify, as a possibility, a favourable finding by the tribunal of fact. In a criminal trial in which the prosecution bear the evidential burden on a particular issue, they must adduce sufficient evidence to prevent the judge from withdrawing that issue from the jury. If the prosecution also bear the legal burden on the same issue, and fail to discharge the evidential burden, they necessarily fail on that issue since the judge refuses to let the issue go before the jury. However, it does not follow that a discharge of the evidential burden necessarily results in a discharge of the legal burden; the issue in question goes before the jury, who may or may not find in favour of the prosecution on that issue. If the accused adduces no evidence in rebuttal, he will not necessarily lose on the issue, although if he takes that course that is a clear risk that he runs.

Like the legal burden, the evidential burden relates to particular facts in issue. The evidential burden in relation to the various issues in a given case may be distributed between the parties to the action. Normally, a party bearing the legal burden in relation to a particular fact at the commencement of the proceedings also bears an evidential burden in relation to the same fact. However, this is not invariably so. Thus although, as we shall see, the prosecution bear the legal burden of negativing all common law defences (except insanity) and certain statutory defences (including the defences of self-defence, duress, and non-insane automatism), such a defence will not be put before the jury unless the accused has discharged the evidential burden in that regard. Equally, and to complicate matters further, the evidential burden borne by the accused in these circumstances may be discharged by *any* evidence in the case, whether given by the accused, a co-accused, or the prosecution, and in this sense the so-called evidential burden is not a burden on the accused at all.[12] If the evidential burden is discharged, whether by defence or prosecution evidence, the prosecution will then bear the legal burden of disproving the defence in question, but if there is no evidence to support the defence, then the judge is entitled to withdraw it from the jury.[13]

As in the case of the legal burden, judges sometimes refer to the 'shifting' of the evidential burden. The evidential burden may sensibly be said to shift on the operation of a rebuttable

---

[11] Per Lord Devlin in *Jayasena v R* [1970] AC 618 PC at 624.

[12] Per Pill LJ in *L v DPP* [2003] QB 137, DC at [23].

[13] *R v Pommell* [1995] 2 Cr App R 607, CA, where it was also held that although normally a judge will not have to decide whether to leave a particular defence to the jury until the conclusion of the evidence, in rare cases where the nature of the evidence to be called is clear, it may be appropriate, in order to save time and costs, for the judge to indicate at an early stage what his ruling is likely to be. See also *R (Cuns) v Hammersmith Magistrates' Court* [2016] EWHC 748, DC, where the accused failed to discharge the evidential burden in respect of his defence of 'needle phobia', having presented no evidence to bring the issue into play.

presumption of law of the 'evidential' variety.[14] However, the phrase has also been employed in other circumstances. Where a party discharges an evidential burden borne by him in relation to a particular fact, his adversary will be under an obligation, referred to as the provisional or tactical burden, to adduce counter-evidence in order to convince the tribunal of fact in his favour. If he chooses not to adduce such counter-evidence, he runs the risk of a finding on that issue in favour of the other party. It is in these circumstances, also, that judges refer to a shifting of the evidential burden.[15] This conjures up a vision of the trial as a ball-game, with the evidential burden as the ball, which is continuously bounced to and fro between the contenders. This is misleading because although examination followed by cross-examination of witnesses often results in swings of fortune for and then against a party, normally in a trial, whether civil or criminal, one party first adduces all of his evidence before his adversary then adduces his. But there is a more important sense in which the phrase misleads. The evidential burden only needs to be considered by the court on two occasions, first at the beginning of a trial, to determine which party starts, and second when, during the trial, the judge determines whether sufficient evidence has been adduced to leave an issue before the tribunal of fact. If the judge decides at the latter stage that insufficient evidence has been adduced, the issue will be withdrawn from the tribunal of fact and further consideration of the evidential burden is unnecessary. But further consideration of the evidential burden is equally unnecessary when the judge allows the issue to go before the tribunal of fact. It is certainly possible to say, at this stage, that the evidential burden has shifted to the opponent and that he, by adducing counter-evidence, may cause the evidential burden to shift back to the first party, and so on, but such observations are of no legal significance. So far as the court is concerned, the evidential burden requires no further consideration; the only burden remaining at this stage is the legal burden.[16]

The incidence of the legal burden

Which party bears the legal burden is determined by the rules of substantive law set out in precedents and statutes. Speaking generally, the determination of where the legal burden falls is a matter of common sense. If certain facts are essential to the claim of, for example, the claimant in civil proceedings or the prosecution in criminal proceedings, that party must prove them. A useful starting-point—although, as we shall see, a far from reliable guide—is

[14] Where a party relying on an 'evidential' presumption has adduced sufficient evidence on the primary or basic fact, his adversary will bear an evidential burden to adduce some evidence to rebut the presumed fact. See further Ch 4.

[15] See, eg, per Lord Goddard CJ in *R v Matheson* [1958] 1 WLR 474, CCA at 478. See also *Rickards and Rickards v Kerrier District Council* (1987) 151 JP 625, DC. See, eg, in relation to the evidential burden shifting on the issue of mental capacity in cases involving wills, contracts and gifts: *Williams v Williams* [2003] WTLR 1371 at 1383; *Gorjat v Gorjat* [2010] EWHC 1537 ChD, at [139]; and *Kicks v Leigh* [2014] EWHC 3926, ChD at [67]. Cf *Dera Commercial Estate v Derya Inc, 'The Sur'* [2018] EWHC 1673 (Comm): where evidence is adduced by an applicant in support of an application to strike out a shipping claim on grounds of the respondent's inordinate and inexcusable delay in bringing the claim (the applicant bearing the legal burden in respect of striking out), it is unhelpful to speak in terms of a 'shifting evidential burden', but it will normally be the respondent that identifies a credible excuse for the delay. See [130]–[150] and [183].

[16] See *Sutton v Sadler* (1857) 3 CBNS 87 (see Ch 4). See for example, *McKeon v DPP* [2008] RTR 14, DC: in respect of the offence of failing to provide a specimen of blood without reasonable excuse under s 7(6) of the Road Traffic Act 1988, the accused bears an evidential burden to show reasonable excuse, and once the burden is satisfied, the prosecution bear the legal burden to prove the absence of reasonable excuse to the criminal standard.

the maxim 'he who asserts must prove' (*ei incumbit probatio qui dicit, non qui negat*). In *Wakelin v London and South Western Rly Co*[17] a widow brought an action in negligence under the Fatal Accidents Act 1846. The only available evidence was that her husband had been found dead near a level crossing at the side of a railway line. Lord Halsbury LC held that the widow bore the burden of proving that her husband's death had been caused by the defendants' negligence; if she could not discharge that burden, she failed. Even assuming that the husband had been knocked down by a train while on the crossing, the evidence adduced was as capable of leading to the conclusion that the husband had been negligent as it was of showing the defendants' negligence and, accordingly, the defendants' negligence was not proved.[18]

A detailed examination of the incidence of the legal burden of proof requires that criminal and civil cases be considered separately.

Criminal cases

Speaking generally, the legal burden of proving any fact essential to the prosecution case rests upon the prosecution and remains with the prosecution throughout the trial, although matters which are distinct from the determination of facts or decisions as to whether a criminal offence has been committed are not subject to the burden and standard of proof simply because they arise in the context of criminal proceedings.[19] Negative as well as positive allegations may be essential to the case for the prosecution. Thus the prosecution bear the legal burden of proving absence of consent on a charge of rape or assault.[20] Generally, therefore, the accused bears no legal burden in respect of the essential ingredients of an offence, whether positive or negative and whether or not he denies any or all of them. In *Woolmington v DPP*[21] the accused, charged with the murder of his wife, gave evidence that he had shot her accidentally. The trial judge directed the jury that once it was proved that the accused had shot his wife, he bore the burden of disproving malice aforethought. The House of Lords held this to be a misdirection and Lord Sankey LC said, in a now famous passage:[22]

> Throughout the web of the English criminal law one golden thread is always to be seen, that it is the duty of the prosecution to prove the prisoner's guilt subject to what I have already said as to the defence of insanity and subject also to any statutory exception . . . No matter what the charge or where the trial, the principle that the prosecution must prove the guilt of the prisoner is part of the common law of England and no attempt to whittle it down can be entertained . . .[23]

The rule enunciated by Lord Sankey is subject to three categories of exception: (i) where the accused raises the defence of insanity; (ii) where a statute expressly places the legal burden on the defence, and (iii) where a statute impliedly places the legal burden on the defence. The statutory

---

[17] (1886) 12 App Cas 41, HL.

[18] Cf *Jones v Great Western Rly Co* (1930) 144 LT 194, HL.

[19] For example, decisions on severance of charges and on whether a witness is eligible for special measures: *Misick v The Queen* [2015] 1 WLR 3215, PC at [35] and [38].

[20] *R v Horn* (1912) 7 Cr App R 200; *R v Donovan* [1934] 2 KB 498. But see also the Sexual Offences Act 2003, ss 75 and 76.

[21] [1935] AC 462, HL.

[22] [1935] AC 462 at 481–2.

[23] Under the principle in *Woolmington v DPP* [1935] AC 462, HL, where, for example, two accused are tried for a crime that must have been committed one of them, if the prosecution fails to discharge the legal burden against one or the other, both must be acquitted. However, concerning offences of causing serious harm or death to children or vulnerable adults, see the Domestic Violence, Crime and Victims Act 2004, ss 5 and 6.

exceptions are often referred to as reverse onus provisions. Since the coming into force of the Human Rights Act 1998, any such provision is open to challenge on the basis of its incompatibility with the presumption of innocence guaranteed by Art 6(2) of the European Convention on Human Rights. This aspect of the topic receives separate treatment later in this chapter.

Insanity

Where an accused raises insanity as a defence,[24] he bears the legal burden of proving it.[25] The justification is based on the difficulty of disproving false claims of insanity, given that the accused may not cooperate with an investigation of his state of mind.[26] Where an accused is charged with murder and raises the issue of either insanity or diminished responsibility, the prosecution, pursuant to s 6 of the Criminal Procedure (Insanity) Act 1964, is allowed to adduce evidence to prove the other of those issues. In this event, the prosecution bear the legal burden of proving the other issue on which they have adduced evidence.[27] If an accused is alleged to be under a disability rendering him unfit to plead and stand trial, the issue may be raised, under s 4 of the 1964 Act, by *either* the prosecution *or* the defence. If the issue is raised by the prosecution, they must prove it and satisfy the jury beyond reasonable doubt;[28] if the issue is raised by the defence, they must prove it, but only on a balance of probabilities, the lower standard of proof.[29]

Express statutory exceptions

A number of statutes expressly place on the accused the legal burden of proving specified issues. The legal burden of proof in relation to all issues other than those so specified remains on the prosecution. For example, s 2(2) of the Homicide Act 1957 places upon the accused the legal burden of establishing the statutory defence of diminished responsibility on a charge of murder.[30] Section 2(2) does not contravene Art 6 of the European Convention on Human Rights.[31] Other examples are considered, in this chapter, under **The burden of proof, Reverse onus provisions and the Human Rights Act 1998.**

Implied statutory exceptions: s 101 of the Magistrates' Courts Act 1980

Section 101 of the Magistrates' Courts Act 1980, formerly s 81 of the Magistrates' Courts Act 1952, provides as follows:

---

[24] Regarding the defence of insanity, see the Law Commission's proposals for reform in *Criminal Liability: Insanity and Automatism, A Discussion Paper*, 23rd July 2013, accessible at http://lawcommission.justice.gov.uk/areas/insanity.htm.

[25] *M'Naghten's Case* (1843) 10 Cl&Fin 200, HL.

[26] For a critique of the justification, see Ashworth, 'Four threats to the presumption of innocence' (2006) 10 E&P 241 at 263–5.

[27] The standard to be met by the prosecution in these circumstances is proof beyond reasonable doubt: *R v Grant* [1960] Crim LR 424.

[28] *R v Robertson* [1968] 1 WLR 1767, CA.

[29] *R v Podola* [1960] 1 QB 325, CCA.

[30] See *R v Wilcocks* [2017] Cr App R 338 (23), CA. Section 2(2) not only dictates which party shoulders the burden of proof once the issue is raised, but also leaves it to the defence to decide whether the issue should be raised at all; if, therefore, the defence does not raise the issue but there is evidence of diminished responsibility, the trial judge is not bound to direct the jury to consider the matter but, at most, should in the absence of the jury draw the matter to the attention of the defence so that they may decide whether they wish the issue to be considered by the jury: per Lord Lane CJ, obiter, in *R v Campbell* (1986) 84 Cr App R 255, CA. For guidance on directions to the jury, see the Crown Court Compendium (July 2019), Part 1, 19–1.

[31] See *R v Wilcocks* [2017] Cr App R 338 (23) CA, applying *R v Foye* (2013) 177 JP 449, CA. For a critique, see Laird, 'Commentary' [2017] Crim LR 707.

Where the defendant to an information or complaint relies for his defence on any exception, exemption, proviso, excuse or qualification, whether or not it accompanies the description of the offence or matter of complaint in the enactment creating the offence or on which the complaint is founded, the burden of proving the exception, exemption, proviso, excuse or qualification shall be on him; and this notwithstanding that the information or complaint contains an allegation negativing the exception, exemption, proviso, excuse or qualification.

Section 81 applies to summary trials but at common law similar principles applied to trials on indictment and it was held by the Court of Appeal in *R v Edwards*,[32] and confirmed by the House of Lords in *R v Hunt*,[33] that the section sets out the common law rule in statutory form. If this were not so, then in the case of an offence triable either way, the incidence of the burden of proof could vary—but for no good reason—according to whether the accused is tried summarily or on indictment.

Implied statutory exceptions within s 101 of the Magistrates' Courts Act 1980 are capable of derogating from Art 6 of the European Convention;[34] and the older cases in which, by virtue of s 101 or the common law principles on which it is based, particular statutory provisions have been construed to impose a legal burden on the accused,[35] must now be read subject to the Human Rights Act 1998 and the cases in which reverse onus provisions have been challenged on the basis of incompatibility with Art 6.[36]

Examples of statutory provisions to which s 101 applies
Section 101 applies to statutory provisions which define a criminal offence and use words such as 'unless', 'provided that', 'except', or 'other than', to set out an exception, proviso, etc which amounts to a defence. The definition of an offence, and the exception or proviso to it, are not always readily distinguishable. However, before considering the kind of statutory provision capable of giving rise to difficulty, reasonably straightforward examples of the kind of provision to which s 101 applies may be given. Section 87(1) of the Road Traffic Act 1988 provides that it is an offence for a person to drive a vehicle on a road otherwise than in accordance with a licence; it is for the accused to prove that he satisfies the proviso of holding a current driving licence.[37] Section 143 of the Road Traffic Act 1988,[38] provides that it is an offence to use a vehicle unless there is in force a certificate of insurance against third party risk; it is for an accused to prove he holds a valid certificate of insurance, although what must be proved is limited to what is clearly stated in the exemption and there is no additional burden to prove that the use was within the scope of the policy.[39] It is an offence for a person, without lawful authority or excuse, to deposit anything whatsoever on a highway in

---

[32] [1975] QB 27.

[33] [1987] AC 352, HL.

[34] See per Clarke LJ in *R (Grundy & Co Excavations Ltd) v Halton Division Magistrates' Court* (2003) 167 JP 387, DC at [61].

[35] See immediately below, under **Examples of statutory provisions to which s 101 applies**.

[36] See, in this chapter, under **Reverse onus provisions and the Human Rights Act 1998**, p 68.

[37] *John v Humphreys* [1955] 1 WLR 325, DC. See also *Leeds City Council v Azam* (1988) 153 JP 157, DC: it is for the accused to prove that he is *exempted* from the need for a licence for the operation of a private hire vehicle under the Local Government (Miscellaneous Provisions) Act 1976, s 75.

[38] As amended by reg 2(2)(a) of the Motor Vehicles (Compulsory Insurance) Regulations 2000.

[39] *DPP v Whittaker* [2016] 1 WLR 1035, DC. See also, Roberts, 'Commentary' [2016] Crim LR 46, where it is argued that driving related information is now easily accessible by the prosecution and so there are good grounds for revisiting the burden of proof in motor insurance and driving licence cases.

consequence of which a user of the highway is injured or endangered; although it is for the prosecution to prove that the thing has been deposited on the highway and that in consequence thereof a user of the highway has been injured or endangered, it is for the accused to raise and prove lawful authority or excuse.[40]

Provisions giving rise to difficulty

The point has been made that in some statutory provisions the definition of an offence and the exception or proviso to it are not always readily distinguishable. Concerning the application of s 101, these kinds of provisions may give rise to difficulty. In *Westminster City Council v Croyalgrange Ltd*,[41] a company which had let premises to a person who used them as a sex establishment without a licence was charged under Sch 3, para 20(1)(a) to the Local Government (Miscellaneous Provisions) Act 1982, whereby a person who knowingly causes or permits the use of premises contrary to Sch 3, para 6 commits an offence. Paragraph 6 provides that no persons shall use any premises as a sex establishment except under and in accordance with a licence. The House of Lords held that s 101 was inapplicable because the exception in question qualified the prohibition created by para 6 and not the offence created by para 20(1)(a). The prosecution bore the burden of proving, inter alia, that the directors of the company knew that no licence had been obtained by the tenant.[42]

Nimmo v Alexander Cowan & Sons Ltd[43] was another case giving rise to difficulty. This was a Scottish case brought by an injured workman under s 29(1) of the Factories Act 1961, which provides that 'every place at which any person has at any time to work . . . shall, so far as is reasonably practicable, be made and kept safe for any person working therein'. The workman alleged that his place of work was not kept safe but did not aver that it was reasonably practicable to make it safe. Section 155(1) of the 1961 Act makes a breach of s 29(1) a summary offence and although the case in question was a civil one, the House of Lords referred to the Scottish equivalent of s 81 of the Magistrates' Courts Act 1952 and Lord Pearson made it clear that the incidence of the burden of proof would be the same whether the proceedings were civil or criminal.[44] The House held, Lords Reid and Wilberforce dissenting, that there was no burden on the plaintiff employee to prove that it was reasonably practicable to keep the premises safe; the defendant employers bore the burden of proving that it was *not* reasonably practicable to keep the premises safe. In reaching this decision, the majority was of the opinion that where, on the face of the statute, it is unclear on whom the burden should lie, a court, in order to determine Parliament's intention, may go beyond the mere form of the enactment and look to other, policy, considerations such as the mischief at which the Act was aimed and the ease or difficulty that the respective parties would encounter in discharging

[40] Per Lord Parker CJ in *Gatland v Metropolitan Police Comr* [1968] 2 QB 279. This was a decision under the Highways Act 1959, s 140(1), re-enacted in the Magistrates' Courts Act 1980, s 161(1). Cf Offences Against the Person Act 1861, s 16: a person who without lawful excuse makes to another a threat, intending that the other would fear it would be carried out, to kill that other or a third person shall be guilty of an offence. In *R v Cousins* [1982] QB 526, CA, it was held that on a charge under s 16, the onus is on the prosecution to prove absence of lawful excuse for making the threat.

[41] (1986) 83 Cr App R 155, HL.

[42] See also, construing s 33(1)(a) of the Environmental Protection Act 1990, *Environment Agency v ME Foley Contractors Ltd* [2002] 1 WLR 1754, DC; and construing regs 12 and 38 of the Environmental Permitting (England and Wales) Regulations 2007, see *R v Walker* [2014] PTSR 929, CA.

[43] [1968] AC 107, HL.

[44] Ibid at 134. Although Lord Reid dissented, his opinion on this point, at 115, was the same.

the burden. Given that the defendant was better able to discharge the legal burden than the plaintiff, the construction of the majority, it is submitted, best achieved the object of the enactment in question, namely to provide a safe place of work.

Implied statutory exceptions: trials on indictment

On its wording, s 101 applies to summary trials. Concerning trials on indictment, the leading authorities are *R v Edwards*[45] and *R v Hunt*.[46] In *R v Edwards* the accused was convicted on indictment of selling intoxicating liquor without holding a justices' licence authorizing such sale contrary to s 160(1)(a) of the Licensing Act 1964. Edwards appealed, one of his grounds being that the prosecution had not called any evidence to prove that he did not hold a licence. It was submitted, on his behalf, that at common law the burden of proving an exception, exemption, proviso, excuse, or qualification fell on the defence only when the facts constituting it were peculiarly within the defendant's own knowledge[47] and that in the instant case they were not. The clerk to the licensing justices for any district is statutorily bound to keep a register of local licences and accordingly the police had access to a public source of knowledge. The Court of Appeal held that the legal burden of proving that the accused was the holder of a justices' licence rested on the defence and not the prosecution. After an extensive review of the authorities, Lawton LJ continued:[48]

> In our judgment this line of authority establishes that over the centuries the common law, as a result of experience and the need to ensure that justice is done both to the community and to the defendants, has evolved an exception to the fundamental rule of our common law that the prosecution must prove every element of the offence charged. This exception . . . is limited to offences arising under enactments which prohibit the doing of an act save in specified circumstances or by persons of specified classes or with specified qualifications or with the licence or permission of specified authorities. Whenever the prosecution seeks to rely on this exception, the court must construe the enactment under which the charge is laid. If the true construction is that the enactment prohibits the doing of acts, subject to provisos, exemptions and the like, then the prosecution can rely upon the exception.
>
> In our judgment its application does not depend upon either the fact, or the presumption, that the defendant has peculiar knowledge enabling him to prove the positive of any negative averment.

In *R v Hunt*[49] the accused was charged with the unlawful possession of morphine contrary to s 5 of the Misuse of Drugs Act 1971. Under the Misuse of Drugs Regulations 1973, it is provided that s 5 shall not have effect in relation to, inter alia, any preparation of morphine containing not more than 0.2 per cent of morphine. At the trial the defence submitted that there was no case to answer because the prosecution had adduced no evidence as to the proportion of morphine in the powder which had been found in Hunt's possession. The judge rejected the submission and Hunt changed his plea to guilty. His appeal to the Court of Appeal was dismissed, but on a further appeal to the House of Lords, two arguments were raised: (i) *R v Edwards* was wrongly decided; and (ii) on the true construction of the provisions

---

[45] [1975] QB 27, CA.

[46] [1987] AC 352, HL.

[47] See *R v Turner* (1816) 5 M&S 206 at 211, followed in *R v Oliver* [1944] KB 68 (dealing in sugar without a licence) and *John v Humphreys* [1955] 1 WLR 325, DC (driving without a licence). See also *R v Ewens* [1967] 1 QB 322, CCA (possessing drugs without a prescription).

[48] [1975] QB 27 at 39–40.

[49] [1987] AC 352, HL.

in question, the prosecution bore the burden of proving that the facts fell outside the 'exception' contained in the Misuse of Drugs Regulations 1973. The prosecution submitted that *R v Edwards* did apply and the burden was on the accused to show that the facts fell within the 'exception'.

The House of Lords allowed the appeal. The reasoning was as follows:

1. When, in *Woolmington v DPP*,[50] Lord Sankey used the phrase 'any statutory exception', he was not referring *only* to statutory exceptions in which Parliament has placed the burden of proof on the accused expressly. A statute can place the legal burden of proof on an accused either expressly or by implication, that is, on its true construction.[51]

2. Where a statute places the legal burden on the accused by implication, that burden is on the accused whether the case be tried summarily or on indictment; s 101 of the Magistrates' Courts Act 1980 reflects and applies to summary trials the rule relating to the incidence of the burden of proof evolved by judges on trials on indictment.

3. *R v Edwards* was decided correctly subject to one qualification: on occasions, albeit rarely, a statute will be construed as imposing the legal burden on the accused although it is outside the ambit of the formula given by Lawton LJ. The present case did not come within the formula, which was 'limited to offences arising under enactments which prohibit the doing of an act save in specified circumstances or by persons of specified classes or with specified qualifications or with the licence or permission of specified authorities'. The formula, although 'a helpful approach'[52] and 'an excellent guide to construction',[53] was not intended to be and is not exclusive in its effect.

4. Ultimately, each case must turn on the construction of the particular legislation. If the linguistic construction of a statute does not clearly indicate on whom the burden should lie, the court, in construing it, is not confined to the form of wording of the provision but, as in *Nimmo v Alexander Cowan & Sons Ltd*,[54] may have regard to matters of policy including practical considerations and in particular the ease or otherwise that the respective parties would encounter if required to discharge the burden.[55] Parliament, however, can never lightly be taken to have imposed the duty on an accused to prove his innocence in a criminal case and the courts should be very slow to draw any such inference from the language of a statute.[56]

5. Policy, in the present case, pointed to the legal burden being on the prosecution. This would not be an undue burden because in most cases the substance in question would

---

[50] [1935] AC 462, HL.

[51] See per Lords Griffiths and Ackner [1987] AC 352 at [6]–[7] and [15] respectively.

[52] Per Lord Ackner at [19].

[53] Per Lord Griffiths at [11].

[54] [1968] AC 107, HL.

[55] On this basis it is possible to explain cases formerly difficult to reconcile with *R v Edwards* such as *R v Putland and Sorrell* [1946] 1 All ER 85, CCA; *R v Cousins* [1982] QB 526, CA; *R v Curgerwen* (1865) LR 1 CCR 1; and *R v Audley* [1907] 1 KB 383. See also *R v K(M)* [2019] QB 86, CA: policy reasons underlie the Modern Slavery Act 2015, justifying a legal burden on the prosecution in respect of the defence under s 45 of the Act, a defence which applies in respect of any offence the accused says was committed as a result of compulsion attributable to slavery or exploitation; where the accused seeks to rely on the defence, he bears an evidential burden to show compulsion in respect of every element of the offence charged and the prosecution bear the legal burden of disproof.

[56] Per Lord Griffiths [1987] 1 All ER 1 at 11.

have been analysed before a prosecution was brought and therefore there would be no difficulty in producing evidence to show that it did contain a certain percentage of morphine. If the burden was on the accused, however, he would have real practical difficulties because the substance is usually seized by the police and he has no statutory entitlement to a proportion of it. Moreover, the substance may already have been analysed by the police and destroyed in the process.

6. The question of construction being one of obviously real difficulty and offences involving the misuse of hard drugs being among the most serious of offences, any ambiguity should be resolved in favour of the accused.

In its 11th report, the Criminal Law Revision Committee was strongly of the opinion that both on principle and for the sake of clarity and convenience in practice, burdens on the defence should be evidential only.[57] In *R v Hunt*, Lord Griffiths thought that such a fundamental change was a matter for Parliament and not a decision for the House of Lords.[58]

Reverse onus provisions and the Human Rights Act 1998
Since the coming into force of the Human Rights Act 1998, any reverse onus provision is open to challenge on the basis of its incompatibility with Art 6(2) of the European Convention on Human Rights, under which 'Everyone charged with a criminal offence shall be presumed innocent until proved guilty according to law'.[59] Clearly, a reverse onus provision will not inevitably give rise to a finding of incompatibility,[60] but if a provision does unjustifiably infringe Art 6(2), the further issue will arise whether it should be read down, in accordance with the obligation under s 3 of the Human Rights Act 1998, so as to impose an evidential and not a legal burden on the accused.

The underlying rationale of the presumption of innocence in both domestic law and the Convention is that it is repugnant to ordinary notions of fairness for a prosecutor to accuse an accused of a crime and for the accused then to be required to disprove the accusation on pain of conviction and punishment if he fails to do so.[61] Under domestic law, as will be apparent from the foregoing text, Parliament does not regard the presumption as an absolute or unqualified right. Equally, the Art 6(2) right is neither absolute nor unqualified. In reaching a decision on the question of incompatibility, the test is whether the modification or limitation of the Art 6(2) right pursues a legitimate aim and whether it satisfies the principle of proportionality: a balance has to be struck between the general interest of the community and the protection of the fundamental rights of the individual.[62] In *Sheldrake v DPP*[63] Lord Bingham

---

[57] Subject to two minor exceptions: see Cmnd 4991, paras 140–1.

[58] [1987] 1 All ER 1 at 12.

[59] Article 6(2) does not apply to confiscation proceedings pursuant to the Drugs Trafficking Act 1994, Pt I, since the defendant has already been proved guilty of the offences to which the proceedings relate: *R v Briggs-Price* [2009] 1 AC 1026, HL. Civil proceedings which are penal in nature and could expose a party to prosecution may engage Art 6(2): *Watkins v Woolas* [2010] EWHC 2702, QB. Hearings in family proceedings which involve findings of fact as to whether a party has committed a crime will engage Art 6(2): *Re E (a child)(family proceedings: evidence)* [2016] 4 WLR 473, CA and *Re W* [2010] 1 WLR 701, SC.

[60] Per Lord Hope in *R v Lambert* [2002] 2 AC 545, HL at [87].

[61] Per Lord Bingham in *Sheldrake v DPP* [2005] 1 AC 264, HL at [9].

[62] Per Lord Hope in *R v Lambert* [2002] 2 AC 545, HL at [88].

[63] [2005] 1 AC 264, HL at [21].

considered the scope of the presumption under the Convention. After an extensive review of the jurisprudence of the European Court, including the leading authority of *Salabiaku v France*,[64] his Lordship summarized the relevant principles to be derived from the Strasbourg case law:

> The overriding concern is that a trial should be fair, and the presumption of innocence is a fundamental right directed to that end. The Convention does not outlaw presumptions of fact or law[65] but requires that these should be kept within reasonable limits and should not be arbitrary. It is open to states to define the constituent elements of a criminal offence, excluding the requirement of *mens rea*. But the substance and effect of any presumption adverse to a defendant must be examined, and must be reasonable. Relevant to any judgment on reasonableness or proportionality will be the opportunity given to the defendant to rebut the presumption, maintenance of the rights of the defence, flexibility in application of the presumption, retention by the court of a power to assess the evidence, the importance of what is at stake and the difficulty which a prosecutor may face in the absence of a presumption. Security concerns do not absolve member states from their duty to observe basic standards of fairness. The justifiability of any infringement of the presumption of innocence cannot be resolved by any rule of thumb, but on examination of all the facts and circumstances of the particular provision as applied in the particular case.

Consideration is now given to some of the leading authorities on reverse onus provisions.

R v Lambert

In *R v Lambert*,[66] L, found in possession of a duffle bag containing two kilograms of cocaine, was convicted of possession of cocaine with intent to supply, contrary to s 5(3) of the Misuse of Drugs Act 1971. L had relied upon s 28 of the 1971 Act, asserting that he did not believe or suspect or have reason to suspect that the bag contained cocaine or any controlled drug. The trial judge had directed the jury that in order to establish possession of a controlled drug, the Crown need only prove that L had the bag in his possession and that it contained a controlled drug. Thereafter the burden was on L to bring himself within s 28 and 'to prove', on a balance of probabilities, that he did not know that the bag contained a controlled drug. The House of Lords held, by majority, that since the trial had taken place before the coming into force of the Human Rights Act 1998, L was not entitled to rely on an alleged breach of his rights under the European Convention. However, the House was of the view (Lord Hutton dissenting) that s 28 is not compatible with Art 6(2) and, under s 3 of the 1998 Act, may be read as imposing no more than an evidential burden on the accused.

Lord Steyn approached the question of compatibility by applying a three-stage test:

1. whether there has been a legislative interference with the presumption in Art 6(2);

2. if so, whether there is an objective justification for such interference; and

3. if so, whether the interference is proportionate, ie no greater than is necessary.

As to the first stage, it was held that, taking account of the fact that under s 28 an accused will be denying moral blameworthiness and that the maximum penalty for the offence is life imprisonment, knowledge of the existence and control of the contents of the container is the

---

[64] (1988) 13 EHRR 379, ECHR.
[65] See Ch 4.
[66] [2002] 2 AC 545, HL.

gravamen of the offence, and therefore s 28 derogates from the presumption of innocence. Lord Steyn also reached this conclusion on broader grounds. His Lordship noted that the distinction between constituent elements of the crime and defensive issues will sometimes be unprincipled and arbitrary: a true constituent element may not be within the definition of the crime but cast as a defensive issue and conversely a definition of the crime may be so formulated as to include all possible defences within it. It is necessary, therefore, to concentrate not on technicalities and niceties of language, but on matters of substance. A defence may be so closely linked with *mens rea* and moral blameworthiness that it will derogate from the presumption of innocence to place the burden of proving that defence on the accused.[67] Accordingly, the issues under s 28, even if regarded as a pure defence, bore directly on the moral blameworthiness of the accused and therefore derogated from the presumption of innocence.

As to the second stage, Lord Steyn was satisfied that there is an objective justification for the legislative interference with the presumption of innocence, namely that sophisticated drug smugglers, dealers, and couriers typically secrete drugs in some container, thereby enabling the person in possession of the container to say that he was unaware of the contents. Such a defence is commonplace and poses real difficulties for the police and prosecuting authorities.

As to the third stage, it was held that the burden is on the state to show that the legislative means adopted were no greater than necessary. The principle of proportionality required the House to consider whether there was a pressing necessity to impose a legal rather than an evidential burden. The obligation to show that only a reverse legal burden can overcome the difficulties of the prosecution in drugs cases is strong. In a case of possession of controlled drugs with intent to supply, although the prosecution must establish that controlled drugs were in the possession of the accused and that he knew that the package contained something, under s 28 the accused must prove on a balance of probabilities that he did not know that the package contained controlled drugs. If the jury is not satisfied of this on a balance of probabilities, or considers that the accused's version is as likely to be true as not, they must convict him. Thus a guilty verdict may be returned in respect of an offence punishable by life imprisonment even though the jury may consider that it is reasonably possible that the accused has been duped. Consequently, s 28 was a disproportionate reaction to perceived difficulties facing the prosecution in drugs cases. A new realism had significantly reduced the scope of the problems faced by the prosecution. First, possession of the container presumptively suggests, in the absence of exculpatory evidence, that the possessor knew of its contents. Second, s 34 of the Criminal Justice and Public Order Act 1994, enabling a judge to comment on an accused's failure to mention facts when questioned or charged, has strengthened the position of the prosecution.[68] Third, where a 'mixed statement', that is, an out-of-court statement made by the accused which is partly inculpatory and partly exculpatory, is introduced in evidence, and the accused elects not to testify, the judge may point out to the jury that the incriminating parts are likely to be true whereas the excuses do not have the same weight, and may also comment on the election of the accused not to testify.[69] For these reasons, Lord Steyn concluded that s 28 was incompatible with Art 6(2). It was further held

---

[67] However, an evidential burden may well apply as a simple matter of statutory construction: see *Shepherd v Information Commissioner* [2019] 4 WLR 50.

[68] See Ch 16.

[69] See *R v Duncan* (1981) 73 Cr App R 359: see Ch 6.

that under s 3 of the Human Rights Act 1998, where s 28(2) and (3) require the accused to 'prove' the matters specified, the word can be read to mean 'give sufficient evidence', thereby placing only an evidential burden on the accused.

L v DPP

L v DPP[70] involved a charge of being in possession of a lock-knife in a public place contrary to s 139 of the Criminal Justice Act 1988, and the related defence under s 139(4), which provides that it shall be a defence for an accused to prove that he had good reason or lawful authority for having the knife with him in a public place. Distinguishing *R v Lambert*, the court held that, striking a fair balance, s 139(4) does not conflict with Art 6.[71] Six reasons were given. (1) Unlike s 28 of the Misuse of Drugs Act 1971, under s 139 of the Criminal Justice Act 1988 it is for the prosecution to prove that the accused knowingly had the offending article in his possession. (2) There is a strong public interest in bladed articles not being carried in public without good reason. Parliament is entitled, without infringing the Convention, to deter the carrying of bladed or sharply pointed articles in public to the extent of placing the burden of proving a good reason on the carrier. (3) The accused is proving something within his own knowledge. (4) The accused is entitled under Art 6 to expect the court to scrutinize the evidence with a view to deciding if a good reason exists, whether he gives evidence or not. (5) Although there will be cases in which the tribunal of fact may attach significance to where the burden of proof rests, in the great majority of cases it needs to make a value judgement as to whether, upon all the evidence, the reason is a good one, without the decision depending on whether it has to be proved that there is a good reason. (6) In striking the balance, some, albeit limited, weight should be given to the much more restricted power of sentence for an offence under s 139 than for an offence under s 5 of the Misuse of Drugs Act 1971.

R v Drummond

R v Drummond[72] concerned the so-called 'hip flask' defence in s 15 of the Road Traffic Offenders Act 1988, under which it is for the accused to prove that he consumed alcohol after the offence but before providing a specimen.[73] It was held, distinguishing *R v Lambert*, that driving while over the limit and causing death by driving while over the limit are both social evils which Parliament sought to minimize by the legislation and that the legislative interference with the presumption of innocence was not only justified, but no greater than was necessary. Four reasons were given. (1) Conviction follows after a scientific test which

---

[70] [2003] QB 137, DC.

[71] See also *R v Mathews* [2004] QB 690, CA: the court, agreeing with and adopting the reasoning in *L v DPP*, held that neither s 139(4) nor s 139(5) of the Criminal Justice Act 1988 was incompatible with Art 6. Where an accused is charged with breaching, without reasonable excuse, the terms of a criminal behaviour order made under s 30(1) of the Anti-social Behaviour, Crime and Policing Act 2014, it is submitted that the burden in relation to the reasonable excuse is evidential only. This was the position in relation to anti-social behaviour orders before they were replaced by criminal behaviour orders: *R v Charles* [2010] WLR 644, CA. Concerning breach of a restraining order under the Protection from Harassment Act 1997, the burden on the accused is evidential: *R v Evans* [2005] 1 WLR 1435, CA.

[72] [2002] 2 Cr App R 352 (25), CA.

[73] Section 15 applies to trials only. Accordingly, the reverse burden will not apply where an accused pleads guilty but raises the issue in order to mitigate sentence. This issue will be determined in a *Newton* hearing where the burden is on the prosecution and the standard of proof is the criminal standard. See *Goldsmith v DPP* (2010) 174 JP 84, DC.

is intended to be as exact as possible. (2) In most cases the test is exact or, to the extent that it is less than exact, the inexactness works in favour of the accused. (3) It is the accused himself who, by drinking after the event, defeats the aim of the legislature by doing something which makes the scientific test potentially unreliable. In many, perhaps most cases, the accused will have taken the alcohol after the event for the precise purpose of defeating the scientific test. (4) The relevant scientific evidence to set against the result ascertained from the specimen of breath or blood, including the amount which the accused drank after the offence, is all within the knowledge or means of access of the accused.

R v S and R v Johnstone

In *R v S*[74] the Court of Appeal considered s 92(5) of the Trade Marks Act 1994, which provides that it is a defence for a person charged with the unauthorized use of a registered trade mark to show that he believed on reasonable grounds that the use of the sign was not an infringement of the registered trade mark. It was held that s 92(5) imposed a legal burden on the accused and was compatible with Art 6(2).[75]

In *R v Johnstone*[76] the House of Lords, approving *R v S*, was of the same, albeit obiter, view. Lord Nicholls, in a speech endorsed by Lords Hope, Hutton, and Rodger, said:[77]

> for a reverse burden of proof to be acceptable there must be a compelling reason why it is fair and reasonable to deny the accused person the protection normally guaranteed to everyone by the presumption of innocence . . . A sound starting point is to remember that if an accused is required to prove a fact on the balance of probability to avoid conviction, this permits a conviction in spite of the fact-finding tribunal having a reasonable doubt as to the guilt of the accused . . . This consequence of a reverse burden of proof should colour one's approach when evaluating the reasons why it is said that, in the absence of a persuasive burden on the accused, the public interest will be prejudiced to an extent which justifies placing a persuasive burden on the accused. The more serious the punishment which may flow from conviction, the more compelling must be the reasons. The extent and nature of the factual matters required to be proved by the accused, and their importance relative to the matters required to be proved by the prosecution, have to be taken into account. So also does the extent to which the burden on the accused relates to facts which, if they exist, are readily provable by him as matters within his own knowledge or to which he already has access. In evaluating these factors the court's role is one of review. Parliament, not the court, is charged with the primary responsibility for deciding, as a matter of policy, what should be the constituent elements of a criminal offence . . . The court will reach a different conclusion from the legislature only when . . . it is apparent the legislature has attached insufficient importance to the fundamental right of an individual to be presumed innocent until proved guilty.

As to s 92(5), Lord Nicholls had regard to the fact that counterfeiting is a serious problem with adverse economic effects on genuine trade and adverse effects on consumers in terms of quality

---

[74] [2003] 1 Cr App R 602 (35), CA.

[75] Cf *Shephard v Information Commissioner* [2019] 4 WLR: in respect of the offence of unlawfully obtaining personal data under s 55(1) of the Data Protection Act 1998, an evidential burden applies in relation to s 55(2) which provides, in effect, that there is no offence if a person 'shows' he acted in reasonable belief that he had the right in law to obtain the data; a criminal statute must be interpreted narrowly in the interests of the defendant and on a close linguistic analysis of the provision, it could not be said that Parliament intended to impose a legal burden on the accused.

[76] [2003] 1 WLR 1736, HL.

[77] Ibid at [49]–[51].

of goods and, sometimes, on the health or safety of consumers. Further, the s 92(5) defence relates to facts within the accused's own knowledge. Two other factors were considered compelling reasons why s 92(5) should place a legal burden on the accused. First, traders in brand products are aware of the need to be on guard against counterfeit goods. Second, it is generally expected that those who supply traders with counterfeit goods, if traceable at all by outside investigators, are unlikely to be cooperative, so if the prosecution are required to prove that traders acted dishonestly, fewer investigations will be undertaken and there will be fewer prosecutions.

DPP v Barker

The concept of facts within the accused's own knowledge is separate from the concept of ease of proof, but in some cases both will point in the same direction. *DPP v Barker*[78] concerned s 37(3) of the Road Traffic Act 1988, whereby a disqualified driver may hold a provisional licence and drive in accordance with its conditions. In support of the conclusion that it was proportionate for the accused to bear the burden under the subsection, it was said that, as to being the holder of a provisional licence, the burden could easily be discharged by producing the licence and, as to the conditions of the licence, in some cases, in the absence of any information from the accused as to the identity of a passenger, it would be impossible for the prosecution to establish his identity and that he was the holder of a licence and therefore qualified to be supervising the accused.[79]

DPP v Wright

In *DPP v Wright*,[80] by contrast, it was held that it was disproportionate to impose a legal burden on an accused who sought to rely on an exemption under s 1 of the Hunting Act 2004, considering the knowledge of facts required and the difficulty involved. The section makes it an offence for a person to hunt a wild mammal with a dog unless the hunting is exempt under s 2, being within a category of hunting specified in Sch 1 to the Act. The court noted the 'diverse and massive potential content' of the categories in Sch 1, which made it difficult for an accused to know within which category his hunting might come. Further, if the burden was a legal one, an accused would have to prove the substantial (and difficult) issues in the case once the prosecution had proved the prima facie (and easy) fact that he had been in pursuit of a mammal with a dog. Accordingly, the exemption was read down to impose an evidential burden only. Imposition of a legal burden would have been '. . . an oppressive, disproportionate, unfair and, in particular, an unnecessary intrusion upon the presumption of innocence in article 6'.[81]

---

[78] [2004] EWHC 2502 (Admin).

[79] See also, concerning the defence in s 1(5) of the Firearms Act 1982, *R v Williams* [2013] 1 WLR 1200, CA at [42]: a legal burden on the defence to prove lack of knowledge that an imitation firearm was readily convertible into a firearm is proportionate, since it would be a real deterrent to prosecution if the burden to prove knowledge was on the Crown. However, it is not easy to distinguish *R v Williams* from *R v Lambert* [2002] 2 AC 545, HL; it may be that in deciding the burden should not be read down, the court in *R v Williams* was influenced by the fact that the maximum sentence for the offence was 10 years (see at [44]), whereas the maximum sentence for the offence in *R v Lambert* was life imprisonment. See also *R v Makuwa* [2006] 1 WLR 2755, CA, concerning the defence in s 31(1) of the Immigration and Asylum Act 1999: the prosecution will find it difficult, if not impossible, to prove, for the purposes of the defence, that the accused's life or freedom was *not* threatened overseas and that he had *not* presented himself to the UK authorities without delay. See also *R v Clarke* [2008] EWCA Crim 893.

[80] [2010] QB 224, DC.

[81] At [85].

Attorney General's Reference (No 1 of 2004)

In *Attorney General's Reference (No 1 of 2004)*[82] a five-judge Court of Appeal heard five conjoined appeals concerning different reverse onus provisions. In the third appeal (*R v Denton*) the court considered s 1(2) of the Protection from Eviction Act 1977, whereby a person is guilty of an offence if he unlawfully deprives the residential occupier of any premises of his occupation of the premises 'unless he proves that he believed, and had reasonable cause to believe, that the residential occupier had ceased to reside in the premises'. The court gave three reasons to justify this reverse burden: the essence of the offence is unlawful deprivation of occupation, the defence only being available to the accused who can bring himself within a narrow exception; the circumstances relied upon by the accused are peculiarly within his own knowledge;[83] and the public interest in deterring landlords from ejecting tenants unlawfully.

The fourth appeal (*R v Hendley*) concerned s 4 of the Homicide Act 1957. Under s 4(1), it is manslaughter and not murder for a person acting in pursuance of a suicide pact between himself and another to kill the other. Under s 4(2), 'Where it is shown that a person charged with the murder of another killed the other, it shall be for the defence to prove that the person charged was acting in pursuance of a suicide pact between him and the other.' This reverse burden was justified on the basis that it provides protection for society from murder disguised as a suicide pact killing, that the defence only arises once the prosecution have proved murder, and the facts necessary to establish the defence lie within the accused's knowledge.

In the fifth appeal (*R v Crowley*), the court considered s 51 of the Criminal Justice and Public Order Act 1994. Under s 51(1):

> A person commits an offence if:
>
> (a) he does an act which intimidates, or is intended to intimidate another person;
>
> (b) he does the act knowing or believing that the victim is assisting in the investigation of an offence or is a witness or potential witness or a juror or a potential juror in proceedings for an offence; and
>
> (c) he does it intending thereby to cause the investigation or the course of justice to be obstructed, perverted or interfered with.

Under s 51(7), if the matters in s 51(1)(a) and (b) are proved, the accused shall be presumed to have done the act with the intention required by s 51(1)(c) unless the contrary is proved. This reverse burden was justified on the basis that although it related to an ingredient of the offence rather than a special defence, witness and jury intimidation, which continues to increase, is a very serious threat to the proper administration of criminal justice, and in balancing the potential detriment to the accused against the mischief which Parliament is seeking to eradicate, the balance comes down firmly in favour of the prosecution.

---

[82] [2004] 1 WLR 2111, CA.

[83] See also the first appeal concerning the Bankruptcy Act 1986, ss 352 and 353(1): facts relating to the defence were within the accused's knowledge and the imposition of a legal burden did not breach Art 6. Contrast the second appeal: the very wide ambit of the Bankruptcy Act 1986, s 357 made the defence difficult to prove and to impose a legal burden would be a breach of Art 6. See also *R (Griffin) v Richmond Magistrates' Court* [2008] 1 WLR 1525, DC: the defence under s 208(4)(a) of the Insolvency Act 1986 imposes a legal burden on the accused.

In *Attorney General's Reference (No 1 of 2004)*, Lord Woolf CJ noted the significant difference in emphasis between the approaches of Lord Steyn in *R v Lambert* and Lord Nicholls in *R v Johnstone*, and noted in particular the likelihood that 'few provisions will be left as imposing a legal burden on Lord Steyn's approach'.[84] It was held that until clarification by a further decision of the House of Lords, lower courts, if in doubt as to the outcome of a challenge to a reverse burden, should follow the approach of Lord Nicholls. In *Sheldrake v DPP*,[85] however, the House of Lords held that both *R v Lambert* and *R v Johnstone*, unless or until revised or supplemented, should be regarded as the primary domestic authorities on reverse burdens; that nothing said in *R v Johnstone* suggested an intention to depart from or modify *R v Lambert*, which should not be treated as superseded or implicitly overruled; and that the differences in emphasis were explicable by the difference in the subject matter of the two cases.[86] Lord Bingham said that the task of the court is never to decide whether a reverse burden should be imposed on a defendant, but always to assess whether a burden enacted by Parliament unjustifiably infringes the presumption of innocence.[87]

Sheldrake v DPP

In *Sheldrake v DPP*,[88] the House of Lords considered two reverse onus provisions in two conjoined appeals. The first appeal concerned s 5(2) of the Road Traffic Act 1988. Under s 5(2) it is a defence for a person charged with an offence of being in charge of a motor vehicle on a road or other public place after consuming excess alcohol, to prove that at the time he is alleged to have committed the offence, the circumstances were such that there was no likelihood of his driving the vehicle whilst the proportion of alcohol in his breath, blood, or urine remained likely to exceed the prescribed limit. It was held that even on the assumption that s 5(2) infringes the presumption of innocence, it was directed to the legitimate object of preventing death, injury, and damage caused by unfit drivers and met the tests of acceptability identified in the Strasbourg jurisprudence. It was not objectionable to criminalize conduct in these circumstances without requiring the prosecutor to prove criminal intent. The accused has a full opportunity to show that there was no likelihood of his driving, a matter so closely conditioned by his own knowledge at the time as to make it much more appropriate for him to prove the absence of a likelihood of his driving on the balance of probabilities than for the prosecutor to prove such a likelihood beyond reasonable doubt. The imposition of a legal burden therefore did not go beyond what was necessary.[89]

---

[84] [2004] 1 WLR 2111, CA at [38].

[85] [2005] 1 AC 264, HL.

[86] Ibid. See per Lord Bingham at [30] and [32]. Lords Steyn and Phillips concurred with Lord Bingham and Lords Rodger and Carswell appear to endorse these parts of the speech.

[87] Lord Bingham also questioned Lord Woolf's assumption that Parliament would not have made an exception without good reason. Such an assumption may lead the court to give too much weight to the enactment and too little to the presumption of innocence and the obligation imposed on it by s 3 (at [30] and [32]).

[88] *Sheldrake v DPP* [2005] 1 AC 264, HL.

[89] *Sheldrake v DPP* [2005] 1 AC 264, HL, may be contrasted with *AG's Ref (No 4 of 2002)*, the appeal with which it was conjoined and which concerned s 11(1) and (2) of the Terrorism Act 2000. It was held that the defence contained in s 11(2) imposed an evidential burden because the imposition of a legal burden would be an unjustifiable infringement of the presumption of innocence: s 11(1) of the Terrorism Act 2000.

Concerning s 11(1) and (2) of the Terrorism Act 2000: the defence contained in s 11(2) imposed an evidential burden as the imposition of a legal burden would be an unjustifiable infringement of the presumption of innocence.

Regulatory offences

According to the authorities, the imposition of a legal burden on the accused is likely to be more acceptable in the case of offences which are concerned to regulate the conduct of particular action taken in the public interest and which are not regarded as 'truly criminal'. In *R v Lambert*,[90] Lord Clyde said:

> The requirement to have a licence in order to carry on certain types of activity is an obvious example. The promotion of health and safety and the avoidance of pollution are among the purposes to be served by such controls. These kinds of cases may properly be seen as not truly criminal. Many may be relatively trivial and only involve a monetary penalty. Many may carry with them no real social disgrace or infamy.[91]

R v Davies[92] concerned s 40 of the Health and Safety at Work Act 1974, which requires the accused to prove that 'it was not reasonably practicable to do more than was in fact done' to satisfy his health and safety duties. It was held that s 40 is not incompatible with the Convention, but justified, necessary, and proportionate.[93] In reaching this conclusion, the court relied upon the regulatory nature of the 1974 Act and the 'convincing and extremely helpful' analysis of Cory J in the Canadian Supreme Court in *R v Wholesale Travel Group*.[94] Cory J expressed the rationale for the distinction between truly criminal and regulatory offences as follows:

> Regulatory legislation involves the shift of emphasis from the protection of individual interests and the deterrence and punishment of acts involving moral fault to the protection of public and societal interests. While criminal offences are usually designed to condemn and punish past, inherently wrongful conduct, regulatory measures are generally directed to the prevention of future harm through the enforcement of minimum standards of conduct and care. It follows that regulatory offences and crimes embody different concepts of fault. Since regulatory offences are directed primarily not to conduct itself but to the consequences of conduct, conviction of a regulatory offence may be thought to import a significantly lesser degree of culpability than conviction of a true crime. The concept of fault in regulatory offences is based upon a reasonable care standard and, as such, does not imply moral blameworthiness in the same manner as criminal fault. Conviction for breach of a regulatory offence suggests nothing more than that the defendant has failed to meet a prescribed standard of care.

Justifying the distinction by what he called the licensing argument and the vulnerability justification, he continued:

> while in the criminal context the essential question to be determined is whether the accused has made the choice to act in the manner alleged in the indictment, the regulated defendant is by virtue of the licensing argument, assumed to have made the choice to engage in the regulated activity. Those who choose to participate in regulated activities have . . . placed themselves in a responsible relationship to the public . . . and must accept the consequences of that responsibility . . . Regulatory legislation . . . plays a legitimate and vital role in protecting those who are most vulnerable and least able to protect themselves.

---

[90] [2002] 2 AC 545, HL at [154].

[91] See *R v S* [2003] 1 Cr App R 602, CA at [48], where this dictum was applied.

[92] [2003] ICR 586, CA.

[93] See also *R v Chargot Ltd (trading as Contract Services) and others* [2009] 1 WLR 1, HL: the reverse burden in s 40 was not rendered *disproportionate* by the fact that penalties had been increased under the Health and Safety (Offences) Act 2008, s 1(1) and (2) and Sch 1.

[94] (1991) 3 SCR 154.

In *R (Grundy & Co Excavations Ltd) v Halton Division Magistrates' Court*,[95] it was held that the offence of tree felling without a licence contrary to s 17 of the Forestry Act 1967 was a case of the kind which Lord Clyde had in mind in *R v Lambert* and which Cory J had in mind in *R v Wholesale Travel Group*: it was a classic regulatory offence, designed to protect the nation's trees, involving only a monetary penalty and carrying no real social disgrace or infamy and no real moral stigma or obloquy.

Critique

To some, including the authors of this work, it remains repugnant in principle, especially in the case of imprisonable offences, that jurors or magistrates should be under a legal duty to convict if left in doubt as to whether the accused has established his defence, or are of the view that his version of events is as likely to be true as not.[96] In some cases, as we have seen, the courts will rule that the reverse onus provision in question is incompatible with Art 6 and can be read down so as to impose only an evidential burden. However, Parliament has decided not to legislate that all burdens borne by the accused should be evidential only. In previous editions of this work, reference has been made to the views of one distinguished commentator who pointed out that if Parliament did not intervene and therefore the question of compatibility fell to be determined in respect of each reverse onus provision, there would be a long period of uncertainty and much expensive and wasteful litigation, with inconsistent results, because courts would have differing views.[97] That prediction is proving to be all too accurate, and the scale of the problem remains vast because some 40 per cent of the offences triable in the Crown Court purport to impose a legal burden on the accused to prove at least one element of the offence or statutory defence.[98]

For a number of reasons, the various criteria that have been developed to determine compatibility compound the problems of uncertainty and inconsistency. Some courts are clearly adopting a 'pick "n" mix' approach to the criteria; there is no guidance as to the weight to be attached to such important and potentially competing criteria as the seriousness of the potential punishment, the ease of proof, and whether a matter is within the knowledge of the accused; the criterion of deference, albeit limited, to the considered opinion of Parliament is of dubious validity given the very nature of the obligation under s 3 of the Human Rights Act 1998; and the distinction between 'truly criminal' and regulatory offences is inherently tenuous, not least because views are bound to differ as to which particular regulatory offences involve moral fault. In these circumstances, in many cases it will be as easy to draw a rational conclusion of compatibility as incompatibility.[99] As another commentator has put it, in the absence of broader principles for applying the relevant factors, decisions will continue to resemble a 'forensic lottery'.[100]

---

[95] (2003) 167 JP 387.

[96] But see *R v S* [2003] 1 Cr App R 602 (35), CA at [13] ('. . .there are competing considerations') and *Shepherd v Information Commissioner* [2019] 4 WLR 50 at [43] ('. . . a factor which carries some weight in the overall balance, but [is] very much last on the list').

[97] See Professor Sir John Smith's, 'Commentary', *R v DPP, ex p Kebilene* [1999] Crim LR 994.

[98] See Ashworth and Blake 'The Presumption of Innocence in English Criminal Law' [1996] Crim LR 306.

[99] For a good example, see *R v Keogh* [2007] 1 WLR 1500, CA: the Court of Appeal read down the Official Secrets Act 1989, ss 2(3) and 3(4) on the basis that the reverse burden was not a necessary element in the operation of ss 2 and 3, it being 'practicable' to require the prosecution to prove that the accused knew, or had reasonable cause to believe, that the information disclosed related to such matters as defence and that its disclosure would be damaging.

[100] Dennis, 'Reverse Onuses and the Presumption of Innocence: In Search of Principle' [2005] Crim LR 901 at 927. See also Ashworth, 'Four threats to the presumption of innocence' (2006) 10 E&P 241.

Civil cases

The general rule, in civil cases, is that he who asserts must prove. Certain issues are 'essential' to the case of a party to civil proceedings in the sense that they must be proved by him if he is to succeed in the action. The legal burden of proof will generally lie on the party asserting the affirmative of such an issue.[101] For example, in an action for negligence, the claimant bears the legal burden of proving duty of care, breach of such duty, and loss suffered in consequence. The legal burden of proving a defence which goes beyond a simple denial of the claimant's assertions, such as *volenti non fit injuria* or contributory negligence, lies on the defendant. The burden of proving a failure to mitigate is also borne by the defendant.[102] Similarly, the legal burden of proving a contract, its breach, and consequential loss lies on the claimant; and the legal burden of proving a defence which goes beyond a simple denial of the claimant's assertions, such as discharge by agreement or by frustration, lies on the defendant. In a claim for equitable compensation for breach of fiduciary duty, the 'burden is squarely on the applicants to prove the breach and the losses that flow from the breach'.[103]

In *BHP Billiton Petroleum Ltd v Dalmine SpA*[104] it was held that, although in most civil proceedings the statements of case are likely to be a good guide to the incidence of the legal burden of proof, they cannot be definitive, because a party cannot, by poor pleading, take upon himself a burden which the law does not impose on him, or free himself from a burden which the law does impose on him. Thus a party cannot escape a legal burden borne by him on a particular issue essential to his case by drafting his claim or defence, in relation to the issue, by way of a negative allegation. In *Soward v Leggatt*[105] the plaintiff, a landlord, alleged that his tenant 'did not repair' a certain house. The defendant replied that he 'did well and sufficiently repair' the house. Lord Abinger CB, observing that the plaintiff might have pleaded that the defendant 'let the house become dilapidated', held that it was not the form of the issue which required consideration, but its substance and effect. Accordingly, it was for the plaintiff to prove the defendant's breach of covenant.[106]

The incidence of the legal burden of proof in civil cases can often be discovered from the precedents concerned with the issue of substantive law in question. In the absence of such a precedent, however, the courts are prepared to decide not on the basis of any general

[101] See, for example, *Dera Commercial Estate v Derya Inc, 'The Sur'* [2018] EWHC 1673 (Comm): where a party applies to strike out a shipping claim on the basis that, in bringing the claim, there has been an inordinate and inexcusable delay under s 41(3) of the Arbitration Act 1996, the applicant bears the legal burden to prove that the delay was inordinate and the inordinate delay was inexcusable. See also n 15.

[102] *Geest plc v Lansiquot* [2002] 1 WLR 3111, PC, disapproving *Selvanayagam v University of the West Indies* [1983] 1 WLR 585, PC.

[103] *Wessely v White* [2018] EWHC 1499 (Ch) at [50]. However, where the claimant proves the breach of duty but the defendant prevents the claimant from adducing evidence to prove the value of his loss (for example, by conduct to conceal the loss), the burden can be properly put on the defendant to show the loss was zero, and if he fails to do so it can be presumed to be the highest possible (ibid at [51]).

[104] [2003] BLR 271, CA at [28].

[105] (1836) 7 C&P 613.

[106] See also *Arbrath v North Eastern Rly Co* (1883) 11 QBD 440, CA: in an action for malicious prosecution, the plaintiff bore the burden of proving both that the defendant had instituted proceedings and that he had done so without reasonable and probable cause, as, according to Bowen LJ, the assertion of a 'negative' was an essential part of the plaintiff's case. This was affirmed on appeal ((1886) 11 App Cas 247, HL) and applied in *Reynolds v Metropolitan Police Comr* (1984) 80 Cr App R 125, CA (procuring the grant of a search warrant falsely, maliciously, and *without reasonable and probable cause*).

principles but more as a matter of policy given the particular rule of substantive law in question.[107] In *Joseph Constantine Steamship Line Ltd v Imperial Smelting Corpn Ltd*[108] a ship on charter was destroyed by an explosion the cause of which was unclear. The charterers claimed damages from the owners for failure to load. The owners' defence was frustration. The charterers argued that the owners could not rely upon frustration unless they proved that the explosion was not caused by fault on their part. The owners replied that they could rely upon frustration unless the charterers showed that the explosion was caused by their (the owners') fault. The House of Lords held that in order to defeat the defence of frustration, the burden of proof was upon the charterers to prove fault on the part of the owners. Accordingly, the cause of the explosion being unclear, the appeal of the owners was allowed. It is possible to justify this outcome on the basis that it is more difficult to prove absence of fault than it is to prove fault. This justification, however, should not be regarded as an inflexible *rule*: in bailment cases, for example, the bailor having proved bailment, the bailee has the onus of proving that the goods were lost or damaged without fault on his part.[109] Similarly, in an action for conversion, the burden is on the bailee to prove that he dealt with the goods in good faith and without notice.[110] Thus the cases have been decided as a matter of policy on their own merits.[111]

In civil cases, as in criminal cases, the incidence of the legal burden of proof may be determined by statute. For example, whereas it is for the former employee claiming unfair dismissal to prove that he was dismissed, it is for the employer to show the reason for the dismissal and that it constitutes one of the grounds set out in the statute on which a dismissal is capable of being fair. If the employer fails to show such a reason, the dismissal is automatically unfair.[112] Equally, the parties themselves may expressly agree upon the incidence of the burden of proof.[113] The parties may do this, for example, in the case of written contracts, but in the absence of express agreement the matter becomes one of construction for the court. In *Munro, Brice & Co v War Risks Association*[114] an insurance policy covered a ship subject to an exemption in respect of loss by capture or in consequence of hostilities. The ship in question had disappeared for reasons unknown and a claim was made. The question for the court was whether the plaintiffs had to prove that the ship was not lost by reason of enemy action. The court found for the plaintiff on the basis that the defendants bore the burden of proving that the facts fell within the exception and this they had clearly failed to do.[115] However, where a

---

[107] See Stone (1944) 60 LQR 262.

[108] [1942] AC 154, HL.

[109] *Coldman v Hill* [1919] 1 KB 443, CA; cf *Levison v Patent Steam Carpet Cleaning Ltd* [1978] QB 69, CA.

[110] *Marcq v Christie Manson and Woods Ltd* [2002] 4 All ER 1005, QBD.

[111] In some civil cases exposition of the law is rendered difficult by a judicial failure to make clear which burden, legal or evidential, is in contemplation. For example, where rape is pleaded as a defence to adultery, it is unclear whether the legal burden is on the petitioner to prove that the intercourse was consensual or on the respondent to prove that it was non-consensual. In *Redpath v Redpath and Milligan* [1950] 1 All ER 600, CA the judgment of Bucknill LJ suggests the former, that of Vaisey J the latter, although neither distinguished between the legal and evidential burden.

[112] See Employment Rights Act 1996, s 98. A further example is the Consumer Credit Act 1974, s 171(7): if a debtor alleges that a credit bargain is extortionate (within the meaning of ss 137 and 138), it is for the creditor to prove to the contrary.

[113] See, eg, *Levy v Assicurazioni Generali* [1940] AC 791, PC and *Fred Chappell Ltd v National Car Parks Ltd* (1987) The Times, 22 May, QBD.

[114] [1918] 2 KB 78.

[115] Cf *Hurst v Evans* [1917] 1 KB 352.

claimant in these circumstances relies upon a proviso to an exemption clause, the burden of proving that the facts fall within the proviso may well be on him. In *The Glendarroch*[116] the plaintiffs brought an action in negligence for non-delivery of goods, the goods in question having been lost when the boat carrying them sank. Under the bill of lading, there was a clause exempting the defendants in respect of loss or damage caused by perils of the sea provided that the defendants were not negligent. It was held that the plaintiffs bore the burden of proving the contract and non-delivery; that if the defendants relied upon the exemption clause, it was for them to prove that the facts fell within it, that is, that loss was caused by a peril of the sea; but that if the plaintiffs then relied upon the proviso to the exemption clause, it was for them to prove that the facts fell within the proviso, that is, that loss was caused by the negligence of the defendants.

The incidence of the evidential burden

As a general rule in both civil and criminal proceedings, a party bearing the legal burden on a particular issue will also bear the evidential burden on that issue. This rule has given rise to little difficulty or case law in civil proceedings. In civil cases, as in criminal cases, the incidence of the evidential burden may be affected by the operation of a presumption, a matter considered in detail in **Chapter 4**.[117] In criminal cases, where, as we have seen, the prosecution generally bear the legal burden of proving those facts essential to the Crown case, the prosecution normally also bear the evidential burden in relation to those facts. Similarly, where the defence bear the legal burden of proving insanity (as required at common law) or some other issue (pursuant to an express or implied statutory exception), the defence also bear the evidential burden on such issues.

In the case of all common law defences except insanity, the evidential burden is on the defence and, once discharged, the legal burden of disproving the defence is then on the prosecution.[118] However, the evidential burden may be discharged by *any* evidence in the case, whether adduced or elicited by the defence, a co-accused, or the prosecution;[119] and where there is sufficiently cogent evidence of such a defence, then the judge must leave it to the jury, even if it has not been mentioned by the defence[120] or has been expressly disclaimed by them[121] (or they have conveyed to the judge their opinion that he should not leave it to the jury)[122] and notwithstanding that it may be inconsistent with the accused's

---

[116] [1894] P 226, CA.

[117] See, eg, the Bills of Exchange Act 1882, s 30(2). The effect of this provision is that if a party sues on a bill of exchange he only bears the evidential burden on the issue whether he gave value for the bill in good faith if the defendant has adduced prima facie evidence that the acceptance, issue, etc of the bill is affected with fraud, duress, etc. See *Talbot v Von Boris* [1911] 1 KB 854, CA at 866.

[118] This is also the case in relation to a variety of statutory defences. See, eg, the Criminal Law Act 1967, s 3(1) (reasonable force in the prevention of crime, etc) and *R v Cameron* [1973] Crim LR 520, CA and *R v Khan* [1995] Crim LR 78, CA. See also the Sexual Offences Act 2003, s 75, the Terrorism Act 2000, s 118(2), and the Coroners and Justice Act 2009, s 54(5).

[119] *Bullard v R* [1957] AC 635, PC.

[120] *Palmer v R* [1971] AC 814, PC at 823. See also *R v Hopper* [1915] 2 KB 431; *R v Cascoe* [1970] 2 All ER 833, CA; *R v Bonnick* (1977) 66 Cr App R 266, CA; *R v Johnson* [1989] 2 All ER 839, CA; and *DPP (Jamaica) v Bailey* [1995] 1 Cr App R 257, PC.

[121] *R v Kachikwu* (1968) 52 Cr App R 538, CA at 543.

[122] *R v Burgess and McLean* [1995] Crim LR 425, CA and *R v Dhillon* [1997] 2 Cr App R 104, CA. But see also *R v Groark* [1999] Crim LR 669, CA at n 129.

defence,[123] or that the judge may fear that the jury may come to a fanciful or unduly sympathetic verdict.[124] It is incumbent on the judge not to withdraw a defence from the jury by impermissibly making up his own mind on the facts.[125]

The above principles apply to the common law defences of self-defence,[126] duress,[127] non-insane automatism,[128] and drunkenness.[129] The common law defence of provocation, to which these principles also applied,[130] has been replaced by a significantly different and more restrictive statutory defence of loss of control.[131] Under s 55(1) of the Coroners and Justice Act 2009, before the defence can apply, there must be a qualifying trigger, namely that the loss of control was attributable to: the accused's fear of serious violence from the victim of the killing against the accused or another identified person;[132] a thing or things done or said (or both) which constituted circumstances of an extremely grave character and caused the accused to have a justifiable sense of being seriously wronged;[133] or a combination of these matters.[134] Under s 54(5) of the 2009 Act, if 'sufficient' evidence is adduced to raise an issue with respect to the statutory defence, the jury must assume that the defence is satisfied unless the prosecution prove beyond reasonable doubt that it is not.[135] Section 54(6) provides that sufficient evidence is adduced to raise an issue with respect to the defence if evidence is

---

[123] See *R v Newell* [1989] Crim LR 906 and generally Doran, 'Alternative Defences: the "invisible burden" on the trial judge' [1991] Crim LR 878.

[124] Per Moses LJ in *R v Hammond* [2013] EWCA Crim 2709 at [6].

[125] See *R v Hammond* [2013] EWCA Crim 2709 at [6]; see also *R v Lang* [2002] 2 Cr App R (S) 44 (15), CA. For an example of a case where a defence of duress was held to have been properly withdrawn, see *R v Batchelor* [2013] EWCA Crim 2638.

[126] *R v Lobell* [1957] 1 QB 547, CCA and *Chan Kau v R* [1955] AC 206, PC. See also the Criminal Justice and Immigration Act 2008, s 76(7), concerning evidence of reasonable force where self-defence is raised. See also ss 76(3), 76(5)A, and 76(6) of the 2008 Act, where the accused is a householder relying on the defence of self defence against an intruder. See *Collins v Secretary of State for Justice* [2016] 2 WLR 1303, DC at [33]–[34] as to how these provisions should be interpreted and applied where the accused householder has brought the defence into play and the prosecution bear the legal burden to disprove it to the criminal standard.

[127] *R v Gill* [1963] 1 WLR 841, CCA. See also *R v Bone* [1968] 1 WLR 983, CA and *R v Hammond* [2013] EWCA Crim 2709.

[128] *Bratty v A-G for Northern Ireland* [1963] AC 386, HL. See also *R v Stripp* (1978) 69 Cr App R 318, CA at 321 and *R v Pullen* [1991] Crim LR 457, CA. The situation is different in the case of insanity, because that defence places a burden of proof on the accused, although in rare and exceptional cases the judge may of his own volition raise the issue and leave it to the jury: see *R v Thomas (Sharon)* [1995] Crim LR 314, CA.

[129] See *Kennedy v HM Advocate* 1944 JC 171 and *R v Foote* [1964] Crim LR 405. However, in *R v Groark* [1999] Crim LR 669, CA, it was held that if, in a case of wounding with intent, there is evidence of drunkenness which might give rise to the issue whether the accused had the specific intent, but the defence is that the accused knew what was happening and acted in self-defence, if the defence object to a direction on drunkenness in relation to intent, such a direction need not be given.

[130] *Mancini v DPP* [1942] AC 1, HL and *R v Cascoe* [1970] 2 All ER 83, CA. See also *R v Rossiter* [1994] 2 All ER 752, CA and *R v Cambridge* [1994] 2 All ER 760, CA.

[131] *R v Godwin* [2018] 4 WLR 165, CA, at [33](8) and *R v Jovan* [2017] EWCA Crim 1359 at [38]. See also *R v Gurpinar* [2015] 1 WLR 3442, CA.

[132] Section 55(3).

[133] Section 55(4).

[134] Section 55(5). Section 55(6) sets out matters to be disregarded in determining whether the accused's loss of self-control had a 'qualifying trigger'.

[135] Notwithstanding the use in s 54(5) of the phrase 'beyond reasonable doubt', it would appear that the jury should be directed that they must assume the defence is satisfied unless the prosecution make them 'sure' that it is not: see the example in the Crown Court Compendium (July 2019), Part 1, 19–14.

adduced on which, in the opinion of the trial judge, a jury, properly directed, could reasonably conclude that the defence might apply. The existence of a qualifying trigger does not of itself connote 'sufficient evidence'.[136] Whether there is sufficient evidence of loss of control to permit the defence to go to the jury is a question of law to be resolved by the judge.[137] The leading authority on the approach that should be taken is *R v Gurpinar*.[138] The principles stated in *R v Gurpinar* may be summarized as follows.

1. The judge must undertake a more rigorous evaluation of the evidence than was required under the old law of provocation, where *any* rather than *sufficient* evidence was the basis for that defence going to the jury.[139]

2. The quality and weight of the evidence should be considered,[140] and the judge should proceed on the premise that the jury may take a view of the evidence which is different from the view taken by him.[141]

3. The judge must analyse the whole of the evidence, even if the accused has not raised the issue or given evidence. Where the accused gives evidence which does not support the defence that he lost his self-control, this is obviously part of the evidence, but it is only one factor (albeit significant) which the judge should take into account in his overall assessment of the evidence.[142]

4. Assistance must be provided by the advocates in the case. The advocates should raise the issue as early as possible in the management of the case and if at the end of the case there is a possibility that the judge will leave the defence to the jury when it is not part of the defence case, the judge must receive written submissions from the advocates so that he can carefully consider whether the statutory test is met.[143] Where the trial judge has reached a reasoned decision in relation to whether to permit the defence to go to the jury, the appellate court will not readily interfere.[144]

It was held in *R v Goodwin*[145] that where there is sufficient evidence with respect to the defence of loss of control, then the defence should be left to the jury whether or not it has been expressly relied on by the accused at trial.[146] This might occur where the accused relies on the defence of self-defence, but the particular facts relating to that defence also raise an issue of loss of control.[147] However, a judge should not be tempted to leave the defence to the jury in order to avoid providing a ground of appeal.[148] In any appeal on the ground that the defence was not properly left to the jury, the fact that the accused at the

---

[136] *R v Godwin* [2018] 4 WLR 165, CA.

[137] See the Explanatory Notes to the Coroners and Justice Act 2009, para 340.

[138] [2015] 1 WLR 3442, CA.

[139] At [14]. See also *R v Goodwin* [2018] 4 WLR 165, CA, at [33](9).

[140] At [12]. See also *R v Jewell* [2014] EWCA Crim 414 at [51]–[54].

[141] At [12]. See also *R v Goodwin* [2018] 4 WLR 165, CA, at [33](7) and *R v Dawes* [2014] 1 WLR 947, CA, at [46].

[142] At [10]–[11]. See also *R v Dawes* [2014] 1 WLR 947, CA, at [53].

[143] At [15].

[144] At [16].

[145] [2018] 4 WLR 165, CA.

[146] Ibid at [33](2).

[147] As to the relationship between the two defences, see *R v Goodwin* [2018] 4 WLR 165, CA, at [36]. See also *R v Martin* [2017] EWCA Crim 1359.

[148] *R v Goodwin* [2018] 4 WLR 165, CA, at [35]. To do so would be contrary to the scheme and the statute.

trial did not assert loss of control, although not decisive, is a powerful point against the issue arising.[149]

Where the defence of non-insane automatism is raised by an accused, the judge must decide two questions before it can be left to the jury: whether there is a proper evidential foundation for it and whether the evidence shows the case to be one of insane or non-insane automatism. If the judge rules it to be a case of insanity, the jury must then decide whether the accused is guilty or not guilty by reason of insanity.[150] It was held by the Court of Appeal in *R v Burns*[151] that where the issues of both insanity and non-insane automatism arise in the same case, the judge should direct the jury that while the accused bears the legal burden of proving insanity, he bears only the evidential burden in relation to non-insane automatism. The law relating to the above defences is reasonably well settled and clear. It is less clear, however, whether the defence bears the evidential burden in relation to a defence which amounts to nothing more than a denial of the prosecution case and therefore raises no new issue. On one view, an accused should not bear an evidential burden in relation to a defence of, say, alibi or accident, because the onus is already on the prosecution to prove, in the one case, that the accused was present at the scene of the crime and, in the other, that he had the requisite *mens rea*.[152] There are obiter dicta, however, to the effect that the evidential burden, in the case of both of these defences, is on the accused.[153] Moreover, in *R v Bennett*[154] it was held that the accused bore the evidential burden in relation to impossibility on a charge of conspiracy to contravene the provisions of the Misuse of Drugs Act 1971[155] and in *Bratty v A-G for Northern Ireland*, as we have seen, the accused was held to bear the evidential burden on non-insane automatism.

Where the evidential burden alone, in relation to a particular defence, is borne by the accused, the judge, if he decides that insufficient evidence has been adduced on the matter, will direct the jury that the issue must be taken as proved against the accused. If the accused has adduced sufficient evidence, the judge will direct the jury that the prosecution bears the legal burden of negativing the defence in question by proof that makes them sure. However, where the legal burden is borne by the accused, the jury should be directed that it is for the defence to satisfy them on a balance of probabilities and that if they are not so satisfied the

---

[149] Ibid, at [40]. See also *R v Martin* [2017] EWCA Crim 1359, where it was made clear to the judge in discussions that loss of control was not being advanced and it was expressly agreed that the issue did not arise.

[150] *R v Burgess* (1991) 93 Cr App R 41, CA.

[151] (1973) 58 Cr App R 364; cf *Bratty v A-G for Northern Ireland* [1963] AC 386 at 402–3.

[152] See Professor Glanville Williams (1977) 127 NLJ at 157–8 and generally per Lord Hailsham LC in *R v Howe* [1987] 1 All ER 771, HL at 781 ff.

[153] *R v Johnson* [1961] 3 All ER 969, CCA (alibi); *Bratty v A-G for Northern Ireland* [1963] AC 386, HL per Lord Kilmuir LC at 405 (accident). There is no dispute, however, that if the defence do adduce evidence in support of an alibi, the prosecution bear the legal burden of disproof (*R v Helliwell* [1995] Crim LR 79, CA and *R v Fergus* (1993) 98 Cr App R 313, CA) and ideally the judge should give a specific direction on the burden of proof in relation to the alibi (*R v Anderson* [1991] Crim LR 361, CA and *R v Johnson* [1995] Crim LR 242, CA). See also *R v Mussell* [1995] Crim LR 887, CA: a specific direction is needed if the nature of the alibi is that the accused was at a specific place elsewhere, raising the question why he did not call witnesses in support, but not if the evidence amounts to little more than a denial that he committed the crime.

[154] (1978) 68 Cr App R 168, CA.

[155] It was further held that if the prosecution have in their possession evidence which might show that at the time when the agreement was made the carrying out of the agreement would have been impossible, it is the duty of the prosecution either to call the evidence or to make it available to the defence.

issue must be taken as proved against the accused.[156] Accordingly, the judge may direct the jury that if they cannot decide on the evidence whether the defence case is more probable than not, they should find against the accused.

The right to begin

The right to begin adducing evidence is determined by the incidence of the evidential burden. As a general rule, the claimant has the right to begin adducing evidence in civil proceedings and the prosecution in criminal proceedings. In civil cases, the claimant has the right to adduce his evidence first unless the defendant bears the evidential burden on every issue.[157] In *Mercer v Whall*[158] an attorney's clerk brought an action for unliquidated damages for wrongful dismissal. The defendant admitted the dismissal but pleaded justification on the basis of the plaintiff's misconduct. It was held that the plaintiff was entitled to begin because he bore the evidential burden in relation to damages. The defendant would have had the right to begin if the claim had been for a liquidated sum because the only fact in issue would then have been the question of misconduct on which the defendant bore the evidential burden. In criminal cases where there is a plea of not guilty, the prosecution will normally have the right to adduce their evidence first. The reason appears to be that they will almost always bear an evidential burden on at least one issue. However, this may not be the case where the accused has made formal admissions under s 10 of the Criminal Justice Act 1967 or agreed to a statement of facts admitted in evidence under s 9 of the same Act. Where the accused pleads *autrefois acquit* or *convict* and there is a dispute of fact requiring evidence, the accused has the right to begin.

The standard of proof

Appropriate standards of proof

Whether a party to civil or criminal proceedings has discharged a legal burden borne by him in relation to a particular issue is, as we have seen, decided by the tribunal of fact at the end of the case. To discharge the burden and succeed on that issue the evidence adduced by that party must, in the opinion of the tribunal of fact, be more cogent or convincing than that adduced by his opponent. How much more cogent or convincing the evidence is required to be is determined by rules of law relating to the standard of proof. If the evidence adduced by a party is sufficiently cogent or convincing to meet the appropriate standard of proof, the legal burden will be discharged and facts in issue will be proved. As Lord Hoffmann explained in *Re B (children) (sexual abuse)*,[159] 'there is no room for a finding that a fact in issue might have happened; the law operates a binary system in which the fact either happened or it did not.'[160]

The standard of proof required to discharge a legal burden depends upon whether the proceedings are criminal or civil, the standard being higher in the former than in the latter. In criminal proceedings, the standard required of the prosecution before the jury could find

---

[156] See *R v Evans-Jones, R v Jenkins* (1923) 87 JP 115 and *R v Carr-Briant* [1943] KB 607.

[157] See *Pontifex v Jolly* (1839) 9 C&P 202 and *Re Parry's Estate, Parry v Fraser* [1977] 1 All ER 309.

[158] (1845) 14 LJ QB 267.

[159] [2009] 1 AC 11.

[160] *Re B (children) (sexual abuse)* [2009] 1 AC 11, HL at [2].

the accused guilty was previously expressed as proof beyond reasonable doubt.[161] However, the standard is now expressed as proof which makes the jury sure. In civil proceedings, the standard of proof required to be met by either party seeking to discharge a legal burden is proof on a balance of probabilities.

The notion of a third and intermediate standard of proof lying between the standards required in criminal and civil cases has not found favour in the courts.[162]

The standard of proof in criminal cases

The rules prescribing the standard of proof are a matter of law for the judge. Whether the evidence adduced meets the standard is a question for the jury as tribunal of fact. In criminal trials, therefore, the judge must direct the jury on the standard of proof that the prosecution are required to meet.[163] As has been noted, the criminal standard of proof is now expressed as proof which makes the jury sure and judges must no longer direct juries by reference to proof beyond a reasonable doubt. This is because directions which refer to proof beyond a reasonable doubt have the potential to confuse juries. Particular difficulties have arisen, for example, where judges attempt to define and explain the concept of proof beyond a reasonable doubt, sometimes by combining it with the concept of being 'sure' and by drawing distinctions with the concept of being 'certain'.[164] The Crown Court Compendium now provides the following example of how the jury should be directed:[165]

> The prosecution must prove that D is guilty. D does not have to prove anything to you. D does not have to prove that he/she is innocent. The prosecution will only succeed in proving that D is guilty if you have been made sure of D's guilt. If, after considering all of the evidence, you are sure that D is guilty, your verdict must be 'Guilty'. If you are not sure that D is guilty, your verdict must be 'Not Guilty'.

The Compendium also states:[166]

> If reference has been made to 'beyond reasonable doubt' by any advocate, the following may be added: You have heard reference to the phrase 'beyond reasonable doubt'. This means the same as being sure.

---

[161] See *Ferguson v R* [1979] 1 WLR 94, PC, *Woolmington v DPP* [1935] AC 462, HL and *Mancini v DPP* [1942] AC 1, HL.

[162] See, eg, per Lord Tucker in *Dingwall v J Wharton (Shipping) Ltd* [1961] 2 Lloyd's Rep 213, HL at 216.

[163] See Ch 2, **Jury directions and the summing-up**, p 44. The same standard as for the prosecution, also has to be met: (i) by a judge determining the facts for the purpose of sentence, the accused having pleaded guilty and having put forward a version of the facts which differs significantly from the prosecution's version (*R v McGrath and Casey* (1983) 5 Cr App R (S) 460 and *R v Ahmed* (1984) 6 Cr App R (S) 391), although in respect of extraneous facts put forward in mitigation the burden is on the accused and the standard is the civil standard (see *R v Guppy* [1995] 16 Cr App R (S) 25); (ii) by a judge when considering whether the first condition for the making of a criminal behaviour order is met under the Anti-social Behaviour, Crime and Policing Act 2014, s 22(3); and (iii) by a judge determining whether exceptional circumstances exist to justify departing from the requirement to impose a statutory minimum sentence under the Firearms Act 1968, s 51A) (*R v Lashari* [2011] 1 Cr App R (S) 439 (72), CA and also *R v Boetang* [2011] EWCA Crim 861).

[164] See the trial judge's direction in *R v Majid* [2009] EWCA Crim 2563, CA, quoted by Moses LJ at [14]. See also *R v Yap Chuan Ching* (1976) 63 Cr App R 7, CA, where the jury sought clarification of a direction which combined the concepts of 'proof beyond reasonable doubt' and 'sure'; *Ferguson v R* [1979] 1 WLR 94 at 99, where Lord Scarman suggested a direction which conflated the concepts; and *R v Stephens* [2002] EWCA Crim 1529, where an unhelpful distinction was drawn between being sure of guilt and being certain of guilt.

[165] The Crown Court Compendium (July 2019), Part 1, 5, Example 1.

[166] Ibid.

It is submitted that there is potential for juries to be confused by a direction that they must be 'sure'. They may well take 'sure' to mean absolutely (or 100 per cent) certain.[167] Where an advocate has used the phrase 'beyond reasonable doubt', juries are also likely to be confused by a direction that it means the same as being sure: 'sure' can mean 'having *no* doubt', which is plainly at odds with 'beyond *reasonable*' doubt'.

A conviction will not necessarily be rendered unsafe where a jury are told in clear terms they should return a verdict of guilty if they are sure, but the judge omits to say that they should return a *not guilty* verdict if they are *not sure*.[168] However, in this respect, judges would be sensible to follow the standard direction in The Compendium.[169] As to what can justifiably leave the jury 'unsure' for the purposes of the standard of proof, in *S v DPP*[170] it was stated: 'It is axiomatic that a mere possibility that a defendant might not be guilty is sufficient to mean that a jury cannot be "sure" of guilt.'[171]

Where the accused bears the legal burden

In criminal cases, the legal burden is, as we have seen, generally borne by the prosecution. Where the legal burden on a particular issue is borne by the accused, it is discharged by the defence satisfying the jury on a balance of probabilities.[172] The Compendium suggests a direction in the following terms.[173]

> When you are considering {specify} this is for D to prove. D has to show that it is more likely than not that {specify}. D does not have to make you sure of it.

The standard of proof in civil cases

In civil trials, the standard of proof required to be met by either party seeking to discharge the legal burden of proof is on a balance of probabilities.[174] The same standard should also be used in reaching a decision on a submission of no case to answer when the defendant has

---

[167] Such a problem arose in *R v JL* [2018] Crim LR 184. See also *R v Stephens* [2002] EWCA Crim 1529. For a critical analysis of the current direction on standard of proof and the need for a replacement, see Keane and McKeown, 'Time to abandon "beyond reasonable doubt" and "sure": the case for a new direction on the criminal standard and how it should be used', [2019] Crim LR 505.

[168] *R v Blackford* [2009] EWCA Crim 1684.

[169] See *R v Miah* [2018] EWCA Crim 563 where a conviction was unsafe in circumstances where the judge at no stage directed the jury that they had to be sure and, at most, had directed that the prosecution had to 'satisfy' them and 'prove' its case if they were to convict.

[170] [2017] EWHC 1162, DC.

[171] At [23]. Cf *R v Majid* [2009] EWCA Crim 2563 at [12]: where the jury raise an issue about what possibilities can justifiably leave them unsure, it is appropriate for the judge simply to direct them that they should exclude fanciful possibilities and act only on realistic ones.

[172] See *R v Carr-Briant* [1943] KB 607, CCA, especially at 612. See also *Sodeman v R* [1936] 2 All ER 1138, PC at 1140 (insanity) and *R v Wilcocks* [2017] 1 Cr App R 338 (23), CA (diminished responsibility).

[173] The Crown Court Compendium (July), Part 1, 5, Example 2.

[174] The same standard is not necessarily appropriate for interim applications. For example, an application for summary judgment is decided not by application of the normal standard of proof but by application of the test whether the respondent has a case with a real prospect of success: *Royal Brompton Hospital NHS Trust v Hammond* [2001] BLR 297, CA. In applications for injunctions under s 1(1) of the Anti-social Behaviour, Crime and Policing Act 2014, s 1(2) expressly states that the civil standard applies to the first condition which must be met (the respondent has engaged in or threatens to engage in anti-social behaviour). However, no reference to proof is made in s 1(3) concerning the second condition (the court considers that it is just and convenient to grant the injunction for the purpose of preventing the respondent from engaging in anti-social behaviour).

elected not to adduce any evidence.[175] In *Miller v Minister of Pensions*[176] Denning J described as well settled the degree of cogency required to discharge the legal burden in a civil case. He continued:[177]

> It must carry a reasonable degree of probability, but not so high as is required in a criminal case. If the evidence is such that the tribunal can say: 'we think it more probable than not', the burden is discharged, but if the probabilities are equal it is not.

To the general rule on the standard of proof in civil proceedings are a number of clearly defined exceptions. First, the appropriate standard in committal proceedings for civil contempt of court is the criminal standard.[178] Second, the criminal standard may also be required in civil proceedings pursuant to statute.[179] Third, it has been held that an exacting civil standard of proof, which for all practical purposes is indistinguishable from the criminal standard of proof, applies to the following civil proceedings: applications for sex offender orders (in relation to the condition, set out in s 2(1)(a) of the Crime and Disorder Act 1998, that the person against whom the order is sought is a 'sex offender');[180] applications for Sexual Offences Prevention Orders (in relation to the conditions set out in s 104 of the Sexual Offences Act 2003, including that the person is a qualifying offender and his behaviour is such that the order is necessary to protect the public from serious sexual harm);[181] and applications for football banning orders under s 14B of the Football Spectators Act 1989.[182] Where a risk of sexual harm order is made under s 123(4) of the Sexual Offences Act 2003, the consequences of a breach of the order are very serious and can have a significant impact on someone who may never have been convicted of a child sex offence. Accordingly, on an application for a risk of sexual harm order on grounds that the defendant has done an act specified in s 123(3) and that the order is necessary to protect a child, the standard of proof must be the same as for an offence. Even though the 2003 Act is silent on the standard of proof and under it there are a range of cases that are civil, the standard of proof is the criminal standard.[183]

There are only two standards of proof, the civil and the criminal standard. There is no intermediate standard. Nor is the civil standard to be broken down into sub-categories designed to produce one or more intermediate standards. Nor, when applying the standard,

---

[175] *Miller v Cawley* [2002] EWCA Civ 1100.

[176] [1947] 2 All ER 372.

[177] Ibid at 374.

[178] *Re Bramblevale Ltd* [1970] Ch 128, CA; *Dean v Dean* [1987] 1 FLR 517, CA; see also *Re A (a child) (abduction: contempt)* [2009] 1 FLR 1, CA; *Re LW (children) (enforcement and committal: contact)* [2011] 1 FCR 78, CA; and *Aviva v Kovacic* [2017] EWHC 2772 (QB), contempt arising from dishonestly exaggerating the extent of disability to inflate a claim for damages. So also, *Pinkus v Direct Line* [2018] EWHC 1671 (QB).Where contempt is proved, the contemnor bears the burden of proving that he has purged his contempt and the civil standard applies (see *JSC BTA Bank v Solodchenko* [2010] EWHC 2843, (Ch)). Proceedings to bind over for breach of the peace are probably criminal proceedings, but even if properly classified as civil proceedings, call for proof to the criminal standard, because failure to comply with an order to enter into a recognizance may result in imprisonment: *Percy v DPP* [1995] 3 All ER 124, DC.

[179] See *Judd v Minister of Pensions and National Insurance* [1966] 2 QB 580. See also *Watkins v Wollas* [2010] EWHC 2702, QB.

[180] *B v Chief Constable of Avon and Somerset Constabulary* [2001] 1 WLR 340, DC.

[181] See *R (Chief Constable of Cleveland Police) v H* (2010) 174 JP 132, DC.

[182] *Gough v Chief Constable of the Derbyshire Constabulary* [2002] QB 1213, CA.

[183] *Commissioner of Police of the Metropolis v Ebanks* (2012) 176 JP 751, DC.

is it acceptable to use or aggregate percentages values. In *Re A (Care Proceedings: Burden of Proof)*,[184] the local authority applied for care orders in respect of five children following the death of their 10 year old sister, who had sustained injuries to her genitals and a ligature compression injury to her neck. The judge decided that the probability of suicide was 10 per cent and of accident was 45 per cent, and combining the two (55 per cent) held that he could not be satisfied on the balance of probabilities that the little girl had died as a result of a perpetrated act. Allowing the local authority's appeal, the Court of Appeal held that this was not the proper approach to the judicial function in respect of the simple application of the balance of probabilities.[185]

However, although there is a single simple civil standard, it is flexible in its application. In particular, the more serious the allegation or the more serious the consequences if the allegation is proved, the stronger must be the evidence before a court will find the allegation proved on the balance of probabilities.[186] Thus although there are indications in some of the authorities that the flexibility of the standard lies in an adjustment of the degree of probability required for an allegation to be proved,[187] the flexibility does not lie in any such adjustment but in the strength or quality of the evidence required for the allegation to be proved on the balance of probabilities.[188] 'The more serious the allegation the more cogent is the evidence required to overcome the unlikelihood of what is alleged and thus to prove it.'[189] However, dicta of this kind need to be seen in the light of the observation of Baroness Hale in *Re B (Children) (Care Proceedings: Standard of Proof)*[190] that there is no logical or necessary connection between seriousness and probability, factors which can vary according to the other evidence in the case; the seriousness and improbability of allegations are simply factors to be taken into account. As Morris LJ remarked in *Hornal v Neuberger Products Ltd*, 'the very elements of gravity become a part of the whole range of circumstances which have to be weighed in the scale when deciding as to the balance of probabilities'.[191]

Some authorities clearly focus on the seriousness of the allegation rather than the seriousness of the consequences if the allegation is proved, on the reasoning that the more serious

---

[184] 4 WLR 117, CA.

[185] Ibid, at [51]. Nor, when applying the standard, is it correct to evaluate and assess evidence in separate compartments. The correct approach is to exercise an overview of the totality of the evidence: *Re T (Children) (Abuse:Standard of Proof)* [2004] 2 FLR 838 at [33]. For an article which considers an explanation-based approach to legal fact-finding and standards of proof, see Ribeiro, 'Can there be a burden of best explanation?' (2018) 22(2) E&P 91.

[186] See *R (D) v Life Sentence Review Commissioners (Northern Ireland)* [2008] 1 WLR 1499, HL, where it was held that although the civil standard of proof was unvarying, it was flexible in its application. For a conceptual framework for understanding the civil standard of proof, see Redmayne, 'Standards of Proof in Civil Litigation' (1999) 62 MLR 167.

[187] See, eg, per Denning LJ in *Bater v Bater* [1951] P 35 at 37 and in *Hornal v Neuberger Products Ltd* [1957] 1 QB 247.

[188] Per Richards LJ, after an extensive review of the authorities, in *R (on the application of N) v Mental Health Review Tribunal* [2006] QB 468, CA at [60]–[62].

[189] Per Ungoed-Thomas J in *Re Dellow's Will Trusts* [1964] 1 WLR 451, Ch D. See also *Rizan v Hayes* [2016] EWCA Civ 481: the judge should not have made a finding of fraud without giving reasons for the conclusion over and above reasons already given for the dismissal of the less serious claim of negligence. In respect of a conclusion of fraud, reasons should address inherent improbabilities in the conclusion which need to be overcome.

[190] [2009] 1 AC 11, HL at [72].

[191] [1957] 1 QB 247, CA at 266. These words of Morris LJ were approved and adopted by the House of Lords in *Khawaja v Secretary of State for the Home Department* [1983] 1 All ER 765 in relation to the detention pending deportation of persons alleged to be illegal immigrants: see per Lord Scarman at 783–4.

the allegation the less likely it is that the event occurred, and that the inherent probability or improbability of an event is itself a matter to be taken into account.[192] However, this rationalization will take due account of the seriousness of the consequences if an allegation is proved, because in general the seriousness of an allegation is a function of the seriousness of its consequences. Nonetheless, there will be cases where proof of an allegation may have serious consequences even though it cannot be said that the matter alleged is inherently improbable, and in such cases the more serious the consequences, the stronger the evidence required to prove the matter on the balance of probabilities.[193]

Issues calling for flexibility in the application of the civil standard defy comprehensive classification, but will be explored by reference to (i) allegations of crime in civil proceedings; (ii) matrimonial causes; and (iii) a miscellany of different cases.

The standard where there are allegations of crime in civil proceedings

Prior to the decision of the Court of Appeal in *Hornal v Neuberger Products Ltd*,[194] it was unclear, on the authorities, what standard of proof was appropriate in civil cases in which a party made an allegation of criminal conduct. One line of authorities supported the view that the standard was as high as that required of the prosecution in a criminal case.[195] Other authorities took the view that the appropriate standard was the normal civil standard on a balance of probabilities.[196] In *Hornal v Neuberger Products Ltd* the plaintiff claimed damages for breach of warranty or alternatively for fraud. The defendant company had sold a lathe to the plaintiff. The plaintiff alleged that one of the company directors had represented that the lathe had been 'Soag reconditioned'. If the director did so represent, there was clearly a fraudulent misrepresentation because he knew that the machine had not been reconditioned. The question became whether the representation had been made or not. Dismissing the claim for damages for breach of warranty on the grounds that the parties did not intend the director's statement to have contractual effect, the trial judge said that he was satisfied on a balance of probabilities, but not beyond reasonable doubt, that the statement was made and accordingly awarded damages for fraud. On appeal, the Court of Appeal held that on an allegation of a crime in civil proceedings the standard of proof is on a balance of probabilities.

One of the reasons for the decision was put clearly by Denning LJ:[197] 'I think it would bring the law into contempt if a judge were to say on the issue of warranty he finds the statement was made, and that on the issue of fraud he finds it was not made.' In support of his conclusion that the civil standard applied, his Lordship referred to the views which he had expressed in *Bater v Bater*[198] where he said that civil cases must be proved by a preponderance of probability, but there may be degrees of probability within that standard. However, as we have seen, it is now recognized that the flexibility of the civil standard does not lie in an

---

[192] See *Re H (Minors) (Sexual Abuse: Standard of Proof)* [1996] AC 563, followed in *Secretary of State for the Home Department v Rehman* [2003] 1 AC 153.

[193] Per Richards LJ in *R (on the application of N) v Mental Health Review Tribunal* [2006] QB 468, CA at [64].

[194] [1957] 1 QB 247.

[195] See, eg, *Issais v Marine Insurance Co Ltd* (1923) 15 Ll L Rep 186, CA (allegations of arson on the part of the assured in an action on an insurance policy).

[196] See, eg, *Hurst v Evans* [1917] 1 KB 352, KBD (an allegation of theft on the part of the servant of the assured in an action on an insurance policy).

[197] [1957] 1 QB 247 at 258.

[198] [1951] P 35 at 37, CA.

adjustment of the degree of probability but in the strength of the evidence required for serious allegations to be proved.[199]

Against the background of conflicting authorities preceding it, *Hornal v Neuberger Products Ltd* would appear to have settled this area of the law in favour of the normal civil standard. It was applied in *Re Dellow's Will Trusts*,[200] civil proceedings in which the issue was whether a wife feloniously killed her husband. As Ungoed-Thomas J pertinently observed: 'There can hardly be a graver issue than that.' It was also applied in *Post Office v Estuary Radio Ltd*,[201] where an allegation of a criminal offence under the Wireless Telegraphy Act 1949 was made on an application for an injunction under the same Act.[202] Similarly, in *Re B (Children) (Care Proceedings: Standard of Proof)*,[203] the House of Lords held that the normal civil standard applied where allegations of sexual crimes against children were made in care proceedings, notwithstanding that such allegations were grave.[204] In *Re B (children) (care proceedings: standard of proof)*, mentioned earlier, Baroness Hale stated that the seriousness and improbability of allegations were simply factors to be taken into account in deciding where the truth lies and that there was no 'logical or necessary connection' between the seriousness of an allegation and the probability that what is alleged occurred, as a serious allegation can be more or less probable according to the other evidence:[205]

> It may be unlikely that any person looking after a baby would take him by the wrist and swing him against a wall, causing multiple fractures and other injuries. But once the evidence is clear that that is indeed what has happened to the child, it ceases to be improbable. Someone looking after the child at the relevant time must have done it. The inherent improbability of the event has no relevance to deciding who that was. The simple balance of probabilities test should be applied.[206]

It is submitted that Baroness Hale's reasoning is not confined to care proceedings where there are allegations of crime. In *Braganza v BP Shipping*,[207] a case concerning a contract of employment, Baroness Hale made it clear that in respect of *all* civil proceedings, 'there is not a sliding scale of probability to be applied, commensurate with the seriousness of the subject matter or the consequences of the decision. The only question is whether something is more likely than not to have happened.'[208]

[199] See, in this chapter, under **The standard of proof in civil cases**, p 86.

[200] [1964] 1 WLR 451, Ch D.

[201] [1967] 1 WLR 1396, CA.

[202] See also *Piermay Shipping Co SA and Brandt's Ltd v Chester, The Michael* [1979] 1 Lloyd's Rep 55 (an allegation of deliberately scuttling a ship); *Khawaja v Secretary of State for the Home Department* [1983] 1 All ER 765, HL (detention pending deportation of persons alleged to be illegal immigrants), distinguished in *Ali v Secretary of State for the Home Department* [1988] Imm AR 274, CA; *Parks v Clout* [2003] EWCA Civ 893 (an allegation of obtaining letters of administration by fraud); and *Rizan v Hayes* [2016] EWCA Civ 481 (an allegation of fraud in a traffic accident insurance claim).

[203] [2009] 1 AC 11, HL.

[204] Followed in *Re D (Children)* [2009] 2 FLR 668, CA. See also *Smithkline Beecham plc v Avery* [2011] Bus LR D 40 which, drawing on *Re B* [2009] 1 AC 11, HL at [59]–[61], determined that a single civil standard applied in a claim for an injunction to restrain harassment under the Protection From Harassment Act 1994, s 1(1)(A).

[205] [2009] 1 AC 11, HL at [72]. See also *Rizan v Hayes* [2016] EWCA Civ 481 at [34]–[35].

[206] At [73].

[207] [2015] 1 WLR 1661, SC.

[208] Ibid at [34].

The standard in matrimonial causes

In *Ginesi v Ginesi*,[209] it was held that adultery must be proved to the criminal standard, relying upon the fact that adultery was regarded by the ecclesiastical courts as a quasi-criminal offence.[210] In *Preston-Jones v Preston-Jones*,[211] a husband petitioned for divorce on the ground of adultery and proved that his wife had given birth to a normal child 360 days after the last opportunity he could have had for intercourse with her. The House of Lords held that adultery had been proved beyond reasonable doubt, Lord MacDermott stressing the gravity and public importance of the issues involved: 'The jurisdiction in divorce involves the status of the parties and the public interest requires that the marriage bond shall not be set aside lightly or without strict inquiry.'[212] However, because the result of a finding of adultery would have been in effect to render the child illegitimate, it may be that the decision can be treated as an application of the law, as it then stood,[213] that the presumption of legitimacy could only be rebutted by proof beyond reasonable doubt.[214] When the question of the appropriate standard in matrimonial causes next fell to be considered by the House of Lords, in *Blyth v Blyth*,[215] the tide had begun to turn. Lord Denning held that both the grounds for and the bars to divorce may be proved on a preponderance of probability. His Lordship disapproved *Ginesi v Ginesi*, preferring *Wright v Wright*,[216] a decision of the High Court of Australia in the same year, and relied upon his own dicta in *Bater v Bater*[217] and the decision in *Hornal v Neuberger Products Ltd*.[218] In *Bastable v Bastable and Sanders*[219] Wilmer LJ, openly expressing the difficulties of determining what standard of proof should be applied in relation to proof of adultery,[220] adopted the dicta of Lord Denning in *Bater v Bater*, which were approved in *Hornal v Neuberger Products Ltd*, that the court requires a degree of probability proportionate to the subject matter.

Bastable v Bastable, it is submitted, is a decision which accords with the spirit of the then un-enacted Divorce Reform Act 1969,[221] which abolished the old grounds for divorce, largely based on the concept of the matrimonial offence, replacing them with one ground, that the marriage has irretrievably broken down, established if the petitioner 'satisfies' the court of one of five facts. The fact that the ecclesiastical courts regarded adultery as a quasi-criminal offence is, under the present philosophy of divorce law, not a convincing reason for the application of the criminal standard of proof, especially now that the civil standard of proof is held to be appropriate in civil cases in which allegations of crime are made. The matter may be one of statutory construction under the current legislation. The same word 'satisfied' was used in the legislation prior to the Divorce Reform Act 1969 under which the above

---

[209] [1948] P 179, CA.

[210] See also *Bater v Bater* [1951] P 35, CA. However, cf *Briginshaw v Briginshaw* (1938) 60 CLR 336, a decision of the High Court of Australia favouring proof to the civil standard.

[211] [1951] AC 391.

[212] See also *Galler v Galler* [1954] P 252.

[213] See now Family Law Reform Act 1969, s 26, but see also *Serio v Serio* (1983) 13 Fam Law 255, CA (see n 233).

[214] See particularly the speech of Lord Simonds. See also *F v F* [1968] P 506.

[215] [1966] AC 643.

[216] (1948) 77 CLR 191.

[217] [1951] P 35, CA at 37.

[218] [1957] 1 QB 247.

[219] [1968] 1 WLR 1684, CA.

[220] [1968] WLR 1684, CA at 1685.

[221] See now the Matrimonial Causes Act 1973.

decisions were decided. However, it is inconceivable that the criminal standard would ever be re-imposed by way of statutory construction or because of the importance of divorce to the parties and to the state.

Miscellaneous

On various different issues arising in civil cases it has been suggested either (a) that the appropriate standard is higher than the ordinary civil standard (sometimes as high as the criminal standard) or, in any event, (b) that the more improbable the event being alleged, the stronger the evidence required to prove it (on a balance of probabilities). The following examples may be given.

1. A party desiring to prove an intention to change domicile must do so 'clearly and unequivocally'.[222]

2. There is a strong common law presumption that a marriage ceremony celebrated between persons who intended it to constitute a valid marriage is formally valid. Evidence in rebuttal is required to be 'strong, distinct, and satisfactory'[223] or 'evidence which satisfied beyond reasonable doubt that there was no valid marriage'.[224]

3. A party claiming rectification is required to prove his case by 'strong irrefragable evidence'.[225]

4. In cases involving the care of children, the standard is the ordinary civil standard but it had been held that the more serious or improbable an allegation of abuse, the stronger the evidence required to prove both the abuse[226] and the identity of the abuser.[227] However, following *Re B (children) (sexual abuse: standard of proof)*,[228] it is settled law that the standard is the simple balance of probabilities and that the seriousness and probability of an allegation are simply factors to be taken into account when determining where the truth lies.[229]

5. The standard required to make a finding of paternity is a heavy one, commensurate with the gravity of the issue, and although not as heavy as in criminal proceedings, more than the ordinary civil standard of balance of probabilities.[230]

---

[222] *Moorhouse v Lord* (1863) 10 HL Cas 272 at 286. See also *Fuld's Estate (No 3)* [1968] P 675 at 685.

[223] *Piers v Piers* (1849) 2 HL Cas 331 at 389.

[224] *Mahadervan v Mahadervan* [1964] P 233 at 246.

[225] *Countess of Shelburne v Earl of Inchiquin* (1784) 1 Bro CC 338 at 341. See also *Earl v Hector Whaling Ltd* [1961] 1 Lloyd's Rep 459, CA.

[226] See *Re H (Minors) (Sexual Abuse: Standard of Proof)* [1996] AC 563, HL and *Re U (A Child) (Serious Injury: Standard of Proof)* [2005] Fam 134, CA. See also Smith, 'Sexual Abuse: Standard of Proof' [1994] Fam Law 626 and Spencer, 'Evidence in child abuse cases—too high a price for too high a standard?' (1994) 6 JCL 160. Where proceedings involve findings of fact, Art 6 is engaged: see *Re W (Children) (Family Proceedings: Evidence)* [2010] 1 WLR 701, SC and *Re E (A Child) (Family Proceedings: Evidence)* [2016] 4 WLR 105, CA.

[227] *Re G (A Child) (Non-Accidental Injury: Standard of Proof)* [2001] 1 FCR 97, CA. See also *Re M (Children)* [2008] EWCA Civ 1216.

[228] [2009] 1 AC 11, HL.

[229] Per Lord Hoffmann at [70]–[73]. There is no necessary connection between seriousness and probability, as a serious allegation can be more or less probable according to other evidence. It could be rare for a person to harm a child he is looking after, but it ceases to be improbable if other evidence shows that the child sustained injuries at a time when being looked after.

[230] *W v K* [1988] Fam Law 64. See also *Serio v Serio* (1983) 13 Fam Law 255, divorce proceedings in which the paternity of the wife's son was in dispute. The Court of Appeal held that notwithstanding the Family Law Reform Act 1969, s 26, the standard on an issue of paternity is slightly higher than the balance of probabilities.

6. For a court to approve medical treatment for an incompetent mentally ill patient without infringing Art 3 of the European Convention on Human Rights, it must be 'convincingly shown' that the proposed treatment is medically necessary, a standard that may be met notwithstanding that there is a responsible body of opinion against the proposed treatment.[231]

7. Cogent evidence is in practice required to satisfy a mental health review tribunal, on the balance of probabilities, that the conditions for continuing detention under ss 72 and 73 of the Mental Health Act 1983 have been met.[232]

8. The gravity of civil recovery proceedings under Pt V of the Proceeds of Crime Act 2002 is 'very great indeed' and evidence that the property sought to be recovered is or represents property obtained through unlawful conduct must satisfy the court to a standard that is commensurate with the gravity of the case.[233]

As to the example at paragraph 4 (cases involving child sexual abuse), in *Re B(Children)(Sexual Abuse: Standard of Proof)*,[234] Baroness Hale went so far as to '. . . announce loud and clear that the standard of proof. . . is the simple balance of probabilities, no more no less.'[235] It is submitted that all the examples above now need to be seen in the light of both *Re B (Children) (Sexual Abuse: Standard of Proof)* and the dictum of Baroness Hale in *Braganza v BP Shipping*.[236]

That dictum, it will be recalled, is to the effect that in respect of all civil cases there is no sliding scale of probability according to how serious the subject matter or how serious the consequences of the decision; there is only one civil standard of proof which applies, which is the balance of probabilities.[237]

Discharging the evidential burden

Whether a party to civil or criminal proceedings has discharged an evidential burden borne by him in relation to a particular issue is, as we have seen, decided by the judge as opposed to the tribunal of fact. This may account for the dearth of authority on the standard required to discharge the evidential burden. In criminal cases, the standard required to discharge the evidential burden depends upon whether it is borne by the prosecution or defence. We have seen that in criminal trials either party bearing an evidential burden must adduce sufficient evidence to prevent the judge from withdrawing the issue in question from the jury, and this is done when there is sufficient evidence to justify as a possibility a favourable finding by the tribunal of fact. Where the evidential burden is borne by the prosecution, it is discharged by

---

[231] *R (N) v Dr M* [2003] 1 WLR 562, CA.

[232] *R (on the application of N) v Mental Health Review Tribunal* [2006] QB 468, CA.

[233] Per Tugendhat J in *The Assets Recovery Agency v Virtosu* [2009] 1 WLR 2808 at [18]. See also the Proceeds of Crime Act 2002, s 241(3). See also *Gale v Serious Organised Crime Agency* [2011] 1 WLR 2760, SC: although such proceedings involve proof of unlawful conduct, they do not involve the bringing of criminal charges and do not engage Art 6(2) of the European Convention on Human Rights. Accordingly, there is no entitlement to the presumption of innocence and it is correct to apply the civil and not the criminal standard.

[234] [2009] 1 AC 11, HL.

[235] Ibid, at [70].

[236] [2015] 1 WLR 1661, SC.

[237] See earlier in this Chapter under **The standard where there are allegations of crime in civil proceedings**, p 89.

the adduction of 'such evidence as, if believed and if left uncontradicted and unexplained, could be accepted by the jury as proof'.[238] This means that the prosecution must adduce sufficient evidence to justify as a possibility a finding by the tribunal of fact that the legal burden on the same issue has been discharged, discharge of the legal burden, of course, requiring proof such that the jury is sure. However, where the evidential burden is borne by the accused, it is discharged by such evidence as 'might leave a jury in reasonable doubt'.[239] This standard applies only where the defence bear the evidential but not the legal burden on a particular issue, as when the defence is one of self-defence or duress. Where the defence bear both the legal and evidential burden in relation to an issue, as when the defence is one of insanity or diminished responsibility, the evidential burden is discharged by such evidence as *might* satisfy the jury of the probability of that which the accused is called upon to establish.[240] In civil cases, whichever party bears the evidential burden on a particular issue, it is discharged by sufficient evidence to justify as a possibility a finding by the tribunal of fact that the legal burden on the same issue has been discharged, discharge of the legal burden requiring proof on a balance of probabilities.

The burden and standard of proof in a trial within a trial

Preliminary facts are those facts which must be proved as a condition precedent to the admissibility of certain items of evidence. It is for the judge alone, if necessary in a trial within a trial, to determine whether preliminary facts have been proved. The burden of proving such facts is borne by the party who alleges their existence and who seeks to admit the evidence in question.[241] On the question whether a witness is competent to give evidence in criminal proceedings, it is for the party calling the witness to satisfy the court on a balance of probabilities that the witness is competent.[242] Where the prosecution bear the burden of proving preliminary facts, the standard of proof required to discharge the burden is proof beyond reasonable doubt.[243] It would seem to follow that where the burden under discussion is borne by the defendant in criminal proceedings, or by either party to civil proceedings, the appropriate standard is proof on a balance of probabilities.[244] In *R v Ewing*[245] the Court of

---

[238] Per Lord Devlin in *Jayasena v R* [1970] AC 618 at 624.

[239] Per Lord Morris in *Bratty v A-G for Northern Ireland* [1963] AC 386, HL at 419.

[240] See per Humphreys J in *R v Carr-Briant* [1943] KB 607 at 612.

[241] See at common law, *R v Jenkins* (1869) LR 1 CCR 187 (a dying declaration) and now under the Criminal Justice Act 2003, ss 116 (hearsay statements of an unavailable witness) and 118(1)(4) (hearsay statements by a person emotionally overpowered by an event). See also the Police and Criminal Evidence Act 1984, s 76(2) (disputed confessions). See generally Pattenden, 'Authenticating "Things" in English Law: Principles for Adducing Tangible Evidence in Common Law Jury Trials' (2008) 12 E&P 273, especially at 281 and, further, Pattenden, 'The Proof Rules of Pre-verdict Judicial Fact-Finding in Criminal Trials by Jury' [2009] 125 LQR 79. For an example of a preliminary issue in civil proceedings, see *Morris v Davies* [2011] EWHC 1773 (Ch) (domicile of the deceased in the administration of an estate).

[242] Youth Justice and Criminal Evidence Act 1999, s 54(2).

[243] See, at common law, *R v Sartori* [1961] Crim LR 397 in relation to confessions; *R v Jenkins* (1869) LR 1 CCR 187 in relation to dying declarations; and generally *R v Ewing* [1983] 3 WLR 1, CA. By contrast, in Australia, New Zealand, and Canada, the civil standard has been held to apply: see *Wendo v R* (1963) 109 CLR 559; *R v Donohoe* [1963] SRNSW 38; *Police v Anderson* [1972] NZLR 233; and *R v Lee* (1953) 104 CCC 400.

[244] See, in the case of a defence application under the Criminal Justice Act 1988, s 23, *R v Mattey and Queeley* [1995] 2 Cr App R 409, CA.

[245] [1983] 3 WLR 1, CA.

Appeal considered what standard of proof was appropriate to the question whether samples of handwriting, allegedly written by the accused, were 'genuine' for the purposes of s 8 of the Criminal Procedure Act 1865. That section provides as follows:

> Comparison of a disputed writing with any writing proved to the satisfaction of the judge to be genuine shall be permitted to be made by witnesses; and such writings, and the evidence of witnesses respecting the same, may be submitted to the court and jury as evidence of the genuineness or otherwise of the writing in dispute.

In the earlier decision of *R v Angeli*,[246] the Court of Appeal, on the basis that the 1865 Act applied to the criminal courts a provision which had already been in operation in the civil courts, held that the standard of proof under the section, whether applied in criminal or civil proceedings, was the civil one, on the balance of probabilities. In *R v Ewing* the Court of Appeal held that *R v Angeli* was decided *per incuriam* and that when the section is applied in civil cases, the civil standard of proof is used, and when it is applied in criminal cases, the criminal standard should be used.

There are cases similar to, but quite distinct from, those discussed in which the judge, before allowing particular issues to go before the jury, must be satisfied of certain matters by prima facie evidence. For example, if the prosecution seek to admit a confession allegedly made by the accused, the defence case being that the confession was never made, the judge must be satisfied by prima facie evidence that the accused did make the confession.[247] Likewise, if the prosecution seek to adduce an audio recording in evidence, the judge must be satisfied that the prosecution have made out a prima facie case of originality and genuineness by evidence which defines and describes the provenance and history of the recording up to the moment of its production in court.[248] In *R v Robson, R v Harris*[249] it was held that in these circumstances the judge is required to be satisfied to the civil standard, on a balance of probabilities, because application of the higher criminal standard of proof would amount to a usurpation by the judge of the function of the jury. If the judge satisfies himself that the evidence is competent to be considered by the jury and should not be withdrawn from them, the very same issues of originality and genuineness may then fall to be considered by them. The standard of proof is then the criminal standard. It has been convincingly argued, however, that a better approach, also involving no usurpation of the function of the jury, would be for the judge to decide the issue in exactly the same way as he is required to decide whether an evidential burden has been discharged.[250] In other words, the judge should not be required to be satisfied on a balance of probabilities; the test should be whether the party seeking to put the evidence before the jury has adduced sufficient evidence on the facts in issue to justify, as a possibility, a finding by the jury on those facts in that party's favour.

---

[246] [1979] 1 WLR 26, CA.

[247] See, further, *Ajodha v The State* [1981] 2 All ER 193, PC (see Ch 15).

[248] See *R v Rampling* [1987] Crim LR 823, CA for general guidance given by the Court of Appeal upon the use in trials of tape recordings and transcripts of police interviews. See also *R v Emmerson* (1990) 92 Cr App R 284, CA; *R v Riaz* (1991) 94 Cr App R 339, CA; and *R v Tonge* [1993] Crim LR 876, CA (all in Ch 5); the Code of Practice on Audio Recording of Interviews with Suspects, Code E; Criminal Practice Directions,V, 16C; and Baldwin and Bedward, 'Summarising Tape Recordings of Police Interviews' [1991] Crim LR 671.

[249] [1972] 1 WLR 651, CA. Cf *R v Stevenson* [1971] 1 WLR 1.

[250] *Cross & Tapper on Evidence* (12th edn, London, 2010) 184.

ADDITIONAL READING

Dennis, 'Reverse Onuses and the Presumption of Innocence: In Search of Principle' [2005] Crim LR 901.
  An article which reviews issues arising from the placing of burdens of proof on the accused. Particular consideration is given to the issue of the compatibility of reverse burdens with the presumption of innocence in the European Convention on Human Rights. It is argued that the application of the criteria of compatibility is uncertain and inconsistent and that general principles are needed to structure and guide decision-making. A number of principles are identified and discussed. The article concludes by suggesting a three-stage process is followed in making decisions on the issue of the compatibility of reverse burdens with the European Convention.

Harmer, 'The Presumption of Innocence and Reverse Burdens: A Balancing Act' (2007) 66(1) CLJ 142.
  An examination of the case law concerning the compatibility of reverse burdens and Art 6(2). The article sets out to identify the pertinent facts and circumstances from the cases and place them within an integrated framework in order to make more predictable decisions on the compatibility of reverse burdens with Art 6(2).

Keane and McKeown, 'Time to abandon "beyond reasonable doubt" and "sure": the case for a new direction on the criminal standard and how it should be used', [2019] Crim LR 505.
  An article which critically analyses 'beyond reasonable doubt' and 'sure' as descriptions of the criminal standard of proof. The argument is made that the descriptions are not fit for purpose and should be replaced by a more accurate description of 'no realistic doubt'. A new direction is proposed which includes guidance to the jury on how to use the criminal standard when reaching their verdict.

Lippke, 'Justifying the proof structure of criminal trials' (2013) 17(4) E&P 323.
  An examination of justifications for the 'proof structure' in criminal trials whereby the state bears the burden to prove and accused are presumed innocent. Error distribution rationale is considered (ie establishing an optimal ratio of false convictions to false acquittals) as is the individual's right to demand rigorous, independent evaluations of the evidence against him before legal punishment can be imposed. The argument is made against alternative proof structures premised upon making it easier for the state to amass convictions of the guilty.

Mirfield, 'How Many Standards of Proof Are There?' (2009) 125 LQR 31.
  An article which considers the civil standard of proof in the light of the decisions in *Re B (Children) (Care Proceedings: Standard of Proof)* [2009] 1 AC 61, HL and *Re D* [2008] 1 WLR 1499, HL.

QUESTIONS

1. Referring to the relevant case law, critically analyse the test for deciding whether a statutory provision placing a legal burden on the accused is incompatible with Article 6(2) of the European Convention on Human Rights.

2. Referring to the relevant case law, critically analyse what is meant by saying that although there is only one single standard of proof in civil cases, it is flexible in its application.

3. Jim is charged with murdering Asif by stabbing him. He gives oral evidence at trial that he and Asif had an altercation in a car park. Asif suddenly produced a knife and tried to stab him. A fight developed, during which he managed to take the knife from Asif and use it to defend himself. He also says that during the fight his mind went blank and he felt he was 'losing it a bit'.

   Identify and explain the issues in relation to the burden and standard of proof that will arise during the trial. By reference to the evidential burden which applies, might Jim be able to rely on the defence of loss of control?

4. Summerton local authority apply for a care order to remove Mille, aged 5, from her family home where she lives with her parents. The authority believe that she is at serious risk of harm because her brother Archie, aged 8, was recently found dead in his bedroom. Archie had bruises to his arms and legs and a mark on his neck which appeared to be from a ligature. The local authority say Archie's death was non-accidental and likely to be at the hands of the parents. The parents oppose the application, strenuously denying that they had anything to do with Archie's death. They say that his death was likely to have been a terrible accident, pointing out that a cord from a blind in his bedroom may have been caught around his neck or that he may have deliberately put the cord around his neck. They also point out that he was a troubled child who often self-harmed.

   The judge refuses the local authority's application. In giving judgment, she says that it was difficult to make findings of fact on the evidence, so that she must resort to the burden and standard of proof. She states that the local authority had not satisfied the appropriate standard of proof. In respect of Archie's death, she rules that the likelihood of accident could be estimated at 45 per cent and the possibility of suicide or self-harm at 10 per cent. She also observed that because the application involved a very serious allegation, a higher standard of proof was appropriate.

Critically discuss the judge's decision.

 For a note-form answer see the online resources, accessible at www.oup.com/he/keane-mckeown13e.

Proof of facts without evidence   **4**

Key issues

- When, and why, should facts in issue be presumed, in the absence of evidence in rebuttal (rebuttable presumptions of law)?

- When, and why, should a fact be treated as established and not open to any evidence in rebuttal (judicial notice)?

- When, and why, should a party admit a fact in issue so that it ceases to be in issue and therefore evidence of it is neither required nor admissible (formal admissions)?

Facts in issue and relevant facts are treated as established by the courts only insofar as they are proved by evidence. There are three exceptions to this general rule: (i) certain facts may be presumed in a party's favour in the absence of proof or complete proof (presumptions); (ii) no evidence is required to establish facts that are judicially noticed; and, similarly, (iii) no evidence is required to establish facts which are formally admitted.

Presumptions

Definitions and classification

Where a presumption operates, a certain conclusion may or must be drawn by the court in the absence of evidence in rebuttal. The effect of this is to assist a party bearing a burden of proof, the degree of assistance varying from presumption to presumption. In some cases, the proof required to establish the fact in question may be less than it otherwise would have been. In other cases, no proof may be required at all or the other party may be barred from adducing any evidence in rebuttal. Presumptions are based on considerations of common sense and public policy. Certain facts or combinations of fact can give rise to inferences which justify legal rules that in such circumstances a conclusion may or must be drawn. For example, if, after an operation, a swab is found to have been left in a patient's body, it seems reasonable to infer, in the absence of explanation by the surgeon, that the accident arose through his negligence.[1] If a surgeon uses proper care, such an accident does not, in the ordinary course of things, occur; negligence may be presumed. However, presumptions are not necessarily logical; there is another presumption that a person is dead if he has not been heard of for over seven years. There is no logic in the choice of 2,556 days' absence for these purposes as opposed to say 2,560 days' absence.[2]

The law of presumptions is as beset with the problems of terminology and classification as the subjects of burden and standard of proof with which it is closely interrelated.[3] A useful starting point is a conventional classification into rebuttable presumptions of law (*praesumptiones iuris sed non de iure*), irrebuttable presumptions of law (*praesumptiones iuris et de iure*), and presumptions of fact (*praesumptiones hominis*). Consideration of the first of these categories is the principal focus of this chapter. The second comprises rules of substantive law expressed as presumptions. The third consists of a number of examples of circumstantial evidence, also expressed as presumptions. A further category, presumptions without basic facts, comprises a number of rules relating to the incidence of the burden of proof. In the ensuing analysis of these four categories, reference will be made, by way of example, to the more important of the common law and statutory presumptions, some of which are considered in greater depth later in this chapter. There are numerous common law, equitable, and statutory presumptions throughout English law. This chapter deals with the most important of them, comprehensive treatment being beyond its scope.[4]

---

[1] See *Mahon v Osborne* [1939] 2 KB 14, CA.

[2] See per Sachs J in *Chard v Chard* [1956] P 259 at 272.

[3] The law of presumptions cannot be understood without an understanding of the legal burden, the evidential burden, the provisional or tactical burden, and the standards of proof, all of which are considered in Ch 3.

[4] The statutory presumptions arising under ss 11 and 12 of the Civil Evidence Act 1968 and s 74 of the Police and Criminal Evidence Act 1984 are considered in Ch 23 and certain presumptions relating to the due execution of documents are considered in Ch 10.

Rebuttable presumptions of law

How they operate

Where a rebuttable presumption of law applies, on the proof or admission of a fact, referred to as a primary or basic fact, and in the absence of further evidence, another fact, referred to as a presumed fact, must be presumed. The party relying on the presumption bears the burden of establishing the basic fact. Once he has adduced sufficient evidence on that fact, his adversary bears the legal burden of disproving the presumed fact or, as the case may be, an evidential burden to adduce some evidence to rebut the presumed fact. The standard of proof to be met by the party seeking to rebut the presumed fact varies according to the presumption in question.[5] For example, there is a rebuttable presumption of law that a child proved or admitted to have been born or conceived during lawful wedlock (the basic facts) is legitimate (the presumed fact). A party seeking to rebut the presumed fact by evidence of, say, the husband's impotence, is, in civil proceedings, required to meet the ordinary civil standard of proof on a balance of probabilities.[6] Other examples to be considered in detail in this chapter are the presumptions of marriage, death, and, in testamentary cases, sanity, and the maxims *omnia praesumuntur rite esse acta* and *res ipsa loquitur*, the last-mentioned arguably being a presumption of fact.

Where a rebuttable presumption of law places a legal burden on the party against whom it operates, as does, for example, the presumption of legitimacy, it may be referred to as a 'persuasive' or 'compelling' presumption.[7] In such a case, the legal burden of disproving the presumed fact is on the party against whom the presumption operates. Where a rebuttable presumption of law operates to place an evidential burden on that party, as does, for example, the presumption of death, it may be referred to as an 'evidential' presumption.[8] In such a case, the legal burden of proving the presumed fact is borne by the party in whose favour the presumption operates. If he adduces prima facie evidence of the basic facts, an evidential burden is placed on his adversary. The adversary may discharge this burden in the usual way and, if he does so, the effect will be as if the presumption had never come into play at all; the party bearing the legal burden of proof must satisfy the tribunal of fact to the required standard of proof in the usual way.

Criminal proceedings

The terminology of 'persuasive' and 'evidential' presumptions is appropriate only in civil proceedings. Subject to express or implied statutory exceptions and cases in which the accused raises the defence of insanity, in criminal proceedings the prosecution bears the legal burden of proving all facts essential to their case. It follows from this general rule that where a common law presumption operates in favour of the accused, the prosecution will always bear a *legal* burden (requiring them to disprove the presumed fact beyond reasonable doubt).[9] Likewise, although there are a number of statutory presumptions which operate to place on the accused a legal burden of proof (which may be discharged by the adduction of

---

[5] Unfortunately, as we shall see, the authorities are often in conflict as to the amount of evidence required to rebut certain presumptions.

[6] Section 26 of the Family Law Reform Act 1969, considered in this chapter, under **Presumptions, The presumption of legitimacy**.

[7] See Denning, 'Presumptions and Burdens' (1945) 61 LQR 380.

[8] See Glanville Williams, *Criminal Law (The General Part)* (2nd edn, London, 1961) 877 ff.

[9] See *R v Willshire* (1881) 6 QBD 366, in this chapter, under **Conflicting presumptions**, p 116, and *R v Kay* (1887) 16 Cox CC 292, both relating to the presumption of marriage.

such evidence as might satisfy the jury on a balance of probabilities),[10] where a common law presumption operates in favour of the prosecution, the accused will never bear more than an *evidential* burden (which may be discharged by the adduction of such evidence as might leave a jury in reasonable doubt).

Irrebuttable presumptions of law

Where an irrebuttable presumption of law, sometimes referred to as a 'conclusive presumption', applies, on the proof or admission of a basic fact, another fact must be presumed. The party against whom the presumption operates is barred from adducing any evidence in rebuttal. Such presumptions amount to no more than rules of substantive law expressed, somewhat clumsily, in the language pertaining to presumptions. Indeed, there is no valid reason why the rather cumbersome phrase 'irrebuttable presumption of law' could not be applied to every rule of substantive law. The following examples may be given. Section 50 of the Children and Young Persons Act 1933 provides that: 'It shall be conclusively presumed that no child under the age of ten years can be guilty of an offence.' Under s 76 of the Sexual Offences Act 2003, in certain sexual cases, including cases of rape, if it is proved that the accused did the relevant act (intentional penetration of the vagina, anus, or mouth) and that he intentionally deceived the complainant as to the nature or purpose of the act, or intentionally induced the complainant to consent to it by impersonating a person known personally to the complainant, it is conclusively presumed that the complainant did not consent to the act and that the accused did not believe that the complainant consented to it. This is a convoluted way of saying that one of the ways in which rape may be committed is by intentional penetration and the intentional deceit or inducing of the kinds described (ie irrespective of whether the complainant consented and what the accused believed in that regard).[11]

Presumptions of fact

Where a presumption of fact applies, on the proof or admission of a basic fact, another fact *may* be presumed in the absence of sufficient evidence to the contrary. Presumptions of fact are sometimes referred to as 'provisional presumptions' to indicate that a party against whom they operate bears a provisional or tactical burden in relation to the presumed fact. Unlike rebuttable presumptions of law, establishment of the basic fact does not have the effect of placing either an evidential or a legal burden on that party. Thus presumptions of fact amount to nothing more than examples of circumstantial evidence.[12] Certain facts or combinations of facts can give rise to inferences which the tribunal of fact *may* draw, there being no rule of law that such inferences *must* be drawn in the absence of evidence to the contrary. However, presumptions of fact can vary in strength and on the operation of a strong presumption of fact, if no evidence in rebuttal is adduced, a finding by the tribunal of fact against the existence of the presumed fact could, in civil proceedings at any rate, be reversed on appeal. Examples of circumstantial evidence which have recurred so frequently as to attract the label 'presumption of fact' include the presumptions of intention, guilty knowledge (in cases of possession of recently stolen goods), continuance of life, and seaworthiness.[13]

---

[10] For examples, see **Ch 3**.

[11] See also s 13(1) of the Civil Evidence Act 1968 (Ch 23).

[12] See **Chapter 2, Circumstantial evidence, p 14**.

[13] See also *Re W (a minor)* (1992) The Times, 22 May, CA: there is a presumption of fact that a baby's best interests are served by being with the mother, although with *children* the situation might be different.

The presumption of intention

There is a presumption of fact that a man intends the natural consequences of his acts. In criminal proceedings, this presumption was treated as a presumption of fact[14] until the House of Lords in *DPP v Smith*[15] concluded that, in certain circumstances, it constituted a presumption of law. This was reversed by s 8 of the Criminal Justice Act 1967, the effect of which has been to re-establish the presumption as one of fact.[16] The section provides that:

A court or jury, in determining whether a person has committed an offence—

(a) shall not be bound in law to infer that he intended or foresaw a result of his actions by reason only of its being a natural and probable consequence of those actions; but

(b) shall decide whether he did intend or foresee that result by reference to all the evidence, drawing such inferences from the evidence as appear proper in the circumstances.

In civil proceedings it remains unclear whether the presumption of intention is one of fact or law.[17]

The presumption of guilty knowledge

Where an accused is found in possession of goods which have been recently stolen, an explanation is called for and if none is forthcoming the jury are entitled, but not compelled, to infer guilty knowledge or belief and to find the accused guilty of handling stolen goods. Where an explanation is given which the jury are convinced is untrue, likewise the jury are entitled to convict. However, if the explanation given leaves the jury in doubt as to whether the accused knew or believed the goods to be stolen, the prosecution have not proved their case and the jury should acquit.[18] An inference should not be drawn under the presumption unless it is fair to do so in all the circumstances of the case.[19] Generally, the jury should be directed that the burden of proof remains on the prosecution and that if the accused's explanation leaves them in doubt about whether the accused came by the property honestly, they should acquit.[20] The presumption may operate to the same effect in the case of theft.[21]

---

[14] See *R v Steane* [1947] KB 997 and per Lord Sankey in *Woolmington v DPP* [1935] AC 462 at 481.

[15] [1961] AC 290.

[16] See *R v Wallett* [1968] 2 QB 367, CA; *R v Moloney* [1985] AC 905, HL.

[17] See *Kaslefsky v Kaslefsky* [1951] P 38, CA; *Jamieson v Jamieson* [1952] AC 525, HL; *Lang v Lang* [1955] AC 402, PC; *Gollins v Gollins* [1964] AC 644, HL; and *Williams v Williams* [1964] AC 698, HL.

[18] See *R v Schama and Abramovitch* (1914) 11 Cr App R 45; *R v Garth* [1949] 1 All ER 773, CCA; *R v Aves* [1950] 2 All ER 330, CCA; and *R v Hepworth and Fearnley* [1955] 2 QB 600, CCA.

[19] *AB v Crown Prosecution Service* [2017] EWHC 2963 at [27].

[20] See *R v Moulding* [1996] Crim LR 440; *R v Hepworth* [1955] 2 QB 600; *R v Aubrey* (1916) 11 Cr App R 182; *R v Brain* (1919) 13 Cr App R 197; *R v Sanders* (1920) 14 Cr App R 11.

[21] In a case of handling, the prosecution are not obliged to adduce evidence that the goods were handled 'otherwise than in the course of the stealing' (see s 22(1) of the Theft Act 1968): the inference that in the proper case the jury are entitled to draw, namely that an accused was the guilty handler, includes the inference that he was not the thief. However, if the accused is in possession of property so recently after it was stolen that the inevitable inference is that he was the thief, as when he is found within a few hundred yards of the scene of the theft and within minutes after it took place, then if the charge is handling only, the jury should be directed that if they take the view that the accused was the thief, they should acquit him of the handling: *R v Cash* [1985] QB 801, CA, applied in *A-G of Hong Kong v Yip Kai-foon* [1988] 1 All ER 153, PC. See also *Ryan and French v DPP* [1994] Crim LR 457, CA.

The presumption of continuance of life

Where a person is proved to have been alive on a certain date, an inference may be drawn, in the absence of sufficient evidence to the contrary, that he was alive on a subsequent date.[22] The strength of this presumption depends entirely upon the facts of the case in question. In *R v Lumley*,[23] on a woman's trial for bigamy, a question arose as to whether her husband was alive at the date of the second marriage. Lush J said:[24]

> This is purely a question of fact. The existence of a party at an antecedent date may, or may not, afford a reasonable inference that he is living at the subsequent date. If, for example, it was proved that he was in good health on the day preceding the marriage, the inference would be strong, almost irresistible, that he was living on the latter day, and the jury would in all probability find that he was so. If, on the other hand, it were proved that he was then in a dying condition, and nothing further was proved, they would probably decline to draw that inference. Thus, the question is entirely for the jury.

The presumption of seaworthiness

Where a ship sinks or becomes unable to continue her voyage shortly after putting to sea, an inference may be drawn, in the absence of sufficient evidence to the contrary, that she was unseaworthy on leaving port. If, in these circumstances, a tribunal of fact were to find the contrary, it would be such a finding against the reasonable inference to be drawn that it would amount to a verdict against the evidence.[25]

Presumptions without basic facts

All of the presumptions so far defined may be explained in terms of a basic fact on the proof or admission of which another fact may or must be presumed. 'Presumptions without basic facts' come into operation without the proof or admission of any basic fact; they are merely conclusions which must be drawn in the absence of evidence in rebuttal. In other words, they are rules relating to the incidence of the legal and evidential burdens expressed in the language pertaining to presumptions. The following examples may be given. In criminal proceedings, reference is often made to the presumptions of innocence and sanity. Both are more meaningfully expressed in terms of the incidence of the burden of proof. The presumption of innocence is a convenient abbreviation of the rule that the prosecution bear the legal burden of proving any fact essential to their case.[26] Likewise, the presumption of sanity refers to the rule that the accused bears the legal burden of proving insanity when he raises it as a defence.[27] In *Bratty v A-G for Northern Ireland* two members of the House of Lords referred to 'the presumption of mental capacity'.[28] The reference was to the rule that the evidential burden in relation to the defence of non-insane automatism is borne by the accused.

---

[22] See *McDarmaid v A-G* [1950] P 218; *Re Peete, Peete v Crompton* [1952] 2 All ER 599; and *Chard v Chard* [1956] P 259.

[23] (1869) LR 1 CCR 196.

[24] Ibid at 198. See also per Denman CJ in *R v Harborne Inhabitants* (1835) 2 Ad&El 540 at 544–5.

[25] See per Brett LJ in *Pickup v Thames & Mersey Marine Insurance Co Ltd* (1878) 3 QBD 594, CA at 600. See also *Anderson v Morice* (1875) LR 10 CP 609 and *Ajum Goolam Hossen & Co v Union Marine Insurance Co* [1901] AC 362, PC.

[26] *Woolmington v DPP* [1935] AC 462. The presumption of innocence also applies when an allegation of criminal conduct is made in civil proceedings: see *Williams v East India Co* (1802) 3 East 192. Concerning the standard of proof to be met in these circumstances, see *Hornal v Neuberger Products Ltd* [1957] 1 QB 247, CA, in Ch 3.

[27] *M'Naghten's Case* (1843) 10 Cl&Fin 200. In testamentary cases, the presumption of sanity is not a presumption without basic facts but a rebuttable presumption of law: see, in this chapter, under **The presumption of sanity in testamentary cases**, p 114.

[28] [1963] AC 386 per Viscount Kilmuir LC at 407 and per Lord Denning at 413.

A final example of a presumption without basic facts is the presumption that mechanical instruments of a kind that are usually in working order, were in working order at the time when they were used. This conclusion will be drawn by the court in the absence of evidence to the contrary, the party seeking to rebut the presumption bearing an evidential burden. The presumption has been applied in the case of speedometers,[29] traffic lights,[30] breath-test machines,[31] and public weighbridges.[32] The presumption, it is submitted, also applies in the case of computers, with the consequence that a party introducing computer-generated evidence need only produce evidence that the computer was working properly at the relevant time if his opponent introduces some evidence to the contrary.

The presumption of marriage

There are three discernible presumptions of marriage: a presumption of formal validity, a presumption of essential validity, and a presumption of marriage arising from cohabitation.

The presumption of formal validity

The formal validity of a marriage depends upon the *lex loci celebrationis* (the law of the land where the marriage is celebrated). A failure to comply with the formal requirements of the local law may make a marriage void. Under English law, a Church of England marriage (otherwise than by special licence) may be void because of irregularities such as failure duly to publish banns or to obtain a common licence. In the case of other marriages under English law, examples include cases of failure to give due notice to the superintendent registrar and cases in which a certificate and, where necessary, a licence have not been duly issued. However, on the proof or admission of the basic facts that a marriage was celebrated between persons who intended to marry, the formal validity of the marriage will be presumed in the absence of sufficient evidence to the contrary. The authorities almost always include among the basic facts the cohabitation of the parties following the ceremony of marriage[33] but the presumption has been held to apply to death-bed marriages,[34] which obviously suggests the opposite.

The leading case relating to an English marriage is *Piers v Piers*.[35] A marriage ceremony had been celebrated between two persons who had shown their intention, at the time, to marry. The ceremony was performed in a private house but there was no evidence that the bishop of the diocese had granted the necessary special licence. The House of Lords held that the marriage was formally valid.[36] An example of the application of the presumption to a foreign marriage is *Mahadervan v Mahadervan*.[37] Rejecting as irrational legal chauvinism an argument that there was no presumption in favour of a foreign marriage the establishment of which would invalidate a subsequent English one, Sir Jocelyn Simon P applied the presumption and held the foreign marriage to be formally valid.

---

[29] *Nicholas v Penny* [1950] 2 KB 466.

[30] *Tingle Jacobs and Co v Kennedy* [1964] 1 All ER 888n, CA.

[31] *Castle v Cross* [1984] 1 WLR 1372, DC.

[32] *Kelly Communications Ltd v DPP* [2003] Crim LR 479 and 875, DC.

[33] See, eg, per Barnard J in *Russell v A-G* [1949] P 391 at 394.

[34] See *The Lauderdale Peerage Case* (1885) 10 App Cas 692, HL and *Hill v Hill* [1959] 1 All ER 281.

[35] (1849) 2 HL Cas 331.

[36] See also *De Thoren v A-G* (1876) 1 App Cas 686, HL; *Re Shephard, George v Thyer* [1904] 1 Ch 456; and *Russell v A-G* [1949] P 391.

[37] [1964] P 233. See also *Spivack v Spivack* (1930) 46 TLR 243 and *Hill v Hill* [1959] 1 WLR 127, PC.

The standard of proof

In civil proceedings, the presumption operates as a persuasive presumption placing a legal burden on the party seeking to rebut formal validity.[38] The standard of proof to be met by that party is high. In *Piers v Piers* Lord Cottenham cited with approval the words of Lord Lyndhurst in *Morris v Davies*:[39] 'The presumption of law is not lightly to be repelled. It is not to be broken in upon or shaken by a mere balance of probabilities. The evidence for the purpose of repelling it must be strong, distinct, satisfactory, and conclusive.'[40] Lord Campbell said:[41] 'a presumption of this sort in favour of marriage can only be negatived by disproving every reasonable possibility'. In *Mahadervan v Mahadervan* Sir Jocelyn Simon P held that the presumption can only be rebutted by evidence which satisfies beyond reasonable doubt that there was no valid marriage.[42] In relation to matrimonial causes more generally, the authorities, although in conflict, tend to favour the ordinary civil standard[43] and it is likely that in future this lower standard will be applied. When Lord Cottenham in *Piers v Piers* adopted the words of Lord Lyndhurst in *Morris v Davies*, an authority on the presumption of legitimacy, the evidence in rebuttal of that presumption was required to meet a high standard of proof. However, the presumption of legitimacy is now rebuttable by evidence which satisfies the ordinary civil standard on a balance of probabilities.[44] It is submitted that the standard of proof to be met by the party seeking to rebut the presumption of marriage should also be the ordinary civil standard.

The presumption of essential validity

A marriage may be void on the grounds that the parties lacked the capacity to marry. Under English law, for example, the parties may lack the capacity to marry if they are related within the prohibited degrees or if either of them is under the age of 16 or already married. However, on the proof or admission of the basic fact that a formally valid marriage was celebrated, the essential validity of the marriage will be presumed in the absence of sufficient evidence to the contrary. In the words of Pilcher J in *Tweney v Tweney*,[45] 'The petitioner's marriage to the present respondent being unexceptionable in form and duly consummated remains a good marriage until some evidence is adduced that the marriage was, in fact, a nullity.' Although the matter is far from clear, in civil proceedings the presumption would appear to operate as a persuasive rather than evidential presumption, placing a legal burden on the party seeking to rebut it.[46]

The standard of proof

The standard of proof required to rebut the presumption of essential validity is lower than that suggested by some of the authorities in the case of the presumption of formal validity. In

---

[38] In criminal cases where the prosecution bear the legal burden of proving the validity of the marriage, the presumption operates to place an evidential burden on the accused: see *R v Kay* (1887) 16 Cox CC 292.

[39] (1837) 5 Cl&Fin 163 at 265.

[40] The word 'conclusive' hardly seems apposite and its use has been criticized: see Harman LJ in *Re Taylor* [1961] 1 WLR 9, CA.

[41] (1849) 2 HL Cas 331 at 380.

[42] [1964] P 233 at 246.

[43] *Blyth v Blyth* [1966] AC 643 and *Bastable v Bastable and Sanders* [1968] 1 WLR 1684.

[44] See s 26 of the Family Law Reform Act 1969, in this chapter, under **The presumption of legitimacy**, p 107.

[45] [1946] P 180 at 182.

[46] Cf *Axon v Axon* (1937) 59 CLR 395, High Court of Australia.

Gatty and Gatty v A-G[47] it was held that evidence of a valid prior marriage sufficed. A similar conclusion was reached in *Re Peete, Peete v Crompton*.[48] A woman, W, made an application under the Inheritance (Family Provision) Act 1938 as the widow of Y. W had separated from her first husband X prior to 1916 and in 1919 went through a formally valid ceremony of marriage with Y. The question arose as to the essential validity of the subsequent marriage. The court held that the application failed. Although a presumption of essential validity arose in relation to the subsequent marriage, there was some evidence before the court, namely the existence of the first marriage, that in 1919 W lacked the capacity to marry Y. However, where the prior marriage is of doubtful validity, there is authority that the presumption is not rebutted.[49]

Subsequent marriages and conflicting presumptions

In most of the cases where the presumption of essential validity has fallen to be applied by the courts, one of the parties to a marriage has been married previously. The question has been whether the earlier marriage had terminated by the time of the subsequent ceremony. This issue may in turn require consideration of the presumption of death, the presumption of continuance of life, or even the presumption of essential validity in relation to the earlier marriage. Two conflicting presumptions[50] applied to the same facts in *Monckton v Tarr*.[51] A, a woman, married B in 1882. B deserted A in 1887. In 1895, at which time there was no evidence that B was alive, A married C. In 1913, at which time A was still alive, C married a woman, D. D made a claim for workmen's compensation as the widow of C. The employers alleged that the 1913 marriage was void because of the 1895 marriage. D replied that the 1895 marriage was void because of the 1882 marriage. D's claim was dismissed by the Court of Appeal. Although a presumption of essential validity arose in relation to the marriage of 1913, the same presumption applied to the marriage of 1895. These two presumptions cancelling each other out, it was for D to prove C's capacity to marry her and this she could only do by showing that B was alive at the date of the 1895 marriage, something which she had failed to do. A different approach was adopted, however, when a similar problem arose in *Taylor v Taylor*.[52] There was some weak evidence that a woman, W, had married X. Subsequently, in 1928, X married another woman, Y. Y left him and in 1942, when X was still alive, married Z. Z petitioned for a decree of nullity alleging that his marriage to Y was void because of the 1928 marriage. Y replied that the marriage of 1928 was void because of the earlier marriage between W and X. It might have been expected, on the reasoning employed in *Monckton v Tarr*, that the court would have held that the presumptions in favour of the 1928 and 1942 marriages effectively cancelling each other out, it was for Y to prove her capacity to marry Z and that she had failed to do this, the weak evidence adduced to show the marriage between W and X being insufficient for the purpose. However, Cairns J held that the marriage of 1942 was valid, expressing a preference for the preservation of existing unions, rather than their avoidance in favour of doubtful earlier and effectively dead ones. The evidence of the earlier

---

[47] [1951] P 444.

[48] [1952] 2 All ER 599, Ch D.

[49] *Taylor v Taylor* [1967] P 25. Cf *Monckton v Tarr* (1930) 23 BWCC 504, CA.

[50] See later in this chapter under **Conflicting presumptions**, p 116.

[51] (1930) 23 BWCC 504, CA.

[52] [1967] P 25.

marriage of doubtful validity, that is the marriage of 1928, was not sufficient to rebut the presumption of essential validity in relation to the marriage of 1942.[53]

The presumption of marriage arising from cohabitation

On the proof or admission of the basic fact that a man and woman have long cohabited as if man and wife and have acquired the reputation of being husband and wife, it is presumed, in the absence of sufficient evidence to the contrary, that they were living together in consequence of a valid marriage.[54] The authorities suggest that in civil proceedings this presumption operates as a persuasive presumption.[55] Evidence in rebuttal is required to meet a high standard of proof: it must be 'clear and firm'[56] or 'of the most cogent kind'.[57] In *Sastry Velaider Aronegary v Sembecutty Vaigalie*[58] the issue concerned the validity of a marriage ceremony which had taken place between Tamils in Ceylon. The Privy Council was of the opinion that the party in whose favour the presumption operated was under no obligation to prove that the ceremony had complied with the requisite customs. Accordingly, the parties were held to be validly married. Although in that case evidence was given that a ceremony had taken place, it is clear that the presumption may apply in the absence of such evidence.[59] In *Al-Saedy v Musawi*[60] it was held that a party will succeed in rebutting the presumption if he can identify the only known ceremony or event which might have constituted a marriage and can show that it did not have that effect in English law.

The presumption of legitimacy

On the proof or admission of the basic fact that a child was born or conceived during lawful wedlock, it is presumed, in the absence of sufficient evidence to the contrary, that the child is legitimate. A person's legitimacy may be challenged notwithstanding that he is dead and that there has been delay, by the party seeking to rebut the presumption, in the pursuit of his claim.[61] The presumption may be rebutted by evidence showing that the husband and wife did not have sexual intercourse as a result of which the child was conceived.[62] The evidence

---

[53] Cf, in this respect, the available evidence in rebuttal in *Re Peete, Peete v Crompton* [1952] 2 All ER 599, in text at n 48 in this chapter.

[54] In cases where, pursuant to local law, a valid marriage may come into existence by the consent of the parties without a formal ceremony, such consent is presumed: see *Breadalbane Case, Campbell v Campbell* (1867) LR 1 Sc&Div 182.

[55] In criminal proceedings where the prosecution rely on this presumption, the authorities suggest that the presumption, by itself, is insufficient to discharge the evidential burden: see *Morris v Miller* (1767) 4 Burr 2057 and *R v Umanski* [1961] VLR 242. Proof or admission of cohabitation supported by the production of a marriage certificate does suffice for these purposes: *R v Birtles* (1911) 6 Cr App R 177.

[56] *Re Taylor* [1961] 1 WLR 9, CA.

[57] *Re Taplin, Watson v Tate* [1937] 3 All ER 105, Ch D. Some cases suggest an extremely high standard of proof: see, eg, *Re Shephard, George v Thyer* [1904] 1 Ch 456.

[58] (1881) 6 App Cas 364, PC.

[59] *Re Taplin, Watson v Tate* [1937] 3 All ER 105. This remains the case even if the period of cohabitation was short: see *Re Taylor* [1961] 1 WLR 9, CA. Cf *Re Bradshaw, Blandy v Willis* [1938] 4 All ER 143. See also *Breadalbane Case, Campbell v Campbell* (1867) LR 1 Sc&Div 182.

[60] [2010] EWHC 3293 (Fam).

[61] *Re Baronetcy of Pringle of Stichill* [2016] UKPC 16.

[62] See per Sir James Mansfield CJ in the *Banbury Peerage Case* (1811) 1 Sim&St 153. Under s 48(1) of the Matrimonial Causes Act 1973, the evidence of a husband or wife shall be admissible in any proceedings to prove that marital intercourse did or did not take place between them during any period.

in rebuttal may be evidence of: non-access; the husband's impotence;[63] the use of reliable contraceptives; the blood groups of the parties; the results of a DNA test;[64] the minimal nature of the husband's access to the wife; an admission of paternity by another man;[65] the wife's cohabitation with another man for an appropriate period of time before the birth of the child;[66] or the conduct of the wife and illicit partner to the child.[67] Evidence of adultery by the mother will not rebut the presumption in the absence of evidence that at the time of conception sexual intercourse between the husband and wife did not take place.[68]

Either birth or conception during wedlock suffices to give rise to the presumption. Thus where a child is born to a married woman so soon after the marriage ceremony that pre-marital conception is indicated, the presumption applies.[69] Likewise, the presumption applies where a child is born to a woman so soon after the termination of her marriage that conception during the marriage is indicated.[70] In *Re Overbury, Sheppard v Matthews*[71] the presumption was applied in such circumstances notwithstanding the remarriage of the mother prior to the birth of the child. Six months after her first husband's death a woman had remarried, giving birth to a girl two months later. Harman J held that the child was the legitimate daughter of the first husband, there being insufficient evidence to rebut the presumption. In a case such as this, the presumption could have operated in favour of the child's legitimacy by virtue of her birth during the second marriage. However, in cases where *paternity* is in issue, it is obviously correct to treat the date of conception, and not the date of birth, as the determinative factor, so that provided the child can be proved to have been conceived during the first marriage, it will be held to be the legitimate offspring of the first husband, even if born, say, four or six months after the second marriage. In a case where marriage takes place so soon after termination of an earlier marriage that it is unclear whether conception occurred during the first or second marriage, it is submitted that although a presumption operates in favour of the child's legitimacy by virtue of birth during the second marriage, it should not be determinative of paternity, if that is in issue.

The presumption applies, although it may be more easily rebuttable, where there is a maintenance order in force against the husband (unless it contains a non-cohabitation clause),[72] where proceedings for divorce or nullity have been commenced,[73] and even where the husband and wife are living apart, whether or not under a separation agreement.[74] However, the presumption does not apply where a decree of judicial separation or a magistrates' separation

---

[63] *Legge v Edmonds* (1855) 25 LJ Ch 125.

[64] *Re Baronetcy of Pringle of Stichill* [2016] UKPC 16. See also *F v Child Support Agency* [1999] 2 FLR 244, QBD.

[65] *R v King's Lynn Magistrates' Court and Walker, ex p Moore* [1988] Fam Law 393, QBD.

[66] *Cope v Cope* (1833) 1 Mood&R 269 and *Re Jenion, Jenion v Wynne* [1952] Ch 454, CA.

[67] *Morris v Davies* (1837) 5 Cl&Fin 163 and *Kanapathipillai v Parpathy* [1956] AC 580.

[68] *R v Mansfield Inhabitants* (1841) 1 QB 444 and *Gordon v Gordon* [1903] P 141.

[69] *The Poulett Peerage Case* [1903] AC 395, HL.

[70] See *Maturin v A-G* [1938] 2 All ER 214 (termination by divorce) and *Re Heath, Stacey v Bird* [1945] Ch 417 (termination by death of husband).

[71] [1955] Ch 122, Ch D.

[72] *Bowen v Norman* [1938] 1 KB 689.

[73] *Knowles v Knowles* [1962] P 161, where the presumption was applied on a finding of conception as a result of intercourse between the husband and wife at a time after a decree nisi had been granted but before it had been made absolute. Wrangham J was of the opinion that the presumption involved both a presumption of paternity and a presumption as to the date of conception.

[74] *Ettenfield v Ettenfield* [1940] P 96, CA.

order is in force.[75] In such circumstances, it is presumed that the parties did not have sexual intercourse. Accordingly, if the child is born more than nine months after the separation, there is a presumption of illegitimacy rebuttable by evidence of intercourse between the husband and wife.

The burden and standard of proof

The authorities suggest that in civil proceedings the presumption of legitimacy operates as a persuasive presumption. At common law, evidence in rebuttal was required to meet a high standard of proof[76] but the matter is now governed by s 26 of the Family Law Reform Act 1969, which provides that:

> Any presumption of law as to the legitimacy or illegitimacy of any person may in any civil proceedings be rebutted by evidence which shows that it is more probable than not that the person is illegitimate or legitimate as the case may be and it shall not be necessary to prove that fact beyond reasonable doubt in order to rebut the presumption.

Thus the party seeking to rebut the presumption bears the legal burden of proving illegitimacy on a balance of probabilities and, in accordance with general principles, will fail if the evidence is such that legitimacy is as probable as illegitimacy.[77] In the words of Lord Reid in *S v S*,[78] which were adopted and applied in *T (HH) v T (E)*:[79]

> That means that the presumption of legitimacy now merely determines the onus of proof. Once evidence has been led it must be used without using the presumption as a make-weight in the scale of legitimacy. So even weak evidence against legitimacy must prevail if there is no other evidence to counterbalance it. The presumption will only come in at that stage in the very rare case of the evidence being so evenly balanced that the court is unable to reach a decision on it.

The presumption of death

Where there is no acceptable affirmative evidence that a person was alive at some time during a continuous period of seven years or more, on the proof or admission of the basic facts (i) that there are persons who would be likely to have heard of him over that period; (ii) that those persons have not heard of him; and (iii) that all due inquiries have been made appropriate to the circumstances, that person will be presumed to have died at some time within that period.[80] One of the difficulties of this presumption stems from the fact that evidence in rebuttal may be indistinguishable from evidence which negatives one of the basic facts. This was the case in *Prudential Assurance Co v Edmonds*,[81] a decision of the House of Lords which suggests that once the party against whom the presumption operates has adduced sufficient

---

[75] *Hetherington v Hetherington* (1887) 12 PD 112.

[76] See per Lord Lyndhurst in *Morris v Davies* (1837) 5 Cl&Fin 163 at 265, quoted in this chapter, under The presumption of formal validity, p 104.

[77] See per Denning J in *Miller v Minister of Pensions* [1947] 2 All ER 372 at 374. However, if the case involves a finding that someone other than the mother's husband is the father of the child, the standard of proof to make the finding of paternity is a heavy one, commensurate with the gravity of the issue and although not as heavy as in criminal proceedings, more than the ordinary civil standard of balance of probabilities: *W v K* (1986) 151 JP 589.

[78] [1972] AC 24 at 41.

[79] [1971] 1 WLR 429.

[80] See per Sachs J in *Chard v Chard* [1956] P 259 at 272.

[81] (1877) 2 App Cas 487.

evidence for the possibility of the existence of the absent person to be put to the tribunal of fact, the presumption has been rebutted. It would seem that the presumption is of the evidential and not persuasive variety.

The basic facts

In *Chard v Chard*[82] the presumption did not arise because there was no evidence of the first basic fact, that is, of persons likely to have heard of the person whose death was in question.[83]

Prudential Assurance Co v Edmonds[84] concerned the second basic fact, that the person whose death is in question has not been heard of. In a claim on a policy of life assurance, it was alleged that the assured was not dead. Members of the family gave evidence that they had not heard of him for more than seven years but knew that his niece believed that she had seen him in Melbourne, Australia. The niece gave evidence that when she was aged 20, standing in a crowded street in Melbourne, a man passed her whom she recognized as her uncle. She did not speak to him because he was lost in the crowd as she turned to do so but said he resembled her uncle as she remembered him from five years earlier. The House of Lords, being in no doubt that it fell to the tribunal of fact to decide whether or not to accept the niece's evidence, held that if the jury had been satisfied that she was mistaken, the basic facts giving rise to the presumption would have been established.

There is a conflict of authority as to whether the presumption arises without proof or admission of the fact that all due inquiries appropriate to the circumstances have been made.[85] The explanation is probably that the extent of the inquiries to be made depends upon the circumstances of the case in question, and that in some cases the circumstances are not appropriate to the making of any inquiries whatsoever.[86] There is some authority that proof of the third basic fact may render proof of the first unnecessary, presumably on the basis that to adduce evidence that a person has made all due inquiries appropriate to the circumstances is also, in some cases, to adduce evidence of a person who would be likely to have heard of the absent person.[87]

The presumed facts

The presumption of death allows the court to presume the fact of a person's death. However, proof of the mere fact of death may be of little or no assistance to a party seeking to establish that an absent person died unmarried, childless, or without next-of-kin. It is reasonably clear that, although these additional issues are not proved by the basic facts giving rise to the presumption of death, but require additional evidence,[88] the amount of such additional evidence may be less than would have been required if the presumption had not applied.[89]

---

[82] [1956] P 259.

[83] Friends and relatives will not be treated as persons likely to have heard of the absent person where it is shown that the latter did not intend the former to hear of him: see, eg, *Watson v England* (1844) 14 Sim 29 and *Re Lidderdale* (1912) 57 Sol Jo 3.

[84] (1877) 2 App Cas 487.

[85] See *Willyams v Scottish Widows' Fund Life Assurance Society* (1888) 4 TLR 489 and *Chipchase v Chipchase* [1939] P 391. Cf *Bradshaw v Bradshaw* [1956] P 274n.

[86] See *Bullock v Bullock* [1960] 1 WLR 975, DC.

[87] *Doe d France v Andrews* (1850) 15 QB 756.

[88] See *Re Jackson, Jackson v Ward* [1907] 2 Ch 354.

[89] See *Dunn v Snowden* (1862) 32 LJ Ch 104, *Rawlinson v Miller* (1875) 1 Ch D 52 and *Greaves v Greenwood* (1877) 2 Ex D 289, CA.

Proof of the mere fact of death is of limited use to a party seeking to establish death before or after a particular date. It seems clear from the authorities that the presumption establishes only the fact of death, additional evidence being required to prove that the death took place at a particular period.[90] However, there are two views as to the date on which the fact of death may be presumed. One view is that the fact of death may be presumed at the date of the proceedings (ie a continuous period of absence for seven years or more runs back from the date of the proceedings). A second view is that the fact of death may be presumed at the end of a continuous period of absence for seven years (ie a continuous period of absence for seven years runs forward from the date of the disappearance of the absent person). Whichever view is taken, if a party seeks to establish that death occurred on a particular date prior to the date on which the fact of death is presumed, additional evidence will be required. A party seeking to establish that death occurred on a particular date prior to the date of the action, will only be assisted by the second view. Thus if there is no evidence that X was alive during a continuous period of nine years from 2010 to 2019 and a party seeks to establish that X was dead in 2018, the matter coming before the court in 2019, that party will fail on the first view but succeed on the second.

A case which is consistent with both of these views is *Re Phené's Trusts*,[91] but in *Lal Chand Marwari v Mahant Ramrup Gir*[92] the Privy Council interpreted the decision as an authority for the first view. Other decisions, however, such as *Re Westbrook's Trusts*[93] and *Chipchase v Chipchase*[94] are only consistent with the second view. It is submitted that the first and stricter view deprives the presumption of death of so much of its value that the laxer second view is to be preferred.

Statutory provisions
The Presumption of Death Act 2013
When a person disappears, it may be difficult or impossible for those left behind to obtain a death certificate in order to deal with various aspects of the missing person's property and affairs, for example to end a marriage to which he was a party or to obtain a grant of probate to administer his estate. The 2013 Act enables those with a sufficient interest to obtain a declaration from the High Court that the missing person is presumed to have died, including a finding as to the date of the death.

Under s 1(1) and (2) of the Act, in the case of a person who is missing and (a) is thought to have died or (b) has not been known to be alive for a period of at least seven years, a person may apply to the High Court for a declaration that the missing person is presumed to be dead. The court has jurisdiction to hear such an application only if there is a connection with England and Wales, in terms of domicile or habitual residence, on the part of either the missing person or, in the case of an application by a spouse or civil partner of the missing person, the spouse or civil partner.[95] The court must refuse to hear an application if it is made by someone other than the missing person's spouse, civil partner, parent, child, or sibling

---

[90] See per Giffard LJ in *Re Phené's Trusts* (1870) 5 Ch App 139, CA at 144.

[91] (1870) 5 Ch App 139, CA at 144.

[92] (1925) 42 TLR 159 at 160.

[93] [1873] WN 167, criticized in *Re Rhodes, Rhodes v Rhodes* (1887) 36 Ch D 586. See also *Re Aldersey, Gibson v Hall* [1905] 2 Ch 181.

[94] [1939] P 391.

[95] For details of the domicile and residence requirements, see s 1(3) and (4).

and that person does not have a sufficient interest in the determination of the application.[96] Section 2 provides as follows.

(1) On an application under section 1, the court must make the declaration if it is satisfied that the missing person—
   (a) has died, or
   (b) has not been known to be alive for a period of at least 7 years.
(2) It must include in the declaration a finding as to the date and time of the missing person's death.
(3) Where the court—
   (a) is satisfied that the missing person has died, but
   (b) is uncertain at which moment during a period the missing person died, the finding must be that the missing person is presumed to have died at the end of that period.
(4) Where the court—
   (a) is satisfied that the missing person has not been known to be alive for a period of at least seven years, but
   (b) is not satisfied that the missing person has died,
   the finding must be that the missing person is presumed to have died at the end of the period of 7 years beginning with the day after the day on which he or she was last known to be alive.

An example under s 2(1)(a) would be an incident at which people were known to have died as part of a group that was likely to have included the missing person.[97] A declaration, subject to successful appeal,[98] is conclusive of the missing person's presumed death and the date and time of the death.[99] It is also effective against all persons and for all purposes, including for the purposes of the acquisition of an interest in any property and the ending of any marriage or civil partnership to which the missing person is a party.[100] However, provision is also made for the variation or revocation of a declaration.[101]

Section 184 of the Law of Property Act 1925
This section provides that:

> In all cases where, after the commencement of this Act, two or more persons have died in circumstances rendering it uncertain which of them survived the other or others, such deaths shall (subject to any order of the court), for all purposes affecting the title to property, be presumed to have occurred in order of seniority, and accordingly the younger shall be deemed to have survived the elder.

In *Hickman v Peacey*,[102] Lord Simon was of the view that the word 'circumstances' in this section is not confined to deaths occurring as a result of a common disaster. It remains unclear, however, whether the statutory phrase 'where . . . persons have died' refers not only to persons whose deaths have been proved, but also to those whose deaths have been presumed.[103]

---

[96] Section 1(5).
[97] For an example under s 2(1)(b), see *A v H* [2016] EWHC 762 (Fam).
[98] Section 3(3) and (4).
[99] Section 3(1).
[100] Section 3(2).
[101] Section 5.
[102] [1945] AC 304, HL at 314–15.
[103] See *Re Watkinson* [1952] VLR 123.

The proviso to s 57 of the Offences Against the Person Act 1861
After defining the offence of bigamy, s 57 continues:

> Provided that nothing in this section contained shall extend . . . to any person marrying a second time whose husband or wife shall have been continually absent from such person for the space of seven years then last past, and shall not have been known by such person to be living within that time . . .

The prosecution, in order to prove bigamy, must show that the first spouse was alive at the date of the second marriage.[104] Where this has been done, the accused may rely upon the proviso, which amounts to a defence, to secure an acquittal.[105] The prosecution bear the legal burden of proving that the first marriage was valid and that the accused went through a second marriage knowing that the first spouse was alive. *R v Edwards*[106] suggests that the accused bears the legal burden of proving that the first spouse was continually absent for seven years[107] and that he or she did not know that the first spouse was living within that time. However, there is also authority that the prosecution bears the legal burden in relation to the accused's knowledge.[108]

Omnia praesumuntur rite esse acta (presumption of regularity)
On the proof or admission of the basic fact that a public or official act has been performed, it is presumed, in the absence of sufficient evidence to the contrary, that the act has been regularly and properly performed. Likewise, persons acting in public capacities are presumed to have been regularly and properly appointed. In civil proceedings, the maxim operates as an evidential presumption and may be rebutted by some evidence of irregularity. The operation of the presumption may be illustrated by the following authorities. In *R v Gordon*[109] proof that a police officer had acted as such was sufficient on a charge of assaulting a police officer in the course of his duty: evidence of due appointment was not required.[110] In *R v Roberts*,[111] on an indictment for perjury committed in the presence of a deputy county court judge, the judge was presumed, in the absence of evidence to the contrary, to have been duly appointed.[112] In *R v Langton*[113] the presumption applied to establish the due incorporation of a company which had acted as such. In *R v Cresswell*,[114] on proof that a marriage had been celebrated in a building some yards from a parish church, in which building several other marriages had also been celebrated, it was presumed that the building was duly consecrated. In *TC Coombs &*

---

[104] Proof that the first spouse was alive before the second marriage may give rise to an inference that he or she was alive at the date of that marriage: see *R v Lumley* (1869) LR 1 CCR 196.

[105] In Australia, the proviso has been treated as a statutory presumption of death in relation to one party to a marriage on the remarriage of the other: see per Evatt J in *Axon v Axon* (1937) 59 CLR 395 at 413 (HC of A) and *Re Peatling* [1969] VR 214 (Supreme Court of Victoria).

[106] [1975] QB 27, in Ch 3, p 65.

[107] See also *R v Jones* (1883) 11 QBD 118 and *R v Bonnor* [1957] VLR 227.

[108] *R v Curgerwen* (1865) LR 1 CCR 1.

[109] (1789) 1 Leach 515.

[110] See also *Doe d Bowley v Barnes* (1846) 8 QB 1037.

[111] (1878) 14 Cox CC 101, CCR.

[112] See also *R v Verelst* (1813) 3 Camp 432. But there is no presumption that a court or tribunal has jurisdiction in relation to any given matter: see *Christopher Brown Ltd v Genossenschaft Oesterreichischer* [1954] 1 QB 8 per Devlin J at 13.

[113] (1876) 2 QBD 296.

[114] (1876) 1 QBD 446, CCR.

Co (a firm) v IRC[115] it was presumed, in the absence of evidence to the contrary, that a tax inspector, who had served statutory notices requiring delivery of documentary information relevant to tax liability, together with a General Commissioner, who had given his consent to the notices, had both acted within the limits of their authority, with honesty and discretion.

Criminal proceedings

The authorities are in conflict as to the applicability of the presumption in criminal proceedings. Although there are cases in which the prosecution have relied on the presumption to establish part of their case,[116] in *Scott v Baker*,[117] on proof that a breathalyzer had been issued to the police, the court refused to presume that it had been officially approved by the Secretary of State. It was held that the presumption may not be used to establish an ingredient of a criminal offence if the regularity and propriety of the matter in question is disputed at the trial.[118] However, there is also authority that it is insufficient merely to dispute regularity; evidence must be adduced.[119]

The presumption of sanity in testamentary cases

Although in criminal cases the presumption of sanity is a presumption without basic facts, a rule relating to the incidence of the burden of proof, in testamentary cases it operates as a rebuttable presumption of law casting an evidential burden on the party against whom it operates. On the proof or admission of the basic fact that a rational will has been duly executed, it is presumed, in the absence of sufficient evidence to the contrary, that the testator was sane.[120]

Res ipsa loquitur

In the ordinary course of things, bags of flour do not fall from warehouse windows,[121] stones are not found in buns,[122] cars do not mount the pavement,[123] and slippery substances are not left on shop floors[124] unless, in each case, those who have the management of the thing in question fail to exercise proper care. The normal rule, that in negligence actions the claimant bears the legal and evidential burden, is capable of causing injustice in cases such

---

[115] [1991] 3 All ER 623, HL.

[116] See *Gibbins v Skinner* [1951] 2 KB 379, where it was held that on proof that speed limit signs had been placed on a road, the presumption could operate to establish the performance of a local authority's statutory duties pursuant to the Road Traffic Acts; and *Cooper v Rowlands* [1972] Crim LR 53, where a man in police uniform who administered a breath test was presumed to have been duly appointed.

[117] [1969] 1 QB 659, DC, approved by the Court of Appeal in *R v Withecombe* [1969] 1 WLR 84.

[118] See also *Dillon v R* [1982] AC 484, PC. *Scott v Baker* was distinguished in *Public Prosecution Service of Northern Ireland v Elliott* [2013] 1 WLR 1611, SC, in the case of fingerprints taken using an electronic device that had not been, but should have been, officially approved, on the basis that whereas breath tests, like speed guns, are means of measuring something that cannot subsequently be re-measured, fingerprints can be reproduced subsequently and the accuracy of the initial readings, if disputed, can readily be checked by the provision of more samples.

[119] *Campbell v Wallsend Slipway & Engineering Co Ltd* [1978] ICR 1015, DC at 1025.

[120] *Sutton v Sadler* (1857) 3 CBNS 87. On capacity to make an inter vivos gift, see *Re Smith (deceased)* [2014] EWHC 3926 (Ch). As to capacity in relation to issues within the statutory jurisdiction of the Court of Protection, see the Mental Capacity Act 2005, s 1(2).

[121] *Byrne v Boadle* (1863) 2 H&C 722.

[122] *Chapronière v Mason* (1905) 21 TLR 633, CA.

[123] *Ellor v Selfridge & Co Ltd* (1930) 46 TLR 236.

[124] *Ward v Tesco Stores Ltd* [1976] 1 WLR 810, CA.

as these. Although the claimant is able to prove the accident, he cannot show that it was caused by the defendant's negligence, the true cause of the accident, in most cases, being known only to the defendant. In these circumstances, the claimant may be assisted by the principle of *res ipsa loquitur*.[125] Translating into the terminology of presumptions the statement of the principle given by Sir William Erle CJ in *Scott v London & St Katherine Docks Co*,[126] the presumption may be defined as follows: on the proof or admission of the basic facts that (i) something was under the management of the defendant or his employees; and (ii) an accident occurred, being an accident which in the ordinary course of things does not happen if those who have the management use proper care, it may or must be presumed, in the absence of sufficient evidence to the contrary, that the accident was caused by the negligence of the defendant.

Classifications

The foregoing definition allows for three possible classifications of the principle, as a presumption of fact, as an evidential presumption, or as a persuasive presumption, for each of which support may be found in the authorities.

Some authorities suggest that the principle is no more than a presumption of fact: proof of the basic facts gives rise to an inference of negligence which the tribunal of fact may draw in the absence of evidence to the contrary. A party against whom the presumption operates bears the provisional or tactical burden in relation to negligence: if he adduces no evidence, he is not bound to lose but it is a clear risk that he runs and a finding by the tribunal of fact in his favour could be reversed on appeal.[127]

Other authorities suggest that it is an evidential presumption: on proof of the basic facts, negligence must be presumed in the absence of evidence to the contrary, and the party against whom the presumption operates bears the evidential burden: he will lose unless he adduces some evidence but where, on all the evidence before the court, the probability of negligence is equal to the probability of its absence, he will succeed, the plaintiff having failed to discharge the legal burden of proving negligence.[128]

Finally, there are authorities to suggest that the principle is a persuasive or compelling presumption: negligence must be presumed in the absence of evidence to the contrary, the party against whom the presumption operates bears the legal burden of disproving negligence, and he will lose not only where he adduces no evidence but also where on all the evidence before the court the probability of negligence is equal to the probability of its absence. To succeed, he must disprove negligence on a balance of probabilities. The evidence he adduces

---

[125] This phrase has been used despite the strictures of the Court of Appeal in *Fryer v Pearson & Anor* (2000) The Times, 4 April: 'People should stop using maxims or doctrines dressed up in Latin which are not readily comprehensible to those for whose benefit they are supposed to exist.' The authors applaud the attempt to accommodate the lay client, but fear that some doctrines—eg estoppel *per rem judicatam*—will need explanation whatever language they are couched in.

[126] (1865) 3 H&C 596 at 601.

[127] See, eg, per Greer LJ in *Langham v Wellingborough School Governors and Fryer* (1932) 101 LJKB 513 at 518 and per Goddard LJ in *Easson v London & North Eastern Rly Co* [1944] KB 421.

[128] See, eg, *The Kite* [1933] P 154 at 170. See also per Lord Porter in *Woods v Duncan* [1946] AC 401 at 434, HL; per Lord Pearson in *Henderson v Henry E Jenkins & Sons and Evans* [1970] AC 282 at 301, HL; per Lawton LJ in *Ward v Tesco Stores Ltd* [1976] 1 WLR 810 at 814, CA; and *Ng Chun Pui v Lee Chuen Tat* [1988] RTR 298, PC.

must either reveal the true cause of the accident and thereby convince the tribunal of fact that negligence is less probable than its absence or show that he used all reasonable care.[129]

It is submitted that there may be no anomaly in the fact that the courts have adopted such different approaches towards this presumption. Given that the facts calling for the application of the principle vary enormously from case to case so that in some the inference of negligence is slight, in others all but irresistible, efforts aimed at confining the principle to a single category seem ill-founded. At the risk of uncertainty, classification according to the facts of the case in question seems preferable. If the thing speaks for itself, it may do so with degrees of conviction. The hardship caused to the claimant may be remedied by placing the tactical, evidential, or legal burden on the defendant depending on the strength of the basic facts in question.

Conflicting presumptions

Where two presumptions apply to the facts of a case, the court may be required to draw two conclusions, the one conflicting with the other. If the two conflicting presumptions are of equal strength so that each operates to place a legal or, as the case may be, evidential or tactical burden on the party against whom it operates, one obvious and equitable solution is to treat the two presumptions as having cancelled each other out and to proceed, as if no presumption were involved, on the basis of the normal rules relating to the burden and standard of proof. As we have seen,[130] this was the solution adopted in *Monckton v Tarr*,[131] where the same presumption of essential validity applied to two different ceremonies of marriage. However, when a similar conflict of presumptions arose in *Taylor v Taylor*,[132] Cairns J preferred to preserve an existing marriage rather than avoid it in favour of an earlier doubtful one. This approach suggests that the strength of a presumption may be gauged by reference to the comparative likelihood of the two presumed facts, or even to general considerations of public policy, as opposed to the nature of the burden placed on the party against whom it operates. Inherently imprecise, such an approach has the obvious advantage of flexibility compared to any set formula.[133]

In cases where the two presumptions are, by reference to the burden placed on the party against whom they operate, of unequal strength, there is a dearth of authority. To say that the presumption of greater strength should prevail is to acknowledge that the conflict is more apparent than real. Where, for example, the conflict is between a presumption of law and a presumption of fact,[134] the determinative factor is the incidence of the legal burden of proof; whether the presumption of law operates to place a legal or evidential burden on the party

---

[129] See per Lords Simon, Russell, and Simmonds in *Woods v Duncan* [1946] AC 401, HL at 419, 425, and 439 respectively; per Asquith LJ in *Barkway v South Wales Transport Co Ltd* [1948] 2 All ER 460, CA at 471; *Walsh v Holst & Co Ltd* [1958] 1 WLR 800, CA; *Colvilles Ltd v Devine* [1969] 1 WLR 475, HL; the speeches of Lords Reid and Donovan in *Henderson v Henry E Jenkins & Sons and Evans* [1970] AC 282, HL; and, arguably, *George v Eagle Air Services Ltd* [2009] UKPC 21.

[130] See under **Subsequent marriages and conflicting presumptions**, p 106.

[131] (1930) 23 BWCC 504, CA.

[132] [1965] 2 WLR 779.

[133] But see *L v L* [2007] HKCA 210: *Taylor v Taylor* was not concerned with conflicting presumptions but with the quality or sufficiency of the evidence to rebut a presumption; the court decided that the existence of the earlier doubtful marriage was not *sufficient* to rebut the presumption of validity of the subsequent marriage.

[134] Or between a persuasive and an evidential presumption.

against whom it operates, the party bearing the legal burden of proof will lose on the issue in question if he fails to discharge it by adducing sufficient evidence to meet the required standard of proof. *R v Willshire*,[135] often cited as an example of conflicting presumptions, is, it is submitted, properly understood in this sense.

R v Willshire

The accused was convicted of bigamy, having married D in the lifetime of his former wife C. In fact he had gone through four ceremonies of marriage: with A in 1864; with B in 1868; with C in 1879; and with D in 1880. The prosecution, who bore the legal burden of proving the validity of the ceremony in 1879, relied upon the presumption of essential validity. The accused sought to show that the marriage of 1879 was void. He could prove that A was alive in 1868 by virtue of his earlier conviction of bigamy in that year (he married B in the lifetime of A) and he relied upon the presumption of fact as to the continuance of life to establish that A was still alive in 1879. The trial judge did not leave the question whether A was alive in 1879 to the jury but directed them that the defendant bore the burden of adducing other or further evidence of A's existence in 1879. On appeal, this was held to be a misdirection and the conviction was quashed. Lord Coleridge CJ, in the course of his judgment, referred to a conflict between the presumption of essential validity and the presumption of continuance of life. Although the judgment is consistent with the view that the two presumptions had cancelled each other out, it is equally consistent with the ordinary operation of both, the determinative factor being the incidence of the legal burden.[136] The prosecution bore the legal burden of proving the validity of the ceremony of 1879. Once they had proved the basic facts giving rise to the presumption of essential validity of that ceremony, the defendant bore an evidential burden to adduce some evidence in rebuttal.[137] He had successfully discharged this burden by relying on the presumption of the continuance of life and accordingly the jury should have been directed that they could only convict if the prosecution had satisfied them beyond reasonable doubt that the ceremony of 1879 was valid.[138]

Judicial notice

Judicial notice without inquiry

Certain facts are beyond serious dispute, so notorious, or of such common knowledge that they require no proof and are open to no evidence in rebuttal. In criminal and civil proceedings, a court may take judicial notice of such a fact and direct the tribunal of fact to treat it as established notwithstanding the absence of proof by evidence. To require proof of such facts, which in some cases could cause considerable difficulty, would be to waste both time and money and could result in inconsistency between cases in relation to which common sense demands uniformity. Any attempt at a compilation of the numerous facts of which judicial notice has been taken would be pointless. It will suffice to refer to the following

---

[135] (1881) 6 QBD 366, CCR.

[136] There is considerable variance in the reports of the judgment of Lord Coleridge CJ: see 6 QBD 366 and cf 50 LJMC 57.

[137] The presumption of essential validity operates as a *persuasive* presumption only in civil proceedings.

[138] See also *Re Peatling* [1969] VR 214 (Supreme Court of Victoria): the presumption of validity can prevail over that of continuance by virtue of the greater strength of the former.

examples: a fortnight is too short a period for human gestation;[139] the duration of the normal period of human gestation is about nine months;[140] the streets of London are crowded and dangerous;[141] a postcard is the sort of document which might be read by anyone;[142] flick-knives,[143] butterfly knives[144] and knuckle-dusters[145] are made for use for causing injury to the person; and reconstructed trials with a striking degree of realism are one of the popular forms of modern television entertainment.[146] A final example of general application is that the court is taken to know the meaning of any ordinary English expression.[147] In all of these examples, the doctrine of judicial notice was expressly applied, but more often than not judicial notice of a fact is taken without being stated. For example, when evidence is adduced that a burglar was found in possession of skeleton keys, judicial notice is tacitly taken of the fact that skeleton keys are frequently used in the commission of the crime of burglary; the fact is not required to be established by evidence but is taken as established as much as if express judicial notice had been taken of it.

Required by statute

Judicial notice of certain facts is expressly required by statute. Most of these provisions require judicial notice to be taken of the fact that a document has been signed or sealed by the person by whom it purports to have been signed or sealed. This applies to any judicial or official document signed by certain judges.[148] Judicial notice shall be taken of European Union Treaties, the Official Journal of the European Union, and decisions of or opinions by the European Court.[149] Statute also requires judicial notice to be taken of Acts of Parliament; evidence is not required to prove either their contents or that they have been duly passed by both Houses of Parliament. Every Act passed after 1850 is a Public Act and to be judicially noticed as such unless the contrary is expressly provided by the Act.[150] At common law, judicial notice is taken of Public Acts passed before 1851, but in the absence of express provision to the contrary, a private Act passed before 1851 must be proved by evidence.[151] Statutory instruments must also be proved,[152] although some have acquired such notoriety that judicial notice may be taken of them.[153]

---

[139] *R v Luffe* (1807) 8 East 193.

[140] *Preston-Jones v Preston-Jones* [1951] AC 391, HL. A child born to a woman 360 days after the last occasion on which she had intercourse with her husband cannot be his child (per Lord Morton).

[141] *Dennis v White* [1916] 2 KB 1.

[142] *Huth v Huth* [1915] 3 KB 32, CA.

[143] *R v Simpson* [1983] 1 WLR 1494, CA.

[144] *DPP v Hynde* [1998] 1 Cr App R 288, DC.

[145] *DPP v Christof* [2016] 2 Cr App R 56 (6), DC.

[146] *R v Yap Chuan Ching* (1976) 63 Cr App R 7, CA. Judicial notice of this fact related to the formulation by the court of the appropriate direction to be given to the jury on the standard of proof in criminal proceedings. Thus the fact judicially noticed was not a fact in issue but was relevant to the question of law which formed the subject of the appeal.

[147] *Chapman v Kirke* [1948] 2 KB 450 at 454.

[148] Section 2 of the Evidence Act 1845.

[149] Section 3(2) of the European Communities Act 1972.

[150] Section 3 and s 22(1) of, and para 2 of Sch 2 to the Interpretation Act 1978.

[151] Production of a Queen's Printers copy or an HMSO copy suffices for these purposes: s 3 of the Evidence Act 1845 and s 2 of the Documentary Evidence Act 1882: see Ch 10.

[152] See Ch 10.

[153] *R v Jones* (1968) 54 Cr App R 63, CA.

Foreign law

Foreign law is a question of fact, the proof of which normally calls for an expert witness.[154] Generally speaking, therefore, foreign law cannot be the subject of judicial notice.[155] Exceptions include: (i) the common law of Northern Ireland;[156] (ii) Scots law in civil cases, of which judicial notice may be taken by the Supreme Court (on account of its appellate jurisdiction); (iii) the law in relation to maintenance orders in all parts of the United Kingdom;[157] and (iv) in civil but not criminal cases,[158] notorious points of foreign law, for example that roulette is legal in Monte Carlo.[159]

Directions to the jury

Judicial directions to the jury as to the way certain types of evidence are to be approached, particularly in areas where there is a danger of the jury coming to an unjustified conclusion or relying upon stereotypical assumptions, such as directions in relation to visual identification evidence, lies told by the accused, or a complainant's delay in reporting a sexual offence, do not, without more, offend the common law principle that judicial notice can only be taken of facts of sufficient notoriety or common knowledge.[160]

Judicial notice after inquiry

The doctrine of judicial notice also applies to facts which are neither notorious nor of common knowledge. Such facts may be judicially noticed after inquiry. In making inquiries before deciding to take judicial notice, the judge may consult a variety of sources including certificates from ministers and officials, learned treatises, works of reference, and the oral statements of witnesses. Such a procedure resembles but remains distinct from proof by evidence: the judge is not required to make such an inquiry, the rules of evidence do not apply, the results of the inquiry may not be rebutted by evidence to the contrary, and the judge's decision constitutes a precedent in law.[161] Proof by evidence bears none of these characteristics. However, although it is easy to distinguish between the processes of judicial notice after inquiry and proof by evidence, there is clearly a fine line separating non-notorious facts from those requiring proof by evidence in the ordinary way.[162] The matter is of more than theoretical or academic interest. To take judicial notice after inquiry of a non-notorious fact which is indistinguishable from a fact to be proved by evidence in the ordinary way is improperly to usurp the function of the jury as the tribunal of fact. This may be justified, however, where

---

[154] See Ch 2, p 36.

[155] *Brenan and Galen's Case* (1847) 10 QB 492 at 498.

[156] *Re Nesbitt* (1844) 14 LJMC 30 at 33.

[157] Section 22(2) of the Maintenance Orders Act 1950.

[158] *R v Ofori (No 2)* (1993) 99 Cr App R 223, CA.

[159] *Saxby v Fulton* [1909] 2 KB 208, CA.

[160] *R v Miller* [2010] EWCA Crim 1578 at [20]–[24].

[161] An exception exists in the case of judicially noticed facts lacking constancy, eg the Crown's view on the status of a foreign government. If the matter arises in a subsequent case, a fresh ministerial certificate should be obtained.

[162] In *Duff Development Co v Government of Kelantan* [1924] AC 797 the court acted on information supplied by a Secretary of State. It was said that such information was not in the nature of evidence (per Viscount Finlay at 813). Lord Sumner, however, referred to the information as the best evidence (at 824). See also per Lord Denning in *Baldwin and Francis Ltd v Patents Appeal Tribunal* [1959] AC 663 at 691.

the issue is such as to require uniformity of decision. In *McQuaker v Goddard*,[163] the plaintiff having been bitten by a camel while feeding it on a visit to a zoo run by the defendant, the question arose whether a camel was a wild or domestic animal for the purposes of the law relating to liability for animals. Books about camels were consulted and expert witnesses gave conflicting evidence on oath concerning the behaviour of camels. The trial judge, without resort to the doctrine of judicial notice, held that camels were domestic animals. The Court of Appeal, affirming this decision, held that judicial notice could be taken of the matter.

Despite the scope for abuse of the doctrine, the authorities show that, in general, the courts are cautious not to take judicial notice of a fact requiring proof by evidence in the normal way.[164] Thus a court will not take judicial notice of a fact simply because it has been proved in another case.[165] Most of the cases in which judicial notice has been taken after inquiry relate to facts of a political nature. An example is to be found in *Secretary of State for Defence v Guardian Newspapers Ltd*,[166] in which it was held that the classification 'secret' appearing on a document originating in a government office was a matter of public record of which the House of Lords was entitled to take judicial notice: Lord Diplock referred to the Statement on the Recommendations of the Security Commission,[167] presented to Parliament by the Prime Minister in 1982, in which it is stated that 'secret' means that the document contains information and material the unauthorized disclosure of which would cause serious injury to the interests of the nation. In cases of this kind, the source of information, a minister, is treated as indisputably accurate for reasons of public policy, namely the desirability of avoiding conflict between the courts and the executive.

Judicial notice after inquiry has also been taken of customs, professional practices, and a variety of readily demonstrable facts including, for example, historical and geographical facts. Such cases can usually be justified on one of two grounds: the fact in question is either readily demonstrable by reference to sources of virtually indisputable authority or comes before the court so frequently that proof in each case is undesirable for reasons of cost, time, and uniformity of decision. Judges also take judicial notice of the common law of England, the source of information, when necessary, being the reports of previous cases, and of the law and custom of Parliament, including parliamentary privilege.[168]

Political facts

Judicial notice has been taken of the relations between the Government of the United Kingdom and other states, for example the existence of a state of war, the status of foreign sovereigns or governments, the membership of diplomatic suites, and the extent of territorial sovereignty. In *R v Bottrill, ex p Kuechenmeister*,[169] the Court of Appeal took judicial notice of

---

[163] [1940] 1 KB 687, CA.

[164] See, eg, *Deybel's Case* (1821) 4 B&Ald 243; *Collier v Nokes* (1849) 2 Car&Kir 1012; *Kirby v Hickson* (1850) 14 Jur 625; and *R v Crush* [1978] Crim LR 357. But see also *Mullen v Hackney London Borough Council* [1997] 1 WLR 1103, CA, considered, in this chapter, under **Personal knowledge of facts in issue or relevant to the issue, p 122**.

[165] Per Lord Wright in *Lazard Brothers & Co v Midland Bank* [1933] AC 289 at 297–8, applied in *Jankowski v District Court Wroclaw (Poland)* [2016] EWHC 747 (Admin), followed in *Krajewski v Circuit Law Court, Swidnica, Poland* [2016] EWHC 3241 (Admin).

[166] [1985] AC 339, HL per Lord Diplock at 354.

[167] Cmnd 8540, (1982).

[168] See *Stockdale v Hansard* (1839) 9 Ad&El 1.

[169] [1947] KB 41.

the fact that the country was still at war with Germany, accepting as conclusive a certificate of the Foreign Secretary to this effect. In *Duff Development Co v Government of Kelantan*[170] the House of Lords took judicial notice of the fact that Kelantan was an independent state and the Sultan its sovereign ruler, accepting as conclusive information to this effect supplied by the Secretary of State for the Colonies. In *Engelke v Mussmann*[171] the statement of the Foreign Office as to the defendant's membership of the staff of the German ambassador was treated as conclusive. In *The Fagernes*[172] the Court of Appeal, on the instructions of the Home Secretary, accepted that a collision in the Bristol Channel had not occurred within the jurisdiction of the High Court.

Customs and professional practices

Although, as a general rule, judicial notice is not taken of facts proved by evidence in earlier proceedings,[173] there is an exception in the case of general customs. In *Brandao v Barnett*,[174] an action against bankers to recover exchequer bills, the defendants rested their defence upon the general lien of bankers on the securities of their customers. The House of Lords took judicial notice of the custom of bankers' lien; it had been judicially ascertained and established and justice could not be administered if proof by evidence was repeatedly required in each case. After consultation with suitably qualified expert witnesses, judicial notice will also be taken of the professional practices of conveyancers,[175] accountants,[176] and ordnance surveyors. In *Davey v Harrow Corpn*[177] Lord Goddard CJ noted that according to the practice of the ordnance survey, where a boundary hedge is delineated on an ordnance survey map by a line, that line indicates the centre of the existing hedge. The court could take notice of that practice as at least prima facie evidence of what such a line indicated.

Readily demonstrable facts

Certain facts, although not notorious, are readily demonstrable after inquiry. The day of the week that a given date fell on, the longitude and latitude of a given place, and the date and location of a well-known historical event are all readily demonstrable by reference to suitably authoritative almanacs, historical or geographical works, or the oral statements of suitably qualified experts.[178]

Personal knowledge

It is clear that the verdict of a jury must be based upon the evidence adduced at the trial and that they should not look for additional material, for example by undertaking

---

[170] [1924] AC 797. See also *Mighell v Sultan of Johore* [1894] 1 QB 149, CA; *Carl Zeiss Stiftung v Rayner & Keeler Ltd (No 2)* [1967] 1 AC 853, HL; and *GUR Corpn v Trust Bank of Africa Ltd* [1987] QB 599, CA.

[171] [1928] AC 433, HL.

[172] [1927] P 311.

[173] *Roper v Taylor's Central Garages (Exeter) Ltd* [1951] 2 TLR 284. See also n 165.

[174] (1846) 12 Cl&Fin 787, HL. See also *George v Davies* [1911] 2 KB 445 at 448 and *Re Matthews, ex p Powell* (1875) 1 Ch D 501.

[175] *Re Rosher* (1884) 26 Ch D 801.

[176] *Heather v PE Consulting Group* [1973] Ch 189.

[177] [1958] 1 QB 60, CA at 69.

[178] See *Read v Bishop of Lincoln* [1892] AC 644, where reference to suitable works was approved on the question whether the practice of mixing communion wine with water was contrary to the law of the church. Cf *Evans v Getting* (1834) 6 C&P 586.

internet searches.[179] A different issue which has given rise to considerable difficulty is the extent to which a judge or juror is entitled to make use of his *personal* knowledge of facts. For these purposes a useful distinction, albeit not always drawn by the courts, is between personal knowledge used in the evaluation of evidence adduced, a matter quite distinct from the doctrine of judicial notice, and personal knowledge of a fact in issue or relevant to a fact in issue.

The evaluation of evidence

It seems reasonably clear that, in assessing evidence adduced in court, a member of the tribunal of fact is entitled to make use of personal knowledge whether it is of a general or specialized nature. In *Wetherall v Harrison*[180] the issue was whether the defendant had a reasonable excuse for failure to give a blood sample. The defendant gave evidence that he was unable to give a sample because he had had a sort of fit. The prosecution gave evidence that the fit had been simulated. One of the justices, a practising doctor, gave his views on the matter to other members of the bench. The justices also drew on their own wartime experiences of the fear that inoculations can create in certain individuals. An appeal by case stated against the acquittal was dismissed. Concerning the extent to which use could be made of local or personal knowledge, the Divisional Court was of the opinion that judges and arbitrators should be treated separately from justices and jurors. That the latter bring into the courtroom and make use of their manifold experience was seen as an advantage. Stressing that it would be quite wrong if a justice gave evidence to himself or other members of the bench in contradiction of the evidence adduced, Lord Widgery CJ held that it was not improper for a justice to draw on special knowledge of the circumstances forming the background to a case in considering, weighing up, and assessing the evidence adduced.

Personal knowledge of facts in issue or relevant to the issue

It is clear from the dictum of Lord Widgery CJ[181] that a member of the tribunal of fact may not make use of his personal knowledge of facts in issue if this amounts to giving evidence in contradiction of that adduced. However, if the fact is notorious, it seems that notice of it may be taken.[182] In *R v Jones*[183] it was contended that in order to show that the accused had been given an opportunity to provide a specimen of breath for a breath test, it was necessary to prove that the device in question, the Alcotest R 80, was of a type approved by the Secretary of State. Rejecting this argument, Edmund Davies LJ held that the court (including the jury) was entitled to take judicial notice of the fact that the Alcotest R 80 was of an approved type.[184] In the case of facts which are not notorious, a member of a tribunal of fact may not act on his personal knowledge of the matter in question. Rather than supplement or contradict the evidence in this way, he should be sworn as a witness and give evidence, thereafter playing no further part in the proceedings.[185] In some cases, however, the use of personal knowledge has been approved. In *R v Field (Justices), ex p White*,[186] the issue was whether cocoa

---

[179] Written notice of the prohibition is required by Criminal Procedure Rules 2015, SI 2015/1490, r 26(3). It is an offence for a juror to research the case during the trial: Juries Act 1974, s 20A.

[180] [1976] QB 773, DC.

[181] In *Wetherall v Harrison* [1976] QB 773, DC.

[182] This has been referred to as 'jury or magistrate notice'.

[183] [1970] 1 WLR 16, CA.

[184] Ibid at 20.

[185] *R v Antrim Justices* [1895] 2 IR 603.

[186] (1895) 64 LJMC 158.

contained a quantity of foreign ingredients. Despite the absence of evidence to establish the matter, the justices, acting on the knowledge of the subject that some of them had acquired in the navy, found for the accused. Although Wills J observed that, in future, evidence should be heard,[187] the finding was not disturbed. In *Ingram v Percival*[188] the accused was convicted of unlawfully using a net secured by anchors for taking salmon or trout in tidal waters. The only issue being whether the place where the net was fixed was in tidal waters, the justices had acted on their own knowledge. Lord Parker CJ held that justices may and should take into consideration personal knowledge, particularly when it relates to local matters. In *Paul v DPP*[189] it was held that in a case of 'kerb crawling', justices, for the purpose of deciding whether or not the soliciting was 'such . . . as to be likely to cause nuisance to other persons in the neighbourhood',[190] were entitled to take into account their local knowledge that the area in question was a heavily populated residential area, often frequented by prostitutes, with a constant procession of cars at night.

When a *judge* takes judicial notice of a notorious fact, he is making use of his general knowledge. The extent to which a judge may make use of his personal knowledge of facts in issue or relevant to the issue is not clear from the authorities. In *Keane v Mount Vernon Colliery Co Ltd*[191] Lord Buckmaster held that 'properly applied, and within reasonable limits' it was permissible to use knowledge of matters within the common knowledge of people in the locality. Similarly, in *Reynolds v Llanelly Associated Tinplate Co Ltd*[192] Lord Greene MR said that whereas it is improper to draw on knowledge of a particular or highly specialized nature, the use of knowledge on matters within the common knowledge of everyone in the district is unobjectionable. These two cases and others cited in support of the same principle were all decided under the Workmen's Compensation Acts, under which the county court judges sat as arbitrators and could take into account, when assessing compensation, their own knowledge of the labour market, conditions of labour, and wages.[193] However, in *Mullen v Hackney London Borough Council*[194] the Court of Appeal treated the principle as being of general application in any county court case. The judge in that case, in deciding the financial penalty to impose on the council for its failure to carry out an undertaking to the court to repair a council house, took account of the fact that the council had failed to honour previous undertakings to the court in similar cases. On appeal it was held that the judge was entitled to take judicial notice of his own knowledge of the council's conduct in relation to the previous undertakings, since even if not notorious or clearly established, it was clearly susceptible of demonstration by reference to the court records, and there was nothing to suggest that the judge had relied on his local knowledge improperly or beyond reasonable limits. It is submitted that this decision confuses and misapplies the separate principles relating to judicial notice and personal knowledge. As to judicial notice, the facts in question were clearly not notorious or of common knowledge, and bear no resemblance to the kinds of fact of which judicial notice has been held to have been properly taken after inquiry. As to personal knowledge, it appears to

---

[187] Ibid at 159–60.
[188] [1969] 1 QB 548.
[189] (1989) 90 Cr App R 173, DC.
[190] Section 1(1) of the Sexual Offences Act 1985, now repealed.
[191] [1933] AC 309 at 317.
[192] [1948] 1 All ER 140, CA.
[193] See Allen, 'Judicial notice extended' (1998) 2(1) E&P 37.
[194] [1997] 1 WLR 1103.

have been used, without good reason, without notice, and to the unfair disadvantage of the council, as a substitute for evidence.

Formal admissions

It is important to distinguish between formal and informal admissions. An informal admission is a statement of a party adverse to his case and admissible as evidence of the truth of its contents, by way of exception to the rule against hearsay, subject to compliance with the relevant statutory conditions and notice procedure.[195] Unlike a formal admission, it is not conclusive: its maker may adduce evidence at the trial with a view to explaining it away. However, a fact which is formally admitted ceases to be in issue. Evidence of such a fact is neither required nor admissible. Thus a party who makes a formal admission, which is generally conclusive for the purposes of the proceedings, saves his opponent the trouble, time, and expense of proving the fact in question. A party who fails formally to admit facts about which there is no real dispute may be ordered to pay the costs incurred by his adversary in proving them. Legal advisers owe a duty to their clients to consider if any formal admissions can properly be made.

Civil cases

CPR r 14.1(1), (2), and (5) provide as follows:

(1) A party may admit the truth of the whole or any part of another party's case.
(2) The party may do this by giving notice in writing (such as in a statement of case or by letter).[196]
(3) The permission of the court is required to amend or withdraw an admission.[197]

CPR r 14.1A(1) provides as follows:

A person may, by giving notice in writing, admit the truth of the whole or any part of another party's case before commencement of proceedings (a 'pre-action admission').[198]

In civil proceedings, a fact may be formally admitted in a variety of additional ways: by an express admission in a defence,[199] by default, that is, by a defendant failing to deal with an allegation,[200] or by either party in response to a notice to admit facts,[201] or in response to a written request, or court order, to give additional information.[202] Prior to the trial, formal admissions may also be made by letter written by a legal adviser acting on behalf of a client.[203] At the trial itself, a party or his legal adviser may admit facts, thereby rendering any evidence on the matter inadmissible.[204]

---

[195] As to criminal cases, see Ch 12. As to civil cases, see Ch 13, **Evidence formerly admissible at common law, p 429**.

[196] Special provision has also been made for the making of admissions where the only remedy which the claimant is seeking is the payment of money: see CPR rr 14.1(3) and 14.4–14.7.

[197] Paragraph 7.2 of PD 14 contains a non-exhaustive list of factors to which the court must have regard when considering an application to withdraw a Pt 14 admission.

[198] Special provision is made for pre-action admissions made in proceedings falling within the pre-action protocol for personal injuries, for the resolution of clinical disputes, or for disease and illness claims: see r 14.1A(2)–(5).

[199] See CPR r 16.5(1)(c).

[200] See CPR r 16.5(5).

[201] See CPR r 32.18.

[202] See CPR rr 18.1 and 26.5(3), and PD 18.

[203] *Ellis v Allen* [1914] 1 Ch 904.

[204] *Urquhart v Butterfield* (1887) 37 Ch D 357, CA.

Criminal cases

Under s 10(1) of the Criminal Justice Act 1967, a formal admission may be made of 'any fact of which oral evidence may be given in any criminal proceedings', words which make it clear that the section covers only facts and therefore not the opinion of an expert,[205] and cannot be used to admit evidence which would otherwise fall to be excluded because, for example, it is inadmissible hearsay.[206] The admission, which may be made before or at the proceedings in question by or on behalf of the prosecutor or accused, is conclusive evidence in those proceedings of the fact admitted. Ordinarily, it should be put before the jury, unless it contains material which should not be before them.[207] The admission is also treated as conclusive for the purposes of any subsequent criminal proceedings, including an appeal or retrial, relating to the same matter to which the original proceedings related.[208] The admission may, with the leave of the court, be withdrawn.[209] The making of an admission under the section is subject to certain protective restrictions: if made otherwise than in court, it shall be in writing;[210] if made in writing by an individual, it shall purport to be signed by the person making it (in the case of a body corporate the signature being required to be that of a director, manager, secretary, clerk, or other similar officer); if made on behalf of an accused who is an individual, it shall be made by his barrister or solicitor; and if made at any stage before the trial by such an accused, it must be approved by his barrister or solicitor (whether at the time it was made or subsequently) before or at the proceedings in question.[211] Where a party introduces in evidence a fact admitted by another party, or parties jointly admit a fact, then unless the court otherwise directs, a written record must be made of the admission.[212] Section 10 applies in the case of relevant facts in a written schedule which the parties agree to put before the jury, including any such facts that were removed pending a judicial ruling on their admissibility and then reinstated following a ruling in favour of admissibility.[213]

ADDITIONAL READING

Carter, 'Judicial Notice: Related and Unrelated Matters' in Campbell and Waller (eds), *Well and Truly Tried* (Sydney, 1982).
  A critical analysis of the doctrine of judicial notice.

Zuckerman, *The Principles of Criminal Evidence* (Oxford, 1989) Chs 6 and 8.
  Chapter 6 addresses judicial notice and chapter 8 addresses burden of proof and presumptions as risk-allocation techniques.

---

[205] *R v Naylor* [2010] EWCA Crim 1188. However, an expert's conclusions may be admitted under Criminal Procedure Rules 2015, SI 2015/1490, r 19.3(1) and (2): see **Ch 20**.

[206] See *R v Coulson* [1997] Crim LR 886, CA.

[207] *R v Pittard* [2006] EWCA Crim 2028.

[208] Section 10(3).

[209] Section 10(4).

[210] Section 10(2)(b). In court, an advocate may admit a fact *orally*: *R v Lewis* [1989] Crim LR 61, CA. Cf *Tobi v Nicholas* [1987] Crim LR 774, DC.

[211] Section 10(2)(c)–(e).

[212] Criminal Procedure Rules 2015, SI 2015/1490, r 24(6) (magistrates' court) and r 25.13 (Crown Court).

[213] *R v Lunkulu* [2015] EWCA Crim 1350.

Witnesses

5

Key issues

- Which types of witness should be eligible to give evidence and which ineligible?

- Which types of witness, if eligible to give evidence, should the court have the power to compel to give evidence?

- When and why should witnesses be allowed to give evidence through a live television link?

- When and why should parties to litigation be allowed to call additional evidence after the close of their case?

- In civil proceedings, what are the advantages of (a) exchanging witness statements prior to trial; and (b) allowing a statement to stand as a witness's evidence-in-chief?

- When and why should witnesses in criminal proceedings be allowed to give their evidence-in-chief by video recording?

- What measures can be taken to minimize the ordeal and trauma experienced by children and other vulnerable or intimidated witnesses when giving evidence in criminal cases?

- When and why should witnesses be allowed to withhold their names and other identifying details?

- Why is witness training or coaching prohibited, but witness familiarization allowed?

Competence and compellability

A witness is said to be competent if he may be called to give evidence and compellable if, being competent, he may be compelled by the court to do so.[1] A compellable witness who chooses to ignore a witness summons is in contempt of court and faces the penalty of imprisonment.[2] The same applies in the case of a compellable witness who attends court but refuses to testify, although such a witness may be entitled, on grounds of public policy or privilege, to refuse to answer some or all of the questions put to him.[3]

No party has any property in the evidence of a witness. Even if there is a contract between a party and a witness under which the latter binds himself not to give evidence to the court on a matter on which the judge can compel him to give evidence, it is contrary to public policy and unenforceable. Thus an expert witness is compellable if, having inadvertently advised both parties, he is loath to appear on behalf of one of them.[4] However, once a witness in criminal proceedings has given evidence for the prosecution, he cannot be called to give evidence for the defence;[5] an expert witness may not be called by one party if his opinion is based on privileged information, such as communications with the other party, and cannot be divorced from it;[6] and an expert is not as a general rule required to give expert evidence against his wishes if he has no connection with the facts or history of the matter in issue, especially where he could not give the evidence without a breach of confidence or without considerable time and study.[7]

The general rule

At common law, the law of competence and compellability is governed by a general rule with two limbs. The first limb is that anyone is a competent witness in any proceedings. Many former categories of exception to the first limb have been swept away, over the centuries, by judicial and statutory reform.[8] The first limb has now been put on a statutory footing in criminal cases. Section 53(1) of the Youth Justice and Criminal Evidence Act 1999 (the 1999 Act) provides that: 'At every stage in criminal proceedings all persons are (whatever their age) competent to give evidence.' The only remaining exceptions to the first limb of the general rule relate to the accused as a witness for the prosecution, children, and persons with a disorder or disability of the mind.

---

[1] In civil cases, a witness summons may be issued by the court: see CPR r 34.2–34.6. In trials on indictment, the attendance of witnesses may also be secured by means of a witness summons: see Criminal Procedure (Attendance of Witnesses) Act 1965, s 2. For the position in magistrates' courts, see the Magistrates' Courts Act 1980, s 97.

[2] See *R v Yusuf* [2003] 2 Cr App R 488 (32), CA.

[3] See Chs 21 and 22.

[4] *Harmony Shipping Co SA v Saudi Europe Line Ltd* [1979] 1 WLR 1380, CA, where the court noted that many of the communications between the expert and the solicitor would be protected by legal professional privilege, as to which see Ch 22. See also *Meat Corporation of Namibia Ltd v Dawn Meats (UK) Ltd* [2011] EWHC 474 (Ch), where the expert gave an undertaking not to reveal confidential or privileged information; and cf *Bolkiah v KPMG* [1992] 2 AC 222, where the expert was previously engaged in a quasi-solicitor role and, despite an undertaking, there was a risk of the misuse of confidential information.

[5] *R v Kelly* (1985) The Times, 27 July, CA.

[6] *R v Davies* (2002) 166 JP 243, CA. See also *R v R* [1994] 4 All ER 260, CA (see Ch 22).

[7] *Seyfang v GD Searle & Co* [1973] QB 148 at 151 and *Lively Ltd v City of Munich* [1976] 1 WLR 1004, QBD, at 1010.

[8] For details, see earlier editions of this work.

The second limb of the general rule is that all competent witnesses are compellable. The only remaining exceptions to the second limb relate to the accused, his or her spouse or civil partner, heads of sovereign states, diplomats, and, in certain circumstances, bankers.[9]

The accused

For the prosecution

Under s 53 of the 1999 Act, the accused, whether charged solely or jointly, is not competent as a witness for the prosecution. Section 53 provides as follows:

(1) At every stage in criminal proceedings all persons are (whatever their age) competent to give evidence.

(2) Subsection (1) has effect subject to subsections (3) and (4).

(3) A person is not competent to give evidence in criminal proceedings if it appears to the court that he is not a person who is able to—

(a) understand questions put to him as a witness, and

(b) give answers to them which can be understood.

(4) A person charged in criminal proceedings is not competent to give evidence in the proceedings for the prosecution (whether he is the only person, or is one of two or more persons, charged in the proceedings).

(5) In subsection (4) the reference to a person charged in criminal proceedings does not include a person who is not, or is no longer, liable to be convicted of any offence in the proceedings (whether as a result of pleading guilty or for any other reason).

Thus if the prosecution wish to call a co-accused to give evidence for them, they may only do so if, in effect, he has ceased to be a co-accused. This may happen, as s 53(5) indicates, as a result of pleading guilty, even if, in his evidence, he suggests that he was not a participant in the offence, unless the plea is set aside.[10] It may also happen in three other ways: the co-accused may be acquitted, for example where no evidence is offered against him or he makes a successful submission of no case to answer at the close of the prosecution case; an application to sever the indictment may succeed so that he is not tried with the other accused; or the Attorney General may enter a *nolle prosequi*, thereby putting an end to the proceedings against him. In any of these circumstances a former co-accused becomes both a competent and compellable witness for the prosecution.[11]

For himself

The accused is a competent but not compellable witness for the defence in all criminal proceedings. As to competence, the authority is now to be found in s 53(1) of the 1999 Act. As to compellability, s 1(1) of the Criminal Evidence Act 1898 provides that: 'A person charged in criminal proceedings shall not be called as a witness in the proceedings except upon his own application.'

---

[9] The leave of the wardship court is not required to call a ward to give evidence at a criminal trial: *Re K (minors)* [1988] 1 All ER 214, Fam D; and *Re R (minors)* [1991] 2 All ER 193, CA. Concerning interviews with wards by the prosecution or police, see *Criminal Practice Directions* V, Part 17A; and *Re R, Re G (minors)* [1990] 2 All ER 633, Fam D. As to interviews with wards by those representing the accused, see *Re R (minors)* [1991] 2 All ER 193, CA.

[10] *R v McEwan* [2011] EWCA Crim 1026.

[11] An accomplice who is not an accused in the proceedings in question but against whom proceedings are pending should only be called by the prosecution if they have undertaken to discontinue the proceedings against him: *R v Pipe* (1966) 51 Cr App R 17, CA. However, this is a rule of practice only and a matter within the discretion of the judge: *R v Turner* (1975) 61 Cr App R 67, CA.

The phrase in s 53(1), 'at every stage in criminal proceedings', is most likely to be construed in the same way as was the phrase 'at every stage of the proceedings' in the original una-mended version of s 1 of the Criminal Evidence Act 1898, so as to allow the accused to give evidence on the *voir dire*[12] and, after conviction, in mitigation of sentence,[13] as well as during the trial proper.

The accused's right to give evidence if he wishes to, is an essential aspect of the right to a fair trial.[14] Where the accused wishes to give evidence but an issue arises as to whether he is genuinely able to do so because of illness, his advocate should be given proper opportunity to obtain medical evidence to ascertain whether special measures might enable him to give evidence without undue risk to his physical and mental health.[15] Where his advocate makes an application for time to obtain medical evidence, the judge should avoid speculating on what such evidence might show and should not proceed without intermission where the effect is that the accused, against his wishes, does not give evidence.[16] Where the accused, wishing to give evidence, has been genuinely unable to, it is incumbent on the judge to direct the jury about the consequences of that fact, in particular, that they have not been able to hear the accused's first-hand account and assess its credibility, including the extent to which it might conflict or be consistent with the evidence of other witnesses.[17] In addition, the judge should consider the extent to which the jury require guidance on specific significant points not covered in the accused's interview, but which the prosecution has raised in the course of the trial and which the accused has not had the opportunity to address.[18]

If the accused elects to give evidence, he may of course be cross-examined by the prosecution and, even if he has not given evidence against a co-accused, by any co-accused.[19] Indeed, having elected to give evidence, then subject to s 1(2) and (4) of the Criminal Evidence Act 1898, and s 101 of the Criminal Justice Act 2003 (the 2003 Act),[20] he will be treated like any other witness and his evidence will be evidence for all the purposes of the case. Thus the evidence of an accused in his own defence may be used against a co-accused whether such evidence was given in chief[21] or elicited in cross-examination. In *R v Paul*[22] an accused had confined his evidence-in-chief to an admission of his own guilt. A cross-examination of him, which had elicited evidence undermining the defence of a co-accused, was held by the Court of Criminal Appeal to have been properly permitted.[23]

---

[12] *R v Cowell* [1940] 2 KB 49.

[13] *R v Wheeler* [1917] 1 KB 283.

[14] *R v Welland* [2018] EWCA Crim 2036 at [1] and [18].

[15] *R v Welland* [2018] EWCA Crim 2036 at [19] and [21]. The accused had suffered several seizures during the course of the trial apparently induced by stress and when the stage was reached for him to give evidence, and he wished to give evidence, defence and prosecution advocates and the judge considered him to be at great risk of further seizures.

[16] Ibid at [20].

[17] Ibid at [22].

[18] Ibid. When directing the jury, it is inappropriate to say that the accused has the judge's 'permission' not to give evidence since this is not a matter in the gift of the judge.

[19] *R v Hilton* [1972] 1 QB 421, CA.

[20] Described at nn 24–26.

[21] See *R v Rudd* (1948) 32 Cr App R 138; cf *R v Meredith* (1943) 29 Cr App R 40.

[22] [1920] 2 KB 183.

[23] But see *Young v HM Advocate* 1932 JC 63, where the view was expressed that in these circumstances the judge should exercise his discretion to prevent such cross-examination.

Section 1(2) of the Criminal Evidence Act 1898 removes from the accused who testifies the privilege against self-incrimination in respect of any offence with which he is charged. It provides that 'Subject to section 101 of the 2003 Act (admissibility of evidence of defendant's bad character), a person charged in criminal proceedings who is called as a witness in the proceedings may be asked any question in cross-examination notwithstanding that it would tend to criminate him as to any offence with which he is charged in the proceedings.'[24] Section 101 of the 2003 Act sets out the only circumstances in which evidence of the bad character of the accused is admissible.[25]

Section 1(4) of the Criminal Evidence Act 1898 provides that 'every person charged in criminal proceedings who is called as a witness in the proceedings shall, unless otherwise ordered by the court, give his evidence from the witness box or other place from which the other witnesses give their evidence'. The court may 'order otherwise' if the accused is too infirm to walk to the witness box or too violent to be controlled there.[26] Subject to exceptional circumstances of this kind, the proviso does not confer a discretion to direct where evidence should be given from, and it is improper to offer the accused a choice as to whether he wishes to give his evidence from the dock or witness box.[27] If an accused elects not to give evidence, it should be the invariable practice of his advocate to record the decision and to cause the accused to sign the record, giving a clear indication that he has by his own will decided not to testify bearing in mind the advice, if any, given to him by his advocate.[28]

For a co-accused
Competence
It will be clear from s 53(1) of the 1999 Act and s 1(1) of the 1898 Act that an accused is a competent but not compellable witness for a co-accused. A person who has ceased to be an accused is both competent and compellable for a co-accused. This may happen where he has pleaded guilty,[29] where he has been acquitted (for example where no evidence has been offered against him, or he has made a successful submission of no case to answer at the close of the prosecution case),[30] or where an application to sever the indictment has succeeded so that he is not tried with the other accused.[31]

The spouse or civil partner of an accused

For the prosecution
In its 11th Report, the Criminal Law Revision Committee considered to what extent the spouse of the accused should be competent and compellable for the prosecution.[32] Concerning competence, the Committee concluded that the wife should be competent for the prosecution in all cases: 'If she is willing to give evidence, we think that the law would be showing excessive

[24] See also Ch 22, The privilege against self-incrimination, p 713.
[25] See further Ch 19, Evidence of the bad character of the defendant, p 570.
[26] *R v Symonds* (1924) 18 Cr App R 100 at 101.
[27] *R v Farnham Justices, ex p Gibson* [1991] Crim LR 642, DC.
[28] *R v Bevan* (1993) 98 Cr App R 354, CA.
[29] *R v Boal* [1965] 1 QB 402 at 414.
[30] *R v Conti* (1973) 58 Cr App R 387, CA.
[31] *R v Richardson* (1967) 51 Cr App R 381.
[32] Criminal Law Revision Committee, 11th Report, *Evidence (General)*, Cmnd 4991 (1972), para 147.

concern for the preservation of marital harmony if it were to say that she must not do so.'[33] This view was given effect by s 80(1) of the Police and Criminal Evidence Act 1984 (the 1984 Act). Section 80(1) was repealed. The spouse or civil partner of an accused is now competent for the prosecution under s 53(1) of the 1999 Act whereby, as we have seen, subject to s 53(3), in criminal proceedings all persons are competent to give evidence. As we have also seen, s 53(1) is also subject to s 53(4), whereby a person charged in criminal proceedings is not competent to give evidence in the proceedings for the prosecution, whether he is the only person, or one of two or more, charged in the proceedings. Thus if a husband and wife are co-accused, whether charged jointly with the same offence or charged with different offences, neither is competent to give evidence for the prosecution. As s 53(5) indicates, the spouse may only become competent for the prosecution if he or she ceases to be a co-accused. This may happen if the spouse pleads guilty or is acquitted (because no evidence is offered against the spouse or the spouse makes a successful submission of no case to answer), or if one of the spouses makes a successful application to sever the indictment. Section 53(4) and (5) apply in relation to a civil partner of an accused in the same way as they apply to a spouse of an accused.

Compellability

Concerning compellability, the Criminal Law Revision Committee was in favour of maintaining the common law rule, as it then stood, of compellability in the case of offences involving personal violence by the accused against his or her spouse. The reasons included the public interest in the punishment of those committing crimes of violence and the fact that compellability would make it easier for the accused's spouse to counter the effect of possible intimidation by the accused and persuade him or her to give evidence.[34] It was also proposed to make the spouse compellable in the case of offences of a violent or sexual nature against children under the age of 16 belonging to the same household as the accused. Subsequent to the Committee's Report and prior to the 1984 Act, a majority of the House of Lords in *Hoskyn v Metropolitan Police Comr*[35] held that where an accused is charged with an offence of violence against his or her spouse, that spouse is competent but *not compellable* for the prosecution. The majority of their Lordships were reluctant to compel a wife to testify against her husband on a charge of violence, however trivial, and regardless of the consequences to herself, her family, and her marriage. Lord Edmund Davies, the sole dissentient, regarded as extremely unlikely prosecutions based on trivial violence and was of the opinion that cases of serious physical violence by one spouse against the other were too grave to depend upon the willingness of the injured spouse to testify and 'ought not to be regarded as having no importance extending beyond the domestic hearth'. Against this background of differing and strongly held opinion, Parliament not only adopted but extended the proposals of the Criminal Law Revision Committee. The relevant subsections of s 80 of the 1984 Act, as since amended, provide as follows:

(2A) In any proceedings the spouse or civil partner of a person charged in the proceedings shall, subject to subsection (4) below, be compellable

    (a) to give evidence on behalf of any other person charged in the proceedings but only in respect of any specified offence with which that other person is charged; or

    (b) to give evidence for the prosecution but only in respect of any specified offence with which any person is charged in the proceedings.

[33] Ibid, para 148.

[34] Ibid, para 149.

[35] [1979] AC 474, HL.

(3) In relation to the spouse or civil partner of a person charged in any proceedings, an offence is a specified offence for the purposes of subsection (2A) above if

  (a) it involves an assault on, or injury or a threat of injury to, the spouse or civil partner or a person who was at the material time under the age of 16;[36]

  (b) it is a sexual offence alleged to have been committed in respect of a person who was at the material time under that age; or

  (c) it consists of attempting or conspiring to commit, or of aiding, abetting, counselling, procuring or inciting the commission of, an offence falling within paragraph (a) or (b) above.[37]

(4) No person who is charged in any proceedings shall be compellable by virtue of subsection (2) or (2A) above to give evidence in the proceedings.

(4A) References in this section to a person charged in any proceedings do not include a person who is not, or is no longer, liable to be convicted of any offence in the proceedings (whether as a result of pleading guilty or for any other reason).

These subsections apply 'in any proceedings', a phrase which encompasses criminal proceedings brought by one spouse against the other. Thus in the unlikely event of such proceedings being pursued by a spouse who declines to give evidence, then he or she may nonetheless be compellable in accordance with s 80(2A) and (3).

It is submitted that the words 'spouse' and 'civil partner' refer to persons whose marriage or civil partnership, wherever it was celebrated, would be recognized by English law,[38] but not cohabitees (whether heterosexual or same-sex couples). In *Van Der Heijden v The Netherlands*[39] the Grand Chamber of the European Court of Human Rights held, by majority, that to compel a cohabitee with two children from a relationship of 18 years' standing, to give evidence against her partner, would interfere with her right to respect for family life under Art 8 of the Convention, but would be 'necessary . . . for the prevention of . . . crime' under Art 8(2).[40] Concerning the word 'involves', in the phrase 'involves an assault on, or injury or a threat of an injury to', it was held in *R v A(B)*[41] that it means that the offence must have as one of its ingredients, or must encompass the real possibility of, 'an assault . . .' etc and therefore does not cover cases where there is no such legal requirement but the way in which the offence was committed did in fact involve, or is alleged to have involved, 'an assault . . .' etc. In that case, the accused said to his wife that he was going to burn their house down with the children in it and was charged under s 2(a) of the Criminal Damage Act 1971 with making a threat to another, intending the other to fear it would be carried out, to destroy or damage any property. It was held that s 2(a) was directed at property and did not have as an

---

[36] Where the age of any person at any time is material for the purposes of s 80(3), his age at the material time shall 'be deemed to be or to have been that which appears to the court to be or to have been his age at that time': s 80(6).

[37] The reference to incitement has effect as a reference to (or to conduct amounting to) the offences of encouraging or assisting crime under the Serious Crime Act 2007, Pt 2 (s 63(1) and Sch 6 para 9 of the 2007 Act).

[38] See *R v Bala* [2016] EWCA Crim 560, construing the words as used in the Criminal Law Act 1977, s 2(2) and, at common law, *R v Khan* (1987) 84 Cr App R 44, CA and *R v Yacoob* (1981) 72 Cr App R 313, CA.

[39] [2012] ECHR 588.

[40] See also *R v Pearce* [2002] 1 WLR 1553, CA, construing s 80 prior to its amendment by the 1999 Act, and, applying the reasoning in these cases, *R v Suski* [2016] 2 Cr App R 32 (3), construing 'spouse' and 'civil partner' as used in the Criminal Law Act 1977, s 2(2).

[41] [2012] 2 Cr App R 467, CA.

ingredient, or encompass the real possibility of, 'an assault . . .' etc, and therefore the wife was not compellable to give evidence against him. In s 80(3)(b), 'sexual offence' means an offence under the Protection of Children Act 1978, Pt 1 of the Sexual Offences Act 2003 or s 2 of the Modern Slavery Act 2015 (human trafficking) committed with a view to exploitation that consists of or includes behaviour within s 3(3) of that Act (sexual exploitation).[42]

Anomalies

In *R v A(B)*, the Court of Appeal also noted three anomalies to which s 80(2A) and (3) give rise. First, as already noted, the restriction on compellability only applies to spouses and civil partners and does not extend to cohabitees, even if they have been living together for a considerable period of time. Second, the judge has the discretion to admit a hearsay statement of a spouse or civil partner, even if not compellable, under s 114(2) of the Criminal Justice Act 2003.[43] Third, the accused may be charged with two or more offences in respect of only one of which the spouse or civil partner is compellable. It seems from the wording of s 80(2A)(b) that the spouse or civil partner is compellable to give evidence for the prosecution on the one offence, but not the other or others, even where such a distinction is artificial because the evidence is relevant to the other or others. Let us suppose, for example, that in the course of a neighbourhood dispute that develops into a fracas, A assaults both B and B's 15-year-old son. It seems that A's wife would only be compellable to give evidence in relation to the assault on B's son, but her evidence would be likely to be relevant to both offences charged. Presumably, in such a case, A could apply for separate trials for each of the offences, or might apply to exclude the evidence of his wife relying upon s 78(1) of the 1984 Act or the common law discretion to exclude in order to ensure a fair trial. It may be doubted, however, that either application would have much prospect of success.[44]

These are not the only anomalies to which s 80 gives rise. Non-compellability is borne of concern for the preservation of marital harmony, but it operates regardless of the state of the marriage or civil partnership, gives protection for only the spouse or civil partner, but not other family members (whose compulsion could easily disrupt the harmony of the relationship), and, in the case of offences against children, including children of the family, draws an arbitrary distinction between those under and over the age of 16. By reason of these and other anomalies, it has been convincingly argued that, in principle, spousal non-compellability cannot be justified and should be abolished.[45]

Duty to explain non-compellability

There is no requirement, before interviewing a spouse or civil partner who is competent but not compellable for the prosecution in relation to the crime of which her husband or civil partner is suspected, to tell her that she is not compellable.[46] An accused's spouse or civil partner who is called as a competent but not compellable witness for the prosecution but proves adverse for the purposes of s 3 of the Criminal Procedure Act 1865,[47] may be treated

---

[42] Section 80(7).

[43] See *R v L* [2009] 1 WLR 626, CA, Ch 12, p 390 n 262.

[44] See Creighton, 'Spouse Competence and Compellability' [1990] Crim LR 34.

[45] Hoyano, 'Commentary', *R v BA: Witness Compellability—Husband and Wife* [2013] Crim LR 170. For the counter-argument in favour of retention and modification, see Brabyn, 'A Criminal Defendant's Spouse as a Prosecution Witness' [2011] Crim LR 613.

[46] *R v L (R)* [2008] 2 Cr App R 243 (18), CA.

[47] See Ch 6.

as a hostile witness in the normal way. This was established prior to the 1984 Act in *R v Pitt*,[48] an authority which may be assumed to remain good law. The Court of Appeal held that the choice of a wife whether or not to give evidence, being a competent but not compellable witness for the prosecution, is not lost because she makes a witness statement or gives evidence at the committal proceedings.[49] She retains the right of refusal up to the point when she takes the oath in the witness box, and waiver of her right of refusal is effective only if made with full knowledge of her right to refuse. However, if she knowingly waives her right of refusal, she becomes an ordinary witness and, having started her evidence, must complete it, unable to retreat behind the barrier of non-compellability. Accordingly, if the nature of her evidence warrants it, an application may be made to treat her as a hostile witness.[50] For these reasons, the Court of Appeal thought it desirable that the judge should explain to the wife, in the absence of the jury and before she takes the oath, that she has the right not to give evidence but that if she chooses to do so she may be treated like any other witness. In appropriate circumstances the Court of Appeal may upset a verdict if it feels that injustice may have occurred because a wife gave evidence without appreciating that she had a right to refuse to do so.

For the accused

The Criminal Law Revision Committee had no doubt that the accused's spouse should be made competent and compellable for the accused in all cases,[51] a recommendation implemented by the 1984 Act. The spouse or civil partner of an accused is now competent to give evidence on behalf of the accused under s 53(1) of the 1999 Act, and this remains the case even if he or she is also charged in the same proceedings. As to compellability, s 80(2) provides as follows:

> (2) In any proceedings the spouse or civil partner of a person charged in the proceedings shall, subject to subsection (4) below, be compellable to give evidence on behalf of that person.

The only exception to s 80(2) is in cases in which the spouses or civil partners are both charged in the same proceedings.[52]

For a co-accused

Competence

Under the Criminal Evidence Act 1898, the accused's spouse was, with the consent of the accused, competent as a witness for any other person jointly charged with the accused,[53] but not compellable. The Criminal Law Revision Committee recommended that the spouse of an accused should be competent to give evidence on behalf of any co-accused whether or not the accused consents. This recommendation is reflected in s 53(1) of the 1999 Act: the spouse or civil partner of an accused is competent to give evidence on behalf of any person jointly charged with the accused and this is the case even if the spouse or civil partner is also charged in the same proceedings.

---

[48] [1982] 3 All ER 63.

[49] However, if she declines to give evidence, her statement is potentially admissible hearsay: see *R v L* [2009] 1 WLR 626 and *R v Hornsell* [2012] EWCA Crim 227. See also Ch 12, Examples of appropriate use of s 114(1)(d), p 390, n 262.

[50] See Ch 6, Unfavourable and hostile witnesses, p 206.

[51] Criminal Law Revision Committee, 11th Report, para 153.

[52] Section 80(4).

[53] Section 1 and proviso (c) thereto.

Compellability

The more difficult question related to compellability on behalf of a co-accused. The interests of justice would seem to require that the co-accused should be able to compel the spouse if he or she is able to give relevant evidence in his defence. On the other hand, if the spouse is compelled to testify in such circumstances, the prosecution, in cross-examination of him or her, may well elicit evidence incriminating the accused, a result which is inconsistent with the general rule that the prosecution may not compel a spouse to testify for them. Given these competing interests of the accused and the co-accused, the Committee proposed that the spouse should be compellable on behalf of a co-accused in any case where he or she would be compellable on behalf of the prosecution.[54] The substance of these proposals has been enacted in s 80(2A) and (3) of the 1984 Act, which, as amended, provide that in any proceedings the spouse or civil partner of the accused shall be compellable to give evidence on behalf of any other person charged in the proceedings, but only in respect of any specified offence with which that other person is charged.[55] The only exception is in cases in which the spouse or civil partner is charged in the same proceedings.[56] Where co-accused A and B are charged with two or more offences in respect of only one of which the spouse or civil partner of B is compellable to give evidence on behalf of A, then it seems from the wording of s 80(2A)(a) that the spouse or civil partner of B is compellable to give evidence on behalf of A on that offence even if that evidence is also relevant to the other offence(s).

Former spouses or civil partners

In criminal proceedings, a former spouse or civil partner of an accused is competent under s 53(1) of the 1999 Act. Such a person is also compellable. Section 80(5) and (5A) of the 1984 Act provide as follows:

(5) In any proceedings a person who has been but is no longer married to the accused shall be compellable to give evidence as if that person and the accused had never been married.

(5A) In any proceedings a person who has been but is no longer the civil partner of the accused shall be compellable to give evidence as if that person and the accused had never been civil partners.

The effect of these provisions is to render former spouses (or civil partners), after their marriage (or civil partnership) has been dissolved, both competent and compellable to give evidence for either the defence or the prosecution, whether the evidence relates to events which occurred before, during, or after the terminated marriage (or civil partnership).[57] In s 80(5) of the 1984 Act the phrase 'in any proceedings' means any proceedings which took place after s 80(5) came into effect on 1 January 1986, and therefore an ex-spouse is competent and compellable to give evidence in such proceedings about any relevant matter whether it took place before or after that date.[58] The phrase 'is no longer married' is apt to apply where the spouses have been divorced and where their marriage, being voidable, has been annulled. If there is evidence to show that a marriage was void *ab initio*, a legally valid marriage never having existed, the parties to such a union are, in accordance with the general rules, both competent

---

[54] Criminal Law Revision Committee, 11th Report, para 155.

[55] The offences are set out in s 80(3), (see, in this chapter, under **For the prosecution**, p 130).

[56] Section 80(4), (see, in this chapter, under **For the prosecution**, p 130).

[57] See *R v Mathias* [1989] Crim LR 64, CC.

[58] *R v Cruttenden* [1991] 3 All ER 242, CA.

and compellable throughout. Spouses who are judicially separated, although often treated in law as the equivalent of divorced spouses, cannot be said to be 'no longer married' for the purposes of s 80(5). Likewise, the subsection has no application to spouses who are not cohabiting, whether without any arrangement or agreement, or pursuant to a separation agreement, non-cohabitation order, or informal arrangement. The Criminal Law Revision Committee considered whether to provide that judicially separated or non-cohabiting spouses should be treated for the purposes of competence and compellability as if they were unmarried. It is difficult to disagree with their conclusions against such a provision:[59]

> if there is little prospect that they will become reconciled, the spouse in question is likely to be willing to give evidence; and if there is a prospect of reconciliation, it may be better to avoid the risk of spoiling this prospect by compelling the spouse to give evidence when he or she would not have been compellable in the ordinary case.

Children and persons with a disorder or disability of the mind—criminal cases

The test for competence

The competence of all witnesses to give evidence in criminal proceedings is governed by s 53(1)–(3) of the 1999 Act, which provides as follows:

(1) At every stage in criminal proceedings all persons are (whatever their age) competent to give evidence.

(2) Subsection (1) has effect subject to subsections (3) and (4).[60]

(3) A person is not competent to give evidence in criminal proceedings if it appears to the court that he is not a person who is able to—

    (a) understand questions put to him as a witness, and

    (b) give answers to them which can be understood.

In *R v MacPherson*[61] it was held that the words 'put to him as a witness' in s 53(3)(a) mean the equivalent of 'being asked of him in court' and therefore an infant who can only communicate in baby language with its mother will not ordinarily be competent but a child who can speak and understand basic English with strangers will be competent. The court in that case, rejecting a submission to the effect that a judge must decide whether a child appreciates the difference between truth and falsehood, also held that there is no requirement that the child be aware of his witness status and that questions of credibility and reliability are not relevant to competence but go to the weight of the evidence and thus may be considered on a submission of no case to answer. Equally, a child who has no recollection of an event may be a perfectly competent witness.[62] In *R v Barker*[63] it was held that: in each case under s 53, the question is witness and trial specific; there are no presumptions; the witness does not need to understand the special importance of telling the truth in court; the issue is whether the witness can answer the questions, although not necessarily every single question, put to him by both sides,[64] and also provide understandable answers to them; and s 53 requires not

---

[59] Criminal Law Revision Committee, 11th Report, para 156.

[60] As to s 53(4), see, in this chapter, under **For the prosecution**, p 130.

[61] [2006] 1 Cr App R 459 (30), CA.

[62] *DPP v R* [2007] All ER (D) 176 (Jul).

[63] [2010] EWCA Crim 4.

[64] See, eg, *R v IA* [2013] EWCA Crim 1308.

the exercise of a discretion, but the making of a judgment on whether the witness fulfils the statutory criteria—it is not open to the judge to impose additional criteria based on former approaches to the evidence of children. However, it is submitted that where it is clear that a proposed witness, although satisfying the statutory criteria, is unable to distinguish truth from fiction or fact from fantasy, his evidence should be excluded under s 78 of the 1984 Act.[65]

In the case of young children, obviously the younger the child the more likely it is that he or she will be incapable of satisfying the test in s 53(3), and care clearly needs to be taken if the question of competence arises. However, a court cannot properly decide that a child is incapable of satisfying the test simply on the basis that he or she is of or below a certain age.[66] Equally, the fact that a judge or interpreter has difficulties in communicating with a child does not necessarily mean that the child cannot satisfy the test.[67] In *R v Sed*,[68] which concerned the competence of an 81-year-old woman who suffered from Alzheimer's disease, it was said that, depending on the length and nature of the questioning and the complexity of the subject matter, s 53 may not always require 100 per cent, or near 100 per cent, mutual understanding between the questioner and the questioned and that the judge should also make allowance for the fact that the witness's performance and command of detail may vary according to the importance to him of the subject matter, how recent it was, and any strong feelings that it may have engendered.[69]

The procedure

The question whether a witness is competent to give evidence in criminal proceedings may be raised either by a party to the proceedings or by the court of its own motion, but either way must be determined by the court in accordance with s 54 of the 1999 Act.[70] Under s 54(2), the burden is on the party calling the witness to satisfy the court, on a balance of probabilities, that the witness is competent. In determining whether the witness is competent, the court must treat the witness as having the benefit of any special measures directions under s 19 of the 1999 Act[71] which the court has given or proposes to give in relation to the witness.[72] Under s 54(4), any proceedings for the determination of the question shall take place in the absence of the jury (if there is one); under s 54(5), expert evidence may be received on the question (which is always likely to be required in the case of the mentally handicapped);[73] and under s 54(6), any questioning of the witness, where the court considers that necessary, shall be conducted by the court in the presence of the parties.

---

[65] Cf *R v D* (1995) The Times, 15 Nov, CA.

[66] *R v MacPherson* [2006] 1 Cr App R 459 (30), CA and *R v Powell* [2006] 1 Cr App R 468 (31), CA.

[67] *R v F (JR)* [2013] 1 WLR 2143, CA.

[68] [2004] 1 WLR 3218, CA at [45].

[69] The weight to be attached to the evidence given by a mentally handicapped person is for the jury: *R v Hill* (1851) 2 Den CC 254. A person suffering from a mental illness may be a reliable witness in relation to matters not affected by the condition: see *R v Barratt and Sheehan* [1996] Crim LR 495, CA (fixed belief paranoia). See also *R (B) v DPP* [2009] EWHC 106 (Admin). It is wrong, therefore, to direct a jury to treat evidence with caution if there is no medical foundation for regarding it as unreliable: *Milton v R* [2015] UKPC 42.

[70] Section 54(1).

[71] See, in this chapter, under **Witnesses in criminal cases**, p 152.

[72] Section 54(3). See also *R v F (JR)* [2013] 1 WLR 2143, CA at [25]: the competency test is not failed because the forensic techniques of the advocate or the processes of the court have to be adapted to enable the witness to give his best evidence.

[73] In *R v Barratt and Sheehan* [1996] Crim LR 495, CA it was held that the proper course is to adduce expert medical evidence so that it is not normally necessary to call the witness said to suffer from mental illness.

The issue of a child's competence should be decided before he or she is sworn, usually as a preliminary issue at the start of the trial when the judge should watch any videotaped interview of the child[74] and/or ask the child appropriate questions.[75] Where an *Achieving Best Evidence* ('ABE') interview[76] indicates competence, a competence hearing may serve only to cause delay, increase expense, and put unnecessary strain on the witness.[77] Any questioning thought to be necessary under s 54(6) is best conducted, it is submitted, in the spirit suggested in *R v Hampshire*:[78] 'it should be a matter of the judge's perception of the child's understanding demonstrated in the course of ordinary discourse'.

A decision that a child is competent should be kept under review and may need to be reconsidered when his or her evidence is complete. Thus although at the start of a trial a videotaped interview may indicate competence, a ruling to that effect should be reversed if the child is unable to understand questions or give answers which can be understood, which may be the result of a lapse of time and lack of memory.[79] There is a risk that the child will not have an accurate recollection of the events, and a further risk that if shown the video before or during the trial, may recollect only what was said on the video and be incapable of distinguishing that from the events themselves. Effective cross-examination, in such circumstances, would be virtually impossible.[80] However, it does not follow from this that in cases involving very young children, delay on its own automatically requires the court to prevent or stop the evidence of the child from being considered by the jury.[81] Furthermore, it has been doubted that a child's evidence should be excluded where she no longer has a reliably independent memory of the events—it is not infrequent for adults to have no such memory and to be able to say no more than that their statement is accurate.[82]

Evidence on oath or unsworn—criminal cases

A witness who is competent to give evidence in criminal proceedings may be sworn for the purpose of giving his evidence on oath, or may give his evidence unsworn. Section 55(1)–(4) of the 1999 Act provide as follows:

(1) Any question whether a witness in criminal proceedings may be sworn for the purpose of giving evidence on oath, whether raised—
   (a) by a party to the proceedings, or
   (b) by the court of its own motion, shall be determined by the court in accordance with this section.
(2) The witness may not be sworn for that purpose unless—
   (a) he has attained the age of 14, and
   (b) he has a sufficient appreciation of the solemnity of the occasion and of the particular responsibility to tell the truth which is involved in taking an oath.

---

[74] See the 1999 Act, s 27, in this chapter, under **Witnesses in criminal cases**, p 152.

[75] *R v MacPherson* [2006] 1 Cr App R 459 (30), CA.

[76] See Home Office, *Achieving Best Evidence in Criminal Proceedings: Guidance for Vulnerable or Intimidated Witnesses, including Children* considered, in this chapter, under **Video-recorded evidence-in-chief**, p 158.

[77] *R v F (JR)* [2013] 1 WLR 2143, CA at [39].

[78] [1995] 2 All ER 1019, CA.

[79] *R v Powell* [2006] 1 Cr App R 468 (31), CA, applied in *R v Malicki* [2009] EWCA Crim 365.

[80] *R v Malicki* [2009] EWCA Crim 365.

[81] *R v Barker* [2010] EWCA Crim 4. See also *R v MH* [2012] EWCA Crim 2725 at [54]: the child witness will be incompetent not merely because of the fact that time has passed, but because the passage of time has affected his or her competence.

[82] *R v R* [2010] EWCA Crim 2469.

(3) The witness shall, if he is able to give intelligible testimony, be presumed to have a sufficient appreciation of those matters if no evidence tending to show the contrary is adduced (by any party).

(4) If any such evidence is adduced, it is for the party seeking to have the witness sworn to satisfy the court that, on a balance of probabilities, the witness has attained the age of 14 and has a sufficient appreciation of the matters mentioned in subsection (2)(b).

For the purposes of s 55(3), a person is able to give intelligible testimony if he is able to (a) understand questions put to him as a witness; and (b) give answers to them which can be understood.[83] This test is the same as that for testing competence in s 53(3). Thus a witness aged 14 or over who is competent as a witness must be presumed to satisfy the test set out in s 55(2)(b), provided that there is no evidence tending to show the contrary. Under s 55(5), any proceedings for the determination of the question whether a witness may be sworn for the purpose of giving his evidence on oath shall take place in the absence of the jury (if there is one); under s 55(6), expert evidence may be received on the question; and, under s 55(7), any questioning of the witness, where the court considers that necessary, shall be conducted by the court in the presence of the parties.

Section 56(1)–(4) of the 1999 Act provide as follows:

(1) Subsections (2) and (3) apply to a person (of any age) who—
  (a) is competent to give evidence in criminal proceedings, but
  (b) (by virtue of s 55(2)) is not permitted to be sworn for the purpose of giving evidence on oath in such proceedings.

(2) The evidence in criminal proceedings of a person to whom this subsection applies shall be given unsworn.

(3) A deposition of unsworn evidence given by a person to whom this subsection applies may be taken for the purpose of criminal proceedings as if that evidence had been given on oath.

(4) A court in criminal proceedings shall accordingly receive in evidence any evidence given unsworn in pursuance of subsection (2) or (3).

Under the mandatory terms of s 56(2), the evidence of any child under the age of 14 who is competent to testify must be given unsworn; and the same applies to anyone who has attained that age and is competent to testify if (a) evidence is adduced that he does not have a sufficient appreciation of the solemnity of the occasion and of the particular responsibility to tell the truth which is involved in taking an oath; and (b) the party seeking to have him sworn fails to satisfy the court, on a balance of probabilities, that he has such an appreciation.

It is an offence for a person giving unsworn evidence in pursuance of s 56(2) and (3) wilfully to give false evidence in such circumstances that, had the evidence been given on oath, he would have been guilty of perjury;[84] but the mere fact that a child under the age of 10 cannot be prosecuted is not a reason to prevent him from giving unsworn evidence.[85]

---

[83] Section 55(8).
[84] The 1999 Act, s 57.
[85] See *R v N* (1992) 95 Cr App R 256, CA.

Civil cases

Children

At common law, a child who did not understand the nature of an oath was not competent to testify and could not be called as a witness.[86] Section 96 of the Children Act 1989 now provides that:

(1) Subsection (2) applies where a child who is called as a witness in any civil proceedings does not, in the opinion of the court, understand the nature of an oath.
(2) The child's evidence may be heard by the court if, in its opinion—
    (a) he understands that it is his duty to speak the truth; and
    (b) he has sufficient understanding to justify his evidence being heard.

A child, for these purposes, is a person under the age of 18.[87] In deciding, under s 96(1), whether or not a child understands the nature of an oath, it is submitted that the court should be guided by the common law authorities which governed in criminal as well as civil cases prior to parliamentary intervention. The issue is for the court to decide and the judge should put preliminary questions in order to form an opinion.[88] Whether a child warrants such examination is a matter of discretion for the judge. There is no fixed age above which a child should be treated as competent and below which a child should be examined. In *R v Khan*,[89] however, it was held that although much depends on the type of child before the court, as a general working rule, inquiry is necessary in the case of a child under the age of 14. Originally, the competence of children to give sworn evidence depended on 'the sense and reason they entertain of the danger and impiety of falsehood'.[90] On this basis, judges would ask questions designed to discover whether the child was aware of the divine sanction of the oath, such as 'Do you have religious instruction at school?' and 'Do you know what I mean by God?' It was questioning of this kind that led the Court of Appeal in *R v Hayes*[91] to adopt a secular approach. Acknowledging that in the present state of society the divine sanction of the oath is probably not generally recognized amongst the adult population, it was held that the important consideration is:[92]

> whether the child has a sufficient appreciation of the solemnity of the occasion and the added responsibility to tell the truth, which is involved in taking an oath, over and above the duty to tell the truth which is an ordinary duty of normal social conduct.

The court, in *R v Hayes*, also appears to have been of the view that 'the watershed dividing children who are normally considered old enough to take the oath and children normally considered too young to take the oath, probably falls between the ages of eight and ten'.

If, in civil proceedings, a child fails on the secular test in *R v Hayes*, his or her evidence may be given unsworn if, in the opinion of the court, the conditions in s 96(2)(a) and (b) are satisfied. It would appear that 'the duty to speak the truth' under s 96(2)(a) should be taken to mean the duty to tell the truth which is an ordinary duty of normal social conduct.

---

[86] *Baker v Rabetts* (1954) 118 JPN 303.
[87] Children Act 1989, s 105.
[88] *R v Surgenor* (1940) 27 Cr App R 175.
[89] (1981) 73 Cr App R 190, CA. But see also *Bains v DPP* [1992] Crim LR 795, DC.
[90] *R v Brasier* (1779) 1 Leach 199.
[91] [1977] 1 WLR 234.
[92] Ibid at 237.

Special factors bear on the question whether a child should give evidence in family proceedings. Video recordings of ABE interviews,[93] if available, are routinely used in care proceedings and it has been rare for children to be called for examination or cross-examination. However, there is no longer a presumption against a child giving evidence in such proceedings; in deciding whether a particular child should be called, the court must weigh two considerations, the advantages that doing so may bring to the determination of the truth and the damage it may do to the welfare of the child or any other child, and should have regard to a range of factors, including the quality of any ABE interview, the nature of any challenge to the child's evidence, the age and maturity of the child, the length of time since the events in question, and whether the child is willing to give evidence.[94]

Persons with a disorder or disability of the mind

In civil proceedings, in deciding on the competence of a person with a disorder or disability of the mind, it is submitted that the courts should be guided by the common law authorities which governed in criminal as well as civil cases prior to parliamentary intervention. In *R v Hill*[95] a patient of a lunatic asylum, labouring under a delusion that he had a number of spirits about him which were continually talking to him, but with a clear understanding of the obligation of the oath, was held competent to give evidence for the Crown on a charge of manslaughter.[96] Three principles were established in the case:

1. If in the opinion of the judge a proposed witness, by reason of impaired intellect, does not understand the nature and sanction of an oath, he is incompetent to testify.

2. A person of impaired intellect who does understand the nature of an oath may give evidence and it will be left to the jury to attach such weight to his testimony as they see fit.

3. If his evidence is so tainted with insanity as to be unworthy of credit, the jury may properly disregard it.

Since *R v Hill* there has been one important development: the test to be applied by the judge should be the secular one adopted in *R v Hayes*, namely whether the proposed witness has a sufficient appreciation of the seriousness of the occasion and a realization that taking the oath involves something more than the duty to tell the truth in ordinary day-to-day life.[97] Resolution of the question calls for appropriate expert medical evidence: it will not normally be necessary to call the witness said to be suffering from mental illness.[98]

A witness unable to understand the nature of the oath, his intellect being temporarily impaired by reason of drink or drugs, may become competent after an adjournment of suitable length.

---

[93] See, in this chapter, under **Video-recorded evidence-in-chief**, p 158.

[94] *Re W (children) (family proceedings: evidence)* [2010] UK SC 12. See also, in relation to the matters to be taken into account, Working Party of the Family Justice Council, *Guidelines on the issue of Children Giving Evidence in Family Proceedings* [2012] Fam Law 79, *Re X (A child)(evidence)* [2011] EWHC 3401 (Fam), *Re E (a child)* [2016] EWCA Civ 473 and *Re S (children)* [2016] EWCA Civ 83.

[95] (1851) 2 Den 254.

[96] Lord Campbell CJ was doubtless sobered by his observation that any rule to the contrary would have excluded the evidence of Socrates 'for he believed that he had a spirit always prompting him'.

[97] *R v Bellamy* (1985) 82 Cr App R 222, CA.

[98] *R v Barratt and Sheehan* [1996] Crim LR 495, CA.

The Sovereign and diplomats

The Sovereign and heads of other sovereign states are competent but not compellable to give evidence. A number of statutes provide for varying degrees of immunity from compellability in the case of diplomats, consular officials, and certain officers of prescribed international organizations.[99]

Bankers

We shall see in **Chapter 10** that, pursuant to the Bankers' Books Evidence Act 1879, copies of entries in bankers' books are, subject to certain safeguards, admissible as evidence of their contents. To protect bank personnel from the unnecessary inconvenience of either providing the originals of such books or appearing as witnesses, s 6 of the Act provides that:

> A banker or official of a bank shall not, in any legal proceedings to which the bank is not a party, be compellable to produce any banker's book the contents of which can be proved under this Act, or to appear as a witness to prove the matters, transactions, and accounts therein recorded, unless by order of a judge made for special cause.

Oaths and affirmations

Sworn evidence is evidence given by a witness who has either taken an oath or made an affirmation. The general rule in both civil and criminal proceedings is that the evidence of any witness should be sworn.[100] The exceptions in the case of certain children and those with a disorder or disability of the mind have already been considered. There are two other minor exceptions at common law. A witness called only to produce a document may give unsworn evidence provided that the identity of the document is either not disputed or can be established by another witness.[101] An advocate acting for one of two parties who have reached a compromise may give unsworn evidence of its terms.[102] Where a video recording of an interview with a child is admitted in evidence, and the child is at that stage aged 14 or over, the oath should be administered before the start of the cross-examination.[103] However, under s 56(5) of the 1999 Act, where a witness who is competent to give evidence in criminal proceedings has given evidence in such proceedings unsworn, no conviction, verdict, or finding in those proceedings shall be taken to be unsafe, for the purposes of the grounds of appeal set out in ss 2(1), 13(1), or 16(1) of the Criminal Appeal Act 1968, by reason only that the witness was in fact a person falling within s 55(2) of the 1999 Act[104] and accordingly should have given his evidence on oath.

The modern law of oaths and affirmations is governed by the Oaths Act 1978. Section 1(1) provides for the manner of administration of the oath in the case of Christians and Jews.

---

[99] See the Diplomatic Privileges Act 1964, Consular Relations Act 1968, International Organisations Act 1968, and State Immunity Act 1978.

[100] For criminal cases, see r 25.11(3), Criminal Procedure Rules 2015, SI 2015/1490. In civil claims which have been allocated to the small claims track, the court need not take evidence on oath: CPR r 27.8(4).

[101] *Perry v Gibson* (1834) 1 Ad&El 48.

[102] *Hickman v Berens* [1895] 2 Ch 638, CA.

[103] *R v Simmonds* [1996] Crim LR 816, CA, a decision under the Criminal Justice Act 1988, s 32A. See now the 1999 Act, s 27, in this chapter, under **Witnesses in criminal cases, p 152**.

[104] See, in this chapter, under **Children and persons with a disorder or disability of the mind—criminal cases, p 136**.

Unless a person about to take the oath in this form and manner objects thereto, or is physically incapable of so taking the oath, it will be administered without inquiry on the part of the judge.[105] It is therefore incumbent on those of other religious beliefs or those who wish to affirm, to object to the taking of such an oath.[106] In the case of those of other religious beliefs, s 1(3) provides that the oath shall be administered 'in any lawful manner'. Such witnesses usually take the oath upon such holy book as is appropriate to their religious belief. Section 3 of the Oaths Act 1978 expressly permits a witness to be sworn with uplifted hand in the form and manner in which an oath is usually administered in Scotland. Whether an oath is administered in a 'lawful manner' under s 1(3) does not depend on the intricacies of the particular religion which is adhered to by the witness but on whether the oath is one which appears to the court to be binding on the conscience of the witness and, if so, whether it is an oath which the witness himself considers to be binding on his conscience. Both conditions were satisfied in *R v Kemble*,[107] in which a Muslim had taken the oath using the New Testament, whereas under the strict tenets of Islam, no oath taken by a Muslim is valid unless taken on a copy of the Koran in Arabic.

Any person who objects to the taking of an oath shall be permitted instead, the choice being his, to make a solemn affirmation.[108] An affirmation is of the same force and effect as an oath.[109] It is improper, in cross-examination of a Muslim, to ask questions designed to challenge whether he regards himself as bound to tell the truth by virtue of the fact that he affirmed and did not swear on the Koran.[110] However, if there is a real risk that the jury will attach less weight to the evidence of a witness of a particular faith because he has affirmed, rather than taken the oath on the relevant holy book, then the judge has a discretion to allow the witness to be questioned, in a sensitive manner, as to why he did not take the oath on the particular holy book.[111]

Occasionally, a court may find itself unequipped to administer an oath in the manner appropriate to a person's particular religious belief. Accordingly, it is provided that a person may be permitted, and indeed required, to affirm where 'it is not reasonably practicable without inconvenience or delay to administer an oath in the manner appropriate to his religious belief'.[112]

A person who has taken a duly administered oath could with relative ease subsequently allege that it was of no binding effect because at the time of taking it he had no religious belief. Section 4(2) avoids this possibility by providing that the fact that a person had, at the time of taking the oath, no religious belief 'shall not for any purpose affect the validity of the oath'.

A witness who, having taken an oath or made an affirmation, wilfully makes a statement material to the proceedings in question which he knows to be false or does not believe to be true, commits perjury and may be prosecuted accordingly.[113]

---

[105] Oaths Act 1978, s 1(2).

[106] For the arguments against the continued use of religious oaths, see Criminal Law Revision Committee, 11th Report, paras 279–81 and Auld LJ's *Review of the Criminal Courts of England and Wales* (HMSO, 2001) 598–600.

[107] [1990] 3 All ER 116, CA.

[108] Oaths Act 1978, s 5(1). See *R v Bellamy* (1985) 82 Cr App R 222, CA.

[109] Oaths Act 1978, s 5(4).

[110] *R v Majid* [2009] EWCA Crim 2563.

[111] See *R v Mehrban* [2002] 1 Cr App R 561 (40), CA, where one of the accused, a Muslim, had affirmed because 'unclean', not having been able to wash himself in the appropriate way before swearing.

[112] Oaths Act 1978, s 5(2) and (3).

[113] See the Perjury Act 1911, s 1, and the Oaths Act 1978, s 5(4), at n 109.

Live links

Civil proceedings

In civil proceedings, Civil Procedure Rules (CPR) r 32.3 provides that the court may allow a witness to give evidence 'through a video link or by other means'.[114] No defined limit or set of circumstances should be placed upon discretionary exercise of this power to permit video link evidence, which is not confined to cases of 'pressing need', as when a witness is too ill to attend in person. Relevant factors include whether failure to attend is an abuse or contemptuous or designed to obtain a collateral advantage, as well as considerations of cost, time, and inconvenience. The court should also have regard to Art 6 of the European Convention on Human Rights and the need to see that the parties are on an equal footing.[115] In *Polanski v Condé Nast Publications Ltd*[116] the House of Lords held, by a majority, that although special cases may arise, as a general rule a claimant's unwillingness to come to the UK because he is a fugitive from justice is a valid reason, and can be a sufficient reason, for making a video conferencing order, because such a person, despite his status, is entitled to invoke the assistance of the court and its procedures in protection of his civil rights.

Criminal proceedings

In criminal cases, there are three sets of rules governing the use that may be made of live links.[117] First, s 32 of the Criminal Justice Act 1988 provides that, in trials on indictment[118] or proceedings in youth courts,[119] a person other than the accused who is outside the United Kingdom may, with the leave of the court, give evidence through a live television link.[120] Second, under s 24 of the 1999 Act, a special measures direction may provide for a child or other vulnerable witness to give evidence by a live television link. Section 24 is considered, together with other special measures directions, later in this chapter. Third, under Pt 8 of the Criminal Justice Act 2003 (ss 51–56), general provision is made for the use of live links in criminal cases.[121] There is no common law power to permit evidence to be given by live link: the statutory regime provides exclusively for the circumstances in which live link evidence may be used in the course of a criminal trial.[122]

Part 8 of the 2003 Act has been introduced without any indication as to the relationship between its general provisions and the provisions in the 1999 Act, except to state that Pt 8

---

[114] See also CPR Practice Direction (PD) 32, Annex 3, *Videoconferencing Guidance*, and *Black v Pastouna* [2005] EWCA Civ 1389.

[115] *Rowland v Bock* [2002] 4 All ER 370, QBD.

[116] [2005] 1 All ER 945, HL.

[117] For an analysis of whether these provisions breach Art 6(3)(d) of the European Convention on Human Rights (the so-called 'right to confront' witnesses), see Daniele, 'Testimony Through a Live Link in the Perspective of the Right to Confront Witnesses' [2014] Crim LR 189.

[118] Or an appeal to the Court of Appeal (Criminal Division) or the hearing of a reference of a case to the Court of Appeal under the Criminal Appeal Act 1995, s 9.

[119] Or appeals to the Crown Court arising out of such proceedings or hearings of references under the Criminal Appeal Act 1995, s 11 so arising.

[120] A statement made on oath by such a witness shall be treated for the purposes of the Perjury Act 1911, s 1, as having been made in the proceedings in which it is given in evidence: s 32(3). See also *R v Forsyth* [1997] 2 Cr App R 299, CA.

[121] See also the Crime (International Cooperation) Act 2003.

[122] *R (S) v Waltham Forest Youth Court* [2004] 2 Cr App R 335 (21), DC at [86]–[89]. Similarly, there is no common law power, even by consent, to permit evidence to be given by telephone: *R v Diane* [2010] 2 Cr App R 1 (1), CA and *R v Hampson* [2012] EWCA Crim 1807.

is without prejudice to 'any power of a court . . . to give directions . . . in relation to any witness'.[123] Under s 51(1)–(3) of the 2003 Act, a court may, on the application of a party, or of its own motion, direct that a witness, other than the accused, give evidence through a live link in the following criminal proceedings: a summary trial, an appeal to the Crown Court arising out of such a trial, a trial on indictment, and an appeal to the criminal division of the Court of Appeal.[124] A 'live link' means a live television link or other arrangement by which a witness, while at a place in the United Kingdom which is outside the building where the proceedings are being held, is able both to see and hear a person at the place where the proceedings are being held and to be seen and heard by the accused, the judge, the justices, and the jury (if there is one), the legal representatives, and any interpreter or other person appointed by the court to assist the witness.[125] Rules of court may make provision as to the procedure to be followed in connection with an application for a direction to give evidence through a live link and as to the arrangements or safeguards to be put in place in connection with the operation of the link.[126] Under s 51(4)(a), a direction may not be given unless the court is satisfied that it is in the interests of the efficient or effective administration of justice. Under s 51(6), in deciding whether to give a direction, the court must consider all the circumstances. Section 51(7) provides that:

(7) Those circumstances include in particular—
   (a) the availability of the witness,
   (b) the need for the witness to attend in person,
   (c) the importance of the witness's evidence to the proceedings,
   (d) the views of the witness,
   (e) the suitability of the facilities at the place where the witness would give evidence through a live link,
   (f) whether a direction might tend to inhibit any party to the proceedings from effectively testing the witness's evidence.

If the court refuses an application for a direction, it must state its reasons in open court and, if it is a magistrates' court, must cause them to be entered in the register of its proceedings.

   Where a direction has been given, the witness may not give evidence otherwise than through the link,[127] and therefore will also be subject to cross-examination and any re-examination through the link, but the court may rescind a direction if there has been a material change of circumstances since the direction was given.[128] Where the evidence is given through a live link, the court retains the power to exclude evidence at its discretion (whether by preventing questions from being put or otherwise),[129] and the judge may give the jury such direction as he thinks necessary to ensure that the jury gives the same weight to the evidence as if it had been given by the witness in the courtroom.[130]

---

[123] The Criminal Justice Act 2003, s 56(5)(a).

[124] Also the hearing of a reference under the Criminal Appeal Act 1995, s 9 or s 11, a hearing before a magistrates' court or the Crown Court which is held after the accused has entered a plea of guilty, and a hearing before the Court of Appeal under the 2003 Act, s 80 (application for retrial following acquittal): s 51(2).

[125] Section 56(2) and (3). For these purposes, the extent (if any) to which a person is unable to see or hear by reason of any impairment of eyesight or hearing is to be disregarded: s 56(4).

[126] Section 55.

[127] Section 52(2).

[128] Section 52(5) and (6).

[129] Section 56(5)(b).

[130] Section 54.

The time at which evidence should be adduced

In both civil and criminal proceedings, as a general rule of practice rather than law, a party should adduce all the evidence on which he intends to rely before the close of his case.[131] However, in a civil case, the claimant, after the close of the trial but before the judgment has been handed down, may introduce in evidence a document which ought to have been disclosed by the defendant and which the claimant could not have obtained by other means.[132]

Prosecution evidence

If, in a criminal case, evidence becomes available to the prosecution for the first time *after* the close of its case, the question of its admissibility should be referred to and decided by the judge.[133] The evidence may be admitted, even if not strictly of a rebutting character, but the court should take care, in the exercise of its discretion, in case injustice is done to the accused, and should consider whether to grant the defence an adjournment.[134]

Although, in criminal cases, the general rule applies not only to the adducing of evidence, but also to matters to be put in cross-examination of an accused,[135] it is confined to evidence probative of his guilt, rather than evidence going only to his credit.[136] If evidence capable of forming part of the affirmative case for the prosecution case did not form part of the evidence on which the accused was committed for trial, the practice is to give notice of the additional evidence to the defence before it is tendered.[137] The fact that the accused might then trim his evidence is not a reason for withholding the material until he gives evidence, because an accused needs to know in advance the case against him if he is to have a proper opportunity of answering that case to the best of his ability. He is also entitled to such knowledge when deciding whether to testify. It is better in the interests of justice that an accused is not induced, by thinking it is safe to do so, to exaggerate, embroider, or lie. To do so might be to ambush the accused.[138]

To the general rule of practice there are two exceptions and a 'wider discretion' to be exercised outside the two exceptions sparingly. As to the first exception, evidence is allowed in rebuttal of matters arising *ex improviso*, which no human ingenuity could have foreseen.[139] Under this exception, it is for the judge, in his discretion, to determine whether the relevance of the evidence could *reasonably* have been anticipated.[140] If the prosecution can reasonably foresee that the evidence is relevant to their case, it must be adduced as a part of that case and

---

[131] *R v Rice* (1963) 47 Cr App R 79, CCA.

[132] *Stocznia Gdanska SA v Latvian Shipping Co* (2000) LTL 19/10/2000, QBD.

[133] *R v Kane* (1977) 65 Cr App R 270, CA.

[134] *R v Doran* (1972) 56 Cr App R 429, CA and *R v Patel* [1992] Crim LR 739, CA; cf *R v Pilcher* (1974) 60 Cr App R 1, CA.

[135] *R v Kane* (1977) 65 Cr App R 270, CA.

[136] *R v Halford* (1978) 67 Cr App R 318, CA.

[137] *R v Kane* (1977) 65 Cr App R 270, CA.

[138] *R v Phillipson* (1989) 91 Cr App R 226, CA. See also *R v Sansom* [1991] 2 QB 130, CA.

[139] *R v Frost* (1839) 4 State Tr NS 85. The exception may be used by the prosecution to adduce evidence in rebuttal of not only defence *evidence*, but also matters unsupported by evidence but arising by implication from the defence closing speech: *R v O'Hadhmaill* [1996] Crim LR 509, CA.

[140] *R v Scott* (1984) 79 Cr App R 49, CA.

not to remedy defects in that case after it has been closed.[141] In *R v Milliken*,[142] the accused, when giving evidence, for the first time accused officers of a conspiracy to fabricate evidence. Evidence in rebuttal was allowed, because it only became relevant when the accused gave evidence. Equally, the prosecution may rely on this exception where the evidence in rebuttal was not, at the outset, *clearly* relevant, but only marginally, minimally, or doubtfully relevant[143] or where they could not have anticipated that anything said in a statement made by the accused would be repeated in court, because it contained many allegations which were obviously ridiculous and untrue.[144]

Under the second exception, the judge has a discretion to admit evidence which has not been adduced by reason of inadvertence or oversight. Although this exception is usually said to apply only in the case of evidence of a formal or uncontentious nature,[145] the cases show that the evidence may relate to a matter of substance.[146]

In *R v Francis*[147] the prosecution established where a man was standing at a group identification, but failed to call evidence that the man in that position was the accused. After the close of their case, the prosecution were allowed to adduce such evidence. It was held that although the failure was not a mere technicality, but an essential if minor link in the chain of identification evidence, the discretion of the judge to admit evidence after the close of the prosecution case is not confined to the two well-established exceptions: there is a wider discretion, but it should only be exercised outside the two exceptions on the rarest of occasions. In *R v Munnery*[148] it was held that this last proposition could be expanded to include the words 'especially when the evidence is tendered after the case for the defendant has begun'. An example of evidence being admitted even at this late stage is *James v South Glamorgan County Council*.[149] In that case, in which the defence had not made a submission of no case to answer, the prosecution, after the accused had given his evidence-in-chief, were allowed to re-open their case to call their main witness, whose evidence was important, if not essential to their case, the witness having arrived late by reason of transport difficulties and genuine confusion about the location of the court house. *Jolly v DPP*,[150] a decision relating to a summary trial, also supports a wider discretionary approach to admissibility. It was held that it was 'beyond argument' that there was a general discretion to permit the prosecution to call evidence after the close of their case, which, in a magistrates' court, extended up to the time when the bench retired. The court would look carefully at the interests of justice overall and in particular the risk of prejudice to the accused,

---

[141] *R v Day* (1940) 27 Cr App R 168.

[142] (1969) 53 Cr App R 330, CA.

[143] *R v Levy* (1966) 50 Cr App R 198.

[144] *R v Hutchinson* (1985) 82 Cr App R 51, CA.

[145] For example, failure to prove that leave of the Director of Public Prosecutions to bring proceedings has been obtained (*R v Waller* [1910] 1 KB 364, CCA, applied in *Price v Humphries* [1958] 2 All ER 725, DC) or failure to prove a statutory instrument by production of a Stationery Office copy (*Palastanga v Solman* [1962] Crim LR 334 and *Hammond v Wilkinson* [2001] Crim LR 323). See also *R v McKenna* (1956) 40 Cr App R 65.

[146] See, eg, *Piggott v Sims* [1973] RTR 15 (an analyst's certificate); *Matthews v Morris* [1981] Crim LR 495 (a statement by the owner of the property allegedly stolen); and *Middleton v Rowlett* [1954] 1 WLR 831 and *Smith v DPP* [2008] EWHC 771 (Admin) (evidence of identification).

[147] [1991] 1 All ER 225, CA.

[148] (1990) 94 Cr App R 164, CA.

[149] (1994) 99 Cr App R 321, DC. See also (applying *R v Francis*) *R v Jackson* [1996] 2 Cr App R 420, CA.

[150] [2000] Crim LR 471, DC.

as when the defence would have been conducted differently had the evidence been adduced as part of the prosecution case. Thus the discretion would be exercised sparingly, but it was doubted whether it assisted to speak in terms of 'exceptional circumstances'.[151]

In appropriate circumstances, rather than have the prosecution re-open their case, a judge may, in the interests of justice, admit evidence himself. In *R v Bowles*[152] it was held that a judge was justified in calling certain evidence to provide an answer to a question raised by the jury during the defence case: the defence had not closed their case, and the evidence, which was non-controversial and did not contradict that of the accused, helped the jury resolve an issue on the basis of known facts, rather than speculation. In the exercise of his discretion, the judge may also recall or permit the recall of a witness at any stage in the proceedings before the end of his summing-up.[153]

Defence evidence

A judge may permit an accused to be recalled to deal with matters which arose after he gave evidence if he could not reasonably have anticipated them and it appears to be in the interests of justice.[154] A judge may, as a matter of discretion and in the interests of justice, allow an accused to be recalled to clarify some feature of his evidence or to address a possible source of misunderstanding or to be given the opportunity to answer new allegations by a co-accused not put to him under cross-examination. However, it is difficult to imagine a situation in which an accused should be allowed to be recalled to advance a new account of facts contradicting his earlier evidence, which would normally constitute an abuse of process.[155]

Evidence after the retirement of the magistrates or jury

In the magistrates' court, evidence may be called even after the magistrates have retired, provided that there are special circumstances, as when the defence seek to ambush the prosecution by raising an issue for the first time in their closing speech.[156] In the Crown Court, once the jury have retired to consider their verdict on the conclusion of the summing-up, no further evidence may be admitted, whether by the calling or recalling of witnesses,[157] and the jury must not be given any additional matter or material to assist them,[158] either at their own request, or in error.[159] However, this principle has been relaxed in the case of additional evidence put before the jury at the request of the accused because it assists his case.[160]

---

[151] See also *Cook v DPP* [2001] Crim LR 321, DC.

[152] [1992] Crim LR 726, CA. See also *R v Aitken* (1991) 94 Cr App R 85, CA.

[153] *R v Sullivan* [1923] 1 KB 47; *R v McKenna* (1956) 40 Cr App R 65. The witness may be cross-examined on new evidence given: *R v Watson* (1834) 6 C&P 653.

[154] *R v Cook* [2005] EWCA Crim 2011 at [28].

[155] *R v Ikram* [2009] 1 WLR 1419, CA.

[156] *Malcolm v DPP* [2007] 1 WLR 1230, DC.

[157] *R v Owen* (1952) 36 Cr App R 16. In *R v Flynn* (1957) 42 Cr App R 15, evidence in rebuttal was called immediately before the summing-up. In *R v Sanderson* (1953) 37 Cr App R 32, fresh evidence was called after the summing-up but before the jury retired. The Criminal Law Revision Committee proposed that evidence be allowed to be given at any time prior to verdict: see 11th Report, Cmnd 4991 (1972), paras 213–16.

[158] *R v Davis* (1975) 62 Cr App R 194. See also *R v Crees* [1996] Crim LR 830, CA, where the jury were improperly given a ruler which they wished to use as if it were a knife, for the purposes of a re-enactment.

[159] See *R v Gilder* [1997] Crim LR 668, CA.

[160] See *R v Hallam* [2007] EWCA Crim 1495 and *R v Khan* [2008] EWCA Crim 1112; and cf *R v Cadman* [2008] EWCA Crim 1418.

When the jury retire, an exhibit may be taken into the jury room for inspection. Where a silent film or video has been shown in court and the jury, after retirement, ask to see it again, they may do so, but it is better that they do so in open court.[161] Concerning audio recordings, if nothing turns on tone of voice, it will usually suffice for the jury to have a transcript, much of which should be summarized, but where tone of voice is all-important, then, subject to editing out inadmissible material, the jury should have the original recording.[162] If the recording is not played during the trial, the jury may listen to it after retirement, but if there is a risk that they may hear inadmissible material, it should be played in open court.[163] If the prosecution do not rely on parts of a recording, the jury may only hear it as edited.[164] However, if the recording, of which there is an agreed transcript, has already been played in court and does not contain inadmissible material, the judge has a discretion to permit the jury to play it in their retiring room.[165] In the case of a video recording used as a child's evidence pursuant to s 27 of the 1999 Act, if the jury, after they have retired, wish to be reminded of *what* the witness said, the judge should remind them from the transcript or his own notes; but if they wish to be reminded of how the words were spoken, the judge may in his discretion allow the video, or relevant part, to be replayed, provided that the replay takes place in court.[166] Either way, the judge should warn the jury that by reason of hearing the evidence again they should guard against the risk of giving it disproportionate weight and bear well in mind the other evidence in the case, and the judge should remind the jury, from his notes, of the cross-examination and re-examination of the witness.[167]

A jury request for equipment, such as weighing scales, to enable them to carry out unsupervised scientific experiments with exhibits, should not be met.[168]

Witnesses in civil cases

The witnesses to be called

Prior to the Civil Procedure Rules, a party to civil proceedings was under no obligation to call particular witnesses, could call such witnesses to support his case as he saw fit, and could call them in the order of his choice.[169] As to the judge, he had no right to call witnesses

---

[161] *R v Imran* [1997] Crim LR 754, CA.

[162] *R v Emmerson* (1990) 92 Cr App R 284, CA.

[163] *R v Riaz* (1991) 94 Cr App R 339, CA.

[164] See *R v Hagan* [1997] 1 Cr App R 464, CA.

[165] *R v Tonge* [1993] Crim LR 876, CA.

[166] See also, to the same effect in the case of a video recording of an interview with the accused, *R v Minnott* [2016] EWCA Crim 2215. In normal circumstances it is inappropriate for the video to be replayed unless there has been a specific request to that effect from the jury: *R v M* [1996] 2 Cr App R 56, CA.

[167] See, in the case of a reminder from the transcript, *R v McQuiston* [1998] 1 Cr App R 139, CA and *R v Morris* [1998] Crim LR 416, CA; and see, in the case of a replay, *R v Rawlings* [1995] 1 All ER 580, CA, applied in *R v M* [1996] 2 Cr App R 56, CA, *R v B* [1996] Crim LR 499, CA and *R v W* [2011] EWCA Crim 1142. The principles, however, do not lay down an inflexible practice to be followed to the letter in every case: *R v Horley* [1999] Crim LR 488, CA. See, eg, *R v Saunders* [1995] 2 Cr App R 313, CA.

[168] *R v Stewart, R v Sappleton* (1989) 89 Cr App R 273, CA; cf *R v Wright* [1993] Crim LR 607, CA. A magnifying glass, a ruler, or a tape-measure do not normally raise the possibility of such an experiment: *R v Maggs* (1990) 91 Cr App R 243, CA.

[169] *Briscoe v Briscoe* [1966] 1 All ER 465; but cf *Bayer v Clarkson Puckle Overseas Ltd* [1989] NLJR 256.

against the will of the parties,[170] except in cases of civil contempt,[171] but did have the power to recall a witness called by a party.[172] CPR r 32.1(1) now provides that the court may control the evidence by giving directions as to the nature of the evidence which it requires to decide the issues on which it requires evidence, and the way in which the evidence is to be placed before the court; and under r 32.1(2) the court may use its power under the rule to exclude evidence that would otherwise be admissible. In exercising these powers, the judge must seek to give effect to the 'overriding objective' of the rules, which is to enable the court 'to deal with cases justly'.[173] It seems that CPR r 32.1(1) does not empower the court to dictate to a litigant what evidence he should tender. Thus a party who has disclosed a witness statement in accordance with pre-trial directions cannot be ordered by the court to call the witness, although he should notify the other parties of his decision not to call the witness and whether he proposes to put the statement in as hearsay.[174] In appropriate circumstances, however, the judge may take the view that, in order to give effect to the overriding objective, he should give directions under CPR r 32.1(1) as to the order in which witnesses should give their evidence, and as to those witnesses who are not required to decide the issues and whose evidence, therefore, although admissible, should not be heard.

Witness statements

The rules for the exchange of witness statements in civil cases have been designed to promote the fair disposal of proceedings and to save costs: they identify the real issues, encourage the parties to make appropriate admissions of fact, promote fair settlements, remove the element of surprise as to the witnesses each party intends to call, and give to the cross-examining party the advantage of knowing in advance what each witness will say in his examination-in-chief.[175]

A witness statement is a written statement signed by a person which contains the evidence which that person would be allowed to give orally.[176] Under CPR r 32.4(2), the court will order a party to serve on the other parties any witness statement of the oral evidence which the party serving the statement intends to rely on in relation to any issues of fact to be decided at the trial; and under r 32.4(3) the court may give directions as to the order in which the statements are to be served.[177] The court will give directions for the service of witness statements when it allocates a case to the fast track[178] or multi-track.[179] Normally, the court will direct the simultaneous exchange of statements,[180] but sequential exchange may be appropriate where

---

[170] *Re Enoch and Zaretzky, Bock & Co's Arbitration* [1910] 1 KB 327, CA.

[171] *Yianni v Yianni* [1966] 1 WLR 120.

[172] *Fallon v Calvert* [1960] 2 QB 201, CA.

[173] See further Ch 2, Civil cases, p 173.

[174] *Society of Lloyd's v Jaffray* (2000) The Times, 3 Aug, QBD.

[175] For a summary of views on the merits and shortcomings of witness statements as a litigation tool, see Acratopulo, 'Litigation futures', [2018] NLJ, 20 April, 9.

[176] Rule 32.4(1). The statement, therefore, should not contain material which is irrelevant or otherwise inadmissible.

[177] Although CPR Pt 32 (except r 32.1) does not apply to claims which have been allocated to the small claims track (r 27.2(1)), in the case of many such claims directions for the exchange of witness statements will be given nonetheless: see r 27.4 and PD 27.

[178] Rule 28.2, r 28.3 and PD 28.

[179] Rule 29.2 and PD 29.

[180] PD 28, para 3.9 and PD 29, para 4.10.

one party will not know fully or precisely the case he has to answer until he has had sight of his opponent's witness statements. If a party fails to serve witness statements, any other party may apply for an order to enforce compliance or for a sanction to be imposed,[181] and, ultimately, the court has the power to strike out the claim or defence.[182]

A witness statement should be dated.[183] It must, if practicable, be in the intended witness's own words and should be expressed in the first person.[184] It must also indicate which of the statements in it are made from the witness's own knowledge and which are matters of information or belief.[185] The statement is the equivalent of the oral evidence which the witness would, if called, give in evidence, and must include a statement of truth by the intended witness, that is, a signed statement that he believes the facts in it are true.[186] If it is not verified by a statement of truth, then the court may direct that it shall not be admissible as evidence.[187] Equally, if it does not comply with CPR Pt 32 or PD 32 in relation to its form, the court may refuse to admit it as evidence.[188]

CPR r 32.5 provides as follows:

(1) If—
   (a) a party has served a witness statement; and
   (b) he wishes to rely at trial on the evidence of the witness who made the statement, he must call the witness to give oral evidence unless the court orders otherwise or he puts the statement in as hearsay evidence.
(2) Where a witness is called to give oral evidence under paragraph (1), his witness statement shall stand as his evidence in chief unless the court orders otherwise.
(3) A witness giving oral evidence at trial may with the permission of the court—
   (a) amplify his witness statement; and
   (b) give evidence in relation to new matters which have arisen since the witness statement was served on the other parties.
(4) The court will give permission under paragraph (3) only if it considers that there is good reason not to confine the evidence of the witness to the contents of his witness statement.
(5) If a party who has served a witness statement does not—
   (a) call the witness to give evidence at trial; or
   (b) put the witness statement in as hearsay evidence, any other party may put the witness statement in as hearsay evidence.

As to CPR r 32.5(2), it is likely that the court, in deciding whether to order that the statement should not stand as the witness's evidence-in-chief, will have regard to such matters as the

---

[181] See PD 28, para 5.1 and PD 29, para 7.1.

[182] See CPR r 3.4.

[183] Rule 32.8 and PD 32, para 17.2.

[184] Ibid, para 18.1.

[185] Ibid, para 18.2.

[186] PD 32, para 20.1 and r 22.1(6). Proceedings for contempt of court may be brought against a person making a false statement in a document verified by a statement of truth without an honest belief in its truth: r 32.14. It is part of the duty of solicitors to ensure, so far as it is within their power, that statements are taken either by themselves or, if that is not practicable, by somebody who can be relied upon to exercise the same standard as should apply when statements are taken by solicitors: *Aquarius Financial Enterprises Inc v Certain Underwriters at Lloyd's* (2001) NLJ 694, QBD.

[187] Rule 22.3.

[188] PD 32, para 25.1.

extent to which his evidence is likely to be controversial and to go to the heart of the dispute, and the extent to which his credibility will be in issue.[189] An order may well be appropriate if it is alleged that the witness is not merely mistaken, but deliberately lying.[190] As to r 32.5(4), the pertinent factors would seem to be the relevance of the evidence to the issues, any prejudice likely to be caused to the party against whom the evidence is to be used and, in the case of r 32.5(3)(a), the reason why the witness statement did not include the additional material.

Under r 32.9, provision is made for a party who is unable to obtain a witness statement to apply for permission to serve a witness summary instead. Rule 32.9 covers cases where a party knows the name and address of a particular witness, but the witness is reluctant or unwilling to give evidence or, having indicated his willingness to give evidence, changes his mind. A typical example is the employee who is loath to give evidence, on behalf of an ex-employee, against his employer.[191] Rule 32.9 provides as follows:

(1) A party who—
   (a) is required to serve a witness statement for use at trial; but
   (b) is unable to obtain one, may apply, without notice, for permission to serve a witness summary instead.
(2) A witness summary is a summary of—
   (a) the evidence, if known, which would otherwise be included in a witness statement; or
   (b) if the evidence is not known, the matters about which the party serving the witness summary proposes to question the witness.
(3) Unless the court orders otherwise, a witness summary must include the name and address of the intended witness.
(4) Unless the court orders otherwise, a witness summary must be served within the period in which a witness statement would have had to be served.
(5) Where a party serves a witness summary, so far as practicable, rules 32.4 (requirement to serve witness statements for use at trial), 32.5(3) (amplifying witness statements), and 32.8 (form of witness statement) shall apply to the summary.

Under r 32.10, if a witness statement or witness summary is not served in respect of an intended witness within the time specified by the court, then the witness may not be called to give oral evidence unless the court gives permission. In deciding whether to give permission, the relevant factors would appear to be the length of delay, whether there is a good reason for failure to serve the statement or it is a result of incompetence on the part of the legal advisers, the relevance of the evidence, including the risk of injustice to the party seeking to call the witness if permission is not given, and any prejudice likely to be caused to his opponent if permission is given.

Witnesses in criminal cases

Under r 3.3 of the Criminal Procedure Rules 2015,[192] each party to criminal proceedings must (a) actively assist the court in fulfilling its duty to further the overriding objective (that criminal cases be dealt with justly) by actively managing the case, without or if necessary

---

[189] See *Mercer v Chief Constable of the Lancashire Constabulary* [1991] 2 All ER 504, CA, a decision under an earlier version of the rules.

[190] *JN Dairies Ltd v Johal Dairies Ltd* [2010] EWCA Civ 348 at [44].

[191] See further Ch 6, **Unfavourable and hostile witnesses**, p 206.

[192] SI 2015/1490.

with a direction; and (b) apply for a direction if needed to further the overriding objective. Under r 3.10, which relates to readiness for trial, each party, in fulfilling his duty under r 3.3, must, inter alia, take every reasonable step to make sure his witnesses will attend when they are needed; and under r 3.11, in order to manage the trial, the court may require a party to identify (a) which witnesses he wants to give evidence in person; (b) the order in which he wants those witnesses to give their evidence; (c) whether he requires an order compelling the attendance of a witness;[193] and (d) what arrangements are desirable to facilitate the giving of evidence by a witness.

The witnesses to be called

In criminal proceedings, the choice as to which witnesses are called rests primarily with the parties. However, a trial judge is entitled to invite either party to consider putting further evidence before the jury as part of the duty to ensure a fair trial for both sides.[194] A judge also has the right to call a witness not called by either the prosecution or defence, and without the consent of either party if, in his opinion, this course is necessary in the interests of justice.[195] Justices have the same right in summary proceedings.[196] This right may be exercised by the judge even after the close of the case for the defence, but only where a matter has arisen *ex improviso*.[197]

The prosecution are under an obligation to call certain witnesses and to have others available at court to be called by the defence. In the case of trials on indictment, the principles were set out in *R v Russell-Jones*:[198]

1. Generally speaking the prosecution must bring to court all the witnesses 'named on the back of the indictment', a phrase reflecting the old practice, nowadays meaning those whose statements have been served as witnesses on whom the prosecution intend to rely, if the defence want those witnesses to attend.[199]
2. The prosecution have a discretion to call, or to tender for cross-examination by the defence, any witness they require to attend, but the discretion is not unfettered.

---

[193] See n 1. See also *R v Dania* [2019] EWCA Crim 796 at [41]–[42] concerning the role of the judge in applications for orders compelling the attendance of witnesses in the Crown Court. When considering, under s 2 of the Criminal Procedure (Attendance of Witnesses) Act 1965, whether the witness has material evidence to give, the judge should not trespass into the territory of the jury by forming her own view of the witness's credibility. However, the judge is entitled to consider whether the witness can at best give only peripheral evidence echoing what has already been given or adduced in the form of admissions. Additionally, there may be rare situations where there is a clear basis for the judge to decide that the witness is incapable of belief. See also n 197.

[194] Per Hooper LJ in *R v Malcolm* [2011] EWCA Crim 2069 at [83].

[195] *R v Chapman* (1838) 8 C&P 558 and *R v Holden* (1838) 8 C&P 606; cf *R v McDowell* [1984] Crim LR 486, CA. The power may be exercised, eg, where the prosecution exercise improperly their discretion not to call a witness (considered in this chapter at nn 199–202): per Lord Parker CJ in *R v Oliva* [1965] 1 WLR 1028 at 1035–6. However, the power should rarely be exercised: *R v Grafton* (1993) 96 Cr App R 156, CA. If it is, an adjournment may be necessary to enable one of the parties to call evidence in rebuttal: see *R v Coleman* (1987) The Times, 21 Nov, CA.

[196] *R v Wellingborough Magistrates' Court, ex p François* (1994) 158 JP 813 and *R v Haringey Justices, ex p DPP* [1996] 2 Cr App R 119, DC.

[197] See *R v Cleghorn* [1967] 2 QB 584, CA; cf *R v Tregear* [1967] 2 QB 574, CA.

[198] [1995] 3 All ER 239, CA. See also *R v Brown and Brown* [1997] 1 Cr App R 112, CA. Similar principles apply to summary proceedings: see *R v Haringey Justices, ex p DPP* [1996] 2 Cr App R 119, DC.

[199] See also *R v Dania* [2019] EWCA Crim 796 at [37]. Further, the prosecution are under no duty to call the makers of statements which have never formed part of the prosecution case because their statements are inconsistent with it and have been served on the defence as unused material: *R v Richardson* (1993) 98 Cr App R 174, CA.

3. The discretion must be exercised in the interests of justice so as to promote a fair trial.

4. The prosecution should normally call or offer to call all the witnesses who can give direct evidence of the primary facts of the case, even if there are inconsistencies between one witness and another,[200] unless for good reason, in any instance, the prosecutor regards the witness's evidence as unworthy of belief,[201] In *R v Oliva*,[202] for example, it was held that the prosecution were not obliged to call the victim of an offence who gave evidence at the committal proceedings first implicating and then exonerating the accused. The witness had proved himself unworthy of belief and, if called by the prosecution, would have confused the jury.[203] However, if the prosecution are of the view that part of a witness's evidence is capable of belief, even though they do not rely on other parts of his evidence, they are entitled to exercise their discretion to call him, since it would be contrary to the interests of justice to deprive the jury of that part of his evidence which could be of assistance to them.[204]

5. It is for the prosecution to decide which witnesses can give direct evidence of the primary facts.

6. The prosecutor is also the primary judge of whether or not a witness to the material events is unworthy of belief.[205]

7. A prosecutor properly exercising his discretion will not be obliged to proffer a witness merely in order to give the defence material with which to attack the credit of other witnesses on whom the Crown relies.

The order of witnesses

Although in criminal proceedings the parties are generally free to call their witnesses in the order of their choice, at common law the defence was required to call the accused before any of his witnesses: 'He ought to give his evidence before he has heard the evidence and cross-examination of any witness he is going to call.'[206] In *R v Smith*[207] the Court of Appeal approved this rule, subject to 'rare exceptions such as when a formal witness,

---

[200] Reading out the material parts of the statement of a witness may discharge the duty on the prosecution: see *R v Armstrong* [1995] Crim LR 831, CA.

[201] Where the witness is incapable of belief, the witness does not need to be called or tendered for cross-examination because his evidence cannot assist the jury: *R v Dania* [2019] EWCA Crim 796 at [37]. Where a witness summons is sought in a criminal trial in the Crown Court to compel the witness's attendance, the judge may consider, albeit in comparatively rare circumstances, that the witness is incapable of belief and thus does not have material evidence to give for the purposes of s 2 of the Criminal Procedure (Attendance of Witnesses) Act 1965: see *R v Dania* ibid at [42]. See also n 193.

[202] [1965] 1 WLR 1028. Cf *R v Witts and Witts* [1991] Crim LR 562, CA.

[203] See also *R v Nugent* [1977] 3 All ER 662 and *R v Balmforth* [1992] Crim LR 825, CA.

[204] *R v Cairns* [2003] 1 WLR 796, CA. See also *R v Smith* [2019] EWCA Crim 1151 where it was held that no principle of law contradicted the judge's exercise of discretion in allowing the prosecution to adduce evidence which contradicted identification evidence given by their witnesses which the prosecution said was mistaken.

[205] See also *R v Dania* [2019] EWCA Crim 796 at [37]: the prosecution have an obligation 'to keep their evidence under review and are entitled to change their assessment of whether a witness is capable of belief;' evidence that appears to be merely inconsistent at the outset of a trial may become, in the light of other evidence that is given, incapable of belief.

[206] Per Lord Alverstone CJ in *R v Morrison* (1911) 6 Cr App R 159 at 165.

[207] (1968) 52 Cr App R 224.

or a witness about whom there is no controversy, is interposed before the accused person with the consent of the court in the special circumstances then prevailing'. The Criminal Law Revision Committee favoured retaining the rule but was of the opinion that the court should be given a discretion, wider than that stated in *R v Smith*, to call other witnesses before the accused.[208] Section 79 of the 1984 Act, implementing this recommendation, provides that:

> If at the trial of any person for an offence—
>   (a) the defence intends to call two or more witnesses to the facts of the case; and
>   (b) those witnesses include the accused, the accused shall be called before the other witness or witnesses unless the court in its discretion otherwise directs.

Evidence-in-chief by video recording

In his *Review of the Criminal Courts of England and Wales*[209] Auld LJ recommended that, further to the use of video-recorded evidence-in-chief for vulnerable witnesses,[210] video-recorded evidence should also be admissible for the witnesses of all serious crimes. The Government, in adopting this proposal, recognized the two key advantages of allowing the video recording to replace the witness's evidence-in-chief, namely the fact that the witness's recollection of the events in question is likely to have been better at the time of the recording, and the reduction in levels of stress when giving evidence on oath. The danger that the witness may, in the recording, make statements elicited in answer to leading questions, was not thought to be serious given that it would be 'completely evident' whether the witness had been led. Under s 137 of the 2003 Act, therefore, where a video recording of a witness's account of events has been made at a time when the events were fresh in his memory, the court may direct that the recording be admitted as his evidence-in-chief if it appears to the court that his recollection of events is likely to have been significantly better at the time of the recording than it will be when he gives oral evidence and it is in the interests of justice for the recording to be admitted, having regard in particular to certain prescribed matters. Under s 137(2), which effectively side-steps the hearsay rule, the statements in the recorded account are not treated as out-of-court statements admissible as evidence of the matters stated, but shall be treated as if made by the witness in his evidence if, or to the extent that, in his oral evidence he asserts the truth of them. Section 137 has yet to be brought into force.

Special measures directions for vulnerable and intimidated witnesses

Sections 16–33 of the 1999 Act introduced a range of 'special measures' which were proposed in *Speaking Up for Justice*[211] and are designed to minimize the ordeal and trauma experienced by certain types of vulnerable and intimidated witnesses when giving evidence in

---

[208] Criminal Law Revision Committee, 11th Report, Cmnd 4991 (1972), para 107. The Committee gave as an example a witness who is to speak of some event which occurred before the events about which the accused is to give evidence. For a further example, see *R v Mulindwa* [2017] 2 Cr App R 94 (10) (at [45]), considered in Ch 7, p 248.

[209] (HMSO, 2001) 555, accessible at http://www.criminal-courts-review.org.uk.

[210] See immediately below, under **Special measures directions for vulnerable and intimidated witnesses**.

[211] (Home Office, 1998). For a critique of *Speaking up for Justice*, see Fairclough, 'Speaking up for injustice: reconsidering the provision of special measures through the lens of equality' [2018] Crim LR 4.

criminal cases.[212] The provisions in the 1999 Act have been amended by the Coroners and Justice Act 2009.[213] The provisions are sensible modifications to orthodox trial procedures designed to meet the real needs of children and other vulnerable witnesses and most applications for special measures succeed.[214] However, there are six failings. (1) The new statutory scheme is needlessly complex, in parts almost impenetrable. (2) It is unduly inflexible and makes somewhat arbitrary distinctions between (a) sexual offences (together with offences involving the use of firearms, knives, and other weapons) and (b) all other types of serious offence. (3) The accused is excluded from the statutory scheme, except in the case of live link and examination through an intermediary, and in those two cases the eligibility criteria for the accused are different from those that apply to other witnesses, and some of the differences are difficult to justify.[215] (4) The provision relating to the video recording of cross-examination and re-examination has been brought into force only on a pilot basis in proceedings before a small number of Crown Courts.[216] (5) More could be achieved, both in improving the processes for the identification of vulnerable and intimidated witnesses[217] and by the introduction of specific new measures such as improved assessment of individual need, the mandatory visual recording of initial interviews, and the curtailment of inappropriate questioning and cross-examination tactics.[218] (6) The statutory scheme does not apply in civil proceedings, but in family proceedings special measures are available under the Family Procedure (Amendment No 3) Rules 2017.[219]

The judge may give a direction providing for the following special measures to apply to evidence given by vulnerable and intimidated witnesses: screening the witness; giving evidence by live link; giving evidence in private; the removal of wigs and gowns; admitting a video recording of an interview of the witness as the evidence-in-chief of the witness; video

---

[212] See also *Report of the Advisory Group on Video-Recorded Evidence* (Home Office, 1989) (the 'Pigot Report'), Law Commission Consultation Paper No 130, *Mentally Incapacitated and Other Vulnerable Adults: Public Law Protection*, and generally Birch, 'A Better Deal for Vulnerable Witnesses?' [2000] Crim LR 223 and Hoyano, 'Variations on a Theme by Pigot: Special Measures Directions for Child Witnesses' [2000] Crim LR 250 and 'Striking a Balance between the Rights of Defendants and Vulnerable Witnesses: Will Special Measures Directions Contravene Guarantees of a Fair Trial?' [2001] Crim LR 948.

[213] For analysis of the amendments, see Hoyano, 'Special Measures Directions Take Two: Entrenching Unequal Access to Justice?' [2010] Crim LR 345.

[214] See Roberts et al, 'Monitoring success, accounting for failure: The outcome of prosecutors' applications for special measures directions under the Youth Justice and Criminal Evidence Act 1999' (2005) 9 E&P 269.

[215] See generally McEwan, 'Vulnerable Defendants and the Fairness of Trials' [2013] Crim LR 100.

[216] See generally Cooper, 'Pigot Unfulfilled: Video-recorded Cross-examination under Section 28 of the Youth Justice and Criminal Evidence Act 1999' [2005] Crim LR 456. See also Henderson and Lamb, 'Pre-Recording Children's Testimony: Effects on Case Progression' [2017] Crim LR 345.

[217] See Burton et al, 'Implementing Special Measures for Vulnerable and Intimidated Witnesses: The Problem of Identification' [2006] Crim LR 229.

[218] See Burton et al, 'Vulnerable and intimidated witnesses and the adversarial process in England and Wales' (2007) 11 E&P 1; but see also, in relation to the examination and cross-examination of vulnerable witnesses, under **Ch 6, Young and vulnerable witnesses, p 180** and **Ch 7, Young and vulnerable witnesses, p 225**.

[219] SI 2017/1033, Part 3A 1–12. The Family Court has a duty to consider the vulnerability of a witness and to provide assistance to protected witnesses by making 'participation directions' for measures such as intermediaries or live links, to help the witnesses participate and give evidence. The Rules are supplemented by a Practice Direction which provides for the holding of a Ground Rules Hearing: PD 5.2–5.7. See also Gold, 'Civil Way, Procedure & Practice, Family Catch-up', [2017] NLJ, 24 November, 13.

recording the cross-examination and re-examination of the witness and admitting such a recording as the evidence of the witness under cross-examination and on re-examination;[220] the examination of the witness through an intermediary; and the provision of appropriate aids to communication with the witness.

Special measures are only available to 'eligible witnesses', namely (i) witnesses other than the accused eligible for assistance on grounds of age or incapacity, for whom all the above special measures are available, and (ii) witnesses other than the accused eligible for assistance on grounds of fear or distress about testifying, for whom all but the last two of the above special measures are available.[221] It will be convenient to consider in more detail the nature of the special measures available and the types of witness eligible for assistance before turning to consider the circumstances in which a special measures direction may or must be given. Finally, consideration will be given to the special position of the accused.

Special measures directions
Screens
Under s 23(1) of the 1999 Act, a special measures direction may provide for the witness while giving evidence or being sworn in court to be prevented by means of a screen or other arrangement from seeing the accused. However, the screen must not prevent the witness from being able to see, and to be seen by, the judge or justices, the jury (if there is one), legal representatives acting in the case, and any interpreter or other person appointed to assist the witness.[222]

Live link
Under s 24 of the 1999 Act, a special measures direction may provide for the witness to give evidence by a live television link or other arrangement whereby the witness, while absent from the courtroom, is able to see and hear a person there and to be seen and heard by the judge or justices, the jury (if there is one), the legal representatives in the case, and any interpreter or other person appointed to assist the witness. Such a direction may also provide for a specified person to accompany the witness while giving evidence by live link.[223] Where a direction has been given providing for the witness to give evidence by live link, the court may later give permission for the witness to give evidence in some other way, if it appears to be in the interests of justice to do so.[224]

Evidence in private
Under s 25 of the 1999 Act, a special measures direction may provide for the exclusion from the court, during the giving of the witness's evidence, of persons of any description specified in the direction other than the accused, legal representatives acting in the case, or any interpreter or other person appointed to assist the witness.[225] However, such a direction may only

---

[220] This special measure has been introduced only on a pilot basis.

[221] See s 18(1).

[222] Section 23(2). See also, prior to the enactment of s 23, Home Office Circular 61/1990, *Use of Screens in Magistrates' Courts*; and *R v X, Y and Z* (1989) 91 Cr App R 36, CA; *R v Watford Magistrates' Court, ex p Lenman* [1993] Crim LR 388, DC; *R v Cooper and Schaub* [1994] Crim LR 531, CA; and *R v Foster* [1995] Crim LR 333, CA.

[223] Section 24(1A).

[224] Section 24(3).

[225] Where the persons specified are representatives of the media, the direction shall be expressed not to apply to one named person nominated by one or more news gathering or reporting organizations: s 25(3).

be given where the proceedings relate to a sexual offence[226] or a slavery or human trafficking case, or it appears to the court that there are reasonable grounds for believing that any person other than the accused has sought, or will seek, to intimidate the witness in connection with testifying in the proceedings.[227]

Removal of wigs and gowns

Under s 26 of the 1999 Act, provision may be made for the wearing of wigs and gowns to be dispensed with during the giving of the witness's evidence.

Video-recorded evidence-in-chief

Section 27(1)–(3) of the 1999 Act provide as follows:

(1) A special measures direction may provide for a video recording of an interview of the witness to be admitted as evidence in chief of the witness.

(2) A special measures direction may, however, not provide for a video-recording, or part of such a recording, to be admitted under this section if the court is of the opinion, having regard to all the circumstances of the case, that in the interests of justice the recording, or that part of it, should not be so admitted.

(3) In considering, for the purposes of subsection (2) whether any part of a recording should not be admitted under this section, the court must consider whether any prejudice to the accused which might result from that part being so admitted is outweighed by the desirability of showing the whole, or substantially the whole, of the recorded interview.

Section 27(2) allows the court to direct that any part of the recording be excluded, in which case the party admitting the video must then edit it accordingly.[228] The effect of s 27(3) is not to extend the common law rules as to the admissibility of evidence so as to lead to the admission of otherwise inadmissible evidence, for example inadmissible evidence of bad character. Such evidence will normally be edited out. Section 27(3) is designed to cover unusual cases in which the evidence of the witness cannot be given in a way that is coherent and understandable to the listener without the inclusion of the inadmissible material.[229] In such cases, it is submitted, the judge will need to give a direction to the jury—which, in the circumstances, is likely to be difficult for them to comprehend—that the offending material is not evidence of the matters stated.

Where a recording (or part of it) is admitted, then: (a) the witness must be called by the party tendering it in evidence, unless either (i) a special measures direction provides for the witness's evidence on cross-examination to be given in any recording admissible under s 28 of the 1999 Act, or (ii) the parties in the proceedings have agreed that there is no need for the witness to be available for cross-examination; and (b) the witness may not without the permission of the court give evidence-in-chief otherwise than by means of the recording (or part of it) as to any matter which, in the opinion of the court, is dealt with in the witness's recorded testimony (or part of it).[230] The court may give such permission if it appears

---

[226] 'Sexual offence' is defined in the 1999 Act, s 62 as any offence under the Sexual Offences Act 2003, Pt 1 or any relevant superseded offence.

[227] Section 25(4).

[228] See *Criminal Practice Directions* V, Part 16B, which also governs the procedure for production and proof of the recording. The parties themselves may agree on the editing of an ABE interview (considered at nn 236–7) and such an agreement should be adhered to, unless there is very good reason to depart from it: *R v M(A)* [2013] 1 Cr App R 245(17), CA.

[229] *R (on the application of the Crown Prosecution Service Harrow) v Brentford Youth Court* [2004] Crim LR 159 (DC).

[230] Section 27(5) and (6).

to the court to be in the interests of justice to do so either (a) on an application by a party to the proceedings; or (b) of its own motion.[231] Where a special measures direction provides for a recording (or part of it) to be admitted under s 27, the court may nevertheless subsequently make a direction to the contrary if it appears to the court that (i) the witness will not be available for cross-examination (whether conducted in the ordinary way or in accordance with a special measures direction) and the parties have not agreed that there is no need for the witness to be so available, or (ii) any rules of court requiring disclosure of the circumstances in which the recording (or part of it) was made have not been complied with to the satisfaction of the court.[232] Nothing in s 27 affects the admissibility of any video recording which would be admissible apart from the section.[233]

Video-recorded interviews with child witnesses should be conducted in accordance with the guidance given in *Achieving Best Evidence in Criminal Proceedings: Guidance on interviewing victims and witnesses and guidance on using special measures*,[234] a non-statutory code which deals with such matters as leading questions, previous statements, and the bad character of the accused. The guidance should be regarded as expert advice as to what will normally be the best practice to adopt in seeking to ensure that a child's evidence is reliable, and if it is not observed there are grounds for a judge or jury to consider with particular care whether the child is reliable.[235] In *R v K*[236] it was held that, in deciding whether to exclude evidence obtained in breach of the Guidance, the starting point is the statutory wording and the strong presumption in favour of the use of special measures, and the test is 'Could a reasonable jury properly directed be sure that the witness has given a credible and accurate account notwithstanding the breaches?' The prime consideration is reliability, which will normally be assessed by reference to the interview itself, the conditions under which it was held, the age of the child, and the nature and extent of the breaches. There may be cases in which other evidence in the case demonstrates that the breaches did not undermine the credibility or accuracy of the interview, but references to other evidence should be undertaken with considerable caution.

In order to reach a decision under s 27(2), the judge, in most—if not all—cases, must watch the video recording. In the case of interviews with some child witnesses, the court will need to decide upon the competence of the child.[237] If, on viewing the recording, the judge considers that the child is not competent to give evidence, the evidence should not be admitted; but if he concludes that the child is competent, there is no need to investigate the child's competence again at the trial before the playing of the recording. Nonetheless, he still has the power to exclude the evidence if, in the course of it, he forms the view that the child is, after all, not competent.[238]

---

[231] Section 27(7). The court may, in giving permission, direct that the evidence in question be given by the witness by means of a live link: s 27(9). If such a direction is given, the court may also provide for a specified person to accompany the witness while the witness is giving evidence by live link: s 27(9A).

[232] Section 27(4) and (6).

[233] Section 27(11).

[234] (Ministry of Justice, 2011), accessible at http://www.cps.gov.uk/publications/docs/best_evidence_in_criminal_proceedings.pdf.

[235] *R v Dunphy* (1993) 98 Cr App R 393 at 395, CA, a decision under an earlier version of the Guidance.

[236] [2006] 2 Cr App R 175 (10), CA.

[237] In deciding, the court shall treat the witness as having the benefit of any special measures which the court has given, or proposes to give, in relation to the witness: s 54(3).

[238] See *R v Hampshire* [1995] 2 All ER 1019, CA, a decision under the Criminal Justice Act 1988, s 32A.

In *R v Popescu*[239] it was held that: where a video recording has been admitted, any transcript of it should only be given to the jury for good reason,[240] where a transcript is given to the jury, the judge should warn the jury to take care to examine the video as it was shown, not least because of the demeanour of the witness;[241] the transcript should generally be withdrawn from the jury after the video has been shown,[242] but might be retained during cross-examination, in exceptional circumstances, in which case the reason for retention should be explained to the jury; if retained during cross-examination, the transcript should generally be withdrawn from the jury at the conclusion of the witness's evidence, but might be retained when the jury retire, in exceptional circumstances, which would usually only be present if the defence want the jury to have the transcript and the judge is satisfied that there is a good reason for the jury to retire with it.[243] Where the jury are permitted to retire with transcripts, it is incumbent on the judge to give a clear and emphatic warning not to give disproportionate weight to the transcripts.[244]

In *R v R*,[245] it was held that where an issue arises as to whether the jury should have received transcripts in retirement, the Court of Appeal will consider the following questions: (i) what was the approach of the defence to the problem; (ii) did the approach amount to agreement by the defence that the jury should have the transcripts in retirement; (iii) what warnings did the judge give, and were they sufficient; and (iv) how does all of this impact on the safety of the conviction?[246] 'Agreement by the defence' (at (ii)), refers to agreement before or at the time a decision is made that the jury should receive the transcripts, not after they have received them by mistake.[247] Where the defence are placed in a difficult position as a result of the jury having been given transcripts by mistake, acquiescence as a pragmatic response to the mistake is not necessarily 'agreement'.

Video-recorded cross-examination or re-examination
Section 28 of the 1999 Act provides for video-taped cross-examination or re-examination. The section has been brought into force, but only on a pilot basis.[248] Under s 28(1), where a

---

[239] [2010] EWCA Crim 1230. In *R v Sothilingham* [2019] 4 WLR 17, CA at [30], the Court of Appeal acknowledged changes to practice since *R v Popescu* [2010] EWCA Crim 1230 and the context in which the principles in that case now operate. The jury are now trusted with written directions, routes to verdicts, written summaries of agreed facts and jurors themselves take notes. However, the court held that the principles do still apply where the judge allows contentious written material to go before the jury.

[240] As when, eg, a child suffers from a speech disorder, poor articulation, or a strong accent. In addition to the evidence being difficult to follow on the screen (for whatever reason), a 'good reason' might simply be poor audio quality; there will need to be a discussion of the issue between the judge and the advocates: see *R v R* [2017] EWCA Crim 1487 at [48].

[241] There is a risk of disproportionate weight being given to the transcript: see also *R v R* [2017] EWCA Crim 487 at [48], *R v Welstead* [1996] 1 Cr App R 59 at 68, CA, and *R v Morris* [1998] Crim LR 16.

[242] See also the Criminal Practice Directions, VI, 26L, 2.

[243] It is not a good reason, for these purposes, that the jury, on retirement, have with them a transcript of the accused's interview: *R v Sardar* [2012] EWCA Crim 134.

[244] *R v R* [2017] EWCA Crim 1487. See also, the Crown Court Compendium (July 2019), Part 1, 3–6, para 13 and Example 3. Cf *R v Sothilingham* [2019] 4 WLR 17, CA.

[245] [2017] EWCA Crim 1487.

[246] Ibid at [52].

[247] Ibid at [54].

[248] It applies only in proceedings before a limited number of Crown Courts and only in the case of witnesses under the age of 18 at the time of the hearing or eligible for assistance on grounds of incapacity: Youth Justice and Criminal Evidence Act 1999 (Commencement No 13) Order, SI 2013/3236 and (Commencement No 15) Order, SI 2016/1201.

special measures direction provides for a video recording to be admitted as evidence-in-chief of the witness under s 27, the direction may also provide for any cross-examination and any re-examination of the witness to be recorded by means of a video recording and for such a recording, so far as it relates to any such cross-examination or re-examination, to be admitted as evidence of the witness under cross-examination or re-examination. Under s 28(2), such a recording must be made in the presence of such persons as rules of court or the direction may provide, and in the absence of the accused, but in circumstances in which (a) the judge or justices (or both) and legal representatives acting in the proceedings are able to see and hear the examination of the witness and to communicate with those in whose presence the recording is being made; and (b) the accused is able to see and hear any such examination and to communicate with any legal representative acting for him.[249] Where a special measures direction provides for a recording to be admitted under s 28, the court may nevertheless subsequently make a direction to the contrary if any requirement of s 28(2) or rules of court or the direction itself has not been complied with to the satisfaction of the court.[250] Where in pursuance of s 28(1) a recording has been made, the witness may not be subsequently cross-examined or re-examined in respect of any evidence given by the witness (whether or not in any recording admissible under s 27 or s 28) unless the court gives a further special measures direction,[251] but such a further direction may only be given if it appears to the court (a) that the proposed cross-examination is sought by a party to the proceedings as a result of that party having become aware, since the time when the original recording was made, of a matter which that party could not with reasonable diligence have ascertained by then; or (b) that for any other reason it is in the interests of justice to give the further direction.[252]

In *R v Hampson*,[253] the Court of Appeal laid down the following six principles concerning best practice where the court has made an order for special measures under s 28.[254]

1. At the ground rules hearing, the judge should discuss how and when limitations on questioning will be explained to the jury during the trial.
2. If the discussion has not taken place at the ground rules hearing, or matters have changed, it should take place before the recording of the cross-examination is played to the jury.
3. The judge will then be able to give the standard direction required by s 32 of the 1999 Act[255] with a direction on the limitations the judge has placed on questioning,[256] before the recording of the cross-examination is played.
4. The judge should, if necessary, have a further discussion with the advocates before closing speeches concerning limits on questioning and any areas where the limitations have had material effects, so that the advocates will know the jury can be addressed on these areas.

---

[249] Section 28 has no application in relation to any cross-examination of the witness by the accused in person: s 28(7).

[250] Section 28(4).

[251] Section 28(5).

[252] Section 28(6).

[253] [2019] 1 WLR 3243 at [21].

[254] Ibid at [21]. However, failure to follow this best practice will not necessarily render convictions unsafe if the defence have been able to explore fully and fairly all relevant areas with the complainant and rely on other evidence and make submissions to the jury: see [22] and [23].

[255] See later in this chapter under, **The status of video-recorded evidence etc, p 167**. See also the Crown Court Compendium (July 2019), Part 1, 3–6, para 3.

[256] See also the Crown Court Compendium (July 2019), Part 1, 3–6, para 4.

5. The judge should remind the jury in summing-up, of limitations imposed and identify areas where there may have been a material effect.

6. Where written directions are provided to the jury, the judge should include with the standard direction under s 32, a general direction on the limits imposed on cross-examination.

Examination of witness through intermediary

Under s 29 of the 1999 Act, a special measures direction may provide for any examination of the witness (however and wherever conducted) to be conducted through an interpreter or other intermediary approved by the court. The function of the intermediary is to communicate to the witness questions put to the witness, to communicate to the person asking such questions the answers given by the witness in reply, and to explain such questions or answers so far as necessary to enable them to be understood.[257] Any examination under s 29 must take place in the presence of such persons as the Criminal Procedure Rules or the direction may provide, but in circumstances in which (a) the judge or justices (or both) and legal representatives acting in the proceedings are able to see and hear the examination of the witness and to communicate with the intermediary; and (b) the jury, if there is one, are able to see and hear the examination of the witness (except in the case of a video-recorded examination).[258] A special measures direction may provide for a recording of an interview, conducted through an intermediary, to be admitted under s 27, provided that the intermediary has been approved by the court before the direction is given.[259]

Aids to communication

Under s 30 of the 1999 Act, a special measures direction may provide for the witness, while giving evidence (whether in court or otherwise), to be provided with such device as the court considers appropriate with a view to enabling questions or answers to be communicated to or by the witness despite any disability or disorder or other impairment which the witness has or suffers from.

The witnesses eligible for assistance

Witnesses eligible for assistance on grounds of age or incapacity

Section 16(1) and (2) of the 1999 Act provide as follows:

(1) . . . a witness in criminal proceedings (other than the accused) is eligible for assistance by virtue of this section—

(a) if under the age of 18 at the time of the hearing; or

(b) if the court considers that the quality of the evidence given by the witness is likely to be diminished by reason of any circumstances falling within subsection (2).

---

[257] Section 29(2). As to the extent to which s 29 will assist eligible witnesses to give their best evidence or promote more empathic communication during cross-examination, see Ellison, 'The Mosaic Art?: Cross-examination and the Vulnerable Witness' (2001) 21 Legal Studies 353 and 'Cross-examination and the Intermediary: Bridging the Language Divide?' [2002] Crim LR 114. See also Henderson, '"A very valuable tool": Judges, advocates and intermediaries discuss the intermediary system in England and Wales' (2015) 19(3) E&P 154. For examples of the use of intermediaries in the case of the profoundly disabled, see *R v Watts* [2010] EWCA Crim 1824. See also Ch 6, **Young and vulnerable witnesses, p 180.**

[258] Section 29(3).

[259] Section 29(6).

   (2) The circumstances falling within this subsection are—

      (a) that the witness—

         (i)   suffers from mental disorder within the meaning of the Mental Health Act 1983; or

         (ii) otherwise has a significant impairment of intelligence and social functioning;

      (b) that the witness has a physical disability or is suffering from a physical disorder.

In s 16(1)(a), 'the time of the hearing', in relation to a witness, means the time when it falls to the court to decide whether to make a special measures direction.[260] In deciding whether a witness has a physical disability or is suffering from a physical disorder, the court must consider any views expressed by the witness.[261] References to the quality of a witness's evidence, in s 16 and in other sections relating to special measures directions, are to its quality in terms of completeness, coherence, and accuracy; and for this purpose 'coherence' refers to a witness's ability in giving evidence to give answers which address the questions put to the witness and can be understood both individually and collectively.[262]

Witnesses eligible for assistance on grounds of fear or distress about testifying

Under s 17(1) of the 1999 Act, a witness other than the accused is eligible for assistance if the court is satisfied that the quality of evidence given by the witness is likely to be diminished by reason of fear or distress on the part of the witness in connection with testifying in the proceedings. In deciding whether a witness falls within s 17(1), the court must take into account, in particular: (a) the nature and alleged circumstances of the offence to which the proceedings relate; (b) the age of the witness; (c) such of the following matters as appear to the court to be relevant, namely (i) the social and cultural background and ethnic origins of the witness, (ii) the domestic and employment circumstances of the witness, and (iii) any religious beliefs or political opinions of the witness; and (d) any behaviour towards the witness on the part of the accused, members of the family or associates of the accused, or any other person who is likely to be an accused or a witness in the proceedings.[263] In deciding, the court must also consider any views expressed by the witness.[264] A complainant in respect of a sexual offence[265] or one of a number of other specified offences (including offences of murder, manslaughter, and offences against the person involving the use of a firearm or knife and other weapons and firearms offences) who is a witness in proceedings relating to that offence, or to that offence and any other offences, is automatically eligible for assistance unless he or she has informed the court of his or her wish not to be so eligible.[266]

The circumstances in which special measures directions are given

General

A party to the proceedings may make an application for the court to give a special measures direction or the court of its own motion may raise the issue whether such a direction should be given.[267] Section 19(2) provides as follows:

[260] Section 16(3).

[261] Section 16(4).

[262] Section 16(5).

[263] Section 17(2).

[264] Section 17(3).

[265] 'Sexual offence' is defined in the 1999 Act, s 62 as any offence under the Sexual Offences Act 2003, Pt 1 or any relevant superseded offence.

[266] Section 17(4).

[267] Section 19(1).

(2) Where the court decides that the witness is eligible for assistance by virtue of section 16 or 17, the court must then—

    (a) determine whether any of the special measures available in relation to the witness (or any combination of them), would, in its opinion, be likely to improve the quality of evidence given by the witness; and

    (b) if so—

        (i) determine which of those measures (or combination of them) would, in its opinion, be likely to maximise so far as practicable the quality of such evidence; and

        (ii) give a direction under this section providing for the measure or measures so determined to apply to evidence given by the witness.

In deciding whether any special measure or measures would or would not be likely to improve, or to maximize so far as practicable, the quality of evidence given by the witness, the court must consider all the circumstances of the case, including in particular any views expressed by the witness and whether the measure or measures might tend to inhibit such evidence being effectively tested by a party to the proceedings.[268] In the case of rape complainants, there is some research evidence to suggest that a video recording is always 'likely to improve the quality of evidence given by the witness'.[269] If a court decides under s 19 to direct that a video recording should be admitted as the evidence-in-chief of a witness, the speculative possibility that the witness, if he were to give live evidence-in-chief instead, might say something different from what was said in the recording and therefore become open to cross-examination on any such difference, is not, in itself, an adequate reason for refusing to allow the playing of the interview.[270]

Under s 20(1), as a general rule a special measures direction has binding effect from the time it is made until the proceedings for the purposes of which it is made are either determined or abandoned in relation to the accused or (if there is more than one) in relation to each of them. The court may discharge or vary a special measures direction if it appears to the court to be in the interests of justice to do so.[271] The court must state in open court its reasons for giving or varying, or refusing an application for, a special measures direction.[272]

Child witnesses

Section 21 of the 1999 Act makes special provision in the case of child witnesses. In the case of witnesses under the age of 18, in effect it creates a presumption in favour of a special measures direction in accordance with s 27 (video-recorded evidence to be admitted as evidence-in-chief) and, in the case of any evidence given by such witnesses which is not given by means of a video recording, in accordance with s 24 (evidence by live link). Section 21 provides as follows:

(1) For the purposes of this section—

    (a) a witness in criminal proceedings is a 'child witness' if he is an eligible witness by reason of section 16(1)(a) (whether or not he is an eligible witness by reason of any other provision of section 16 or 17);

    . . . and

---

[268] Section 19(3).

[269] In a study comparing the content of video-recorded police interviews with the live evidence-in-chief of the same adult rape complainants, over two-thirds of the details that were central to establishing whether the crime had occurred were later omitted from live evidence: see Westera and Milne, 'Losing Two Thirds of the Story: A Comparison of the Video-Recorded Police Interview and Live Evidence of Rape Complainants' [2013] Crim LR 290.

[270] *R v Davies* [2011] EWCA Crim 1177.

[271] Section 20(2).

[272] Section 20(5).

(c) a 'relevant recording', in relation to a child witness, is a video recording of an interview of the witness made with a view to its admission as evidence in chief of the witness.

(2) Where the court, in making a determination for the purposes of section 19(2), determines that a witness in criminal proceedings is a child witness, the court must—

(a) first have regard to subsections (3) to (4C) below; and

(b) then have regard to section 19(2);

and for the purposes of section 19(2), as it then applies to the witness, any special measures required to be applied in relation to him by virtue of this section shall be treated as if they were measures determined by the court, pursuant to section 19(2)(a) and (b)(i), to be ones that (whether on their own or with any other special measures) would be likely to maximise, so far as practicable, the quality of his evidence.

(3) The primary rule in the case of a child witness is that the court must give a special measures direction in relation to the witness which complies with the following requirements—

(a) it must provide for any relevant recording to be admitted under section 27 (video recorded evidence in chief); and

(b) it must provide for any evidence given by the witness in the proceedings which is not given by means of a video recording (whether in chief or otherwise) to be given by means of a live link in accordance with section 24.

(4) The primary rule is subject to the following limitations—

(a) . . .

(b) the requirement contained in subsection (3)(a) . . . has effect subject to subsection 27(2);[273]

(ba) if the witness informs the court of the witness's wish that the rule should not apply or should apply only in part, the rule does not apply to the extent that the court is satisfied that not complying with the rule would not diminish the quality of the witness's evidence; and

(c) the rule does not apply to the extent that the court is satisfied that compliance with it would not be likely to maximise the quality of the witness's evidence so far as practicable (whether because the application to that evidence of one or more other special measures available in relation to the witness would have the result or for any other reason).

(4A) Where as a consequence of all or part of the primary rule being disapplied under subsection (4)(ba) a witness's evidence or any part of it would fall to be given as testimony in court, the court must give a special measures direction making such provision as is described in section 23 for the evidence or that part of it.

(4B) The requirement in subsection (4A) is subject to the following limitations—

(a) if the witness informs the court of the witness's wish that the rule should not apply, the requirement does not apply to the extent that the court is satisfied that not complying with it would not diminish the quality of the witness's evidence; and

(b) the requirement does not apply to the extent that the court is satisfied that making such a provision would not be likely to maximise the quality of the witness's evidence so far as practicable (whether because the application to that evidence of one or more other special measures available in relation to the witness would have that result or for any other reason).

(4C) In making a decision under subsection 4(ba) or (4B)(a), the court must take into account the following factors (and any others it considers relevant)—

---

[273] Under the 'interests of justice' test in s 27(2), the judge's main focus should be on whether the contents of the ABE interview are likely to be accurate and reliable, but allowance should be made for the fact that a child may have difficulties such as placing events in correct chronological order and that few eyewitnesses, whatever their age, tell a completely accurate and reliable story: *R v Krezolek* [2014] EWCA Crim 2782.

(a) the age and maturity of the witness;

(b) the ability of the witness to understand the consequences of giving evidence otherwise than in accordance with the requirements in subsection (3) or (as the case may be) in accordance with the requirements in subsection (4A);

(c) the relationship (if any) between the witness and the accused;

(d) the witness's social and cultural background and ethnic origins;

(e) the nature and alleged circumstances of the offence to which the proceedings relate.

(8) Where a special measures direction is given in relation to a child witness who is an eligible witness by reason only of section 16(1)(a), then—

(a) subject to subsection (9) below, and

(b) except where the witness has already begun to give evidence in the proceedings, the direction shall cease to have effect at the time when the witness attains the age of 18.

(9) Where a special measures direction is given in relation to a child witness who is an eligible witness by reason only of section 16(1)(a) and

(a) the direction provides—

(i) for any relevant recording to be admitted under section 27 as evidence in chief of the witness, or

(ii) for the special measure available under section 28 to apply in relation to the witness, and

(b) if it provides for that special measure to so apply, the witness is still under the age of 18 when the video recording is made for the purposes of section 28, then, so far as it provides as mentioned in paragraph (a)(i) or (ii) above, the direction shall continue to have effect in accordance with section 20(1) even though the witness subsequently attains that age.[274]

In *R (D) v Camberwell Green Youth Court*,[275] an appeal in relation to s 21 of the 1999 Act prior to its amendment by the Coroners and Justice Act 2009, the House of Lords held that there is nothing in the special measures provisions inconsistent with the principles set out by the European Court of Human Rights in *Kostovski v Netherlands*.[276] All the evidence is produced at the trial in the presence of the accused, some of it in pre-recorded form and some of it by contemporaneous television transmission. The accused can see and hear it all and has every opportunity to challenge and question the witnesses against him at the trial itself. A face-to-face confrontation is missing, but the Convention does not guarantee a right to such a confrontation. The court also has the opportunity to scrutinize the video-recorded interview at the outset and exclude all or part of it. Furthermore, at the trial it has the fallback position of allowing the witness to give evidence in the courtroom or to expand upon the video recording if the interests of justice require this.

Complainants in respect of sexual offences

Section 22A of the 1999 Act makes special provision for complainants in respect of sexual offences. It provides as follows:

(1) This section applies where in criminal proceedings relating to a sexual offence (or to a sexual offence and other offences) the complainant in respect of that offence is a witness in the proceedings.

(2) This section does not apply if the place of trial is a magistrates' court.

---

[274] Section 21(2)–(4) and (4C), so far as relating to the giving of a direction complying with the requirement in s 21(3)(a), also apply to witnesses who were over the age of 18 at the time of the hearing, but who were under that age when a relevant recording was made: see s 22.

[275] [2005] 1 All ER 999, HL.

[276] (1990) 12 EHRR 434 at 447–8.

(3) This section does not apply if the complainant is an eligible witness by reason of section 16(1)(a) (whether or not the complainant is an eligible witness by reason of any other provision of section 16 or 17).

(4) If a party to the proceedings makes an application under section 19(1)(a) for a special measures direction in relation to the complainant, the party may request that the direction provide for any relevant recording to be admitted under section 27 (video recorded evidence in chief).

(5) Subsection (6) applies if—

    (a) a party to the proceedings makes a request under subsection (4) with respect to the complainant, and

    (b) the court determines for the purposes of section 19(2) that the complainant is eligible for assistance by virtue of section 16(1)(b) or 17.

(6) The court must—

    (a) first have regard to subsections (7) to (9); and

    (b) then have regard to section 19(2)

    and for the purpose of section 19(2), as it then applies to the complainant, any special measure required to be applied in relation to the complainant by virtue of this section is to be treated as if it were a measure determined by the court, pursuant to section 19(2)(a) and (b)(i), to be one that (whether on its own or with any other special measures) would be likely to maximise, so far as practicable, the quality of the complainant's evidence.

(7) The court must give a special measures direction in relation to the complainant that provides for any relevant recording to be admitted under section 27.

(8) The requirement in subsection (7) has effect subject to section 27(2).

(9) The requirement in subsection (7) does not apply to the extent that the court is satisfied that compliance with it would not be likely to maximise the quality of the complainant's evidence so far as practicable (whether because the application to that evidence of one or more other special measures available in relation to the complainant would have that result or for any other reason).

(10) In this section 'relevant recording', in relation to a complainant, is a video recording of an interview of the complainant made with a view to its admission as the evidence in chief of the complainant.

The status of video-recorded evidence, etc

Section 31(1)–(4) of the 1999 Act provide as follows:

(1) Subsections (2) to (4) apply to a statement[277] made by a witness in criminal proceedings which, in accordance with a special measures direction, is not made by the witness in direct oral testimony in court but forms part of the witness's evidence in those proceedings.[278]

(2) The statement shall be treated as if made by the witness in direct oral testimony in court; and accordingly—

    (a) it is admissible evidence of any fact of which such testimony from the witness would be admissible;

    (b) it is not capable of corroborating any other evidence given by the witness.

(3) Subsection (2) applies to a statement admitted under section 27 or 28 which is not made by the witness on oath even though it would have been required to be made on oath if made by the witness in direct oral testimony in court.

(4) In estimating the weight (if any) to be attached to the statement, the court must have regard to all the circumstances from which an inference can reasonably be drawn (as to the accuracy of the statement or otherwise).

---

[277] 'Statement' includes any representation of fact, whether made in words or otherwise: s 31(8).

[278] Ie statements given in evidence by live television link or recorded in a video recording admitted as evidence: see *R (S) v Waltham Forest Youth Court* [2004] 2 Cr App R 335 (21) at [76].

Section 32 of the 1999 Act provides that where, on a trial on indictment with a jury, evidence has been given in accordance with a special measures direction, the judge must give the jury such warning (if any) as the judge considers necessary to ensure that the fact that the direction was given in relation to the witness does not prejudice the accused. In the case of the use of screens, for example, it may suffice to say that they must not allow their use by witnesses to prejudice them in any way against the accused.[279]

The accused

The availability of special measures for the accused is of particular importance given that, under Art 6 of the European Convention on Human Rights, an accused has the right to effective participation in his trial. Such participation includes the right to be present and to hear and follow the proceedings.[280] In the case of a child accused, he must be dealt with in a manner that takes full account of his age, level of maturity, and intellectual and emotional capacities, and steps must be taken to promote his ability to understand and participate in the proceedings and to reduce as far as possible his feelings of intimidation and inhibition.[281]

Live link

Under s 33A of the 1999 Act, a provision that appears to be rarely invoked,[282] a court may permit an accused to give his oral evidence through a live link if the conditions in either s 33A(4) or s 33A(5) are met and it is in the interests of justice to do so.[283] The conditions in s 33A(4), which apply to an accused aged under 18, are that (a) his ability to participate effectively as a witness giving oral evidence in court is compromised by his level of intellectual ability or social functioning;[284] and (b) use of a live link would enable him to participate more effectively.[285] The conditions in s 33A(5), which apply where the accused has attained the age of 18, are that (a) he suffers from a mental disorder (within the meaning of the Mental Health Act 1983) or otherwise has a significant impairment of intelligence and social function; (b) he is for that reason unable to participate effectively as a witness giving oral evidence in court; and (c) use of a live link would enable him to participate more effectively.[286]

In *R (S) v Waltham Forest Youth Court*,[287] a decision prior to the amendment of the 1999 Act, it was held that since Parliament had sought to provide exclusively for the circumstances in which a live link might be used in a criminal trial, there was no residual common law power to allow an accused to give evidence by live link. This approach was followed in *R v Ukpabio*,[288] a decision after the amendment but prior to its coming into force, but doubted by

---

[279] See *R v Brown* [2004] Crim LR 1034, CA.

[280] *Stanford v UK* [1994] ECHR 16757/90 at para 26.

[281] *T v UK* (1999) 7 BHRC 659 at paras 84 and 85. See further *SC v UK* (2004) 17 BHRC 607, ECHR.

[282] See Fairclough, 'It doesn't happen . . . and I've never thought it was necessary for it to happen': Barriers to vulnerable witnesses giving evidence by live link in Crown Court trials' (2017) 21(3) E&P 209.

[283] Section 33A(2).

[284] Impaired 'social functioning' does not cover an accused who has a temper and does not like being challenged by authority figures; and evidence on the issue from someone as partisan as the accused's mother is unlikely to be sufficient: see *R v Rahman* [2015] 1 Cr App R 457 (30), CA.

[285] Section 33A(4).

[286] Section 33A(5).

[287] [2004] 2 Cr App R 335 (21), DC.

[288] [2008] 1 WLR 728, CA.

the House of Lords in *R (D) v Camberwell Green Youth Court*,[289] where it was held that the court had wide and flexible inherent powers to ensure that the accused is not at a substantial disadvantage compared with the prosecution and receives a fair trial, including a fair opportunity of giving the best evidence he can.[290] Baroness Hale was of the view that in exceptional circumstances special measures designed to shield a vulnerable or intimidated witness can apply in the case of the accused, giving as a possible example the use of live link by a younger child accused too scared to give evidence in the presence of her co-accused.

Examination of accused through intermediary

Under s 33BA of the 1999 Act, inserted by s 104 of the Coroners and Justice Act 2009, but not yet in force, a court may, on the application of the accused, direct that any examination of the accused be conducted through an intermediary.[291] Such a direction may be given if the conditions in either s 33BA(5) or s 33BA(6) are met and it is necessary in order to ensure that the accused receives a fair trial.[292] The conditions in s 33BA(5) (for an accused aged under 18) and s 33BA(6) (for an accused who has attained that age) are essentially the same as those that apply in respect of live link for an accused, as set out in s 33A(4) and (5) respectively.[293] The function of an intermediary for an accused is the same as for any other witness.[294] Any examination under s 33BA must take place in the presence of such persons as the Criminal Procedure Rules or the direction may provide and in circumstances in which (a) the judge or justices (or both) and legal representatives acting in the proceedings are able to see and hear the examination of the accused and to communicate with the intermediary (b) the jury, if there is one, are able to see and hear the examination of the accused, and (c) where there are two or more accused, each of the other accused is able to see and hear the examination of the accused.[295]

Until s 33BA is brought into force, the courts may use their inherent jurisdiction to direct that an accused be assisted by an intermediary;[296] there is a right, which may in certain circumstances amount to a duty, to appoint an intermediary to assist the accused to follow the proceedings and give evidence if, without assistance, he would not be able to have a fair trial.[297] However, Criminal Practice Direction I, paras 3F.12 and 3F.13 provide that there is no presumption that an accused will be assisted by an intermediary, it will be rare to appoint an intermediary to assist the accused to give evidence (only cases of 'the most pressing' need)

---

[289] [2005] 1 All ER 999.

[290] For example, the court can allow an accused with learning and communication difficulties to have the equivalent of an interpreter to assist with communication, and his written statement can be read to the jury so that they know what he wants to say: see *R v H* [2003] EWCA Crim 1208.

[291] See generally, Cooper and Wurtzel, 'A Day Late and a Dollar Short: In Search of an Intermediary Scheme for Vulnerable Defendants in England and Wales' [2013] Crim LR 4.

[292] Section 33BA(2).

[293] See at nn 285 and 286.

[294] See s 33BA(4) and s 29(2).

[295] Section 33BA(7).

[296] See *R(C) v Sevenoaks Youth Court* [2010] 1 All ER 375 and *R v H* [2003] EWCA Crim 1208.

[297] *R(AS) v Great Yarmouth Youth Court* [2011] EWHC 2059 (Admin), where, without the assistance of an intermediary, the court would not necessarily have realized that the accused, who suffered from ADHD but was able to communicate his evidence to the court, was put in difficulty by complex questions and might react by not answering a question because concentrating on a previous question.

and extremely rare to appoint one to assist with the entire trial.[298] Where the examination of an accused should be conducted through an intermediary, fairness requires the availability of a registered intermediary, that is, an intermediary of the kind available for victims and non-defendant witnesses who works through the Witness Intermediary Scheme ('WIS') run by the Ministry of Justice, and not merely a private and unregistered intermediary.[299] Where a judge directs that an intermediary should be made available, but every step to identify an available intermediary has been unsuccessful, the judge should make an informed assessment whether the absence of an intermediary would make the trial unfair or whether the specific communication problems could be dealt with by procedural modifications to the ordinary trial process, such as the use of simply phrased questions, short periods of evidence, and breaks to allow the advocate for the defence to summarize the evidence and to take further instructions.[300]

Other special measures

In the case of a witness who is not an eligible witness under the statutory scheme, the scheme has no effect on the powers of the court in the exercise of its inherent jurisdiction,[301] for example the powers to provide for the use of screens or the removal of wigs and gowns. Judges are expected to deal with specific communication problems faced by an accused (or other witness) as part and parcel of their ordinary control of the judicial process, when necessary adapting the processes to ensure that a particular individual is not disadvantaged as a result of personal difficulties, whatever form they may take; the overall responsibility of the judge for the fairness of the trial has not been altered by the availability of the statutory special measures.[302]

Witness anonymity

In some cases, witnesses will be in genuine and justified fear of serious consequences should their true identity become known. If such witnesses do not give evidence, criminals may walk free and the innocent may be convicted. To ensure the safety of such witnesses and induce them to give evidence, various measures can be taken, including the use of a pseudonym, the withholding from the defence of any particulars which might identify them, the banning of any questions in cross-examination of the witnesses which might enable any of them to be identified, and the giving of evidence behind screens.[303] The obvious danger, however, is the potential or actual disadvantage to the accused, which has been likened to taking blind shots at a hidden target,[304] and the concomitant risk of an unfair

---

[298] For an example of an appointment in relation to the accused's evidence but not the entire trial, see *R v Rashid* [2017] 1 WLR 2449. Cf *R v Biddle* [2019] 2 Cr App R 209 (20), CA. For criticism of these provisions of the Practice Direction, see Hoyano and Rafferty, 'Rationing Defence Intermediaries under the April 2016 Criminal Practice Direction' [2017] Crim LR 93.

[299] *R (OP) v Secretary of State for Justice* [2014] EWHC 1944 (Admin). But see Criminal Practice Direction I, para 3F.15: the WIS is not presently available to identify intermediaries for defendants and therefore non-registered intermediaries must be appointed.

[300] *R v Cox* [2012] 2 Cr App R 63 (6), CA. See also *R v Biddle* [2019] 2 Cr App R 209 (20), CA at [35]; and *R v Rashid* [2017] 1 WLR 2449 at [80] and [82].

[301] Section 19(6).

[302] *R v Cox* [2012] 2 Cr App R 63 (6), CA at [29].

[303] The alternative or supplementary measure of secret relocation of witnesses and their families, which has found favour in the US, is costly and effectively penalizes not only the witness, for doing his civic duty, but also his family.

[304] *R v Davis* [2008] 3 All ER 461, per Lord Bingham at [32].

trial. In *R v Davis*[305] the House of Lords held that the use of such measures, in the circumstances of the case, hampered the conduct of the defence in a manner and to an extent which was unlawful and rendered the trial unfair. Their Lordships were in agreement that it was a long-established principle of the English common law that subject to certain exceptions and statutory qualifications, the accused should be confronted by his accusers in order that he may cross-examine them and challenge their evidence. Article 6(3)(d) of the European Convention, guaranteeing the accused the right to examine or have examined witnesses against him, had not added anything of significance to English law. The Strasbourg case law has established that no conviction should be based solely or to a decisive extent upon the statements or testimony of anonymous witnesses, because it results from a trial which cannot be regarded as fair. However, their Lordships did not doubt that the problem of witness intimidation was real and prevalent and might well call for urgent attention by Parliament.

The parliamentary response was swift and decisive, not least because the decision in *R v Davis* was bound to lead to the collapse of numerous trials, including a number of murder trials, in which applications had been or were being made for witness anonymity orders. The Criminal Evidence (Witness Anonymity) Act 2008 abolished the common law rules and provided for the making of witness anonymity orders in relation to witnesses in criminal proceedings. The 2008 Act had a 'sunset clause', and expired, but the Coroners and Justice Act 2009 re-enacted the provisions of the 2008 Act, subject to relatively minor amendment.[306]

The relevant provisions of the 2009 Act may be summarized as follows.[307] A witness, for the purposes of an anonymity order, is any person called or proposed to be called, to give evidence at the trial or hearing.[308] The measures that can be taken under a witness anonymity order are (a) the withholding, and removal from materials disclosed to any party to the proceedings, of the witness's name and other identifying details; (b) use of a pseudonym; (c) not permitting the witness to be asked questions that might lead to his identification; (d) screening the witness, but not to the extent that the witness cannot be seen by the judge or jury; or (e) subjecting the witness's voice to modulation, but not to the extent that his natural voice cannot be heard by the judge or jury.[309] Application for an order may be made by the prosecution or defence;[310] where it is made by the prosecution, they must inform the court of the identity of the witness, but are not required to disclose either identity or information that may lead to identification to any other party to the proceedings or his lawyers;[311] and where it is made by the defence, they must inform the court and the prosecutor of the identity of

---

[305] [2008] 1 AC 1128, HL per Lord Bingham at [32].

[306] The 2009 Act also provides for investigation anonymity orders (ss 74–85), ie orders prohibiting the disclosure of information identifying an individual as having aided an investigation into an offence of murder or manslaughter caused by a firearm or knife. The circumstances in which such orders can be made are tightly circumscribed.

[307] See also the Attorney General's guidelines on the prosecutor's role in applications for witness anonymity orders; Criminal Procedure Rules 2015, rr 18.18–18.22; and *Criminal Practice Directions* V, Part 18D. For a detailed analysis of the provisions of the 2009 Act, see Ormerod et al, 'Coroners and Justice Act 2009: the "Witness Anonymity" and 'Investigation Anonymity' Provisions' [2010] Crim LR 368.

[308] Section 97. The Act does not apply to extradition proceedings, but in such proceedings the court has an inherent power to admit anonymous evidence: *R (B) v Westminster Magistrates' Court* [2014] UKSC 59.

[309] Section 86.

[310] Section 87(1).

[311] Section 87(2).

the witness, but are not required to disclose either identity or information that might lead to identification to any other accused or his lawyers.[312] Every party must be given the opportunity to be heard on an application for an order, except that the court may hear one or more parties in the absence of an accused and his lawyers if it appears to the court appropriate to do so.[313]

Under s 88 of the Act, the court may only make an order if satisfied that Conditions A to C are met. Condition A is that the proposed order is necessary (a) in order to protect the safety of the witness or another or to prevent any serious damage to property (and in deciding the question of necessity in this respect, the court must have regard in particular to any reasonable fear on the part of the witness that, if identified, he or another would suffer death or injury or there would be serious damage to property); or (b) in order to prevent real harm to the public interest. Condition A will not be met if the witness's identity is already known to the accused, because an anonymity order cannot reasonably serve to protect the witness and is therefore not necessary for that purpose.[314] Condition B is that, having regard to all the circumstances, the effect of the proposed order would be consistent with the accused receiving a fair trial. Condition C is that the importance of the witness's testimony is such that in the interests of justice the witness ought to testify and (a) the witness would not testify if the proposed order were not made or (b) there would be real harm to the public interest if the witness were to testify without the proposed order being made. When deciding whether Conditions A to C are met, the court must have regard to the considerations set out in s 89(2) and such other matters as the court considers relevant. The considerations in s 89(2) are:

(a) the general right of an accused to know the identity of a witness;
(b) the extent to which the credibility of the witness would be a relevant factor when assessing the weight of his evidence;
(c) whether the evidence given by the witness might be the sole or decisive evidence implicating the accused;
(d) whether the witness's evidence could be properly tested (on grounds of credibility or otherwise) without his identity being disclosed;
(e) whether there is any reason to believe that the witness (i) has a tendency to be dishonest, or (ii) has any motive to be dishonest in the circumstances of the case, having regard in particular to any previous convictions and to any relationship between him and the accused or any of his associates; and
(f) whether it would be reasonably practicable to protect the witness by any means other than by making a witness anonymity order specifying the measures under consideration by the court.

Under s 90 of the Act, in jury trials the judge must give the jury such warning as he considers appropriate to ensure that the fact that the order was made does not prejudice the accused. Under s 91, where an order has been made, the court may discharge or vary the order on an

---

[312] Section 87(1)–(3). Art 6(3) of the European Convention on Human Rights and s 3 of the Human Rights Act 1998 do not require s 87(3) to be read so as to include the words 'unless to inform the prosecution would deprive the accused of a fair trial' because that would be to deprive the prosecution of the essential ability to do the same research in relation to defence witnesses as is required in relation to any witness whom they wish to call anonymously: *R v Sardar* [2017] 1 WLR 917, CA.

[313] Section 87(6) and (7).

[314] *R v Willett* [2011] EWCA Crim 2710.

application by a party to the proceedings or on its own initiative if there has been a material change to the circumstances since the relevant time and where it is appropriate to do so in view of the provisions of s 88 and 89.[315]

R v Mayers[316] provided detailed guidance on the meaning and application of the provisions of the Criminal Evidence (Witness Anonymity) Act 2008. It is submitted that the guidance remains valid despite the amendments made by the 2009 Act. In the summary of the guidance that follows, for convenience reference has been made to the relevant statutory provisions of the 2009 Act.

1. Save in the exceptional circumstances permitted by the Act, the ancient principle that the accused is entitled to know the identity of the witnesses who incriminate him is maintained.

2. The Act seeks to address the provisions of the European Convention and the relevant jurisprudence of the European Court by seeking to preserve the delicate balance between the rights of the accused, including his entitlement to a fair trial and public hearing, and to examine or have the witnesses who inculpate him properly examined (Art 6) and the witness's right to life (Art 2) and physical security (Art 3) and the right to respect for his private life (Art 8).

3. Bearing in mind other provisions such as special measures under the 1999 Act[317] and the admissibility of evidence under s 116 of the 2003 Act where a witness is unavailable,[318] an anonymity order should be regarded as a special measure of last practicable resort.

4. The principles which govern the use of 'special counsel' for public interest immunity purposes[319] should be adapted when the use of such 'counsel' arises in the context of witness anonymity, when the issue will be whether sufficient and complete investigation and consequential disclosure have taken place. A detailed investigation into the background of each potential anonymous witness will almost inevitably be required.

5. The judge should normally reflect both at the close of the prosecution and when the defence evidence is concluded, whether properly directed and in the light of the evidence as a whole, the case can safely be left to the jury.

6. The s 90 warning must be sufficient to ensure that the jury do not make any assumptions adverse to the accused or favourable to the witness and, in particular, do not draw an inference of guilt against the accused.

7. None of the s 89(2) considerations outweighs any of the others, none is conclusive on the question whether the individual accused will receive a fair trial, and none precludes the possibility of an order.

---

[315] See *R v Aziz* [2018] EWCA Crim 2412, where the judge was correct to refuse an application to vary anonymity orders, in respect of two undercover police officers, made on the basis that they had been discredited during cross-examination. Submissions concerning evidence allegedly planted were wholly speculative; there was no arguable basis for thinking that evidence relating to past complaints against the officers would pass the threshold for admissibility under s 100 of the Criminal Justice Act 2003 as evidence of bad character relevant to credibility; and the anonymity orders had not prevented the accused from making points they would otherwise not have been able to make.

[316] [2009] 1 WLR 1915, CA.

[317] See, in this chapter, under **Special measures directions for vulnerable and intimidated witnesses**, p 155.

[318] See Ch 12.

[319] See Ch 21.

8. Section 89(2)(a) restates the common law principle that the accused is normally entitled to know the identity of any witness who gives incriminating evidence against him and s 89(2)(f) confirms that an order represents the last resort.

9. Concerning the considerations in s 89(2)(b)(d) and (e), the process of investigation and disclosure is crucial. The three considerations are distinct but linked and are likely to require an overall view of the potential impact of the witness on the trial. Thus, for example, there may be no reason to doubt the integrity or motive or credibility of a witness; the issue may be his accuracy, which may be fully tested without disclosure of his identity.

10. Concerning the consideration in s 89(2)(c), which addresses the jurisprudence of the European Court, the fact that a witness provides the sole or decisive evidence against the accused is not conclusive whether conditions A, B, and C are met, but does directly impinge on the question whether condition B may be met. Whether the evidence is sole or decisive raises two separate questions, but if the evidence is both sole and decisive condition B may be harder to meet. The court should examine whether the evidence is supported extraneously. The more facts independent of the witness which tend to support him (and which may derive from the conduct of the accused himself), the safer it is to admit anonymous evidence.[320] Where there are a number of anonymous witnesses who incriminate the accused, whether there is a link between them, and if so its nature, should be investigated, addressing any question of possible improper collusion or cross-contamination. Suspicion is less likely to be engendered about the integrity of witnesses who immediately or virtually immediately are identified or identify themselves, before a sufficient opportunity to engineer a sophisticated conspiracy, than witnesses who turn up late and 'out of the blue'.

11. Condition C should probably be addressed first. The order should not be made where the oral testimony of the witness is not potentially important or where the proposed anonymous evidence could be addressed by admissions or agreed facts or, subject to proper editing, is capable of being read. In relation to Condition C(a), it must be clear that, notwithstanding the powers invested in the court in relation to contempt, the witness 'would not testify' without the order: it is insufficient that the witness might prefer not to testify or would be reluctant or unhappy at the prospect. However, the court may conclude that the witness would not testify if the circumstances of the offence justify the inference.

12. Condition A does not require the risk to the safety to the witness to be attributable to the action of the accused personally: the threat may come from any source. Under Condition A, the order must be necessary, which goes well beyond what may be described as desirable or convenient. A specific problem arises in relation to police witnesses, especially those working undercover, for there are often sound operational reasons for maintaining anonymity; the court would normally be entitled to follow the unequivocal assertion by an undercover officer that without an order he would not be prepared to testify. The

---

[320] Cf Lord Phillips in *R v Horncastle* [2010] 2 AC 373, SC at [50]: the extent of the disadvantage for the accused will depend on the facts of the particular case.

witnesses may well be known to the accused by a false identity, and the accused may be able to advance criticisms of their evidence or conduct without being disadvantaged by ignorance of their true identities. Condition A covers a potentially very wide group, ranging from undercover officers working in areas of terrorism to test purchase officers. It is worth identifying the public interest which is involved in the deployment of these witnesses. At the most dangerous level, extreme measures might be taken to discover the identity of undercover officers who have penetrated criminal associations, not merely out of revenge, but to prevent their use as witnesses and compromise or damage sensitive covert techniques or to discourage them or others from continuing with their activities (all of which serve a valuable public interest).

13. Condition B appears to be focused on the *accused* receiving a fair trial, even when it is the accused seeking the anonymity order. Condition B is fact-specific. In the vast majority of cases, all of the s 89(2) considerations will require attention.

14. The Act is silent about the use of anonymous *hearsay* evidence, or evidence in the form of a statement by an unidentified witness. Such evidence is not admissible under s 116 of the 2003 Act.[321]

Witness anonymity orders may be a 'last resort' to be used sparingly, but they are unlikely to be rare. As the Court of Appeal observed in *R v Powar*:[322] '. . . the calling of anonymous witnesses must not become a routine event in the prosecution of serious crime but we reject the submission that witness anonymity orders should be confined to cases of terrorism or gangland killings. The intimidation of witnesses has become an ugly feature of contemporary life'.

Witness training and witness familiarization

Criminal cases

The Court of Appeal in *R v Momodou*[323] made it clear that in criminal proceedings, witness training or coaching is prohibited, but witness familiarization is permitted. The following reasons were given for the ban on training or coaching. It reduces the possibility that a witness may tailor his evidence in the light of what anyone else has said. Even if the training takes place one-to-one with someone completely remote from the facts of the case, the witness may come, even unconsciously, to appreciate which aspects of his evidence are not quite consistent with what others are saying or not quite what is required of him. An honest witness may alter the emphasis of his evidence. A dishonest witness will very rapidly calculate how his evidence may be 'improved'. Where a witness is jointly trained with other witnesses to the same events, the dangers dramatically increase: recollections change, memories are contaminated, and witnesses bring their respective accounts into what they believe to be better alignment with others. They may even collude deliberately.

---

[321] See Ch 12, Cases where a witness is unavailable, p 373. See also, *R v Brown* [2019] EWCA Crim 1143: where the witness is untraceable, the evidence may be potentially admissible under the *res gestae* principle and under s 114(1)(d). See also Ch 14, Statements forming part of the *res gestae*, p 442 and Ch 12, Admissibility in the interests of justice, p 386.

[322] [2009] EWCA Crim 594.

[323] [2005] 2 All ER 571, CA.

The ban on witness training or coaching, however, does not preclude pre-trial arrange-ments, usually in the form of a visit to the court, to familiarize witnesses with the court layout, the likely sequence of events, and a balanced appraisal of the different responsibilities of the various participants. Such arrangements are welcomed because witnesses should not be disadvantaged by ignorance of the process nor, when they come to give evidence, be taken by surprise at the way it works.[324] None of this involves discussions about proposed evidence. Equally, the ban does not prohibit the out-of-court training of expert and similar witnesses in, for example, the technique of giving comprehensive evidence of a specialist kind to a jury, both in examination-in-chief and in cross-examination, and developing the ability to resist the inevitable pressure of going further in evidence than matters covered by the witness's specific expertise. However, such training should not be arranged in the context of, nor be related to, any forthcoming trial.

It was also held in *R v Momodou* that where arrangements are to be made for familiarization in the case of prosecution witnesses by outside agencies, the Crown Prosecution Service (CPS) should be informed in advance and the proposals should be reduced into writing so that they can be amended if they breach the permitted limits. If the defence engage in the process, it is wise to seek the advice of the defence advocate in advance, and in any event the trial judge and the CPS should be informed of any familiarization process organized using outside agencies. The familiarization process itself should normally be supervised or conducted by a solicitor or barrister, but no one involved should have any personal knowledge of the matters in issue, none of the material should bear any similarity whatever to the issues in the trial, nothing in it should play on or trigger the witness's recollection of events, and if discussion of the trial begins, it must be stopped. Records should be maintained of all those present and the identity of those responsible for the process. All documents used in the process should be retained and handed to the CPS or, in the case of defence witnesses, should be produced to the court.

As to witness familiarization by prosecutors at or before trial with a view to ensuring that prosecution witnesses give their best evidence, the Crown Prosecution Service has issued guidance.[325]

Civil cases

In *Ultraframe (UK) Ltd v Fielding*[326] Lewison J, while noting the significant differences between civil and criminal procedure, including in particular that in civil cases evidence-in-chief generally takes the form of a pre-prepared witness statement, declined to give guidance on the permissible limits of witness familiarization and appeared to endorse the principles established for criminal cases in *R v Momodou*. However, in *Republic of Djibouti v Boreh*[327]

---

[324] For the potential positive effects of written guidance about the nature of cross-examination, including enhanced witness accuracy, see Ellison and Wheatcroft, '"Could You Ask Me That in a Different Way Please?" Exploring the Impact of Courtroom Questioning and Witness Familiarisation on Adult Witness Accuracy' [2010] Crim LR 823.

[325] CPS, *Speaking to Witnesses at Court* (2015), accessible at http://www.cps.gov.uk/publications/prosecution/speaking-to-witnesses-at-court-guidance-mar-2016.pdf and Padfield, 'When Does Speaking to Witnesses Become Coaching?' [2015] Crim LR 309.

[326] [2005] EWHC 1638 (Ch) at [22]–[23].

[327] [2016] EWHC 405 (Comm) at [65] and [67].

the evidence of witnesses who had received witness training was approached with consider-able caution and the court, although declining to suggest that witness training as opposed to coaching was improper, said that it was to be discouraged since it tended to reflect badly on the witness who, perhaps through no fault of her own, may appear evasive because 'trained' to give evidence in a particular way.

ADDITIONAL READING

Burton et al, 'Implementing Special Measures for Vulnerable and Intimidated Witnesses: The Problem of Identification' [2006] Crim LR 229.
The proportion of vulnerable and intimidated witnesses is significantly higher than official estimates. A discussion of the extent to which criminal justice agencies identify such witnesses, at what stage, and why they have difficulties in identifying them. The usual distinction between 'normal' and 'vulnerable and intimidated' witnesses is questioned.

Burton et al, 'Vulnerable and intimidated witnesses and the adversarial process in England and Wales' (2007) 11 E&P 1.
Use of findings from empirical research into the implementation of special measures for vulnerable and intimidated witnesses to examine the argument that features of the adversarial process inevitably prevent such witnesses from giving their best evidence, whatever modifications are made to accommodate them. Suggestions are made for further steps that might be taken to address the problems such witnesses experience.

Cooper and Mattison, Intermediaries, vulnerable people and the quality of evidence: an international comparison of three versions of the English intermediary model' (2017) 21(4) E&P 351.
A review of intermediary models in three jurisdictions—England and Wales, Northern Ireland, and New South Wales in Australia. Aspects of law and procedure are compared, for example, statutory tests for eligibility, the test being widest in Northern Ireland because it includes vulnerable accused. The authors observe that little scientific research has been done into the extent to which intermediaries facilitate the completeness, accuracy, and coherence of testimony. Research will be needed to justify the cost of developing intermediary schemes and using them more widely.

Ellison and Wheatcroft, 'Could You Ask Me That in a Different Way Please?' Exploring the Impact of Courtroom Questioning and Witness Familiarisation on Adult Witness Accuracy' [2010] Crim LR 823.
Discussion of the findings of a study in which participants reviewed a video of an event and were then 'cross-examined' by a barrister about its contents. Some were given written guidance about the nature of cross-examination and questioning techniques used by lawyers while others were given no guidance.

Fairclough, 'Speaking up for injustice: reconsidering the provision of special measures through the lens of equality' [2018] Crim LR 4.
An article which considers the law's commitment to the principle of equality in respect of special measures. The argument is made that in respect of vulnerable accused, there is a lack of equality in law and practice which significantly jeopardizes fair trial rights.

Hoyano, 'Variations on a Theme by Pigot: Special Measures Directions for Child Witnesses' [2000] Crim LR 250.
The principles established by the Pigot Committee dictated that children should have their entire testimony videotaped before trial, but the Government opted for a diluted version, 'half-Pigot'. This article identifies the difficulties to which this has given rise and evaluates how these problems have been addressed by the special measures introduced by the Youth Justice and Criminal Evidence Act 1999.

Kirkby, 'Effectively engaging victims, witnesses and defendants in the criminal courts: a question of "court culture"?' [2017] Crim LR 949.
An article which draws on the findings of two empirical studies to explore 'court culture': First, a study of the public's experiences in the Crown Court and, second, a review of advocacy in youth court proceedings. Three features of court culture are identified which, it is argued, undermine policy and legislative reforms aimed at meaningful participation in proceedings. The features are: (i) the ritualized and formal nature of court proceedings; (ii) the presence of a 'them and us' factor in the relationship between court-users and legal professionals; and (iii) the organized yet chaotic nature of court proceedings. The article advocates the promotion of respectful, considerate, and empathetic interactions and notes signs of improved communication on the part of legal professionals, judges, and magistrates.

McEwan, 'Vulnerable Defendants and the Fairness of Trials' [2013] Crim LR 100.
Consideration of the extent to which criminal courts in England and Wales are enabling the participation in their own trials of accused who are vulnerable by dint of their youth or mental condition. Consideration is also given to the campaign to clarify issues before trial and to bring accused to trial more quickly and its potential to derail the momentum to ensure compliance with the rights of accused under Art 6 of the European Convention on Human Rights to effective participation in their trials.

Ormerod et al, 'Coroners and Justice Act 2009: the "Witness Anonymity" and "Investigation Anonymity" Provisions' [2010] Crim LR 368.
A critical analysis of the statutory powers to give evidence anonymously, suggesting that they are likely to be of symbolic rather than practical significance.

Pigot, 'Advisory Group on Video-Recorded Evidence' (or 'the Pigot Report') (Home Office, London, 1989).
The report of the Group with the following terms of reference: 'to look in greater depth than has so far been possible at the idea that video recordings of interviews with child witnesses (and possibly other victims of crime) should be readily admissible as evidence in criminal trials.'

Plotnikoff and Woolfson, 'Making Best Use of the Intermediary Special Measure at Trial' [2008] Crim LR 91.
A presentation of the findings from an evaluation of the intermediary scheme, describing benefits from the use of intermediaries at trial and highlighting a range of obstacles to be overcome in achieving effective national roll out of the scheme.

Spencer and Flin, *The Evidence of Children* (2nd edn, Blackstone, London, 1993).
The rules of civil and criminal evidence affecting children in England, Scotland, and Northern Ireland are set out and reviewed in the light of the findings of psychologists and social scientists, with proposals for reform.

Starmer, 'Human rights, victims and the prosecution of crime in the 21st century' [2014] Crim LR 777.
A thesis that victims' rights present a fundamental challenge to the basic criminal justice model in place in most common law countries, that key developments in such rights would not have taken place without the positive approach of human rights law, but that the readjustment of criminal justice arrangements to accommodate victims' rights is far from complete.

Examination-in-chief 6

Key issues

- What restrictions should be placed on the way evidence is elicited from witnesses in their evidence-in-chief?

- Should a party calling a witness be permitted to ask questions which suggest the answer sought?

- In what circumstances should a witness be permitted to refresh his memory from a record containing his earlier recollection of an event about which he is called to give evidence?

- What evidential status should be given to a document used by a witness to refresh his memory?

- When and why should a party calling a witness be permitted to adduce evidence of a statement made by him on a previous occasion consistent with his testimony at trial?

- What steps should be open to a party calling a witness if the witness fails to come up to proof or gives evidence supporting another party?

- What steps should be open to a party calling a witness if the witness shows no desire to tell the truth?

The general rule, in both civil and criminal trials, is that any fact which needs to be proved by the evidence of witnesses is to be proved by their oral evidence, given in public.[1] The questioning of witnesses, which generally falls into three stages known as examination-in-chief, cross-examination and re-examination, is central to the English adversary system of justice. The first stage, examination-in-chief, is the questioning of a witness by the party calling him. In examination-in-chief, the party calling a witness, or that party's advocate on his behalf, will seek to elicit evidence which supports his version of the facts in issue. This chapter concerns the rules governing the manner in which this may be done.

Young and vulnerable witnesses

Under para 3E.4 of the Criminal Practice Directions, all witnesses, including the accused and defence witnesses, should be enabled to give the best evidence they can.[2] Children and otherwise vulnerable witnesses, including people with learning disabilities or disabilities of the mind, older adults, victims of sexual assaults, and those who have experienced a traumatic event, have particular needs when appearing as witnesses.

With a view to enabling young witnesses to give their 'best evidence', the *Judicial College Bench Checklist: Young Witness Cases*[3] lists the various matters to be considered in this respect at the first hearing in a magistrates' court or the preliminary or Plea and Trial Preparation Hearing in the Crown Court.[4] They include: the provision of information about the child's development, health, and concentration span; whether the child is unlikely to recognize a problematic question or say that he or she has not understood and whether, in this respect, an intermediary is needed;[5] time estimates; and the need to schedule a 'ground rules' hearing about questioning, which should be held in every case where there is a young or vulnerable witness.[6] In *R v Lubemba*[7] it was said that a 'ground rules' hearing should cover, inter alia, the length of questioning, the frequency of breaks, and the nature of the questions to be asked. The *Checklist* also sets out the directions that may be given at a 'ground rules' discussion to the advocates appearing for both sides. They include the following: adapt questions to the child's developmental stage; ask short, simple questions (one idea at a time); follow

---

[1] In civil cases this is subject to any provision to the contrary or to any order of the court: CPR r 32.2. A civil court, in exercise of its power under r 32.1 to control evidence, may direct that, in order to decide a particular issue, it only requires evidence in written form. As to giving evidence in private in criminal cases, see the Youth Justice and Criminal Evidence Act 1999, s 25, **Ch 5, Special measures directions for vulnerable and intimidated witnesses, p 155.**

[2] As to evidence given under cross-examination, see **Ch 7, Young and vulnerable witnesses, p 225.**

[3] Accessible at https://www.judiciary.gov.uk/publications/jc-bench-checklist-young-wit-cases.

[4] See also, the Crown Court Compendium (July 2019), Part 1, 10–5, para 12.

[5] The role of an intermediary is to provide a report, and if required, to provide assistance to a witness or defendant as directed by the judge: *R v Grant-Murray* [2017] EWCA Crim 1228 at [199]. See also Criminal Practice Directions, para 3F.1: '. . . they commonly advise on the formulation of questions to avoid misunderstanding. They will on occasion actively assist and intervene during questioning.' See also **Ch 5, Examination of witness through intermediary, p 162,** and also **Examination of accused through intermediary, p 169.**

[6] The Crown Court Compendium (July 2019), Part 1, 10–5, para 15. See also Criminal Practice Directions, para 3F.27 to the effect that where the court has directed that questioning will be conducted through an intermediary, the intermediary should be present at the ground rules hearing to make representations in accordance with CrimPR 3.9(7)(a). And to similar effect, see Criminal Practice Directions, para 3E.2.

[7] [2015] 1 WLR 1579, CA.

a logical sequence; speak slowly and allow enough time for questions to be processed; and use a body diagram rather than ask a child to demonstrate intimate touching on his or her body.[8] The *Checklist* also refers to the more detailed guidance provided by Plotnikoff and Woolfson in *Measuring Up? Evaluating implementation of Government commitments to young witnesses in criminal proceedings*, Annexes A and B,[9] which includes, for example, the need to avoid negatives and restricted choice questions, and to recognize that children, even adolescents, cannot be relied upon to say that they have not understood a question. 'Toolkits' to assist advocates as they prepare to question vulnerable people at court are available through the *Advocate's Gateway*[10] managed by the Inns of Court College of Advocacy (formerly the Advocacy Training Council). These toolkits represent best practice; advocates should consult and follow the relevant guidance whenever they prepare to question a young or otherwise vulnerable witness or accused.[11]

Similar guidance has been drawn up by the Family Justice Council in relation to children giving evidence in family proceedings.[12]

Leading questions

An advocate calling a witness and seeking to elicit evidence supporting his case may face a witness who, although favourable, is not particularly forthcoming. The advocate may be tempted to suggest to him what he wants him to say. In both examination-in-chief and re-examination, however, the general rule is that a witness may not be asked leading questions.[13] Evidence elicited by leading questions is not inadmissible but the weight to be attached to it may be reduced.[14] Leading questions are usually those framed in such a way as to suggest the answer sought. Thus it would be a leading question if the prosecution advocate, seeking to establish an assault, asked the victim, 'Did X hit you in the face with his fist?' The proper course would be to ask, 'Did X do anything to you?' and, if the witness then gives evidence of having been hit, to ask, 'Where did X hit you?' and 'How did X hit you?' Questions are also leading if framed in a way which assumes the existence of facts yet to be established. If evidence has yet to be given of the assault, it would be improper, for example, to ask, 'What were you doing immediately before X hit you?' These examples are reasonably straightforward, but in practice the avoidance of leading questions often requires considerable skill and experience. An over-strict adherence to the rule against leading questions would render examination-in-chief extremely difficult. The question 'Did X do anything to you?', even if it does not suggest that X hit the witness, suggests that X did something, whereas in fact he

---

[8] See also Criminal Practice Directions, para 3E.6. According to experimental research, the use of props such as diagrams and toys can adversely affect the quality of the evidence of children: see Bruck, Kelly, and Poole, 'Children's Reports of body touching in Medical Examinations: The benefits and risks of using body diagrams', (2016) 22 Psychology, Public Policy, and Law 1.

[9] Accessible at https://www.nspcc.org.uk/globalassets/documents/research-reports/measuring-up-report.pdf.

[10] Accessible at http://www.theadvocatesgateway.org.

[11] Criminal Practice Directions, para 3D.7. See also *R v Lubemba* [2015] 1 WLR 1579, CA at [40]: 'They [the tool-kits] provide excellent practical guides and are to be recommended.'

[12] Accessible at https://www.judiciary.gov.uk//wp-content/uploads/2014/10/fjc_guidelines_-in_relation_children_-giving_evidence_-in_-family_-proceedings_dec2011.pdf.

[13] For critical analysis of the rationale, scope, and complexity of the rule, see Keane and Fortson, 'Leading Questions: A Critical Analysis' [2011] Crim LR 280.

[14] *Moor v Moor* [1954] 1 WLR 927, CA.

might have been asleep at the relevant time. 'And what happened next?' is a solution often resorted to, although there is a risk, with such a question, that it will not elicit what the advocate has in mind, but rather something that happened later on in time. In practice, the judge, and the advocate for the other side, will not always demand strict adherence to the rule, and for good reason: '"leading" is a relative, not an absolute term.'[15]

To the general prohibition on leading questions there are frequently recurring 'exceptions'. A witness may be asked leading questions on formal and introductory matters, such as his name and occupation. Leading questions are also permissible on facts which are not in dispute, and the advocate for the other side may well indicate, in the case of any witness, those matters on which he has no objection to such questions being put. Leading questions may also be put to a witness called by a party who has been granted leave to treat him as hostile.[16] Leading questions may be put in cross-examination,[17] when they are usually used extensively.

Judicial interventions

During the course of the questioning of a witness by an advocate in examination-in-chief, it is not uncommon for judges to intervene and ask questions of the witness. This is perfectly acceptable where the purpose is to clarify the witness's answer. However, judges must avoid giving the appearance of 'entering the arena' or intervening in examination-in chief in such a manner as to affect the witness's ability to give his or her evidence in the best way possible.[18] In *R v Inns*,[19] the Court of Appeal laid down the following principles concerning judicial interventions during examination-in-chief:[20]

1. The tribunal of fact in a criminal trial in the Crown Court is the jury and no one else.

2. The system is adversarial, not inquisitorial, so the role of the judge is that of a neutral umpire to ensure a fair trial between the prosecution and the defence.[21] It is well established that the judge should not enter the arena so as to appear to be taking sides.

3. There is nothing wrong with the judge asking questions in order to assist the jury, which is one of the functions of a judge. For example, the judge may ask questions to clarify a point in a document or in an immediate response to a witness's answer. However, it may be appropriate to wait until the end of examination-in-chief, to see if matters have become clearer: matters which are not clear at the time, may become clearer later.

4. Under an adversarial system, it is for the prosecution to prove its case and it will have the opportunity to cross-examine the accused if the accused gives evidence. This

---

[15] Best, *Law of Evidence* (12th edn, London, 1922) 562.

[16] See, in this chapter, under **Hostile witnesses**, p 207.

[17] *Parkin v Moon* (1836) 7 C&P 408.

[18] See *R v Alves* (1997) 1 Cr App R 78, CA; *R v Gunning* (1994) 98 Cr App R 303, CA; and *R v Hamilton* [1969] Crim LR 486, CA.

[19] [2019] 1 Cr App R 61(5), CA.

[20] Ibid per Singh LJ at [33]–[38]. See also *R v Marchant* [2019] 1 WLR 20, CA where these principles are cited (at [14]). When deciding whether the nature and frequency of interventions amount to a breach of Art 6, the European Court of Human Rights will look at proceedings as a whole, including the appellate proceedings: see *CG v United Kingdom* (2002) 34 EHRR 31 at [35]–[42]. (See also *R v Forbes* [2001] 1 AC 473, HL at [24]: where there *has been* a breach of Art 6, a conviction will be unsafe.)

[21] See also *R v Alves* (1997) 1 Cr App R 78, CA.

means it will often be unnecessary for the judge to ask questions during the accused's examination-in-chief and it is certainly not the role of the judge to cross-examine the accused.

5. It is crucial that the accused has the opportunity to give his or her account to the jury in the way he or she would like it to come out, elicited through questions from their own advocate. Constant interruptions during examination-in-chief means there is a risk that the accused will not be able to do this.[22]

6. This is the case irrespective of the accused's defence appearing implausible or even fanciful. Where a defence appears to be 'truly incredible', its deficiencies may be expected to be exposed by the prosecution in cross-examination and unwarranted intervention may be simply counter-productive.

Jury notes

During the course of a witness's evidence-in-chief, the jury may send notes to the judge requesting clarification of some matter. In *R v Inns*,[23] the Court of Appeal provided guidance on the correct approach to take, which can be summarized as follows:[24] (i) the trial judge is best placed to deal with notes because she will often have to take quick decisions in the context of the questioning and will also understand the entirety of the evidence given thus far; (ii) however, normal practice is to show jury notes to the advocates and reach agreement on how best to address the jury's question; (iii) it may then be appropriate to deal with the matter straight away by allowing the advocate to put the jury's question to the witness, or to deal with it at the end of the witness's evidence; (iv) other ways to deal with the question may include the advocates agreeing a fact or an answer being given by the judge; (v) sometimes the contents of the note may need to be discussed in the absence of the jury because it raises a matter of law; and (vi) where the accused is giving evidence, it is undesirable if the frequency of notes sent interrupts the flow of evidence to the extent that the accused is prevented from giving his or her account in a complete or fair way. In respect of (iii), it is submitted that if the decision is made to deal with the question at the end of the witness's evidence, the jury should be told that this will happen but that for now they should focus their minds on the evidence which is about to continue.

Refreshing the memory

Witnesses often experience difficulty in recollecting the events to which their evidence relates, especially when the events took place a long time ago. In consequence, common law rules have evolved to allow a witness to refresh his memory from a document made or verified by him at an earlier time. The common law rules have been supplemented and, to a large extent, superseded by, statutory provisions. The scope for use of the memory-refreshing

---

[22] The accused's ability to give her account may be affected not only by interruptions during examination-in-chief, but by the judge's conduct in the absence of the jury where it is hostile or intimidating to the accused, or otherwise leads the accused to believe she will not get a fair trial. See, for example, *R v Myers* [2019] Crim LR 181. See also *R v Tedjame-Mortty* [2011] EWCA Crim 950 and *R v Cordingley* [2007] EWCA Crim 2174.

[23] [2019] 1 Cr App R 61 (5).

[24] Ibid at [40]–[41].

rules has also diminished by reason of the growth in the categories of admissible hearsay[25] and the introduction of rules permitting a witness statement to stand as a witness's evidence-in-chief.[26]

Refreshing the memory in court

The rules

Common law

At common law, a witness in either civil or criminal proceedings, in the course of giving his evidence, may refer to a document, such as a diary, log-book, or account-book, in order to refresh his memory. The conditions are that the document (i) was made or verified by him either contemporaneously with the events in question or so shortly thereafter that the facts were still fresh in his memory; (ii) is, in prescribed cases, the original; and (iii) is produced for inspection by either the court or the opposite party.

Criminal proceedings

In criminal proceedings, this common law rule has not been repealed, but has in effect been replaced, and relaxed, by s 139(1) of the Criminal Justice Act 2003 (the 2003 Act). Section 139(1) substitutes for the requirement of contemporaneity, or that the facts were still fresh in the memory, two different conditions. The first is that the witness testifies that the document records his recollection at the time when he made it. The second is that his recollection is likely to have been significantly better at that time than at the time of his oral evidence. The common law rule has also been supplemented by s 139(2), which provides for the refreshing of memory from a transcript of a sound recording, a provision designed to avoid the practical difficulties that would otherwise be encountered in refreshing the memory from the sound recording itself. Section 139 states as follows:

> (1) A person giving oral evidence in criminal proceedings about any matter may, at any stage in the course of doing so, refresh his memory of it from a document made or verified by him at an earlier time if—
>   (a) he states in his oral evidence that the document records his recollection of the matter at that earlier time, and
>   (b) his recollection of the matter is likely to have been significantly better at that time than it is at the time of his oral evidence.
> (2) Where—
>   (a) a person giving oral evidence in criminal proceedings about any matter has previously given an oral account, of which a sound recording was made, and he states in that evidence that the account represented his recollection of the matter at that time,
>   (b) his recollection of the matter is likely to have been significantly better at the time of the previous account than it is at the time of his oral evidence, and
>   (c) a transcript has been made of the sound recording,
>   he may at any stage in the course of giving his evidence, refresh his memory of the matter from that transcript.

---

[25] In civil proceedings, see the Civil Evidence Act 1995, s 6(2)(a) (the previous documentary statement of a witness) (Ch 13). In criminal proceedings, see the Criminal Justice Act 2003, s 117 (trade, business, and professional records) and s 114(1)(d) (hearsay admissible in the interests of justice) (Ch 12).

[26] See CPR r 32.5 (witness statements) (Ch 5). See also, in criminal proceedings, the Criminal Justice Act 2003, s 137 (video recordings), which has yet to be brought into force, considered in **Ch 5, Evidence-in-chief by video recording, p 155.**

Application to refresh memory

An application for a witness to refresh his memory will normally be made by the party calling the witness, but it is a proper function of the judge, where it is in the interests of justice,
to suggest that a witness, including in a criminal case, a witness for the prosecution, refresh
his memory.[27] Both s 139(1) and s 139(2) refer to 'a person giving oral evidence', that is, any
person giving oral evidence, including, as at common law, the accused.[28] Both subsections
also permit the witness to refresh his memory 'at any stage' in the course of giving his evidence. Thus, as at common law, although a witness will normally refresh his memory in
examination-in-chief, there is nothing wrong in principle in allowing him to do so during
re-examination.[29]

Whether the condition in s 139(1)(b) is met is ultimately a decision for the judge, whatever
the witness's view of the matter;[30] but the judge has a residual discretion to refuse an application under s 139 even if the statutory conditions are met.

Present recollection revived and past recollection recorded

The common law rule on refreshing memory applies in the case of both 'present recollection
revived' and 'past recollection recorded'.[31] 'Present recollection revived' is a phrase used to
describe the genuine refreshing of memory on sight of the document. In this case, both at
common law and under s 139, it is the oral testimony of the witness whose memory has been
refreshed, and not the document, which constitutes the evidence in the case.[32] 'Past recollection recorded' refers to the situation in which the witness, although he has no current
recollection of the events, his memory being a perfect blank, is prepared to testify as to the
accuracy of the contents of the document. A typical example is when a police officer, with
no recollection of the relevant events, simply reads from his notes. In *Maugham v Hubbard*[33]
a witness, called to prove that he had received a sum of money, looked at an unstamped
acknowledgment signed by himself and thereupon gave evidence that he had no doubt
that he had received the money although he had no recollection of having done so. It was
held that the witness's oral evidence sufficed to establish receipt of the money, the written
acknowledgment not being evidence in the case because it was unstamped.[34] It has always
been inaccurate to describe the witness in such a case as having 'refreshed his memory'.[35]
However, at common law, cases of 'past recollection recorded' are treated in the same way as
cases of 'present recollection revived' in that the oral evidence of the witness, and not the
document, constitutes the evidence in the case.[36]

---

[27] *R v Tyagi* (1986) The Times, 21 July, CA.

[28] See *R v Britton* [1987] 1 WLR 539, CA.

[29] *R v Harman* (1984) 148 JP 289, CA and *R v Sutton* (1991) 94 Cr App R 70, CA.

[30] *R v Mangena* [2009] EWCA Crim 2535. The judge's decision should be upheld unless obviously wrong, unreasonable, or perverse: *R v McAfee* [2006] EWCA Crim 2914.

[31] See Wigmore, *Evidence in Trials at Common Law*, vol 3 (rev Chadbourn) (Boston, 1970) ch 28.

[32] See *DPP v Sugden* [2018] 2 Cr App R 101 (8), (Admin) at [26]: 'A document does not become evidence in the
case merely by being relied on by the witness during evidence-in-chief, for the purpose of refreshing memory.'

[33] (1828) 8 B&C 14.

[34] See also *R v Simmonds* [1969] 1 QB 685 CA.

[35] See per Hayes J in *Lord Talbot de Malahide v Cusack* (1864) 17 ICLR 213 at 220.

[36] See *Maugham v Hubbard* (1828) 8 B&C 14, but see also *R v Sekhon* (1986) 85 Cr App R 19 CA (considered at nn
61, 62, and 64) and *R v Virgo* (1978) 67 Cr App R 323, CA. See also *R v Sugden* [2018] 2 Cr App R 101 (8), (Admin).

Admissibility of statements by witnesses with no recollection

In principle, where witnesses have no recollection, it would be better to regard their out-of-court documentary statements as a variety of potentially admissible hearsay evidence, which is the case, in criminal proceedings, under s 120 of the 2003 Act. Under s 120, a previous statement of a witness, which may be a statement made orally or a statement made in a document,[37] is admissible as evidence of any matter stated, provided that the witness testifies that to the best of his belief he made the statement and it states the truth, and that he does not remember the matters and cannot reasonably be expected to do so. Section 120(1), (4), and (6) of the 2003 Act provide as follows:

> (1) This section applies where a person (the witness) is called to give evidence in criminal proceedings.
>
> . . .
>
> (4) A previous statement by the witness is admissible as evidence of any matter stated of which oral evidence by him would be admissible, if—
>
> (a) any of the following three conditions is satisfied, and
>
> (b) while giving evidence the witness indicates that to the best of his belief he made the statement, and to the best of his belief it states the truth.
>
> . . .
>
> (6) The second condition is that the statement was made by the witness when the matters stated were fresh in his memory but he does not remember them, and cannot reasonably be expected to remember them, well enough to give oral evidence of them in the proceedings.

Section 120(4) only applies in the case of a statement *made* by the witness, and has no application, therefore, in the case of a statement *verified* by him.

The following principles relating to s 120(4) and (6) derive from *R v Chinn*.[38]

1. The subsections are not limited to statements about 'routine' matters.

2. If any matter in s 120(6) is disputed, the judge must decide the issue.

3. If there is a dispute about whether the witness cannot reasonably be expected to remember the matters stated well enough to give oral evidence of them, the judge must decide the matter objectively, taking into account all relevant factors, including, for example, the characteristics of the witness and the nature and circumstances of the incident and what has happened to the witness thereafter.

4. When a witness gives evidence that satisfies the condition in s 120(6), but this is disputed, then in the absence of the jury he can be asked why he does not recall the matters and may be cross-examined on the issue.

5. Arguments about discretionary exclusion under s 78 of the Police and Criminal Evidence Act 1984 should also be addressed at this stage.

6. If the previous statement is ruled admissible, the judge should explain to the jury, when he sums up, that they may consider it because the witness could not reasonably be expected to remember the matters well enough to give oral evidence of them.

---

[37] *R v Chinn* [2012] 1 WLR 3401, CA.

[38] Ibid.

7. The judge should also direct the jury to consider the reliability of the witness's earlier recollection and emphasize that it is for them to decide what weight to give to the evidence.

As to the question whether a witness's evidence that he does not remember the matters in the previous statement can render the previous statement an *inconsistent statement* for the purposes of s 119 of the Criminal Justice Act 2003, see later in this chapter under **Previous inconsistent statements**.

The conditions for memory refreshing

A document

At common law a document includes a tape recording,[39] but in criminal proceedings, for the purposes of s 139(1) of the 2003 Act, it means anything in which information of any description is recorded, but not including any recordings of sounds or moving images.[40]

Made or verified

Both at common law and under s 139(1) of the 2003 Act, a witness may refresh his memory either from a document made by himself or by another, provided that, if made by another, the witness verified the document, that is, checked the contents of the document, while the events were still fresh in his memory, and satisfied himself as to their accuracy.[41] For example, in *Anderson v Whalley*,[42] a common law authority, entries in a ship's log-book made by the mate and verified by the captain about a week later could be used to refresh the memory of the latter. It is submitted that under s 139(1), as at common law, verification can be either visual or aural. In *R v Kelsey*,[43] another common law authority, H, a witness called for the prosecution, was allowed to refresh his memory as to the registration number of a car from a note which he had dictated to a police officer. The officer had read his note back aloud and H had confirmed that it was correct. Although H had seen the officer making the note, he had not read it himself. The officer gave evidence that the note used in court was the one that the witness saw him make. The Court of Appeal held that verification could be either visual or aural, the important matter being that the witness satisfies himself, while the matters are fresh in his mind, (i) that a record has been made; and (ii) that it is accurate.[44] However, where a witness dictates a note to another, hears it read back, and confirms its accuracy without reading it himself, another witness must be called to prove that the note used in court is the one that was dictated and read back. The officer in the instant case had given evidence to that effect.[45] The principles in *R v Kelsey* were applied in *Cummings v CPS*,[46] a case which considered memory refreshing under s 139(1). A police officer, in the course of giving evidence that the accused had refused a breath test, was permitted to refresh his memory from a form recording the refusal, which had been completed by another officer. The officer giving

---

[39] *R v Bailey* [2001] EWCA Crim 733.

[40] The 2003 Act, s 140.

[41] See *Burrough v Martin* (1809) 2 Camp 112 and *R v Langton* (1876) 2 QBD 296, CCR.

[42] (1852) 3 Car&Kir 54. See also *R v Sekhon* (1986) 85 Cr App R 19, CA and cf *R v Eleftheriou* [1993] Crim LR 947, CA.

[43] (1982) 74 Cr App R 213.

[44] Ibid at 217.

[45] Cf *R v Mills* [1962] 1 WLR 1152, CCA at 1156, per Winn J, obiter. The officer's note, in *R v Kelsey*, would now be admissible as evidence of the matters stated under the 2003 Act, s 117 (business and other documents): see Ch 12.

[46] [2016] EWHC 3624 (Admin).

evidence was able to verify the form to the court's satisfaction because he was present when the accused refused the test and the other officer completed the form.[47] Whether verification has actually occurred for the purposes of s 139(1) is invariably a question of fact.[48]

Contemporaneity
At common law, but not under s 139 of the 2003 Act, the document, whether made or verified by the witness, 'must have been written either at the time of the transaction or so shortly afterwards that the facts were fresh in his memory'.[49] Commenting on this definition, the Court of Appeal has observed that it provides 'a measure of elasticity and should not be taken to confine witnesses to an over-short period'.[50] The question is a matter of fact and degree;[51] the permitted gap between the date of the statement and that of the events to which it relates cannot be fixed with precision. The precedents are therefore of very limited value.[52]

Originals and secondary documents
There is no requirement, either at common law or under s 139(1) of the 2003 Act, that the memory-refreshing document be the first or only document made or verified by the witness recording his recollection of the matters in question. A witness, therefore, may refresh his memory from a document which is based on original notes[53] or a tape recording made by him.[54] A witness may also refresh his memory from a copy of his original document, provided that the court is satisfied that the copy is accurate or substantially reproduces the contents of the original.[55] In *DPP v Sugden*[56] it was held that memory refreshing under s 139(1) may be from a secondary document (a copy of an original document or a document derived from the original) provided that the secondary document is likely to be an accurate reflection of the contents of the original and the witness verified it at a time when his recall was better than at the time of giving oral evidence.[57]

Production of the document
A document used to refresh memory in court must be produced for inspection by the opposite party who may wish to cross-examine the witness on its contents.[58] At the request of the opposite party, the document may also be shown to the jury, if this is necessary to their determination of a point in issue in the case. In *R v Bass*[59] the only evidence against the appellant was a confession allegedly made to two police officers. They read identical accounts of the

[47] Ibid at [32].
[48] *Sugden v DPP* [2018] 2 Cr App R 101 (8), (Admin) at [31]–[34], citing *CPS v Cummings* [2016] EWHC 3624 (Admin) at [16]–[18].
[49] See *Phipson on Evidence* (11th edn, London, 1970) 634, para 1528.
[50] *R v Richardson* [1971] 2 QB 484.
[51] *R v Simmonds* [1969] 1 QB 685, CA.
[52] *R v Woodcock* [1963] Crim LR 273, CCA (three-month gap treated as too long); *R v Graham* [1973] Crim LR 628, CA (one-month gap regarded as doubtful); *R v Fotheringham* [1975] Crim LR 710, CA (21-day gap accepted).
[53] See, at common law, *A-G's Reference (No 3 of 1979)* (1979) 69 Cr App R 411 and *R v Cheng* [1976] 63 Cr App R 20.
[54] See, at common law, *R v Mills* [1962] 1 WLR 1152, CCA.
[55] *Topham v McGregor* (1844) 1 Car&Kir 320. See, eg, *R v Chisnell* [1992] Crim LR 507, CA. However, in cases of 'past recollection recorded', in which the original has *not* been lost or destroyed, there is old authority that the original document must be used: *Doe d Church and Phillips v Perkins* (1790) 3 Term rep 749.
[56] [2018] 2 Cr App R 101 (8), (Admin).
[57] [2018] 2 Cr App R 101 (8), (Admin) at [38] sub para 7.9.
[58] *Beech v Jones* (1848) 5 CB 696.
[59] [1953] 1 QB 680, CCA; cf *R v Fenlon* (1980) 71 Cr App R 307, CA.

interview with the appellant but denied that they had been prepared in collaboration. The trial judge refused a defence application that the jury be allowed to examine the notebooks. The Court of Criminal Appeal, allowing the appeal, held that the jury, by an inspection of the notebooks, might have been assisted in their evaluation of the credibility and accuracy of the officers.[60] Similarly, in cases in which the witness's evidence is long and involved, it may be convenient for the jury to use the document as an aide-memoire as to that evidence, but care should be exercised in adopting this course in cases where the evidence is bitterly contested, because of the danger that the jury will improperly regard the document as constituting evidence in the case.[61]

Cross-examination on the document

In the majority of cases, the fact that there is cross-examination on the basis of a document used to refresh memory in court will neither entitle the jury to inspect the document nor make it evidence in the case.[62] The advocate cross-examining may inspect the document without thereby making it evidence and may cross-examine on it without thereby making it evidence, provided that his cross-examination goes no further than the parts which were used by the witness to refresh his memory. However, cross-examination on new matters deriving from other parts of the document entitles the party calling the witness to put the document in evidence and to let the tribunal of fact see the document upon which such cross-examination is based.[63] Two other situations have been identified in which the document may be admitted in evidence.[64] First, where the nature of the cross-examination involves a suggestion that the witness has subsequently fabricated his evidence, which will usually involve the allegation that the record is concocted, the document is admissible to rebut this suggestion and, if the document assists as to this, to show whether or not it has the appearance of being a contemporaneous record which has not subsequently been altered.[65] Second, where the document is inconsistent with the evidence, the document is admissible as evidence of this inconsistency.

[60] The court also made it clear that it is not improper for two or more police officers to refresh their memories from notes in the making of which they have collaborated. See also *R (Saunders) v Independent Police Complaints Commission* [2009] 1 All ER 379 where the Divisional Court acknowledged the risks of innocent contamination and deliberate collusion, but asserted that the pooling of recollections could also improve the accuracy of an officer's notes. Moreover, a prohibition on the practice would have serious operational disadvantages. For a critical analysis of police practice in respect of note taking, see three inter-related articles by Wolchover and Heaton-Armstrong, 'Casting the police as criminals?' [2019] NLJ 22 February 12, 1 March 11, and 5 April 15. Concerning non-police witnesses, the general rule is that discussions as to the evidence they will give should not take place: *R v Skinner* (1993) 99 Cr App R 212, CA. See also *R v Momodou* [2005] 1 WLR 3442, CA at [61] where Judge LJ alluded to, '. . . the well known principle that discussions between witnesses should not take place and proofs of one witness should not be disclosed to any other witness.' If a discussion may have led to fabrication, it may be unsafe to leave any of the evidence to the jury. In other cases it may suffice to direct the jury on the implications of such conduct in relation to the reliability of the evidence: see *R v Arif* (1993) The Times, 17 June, CA.

[61] Per Woolf LJ in *R v Sekhon* (1986) 85 Cr App R 19, CA at 23: the document may also be put before the jury where it is difficult for them to follow the *cross-examination* of the witness who has refreshed his memory. But cf *R v Dillon* (1983) 85 Cr App R 29, CA.

[62] Per Woolf LJ in *R v Sekhon* (1986) 85 Cr App R 19, CA at 22.

[63] *Gregory v Tavernor* (1833) 6 C&P 280; *Senat v Senat* [1965] P 172 P, D and Admlty per Sir Jocelyn Simon P at 177; and *R v Britton* [1987] 1 WLR 539, CA.

[64] *R v Sekhon* (1986) 85 Cr App R 19, CA at 22–3.

[65] Cf *R v Fenlon* (1980) 71 Cr App R 307, CA and *R v Dillon* (1983) 85 Cr App R 29, CA.

Where, as a result of cross-examination, a memory-refreshing document is admitted in evidence, it is admitted as evidence of any matter stated. Under s 1 of the Civil Evidence Act 1995 (the 1995 Act), in civil proceedings evidence shall not be excluded on the ground that it is hearsay. Section 6(4) and (5) of the 1995 Act provide as follows:

> (4) Nothing in this Act affects any of the rules of law as to the circumstances in which, where a person called as a witness in civil proceedings is cross-examined on a document used by him to refresh his memory, that document may be made evidence in the proceedings.
>
> (5) Nothing in this section shall be construed as preventing a statement of any description referred to above from being admissible by virtue of s 1 as evidence of the matters stated.

Although s 6(5) refers to 'a statement of any description referred to above' and s 6(4) makes no reference to a 'statement' as such, it seems reasonably clear that the parliamentary intention was to perpetuate the rule formerly stated with clarity in s 3(2) of the Civil Evidence Act 1968, that is, that where a memory-refreshing document is made evidence in civil proceedings, any statement made in the document is admissible as evidence of any matter stated therein. As to criminal proceedings, s 120(1) and (3) of the 2003 Act provide as follows:

> (1) This section applies where a person (the witness) is called to give evidence in criminal proceedings.
>   . . .
> (3) A statement made by the witness in a document—
>   (a) which is used by him to refresh his memory while giving evidence,
>   (b) on which he is cross-examined, and
>   (c) which as a consequence is received in evidence in the proceedings,
>   is admissible as evidence of any matter stated of which oral evidence by him would be admissible.

Section 120(1) and (3) provide not for the circumstances in which a documentary statement may be received in evidence, but merely for the evidential status of a document where it is received in evidence.[66]

In *R v Chinn*,[67] the Court of Appeal, construing s 120(3) of the 2003 Act, held that: the word 'which' refers back to 'a document'; s 120(3)(a) contemplates use of the document by the witness to refresh his memory while giving evidence-in-chief; his evidence about the facts of which he has refreshed his memory is admissible oral evidence; the 'statement' in the document used to refresh memory also becomes evidence of the matters stated; and if the witness fails to refresh his memory, the situation is covered not by s 120(3) but by ss 120(4) and 120(6).[68]

Section 120 does not apply in the case of a statement *verified* by a witness which, as a result of cross-examination, is admitted in evidence. In criminal proceedings, therefore, such a statement is not admitted as evidence of any of the matters stated in it, but as evidence of the witness's consistency or inconsistency, going only to his credit.

Use of exhibited document by jury

If, in a trial before a judge and jury, a statement made in a document is admitted in evidence under s 120, and the document or a copy of it is produced as an exhibit, the exhibit must

---

[66] *R v Pashmfouroush* [2006] EWCA Crim 2330.

[67] [2012] 1 WLR 3401, CA.

[68] See, in this chapter, under **Present recollection revived and past recollection recorded**, p 185.

not accompany the jury when they retire to consider their verdict unless the court considers it appropriate or all the parties to the proceedings agree that it should accompany the jury.[69]

Refreshing the memory out of court

It is a routine practice, in both civil and criminal proceedings, for witnesses, before going into the witness box, to look at and refresh their memories from their own previous statements.[70] Such a statement may have been made by a witness for some personal reason, may constitute a 'proof of evidence' made at the request of the solicitor for the party calling him or, in the case of a prosecution witness, may be a signed statement which he made to the police.[71] Whatever form it takes, however, it would appear that the conditions on which a witness may refresh his memory while giving evidence do not apply to the witness who refreshes his memory outside the witness box.[72] In *R v Richardson*[73] the Court of Appeal approved the following two observations of the Supreme Court of Hong Kong in *Lau Pak Ngam v R*:[74]

1. Testimony in the witness box becomes more a test of memory than of truthfulness if witnesses are deprived of the opportunity of checking their recollection beforehand by reference to statements or notes made at a time closer to the events in question.

2. Refusal of access to statements would tend to create difficulties for honest witnesses but be likely to do little to hamper dishonest witnesses.

However, it was also observed in *R v Richardson* that it would obviously be wrong for several witnesses to be handed statements in circumstances enabling one to compare with another what each had said. Equally, as a general rule, discussions between witnesses, particularly just before going into court to give evidence, should not take place, and statements or proofs should not be read to witnesses in each other's presence.[75] It is incumbent on prosecuting authorities and judges to ensure that witnesses are informed that they should not discuss cases in which they are involved.[76]

In *R v Da Silva*[77] it was held that it is open to the judge, in the exercise of his discretion and in the interests of justice, to permit a witness who has begun to give his evidence, to withdraw and refresh his memory from a statement made near to the time of the events in question, even if not 'contemporaneous', provided he is satisfied that: (i) the witness indicates that he cannot now recall the details of the events because of the lapse of time; (ii) he made a statement much nearer the time of the event,[78] the contents of which represented his recollection at the time he made it; (iii) he has not read the statement before giving evidence; and

---

[69] The Criminal Justice Act 2003, s 122.

[70] See also Crim PD V, para 18C.1: 'Witnesses are entitled to refresh their memory from their statement or visually recorded interview.'

[71] Witnesses should be shown their witness statements so that they can refresh their memories before giving evidence: see the guidance issued by the Crown Prosecution Service, accessible at: https://www.cps.gov.uk/legal-guidance/witness-statements-and-memory-refreshing.

[72] See also *Owen v Edwards* (1983) 77 Cr App R 191, DC, at n 86.

[73] [1971] 2 QB 484.

[74] [1966] Crim LR 443.

[75] *R v Skinner* (1993) 99 Cr App R 212, CA at 216.

[76] *R v Shaw* [2002] EWCA Crim 3004.

[77] [1990] 1 WLR 31, CA.

[78] In *R v Da Silva* itself, the statement was made one month after the events to which it related.

(iv) he wishes to read the statement before he continues to give evidence. It does not matter whether the witness withdraws from the witness box to read his statement or reads it in the witness box, but if the former course is adopted, no communication must be had with the witness other than to see that he can read the statement in peace. If either course is adopted, the statement must be removed from him when he continues to give his evidence and he should not be permitted to refer to it again. In criminal proceedings, however, the witness may be permitted to make further use of the document to refresh his memory in the witness box, provided that the conditions of s 139 of the 2003 Act are met.[79]

In *R v South Ribble Magistrates' Court, ex p Cochrane*[80] it was held that *R v Da Silva* does not lay down as a matter of law that all four conditions to which it refers must be satisfied, because the court has a 'real discretion', that is, a choice free of binding criteria, whether to permit a witness to refresh his memory from a non-contemporaneous statement. In that case it was held that a witness who had read his statement before giving evidence, but who had not taken it in properly, and therefore did not satisfy condition (iii), had been properly permitted to refresh his memory. The discretion is a broad fact-sensitive discretion to be exercised in the interests of fairness and justice.[81]

Memory refreshing and the weight of evidence

The fact that a witness has refreshed his memory out of court and before entering the witness box may be relevant to the weight which can properly be attached to his evidence, so that in a criminal case injustice may be caused to the accused if the matter is not brought to the attention of the jury.[82] For this reason, the Court of Appeal in *R v Westwell*[83] held that the prosecution, if aware that statements have been seen by their witnesses, should inform the defence. Informing the defence, however, is 'desirable but not essential'[84] and 'if for any reason this is not done, the omission cannot of itself be a ground for acquittal'.[85] *R v Westwell* left undecided the question whether a party may call for, inspect, and cross-examine on a document which a witness called by the opposite party has used to refresh his memory outside court but has not used while giving evidence. The issue arose in *Owen v Edwards*.[86] A policeman, outside the courtroom and before giving evidence for the prosecution, refreshed his memory from a notebook which he did not use in the witness box. The Divisional Court held that the advocate for the defence was entitled not only to inspect the notebook but also to cross-examine the witness upon relevant matters contained in it. It was further held that although the advocate for the defence may cross-examine upon the material in the

[79] See, in this chapter, under **The rules, p 184.**

[80] [1996] 2 Cr App R 544, DC.

[81] *R v Gordon* [2002] EWCA Crim 412, where a witness who was dyslexic and unable to read the statement himself, adopted it after it had been read out to him, by the advocate for the party calling him, in the absence of the jury.

[82] Crown Prosecution Service guidance, 'Witness Statements and Memory Refreshing', identifies the possibility of collusion and of the witness seeking to 'learn' their statement to ensure their evidence is consistent with a false statement or to otherwise give a false impression of truthfulness. Accessible at: https://www.cps.gov.uk/legal-guidance/witness-statements-and-memory-refreshing.

[83] [1976] 2 All ER 812. See also *Worley v Bentley* [1976] 2 All ER 449, DC.

[84] See also the guidance of the CPS accessible at https://www.cps.gov.uk/legal-guidance/witness-statements-and-memory-refreshing.

[85] See also, *sed quaere, R v H* [1992] Crim LR 516, CA: child victims of sexual offences should only refresh their memory out of court with the *consent* of the defence.

[86] (1983) 77 Cr App R 191.

notebook from which the witness has refreshed his memory without the notebook being made evidence in the case, if he cross-examines on material in the notebook which has not been referred to by the witness, he runs the risk of the notebook being put in evidence. As we have seen, in civil cases the document will be admitted as evidence of the matters stated. The same applies in criminal cases, but only in the case of statements made, as opposed to verified, by the witness. The weight to be attached to the documentary evidence will obviously vary according to the precise circumstances, but a note made a long time after the events in question may be viewed by the tribunal of fact with considerable caution, if not suspicion.

Refreshing the memory from visually recorded interviews

Where the evidence in chief of a young or vulnerable witness is contained in a visually recorded interview which will played to the jury prior to the cross-examination of the witness, the Criminal Practice Directions[87] make provision for the witness to refresh his memory as to what he said in the interview, by viewing the recording. The reason for this is that, 'The witness's first viewing of the visually recorded interview can be distressing or distracting [and] it should not be seen for the first time immediately before giving evidence.'[88] The Criminal Practice Directions, V, 18C.4 and 5 provide as follows:

> . . . 18C.4 There is no legal requirement that the witness should watch the interview at the same time as the trial bench or jury. Increasingly, this is arranged to occur at a different time, with the advantages that breaks can be taken as needed without disrupting the trial, and cross-examination starts while the witness is fresh. An intermediary may be present to facilitate communication but should not act as the independent person designated to take a note and report to the court if anything is said.[89]

> 18C.5 Where the viewing takes place at a different time from that of the trial bench or jury, the witness is sworn (or promises) just before cross-examination and, unless the judge otherwise directs: (a) it is good practice for the witness to be asked by the prosecutor, (or the judge/magistrate if they so direct), in appropriate language if, and when, he or she has watched the recording of the interview; (b) if, in watching the recording of the interview or otherwise the witness has indicated that there is something he or she wishes to correct or to add then it is good practice for the prosecutor (or the judge/magistrate if they so direct) to deal with that before cross-examination provided that proper notice has been given to the defence.

Previous consistent or self-serving statements

The general rule

There is a general common law rule that a witness may not be asked in examination-in-chief about former oral or written statements made by him and consistent with his evidence in the proceedings. Evidence of the earlier statement may not be given either by the witness who made it or by any other witness. The reason usually given for the rule is the danger of manufactured evidence.[90] A resourceful witness, minded to deceive the court, could with

---

[87] Accessible at https://www.judiciary.uk/wp-content/uploads/2019/03/crim-pd-amendment-no-8-consolidated-mar2019.pdf.

[88] Criminal Practice Directions, V, 18C.1.

[89] As to the role of intermediaries, see earlier in this chapter under **Young and vulnerable witnesses, p 180** and n 5. See also Ch 5, **Video-recorded evidence-in-chief, p 158**.

[90] See, eg, per Humphreys J in *R v Roberts* [1942] 1 All ER 187, CCA at 191.

ease deliberately repeat his version of the facts to a number of people prior to trial with a view to showing consistency with the story he tells in the witness box, thereby bolstering his credibility. Of course, this objection could be overcome if the possibility of deceit could be ruled out because the previous statement had been obtained by a scientific method that could establish its reliability. However, English courts have shown no interest in admitting polygraph (lie-detector) tests, presumably on the basis that such technologies cannot be shown to be reliable and trespass upon the role of the fact-finder, notwithstanding that they may have comparative advantages over the traditional methods used to test credibility. It has been said that, as a matter of principle, evidence produced by administration of some mechanical, chemical, or hypnotic truth test on a witness is inadmissible to show the veracity or otherwise of that witness.[91]

The rule against previous consistent statements also applies to re-examination. Thus the credibility of a witness may not be bolstered by evidence of a previous consistent statement merely because his testimony has been impeached in cross-examination.[92] This remains the case 'even if the impeachment takes the form of showing a contradiction or inconsistency between the evidence given at the trial and something said by the witness on a former occasion'.[93] However, the court does have a residual discretion to permit re-examination to show consistency by reference to a previous statement to ensure that the jury is not positively misled by the cross-examination as to the existence of some fact or the terms of an earlier statement.[94]

Evidence of consistency, not matters stated

The rule is distinct from the common law rule against hearsay, whereby an out-of-court statement is inadmissible as evidence of the matters stated. A previous consistent or self-serving statement of a witness is excluded as evidence of his consistency. The distinction may be illustrated by the following two cases. In *Corke v Corke and Cook*[95] a husband petitioned for divorce on the ground of adultery. Late one night he had accused his wife of having recently committed adultery with a lodger. The Court of Appeal held that the wife, who denied adultery, had been improperly permitted to give evidence that some 10 minutes after the husband's accusation she had telephoned her doctor and asked him to examine her and the lodger with a view to showing that there had been no recent sexual intercourse. In *R v Roberts*[96] the accused was convicted of the murder of a girl by shooting her. His defence was that the gun went off accidentally while he was trying to make up a quarrel with the girl. Evidence that two days after the event the accused had told his father that his defence would be accident was held by the Court of Criminal Appeal to have been properly excluded. In both of these

---

[91] *Fennell v Jerome Property Maintenance Ltd* (1986) The Times, 26 Nov, QBD; and see *R v McKay* [1967] NZLR 139, NZCA: a psychiatrist is not permitted to give evidence of statements made by the accused while under the influence of a truth drug and consistent with his evidence. See also Danaher, 'The comparative advantages of brain-based lie detection: the P300 concealed information test and pre-trial bargaining' (2015) 19 E&P 52.

[92] *R v Coll* (1889) 25 LR Ir 522.

[93] Per Holmes J (1889) 25 LR Ir 522 at 541. See also *R v Weekes* [1988] Crim LR 244, CA; *R v Beattie* (1989) 89 Cr App R 302, CA per Lord Lane CJ at 306–7; and *R v P (GR)* [1998] Crim LR 663, CA. Contrast, *sed quaere*, *Ahmed v Brumfitt* (1967) 112 Sol Jo 32, CA.

[94] *R v Ali* [2004] 1 Cr App R 501 (39), CA.

[95] [1958] P 93.

[96] [1942] 1 All ER 187.

cases the evidence in question was hearsay and inadmissible as evidence of the facts stated, that is to show in the one case that there was no sexual intercourse and in the other that the gun went off accidentally. But it was also inadmissible, by reason of the rule against previous consistent statements, to bolster the credibility of the witnesses in question by demonstrating their consistency.

When admitted as hearsay

When a previous statement of a witness is admitted as hearsay, that is, as evidence of the matters stated, it will also be received as evidence of consistency. Thus a decision such as *Corke v Corke and Cook* might be decided differently today, because in civil proceedings the previous statements of a witness may be admitted, with the leave of the court, both as evidence of the matters stated, and also, therefore, as evidence of consistency, under s 6(2) of the Civil Evidence Act 1995.[97] Similarly, if a previous statement of a witness is admitted in criminal proceedings as evidence of the matters stated under s 114(1)(c) of the 2003 Act, that is, where all parties agree to it being admissible, or under s 114(1)(d) of that Act, that is, where the court is satisfied that it is in the interests of justice for it to be admissible, then it will also be received as evidence of consistency. Where evidence of a previous consistent statement is admitted in evidence, it is not a necessary indicator of truthfulness and, in appropriate cases, a judge may need to direct the jury to this effect.[98]

The common law exceptions

To the rule against previous consistent statements, there are a number of common law exceptions. The statutory categories of admissible hearsay now embrace almost all of the varieties of statement admissible by way of these common law exceptions to the rule against previous consistent statements, in some cases expanding their scope. The justification for separate treatment of the common law exceptions is that: (a) the overlap is not total (wholly exculpatory statements made on accusation, for example, are not admissible as evidence of the matters asserted); (b) Parliament has elected not to repeal any of the common law exceptions; and (c) in some cases (statements admissible to rebut allegations of recent fabrication and statements in documents used to refresh the memory and received in evidence), Parliament, rather than give the common law exception a statutory formulation, has chosen to identify it as a category of hearsay by simply referring to the circumstances in which the statement may be admitted at common law.

Complaints in sexual cases

If, in the case of sexual offences, the complainant made a voluntary complaint shortly after the alleged offence, the person to whom the complaint was made may give evidence of the particulars of that complaint in order to show the consistency of that conduct with the complainant's evidence and, in cases in which consent is in issue, as evidence inconsistent with such consent. Section 120(7) of the 2003 Act has extended the principle to cover a previous statement by a person against whom *any* offence has been committed, provided that: it is an offence to which the proceedings relate; that the statement consists of a complaint about conduct which would, if proved, constitute the offence; and the complainant, in giving evidence, indicates that to the best of his belief, he made the statement and it states the truth.

---

[97] See Ch 13.
[98] The Crown Court Compendium (July 2019), Part 1, 20–1, para 10(2), and Example 4.

A statement received under s 120(7) is admissible as evidence of the matters stated and, provided that the evidence is given by the person to whom the complaint was made,[99] also goes to the consistency of the witness. Section 120(7), which is considered in **Chapter 11**, is much wider than the common law exception. The common law exception, therefore, is likely to be invoked only rarely and falls to be considered in outline only.

The common law exception applies to written, as well as oral, complaints, and even extends to a written note given to a friend by mistake.[100] Where the exception applies, it is essential to direct the jury that the complaint is not evidence of the facts complained of, and cannot be independent confirmation of the complainant's evidence since it does not come from a source independent of her, but may assist in assessing her veracity.[101]

In *White v R*[102] it was held that if the person to whom the complaint was made does not give evidence, the complainant's own evidence that she made a complaint cannot assist in either proving her consistency or negativing consent because, without independent confirmation, her own evidence that she complained takes the jury nowhere in deciding whether she is worthy of belief.

Sexual offences

The common law exception applies only in the case of sexual offences, but is not restricted to sexual offences where absence of consent is among the facts in issue.[103] Nor is the exception confined to sexual offences against females.[104]

The fact and the particulars of the complaint

There is a two-stage test for the jury to follow, first to decide whether the recent complaint was in fact made and, if so, second to decide whether it is consistent with the complainant's evidence.[105] In *R v Lillyman*,[106] it was held that the person to whom the complaint was made can give detailed evidence as to what the complainant said, rather than simply evidence of the bare fact that the complaint was made, in order that the jurors can judge for themselves whether the complaint in question is consistent with the complainant's evidence.

Consistency is a question of degree. In *R v S*[107] it was held that evidence of a recent complaint will be admissible where it is sufficiently consistent that it can, depending on the view of the evidence taken by the jury, support or enhance the credibility of the complainant. Whether the complaint is sufficiently consistent must depend on the facts.[108] It is not necessary that the complaint discloses the ingredients of the offence, but it is usually necessary that it discloses evidence of material and relevant unlawful sexual conduct on the part of the accused which can support the complainant's credibility.

---

[99] See *White v R* [1999] 1 Cr App R 153, PC.

[100] *R v B* [1997] Crim LR 220, CA.

[101] *R v Islam* [1999] 1 Cr App R 22, CA, applied in *R v NK* [1999] Crim LR 980, CA.

[102] [1999] 1 Cr App R 153, PC.

[103] *R v Osborne* [1905] 1 KB 551, CCR.

[104] *R v Camelleri* [1922] 2 KB 122, CCA. See also *R v Wannell* (1924) 17 Cr App R 53, CCA.

[105] *R v Hartley* [2003] EWCA Crim 3027.

[106] [1896] 2 QB 167, CCR.

[107] [2004] 1 WLR 2940, CA.

[108] There may be sufficient consistency even if the complaint is, in parts, inconsistent with the evidence of the complainant: see *R v S* [2004] 1 WLR 2940, CA.

Voluntariness

It is a condition of the admissibility of a complaint in a sexual case that it should have been made voluntarily, and not in reply to questions of a suggestive, leading, or intimidating character.[109]

The time of complaint

A complaint is only admissible in evidence under the exception if 'it was made at the first opportunity after the offence which reasonably offered itself'[110] and was 'recent'.[111] Whether a complaint was made as soon as was reasonably practicable after the occurrence of the offence is a question of fact and degree.[112] The answer will depend on the circumstances, including the character of the complainant and the relationship between the complainant and the person to whom she might have complained but did not do so. Victims often need time before they can bring themselves to tell what has happened, and whereas some will find it impossible to complain to anyone other than a parent or member of their family, others may feel it impossible to tell their parents or members of their family.[113] As to 'recency', in *R v Birks*[114] it was held, albeit reluctantly, that a complaint made, at the earliest, two months after the alleged offences, was inadmissible notwithstanding that the complaint was made spontaneously and that the accused had allegedly threatened her by saying that if she told her mother she would be put in a home.

Admissibility to show consistency

At common law, the complaint is not evidence of the facts complained of and may be used only as evidence of the consistency of the complaint with the testimony of the complainant and, in cases where consent is in issue, as evidence inconsistent with consent. Thus if the terms of the complaint are not ostensibly consistent with the terms of the complainant's testimony, the introduction of the complaint has no purpose.[115] Likewise, in cases where the complainant does not testify, there being no evidence with which the complaint may be consistent, the particulars of the complaint are inadmissible.[116]

Statements admissible to rebut allegations of recent fabrication

If, in cross-examination, it is suggested to a witness that her account of some incident or set of facts is a recent invention or fabrication, evidence of prior statements made by her to the same effect is admissible to support her credit.[117] Evidence of such prior statements will normally be elicited in re-examination. In *R v Oyesiku*[118] the accused was convicted of assaulting a

---

[109] *R v Osborne* [1905] 1 KB 551, CCR at 556.

[110] Per Ridley J in *R v Osborne* [1905] 1 KB 551, CCR at 561. See also *R v Cummings* [1948] 1 All ER 551, CCA. However, the fact that the complaint was not the first to be made is not, per se, sufficient to exclude it: *R v Wilbourne* (1917) 12 Cr App R 280, CCA.

[111] *R v Birks* [2003] 2 Cr App R 122(7), CA.

[112] A complaint made one week after the offence was admitted in *R v Hedges* (1910) 3 Cr App R 262, CCA.

[113] *R v Valentine* [1996] 2 Cr App R 213, CA.

[114] [2003] 2 Cr App R 122 (7), CA.

[115] *R v Wright* and *R v Ormerod* (1987) 90 Cr App R 91, CA.

[116] See, eg, *R v Wallwork* (1958) 42 Cr App R 153, CCA.

[117] Evidence of a complaint in a sexual case may be admissible on this basis notwithstanding that it was not made at the first reasonably practicable opportunity (see, in this chapter, under **The time of complaint, p 197**): *R v Tyndale* [1999] Crim LR 320, CA.

[118] (1971) 56 Cr App R 240. See also *R v Benjamin* (1913) 8 Cr App R 146, CCA; *Flanagan v Fahy* [1918] 2 IR 361, Ir KBD; and *Fox v General Medical Council* [1960] 1 WLR 1017, PC.

police officer. In cross-examination, it was put to the accused's wife, who had given evidence that the police officer was the aggressor, that her evidence had been recently fabricated. The Court of Appeal held that the trial judge had improperly refused to admit evidence of a previous statement consistent with her testimony and made by her to a solicitor after her husband's arrest but before she had seen him. Karminski LJ, giving the judgment of the court, accepted as a correct statement of the law the judgment of Dixon CJ in *Nominal Defendant v Clement*,[119] from which the following propositions derive. The exception is brought into play where it is suggested in cross-examination that the witness's account 'is a late invention or has been recently reconstructed, even though not with conscious dishonesty'. The prior statement is admissible 'if it was made by the witness contemporaneously with the event or at a time sufficiently early to be inconsistent with the suggestion that his account is a late invention or reconstruction'. The judge, in determining whether the exception has been brought into play, should assure himself: (i) 'that the account given by the witness in his testimony is attacked on the ground of recent invention or reconstruction or that a foundation for such an attack has been laid'; (ii) 'that the contents of the statement are in fact to the like effect as his account given in his evidence'; and (iii) 'that having regard to the time and circumstances in which it was made, it (the statement) rationally tends to answer the attack'.

'Recent' in this context should not be confined within a temporal straitjacket but is an 'elastic' description designed to assist in the identification of circumstances in which a previous consistent statement should be admitted where there is a rational and cogent basis on which it could assist the tribunal of fact in determining where the truth lies.[120] *R v MH*[121] provides a good example. MH alleged that his son had been coached by his mother to give false evidence against him to prevent him from seeing his children. He asserted that she was also motivated by the financial dispute between them following their separation. It was held that evidence of the son's complaints to the mother prior to the breakdown of the marriage was admissible in rebuttal, but not evidence of complaints made at a time when MH was not permitted to see his children and when he and his wife were in financial dispute.

Admissibility as evidence of matters stated

In both civil and criminal proceedings, the previous consistent statement is now admissible both to negative the suggestion of invention or reconstruction, thereby confirming the witness's credit, and as evidence of the matters stated. Under s 1 of the Civil Evidence Act 1995, in civil proceedings evidence shall not be excluded on the ground that it is hearsay. Section 6(2) and (5) of the 1995 Act provide as follows:

(2) A party who has called or intends to call a person as a witness in civil proceedings may not in those proceedings adduce evidence of a previous statement made by that person, except—

. . .

(b) for the purposes of rebutting a suggestion that his evidence has been fabricated.

. . .

(5) Nothing in this section shall be construed as preventing a statement of any description referred to above from being admissible by virtue of section 1 as evidence of the matters stated.

---

[119] (1961) 104 CLR 476, High Court of Australia. The extracts given in the text are at 479.
[120] *R v Athwal* [2009] 1 WLR 2430, CA at [58].
[121] [2012] EWCA Crim 2725.

In criminal proceedings, s 120(1) and (2) of the 2003 Act provide as follows:

(1) This section applies where a person (the witness) is called to give evidence in criminal proceedings.
(2) If a previous statement by the witness is admitted as evidence to rebut a suggestion that his oral evidence has been fabricated, that statement is admissible as evidence of any matter stated of which oral evidence by the witness would be admissible.

Section 120(1) and (2) do not provide for the circumstances in which a previous statement by a witness may be received in evidence, but merely regulate the use to which such evidence, once admitted, may be put.[122] It follows that although s 120(2) omits reference to the recency of the fabrication, this omission does not mean that it is no longer a requirement for admissibility.

Statements made on accusation

Exculpatory statements

Provided that the conditions of admissibility are satisfied, and subject to the exclusionary discretion of the court, an admission made by an accused is admissible, by way of exception to the general rule against hearsay, as evidence of the facts contained in it.[123] There is also, however, a well-established practice on the part of the prosecution, approved by the Court of Appeal,[124] 'to admit in evidence all unwritten and most written statements made by an accused person to the police whether they contain admissions or whether they contain denials of guilt'. If such statements are wholly exculpatory, they are not admitted as evidence of the facts stated. In *R v Storey*,[125] the police having found a large quantity of cannabis in the accused's flat, she explained that it belonged to a man who had brought it there against her will. The Court of Appeal held that this statement was not evidence of the facts contained in it, but admissible 'because of its vital relevance as showing the reaction of the accused when first taxed with the incriminating facts'.[126] It does not follow from these words, however, that the only statements admissible as evidence of reaction are those which the accused made on the first encounter with his accusers. In *R v Pearce*[127] the Court of Appeal decided that statements subsequently made are also admissible, although 'the longer the time that has elapsed after the first encounter the less the weight which will be attached to the denial', a matter on which the judge may direct the jury. Thus, in that case it was held that a judge had improperly excluded self-serving statements made by the accused to the police after his arrest, which took place two days after he was first taxed by his employer's security officer with incriminating facts.

However, this principle cannot be relied upon to admit a statement which adds nothing to evidence of reaction which has already been admitted. In *R v Tooke*[128] the accused made an exculpatory statement shortly after the time of the offence. Some 40 minutes later, he went to the police station and made a spontaneous exculpatory witness statement. The first statement

---

[122] *R v T* [2008] EWCA Crim 484. See also *R v Athwal* [2009] 1 WLR 2430, CA.
[123] See **Ch 15**.
[124] *R v Pearce* (1979) 69 Cr App R 365, CA at 368 and 370.
[125] (1968) 52 Cr App R 334.
[126] See per Widgery LJ, (1968) 52 Cr App R at 337.
[127] (1979) 69 Cr App R 365 at 369.
[128] (1989) 90 Cr App R 417, CA.

was admitted, but the defence were not permitted to cross-examine a constable to prove the statement made at the station. The fact that it was a witness statement and not a statement in answer to a charge made no difference, because the same test applied. It was inadmissible because it added nothing to the evidence of reaction already before the jury.

Impromptu exculpatory statements made on accusation are admissible as evidence of consistency in the case of an accused who testifies. In a case where the accused give no evidence, it would appear that the judge, in his summing-up, should remind the jury of any entirely exculpatory statement, and that it is admissible not as evidence of matters stated, but as evidence of the accused's reaction.[129] Moreover, the accused will not be permitted to take unfair advantage of the practice:

> Although in practice most statements are given in evidence even when they are largely self-serving, there may be a rare occasion when an accused produces a carefully prepared written statement to the police, with a view to it being made a part of the prosecution evidence. The trial judge would probably exclude such a statement as inadmissible.[130]

'Mixed' statements

A distinction needs to be drawn between a purely exculpatory statement and a 'mixed' statement, that is, a statement containing both inculpatory and exculpatory parts, such as 'I killed X. If I had not done so, X would certainly have killed me there and then.'[131] When the prosecution admit in evidence a statement relied upon as an admission, the whole statement, including qualifications, explanations, and other exculpatory parts of it favourable to the accused, becomes admissible. Any other course would be unfair and misleading.[132] The jury must decide whether the statement viewed as a whole constitutes an admission. As to the question whether the judge should then direct the jury (a) that the statement is not evidence of the facts contained in it except insofar as it constitutes an admission (the 'purist' approach); or (b) that the whole statement is evidence of the truth of the facts it contains (the 'common sense' approach), in *R v Duncan*[133] the Court of Appeal came down firmly in favour of the latter approach. Lord Lane CJ, in a dictum which was subsequently applied by the Court of Appeal in *R v Hamand*[134] and unanimously endorsed by the House of Lords in *R v Sharp*,[135] said:[136]

> Where a 'mixed' statement is under consideration by the jury in a case where the defendant has not given evidence, it seems to us that the simplest, and, therefore, the method most likely to produce a just result, is for the jury to be told that the whole statement, both the incriminating parts and the excuses or explanations, must be considered by them in deciding where the truth lies. It is, to say the least, not helpful to try to explain to the jury that the exculpatory parts of the statement are something less than evidence of the facts they state.

---

[129] *R v Barbery* (1975) 62 Cr App R 248, CA. Cf *R v Donaldson* (1977) 64 Cr App R 59, CA at 69.

[130] *R v Pearce* (1979) 69 Cr App R 365, CA at 370. See, eg, *R v Newsome* (1980) 71 Cr App R 325, CA. Such a statement remains inadmissible notwithstanding that access to the solicitor is delayed by the police in exercise of their right to do so under the Police and Criminal Evidence Act 1984, s 58: *R v Hutton* (1988) The Times, 27 Oct, CA.

[131] See per Lord Lane CJ in *R v Duncan* (1981) 73 Cr App R 359, CA at 364.

[132] *R v Pearce* (1979) 69 Cr App R 365, CA at 369–70.

[133] (1981) 73 Cr App R 359.

[134] (1985) 82 Cr App R 65, CA.

[135] [1988] 1 WLR 7. See also *R v Aziz* [1995] AC 41, HL.

[136] (1981) 73 Cr App R 359 at 365.

Equally, where appropriate, as it usually will be, the judge may, and should, point out that the incriminatory parts are likely to be true (otherwise why say them?) whereas the excuses do not have the same weight.

The requirement to give such a direction on weight, it is submitted, is to introduce a new and different source of potential confusion for the jury.[137] In *R v Rojas*[138] the Supreme Court of Canada refused to adopt the direction on the ground that in most circumstances expounding the rationale for an evidentiary rule may only serve to confuse the jury unnecessarily or risk encroaching unduly upon their role as fact finders. Such observations may be better left to the advocacy of advocates.

The principle established in *R v Duncan* applies whether the 'mixed' statement is a written statement or a record of questions and answers at an interview.[139] In the case of a suspect who asserts his innocence, his answers in interview will almost always contain *some* admissions of relevant fact, but statements will only be treated as 'mixed' for the purposes of the principle if they contain an admission of fact which is 'significant' in relation to an issue in the case, that is, capable of adding some degree of weight to the prosecution case on an issue which is relevant to guilt.[140] The admission in interview of an ingredient of the offence will often constitute a significant admission.[141] However, there is no requirement that any act admitted be unlawful per se.[142] Whether a mixed statement is 'significant' in relation to an issue in the case can only be determined by reference to what happens at trial and, therefore, can only be finally resolved at the close of the evidence. In particular, the greater the reliance the prosecution place on the inculpatory parts of the statement at trial, the more likely it is that the jury should be told that the exculpatory parts are also evidence in the case.[143] It remains unclear whether the principle applies if the statement is not relied on by the prosecution. On one view, the self-serving parts of the statement are only admissible for their truth if the prosecution elect to rely on the statement as containing an admission.[144] However, it is submitted that there are compelling reasons against any such additional requirement. As Butterfield J pointed out in *Western v DPP*,[145] whether a statement is mixed or not should not depend on the accident of what other evidence is available to the prosecution; and in cases in which the statement is *not* relied on by the prosecution, the view advanced would mean reviving the unintelligible direction, repudiated in *R v Duncan*, to the effect that although the admission is evidence of the facts stated, the self-serving parts of the statement are only evidence of reaction.[146] Where the accused does not give evidence and does not call evidence, it is the duty of the judge, when directing the jury, to set out the defence case insofar as it can

---

[137] The question of weight in respect of 'excuses' continues to feature in the Crown Court Compendium (July 2019), Part 1, 16–1, para 3. In respect of good character directions where the accused has made a mixed statement, see Ch 18, **The meaning of 'pre-trial answers or statements'**, p 542.

[138] [2008] SCC 56; [2009] Crim LR 130.

[139] *R v Polin* [1991] Crim LR 293, CA.

[140] *R v Garrod* [1997] Crim LR 445, CA. See also *R v Papworth* [2008] 1 Cr App R 439 (36), CA and *R v Shirley* [2013] EWCA Crim 1990.

[141] *R v Papworth* [2008] 1 Cr App R 439 (36), CA.

[142] *R v McCleary* [1994] Crim LR 121, CA.

[143] *R v Papworth* [2008] 1 Cr App R 439 (36), CA.

[144] See per Lord Steyn in *R v Aziz* [1995] AC 41, HL at 50.

[145] [1997] 1 Cr App R 474, DC at 484–5.

[146] See generally Birch, 'The Sharp End of the Wedge: Use of Mixed Statements by the Defence' [1997] Crim LR 416.

be determined from the mixed statement, the mixed statement being admissible as evidence of matters stated.[147]

The common law rule relating to the admissibility of mixed statements as evidence of the matters stated is among the common law rules preserved by s 118 of the 2003 Act.[148]

Statements made on discovery of incriminating articles

In cases of handling and theft, if it is shown that the accused was found in possession of recently stolen goods, but failed to give a credible innocent explanation, the jury *may* infer guilty knowledge or belief and return a finding of guilt.[149] Any explanation which is given by the accused is admissible, if the accused testifies to the same effect, as evidence of consistency.[150]

Previous identification

Where, in criminal proceedings, a witness gives evidence identifying the accused as the person who committed the offence charged, evidence of a previous identification of the accused by that witness may be given, as evidence of consistency, either by the witness himself or by any other person who witnessed the previous identification,[151] for example a police officer who conducted a formal identification procedure such as a video identification or an identification parade.[152] Section 120(5) of the 2003 Act, when read in conjunction with section 120(1) and (4) of the 2003 Act, has extended the principle to cover a previous statement of a witness which identifies *or describes* a person, *object or place*, provided that the witness, while giving evidence, indicates that to the best of his belief, he made the statement and it states the truth. A statement received under s 120(5) is admitted as evidence of any matter stated, and will also be evidence of the witness's consistency. Section 120(5) is considered in **Chapter 12**. The text which follows relates to the common law principle.

The admissibility of evidence of previous identification of the accused has been justified on the ground that:

> In cases where there has been a considerable lapse of time between the offence and the trial, and where there might be a danger of the witness's recollection of the prisoner's features having become dimmed, no doubt it strengthens the value of the evidence if it can be shown that in the meantime, soon after the commission of the offence, the witness saw and recognized the prisoner.[153]

---

[147] *R v Curley* [2004] EWCA Crim 2395.

[148] Section 118(1)5.

[149] See **Ch 4, The presumption of guilty knowledge**, p 102.

[150] See *R v Abraham* (1848) 3 Cox CC 430. For further authorities and discussion, see Gooderson, 'Previous Consistent Statements' (1968) CLJ 64 at 70–73.

[151] For the difficulties which arise where the witness fails to identify the accused in court, having previously identified him outside court, see *R v Osborne* and *R v Virtue* [1973] QB 678, CA and *R v Burke and Kelly* (1847) 2 Cox CC 295.

[152] The detailed rules governing the proper conduct of formal identification procedures, which are contained in the Code of Practice issued by the Home Secretary pursuant to the Police and Criminal Evidence Act 1984, s 66 are beyond the scope of this book. Failure on the part of the police to observe the provisions may be taken into account by the court when deciding whether to exclude identification evidence and by the jury when assessing the weight of such evidence: see **Ch 11**.

[153] Per Ferguson J in *R v Fannon* (1922) 22 SRNSW 427 at 430.

In *R v Christie*[154] the accused was convicted of indecent assault on a boy. The boy gave unsworn evidence in which he described the assault, and identified the accused, but made no reference to any previous identification. The House of Lords, by a majority, held that both the boy's mother and a constable had been properly allowed to give evidence that shortly after the alleged act they saw the boy approach the accused, touch his sleeve, and identify him by saying, 'That is the man'. Evidence of the previous identification was admissible as evidence of the witness's consistency, 'to show that the witness was able to identify at the time' and 'to exclude the idea that the identification of the prisoner in the dock was an afterthought or mistake'.[155]

Evidence that a witness previously identified the accused from a photograph is also admissible for these purposes provided that the photograph does not come from police files or, if it does, cannot be identified as such.[156] Thus, evidence of identification from a photograph which forms part of an album of police photographs[157] or which shows the accused wearing prison clothes[158] should be excluded, unless the jury have been or will be made aware of the accused's record for some other good reason.[159] The accused should not be prejudiced by the jury being informed or allowed to suspect that he has previous convictions.[160]

Dock identifications

The evidence of a witness who identifies the accused for the first time in court is properly treated with considerable suspicion. There are no safeguards of the kind offered by a formal identification procedure.[161] There is the obvious danger stemming from delay. There is also the real risk of prejudice, because a witness, asked if he sees in court the person who committed the offence, might all too readily point to the person standing in the dock, overriding any doubts in his mind, especially in cases where he gave a description to the police, by the thought: 'Surely the police would not have brought the wrong person to court?'[162] For these reasons, it is undesirable to invite a witness to make a 'dock identification', that is to identify the accused for the first time in court;[163] the normal and proper practice should be to hold

---

[154] [1914] AC 545.

[155] Ibid at 551 per Viscount Haldane LC.

[156] Such a photograph may also be used to show that between commission of the offence and arrest, the accused had strikingly changed his appearance and thereby thwarted an attempt by the identifying witness to pick him out of an identification parade: *R v Byrne and Trump* [1987] Crim LR 689, CA.

[157] *R v Wainwright* (1925) 19 Cr App R 52, CCA.

[158] *R v Dwyer* and *R v Ferguson* [1925] 2 KB 799, CCA. See also *R v Varley* (1914) 10 Cr App R 125, CCA.

[159] See, eg, *R v Allen* [1996] Crim LR 426, CA.

[160] But see also *R v Governor of Pentonville Prison, ex p Voets* [1986] 1 WLR 470, QBD: such photographs are admissible in law and their exclusion discretionary. The police should not show photographs, including that of a suspect, to potential witnesses where the suspect is already under arrest: *R v Haslam* (1925) 19 Cr App R 59, CCA. Such witnesses should not be shown photographs of an accused whom they will be asked to identify in court: *R v Dwyer* and *R v Ferguson* [1925] 2 KB 799, CCA. However, the police, if in doubt as to the identity of a criminal, may show photographs to potential witnesses in order to discover who the offender is: *R v Palmer* (1914) 10 Cr App R 77, CCA. See also *R v Crabtree* [1992] Crim LR 65, CA: it is permissible for officers to identify the accused from photographs taken as part of a surveillance operation and shown to them before the offence was committed. As to the rules to be observed when a witness is shown photographs for identification purposes, see paras 3.3 and 3.28 of, and Annex E to, Code D, the Code of Practice on Identification issued pursuant to the Police and Criminal Evidence Act 1984, s 66.

[161] See Ch 9, **Pre-trial procedure**, p 290.

[162] See generally *Holland v Her Majesty's Advocate* [2005] HRLR 25, PC at [47].

[163] *R v Cartwright* (1914) 10 Cr App R 219, CCA.

a formal identification procedure;[164] and the usual practice, in cases where there has been a prior out-of-court identification, is to elicit evidence on this *before* asking a question such as, 'Is that person in court today?'

The making of a dock identification is not, by its very nature, incompatible with the right to a fair trial in Art 6(1) of the European Convention on Human Rights, but may be incompatible depending on all the circumstances of the case.[165] In *Tido v R*,[166] the Privy Council held that although a dock identification is not inadmissible per se, and that admission of such evidence is not to be regarded as permissible in only the most exceptional circumstances, a trial judge should always consider whether admission might imperil the fair trial of the accused. The judge should consider all the relevant circumstances, including any reason for not holding a formal identification procedure.[167] A dock identification may be justified if the suspect has refused to take part in a formal identification procedure,[168] but as was observed in *Tido v R*,[169] given the variety of formal identification procedures available in England and Wales, even if the accused is unwilling to participate, dock identifications are rare. A dock identification is justified if the identifying witness claims to recognize the suspect as a person he already knows well.[170] However, a formal identification procedure is necessary when the witness has seen the suspect only once, or on a few occasions, before.[171]

In *Tido v R*,[172] it was also held that where there has been a dock identification, the jury should always be given a careful direction as to the danger of relying on it and also a particular warning of the disadvantages to the accused of having been denied a formal identification procedure, including the possibility of an inconclusive result which the defence could have used to cast doubt on the accuracy of a subsequent identification. The jury should also be reminded of the obvious danger that an accused in the dock might automatically be assumed by even a well-intentioned witness to be the person who had committed the crime. Where a dock identification is made but not solicited by the prosecution, it is insufficient for the judge merely to direct the jury that such an identification is abnormal and unfair—they should probably be told to disregard it altogether.[173]

The usual two criticisms of a dock identification are that it lacks the safeguards offered by an identification procedure and, by reason of the accused's position in the dock, positively increases the risk of a wrong identification. These criticisms are most compelling when there has been an identification procedure and a witness who was unable to identify the accused at that procedure, makes a dock identification.[174] In such circumstances, the judge should warn the jury of this heightened risk of a false identification.[175]

---

[164] *Neilly v R* [2012] 2 Cr App R 248 (20), PC at [31].

[165] *Holland v Her Majesty's Advocate* [2005] HRLR 25, PC. See also *Young v Trinidad and Tobago* [2008] UKPC 27.

[166] [2011] 2 Cr App R 336, PC.

[167] *Neilly v R* [2012] 2 Cr App R 248 (20), PC at [32].

[168] *R v John* [1973] Crim LR 113, CA.

[169] [2012] 1 WLR 115, PC at [22].

[170] See para 3.12(ii) of Code D and *R v France* [2012] UKPC 28.

[171] *R v Fergus* [1992] Crim LR 363, CA.

[172] [2012] 1 WLR 115, PC.

[173] *R v Thomas* [1994] Crim LR 128, CA. Cf *R v Abdullah* [2019] EWCA Crim 1137 where, in the circumstances, a direction to place 'little or no reliance' on the dock identification was held to have been sufficient.

[174] Per Lord Rodger in *Holland v Her Majesty's Advocate* [2005] HRLR 25 at [48].

[175] *Lawrence v R* [2014] UKPC 2.

Although it has been held that it would be wrong to apply one approach to dock identifica-tions for minor offences and another for more serious offences,[176] in *Barnes v Chief Constable of Durham*,[177] the Divisional Court held that dock identifications were customary in mag-istrates' courts, in relation to driving offences at least, and that if, in every case where the defendant did not distinctly admit driving there had to be a formal identification procedure, the whole process of justice in a magistrates' court would be severely impaired. This approach was followed in *Karia v DPP*,[178] a case of speeding and failing to produce insurance and other documents, where the court rejected a submission that *Barnes v Chief Constable of Durham* could be distinguished on the basis that in that case the defendant had been arrested and interviewed, whereas Karia was summonsed and had had no opportunity to explain that he was not the driver.

Statements admissible as part of the res gestae

The common law principle of *res gestae*, which is considered in Chapter 14, renders admis-sible all those events and statements which may be said to constitute a part of a transac-tion which is in issue. For example, in *R v Fowkes*[179] the accused, charged with murder, was commonly known, in the circumstances somewhat unfortunately it may be thought, as 'the butcher'. The son of the deceased gave evidence that he was sitting in a room with his father and a police officer, that a face appeared at the window through which a shot was fired, and that he thought the face was that of the accused. Both the son and the police officer, who had not seen the face, were allowed to give evidence that the son, on seeing the face, had shouted, 'There's Butcher'. A statement forming part of the *res gestae* is admissible at common law as evidence of the matters stated and also as evidence of consistency insofar as it confirms testimony given by the witness to the same effect. In criminal proceedings the common law rules in this regard have been preserved by the 2003 Act.[180] In civil pro-ceedings, a previous statement forming part of the *res gestae* may only be adduced with the leave of the court.[181]

Statements in documents used to refresh the memory and received in evidence

As we have seen earlier in this chapter, where a party, or his advocate on his behalf, cross-examines a witness on a document used by him to refresh his memory, and goes beyond the parts relied upon by the witness, the document may be received in evidence. As we have also seen, in civil proceedings, statements in the document are admitted as evidence of the matters stated; and the same applies in criminal proceedings, provided that the state-ment was made, as opposed to verified, by the witness. Where such statements are received in evidence, they may also go to the consistency of the witness.

Previous inconsistent statements

Where a witness during examination-in-chief (or during cross-examination) admits making a previous oral or written inconsistent statement, under s 119 of the Criminal Justice Act

---

[176] See *North Yorkshire Trading Standards Dept v Williams* (1994) 159 JP 383, DC.

[177] [1997] 2 Cr App R 505, DC.

[178] (2002) 166 JP 753, QBD.

[179] (1856) The Times, 8 Mar, Assizes.

[180] Section 118(1)4.

[181] See the Civil Evidence Act 1995, s 6(2)(a) (see Ch 13).

2003, the statement is admissible as evidence of any matter stated of which oral evidence by him would be admissible. Section 119 states as follows:

(1) If in criminal proceedings a person gives oral evidence and—
    (a) he admits making a previous inconsistent statement,[182] or
    (b) a previous inconsistent statement made by him is proved by virtue of section 3, 4 or 5 of the Criminal Procedure Act 1865 (c. 18),
the statement is admissible as evidence of any matter stated of which oral evidence by him would be admissible.

The fact that a witness has made a previous statement but gives evidence that he cannot remember the matters in the statement does not necessarily render the statement a previous *inconsistent* statement.[183] The conclusion that the witness's statement is inconsistent with his evidence obviously cannot be reached where the witness stands by what he said in his earlier statement even though he is unable to remember the matters contained in it.[184] However, it is submitted that such a conclusion could be reached if the witness denies the truth of the previous statement, in which case 'he admits making a previous inconsistent statement' for the purposes of s 119(1)(a), or he is treated as a hostile witness on the basis that he is likely to be able to remember the matters in question and by claiming not to do so he is not willing to tell the truth.[185]

Unfavourable and hostile witnesses

The rule against a party impeaching the credit of his own witness

A party seeking to elicit evidence in support of his version of the facts in issue may call a witness who, in the witness box, fails to come up to proof or gives evidence in support of the other party's version of the facts in issue. In order to remedy this, the party may understandably wish to change course and attack the credibility of the witness. The general rule at common law, however, is that a party is not permitted to impeach the credit of a witness he calls: the party may neither question the witness about, nor call evidence concerning, his bad character,[186] convictions, prior inconsistent statements, or bias. Thus if the witness gives adverse evidence, the party may not turn round and cross-examine him as if he were a witness for the opposite party: 'It would be repugnant to principle, and likely to lead to abuse, to enable a party, having called a witness on the basis that he is at least in general going to tell the truth, to question him or call other evidence designed to show that he is a liar.'[187]

---

[182] The effect of the 2003 Act, s 119(1)(a) is to make a prior statement admissible for the truth of the matter stated where a witness admits having made the prior statement without an application having been made to treat him as hostile. See *R v Joyce* [2005] EWCA Crim 1785.

[183] See also under Hostile witnesses, p 207.

[184] See *R v Chinn* [2012] 1 WLR 3401, CA.

[185] See *R v Bennet* [2008] EWCA Crim 248. Cf *Griffiths v CPS* [2018] EWHC 3062 (Admin), considered below under Hostile witnesses, p 207.

[186] It appears that a party is permitted to adduce evidence of the witness's bad character where the evidence is relevant to an issue in the case but does not discredit him or his credibility in relation to the discrete issue on which he gives evidence: *R v Ross* [2008] Crim LR 306, CA.

[187] Criminal Law Revision Committee, 11th Report, Cmnd 4991 (1972), para 162.

Unfavourable witnesses

An unfavourable witness may be defined as a witness who displays no hostile 'animus', ie no hostile spirit or attitude, to the party calling him, but fails to come up to proof or gives evidence unfavourable to the case of that party.[188] At common law, a party is not permitted to impeach the credit of an unfavourable witness by any of the means outlined in the preceding paragraph but may call other witnesses to give evidence of those matters in relation to which the unfavourable witness failed to come up to proof. Thus in *Ewer v Ambrose*,[189] the defendant having called a witness to prove a partnership and the witness having testified to the contrary, it was held that while the defendant could not adduce general evidence to show that the witness was not to be believed on his oath, he was entitled to contradict him by calling other witnesses. If the rule were otherwise, undue importance would attach to the order in which witnesses are called. As Littledale J observed, 'if a party had four witnesses upon whom he relied to prove his case, it would be very hard that, by calling first the one who happened to disprove it, he should be deprived of the testimony of the other three'.

Hostile witnesses

A hostile witness is a witness who, in the opinion of the judge, shows no desire to tell the truth at the instance of the party calling him, to whom he displays a hostile animus.[190] In a civil case, it seems that a party may call a person even if he has shown signs that he is likely to be a hostile witness by refusing to make a statement.[191] In a criminal case, it appears that if a person refuses to assist the prosecution or court, or claims to be no longer able to remember anything, the judge has a discretion to hold a *voir dire* in order to decide whether to prevent him from being called.[192] However, it has also been held that the prosecution may call a person who has shown signs that he is likely to be a hostile witness, for example by retracting a statement, or making a second statement, prior to the trial.[193] In *R v Mazekelua*[194] the prosecution called a person who had shown every sign that he would be a hostile witness, had him treated as a hostile witness, and cross-examined him on the contents of a video recording of an interview that the judge had earlier ruled should not stand as his evidence-in-chief because it was not in the interests of justice for that to happen.[195] It has also been held that where an accused calls a witness to give evidence against a co-accused, he may, if appropriate, apply to have him treated as hostile notwithstanding that he was expected to resile from what he said previously, and the previous inconsistent statement, if proved, will be evidence of the truth of its contents under s 119 of the Criminal Justice Act 2003.[196]

---

[188] See for example *R v Smith* [2019] EWCA Crim 1151.

[189] (1825) 3 B&C 746. See also *Bradley v Ricardo* (1831) 8 Bing 57; cf Hamilton J in *Sumner and Leivesley v John Brown & Co* (1909) 25 TLR 745, Assizes.

[190] See Stephen, *Digest of the Law of Evidence* (12th edn, London, 1948) Art 147.

[191] See CPR r 32.9, whereby a party unable to obtain a witness statement may seek permission to serve a witness summary instead (see Ch 5).

[192] *R v Honeyghon and Sayles* [1999] Crim LR 221, CA. See also *R v Dat* [1998] Crim LR 488, CA.

[193] See *R v Mann* (1972) 56 Cr App R 750, CA; *R v Vibert* (21 Oct 1974, unreported), CA; and *R v Dat* [1998] Crim LR 488, CA.

[194] [2011] EWCA Crim 1458.

[195] See Youth Justice and Criminal Evidence Act 1999, s 27 (see Ch 5).

[196] *R v Osborne* [2010] EWCA Crim 1981. Cf, in the case of a prosecution witness, *R v Dat* [1998] Crim LR 488, CA: the prosecution should limit the damage which might occur as a result of wide-ranging cross-examination on the previous statement. See also in respect of s 119(1)(a), n 217.

In criminal cases, although the question whether a witness is hostile is for the judge alone, the evidence and demeanour of the potentially hostile witness should usually be tested in the presence of the jury.[197] It is only in very exceptional cases that a *voir dire* should be held to decide whether or not a witness who has yet to be called might prove to be hostile.[198] Equally, once a witness has started to give his evidence, a *voir dire* before a decision on whether to treat him as hostile is only appropriate in exceptional circumstances, because the jury may see the witness apparently giving evidence in one frame of mind and then see a complete turn-around after events which have taken place in their absence.[199]

At common law a judge may allow cross-examination of a hostile witness by the party calling him.[200] An application to treat a witness as hostile may be made at any time during the witness's evidence, even at the late stage of re-examination.[201] Even though, during the course of examination-in-chief, the grounds for treating a witness as hostile are plain, it is inappropriate to begin to cross-examining the witness without making an application.[202] As to the judge's discretion whether to grant leave to cross-examine, his decision will seldom be challenged successfully on appeal.[203] In deciding whether a witness is not merely unfavourable but should be treated as hostile, the judge may take into account the attitude and demeanour displayed by the witness, his willingness to cooperate, and the extent to which any prior statement made by him is inconsistent with his testimony. If a hostile witness gives evidence contrary to an earlier statement, or fails to give the evidence expected, the party calling him and the trial judge should first consider inviting him to refresh his memory from material which it is legitimate to use for that purpose, and should not immediately proceed to treat him as hostile, unless he displays such an excessive degree of hostility that that is the only appropriate course.[204] In *R v Fraser* and *R v Warren*[205] Lord Goddard CJ went so far as to state, and it is best regarded as an over-statement, that if the prosecution have in their possession a previous statement 'in flat contradiction' of the witness's testimony, they are *entitled* to cross-examine and should apply for leave to do so.

If a witness is treated as hostile, the party calling him may ask leading questions[206] but may neither cross-examine him on his previous misconduct or convictions, nor adduce evidence to show that he is not to be believed on oath. At common law, it was doubtful whether the

---

[197] *R v Darby* [1989] Crim LR 817, CA. Cf *R v Jones* [1998] Crim LR 579, CA.

[198] *R v Olumegbon* [2004] EWCA Crim 2337.

[199] *R v Khan* [2003] Crim LR 428, CA. *R v Hopes* [2011] EWCA Crim 1869 appears to be an example of exceptional circumstances justifying a *voir dire*. The witness said he was unable to recall events and when the prosecution advocate sought to refresh his memory using his statement, he began to deny having made some parts of the statement. The court held (at [19]) that the jury should have been sent out, and, if necessary, the witness too.

[200] It appears that the party calling the witness retains the right to *re-examine* him on any new matters arising out of cross-examination by the other party to the action: *R v Wong* [1986] Crim LR 683 (Crown Court).

[201] *R v Powell* [1985] Crim LR 592, CA.

[202] See *R v Hopes* [2011] EWCA Crim 1869 at [19]: it is important that the procedures are undertaken with the proper formality; absent due formality, the separate processes of memory refreshing and cross-examination become blurred with a risk of unfairness to the defence.

[203] *Rice v Howard* (1886) 16 QBD 681 and *Price v Manning* (1889) 42 Ch D 372, CA.

[204] *R v Maw* [1994] Crim LR 841, CA.

[205] (1956) 40 Cr App R 160, CCA.

[206] *R v Thompson* (1976) 64 Cr App R 96, CA.

party could prove prior statements made by the witness and inconsistent with his testimony, a matter which is now governed by s 3 of the Criminal Procedure Act 1865.[207] Section 3 provides that:

> A party producing a witness shall not be allowed to impeach his credit by general evidence of bad character, but he may, in case the witness shall, in the opinion of the judge, prove adverse, contradict him by other evidence, or, by leave of the judge, prove that he has made at other times a statement inconsistent with his present testimony; but before such last mentioned proof can be given the circumstances of the supposed statement, sufficient to designate the particular occasion, must be mentioned to the witness, and he must be asked whether or not he has made such statement.

Section 3 was not drafted with felicity.[208] In *Greenough v Eccles*[209] it was held that the word 'adverse' in the section means 'hostile' and not 'unfavourable'. In assessing whether a witness is hostile for the purposes of s 3, a judge will consider a large number of factors, including whether the witness can assist, whether he has indicated a willingness to assist, any previous accounts given by him, and his demeanour in the witness box. The issue does not depend solely on whether he has made a previous inconsistent statement.[210]

Section 3 may be analysed in terms of three rules governing a party's entitlement to discredit his own witness. The first is that he is not entitled to impeach the witness's credit by general evidence of his bad character. In other words, he may neither cross-examine the witness on his previous misconduct or convictions nor adduce evidence of a general nature to show that the witness is not to be believed on oath. This rule applies to both unfavourable and hostile witnesses and amounts to no more than a statutory restatement of the common law. The second rule, that the party may contradict the witness by other evidence, applies under the statute only to hostile witnesses. The section suggests that this rule does not apply to unfavourable witnesses, but in *Greenough v Eccles*, Williams and Willes JJ held that the section has not affected the rule at common law that a party may contradict an unfavourable witness by calling other witnesses.[211] The third rule, that the party may, with the leave of the judge,[212] prove that the witness made at other times a statement inconsistent with his present testimony, applies only in the case of hostile witnesses.[213] In this connection, it remains to note that section 3 has not removed the common law right of the judge, in his discretion, to allow cross-examination when a witness proves hostile. In *R v Thompson*[214] the accused was

---

[207] Section 3 applies to both civil and criminal proceedings. In civil proceedings the prior statement of any witness may with the leave of the court be admitted as evidence of the facts contained in it: see the Civil Evidence Act 1995, s 6(2)(a) (see Ch 13). The evidential status of a prior inconsistent statement of a hostile witness in civil proceedings is governed by the 1995 Act, s 6(3) and (5): see text which follows reference to this note, n 216.

[208] 'Section 3 of the 1865 Act certainly requires thorough revision': Criminal Law Revision Committee, 11th Report, Cmnd 4991 (1972), para 161. See also cl 11 of the draft Bill.

[209] (1859) 5 CBNS 786, a decision on the construction of the Common Law Procedure (Amendment) Act 1856, s 22, which was repealed but re-enacted by the 1865 Act, s 3.

[210] *R v Hengari-Ajufo* [2016] EWCA Crim 1913 at [59].

[211] See *Ewer v Ambrose* (1825) 3 B&C 746, at n 189.

[212] The need for leave cannot be circumvented by reliance on s 4 of the Act (as to which, see Ch 7, **Section 4 of the 1865 Act, p 222**): *R v Booth* (1981) 74 Cr App R 123.

[213] Acceptance by the witness that he made some parts of the statement and signed it may constitute proof for these purposes: see *R v Baldwin* [1986] Crim LR 681, CA.

[214] (1976) 64 Cr App R 96, CA.

convicted of indecent assault and incest. His daughter, who had given a statement to the police implicating him, was called into the witness box but stood mute of malice, refusing to give evidence. The judge gave leave to treat her as a hostile witness, and she was then asked leading questions and her former statement was put to her. On appeal, it was argued that since the girl had given no 'testimony', the case did not fall within s 3. Dismissing the appeal, Lord Parker CJ held it unnecessary to decide whether s 3 applied, since there was authority at common law for what the judge had done.[215]

If a hostile witness, on being cross-examined on a previous inconsistent statement, adopts and confirms the contents (or part of them), then what he says becomes part of his evidence and, subject to the assessment of his credibility by the tribunal of fact, it is capable of being accepted.[216] However, even if the witness does not admit the truth of the previous statement, it is admissible in both civil and criminal proceedings as evidence of the matters stated. Under s 1 of the 1995 Act, in civil proceedings evidence shall not be excluded on the ground that it is hearsay. Section 6(3) and (5) of the 1995 Act provide as follows:

(3) Where in the case of civil proceedings sections 3, 4 or 5 of the Criminal Procedure Act 1865 applies, which make provision as to—
   (a) how far a witness may be discredited by the party producing him, . . . this Act does not authorise the adducing of evidence of a previous inconsistent or contradictory statement otherwise than in accordance with those sections.

   . . .

(5) Nothing in this section shall be construed as preventing a statement of any description referred to above from being admissible by virtue of section 1 as evidence of the matters stated.

As to criminal proceedings, s 119 of the 2003 Act has been considered earlier in this chapter under **Previous inconsistent statements.** The effect of s 119 is that a previous inconsistent statement is admissible as evidence of matters stated.[217]

In both civil and criminal cases, therefore, the tribunal of fact may accept as the truth of the matter the previous statement of a witness who has been declared hostile. However, s 119 does not apply to a witness who, once sworn, stands mute of malice because the provision only applies where a witness 'gives oral evidence'.[218] Section 119 was invoked in *Griffiths v CPS*,[219] a case of domestic violence where the complainant began her evidence-in-chief by confirming that the two previous witness statements she had made were true, but went on to say that she did not want to be in court because she and her partner 'had both done wrong that day'. The prosecution put both her previous statements to her, pursuant to s 119. The first contained details of the alleged assault and the second was a retraction statement in which she said that she did not want to go to court. However, it is not easy to see

---

[215] Reliance was placed upon *Clarke v Saffery* (1824) Ry&M 126 and *Bastin v Carew* (1824) Ry&M 127. It remains unclear whether if, in circumstances such as those in *R v Thompson*, the witness denies making the previous statement, it can be proved at common law.

[216] *R v Maw* [1994] Crim LR 841, CA. See also *R v Gibbons* [2009] Crim LR 197, CA.

[217] The effect of s 119(1)(a) is to make a prior statement admissible for the truth of the matter stated where a witness admits having made the prior statement without an application having been made to treat him as hostile. See *R v Joyce* [2005] EWCA Crim 1785.

[218] However, in such circumstances it would be open to the court to admit the statement as evidence of the truth of the matter stated under the 2003 Act, s 114(1)(d) (see Ch 12).

[219] [2018] EWHC 3062 (Admin).

how the conditions in s 119(1)(a) and (b) were satisfied in these circumstances: there do not appear to be inconsistencies between the complainant's two previous statements and her oral evidence—she said both previous statements were true.[220]

Section 119 of the 2003 Act, by allowing previous inconsistent statements to be admitted for the truth of the matter stated, has changed the landscape of the criminal trial. Protection for defendants is contained in the court's powers to exclude evidence,[221] to direct an acquittal or discharge the jury where the evidence provided by the statement is unconvincing,[222] and to give appropriate directions to the jury.[223]

At one time it was thought that, in the case of a hostile witness who had made a previous inconsistent statement, the judge should direct the jury that his evidence should be regarded as unreliable.[224] However, it has since been said that it is not always necessary or appropriate, as an inflexible rule, to give such a direction.[225] In some cases, the evidence given by the witness may be regarded as reliable notwithstanding his prior inconsistent statement—for example when the witness is able to give a convincing explanation of the inconsistency. In *R v Joyce*,[226] which was decided under the 2003 Act, it was held that the jury may accept what the witness said either on the previous occasion or when giving evidence. As to the strength of the direction on the weight to be attached to the witness's evidence or previous statement, it is submitted that it should vary according to the particular circumstances of the case in question. The jury should not be directed that a previous statement is just as much evidence as the witness's testimony in court because the jury may take the direction to mean that they are obliged to give both the same evidential weight.[227] However, it is necessary for the jury to consider whether a hostile witness should be treated as creditworthy at all. The judge should give a clear warning about the dangers of a witness who has contradicted himself. It is insufficient to tell the jury to approach the evidence with great caution and reservation. Before the jury may rely on either the witness's evidence or prior statement as evidence of truth supporting the prosecution case, they must be sure that it is true.[228] However, where it is exculpatory of the accused, it is sufficient if the jury are persuaded that it may be true.[229] Where a witness is declared hostile but subsequently

---

[220] See Commentary, [2019] Crim LR 358. Perhaps the decision might be best justified on this basis—the retraction did not contradict the first statement, but the point of the retraction was to prevent the court convicting her partner, which was in effect a denial of truth of the first statement and therefore admissible as an inconsistent statement to contradict her.

[221] See, eg, *R v Coates* [2008] 1 Cr App R 52 (3), CA.

[222] The Criminal Justice Act 2003, s 125.

[223] See *R v Joyce* [2005] EWCA Crim 1798 and *R v Bennett* [2008] EWCA Crim 248.

[224] *R v Golder* [1960] 1 WLR 1169, CCA at 1172–3, approved in *R v Oliva* [1965] 1 WLR 1028, CCA at 1036–7.

[225] *Driscoll v R* (1977) 137 CLR 517, High Court of Australia, a view supported by *R v Pestano* [1981] Crim LR 397, CA; *Alves v DPP* [1992] 4 All ER 787, HL; and *R v Goodway* [1993] 4 All ER 894, CA at 899. See also *R v Billingham* [2009] 2 Cr App R 341 (20), CA. See also *Himanshu @ Chintu v State of NCT of Delhi* 2011 STPL (Web) 6 SC, 4 Jan 2011, Supreme Court of India: the fact that a prosecution witness is hostile does not prevent the prosecution from relying on his evidence to the extent that it supports their case.

[226] [2005] EWCA Crim 1785 at [29]–[30].

[227] *R v Billingham* [2009] 2 Cr App R 341 (20), CA.

[228] See, eg, *R v Parvez* [2010] EWCA Crim 3229: where it is alleged that an earlier statement was retracted through fear, the proper direction is whether the jury are sure that the statement is true and was retracted through fear, in which case, subject to caution, they may act on it.

[229] *R v Billingham* [2009] 2 Cr App R 341 (20), CA; see also *R v Maw* [1994] Crim LR 841, CA.

reverts to his original account, the trial judge is still obliged to warn the jury to approach his evidence with caution, the precise nature of the direction depending on the particular circumstances of the case.[230]

Under s 122 of the 2003 Act, if in a jury trial a statement made in a document is admitted under s 119 and produced as an exhibit, it must not accompany the jury when they retire to consider their verdict unless the court considers it appropriate or all parties agree that it should accompany them. The reason for the general rule in s 122 is the risk that the jury, by having the document in front of them, will place disproportionate weight on its contents as compared with the oral evidence. Normally, in the absence of some special feature of the document, it is sufficient for the judge to give a reminder in the summing-up of the contents of the statement and anything said by the witness about the document and the circumstances in which it was made. In cases where it is appropriate for the jury to take the document with them, the judge should not only give the general direction about a hostile witness, but also impress upon the jury the reason why they are being given the document and the importance of not attaching disproportionate weight to it simply because they have it before them.[231]

ADDITIONAL READING

Andrews and Lamb, 'Cross-examining young alleged complainers in Scottish criminal cases' [2018] Crim LR 34.
This article presents the findings of research into the features of questions used by criminal lawyers in Scotland (question type, complexity, repetition, and content), the effect of their questioning techniques on children's responses, and the effect of children's ages on responses. It highlights the need for improved practitioner training on questioning, which should be based on methods scientifically proven to work, should explain the research base for best practice to recipients, and should be continuous and ongoing. Consideration is given to improvements made in England and Wales, including the use of intermediaries (although the point is made that the effectiveness of the special measure of intermediaries has not been objectively or systematically evaluated).

Keane and Fortson, 'Leading Questions: A Critical Analysis' [2011] Crim LR 280.
A critical analysis of the rules relating to leading questions, their rationale, scope, and potential complexity, having regard in particular to the relevant psychological literature. Proposals are made for clarification and reform.

Lewis, 'Delayed complaints in childhood sexual abuse prosecutions—a comparative evaluation of admissibility determinations and judicial warnings' (2006) 10 E&P 104.
A review of legal responses to delayed complaints in child sexual abuse prosecutions in Australia, Canada, the United States, Ireland, and England and Wales, focusing on legislative and judicial modifications to the historical common law requirement for early or recent complaint. Consideration is given to three legal mechanisms regulating the jury's access to information about delayed complaints: cross-examination of the complainant on the issue of delay, the admissibility of a late complaint for the prosecution, and judicial warnings about late complaints.

Wheatcroft et al, 'Rethinking Leading: The Directive, Non-Directive Divide' [2015] Crim LR 340.
Drawing upon psychological studies which suggest that questioning in the directive form (ie 'tag' questions) may negatively affect accuracy, an argument for a ban on such questioning in cross-examination.

---

[230] *R v Greene* (2009) The Times, 28 Oct.
[231] *R v Hulme* [2007] 1 Cr App R 334 (26), CA.

QUESTION

Dan is charged with armed robbery. The offence took place at midday at a jewellery shop, Glitters, in Hatton Garden, London. Dan's defence is mistaken identity. Dan is bald, 6 foot 6 inches tall, and weighs 20 stone.

Ella, an 8-year-old girl, and Frieda, her mother, were outside Glitters at the time of the offence. Ella told Frieda that she had just seen a big fat bald man with a gun run out of Glitters and jump into a black car. Frieda used her mobile phone to take a picture of the registration number of the car. Later that day, Frieda used the picture to include the registration number of the car in her written police statement.

The police, using the registration number in Frieda's statement, traced the car to Gil. Gil, when questioned by the police, initially told them that on the date of the robbery, the car had been in his garage all day, but later, in his written police statement, said that on that date, Dan had borrowed it between 10am and 2pm.

The police interviewed Dan. When it was suggested to him that he was the robber, he said, 'No—I may have been in Hatton Garden, but you've got the wrong man'.

A week before the trial, 9 months after the robbery, Frieda says that she cannot remember the registration number of the car and Gil tells the police that the contents of his police statement are not true.

What evidential issues are likely to arise at or before the trial and how are they likely to be resolved?

 For a note-form answer see the online resources, accessible at
www.oup.com/he/keane-mckeown13e.

Cross-examination and re-examination

7

Key issues

- When should cross-examination by an accused be prohibited?

- What is the object of cross-examination?

- What restrictions should be placed on the form of questioning in cross-examination?

- What are the consequences for a party to litigation who fails to cross-examine a witness?

- When and why is a party to litigation permitted to prove that a witness called by another party has made a prior inconsistent statement?

- In proceedings for sexual offences, when and why should questions or evidence concerning the previous sexual experiences of the complainant be allowed?

- If a witness denies a matter under cross-examination, when and why should the cross-examining party be permitted to call evidence in rebuttal?

- What is the object of re-examination?

Cross-examination

Cross-examination is the questioning of a witness, immediately after his examination-in-chief, by the legal representative of the opponent of the party calling him, or by the opposing party in person, and by the legal representative of any other party to the proceedings or by any other party in person. Thus if an accused elects to testify, he will be open to cross-examination not only by the prosecution but also by a co-accused; and the co-accused is entitled to cross-examine him whether he has given evidence unfavourable to the co-accused or has merely given evidence in his own defence.[1] The order of cross-examination where two or more are jointly indicted and separately represented is the order in which their names appear on the indictment or as directed by the court.[2]

In general, when cross-examination is being conducted with competence, a judge should not intervene, except to clarify matters he does not understand or thinks the jury may not understand.[3] However, a judge has specific powers and duties to intervene in the case of young and vulnerable witnesses.[4]

Liability to cross-examination

The general rule is that all witnesses are liable to be cross-examined. If a witness dies before cross-examination, his evidence-in-chief is admissible, though little weight may attach to it.[5] If a prosecution witness, during cross-examination, becomes incapable through illness of giving further evidence, the judge may allow the trial to continue on the basis of the evidence already given, subject to an appropriate direction to the jury to acquit if they feel that the truncated cross-examination prevented them from judging fairly the witness's credibility.[6] The critical issue is whether the accused can have a fair trial if the cross-examination is cut short and, on this issue, regard can be had to the extent to which the defence has been explored with the witness, whether previous inconsistent statements can be reduced to agreed facts and put before the jury in writing, and whether there is other evidence against the accused.[7]

To the general rule that all witnesses are liable to cross-examination, there are three minor exceptions in the case of: (i) a witness who is not sworn, being called merely to produce a document;[8] (ii) a witness called by mistake, because he is unable to speak as to the

---

[1] *R v Hilton* [1972] 1 QB 421, CA.

[2] Criminal Procedure Rules 2015, SI 2015/1490, r 25.11(4)(c)(i).

[3] *R v Sharp* [1994] QB 261, CA. See also *R v Roncoli* [1998] Crim LR 584, CA and *R v Zarezadeh* [2011] EWCA Crim 271. Interventions which may raise an eyebrow do not necessarily result in an unfair trial: *R v Denton* [2007] All ER (D) 492 (Apr), [2007] EWCA Crim 1111. However, interventions carry the risk of depriving the judge of the advantage of calm and dispassionate observation and lengthy interrogation may so hamper his ability properly to evaluate and weigh the evidence as to impair his judgment and render the trial unfair: *Southwark London Borough Council v Kofi-Adu* [2006] HLR 33, CA. Concerning interventions during examination-in-chief, see Ch 6, Judicial interventions, p 182.

[4] See, in this chapter, under **Young and vulnerable witnesses**, p 225.

[5] *R v Doolin* (1882) 1 Jebb CC 123, IR.

[6] *R v Stretton* and *R v McCallion* (1986) 86 Cr App R 7, CA. See also *R v Wyatt* [1990] Crim LR 343, CA, where the judge halted the examination of a 7-year-old victim of an indecent assault by reason of her distress.

[7] *R v Pipe* [2014] EWCA Crim 2570. If the only direct evidence on one important part of the prosecution case is given by a witness who, at the end of his examination-in-chief, is unable to give further evidence, it is at least doubtful whether any direction to the jury, however strongly expressed, can overcome the powerful prejudice of his evidence going wholly untested by cross-examination: *R v Lawless* (1993) 98 Cr App R 342, CA.

[8] *Summers v Moseley* (1834) 2 Cr&M 477. Nor may such a witness be cross-examined if he was sworn unnecessarily: *Rush v Smith* (1834) 1 Cr M&R 94.

matters supposed to be within his knowledge, where the mistake is discovered before the examination-in-chief has begun but after the witness has been sworn;[9] and (iii) a witness called by the judge, in which case neither party is entitled to cross-examine him without the leave of the judge, although such leave should be given if the evidence is adverse to either party.[10]

Cross-examination by accused in person

Cross-examination may be conducted by a legal representative or by a party in person. In criminal cases, as a general rule, an unrepresented accused is entitled to cross-examine in person any witness called by the prosecution. However, there are common law restrictions on this rule, as well as statutory exceptions to it. As to the former, the judge is not obliged to give an unrepresented accused the right to ask whatever questions, at whatever length, he wishes.[11] Where the accused is not represented, the judge may ask a witness any question necessary in the accused's interests;[12] and it is generally desirable for the judge to ask such questions as he sees fit to test the reliability and accuracy of the witness.[13] Sections 34–39 of the Youth Justice and Criminal Evidence Act 1999 (the 1999 Act) protect three categories of witness from cross-examination by an accused in person.[14] Under s 34, no person charged with a sexual offence[15] may cross-examine in person the complainant, either in connection with the offence, or in connection with any other offence (of whatever nature) with which that person is charged in the proceedings. Under s 35, no person charged with one of a number of specified offences[16] may cross-examine in person a 'protected witness', either in connection with the offence, or in connection with any other offence (of whatever nature) with

---

[9] However, if an advocate seeks to withdraw a witness who can give relevant evidence because he might also reveal other inconvenient matters, the witness is liable to cross-examination: *Wood v Mackinson* (1840) 2 Mood&R 273.

[10] *Coulson v Disborough* [1894] 2 QB 316, CA; *R v Cliburn* (1898) 62 JP 232, CCC. See also *R v Tregear* [1967] 2 QB 574, CA at 580.

[11] *R v Brown* [1998] 2 Cr App R 364, CA.

[12] Criminal Procedure Rules 2015, r 25.11(6)(b). See also, in relation to family proceedings, s 31G(6), Matrimonial and Family Proceedings Act 1984. Where an accused has made an application for legal aid which has not yet been determined, the court may appoint a 'cross-examination advocate' contingently under s 38(4) of the Youth Justice and Criminal Evidence Act 1999, 'the appointment to come into force only if, and when, it is established that the defendant will not be represented for the purposes of the case generally': Criminal Practice Directions 2015 (Amendment No 6), 6, 23A.1.

[13] *R v De Oliveira* [1997] Crim LR 600, CA.

[14] As to the need for similar statutory protection in civil cases, see per Wood J in *H v L and R, Re* [2007] 2 FLR 162, Fam D.

[15] A 'sexual offence' is defined in s 62 as any offence under the Sexual Offences Act 2003, Pt 1, any relevant superseded offence or any offence under the Modern Slavery Act 2015, s 2 (human trafficking) which is committed with a view to sexual exploitation. 'Relevant superseded offence' means rape or burglary with intent to rape, an offence under any of ss 2–12 and 14–17 of the Sexual Offences Act 1956, an offence under the Mental Health Act 1959, s 128, an offence under the Indecency with Children Act 1960, s 1 (indecent conduct towards child under 14), and an offence under the Criminal Law Act 1977, s 54 (incitement of child under 16 to commit incest).

[16] The offences are any offence under any of ss 33–36 of the Sexual Offences Act 1956, the Protection of Children Act 1978, the Sexual Offences Act 2003, Pt 1, any of ss 1–32 of the Sexual Offences Act 1956, the Indecency with Children Act 1960, the Sexual Offences Act 1967, or the Criminal Law Act 1977, s 54 (s 35(3)(a)); and kidnapping, false imprisonment, or an offence under the Child Abduction Act 1984, s 1 or s 2, any offence under the Children and Young Persons Act 1933, s 1, and any offence (not already listed) which involves an assault on, or injury, or a threat of injury to, any person (s 35(3)(b), (c), and (d)).

which that person is charged in the proceedings. A 'protected witness' is a witness[17] who (a) is the complainant or is alleged to have been a witness to the commission of the offence; and (b) either is a child or falls to be cross-examined after giving evidence-in-chief (i) by means of a video recording made for the purposes of s 27 of the 1999 Act (video-recorded evidence admitted as evidence-in-chief)[18] at a time when the witness was a child, or (ii) in any other way at any such time.[19]

Section 36 gives the court a general power, in a case where neither s 34 nor s 35 operates, to give a direction prohibiting the accused from cross-examining a witness in person.[20] Under s 36(2), such a direction may be given if it appears to the court that (a) 'the quality of evidence[21] given by the witness on cross-examination—(i) is likely to be diminished if the cross-examination . . . is conducted by the accused in person, and (ii) would be likely to be improved if a direction were given . . .' and (b) it would not be contrary to the interests of justice.[22]

Where an accused is prevented from cross-examining a witness in person under s 34, s 35, or s 36, the court must invite the accused to arrange for a legal representative to act for him for the purpose of the cross-examination, and if the invitation is not taken up, must consider whether it is necessary in the interests of justice for the witness to be cross-examined by a legal representative, chosen and appointed by the court, to represent the interests of the accused.[23]

The permitted form of questioning in cross-examination

The permitted form of questioning in cross-examination is conveniently considered by reference to the aims of cross-examination. These are twofold: the cross-examiner will seek (i) to elicit evidence which supports his version of the facts in issue and (ii) to cast doubt upon the witness's evidence. Before giving further consideration to these aims, it is useful to note four general matters. First, a witness under cross-examination may be asked leading questions. Such questions may be asked even if he appears to be more favourable to the cross-examiner than to the party who called him, and whether the questions are directed to either the first or second of the two objects of cross-examination.[24] Second, there are special restrictions on the cross-examination of young and vulnerable witnesses and also of complainants in proceedings for sexual offences. The restrictions are considered later in this chapter. Third,

---

[17] A 'witness' includes a witness who is a co-accused: s 35(5) and *R (S) v Waltham Forest Youth Court* [2004] 2 Cr App R 335 (21), DC at [27].

[18] See **Ch 5**.

[19] Section 35(2). Child means, where the offence falls within s 35(3)(a), a person under the age of 18; or, where the offence falls within s 35(3)(b), (c), or (d), a person under the age of 14. See **n 16**.

[20] A 'witness', for these purposes, does not include a co-accused: s 36(4)(a).

[21] 'The quality of evidence' is to be construed in accordance with s 16(5) (s 36(4)(b)): see **Ch 5, Special measures directions for vulnerable and intimidated witnesses, p 155**.

[22] As to the matters to be taken into account, in deciding whether s 36(2)(a) applies, see s 36(3).

[23] Section 38(1)–(5). The duty of the court-appointed advocate is to cross-examine a particular witness and to ensure that he is in a position to do so, and therefore the duty may include, for example, applications to admit evidence of the bad character of the witness: *Abbas v CPS* [2015] EWHC 579. As to warning the jury to prevent prejudice to the accused, see s 39. As to the need for statutory provision to appoint legal representatives in civil cases, see per Lord Dyson MR in *Re K and H* [2015] EWCA Civ 543 at [62].

[24] *Parkin v Moon* (1836) 7 C&P 408.

many other witnesses may require assistance: the court must take every reasonable step to facilitate their participation, which includes enabling witnesses or accused to give their best evidence.[25] Fourth, all cross-examination is subject to a general constraint which applies whether the questions to be put to the witness go to matters in issue or to credit only. This is the discretion of the judge to prevent any questions which in his opinion are unnecessary, improper, or oppressive. Cross-examination, a powerful weapon entrusted to an advocate, should be conducted with restraint and with a measure of courtesy and consideration to the witness.[26] Thus an advocate will be restrained from embarking on lengthy cross-examination on matters that are not really in issue[27] and from framing his questions in such a way as to invite argument rather than elicit evidence on the facts in issue.[28] In criminal cases, entitlement to a fair trial is not inconsistent with proper judicial control over the use of time as part of the judge's responsibility to manage the trial.[29] It should not become a routine feature of trial management to impose time limits for cross-examination (or examination-in-chief), but if the advocate cross-examining indulges in prolix and repetitious questioning, judges are obliged to impose reasonable time limits; the advocate has a duty to put his client's case fearlessly but also to avoid wasting time.[30] The court does have power, whenever appropriate, to impose time limits in the case of children and otherwise vulnerable witnesses.[31] In civil proceedings, CPR r 32.1(3) bluntly provides that: 'The court may limit cross-examination.' When exercising this power, the judge must seek to give effect to the 'overriding objective', which is to enable the court 'to deal with cases justly',[32] and in deciding how long cross-examination should last in the interests of justice, for both parties and the witness, the judge may take into account any medical condition which the witness may have.[33]

Cross-examination as to matters in issue

The questions of the cross-examiner are not restricted to matters proved in examination-in-chief but may relate to any fact in issue or relevant to a fact in issue. This does not mean that evidence which is otherwise inadmissible can become admissible by being put to a witness in cross-examination: the ordinary rules relating to the inadmissibility of certain types of evidence operate to prevent such evidence from being elicited in cross-examination as well as in examination-in-chief. Thus an accused cannot be cross-examined upon inadmissible confessions inconsistent with his testimony.[34] Similarly, a party is unable to admit an inadmissible

---

[25] Criminal Practice Directions, para 3D.2.

[26] See per Sankey LC in *Mechanical & General Inventions Co Ltd v Austin* [1935] AC 346, HL at 360. See also r C7.1 of the Code of Conduct for barristers in the Bar Standards Handbook: '. . . you must not make statements or ask questions merely to insult, humiliate or annoy a witness . . .'

[27] *R v Kalia* [1975] Crim LR 181, CA and *Mechanical & General Inventions Co Ltd v Austin* [1935] AC 346, HL at 359.

[28] See per Lord Hewart CJ in *R v Baldwin* (1925) 18 Cr App R 175, CCA. Thus an advocate should not put to a witness what somebody else has said or is expected to say (at 178–9). Nor should the judge put such questions: *R v Wilson* [1991] Crim LR 838, CA.

[29] *R v Chaaban* [2003] Crim LR 658, CA and the Criminal Procedure Rules 2015, paras 1.1(2)(e), 3.2(2)(e), and 3.2(3).

[30] *R v B* [2006] Crim LR 54, CA.

[31] See, in this chapter, under **Young and vulnerable witnesses**, p 225.

[32] CPR r 1.1. See further Ch 2, Civil cases, p 173.

[33] *Three Rivers District Council v Bank of England* [2005] CP Rep 46, CA.

[34] *R v Treacy* [1944] 2 All ER 229, CCA. See also *R v Thomson* [1912] 3 KB 19, CCA and *R v Windass* (1988) 89 Cr App R 258, CA (inadmissible hearsay); *Re P* [1989] Crim LR 897, CA (inadmissible complaint in a sexual case); and *R v Gray* [1998] Crim LR 570, CA (interview with a co-accused inadmissible as against the accused). In civil proceedings, see *Beare v Garrod* (1915) 85 LJKB 717, CA and *Sharp v Loddington Ironstone Co Ltd* (1924) 132 LT 229, CA.

hearsay statement contained in a document by handing it to a witness under cross-examination and requiring him to read it aloud. The advocate may, of course, properly produce the document to the witness and ask him if he accepts the contents as true,[35] and, if the witness does, the contents of the document become evidence in the case. However, if the witness does not accept the contents as true, it would be improper for the advocate to request the witness to read aloud from the document, the contents of which remain inadmissible hearsay.[36]

The principle that an accused cannot be cross-examined by the *prosecution* in such a way as to reveal that he made a confession which has been ruled inadmissible also obtains in favour of any co-accused of the maker of such a confession.[37] However, where an accused has made a confession which has been ruled inadmissible but which is relevant to the defence of a co-accused, then if the accused gives evidence which is inconsistent with his statement, he may be cross-examined on it by the *co-accused*, provided that the judge directs the jury not to treat it as evidence of its maker's guilt.[38]

Cross-examination as to credit

Concerning the second object of cross-examination, at common law there is a wide variety of ways in which the cross-examining party may seek to cast doubt upon the witness's evidence-in-chief and to show that the witness ought not to be believed on his oath. He may cross-examine him about omissions or inconsistencies in previous statements, if either will affect his likely standing with the tribunal of fact;[39] he may question him about his means of knowledge of the facts to which he has testified; he may challenge the quality of his memory[40] and his powers of perception; he may ask him about his unreliability by reason of any physical or mental disability; and he may ask him to explain any delay in reporting the offence[41] as well as any omissions, mistakes, or inconsistencies in his evidence insofar as they militate against his veracity or plausibility. As to omissions, for example, where an accused is charged with a sexual offence and asserts fabrication on the part of the complainant, he may

---

[35] He should not, however, describe the nature or contents of the document to the court: see *R v Yousry* (1914) 11 Cr App R 13, CCA.

[36] *R v Gillespie* and *R v Simpson* (1967) 51 Cr App R 172, CA, applied in *R v Cooper* (1985) 82 Cr App R 74, CA; and *R v Cross* (1990) 91 Cr App R 115, CA.

[37] Per Winn J in *R v Rice* [1963] 1 QB 857, CCA at 868–9.

[38] *R v Rowson* [1986] QB 174, CA, followed in *Lui-Mei Lin v R* [1989] AC 288, PC and *R v Corelli* [2001] Crim LR 913, CA. See also *R v O'Boyle* (1990) 92 Cr App R 202, CA. The co-accused may also cross-examine prosecution witnesses on the confession if to do so will affect the cogency of the prosecution evidence against him: *R v Beckford* (1991) 94 Cr App R 43, CA. See also *R v Myers* [1998] AC 124, HL (Ch 15).

[39] He may do so even if evidence of the making of the statement would not be allowed because it is not 'relative to the subject matter of the indictment or proceeding' for the purposes of the Criminal Procedure Act 1865, s 4: *R v Funderburk* [1990] 1 WLR 587, CA. Section 4 of the 1865 Act is considered, in this chapter, under **Section 4 of the 1865 Act**, p 222.

[40] For a consideration of issues relating to memory as they arise in legal proceedings, see: The British Psychological Society Memory and the Law Working Party, *Guidelines on Memory and the Law: Recommendations from the Scientific Study of Human Memory* (British Psychological Society, 2008).

[41] The trauma of serious sexual assault may cause feelings of shame and guilt leading to a delayed complaint and therefore a judge may direct a jury that a late complaint is not necessarily false: see *R v D* [2008] EWCA Crim 2557; *R v Miller* [2010] EWCA Crim 1578; and *R v GJB* [2011] EWCA Crim 867. For directions on this and other potentially unwarranted assumptions that juries may make, or be invited by advocates to make, in sexual cases, see Part 1 of the Crown Court Compendium, 20–1.

be cross-examined as to what facts are known to him that might explain why the complainant would make a false accusation against him.[42] Questions about omissions or inconsistencies in previous statements, often relating to matters of less than central importance, are the stock-in-trade of cross-examination with a view to discrediting a witness by implying his unreliability or untruthfulness. However, as to omissions, research shows that, in the case of stressful events, central details are more likely to be remembered than peripheral details; equally, as to inconsistency, research shows that variability of memory is the norm, and can be exacerbated both by the impact of trauma, such as that experienced by victims of sexual assaults and, in the case of children, by under-developed communication skills.[43]

The cross-examining party may also ask questions about the witness's bad character and previous misconduct, including questions about previous convictions and questions with a view to showing his prejudice or bias. However, s 99 of the Criminal Justice Act 2003 (the 2003 Act) abolishes the common law rules governing the admissibility of evidence of 'bad character' in criminal proceedings and the intention appears to be to abolish not only the rules as to the introduction of such evidence, but also the rules governing cross-examination about conduct that comes within the statutory definition of 'bad character' in s 98 of the 2003 Act. The effect is that in criminal cases such cross-examination is only permitted if it comes within one of a number of specified categories of admissibility set out in s 100 (non-defendant's bad character) or s 101 (defendant's bad character). Evidence of bad character, for the purposes of these provisions, is evidence of, or a disposition towards, misconduct, other than evidence which 'has to do' with the alleged facts of the offence charged or evidence of misconduct in connection with the investigation or prosecution of that offence. Section 108 of the 2003 Act imposes an additional restriction in relation to offences committed by the accused when a child. Finally, under s 41 of the Youth Justice and Criminal Evidence Act 1999, in the case of sexual offences, except with the leave of the court, no question may be asked in cross-examination about any sexual behaviour of the complainant.[44]

Hobbs v Tinling[45] and *R v Sweet-Escott*[46] set out the general principles as to the propriety of cross-examining a witness as to his credit. They apply fully in civil proceedings but in criminal proceedings apply only insofar as the cross-examination relates to conduct which falls short of the statutory definition of 'bad character' in s 98 of the 2003 Act. In *Hobbs v Tinling*, Sankey LJ held that the court, in the exercise of its discretion to disallow questions as to credit in cross-examination, should have regard to the following considerations:

1. Such questions are proper if they are of such a nature that the truth of the imputation conveyed by them would seriously affect the opinion of the court as to the credibility of the witness on the matter to which he testifies.

---

[42] *R v B* [2003] 1 WLR 2809, CA, preferring *R v T* [1998] 2 NZLR 257 (New Zealand Court of Appeal) to *R v Palmer* (1998) 193 CLR 1 (Australian High Court).

[43] See Ellison, 'Closing the credibility gap; The prosecutorial use of expert witness testimony in sexual assault cases' (2006) 9 E&P 239 at 241–8, which cross-refers to much of the psychological and other research literature.

[44] The restrictions in the 2003 Act are considered in Ch 19. The restriction in the 1999 Act, s 41 is considered, in this chapter, under **The restriction**, p 231.

[45] [1929] 2 KB 1 at 51, CA.

[46] (1971) 55 Cr App R 316, Assizes.

2. Such questions are improper if the imputation which they convey relates to matters so remote in time, or of such a character, that the truth of the imputation would not affect, or would affect in a slight degree, the opinion of the court as to the credibility of the witness on the matter to which he testifies.

3. Such questions are improper if there is a great disproportion between the importance of the imputation made against the witness's character and the importance of his evidence.

In *R v Sweet-Escott* Lawton J posed the question: 'How far back is it permissible for advocates when cross-examining as to credit to delve into a man's past and to drag up such dirt as they can find there?' It was held that:

> Since the purpose of cross-examination as to credit is to show that the witness ought not to be believed on oath, the matters about which he is questioned must relate to his likely standing after cross-examination with the tribunal which is trying him or listening to his evidence.[47]

Putting one's case and the consequences of not doing so

A party may decide that there is no need to cross-examine at all, especially if the witness in question has become unfavourable or even hostile to the party calling him. A party's failure to cross-examine, however, has important consequences. It amounts to a tacit acceptance of the witness's evidence-in-chief. A party who has failed to cross-examine a witness upon a particular matter in respect of which it is proposed to contradict his evidence-in-chief or impeach his credit by calling other witnesses, will not be permitted to invite the jury or tribunal of fact to disbelieve the witness's evidence on that matter.[48] A cross-examiner who wishes to suggest to the jury that the witness is not speaking the truth on a particular matter must lay a proper foundation by putting that matter to the witness so that he has an opportunity of giving any explanation which is open to him.[49] The rule, however, is not absolute or inflexible. Thus if it is proposed to invite the jury to disbelieve a witness on a matter, it is not always necessary to put to him explicitly that he is lying, provided that the overall tenor of the cross-examination is designed to show that his account is incapable of belief.[50] In other cases, the story told by a witness may be so incredible that the matter upon which he is to be impeached is manifest, and in such circumstances it is unnecessary to waste time in putting questions to him upon it.[51] The most effective cross-examination in such a situation would be, in the words of Lord Morris, 'to ask him to leave the box'. The rule has also been held to be unsuitable in the case of proceedings in magistrates' courts.[52] It could be argued[53] that the rule should not apply in any criminal case, because there is no obligation on the accused to put his case by adducing evidence, but there is no authority to that effect.

---

[47] (1971) 55 Cr App R 316, Assizes at 320.

[48] Evidence to contradict a witness which was not put to the witness in cross-examination may still be admitted, provided that the witness is recalled and cross-examination of him reopened in order to put the new evidence to him: *R v Cannan* [1998] Crim LR 284, CA.

[49] *Browne v Dunn* (1893) 6 R 67, HL. See also *R v Hart* (1932) 23 Cr App R 202, CCA; *R v Bircham* [1972] Crim LR 430, CA; and *R v Fenlon* (1980) 71 Cr App R 307, CA. See also r C7.2 of the Code of Conduct for barristers in the Bar Standards Handbook.

[50] *R v Lovelock* [1997] Crim LR 821, CA.

[51] *Browne v Dunn* (1893) 6 R 67, HL.

[52] *O'Connell v Adams* [1973] Crim LR 313, DC. See also *Wilkinson v DPP* [2003] EWHC 865 (Admin).

[53] As in *R v Livirtis* [2004] NSWCCA 287.

In the case of a young or otherwise vulnerable witness, the court may impose restrictions on an advocate 'putting his case' in cross-examination.[54]

Cross-examination on documents

In civil proceedings, where a witness is called to give evidence at trial, he may be cross-examined on his witness statement,[55] whether or not the statement or any part of it was referred to during his evidence-in-chief.[56] An advocate cross-examining may also put to an opposing witness a statement taken on behalf of the cross-examiner's own client, but may not, it seems, cross-examine a witness called by an opposing party by reference to a statement of another witness who may or may not be called in the future by that opposing party or by someone other than the party on whose behalf the cross-examination is being conducted.[57]

The law relating to the cross-examination of a witness upon a previous statement made by him relative to the subject matter of the indictment or proceeding and inconsistent with his testimony is governed by ss 4 and 5 of the Criminal Procedure Act 1865 (the 1865 Act).[58] The common law and statutory rules on the cross-examination of a witness upon a document used by him to refresh his memory are considered in **Chapter 6.**

Previous inconsistent statements

If it is put to a witness,[59] in cross-examination, that he has made a previous oral or written statement inconsistent with his testimony, and the witness admits that he has made such a statement, no further proof of the making of the statement is needed or permitted.[60] However, if the witness denies making the statement, or does not distinctly admit that he made it, and the statement is 'relative to the subject matter of the indictment', then it may be proved against him. The proof of such a statement in both civil and criminal proceedings is governed by ss 4 and 5 of the 1865 Act. Section 5 applies only to written statements, whereas s 4 applies to both oral and written statements.[61] Additional restrictions may be applied in the case of young or otherwise vulnerable witnesses.[62]

Section 4 of the 1865 Act

Section 4 provides that:

> If a witness, upon cross-examination as to a former statement made by him relative to the subject matter of the indictment or proceeding, and inconsistent with his present testimony, does not distinctly admit that he has made such a statement, proof may be given that he did in fact make it; but before such proof can be given, the circumstances of the supposed statement, sufficient to designate the particular occasion, must be mentioned to the witness, and he must be asked whether or not he has made such statement.

---

[54] See, in this chapter, under **Young and vulnerable witnesses**, p 225.

[55] See Ch 5.

[56] CPR r 32.11.

[57] *Fairfield-Mabey Ltd v Shell UK Ltd* [1989] 1 All ER 576, QBD, a decision on an earlier version of the rules.

[58] See below, under **Section 4 of the 1865 Act** and **Section 5 of the 1865 Act.**

[59] In the case of hostile witnesses, see Ch 6, **Hostile witnesses**, p 207.

[60] *R v P (GR)* [1998] Crim LR 663, CA.

[61] *R v Derby Magistrates' Court, ex p B* [1996] AC 487, HL, per Lord Taylor CJ at 498.

[62] See, in this chapter, under **Young and vulnerable witnesses**, p 225.

This section assumes, correctly, the existence of a common law right to cross-examine a witness about a former inconsistent statement. It is not confined to previous statements made on oath.[63] The section refers to a witness who 'does not distinctly admit' his previous statement and accordingly applies not only to a witness who clearly denies the statement but also to a witness who, neither denying nor admitting the statement, is equivocal, asserts that he has no recollection of it, or refuses to answer.

Whether a statement is 'relative to the subject matter of the indictment or proceeding' is a matter within the discretion of the judge.[64] In *R v Funderburk*[65] F was charged with counts of sexual intercourse with a girl of 13. She gave evidence of a number of acts of intercourse with F, and her evidence of the first act clearly described the loss of her virginity. The defence claimed that she was lying and in order to explain how a girl of her age, if lying, could have given such detailed and varied accounts of the acts of intercourse, wished to show that she was sexually experienced and had either transposed to F experiences with others or fantasized about experiences with F. They wished (a) to put to her that she had told a Miss P that, before the first incident complained of, she had had sexual intercourse with two men; and, if she denied making this previous inconsistent statement, (b) to call P to prove the conversation. As to (a), it was held that the proper test for cross-examination as to credit was not the test set out in the 1865 Act, but that suggested by Lawton J in *R v Sweet-Escott*,[66] and that the cross-examination should have been allowed because the jury might then have wished to reappraise the girl's evidence about the loss of her virginity. As to (b), it was held that the conversation, if denied, could have been proved, because the previous statement did not merely go to credit but was also 'relative to the subject matter of the indictment': where the disputed issue is a sexual one between two persons in private, the difference between questions going to credit and questions going to the issue is reduced to vanishing point.[67] This principle, as we shall see, is not confined to sexual cases.[68]

Section 5 of the 1865 Act

Unlike s 4, s 5 applies only to previous written statements. It provides that:

> A witness may be cross-examined as to previous statements made by him in writing or reduced into writing relative to the subject-matter of the indictment or proceeding, without such writing being shown to him; but if it is intended to contradict such witness by the writing, his attention must, before such contradictory proof can be given, be called to those parts of the writing which are to be used for the purpose of so contradicting him; provided always, that it shall be competent for the judge, at any time during the trial, to require the production of the writing for his inspection, and he may thereupon make such use of it for the purposes of the trial as he may think fit.

Section 5 expressly permits the cross-examination of a witness about a previous statement contained in a document without that document being shown to him, but because the judge, pursuant to s 5, may require production of the document and make such use of it as he may think

---

[63] *R v Hart* (1957) 42 Cr App R 47, CCA; *R v O'Neill* [1969] Crim LR 260, CA.

[64] See per Veale J in *R v Bashir and Manzur* [1969] 1 WLR 1303, Assizes at 1306.

[65] [1990] 1 WLR 587, CA. Cf, *sed quaere, R v Gibson* [1993] Crim LR 453, CA.

[66] (1971) 55 Cr App R 316, CA (see n 47).

[67] See also *R v Nagrecha* [1997] 2 Cr App R 401, CA; and cf *R v Neale* [1998] Crim LR 737, CA.

[68] See, in this chapter, under **Finality of answers to collateral questions**, p 242.

fit, the cross-examining party must have the document with him even if he does not intend to contradict the witness with it.[69] If that party wishes to contradict the witness, he should, without reading the contents of the document aloud, hand it to the witness, direct his attention to the relevant part of its contents, ask him to read that part of the document to himself, and then inquire whether he still wishes to stand by the evidence which he has given. If the witness adopts the previous statement, it becomes part of his evidence, which has therefore changed, and to that extent his credibility will have been impeached. If the witness adheres to his original evidence, there is no obligation on the cross-examining party to put the document in evidence, a course which he may well wish to avoid if the discrepancy is minor or the document, taken as a whole, tends to confirm rather than contradict the witness.[70] The cross-examining party, therefore, may simply accept the answer given and move on to some other matter. However, if the cross-examining party does wish to contradict the witness, he must then prove the document and put it in evidence.[71] After reading aloud the relevant parts of the previous statement, or inviting the witness to do so, the cross-examining party will put it to the witness that the truth of the matter is contained in the earlier statement as opposed to his evidence. Once the document has been put in evidence, the tribunal of fact may inspect it in its entirety, looking at those passages, if any, which are consistent, as well as those which are inconsistent with the evidence given by the witness. However, although the *whole* document may be put before the jury, because under s 5 the judge may 'make such use of it for the purposes of the trial as he may think fit', he has a discretion to permit the jury to see only those parts on which the cross-examination was based, and not other parts relating to other unconnected matters.[72]

Admissibility as evidence of the matter stated

Where a prior inconsistent statement has been put in evidence under s 4 or s 5 of the 1865 Act, in both civil and criminal proceedings it is admitted as evidence of inconsistency *potentially* going to credit: it is not a necessary indicator of untruthfulness and, in appropriate cases, the judge may need to direct the jury to this effect.[73] It is also admitted as evidence of the matters stated. Under s 1 of the Civil Evidence Act 1995, in civil proceedings evidence shall not be excluded on the ground that it is hearsay. Section 6(3) and (5) of the 1995 Act provide as follows:

(3) Where in the case of civil proceedings section . . . 4 or 5 of the Criminal Procedure Act 1865 applies, which make provision as to—

. . .

(b) the proof of contradictory statements made by a witness, and

(c) cross-examination as to previous statements made in writing, this Act does not authorise the adducing of evidence of a previous inconsistent or contradictory statement otherwise than in accordance with those sections. . ..

(5) Nothing in this section shall be construed as preventing a statement of any description referred to above from being admissible by virtue of s 1 as evidence of the matters stated.

---

[69] *R v Anderson* (1930) 21 Cr App R 178, CCA.

[70] For an example of a case where the admission of a prior inconsistent statement must have been, at best, a mixed blessing, see *R v Askew* [1981] Crim LR 398, CA, where the advocate for the defence cross-examined the victim of an alleged rape on a statement made to the police in which she had incriminated the appellant. But see *R v Beattie* (1989) 89 Cr App R 302, CA (see n 72).

[71] Per Channell B in *R v Riley* (1866) 4 F&F 964; *R v Wright* (1866) 4 F&F 967.

[72] *R v Beattie* (1989) 89 Cr App R 302, CA.

[73] The Crown Court Compendium (July 2019), Part 1, 20–1, para 10(1) and Example 4.

As to criminal proceedings, s 119(1) of the Criminal Justice Act 2003, which is considered further in **Chapter 12**, provides as follows:

(1) If in criminal proceedings, a person gives oral evidence and—
   (a) he admits making a previous inconsistent statement, or
   (b) a previous inconsistent statement made by him is proved by virtue of section 3, 4 or 5 of the Criminal Procedure Act 1865,
   the statement is admissible as evidence of any matter stated of which oral evidence by him would be admissible.

In both civil and criminal cases, therefore, the tribunal of fact will have to decide whether the truth is to be found in what the witness said on oath, in what he said in the previous statement but denied on oath, or is to be found elsewhere because neither version can be accepted as the truth of the matter.[74] By allowing a previous inconsistent statement to be put before the tribunal of fact for the truth of the matter stated, s 119 of the 2003 Act has introduced a significant change to criminal proceedings which can operate unfairly to the prejudice of the accused. Protection is contained in the court's powers to exclude evidence,[75] to direct an acquittal, or discharge the jury where the evidence provided by the statement is unconvincing,[76] and to give appropriate directions to the jury.[77]

Young and vulnerable witnesses

In **Chapter 6**, consideration was given to the particular needs of young and otherwise vulnerable witnesses and the general action that needs to be taken, before trial, to ensure that they give their 'best evidence'. As to cross-examination, traditional cross-examination techniques can confuse such witnesses, reducing their ability to understand the questions and the accuracy of their answers.[78] Belated recognition of the issue has resulted in a range of new law, including various judicial dicta, Criminal Practice Directions, a Judicial College Checklist, and guidance from the Inns of Court College of Advocacy (formerly the Advocacy Training Council), all of which, in their detail, overlap to a considerable extent.

The Criminal Practice Directions

Paragraphs 3E.1, 3E.4, and 3E.5 of the Criminal Practice Directions provide as follows:

3E.1 The judiciary is responsible for controlling questioning. Over-rigorous or repetitive cross-examination of a child or vulnerable witness should be stopped . . .

---

[74] In criminal proceedings, before the jury may rely on either the witness's evidence or prior statement as evidence of truth supporting the prosecution case, they must be sure that it is true. Where it is exculpatory of the defendant, it is sufficient if the jury are persuaded that it *may* be true: *R v Billingham* [2009] 2 Cr App R 341 (20), CA.

[75] See, eg, *R v Coates* [2008] 1 Cr App R 52 (3), CA.

[76] The 2003 Act, s 125.

[77] See *R v Joyce* [2005] EWCA Crim 1785 and *R v Bennett* [2008] EWCA Crim 248.

[78] On the need for new systems for the training and accreditation of advocates in this respect, see Keane, 'Cross-examination of vulnerable witnesses—towards a blueprint for re-professionalisation' (2012) 16 E&P 153. See also Henderson, 'Communicative Competence? Judges, Advocates and Intermediaries Discuss Communication Issues in the Cross-examination of Vulnerable Witnesses' [2015] Crim LR 659.

3E.4   All witnesses, including the defendant and defence witnesses should be enabled to give the best evidence they can.[79] In relation to young and/or vulnerable people, this may mean departing radically from traditional cross-examination. The form and extent of appropriate cross-examination will vary from case to case. For adult non vulnerable witnesses an advocate will usually put his case so that the witness will have the opportunity of commenting upon it and/or answering it. When the witness is young or otherwise vulnerable, the court may dispense with the normal practice and impose restrictions on the advocate 'putting his case'[80] where there is a risk of a young or otherwise vulnerable witness failing to understand, becoming distressed or acquiescing to leading questions.[81] Where limitations on questioning are necessary and appropriate, they must be clearly defined. The judge has a duty to ensure that they are complied with and should explain them to the jury and the reasons for them. If the advocate fails to comply with the limitations, the judge should give relevant directions to the jury when that occurs and prevent further questioning that does not comply with the ground rules settled upon in advance.[82] Instead of commenting on inconsistencies during cross-examination, following discussion between the judge and the advocates, the advocate or judge may point out important inconsistencies after (instead of during) the witness's evidence.[83] The judge should also remind the jury of these during summing-up. The judge should be alert to alleged inconsistencies that are not in fact inconsistent, or are trivial.

[79] In *R v Grant-Murray* [2017] EWCA Crim 1228, a case which concerned vulnerable accused who were children, the Court of Appeal emphasized and confirmed ('if confirmation was needed') that the principles in *R v Lubemba* [2015] 1 WLR 1579 (which endorsed the criminal practice directions) applied to defendants as much as to any other witnesses (see [113] and [226]). See also n 92. For an example of objectionable questioning of a vulnerable accused, the vulnerability being significant learning difficulties which may not have been apparent to the jury, see *R v Jones* [2018] EWCA Crim 2816. Many questions were charged, rhetorical and involved comment, and would have been objectionable whether the accused was vulnerable or not (at [99]).

[80] For the first reported example, see *R v E* [2011] EWCA Crim 3028. As to the correctness of the decision and how use could have been, but was not, made of evidential human rights norms developed under Art 6.1 and 6.3(d) of the European Convention on Human Rights, see Keane, 'Towards a Principled Approach to the Cross-examination of Vulnerable Witnesses' [2012] Crim LR 407.

[81] Where there is a real possibility that a young child appearing for the prosecution has assented to a suggestion to please or to bring questioning to an end, or a speedier end, making it very difficult to tell whether he is truly changing his account or just taking the line of least resistance, it may lead to a successful submission of no case to answer if the evidence, taken at its highest, is such that no jury could safely be sure of guilt, but not where the jury can conclude, particularly in the light of other evidence, that the child was not agreeing in any meaningful way: *R v W* [2010] EWCA Crim 126. However, concerning the duty to put the accused's case, see immediately below in this chapter under, **Duty to put the accused's case, p 227.**

[82] See also, to similar effect, *R v Wills* [2012] 1 Cr App R 16 (2).

[83] See also per Lord Judge CJ in *R v Barker* [2012] EWCA Crim 4: '. . . the advocate may have to forego much of the kind of contemporary cross-examination which consists of no more than comments on matters which will be before the jury in any event from different sources . . . Comment on the evidence, including comment on evidence which may bear adversely on the credibility of the child, should be addressed after the child has finished giving evidence'. In *R v Wills* [2012] 1 Cr App R 16 (2) at [39], this was taken to mean, in the case of important inconsistencies at any rate, immediately after the child has given evidence. See also *R v M* [2019] 2 Cr App R 39 (5), CA at [21]: 'If any specific issues of content have been identified that the cross-examiner cannot explore, the judge may wish to direct the jury about them after the cross-examination is completed. On any view, the judge should direct the jury about them in the summing-up.'

3E.5 If there is more than one defendant, the judge should not permit each advocate to repeat the questioning of a vulnerable witness. In advance of the trial, the advocates should divide the topics between them, with the advocate for the first defendant leading the questioning, and the advocate(s) for the other defendant(s) asking only ancillary questions relevant to their client's case, without repeating the questioning that has already taken place on behalf of the other defendant(s).[84]

Limitations on cross-examination

In paragraph 3E.4 above, it is stated that, 'Where limitations on questioning are necessary and appropriate, they must be clearly defined'. In *R v M*,[85] the court of Appeal observed that: '. . .the identification of any limitations on cross-examination should take place at an early stage. We assume this will occur at the ground rules hearing where the judge will discuss with the advocates the nature and extent of the limitations and whether they are simply as to style or also relate to content'.[86] As to the process by which limitations are defined, it was said in *R v Lubemba*[87] that, '. . . it would be an entirely reasonable step for a judge . . . to invite defence advocates to reduce their questions to writing in advance.'[88] It is submitted that this applies equally to prosecution advocates intending to cross-examine a vulnerable accused or vulnerable witnesses for the accused.[89] Advocates may be required to submit a list of questions not only where cross-examination will be live, but also where recorded cross-examination has been ordered under s 28 of the Youth Justice and Criminal Evidence Act 1999.[90] The value of a written list of questions is that it may ensure that advocates ask more focused and effective questions during cross-examination.[91]

Duty to put the accused's case

It is also stated in paragraph 3E.4 above that the court may dispense with the normal practice and impose restrictions on the advocate 'putting his case'. In *R v Lubemba*[92] the Court of Appeal cast doubt on the right of an advocate to put her case at all: 'If there is a right to "put one's case" (about which we have our doubts) it must be modified for young or vulnerable witnesses. It is perfectly possible to ensure the jury are made aware of the defence case and of significant inconsistencies without intimidation or distressing a witness . . .' The effect may have been to encourage what the Court of Appeal in *R v RK*[93] were told was 'an increasing practice' for defence advocates not to cross-examine vulnerable witnesses, particularly child witnesses, to protect the child or avoid any suggestion of confronting the child.[94] Under

[84] Compliance with para 3E.5 will not, without more, result in an unfair trial: see *R v Jonas* [2015] EWCA Crim 562.

[85] [2019] 2 Cr App R 39 (5), CA.

[86] At [21].

[87] [2015] 1 WLR 1579, CA.

[88] At [43].

[89] See *R v Grant-Murray* [2017] EWCA Crim 1228 at [113] and [226] and n 81.

[90] See *R v Dinc* [2017] EWCA Crim 1206. See also Ch 5, Video-recorded cross-examination and re-examination, p 160.

[91] See *R v Dinc* [2017] EWCA Crim 1206 at [21]. See also *R v Usayi* [2017] EWCA Crim 1394. Only one point was flagged in the ground rules hearing and consequently the judge had not focused on reducing the cross-examination into writing. The court observed (at [38]) that the 'case stands as a reminder of the benefits of establishing the scope of cross-examination of a vulnerable witness giving evidence'.

[92] [2015] 1 WLR 1579 at [45].

[93] [2018] EWCA Crim 603.

[94] Ibid at [27].

the practice, defence advocates may, for example, ask the prosecutor and the judge to agree that the defence case may be adequately put by cross-examining another witness. In *R v RK*, the court questioned the practice of not cross-examining a vulnerable witness and re-affirmed the duty on defence advocates to put the accused's case, where possible: 'Although this court has in the past doubted the *right* to put every aspect of the defence case to a vulnerable witness, whatever the circumstances, it has not questioned the general *duty* to ensure the defence case is put fully and fairly and the witness challenged, where this is possible.'[95] Accordingly, where a child is assessed as competent the court would generally expect the child to be called and cross-examined with the benefit of a range of special measures. Where the defence propose not to cross-examine a vulnerable witness who gives evidence-in-chief by video recording, the prosecutor should think very carefully before agreeing to this and the judge should think carefully before approving it.[96]

Judicial College Bench Checklist: Young Witness Cases
Concerning children, the *Judicial College Bench Checklist: Young Witness Cases*[97] also seeks to ensure that young witnesses give their 'best evidence' and lists the directions that may be given to the advocates appearing for both sides at a 'ground rules' discussion. Many of the directions relate to both examination-in-chief and cross-examination and are considered in **Chapter 6**. The list includes the following three additional directions, which relate to cross-examination.

1. Avoid types of question which may produce unreliable answers. 'Tag' questions are particularly complex. A 'tag' question is a positive or negative statement followed by a question inviting acceptance that the statement is true, such as 'He was kind to you, wasn't he?' and 'He didn't touch you, did he?' The question should be put more directly, for example 'Did Jim touch you?' and, if the answer is 'Yes', 'How did Jim touch you?' (using Jim's name and not the pronoun 'he').[98]

2. Avoid allegations of misconduct without reasonable grounds. Being accused of lying, particularly if repeated, may cause a child to give inaccurate answers or to agree simply to bring questioning to an end.

3. In putting the defence case to younger children, inform the jury of the evidence believed to undermine credibility, which does not necessarily need to be covered in detail in cross-examination.

The Checklist also refers to the further and more detailed guidance provided by Plotnikoff and Woolfson in *Measuring Up? Evaluating implementation of Government commitments to young witnesses in criminal proceedings, Annexes A and B.*[99] That guidance states that prefatory phrases such as 'I suggest to you that . . .' and 'Isn't it a fact that . . .' are wholly inappropriate for

---

[95] Ibid at [27]. See also The Bar Standards Board Handbook, The Code of Conduct, rC15.1: 'you must promote fearlessly and by all proper and lawful means the *client's* best interests.'

[96] Ibid at [29].

[97] Accessible at https://www.judiciary.gov.uk/publications/jc-bench-checklist-young-wit-cases.

[98] In *R v Grant-Murray* [2017] EWCA Crim 128 at [114]–[115] and [194], the Court of Appeal noted that although it is particularly important to avoid tag questions because they are 'powerfully suggestive and linguistically complex', this does not mean that all tag questions will have an adverse effect on the witness; questions with two positives (eg, 'You hit her, did you?') are not necessarily complex or difficult to follow and even those with a positive and a negative (eg, 'You hit her, didn't you?') may not trouble a particular witness.

[99] Accessible at https://www.nspcc.org.uk/globalassets/documents/research-reports/measuring-up-report.pdf.

children, because when an adult in a powerful position formally suggests that something is a fact, it becomes extremely difficult for children—even those aged 11 and 12—to know how to disagree if necessary. The guidance also says that tag questions of all kinds should be avoided, because they are one of the most powerfully suggestive forms of speech and children often answer 'Yes' to a negative 'tag' question because it indicates cooperation and is often perceived to be the answer that the adult wants.

The Checklist also recommends judicial monitoring of the questioning of young witnesses with a view to ensuring that the tenor, tone, language, and duration of the questioning is developmentally appropriate to the particular child, preventing questioning that lacks relevance or is repetitive, oppressive, or intimidating, and identifying possible difficulties in understanding and asking the advocate to re-phrase.[100]

Other guidance

Further detailed guidance on how to conduct a 'ground rules' hearing and how to question vulnerable witnesses is to be found in Part I of the Crown Court Compendium, 10–5, on *The Advocate's Gateway* website,[101] in the report of the Inns of Court College of Advocacy (formerly the Advocacy Training Council), *Raising the Bar: The handling of vulnerable witnesses, victims and defendants in court,*[102] which was endorsed by the Court of Appeal in *R v Wills,*[103] and in the Criminal Bar Association's film, *A Question of Practice.*[104]

Witness distress while giving evidence

In *R v SG*[105] the following guidance was given in relation to witnesses who become distressed while giving evidence.

1. Very often a break will result in the witness becoming better able to give evidence.

2. In deciding on the right course of action, the court should balance the importance of a witness being able to give the best evidence she can without being harassed against the interest of an accused to properly challenge her account.

3. There may be a number of reasons for signs of distress, for example the stress of giving evidence or being caught out in a lie.

4. A witness exhibiting signs of distress is not necessarily a vulnerable witness.

5. If the witness is vulnerable, it may not be necessary to require the defence to prepare a list of further questions; a judge can intervene to prevent over-rigorous or repetitive questioning. The court should bear in mind the disadvantage of prepared questions, especially insofar as they may inhibit the development of cross-examination in response to a particular answer.

6. If the witness has no difficulty in understanding questions, requiring the preparation of a list of questions during cross-examination should be exceptional.

---

[100] See also *R v Lubemba* [2015] 1 WLR 1579, CA at [44]: 'The judge has a duty to intervene . . . if an advocate's questioning is confusing or inappropriate'. For a qualitative study, see Henderson, 'Taking Control of Cross-examination: Judges, Advocates and Intermediaries Discuss Judicial Management of the Cross-examination of Vulnerable People' [2016] Crim LR 181.

[101] https://www.theadvocatesgateway.org.

[102] Accessible at http://www.icca.ac.uk/advocacy-the-vulnerable/raising-the-bar.

[103] [2012] 1 Cr App R 16 (2).

[104] Accessible at http://www.criminalbar.com.

[105] [2017] EWCA Crim 617.

Vulnerable witness training and professional conduct

In *R v Grant-Murray*,[106] the Court of Appeal confirmed the importance of training for the profession in the questioning of vulnerable witnesses, emphasizing that '. . . it is, of course, generally misconduct for an advocate to take on a case where the advocate is not competent. . . [and] it would be difficult to conceive of an advocate being competent to act in a case involving young witnesses or defendants unless the advocate had undertaken specific training.'[107]

Complainants in proceedings for sexual offences

The rationale

In cases of rape and other sexual offences, whether, and to what extent, evidence may be adduced, or the complainant cross-examined, by or on behalf of the accused, about sexual experience with the accused or any other person, is now governed by ss 41–43 of the Youth Justice and Criminal Evidence Act 1999. These provisions, which restrict the use that the accused can make of evidence of the complainant's sexual history, reflect a recognition that it is bad for society if victims of sexual crimes do not complain for fear that they will be harassed unfairly at trial by questions about their previous sexual experiences, because in consequence the guilty may escape justice.[108] The intention underlying the provisions is also to counter what in the Canadian jurisprudence has been described as the twin myths that unchaste women are more likely to consent to intercourse and in any event are less worthy of belief.[109] Lord Steyn, in the leading case of *R v A (No 2)*, said:[110]

> Such generalized, stereotyped and unfounded prejudices ought to have no place in our legal system. But even in the very recent past such defensive strategies were habitually employed. It resulted in an absurdly low conviction rate in rape cases. It also inflicted unacceptable humiliation on complainants in rape cases.

Prior to the 1999 Act, a distinction was drawn between evidence of previous sexual experiences with the accused, which was admissible as rendering it more likely that the complainant consented on the occasion under investigation, and evidence of previous sexual experiences with others, which, under s 2 of the Sexual Offences (Amendment) Act 1976, now repealed, was only admissible if the judge was satisfied that it would be unfair to the accused to refuse its admission. No such distinction exists, in terms, under the 1999 Act, but a number of new and difficult distinctions have been introduced and have given rise to lively academic debate.[111] However, the impact of the provisions of the Act on the use of sexual

---

[106] [2017] EWCA Crim 1228.

[107] Ibid at [226]. See also *R v M* [2019] 2 Cr App R 39 (5) at [21] : '. . . every advocate (and the trial judge) is expected to ensure that they are up to date with the current best practice in the treatment of vulnerable witnesses.' See also, 'The Code of Conduct for Barristers' in *The Bar Standards Handbook*, r C 21.8 : 'You must not accept instructions to act in a particular matter if : . . . you are not competent to handle the matter or otherwise do not have enough experience to handle the matter. . .'

[108] As to the need for additional provision to regulate disclosure of a complainant's personal records, such as social work, counselling, and therapeutic medical or educational records, see Leahy, 'Too Much Information? Regulating Disclosure of Complainants' Personal Records in Sexual Offence Trials' [2016] Crim LR 229.

[109] See per McLachlin J in *R v Seaboyer* [1991] 2 SCR 577 (Supreme Court of Canada) at 604 and per Lords Steyn and Hutton in *R v A (No 2)* [2002] 1 AC 45, HL at [27] and [147] respectively.

[110] [2002] 1 AC 45, HL at [27].

[111] For relevant articles, see under **Additional Reading** at the end of this chapter.

history evidence appears to have been limited and the conviction rate for rape continued to fall after their implementation; there is certainly scope for strengthening the legislation.[112]

The restriction

Section 41(1) of the 1999 Act provides as follows:

> (1) If at a trial a person is charged with a sexual offence, then, except with the leave of the court—
> (a) no evidence may be adduced, and
> (b) no question may be asked in cross-examination,
> by or on behalf of any accused at the trial, about any sexual behaviour of the complainant.

Section 41 applies to a number of other proceedings, as it applies to a trial, including any hearing held, between conviction and sentencing, for the purposes of deciding matters relevant to the court's decision as to how the accused is to be dealt with, and the hearing of an appeal; and references in s 41 to a person charged with an offence accordingly include a person convicted of an offence.[113] 'Sexual offence' is to be construed in accordance with s 62.[114] 'Sexual behaviour' is defined in s 42(1)(c), which provides as follows:

> (c) 'sexual behaviour' means any sexual behaviour or other sexual experience, whether or not involving any accused or other person, but excluding (except in s 41(3)(c)(i) and (5)(a)) anything alleged to have taken place as part of the event which is the subject matter of the charge against the accused.

Such a definition, it is submitted, covers not only physical advances of a sexual nature, but also verbal advances.[115] The definition covers the viewing of pornography, sexually charged internet messaging, and answering questions in a sexually explicit quiz.[116] It also covers sexual behaviour or sexual experience even if it does not involve any other person, for example the use of a vibrator, which could be relevant as evidence of the possible cause of the ruptured state of a complainant's hymen.[117] Whether behaviour or experience is 'sexual' cannot depend upon the perception of the complainant, because that would result in many vulnerable people, including children and those with learning difficulties, losing the protection of s 41.[118] A question about an abortion may amount to a question about sexual behaviour, but not a question about the complainant's conduct in accepting from the accused emotional and financial support in relation to an abortion performed after the offence, when relevant as tending to detract from her claim that she regarded him with distaste because of the sexual abuse.[119]

In *R v B*[120] it was held that there is no difference in substance between questions of a female complainant about her suggested sexual habits or promiscuity or frequency of casual sexual

---

[112] For an evaluation of the impact of s 41 and recommendations for improvement, see the study commissioned by the Home Office, Kelly et al, *Section 41: an evaluation of new legislation limiting sexual history evidence in rape trials*, Home Office Online Report 20/06. Cf Wolchover and Heaton-Armstrong, 'Debunking rape myths' (2008) 158 NLJ 117.

[113] Section 42(3).

[114] See s 42(1)(d), s 42(2) and n 15.

[115] See *R v Hinds* [1979] Crim LR 111 (Crown Court) and *R v Viola* [1982] 1 WLR 1138, CA, both decided under the Sexual Offences (Amendment) Act 1976.

[116] *R v Ben-Rejab* [2012] 1 WLR 2364, CA.

[117] Cf *R v Barnes* [1994] Crim LR 691, CA.

[118] *R v E* [2005] Crim LR 227, CA.

[119] *R v P(R)* [2014] 1 WLR 3058, CA; and cf *R v K(P)* [2008] EWCA Crim 434.

[120] [2007] Crim LR 910, CA.

engagement and questions of a male complainant about his suggested homosexuality and casual homosexual encounters. In each case the questions are predicated on the proposition that previous consent is evidence of present consent and fall squarely within the restriction in s 41(1).

False statements or failure to complain

In *R v T*[121] it was held that, normally, questions or evidence about the complainant's past false statements about sexual assaults, or about a failure to complain about the assault which is the subject matter of the charge at the time when she complained about sexual assaults by others, are not 'about' any sexual behaviour of the complainant, because they relate not to her sexual behaviour but to her past statements or her past failure to complain, and the purpose of the 1999 Act was not to exclude such evidence. However, it was also held, *per curiam*, that if the defence wish to put questions about previous false complaints, they should seek a ruling from the judge that s 41 does not exclude them. It would be improper to put such questions as a device to smuggle in evidence about the complainant's past sexual behaviour. In any such case, the defence must have a proper evidential basis for asserting that the previous statement was both made and untrue. Without such a basis, the questions are not about lies but about sexual behaviour within the meaning of s 41(1).[122] Whether there is a 'proper evidential basis' is a fact-sensitive exercise of judgment rather than discretion.[123] In *R v M*[124] it was held that a 'proper evidential basis' is less than a strong factual foundation for concluding that the previous complaint was false, but must comprise some material from which that conclusion can properly be reached. Similarly, it has been held that the defence must be able to point to material that is capable of supporting, and not which must inevitably support, the inference of falsity.[125] However, in *R v D*[126] it was held, confusingly, that the earlier authorities are not to be taken as authorizing the use of a trial to investigate the truth or falsity of a previous allegation merely because there is some material which could be used to try and persuade a jury that it was in fact false. The mere fact that a complaint is raised and not pursued does not necessarily mean that it is false, even where this has happened more than once.[127] However, where there is evidence of a complaint, a 'proper evidential basis' for falsity may, depending on the circumstances, derive from the complainant's subsequent failure to cooperate with the police,[128] unless, it is submitted, there is evidence to establish reasons for non-cooperation other than fabrication, such as fear of the criminal process itself. The mere fact that the police decided that there was insufficient evidence to prosecute does not provide a 'proper evidential basis' for falsity;[129] and the decision of the Crown Prosecution Service not to prosecute is irrelevant—it is for the court to decide whether there is a 'proper evidential basis'.[130] Where there is a 'proper evidential basis', there is an additional hurdle:

---

[121] [2002] 1 WLR 632, CA.

[122] Applied in *R v E* [2005] Crim LR 227, CA.

[123] *R v All-Hilly* [2014] 2 Cr App R 530 (33).

[124] [2009] EWCA Crim 618; see also *R v Garaxo* [2005] Crim LR 883, CA.

[125] *R v E* [2009] EWCA Crim 2668. The number of previous allegations, by itself, will not entitle the defence to explore the possibility of their falsity: *R v A* [2012] EWCA Crim 1273.

[126] [2009] EWCA Crim 2137.

[127] *R v All-Hilly* [2014] 2 Cr App R 530 (33).

[128] *R v V* [2006] EWCA Crim 1901 and *R v Garaxo* [2005] Crim LR 883, CA.

[129] *R v D* [2009] EWCA Crim 2137.

[130] *Davarifar v R* [2009] EWCA Crim 2294.

leave is required under s 100(1) of the 2003 Act,[131] because questioning about previous false complaints would relate to the bad character of the complainant.[132] However, leave may not be required if the complaint was not a deliberate lie but, for example, the product of alcoholism and personality problems and so is not 'reprehensible behaviour' and therefore not misconduct as defined in s 98 of the 2003 Act.[133]

The principle established in *R v T* has no application where an accused seeks to adduce evidence of the fact that a statement was made by the complainant about her previous sexual experience simply to show that the statement was made, rather than that it was false, as when it is argued that it is relevant to a defence of belief in consent: such evidence falls within s 41(1).[134] Nor does the principle apply to evidence or questions about the complainant's false denials concerning her previous sexual experiences because the falsity of the denial can only be exposed if the complainant's sexual behaviour is established.[135]

Evidence adduced by the prosecution

Section 41 only applies to evidence to be adduced or questions to be put 'by or on behalf of any accused at the trial'. In appropriate circumstances, therefore, evidence of the complainant's sexual behaviour may be adduced by the prosecution, as in *R v Soroya*,[136] where the evidence was relevant to the issue of consent because it showed that the complainant had *falsely* told the accused that she was a virgin in the hope that this might cause him to desist from the assault on her. The court rejected the argument that because such evidence cannot be introduced by the defence, its admission infringes the principle of equality of arms between the defence and prosecution in breach of the right to a fair trial under Art 6 of the European Convention on Human Rights, observing that, where appropriate, s 78 of the Police and Criminal Evidence Act 1984 can be deployed.

When the restriction may be lifted

Under s 41(2) of the 1999 Act, the court may not give leave in relation to any evidence or question unless satisfied that (a) the evidence or question is of the kind specified in s 41(3) or (5) and (b) a refusal of leave might render unsafe a conclusion of the jury or court on any 'relevant issues in the case', that is, any issue falling to be proved by the prosecution or defence in the trial of the accused.[137] Subsection (3) covers evidence or questions relating to a relevant issue in the case and draws an important distinction between cases in which that issue is not an 'issue of consent' and cases in which it is. An 'issue of consent', for these purposes, means any issue whether the complainant in fact consented to the conduct constituting the offence with which the accused is charged (and accordingly does not include any issue as to the belief of the accused that the complainant so consented).[138] Subsection (5) covers evidence or questions to rebut or explain evidence adduced by the prosecution about any sexual behaviour of the complainant.

---

[131] See Ch 19.
[132] *R v V* [2006] EWCA Crim 1901.
[133] *Davarifar v R* [2009] EWCA Crim 2294.
[134] *R v W* [2005] Crim LR 965, CA.
[135] *R v Winter* [2008] Crim LR 971, CA.
[136] [2007] Crim LR 181, CA.
[137] Section 42(1)(a).
[138] Section 42(1)(b).

Where leave is given to lift the restriction and under cross-examination the complainant denies the sexual behaviour, the rule of finality of answers to questions on collateral matters[139] does not apply so as to prevent the admissibility of evidence to contradict her, because (i) if the evidence or question goes solely or mainly to the complainant's credibility, it will be inadmissible under s 41(4)[140] and (ii) where leave is given, the statute clearly provides for both the asking of questions and the calling of evidence.[141]

Section 41(2) to (8) provide as follows:

(2) The court may give leave in relation to any evidence or question only on an application made by or on behalf of an accused, and may not give such leave unless it is satisfied—

(a) that subsection (3) or (5) applies; and

(b) that a refusal of leave might have the result of rendering unsafe a conclusion of the jury or (as the case may be) the court on any relevant issue in the case.

(3) This subsection applies if the evidence or question relates to a relevant issue in the case and either—

(a) that issue is not an issue of consent; or

(b) it is an issue of consent and the sexual behaviour of the complainant to which the evidence or question relates is alleged to have taken place at or about the same time as the event which is the subject matter of the charge against the accused; or

(c) it is an issue of consent and the sexual behaviour of the complainant to which the evidence or question relates is alleged to have been, in any respect, so similar—

(i) to any sexual behaviour of the complainant which (according to evidence adduced or to be adduced by or on behalf of the accused) took place as part of the event which is the subject matter of the charge against the accused, or

(ii) to any other sexual behaviour of the complainant which (according to such evidence) took place at or about the same time as that event, that the similarity cannot reasonably be explained as a coincidence.

(4) For the purposes of subsection (3) no evidence or question shall be regarded as relating to a relevant issue in the case if it appears to the court to be reasonable to assume that the purpose (or main purpose) for which it would be adduced or asked is to establish or elicit material for impugning the credibility of the complainant as a witness.

(5) This subsection applies if the evidence or question—

(a) relates to any evidence adduced by the prosecution about any sexual behaviour of the complainant; and

(b) in the opinion of the court, would go no further than is necessary to enable the evidence adduced by the prosecution to be rebutted or explained by or on behalf of the accused.

(6) For the purposes of subsections (3) and (5) the evidence or question must relate to a specific instance (or specific instances) of alleged sexual behaviour on the part of the complainant (and accordingly nothing in those subsections is capable of applying in relation to the evidence or question to the extent that it does not so relate).

(7) Where this section applies in relation to a trial by virtue of the fact that one or more of a number of persons charged in the proceedings is or are charged with a sexual offence—

(a) it shall cease to apply in relation to the trial if the prosecutor decides not to proceed with the case against that person or those persons in respect of that charge; but

---

[139] See, in this chapter, under **Finality of answers to collateral questions, p 242.**

[140] See, in this chapter, under **Section 41(4)—where the purpose is to impugn credibility, p 240.**

[141] *R v Evans* [2016] EWCA Crim 452.

(b) it shall not cease to do so in the event of that person or those persons pleading guilty to, or being convicted of, that charge.

(8) Nothing in this section authorises any evidence to be adduced or any question to be asked which cannot be adduced or asked apart from this section.

The test in s 41(2)(b)

Before leave can be granted, the test in s 41(2)(b) must always be met. It would seem that 'a refusal of leave might have the result of rendering unsafe a conclusion of the jury . . . on any relevant issue' (which typically, in a rape case, will be the issue of consent or mistaken belief in consent), where to disallow the evidence or question would prevent the jury (or court) from hearing (taking into account) something which might cause them to change their minds on that issue. This hurdle, therefore, is not particularly high: the court need only be satisfied that a refusal of leave *might* have the consequence specified, not that such a consequence is probable. The last point is of particular significance where s 41(3)(a) applies, that is, where the evidence or question relates to a relevant issue in the case other than whether the complainant in fact consented, because in such cases s 41(2)(b) is the *only* condition to be met.

Exercise of judgment, not discretion

The operation of s 41 involves not the exercise of judicial discretion but making a judgment whether to admit evidence said by the defence to be relevant. The judge has no discretion to exclude evidence admissible under s 41 and therefore cannot exclude it, for example, on the basis that it has been raised without advance notice, which goes to weight, not admissibility.[142] Equally, although a judge must ensure that a complainant is not unnecessarily humiliated or cross-examined with inappropriate aggression, and is treated with proper courtesy, this does not permit him, by way of general discretion, to exclude evidence admissible under s 41 merely because it comes in a stark, uncompromising form.[143]

Section 41(3)(a)—an issue other than consent

The following examples may be given of issues falling within s 41(3)(a): (i) the defence of reasonable belief in consent; (ii) that the complainant was biased against the accused or had a motive to fabricate the evidence;[144] (iii) that there is an alternative explanation for the physical conditions on which the Crown relies to establish that intercourse took place; and (iv) especially in the case of young complainants, that the detail of their account must have come from some other sexual activity before or after the event which provides an explanation for their knowledge of that activity.[145]

As to (i), in *R v Steltner*,[146] it was held that the mere fact that a complainant may have experienced sexual activity in the past does not support an accused's assertion that she would

---

[142] *R v T* [2012] EWCA Crim 2358.

[143] *R v F* [2005] 1 WLR 2848, CA (videotapes of the complainant stripping and masturbating).

[144] In a case with counts of indecent assault, as well as rape, evidence showing bias or a motive to fabricate in relation to the rape may also be relevant to the charges of indecent assault, if they are sufficiently intertwined with the rape: see *R v DGF* [2008] EWCA Crim 2859 and cf *R v L* [2015] EWCA Crim 741.

[145] See per Lord Hope in *R v A (No 2)* [2002] 1 AC 45 at [79]. As to (i), Lord Hope referred to the defence of 'honest' belief in consent, but see now the Sexual Offences Act 2003, ss 1(1)(c) and 75–7.

[146] [2018] EWCA Crim 1479 at [23].

consent to similar activity with him.[147] In *R v Barton*[148] it was stressed that, when considering the effect of the complainant's past sexual behaviour on the accused's belief in consent, whereas evidence of his belief that the complainant was consenting to intercourse is relevant, evidence of his belief that the complainant would consent if advances were made is irrelevant. Although *R v Barton* was a decision under s 2 of the Sexual Offences (Amendment) Act 1976 relating to a defence of *mistaken* belief in consent, the distinction was subsequently approved by the Court of Appeal in *R v Winter*[149] in relation to a decision under s 41 of the 1999 Act relating to a defence of *reasonable* belief in consent under the Sexual Offences Act 2003. However, belief that the complainant will consent may be 'a relevant issue in the case' for the purposes of s 41, for example when, without evidence of the complainant's sexual behaviour, the jury may infer from the other evidence that the intention of the accused, from the outset, was to have intercourse with or without consent.[150] As to (ii), in *R v T*,[151] evidence of a photograph allegedly sent to the accused around Valentine's day, and showing the complainant scantily dressed, went to a relevant issue other than consent, the defence case being that the complainant was interested in him, he was not interested in her, and the motive for her false allegation was her affront at his lack of interest.[152]

An issue of consent

Subsections (3)(b) and (c) were designed to reverse the decision in *R v Riley*.[153] Under these provisions, therefore, in a case where consent is in issue, leave will not be granted in relation to evidence or questions about sexual behaviour of the complainant *simply* because the behaviour in question is previous voluntary sexual intercourse with the accused.[154] In many cases, however, the jury will be likely to infer such behaviour by virtue of the other evidence in the case, as when evidence is introduced that the accused and the complainant are married or have cohabited for a period of time, and in this situation, it is submitted, the judge, rather than simply ignore the likelihood of such an inference being drawn, should direct the jury that any such inference can have no bearing on the issues to be decided.

Section 41(3)(b)—behaviour at or about the same time

To come within s 41(3)(b), the evidence or question must relate to sexual behaviour alleged to have taken place at or about the same time as the event which is the subject matter of the charge, other than anything alleged to have taken place as part of that event.[155] The distinction between sexual behaviour which took place at the same time as the event, and sexual behaviour which took place as part of the event, is not readily apparent. The meaning of

---

[147] The complainant, who was 14 years old, only revealed to the accused that she had once been digitally penetrated in response to questions asked by the accused, gave her answer reluctantly and did not engage in flirtatious behaviour.

[148] (1986) 85 Cr App R 5, CA.

[149] [2008] Crim LR 971, CA.

[150] *R v Gjoni* [2014] EWCA Crim 457 at [25].

[151] [2012] EWCA Crim 2358.

[152] See also *R v F* [2005] 1 WLR 2848, CA and cf *R v Mokrecovas* [2002] 1 Cr App R 226 (20), CA. Cf *R v Moody* [2019] EWCA Crim 1222 where the questioning went to motive for fabrication, but was extremely speculative, lacked an evidential basis and was 'precisely the sort of thing s 41 was designed to exclude' (at [21]).

[153] (1887) 18 QBD 481, CCR.

[154] See further, in this chapter, under **Subsection 41(3)(c)—similar behaviour**, p 237.

[155] Section 42(1)(c).

'the event which is the subject matter of the charge' is also unclear, but seems designed to embrace more than 'the conduct constituting the offence'.[156] The phrase 'at or about the same time as the event', although it provides a degree of elasticity, is a narrow temporal restriction and prima facie prohibits questions both as to a continuous period of cohabitation or sexual activity, and as to individual events more than a very limited period before or after the 'event', generally no more than 24 hours before or after the offence.[157] Section 41(3)(b) could cover behaviour such as any sexual advances made by the complainant towards the accused or other men shortly before or after 'the event' and other behaviour relevant to the issue of consent. An example would be an allegation that the complainant invited the accused to have sexual intercourse with her earlier in the evening.[158]

Subsection 41(3)(c)—similar behaviour

Subsection (3)(c) covers the sexual behaviour of the complainant with the accused (or another man) on another occasion, provided that it is sufficiently similar in nature to her behaviour during, or shortly before or after, the event which is the subject matter of the charge. It was included in the Act in response to the *Romeo and Juliet* scenario advanced by Baroness Mallalieu.[159] She envisaged a complainant in a rape case who says that the accused climbed up on to her balcony and into her bedroom, but who, on occasions both before and after the alleged rape—but not 'at or about the same time as the event' under s 41(3)(b)—invited men to re-enact the *Romeo and Juliet* balcony scene prior to consensual sexual intercourse. Such evidence is introduced under s 41(3)(c) not so much to show that history has been repeated as to indicate a state of mind on the part of the complainant which is potentially highly relevant to her state of mind on the occasion in question.[160] A comparison could be made between the wording of s 41(3)(c) and the concept of similar fact evidence as formulated by Lord Salmon in *DPP v Boardman*:[161] 'The similarity would have to be so unique or striking that common sense makes it inexplicable on the basis of coincidence.' However, as Lord Clyde said in *R v A (No 2)*[162] the phrase 'striking similarity' is not used in s 41(3)(c)—the standard is something short of a striking similarity. Elaborating on this, Lord Clyde said:[163]

> It is only a similarity that is required, not an identity. Moreover the words 'in any respect' deserve to be stressed. On one view any single factor of similarity might suffice to attract the application of the provision, provided that it is not a matter of coincidence . . . the similarity must be such as cannot reasonably be explained as coincidence. To my mind that does not necessitate that the similarity has to be in some rare or bizarre conduct.

---

[156] A phrase also used in s 42(1): see s 42(1)(b).

[157] *R v A (No 2)* [2002] 1 AC 45, per Lords Slynn, Steyn, and Hope at [9], [40], and [82] respectively. But see also per Lord Clyde at [132], who was of the view that it is undesirable to prescribe any test in terms of days or hours, while accepting that it may be difficult to extend the period to 'several days'. In *R v Aidarus* [2018] EWCA Crim 2073, the judge was 'unquestionably' entitled to reject an application to admit sexual behaviour evidence which post-dated the alleged offence by two years and was in a 'wholly different context'.

[158] *R v A (No 2)* [2002] 1 AC 45 per Lord Steyn at [40]. Cf the example furnished by *R v Mukadi* [2004] Crim LR 373, CA, which is hard to justify.

[159] House of Lords Committee Stage, Hansard, 1 Feb 1999, col 45.

[160] Per Lord Clyde in *R v A (No 2)* at [133].

[161] [1975] AC 421, HL at 462.

[162] [2002] 1 AC 45 at [133].

[163] Ibid at [135].

An example of evidence of the kind specified in s 41(3)(c), provided by Lord Steyn in *R v A (No 2)*,[164] is, in a rape case in which the accused says that after consensual intercourse the complainant tried to blackmail him by alleging rape, evidence of a previous occasion when she similarly tried to blackmail him. A reported example is *R v T*[165] where the alleged offence took place in a climbing frame in a park and there was evidence that three to four weeks earlier the accused and the complainant had had consensual intercourse in the same climbing frame and had adopted the same position, both standing and the complainant facing away from the accused.[166] In *Rv MM*[167] the test was not met. The alleged rape occurred in the complainant's bedroom while other members of her family were in other parts of the house; four months earlier she had sent her brother out of the house before engaging in consensual sexual intercourse with the accused in her bedroom.

In appropriate cases in which there has been a sexual relationship between the accused and the complainant, the test in s 41(3)(c) can be subordinated to broader conditions of relevance. In *R v A (No 2)* the House of Lords recognized that as a matter of common sense a prior sexual relationship between the accused and the complainant may, depending on the circumstances, be relevant to the issue of consent, as a species of prospective evidence which, although it cannot prove consent on the occasion in question, may throw light on the complainant's state of mind.[168] Recognizing further that s 41 is therefore prima facie capable of preventing an accused from putting forward relevant evidence which may be critical to his defence, whether one of consent or belief in consent, the House was of the unanimous view that it is possible under s 3 of the Human Rights Act 1998 to read s 41 of the 1999 Act, and in particular s 41(3)(c), as subject to the implied provision that evidence or questioning which is required to ensure a fair trial under Art 6 of the European Convention on Human Rights should not be treated as inadmissible. The result is that sometimes logically relevant evidence of sexual experience between a complainant and an accused may be admitted under section 41(3)(c). Lord Steyn said:[169] 'section 3 of the 1998 Act requires the court to subordinate the niceties of the language of section 41(3)(c) of the 1999 Act, and in particular the touchstone of coincidence, to broader considerations of relevance judged by logical and commonsense criteria of time and circumstances'. Members of the House were agreed as to the effect of its decision, namely that:

> under s 41(3)(c) of the 1999 Act, construed where necessary by applying the interpretative obligation under s 3 of the 1998 Act, and due regard always being paid to the importance of seeking to protect the complainant from indignity and from humiliating questions, the test of admissibility is whether the evidence (and questioning in relation to it) is nevertheless so relevant to the issue of consent that to exclude it would endanger the fairness of the trial under art 6 of the Convention. If this test is satisfied, the evidence should not be excluded.[170]

---

[164] Ibid at [42].

[165] [2004] 2 Cr App R 32, CA.

[166] In *R v Harris* [2010] Crim LR 54 the Court of Appeal said that *R v T* was an easy case, the similarity being so clear that it was not disputed. The court indicated that in more difficult cases it would not interfere where the judge adopted a view on similarity which was open to him within the margin of judgment open to a decision-maker.

[167] [2011] EWCA Crim 1291.

[168] [2002] 1 AC 45 per Lord Steyn at [31].

[169] Ibid at [45].

[170] Ibid per Lord Steyn at [46].

Thus where there has been a recent close and affectionate relationship between the complainant and the accused, it is probable that the evidence will be relevant and admissible, not to prove consent, but to show the complainant's specific mindset towards the accused, namely her affection for him. But where, as in *R v A (No 2)* itself, there have only been some isolated acts of intercourse, even if fairly recently, without the background of an affectionate relationship, it is probable that the evidence will not be relevant. It is not possible to state with precision where the line is to be drawn—it will depend on the facts of the individual case as assessed by the trial judge.[171] *R v A (No 2)* was applied in *R v R*[172] where it was held that permission should have been given to the defence to cross-examine the complainant about both a previous consensual sexual relationship with the accused and consensual sexual intercourse with the accused occurring some 11 months after the alleged offence.[173] However in *R v G*[174] there was no 'sufficient chronological nexus' to justify admissibility, the consensual sexual intercourse having taken place about a year before and several weeks after the alleged offence. In *R v C*,[175] in which the complainant and the accused had been in a relationship for about twelve months at the time of the offence, it was held that evidence of consensual sexual activity with the accused some seven months after the offence had been properly excluded; to admit such evidence risked reinforcing the stereotypical and potentially false view that in a complex relationship no victim of a serious sexual assault would subsequently instigate and engage in consensual sexual activity.

It is very much more difficult to show relevance to the issue of consent in the case of evidence of the complainant's sexual behaviour with men other than the accused than in the case of evidence of sexual behaviour with the accused himself.[176] In *R v White*,[177] W denied rape and said that the complainant had asked him for money which he had refused to give her, and that after consensual intercourse he had woken up to find her with his wallet. It was held that the judge had properly refused an application to cross-examine the complainant on her previous and ongoing activities as a prostitute. A prostitute was as entitled as any other person to say 'no' to sex and the fact that the complainant was a prostitute did not mean that she was more ready than any other to say 'yes'. The bare fact that the complainant was a prostitute was therefore irrelevant to the issue of consent. There had to be something about the specific circumstances that satisfied the test in s 41(3)(c). *R v A (No 2)*, it was held, could be distinguished, since it did not concern the introduction of evidence of sexual behaviour with men other than the accused, and it would take a very special case to admit such evidence in circumstances where it could not be admitted by an ordinary reading of s 41. *R v Evans*[178] appears to be an example of such a special case. E was charged with rape on the basis that X was incapable of consent. Both had been drinking. X could not remember what had happened and did not allege that she had been raped or was incapable of consent. E volunteered

---

[171] Ibid per Lord Hutton at [152].

[172] [2003] EWCA Crim 2754.

[173] Cf *R v S* [2010] EWCA Crim 1579 where, the jury being aware of a previous consensual sexual relationship, evidence of the fact that the last act of intercourse had taken place nine days before the alleged rape was of no relevance to the issue of consent.

[174] [2016] EWCA Crim 1633.

[175] [2016] EWCA Crim 1631.

[176] See per Lord Clyde in *R v A (No 2)* at [125]–[127].

[177] [2004] EWCA Crim 946.

[178] [2016] EWCA Crim 452.

that intercourse had taken place, his defence being consent or reasonable belief in consent. On appeal against conviction, there was fresh evidence from two other men concerning similar sexual behaviour by X with each of them, separately, before and after the alleged rape by E. On each occasion, X had been drinking, had instigated sexual activity, had directed them into the same position, and had used the same sort of words of encouragement. The precise ratio of the court is far from clear. It was held that the evidence was 'arguably' sufficiently similar to be covered by s 41(3)(c). However, it was also held that it was 'potentially' an example of a rare case in which evidence of sexual activity with someone other than the accused would be relevant. It would seem to be an *actual* example of such a case—the conclusion of the court was to apply the principle in *R v A (No 2)* that the requirements of s 41 should give way to the requirements of a fair trial.

Section 41(4)—where the purpose is to impugn credibility

Section 41(4) operates where 'the purpose' or the 'main purpose' for adducing the evidence or asking the question is to impugn the credibility of the complainant. *R v Sunny Islam*[179] illustrates its application. On a charge of rape, the defence being consent, it was held that the defence had been properly prevented from questioning the complainant about her flirtatious behaviour towards other men in a bar a few hours before the alleged offence, in order to suggest that she was 'up for sex'. The Court of Appeal upheld the ruling of the trial judge that the questions did not pass the test under s 41(2) and fell foul of s 41(4), having as their main purpose impugning the credibility of the complainant by reason of her unchaste behaviour. In *R v Martin*,[180] on the other hand, a case of indecent assault involving enforced oral sex, in which M alleged that the complainant had fabricated her evidence because he had rejected her advances, it was held that the defence should have been allowed to question her about his allegation that two days earlier she had not merely pestered him for sex, but performed an act of oral sex upon him, after which he had rejected her. It was held that although one purpose of the questioning was to impugn the credibility of the complainant, it also went to the accused's credibility and strengthened the defence case of fabrication, because the jury might have interpreted a rejection after the performance of oral sex as more hurtful than rejection after mere verbal advances.

Following *R v Martin*, it has been properly observed that merely because evidence may impugn the complainant's credibility, it does not follow that the purpose or main purpose for deploying it is to do so.[181] However, the application of s 41(4) is, it is submitted, bound to give rise to real difficulties in the many cases where, as we have seen, the difference between questions going to credit and those going to the issue is reduced to vanishing point.[182] As Lord Hutton observed in *R v A (No 2)*, in the context of the issue of consent:[183] 'Issues of consent and issues of credibility may well run so close to each other as almost to coincide. A very sharp knife may be required to separate what may be admitted from what may not'.

---

[179] [2012] EWCA Crim 3106.
[180] [2004] 2 Cr App R 354 (22), CA.
[181] Per Judge LJ in *R v F* [2005] 1 WLR 2848, CA at [27].
[182] See *R v Funderburk* [1990] 1 WLR 587, CA (see **n 67**).
[183] [2002] 1 AC 45, HL at [138].

Section 41(5)—evidence in rebuttal or explanation

Section 41(4) applies only for the purposes of s 41(3) and not for the purposes of s 41(5), which concerns evidence, or a question, in rebuttal or explanation of evidence adduced by the prosecution about *any* sexual behaviour of the complainant, including anything alleged to have taken place as part of the event which is the subject matter of the charge.[184] Thus, in *R v F*[185] where the complainant gave evidence that she had been raped by her mother's partner, that she had subsequently become pregnant but had not been sexually active with anyone else at the time, the Court of Appeal held that the accused ought to have been permitted to ask questions about the complainant's medical notes which recorded that to her doctor she had attributed her pregnancy to a 'condom accident' with her boyfriend and that subsequently she had been prescribed oral contraceptives. However, in *R v Winter*,[186] where the complainant, who claimed that she had been raped by the accused, sought to give evidence that at the time of the alleged offence she was in a happy long-term relationship with her partner, the statement was held not to be so misleading that evidence of an affair with another man was admissible in rebuttal. Similarly, in *R v Steltner*,[187] where the 14-year-old complainant was referred to by the prosecution as a 'virgin', the defence were properly prevented from admitting evidence contained in WhatsApp messages where she answered the accused's questions about her sexual experience by saying that she had on one occasion in the past been 'fingered' (digitally penetrated). In the circumstances of the case, this evidence would have had no relevance to the jury's overall assessment of the complainant, her consent, or the accused's belief in the consent.[188]

In *R v Aidarus*,[189] evidence towards the outset of the complainant's Achieving Best Evidence (ABE) interview was that just before she was raped, there was an exchange with the accused during which he asked her for oral sex and also asked if she had performed oral sex before, to which she replied that she had not. The accused sought to admit evidence that she did have prior experience of oral sex in order to rebut a misleading impression she had given in this part of the ABE. The Court of Appeal held that in the particular circumstances of the case, the trial judge was entitled to refuse to admit the evidence. The accused's defence was that she had consented and that there was no such exchange. The judge was therefore justified in his reasoning that the evidence neither rebutted nor explained the evidence that the exchange had taken place.

'Evidence adduced by the prosecution' refers to evidence placed before the jury by prosecution witnesses in the course of their evidence-in-chief and by other witnesses in the course of cross-examination by the advocate prosecuting and, where it is necessary to ensure a fair trial, may also include something said by a prosecution witness in cross-examination about the complainant's sexual behaviour which was not deliberately elicited by the advocate for the defence and is potentially damaging to the accused's case.[190] However, where the evidence is elicited by questions from the judge, s 41(5) does not apply. Where such questioning

---

[184] See s 42(1)(c).

[185] [2008] EWCA Crim 2859.

[186] [2008] Crim LR 971, CA.

[187] [2018] EWCA Crim 1479.

[188] Ibid, at [24]–[25]. The jury were told that the fact that she was a virgin did not carry with it the implication that she would not consent to sex and indeed she had said that she would consent in certain circumstances.

[189] [2018] EWCA Crim 2073.

[190] *R v Hamadi* [2008] Crim LR 635, CA.

and evidence is seriously prejudicial to the defence this could lead to the jury being discharged but not, it appears, to leave being granted to question the complainant on her sexual history.[191]

Section 41(5) only allows the defence to rebut *evidence* adduced by the prosecution about the sexual behaviour of the complainant, and not, it seems, inferences about her sexual behaviour that may reasonably be drawn from evidence adduced by the prosecution.

Section 41(6)—specific instances of behaviour

Section 41(6) would rule out, for example, evidence or questions revealing the complainant to be, for example, a prostitute or of a promiscuous nature. Nor will the requirements of s 41(6) be met, in the case of a prostitute, by the information contained in a list of previous convictions for prostitution.[192] However, in some cases, of course, evidence or questions relating to specific instances may well allow the jury to infer that the complainant was a prostitute or promiscuous, as would happen, for example, if evidence were to be introduced that she had, on a number of previous occasions, agreed to sleep with men for money.

The procedure on applications under s 41

Where the defence wish to make use of s 41, they must apply in writing pre-trial, identifying the issue to which the sexual behaviour is relevant and the exception to the general prohibition on which they rely and giving particulars of the evidence they want to introduce or the questions they want to ask; and a party who wishes to make representations about such an application must also do so in writing.[193] An application for leave under s 41 shall be heard in private and in the absence of the complainant.[194] Where the court allows the cross-examination of a witness, the court must give directions for the appropriate treatment and questioning of that witness by setting ground rules for the conduct of questioning.[195] The defence should identify individual questions for the judge, merely identifying a topic is insufficient.[196] After the court has reached its decision, it must state in open court, but in the absence of the jury (if there is one), its reasons for giving or refusing leave and, if it gives leave, the extent to which evidence may be adduced or questions asked in pursuance of the leave.[197]

Finality of answers to collateral questions

The rule

A party eliciting from a witness under cross-examination evidence unfavourable to his case, may understandably seek to adduce evidence in rebuttal. To allow that party to adduce such evidence without restriction, however, would lead to a multiplicity of issues, some of which might

---

[191] See *R v JG* [2018] EWCA Crim 1318 (4) at [35].

[192] *R v White* [2004] EWCA Crim 946.

[193] See the Criminal Procedure Rules 2015, SI 2015/1490, r 10 and Sch. and The Criminal Practice Directions V, 22A.3 Concerning the prosecutor's duties toward the complainant where the court allows introduction of or cross-examination about her sexual behaviour, and the court's obligation to determine see r 22.3(1) of the Criminal Procedure Rules 2015 (SI 2015/1490). Failure to comply with the rules makes it more likely that things will go wrong at the trial: *R v Crossland* [2013] EWCA Crim 2313 at [28]. See, eg, *R v Andrade* [2015] EWCA Crim 1722.

[194] Section 43(1).

[195] See Rule 22.7(3) of the Criminal Procedure 2015, SI 2015/1490.

[196] Ibid.

[197] Section 43(2). A magistrates' court must also cause such matters to be entered in the register of its proceedings: s 43(2). See also the Criminal Practice Directions 2015, V, 22A.4.

be of minimal relevance to the facts in issue in the case, and thereby prolong the trial unnecessarily. As a general rule, therefore, the answers given by a witness under cross-examination to questions concerning collateral matters, that is, matters which are irrelevant to the issues in the proceedings, must be treated as final. Finality for these purposes does not mean that the tribunal of fact is obliged to accept the answers as true, but simply that the cross-examining party is not permitted to call further evidence with a view to contradicting the witness.[198]

Whether a question is collateral is not always easy to decide. According to the often cited test formulated by Pollock CB in *A-G v Hitchcock*,[199] if the witness's answer is a matter on which the cross-examining party would be allowed to introduce evidence-in-chief, because of its connection with the issues in the case, then the matter is not collateral and may be rebutted.[200] Relevance, however, is a question of degree, the answer to which may turn on whether the matter which the cross-examining party seeks to prove is a single fact which is easy of proof or a broad issue which will require the jury to embark on a difficult and complex task.[201] Questions which go merely to the credit of the witness are clearly collateral. However, where the disputed issue is a sexual one between two persons in private, the difference between questions going to credit and questions going to the issue is reduced to vanishing point because sexual intercourse, whether or not consensual, most often takes place in private and leaves few visible traces of having occurred, so that the evidence is often effectively limited to that of the parties, and much is likely to depend upon the balance of credibility between them.[202] This principle, however, is not confined to cases involving sexual intercourse.[203]

In *R v Burke*[204] an Irish witness who gave evidence through an interpreter and was cross-examined about his knowledge of English, denied that he was able to speak the language. The witness's ability to speak English being irrelevant to any matter directly in issue in the proceedings, it was held that evidence in rebuttal was inadmissible. In *A-G v Hitchcock*[205] a maltster was charged with the use of a cistern in breach of certain statutory requirements. A prosecution witness, who gave evidence that the cistern had been used, was asked in cross-examination whether he had not said to one Cook that the Excise officers offered him £20 to give evidence that the cistern had been used. The witness denied this allegation and it was held that the advocate for the defence was not permitted to call Cook to give evidence in rebuttal of what the witness had said. Pollock CB said:[206]

> it is totally irrelevant to the matter in issue, that some person should have thought fit to offer a bribe to the witness to give an untrue account of a transaction, and it is of no importance whatever, if that bribe was not accepted.

---

[198] For an argument that the collateral evidence rule should be repealed on the basis that it does not achieve its aim, can lead to injustice and is, in any event, unnecessary, see Keane, 'The collateral evidence rule: a sad forensic fable involving a circus, its sideshow, confusion, vanishing tricks and alchemy' (2015) 19 E&P 100.

[199] (1847) 1 Exch 91 at 99.

[200] The test seems to be circular, but its utility may lie in the fact that the answer is an instinctive one, based on the sense of fair play of the prosecutor and the court rather than any philosophic or analytic process: per Henry J in *R v Funderburk* [1990] 1 WLR 587, CA at 598. But see also per Evans LJ in *R v Neale* [1998] Crim LR 737, CA: the decision is ultimately a matter of common sense and logic.

[201] *R v S* [1992] Crim LR 307, CA.

[202] Per Henry J in *R v Funderburk* [1990] 1 WLR 587, CA at 597, citing *Cross on Evidence* (6th edn, London, 1985) 295.

[203] See *R v Nagrecha* [1997] 2 Cr App R 401, CA, a case of indecent assault, and *R v David R* [1999] Crim LR 909, CA.

[204] (1858) 8 Cox CC 44.

[205] (1847) 1 Exch 91; cf *R v Phillips* (1936) 26 Cr App R 17, CCA, at n 229.

[206] (1847) 1 Exch 91 at 101.

Many of the criminal authorities as to the application of the rule, for example *R v Edwards*,[207] must be treated with caution insofar as they involved questioning the witness about his previous misconduct or disposition towards such misconduct; in criminal proceedings, the asking of questions about a witness's bad character is governed by ss 100 and 101 of the 2003 Act, which are considered in **Chapter 19.**

The exceptions

To the general rule on the finality of answers to collateral questions there are three exceptions, although it may be that the categories of exception are not closed.[208]

Previous convictions

Under s 6 of the Criminal Procedure Act 1865:

> If, upon a witness being lawfully questioned as to whether he has been convicted of any felony or misdemeanour, he either denies or does not admit the fact, or refuses to answer, it shall be lawful for the cross-examining party to prove such conviction.[209]

Section 6 applies to both civil and criminal proceedings. In criminal proceedings, a witness will only be 'lawfully questioned' as to his previous convictions where the questions are lawful having regard to the relevant provisions of the 2003 Act, namely s 100 in the case of the previous convictions of a non-defendant and s 101 in the case of the previous convictions of the defendant. In civil proceedings, cross-examination of any witness about 'spent' convictions is prohibited by s 4(1) of the Rehabilitation of Offenders Act 1974, unless the judge is satisfied that it is not possible for justice to be done except by admitting the convictions.[210] This section does not apply in criminal proceedings, but when considering bad character applications under the 2003 Act, regard should always be had to the general provisions of the 1974 Act.[211]

There is authority to suggest that, in civil proceedings, subject to s 4(1) of the Rehabilitation of Offenders Act 1974, s 6 permits a witness to be cross-examined about his convictions irrespective of their relevance to his credibility or the issues in the case.[212] It seems clear, however, that cross-examination about a witness's previous convictions is subject to the general power of the judge to restrain unnecessary, irrelevant, or unduly oppressive questions in cross-examination.[213] In civil proceedings, a judge may use the general exclusionary discretion under CPR r 32[214] to limit cross-examination on previous convictions to the convictions for offences of dishonesty, although where sitting with a jury should be more hesitant in exercising the discretion.[215]

---

[207] [1991] 1 WLR 207, CA. See also *R v Clancy* [1997] Crim LR 290, CA and *R v Irish* [1995] Crim LR 145, CA.

[208] *R v Funderburk* [1990] 1 WLR 587, CA, per Henry J at 599.

[209] However, if the witness accepts the conviction but claims his innocence, the cross-examining party may be prevented from adducing evidence in rebuttal: see *R v Irish* [1995] Crim LR 145, CA.

[210] Section 7(3). Evidence of the conviction may be admitted under s 7(3) not only if relevant to an issue in the case, but also if relevant merely to the credit of the witness, but the judge should weigh its relevance and its prejudicial effect and only admit it if satisfied that otherwise the parties would not have a fair trial or the witness's credit could not be fairly assessed: *Thomas v Metropolitan Police Comr* [1997] QB 813, CA.

[211] Criminal Practice Directions V, para 21A.2. See also the 2003 Act, s 108, Ch 19.

[212] *Clifford v Clifford* [1961] 1 WLR 1274 P, D and Admlty at 1276.

[213] See, eg, per Lawton J in *R v Sweet-Escott* (1971) 55 Cr App R 316, Assizes.

[214] See Ch 2, Civil cases, p 173.

[215] *Watson v Chief Constable of Cleveland Police* [2001] EWCA Civ 1547.

In criminal proceedings, s 101(1)(g) of the 2003 Act operates as a powerful disincentive to the use of s 6 by an advocate for the defence in cross-examination of prosecution witnesses. We shall see in **Chapter 19** that, under s 101(1)(g), the accused, by making an attack on another person's character, thereby renders admissible evidence of his own bad character.

Bias

'It has always been permissible to call evidence to contradict a witness's denial of bias or partiality towards one of the parties and to show that he is prejudicial so far as the case being tried is concerned.'[216] Thus where a female servant of the claimant is called as his witness and denies in cross-examination that she is his kept mistress, the defendant may call evidence to contradict her.[217] Under s 99 of the 2003 Act, this common law principle has been abolished in criminal proceedings to the extent that it allows the introduction of evidence of the witness's bad character, that is, evidence of, or of a disposition towards, misconduct on his part. However, much evidence of bias is likely to remain admissible at common law, because outside the statutory definition of evidence of bad character in s 98 of the 2003 Act, which excludes 'evidence of, or of a disposition towards misconduct . . . which has to do with the alleged facts of the offence with which the defendant is charged, or is evidence of misconduct in connection with the investigation or prosecution of that offence'. Alternatively, to the extent that the evidence is not admissible on that basis, it is likely to be admitted under s 100(1)(b) of the 2003 Act, that is, as evidence of the bad character of a person other than the defendant which has substantial probative value in relation to a matter which is in issue in the proceedings and of substantial importance in the context of the case as a whole.[218] Thus the *outcome* in each of the following examples of the common law doctrine is likely to remain the same.

In *R v Shaw*[219] it was held that the accused may call evidence to contradict a prosecution witness who, in cross-examination, denies having threatened to take revenge on the accused following a quarrel with him. In *R v Mendy*,[220] during a trial for assault, and while a detective was giving evidence, a man in the public gallery was observed to be taking notes. The man was seen to leave the court and hold a conversation, apparently concerning the detective's evidence, with the accused's husband, who, as a prospective witness, had been kept out of court in accordance with the normal practice. The husband subsequently gave evidence and under cross-examination denied that he had spoken to the man in question. The Court of Appeal held that the trial judge had properly allowed evidence to be given in rebuttal. The jury were entitled to know that, in order to deceive them and help the accused, the witness was prepared to cheat.

The line dividing questions put to a witness in cross-examination concerning facts tending to show prejudice or bias, and those concerning collateral facts on which the witness's answers must be treated as final, is often a very fine one. Although in *A-G v Hitchcock*,[221] as we have seen, it was held that the witness's denial of an alleged statement by him that he had been *offered* a bribe, being a collateral matter, could not be contradicted, the court acknowledged

[216] Per Geoffrey Lane LJ in *R v Mendy* (1976) 64 Cr App R 4, CA at 6.

[217] *Thomas v David* (1836) 7 C&P 350.

[218] Sections 99 and 100 of the 2003 Act are considered in Ch 19.

[219] (1888) 16 Cox CC 503, Assizes.

[220] (1976) 64 Cr App R 4.

[221] (1847) 1 Exch 91.

that where a witness denies *acceptance* of a bribe to testify, a matter tending to show his partiality, evidence in rebuttal is admissible. *R v Phillips*[222] also falls to be contrasted with the actual
decision in *A-G v Hitchcock*. The accused was charged with incest. His defence was that the
principal prosecution witnesses, his two daughters, had been 'schooled' by their mother into
giving false evidence. In cross-examination, the girls denied that their testimony was no more
than a repetition of what their mother had told them to say. The girls also denied that on separate occasions each of them had admitted to another person that their evidence in previous
criminal proceedings against their father for indecent assault had been false. The trial judge
refused to allow the advocate for the defence to call two women to whom these admissions
were alleged to have been made. The Court of Criminal Appeal, quashing the conviction, held
that this evidence was admissible on the grounds that the questions were directed not to the
credibility of the two girls but went to the very foundation of the accused's defence.

In *R v Busby*[223] police officers were cross-examined on the basis that they had made up statements attributed to the accused and indicative of his guilt, and had threatened, a potential
witness for the defence, to stop him giving evidence. The allegations were denied. The trial
judge ruled that W, who was subsequently called for the defence, could not give evidence that
he had been threatened by the officers, because this would go solely to their credit. The Court
of Appeal, allowing the appeal against conviction, held that the judge had erred: W's evidence
was relevant to an issue which had to be tried, in that, if true it showed that the police were
prepared to go to improper lengths in order to secure a conviction, and this would have supported the accused's case that the statements attributed to him had been fabricated. In *R v
Funderburk*[224] *R v Busby* was treated as having created a new exception to the rule against finality, but in *R v Edwards*[225] it was held that the facts came within the exception of bias and that
if the case could not be explained on that basis, it was inconsistent with the general rule itself.

Evidence of physical or mental disability affecting reliability
The credibility of a witness may be impeached by expert medical evidence which shows that
he suffers from some physical or mental disability that affects the reliability of his evidence.[226]

> If a witness purported to give evidence of something which he believed that he had seen at a
> distance of 50 yards, it must surely be possible to call the evidence of an oculist to the effect that
> the witness could not possibly see anything at a greater distance than 20 yards, or the evidence
> of a surgeon who had removed a cataract from which the witness was suffering at the material
> time and which would have prevented him from seeing what he thought he saw. So, too, must it
> be allowable to call medical evidence of mental illness which makes a witness incapable of giv-
> ing reliable evidence, whether through the existence of delusions or otherwise.

These examples were given by Lord Pearce in *Toohey v Metropolitan Police Comr.*[227] Toohey
was convicted with others of an assault with intent to rob. The defence was that the alleged

---

[222] (1936) 26 Cr App R 17.

[223] (1981) 75 Cr App R, CA.

[224] [1990] 1 WLR 587, CA at 591.

[225] [1991] 1 WLR 207, CA at 215.

[226] For a critique of the use of psychiatric evidence in rape trials, see Ellison, 'The use and abuse of psychiatric
evidence in rape trials' (2009) 13 E&P 28.

[227] [1965] AC 595 at 608. See also *R v Eades* [1972] Crim LR 99, Assizes. However, as to medical evidence of mental
illness, the analogy with physical disease is neither appropriate nor apt, because whereas a cataract would prevent
the witness from seeing what he purported to see, the fact of mental ill health does not mean that a witness *cannot*
be accurately describing what happened: see *R v H* [2014] EWCA Crim 1555 at [26].

victim had been drinking and that while the accused were trying to help him by taking him home, he became hysterical and accused them of the offence charged. The trial judge held that, although a doctor called for the defence could give evidence that when he examined the victim he was hysterical and smelt of alcohol, he could not give evidence that in his opinion drink could exacerbate hysteria and that the alleged victim was more prone to hysteria than a normal person. The Court of Criminal Appeal dismissed the appeal, but the House of Lords, quashing the convictions, held that the doctor's evidence had been improperly excluded. Lord Pearce, in a speech with which the other members of the House concurred, held that the evidence was admissible not only because of its relevance to the facts in issue, regardless of whether or not it affected the credibility of the alleged victim as a witness, but also to show that the evidence of the alleged victim was unreliable.

> Medical evidence is admissible to show that a witness suffers from some disease or defect or abnormality of mind that affects the reliability of his evidence. Such evidence is not confined to a general opinion of the unreliability of the witness but may give all the matters necessary to show, not only the foundation of and reasons for the diagnosis, but also the extent to which the credibility of the witness is affected.[228]

Expert opinion evidence is admissible in relation to matters requiring special knowledge or expertise, not matters within the ordinary experience and knowledge of the tribunal of fact. Thus expert medical evidence on the reliability of a witness will only be admissible if the disability from which the witness suffers is a proper subject of such evidence. As Lord Pearce observed in *Toohey v Metropolitan Police Comr*:[229]

> Human evidence . . . is subject to many cross-currents such as partiality, prejudice, self-interest and above all, imagination and inaccuracy. Those are matters with which the jury, helped by cross-examination and common sense, must do their best. But when a witness through physical (in which I include mental) disease or abnormality is not capable of giving a true or reliable account to the jury, it must surely be allowable for medical science to reveal this vital hidden fact to them.

In *R v MacKenney*[230] the accused were convicted of murder. At their trial, they had alleged that the chief prosecution witness had fabricated his evidence and wished to call a psychologist by whom the witness had refused to be examined. The psychologist had watched the witness give his evidence and as a result had formed the opinion that he was a psychopath who was likely to be lying and whose mental state was such that his demeanour and behaviour when giving evidence would not convey the usual indications to the jury as to when he was lying. The evidence of the psychologist was ruled inadmissible. The convictions were upheld on appeal. On referral to the Court of Appeal by the Criminal Cases Review Commission, there was fresh evidence from a psychiatrist. He, too, had not examined the witness. His opinion was very similar to that of the psychologist who had attended the trial. It was held that the evidence of the psychologist would now be admissible and that the absence of an examination by the expert went to the weight to be attached to his opinion, not its admissibility. Deciding the reference on the fresh evidence, the conviction was quashed.

---

[228] [1965] AC 595 at 609.
[229] Ibid at 608.
[230] [2004] 2 Cr App R 32 (5), CA.

In *R v Robinson*[231] it was held that although a party, A, cannot call a witness of fact, W, and then, without more, call a psychologist or psychiatrist to give reasons why the jury should regard W as reliable, if the other party, B, proposes to call an expert to say that W should be regarded as unreliable due to some mental abnormality outside the jury's experience, then A may call an expert in rebuttal or even, anticipating B's expert, as part of his own case. Where B does not call an expert, but puts a case in cross-examination that W is unreliable by reason of mental abnormality, this may also be open to rebuttal by expert evidence, although much may depend on the nature of the abnormality and of the cross-examination. If such expert evidence is admitted, it must be restricted to the specific challenge, and should not extend to 'oath-helping'. Thus on the facts of that case, since B had not called evidence impugning W's reliability and had not put a specific case in cross-examination that W was peculiarly suggestible or liable to fantasize as a result of her mental impairment, expert evidence to suggest the opposite was inadmissible.

R v Robinson was distinguished in *R v S*,[232] where it was held that the judge had not erred in allowing an expert to make a general observation that it would be unlikely for an autistic person, as the victim was, to have invented such an account as that given by her, leaving it to the jury to decide whether the victim was capable of belief. Similarly in *R v Mulindwa*[233] it was held that in rare cases, before evidence is given by an accused suffering from a recognized mental disorder which may affect the way in which he will present his evidence, a psychiatrist or psychologist may give evidence about the matter, for example explaining that certain ways of behaving or responding to questions are a feature of the disorder, in order to enhance the ability of the jury to form a view on his reliability, which is a matter exclusively for them. In *R v Eden*[234] where, on charges of numerous sexual offences against the complainant over a period of six years, E denied the offences and claimed that the complainant was simply lying, it was held that evidence of a psychologist that the complainant had symptoms which could be consistent with extensive child abuse or some other repeated prolonged trauma did not fall to be excluded as 'oath-helping' but was admissible as evidence of a psychological injury consistent with the complainant's allegations and relevant to the issue of where the truth lay.

The rule against 'oath-helping' will not necessarily prevent a non-expert from giving evidence as to the good character of a witness from which his likely reliability may be inferred. In *R v Tobin*,[235] a case of indecent assault on a girl, the defence claimed that the sexual activity had been initiated by the girl. The accused gave evidence that he was a married man with no previous convictions for sexual offences and called five character witnesses. The girl's mother was allowed to give evidence that she had never had problems with her daughter, who had done well at school, got on well with her siblings, was very polite and quiet, and had been brought up to respect people. It was held that the evidence did go to boost the claimant's credibility, but since full evidence had been given about the accused's character, the court's sense of fair play was not offended by admission of the evidence as to the complainant's character.[236]

---

[231] [1994] 3 All ER 346, CA. See also *R v Beard* [1998] Crim LR 585, CA.

[232] [2006] EWCA Crim 2389.

[233] [2017] 2 Cr App R 94 (10), CA.

[234] [2011] EWCA Crim 1690.

[235] [2003] Crim LR 408, CA.

[236] In trials of sexual offences in which there is a direct conflict between the evidence of the accused and the victim, there is a compelling case that the same rules as to the admissibility of good character evidence should apply to both: see Buxton, 'Victims as Witnesses in Trials of Sexual Offences: Towards Equality of Arms' [2015] Crim LR 679. See also *R v Mader* [2018] EWCA Crim 2454 (considered in **Ch 18**). Cf *R v G(T)*, [2018] 1 Cr App R 405 (30), CA.

Re-examination

A witness who has been cross-examined may be re-examined by the party who called him.[237] The object of re-examination is, in broad terms, to repair such damage as has been done by the cross-examining party insofar as he has elicited evidence from the witness supporting his version of the facts in issue and cast doubt upon the witness's evidence-in-chief.

The cardinal rule of re-examination is that it must be confined to such matters as arose out of the cross-examination.[238] Thus although the witness may be asked to clarify or explain any matters, including evidence of new facts, which arose in cross-examination, questions on other matters may only be asked with the leave of the judge. In *Prince v Samo*[239] Lord Denman CJ held that where a witness under cross-examination has given evidence of part of a conversation, evidence may not be given in re-examination about everything that was said in that conversation, but only about so much of it as is in some way connected with the evidence given in cross-examination. For example, the witness may be re-examined about things said which qualify or explain the statement on which he was cross-examined, but not about things said on other distinct and unrelated matters.

Evidence which was not admissible in examination-in-chief may become admissible in re-examination as a result of the nature of the cross-examination. Thus although in criminal proceedings an earlier statement of a witness which is consistent with his testimony on a particular matter is generally inadmissible in chief, it will become admissible in re-examination if, in cross-examination, it is suggested to him that his evidence on that matter is a recent fabrication.[240] It remains to note that leading questions may be asked in re-examination to the same limited extent as in examination-in-chief.

ADDITIONAL READING

Andrews and Lamb, 'Cross-examining young alleged complainers in Scottish criminal cases', [2018] Crim LR 34.
See Ch 6, Additional reading.

Birch, 'Rethinking Sexual History Evidence: Proposals for Fairer Trials' [2002] Crim LR 531.
An argument that s 41 of the Youth Justice and Criminal Evidence Act 1999 has created serious problems for the fairness of trials; that the decision in *R v A (No 2)* [2002] 1 AC 45 has resolved some of them; but that a better solution is to rethink the legislation.

Birch, 'Untangling Sexual History Evidence: A Rejoinder to Professor Temkin' [2003] Crim LR 370.
A reply to Professor Temkin's arguments—see later in this section.

Cohen, 'Errors of Recall and Credibility: Can omissions and discrepancies in successive statements reasonably be said to undermine credibility of testimony?' (2001) 69 (1) Med Leg J 25.
An article that questions whether omissions and discrepancies in successive statements made by asylum-seekers can fairly be treated as casting doubt on their credibility, in the light of research findings relating to variability of true memories and the likely impact of traumatic experiences.

---

[237] Even a hostile witness, apparently, may be re-examined by the party who called him (on any new matters which arose out of cross-examination by the other party to the action): *R v Wong* [1986] Crim LR 683 (Crown Court).

[238] The rule applies in the case of someone whose statement has been served as a witness on whom the prosecution intend to rely but who has been called by the prosecution merely to allow the defence to cross-examine him: *R v Beezley* (1830) 4 C&P 220.

[239] (1838) 7 Ad&El 627. See also *Queen Caroline's Case* (1820) 2 Brod&Bing 284.

[240] See, eg, *R v Oyesiku* (1971) 56 Cr App R 240, CA (see Ch 6, **Statements admissible to rebut allegations of recent fabrication, p 197**).

Dent and Paul, 'In Defence of Section 41' [2017] Crim LR 613.
An analysis of the media commentary surrounding *R v Evans* [2016] EWCA Crim 452 and the re-trial of the accused, in particular the proposals for a 'rape shield' which would preclude any questioning of a complainant about previous sexual behaviour in a sexual offence trial.

Ellison and Munro, 'Better the devil you know? "Real rape" stereotypes and the relevance of a previous relationship in (mock) juror deliberations' (2013) 17 E&P 299.
Commentary on the deliberations of jurors in a 'trial' involving an alleged rape by the complainant's ex partner, shedding light on the 'real rape' stereotype, a stereotype dominated by the imagery of a sudden surprise attack by an unknown assailant.

Henderson, 'Bigger fish to fry: should the reform of cross-examination be expanded beyond vulnerable witnesses?' (2015) 19 E&P 83.
A summary of the research into adult comprehension of typical cross-examination language, adult suggestibility, and the reliability of demeanour evidence, suggesting that it may be time to consider an extension of the restrictions on cross-examination in the case of vulnerable witnesses to all witnesses.

Hoyano, 'Cross-examination of sexual assault complainants on previous sexual behaviour: views from the barristers' row' [2019] Crim LR 77.
A summary of the largest empirical study of the use of evidence of past sexual behaviour in sexual offences trials in England and Wales. The study examined data from cases and views from anonymous barristers directly involved. Conclusions relate to whether s 41 is working in the interests of justice, how sexual behaviour evidence is handled in practice, how the prosecution should respond to s 41 applications, the need to limit prejudiced reasoning, and the impact of inaccurate information about the aims and operation of s 41.

Hoyano, 'Reforming the Adversarial Trial for Vulnerable Witnesses and Defendants' [2015] Crim LR 107.
An argument that radical proposals relating to vulnerable witnesses (proposals for the exclusion of advocates from cross-examination, the requirement of prior approval by a non-judicial figure for every question in cross-examination, and allowing independent legal representation for the complainant) encounter serious difficulties, especially for equality of arms and effective participation by the accused. An alternative package of more modest proposals is set out.

Keane, 'Towards a Principled Approach to the Cross-examination of Vulnerable Witnesses' [2012] Crim LR 407.
An argument that the courts need to take a more principled approach, when restrictions are imposed in the case of vulnerable witnesses appearing on behalf of the prosecution, so as to enable a transparent balancing of the rights and needs of such witnesses against those of the accused and to ensure a fair trial in accordance with Art 6.1 and 6.3(d) of the European Convention on Human Rights.

Keane, 'The collateral evidence rule: a sad forensic fable involving a circus, its sideshow, confusion, vanishing tricks and alchemy' (2015) 19 E&P 100.
A critical analysis of the collateral evidence rule, having regard to the other rules that impinge on its ambit and to the way in which it has been applied and modified in a number of jurisdictions, that argues for abolition of the rule without replacement.

Kibble, 'Judicial Perspectives on the Operation of s 41 and the Relevance and Admissibility of Prior Sexual History Evidence: Four Scenarios' [2005] Crim LR 190.
A discussion of findings from a research project which had as its main purpose an examination of judicial perspectives on s 41 of the Youth Justice and Criminal Evidence Act 1999 and on the relevance and admissibility of the complainant's previous sexual behaviour in sex offence cases.

McGlynn, 'Challenging the law on sexual history evidence: a response to Dent and Paul' [2018] Crim LR 216.
A response to Dent and Paul, 'In Defence of Section 41'—see above. The author challenges the current interpretation of the law on the admissibility of sexual history evidence and argues that significant reform is needed.

Redmayne, 'Myths, relationships and coincidences: The new problems of sexual history' (2003) 7 E&P 75.
An article that questions the justifications for the view that the complainant's sexual history with third parties is generally irrelevant to the issue of consent in rape trials; that suggests that the relevance of sexual history is a more complex issue than is usually acknowledged; and that questions the way in which concepts drawn from the law on similar fact evidence have been used in relation to the admissibility of evidence of sexual history.

Spencer and Lamb, eds, *Children and Cross-examination, Time to Change the Rules?* (Hart, 2012).
The Pigot Committee proposed a scheme under which the whole of a young child's evidence would be obtained out of court and in advance of trial. The proposal was implemented in Western Australia and similar schemes

operate in a number of European jurisdictions. This book of essays considers some of these schemes and argues the case for reform in the United Kingdom.

Temkin, 'Sexual History Evidence—Beware the Backlash' [2003] Crim LR 217.
An article that seeks to defend ss 41–43 of the Youth Justice and Criminal Evidence Act 1999 against the attacks of several critics and argues that it would be ill-advised to return to a 'discretionary' system.

Ward, 'Usurping the role of the jury? Expert evidence and witness credibility in English criminal trials' (2009) 13 E&P 83.
An argument that, particularly in rape and sexual abuse cases, there are good reasons for admitting some forms of expert evidence of credibility and that concerns about usurping the jury's role do not justify the British government's apparent abandonment of proposals to make such evidence more widely admissible in rape trials.

QUESTIONS

1. Critically evaluate the interpretation by the House of Lords in *R v A (No 2)* [2002] 1 AC 45 of s 41 of the Youth Justice and Criminal Evidence Act 1999.

2. Charlie, a failed businessman, is suing Damian for damages for breach of an oral contract allegedly made in 2017. Damian denies having entered into any such contract. At the trial, may Damian cross-examine Charlie about the following facts and, if necessary, prove them?

   (a) As a teenager, Charlie was cautioned by the police for being drunk and disorderly.

   (b) Charlie has recently been receiving treatment as a recovering alcoholic.

   (c) In a letter dated July 2018 written by Charlie to Ed, a mutual friend of Charlie and Damian, Charlie wrote: 'Have you heard from Damian recently? I lost contact with him many years ago.'

   (d) Fred, a business rival of Damian, offered to give Charlie tickets for the men's final of the 2018 Wimbledon tennis tournament if Charlie were to start the civil proceedings against Damian that have now been brought.

   (e) Some years ago, Charlie became bankrupt and was convicted of fraudulently failing to inform the official receiver of the disposal of certain valuable property comprised in his estate.

 For a note-form answer see the online resources, accessible at www.oup.com/he/keane-mckeown13e.

Corroboration and care warnings

8

Key issues

- When a witness in a criminal trial gives evidence against the accused, why might it be desirable to have additional independent evidence by way of confirmation or support?

- In a criminal trial, when should the judge warn the jury to exercise caution before acting on the unsupported evidence of (a) an alleged accomplice or (b) in a sexual case, the complainant?

- If a prosecution witness gives evidence of a confession by the accused made when he and the accused were both in custody, when should the judge warn the jury to treat the evidence with caution?

- When an accused who is mentally handicapped makes a confession, when and why is there a special need for caution before convicting him in reliance on the confession?

- Should there be a prosecution for murder in a case involving a number of sudden infant deaths in the same family, if there is a conflict between experts as to the likely cause of the deaths and there is no other evidence additional to the expert evidence to support the prosecution case?

General rule and exceptions

'Any risk of the conviction of an innocent person is lessened if conviction is based upon the testimony of more than one acceptable witness.'[1] In civil, as well as criminal, cases it would not be unreasonable to expect a general rule requiring a party, who seeks to prove certain facts by the testimony of a single witness, to adduce additional independent evidence, by way of confirmation or support, so that the tribunal of fact is double-sure before it makes a particular finding, or gives judgment, in that party's favour. Although this is the case in most civil law jurisdictions, there is no general rule to this effect in English law. Thus in a criminal trial, provided that the jury are sure of the guilt of the accused, a conviction may be based on the testimony of a single prosecution witness who swears that he saw the accused commit the crime in question, and this remains the case even if part or all of his evidence is contradicted by the testimony of one or more witnesses called by the defence.[2] A party is, of course, free to adduce evidence which corroborates or supports the other evidence that he has tendered,[3] and to the extent that this would strengthen an otherwise weak case, as a matter of common sense he would be well advised to do so. As a general rule, however, there is no requirement (a) that evidence be corroborated; or (b) that the tribunal of fact be warned of the danger of acting on uncorroborated evidence.

This chapter is concerned with the exceptions to the general rule. There are three categories of exception. The first is where corroboration (probably in a technical sense) is required as a matter of law. In cases falling within this category, the ambit of which is clearly defined, comprising as it does of four cases governed by statute (perjury, treason, speeding, and attempts to commit such offences), a conviction cannot be based on uncorroborated evidence and, if it is, will be reversed on appeal. Thus in the absence of such corroboration, the judge should direct an acquittal. Depending on the statute in question, the corroboration may be required to take a particular form, such as the evidence of another witness, or may be permitted to take any form, whether testimony, real evidence, or documentary evidence.[4]

In the second category, which comprises a miscellany of different cases, neither corroboration in a technical sense nor supportive evidence is required as a matter of law, but in appropriate circumstances the tribunal of fact should be warned to exercise caution before acting on the evidence of certain types of witness, if unsupported. The witnesses in question include: (i) accomplices giving evidence for the prosecution; (ii) complainants in sexual cases; (iii) other witnesses whose evidence may be tainted by an improper motive; (iv) children; (v) anonymous witnesses; (vi) certain witnesses in matrimonial cases; and (vii) witnesses advancing claims against the estate of a deceased person. Whether a warning is given at all

---

[1] Per Lord Morris in *DPP v Hester* [1973] AC 296, HL at 315.

[2] However, a conviction in such circumstances may be set aside where it is unsafe: see *R v Cooper* [1969] 1 QB 267, CA at 271. In civil cases, a new trial may be ordered where the verdict of the jury is against the weight of the evidence: see per Lord Selborne in *Metropolitan Rly Co v Wright* (1886) 11 App Cas 152, HL at 153.

[3] Subject to the inherent power of the court to prevent the admission of superfluous evidence.

[4] It is very rare for statute to impose a corroborative requirement on an accused. Under s 1(1) of the Criminal Procedure (Insanity and Unfitness to Plead) Act 1991, a jury shall not acquit the accused on grounds of insanity except on the written evidence of two or more medical practitioners, at least one of whom has been duly approved as having special experience in the diagnosis or treatment of mental disorder. Section 4(6) of the 1991 Act contains an identical requirement of medical evidence where the jury are determining whether the accused is fit to be tried. Neither provision requires corroboration in the technical sense.

is a matter of judicial discretion dependent on the circumstances of the case, and therefore failure to give a warning will not necessarily furnish a good ground of appeal. Where a warning is given, the strength of the warning and the extent to which the judge should elaborate upon it, for example by referring to the potentially supportive material, also depends upon the particular circumstances of the case.

The third category comprises five cases in which corroboration in a technical sense is not required as a matter of law, and there is no obligation to warn the tribunal of fact of the danger of acting on the evidence in question *simply* by reason of the fact that it is uncorroborated or unsupported, but there is a special need for caution which has led to requirements analogous to, but distinct from, those relating to the first two categories. Three of the five cases are considered in this chapter. They are confessions by mentally handicapped persons, lip-reading evidence, and cases of Sudden Infant Death Syndrome (colloquially 'cot deaths'). The fourth case, identification evidence, merits the discrete treatment given to it in **Chapter 9**. The fifth case, unconvincing hearsay, is governed by s 125 of the Criminal Justice Act 2003, which is considered in **Chapter 12**.[5]

The meaning of corroboration

At common law a trial judge was required as a matter of law to warn the jury of the danger of acting on certain types of evidence if uncorroborated. Corroboration, for these purposes, bore a technical meaning. Corroboration, where required by statute, probably bears the same technical meaning. This appears to have been the view of Lord Reading CJ in *R v Baskerville*.[6] It has been held that corroboration in the technical sense is required in the case of the statutory provision relating to perjury;[7] and although, as we shall see, neither the perjury provision nor the provisions relating to treason and speeding expressly require 'corroboration', the wording of s 2(2)(g) of the Criminal Attempts Act 1981 suggests that that is exactly what they require.[8] Therefore before considering the statutory provisions requiring corroboration, it is necessary to consider first the meaning of corroboration in the technical sense.

To be capable of amounting to corroboration in the technical sense, evidence must be: (i) relevant; (ii) admissible; (iii) credible; (iv) independent; and (v) evidence which implicates the accused in the way that the specific statute requires. The first two requirements[9] apply to evidence generally and need no further explanation in the present context. As to

---

[5] See Ch 12, Stopping the case where the evidence is unconvincing, p 400.

[6] [1916] 2 KB 658 at 667.

[7] See para 3.9, Law Commission Working Paper No 115 (1990), citing *R v Hamid* (1979) 69 Cr App R 324, CA.

[8] Section 2(1) of the Criminal Attempts Act 1981 states, 'Any provision to which this section applies shall have effect with respect to an offence under section 1 above of attempting to commit an offence as it has effect with respect to the offence attempted.' Section 2(2)(g) of the Act states, ' provisions whereby a person may not be convicted or committed for trial on the uncorroborated evidence of one witness (including any provision requiring the evidence of not less than two credible witnesses)'. It may be that the draftsmen of the 1981 Act were, to some extent, influenced by the Children and Young Person's Act 1933, s 38(1), which expressly required corroboration in respect of the unsworn evidence of a child witness called by the prosecution. Section 38(1) has been repealed. See further in this chapter under **Children, p 267**.

[9] See per Scarman LJ in *R v Scarrott* [1978] QB 1016, CA at 1021.

the third requirement: 'Corroboration can only be afforded . . . by a witness who is otherwise to be believed. If a witness's testimony falls of its own inanition, the question of his . . . being capable of giving corroboration does not arise.'[10] Under the fourth requirement, independence, the evidence must emanate from a source other than the witness who is to be corroborated.[11] The fifth requirement, implication, is best explored by reference to the statutory provisions themselves. Before turning to them, it remains to note the respective functions of the judge and jury.[12] Where a judge does give a direction to the jury on corroboration, he must explain what it is. No particular form of words is necessary and there is no need even to use the word 'corroboration' provided that the requirements of credibility, independence, and implication are made clear.[13] The judge should also indicate what evidence is (and is not) capable of being corroboration.[14] Having directed the jury as to what evidence is capable in law of amounting to corroboration, the judge should explain that it falls to them, as the tribunal of fact, to decide whether the evidence does in fact constitute corroboration.[15]

Corroboration required by statute

Perjury

The rationale for the requirement of corroboration in relation to offences of perjury is not entirely clear. Historically, perjury was first punished in the Star Chamber, which usually required a second witness. Prior to the statutory provisions, the requirement at common law was held to be justified 'else there is only oath against oath'.[16] This argument did not seem strong to the Criminal Law Revision Committee 'as there may be more than oath against oath when the falsity of the accused's evidence is corroborated although not by a second witness'. Furthermore, 'there are many cases where corroboration is not required but the decision depends on the choice between two pieces of sworn evidence'. However, a majority of the Committee felt that to make a prosecution for perjury too easy might discourage persons from giving evidence and create the danger of a successful party to litigation, his evidence having been preferred, seeking to have his adversary, or his adversary's witnesses, prosecuted for perjury.[17]

---

[10] Per Lord Hailsham in *DPP v Kilbourne* [1973] AC 729 at 746. See also per Lord Morris in *DPP v Hester* [1973] AC 296 at 315 ('Corroborative evidence will only fill its role if it itself is completely credible') and *R v Thomas* (1985) 81 Cr App R 331, CA.

[11] See, eg, *R v Whitehead* [1929] 1 KB 99, CCA.

[12] It is submitted that the authorities that follow, which mainly related to common law corroboration requirements, also apply where corroboration is required by statute.

[13] See *R v Fallon* [1993] Crim LR 591, CA.

[14] *R v Charles* (1976) 68 Cr App R 334n; *R v Cullinane* [1984] Crim LR 420, CA; and *R v Webber* [1987] Crim LR 412, CA. If the judge fails to do so, this is unlikely to result in a successful appeal if there was in fact ample corroboration and the Court of Appeal is in no doubt that if a proper direction had been given, the jury would still have convicted: see *R v McInnes* (1989) 90 Cr App R 99, CA.

[15] *R v Tragen* [1956] Crim LR 332; *R v McInnes* (1989) 90 Cr App R 99, CA.

[16] *R v Muscot* (1713) 10 Mod Rep 192.

[17] Criminal Law Revision Committee, 11th Report, Cmnd 4991 (1972), paras 178 and 190.

Section 13 of the Perjury Act 1911 provides that:

A person shall not be liable to be convicted of any offence against this Act, or of any other offence declared by any other Act to be perjury or subornation of perjury, or to be punishable as perjury or subornation of perjury, solely upon the evidence of one witness as to the falsity of any statement alleged to be false.

The judge is therefore required to direct the jury that, before a conviction of perjury can be recorded, there must be evidence before them, which they accept, of more than one witness, that is, either evidence of at least one other witness or some other supporting evidence, by way of confession or otherwise, which is independent of the evidence given by the witness[18] and which supplements it.[19] The requirements of s 13 will be met, for example, by two witnesses hearing the accused admit to the falsity of the statement on the same occasion.[20] The section requires corroboration not only in relation to the offence of perjury in judicial proceedings, but also in relation to the many other offences under the Perjury Act of making false statements, on oath, in statutory declarations or otherwise, but not in judicial proceedings.[21] The corroboration need relate only to the *falsity* of the statement in question. Thus if the accused admits that the statement was untrue, the prosecution need call no evidence to prove this fact and s 13 does not apply.[22] Nor does the section apply to allegations of perjury contrary to s 1(1) of the 1911 Act when the falsity of the statement forms no part of the prosecution case: under s 1(1), if any person lawfully sworn as a witness wilfully makes a statement material in the proceedings which he knows to be false *or does not believe to be true*, he shall be guilty of an offence.[23]

Treason

Section 1 of the Treason Act 1795 requires corroboration in the form of evidence given by a second witness. It provides that a person charged with the offence of treason by compassing the death or restraint of the Queen or her heirs shall not be convicted except on 'the oaths of two lawful and credible witnesses'. The Criminal Law Revision Committee recommended the repeal of this provision.[24]

Speeding

The opinion evidence of non-experts is generally inadmissible.[25] One of the exceptions to this rule is opinion evidence relating to speed. Section 89(2) of the Road Traffic Regulation Act 1984, in recognition of the danger of such evidence being inaccurate, provides that a

---

[18] See *R v Cooper* [2010] 1 WLR 2390, CA: business documents compiled by the witness himself, who is the single source of the document, will not qualify as corroboration for the purposes of s 13.

[19] See *R v Hamid* (1979) 69 Cr App R 324, CA and *R v Carroll* (1993) 99 Cr App R 381, CA. Failure to direct the jury in accordance with s 13 may afford grounds for a successful appeal: see *R v Rider* (1986) 83 Cr App R 207, CA.

[20] *R v Peach* [1990] 2 All ER 966, CA. See also *R v Threlfall* (1914) 10 Cr App R 112: a letter suborning another to commit perjury in relation to the same matter in respect of which the false statement was made may constitute corroboration.

[21] The Criminal Law Revision Committee and the Law Commission (para 45, Published Working Paper No 33, *Perjury and Kindred Offences*) saw no need to preserve the latter requirement.

[22] *R v Rider* (1986) 83 Cr App R 207, CA.

[23] Ibid.

[24] Criminal Law Revision Committee, 11th Report, Cmnd 4991 (1972), para 195.

[25] See Ch 20.

person charged with an offence of driving a motor vehicle on a road at an excessive speed 'shall not be liable to be convicted solely on the evidence of one witness to the effect that in the opinion of the witness the person prosecuted was driving the vehicle at a speed exceeding a specified limit'. The opinion evidence of two or more people that a vehicle was exceeding the speed limit is sufficient to justify a conviction under this provision provided that their evidence relates to the speed of the vehicle at the same place and time.[26] The provision only applies to evidence of mere opinion and not to evidence of fact.[27] Speedometers and other similar devices[28] will be presumed, in the absence of evidence to the contrary, to have been working properly at the material time and to be capable of providing evidence of fact.

In *Crossland v DPP*[29] Bingham LJ said: 'It is plain . . . that the subsection is intended to prevent the conviction of a defendant on evidence given by a single witness of his unsupported visual impression of a defendant's speed.' An expert in accident reconstruction testified that he had inspected the scene of a road traffic accident, including skid marks and damage to the defendant's car, carried out speed and braking tests on the car, and calculated that its speed had been not less than 41 mph. It was held that this was not just the opinion evidence of one witness: the expert had also described the objectively determined phenomena on which his opinion was based.

Attempts

Under s 2(2)(g) of the 1981 Act, any provision whereby a person may not be convicted on the uncorroborated evidence of one witness (including any provision requiring the evidence of not less than two credible witnesses) shall have effect with respect to an offence under s 1 of the Act of attempting to commit an offence as it has effect with respect to the offence attempted.

Care warnings

Accomplices testifying for the prosecution and complainants in sexual cases

The background

Prior to the Criminal Justice and Public Order Act 1994 there existed at common law a category of exception to the general rule under which, although corroboration (in the technical sense) was not required as a matter of law, the tribunal of fact had to be warned, as a matter of law, of the danger of acting on evidence if not corroborated (in the technical sense). This obligatory warning was required in respect of the evidence of (a) accomplices testifying on behalf of the prosecution; and (b) complainants in sexual cases.[30] As to the former, accomplices were defined as: (i) parties to the offence in question; (ii) handlers of stolen goods, in the case of thieves from whom they receive, on the trial of the latter for theft; and (iii) parties

---

[26] *Brighty v Pearson* [1938] 4 All ER 127.

[27] See *Nicholas v Penny* [1950] 2 KB 466 where it was held that magistrates could convict on the evidence of a police officer who had checked his speedometer and driven at an even distance behind the accused's car. However, see *Iaciofano v DPP* [2011] RTR 15, DC. See also *Connell v The Crown Prosecution Service* (2011) 175 JP 151, DC.

[28] See *Collinson v Mabbott* (1984) The Times, 10 Oct, DC (corroboration by radar gun); and *Burton v Gilbert* [1984] RTR 162, DC (corroboration by radar speed meter).

[29] [1988] 3 All ER 712 at 714.

[30] The need for such a warning was not confined to criminal proceedings: see *Mattouk v Massad* [1943] AC 588.

to another offence committed by the accused in respect of which evidence is admitted under the similar fact evidence doctrine.[31] Whether a particular witness was an accomplice was a question usually answered by the witness himself, by confessing to participation, by pleading guilty to it, or by being convicted of it. If not answered by the witness himself, the question whether he was in fact an accomplice was for the jury, provided that there was evidence on which a reasonable jury could have concluded that the witness was an accomplice.[32] As to complainants in sexual cases, the warning was required in respect of the victims, whether male or female,[33] of sexual offences.[34]

There were only two exceptions to the requirement that a warning be given: first, where an accomplice gave evidence, on behalf of the prosecution, which was mainly favourable to the accused and more harm would have been done to the accused by giving the warning than by not giving it;[35] second, in sexual cases in which identification was in issue, but not the commission of the offence itself.[36] Subject to these exceptions, failure to give the warning furnished a good ground of appeal. The warning to be given to the jury (the 'full' warning) comprised four parts:

1. The warning itself, that is, that it was dangerous to convict on the uncorroborated evidence of the 'suspect' witness but that if they, the jury, were satisfied of the truth of such evidence, they might nonetheless convict.

2. An explanation of the meaning of corroboration in the technical sense.

3. An indication of what evidence was (and was not) capable in law of amounting to corroboration.

4. An explanation that it fell to the jury, as the tribunal of fact, to decide whether that evidence did in fact constitute corroboration.

By reason of s 32 of the 1994 Act, full warnings are no longer required. In order to understand the effect of s 32, it is important to consider first both the justification for the rules requiring a full warning and the reasons for their abolition. The justification given for the requirement of a warning in the case of an accomplice giving evidence for the prosecution was that such a witness may have a purpose of his own to serve: he may give false evidence against the accused out of spite, to exaggerate or even invent the accused's role in the crime, or with a view to minimizing the extent of his own culpability. Concerning sexual offences (as in

---

[31] *Davies v DPP* [1954] AC 378, HL. An accomplice, for these purposes, also included a thief from whom a handler has received goods, on the trial of the latter for receiving (*R v Vernon* [1962] Crim LR 35) but not an agent provocateur (*R v Mullins* (1848) 3 Cox CC 526), a child victim of a sexual offence (*R v Pitts* (1912) 8 Cr App R 126), or a woman upon whose immoral earnings the accused was charged with having lived (per Lord Reading CJ in *R v King* (1914) 10 Cr App R 117, CCA) unless, on the facts, there was evidence of aiding and abetting the accused, eg evidence of collecting money on behalf of the accused from other prostitutes (as in *R v Stewart* (1986) 83 Cr App R 327, CA).

[32] *Davies v DPP* [1954] AC 378.

[33] *R v Burgess* (1956) 40 Cr App R 144, CCA.

[34] The rule did not apply to other kinds of offence, even if their commission was allegedly accompanied by some form of sexual activity on the part of the accused: *R v Simmons* [1987] Crim LR 630, CA.

[35] See *R v Royce-Bentley* [1974] 1 WLR 535, CA.

[36] See *R v Chance* [1988] 3 All ER 225, CA.

procuration cases), the requirement of a warning stemmed from an assumption that such a charge is easy to make but difficult to refute. There is also 'the danger that the complainant may have made a false accusation owing to sexual neurosis, jealousy, fantasy, spite or a girl's refusal to admit that she consented to an act of which she is now ashamed'.[37] Such a danger may be hidden, yet the nature of the evidence may well make jurors sympathetic to the complainant and so prejudice them against the accused.

The reasons in favour of the abolition of mandatory corroboration warnings were compelling.[38] The first and most serious objection was that the rules applied on a class basis, that is, irrespective of the circumstances of the particular case and the credibility of the particular witness. Thus even if there was no danger of the 'suspect' witness giving false evidence, the judge still had to give the warning. Second, since many sexual offences are committed in circumstances in which corroboration is difficult if not impossible to obtain, the requirement was capable of resulting in the acquittal of the guilty. In cases involving the sexual abuse of children, the mandatory warning simply compounded the difficulty of securing a conviction.[39] Third, the full warning had become extremely complex, not least because of the technical rules on what constituted corroboration, and this often led to successful appeals. Fourth, there was an element of self-contradiction in directing jurors that it was 'dangerous' to convict on uncorroborated evidence and then proceeding to direct them that they could nonetheless do so. Finally, there was some evidence to suggest that where a warning was given, far from operating as a safeguard for the accused, the jury were more likely to convict.[40]

Section 32 of the Criminal Justice and Public Order Act 1994

Section 32 of the 1994 Act provides as follows:

1. Any requirement whereby at a trial on indictment it is obligatory for the court to give the jury a warning about convicting the accused on the uncorroborated evidence of a person merely because that person is—
   (a) an alleged accomplice of the accused, or
   (b) where the offence charged is a sexual offence, the person in respect of whom it is alleged to have been committed,
   is hereby abrogated . . .
2. Any requirement that—
   (a) is applicable at the summary trial of a person for an offence, and
   (b) corresponds to the requirement mentioned in subsection (1) above . . .
   is hereby abrogated.

Thus in cases involving the evidence of an alleged accomplice or of a complainant in a sexual case, s 32 has simply abrogated any requirement whereby it was *obligatory* for the tribunal of

---

[37] Criminal Law Revision Committee, 11th Report, Cmnd 4991 (1972), para 186.

[38] See generally Criminal Law Revision Committee, 11th Report, Cmnd 4991 (1972), paras 183–6; Law Commission Working Paper No 115 (1990); Law Commission Report No 202, Cm 1620 (1991); and Royal Commission on Criminal Justice, Cm 2263 (1993), Ch 8. Although note the Canadian case of *R v Khela* 2009 SCC 4, in which views to the contrary were expressed. For comment on this case, see Pattenden, 'Case Commentaries' (2009) 13 E&P 243.

[39] See *Report of the Advisory Group on Video Evidence* (Home Office, 1989), para 5.17.

[40] See Law Commission Working Paper No 115, paras 2.9 and 2.18 and *Vetrovec v R* (1982) 136 DLR (3d) 89 at 95.

fact to be given a full warning—the judge still has a discretion to give some form of warning whenever he considers it necessary to do so. The leading authority on s 32 is *R v Makanjuola*,[41] in which Lord Taylor CJ summarized the relevant principles:[42]

1. Section 32(1) abrogates the requirement to give a corroboration direction in respect of an alleged accomplice or a complainant of a sexual offence simply because a witness falls into one of those categories.

2. It is a matter for the judge's discretion what, if any, warning he considers appropriate in respect of such a witness, as indeed in respect of any other witness in whatever type of case. Whether he chooses to give a warning and in what terms will depend on the circumstances of the case, the issues raised, and the content and quality of the witness's evidence.

3. In some cases, it may be appropriate for the judge to warn the jury to exercise caution before acting upon the unsupported evidence of a witness. This will not be so simply because the witness is a complainant of a sexual offence nor will it necessarily be so because a witness is alleged to be an accomplice. There will need to be an evidential basis for suggesting that the evidence of the witness may be unreliable. An evidential basis does not include mere suggestions by cross-examining counsel.

4. If any question arises as to whether the judge should give a special warning in respect of a witness, it is desirable that the question be resolved by discussion with counsel in the absence of the jury before final speeches. (The judge will often consider that no special warning is required at all. Where, however, the witness has been shown to be unreliable, he or she may consider it necessary to urge caution.[43] In a more extreme case, if the witness is shown to have lied, to have made previous false complaints, or to bear the defendant some grudge, a stronger warning may be thought appropriate and the judge may suggest it would be wise to look for some supporting material before acting on the impugned witness's evidence.[44] We stress that these observations are merely illustrative of some, not all, of the factors which judges may take into account in measuring where a witness stands in the scale of reliability . . .).[45]

5. Where the judge does decide to give some warning in respect of a witness, it will be appropriate to do so as part of the judge's review of the evidence and his comments as to how the jury should evaluate it rather than a set-piece legal direction.

6. Where some warning is required, it will be for the judge to decide the strength and terms of the warning. It does not have to be invested with the whole florid regime of the old corroboration rules.

---

[41] [1995] 1 WLR 1348, CA.

[42] Ibid at 1351–2. See also Lewis, 'A Comparative Examination of Corroboration and Care Warnings in Prosecutions of Sexual Offences' [2006] Crim LR 889.

[43] eg when a complainant's evidence is internally inconsistent or there are previous inconsistent statements: see *R v Walker* [1996] Crim LR 742, CA.

[44] Delay in complaining will not, by itself, require either the 'stronger direction' or the urging of 'caution': see *R v R* [1996] Crim LR 815, CA and *R v Fallis* [2004] EWCA Crim 923.

[45] The bracketed material is set out in an earlier part of the judgment (at 732).

7. It follows that we emphatically disagree with the tentative submission [that if a judge does give a warning, he should give a full warning and should tell the jury what corroboration is in the technical sense and identify the evidence capable of being corroborative]. Attempts to re-impose the straitjacket of the old corroboration rules are strongly to be deprecated.

8. Finally, this court will be disinclined to interfere with a judge's exercise of his discretion save in a case where that exercise is unreasonable in the *Wednesbury* sense.[46]

'*Supporting material*'

Following *R v Makanjuola*, if there is an evidential basis for suggesting that the witness may be unreliable, and the trial judge therefore decides to direct the jury that it would be wise to look for some 'supporting material', the judge is no longer required to identify for the jury what evidence is and is not capable of being corroboration in the technical sense. However, once such a direction is given, it has been held that it is then incumbent on the judge to identify any 'independent supporting evidence'.[47] It seems reasonably clear that such evidence may be furnished by the accused himself, as when evidence is given of an out-of-court confession or the accused makes a damaging admission in the course of giving his evidence.[48] It seems equally clear that it may be furnished by (i) the accused's lies, whether told in or out of court; (ii) his silence; (iii) his refusal to consent to the taking of samples; or (iv) his misconduct. It will be convenient to consider, briefly, these examples before turning to some items of evidence which, arguably, cannot constitute 'supporting material'.

Lies by the accused may amount to 'supporting material' depending on the nature of the lie and the nature of the other evidence in the case. It is submitted that the criteria for determining whether a lie constitutes 'supporting material' are the same as those previously employed for determining whether a lie amounted to corroboration in the technical sense. Those criteria, applicable to lies whether told in or out of court, were established in *R v Lucas*:[49]

> To be capable of amounting to corroboration the lie . . . must first of all be deliberate.[50] Secondly it must relate to a material issue. Thirdly the motive for the lie must be a realisation of guilt and a fear of the truth. The jury should in appropriate cases be reminded that people sometimes lie, for example, in an attempt to bolster up a just cause, or out of shame or out of a wish to conceal disgraceful behaviour from their family. Fourthly the statement must clearly be shown to be a lie by evidence other than that of the [witness] who is to be corroborated, that is to say by admission or by evidence from an independent witness.

Thus where an accused, charged with a sexual offence, tells the police that on the evening in question he did not leave his house, but subsequently admits that this statement was false, his lie may be used to support the evidence of the victim that the offence had taken place near to the accused's home,[51] because 'a false statement . . . may give to a proved opportunity

---

[46] See *Associated Provincial Picture Houses Ltd v Wednesbury Corpn* [1948] 1 KB 223. This is a heavy burden for an appellant to discharge: see *R v R* [1996] Crim LR 815, CA.

[47] *R v B (MT)* [2000] Crim LR 181, CA.

[48] See *R v Dossi* (1918) 13 Cr App R 158, CCA: on a charge of indecently assaulting a girl, an admission by the accused, in court, that he had innocently fondled her, is some corroboration of her evidence.

[49] [1981] QB 720, CA at 724.

[50] A lie being an *intentional* false statement, the meaning of the first requirement is obscure.

[51] See *Credland v Knowler* (1951) 35 Cr App R 48, DC. For an example of a lie told in court, see *Corfield v Hodgson* [1966] 2 All ER 205.

a different complexion from what it would have borne had no such false statement been made'.[52] *R v Lucas* itself concerned the fourth criterion. The appeal was allowed because the jury had been invited to prefer the evidence of an accomplice to that of the accused and then to use their disbelief of the accused as corroboration of the accomplice. The direction was erroneous because the 'lie' told by the accused was not shown to be a lie by evidence other than that of the accomplice who was to be corroborated.[53]

Where a person is accused of a crime, by a person speaking to him on even terms, in circumstances such that it would be natural for him to reply, evidence of his silence may be admitted, at common law, to show that he admits the truth of the charge made[54] and may constitute 'supporting material'.[55] Such material, it is submitted, may also be derived from inferences properly drawn from (i) the accused's failure to mention facts when questioned by a constable or on being charged with an offence; (ii) his silence at trial; (iii) his failure or refusal to account for objects, substances, marks, or presence at a particular place;[56] or (iv) his refusal to consent to the taking of 'intimate samples'.[57] Supporting material may also take the form of evidence of the accused's misconduct on some other occasion admitted under the similar fact evidence doctrine as evidence relevant to the question of guilt on the charge before the court.[58]

Whether a given item of evidence is capable of amounting to 'supporting material' is not always as easy as the above examples might suggest. For example, in a case of rape in which the complainant is shown to have made previous false complaints and a warning is properly given, should any of the following items be treated as 'supporting material', and in any event, how should the judge direct the jury in their regard: (i) evidence of recent complaint;[59] (ii) evidence of the distressed condition of the complainant; and (iii) medical evidence showing that someone had had intercourse with the complainant at a time consistent with her evidence? There are compelling reasons to suggest that each of these items, by itself, should not be treated as 'supporting material' and the judge should direct the jury accordingly. As to a recent complaint, the trial judge should, at the least, explain to the jury that the evidence emanates from the complainant herself.[60] As to evidence of distress, the same point could be made, but such a direction would be inappropriate if, for example, the distress was witnessed shortly after the offence, the complainant was unaware that she was being observed, and there is nothing to suggest that she put on an act and simulated distress.[61] However, in appropriate cases the jury should be alerted to the risk that distress may have

---

[52] Per Lord Dunedin in *Dawson v McKenzie* (1908) 45 SLR 473.

[53] See also per Lord MacDermott in *Tumahole Bereng v R* [1949] AC 253 at 270.

[54] See *R v Mitchell* (1892) 17 Cox CC 503; *R v Chandler* [1976] 1 WLR 585, CA; *Parkes v R* [1976] 1 WLR 1251; and generally Ch 15.

[55] See *R v Cramp* (1880) 14 Cox CC 390, a decision on corroboration in the technical sense.

[56] See Criminal Justice and Public Order Act 1994, ss 34–7 (see Ch 16).

[57] See *R v (Robert William) Smith* (1985) 81 Cr App R 286, CA and Police and Criminal Evidence Act 1984, s 62(10) (Ch 16).

[58] See Ch 19.

[59] See the Criminal Justice Act 2003, s 120(7), Ch 12.

[60] Such evidence was not corroboration in the technical sense because not independent of the witness requiring to be corroborated: see *R v Whitehead* [1929] 1 KB 99, CCA.

[61] Evidence of distress could amount to corroboration in the technical sense, but juries had to be warned that except in special circumstances little weight should be given to it: see per Lord Parker CJ in *R v Knight* [1966] 1 WLR 230 at 233. For examples, see *R v Redpath* (1962) 46 CR App R 319, CCA; *R v Chauhan* (1981) 73 Cr App R 232, CA; and *R v Dowley* [1983] Crim LR 168, CA.

been feigned.[62] In respect of the complainant's own evidence as to her distress, as opposed to evidence of her distress from a third party, this is not independent evidence. A direction which stated that such evidence is capable of being supporting evidence would plainly be in error.[63] Where evidence of distress relates to distress some considerable time after the alleged incident, or distress which occurs over a particular period of time, generally it may not be of much assistance, but if it is, both its admissibility and any direction has to be considered very carefully.[64] Where there is evidence of contemporaneous distress or distress very shortly after the offence, and evidence of distress some time later, the judge, when directing the jury, should separate out and distinguish it and not treat all the pieces of evidence of distress in the same way.[65] Concerning medical evidence of intercourse, the trial judge might sensibly direct the jury that it does not, by itself, show that intercourse took place without consent or that the accused was a party to it.[66] It is to be hoped that commonsensical guidance and helpful directions of this kind will not be regarded as 'attempts to re-impose the straitjacket of the old corroboration rules'. It would be a pity if the baby of common sense were to be thrown out with the corroboration bath water.

Sexual cases in which identification is in issue

There is nothing to suggest that the principles established in *R v Makanjuola* should not apply to sexual cases in which identification is in issue. However, if the identity of the offender is in issue, but the fact that someone committed the offence is not in issue, either because formally admitted by the accused or, if not formally admitted, because there has been no suggestion by the defence that there is any doubt as to the commission of the offence, it will normally suffice to direct the jury, in accordance with *R v Turnbull*,[67] about the need for

---

[62] *R v Romeo* [2004] 1 Cr App R 418 (30), CA. Conversely, an issue that has not uncommonly arisen in sexual cases has been a complainant's apparent lack of distress, inferred from such things as delay in reporting and demeanour after the offence and in the witness box. Where such an issue does arise, a careful direction should be given to the jury that the trauma of a serious sexual assault means that there is no one classic response. See *R v D* [2008] EWCA Crim 2557 and Neil Kibble's 'Commentary' [2009] Crim LR 591. See also the Crown Court Compendium (July 2019), Part 1, 20–1 (erroneous assumptions about complainants in sexual cases). See also *R v Beale* [2019] 2 Cr App R 194 (19), CA, where it was held that the guidance on myths and stereotypes about complainants in sexual cases may be appropriate to benefit an accused charged with perjury by making false allegations of sexual offences (although not in the case itself). For a critical reflection on educational jury directions in sexual cases and an argument that there should be an educational direction specifically for cases involving 'domestic' or intimate partner rape, see Ellison, 'Credibility in context: jury education and intimate partner rape', E & P (2019) 23(3), 263.

[63] See *R v Zala* [2014] EWCA Crim 2181 at [24].

[64] *R v Miah* [2014] EWCA Crim 938.

[65] See *R v Zala* [2014] EWCA Crim 1281 at [25].

[66] For these reasons, such evidence was not corroboration in the technical sense: *James v R* (1970) 55 Cr App R 299, PC. However, if there was *also* evidence that the accused alone had been with the complainant at the relevant time, and evidence that her underclothing was torn and that she had injuries to her private parts, the combined effect of all the evidence was capable of amounting to corroboration: see per Lord Lane CJ in *R v Hills* (1987) 86 Cr App R 26, CA at 31. Where the only issue is consent, it would seem that evidence of injuries is, by itself, capable of supporting the complainant's assertion of lack of consent. However, where two or more accused are charged with successive acts of rape, the question whether the material can support the complainant's case against more than one of them will turn on the particular circumstances of the case: see *R v Pountney* [1989] Crim LR 216, CA and *R v Franklin* [1989] Crim LR 499, CA, decisions on corroboration in the technical sense. See also *R v Ensor* [1989] 1 WLR 497, CA.

[67] [1977] QB 224, CA (see **Ch 9, Visual identification, p 278**).

caution before convicting on identification evidence; a further warning about the complainant's evidence as to the *offence* is only required where there is an evidential basis for suggesting that her evidence in that regard is unreliable.[68]

Other witnesses whose evidence may be tainted by an improper motive

There are a number of common law authorities to the effect that the jury should be warned to exercise caution before acting on the evidence of a witness who may have a purpose of his own to serve. These authorities are considered in the paragraphs that follow. Some of the authorities preceding *R v Makanjuola* suggested that in some circumstances, at any rate, the warning was obligatory. It is now clear, from the decision in *R v Muncaster*,[69] that all such authorities need to be looked at afresh in the light of *R v Makanjuola*. It was held that the guidance in *R v Makanjuola* must be read as applying generally to all cases in which a witness may be suspect because he falls into a certain category.

An accomplice who is a co-accused

An accomplice who is a co-accused may incriminate another co-accused when giving evidence in his own defence. Because, in these circumstances, an accomplice may be regarded as having some purpose of his own to serve, it has been held that it is desirable, but only as a matter of practice, to warn the jury of the danger of acting on his unsupported evidence, and that every case must be looked at in the light of its own facts.[70] In *R v Cheema*,[71] following a full review of the authorities, Lord Taylor CJ said:

> although a warning in suitable terms as to the danger of a co-defendant having an axe to grind is desirable, there is no rule of law or practice requiring a full corroboration direction . . . what is required when one defendant implicates another in evidence is simply to warn the jury of what may very often be obvious—namely that the defendant witness may have a purpose of his own to serve.[72]

Following *R v Makanjuola*, it is clear that whether a warning is given, and if so, its strength, remain matters of judicial discretion dependent on the circumstances of the case.[73] In *R v Jones*[74] it was held that in the case of cut-throat defences, including mirror-image cut-throat defences, a warning should normally be considered and given and, if given, should at least warn the jury to examine the evidence of each accused with care because each has or may have an interest of his own to serve.[75] There is a particular need for some such warning where,

---

[68] Cf *R v Chance* [1988] 3 All ER 225, CA, regarding corroboration in the technical sense.

[69] [1999] Crim LR 409, CA.

[70] *R v Prater* [1960] 2 QB 464, CCA at 466. See also *R v Knowlden* (1983) 77 Cr App R 94, CA; *R v Stannard* [1964] 1 All ER 34 at 40, per Winn J; and *R v Whitaker* (1976) 63 Cr App R 193, CA at 197, per Lord Widgery. However, if the evidence incriminates the accused in one material respect but otherwise exonerates him, there is no need for a warning (which could operate to the *disadvantage* of the accused): see *R v Perman* [1995] Crim LR 736, CA.

[71] [1994] 1 WLR 147, CA at 156–7.

[72] See also *R v Sargent* [1993] Crim LR 713, CA: the defendant witness may well have a 'row of his own to hoe'.

[73] *R v Muncaster* [1999] Crim LR 409, CA.

[74] [2004] 1 Cr App R 60, CA.

[75] Contrast *R v Burrows* [2000] Crim LR 48, CA, where, according to *R v Jones*, the court was heavily influenced by the particular facts.

as in *R v Jones* itself, one of the accused has refused to answer questions in interview and is therefore able, if he wishes, to tailor his defence to the facts in evidence. It was further held that, subject to what justice demands on the particular facts of each case, in many or most cases a judge might consider four points to put to the jury: (1) to consider the case for and against each accused separately; (2) to decide the case on all the evidence, including the evidence of each co-accused; (3) when considering the evidence of each co-accused, to bear in mind that he may have an interest to serve or 'an axe to grind'; and (4) to assess the evidence of co-defendants in the same way as the evidence of any other witness in the case.[76]

Cell confessions

Where a witness seeks to give evidence of a confession made by the accused when they were both in custody (a 'cell confession'), there are no special conditions of admissibility and no requirement for corroboration.[77] However, in *Pringle v R*[78] it was held that a judge must always be alert to the possibility that the evidence of one prisoner against another is tainted by an improper motive, especially where a prisoner who has yet to face trial gives evidence that the other prisoner has confessed to the crime for which he is being held in custody. The indications that the evidence may be tainted by an improper motive must be found in the evidence—described as 'not an exacting test'—and the surrounding circumstances may justify the inference that his evidence is so tainted. This approach was followed in *Benedetto v R*,[79] where the Privy Council observed that the prisoners giving the evidence will almost always have strong reasons of self-interest for seeking to ingratiate themselves with those who may be in a position to reward them for volunteering the evidence, and that the accused is always at a disadvantage because he has none of the usual protections against the inaccurate recording or invention of words when interviewed by the police, and if the informer has a bad character, it may be difficult for him to obtain information needed to expose it fully. However, a much more flexible approach was adopted in *R v Stone*,[80] where the Court of Appeal held as follows.

1. Not every case involving a cell confession requires the detailed directions discussed in *Pringle v R* and *Benedetto v R*. Such cases prompt the most careful consideration by the trial judge, but that consideration is not trammelled by fixed rules; the trial judge is best placed to decide the strength of any warning and any accompanying analysis.

2. In the case of a 'standard two-line confession', there would generally be a need to point out that such confessions are often easy to concoct and difficult to disprove and that experience has shown that prisoners may have many motives to lie. Further, if the informant has a significant criminal record or history of lying, this should usually be pointed out, explaining why it gives rise to a need for great care.

---

[76] *R v Jones* was followed in *R v Petkar* [2004] 1 Cr App R 270 (22), CA. However, in *Petkar*, Rix LJ voiced two concerns about *Jones*: first, the warning could devalue the evidence of both co-accused in the eyes of the jury and second, point (3) in *Jones* did not appear to lie easily with point (4).

[77] For an analysis of the issues, see Jeremy Dein, 'Non Tape Recorded Cell Confession Evidence—On Trial' [2002] Crim LR 630.

[78] [2003] UKPC 9.

[79] [2003] 1 WLR 1545, PC.

[80] [2005] Crim LR 569, CA. See also *R v Cundell* [2009] EWCA Crim 2072, where, notwithstanding the more flexible approach in *Stone*, the judge should have given a warning in respect of the evidence of two prisoners awaiting sentence and one prisoner who hoped to be moved to an open and more local prison.

3. However, a summing-up should be tailored to the circumstances of the particular case. Where an alleged confession would not be easy to invent, it would be absurd to give a direction on the ease of concoction. Similarly, where the defence deliberately do not cross-examine the complainant about the motive of hope of obtaining advantage, there is no requirement to tell the jury that the informant being a prisoner, there might, intrinsically, have been such a motive.

4. There will be cases where the prisoner has witnessed the acts constituting the offence in which it will be appropriate to treat him as an ordinary witness about whose evidence nothing out of the usual needs to be said.

5. Indications that the prison informant's evidence may be tainted by an improper motive have to be found in the evidence.

Other examples

In *R v Beck*[81] it was argued that an accomplice warning should be given in cases where a witness has a substantial interest of his own for giving false evidence even though there is no material to suggest any involvement by the witness in the crime. Although rejecting the argument, Ackner LJ said that the court did not wish to detract from 'the obligation on a judge to advise a jury to proceed with caution where there is material to suggest that a witness's evidence may be tainted by an improper motive', continuing, 'and the strength of that advice must vary according to the facts of the case'.[82] Thus a warning may be given where there is evidence to suggest that a witness is acting out of spite or malevolence, has a financial or other personal interest in the outcome of the proceedings, or is otherwise biased or partial.[83] Where a witness, awaiting sentence, gives evidence for the prosecution in another case in circumstances in which he knows that at the very least by doing so he stands a chance of having his sentence reduced, it has been held that the potential fallibility of his evidence should be put squarely before the jury.[84] In *R v Asghar*[85] a group of men became involved in a fight in which someone was fatally stabbed. A was charged with murder. Three others from the group pleaded guilty to affray and gave evidence for the prosecution against A. It was held that the judge should have exercised his discretion to direct the jury on the danger of convicting A on the evidence of the other three without some independent supporting evidence because: (i) the defence case was that the three had put their heads together with others to fabricate a story incriminating A in order to protect one of their number; (ii) this suggested the motive for their alleged lies was directly linked with the murder charge and did not arise from some unconnected cause; and (iii) the three were not on trial with A and not at risk, their position being akin to those of accomplices in the strict sense.[86] Equally, where a witness, having entered into an agreement to assist the authorities under s 73 of the

---

[81] [1982] 1 WLR 461, CA.

[82] Ibid at 469. See also *R v Witts and Witts* [1991] Crim LR 562, CA.

[83] A warning is unnecessary, however, if it would do more harm than good, as when it is obvious to the jury, from the circumstances of the case, that a witness is suspect: *R v Lovell* [1990] Crim LR 111, CA.

[84] *Chan Wai-Keung v R* [1995] 2 All ER 438, PC.

[85] [1995] 1 Cr App R 223, CA.

[86] Although the final reason is no longer compelling (see, in this chapter, under **Section 32 of the Criminal Justice and Public Order Act 1994**, p 259), it is submitted that in such a case the need for some form of warning remains. See, further, the judgment of Lord Reading CJ in *R v King* (1914) 10 Cr App R 117; and cf *R v Hanton* (1985) The Times, 14 Feb, CA; and *R v Evans* [1965] 2 QB 295. See also *R v Blackburn* [2008] 2 Cr App R (S) 16 (5), CA and *Krishna v Trinidad & Tobago* [2011] UKPC 18: a witness does not cease to be an accomplice on the basis that he has agreed to and does give evidence as a prosecution witness.

Serious Organized Crime and Police Act 2005, gives evidence in return for a reduced sentence, a warning is called for to address the obvious risk that he is serving his own ends and not those of justice. In *R v Daniels*,[87] it was held that a carefully worded warning is the proper way to address this risk since, given the overwhelming public interest that major criminals should be convicted, there could be no objection to the admissibility of such evidence purely because the witness had 'self-interestedly done a deal or entered into a . . . Faustian pact'.[88]

R v Spencer, R v Smails[89] may be regarded as a further example. In that case, nursing staff at a secure hospital were charged with ill-treating patients convicted of crimes and suffering from mental disorders. The prosecution case consisted of the evidence of patients who were characterized as being mentally unbalanced, of bad character, anti-authoritarian, and prone to lie or exaggerate and who could have had old scores to settle. The House of Lords held that where the only evidence for the prosecution is that of a witness who, by reason of his particular mental condition and criminal connection, fulfils criteria analogous to those which (formerly) justified a full corroboration warning (accomplices testifying for the prosecution and complainants in sexual cases), the judge should warn the jury that it is dangerous to convict on his uncorroborated evidence, but such a warning need not amount to the full warning.[90] Thus while it may often be convenient to use the words 'danger' or 'dangerous', the use of such words is not essential to an adequate warning, so long as the jury are made fully aware of the dangers of convicting on such evidence, and the extent to which the judge should refer to the corroborative material, if any exists, depends on the facts of each case.[91] It may be doubted whether 'corroborative material', for these purposes, was ever intended to mean corroboration in the strict sense; and it is submitted that, notwithstanding the analogy drawn with cases which (formerly) justified a full corroboration warning (which, in the light of s 32 of the 1994 Act, would suggest that a warning is no longer obligatory), a warning of the kind indicated in *R v Spencer, R v Smails* should still be given in respect of witnesses sharing the same unfortunate characteristics as the witnesses in that case. Following *R v Makanjuola*, however, it is clear that where a warning is given, its terms will depend on the precise circumstances of the particular case.[92]

Children

Under the proviso to s 38(1) of the Children and Young Persons Act 1933, where the unsworn evidence of a child was given on behalf of the prosecution, the accused was not liable to be convicted unless that evidence was corroborated by some other material evidence implicating him; and at common law, the sworn evidence of a child required a corroboration warning as a matter of law.[93] Section 38(1) has been repealed[94] and s 34(2) of the Criminal Justice Act 1988[95] provides that: 'Any requirement whereby at a trial on indictment it is obligatory for the court to give the jury a warning about convicting the accused on the uncorroborated evidence of a child

---

[87] [2011] 1 Cr App R 228 (18), CA.

[88] Per Richards LJ at [40], quoting from a ruling of Langstaff J in the trial of the appellants.

[89] [1986] 2 All ER 928, HL.

[90] Overruling, in this respect, *R v Bagshaw* [1984] 1 WLR 477, CA.

[91] See also, in this chapter, concerning confessions made by the mentally handicapped, *R v Bailey* [1995] 2 Cr App R 262, CA and Police and Criminal Evidence Act 1984, s 77, under **Confessions by the mentally handicapped**, p 269.

[92] See *R v Causley* [1999] Crim LR 572, CA.

[93] See, eg, *R v Cleal* [1942] 1 All ER 203, CCA.

[94] Criminal Justice Act 1991, s 101(2) and Sch 13.

[95] As amended by the Criminal Justice and Public Order Act 1994, s 32(2).

is abrogated.' The rationale underlying the proviso to s 38(1) and the common law rule was the danger that the evidence of a child, especially if unsworn, but even if sworn, may be unreliable by reason of childish imagination, suggestibility, or fallibility of memory. These dangers have doubtless been exaggerated,[96] but in some cases may remain. Although in *R v Pryce*[97] it was held that a direction to treat the evidence of a 6-year-old girl with caution was not required, because this would amount to a re-introduction of the abrogated rule, it is clear, following *R v Makanjuola*, that judges do retain a discretionary power to give such a direction. Whether such a direction should be given, and if so, its precise terms, are matters dependent on the circumstances of the case.[98] In the case of children, the relevant factors include the age and intelligence of the child, whether the evidence is given on oath, and, if the evidence is unsworn, how well the child in question understands the duty of speaking the truth. In *R v Pryce* itself, the Court of Appeal thought that it was sufficient for the trial judge to have told the jury to take into account the fact that the witness was a child. In other cases, a stronger direction may be called for.

Anonymous witnesses

In criminal cases witnesses may give evidence anonymously under the Coroners and Justice Act 2009,[99] provided certain express pre-conditions are satisfied.[100] Previously, at common law, the Court of Appeal had held in *R v Davis*[101] that where the prosecution rely on the evidence of anonymous witnesses, the judge 'would probably' suggest that the jury should consider whether there is any independent, supporting evidence tending to confirm their credibility and the incriminating evidence that they have given. Under s 90 of the Act, the judge is required to give the jury a 'judicial warning' to ensure that an accused is not prejudiced by the fact that a witness has given evidence anonymously.[102] According to the Crown Court Compendium,[103] 'the jury will need a careful direction to ensure that: (1) no unfair prejudice to the defendant is drawn from the use of such measures; and (2) the disadvantages faced by the defendant because of the inability to know the identity of the witness are highlighted.'[104] It is submitted that any warning should also invite the jury to consider the existence or absence of independent supporting evidence confirming the credibility of the anonymous witness and the evidence given.

---

[96] See the forceful observations of Lord Judge LCJ in *R v B* [2010] EWCA Crim 4, CA. His Lordship stated that: '. . . Many accreted suspicions and misunderstandings about children and their capacity to understand the nature and purpose of an oath and to give truthful and accurate evidence at a trial have been swept away . . .'. (at [33]). He went on to say (at [40]): 'We emphasise that in our collective experience the age of a witness is not determinative on his or her ability to give truthful and accurate evidence . . .' See also 'Commentary', *R v B* [2011] Crim LR 23. See also Spencer, 'Children's Evidence: the Barker case, and the case for Pigot' [2010] Arch Rev 3, 5–8.

[97] [1991] Crim LR 379, CA.

[98] See *R v L* [1999] Crim LR 489, CA.

[99] The 2009 Act replaced the Criminal Evidence (Witness Anonymity) Act 2008.

[100] See Ch 5, **Witness anonymity, p 170.**

[101] [2006] 1 WLR 3130, CA, per Sir Igor Judge, P, at [61]. The decision was overturned by the House of Lords (see *R v Davis* [2008] 1 AC 1128, HL). See also *R v Myers and others* [2009] 1 WLR 1519, CA.

[102] According to the Explanatory Notes of the 2009 Act at [475], s 90 is based on the Youth Justice and Criminal Evidence Act 1999, s 32 which provides for jury warnings in cases where special measures have been enacted for vulnerable witnesses. See Ch 5, **The status of video-recorded evidence, etc, p 167.**

[103] The Crown Court Compendium (July 2019), Part 1, 3–8, para 5 and Example.

[104] For example, whether the accused has been deprived of making enquiries about the background and reputation of the witness which might have provided a basis for testing his evidence and reliability.

Matrimonial cases

Where a matrimonial 'offence' is alleged, whether in proceedings in the High Court or in a summary court, the gravity of the consequences of proof of such an allegation and the risk of a miscarriage of justice in acting on the uncorroborated evidence of a spouse have led the courts to acknowledge the desirability of corroboration. Corroboration is sought as a matter of practice rather than as a matter of law. Thus the court may act on the uncorroborated evidence of a spouse if in no doubt where the truth lies.[105] However, in cases where sexual misconduct is alleged, or the evidence of adultery is that of a willing participant,[106] the appellate court will intervene unless the trial court expressly warned itself of the danger of acting on uncorroborated evidence.[107]

Section 4 of the Affiliation Proceedings Act 1957 provides that in affiliation proceedings the court shall not adjudge the defendant to be the putative father of the child, in a case where evidence is given by the mother, unless her evidence is corroborated in some material particular. Despite the abolition of affiliation proceedings by s 17 of the Family Law Reform Act 1987, the question of paternity will continue to arise in family and other proceedings. What corroboration requirement, if any, remains? The justification for the corroboration requirement in s 4, which was the comparative ease with which a false allegation as to paternity could be made, and the difficulty of rebutting it, is no longer convincing. Section 20 of the Family Law Reform Act 1969 provides that, in any civil proceedings in which the parentage of any person falls to be determined, the court may direct the genetic paternity testing of that person, the mother of that person, and any party alleged to be the father of that person. Presumably, although there is no longer any requirement for corroboration, or even a warning, it is likely that the courts will be aware of the need for caution, if only in those cases in which, no direction having been given under s 20, the mother adduces no material in support of her allegation.

Claims against the estate of a deceased person

Where a claim is advanced by a person against the estate of a deceased person, it is natural to look for corroboration in support of the claimant's evidence, but there is no rule of law which prevents the court from acting on the claimant's uncorroborated evidence, if it is convincing.[108]

Cases where special need for caution

Confessions by the mentally handicapped

In *R v MacKenzie*[109] Lord Taylor CJ, applying the guidance given in *R v Galbraith*[110] to cases involving confessions by the mentally handicapped, held that where (i) the prosecution case depends wholly on confessions; (ii) the defendant suffers from a significant degree

---

[105] See *Curtis v Curtis* (1905) 21 TLR 676.

[106] See *Galler v Galler* [1954] P 252, CA and *Fairman v Fairman* [1949] P 341.

[107] However, see also *Joseph v Joseph* [1915] P 122 and *Alli v Alli* [1965] 3 All ER 480.

[108] *Re Hodgson, Beckett v Ramsdale* (1885) 31 Ch D 177, CA; *Re Cummins* [1972] Ch 62, CA.

[109] [1993] 1 WLR 453, CA.

[110] [1981] 1 WLR 1039, CA (see **Ch 2**).

of mental handicap; and (iii) the confessions are unconvincing to a point where a jury properly directed could not properly convict on them, then the judge, assuming he has not excluded the confessions earlier, should withdraw the case from the jury. It was held that confessions may be unconvincing, for example because they lack the incriminating details to be expected of a guilty and willing confessor, they are inconsistent with other evidence, or they are otherwise inherently improbable. In a case which is not withdrawn from the jury, the fact that the confession was made by a mentally handicapped person may be taken into account by the judge not only for the purpose of deciding whether it should be excluded as a matter of law (under s 76 of the Police and Criminal Evidence Act 1984 (the 1984 Act)), but also in deciding whether to exercise his discretion to exclude (under s 82(3) or s 78(1) of that Act).[111] Thus in *R v Moss*[112] it was held that confessions made by an accused on the borderline of mental handicap, in the absence of a solicitor or any other independent person, in the course of nine interviews held over nine days, should have been excluded under s 76(2)(b).

Where the confession of a mentally handicapped person *is* admitted in evidence, s 77 of the 1984 Act imposes on the court a duty, in certain circumstances, to warn the tribunal of fact of the dangers of convicting such a person in reliance on his confession. It provides that:

1. Without prejudice to the general duty of the court at a trial on indictment with a jury to direct the jury on any matter on which it appears to the court appropriate to do so, where at such a trial—
   (a) the case against the accused depends wholly or substantially on a confession by him; and
   (b) the court is satisfied—
       (i)   that he is mentally handicapped; and
       (ii) that the confession was not made in the presence of an independent person,
   the court shall warn the jury that there is a special need for caution before convicting the accused in reliance on the confession, and shall explain that the need arises because of the circumstances mentioned in paragraphs (a) and (b) above.
2. In any case where at the summary trial of a person for an offence it appears to the court that a warning under subsection (1) above would be required if the trial were on indictment with a jury, the court shall treat the case as one in which there is a special need for caution before convicting the accused on his confession.[113]

Concerning the 'general duty' referred to in s 77(1), in *R v Bailey*[114] it was held that in cases where the accused is significantly mentally handicapped and the prosecution would not have a case in the absence of the accused's confessions, the judge should give a full and proper statement of the accused's case against the confessions being accepted by the jury as true and accurate, which should include not only the points made on the accused's behalf, but also any points which appear to the judge to be appropriate. The matters which in that case should have been put before the jury[115] included: (i) that the experience of the courts has shown that people with significant mental handicap do make false confessions for a variety

---

[111] See generally **Ch 15**.
[112] (1990) 91 Cr App R 371, CA. See also *R v Cox* [1991] Crim LR 276, CA and *R v Wood* [1994] Crim LR 222, CA.
[113] Section 2A makes the warning under s 77(1) a requirement in trials on indictment without a jury.
[114] [1995] 2 Cr App R 262, CA.
[115] The court held that nothing in its judgment was to be taken as of general application.

of reasons; (ii) the various possible reasons for the accused having made false confessions; and (iii) that without the confessions, there was no case against the accused.

Concerning s 77(1)(a), the word 'substantially' should not be given a restricted meaning: s 77 is not confined to cases where either the whole or 'most of the case' depends on the confession.[116] In deciding whether a case depends 'substantially' on the confession, the test to be applied is whether the case for the Crown is substantially less strong without the confession, a test which may not be satisfied if there is other prosecution evidence such as identification evidence and evidence of another confession which was made in the presence of an independent adult.[117]

Although para (a) of s 77(1), unlike para (b), does not expressly state that it is for the court to be satisfied of the circumstances mentioned therein, it seems clear that the need for a direction to the jury can only arise where the *judge* is satisfied as to the circumstances mentioned in para (a) as well as para (b), since the judge, when a warning is given, must explain that the need for caution arises because of the circumstances mentioned in both paragraphs.[118] Accordingly, the judge should not direct the jury that a special need for caution *may* arise if *they* are satisfied of the circumstances mentioned in the paragraphs, but that there is a special need for caution which has arisen because the case against the accused *does* depend wholly or substantially on a confession, the accused is mentally handicapped, and the confession *was not* made in the presence of an independent person.

In *R v Campbell*[119] it was held that, as to the 'warning', the judge does not have to follow any specific form of words, but would be wise to use the phrase 'special need for caution', and as to the 'explanation', the judge should explain that persons who are mentally disordered or mentally handicapped may, without wishing to do so, provide information which is unreliable, misleading, or self-incriminating. The explanation should be tailored to the particular evidence in the case, for example evidence that the accused is particularly suggestible or prone to acquiesce, comply, or give in to pressure. The judge should then explain that the function of the appropriate adult is designed to minimize the risk of the accused giving unreliable information by seeing that the interview is conducted properly and fairly and facilitating, if need be, communication between the police and the suspect.

A person is mentally handicapped if 'he is in a state of arrested or incomplete development of mind which includes significant impairment of intelligence and social functioning'.[120] An 'independent person' is defined negatively as not including a police officer or a person employed for, or engaged on, 'police purposes'[121] and could include, for example, a relative or friend of the accused or his solicitor.[122] Should a dispute arise on the issue whether the

---

[116] *R v Bailey* [1995] Crim LR 723, CA.

[117] See *R v Campbell* [1995] 1 Cr App R 522, CA.

[118] But as to para (b), at any rate, it seems that the issue is also for the jury. See *R v Lamont* [1989] Crim LR 813, CA: the judge should have directed the jury to exercise the caution called for if *they* accepted the evidence of mental handicap.

[119] [1995] 1 Cr App R 522, CA.

[120] Section 77(3).

[121] Section 77(3). For the meaning of 'police purposes' see the Police Act 1964, s 64.

[122] Although the definition of an 'independent person' suggests that s 77 only applies in the case of questioning by police officers, in *R v Bailey* [1995] Crim LR 723, CA it was held that a s 77 warning should have been given in respect of a confession made to a member of the public.

accused is mentally handicapped (or whether his confession was made in the presence of an independent person), evidence, if necessary expert medical evidence, may be adduced to enable the judge to come to a decision. In these circumstances, the section is silent as to the incidence of the burden of proof. Presumably, the onus is on the defence to prove the circumstances mentioned in s 77(1)(b) on a balance of probabilities, rather than on the prosecution to prove their non-existence beyond reasonable doubt.

The number of cases in which a s 77 warning will be required is likely to be very small. The possibilities of withdrawing the case from the jury or excluding the confession under ss 76, 78, or 82(3) have already been mentioned. It should also be noted that, under Code C, a person who is mentally handicapped must not be interviewed in the absence of an 'appropriate adult' (a concept which in large measure overlaps with that of an 'independent person' for the purposes of s 77)[123] unless an officer of the rank of superintendent or above considers that delay would be likely (a) to lead to (i) interference with or harm to evidence, or (ii) interference with or physical harm to other people, or (iii) serious loss of or damage to property; (b) to lead to the alerting of other people suspected of having committed an offence but not yet arrested for it; or (c) to hinder the recovery of property obtained in consequence of the commission of an offence.[124] Thus it seems that s 77 is confined to cases in which the confession was made either in an interview conducted in breach of the Code or in an 'urgent interview'.[125] In the rare cases in which s 77 does apply, however, failure to warn the jury as required is grounds for a successful appeal.[126]

Lip-reading evidence

An expert lip-reader who has viewed a video or CCTV recording of a person talking may give expert opinion evidence as to what was said, notwithstanding that such evidence is always, to some extent, unreliable, because not all words can be identified by vision alone, single-syllable words with little context are very difficult to interpret, and even when the words are presented in clearly spoken sentences, the best lip-readers can only achieve up to 80 per cent correctness. In *R v Luttrell*[127] the Court of Appeal considered two issues: when such evidence should be excluded; and, where such evidence is admitted, the nature of the special warning that the judge must give to the jury. As to the former, Rose LJ said:[128]

> The decision in each case is likely to be highly fact sensitive. For example, a video may be of such poor quality or the view of the speaker's face so poor that no reliable interpretation is possible. There may also be cases where the interpreting witness is not sufficiently skilled. A judge may properly take into account: whether consistency with extrinsic facts confirms or inconsistency casts doubt on the reliability of an interpretation; whether information provided to the lip reader might have coloured the reading; and whether the probative effect of the evidence depends on

---

[123] It is defined to include, inter alia, a relative, guardian, or other person responsible for his care or custody: see para 1.7(b), Code C. See also *R v Lewis* [1996] Crim LR 260, CA.

[124] Paras 11.15 and 11.18 and Annex E, Code C.

[125] See per Taylor LJ in *R v Moss* (1990) 91 Cr App R 371, CA at 377.

[126] See *R v Lamont* [1989] Crim LR 813, CA: such a direction was not a matter of prudence, but an essential part of a fair summing-up. However, see also *R v Qayyum* [2007] Crim LR 160, CA, where it was held that giving a formal warning would have made no difference to the jury's approach.

[127] [2004] 2 Cr App R 520 (31), CA. For case comment, see *Rees and Roberts* [2004] Crim LR 939.

[128] [2004] 2 Cr App R 520 (31), CA at [38].

the interpretation of a single word or phrase or on the whole thrust of the conversation. In the light of such considerations, (which are not intended to be exhaustive) a judge may well rule on the *voir dire* that any lip-reading evidence proffered should not be admitted before the jury.

The court was in no doubt that where the evidence is admitted, it requires a warning from the judge as to its limitations and the concomitant risk of error, not least because the expert may fall significantly short of complete accuracy. Rose LJ said:[129]

> As with any 'special warning', its precise terms will be fact-dependent, but in most, if not all cases, the judge should spell out to the jury the risk of mistakes as to the words that the lip reader believes were spoken; the reasons why the witness may be mistaken; and the way in which a convincing, authoritative and truthful witness may yet be a mistaken witness. Furthermore, the judge should deal with the particular strengths and weaknesses of the material in the instant case, carefully setting out the evidence, together with the criticisms that can properly be made of it because of other evidence. The jury should be reminded that the quality of the evidence will be affected by such matters as the lighting at the scene, the angle of the view in relation to those speaking, the distances involved, whether anything interfered with the observation, familiarity on the part of the lip-reader with the language spoken, the extent of the use of single syllable words, any awareness on the part of the expert witness of the context of the speech and whether the probative value of the evidence depends on isolated words or phrases or the general impact of long passages of conversation.

However, the court was also of the view that there was no reason in principle why lip-reading evidence adduced by the prosecution should not establish a prima facie case, although in reaching this conclusion the court may have been influenced by its own—and, it is submitted, questionable—observation that it is highly unlikely that lip-reading evidence will ever stand alone.

Sudden infant death syndrome

Infant deaths are attributed to Sudden Infant Death Syndrome (SIDS), known colloquially as 'cot deaths', where the immediate cause of death is apnoea, loss of breath or cessation of breathing occurring naturally, the underlying cause or causes being as yet unknown. Infant deaths cannot be attributed to SIDS, therefore, if they are clinically explicable or consequent on demonstrable trauma.

In *R v Cannings*[130] the appellant had been convicted of the murder of two of her four children, J who had died six weeks after his birth and M who had died 18 weeks after his birth. Her eldest child, G, had died 13 weeks after her birth. The Crown's case, for which there was no direct evidence, was that the accused had smothered all three of the children and that the deaths of J and M formed part of an overall 'pattern'. Their case depended on expert evidence that the conclusion of smothering could be drawn from the extreme rarity of three separate infant deaths in the same family. The appellant's case was that the deaths were attributable to SIDS and at the appeal she relied on fresh expert evidence to the effect that infant deaths occurring in the same family can and do occur naturally, even when unexplained. Allowing the appeal, it was held that where three infant deaths have occurred in the same family, each apparently unexplained, and for each of which there is no evidence

---

[129] Ibid at [44].
[130] [2004] 1 WLR 2607, CA.

extraneous to the expert evidence that harm was or must have been inflicted—for example, indications or admissions of violence or a pattern of ill-treatment—the proper approach is to start with the fact that three unexplained deaths in the same family are indeed rare, but to proceed on the basis that if there is nothing to explain them, in our current state of knowledge they remain unexplained and, despite the known fact that some parents do smother their infant children, possible natural deaths. Whether there are one, two, or even three deaths, the exclusion of currently known natural causes of infant death does not establish that the death or deaths resulted from the deliberate infliction of harm. If, on examination of all the evidence, every possible cause has been excluded, the cause remains unknown. It was further held that, for the time being, where a full investigation into two or more sudden unexplained infant deaths in the same family is followed by a serious disagreement between reputable experts about the cause of death, and a body of such expert opinion concludes that natural causes, whether explained or not, cannot be excluded as a reasonable (and not a fanciful) possibility, a prosecution for murder should not be started or continued unless there is additional cogent evidence, extraneous to the expert evidence tending to support the conclusion that one of the infants was deliberately harmed, such as indications or admissions of violence or a pattern of ill-treatment.

R v Cannings should be seen alongside R v Kai-Whitewind.[131] In R v Kai-Whitewind, it was held that when there is a genuine conflict between expert witnesses, it did not always follow that a prosecution should not proceed in the absence of evidence independent of the evidence of the experts. This would only apply to cases such as R v Cannings where the prosecution relied solely on inferences drawn against the accused based on coincidence or the unlikelihood of multiple infants suffering unexplained acute or apparent life-threatening events. R v Kai-Whitewind concerned a single infant death where no inference could be drawn against the accused from previous incidents involving other children. Evidence of two episodes of upper airway obstruction was found on the post-mortem examination and the dispute between the experts concerned the interpretation of this evidence. Distinguishing R v Cannings, it was held that it was for the jury to assess the expert evidence, the results of the post-mortem examination, and additional evidence adduced by the prosecution.

The impact of the decision in R v Cannings in care proceedings was considered in In re U (a child) (serious injury: standard of proof).[132] It was held that although R v Cannings had provided a useful warning to judges in care proceedings against ill-considered conclusions or conclusions resting on insufficient evidence, a local authority should not refrain from proceedings or discontinue proceedings in any case where there is a substantial disagreement among the medical experts. However, there were considerations emphasized by the judgment in R v Cannings that were of direct application in care proceedings: (i) the cause of an injury or episode that cannot be explained scientifically remains equivocal; (ii) recurrence is not of itself probative; (iii) particular caution is necessary where medical experts disagree, with one opinion declining to exclude a reasonable possibility of natural cause; (iv) the court has to be on its guard against the over-dogmatic expert, an expert whose reputation or amour propre is at stake or one who has developed a scientific prejudice; and (v) it should never be forgotten that today's medical certainty may be discarded by the next generation of experts or that scientific research will throw light into corners that are, at present, dark.

---

[131] [2005] 2 Cr App R 457 (31), CA.
[132] [2005] Fam 134, CA.

ADDITIONAL READING

Dein, 'Non Tape Recorded Cell Confession Evidence—On Trial' [2002] Crim LR 630.

> A critical analysis of issues relating to the admissibility of non-tape recorded cell confession evidence. The article considers both the case for admitting and excluding such evidence. Safeguards alternative to those available at the time the article was written are also considered. It is argued that the law requires urgent attention to avoid the risk of wrongful conviction in trials which have featured this type of evidence.

Ellison, 'Credibility in context: jury education and intimate partner rape' E & P (2019) 23(3), 263.

> A critical reflection on educational jury directions in sexual cases. The argument is made that there should be an educational direction specifically for cases involving 'domestic' or intimate partner rape. (See also **n 62** in the text.)

Leahy, 'The Corroboration Warning' (2014) 18 E&P 41.

> The article examines the discretion to give a 'corroboration warning' in respect of complainants in sexual cases. The current law relating to corroboration in Ireland and England is considered. The argument is made against rules which place complainants in sexual cases in a special category. Suggestions are made for the reform of the rules.

Lewis, 'A Comparative Examination of Corroboration and Caution Warnings in Prosecutions of Sexual Offences' [2006] Crim LR 889.

> An examination of the requirements for corroboration or caution warnings which, historically, arose from concerns about the reliability of the complainant in sexual offences cases. The history of corroboration warnings and their subsequent abolition is briefly examined. The position in other jurisdictions is considered. There is a discussion of the discretionary approach to warnings, which has replaced the mandatory requirement.

QUESTION

Section 32 of the Criminal Justice and Public Order Act 1994 abrogated any requirement whereby it is obligatory to give a 'full warning' in the case of the uncorroborated evidence of a person merely because that person is an alleged accomplice or the alleged victim of a sexual offence. Critically examine how the law has developed in consequence of s 32.

 For a note-form answer see the online resources, accessible at
www.oup.com/he/keane-mckeown13e.

Visual and voice identification

9

The risk of mistake

The risks associated with evidence of visual identification are well accepted and there have been many instances of wrongful convictions based on such evidence.[1] A specific danger is that an honest witness who is mistaken in his identification of the accused may be very convincing to a jury, in spite of any cross-examination to the effect that he was mistaken. In the Devlin Report on *Evidence of Identification in Criminal Cases*, an underlying problem of visual identification was explained:[2]

> The problem peculiar to identification . . . is that the value of the evidence is very difficult to assess. The weapon of cross-examination is blunted. The witness says he recognises the man and that is that or almost that. There is no story to be dissected, just a simple assertion to be accepted or rejected. If a witness thinks he has a good memory for faces when in fact he has a poor one, there is no way of detecting that.

As to why an honest witness might be mistaken, there are a variety of possible contributing factors. These factors, which cannot be controlled,[3] include the length of the observation of the perpetrator by the witness; environmental factors such as distance, obstructions, and light; whether a weapon was present;[4] whether the perpetrator was of different ethnicity;[5] whether there was more than one perpetrator; stress;[6] and the complex process of encoding, storing, and retrieving the memory of what has been witnessed.[7] In respect of identification by voice, it is generally accepted that this is more difficult for a witness than identification by sight, and the risks of mistake are greater.[8] Many of the factors which affect the reliability of visual identification also affect the reliability of voice identification, but the process of recognizing a voice is obviously different and, as we shall see, there are additional factors to consider, such as the variety and distinctiveness of speech heard by the witness.

---

[1] See the Devlin Committee Report: *Report of the Committee on Evidence of Identification in Criminal Cases*, 1976 Cmnd 338 134/135, accessible at https://www.gov.uk/government/uploads/system/uploads/attachment_data/file/228523/0338.pdf. See, in particular, p 78, para 4.33 and Appendix H Table VI of the report.

[2] Ibid, p 7, 1.24.

[3] In the psychology of eyewitness identification, such factors are known as 'estimator variables'.

[4] Loftus, Loftus, and Messo, 'Some Facts about Weapon Focus' (1987) 11 Law and Human Behavior 55–62. Compare Yuille and Cutshall, 'A Case Study of Eyewitness Memory of a Crime', (1986) 71 Journal of Applied Psychology 291–301.

[5] Yuille and Cutshall, 'A Case Study of Eyewitness Memory of a Crime', (1986) 71 Journal of Applied Psychology 291–301.

[6] See Yuille and Cutshall, 'A Case Study of Eyewitness Memory of a Crime' (1986) 71 Journal of Applied Psychology 291–301: there was some evidence that stress may enhance recall. However, other studies have shown that stress has a significant negative impact on the accuracy of visual identification: see Ihlebæk et al, 'Memory for a Staged Criminal Event Witnessed Live and on Video' (2003) 11 Memory 319–27 and Valentine and Mesout, 'Eyewitness Identification under Stress in the London Dungeon' (Goldsmiths, University of London, 2008) accessible at http://www.valentinemoore.co.uk/trv/londondungeon.pdf.

[7] See the British Psychological Society, 'Guidelines on Memory and the Law', 'Recommendations from the Scientific Study of Human Memory', (The Research Board, 2008) accessible at https://www.judcom.nsw.gov.au/publications/benchbks/sexual_assault/british-guidelines_on_memory_and_the_law.html. See also Keane, 'The Use at Trial of Scientific Findings Relating to Human Memory' [2010] Crim LR 19.

[8] *R v Roberts* [2000] Crim LR 183, CA.

This chapter considers the principles which apply to the admissibility and use at trial of evidence of visual and voice identification.[9] It is convenient to consider visual identification first. As we shall see, the guidelines in *R v Turnbull*[10] provide guidance on how the courts should deal with visual identification evidence, including when a case based wholly or mainly on this type of evidence should be stopped and, where a case goes to the jury, the nature of the warning required. However, it is not in every case involving identification evidence that a warning is required under the *Turnbull* guidelines; we will consider situations where a warning is not necessarily required, including some situations in which the jury themselves are invited to identify the accused. In addition to the *Turnbull* guidelines, pre-trial procedure will be considered, including formal identification procedures held under Code D issued pursuant to the Police and Criminal Evidence Act 1984 where a suspect is known and unknown, identification from film and photographs in 'controlled' circumstances (ie where formal arrangements are made for viewing images), and 'uncontrolled' circumstances (ie where the witness identifies the accused by informally viewing images, for example by looking at images on social media).

As to voice identification, where the risk of mistake is greater, we shall see that the law draws on the guidelines in *R v Turnbull*. However, where evidence of voice identification is admitted before the jury, a more stringent warning is called for about the dangers of mistake; and juries need careful guidance where voice identification evidence is in the form of recognition evidence provided by a 'lay listener' (non-expert), or by an expert using phonetic or acoustic analysis. In relation to pre-trial procedures for voice identification, as we shall see, Code D makes almost no provision and 'minimal safeguards' are contained in case law.[11]

Visual identification

In *R v Turnbull*[12] Lord Widgery CJ, giving the judgment of the Court of Appeal, laid down important guidelines relating to evidence of allegedly mistaken visual identification of the accused.[13] Mistaken identification of the accused, especially in cases of visual identification, may be regarded as the greatest cause of wrong convictions.[14] The guidelines in *R v Turnbull* were designed to lessen this danger. The Court of Appeal attempted to follow the recommendations in the Devlin Report.[15] The Committee had recommended the enactment of a general rule precluding a conviction in any case in which the prosecution relies wholly or mainly on evidence of visual identification by one or more witnesses, but the guidelines fall considerably short of the Committee's proposals.

---

[9] Some aspects of identification are dealt with more conveniently elsewhere: the admissibility of previous identifications and dock identifications (Ch 6); identification by inference from refusal to consent to the taking of samples (Ch 16); aspects of identification by photographs, films and photofits, and sketches (Ch 10); and expert evidence on identification by voice (Ch 20).

[10] [1977] QB 224, CA.

[11] *R v Flynn* [2008] 2 Cr App R 266 (20), CA.

[12] [1977] QB 224.

[13] As to the importance of pre-trial procedures relating to identification evidence, see Roberts, 'The problem of mistaken identity: Some observations on process' (2004) 8 E&P 100.

[14] See Criminal Law Revision Committee, 11th Report, Cmnd 4991 (1972), para 196.

[15] Cmnd 338 (1976).

Failure to follow the guidelines is likely to result in a conviction being quashed if, on all the evidence, the verdict is unsafe.[16] It will be otherwise, however, if the Court of Appeal is convinced that had the jury been directed correctly, they would nevertheless have come to the same conclusion.[17] Privy Council authority is to the same effect, so that in 'exceptional circumstances' a conviction based on unsupported identification evidence might be upheld even though a *Turnbull* direction was not given.[18] In *Freemantle v R*[19] the trial judge failed to give a *Turnbull* direction. The identification, which was by way of recognition evidence, was of exceptionally good quality: both identification witnesses had more than a fleeting glance at the accused and one of them said to the accused that he recognized him, to which the accused had replied in a way which appeared to acknowledge that he had been correctly identified. The Board was of the opinion that 'exceptional circumstances' include the fact that the evidence of identification is of exceptionally good quality and accordingly held that application of a proviso similar in its terms to s 2(1) of the Criminal Appeal Act 1968 was justified.

It is advisable, in every case in which a *Turnbull* direction may be required, for there to be a discussion between the judge and advocates, prior to the closing speeches and the summing-up, as to how identification issues will be addressed.[20]

The *Turnbull* guidelines are extensive. It will be convenient to consider separately seven extracts from the judgment of the Court of Appeal, together with subsequent developments in relation to each.

The special need for caution

Whenever the case against an accused depends wholly or substantially on the correctness of one or more identifications of the accused which the defence alleges to be mistaken, the judge should warn the jury of the special need for caution before convicting the accused in reliance on the correctness of the identification or identifications. In addition, he should instruct them as to the reason for the need for such a warning and should make some reference to the possibility that a mistaken witness can be a convincing one and that a number of such witnesses can all be mistaken. Provided that this is done in clear terms, the judge need not use any particular form of words.

Although Lord Widgery CJ himself said that *Turnbull*'s case 'is intended primarily to deal with the ghastly risk run in cases of fleeting encounters . . .',[21] the warning should be given even if the opportunities for observation were good and the identifying witness is convinced that he has correctly identified the accused.[22] A warning must also be given notwithstanding that the identifying witness has picked out the accused at a formal identification procedure

---

[16] *R v Kane* (1977) 65 Cr App R 270, CA. See also *R v Tyson* [1985] Crim LR 48, CA.

[17] *R v Hunjan* (1978) 68 Cr App R 99, CA, where the conviction was in fact quashed; and cf *R v Clifton* [1986] Crim LR 399, CA, where the prosecution case was exceptionally strong.

[18] See *Reid v R* (1989) 90 Cr App R 121 at 130, PC and also the judgment of Lord Griffiths, in *Scott v R* [1989] AC 1242, PC, at 1261. However, see also Lord Ackner in *Reid v R* (1989) 90 Cr App R 121 at 130.

[19] [1994] 3 All ER 225, PC.

[20] *R v Stanton* [2004] EWCA Crim 490.

[21] *R v Oakwell* (1978) 66 Cr App R 174 at 178.

[22] *R v Tyson* [1985] Crim LR 48, CA.

such as a video identification procedure.[23] It is of the utmost importance to give a warning where the sole evidence of identification is contained in the deposition of a deceased witness and the identification may have been based on a fleeting glance.[24]

Identification of persons with the accused

Where identification is in issue and there is strong prosecution evidence that the accused was with some other person at the relevant time, then the evidence identifying that other, unless unchallenged by the defence, should normally be the subject of a *Turnbull* direction.[25]

Where the issue is not identification but what the accused did

According to *R v Slater*,[26] where there is no issue as to the presence of the accused at or near the scene of the offence, but the issue is as to what he was doing, whether a *Turnbull* direction is necessary will depend on the circumstances of the case. It was held that it will be necessary where, on the evidence, the possibility exists that the identifying witness may have mistaken one person for another, for example because of similarities in face, build, or clothing between two or more people present,[27] but where there is no possibility of such a mistake there is no need to give a *Turnbull* direction. On the facts, the accused was six foot six inches tall and there was no evidence to suggest that anyone else present was remotely similar in height. It was therefore held that there was no basis for any mistake: the issue in the case was not identification, but what the accused did, and accordingly a *Turnbull* direction was not required. The court observed that in some cases, where presence is admitted but conduct disputed, it would be contrary to common sense to require a *Turnbull* direction, as when a black man and a white man are present and the complainant says that it was the white man.[28]

Where the evidence is a description rather than identification

It has also been said that a full direction is not required if none of the identifying witnesses purports to identify the accused, their evidence merely serving to provide a description which is not inconsistent with the appearance of the accused and forming only one part, albeit a very important part, of all the evidence, because such a case does not depend wholly or substantially upon the correctness of their evidence.[29] In *R v Constantinou*,[30] where none of the witnesses purported to identify the accused but merely gave descriptions which might have been consistent with his appearance, and a photofit was admitted which also might

---

[23] Per Lord Griffiths in *Scott v R* [1989] AC 1242, PC, at 1260. Where the witness picks out a volunteer, there is no obligation to give a 'reverse *Turnbull* direction', ie that the witness may be honest but mistaken in identifying the volunteer, because the purpose of the *Turnbull* direction is to lessen the danger of a wrongful conviction, not a wrongful acquittal: see *R v Trew* [1996] Crim LR 441, CA. For the special issues that arise where there has been a qualified identification, see *R v George* [2003] Crim LR 282, CA and Roberts, 'The perils and possibilities of qualified identification: *R v George*' (2003) 7 E&P 130. A qualified identification cannot on its own be the basis of a conviction: *R v Howe* [2017] EWCA Crim 2400 at [20], citing *R v George* [2002] EWCA Crim at [35].

[24] *Scott v R* [1989] 2 All ER 305 at 314–15.

[25] *R v Bath* [1990] Crim LR 716, CA. A *Turnbull* direction is not required in relation to the identification of cars: *R v Browning* (1991) 94 Cr App R 109, CA.

[26] [1995] 1 Cr App R 584, CA.

[27] See, eg, *R v Thornton* [1995] 1 Cr App R 578, CA, where the appellant and others were similarly dressed.

[28] See also *R v Conibeer* [2002] EWCA Crim 2059 and cf *R v O'Leary* [2002] EWCA Crim 2055, CA.

[29] *R v Browning* (1991) 94 Cr App R 109. Cf *R v Andrews* [1993] Crim LR 590, CA.

[30] (1989) 91 Cr App R 74, CA.

have been consistent with his appearance, it was held that no *Turnbull* warning was required in respect of the photofit. This decision, it is submitted, is in need of review because descriptions may be as unreliable as identifications, considering that the sorts of factors which affect the reliability of identifications may equally affect descriptions. Such factors include the circumstances of the observation, its length, and the interval between the observation and the witness giving the description.

The terms of the direction

As to the terms of the direction, *R v Turnbull* is not a statute and does not require an incantation of a formula or set form of words: provided that the judge complies with the sense and spirit of the guidance given, he has a broad discretion to express himself in his own way.[31] Thus as to the reason for the warning, failure to use the word 'convincing' ('a mistaken witness can be a convincing one') need not be fatal to the summing-up.[32] Indeed, even prefacing the warning with advice to guard against 'allowing an oversophisticated approach to evidence relating to identification to become . . . a "mugger's charter"' was not fatal in *R v Shervington*[33] because, in the round, the judge did set out the direction sufficiently. Nonetheless, to depart from the standard form of the direction was 'singularly unwise' and the use of the words 'mugger's charter' was plainly inappropriate.[34] In relation to the general risk of mistaken identification, it is insufficient merely to say that 'even an honest witness may be mistaken': the judge should explain that evidence of visual identification is a category of evidence which experience has shown to be particularly vulnerable to error, in particular by honest and impressive witnesses, and that this has been known to result in wrong convictions.[35] There is a requirement to make clear that the need for special caution is rooted in the court's actual experience of miscarriages of justice.[36]

The circumstances of the identification and specific weaknesses in the identification evidence

The judge should direct the jury to examine closely the circumstances in which the identification by each witness came to be made.[37] How long did the witness have the accused under observation? At what distance? In what light? Was the observation impeded in any way, as for example by passing traffic or a press of people? Had the witness seen the accused before? How often? If only occasionally, had he any special reason for remembering him? How much time

---

[31] Per Lord Steyn in *Mills v R* [1995] 3 All ER 865, PC at 872.

[32] See *Rose v R* [1995] Crim LR 939, PC. See also *France v The Queen* [2012] UKPC 28 at [18] and *R v Alexander* [2013] 1 Cr App R 334 (26), CA at [38]–[39].

[33] [2008] Crim LR 581, CA.

[34] *R v Shervington* [2008] EWCA Crim 658 at [25] and [28].

[35] Per Lord Ackner in *Reid v R* (1989) 90 Cr App R 121 at 134–5.

[36] *R v Nash* [2005] Crim LR 232, CA. However, it has also been held that failure to refer to past miscarriages of justice is not fatal: *R v Tyler* [1993] Crim LR 60, CA. Indeed, in jurisdictions in which there is no history of well-publicized miscarriages of justice, eg Jamaica, such a reference would be unnecessary and unhelpful: *Amore v R* (1994) 99 Cr App R 279, PC.

[37] See the Crown Court Compendium (July 2019), Part 1, 15–1, para 9. See also *R v Cole* [2013] EWCA Crim 1149 at [72]: it would be a misdirection to direct the jury in such a way as to suggest that evidence of an identification '. . . could or should be compartmentalised and the decision about its accuracy made without reference to extraneous circumstantial evidence which supported or undermined confidence in its reliability.'

elapsed between the original observation and the subsequent identification to the police? Was there any material discrepancy between the description of the accused given to the police by the witness when first seen by him and his actual appearance? If in any case the prosecution have reason to believe that there is such a material discrepancy, they should supply the accused or his legal advisers with particulars of the description the police were first given.[38] Finally, he should remind the jury of any specific weaknesses which had appeared in the identification evidence.

Simply paying lip service to the guidelines, without reference to the particular circumstances relevant to the accuracy of the identification will not suffice.[39] Nor is it sufficient for the judge simply to invite the jury to take into account what the advocate for the defence has said about 'specific weaknesses': the judge must fairly and properly summarize for the jury any such weaknesses which can arguably be said to have been exposed in the evidence.[40] However, provided that the judge does identify all the specific weaknesses, there is no obligation to do so in a particular way, for example by bringing them together and listing them, rather than by dealing with them in context when reviewing the evidence in the case.[41] The extent of the duty to cover specific weaknesses depends entirely on the state of the evidence in the individual case and the judge 'is not required in effect to make a second speech for the defendant.'[42] If the judge does identify specific points relied on by the defence, she should also normally remind the jury of all the evidence affecting such points. This may include evidence negatively affecting their worth.[43] In the case of minor discrepancies between what the identifying witnesses have said, it is a matter for the judge's discretion whether simply to refer to them in her review of the evidence, or to categorize them specifically as potential weaknesses.[44]

The same rules apply to police officers as to other identifying witnesses, but sometimes an officer pays particular attention to the identity of a person, even in a fleeting glance type case. Where this issue arises, the judge should specifically direct the jury as to the likelihood of the officer being correct, when a 'mere casual observer' might not be, because an officer has a greater appreciation of the importance of identification, is trained, and is less likely to be affected by the excitement of the situation.[45]

Recognition

Recognition may be more reliable than identification of a stranger; but even when the witness is purporting to recognize someone whom he knows, the jury should be reminded that mistakes in recognition of close relatives and friends are sometimes made.

---

[38] See Code D 3.1. See also *R v Cole* [2013] EWCA Crim 1149, where, in clear breach of Code D, a record of the witness's first description of the accused was not provided to the accused or his legal advisers before the accused's participation in an identification parade.

[39] *R v Graham* [1994] Crim LR 212, CA, applied in *R v Allen* [1995] Crim LR 643, CA, where the trial judge took no steps to remove the possible prejudice resulting from an improper refusal to hold an identification parade. See also *R v I* [2007] 2 Cr App R 316 (24), CA. Cf *R v Doldur* [2000] Crim LR 178, CA.

[40] *R v Fergus* (1993) 98 Cr App R 313, CA.

[41] *R v Mussell* [1995] Crim LR 887, CA; *R v Barnes* [1995] 2 Cr App R 491, CA; and *R v Qadir* [1998] Crim LR 828, CA. Cf *R v Pattinson* [1996] 1 Cr App R 51, CA.

[42] *R v Stoutt* [2014] UKPC 14 at [23].

[43] Ibid.

[44] *R v Barnes* [1995] 2 Cr App R 491 at 500, CA.

[45] *R v Ramsden* [1991] Crim LR 295, CA; *R v Tyler* [1993] Crim LR 60, CA. Cf per Lord Ackner in *Reid v R* (1989) 90 Cr App R 121 at 137: 'experience has undoubtedly shown that police identification can be just as unreliable [as that of an ordinary member of the public].'

Many people experience seeing someone in the street whom they know, only to discover that they are wrong. The expression 'I could have sworn it was you' indicates the sort of warning which a judge should give, because that is exactly what a witness does—he swears that it was the person he thinks it was. In the field of recognition, there are degrees of danger, but perhaps less where the parties have known each other for many years or where there is no doubt that the person identified was at the scene at the time. Even here, it is at least advisable to alert the jury to the possibility of honest mistake and to the dangers, and the reasons why such dangers exist.[46]

In *Beckford v R*[47] the Privy Council held as follows. (1) A general warning on *Turnbull* lines *must* normally be given in recognition cases and failure to do so will nearly always *by itself* suffice to invalidate a conviction substantially based on identification evidence. (2) Such a warning should be given even if the sole or main thrust of the defence is directed to the issue of the identifying witness's credibility, that is, whether his evidence is true or false as distinct from accurate or mistaken. The first question for the jury is whether the witness is honest, and if the answer to that question is Yes, the next question is whether he could be mistaken. (3) This 'strong general rule' is subject to only very rare exceptions:

> If, for example, the witness's identification evidence is that the accused was his workmate whom he has known for 20 years and that he was conversing with him for half an hour face to face in the same room and the witness is sane and sober, then, if credibility is the issue, it will be the only issue.[48]

However, in *Capron v R*[49] the Privy Council deprecated the use of phrases such as 'wholly exceptional' or 'very rare' to describe the situations in which the court can dispense with a *Turnbull* direction on the basis that the sole or main issue is the credibility of the identification witness or witnesses; what matters, it was said, is the nature of the identification evidence in each case. In *R v Giga*,[50] the Court of Appeal, affirming this approach, held that each case must turn on its own facts. In *Duporte v The Queen*,[51] the judge, in giving a *Turnbull* direction, did not specifically address the jury on the issue of identification where it involved recognition. However, the case against the appellant was strong, it had not been disputed in cross-examination that the witnesses who recognized the appellant, knew him, and overall the summing-up was sufficient for its purpose.[52]

The 'strong general rule' referred to in *Beckford* means that in many cases where evidence of recognition is adduced, failure to warn the jury about its inherent dangers will be fatal to a conviction. In *R v Ali*,[53] the importance of the warning was stressed. In *R v Ali*, a 'steaming robbery' whereby a train passenger was surrounded by a group and robbed, the accused was identified as a participant by the passenger. In addition to the evidence of identification given by the passenger, a police officer gave evidence that he recognized the accused from

---

[46] *R v Bentley* (1991) 99 Cr App R 342, CA; *R v Bowden* [1993] Crim LR 379, CA. Cf *R v Curry* [1983] Crim LR 737 and *R v Oakwell* (1978) 66 Cr App R 174, CA.

[47] (1993) 97 Cr App R 409, PC.

[48] Ibid at 415, applied in *Shand v R* [1996] 1 All ER 511, PC. Cf *R v Courtnell* [1990] Crim LR 115, CA and *R v Ryder* [1994] 2 All ER 859, CA (see n 57).

[49] [2006] UKPC 34.

[50] [2007] Crim LR 571, CA.

[51] [2015] UKPC 18.

[52] Ibid at [50].

[53] [2008] EWCA Crim 1522; [2009] Crim LR 40, CA.

a CCTV 'still image' of a group of males on the platform of the station where the train had stopped. Although the judge provided a *Turnbull* warning in respect of the evidence of the passenger's identification, none was provided in respect of the evidence of the police officer's recognition. In quashing the conviction, the Court of Appeal observed that even with recognition, the risk of mistaken identification remains and a direction is required which brings home fully to the jury that an identifying witness can make a mistake when purporting to recognize someone he knows.[54] In this case, not only had the judge failed to warn the jury, but he had directed them in such a way as to suggest that the correctness of the police officer's recognition could be treated as an established fact.[55]

In a case where identification, including recognition, is in issue but the defence is that the identifying witness is lying, rather than mistaken, a *Turnbull* direction may not be required. In *R v Courtnell*[56] the defence was one of alibi and it was alleged that the purported identification, by someone who had known the accused for a week, was a fabrication. It was held that the trial judge had properly withdrawn the issue of mistaken identity from the jury: the sole issue was the veracity of the identifying witness and therefore a *Turnbull* direction would only have confused the jury.[57]

Recognition by police officers

It will be apparent from the facts in *Ali* that there is no general rule excluding evidence of recognition by police officers including recognition evidence based on viewing images recorded by a CCTV camera, even though the jury may then infer that the accused has previously been in trouble with the police. This is because the fact of the officers' knowledge is of critical significance to the quality of the identification, and to exclude the evidence would unfairly advantage those with criminal records.[58] However, the jury must still be warned of the general dangers of mistaken recognition, from which police officers are not immune.[59] In relation to recognition from CCTV footage, consideration should be given to the circumstances of the event recorded and the quality of the footage.[60] The jury should also be directed that although a witness has had time to study the footage, the images are not three dimensional and watching CCTV footage is not the same as actually observing a person and an event.[61]

---

[54] *R v Ali* [2008] EWCA Crim 1522 at [35]. See also the Crown Court Compendium (July 2019), Part 1, 15–3.

[55] Code D is now directly applicable to recognition by film, photographs and other images, both where the recognition occurs in circumstances where the viewing by the witness is controlled and supervised, and where it is not. See, in this chapter, under **Pre-trial procedure**, p 290.

[56] [1990] Crim LR 115, CA.

[57] See also, applying *R v Courtnell, R v Cape* [1996] 1 Cr App R 191, CA and *R v Beckles and Montague* [1999] Crim LR 148, CA; and *R v Ryder* [1994] 2 All ER 859, CA, *Capron v R* [2006] UKPC 34, and *R v Giga* [2007] Crim LR 571, CA, cases of recognition. But see further *Beckford v R* (1993) 97 Cr App R 409, PC, applied in *Shand v R* [1996] 1 All ER 511, PC—see text accompanying **nn 54 and 55**.

[58] See *R v Crabtree* [1992] Crim LR 65, CA and *R v Caldwell* (1993) 99 Cr App R 73, CA; and cf *R v Fowden and White* [1982] Crim LR 588, CA. The defence then face difficulties in challenging the extent of the officers' knowledge of the accused. In *R v Caldwell* the Court of Appeal thought the difficulty was 'manageable', approving the sensitive ruling of the trial judge that the officers should not refer to any convictions or criminal associations of the accused, their families, etc.

[59] See *R v Ali* [2008] EWCA Crim 1522.

[60] Concerning CCTV stills, see *R v Walters* [2013] EWCA Crim 1361: the jury should always be directed as to the factors which might render unreliable, a recognition from still images.

[61] See the Crown Court Compendium (July 2019), Part 1, 15–4, para 8.

Identification evidence of good quality

When the quality [of the identification evidence] is good, as for example when the identification is made after a long period of observation, or in satisfactory conditions by a relative, a neighbour, a close friend, a workmate, and the like, the jury can safely be left to assess the value of the identifying evidence even though there is not other evidence to support it: provided always, however, that an adequate warning has been given about the special need for caution.[62]

Where the quality of the identification evidence is such that the jury can be safely left to assess its value, even though there is no other evidence to support it, then the judge is fully entitled, if so minded, to direct the jury that an identification by one witness can constitute support for the identification by another, *provided* that he warns them in clear terms that even a number of honest witnesses can all be mistaken.[63]

Identification evidence of poor quality

When, in the judgment of the trial judge, the quality of the identifying evidence is poor, as for example when it depends solely on a fleeting glance or on a longer observation made in difficult conditions, the situation is very different. The judge should then withdraw the case from the jury and direct an acquittal unless there is other evidence which goes to support the correctness of the identification. This may be corroboration in the technical sense that lawyers use that word,[64] but it need not be so if its effect is to make the jury sure that there has been no mistaken identification.

However, where the issue is raised that the identification evidence is of poor quality, the judge should take into account the prosecution evidence as a whole and not focus solely on the quality of the evidence, and should be careful to avoid conflating the principle of no case to answer and the standard of proof required for conviction.[65]

Under the guideline, a case is withdrawn from the jury not because the judge considers that the witness is lying, but because the evidence, even if taken to be honest, has a base which is so slender that it is unreliable and therefore insufficient to found a conviction. The jury are protected from acting upon the type of evidence which, even if believed, experience has shown to be a possible source of injustice.[66]

In the absence of a submission, the judge is under a duty to invite submissions when, in his view, the identification evidence is poor and unsupported.[67] Moreover, *R v Turnbull* plainly contemplates that the position must be assessed not only at the end of the prosecution case, but also at the close of the defence case.[68] In exceptional cases, a ruling can be made even before the close of the prosecution case, on the depositions, but apparently in any event a *voir dire* should not be held.[69] A judge should not direct a jury that he would have withdrawn the

---

[62] *R v Turnbull* [1977] QB 224 at 229.

[63] Per Lord Lane CJ in *R v Weeder* (1980) 71 Cr App R 228, CA at 231. In *R v Breslin* (1984) 80 Cr App R 226, CA it was held that this direction (and warning) should be given in all identification cases to which it applies.

[64] See Ch 8.

[65] *DPP v Jobling*, 26 May 2016, DC, unreported.

[66] Per Lord Mustill in *Daley v R* [1993] 4 All ER 86, PC at 94.

[67] *R v Fergus* (1994) 98 Cr App R 313, CA.

[68] Ibid, citing *R v Turnbull* [1977] QB 224 at 228–9.

[69] See *R v Flemming* (1987) 86 Cr App R 32, CA and cf *R v Beveridge* [1987] Crim LR 401, CA.

case from them on a submission of no case to answer, had he thought that there was insufficient identification evidence, because the jury may mistakenly take this to mean that the evidence is sufficiently strong for them to convict.[70]

Supporting evidence

The trial judge should identify to the jury the evidence which he adjudges is capable of supporting the evidence of identification.[71] If there is any evidence, or there are circumstances, which the jury might think was supporting, when the evidence or circumstances did not have this quality, the judge should say so.[72]

It is essential for the judge to make clear to the jury that although he has adjudged that certain evidence is capable of supporting the evidence of identification, it is for them to decide, if they accept it, whether it does in fact support the evidence of identification.[73] The support may be provided by a variety of evidence or circumstances depending on the facts, including evidence of the accused's association with other suspects who have been identified,[74] evidence that the identifying witness correctly identified another suspect seen with the accused at the relevant time,[75] evidence that another witness has also identified the accused at the relevant time,[76] or evidence of a description if the jury are sure that it comes from a witness who is honest and independent.[77]

In a case of purported recognition in circumstances such that, had it been a case of identification by a stranger, the quality of the evidence would have been poor, the fact that it was a recognition may itself form part of the evidence in support.[78] However, it is doubtful that purported recognition of a suspect by a police officer would be supporting evidence for another witness's identification where the officer was not an expert and his recognition was based on viewing recorded images in which the suspect's face was partially hidden.[79] Further, it has been held that the physical appearance of an accused, however singular, and however closely it corresponds with the evidence of a witness describing the criminal, cannot amount without more to corroboration of that evidence because it does not establish the reliability of the witness's evidence that the criminal had such an appearance.[80]

---

[70] *R v Smith and Doe* (1986) 85 Cr App R 197, CA. See also *R v Akaidere* [1990] Crim LR 808, CA: a judge should not direct the jury that the identification evidence is so poor that he would have stopped the case if it had stood alone.

[71] See also the Crown Court Compendium (July 2019), Part 1, 15–1, para 11.

[72] Absence from the witness box may be supportive: s 35 of the Criminal Justice and Public Order Act 1994 (see Ch 16). Contrast at common law, *R v Forbes* [1992] Crim LR 593, CA.

[73] *R v Akaidere* [1990] Crim LR 808, CA.

[74] *R v Penny* (1991) 94 Cr App R 345, CA.

[75] *R v Hussain* [2004] EWCA Crim 1064.

[76] *R v Weeder* (1980) 71 Cr App R 228; *R v Castle* [1989] Crim LR 567, CA; and *R v Jones (Terence)* [1992] Crim LR 365, CA. See also *R v Brown* [1991] Crim LR 368, CA.

[77] See the Crown Court Compendium (July 2019), Part 1, 15–1, para 13.

[78] *R v Turnbull* [1977] QB 224.

[79] See *R v Ali* [2009] EWCA Crim 1522, CA. However, see also *R v Clare, R v Peach* [1995] 2 Cr App R 333, CA: an officer could acquire special knowledge which the court did not possess obtained by, eg, spending a long time analysing material from the crime scene.

[80] *R v Willoughby* (1988) 88 Cr App R 91, CA. Cf *R v McInnes* (1989) 90 Cr App R 99, CA, where a kidnapping victim's detailed knowledge of the inside of the alleged kidnapper's car was independent corroboration. See also *R v Nagy* [1990] Crim LR 187, CA.

It is for the jury to decide whether evidence is in fact supportive of the identification, and although there may be cases where in the light of the evidence that has unfolded the jury should be directed not to convict on the identification evidence alone, there is no general requirement to give such a direction.[81]

Evidence of the accused's bad character may also provide support for an identification, for example where the evidence has sufficient probative force in showing the improbability of the witness mistakenly identifying an accused with propensity to commit the offence charged.[82] However, as one commentator has observed, 'Although . . . evidence of previous convictions are [sic] commonly relied upon to support the accuracy of an identification of the defendant by an eyewitness . . . the principles that determine admissibility have not been adequately articulated. How does the use of evidence of previous convictions for this purpose differ from use as the foundation for an inference that goes directly to evaluation of the defendant's guilt?'[83]

Where a witness has purported to identify the accused from CCTV footage and other images and the prosecution invite the jury to make their own comparison of the footage or images with the accused, the Crown Court Compendium states that the 'evidence capable of supporting the evidence of identification may include the jury's own comparison of [the accused] with the suspect shown in the CCTV footage/images and vice versa . . .'[84] The Compendium also states that, 'When the prosecution relies both upon the evidence of a witness who recognises D and the jury's own ability to compare the photographic evidence with D in person, the jury may be directed that the evidence may be mutually supportive. If so, they should be reminded of the danger that several witnesses can make the same mistake.'[85] However, where a non-expert witness purports to recognize the accused from CCTV footage or an image which is not of sufficient quality to permit a reliable recognition, it is submitted that the recognition evidence of the witness is unlikely to constitute supporting evidence of the jury's own comparison. In *R v Ali*,[86] for example, it was doubted that recognition of the accused from CCTV footage by a police officer could be supporting evidence for the jury's comparison in circumstances where the suspect's face was partially obscured and the police officer was not giving evidence as an expert.

False alibis

Care should be taken by the judge when directing the jury about the support for an identification which may be derived from the fact that they have rejected an alibi. False alibis may be put forward for many reasons: an accused, for example, who has only his own truthful evidence to rely on may stupidly fabricate an alibi and get lying witnesses to support it out

---

[81] *R v Ley* [2007] 1 Cr App R 325 (25), CA.

[82] See *R v Blake* [2006] EWCA Crim 871; *R v Randall* [2006] EWCA Crim 1413; *R v Miller* [2009] EWCA Crim 2890; *R v Richardson* [2014] EWCA Crim 1785; and *R v N* [2014] EWCA Crim 506. See also *R v Howe* [2017] EWCA Crim 2400 and *R v Holmes* [2014] EWCA Crim 420.

[83] See Roberts, 'Commentary', Crim LR [2015] 443. The use of evidence of similar-fact evidence to prove identity is further considered in Ch 19, **Misconduct to prove identity**, p 595.

[84] The Crown Court Compendium (July 2019), Part 1, 15–3, para 8. See also the Compendium at 15–4, para 1 and *R v Caldwell* [1994] 99 Cr App R 73, CA.

[85] The Crown Court Compendium (July 2019), Part 1, 15–3, para 8.

[86] See *R v Ali* [2008] EWCA 1522 at [34]; [2009] Crim LR 40.

of fear that his own evidence will not be enough. Further, alibi witnesses can make genuine mistakes about dates and occasions just as any other witnesses can. Only when the jury are satisfied that the sole reason for the fabrication was to deceive them and there is no other explanation for its being put forward can fabrication provide any support for identification evidence. The jury should be reminded that proving the accused has told lies about where he was at the material time does not by itself prove that he was where the identifying witness says he was. Such a direction should be given even if the prosecution have not relied on the collapse of the alibi as part of the material supporting their case.[87]

Visual identification by the jury

In a case in which the jurors themselves are asked to 'identify' the accused, whom they have seen in court, from a film, photograph, or other image of the offender committing the offence, generally speaking they should be warned of the risk of mistaken identity and of the need to exercise particular care in any identification which they make.[88] Concerning identification by the jury using CCTV recordings, the following guidance has been provided by the Crown Court Compendium:[89] where a CCTV recording is presented as real evidence and is virtually a direct observation,[90] the jury should be warned of the dangers of mistaken identification and of the need for great care when attempting their identification;[91] the CCTV recording must be sufficiently clear;[92] where the appearance of the accused is different, an image of him at the time of the CCTV recording should be provided to the jury; the jury's attention should be drawn to factors which might affect the reliability of their identification, such as how much of the suspect's face is visible and how long the jury have had to look at the accused in court; and any other factors that might make recognition from CCTV stills unreliable.[93] It is submitted that another important factor to consider is contamination, and the extent to which jurors might influence each other in their individual identifications.

A full *Turnbull* warning is inappropriate where the jury attempt their own identification from a photograph. This is because the process of identifying a person from a photograph is a commonplace and everyday event and some things are obvious from the photograph itself. However, in *R v Shanmugarajah*,[94] it was noted that there appeared to be a conflict between the judgments in *R v Downey*[95] and *R v Blenkinsop*.[96] In *R v Downey*, the Court of Appeal held that the authority of *R v Dodson and Williams*[97] did not lay down an invariable or inflexible rule that a judge should direct the jury expressly about the dangers of mistaken identification, and that *they* might make a mistaken identification. However, in

---

[87] See *R v Duncan* (1992) The Times, 24 July, CA and *R v Pemberton* (1993) 99 Cr App R 228, CA.

[88] *R v Dodson and Williams* [1984] 1 WLR 971, CA.

[89] The Crown Court Compendium (July 2019), Part 1, 15–2, paras 6–9.

[90] Ibid, para 4. See also *R v Najjar* [2014] EWCA Crim 1309 at [17].

[91] The Crown Court Compendium (July 2019), Part 1, 15–2, para 6. See also *R v Dodson and Williams* [1984] 1 WLR 971, CA.

[92] The Crown Court Compendium (July 2019), Part 1, 15–2, para 7. See also *R v West* [2005] EWCA Crim 3034 at [14].

[93] The Crown Court Compendium, Part 1 (July 2019), 15–2, para 7–8. *R v Walters* [2013] EWCA Crim 1361.

[94] [2015] 2 Cr App R 215 (14), CA.

[95] [1995] 1 Cr App R 547, CA.

[96] [1995] 1 Cr App R 7, CA.

[97] [1984] 1 WLR 971, CA.

the subsequent case of *R v Blenkinsop*, heard only a few days after *R v Downey*, it was held that there *was* a general and invariable rule. The Court of Appeal in *R v Shanmugarajah* preferred the decision in *R v Downey* and held there was no invariable or inflexible rule in every case. The court referred to the judgment of Watkins LJ in *R v Dodson and Williams*,[98] in which His Lordship said the task the jury are being asked to perform is a perfectly straightforward one and it is a statement of the obvious that they must be careful. Modern practice in the Court of Appeal is not to require trial judges to direct the jury as to the obvious. For example, the jury do not need to be told that the photograph is of good quality or poor, nor whether the person is shown in close-up or was distant from the camera, or was alone or part of a crowd.[99]

Where the jury are attempting their own visual identification, the accused who has elected not to testify is under no obligation to meet any request by them to stand up and turn around, so that they might have a better view of him; no inference should be drawn against him for his refusal and to direct the jury otherwise would reverse the burden of proof.[100]

Evidence of analysis of films, photographs, and images

In *Attorney General's Reference (No 2 of 2002)*[101] the Court of Appeal set out four sets of circumstances in which evidence of analysis of photographic images from the scene of the crime is admissible, subject to the discretion to exclude, to show that the accused committed the offence. Upon hearing such evidence, the jury may, with appropriate directions, be invited to conclude, on the basis of the images, that the accused committed the offence. The circumstances are: (i) where the image was clear enough to make a comparison with the accused;[102] (ii) where the accused was recognized in the image by someone who knew him sufficiently well; (iii) where a witness has acquired through hours of examination of photographic images familiarity with the material, he may make the comparison with a known and reasonably contemporary photograph, provided the evidence can be tested by the jury's own examination of the images; and (iv) where the accused has been identified in the image by an expert in facial mapping[103] or with some other relevant expertise. Concerning (iv), other relevant

[98] *R v Shanmugarajah* [2015] 2 Cr App R 215 (14), CA, at 228.

[99] *R v Blenkinsop* [1995] 1 Cr App R 7, CA. See also *Taylor v Chief Constable of Cheshire* [1987] 1 All ER 225, DC (see **Ch 12**); see also *R v Najjar* [2014] EWCA Crim 1309. Research, however, shows that there are dangers: see Bruce, 'Fleeting Images of Shade' (1998) *The Psychologist* 331 and Henderson et al, 'Matching the Faces of Robbers Captured on Video' (2001) 15 *Applied Cognitive Psychology* 445.

[100] *R v McNamara* [1996] Crim LR 750, CA.

[101] [2003] 1 Cr App R 321 (21).

[102] For an example of images not clear enough to make a meaningful comparison, see *R v Ali* [2009] Crim LR 40, CA. The trial judge in that case also failed to give the full and careful direction required when he invited the jury to, 'use your own eyes' (*R v Ali* [2008] EWCA 1522 at [40]–[41]).

[103] For a study which suggests that training and experience in facial analysis will produce more reliable and accurate facial identification, see Wilkinson and Evans, 'Are Facial Image Analysis Experts any Better than the General Public at Identifying Individuals from CCTV Images?' (2009) 49(3) *Science and Justice* 191–6. For guidance on using and interpreting facial image comparison evidence, see 'Forensic Image Comparison and Interpretation Evidence: Guidance for Prosecutors and Investigators', Issue 1, Forensic Science Regulator, 16 January 2015, accessible at https://www.gov.uk/government/uploads/system/uploads/attachment_data/file/405528/Image_Comparison_and_Interpretation_Guidance_Issue_1_160115.pdf.

expertise has included, in relation to CCTV images, expertise in forensic gait analysis[104] and expertise in 'image addition', 'image subtraction', and 'blink comparison' techniques which involve superimposing an image of the accused on an image of the perpetrator or switching between the images for comparison.[105] In the case of evidence from an expert using new techniques, the court should approach the evidence with caution and a full and careful direction will be required.[106]

Pre-trial procedure

The purpose of Code D of the Police and Criminal Evidence Act 1984 is to enable the accused to test the reliability of a witness's identification and provide safeguards for the accused against the very real risk that the witness identification may be mistaken.[107] Code D, Para 3, Part A concerns identification by an eyewitness, where the witness sees a person committing a crime and subsequently attempts to identify that person in a formal identification procedure. Para 3, Part B concerns recognition from films, photographs and images where the witness views them in 'controlled circumstances' under supervision. Para 3, Part C also concerns recognition from films, photographs and images, but in 'uncontrolled and unsupervised circumstances', for example, where a witness recognizes a person by looking at images on social media at home.

Code D, Para 3, Part A: eyewitnesses

Code D, para 3.1 states that there is a duty to make and keep a record of the first description given by the witness. This is of obvious importance because it enables the accused to challenge the reliability of the identification by pointing out inconsistencies between the witness's first description and any subsequent description, and between any description and his actual appearance. Concerning identification procedures, Code D para 3.12 provides that whenever a suspect is known and (i) a witness has identified or purported to identify a suspect; or (ii) there is a witness available who expresses an ability to identify the suspect, or there is a reasonable chance of the witness being able to do so, and the suspect disputes the identification, an identification procedure shall be held, that is, a video identification, an identification parade, or a group identification. The exception is where an identification procedure is not practicable or it would serve no useful purpose, for example when it is not disputed that the suspect is already well known to the witness.[108] The Code also provides obligations concerning the arrangement of procedures themselves, for example in

---

[104] For a study which suggests that individuals with experience in gait analysis perform well in the comparative identification of suspects from CCTV footage, and so have a role to play as expert witnesses in this field, see Birch et al, 'The Identification of Individuals from Observational Gait Analysis Using Closed Circuit Television Footage', (2013) 53(3) *Science and Justice* 339–42.

[105] *R v Gardener* [2004] EWCA Crim 1693.

[106] Ibid at [48].

[107] Code D (2017), para 1.2. As to the importance of pre-trial procedures relating to identification evidence, see Roberts, 'The problem of mistaken identity: Some observations on the process' (2008) 8 E&P 100.

[108] For the issues that arise where a suspect admits his presence at the scene of the offence, but denies committing the offence, see Roberts, 'Questions of "Who was there?" and "Who did what?": The Application of Code D in Cases of Dispute as to Participation but not Presence' [2003] Crim LR 709.

relation to the duties of 'identification officers' in selecting procedures[109] and in providing information to suspects and recording details of the procedure conducted.[110] Where the suspect is not known, Code D provides that the witness may be taken to a place to see if he can identify the person he saw on a previous occasion. In this situation various obligations arise: to make a record of the witness's first description;[111] to avoid providing information to the witness which might direct his attention to an individual unless, in the circumstances, this is unavoidable;[112] to make every effort to separate witnesses, where there are two or more;[113] and to make a comprehensive record of the details of the identification.[114] The obligation to hold a formal identification procedure under Code D, para 3.12 unless it would be impracticable to do so or would serve no useful purpose, applies even where an informal recognition has already occurred. The reasons for this were given in *R v Forbes*:[115] (i) a recognition may take place in informal circumstances over which the investigator has little or no control; (ii) a formal procedure holds a useful purpose because it allows the witness to entertain doubts about the informal recognition; and (iii) when an identification occurs on both occasions, the jury will receive assistance as to the value of the evidence.[116] In *R v Lariba*,[117] it was held that the reasoning in *R v Forbes* applies with equal force to identifications based on recognition from CCTV.[118] In *R v McCullough*[119] it was held that where the accused is identified at a formal procedure, a prior informal identification is capable of having a substantial effect on the *weight* of the subsequent identification rather than its *admissibility*.[120]

Code D, Para 3, Part B: recognition by formal viewing of film, photographs and images

Code D, paras 3.34–3.37 set out the pre-trial procedure applicable to recognition by viewing films, photographs and images where the viewing takes place in circumstances which are formally controlled and supervised.[121] A detailed contemporaneous record must be kept of the circumstances in which the recognition took place and of any comments (such as expressions of doubt) made by the witnesses, so that the accused is able to test its reliability.[122]

---

[109] Code D, paras 3.14–3.16.

[110] Ibid, paras 3.17–3.20.

[111] Ibid, para 3.2 (a).

[112] Ibid, para 3.2 (b).

[113] Ibid, para 3.2 (c).

[114] Ibid, para 3.2 (d)–(e).

[115] [2001] 1 AC 473, HL.

[116] However, the forensic value of a formal identification following an informal identification is doubtful and arguably one should only be held if requested by the suspect: see Roberts, 'Commentary' [2017] Crim LR 801.

[117] [2015] EWCA Crim 478.

[118] See also *R v Byrne* [2016] EWCA Crim 2124, where a police officer, out of curiosity, looked at an image in another officer's 'graphic pack' and recognized the accused.

[119] [2011] EWCA Crim 1413.

[120] At [13]. The prior informal identification was by Facebook. See also *R v LT* [2019] 4 WLR 51, CA.

[121] The provisions supersede the guidance given in *R v Smith* [2009] 1 Cr App R 521 (36), CA.

[122] Code D, para 3.36. See also *R v Byrne* [2016] EWCA Crim 2124.

Code D, Para 3, Part C: recognition by informal viewing of film, photographs and images

A recognition is not invalidated because it takes place in informal circumstances, such as an informal viewing of images on a social networking site such as Facebook[123] or broadcast on national or local media. However, such recognitions carry a clear risk of contamination and in *R v Alexander*,[124] which concerned an identification using Facebook, the Court of Appeal said that pre-trial procedure was a matter requiring urgent consideration by relevant statutory and professional bodies, 'so that *short* and *simple* guidance can be given in short order . . .'[125] Guidance in Code D, paras 3.38–3.41 now covers informal recognitions in situations where films, photographs, and images are shown to the public through national or local media (including social media), or are circulated for viewing by police officers and staff through police communication systems. Where a witness (including a police officer or a member of police staff) indicates that as a result of an informal (or 'uncontrolled') viewing, he may have information as to the identity of a person seen, he should be asked to give details of the circumstances and conditions of the viewing (subject to his recollection) and a record should be made which accords with the record required to be made where the viewing of images is in controlled circumstances. In addition, any material released should be kept and the accused and his representative should be permitted to see it before any formal identification procedure is held (unless this would unreasonably delay the investigation). After any formal procedure, witnesses must be asked if they previously saw any film, photograph, or other image or any description broadcast and their reply should be recorded, as should details of the circumstances of the viewing.

Where there has been an informal identification using Facebook, it was held in *R v Alexander*[126] that it is incumbent on the police to obtain, in as much detail as possible, evidence about the circumstances of the identification. This should include the images that were looked at and a statement from the witness, so that the jury are able to properly assess how the identification occurred[127] and the defence are able to test its reliability. As to the direction to be given to the jury, the court held that the judge will need to direct the jury carefully on the circumstances of the identification and specific factors which could affect its reliability, including: (i) whether the witness obtained in advance the name of the person he identified; (ii) whether the witness read information about the person he identified, for example in 'personal profiles' or comments left on web pages; (iii) whether other persons were present (or in contact) who prompted the witness; and (iv) the nature and quality of the images viewed. Guidance to this effect now appears in the Crown Court Compendium and applies to all identifications from social media, not just Facebook.[128]

---

[123] See *R v LT* [2019] 1 WLR 51, CA; *R v Alexander* [2013] 1 Cr App R 334 (26), CA; and *R v McCullough* [2011] EWCA Crim 1413.

[124] [2013] 1 Cr App R 334 (26), CA. Although in this case the court held that no remarks had been made to the identifying witness which might have contaminated the identification. See also *R v LT* [2019] 1 WLR 51, CA.

[125] At [23].

[126] [2013] 1 Cr App R 334 (26), CA.

[127] Ibid at [22].

[128] The Crown Court Compendium (July 2019), Part 1, 15–1, para 6.

Breaches of Code D and exclusion

A breach of Code D provides a basis for the exclusion of identification evidence under s 78 of the Police and Criminal Evidence Act 1984.[129] However, a breach will not necessarily result in the exclusion of the evidence obtained as a result of the breach, or of other evidence of identification, of which there may be an abundance.[130] The critical issue is the impact of the breach on the fairness of the trial.[131] Thus in *R v Samms*,[132] where it was not shown that it was impracticable to hold a parade (or group identification),[133] it was held that it would be unfair to admit the evidence of identification of the suspect by confrontation because the confrontation that occurred partook of the dangers sought to be prevented by a parade (or group identification).[134] It will be unfair to make use of identification evidence obtained by a video identification procedure which uses images of persons bearing an insufficient resemblance to the accused.[135] It will also be unfair to use the CCTV recognition evidence of an officer where there has been a wholesale breach of Code D, involving another officer's improper indication as to the suspect's identity and a failure to keep a proper record of the recognition.[136] On the other hand, in *R v Grannell*[137] it was held that no unfairness arose from the failure, in breach of what is now para 3.17 of the Code, to explain to the suspect prior to an identification procedure such matters as the purpose of the identification and the procedures for holding it; and in *R v Ryan*[138] it was held that a clear breach of what is now para 3.11 of the Code—an officer involved with the investigation of the case took part in the identification procedures—had caused no prejudice to the accused.[139] Thus in deciding whether to exclude the evidence of

---

[129] See Ch 11.

[130] See *R v McEvoy* [1997] Crim LR 887, CA, a decision under an earlier version of para 3.12.

[131] This remains the case where the identification is not strictly governed by Code D at all (see *R v Hickin* [1996] Crim LR 584, CA) or where the evidence of identification has come into existence abroad as a result of arrangements made by a foreign police force (see *R v Quinn* [1990] Crim LR 581, CA).

[132] [1991] Crim LR 197, CC.

[133] See also *R v Johnson* [1996] Crim LR 504, CA (confrontation by video).

[134] See Code D, paras 3.9–3.10 and Annex C. See also *R v Martin and Nicholls* [1994] Crim LR 218, CA (evidence of informal identification by young witnesses a very long time after the offence and in unsatisfactory conditions outside the court while the accused and witnesses were awaiting allocation of the case to a court). Cf *R v Tiplady* [1995] Crim LR 651, CA (a group identification in the foyer of a magistrates' court where T had been bailed to attend). It was held that the venue was not inappropriate and *Martin and Nicholls* was distinguished on the basis that whereas in that case there were striking limitations on the choice open to the identifying witnesses (the accused wore 'funky dreads'), in *Tiplady* at any one time between 20 and 30 people had been present, most of them in T's age group. Cf also *R v Quinn* [1990] Crim LR 581, CA: evidence of an informal identification as a result of a chance meeting would be admissible. See also *R v Oscar* [1991] Crim LR 778, CA, and *R v Rogers* [1993] Crim LR 386, CA.

[135] See *R v Marcus* [2005] Crim LR 384, CA. See also *R v Preddie* [2011] EWCA Crim 312 (improper street identification that rendered valueless a later video identification procedure).

[136] See *R v Deakin* [2012] EWCA Crim 2637 and paras 3.35 and 3.36 of Code D and cf *R v Lariba* [2015] EWCA Crim 478.

[137] (1989) 90 Cr App R 149, CA.

[138] [1992] Crim LR 187, CA. See also *R v Jones (Terence)* [1992] Crim LR 365, CA and *R v Khan* [1997] Crim LR 584, CA; and cf *R v Gall* (1989) 90 Cr App R 64, CA and *R v Finley* [1993] Crim LR 50, CA.

[139] See also, *sed quaere*, *Marsh v DPP* [2007] Crim LR 163 (failure, in breach of para 3.1(b), to make a record of a witness's description of a suspect before participation in any identification procedure), and *R v Cole* [2013] EWCA Crim 1149.

identification, the judge will consider the seriousness of the breach[140] and whether there is other evidence sufficient to enable the reliability of the evidence to be tested.[141]

Where evidence of a formal identification procedure at which the accused was identified is central to the prosecution case but the judge, notwithstanding breaches of Code D, properly decides not to exercise his discretion to exclude it, any breach will be a 'specific weakness in the identification evidence' which, applying the *Turnbull* guidelines, the jury must be directed on. Accordingly, the judge should make specific references to the breaches and leave it to the jury to consider what their approach should be in the light of them.[142] According to the Court of Appeal in *R v Gojra*,[143] the jury should be told that a failure to hold an identification procedure in breach of Code D is a breach of a positive obligation; to merely tell them that holding a procedure would have been 'desirable' is not sufficient. The Crown Court Compendium provides an example of how the jury should be directed where there has been no identification procedure in breach of Code D:[144]

> The fact that no identification procedure took place broke the rules that should be followed in cases involving disputed identification. These rules . . . are designed to provide safeguards for a suspect whom a witness says he can identify, and to test the ability of the witness to identify the suspect. The failure to hold a formal identification procedure has deprived [the accused] of an important safeguard which would have tested the witness's ability to make an identification under normal and fair conditions. You must bear that in mind when considering the reliability of the witness's identification.

However, in *R v Forbes*,[145] applied in *R v Gojra*,[146] it was held that a failure to direct the jury about a breach of Code D will not necessarily infringe an accused's right to a fair trial or render a conviction unsafe. In *R v Byrne*,[147] where a police officer failed to make a record of the circumstances of his own informal recognition, it was held that although the judge did not direct the jury in express terms that there had been a breach of Code D, what was said to the jury was sufficient to convey that the accused had lost the benefit of a safeguard which enabled him to put the reliability of the police officer's recognition to the test.[148]

---

[140] See *R v D* (2013) 177 J P 158, CA, where the evidence should have been excluded in the light of a 'wholesale breach of Code D' which was 'lamentable'. The court was particularly concerned by 'highly suggestive' comments made by a police officer to the witness (another police officer), namely that she believed the accused appeared in the CCTV footage which the witness was about to view.

[141] See *R v Moss* [2011] EWCA Crim 252, where an off-duty police officer had gone to a police station to check his emails and on passing by a computer screen recognized the suspect in an image from CCTV footage of a burglary. Although there had been a breach of Code D, it was held that the defence could test the reliability of the recognition because of evidence that the officer had reported it to his superior at the time and made a note in his notebook when he returned to work a week later. See also *R v Selwyn* [2012] EWCA Crim 2968; *R v Singh* [2013] EWCA Crim 669; and *R v Lariba* [2015] EWCA Crim 478.

[142] See the Crown Court Compendium (July 2019), Part 1, 15–1, para 11(2). See also *R v Quinn* [1995] 1 Cr App R 480, CA; and *R v Preddie* [2011] EWCA Crim 312, where the judge should have exercised his discretion to exclude.

[143] [2010] EWCA Crim 1939.

[144] The Crown Court Compendium (July 2019), Part 1, 15–1, Example.

[145] [2001] 1 AC 473, HL.

[146] [2010] EWCA Crim 1939.

[147] [2016] EWCA Crim 2124.

[148] At [39]. See also Code D, para 3.36.

Voice identification

In *R v Roberts*,[149] the Court of Appeal acknowledged that according to the expert research, voice identification is more difficult than visual identification, especially in the case of a stranger, and therefore should attract an even more stringent warning than that given in the case of visual identification.[150] Indeed the difficulties of voice identification were considered to be such that in *R v Chenia*[151] the Court of Appeal held that where evidence of a recording of a voice alleged to be the accused was admitted in evidence without the assistance of an expert in phonetics, the jury should not be asked to compare what they hear on a recording with either what they hear on another recording or the voice of the accused when giving evidence. However, *R v Chenia*, in this respect, has been superseded by *R v Flynn*.[152] In *R v Flynn*, the Court of Appeal concluded that, apart from *R v Chenia*, there was no other authority for the proposition that juries could only make a voice comparison with expert assistance. It was therefore wrong to direct the jury not to make their own comparison between the voices heard on a covert recording and the voices of the accused when giving evidence where, during the trial, recognition evidence identifying the accused had been given by police officers as 'lay listeners'. A jury may make a voice comparison provided that they have received guidance from *either* experts or lay listeners. Nonetheless, the court decided that the evidence should have been excluded because its prejudicial effect outweighed its probative value.[153] The court stated that: mistakes can still be made by lay listeners even where they have considerable familiarity with a voice and have listened to a clear recording;[154] the increasing use of police officers to conduct 'lay listener' identifications of voice recordings was to be treated with 'great care and caution';[155] and the jury must be given a careful direction on the dangers of mistake in all cases where the prosecution rely on voice identification, whether by a lay listener or expert, or both.[156]

The warning to be given

Important guidance on directing juries in cases where the prosecution rely on voice identification evidence is now contained in the Crown Court Compendium.[157] Citing *R v Flynn*[158] as the leading authority on identification by voice, the Compendium states that in cases of voice identification an explicit modified *Turnbull* direction is required and that where juries are allowed to conduct their own identification by listening to recordings, they should be reminded of the evidence of witnesses who gave evidence of voice recognition and warned of the dangers of relying on their own untrained ears.[159] The direction itself need not follow a

---

[149] [2000] Crim LR 183, CA.

[150] See also *R v Chenia* [2004] 1 All ER 543, and *R v Hersey* [1998] Crim LR 281, CA where it was stated that a warning based on the guidelines in *R v Turnbull* should be given, but tailored for the purposes of voice identification.

[151] [2004] 1 All ER 543, CA at [106] and [107]. Cf *R v O'Doherty* [2003] 1 Cr App R 77 (5): the Northern Ireland Court of Appeal held that auditory analysis is inadmissible because it is not sufficiently reliable. See also Ch 20.

[152] [2008] 2 Cr App R 266 (20), CA, at [56].

[153] At [52].

[154] At [51].

[155] At [63].

[156] At [64].

[157] See the Crown Court Compendium (July 2019), Part 1, 15–7.

[158] [2008] 2 Cr App R 266 (20), CA.

[159] See the Crown Court Compendium (July 2019), Part 1, 15–7, paras 3 and 8.

precise form of words provided the essential elements of the modified warning are included.[160] As to the reliability of a voice identification, the Compendium provides the following 'non-exhaustive list of possible considerations'.[161]

(1) Identification by voice recognition is more difficult than visual identification.

(2) As with visual identification, a genuine, honest and convincing witness who purports to identify a voice may be mistaken and a number of such witnesses may all be mistaken. This is so even when the witness [or] witnesses are very familiar with the known voice . . .

(3) [Non-expert evidence is admissible], but the ability of a lay listener correctly to identify voices is subject to a number of variables which require such evidence to be treated with great caution and great care having regard to, inter alia, these factors: (a) the quality of the recording of the disputed voice; (b) the length of time between the listener hearing the known voice and his attempt to recognise the disputed voice; (c) the extent of the listener's familiarity with the known voice; (d) the nature, duration and amount of speech which it is sought to identify; (e) the nature and integrity of the process by which the purported identification was made, in particular whether or not a voice comparison exercise in which the disputed voice is put with the voices of several others (similar to an identification procedure) was used.

(4) Voice identification is likely to be more reliable when carried out by (i) an expert listener using auditory phonetic analysis and/or (ii) an expert in voice analysis using acoustic recording and measurement (quantitative acoustic analysis).

(5) Evidence which is capable of supporting/not capable of supporting/capable of undermining such evidence must be drawn to the attention of the jury.

(6) Any direction must be modified if two or more experts with differing views give evidence on this topic. In particular their relative levels of qualification and experience, the steps which each took to compare the recordings, their findings and their opinions should be identified in such a way that their differences are made clear to the jury.

In respect of (4) and (6), it is submitted that guidance provided in the Compendium's precursor, the Crown Court Bench Book, remains valid, namely that judicial comment is likely to be made where the expert evidence adduced is based solely on auditory phonetic analysis rather than quantitative acoustic analysis, the former being unable to distinguish between the vocal mechanisms of voices.[162] As to paragraph (5), the Compendium lists a number of factors which may need to be addressed:[163] how audible the speech was; environmental conditions which might affect the witness's ability to hear the speech; the length of time of the hearing of the speech; how many voices were heard; whether speech was heard directly or by phone or other indirect means; any attempt to disguise the voice;[164] any disability

---

[160] *Phipps v DPP* [2012] UKPC 24. But see *R v Putland* [2010] EWCA Crim 459: a conviction was not unsafe where evidence of voice and visual identification was adduced and the judge gave a standard *Turnbull* warning with no specific reference to the risks of identification by voice. Cf *Karsten v Wood Green Crown Court* [2014] EWHC 2900, DC, where the Crown Court had directed itself correctly in accordance with *Turnbull*, had taken expert evidence into account and was aware of the more stringent test required for voice identification.

[161] The Crown Court Compendium (July 2019), Part 1, 15–7, para 11.

[162] See the Crown Court Bench Book 2010, 132, 6.

[163] The Crown Court Compendium (July 2019), Part 1, 15–7, para 4.

[164] See generally, Bull and Clifford, 'Earwitness Testimony' in Heaton-Armstrong et al (eds), *Analysing Witness Testimony* (London, 1999) ch 13.

affecting hearing; the variety of speech; how familiar the hearer was with the known voice; whether the speech was distinctive or with an accent; whether the speech was in the speaker's first language; and the length of time between the hearing of the speech and the identification. In addition to those factors, it is submitted that detailed guidance is also required, in relation to audibility, on the effect of words being shouted[165] and, more generally, the effect of stress.

Pre-trial procedure

Code D says little about pre-trial procedures for voice identification: it simply states that the Code does not preclude the police from making use of aural identification procedures, such as a 'voice identification parade', where they judge that appropriate.[166] Such a parade was held in *R v Hersey*.[167] Eleven volunteers and the accused, H, read out a passage of text from an unrelated interview with H. This was listened to by the 'earwitness' who had heard considerable speech by two masked robbers during the robbery of his shop. On a *voir dire* an expert gave evidence that twelve voices was too many, that almost all of the volunteers' voices were of a pitch higher than that of H, and only H had read the passage in a way which made sense. He also gave evidence of the effect of stress on pitch. The trial judge decided not to exclude the identification evidence under s 78 of the Police and Criminal Evidence Act 1984, and ruled that the evidence of the expert was not admissible before the jury. The Court of Appeal held that evidence of the parade had been properly admitted and that the jurors did not require the assistance of the expert, who had dealt with matters which were within their own experience and competence.[168] It has been made clear since *R v Hersey* that there is no duty to hold a voice identification procedure under Code D, which relates only to visual identification, and that the matter is properly dealt with by a suitably adapted *Turnbull* warning.[169] However, there is an obvious need for a pre-trial procedure and not one crudely modelled on the procedures used in the case of visual identification, because that would be to duck important issues of the kind raised by the expert in *R v Hersey*, for example questions relating to the number of voices that should be heard, the nature of the text that should be used, and the method by which the police should select those whose voices, so far as possible, resemble that of the accused.[170] Although para 1.2 of Code D refers to the police being able to make use of a voice identification parade where they judge that to be appropriate,[171] which seems broad enough to cover the kind of procedure adopted in *R v Hersey*, it refers to Note

---

[165] See *R v Hussain* [2010] EWCA Crim 1327, CA: the evidence of voice recognition by hearing a small number of words shouted was on the borderline of admissibility.

[166] Para 1.2. However, para 1.2 refers to Note 1B which refers, in turn, to the Home Office Circular 57/2003, considered in this chapter: see text accompanying nn 172–5. See also para 18, Annex B, where a witness at a visual identification parade wishes to hear any parade member speak.

[167] [1998] Crim LR 281, CA.

[168] See *R v Turner* [1975] QB 834, CA (see Ch 20).

[169] *R v Gummerson and Steadman* [1999] Crim LR 680, CA.

[170] See Ormerod, 'Sounds Familiar?—Voice Identification Evidence' [2001] Crim LR 595.

[171] Code D 1.2.

1B of the Note for Guidance, which refers, in turn, to the Home Office Circular prepared in 2003 as part of 'work to develop reliable procedures for voice identification, in contemplation that it might ultimately go forward for inclusion in Code D . . .'[172] The Circular, states that, 'Under no circumstances should an attempt be made to conduct a live voice identification procedure, using live suspect and foils'.[173] This strong warning against live parades, along with other suggestions in the Circular concerning the preparation of material for a voice identification procedure, were recommendations for good practice.[174] However, their precise status is unclear. Although in Code D there is an electronic link to the Circular, the Circular itself has been archived.[175]

In *R v Flynn*[176] the Court of Appeal provided the following 'minimal safeguards' in respect of pre-trial procedure for 'lay listener' voice identification:

1. The evidence-gathering procedure should be properly recorded, in particular the amount of time spent in contact with the accused should be recorded as it is highly relevant to the issue of the officer's familiarity with the accused when identifying his voice.

2. The date and time spent by the police officer compiling a transcript of a covert recording must be noted and annotated with the officer's views as to who is speaking on the recording.

3. Before attempting to make a voice identification the police officer should not be supplied with a copy of a transcript bearing another officer's annotations of who he believes is speaking.

4. A voice identification should be carried out by someone other than an officer involved in investigating the case because of the risk that the identification might be influenced by knowledge already gained in the course of the investigation.

Valuable though these safeguards are, much more is needed in terms of pre-trial procedure.[177] Given that many years have passed since the Court of Appeal acknowledged in *R v Roberts*[178] that voice identification was more difficult than visual identification, it is troubling to the authors of this work that, at the time of writing, not even minimal safeguards of the kind suggested in *R v Flynn*[179] appear in Code D.

---

[172] Home Office Circular 57/2003, 'Advice on the use of voice identification parades,' accessible at https://webarchive.nationalarchives.gov.uk/20130308000037 and http://www.homeoffice.gov.uk/about-us/corporate-publications-strategy/home-office-circulars/circulars-2003/057-2003/.

[173] Para 7 of the Circular.

[174] See paras 6–11 of the Circular. For an article which argues in favour of procedures, see, Robson, 'A fair hearing? The use of voice identification parades in criminal investigations in England and Wales' [2017] Crim LR 36.

[175] Archived on 25th January 2013.

[176] [2008] 2 Cr App R 266 (20), CA, at [53].

[177] See Warburton and Lewis, 'Opinion evidence; admissibility of ad hoc expert voice recognition evidence: *R v Flynn*' (2009) 13 E&P 50.

[178] *R v Roberts* [2000] Crim LR 183, CA.

[179] [2008] 2 Cr App R 266 (20), CA.

ADDITIONAL READING

Bruce, 'Fleeting Images of Shade' [1988] *The Psychologist* 331, accessible at https://thepsychologist.bps.org.uk/volume-11/edition-7/fleeting-images-shade-identifying-people-caught-video.
An article which considers the problems with eyewitness and video-witness testimony, issues affecting the ability to match unfamiliar faces, the effect of movement, and issues in recognition of faces from CCTV.

Bull and Clifford, 'Earwitness Testimony' in Heaton-Armstrong et al (eds), *Analysing Witness Testimony* (London, 1999), ch 13.
A chapter which identifies issues affecting the reliability of earwitness testimony.

Costigan, 'Identification from CCTV: The Risk of Injustice' [2007] Crim LR 591.
An examination of the law relating to identification from photographic images by reference to the findings of psychological research. Evidence of recognition from CCTV images is discussed. Issues around identification of unfamiliar faces are considered, including the unreliability of such identifications, jury directions and prosecution strategies of using ad hoc experts, facial mapping, and image comparison to bolster evidence of images which are of poor quality.

Henderson et al., 'Matching the Faces of Robbers Captured on Video' (2001) 15 Applied Cognitive Psychology 445.
This article covers the methodology and results of five experiments conducted to test the ability of subjects to match the unfamiliar faces of participants in a staged bank robbery, using CCTV images and photographs of differing quality. Performance was found to be highly error prone even where the matching tasks were very simple. The legal implications of the results are discussed.

McGorrery and McMahon, 'A fair "hearing": earwitness identification and voice identification parades' (2017) 21(3) E&P 262.
An article which proposes 'best practice' for conducting voice identification parades. The authors critically examine voice identification procedures in criminal cases reported in Australia and the argument is made that procedures used are out of step with current scientific knowledge of auditory memory and identification by voice and that the courts are not addressing the risks associated with this type of evidence.

O'Floinn and Ormerod, 'Social Networking Material as Criminal Evidence' [2012] Crim LR 486 at 499–501.
The article considers problems related to the use of evidence from Social Networking Sites in criminal trials. This short section of the article considers the admissibility evidence of identification from images displayed on such sites.

Ormerod, 'Sounds Familiar?—Voice Identification Evidence' [2001] Crim LR 595.
A comprehensive analysis of the dangers of using voice identification and recognition evidence which proposes safeguards for the use of such evidence in the pre-trial and trial procedure. The article considers identification and recognition, the utility of voice identification evidence, scientific findings and their application, pre-trial procedures, and trial procedures. The article concludes that it is 'incumbent on English law to formulate appropriate safeguards and procedures to ensure that an efficient and reliable system is established for pre-trial and trial uses of voice identification evidence.'

Ormerod, 'Sounding Out Expert Voice Identification' [2002] Crim LR 771.
An article which considers expert evidence of voice identification and argues that the technique of acoustic analysis of voice samples is superior to auditory analysis. The article considers the Northern Irish case of *R v O'Doherty* [2002] NI 26, NICA, which expressed a strong preference for the former technique, and the English case of *R v Robb* (1991) 93 Cr App R 161, which gave qualified approval to the latter.

Robson and Smith, 'Can we have faith jurors listen without prejudice?: Likely sources of inaccuracy in voice-comparison exercises' [2019] Crim LR 115.
An examination of the question whether juries should be permitted to make their own identifications based on listening to evidence of audio recordings. The current law in England and Wales and other jurisdictions (Northern Ireland, Australia, and the United Sates) is reviewed. Factors which may affect the reliability of voice identification are considered (estimator and system variables). An approach to voice identification, which takes these factors into account, is suggested for the courts.

Warburton and Lewis, 'Opinion evidence; admissibility of ad hoc expert voice recognition evidence: *R v Flynn*' (2009) 13 E&P 50.
A commentary on the case of *R v Flynn* [2008] 2 Cr App R 20, CA, and the admissibility and use of ad hoc expert evidence of voice recognition.

QUESTIONS

1. In criminal cases, does the risk still exist of a miscarriage of justice by reason of a mistaken visual identification? Give reasons for your answer and refer to any relevant case law.

2. Critically discuss the law relating to the admissibility of voice identification evidence.

3. Jim is involved in an altercation with another man in a car park. During the altercation the man suddenly and viciously punches Jim in the face. The man then gets into his car and drives off. Jim, shaken, contacts the police and makes a statement. The statement includes a detailed description of the man. Jim also tells a friend, Andy, what happened and describes the man to him. A day later Jim goes to Andy's house and as soon as he arrives, Andy says, 'Look at this.' He passes Jim his mobile phone which shows an image of two men. Jim immediately says, 'The one on the left. I think that's him. It looks quite like him'. Andy says, 'Yeah, I thought you might say that. I did some digging on Facebook. This is just like something that guy would do.' Jim then says, 'Yeah, it's him alright. I'm 100% sure'.

    Jim sends the image to the police who visit both Jim and Andy. They obtain a full record of what was said when Andy showed the image to Jim and obtain full details from Andy about his searches on Facebook. They then identify and arrest Steve. He strongly denies that he was the person who assaulted Jim and says Jim has mistakenly identified him. He points out discrepancies between the description Jim gave and his own appearance, and he asks for an identification procedure. However, the officer tells Steve that he will not be holding a procedure because Jim has already identified him.

    In respect of the identification evidence, what issues are likely to arise at Steve's trial and how might they be resolved.

 For a note-form answer see the online resources, accessible at www.oup.com/he/keane-mckeown13e.

Documentary and real evidence

10

Documentary evidence

Admissibility

Statements contained in documents, like oral statements, are subject to the general rules of evidence on admissibility considered throughout this book.[1] This chapter concerns two additional requirements relating to the proof of documents on the contents of which a party seeks to rely. The first relates to proof of the contents of a document, for example proof of the length of a tenancy or the amount of rent as set out in a lease. The essential question relating to proof of contents is whether the party relying on the document must produce primary evidence, for example the original, as opposed to secondary evidence, for example a copy of the original. The second relates to proof of the fact that the document was properly executed, ie cases in which it becomes necessary to prove that a document was written, signed or attested by the person by whom it purports to have been written, signed or attested.[2]

Meaning of 'document'

In *R v Daye*[3] Darling J defined a document as 'any written thing capable of being evidence', whether the writing is on paper, parchment, stone, marble, or metal. Nowadays, a 'document' may be in electronic form, contained in a file stored on a computer or a portable device, or it may be a disc, a tape, or film and convey information by symbols, diagrams, and pictures as well as by words and numbers. It is clear from the modern authorities, however, that the definition of a document varies according to the nature of the proceedings and the particular context in question. Concerning proof of a document in criminal proceedings, the word has been narrowly defined. In *Kajala v Noble*[4] Ackner LJ, referring to the rule that if an original document is available in a party's hands, that party must produce it and cannot give secondary evidence by producing a copy, concluded: 'the old rule is limited and confined to written documents in the strict sense of the term, and has no relevance to tapes or films'.[5]

In civil proceedings, by contrast, 'document', for the purposes of the rules on the disclosure and inspection of documents, means 'anything in which information of any description is recorded',[6] a definition wide enough to cover not only documents in writing, but also maps, plans, graphs, drawings, discs, audio tapes, soundtracks, photographs, negatives, videotapes, and films. The same definition is used in relation to documents, including computer-produced documents, containing hearsay statements admissible under the Civil Evidence Act 1995 (the 1995 Act) or the Criminal Justice Act 2003 (the 2003 Act).[7]

---

[1] Principal among these, in criminal cases, is the rule against hearsay. See Chs 12–14.

[2] A third issue, relating to the admissibility of extrinsic evidence for the purpose of explaining, contradicting, varying, or adding to the terms of a document, is beyond the scope of this work.

[3] [1908] 2 KB 333 at 340.

[4] (1982) 75 Cr App R 149, CA.

[5] Ibid at 152. As an authority on the *proof of contents* in a criminal case, this decision should now be read subject to the Criminal Justice Act 2003, s 133: see, in this chapter, under General statutory provisions, p 303.

[6] CPR r 31.4.

[7] The 1995 Act, s 13 and the 2003 Act, s 134(1).

Proof of contents

General statutory provisions

Proof of the contents of a document on which a party seeks to rely is now largely governed, in criminal cases, by s 133 of the 2003 Act and s 71 of the Police and Criminal Evidence Act 1984,[8] and in civil cases by ss 8 and 9 of the 1995 Act. Section 133 of the 2003 Act provides that:

> Where a statement in a document is admissible as evidence in criminal proceedings, the statement may be proved by producing either—
>
> (a) the document, or
>
> (b) (whether or not the document exists) a copy of the document or of the material part of it, authenticated in whatever way the court may approve.[9]

Under s 71 of the Police and Criminal Evidence Act 1984, in any criminal proceedings the contents of a document may (whether or not the document is still in existence) be proved by the production of an enlargement of a microfilm copy of that document or the material part of it, authenticated in such manner as the court may approve.

Section 8 of the 1995 Act is cast in terms similar to those of s 133 of the 2003 Act. Under s 9(1) and (2) of the 1995 Act, a document which is certified as forming part of the records of a business or public authority may be received in evidence in civil proceedings without further proof; and under s 9(3) of that Act, the *absence* of an entry in the records of a business or public authority may be proved by the affidavit of an officer of the business or authority.[10]

Section 133 of the 2003 Act and s 8 of the 1995 Act appear to be of general application, that is, to apply to *any* statement contained in a document, and thus not confined to hearsay statements in documents admissible under the 2003 Act or the 1995 Act. Likewise, s 9 of the 1995 Act appears to apply to *any* document forming part of the records of a business or public authority and not merely documents containing hearsay statements admissible under the 1995 Act. On this reading, these provisions have reversed completely the general common law rule that a party seeking to rely on the contents of a document must adduce primary evidence (usually the original). Pending a definitive ruling to this effect, the general common law rule,[11] may continue to apply to non-hearsay, a conclusion that has been described as 'absurd'.[12] In any event, s 133 of the 2003 Act is permissive as to the means of proof and therefore cannot be taken to have overridden (i) the common law rule that where secondary evidence of the contents of a private document is admissible, it may take the form of *oral* evidence (use of which is not sanctioned by s 133);[13] (ii) a number of statutory provisions, mainly relating to public

---

[8] In the case of tape recordings and transcripts of police interviews sought to be introduced in criminal proceedings, see also the Code of Practice on Audio Recording Interviews with Suspects (Code E) and Criminal Practice Directions V, Part 16C.

[9] For the meaning of the words 'statement', 'document', and 'copy', see s 115(2) and s 134(1) of the 2003 Act (see Ch 12). Where the document is sought to be used by a witness only to refresh her memory during the course of oral evidence, the document must be made by the witness, or if it is a copy, 'verified' by the witness at an earlier time: s 139(1) of the Act. As to verification, the focus will be on the accuracy of the copy: see *DPP v Sugden* [2018] 2 Cr App R 101 (8), (Admin). See further Ch 6, The conditions for memory refreshing, p 187.

[10] See further Ch 13.

[11] Considered, in this chapter, under The general rule at common law—primary evidence, p 304.

[12] R Pattenden, 'Authenticating "things" in English law: principles for adducing tangible evidence in common law jury trials' (2008) 12 E&P 273 at 294.

[13] *R v Nazeer* [1998] Crim LR 750, CA.

documents, which provide for proof of their contents by copies required to take a particular form, such as an examined copy (ie a copy proved by oral evidence to correspond with the original) or a certified copy (ie a copy certified to be accurate by an official who has custody of the original); or (iii) the Bankers' Books Evidence Act 1879, whereby provision is made for the admission of copies of entries in a banker's book, subject to the fulfilment of certain conditions, one of which is that some person proves that he has examined the copy with the original and that it is correct.[14] The same may be said, concerning civil cases, of ss 8 and 9 of the 1995 Act. Section 14 of that Act provides that nothing in the Act affects (i) the proof of documents by means other than those specified in ss 8 or 9;[15] or (ii) the operation of certain statutory provisions governing the means of proving certain public and official documents.[16]

The general rule at common law—primary evidence

The general rule is that a party seeking to rely upon the contents of a document must adduce primary evidence of those contents. The rule, often regarded as the only remaining instance of the 'best evidence rule',[17] under which a party must produce the best evidence that the nature of the case will allow, may be justified as a means of reducing the risks of fraud, mistake, and inaccuracy which might result from proof by either production of a copy of a document or oral evidence of its contents.

There are three recognized categories of primary evidence of the contents of a document: the original, copies of enrolled documents, and admissions made by parties. The best kind of primary evidence is the original document in question. Although the original is usually identifiable with ease, some cases do occasion difficulty. Where documents are produced in duplicate, each of them may constitute an original. Thus the duplicates of a deed which have been executed by all parties are all originals.[18] A copy of a document, however, whether produced by carbon, photocopier, scanner or otherwise, is not original unless signed or otherwise duly executed. In the case of telegrams,[19] the original, if tendered against the receiver, is the message he received; the original, if tendered against the sender, is the message that was handed in or recorded at the Post Office.[20] A counterpart lease executed by the lessee alone is the original if tendered against him, whereas the other part is the original if tendered against the lessor.[21] Where a private document is required to be enrolled, that is officially filed in either a court or some other public office, a copy issued by the court or office in question is treated as an original. Thus where executors obtain a grant of probate, the probate copy of the will is treated as primary evidence of the contents of the will.[22] Where a party to litigation

---

[14] All three matters are considered, in this chapter, under **Public documents**, p 308, and **Bankers' books**, p 309.

[15] Section 14(2).

[16] Section 14(3). It is unclear, however, why only some of the many statutory provisions governing the proof of various types of document have been specified. Those referred to in s 14(3) include the Documentary Evidence Act 1868, s 2 and the Documentary Evidence Act 1882, s 2 (see under **Public documents**, p 308, in this chapter); the Evidence (Colonial Statutes) Act 1907, s 1 (see **Ch 20**); and the Evidence (Foreign, Dominion and Colonial Documents) Act 1933, s 1 (see **Chs 2** and **14**).

[17] In fact it pre-dates the best evidence rule.

[18] *Forbes v Samuel* [1913] 3 KB 706.

[19] At the time of writing, it is still possible to send a telegram.

[20] *R v Regan* (1887) 16 Cox CC 203.

[21] *Doe d West v Davis* (1806) 7 East 363.

[22] If a question arises concerning construction of the will, however, the court may examine the original: see *Re Battie-Wrightson, Cecil v Battie-Wrightson* [1920] 2 Ch 330.

has made an informal admission concerning the contents of a document, his admission constitutes primary evidence of the contents and is admissible in evidence against him.[23]

The general rule applies in any case where a party seeks to rely upon the actual contents of a document.[24] However, in cases where it is unnecessary to place reliance upon the contents of a document because the fact or matter in issue, even if recorded in a document, can be proved by other evidence, the general rule has no application. Thus, whereas production of a lease is necessary in order to prove the length of a tenancy[25] or the amount of rent due thereunder,[26] proof of the existence or fact of a tenancy, albeit created by a lease, may be proved by other evidence. In *R v Holy Trinity, Hull (Inhabitants)*,[27] the fact of a tenancy, created by a lease which defined its terms, could be proved without production of that lease; oral evidence, such as evidence on the payment of the rent, sufficed.[28] Likewise, the rule has no application where reference is made to a document merely for the purpose of establishing the bare fact of its existence. In *R v Elworthy*[29] the accused, a solicitor, was charged with perjury. It was alleged that he had falsely sworn that there was no draft of a certain statutory declaration which he had prepared. It was held that although secondary evidence of the contents of the draft and of certain alterations made in it was inadmissible, the prosecution could properly adduce oral evidence that such a draft existed and was in the possession of the accused.[30] Nor does the general rule apply when the contents of a document are referred to merely in order to identify it. Thus it has been said that 'in an action of trover for a promissory note, the contents of the promissory note may be stated verbally by a witness'.[31] Nor does the general rule apply where the document is a witness statement used only for the purposes of memory refreshing.[32]

Although both the general rule and the common law exceptions to it are well established, in *Springsteen v Flute International Ltd*[33] the Court of Appeal favoured a more generalized discretionary approach to admissibility. It held as follows. (1) The best evidence rule, long on its deathbed, had finally expired. (2) In every case where a party seeks to adduce secondary evidence of the contents of a document, it is a matter for the court to decide, in the light of all the circumstances of the case, what, if any, weight to attach to the evidence. (3) Where such a party can readily adduce the document, it may be expected that, absent some special circumstances, the court will decline to admit the secondary evidence on the ground that it is worthless. (4) At the other extreme, where such a party genuinely cannot produce the document, it may be expected that, absent some special circumstances, the court will admit the secondary evidence and attach such weight to it as it considers appropriate. (5) In cases

---

[23] *Slatterie v Pooley* (1840) 6 M&W 664. But see now Civil Evidence Act 1995, s 7(1) (see Ch 13).

[24] *MacDonnell v Evans* (1852) 11 CB 930.

[25] *Twyman v Knowles* (1853) 13 CB 222.

[26] *Augustien v Challis* (1847) 1 Exch 279.

[27] (1827) 7 B&C 611.

[28] See also *Alderson v Clay* (1816) 1 Stark 405 (proof of the fact of a partnership).

[29] (1867) LR 1 CCR 103.

[30] The Crown had not given notice to the accused to produce the original. Had they done so, secondary evidence of the contents of the draft would have been admissible (see, in this chapter, under **The exceptions—secondary evidence**, p 306).

[31] Per Martin B in *Boyle v Wiseman* (1855) 11 Exch 360 at 367, citing *Whitehead v Scott* (1830) 1 Mood&R 2.

[32] See, for example, *DPP v Sugden* [2018] 2 Cr App R 101 (8), (Admin).

[33] [2001] EMLR 654, CA.

falling between these two extremes, it is for the court to make a judgment as to whether in all the circumstances any weight should be attached to the secondary evidence.[34]

The exceptions—secondary evidence

Public documents, which constitute one of the exceptions to the general rule, are considered later in this chapter.[35] In the case of private documents, secondary evidence of their contents, where admissible, may take the form of a copy, a copy of a copy,[36] or oral evidence. Where a copy is produced, proof is required that it is a true copy of the original and in the same terms.[37] In *DPP v Sugden*,[38] a criminal case, the court observed that where a party seeks to admit a copy of a document and the other party asks why the original is not available and there is no answer, issues of accuracy may arise in respect of the copy. In these circumstances, the court will balance the probative value of the copy against the prejudicial effect of admitting it. However, there will be no prejudice where there is nothing to suggest that the copy is not a true copy and the accuracy of the copy can be explored by the accused through cross-examination.[39]

Where secondary evidence is admissible, there is a general rule that 'there are no degrees of secondary evidence'.[40] Thus although less weight may attach to inferior forms of secondary evidence, there is no obligation to tender the 'best' copy, rather than an inferior copy or a copy of a copy, and oral evidence of the contents is admissible even if a copy or some other more satisfactory type of secondary evidence is available. To this general rule there is a variety of exceptions. The contents of a will admitted to probate may not be proved by oral evidence if the original or probate copy exists. Judicial documents and bankers' books[41] are generally proved not by oral evidence but by office copies and examined copies respectively. Finally, many public documents may be proved by oral evidence only if examined, certified, or other copies are unavailable.[42]

Hearsay statements admissible by statute

Where the contents of a document are admissible hearsay under the 2003 Act, they may be proved in accordance with s 133 of that Act and s 71 of the Police and Criminal Evidence Act 1984; and where the contents of a document are admissible hearsay under the 1995 Act, they may be proved in accordance with ss 8 and 9 of that Act.[43]

Failure to produce after notice

A party seeking to rely upon a document may prove its contents by secondary evidence if the original is in the possession or control of another party to the proceedings who, having been served with a notice to produce it, has failed to do so. The purpose of serving such a notice is

---

[34] See also *Post Office Counters Ltd v Mahida* [2003] EWCA Civ 1583 (see Ch 2).

[35] See under **Public documents**, p 308.

[36] *Lafone v Griffin* (1909) 25 TLR 308; *R v Collins* (1960) 44 Cr App R 170. Contrast *Everingham v Roundell* (1838) 2 Mood&R 138.

[37] *R v Collins* (1960) 44 Cr App R 170; cf *R v Wayte* (1982) 76 Cr App R 110, CA.

[38] [2018] 2 Cr App R 101 (8), Admin; Crim LR [2018] 752.

[39] At [38](1)–(5).

[40] Per Lord Abinger CB in *Doe d Gilbert v Ross* (1840) 7 M&W 102. See also *DPP v Sugden* [2018] 2 Cr App R 101 (8), (Admin) at [24].

[41] See, in this chapter, under **Bankers' books**, p 309.

[42] See, in this chapter, under **Public documents**, p 308.

[43] See, in this chapter, under **General statutory provisions**, p 303 and see Chs 12 and 13.

not to notify the other party that reliance will be placed on a document so that he can prepare evidence to explain or confirm it, but merely to give him sufficient opportunity to produce it if he wishes or, if he does not, to enable the first party to adduce secondary evidence. Thus it has been held that where the original is in court, secondary evidence is admissible even where a party fails to comply with a notice to produce served during the course of the trial.[44]

It is assumed that the foregoing principles remain good law notwithstanding that the Civil Procedure Rules make no provision for formal service of a notice to produce.[45]

A notice to produce has never *compelled* production of a document. A party to civil proceedings who wishes to rely at the trial on the original of a document should serve a witness summons requiring a witness to produce the document to the court.[46]

A stranger's lawful refusal to produce

Secondary evidence of the contents of a document may be given when the original is in the possession of a stranger to the litigation who, having been served with a witness summons requiring her to produce it,[47] has lawfully refused to produce it, for example by reason of a claim to privilege[48] or diplomatic immunity[49] or because she is outside the jurisdiction and therefore cannot be compelled to produce it.[50] However, if the stranger, in unlawful disobedience of the summons, refuses to produce the original, secondary evidence is inadmissible because she is bound to produce it and is punishable for contempt if she refuses to do so.[51] The effect of these rules is to place a duty on the party who seeks to rely on the document, to compel the stranger to produce the original. This eliminates the risk of unreliable secondary evidence being admitted in consequence of their collusion.

Lost documents

Secondary evidence of the contents of a document is admissible on proof that the original has been destroyed or cannot be found after due search. The quality of evidence required to show the loss or destruction varies according to the nature and value of the document in question. In *Brewster v Sewell*[52] the plaintiff was unable to produce a policy of insurance against loss by fire on which a claim had been paid. Subsequent to the fire, which had occurred some years before the proceedings, a fresh policy had been issued. Evidence was given of a thorough but unsuccessful search for the earlier policy. It was held that, in the circumstances, the original policy had become 'mere waste paper' and that sufficient evidence of due search had been given to allow proof of its contents by secondary evidence. Bayley J said:[53]

> The presumption of law is that a man will keep all those papers which are valuable to himself, and which may, with any degree of probability, be of any future use to him. The presumption on the contrary is that a man will not keep those papers which have entirely discharged their duty, and which are never likely to be required for any purpose whatever.

---

[44] *Dwyer v Collins* (1852) 21 LJ Ex 225.

[45] See, formerly, RSC Ord 24, r 10.

[46] See CPR r 34.2.

[47] Ibid.

[48] *Mills v Oddy* (1834) 6 C&P 728.

[49] *R v Nowaz* [1976] 3 All ER 5, CA.

[50] *Kilgour v Owen* (1889) 88 LT Jo 7.

[51] *R v Llanfaethly (Inhabitants)* (1853) 2 E&B 940.

[52] (1820) 3 B&Ald 296. See also *R v Wayte* (1982) 76 Cr App R 110, CA.

[53] (1820) 3 B&Ald 296 at 300.

Production of original impossible

Secondary evidence is admissible where production of the original is either physically impossible, for example because it is an inscription upon a tombstone or wall,[54] or legally impossible, for example because the document in question is a notice which is required by statute to be constantly affixed at a factory or workshop.[55]

Public documents

At common law, secondary evidence of the contents of a wide variety of public documents is admissible on the grounds that production of the originals would entail a high degree of public inconvenience.[56] Under the modern law, there is a large number of statutes which also provide for the proof of public documents by secondary evidence. Secondary evidence for these purposes is usually required to take the form of an examined, authenticated, certified, office, Queen's Printer's, or Stationery Office copy. Under s 7 of the Evidence Act 1851, for example, the contents of all proclamations, treaties, and other acts of state of any foreign state or of any British colony, and all judgments, decrees, orders, and other judicial proceedings of any court of justice in any foreign state or in any British colony may be proved by an examined copy, which is a copy proved by oral evidence to correspond with the original, or by copies authenticated with the seal of the foreign state, British colony, or foreign or colonial court, as the case may be.[57] Certified copies are copies certified to be accurate by an official who has custody of the original.[58] They are employed to prove byelaws and records kept in the Public Record Office.[59] They are also used to prove a birth or death,[60] an adoption,[61] and a marriage[62] or civil partnership.[63] Under s 14 of the Evidence Act 1851, certified or examined copies may be used to prove the contents of any document provided that it is of such a public nature that it is admissible in evidence on production from proper custody and no other statute provides for proof of its contents by means of a copy. Office copies, which are prepared by officials who have custody of original judicial documents and are authenticated with the seal of the court, may be used to prove judgments, orders, and other judicial documents. Queen's

---

[54] Per Alderson B in *Mortimer v M'Callan* (1840) 6 M&W 58. See also, *sed quaere, R v Hunt* (1820) 3 B&Ald 566 (inscriptions on flags or banners).

[55] *Owner v Bee Hive Spinning Co Ltd* [1914] 1 KB 105, DC. See also *Alivon v Furnival* (1834) 1 Cr M&R 277 (document in custody of foreign court).

[56] See, eg, *Mortimer v M'Callan* (1840) 6 M&W 58 (books of the Bank of England).

[57] In the case of a foreign conviction, it remains necessary to establish that the examined copy relates to the person said to have been convicted, which may be achieved by the admission of any relevant evidence, including, eg, fingerprint evidence: *R v Mauricia* [2002] 2 Cr App R 377 (27), CA.

[58] Where a statute provides for proof of a document by a certified, sealed, or stamped copy, the copy, provided it purports to be signed, sealed, or stamped, is admissible without any proof of the sign, seal, or stamp, as the case may be: Evidence Act 1845, s 1.

[59] Local Government Act 1972, s 238 (the clerk to the local authority) and Public Records Act 1958, s 9 (the Keeper of Public Records).

[60] Births and Deaths Registration Act 1953, s 34 and, in the case of deaths in the Register of Presumed Deaths, the Presumption of Death Act, 2013, Sch 1, paras 3 and 4.

[61] Adoption and Children Act 2002, s 77(4).

[62] Marriage Act 1949, s 65(3).

[63] Civil Partnership (Registration Provisions) Regulations 2005, SI 2005/3176, regs 13(4) and 14(4).

Printer's copies are used to prove private Acts of Parliament and journals of either House of Parliament,[64] royal proclamations, orders, and statutory instruments.[65]

Bankers' books

In both civil and criminal proceedings, it is often necessary to adduce evidence of the contents of bankers' books. In order to avoid the inconvenience that production of the originals would entail, the Bankers' Books Evidence Act 1879 (the 1879 Act) provides for the admission of copies. Section 3, an exception to the rule against hearsay, reads as follows:

> Subject to the provisions of this Act, a copy of an entry in a banker's book shall in all legal proceedings be received as prima facie evidence of such entry, and of the matters, transactions, and accounts therein recorded.

'Banker' is defined as a 'deposit-taker' or the National Savings Bank.[66] 'Bankers' books' were originally defined to include 'ledgers', 'day books', 'cash books', and 'account books'. The definition has since been extended to include 'other records used in the ordinary business of the bank, whether those records are in written form or are kept on microfilm, magnetic tape, or any other form of mechanical or electronic data retrieval mechanism'.[67] 'Other records used in the ordinary business of the bank' has to be read *eiusdem generis* with 'ledgers, day books, cash books', and 'account books', which are the means by which banks record day-to-day financial transactions. Therefore, 'other records...' does not cover bank records of conversations between its employees and customers or others, or internal memoranda.[68] Paid cheques and paying-in slips retained by a bank after the conclusion of a banking transaction to which they relate have been held not to be bankers' books on the same basis or on the grounds that even if bundles of such documents can be treated as 'records used in the ordinary business of the bank', the addition of an individual cheque or paying-in slip cannot be regarded as making an 'entry' in those records.[69] The same reasoning may be used to justify the decision,

---

[64] Evidence Act 1845, s 3 and Documentary Evidence Act 1882, s 2. Stationery Office copies may also be used. The Interpretation Act 1978, s 3 provides that: 'Every Act is a public Act to be judicially noticed as such, unless the contrary is expressly provided by the Act.' This section applies to all Acts passed after 1850. At common law, judicial notice is taken of earlier enactments, if public: see **Ch 4**.

[65] Evidence Act 1845, s 3 and Documentary Evidence Act 1868, s 2. Such documents may also be proved by a copy of the Gazette containing them or by a copy certified to be true by the appropriate official. They may also be proved by a photocopy from a commercial publication, provided that there is no suggestion of any inaccuracy in the version before the court: *R v Koon Cheung Tang* [1995] Crim LR 813, CA. An 'order' under the 1868 Act, s 2 covers any executive act of government performed by the bringing into existence of a public document for the purpose of giving effect to an Act of Parliament: *R v Clarke* [1969] 2 QB 91 at 97. See also *West Midlands Probation Board v French* [2009] 1 WLR 1715, DC (a licence issued by the governor of a prison on behalf of the Secretary of State for the Home Office).

[66] Section 9(1). A 'deposit taker' will normally be someone with permission under the Financial Services and Markets Act 2000, Pt 4 to accept deposits: see s 9(1A)–(1C).

[67] Section 9(2).

[68] *Re Howglen Ltd* [2001] 1 All ER 376, Ch D.

[69] *Williams v Williams* [1987] 3 All ER 257, CA. In civil proceedings, if such documents relate to the bank account of the other party to the action, an order for disclosure may be made and the bank, as agent holding the documents on that party's behalf, may then be required to disclose them. In other cases, the party seeking disclosure of specific documents may be able to make use of CPR r 31.17, which provides for disclosure by a person who is not a party to the proceedings, or CPR r 34.2, which empowers the court to issue a witness summons requiring a witness to produce documents to the court.

reached prior to the extension of the definition of 'bankers' books', that copies of letters written by a bank and contained in a file of its correspondence do not constitute bankers' books.[70]

A copy is only admissible under s 3 of the 1879 Act if: (i) a partner or officer of the bank proves, by oral evidence or affidavit, that the book was at the time of the making of the entry one of the ordinary books of the bank, the entry was made in the usual and ordinary course of business, and the book is in the custody or control of the bank;[71] and (ii) some person proves, by oral evidence or affidavit, that he has examined the copy with the original and that it is correct.[72] Section 7 provides for any party to legal proceedings to apply to a court[73] or judge for an order to be at liberty to inspect and take copies of entries in bankers' books for the purposes of those proceedings. The order may be made without summoning the bank or any other party and shall be served on the bank three clear days before it is to be obeyed, unless the court or judge otherwise directs.[74] An order may be made under s 7 to inspect the account of a person not a party to the proceedings, even if that person is not compellable as a witness,[75] but in criminal cases such an order should be made only in exceptional circumstances and where the private interest in keeping a bank account confidential is outweighed by the public interest in assisting a prosecution.[76]

In civil proceedings, an application under s 7 to inspect entries in the bank account of a third party will only be granted if (i) the court is satisfied that the account is in fact the account of the other party to the action or an account with which he is so much concerned that items in it would be evidence against him; and (ii) the applicant shows very strong grounds for suspicion, almost amounting to certainty, that there are items in the account which would be material evidence against the other party.[77] A foreign bank which is not a party to the proceedings, even if it carries on business within the jurisdiction, should not, save in exceptional circumstances, be ordered to produce documents which are outside the jurisdiction and concern business transacted outside the jurisdiction, because an order under the 1879 Act is an exercise of sovereign authority to assist in the administration of justice, and foreign banks owe their customers a duty of confidence regulated by the law of the country where the documents are kept.[78] Although in criminal proceedings an order will not be refused on the

---

[70] *R v Dadson* (1983) 77 Cr App R 91, CA. See also *Barker v Wilson* [1980] 1 WLR 884, DC.

[71] Section 4.

[72] Section 5.

[73] Justices constitute a court for these purposes: *R v Kinghorn* [1908] 2 KB 949.

[74] Although the Act allows an application to be made without notice, there is much to be said for notice being given: per Widgery LJ in *R v Marlborough Street Magistrates' Court, ex p Simpson* (1980) 70 Cr App R 291, DC at 294. In an application in respect of accounts of a person who is not a party to the proceedings, the order either should not be made until the account owner has been informed and given an opportunity to be heard or should be made in the form of an order nisi, allowing a period for the person affected to show cause why the order should not take effect: per Oliver LJ in *R v Grossman* (1981) 73 Cr App R 302, CA at 309.

[75] *R v Andover Justices, ex p Rhodes* [1980] Crim LR 644, DC.

[76] *R v Grossman* (1981) 73 Cr App R 302 at 307, CA.

[77] *South Staffordshire Tramways Co v Ebbsmith* [1895] 2 QB 669, CA (a pre-trial application) and *D B Deniz Nakliyati TAS v Yugopetrol* [1992] 1 All ER 205, CA (an application against a judgment debtor).

[78] *MacKinnon v Donaldson Lufkin and Jenrette Securities Corpn* [1986] 1 All ER 653, Ch D, applying *R v Grossman* (1981) 73 Cr App R 302, CA (a decision acknowledged to have been given *per incuriam*, the proceedings in the case being criminal and the Court of Appeal, therefore, having no jurisdiction). However, a party seeking to obtain documents from a foreign bank in these circumstances may apply to a master under CPR r 34.13 for the issue of letters of request to the courts of the country in question specifying the documents to be produced, or may apply directly to a court in that country under the relevant local provisions, having first obtained the permission of the English court on an application with notice.

grounds that it incriminates the party against whom it is made,[79] it is a serious interference with the liberty of the party and the court should satisfy itself that the application is more than a mere fishing expedition by considering whether the prosecution has other evidence to support the charge.[80] In *R v Nottingham City Justices, ex p Lynn*[81] an order made by justices against an accused charged with drug smuggling, for the inspection of accounts over a three-year period, was amended by the Divisional Court to cover a period of six months, there being insufficient evidence to link the accused with offences during most of the three years.

An order under s 7 is not a necessary pre-condition of producing evidence under s 3; an order enables bankers' books to be inspected and copied despite the duty of confidentiality owed by banker to customer and is clearly unnecessary if the customer waives the right to confidentiality and the bank agrees to the inspection and copying.[82]

Proof of due execution

The general rule, in both civil and criminal proceedings, is that a document will only be admitted in evidence on proof of due execution. An exception exists in the case of public documents covered by statutes of the kind previously referred to in this chapter,[83] most of which not only provide for the proof of contents by secondary evidence, but also exempt from proof of due execution. In the case of a private document, proof of due execution may be admitted or presumed, but otherwise usually involves proof of handwriting or a signature and, sometimes, proof of attestation. In some cases, documents are required to be stamped for the purposes of stamp duty. Each of these matters now falls to be considered further.

Proof of handwriting

Proof of the due execution of a private document usually involves showing that it was written or signed by the person by whom it purports to have been written or signed. For these purposes, direct oral evidence that the signatory signed in a particular name may be given by the signatory himself or by any other person who witnessed the execution of the document. Proof may also be effected by admissible hearsay assertions to the same effect; or by the opinion evidence of someone who, although not a witness to the execution of the document, is acquainted with the handwriting of the person in question.[84] It is clear, however, that the weight to be attached to such opinion evidence will vary according to the circumstances.

A final method of proving handwriting or a signature is by comparing the document in question with another document which is proved or admitted to have been written by the person in question. Section 8 of the Criminal Procedure Act 1865 provides that:

Comparison of a disputed writing with any writing proved to the satisfaction of the judge to be genuine shall be permitted to be made by witnesses;[85] and such writings, and the evidence of

---

[79] In civil proceedings the Act may not be used to compel disclosure of incriminating material: see *Waterhouse v Barker* [1924] 2 KB 759, CA and *Re Bankers' Books Evidence Act 1879, R v Bono* (1913) 29 TLR 635.

[80] *Williams v Summerfield* [1972] 2 QB 512, DC.

[81] [1984] Crim LR 554.

[82] *Wheatley v Commissioner of Police of the British Virgin Islands* [2006] 1 WLR 1683, PC, a decision under the equivalent statutory provisions of the British Virgin Islands.

[83] See under **The exceptions—secondary evidence, Public documents,** p 308.

[84] *Doe d Mudd v Suckermore* (1837) 5 Ad&El 703 at 705.

[85] A witness who has not seen the original 'disputed writing' (because, eg, it is lost) may use a photocopy of it to make the comparison: *Lockheed-Arabia Corpn v Owen* [1993] 3 All ER 641, CA.

witnesses respecting the same, may be submitted to the court and jury as evidence of the genuineness or otherwise of the writing in dispute.

The section applies to both civil and criminal proceedings but whereas in the former the court must be satisfied as to the genuineness of the specimen handwriting only on a balance of probabilities, proof beyond reasonable doubt is the appropriate standard for the prosecution in criminal cases.[86] The tribunal of fact, in comparing the disputed and specimen handwriting, may be assisted by the evidence of someone who, although not an expert, is familiar with the handwriting in question[87] or by the opinion evidence of an expert in handwriting, whether his skill has been acquired professionally or otherwise.[88] As a general rule, in criminal cases the jury should not be left to draw their own unaided conclusion from a comparison without the assistance of an expert.[89] However, where an expert is called, it is his function to point out similarities or differences between the documents, leaving it to the tribunal of fact to draw their own conclusion.[90] In cases where the documents are placed before the jury as exhibits or for some proper purpose other than making a comparison and an expert is not called, the jury should be warned very carefully not to make a comparison.[91]

Any of the above forms of proof of handwriting may be used in the case of a document which, although not required by law to be attested, was in fact attested. Section 7 of the Criminal Procedure Act 1865 provides that such a document may be proved 'as if there had been no attesting witness thereto'.

Proof of attestation

Proof of due execution sometimes requires evidence of attestation. It will be convenient to consider first the proof of wills and other testamentary documents. Except where probate is sought in common form, in order to prove the due execution of a will, one of the attesting witnesses, if available, must be called. Witnesses to the execution of a will are treated as the court's witnesses and may be cross-examined by the party seeking to prove due execution.[92] If the witness denies the execution[93] or refuses to give evidence,[94] other evidence becomes admissible. If all of the attesting witnesses are dead, insane, beyond the jurisdiction, or untraceable, secondary evidence of attestation by proof of the handwriting of one of the attesting witnesses is required. If, despite every effort to do so, it is impossible to prove the handwriting of one of the attesting witnesses, other evidence of due execution is admissible, for example that of a non-attesting witness to the execution.[95]

Although at one time it was necessary in the case of any document required by law to be attested to call one of the attesting witnesses (unless they were all unavailable), s 3 of the Evidence Act 1938 provides that, except in the case of a will or other testamentary document, any document required by law to be attested 'may, instead of being proved by an attesting

---

[86] *R v Ewing* [1983] 2 All ER 645, CA (see **Ch 3**).

[87] *Fitzwalter Peerage Claim* (1844) 10 Cl&Fin 193, HL.

[88] *R v Silverlock* [1894] 2 QB 766 (see **Ch 20**).

[89] *R v Tilley* [1961] 1 WLR 1309, CCA; *R v Harden* [1963] 1 QB 8, CCA.

[90] *Wakeford v Bishop of Lincoln* (1921) 90 LJPC 174. See further **Ch 20**.

[91] *R v O'Sullivan* [1969] 1 WLR 497, CA.

[92] *Oakes v Uzzell* [1932] P 19.

[93] *Bowman v Hodgson* (1867) LR 1 P&D 362.

[94] *Re Oven's Goods* (1892) 29 LR Ir 451.

[95] *Clarke v Clarke* (1879) 5 LR Ir 47.

witness, be proved in the manner in which it might be proved if no attesting witness were alive', that is, by evidence of the handwriting of an attesting witness or, if this is unobtainable, by other evidence.

Admissions and presumptions

In practice, due execution is frequently admitted or presumed, rendering proof of handwriting and attestation unnecessary. Due execution may be formally admitted both in civil proceedings and, under s 10 of the Criminal Justice Act 1967, in criminal proceedings. Under CPR r 32.19(1), a party shall be deemed to admit the authenticity of a document disclosed to him under Pt 31 of the Rules (disclosure and inspection of documents) unless he serves notice that he wishes the document to be proved at trial. Proof of due execution is also unnecessary when the document in question is in the possession of an opponent who refuses to comply with a notice to produce it.[96]

A document which is more than 20 years old[97] and comes from proper custody is presumed to have been duly executed. Although proper custody, for these purposes, does not mean that the document should be found in 'the best and most proper place of deposit', if the document is found in some other place, the court must be satisfied that such custody was 'reasonable and natural' in the circumstances of the case. This was the view of Tindal CJ in *Meath (Bishop) v Marquis of Winchester*,[98] who accordingly held that certain documents relating to a bishopric had been produced from proper custody despite having been found among the papers of a deceased bishop rather than in the custody of his successor, which was the best place of deposit.

There are four other presumptions relating to documents. They are: (i) that a document was made on the date which it bears;[99] (ii) that an alteration or erasure in a deed was made before execution, in a will after execution (on the grounds that a deed, not a will, would be invalidated if presumed to have been altered after execution);[100] and (iii) that a deed was duly sealed.[101]

Stamped documents

Certain documents are required to be stamped for the purposes of stamp duty. Although in criminal proceedings such a document is admissible if unstamped, in civil proceedings a document requiring a stamp shall not be given in evidence unless it is duly stamped in accordance with the law in force at the time when it was first executed or, the court having objected to the omission or insufficiency of the stamp, and the document being one which may be legally stamped after its execution, payment is made of the amount of unpaid duty, together with any penalty payable on stamping, and a further sum of one pound.[102] The parties cannot waive these rules.[103] If a document requiring a stamp cannot be found or is not

---

[96] *Cooke v Tanswell* (1818) 8 Taunt 450.

[97] The Evidence Act 1938, s 4.

[98] (1836) 3 Bing NC 183, HL; cf *Doe d Lord Arundel v Fowler* (1850) 14 QB 700.

[99] *Anderson v Weston* (1840) 6 Bing NC 296.

[100] Per Lord Campbell CJ in *Doe d Tatum v Catomore* (1851) 16 QB 745. An alteration in a will is only valid and effective if executed in like manner as is required for the execution of the will: Wills Act 1837, s 21.

[101] *Sed quaere*: see *Re Sandilands* (1871) LR 6 CP 411.

[102] Stamp Act 1891, s 14.

[103] *Bowker v Williamson* (1889) 5 TLR 382.

produced after notice to do so, it is presumed to have been duly stamped. However, if there is evidence to show that the document was not duly stamped, it is presumed, in the absence of evidence to the contrary, that this remained the case.[104]

Real evidence

Real evidence usually takes the form of some material object examined by the tribunal of fact as a means of proof. This and other varieties of real evidence are considered separately as follows.

Material objects

Where the existence, nature, condition, or value of some material object is in issue or relevant to an issue, it may be produced for inspection by the tribunal of fact. Thus where a purchaser alleges that certain goods do not answer the vendor's description, the goods in question may be produced to the judge so that she may act on her own perception. Likewise, a jury may inspect a knife alleged to have been used in the commission of a murder. Material objects, however, call for accompanying testimony. Thus in the examples given, the goods would require to be identified and the knife, as an item of evidence, would be of no value in the absence not only of some testimony connecting it with the accused, for example evidence that it was found in his possession, but also of expert testimony that it was capable of causing the injuries sustained by the victim.[105]

There is no rule of law that unless a material object is produced, or its non-production excused, oral evidence in respect of it is inadmissible. Thus in *Hocking v Ahlquist Bros Ltd*,[106] the issue concerning the method by which certain garments had been made, it was held that although the garments were not produced at the trial, the evidence of witnesses who had seen them and could speak to their condition was not inadmissible. However, non-production of the object in question may go to the weight of the oral evidence adduced[107] and give rise to an inference adverse to the party failing to produce. Thus, in *Armory v Delamirie*[108] an action in trover against a goldsmith who failed to produce certain stones which he had removed from a jewel found by a chimney sweeper's boy, Pratt CJ directed the jury to assess damages on the basis that the stones were of the first water.

The appearance of persons and animals

Real evidence may take the form of a person's physical appearance. Thus it may be relevant, for identification or some other purpose, to have regard to a person's physical characteristics such as his height or colour of eyes or the fact that he is left-handed or bears some scar or other distinguishing feature. His accent, as opposed to the actual words he utters, also constitutes real evidence. Personal injuries may be examined on a question of causation or quantum of damages. Although in many cases little weight should be attached to it, the

---

[104] *Closmadeuc v Carrel* (1856) 18 CB 36.

[105] In some cases, the tribunal of fact may not draw its own unaided conclusion without the assistance of an expert witness: *R v Tilley* [1961] 1 WLR 1309 (comparison of handwriting). See also *Anderson v R* [1972] AC 100, PC.

[106] [1944] KB 120. See also *R v Uxbridge Justices, ex p Sofaer* (1986) 85 Cr App R 367.

[107] Per Lord Coleridge CJ in *R v Francis* (1874) LR 2 CCR 128 at 133.

[108] (1722) 1 Stra 505.

facial resemblance of a child to its alleged father and mother may be relevant to the issue of legitimacy.[109] For the purposes of contempt of court, a person's misconduct in court may constitute real evidence. Real evidence may also take the form of an animal, as in *Line v Taylor*,[110] where a dog of allegedly vicious disposition was brought into court and examined by the jury.

The demeanour of witnesses

The way in which a witness gives his evidence is often just as important as what he actually says. While some witnesses may appear to be forthright and frank, others may present themselves as hesitant, equivocal, or even hostile. Whatever form it takes, the demeanour and attitude of a witness in the course of giving his evidence is real evidence which is relevant to his credit and the weight to be attached to the evidence he gives.[111]

Lip-reading and facial mapping

Where an expert lip-reader, after viewing a CCTV recording of a person talking, gives opinion evidence as to what that person said, he is providing expert assistance to the jury in their interpretation of a species of real evidence.[112] Expert opinion evidence of facial mapping may be regarded in the same way.[113]

Documents

A document may be tendered in evidence for a variety of purposes. If it is produced by a party relying upon the statements it contains, whether that party is relying upon them as evidence of their truth, by way of exception to the hearsay rule, or simply as original evidence, for example to show that they were made,[114] it constitutes documentary evidence and is subject to the rules considered in this chapter.[115] However, if the document is tendered in evidence as a material object, regardless of the words contained in it, for instance to show the bare fact of its existence, the substance of which it is made (eg whether parchment or paper), or the condition that it is in (eg whether crumpled or torn), it constitutes real evidence.[116]

Tape recordings, films, and photographs

Tape recordings, films, and photographs are, as we have seen,[117] sometimes treated as documentary evidence. By playing over an audio recording in court, a statement recorded on it may be admitted as evidence of the truth of its contents, by way of exception to the hearsay

---

[109] *C v C* [1972] 3 All ER 577; cf *Slingsby v A-G* (1916) 33 TLR 120, HL at 122–3.

[110] (1862) 3 F&F 731.

[111] For a critical analysis of demeanour as a test of credibility, see Ekman, *Telling Lies* (3rd edn, New York, 2002) and Stone, 'Instant Lie Detection? Demeanour and Credibility in Criminal Trials' [1991] Crim LR 821.

[112] *R v Luttrell* [2004] 2 Cr App R 520 (31), CA at 539. See Ch 8, Lip-reading evidence, p 272.

[113] *R v Clarke* [1995] 2 Cr App R 425, CA at 429.

[114] See Ch 12.

[115] But this is not the case if the contents are referred to merely for the purpose of identifying the document: see under The general rule at common law—primary evidence, p 304.

[116] But see *R v Rice* [1963] 1 QB 857, CCA (see Ch 12).

[117] Under Meaning of 'document', p 302, in this chapter.

rule,[118] or as original evidence, for example merely to show that it was made. To the extent, however, that the recording also reveals the way in which the person in question spoke, his accent, accentuation, tone, intonation, etc, it is real evidence.[119]

In *The Statue of Liberty*,[120] an action concerning a collision between two ships, the plaintiff sought to admit in evidence a cinematograph film of radar echoes recorded by a shore radar station. The defendants argued that the evidence, having been produced mechanically and without human intervention, was inadmissible hearsay. Rejecting this submission, Sir Jocelyn Simon P said:[121]

> If tape-recordings are admissible, it seems that a photograph of radar reception is equally admissible—or indeed, any other type of photograph. It would be an absurd distinction that a photograph should be admissible if the camera were operated manually by a photographer, but not if it were operated by a trip or clock mechanism. Similarly, if evidence of weather conditions were relevant, the law would affront commonsense if it were to say that those could be proved by a person who looked at a barometer from time to time, but not by producing a barograph record. So, too, with other types of dial recording. Again, cards from clocking-in-and-out machines are frequently admitted in accident cases.[122]

It is tempting, on reading this passage, to conclude that photographs and films, the relevance of which can be established by the testimony of someone with personal knowledge of the circumstances in which they were taken or made, are admissible as items of real evidence and can never give rise to problems of a hearsay nature. If the evidence of a witness to certain events is admissible, it may be reasoned, then photographs or films recording those same events should be no less admissible. Thus in *R v Dodson; R v Williams*[123] the Court of Appeal entertained no doubt that photographs taken by security cameras installed at a building society office at which an armed robbery was attempted, were admissible in evidence, being relevant to the issues of both whether an offence was committed and, if so, who committed it.[124] As to the latter issue, the jury were entitled to compare the photographic images with the accused sitting in the dock;[125] and that the jury can do this will not prevent the calling

---

[118] As in *R v Senat; R v Sin* (1968) 52 Cr App R 282, CA, where tape recordings of incriminating telephone conversations were held to have been properly admitted. See also *R v Maqsud Ali* [1966] 1 QB 688, CCA at 701: provided the jury are guided by what they hear, there is no objection to a properly proved transcript being put before them. As to audio recordings and transcripts of police interviews sought to be adduced in criminal proceedings, see also *R v Rampling* [1987] Crim LR 823, CA and the Code of Practice on Audio Recording Interviews with Suspects (Code E). See also the Code of Practice on Visual Recording with Sound of Interviews with Suspects (Code F) and *Criminal Practice Directions* V, Part 16C.

[119] See, eg, *R v Emmerson* (1991) 92 Cr App R 284, CA (tone of voice). Before it is played over to the jury, the judge must satisfy himself that there is a prima facie case that it is both original and authentic: see *R v Stevenson* [1971] 1 WLR 1 and *R v Robson, R v Harris* [1972] 1 WLR 651 (see **Ch 3, The burden and standard of proof in a trial within a trial, p 94**).

[120] [1968] 1 WLR 739.

[121] [1968] 1 WLR 739 at 740.

[122] Cf *R v Wood* (1983) 76 Cr App R 23, CA: a computer printout is an item of real evidence and not hearsay if the computer in question is used as a calculator, a tool which does not contribute its own knowledge but merely does calculations which can be performed manually (see **Ch 12**).

[123] [1984] 1 WLR 971, CA.

[124] See also *Kajala v Noble* (1982) 75 Cr App R 149, CA; *R v Thomas* [1986] Crim LR 682; and *Taylor v Chief Constable of Cheshire* [1987] 1 All ER 225, DC (**Ch 12**).

[125] However, this will not be allowed if the images are of insufficient quality to permit such a comparison: see *R v Lariba* [2015] EWCA Crim 478. See also **Ch 9, Visual identification by the jury, p 288**.

of a witness who was not present at the scene of the crime, but who knows the person shown in the photograph, video, or film, to give evidence as to his identity.[126] It is clear, however, that a photograph or film is as capable of containing an out-of-court statement as a tape or a document made of paper. Both the 1995 Act and the 2003 Act operate on this assumption by catering for the admissibility of a statement contained in a 'document', which is defined as 'anything in which information of any description is recorded',[127] a definition wide enough to cover not only audio tapes, but also photographs, videotapes, and films. Indeed, the film in *The Statue of Liberty*, which may be regarded as having constituted a statement as to the paths taken by the two ships, would now be admissible for the truth of its contents under the 1995 Act. In cases falling outside these statutory provisions, however, it would seem that a photograph or film, even if it contains, or can itself be treated as the equivalent of, an out-of-court statement, will, if relevant, be admitted as an item of real evidence rather than excluded as hearsay. Indeed, in *R v Cook*[128] Watkins LJ went so far as to state that the photograph, together with the sketch and the photofit, are in a class of evidence of their own to which neither the rule against hearsay nor the rule against previous consistent or self-serving statements applies.

For the purposes of disclosure in civil proceedings, a video, film, or recording is a document within the extended meaning contained in CPR r 31.4 and therefore a party proposing to use it is subject to all the rules as to disclosure and inspection of documents contained in CPR r 31. Equally, if it is disclosed in accordance with r 31, the other party will be deemed to admit its authenticity unless notice is served that he wishes it to be proved at trial.[129] If he does serve such notice, the first party will be obliged to serve a witness statement by the person who took the video, film, or recording in order to prove its authenticity. If authenticity is not challenged, in the absence of any ruling by the court to the contrary, it is available for use by the first party, which includes using it in cross-examination of the other party and his witnesses.[130]

Views and demonstrations

A view is an inspection out of court of the *locus in quo* (ie 'scene of the event') or of some object which it is inconvenient or impossible to bring to court.[131] There is some dispute whether out-of-court demonstrations or re-enactments are properly to be regarded as real evidence or as the equivalent of testimonial evidence. If the latter, it is arguable that the demonstrator should take the oath and thereby offer himself for cross-examination. On balance,

---

[126] See *R v Fowden and White* [1982] Crim LR 588, CA; *R v Grimer* [1982] Crim LR 674, CA; and *Attorney General's Reference (No 2 of 2002)* [2003] 1 Cr App R 321 (21), CA. See also *R v Clare and Peach* [1995] 2 Cr App R 333, CA, where a witness who did *not* know the people shown in a video recording, but had spent time analysing the photographic images, thereby acquiring special knowledge that the jury lacked, was permitted to identify them as the same people shown in a film and still photographs of the accused; and *R v Clarke* [1995] 2 Cr App R 425, CA, where the witness was an expert in facial identification who, using the technique of video superimposition, had compared photographs of a bank robber taken by an automatic camera with police identification photographs of the accused.

[127] The 1995 Act, s 13 and the 2003 Act, s 134(1).

[128] [1987] QB 417, CA at 425. See also, in the case of photofits, *R v Constantinou* (1990) 91 Cr App R 74, CA.

[129] See CPR r 32.19(1).

[130] *Rall v Hume* [2001] 3 All ER 248, CA at [16].

[131] See, eg, *London General Omnibus Co Ltd v Lavell* [1901] 1 Ch 135, CA (an omnibus).

the authorities would appear to favour the former view. In *Buckingham v Daily News Ltd*,[132] a negligence action concerning a machine, the judge inspected the machine, watched the plaintiff demonstrate what he had done and gave judgment for the defendants. On appeal, it was argued that the judge had acted improperly by substituting his own opinion, based on the impression which he had gained at the view, for the plaintiff's oral evidence. Rejecting this argument, the Court of Appeal held that what the judge had seen was as much a part of the evidence as if the machine had been brought into the well of the court and the plaintiff had there demonstrated what took place.[133] As to expert evidence of a reconstruction of an event, this may be presented in-court, for example, in the form of a plan prepared from an out-of-court inspection by the expert of the *locus in quo*, accompanied by the expert's testimonial evidence.[134]

In a criminal case, before the court embarks on a view, the judge should produce ground rules, detailing what the jury will be shown and in what order and who, if anyone, will be permitted to speak and what will be said, and also making provision for the jury to ask questions.[135] It is critical that there is clarity about precisely what is to happen, who is to stand where, what, if any, objects should be placed where, and who will do what. These matters should not be decided at the scene of the view, which should be conducted without discussion.[136] As a general rule, a view should be attended by the judge, the tribunal of fact, the parties, the advocates, a shorthand writer and the ushers.[137] In civil proceedings, each of the parties must be given the opportunity of being present at a view and a failure to do so may result in a retrial.[138] In a summary trial, as a general rule, a view by magistrates of the scene of the alleged offence should take place before the conclusion of the evidence and in the presence of the parties or their representatives so as to afford them an opportunity of commenting on any feature of the locality which has altered since the time of the incident or any feature not previously noticed by the parties which impresses the magistrates.[139] The presence of the accused at a view is important because he may be able to point out some important matter of which his legal adviser is ignorant or about which the magistrates are making a

---

[132] [1956] 2 QB 534, CA.

[133] The court approved, in this respect, the views of Denning LJ in *Goold v Evans & Co* [1951] 2 TLR 1189, CA. But cf per Hodson LJ in the same case at 1191–2 and per Barwick CJ in *Railway Comr v Murphy* (1967) 41 ALJR 77, HC of A at 78.

[134] In *R v Moore* [2017] EWCA Crim 1304, the Court of Appeal heard, *de bene esse* (ie 'provisionally'), fresh evidence comprising four three-dimensional plans of a murder scene and testimony from the expert who prepared the plans. Having heard the evidence however, the court held that the plans lacked probative value and were not admissible. See also **Ch 20**.

[135] CPD VI, para 26J.1.

[136] *M v DPP* [2009] EWHC 752 (Admin).

[137] The Crown Court Compendium (July 2019), Part 1, 2–5, which also gives detailed guidance on procedure in relation to planning and travel and at the view.

[138] *Goold v Evans & Co* [1951] 2 TLR 1189, CA. But see per Widgery LJ in *Salsbury v Woodland* [1970] 1 QB 324, CA at 343–4: although a judge attending a demonstration at which the events in question are reconstructed or simulated should be accompanied by representatives of both parties, he may visit the *locus in quo* in order to see that which has previously been represented to him in court by plan and photograph on his own and without reference to the parties at all.

[139] *Parry v Boyle* (1986) 83 Cr App R 310, DC.

mistake.[140] In a criminal trial by jury, the judge should always be present at a view, whether or not any witness is present for the purposes of a demonstration,[141] in order to control the proceedings. In particular, she should take precautions to prevent any witnesses who are present from communicating, except by way of demonstration, with the jury.[142] Because the jury should remain together at all times when evidence is being received, it is improper for one juror to attend a view and report back to the others what he observed.[143]

ADDITIONAL READING

Hollander, *Documentary Evidence* (London, 2015).
A comprehensive guide to the legal obligations of disclosure in civil proceedings.

Porter, 'A new theoretical framework regarding the application and reliability of photographic evidence' (2011) 15 E&P 26.
An examination of the critical concepts relating to the reliability of photographic evidence, with a proposal for a new theoretical framework to provide a basis to form reliability norms and standards for such evidence.

---

[140] *R v Ely Justices, ex p Burgess* [1992] Crim LR 888, DC.

[141] *R v Hunter* [1985] 2 All ER 173, CA. Cf *Tameshwar v R* [1957] AC 476, PC. See also *R v Turay* [2007] EWCA Crim 2821, where there was no disadvantage to the defence. Where an inspection of the *locus in quo* is carried out, not by the court, but by an expert in order to prepare a plan reconstructing an event, relevant witnesses may need to be present at the inspection and given the opportunity to comment, and their comments recorded accurately on the plan. Failure to do this may affect the probative value and admissibility of the plan. See for example, *R v Moore* [2017] EWCA Crim 1304 at [19] and [70]–[73].

[142] *R v Martin* (1872) LR 1 CCR 378; *Karamat v R* [1956] AC 256, PC.

[143] *R v Gurney* [1976] Crim LR 567, CA.

Evidence obtained by illegal or unfair means

11

Key issues

- When and why should relevant evidence obtained illegally, improperly, or unfairly be admitted at trial?

- When and why should relevant evidence obtained illegally, improperly, or unfairly be excluded at trial?

- Should the law of evidence admit or exclude relevant evidence obtained by (a) torture; (b) inhuman or degrading treatment; (c) entrapment; and (d) undercover operations?

- Should decisions on the above issues be governed by rules of law or the exercise of judicial discretion?

- When and why should the law of evidence, in dealing with the above issues, differentiate between criminal and civil cases?

This chapter concerns the circumstances in which relevant evidence can be excluded, as a matter of law or discretion, on the grounds that it was obtained illegally, improperly, or unfairly. It also considers a related matter, namely the circumstances in which criminal proceedings should be stayed, ie stopped, as an abuse of the court's process where, having regard to the way in which evidence was obtained, a trial would undermine public confidence in the criminal justice system and bring it into disrepute.

Evidence may be obtained illegally, for example by a crime, tort, or breach of contract, or in contravention of statutory or other provisions governing the powers and duties of the police or others involved in investigating crime. Evidence may also be obtained by other improper or unfair means, for example by trickery, deception, bribes, threats, or inducements. At one extreme, the view could be taken that evidence which is relevant and otherwise admissible should not be excluded because of the means by which it was obtained, whether illegal, improper, or unfair; to exclude it would, in some cases, result in injustice, including the acquittal of the guilty. On this view, all evidence which is necessary to enable justice to be done would be admitted; and those responsible for the illegality or impropriety could be variously prosecuted (in the case of crime), sued (in the case of actionable wrongs), or disciplined (in the case of conduct amounting to breach of some statutory, professional, or other code of conduct). The view at the other extreme would be that illegally or improperly obtained evidence should always be excluded; to admit it might encourage the obtaining of evidence by such means or at any rate bring the administration of justice into disrepute. On this view, all such evidence would be excluded, even if this would sometimes result in injustice, including the guilty going free, in order that those responsible for the illegality or impropriety are in future compelled to respect, and deterred from invading, the civil liberties of the citizen and the rights of the suspect.

The modern law of evidence in this country represents a compromise between these two extreme views. Thus although at common law there is a general rule of law that relevant and otherwise admissible evidence should not be excluded because of the means by which it was obtained, there are both exceptions to the rule and discretionary powers to exclude.[1] It is useful, before turning to consider the exceptions and discretionary powers, to consider first the theoretical principles for exclusion.

Principles for exclusion

There are four principles that may be used to justify the exclusion of evidence obtained illegally or unfairly. The first is the reliability principle—perhaps better described as the unreliability principle—under which evidence should be excluded where its reliability has been impaired, or the accused's ability to test its reliability has been impaired, by reason of the way in which it was obtained. An example would be where the police take a statement from a suspect in breach of safeguards specifically designed to ensure the reliability of such a statement. The second principle is the integrity principle, under which the court excludes evidence to disassociate itself from the way in which it was obtained and to maintain the

---

[1] For an interesting analysis of the question whether to admit illegally obtained evidence and the shortcomings of the exclusionary principle, see *Zuckerman, The Principles of Criminal Evidence* (Oxford, 1989) Ch 16. See also *Mirfield, Silence, Confessions and Improperly Obtained Evidence* (Oxford, 1998).

integrity of the criminal justice process. The third is the disciplinary principle, under which the court excludes evidence obtained illegally or improperly to 'discipline' the police and discourage them from obtaining evidence in such a way. The fourth is the 'rights-based' or 'protective' principle, under which the court excludes evidence obtained in breach of the rights that suspects have been granted. This principle is probably no different, except in name, from the remedial principle, under which evidence is excluded as a 'remedy' for breach of the rights of the suspect.

These four principles overlap in their operation, so that to use one may well be to give effect to another. Thus, for example, to exclude evidence under the reliability or rights-based principle, and not the disciplinary principle, may nonetheless have the effect of 'disciplining' the police.

Law

Staying proceedings as an abuse of process

In English law, it is well established that the powers of a court to stay proceedings, ie to stop them, as an abuse of its process may be exercised in two categories of case.[2] The first, which is beyond the proper scope of this book, is where it will be impossible to give the accused a fair trial. The second, which is clearly underpinned by the integrity principle, was described by Sir John Dyson SCJ in *R v Maxwell*[3] in the following terms:

> In the second category of case, the court is concerned to protect the integrity of the criminal justice system. Here a stay will be granted where the court concludes that in all the circumstances a trial will 'offend the court's sense of justice and propriety' (per Lord Lowry in *R v Horseferry Road Magistrates' Court, ex p Bennett* [1993] 3 All ER 138 at 161, [1994] 1 AC 42 at 74) or will 'undermine public confidence in the criminal justice system and bring it into disrepute' (per Lord Steyn in *R v Latif, R v Shahzad* [1996] 1 All ER 353 at 360, [1996] 1 WLR 104 at 112).

The second category calls for a balancing exercise. Some of the factors frequently taken into account when carrying out the exercise are: the seriousness of any violation of the rights of the accused or a third party; whether the police have acted in bad faith or maliciously, or with an improper motive; whether the misconduct was committed in circumstances of urgency, emergency, or necessity; the availability or otherwise of a direct sanction against the person responsible for the misconduct; and the seriousness of the offence with which the accused is charged.[4] In *Warren v Attorney General for Jersey*[5] Lord Dyson held that how the discretion will be exercised will depend on the particular circumstances of the case; that in abduction and entrapment cases, the court will generally conclude that the balance favours a stay,[6] but rigid classifications are undesirable; and that whether a stay should be granted will not always, or even in most cases, be necessarily determined by the test of whether,

---

[2] *R v Beckford* [1996] 1 Cr App R 94, CA.

[3] [2011] 1 WLR 1837, SC.

[4] Choo, *Abuse of Process and Judicial Stays of Criminal Proceedings* (2nd edn, New York, 2008) 132, endorsed as a 'useful summary' by Lord Dyson in *Warren v Attorney General for Jersey* [2012] 1 AC 22, PC at [25].

[5] [2012] 1 AC 22, PC.

[6] As to entrapment cases, see later in this chapter, under **Entrapment and undercover operations**, p 339.

but for an abuse of executive power, the accused would never have been before the court at all.[7] When considering a stay in entrapment cases, a distinction will be drawn between the conduct of state agents and private citizens who have acted on their own initiative as 'agents provocateurs'.[8] The issue will be the same however, namely whether the prosecution would be 'deeply offensive to ordinary notions of fairness' or 'an affront to the public conscience', or 'so seriously improper as to bring the administration of justice into disrepute'.[9] Thus in principle it could be an abuse of the process of the court where there has been misconduct by private citizens which is so serious that reliance on evidence obtained by them would compromise the court's integrity. However, 'the situations in which that might occur would be very rare indeed.'[10] A stay may be justified where intrusive covert surveillance has interfered significantly with an accused's right to legal professional privilege.[11]

The general rule of law

Where proceedings have not been stayed as an abuse of process, then, subject to exceptions, the rules of English *law* make no provision for the exclusion of relevant evidence on the grounds that it was obtained illegally or improperly. However, as we shall see, such evidence is open to exclusion by the exercise of *discretion*. The general rule of *law* is accurately represented by the following words of Crompton J in *R v Leatham*:[12] 'It matters not how you get it; if you steal it even, it would be admissible in evidence.' Thus evidence remains admissible in law if obtained by the use of agents provocateurs,[13] or by invasion of privacy,[14] or by the unlawful search of persons[15] or premises.[16]

The exceptions

Theft of privileged documents in court

One exception to the general rule concerns privileged documents. Although there is a general rule allowing secondary evidence of privileged documents to be adduced, even though obtained illegally or improperly,[17] a party to litigation who obtains by a trick documents belonging to the other party and brought into court by him will not be permitted to adduce copies of those documents, because the public interest in the ascertainment of truth in litigation is outweighed by the public interest that litigants should be able to bring their documents into court without fear that they may be filched by their opponents.[18]

---

[7] [2012] 1 AC 22, PC at [30].

[8] See *R v L* [2018] EWCA Crim 1821 (evidence of sexual grooming obtained by 'paedophile hunters'). See also *R v Marriner* [2002] EWCA Crim 2855, *R v Shannon* [2001] 1 WLR 51, CA and *R v Hardwicke* [2001] Crim LR 220 (examples of evidence obtained by undercover journalists).

[9] *R v L* [2018] EWCA Crim 1821 at [32].

[10] Per Goldring J in *Council for the Regulation of Healthcare Professionals v General Medical Council* [2007] 1 WLR 3094, (Admin) at [81], cited in *R v L* [2018] EWCA Crim 1821 at [32].

[11] *R v Turner* [2013] EWCA Crim 642 at [28]. As to legal professional privilege, see Ch 22.

[12] (1861) 8 Cox CC 498 at 501.

[13] *R v Sang* [1980] AC 402, HL. Agents provocateurs may be state agents or non-state actors (see n 8).

[14] *R v Khan (Sultan)* [1997] AC 558, HL.

[15] See *Jones v Owens* (1870) 34 JP 759 and *Kuruma, Son of Kaniu v R* [1955] AC 197, PC.

[16] See *Jeffrey v Black* [1978] QB 490.

[17] See per Parke B in *Lloyd v Mostyn* (1842) 10 M&W 478, applied by Lindley MR in *Calcraft v Guest* [1898] 1 QB 759, CA at 764 (see Ch 22).

[18] *ITC Film Distributors v Video Exchange Ltd* [1982] Ch 431. Cf *R v Tompkins* (1977) 67 Cr App R 181, CA (see Ch 22).

Improperly obtained confessions

A second exception relates to a confession made by an accused that was or may have been obtained by oppression or in consequence of anything said or done which was likely, in the circumstances, to render unreliable any confession which might be made by him in consequence thereof.[19] Oppression, for these purposes, is defined to include torture,[20] in respect of which there is a broader common law exclusionary principle.

Evidence obtained by torture

In *A v Secretary of State for the Home Department (No 2)*[21] it was held that as a matter of constitutional principle evidence obtained by torture may not lawfully be admitted against a party to proceedings in a British court, irrespective of where, or by whom, or on whose authority the torture was inflicted. Such evidence falls to be excluded both at common law and in accordance with the European Convention on Human Rights, which takes account of the United Nations Convention Against Torture and Other Cruel, Inhuman or Degrading Treatment or Punishment 1987.[22] Article 15 of the Torture Convention requires states to ensure that statements made as a result of torture shall not be invoked as evidence in any proceedings.

In reaching this decision, some of their Lordships relied explicitly upon the integrity principle.[23] However, their Lordships declined to accept that the exclusionary rule should extend beyond torture to inhuman or degrading treatment, a distinction that is difficult to justify. As one commentator has observed: '. . . if torture evidence is an affront to civilised values, so too will [sic] evidence procured by inhuman treatment, albeit to a lesser extent'.[24]

Distinctions that are difficult to defend have also been drawn, in the European jurisprudence, between cases of torture and cases of inhuman or degrading treatment. In *Jalloh v Germany*[25] the Grand Chamber of the European Court of Human Rights held that evidence obtained by torture should be automatically excluded. The court expressly left open the question whether there should also be automatic exclusion for evidence obtained by inhuman or degrading treatment, but on the facts held that the admission of such evidence did violate the accused's rights under Art 6.[26] In *Gäfgen v Germany*[27] it was held that incriminating real evidence recovered as a direct result of torture should always be excluded, but if it is obtained as a result of statements obtained by inhuman treatment, it may be admitted, provided that it is not necessary to secure a conviction.

There is an argument for the exclusion of evidence obtained as a result of secret detention, but it is not as strong as in the case of torture, there being no equivalent of Art 15 of the Torture Convention.[28]

---

[19] Police and Criminal Evidence Act 1984 (the 1984 Act), s 76(2) (see Ch 15).

[20] The 1984 Act, s 76(8).

[21] [2005] 3 WLR 1249, HL.

[22] See per Lord Bingham at [51] and [52]. The definition of torture for these purposes appears to be that adopted in the Criminal Justice Act 1988, s 134, namely the infliction of severe pain or suffering by a public official in the performance or purported performance of his official duties: see per Lord Hoffmann at [97].

[23] See per Lord Hoffmann at [87] and per Lord Carson at [150].

[24] Rasiah, '*A v Secretary of State for the Home Department (No 2)*: Occupying the Moral High Ground?' (2006) 69 MLR 995 at 1003.

[25] (2007) 44 EHRR 32.

[26] See also *R v Ahmed* [2011] EWCA Crim 184.

[27] Application No 22978/05, 30 June 2008, [2010] Crim LR 865, ECHR.

[28] Per Richards LJ, obiter, in *XX v Secretary of State for the Home Department* [2012] 4 All ER 692, CA at [39].

Intercepted evidence

Section 56(1) of the Investigatory Powers Act 2016 makes provision for the exclusion of the content of intercepted communications which have been unlawfully or improperly obtained. Under the section, exclusion may cover 'secondary data' (material) obtained from such communications. Section 56(1) states as follows:

56 Exclusion of matters from legal proceedings etc.

(1) No evidence may be adduced, question asked, assertion or disclosure made or other thing done in, for the purposes of or in connection with any legal proceedings or Inquiries Act proceedings which (in any manner)—

    (a) discloses, in circumstances from which its origin in interception-related conduct may be inferred—

        (i)   any content of an intercepted communication, or

        (ii) any secondary data obtained from a communication, or

    (b) tends to suggest that any interception-related conduct has or may have occurred or may be going to occur.

This is subject to Schedule 3 (exceptions).[29]

Under 56(2)(a)–(e), 'interception-related conduct' means conduct which would constitute an offence of unlawful interception contrary to s 3(1) of the Act; a breach of the prohibition under s 9 (concerning the restriction on requests for interception by overseas authorities); a breach of the prohibition imposed by s 10 (concerning the restriction on requests for assistance under mutual assistance agreements etc); conduct which involves the making of an application for a warrant or the issue of a warrant under Chapter 1, Part 2 of the Act; or involves imposing any requirement on a person to provide assistance in effecting a targeted interception warrant or a mutual assistance warrant.[30]

Discretion

Civil cases

Prior to the introduction of the Civil Procedure Rules, such authority as there was suggested that in civil proceedings there was no discretion to exclude evidence obtained illegally or improperly.[31]

Under CPR r 32.1(2) the court may now exclude evidence that would otherwise be admissible and, in deciding whether to do so, must seek to give effect to the overriding objective of enabling the court to deal with cases justly.[32] It is submitted that, in appropriate circumstances, therefore, the court may exercise the discretionary power to exclude evidence

---

[29] Under Sch 3 para 5, for example, s 56(1) does not apply to proceedings before the Special Immigration Appeals Commission. Nor, by virtue of Sch 3, para 7, does it apply to Closed Material Proceedings (see further, Ch 21, **Closed material procedures**, p 702 and see also in Ch 21, **The Justice and Security Act 2013**, p 704).

[30] Under s 56(4) 'interception-related conduct' also covers conduct which occurred before s 56(1) came into force and would have amounted to an offence or otherwise have been improper under provisions contained in the Regulation of Investigatory Powers Act 2000 and the Interception of Communications Act 1985.

[31] See per Lord Denning MR in *Helliwell v Piggott-Sims* [1980] FSR 582.

[32] See Ch 2, Civil cases, p 173.

which, although relevant, has been obtained illegally or improperly. In *Jones v University of Warwick*,[33] a claim for damages for personal injuries, the defendant was allowed to introduce a video of the claimant obtained by trespass and in breach of Art 8 of the European Convention on Human Rights (the right of respect for private and family life). Inquiry agents acting for the defendant's insurers had gained access to the claimant's home by deception and filmed her without her knowledge. It was held that the court should consider two conflicting public interests, on the one hand the achieving of justice in the particular case and on the other, considering the effect of its decision upon litigation generally, the risk that if the improper conduct goes uncensored, improper practices of the type in question will be encouraged. The weight to be attached to each public interest will vary according to the circumstances. The significance of the evidence will differ as will the gravity of the breach of Art 8, and the decision will depend on all the circumstances. In the case before it, the Court of Appeal held that the conduct of the insurers was not so outrageous that the defence should be struck out and that it would be artificial and undesirable to exclude the evidence, which would involve the instruction of fresh medical experts from whom relevant evidence would have to be concealed. However, it was also held that the conduct of the insurers was improper and unjustified and that the trial judge should take it into account when deciding the appropriate order for costs.[34]

Exclusion of evidence will be justified if its admission would amount to a breach of the right to a fair trial under Art 6 of the European Convention on Human Rights. In *Re E (A Child) (Family Proceedings:Evidence)*[35] the judge found as a fact that a teenage boy A and his father E had sexually abused three children of another family. At the hearing, evidence of the interviews of complainants was admitted notwithstanding multiple substantial breaches of the guidance for conducting Achieving Best Evidence (ABE) interviews. These included conducting parts of the interviews 'off camera' and making no written record of them, conducting irregular 'fast track' interviews at the complainants' homes, failing to complete any pro forma written record of the ABE process and the use of leading questions, including leading questions to introduce key elements of the narrative.[36] Further, the judge had directed A's guardian to file a statement giving evidence about matters protected by legal professional privilege. Allowing the appeal, the Court of Appeal held that there had been a wholesale failure to acknowledge and analyse the many significant departures from best or acceptable practice.[37] In the circumstances, A's right to a fair trial under Art 6 had been substantially breached, as had his right to the protection of legal professional privilege.

Criminal cases—common law

That a judge, in criminal proceedings, has a discretionary power to exclude otherwise admissible evidence on the grounds that it was obtained improperly or unfairly was, until *R v Sang*,[38] only clearly established in relation to evidence of admissions and confessions. The power to

---

[33] [2003] 1 WLR 954, CA.

[34] See also *Niemietz v Germany* (1992) 16 EHRR 97; *Halford v UK* (1997) 24 EHRR 523; and *Imerman v Tchenguiz* [2011] Fam 116, CA.

[35] [2016] 4 WLR 105, CA.

[36] At [36].

[37] At [98(i)].

[38] [1980] AC 402, HL.

exclude, as a matter of discretion, an otherwise admissible admission or confession is a large and complex topic which is considered separately in **Chapter 15**. Admissions and confessions apart, there was also an unbroken series of dicta from a variety of impressive sources to suggest that in criminal proceedings the trial judge also has a general discretion to exclude prosecution evidence which has been obtained oppressively, improperly, or unfairly[39] or as a result of the activities of an agent provocateur.[40] However, despite weighty dicta, this discretion was rarely exercised. A rare reported example is *R v Payne*[41] where the accused, charged with drunken driving, agreed to a medical examination to see if he was suffering from any illness or disability on the understanding that the doctor would not examine him to assess his fitness to drive. At the trial, the doctor gave evidence of the accused's unfitness to drive and the Court of Criminal Appeal quashed the conviction on the grounds that the trial judge should have exercised his discretion to exclude the doctor's evidence. In *R v Sang*[42] Lords Diplock, Fraser, and Scarman regarded the decision as based on the maxim *nemo tenetur se ipsum prodere* ('no man is to be compelled to incriminate himself') and analogous, therefore, to cases in which an accused is unfairly induced to confess to, or make a damaging admission in respect of, an offence.[43]

In *R v Sang* the House of Lords held that the judicial discretion to exclude admissible evidence does not extend to excluding evidence of a crime on the grounds that it was instigated by an agent provocateur, because if it did it would amount to a procedural device whereby the judge could avoid the substantive law under which it is clearly established that there is no defence of entrapment.[44] The primary importance of *R v Sang*, however, is the obiter answer given to the certified point of law of general importance, namely: 'Does a trial judge have a discretion to refuse to allow evidence, being evidence other than evidence of an admission, to be given in any circumstances in which such evidence is relevant and of more

---

[39] See per Lord Goddard CJ in *Kuruma, Son of Kaniu v R* [1955] AC 197, PC at 203–4 (evidence obtained 'by a trick'); per Lord Parker CJ in *Callis v Gunn* [1964] 1 QB 495, DC at 505 (evidence obtained 'oppressively, by false representations, by a trick, by threats, by bribes, anything of that sort'); and per Lord Widgery CJ in *Jeffrey v Black* [1978] QB 490, DC at 497–8 (exceptional cases where 'not only have the police officers entered without authority, but they have been guilty of trickery, or they have misled someone, or they have been oppressive, or they have been unfair, or in other respects they have behaved in a manner which is morally reprehensible'). See also per Lord Hodson in *King v R* [1969] 1 AC 304, PC at 319.

[40] See per Lord McDermott CJ in *R v Murphy* [1965] NI 138, C-MAC, a case decided before the rejection of entrapment as a defence. See also *R v Foulder, Foulkes and Johns* [1973] Crim LR 45; *R v Burnett and Lee* [1973] Crim LR 748; and *R v Ameer and Lucas* [1977] Crim LR 104, CA.

[41] [1963] 1 WLR 637, CCA.

[42] [1980] AC 402.

[43] At 435, 449, and 455 respectively. Cf *R v McDonald* [1991] Crim LR 122, CA, a decision under the Police and Criminal Evidence Act 1984, s 78: it is not unfair for a psychiatrist to give evidence of an admission made by the accused on a non-medical issue in the course of a psychiatric examination. *R v McDonald* was followed in *R v Gayle* [1994] Crim LR 679, CA and, in the case of confessions to probation officers, *R v Elleray* [2003] 2 Cr App R 165 (11), CA.

[44] See *R v McEvilly; R v Lee* (1973) 60 Cr App R 150, CA; and *R v Mealey; R v Sheridan* (1974) 60 Cr App R 59, CA. However, as to the discretion to exclude under the Police and Criminal Evidence Act 1984, s 78, see *R v Looseley* [2001] 1 WLR 2060, HL, considered, in this chapter, under **Entrapment and undercover operations**, p 339.

than minimal probative value?' On that wider issue, the House was of the unanimous opinion that: (i) a trial judge always has a discretion to exclude prosecution evidence where its prejudicial effect outweighs its probative value;[45] but (ii) since the court is not concerned with how prosecution evidence has been obtained, but with how it is used by the prosecution at the trial, a judge has no discretion to refuse to admit admissible evidence on the grounds that it was obtained by improper or unfair means except in the case of admissions, confessions, and evidence obtained from the accused after the commission of the offence. Although the judgment in this respect was obiter, Lord Roskill declared later that it would be a retrograde step to enlarge the narrow limits of, or to engraft an exception on, the discretion to exclude as defined in *R v Sang*.[46] Unfortunately, however, the scope of the discretion defined, despite their Lordships' apparent unanimity, is far from clear, particularly insofar as it extends to 'evidence obtained from the accused after the commission of the offence'. For Lord Diplock, that phrase seems to refer to evidence tantamount to a self-incriminating admission obtained from the accused by means which would justify a judge in excluding an actual confession which had the like self-incriminating effect.[47] Lord Diplock was also of the view that there is no discretion to exclude evidence discovered as the result of an illegal search.[48] For Lord Salmon, the decision whether to exclude being dependent upon the 'infinitely variable' facts and circumstances of each particular case, the category of cases in which evidence could be rejected on the grounds that it would make a trial unfair was not closed and never could be closed except by statute.[49] Lord Fraser appears to have understood the phrase as referring to evidence and documents obtained from an accused or from premises occupied by him, but also said that their Lordships' decision would leave judges with a discretion to be exercised in accordance with their individual views of what is unfair, oppressive, or morally reprehensible.[50] For Lord Scarman, it referred exclusively to the obtaining of evidence from the *accused*.[51]

Subsequent case law has done little to clarify the meaning of the phrase 'evidence obtained from the accused after the commission of the offence' but has put a major gloss on *R v Sang* to the effect that the discretion should not be exercised if those who obtained such evidence unlawfully did so on the basis of a bona fide mistake as to their powers.[52]

---

[45] See Ch 2, Criminal cases, p 49.

[46] *Morris v Beardmore* [1981] AC 446, HL at 469.

[47] See *R v Payne* [1963] 1 WLR 637, CCA at n 38. Following *R v Sang*, see *R v Trump* (1979) 70 Cr App R 300, CA: a specimen of blood may be subject to the discretion; but contrast *R v Apicella* (1985) 82 Cr App R 295, CA: an incriminating sample of body fluid is not the physical equivalent of an oral confession; and cf *R v Khan (Sultan)* [1997] AC 558, HL: evidence of an admission obtained by a covert surveillance device is not covered by the phrase because the accused has not been induced to make it.

[48] *R v Sang* [1980] AC 402, HL at 436. But see, following *R v Sang*, *R v Adams* [1980] QB 575, CA: the discretion should not be used to exclude articles obtained by means of unlawful entry, search, and seizure *in the absence of oppressive conduct*.

[49] *R v Sang* [1980] AC 402 at 445. See also per Lord Fraser at 450.

[50] *R v Sang* [1980] AC 402 at 450.

[51] *R v Sang* [1980] AC 402 at 456.

[52] See *R v Trump* (1979) 70 Cr App R 300, CA and *R v Fox* [1986] AC 281, HL, both relating to evidence of specimens obtained improperly but in good faith.

Criminal cases: s 78 of the Police and Criminal Evidence Act 1984

The narrow and confusing common law approach to the discretionary exclusion of improperly obtained evidence has been buttressed by the much more extensive power contained in s 78 of the 1984 Act. It provides as follows:

(1) In any proceedings the court may refuse to allow evidence on which the prosecution proposes to rely to be given if it appears to the court that, having regard to all the circumstances, including the circumstances in which the evidence was obtained, the admission of the evidence would have such an adverse effect on the fairness of the proceedings that the court ought not to admit it.

(2) Nothing in this section shall prejudice any rule of law requiring a court to exclude evidence.

The effect of s 78(2) is that if an item of evidence is inadmissible by virtue of any of the exclusionary rules of evidence, it *must* be excluded. As to the discretionary power to exclude under s 78(1), the question of exclusion may be raised by any accused against whom the evidence is to be used or by the court on its own motion.[53] However, if the accused is represented by an apparently competent advocate, who does not raise the issue, perhaps for tactical reasons, the judge is under no duty to exercise the discretion of her own motion, even in the case of a flagrant abuse of police power, although she may make a pertinent enquiry of the advocate in the jury's absence.[54] Section 78(1) refers to evidence on which the prosecution *proposes* to rely. Thus in *R v Harwood*[55] it was doubted whether s 78(1) empowers a judge to exclude evidence, after it has been adduced, in the absence of any submission to exclude before it was adduced. At trials on indictment, if there is a dispute as to the circumstances in which the evidence was obtained, it would seem to be necessary to hold a trial within a trial.[56] Thus if the accused disputes that he was cautioned, it is the duty of the judge to hold a *voir dire* and make a finding on the issue.[57] However, concerning the admissibility of identification evidence, it has been held that although there may be rare occasions when it will be desirable to hold a *voir dire*, in general the judge should decide on the basis of the depositions, statements, and submissions of the advocates.[58] It is not clear under s 78(1) where the burden of proof lies.[59] If there is a dispute as to the circumstances in which the evidence was obtained, it is submitted that, in principle, there should be an evidential burden on the accused in relation to his version of events, on the discharge of which there should be a legal burden on the prosecution to disprove the accused's version beyond reasonable doubt.[60] However, it was said in *Re Saifi*,[61] in the context of extradition proceedings, that the words of s 78 provide no support for such a contention, and that the absence from s 78 of words

---

[53] *Re Saifi* [2001] 4 All ER 168, DC at [52].

[54] *R v Raphaie* [1996] Crim LR 812, CA.

[55] [1989] Crim LR 285, CA.

[56] Concerning proceedings before magistrates, see **Ch 2, The functions of the judge and jury, p 34.**

[57] *R v Manji* [1990] Crim LR 512, CA.

[58] *R v Beveridge* [1987] Crim LR 401, CA (identification parade evidence); and *R v Martin and Nicholls* [1994] Crim LR 218, CA (evidence of informal identification). Cf *R v Flemming* (1987) 86 Cr App R 32, CA. Concerning confessions, see also *R v Keenan* [1990] 2 QB 54, CA (see **Ch 15**).

[59] Acknowledged, *per curiam*, in *R v Anderson* [1993] Crim LR 447, CA.

[60] See generally **Ch 3.**

[61] [2001] 4 All ER 168, DC at [50]–[61].

suggesting that facts are to be established or proved to any particular standard is deliberate, leaving the matter open and untrammelled by rigid evidential considerations. Similarly, it was said in *Misick v The Queen*:[62] 'Whilst often loosely referred to as conferring a judicial discretion, what this power actually calls for is not simple discretion but an exercise of judgment after weighing all relevant factors. It is plain that its exercise cannot be analysed in terms of a standard of proof.'[63]

Scope

Concerning the scope of s 78(1), it applies to *any* evidence on which the prosecution propose to rely, whether tendered by the prosecution or (presumably) a co-accused. Thus it may be used to attempt to exclude, inter alia, the following types of otherwise admissible evidence: hearsay evidence, including depositions and documentary records[64] and admissions and confessions;[65] evidence of the defendant's bad character admissible under s 101(1)(c) or (f) of the Criminal Justice Act 2003 as explanatory evidence or evidence to correct a false impression;[66] evidence of opinion, including identification evidence;[67] and evidence of an intoximeter reading.[68] Insofar as s 78(1) may be used to exclude evidence obtained by improper or unfair means, it is *not* confined, as is the common law power described in *R v Sang*, to admissions, confessions, and evidence obtained from the accused after the commission of the offence—it extends to any evidence on which the prosecution propose to rely, whenever it was obtained and whether it was obtained from the accused, his premises, or any other source.[69]

'. . . having regard to all the circumstances . . .'

In deciding whether or not to exercise the discretion, s 78(1) directs the court to have regard to all the circumstances, including those in which the evidence was obtained. In particular, the court may be invited to take into account any illegality, impropriety, or unfairness by means of which the evidence was obtained, including conduct in breach of the European Convention on Human Rights, or any abuse by the police of their powers under the 1984 Act, and the Codes of Practice issued pursuant to that Act, including those relating to stop and search (Code A), the search of premises and the seizure of property (Code B), detention, treatment, and questioning (Code C), identification (Code D), and

---

[62] [2015] 1 WLR 3215, PC.

[63] At [39]. In *R v Thompson* [2018] EWCA Crim 2082 at [48], it was said that general remarks made by Sir Igor Judge P in *R v Renda* [2006] 1 WLR 2948, CA at [3] concerning the exercise of the exclusionary discretion under s 101(3) of the Criminal Justice Act 2003, applied equally when considering the exercise of discretion under s 78. See Ch 19, The role of the trial judge and the Court of Appeal, p 562. See also in Ch 18, Common law and s 78 of the Police and Criminal Evidence Act 1984, p 576.

[64] *R v O'Loughlin* [1988] 3 All ER 431, CCC.

[65] *R v Mason* [1988] 1 WLR 139, CA.

[66] See Ch 19, Common law and s 78 of the Police and Criminal Evidence Act 1984, p 576. See also *R v Thompson* [2018] EWCA Crim 2082, where the judge was correct not to exercise her discretion under s 78 in respect of evidence admissible under s 101(1)(f) (see [46]–[48]).

[67] *R v Nagah* (1990) 92 Cr App R 344, CA. See also *R v Deenik* [1992] Crim LR 578, CA (voice identification).

[68] *McGrath v Field* [1987] RTR 349, DC.

[69] The dictum of Watkins LJ in *R v Mason* [1987] 3 All ER 481 at 484, that 's 78 . . . does no more than restate the power which judges had at common law before the 1984 Act was passed', is best regarded as having been made *per incuriam*.

audio recording of interviews (Code E).[70] When breaches of an earlier Code are considered, the provisions of the current version may well be relevant to the question of unfairness under s 78, because they reflect current thinking as to what is fair.[71]

'. . . the fairness of the proceedings . . .'

Section 78 can only be exercised if in all the circumstances admission of the evidence would have an adverse effect on the fairness of the 'proceedings'. The first use of the word 'proceedings' in s 78(1) suggests that it means 'court proceedings' rather than both the investigative and trial process. Section 78(3), since repealed, which referred to 'proceedings before a magistrates' court' supports such an interpretation.

As to 'fairness', trial judges, as we have seen, already have a duty to ensure that the accused receives a fair trial, in the exercise of which they may exclude any evidence the prejudicial effect of which outweighs its probative value. Section 78(1), however, goes further. Thus although the fact that evidence was obtained improperly or unfairly will not by itself automatically have such an adverse effect on the fairness of the proceedings that the court should not admit it, it is implicit in the wording of the subsection that the circumstances in which the evidence was obtained *may* have such an adverse effect.[72]

It is, of course, impossible to catalogue, precisely or at all, the kinds of impropriety which will be treated as having an adverse effect on the fairness of the proceedings. As we shall see, a breach of the 1984 Act or of the Codes does not mean that any statement made by an accused after such breach will necessarily be excluded—every case has to be determined on its own particular facts.[73] Equally, the fact that evidence has been obtained by conduct which may be 'oppressive' will not automatically result in exclusion, because oppressive conduct, depending on its degree and actual or possible effect, may or may not affect the fairness of admitting particular evidence.[74]

A judge's exercise of her discretion under the subsection can be impugned if it is perverse according to *Wednesbury* principles,[75] that is, a decision to which no reasonable trial judge could have come, in which case the Court of Appeal will exercise its own discretion.[76] The Court of Appeal will also interfere if the trial judge exercised her discretion on a wrong

---

[70] Even where the evidence in question was obtained by someone other than a police officer (or a person charged with the duty of investigating offences or charging offenders—see the 1984 Act, s 67(9) (see Ch 15)), the principles underlying Code C may be of assistance in considering the discretion to exclude under s 78(1): *R v Smith* (1995) 99 Cr App R 233, CA. Regard may also be had to the guidance set out in Ministry of Justice, *Achieving Best Evidence in Criminal Proceedings: Guidance on Interviewing Victims and Witnesses, and Guidance on Using Special Measures* (2011): see *F v CPS* [2015] EWHC 2527, DC and *R v Dunphy* (1994) 98 Cr App R 393, CA, a decision on a precursor to the current ABE guidance. See also Keenan et al, 'Interviewing Allegedly Abused Children' [1999] Crim LR 863.

[71] *R v Ward* (1993) 98 Cr App R 337, CA at 340.

[72] Per Woolf LJ in *Matto v Crown Court at Wolverhampton* [1987] RTR 337.

[73] Per Lord Lane CJ in *R v Parris* (1989) 89 Cr App R 68, CA at 72. See also per Hodgson J in *R v Keenan* [1990] 2 QB 54 at 69.

[74] *R v Chalkley and Jeffries* [1998] QB 848, CA at 873–4. Under the Police and Criminal Evidence Act 1984, s 76(2)(a), a confession obtained by oppression will be excluded whether or not it is unreliable. See Ch 15.

[75] *Associated Provincial Picture Houses Ltd v Wednesbury Corpn* [1948] 1 KB 223.

[76] *R v O'Leary* (1988) 87 Cr App R 387 at 391, CA; *R v Christou* [1992] QB 979, CA; *R v Dures* [1997] 2 Cr App R 247, CA; and *R v Khan* [1997] Crim LR 508, CA. See also Tucker J, *per curiam*, in *R v Grannell* (1989) 90 Cr App R 149, CA: the citation of decisions of judges or recorders of the Crown Court, not being High Court judges, is of no assistance to the Court of Appeal in deciding whether a judge has exercised his discretion properly.

basis, for example by adverting to an out-of-date version of a relevant Code of Practice.[77] Circumstances vary infinitely, and for this reason it has been said that it is undesirable to attempt any general guidance on the way in which the discretion should be exercised.[78] However, some such guidance is available from the reported decisions. They show, with a reasonable degree of clarity, that the purpose of s 78(1) is to give effect to the reliability principle.

The reliability principle

Section 78 has spawned much appellate authority and most of it indicates that the section should be taken to have been designed primarily to give effect to the reliability principle.[79] The prevailing view is summarized well by Lord Nicholls in *R v Looseley; Attorney General's Reference (No 3 of 2000)*[80] who said that the phrase 'fairness of the proceedings' is 'directed primarily at matters going to fairness in the actual conduct of the trial; for instance the reliability of the evidence and the defendant's ability to test its reliability'.[81] Thus in *R v Cooke*,[82] a rape case, it was said, obiter, that where a sample of hair is not taken in accordance with the relevant statutory provisions but obtained by an assault, and is then used to prepare a DNA profile implicating the accused, the evidence will be admitted on the basis that the means used to obtain the evidence have done nothing to cast doubt on its reliability and strength.[83]

On its wording, however, s 78 does not indicate that it is underpinned by the reliability principle, and for that reason, most probably, some of the authorities, especially the earlier authorities, seem to have been decided in reliance on the disciplinary principle or the rights-based principle.[84] It will be useful, therefore, to consider some of these decisions before turning to the various types of illegality and impropriety that have fallen to be considered under s 78.

The disciplinary principle

There are rare cases in which it has been held that *reliable* evidence could or should have been excluded where the police acted mala fide, deliberately flouting the law or wilfully abusing their powers. An example is *Matto v Crown Court at Wolverhampton*.[85] In that case the accused was convicted of driving with excess alcohol. Police officers, when requesting a specimen of breath on the accused's property, had realized that they were acting illegally. Having obtained a positive specimen, they arrested the accused, who then provided another positive

---

[77] See *R v Miller* [1998] Crim LR 209, CA.

[78] Per Hodgson J in *R v Samuel* [1988] QB 615, CA.

[79] For the disparate views of *trial judges* as to how s 78 should be exercised, see Hunter, 'Judicial Discretion: Section 78 in Practice' [1994] Crim LR 558.

[80] [2001] 1 WLR 2060, HL.

[81] Lord Hutton, in *Attorney General's Reference (No 3 of 1999)* [2001] 1 All ER 577, HL at 590, was of the obiter view that in cases involving the commission of a very grave crime, the interests of the victim and the public must be considered, as well as the interests of the accused. Balancing exercises of this kind have found little favour in subsequent authorities, except in the context of police undercover operations, considered, in this chapter, under **Entrapment and undercover operations**, p 339.

[82] [1995] 1 Cr App R 318, CA.

[83] See also *Attorney General's Reference (No 3 of 1999)* [2001] 1 All ER 577, HL, another rape case in which there was no question as to the reliability of the DNA evidence, the admissibility of which was in dispute.

[84] See Ormerod and Birch, 'The Evolution of the Discretionary Exclusion of Evidence' [2004] Crim LR 767 at 779.

[85] [1987] RTR 337.

specimen of breath at the police station. Allowing the appeal, it was held that the officers, having acted mala fide and oppressively, the circumstances were such that if the Crown Court had directed itself properly it could have exercised its discretion to exclude the evidence under s 78.

Another example is *R v Nathaniel*.[86] In that case a DNA profile taken from the appellant's blood in relation to charges of raping A and B, of which he was acquitted, was not destroyed in accordance with s 64 of the 1984 Act, but formed the main prosecution evidence on a charge of raping C. It was held that the evidence should have been excluded. The accused was misled, in consenting to give the blood sample, by statements and promises which were not honoured. He was told that it was required for the purposes of the case involving A and B; that it would be destroyed if he was prosecuted in relation to A and B and acquitted; and that if he refused without good cause to give the sample, the jury, in any proceedings against him for the rape of A and B, could draw inferences from his refusal.[87] Similarly, in *R v Alladice*,[88] in which, despite improper denial of the right of access to a solicitor under s 58 of the 1984 Act, it was held that a confession should not be excluded. However, it was also held that if the police had acted in bad faith, the court would have had little difficulty in ruling any confession inadmissible. The Court of Appeal has also deplored police ignorance of the provisions of the Codes[89] and lamented deliberate, cynical, and flagrant breaches of such provisions.[90]

However, despite these decisions and dicta, it seems clear that although deliberate or wilful misconduct on the part of the police may make exclusion more likely, it should not by itself be used as the basis for exclusion. Thus it has been said that the court cannot exclude simply as a mark of its disapproval of the way in which evidence was obtained[91] or simply in order to punish the police for failure to observe the Codes of Practice.[92] Watkins LJ put the matter clearly in *R v Mason*:[93] the *effect* of excluding relevant evidence which has been obtained improperly or unfairly may be to discourage the police from obtaining evidence in such a way, but a decision to exclude under s 78 should not be taken *in order to* discipline or punish the police. However, evidence should be excluded where deliberate misconduct has rendered evidence potentially unreliable, as *R v Mason* itself illustrates. A confession had been made, after the police had deceived the accused and his solicitor by saying that they had incriminating fingerprint evidence which they did not in fact have. It was held that the trial judge should have excluded the evidence under s 78.[94] It does not follow from *R v Mason*, of course, that s 78 can be used only in the case of deliberate misconduct. If the reliability of the evidence has been impaired by misconduct, the discretion may be exercised on this basis whether the misconduct was wilful or merely ignorant.

---

[86] [1995] 2 Cr App R 565, CA.

[87] See now the 1984 Act, s 62(10).

[88] (1988) 87 Cr App R 380, CA, considered more fully, in this chapter, under **The rights-based principle, p 334**.

[89] See per Hodgson J in *R v Keenan* [1990], 2 QB 54, CA at 61.

[90] See per Lord Lane CJ in *R v Canale* [1990] 2 All ER 187, CA at 190 and 192.

[91] Per Auld LJ in *R v Chalkley and Jeffries* [1998] QB 848, CA at 876.

[92] Per Lord Lane CJ in *R v Delaney* (1989) 88 Cr App R 338, CA at 341.

[93] [1988] 1 WLR 139, CA.

[94] See also *R v Alladice* (1988) 87 Cr App R 380, CA at **n 99** and *R v Canale* [1990] 2 All ER 187, CA at **n 123**; and cf *R v Christou* [1992] QB 979, CA at **n 175**.

The rights-based principle

There are very rare instances of exclusion under s 78 *simply* on the basis of a substantial breach of a suspect's rights, that is, where the breach has had no effect on the reliability of the evidence obtained.[95] The Court of Appeal has also used language that might suggest that s 78 is underpinned by the rights-based principle, for example its description of the right to legal advice under s 58 of the 1984 Act as 'one of the most important and fundamental rights of a citizen'[96] and references to 'significant and substantial breaches' of Code C.[97] This language is apt to mislead: it is very clear from the authorities that ultimately what matters is not how important or significant any particular provision is thought to be, but the effect, if any, of its breach on the fairness of the trial. This is illustrated well by cases involving breaches of s 58 of the 1984 Act.

It has been held that significant and substantial breaches of s 58 (or the provisions of Code C) will, prima facie, have an adverse effect on the fairness of the proceedings.[98] Breach of the section, however, is no guarantee of the exclusion of any statement made thereafter. In *R v Alladice*,[99] for example, it was held that if the trial judge had considered s 78, he would not have been obliged to exclude the confession, because the circumstances showed that the accused was well able to cope with the interviews, understood the cautions that he had been given, at times exercising his right to silence, and was aware of his rights, so that, had the solicitor been present, his advice would have added nothing to the knowledge of his rights which the accused already had.[100] In *R v Parris*,[101] on the other hand, another case involving breach of s 58, it was held that evidence of a confession should have been excluded because, had a solicitor been present, the accused would probably have accepted his advice to remain silent. Furthermore, the solicitor could have given evidence on whether the police had fabricated the confession; alternatively, his presence would have discouraged any such fabrication.[102] Denial of access to a lawyer may also result in a breach of Art 6(1) and (3)(c) (the right to legal advice),[103] unless there are compelling reasons. In *Ibrahim v UK*,[104] the Grand Chamber of the European Court of Human Rights considered whether a breach of Art 6 occurs where a person is arrested under s 41 of the Terrorism Act 2000 and questioned without a lawyer in a

---

[95] See *DPP v Goodwin* [1991] RTR 303, in the case of evidence of a positive breath specimen obtained following an unlawful arrest.

[96] Per Hodgson J in *R v Samuel* [1988] QB 615, CA. Cf *Brennan v UK* (2002) 34 EHRR 18, ECHR (the right to consult with a lawyer *in private* is part of the basic requirements of a fair trial and follows from Art 6(3)(c) of the European Convention on Human Rights) and *Salduz v Turkey* (2008) 49 EHRR 421, ECHR (it is of fundamental importance to provide access to a lawyer where the person in custody is a minor).

[97] *R v Keenan* [1990] 2 QB 54, CA.

[98] Per Saville J in *R v Walsh* (1989) 91 Cr App R 161, CA at 163. However, in the case of drink-driving offences, the public interest requires that the obtaining of specimens should not be delayed to any significant extent to enable a suspect to take legal advice: *Kennedy v DPP* [2003] Crim LR 120, DC. See also *Campbell v DPP* [2003] Crim LR 118, DC; *Kirkup v DPP* [2004] Crim LR 230, DC; and *Whitley v DPP* [2003] EWHC 2512 (Admin). Similarly, in the case of juveniles, there is no reason to delay the obtaining of specimens in order for an 'appropriate adult' to be present: *DPP v Evans* [2003] Crim LR 338, DC.

[99] (1988) 87 Cr App R 380, CA.

[100] See also, to similar effect, *R v Dunford* (1990) 91 Cr App R 150, CA.

[101] (1989) 89 Cr App R 68, CA. See also *R v Walsh* (1990) 91 Cr App R 161.

[102] This argument was not employed in *R v Alladice* (1988) 87 Cr App R 380, CA, where fabrication was also alleged.

[103] *Salduz v Turkey* (2009) 49 EHRR 19, GC.

[104] [2016] ECHR 750, GC.

safety interview held pursuant to Schedule 8 of the Act, which permits the police to delay the right to legal advice on urgent public safety grounds.[105] It was held that provided the statutory requirements of the Act are met and compelling reasons exist for temporarily restricting the right, such as an urgent need to protect the life and physical integrity of the public, there will be no breach of Art 6(1) and (3)(c). In *Bueze v Belgium*, the Grand Chamber stated that the criterion of 'compelling reasons' to justify any restriction is stringent, the restriction being permissible only in exceptional circumstances, and only if it is temporary and based on an individual assessment of the circumstances of the case.[106] However, the lack of compelling reasons does not automatically result in a breach of Art 6, the real question being whether the accused nevertheless had a fair trial overall. Where there are no compelling reasons, the onus will be on the authorities to demonstrate convincingly why the overall fairness of the criminal proceedings was not irretrievably prejudiced by the restriction.[107]

Breaches of Code B (search of premises)

The reliability principle serves to explain the admission in evidence of the fruits of an improper search in *R v Stewart*,[108] where, following an entry involving a number of breaches of Code B, the accused was found in possession of apparatus to divert the gas and electricity supplies so as to bypass the meters. The outcome was the same in *R v Sanghera*[109] where, a search having been conducted without written consent in breach of the Code, there was no issue as to the reliability of the evidence as to what had been discovered. However, it should be otherwise if the means used to obtain the evidence could have affected its quality, for example a case in which the accused, following a search of his premises during which he was improperly kept out of the way, claims that the property found was 'planted'.[110] Equally, although officers are entitled to delay taking a suspect to a police station in order that a search may be conducted with his assistance, if they abuse that entitlement to ask questions, beyond those necessary to the search, on matters which properly ought to be asked under the rules of Code C applying at a police station, the answers may be excluded on the grounds of unfairness.[111]

Breaches of Code C (detention, treatment, and questioning)

It is clear that the outcome, in the case of breaches of Code C, as in all cases, depends upon the precise facts. In *R v Pall*[112] it was said that the absence of a caution[113] was bound to be significant in most circumstances, and in *R v Nelson and Rose*[114] it was held that a failure to

---

[105] The Terrorism Act 2003, Schedule 8(4)(a)–(g).

[106] (2019) 69 EHRR 1, GC, at [142]. See also *Ibrahim v UK* [2016] ECHR 750, GC at [258].

[107] *Beuze v Belgium* (2019) 69 EHRR 1, GC at [145]. See also *Ibrahim v UK* [2016] ECHR 750, GC at [235] and [260]–[265]. The decision in *Beuze v Belgium* (2019) 69 EHRR 1, GC, has been criticized for diluting the principle laid down in *Salduz v Turkey* (2009) 49 EHRR 19, GC, to the effect that restricting access to a lawyer without compelling reasons *does* automatically violate Art 6 : see *Beuze V Belgium* [2019] Crim LR 233 ; and Celiksoy, 'Ibrahim and Others v. UK: Watering down the Salduz principles?' accessible at https://journals.sagepub.com/doi/pdf/10.1177/2032284418778149, accessed 19th June 2019.

See further, the Joint Concurring Opinion in *Bueze v Belgium* (2019) 69 EHRR 1, GC at [B–F].

[108] [1995] Crim LR 500, CA. See also *R v McCarthy* [1996] Crim LR 818, CA.

[109] [2001] 1 Cr App R 299 (20), CA.

[110] But cf *R v Wright* [1994] Crim LR 55, CA, and see also *R v Khan* [1997] Crim LR 508, CA.

[111] *R v Khan* [1993] Crim LR 54, CA, applied in *R v Raphaie* [1996] Crim LR 812, CA.

[112] (1991) 156 JP 424, CA.

[113] See now paras 10.1–10.9 of Code C.

[114] [1998] 2 Cr App R 399, CA.

caution should have led to the exclusion of the whole of an interview. However, in *R v Hoyte*[115] a confession was admitted, despite a failure to caution, on the basis that the police had acted in good faith and in the particular circumstances there could have been no unfairness.[116] Similarly in *R v Gill*[117] it was held that lies told during an Inland Revenue investigation of tax fraud were admissible, despite a failure to caution. Clarke LJ said that the principal purpose of the caution was to ensure, so far as possible, that interviewees do not make admissions unless they wish to do so and are aware of the consequences, and not to prevent interviewees from telling lies. Although lies may be excluded where there has been a failure to caution, each case depends on its own facts. On the facts, the Revenue had not acted in bad faith and the appellants were aware that criminal proceedings were in prospect and must have known that they were not obliged to answer the questions.[118] In *R v Aspinall*[119] the accused, a schizo-phrenic, was interviewed, about 13 hours after his arrest, without an 'appropriate adult', in breach of what is now para 11.15 of Code C, and without a solicitor. It was held that an accused of this kind may not be able to judge for himself what is in his best interests, which may put him at a considerable disadvantage, not least because the record of the interview may not seem unreliable to a jury. However, in appropriate circumstances the confession of a mentally disordered accused may be properly admitted notwithstanding that it was made in breach of para 11.15.[120]

In *R v Konscol*[121] the trial judge admitted evidence of an interview with K, containing lies, conducted by a Belgian customs officer. There was no dispute that K had said what was recorded, and that the interview was conducted fairly according to Belgian law, but K was neither cautioned nor advised that he could have a lawyer present. The Court of Appeal dis-missed the appeal and—unhelpfully—declined to lay down guidelines as to when a court should admit a statement made overseas according to rules which did not coincide with the provisions of the 1984 Act.[122] The obvious guideline, it is submitted, is that however fair, according to foreign law, the means by which the evidence was obtained, the outcome should be determined by reference to the effect of those means on the fairness of the domestic criminal proceedings. In *R v Keenan*[123] records of an interview with the accused were compiled in plain breach of Code C: the record was not made during the course of the interview; the reason for not completing it at that time was not recorded in the officer's pocket book; and the accused was not given the opportunity to read it and to sign it as cor-rect or to indicate the respects in which he considered it inaccurate. The accused's defence, unknown to the trial judge at the time when the submission on admissibility was made,

---

[115] [1994] Crim LR 215, CA.

[116] See also *Ibrahim v UK* [2014] ECHR 1492.

[117] [2004] 1 WLR 49, CA.

[118] See also *R v Senior* [2004] 3 All ER 9, CA, applied in *R v Rehman* [2007] Crim LR 101, CA (questioning by customs officers to establish ownership of a suspicious baggage, prior to administering a caution) and *R v Devani* [2008] 1 Cr App R 65 (questioning of a suspect, who was a solicitor, without a caution, but in the presence of her principal).

[119] [1999] Crim LR 741, CA.

[120] See *R v Law-Thompson* [1997] Crim LR 674, CA.

[121] [1993] Crim LR 950.

[122] See also *R v Quinn* [1990] Crim LR 581, CA and *R v McNab* [2002] Crim LR 129, CA.

[123] [1990] 2 QB 54, CA.

was that the interview had been fabricated. The judge, ruling that any unfairness to the accused could be cured by the accused going into the witness box and giving his version of the interview, admitted the evidence. On appeal, it was held that the relevant provisions of Code C[124] are designed to make it difficult for detained persons to make unfounded allegations against the police which might otherwise appear credible and to provide safeguards against the police inaccurately recording or inventing the words used in questioning a detained person. Where there have been significant and substantial breaches of the 'verballing' provisions, evidence so obtained should be excluded, because if the other evidence in the case is strong, then it may make no difference to the eventual result if the evidence in question is excluded, and if the other evidence is weak or non-existent, that is just the situation where the protection of the rules is most needed. It was wrong to assume that any unfairness could be cured by the accused going into the witness box: if he intended not to testify if the evidence was excluded, then its admission unfairly robbed him of his right to remain silent; if the defence case was to be (as it turned out to be) that the evidence was concocted, then its admission forced the accused to give evidence and also, by attacking the police, to put his character in issue; and if the defence was to be that the interview was inaccurately recorded, it placed the accused at a substantial disadvantage because he had been given no contemporaneous opportunity to correct any inaccuracies. For these reasons, the conviction was quashed.[125]

In *R v Canale*[126] the way in which records of two interviews with the accused were obtained involved breaches very similar to those which occurred in *R v Keenan*. In this case, however, at two subsequent and contemporaneously recorded interviews, the accused repeated admissions allegedly made in the first two interviews. On the *voir dire* and in evidence the accused admitted that he had made the admissions but said that they were untrue and that the police had induced him to make them by a trick. The Court of Appeal held that by reason of the flagrant and cynical breaches of the Code, the judge was deprived of the very evidence which would have enabled him to reach a more certain conclusion on the question of admissibility and, had he ruled in favour of admission, the jury would have been deprived of the evidence necessary to decide the truth of the accused's denial of the offence. The initial breaches affected the whole series of alleged admissions, all of which should have been excluded.[127]

Breaches of Code D (identification)
Many of the reported decisions under s 78 have involved breaches of Code D (identification). These decisions are more conveniently covered in **Chapter 9**.[128]

---

[124] See now para 11.13 of Code C.

[125] See also *R v Williams* [2012] EWCA Crim 264. Cf *R v Harper* [2019] EWCA Crim 343 concerning an unsolicited admission to a prison officer.

[126] [1990] 2 All ER 187, CA.

[127] See also *R v Absolam* (1988) 88 Cr App R 332, CA, and *R v Sparks* [1991] Crim LR 128, CA; and cf *R v Langiert* [1991] Crim LR 777, CA (failure to record the reason for not making a contemporaneous record), and *R v Rajakuruna* [1991] Crim LR 458, CA (failure to inform a person not under arrest that he is not obliged to remain with the officer).

[128] **Chapter 9**, Breaches of Code D and exclusion, p 293.

Covert recording and filming

In *R v Bailey*[129] two co-accused, having exercised their right to silence when interviewed, were charged and placed in the same bugged cell by officers who, in order to lull them into a false sense of security, pretended that they had been forced to put them in the same cell by an uncooperative custody officer. Evidence of incriminating conversations obtained by this subterfuge was held to be admissible. In *R v King*[130] evidence of incriminating conversations was obtained when the accused, after their arrest, were put in a police vehicle fitted with recording equipment. The evidence was held to be admissible: the officers did not engage the accused in conversation or trick them into speaking and although the recording took place before interview under caution, that placed the accused at no greater disadvantage than if they had been covertly recorded after such an interview.

In *R v Khan (Sultan)*[131] the House of Lords held that the fact that evidence has been obtained in circumstances which amount to a breach of Art 8 of the European Convention on Human Rights (the right to respect for private life, home, and correspondence) may be relevant to exercise of the s 78 power, but the significance of the breach turns on its effect on the fairness of the proceedings. The police had made a recording of an incriminating conversation relating to the importation of heroin, using an electronic surveillance device attached to a house without the knowledge or consent of the owner or occupier. It was held that the judge had been entitled to conclude that the circumstances in which the evidence had been obtained, even if they constituted a breach of Art 8, were not such as to require its exclusion.[132] The European Court of Human Rights subsequently held that although the recording was obtained in breach of Art 8, its use at the trial did not conflict with the right to a fair hearing under Art 6, because there was no risk of the recording being unreliable, the accused had the opportunity to challenge its admissibility, and if its admission would have given rise to substantive unfairness, the domestic court could have excluded it under s 78.[133] The European Court has reached similar conclusions in relation to evidence obtained in breach of Art 8 by the unlawful installation of a listening device in the accused's home[134] and, in *PG and JH v United Kingdom*,[135] by the unlawful use of covert listening devices in police cells.[136] In *PG and JH v United Kingdom*, the recordings did not contain any incriminating statements, but were used at trial as a control to identify the voices of the accused on other tapes. It was held that they could be regarded as akin to blood, hair, or other physical or objective specimens used in forensic analysis and to which the privilege against self-incrimination does not apply. In that case the European Court also reiterated that:

---

[129] [1993] 3 All ER 513, CA.

[130] [2012] EWCA Crim 805.

[131] [1997] AC 558.

[132] See also *R v Plunkett* [2013] 1 WLR 3121, CA (covert recordings authorized under the Regulation of Investigatory Powers Act 2000), followed in *R v Khan* [2013] EWCA Crim 2230 (a covert recording *not* covered by the authorization granted under the 2000 Act).

[133] *Khan v United Kingdom* (2001) 31 EHRR 1016.

[134] *Chalkley v United Kingdom* [2003] Crim LR 51.

[135] [2002] Crim LR 308.

[136] See also *R v Mason* [2002] 2 Cr App R 628 (38), CA; and *R v Button* [2005] Crim LR 571, where the 'startling proposition' that the court is bound to exclude any evidence obtained in breach of Art 8 because otherwise it would be acting unlawfully was rejected on the basis that any breach of Art 8 is subsumed by the Art 6 duty to ensure a fair trial.

Whilst Article 6 guarantees the right to a fair hearing, it does not lay down any rules on the admissibility of evidence as such, which is therefore primarily a matter for regulation under national law . . . It is not the role of the court to determine, as a matter of principle whether particular types of evidence, for example unlawfully obtained evidence—may be admissible or, indeed, whether the applicant was guilty or not. The question which must be answered is whether the proceedings as a whole, including the way in which the evidence was obtained, were fair.[137]

The European Court has followed the same approach in relation to covert filming. In *Perry v United Kingdom*,[138] the applicant having failed to attend identification parades, the police, infringing official guidelines, filmed him covertly for the purposes of a video identification of which neither he nor his solicitor was aware. It was held that the application was manifestly ill-founded on the grounds that the use of evidence obtained without a proper legal basis or through unlawful means will not generally contravene Art 6(1) so long as proper procedural safeguards are in place and the source of the material is not tainted.[139]

In *R v P*[140] it was argued that although telephone intercept evidence was properly obtained in accordance with the Convention and the law of a country overseas, its use in an English trial was contrary to Art 6 and the policy of the English law. Rejecting this argument, the House of Lords held that: the fair use of intercept evidence at a trial is not a breach of Art 6; that even if it was unlawfully obtained, the criterion of fairness in Art 6 is the criterion to be applied by the judge under s 78; and there is no principle of exclusion of intercept evidence independently of the statutory provisions.[141] The House has also held that where intercept evidence is inadmissible pursuant to statutory provisions, there is no rule prohibiting the use of the intercepts at police interviews and, subject to s 78, such use will not render the interview evidence inadmissible, although the interview transcript will need to be edited to remove any direct or indirect references to the intercept.[142]

Entrapment and undercover operations

R v Looseley and Attorney General's Reference (No 3 of 2000)

R v Looseley and *Attorney General's Reference (No 3 of 2000)*[143] are the leading authorities on the circumstances in which criminal proceedings should be stayed, or evidence excluded, on the grounds of entrapment.[144] Hearing both appeals together, the House of Lords held as follows:

1. Entrapment is not a substantive defence, but where an accused can show entrapment the court may stay the proceedings as an abuse of the court's process or it may exclude evidence under s 78.

---

[137] For a fuller examination of approaches to exclusion of evidence obtained in breach of Art 8, see Ormerod, 'ECHR and the Exclusion of Evidence: Trial Remedies for Article 8 Breaches' [2003] Crim LR 61. See also Mahoney, 'Abolition of New Zealand's Prima Facie Exclusionary Rule' [2003] Crim LR 607.

[138] [2003] Crim LR 281.

[139] See also *R v Loveridge* [2001] 2 Cr App R 591 (29), CA, where the accused were covertly filmed in court, which was both unlawful and in breach of Art 8, to enable comparison with pictures of the crime as recorded on a CCTV film; *R v Marriner* [2002] EWCA Crim 2855, where the accused were covertly recorded on video and tape by undercover journalists; and *R v Rosenberg* [2006] Crim LR 540, CA, where the accused and the police were aware of surveillance by the accused's neighbour that had been neither initiated nor encouraged by the police.

[140] [2002] 1 AC 46, HL.

[141] See now the surveillance provisions of the Investigatory Powers Act 2016.

[142] *R v Sargent* [2003] 1 AC 347, HL.

[143] [2001] 1 WLR 2060, HL.

[144] See Ashworth, 'Redrawing the Boundaries of Entrapment' [2002] Crim LR 161.

2. As a matter of principle, a stay of the proceedings rather than exclusion of evidence should normally be regarded as the appropriate response. A prosecution founded on entrapment would be an abuse of the court's process. Police conduct which brings about state-created crime is unacceptable and improper and to prosecute in such circumstances would be an affront to the public conscience.[145]

3. In deciding whether conduct amounts to state-created crime, the existence or absence of a predisposition on the part of the accused to commit the crime is not the criterion by which the acceptability of police conduct is to be decided, because it does not make acceptable what would otherwise be unacceptable conduct on the part of the police or negative misuse of state power.[146]

4. A useful guide is to consider whether the police did no more than present the accused with an unexceptional opportunity to commit a crime. The yardstick for these purposes is, in general, whether the police conduct preceding the commission of the offence was no more than might have been expected from others in the circumstances. 'The State can justify the use of entrapment techniques to induce the commission of an offence only when the inducement is consistent with the ordinary temptations and stratagems that are likely to be encountered in the course of criminal activity . . . But once the State goes beyond the ordinary, it is likely to increase the incidence of crime by artificial means.'[147] Of its nature, the technique of providing an opportunity to commit a crime is intrusive. The greater the degree of intrusiveness, the more closely will the courts scrutinize the reason for using it.[148]

5. Usually, a most important factor, but not necessarily decisive, will be whether an officer can be said to have caused the commission of the offence, rather than merely providing an opportunity for the accused to commit it with an officer rather than in secrecy with someone else. A good example of the latter situation is furnished by *Nottingham City Council v Amin*[149] where a taxi driver who was not licensed to ply for hire in a particular district, and was flagged down by plain-clothes officers in that district, took them to their stated destination. Lord Bingham CJ said:[150]

> it has been regarded as unobjectionable if a law enforcement officer gives a defendant an opportunity to break the law, of which the defendant freely takes advantage, in circumstances where it appears that the defendant would have behaved in the same way if the opportunity had been offered by anyone else. . .

In other words, the officers behaved like ordinary members of the public in flagging the taxi down. They did not, for example, wave £50 notes or pretend to be in distress.

---

[145] The possibility of a stay on the basis of entrapment by non-state agents, eg journalists, seems to be remote: see *Council for the Regulation of Health Care Professionals v General Medical Council* [2007] 1 WLR 3094 at [81]. But see Dyer, 'The Problem of Media Entrapment' [2015] Crim LR 311, where it is argued that a stay should be available on the basis of a breach of Art 6(1) of the European Convention on Human Rights or the rule of law. And see earlier in this Chapter under **Staying proceedings as an abuse of process**, p 322.

[146] Cf *R v Moon* [2004] All ER (D) 167 (Nov), CA, where the absence of predisposition on the part of M to deal with or supply heroin was a critical factor in concluding that a test purchase by an undercover officer, who claimed that she was suffering from heroin withdrawal symptoms, was an abuse of process.

[147] Per McHugh J in *Ridgeway v The Queen* (1995) 184 CLR 19 at 92.

[148] For an example of 'unexceptional opportunity', see *R v Palmer* [2014] EWCA Crim 1681.

[149] [2000] 1 WLR 1071, DC. See also *East Riding of Yorkshire Council v Dearlove* [2012] RTR 29, DC.

[150] At 1076–7.

The test of whether a police officer acted like an ordinary member of the public works well and is likely to be decisive in many cases of regulatory offences committed with ordinary members of the public, such as selling liquor without a licence, but ordinary members of the public do not become involved in large-scale drug dealing, conspiracy to rob, or hiring assassins. The appropriate standards of behaviour in such cases are more problematic; and even in the case of offences committed with ordinary members of the public, other factors may require a purely causal test to be modified.

6. The causal question cannot be answered by a mechanical application of a distinction between 'active' and 'passive' conduct on the part of the undercover policeman. For example, drug dealers can be expected to show some wariness about dealing with a stranger and therefore some protective colour in dress or manner as well as a certain degree of persistence may be necessary.[151] Equally, undercover officers who infiltrate conspiracies to murder, rob, or commit terrorist offences could hardly remain concealed unless they showed some enthusiasm for the enterprise. A good deal of active behaviour may therefore be acceptable without crossing the boundary between causing the offence to be committed and providing an opportunity for the accused to commit it.

7. Ultimately the overall consideration is always whether the conduct of the police was so seriously improper as to bring the administration of justice into disrepute. Other formulations substantially to the same effect are: a prosecution which would affront the public conscience[152] or conviction and punishment which would be deeply offensive to ordinary notions of fairness.[153] In applying these formulations, the court has regard to all the circumstances of the case. One cannot isolate any single factor or devise any formula that will always produce the correct answer. There are a cluster of relevant factors but their relevant weight and importance depends on the particular facts of the case. The following are of particular relevance.

(a) The nature of the offence. The use of proactive techniques is more appropriate in the case of some offences, for example dealing in unlawful substances, offences with no immediate victim, such as bribery, offences which victims are reluctant to report, and conspiracies. The secrecy and difficulty of detection, and the manner in which the criminal activity is carried on, are relevant considerations. However, the fact that the offence is a serious one is not in itself a sufficient ground for the police to ignore the provisions of the Undercover Operations Code of Practice (issued jointly by all UK police authorities and HM Customs and Excise in response to the Human Rights Act 1998)[154] or for the courts to condone their actions by allowing the prosecution to proceed.[155]

---

[151] See, eg, *R v Jones* [2010] 2 Cr App R 69 (10), a case of incitement to produce cannabis, and *R v Moore* [2013] EWCA Crim 85.

[152] Per Lord Steyn in *R v Latif* [1996] 1 WLR 104, HL at 112.

[153] Per Lord Bingham in *Nottingham City Council v Amin* [2000] 1 WLR 1071, DC at 1076. See also *R v L* [2018] EWCA Crim 821 at [32]. And see earlier in this chapter under **Staying proceedings as an abuse of process, p 322**.

[154] Regulation of the deployment of undercover officers is governed by the Regulation of Investigatory Powers Act 2000 and the revised *Covert Human Intelligence Sources Code of Practice*, issued under s 71 of the 2000 Act and accessible at https://assets.publishing.service.gov.uk/government/uploads/system/uploads/attachment_data/file/742042/20180802_CHIS_code_.pdf.

[155] For an example of an undercover officer going far beyond his authority, see *R v Barkshire* [2011] EWCA Crim 1885.

(b) The reason for the particular police operation and supervision. As to the former, the police must act in good faith. Having reasonable grounds for suspicion is one way good faith may be established. It is not normally considered a legitimate use of police power to provide people not suspected of any criminal activity with the opportunity to commit crimes.[156] However, having grounds for suspicion of a particular individual is not always essential. The police may, in the course of a bona fide investigation into suspected criminality, provide an opportunity for the commission of an offence which is taken by someone to whom no suspicion previously attached, as in *Williams v DPP*.[157] This can happen when a human or inanimate decoy is used in the course of the detection of crime which has been prevalent in a particular place. Sometimes, random testing may be the only way of policing a particular trading activity. As to supervision, to allow officers or controlled informers to undertake entrapment activities unsupervised carries great danger, not only that they will try to improve their performances in court, but of oppression, extortion, and corruption.

(c) The nature and extent of police participation in the crime. The greater the inducement held out by the police, and the more forceful or persistent their overtures, the more readily may a court conclude that they overstepped the boundary.[158] In assessing the weight to be attached to the police inducement, regard is to be had to the accused's circumstances, including his vulnerability. It will not normally be regarded as objectionable for the police to behave as would an ordinary customer of a trade, whether lawful or unlawful, being carried on by the accused.

(d) The accused's criminal record. This is unlikely to be relevant unless it can be linked to other factors grounding reasonable suspicion that he is engaged in criminal activity.

8. A decision on whether to stay the proceedings is distinct from a decision on the fairness of admitting evidence.[159] Different tests are applicable to these two decisions. If an application under s 78 is in substance a belated application for a stay, it should be treated as such and decided according to the principles appropriate to the grant of a stay. If the court is not satisfied that a stay should be granted, the question under s 78 is not whether the proceedings should have been brought but, as Potter LJ held in *R v Shannon*:[160]

> It is whether the fairness of the proceedings will be adversely affected by admitting the evidence of the agent provocateur or evidence which is available as the result of his action or activities. So, for instance, if there is good reason to question the credibility of evidence given by an agent provocateur, or which casts doubt on the reliability of other evidence procured by or resulting from his actions, and that question is not susceptible of being properly or fairly resolved in the course of the proceedings from available, admissible and 'untainted' evidence, then the judge may readily conclude that such evidence should be excluded.

---

[156] See, eg, *Ramanauskas v Lithuania* [2008] Crim LR 639, where an officer acted on mere rumours about a prosecutor's openness to bribery.

[157] [1993] 3 All ER 365. See at **n 170**. See also *R v Moore* [2013] EWCA Crim 85.

[158] See also *R v M* [2011] EWCA Crim 648 at [18]: in the absence of persuasion or pressure or the offer of a significant inducement, it will not generally amount to an abuse of process for an officer to so insinuate himself into the confidence of the accused as to offer him an opportunity to commit a crime.

[159] Citing *R v Chalkley* [1998] QB 848, CA at 874.

[160] [2001] 1 WLR 51, CA at 68.

9. Neither s 78 nor the power to stay proceedings has been modified by Art 6 of the European Convention on Human Rights and the jurisprudence of the European Court of Human Rights. There is no appreciable difference between the requirements of Art 6, or the Strasbourg jurisprudence on Art 6, and the English law. Nor is there anything in *Teixeira de Castro v Portugal*[161] which suggests any difference from the current English approach to entrapment.

R v Smurthwaite and Gill

In *R v Smurthwaite and Gill*[162] the Court of Appeal considered the application of s 78(1) to evidence obtained as a result of police undercover operations. It was held that the relevant factors include:

1. whether the undercover officer was acting as an agent provocateur, that is, enticing the accused to commit an offence he would not otherwise have committed;

2. the nature of any entrapment;

3. whether the evidence consists of admissions to a completed offence or relates to the actual commission of an offence;

4. how active or passive the officer's role was in obtaining the evidence;

5. whether there is an unassailable record of what occurred or whether it is strongly corroborated; and

6. whether the officer abused his role to ask questions which ought properly to have been asked as a police officer and in accordance with the Codes.[163]

Both *Smurthwaite* and *Gill* were trials for soliciting to murder. In each case the person solicited was an undercover police officer posing as a contract killer and the prosecution case depended upon secret tape recordings of meetings held between the undercover officer and the accused. In S's case, the Court of Appeal was not persuaded that the officer was an agent provocateur. There was an element of entrapment and a trick. However, the tapes recorded not admissions about some previous offence but the actual offence being committed; they showed that S made the running and that the officer had taken a minimal role in the planning and had used no persuasion towards S; they were an accurate and unchallenged record; and the officer had not abused his role to ask questions which ought properly to have been asked as a police officer. In these circumstances, the judge's decision not to exclude the evidence was upheld. The outcome was the same in G's case: the facts were very similar and although the first meeting between G and the officer was not recorded and there was a stark conflict of evidence as to what was said at that meeting, the existence of a total record was only one factor, and both the contents of the subsequent taped conversations and statements made by G in her formal police interviews supported the officer's account of the first meeting.[164]

---

[161] (1998) 28 EHRR 101.

[162] [1994] 1 All ER 898, CA.

[163] The same factors also apply in the case of evidence obtained by undercover journalists acting on their own initiative and not on police instructions: *R v Shannon* [2001] 1 WLR 51, CA and *Shannon v UK* [2005] Crim LR 133, ECHR. See also Hofmeyr, 'The Problem of Private Entrapment' [2006] Crim LR 319. As to the sixth factor, see also *R v Christou* [1992] QB 979, CA and *R v Bryce* [1992] 4 All ER 567, CA.

[164] Cf *Re Proulx* [2001] 1 All ER 57, DC.

Where the means of entrapment are an offence under foreign law

R v Governor of Pentonville Prison, ex p Chinoy[165] concerned the setting up of a bank account to facilitate the laundering of money alleged to be the proceeds of drug trafficking. The Divisional Court held that the fact of entrapment was one of the circumstances which should be taken into account when carrying out the balancing exercise under s 78(1), but concluded that the circumstances did not require the exclusion of the evidence. It was held that the detection and proof of certain types of criminal activity may necessitate the employment of underhand and even unlawful means. On the facts, although the evidence was obtained by means which were criminal in France and, according to French law, in breach of the European Convention on Human Rights, there was no breach of English law and the means employed by the undercover agents were appropriate to the situation they were investigating and did not require the exclusion of the evidence they obtained. In *R v Latif*[166] S was convicted of being knowingly concerned in the importation of drugs which had been brought into the country by an undercover customs officer. Although S had been lured into England by the deceit of an informer, and both he and the undercover officer had possibly committed the offence of possessing heroin in Pakistan, the House of Lords upheld the judge's refusal to either stay the proceedings or exclude the informer's evidence under s 78.[167]

Giving an accused an opportunity to break the law

An application under s 78 will not succeed where a police officer gives an accused an opportunity to break the law, of which the accused freely takes advantage, in circumstances in which the accused would have behaved in the same way if the opportunity had been offered by anyone else. An example is *DPP v Marshall*,[168] where, on a charge of selling alcohol without a licence, evidence was received of purchases made by plain clothes officers. The same approach was adopted in *Ealing London Borough v Woolworths plc*,[169] in which it was held that, on a charge under s 11(1) of the Video Recordings Act 1984, justices were in error in excluding evidence that a boy aged 11, acting under instructions of officers of the Trading Standards Department, had entered the store and purchased an 18-category video film. In *Williams v DPP*,[170] the trick, based on the expectation that someone might act dishonestly, was to leave in a busy street an insecure van containing an apparently valuable load, a stratagem which, it was held, left the accused free whether to succumb or not.

Using, as agent provocateurs, informers not called as witnesses

It seems that the police cannot circumvent s 78(1) by using, as agents provocateurs, informants who will not be called as witnesses. Thus if an informant, C, acting on police instructions rather than on his own initiative, incites or entraps an accused, D, into committing an offence (the supply of drugs, say) and D is then approached by E, an undercover police officer, in whose presence the offence is committed (D supplies E with drugs), this may form the basis of a submission to exclude E's evidence under s 78(1) notwithstanding that E,

---

[165] [1992] 1 All ER 317, DC.

[166] [1996] 1 WLR 104, HL.

[167] See also *R v Pattemore* [1994] Crim LR 836, CA and *R v Morley* [1994] Crim LR 919, CA.

[168] [1988] 3 All ER 683, DC.

[169] [1995] Crim LR 58, DC.

[170] [1993] 3 All ER 365, DC.

by reference to the relevant factors as set out in *R v Smurthwaite and Gill*, behaved throughout with perfect propriety.[171]

No difference from Strasbourg law

In *R v Syed*,[172] the Court of Appeal stated that working definitions of entrapment in Strasbourg jurisprudence and English law are essentially the same; that although there may be distinctions in the language used, they are not material distinctions; and that efforts to construct differences between the approaches using unduly literal reading of the language of judgments are misplaced and discouraged.[173] The court rejected, for example, an argument that Strasbourg authorities had laid down the principle (not found in English law) that once an arguable allegation of 'incitement' (or entrapment) had been made, the burden of proof was on the state to disprove it.[174]

Undercover operations after commission of an offence

In *R v Christou*[175] the police set up a shop staffed by two undercover police officers who purported to be willing to buy stolen jewellery. Transactions in the shop were recorded, the object being to recover stolen property and obtain evidence against thieves or receivers. The accused, charged as a result of the operation, unsuccessfully sought to exclude all the evidence obtained thereby. It was argued that the evidence was obtained by a trick designed to deprive visitors to the shop of their privilege against self-incrimination and that a caution should have been administered. The Court of Appeal, distinguishing *R v Payne*[176] and *R v Mason*,[177] held that the accused had voluntarily applied themselves to the trick (in the sense that what they did in the shop was exactly what they intended to do) and this had resulted in no unfairness.[178] Concerning the absence of a caution, the court acknowledged that the officers had grounds to suspect the accused of an offence, but held that Code C was not intended to apply in the present context. The Code was intended to protect suspects who are vulnerable to abuse or pressure from officers or who may believe themselves to be so. Where a suspect, even if not in detention, is being questioned by an officer, acting as such, for the purpose of obtaining evidence, the officer and the suspect are not on equal terms: the officer is perceived to be in a position of authority and the suspect may be intimidated or undermined. On the facts, however, the accused were not questioned by officers acting as such, conversation was on equal terms, and there was no question of pressure or intimidation.

In *Christou* the court held that it *would* be wrong for the police to adopt an undercover pose or disguise to enable them to ask questions about an offence uninhibited by the Code and with the effect of circumventing it, and it would then be open to a judge to exclude under s 78. On the facts, however, the questions and comments of the officers were, for the most part, simply those necessary to conduct the bartering and to maintain their cover, and not questions about the offence. Thus, although officers had asked questions about the origin of the goods,

---

[171] See *R v Smith (Brian)* [1995] Crim LR 658, CA and cf *R v Mann* [1995] Crim LR 647, CA.

[172] [2019] 1 Cr App R 267 (21), CA.

[173] Ibid at [109]–[110].

[174] Ibid at [112].

[175] [1992] QB 979, CA.

[176] [1963] 1 WLR 637, CCA.

[177] [1988] 1 WLR 139, CA.

[178] Similar reasoning was applied in *R v Maclean* [1993] Crim LR 687, CA and *R v Cadette* [1995] Crim LR 229, CA, considered at **n 181**. See also *R v Deenik* [1992] Crim LR 578, CA (police evidence of voice identification, D not having been warned that an officer was listening).

they had formed a part of their undercover pose as receivers: receivers need such information to prevent them from re-selling goods in the area from which they were stolen.[179] In *R v Bryce*,[180] on the other hand, in which an undercover officer, posing as a potential buyer of a car, asked B how recently the car had been stolen, it was held that evidence of the answers should have been excluded. The questions were not necessary to the maintenance of the undercover pose. They went directly to the issue of guilty knowledge, they were hotly disputed, and there had been no caution and no contemporary record.

Use of accomplices and informers

In a number of cases, the trickery or subterfuge has involved the use of an accomplice. In *R v Cadette*[181] B, arrested as a suspected drugs courier, was asked by customs officers to telephone C, in accordance with an arrangement previously made between B and C, but to pretend that she had not been arrested and to try to persuade C to come to the airport. Evidence of their conversation, which was recorded, was held to have been properly admitted. The court observed that, in practical terms, there comes a point when officers move from following up available lines of inquiry to obtain evidence against others involved to a stage where they seek in effect to deprive a suspect of the protection afforded by the 1984 Act and the Codes, but held that the officers had not crossed the line. The provisions of the 1984 Act did not apply; there was a reliable record of the conversation; and the ruse, of itself, did not give rise to unfairness for the purposes of s 78.[182]

The line was crossed, however, in *Allan v United Kingdom*.[183] A, suspected of murder, was interviewed by officers on several occasions but, acting on legal advice, consistently refused to answer questions. H, an experienced informer, who had undergone coaching by police informers, was fitted with recording devices and placed in A's cell for the specific purpose of questioning him to obtain information about the murder. At the trial H gave evidence, which proved to be decisive, that A had admitted his presence at the scene of the murder, but this conversation had not been recorded on tape. A was convicted. The European Court of Human Rights was satisfied that using statements obtained in a manner which effectively undermines a suspect's right to make a meaningful choice whether to speak to the authorities or to remain silent infringes procedural rights inherent in Art 6. The court acknowledged that whether the right to silence is undermined to such an extent as to invoke Art 6 will depend upon the circumstances of the case, but, distinguishing *Khan v United Kingdom*,[184] was satisfied that evidence of the conversation had been obtained without sufficient regard to fair trial guarantees:

> the admissions allegedly made by the applicant to H . . . were not spontaneous and unprompted statements volunteered by the applicant, but were induced by the persistent questioning of H who, at the instance of the police, channelled their conversations into discussions of the murder in circumstances which can be regarded as the functional equivalent of interrogation, without any of the safeguards which would attach to a formal police interview, including the attendance of a solicitor and the issuing of the usual caution.[185]

---

[179] See also *R v Lin* [1995] Crim LR 817, CA.

[180] [1992] 4 All ER 567, CA.

[181] [1995] Crim LR 229, CA.

[182] See also *R v Jelen; R v Katz* (1989) 90 Cr App R 456, CA and *R v Edwards* [1997] Crim LR 348, CA.

[183] (2002) 36 EHRR 143.

[184] (2001) 31 EHRR 1016. See at n 133.

[185] At para 52. Cf *Bykof v Russia* [2010] Crim LR 413, ECHR.

The conviction was subsequently quashed by the Court of Appeal[186] on the basis that H was a 'police stooge' carrying out the equivalent of interrogation after A had exercised a right of silence, impinging on that right and the privilege against self-incrimination

ADDITIONAL READING

Bunning v Cross (1978) 141 CLR 54, accessible via: http://www.austlii.edu.au/au/cases/cth/HCA/.
A leading Australian authority on unlawfully obtained evidence.

R v Harrison [2009] 2 SCR 494, accessible at: https://scc-csc.lexum.com/scc-csc/scc-csc/en/item/7801/index.do.
A leading Canadian authority on unlawfully obtained evidence.

Ashworth, 'Redrawing the Boundaries of Entrapment' [2002] Crim LR 161.
An exploration of the questions to be answered about the limits of proactive policing and the boundaries of entrapment following the decision of the House of Lords in *R v Looseley and Attorney General's Reference (No 3 of 2000)* [2001] 1 WLR 2060.

Choo and Nash, 'Improperly obtained evidence in the Commonwealth: lessons for England and Wales?' (2007) 11 E&P 75.
A selective review of comparative approaches to the admissibility of improperly obtained evidence in Australia, Canada, and New Zealand from which general principles are derived to guide future development of English law in conformity with the European Convention on Human Rights.

Giannoulopoulos, 'The exclusion of improperly obtained evidence in Greece: putting constitutional rights first' (2007) 11 E&P 181.
An examination of the Greek rules for the automatic exclusion of improperly obtained evidence that sheds light on the protection of constitutional rights as a rationale for exclusion.

Guo, 'Exclusion of illegally obtained confessions in China: an empirical perspective' (2017) 21 E&P 30.
An article based on a comprehensive empirical survey of the implementation of the exclusionary rule contained in China's Criminal Procedure Law. The article addresses three key issues prominent in the empirical survey: (i) how an illegally obtained confession is defined; (ii) proving that confessions are obtained by illegal means; and (iii) hearings to suppress the use of illegally obtained evidence.

Mahoney, 'Abolition of New Zealand's Prima Facie Exclusionary Rule' [2003] Crim LR 607.
A critical review of the evolution in New Zealand's handling of improperly obtained evidence from a prima facie exclusionary rule to a 'balancing approach' which considers a variety of factors in determining admissibility.

Ormerod, 'ECHR and the Exclusion of Evidence: Trial Remedies for Article 8 Breaches' [2003] Crim LR 61.
An examination of the extent to which breaches of Art 8 of the European Convention on Human Rights in a criminal investigation should render inadmissible the evidence obtained as a result.

Privy Council Review of Intercept as Evidence, Cm 7324 (2008), accessible at: http://www.official-documents.gov.uk/document/cm73/7324/7324.pdf.
The outcome of a Privy Council review with the following terms of reference: 'To advise on whether a regime to allow the use of intercepted material in court can be devised that facilitates bringing cases to trial while meeting the overriding imperative to safeguard national security'.

Rasiah, '*A v Secretary of State for the Home Department (No 2)*: Occupying the Moral High Ground?' (2006) 69 MLR 995.
A critical review of the leading English authority on evidence obtained by torture.

Zuckerman, *The Principles of Criminal Evidence* (Oxford, 1989) Ch 16.
This chapter analyses the nature of the problem posed by improperly obtained evidence, the shortcomings of the exclusionary principle, the principle of legitimacy, the English approach, and a policy of accountability.

---

[186] *R v Allan* [2005] Crim LR 716, CA.

QUESTION

One evening, Dave, in his local pub, started a conversation at the bar with Pete, whom he had never met before. Pete was a police officer, but Dave was unaware of this. Pete was off duty and not wearing his uniform. Dave said that he was about to divorce his wife but was angry that he would be likely to have to pay her monthly maintenance payments of about £2,000 even though it was she who had brought the marriage to an end by having an adulterous relationship. Pete then said, 'Well, I can get rid of her, and her lover as well. If that's what you want, meet me here tomorrow at 7pm'.

At 7pm on the following evening, Dave joined Pete in the pub. Pete secretly tape-recorded the conversation, which proceeded as follows.

Pete: 'So, can you get me the address of your wife's lover and £30,000 in cash?'

Dave: 'Yeah.'

Pete: 'Then I will shoot the pair of them at a time when you are a long way away in a public place and with a lot of friends.'

Dave: 'Do you need a gun? I've got one that's ideal for the job.'

Pete: 'No, I've got my own. Have we got a deal?'

Dave: 'It's a deal.'

At that point, Pete revealed that he was a police officer and arrested Dave for soliciting to murder.

What evidential issues are likely to arise at the trial and how are they likely to be resolved?

For a note-form answer see the online resources, accessible at
www.oup.com/he/keane-mckeown13e.

Hearsay in criminal cases

12

Key issues

- In criminal proceedings, when and why should hearsay (a statement made out of court and tendered as evidence of facts asserted) be excluded or admitted?

- If a statement is made out of court but is *not* tendered as evidence of facts asserted, when and why should it be admitted in criminal proceedings?

- Should the definition of hearsay cover:

  - assertions that may be inferred from a person's out-of-court statement;

  - out-of-court statements tendered as evidence of the non-existence of a fact; and

  - statements produced by computers or machines?

- To what extent is the admission of hearsay compatible with Article 6 of the European Convention on Human Rights?

- Where hearsay is admissible, what safeguards may be needed to address risks of unfair prejudice?

Background and rationale

This chapter covers the meaning of hearsay in criminal proceedings. It also deals with all but one of the categories of hearsay admissible by statute in such proceedings. The exceptional category, confessions, merits the discrete treatment given to it in **Chapter 15**. It is also convenient to consider separately the subsisting common law rules governing the admissibility of hearsay evidence in criminal proceedings. They are considered in **Chapter 14**.

Under the common law rule against hearsay, any assertion, other than one made by a person while giving oral evidence in the proceedings, was inadmissible if tendered as evidence of the facts asserted.[1] The rule operated to prevent advocates from eliciting such evidence from any witness, whether in examination-in-chief or cross-examination[2] and applied to assertions in documents as well as oral assertions. The rule is perhaps best explained by way of example. Suppose that A, who witnessed an act of dangerous driving, some weeks later said to B that the car in question was blue and at that time also made a written note to this effect. B reported to C what A had said to him. If A is called as a witness in proceedings concerned with the incident, he may of course make a statement from the witness box when giving his evidence that the colour of the car he saw was blue. However, evidence may not be given by A, B, or C, to establish the colour of the car, of the earlier oral statement which A made out of court. Nor would A's earlier *written* statement be admissible to establish the colour of the car. In respect of B or C, neither could give evidence of the colour of the car because they themselves had not seen it, and this remains the case whether or not they disclose that they had no first-hand knowledge of the colour of the car.[3]

The example given may be simple enough, but the common law rule against hearsay was highly complex, technical, difficult to describe with accuracy, and unclear in its scope. It was also subject to a variety of common law and statutory exceptions, and these too were often complex and technical in nature, and some were ill-considered and subject to frequent amendment.[4] In criminal cases, the meaning of hearsay and the circumstances in which it is admissible, are now governed by Chapter 2 of Pt 11 of the Criminal Justice Act 2003 (the 2003 Act).

A number of reasons have been advanced to justify the rule against hearsay, including the danger of manufactured evidence and, in respect of oral hearsay, especially multiple oral hearsay (eg C testifies as to what B told him A had said), the danger of inaccuracy or mistake by reason of repetition. The principal rationale of the common law rule was summarized by Lord Bridge in *R v Blastland*:[5]

> Hearsay evidence is not excluded because it has no logically probative value . . . The rationale of excluding it as inadmissible, rooted as it is in the system of trial by jury, is a recognition of the great difficulty, even more acute for a juror than for a trained judicial mind, of assessing what,

---

[1] Per Lord Havers in *R v Sharp* [1988] 1 WLR 7, HL and per Lords Ackner and Oliver in *R v Kearley* [1992] 2 AC 228, HL at 255 and 259 respectively. The rule also extended to out-of-court statements of otherwise admissible *opinion* (see Ch 20).

[2] *R v Thomson* [1912] 3 KB 19, CCA (see Ch 7, p 218).

[3] Cf *R v Rothwell* (1994) 99 Cr. App. R. 388, CA.

[4] See the Criminal Evidence Act 1965, replaced by ss 68–72 of the Police and Criminal Evidence Act 1984, in turn replaced by ss 23–28 of the Criminal Justice Act 1988, which contained serious drafting errors and were subsequently repealed by s 136 of the Criminal Justice Act 2003.

[5] [1986] AC 41, HL at 53 and 54.

if any, weight can properly be given to a statement by a person whom the jury have not seen or heard and who has not been subject to any test of reliability by cross-examination . . . The danger against which this fundamental rule provides a safeguard is that untested hearsay evidence will be treated as having a probative force which it does not deserve.

On the other hand, evidence of virtually unquestionable reliability had been excluded under the rule; cross-examination has been said to be arguably the poorest technique employed to elicit accurate testimony;[6] and there are dangers in deciding veracity on the basis of demeanour.[7] That the danger to which Lord Bridge referred can be overstated was recognized in the Report of the Royal Commission of Criminal Justice.[8] A reference to the Law Commission led to a consultation paper[9] and a final report.[10] The Commission favoured retention of the rule but proposed a statutory formulation of both the rule and some of the exceptions to it, an expansion of the exceptions, and a 'safety valve' discretion to admit sufficiently reliable hearsay evidence not covered by any of the exceptions.[11] Subsequently, the Auld Report[12] recommended an alternative approach, that hearsay should be admissible if the original source or 'best evidence' is not available. This approach would have placed much greater trust in the fact finders to give hearsay evidence the weight it deserves. 'Many are of the view that both [judges and magistrates] are already more competent than we give them credit for assessing the weight of the evidence, including hearsay evidence.'[13] Greater trust in the fact finders would also have followed if the Government had accepted the plea, made during the passage of the 2003 Act through the House of Lords, for a simple rule giving judges a wide discretionary power. Lord Ackner referred to a paper, written by Lord Chief Justice Woolf and supported by all the judges of the criminal division of the Court of Appeal, in which he said:[14]

> If we have got to the stage where it is considered that it is safe to allow juries to hear hearsay evidence, then we must be accepting that they can be trusted to use that evidence in accordance with the directions of the judge. Instead of the detailed and complex provisions which are contained in Chapter 2, what is needed is a simple rule putting the judge in charge of what evidence is admissible and giving him the responsibility of ensuring that the jury use the evidence in an appropriate manner.

The Government rejected both this plea and the approach favoured by Auld LJ. The provisions relating to hearsay in Chapter 2 of Pt 11 of the 2003 Act are, in very large measure, based on the proposals of the Law Commission.[15]

---

[6] Australian Law Reform Commission Research Paper No 8 (1982), *Manner of Giving Evidence* ch 10, para 5. See also Law Commission Consultation Paper No 138 (1995), *Evidence in Criminal Proceedings: The Hearsay Rule and Related Topics*, paras 6.49 and 6.62.

[7] See Law Commission Consultation Paper No 138, paras 6.22 and 6.27.

[8] Cm 2263 (1993).

[9] Consultation Paper No 138 (see n 7).

[10] Law Com No 245, *Evidence in Criminal Proceedings: Hearsay and Related Topics*, Cm 3670 (1997).

[11] For a critique of the Report, see Tapper, 'Hearsay in Criminal Cases: An Overview of Law Commission Report No 245' [1997] Crim LR 771.

[12] *Review of the Criminal Courts of England and Wales* (2001).

[13] Ibid, ch 11, para 98.

[14] Hansard HL vol 654 cols 752–3 (4 Nov 2003).

[15] For a critique of the statutory framework, see Birch, 'Criminal Justice Act 2003 (4) Hearsay: Same Old Story, Same Old Song?' [2004] Crim LR 556.

Admissibility of hearsay under the Criminal Justice Act 2003

Overview of the statutory scheme

The only heads under which hearsay is admissible in criminal proceedings are set out in s 114(1) of the 2003 Act. Section 114(1), which is subject to discretionary powers to exclude hearsay,[16] provides as follows:

(1) In criminal proceedings[17] a statement not made in oral evidence in the proceedings is admissible as evidence of any matter stated if, but only if—

    (a) any provision of this Chapter or any other statutory provision makes it admissible,

    (b) any rule of law preserved by s 118 makes it admissible,

    (c) all parties to the proceedings agree to it being admissible, or

    (d) the court is satisfied that it is in the interests of justice for it to be admissible.

Concerning the first part of s 114(1)(a), the categories of hearsay rendered admissible under the provisions of Chapter 2 of Pt 11 of the 2003 Act are (i) statements made by persons who are not available as witnesses (s 116); (ii) statements in business and other documents (s 117); (iii) certain inconsistent and other previous statements of witnesses (s 120); (iv) statements on which an expert will in evidence base an opinion (s 127); and, by virtue of s 128(1) of the 2003 Act, (v) confessions admissible on behalf of a co-accused.[18] Concerning the second part of s 114(1)(a), the phrase 'any other statutory provision' means any provision contained in, or in an instrument made under, the 2003 Act or any other Act, including any Act passed after the 2003 Act.[19] These statutory provisions are considered in this chapter,[20] except those relating to confessions, which are considered in **Chapter 15**.

As to s 114(1)(b), the rules of law preserved by s 118 are most, but not all, of the common law rules providing for the admissibility of various categories of hearsay. With the exception of the rules preserved by s 118, the common law rules governing the admissibility of hearsay evidence in criminal proceedings are abolished.[21] The statute abolishes the common law rule as well as the exceptions which it does not preserve.[22] Some of the rules preserved by s 118—statements in public documents, works of reference, evidence of age, evidence of reputation, and statements forming part of the *res gestae*—are considered in **Chapter 14**. It is convenient to consider the remainder of the preserved rules in other parts of this work: mixed statements in **Chapter 6**; confessions, admissions by agents, and statements made by a party to a common enterprise in **Chapter 15**; and the rule whereby an expert may draw on the body of expertise relevant to his field in **Chapter 20**.

---

[16] See s 126, considered, in this chapter, under **Discretion to exclude**, p 401.

[17] 'Criminal proceedings' means criminal proceedings in relation to which the strict rules of evidence apply: s 134(1). These include proceedings under the Criminal Procedure (Insanity) Act 1964, s 4A: *R v Chal* [2008] 1 Cr App R 247 (18), CA.

[18] See s 76A, Police and Criminal Evidence Act 1984, Ch 15. Section 128(2) of the 2003 Act provides that, subject to s 128(1), nothing in Ch 2 of Pt 11 makes a confession by an accused admissible if it would not be admissible under the Police and Criminal Evidence Act 1984, s 76.

[19] The 2003 Act, s 134(1).

[20] See, in this chapter, under **Written statements under s 9 of the Criminal Justice Act 1967**, p 409 and **Depositions of vulnerable children and young persons under section 43 of the Children and Young Persons Act 1933**, p 410.

[21] The 2003 Act, s 118(1)2.

[22] *R v Singh* [2006] 1 WLR 1564, CA.

Section 114(1)(c) permits hearsay to be admissible where the prosecution, the accused, and any co-accused agree to it being admissible.[23] Finally, s 114(1)(d) provides for the admissibility of hearsay which it would be in the interests of justice to admit, that is, hearsay admissible by exercise of the inclusionary discretion.

Under s 114(3):

Nothing in this Chapter affects the exclusion of evidence of a statement on grounds other than the fact that it is a statement not made in oral evidence in the proceedings.

Thus if hearsay evidence falls to be excluded because it is irrelevant or inadmissible on grounds of public policy, privilege or because of any other exclusionary rule of evidence, it will still fall to be excluded notwithstanding that it is otherwise admissible hearsay.

The statutory scheme provides safeguards where hearsay is sought to be admitted under s 114(1): (i) the right under s 123 to admit evidence which casts doubt on the *capability* of the maker of the statement; (ii) the right under s 124 to admit evidence which casts doubt on the *credibility* of the maker of the statement; (iii) the power of a judge under s 127 to stop a case where he is satisfied that the hearsay evidence is unconvincing to the extent that it might render a conviction unsafe; and (iv) a discretionary power to exclude evidence under s 126. These safeguards are also considered in this chapter.

The statutory scheme and Art 6 of the European Convention on Human Rights

Before looking at the statutory scheme in detail, it is necessary to consider, in relation to hearsay statements of absent witnesses, its compatibility with Art 6(3)(d) of the European Convention on Human Rights. Article 6(3)(d) states that an accused has the right to examine witnesses against him as part of his right to a fair and public hearing under Art 6(1).[24] The relationship between the hearsay provisions of the 2003 Act and Art 6 has been considered, in this respect, in a number of important cases in both the domestic courts and the European Court of Human Rights, and important principles have been laid down.

'A statement' to which Art 6 applies

Concerning statements to which Art 6 applies, in none of the decided cases in Strasbourg jurisprudence has the expression 'witness' (in Art 6(3)(d)) been extended beyond persons who have provided statements to the authorities as part of the prosecutorial process. It is doubtful

---

[23] However, the leave of the judge may be required to ensure that potential public interest immunity issues are properly considered. See *R v DJ* [2010] 2 Cr App R 8 (2), CA, (social security files relating to a person other than the accused).

[24] By virtue of ss 2 and 3 of the Human Rights Act 1998, domestic courts must take into account judgments of the European Court of Human Rights and domestic legislation must be read and given effect in a way which is compatible with rights set out in the European Convention on Human Rights. See also *R (Hicks) v Commissioner of Police of the Metropolis* [2014] EWCA Civ 3: the domestic courts have a general duty to enforce domestically enacted Convention Rights and to follow an interpretation of the Grand Chamber of the European Court of Human Rights unless it is apparent that it has misunderstood or overlooked a significant feature of domestic law which, properly explained, would lead to that interpretation being reviewed by the Strasbourg Court in relation to domestic circumstances. The duty also applies where there is a 'clear and consistent' line of decisions of the Strasbourg court, other than a decision of the Grand Chamber.

then whether the admission of statements less formal than a witness statement, deposition, or business documents would infringe the rights of the accused under Art 6(3)(d). The jurisprudence on Art 6(3)(d) is therefore of principal relevance where the prosecution seek to admit hearsay evidence under s 116 or s 114(1)(d).[25]

Article 6 and statements of absent witnesses

Article 6 of the European Convention on Human Rights provides:

> (1) In the determination . . . of any criminal charge against him, everyone is entitled to a fair and public hearing . . .
>
> (3) Everyone charged with a criminal offence has the following minimum rights:
>
> . . .
>
> (d) to have examined witnesses against him and to obtain the attendance and examination of witnesses on his behalf under the same conditions as witnesses against him.

The leading domestic authority on the relationship between Art 6 and the hearsay provisions of the 2003 Act is *R v Horncastle*.[26] In *R v Horncastle*, the Supreme Court dealt with two appeals. In the first, *R v Horncastle and Blackmore*, the hearsay statement of the victim of a serious assault was admitted under s 116(2)(a) of the 2003 Act because he had died before the trial for reasons unconnected to the assault. In the second appeal, *R v Marquis and Graham*, the hearsay statement of a witness was admitted under s 116(2)(e) because the witness was too frightened to attend to give evidence. In both appeals, the Supreme Court concluded that there had been no violation of the appellants' rights under Art 6 by admitting the statements, even though in the first appeal the hearsay evidence was 'to a decisive degree the basis upon which the appellants were convicted.'[27] The Supreme Court affirmed the earlier decision of the Court of Appeal in *R v Horncastle*,[28] in which the following principles were stated:

1. The admissibility of evidence is a matter for the national court.

2. The ordinary rule, sometimes known as the right of confrontation, is that a witness must be examined in court.

3. The term 'witness' has an autonomous meaning for the purposes of Art 6, which includes a person who has given information to the police which is relied on in the trial process.

4. The right in Art 6(3)(d) is not absolute or unqualified and there may be circumstances which justify a departure from it. Thus, to use as evidence witness statements or depositions obtained at the pre-trial stage, whether by police or an investigating judge, is not in itself inconsistent with Art 6(1) and (3)(d).

---

[25] See, eg, *R v L* [2009] 1 WLR 626, CA. Where hearsay evidence takes the form of a statement made by a person who is also called to give evidence at trial, for example, because it is admitted under s 119 or s 120, and is therefore available for questioning, it is submitted that there can be no question of its admission being in breach of Art 6(3)(d). See, eg, *R v Xhabri* [2006] 1 Cr App R 413 (26), CA, at [44].

[26] [2010] 2 AC 373, SC.

[27] At [110].

[28] *R v Horncastle* [2009] 2 Cr App R 230 (15), CA.

5. In departing from the Art 6(3)(d) right, the Convention rights of witnesses are engaged and material. Contracting states should organize their criminal proceedings in such a way that those rights are not unjustifiably imperilled.

6. Departure from the right to confrontation must not be taken without careful consideration, thought and analysis of (a) the circumstances in which the statements to be relied upon were made; and (b) the reasons for the witness not being called and made available for examination. Any departure from the right must then be justified.[29]

7. Where evidence is relied upon which is not given orally by the witness who is available to be examined by the accused, the rights of the defence must be respected. There is a requirement for 'counterbalancing measures' sufficient to compensate for the restrictions placed on the defence. However, where the evidence in question is only part of the evidence relied upon there need be no counterbalancing measures.

Article 6 and statements of witnesses which are 'sole or decisive'

In *R v Horncastle*, the Supreme Court addressed a difficult question which had arisen in both Strasbourg and domestic jurisprudence, namely whether a breach of Art 6 occurs where a conviction is based solely or to a decisive degree on depositions or statements made by someone whom the accused has had no opportunity to question. The Court of Appeal in *R v Horncastle*[30] had declined to follow the Strasbourg court's decision in *Al Khawaja and Tahery v UK*,[31] in which the Strasbourg court doubted that a breach of Art 6 could ever be avoided by counterbalancing measures in a situation where an untested statement was the 'sole or decisive' basis for a conviction.[32] The Court of Appeal in *R v Horncastle* held that Chapter 2 of Pt II of the 2003 Act contained a 'crafted code' intended to ensure that hearsay evidence—including evidence that might be referred to as 'sole or decisive' in Strasbourg jurisprudence—is admitted only when it is fair to do so.[33] The 2003 Act, the court said, allowed the defence to test the credibility of evidence (s 124) and contained an overriding safeguard in the power of the judge to stop a trial where the evidence is unconvincing (s 125). Therefore, provided the provisions of the Act are properly applied, there is no breach of Art 6 or in particular Art 6(3)(d), even if the conviction is based solely or to a decisive degree on hearsay.[34] The Supreme Court[35] affirmed this decision and Lord Phillips' conclusions may be summarized as follows:

1. Long before the Convention of 1953, the common law had by the hearsay rule addressed that aspect of a fair trial which Art 6(3)(d) was designed to ensure.

---

[29] See also *R v Jones* [2015] EWCA Crim 1317: courts have a duty to follow due process before the admission of hearsay evidence in order to ensure the accused's rights under Art 6 are respected, even where the accused's defence is fanciful.

[30] [2009] 2 Cr App R 230 (15).

[31] (2009) 49 EHRR 1. The Strasbourg court relied on *Luca v Italy* (2003) EHHR 807.

[32] See also *Doorson v Netherlands* (1996) 22 EHRR 330 at [76].

[33] *R v Horncastle* [2009] 2 Cr App R 230 (15) at [16].

[34] See also *R v Xhabri* [2006] 1 Cr App R 413 (26).

[35] *R v Horncastle* [2010] 2 AC 373, SC.

2. Parliament has since enacted exceptions to the hearsay rule required in the interests of justice which are not subject to a 'sole or decisive' rule, such a rule being unnecessary because of safeguards in the regime enacted in Parliament.

3. The European procedure has not, by contrast, addressed that aspect of a fair trial which Art 6(3)(d) was designed to ensure.

4. The Strasbourg court itself has recognized that exceptions to Art 6(3)(d) are required in the interests of justice.

5. The manner in which the Strasbourg court has approved those exceptions has resulted in jurisprudence which lacks clarity.

6. The sole or decisive rule has been introduced into the Strasbourg jurisprudence without discussion of the principle underlying it or full consideration of whether there was justification for it as an overriding principle which applied equally to continental and common law jurisdictions.

7. Although English law does not include the sole or decisive rule it would, in almost all cases, have reached the same result in those cases where the Strasbourg court had invoked the rule.

8. The decision in *Al Khawaja and Tahery v UK* does not establish that it is necessary to apply the sole or decisive rule in this jurisdiction.

Following this and pursuant to a request by the United Kingdom Government, the decision in *Al Khawaja and Tahery v UK*[36] was referred to the Grand Chamber of the European Court of Human Rights. In *Al Khawaja and Tahery v UK*,[37] the Grand Chamber held that the same standard of review under Art 6(1) and 6(3)(d) applies 'irrespective of the legal system from which a case emanates'[38] and the primary concern under Art 6(1) is to evaluate the overall fairness of proceedings, taking into account the rights of the defence, the interests of the public and victims who expect crimes to be prosecuted, and, where necessary, the rights of witnesses.[39] The Grand Chamber stated that the general rule under Art 6(3)(d) is that before an accused can be convicted, all the evidence against him must normally be produced in his presence at a public hearing so that it can be challenged.[40] Exceptions to the general rule were possible, but this was subject to two requirements. First, there must be a good reason for the non-attendance of the witness. Second, when a conviction is based solely or to a decisive degree on statements, whether during investigation or at the trial, rights of the defence may not be restricted to an extent that it is incompatible with the guarantees provided by Art 6 (the so-called, 'sole or decisive' rule).[41] Defining 'sole or decisive' hearsay, the Grand Chamber stated that a conviction based 'solely' on hearsay evidence is a conviction where hearsay was the only evidence in the case, while a conviction based to a 'decisive degree' on hearsay evidence occurs where the evidence is of such significance, it is likely to be determinative of the outcome of the case. Where the hearsay evidence is supported by other corroborative evidence, whether it is 'decisive' will depend on the strength of the supportive evidence: the

---

[36] (2009) 49 EHRR 1.

[37] (2012) 54 EHRR 23, Crim LR [2012] 375.

[38] (2012) 54 EHRR 23 at [130].

[39] Ibid at [118]. See also *Price v UK* [2016] ECHR 55287/10 at [113].

[40] (2012) 54 EHHR 23 at [118].

[41] Ibid at [119].

stronger the corroborative evidence, the less likely that the evidence will be decisive.[42] In relation to the so-called 'sole or decisive rule' itself, the Grand Chamber held that justifications for the rule remain valid (hearsay may be 'designedly untruthful or simply erroneous' and the accused may be unable to challenge the case against him effectively),[43] but the rule is not an absolute rule and may operate flexibly. Accordingly, a conviction based solely or decisively on hearsay may not necessarily breach an accused's rights under Art 6(3)(d) if there are sufficient counterbalancing factors, including strong procedural safeguards and measures that permit a fair and proper assessment of the reliability of that evidence.[44] The Grand Chamber recognized that the safeguards contained in the Criminal Justice Act 2003, supported by those contained in the Police and Criminal Evidence Act 1984 and the common law, are, in principle, strong safeguards designed to ensure fairness.[45]

Any difference between Horncastle and Al Khawaja?

As a result of the decision of the Grand Chamber in *Al Khawaja and Tahery v UK*, Strasbourg jurisprudence accommodates *R v Horncastle* in respect of hearsay statements admitted under the 2003 Act which are sole or decisive. Indeed, many of the principles stated by the Grand Chamber in its judgment in *Al Khawaja and Tahery v UK* are in essence the same as the principles stated in the judgment in *R v Horncastle*, albeit that they may be expressed in a different way and albeit that in the two judgments there were disagreements about the justification for the sole or decisive rule, its precision, and its practicality in English criminal proceedings.[46]

That differences between the principles stated in *R v Horncastle* and *Al Khawaja and Tahery v UK* may be more a matter of form than substance was recognized in *R v Riat*.[47] In *R v Riat*, the Court of Appeal set down five 'central' propositions to be adhered to by the Crown Courts in England and Wales when dealing day to day with hearsay evidence: (i) the law is and must be accepted to be, as stated in UK statute, namely the Criminal Justice Act 2003; (ii) where there is any difference between the judgments in *R v Horncastle* and *Al Khawaja and Tahery v UK*, the obligation is to follow *R v Horncastle*; (iii) both decisions state the same principle that the importance of the hearsay evidence is a vital consideration regarding its admissibility and treatment, but there is no over-arching rule in Strasbourg law or English law that 'sole or decisive' hearsay is automatically inadmissible; (iv) a Crown Court judge need not ordinarily concern himself or herself with close analysis of the relationship between the two

---

[42] Ibid at [131]. For examples of decisive hearsay in domestic case law, see *R v Ibrahim* [2012] 2 Cr App R 420 (32), CA, *R v Tahery* [2013] EWCA Crim 1053, and *R v Lawrence* [2014] 1 Cr App R 33 (5), CA. For examples of hearsay which was not decisive because of other supportive evidence, see *R v J* [2011] EWCA Crim 3021, *R v Horsnell* [2012] EWCA Crim 227, *R v M* [2014] EWCA Crim 1457, *R v Harvey* [2014] EWCA Crim 54, and *R v Friel* [2012] EWCA Crim 2871 (multiple hearsay).

[43] A justification stated previously in *Kotovski v Netherlands* (1989) 12 EHRR 434. To emphasize the justification, the Grand Chamber cited, at [142], a passage from the judgment of Sedley LJ in *Secretary of State for the Home Department* v *AF* [2009] 2 WLR 423, CA(Civ) at [113]: '[it] is seductively easy to conclude that there can be no answer to a case of which you have heard only one side . . . experience shows that the reliability of evidence, including evidence which appears cogent and convincing, may look very different when subject to a searching examination [and the] dangers in allowing untested hearsay to be adduced are all the greater if that evidence is the sole or decisive evidence against the defendant.'

[44] (2012) 54 EHRR 23 at [146]–[147]. See also *Price v UK* [2016] ECHR 15602/07 at [114](vii).

[45] (2012) 54 EHRR 23 at [151].

[46] See *R v Horncastle* [2010] 2 AC 373 at [87]–[90] and *Al Khawaja and Tahery v UK* (2012) 54 EHRR 23 at [129]–[146].

[47] [2013] 1 WLR 2592, CA.

strands of jurisprudence and generally need look no further than *R v Horncastle*; (v) neither under statute, nor under *Horncastle*, can hearsay simply be treated as if it were first-hand evidence and automatically admissible.[48] These five propositions are addressed to the Crown Courts; in relation to the approach to be taken by the Court of Appeal, in *R v Ibrahim*,[49] it was stated that the obligation is also to follow *R v Horncastle*, other than in wholly exceptional circumstances.[50]

Article 6 and statements which may or may not be sole or decisive

In *Schatschaschwili v Germany*,[51] the Grand Chamber stated that counterbalancing factors should also be considered where it is unclear whether the evidence is sole or decisive, but the evidence nevertheless carries significant weight and might handicap the accused in his defence.[52] In relation to counterbalancing factors, they must permit a fair and proper assessment of the reliability of the evidence, but, relative to the importance of the evidence, where there are sufficient factors, there will be no breach of Art 6.[53] It is submitted that this principle is obviously of general relevance to the admissibility of statements under the hearsay provisions of the 2003 Act, where the statements are significant but it is unclear whether they are sole or decisive. In *Price v UK*[54] for example, the Strasbourg court held that there had been no breach of Art 6 where the accused was convicted of drugs importation after a trial in which the hearsay statements of a witness were admitted under s 116(2)(e), the witness being absent due to fear. Although it was not in a position to reach a firm conclusion on whether there was a good reason for the witness's non-attendance, the court held that this was not the only consideration.[55] Other substantial evidence supported the witness's statements and incriminated the accused, and, relative to the importance of the evidence, there were sufficient procedural safeguards and counterbalancing factors.[56] These included the procedural safeguards in the statutory scheme and the judge's careful summing-up in which he expressly cautioned the jury about the limitations of the evidence of the absent witness.[57]

Article 6 and the reasons for non-attendance

In *Al Khawaja and Tahery v UK*, the Grand Chamber stated that before a hearsay statement can be admitted, the first requirement is that there must be a good reason for the non-attendance of the witness.[58] However, in a significant retreat from this principle, the Grand Chamber

---

[48] At [2]. See also *R(RJM) v SSWP* [2009] 1 AC 311 at [64]; *R v Ibrahim* [2012] 2 Cr App R 420 (32), CA at [87]; and *R v Tahery* [2013] EWCA Crim 1053 at [6].

[49] [2012] 2 Cr App R 420 (32).

[50] At [87].

[51] [2015] ECHR 1113.

[52] At [115]–[116]. See also *Price v UK* [2016] ECHR 15602/07 at [115]–[116].

[53] See *Schatschachswili v Germany* [2015] ECHR 1113 at [116].

[54] [2016] ECHR 15602/07.

[55] At [121].

[56] At [124]–[127].

[57] At [128]–[130].

[58] (2012) 54 EHRR 23 at [119].

in *Schatschaschwili v Germany*[59] stated that the admission of hearsay where there is no good reason for the non-attendance of a witness is a very important factor, but is not conclusive of a breach of Art 6.[60] Additionally, it was not always necessary to address this question first, especially if other questions concerning the importance of the evidence and the strength of counterbalancing factors appear to be particularly conclusive of the fairness or unfairness of proceedings.[61]

The principle was applied in *Seton v UK*,[62] a gang and drugs related murder where the statement of a 'reluctant witness' was admitted in the interests of justice under s 114(1)(d) of the Criminal Justice Act 2003. The accused's defence was that he had not committed the murder and that P, a serving prisoner, was responsible. In a recorded telephone call from prison, P strongly refuted this and expressed outrage that he had been implicated, but made no comment when interviewed by the police and made it clear that he would not give evidence. The judge ruled that a transcript of P's telephone call was admissible under s 114(1)(d) to rebut the defence that P had committed the murder and the Court of Appeal held that the judge had been entitled to do so. Concerning whether a breach of Art 6 had occurred, the Strasbourg court held that this was not a case where the witness P was *unable* to attend, and the court was not persuaded that all reasonable efforts had been made to secure his attendance because, despite the witness's reluctance, it would have been possible to compel his attendance and if he refused to give evidence, the jury would still have been able to see him in the witness box and judge his demeanour.[63] However, applying *Schatschaschwili v Germany*,[64] the Strasbourg court stated that absence of a good reason, although a very important factor, was not conclusive of the fairness of the trial. Considering other relevant factors, the evidence against the accused was not sole or decisive and indeed the court noted that the Court of Appeal had found other evidence to be overwhelming.[65] In these circumstances, relative to the importance of the evidence of the absent witness, the court held there were sufficient counterbalancing measures to ensure a fair trial, namely procedural safeguards in the statutory scheme and the judge's warnings to the jury. Accordingly, no breach of Art 6 occurred. However, the decisions of both the Strasbourg court and the Court of Appeal in this case are difficult to reconcile with the decision of the Court of Appeal in *R v Freeman*,[66] where, applying *R v Horncastle*[67] and *R v Y*,[68] it was clearly stated that allowing s 114(1)(d) to be used to circumvent the requirements of s 116 would be contrary to the statutory scheme,[69] and that reluctance is not a ground for failing to make a witness attend and reading their statement is not an acceptable alternative.[70]

---

[59] [2015] ECHR 1113.

[60] At [112]–[113].

[61] At [117]–[118].

[62] [2016] ECHR 318. See also *R v Seton* [2010] EWCA Crim 450.

[63] At [62].

[64] [2015] ECHR 1113.

[65] [22]–[29] and [38]. See *R v Seton* [2010] EWCA Crim 450 at [28]–[29].

[66] [2010] EWCA Crim 1997.

[67] [2010] 2 WLR 47 at [31].

[68] [2008] EWCA Crim 10 at [58]–[59].

[69] *R v Freeman* [2010] EWCA Crim 1997 at [26].

[70] Per Moses LJ at [33]. See also Karl Laird, 'Commentary', *Seton v United Kingdom* [2016] Crim LR 653, ECHR at 655. See also n 233.

The meaning of hearsay in the Criminal Justice Act 2003

Original evidence

Under s 114(1) of the 2003 Act, hearsay is a statement not made in oral evidence in the proceedings 'admissible as evidence of any matter stated'. Statements not made in oral evidence which are hearsay fall to be distinguished from statements which are so called 'original evidence'. Statements not made in oral evidence which are admissible for any relevant purpose *other* than that of establishing any matter stated, are 'original evidence'. This distinction is difficult, but important, because whereas hearsay must meet the requirements of the 2003 Act to be admissible, original evidence is admissible simply on the basis that it is sufficiently relevant. Examples of original evidence may be classified according to whether they are admitted (i) simply to show that the statement was made, because that is a fact in issue in the proceedings; or (ii) because of their relevance to some other fact in issue in the proceedings.

The making of the statement as a fact in issue

If the making of a statement is itself a fact in issue in the proceedings, that statement, even if inadmissible as evidence of any matter stated, may be admitted as evidence of the fact that it was made.[71] For instance, on a charge of making a threat to kill, the victim may give evidence of the fact that the accused said to her, 'I am going to kill you'.[72]

The statement as evidence relevant to some other fact in issue

A statement may also be admissible as evidence of a fact relevant to some other fact in issue in the proceedings notwithstanding that the statement is inadmissible as evidence of any matter stated. Some examples follow.

The statement as evidence relevant to the state of mind of the person who makes it

In some cases the statement is admitted as evidence of the state of mind of its maker. Thus a man's assertion today that he is Napoleon, Emperor of France, may be tendered for the purpose of showing his insanity. In *Ratten v R*,[73] Ratten was convicted of murdering his wife by shooting her. His defence was that a gun went off accidentally while he was cleaning it. Evidence established that the shooting happened between 1.12pm and about 1.20pm, and a telephonist from the local exchange gave evidence that at 1.15pm she received a call from Ratten's house from a woman who was sobbing and who in an hysterical voice said, 'Get me the police please'. The Privy Council held that this evidence was not hearsay. It was relevant (i) to show that a call had been made, contrary to Ratten's denial that his wife had made a call; and (ii) as possibly showing that the wife was in a state of emotion or fear at an existing or impending emergency, which could rebut Ratten's defence that the shooting was

---

[71] But see *West Midlands Probation Board v French* [2009] 1 WLR 1715, DC concerning proceedings for breach of a licence issued to a serving prisoner on his release from imprisonment, in which the Divisional Court held that the licence was hearsay. It is submitted that this decision is incorrect as the licence was adduced not as evidence *of* the matters stated but simply as evidence of the fact that the matters *were* stated in the licence. See also Ormerod, 'Commentary' [2009] Crim LR 283.

[72] In *R v Rizwan Mawji* [2003] EWCA Crim 3067, where such a threat was contained in an e-mail sent from the accused's e-mail address, it was held that whether the jury accepted a printout of the e-mail as genuine was a matter manifestly for them.

[73] [1972] AC 378.

accidental.[74] *R v Ratten* was distinguished in *R v Blastland* where, on the facts of the case, statements showing knowledge of a third party were not relevant.[75] In *R v Blastland*, the House of Lords held that the accused, convicted of buggery and murder, had been properly prevented from adducing evidence of statements made by a third party indicating what *he* (the third party) knew of the murder before the body was found, in order to incriminate the third party. The only issue was whether the accused had committed the crimes and what was relevant to that issue was not the third party's knowledge but how he had acquired it; since he could have done so in a number of different ways, there was no rational basis on which the jury could infer that he, rather than the accused, was the murderer.

The statement as evidence relevant to the state of mind of the person who hears or reads it

In some cases, the statement is admitted as evidence of the state of mind of the person who heard or read it, that is, to show what the person who heard or read it, knew, thought, or believed. If A is charged with the murder of B, evidence of a statement by C to A that B was having an adulterous relationship with A's spouse, even if not admissible as evidence of the adulterous relationship, has an obvious relevance on the question of A's motive. In *Subramaniam v Public Prosecutor*[76] the accused was convicted of being in unlawful possession of ammunition. His defence was that he had been threatened by terrorists and acted under duress, but evidence of what the terrorists had said was excluded by the trial judge as inadmissible hearsay. Quashing the conviction, the Privy Council held that statements could have been made by the terrorists which, even if not admissible as evidence of matters stated, might reasonably have induced in the accused, if he believed them, an apprehension of instant death if he failed to conform to their wishes. Accordingly, the statements were admissible as potentially cogent evidence of duress.[77]

The statement as evidence of the fact that it is false

A statement may be admitted as original evidence where it is tendered for the purpose of allowing the tribunal of fact to conclude that its contents are false and to draw inferences from the falsity of those contents. An old but useful example is *A-G v Good*,[78] where the demonstrably false statement of a debtor's wife that her husband was not at home was admissible to show her husband's intention to defraud his creditors. If an unreasonable time had intervened between the demand for entrance and the opening of the door, that would have been a fact relevant to the issue, and the untrue statement of the wife was relevant in the same way. In *Mawaz Khan v R*[79] the appellants were convicted of murder.

---

[74] See also *R v Gilfoyle* [1996] 3 All ER 883, CA (suicide notes admissible as evidence of a woman's suicidal frame of mind and further statements made by her which showed that when she wrote the notes she had no intention of taking her own life) and *R v Gregson* [2003] 2 Cr App R 521 (34), CA (evidence that G had expressed concerns about how to dispose of a quantity of ecstasy tablets he had purchased admissible in relation to his intent to supply, the defence case being that he believed he was acquiring a much smaller amount).

[75] [1986] AC 41.

[76] [1956] 1 WLR 965, PC. See also *R v Willis* [1960] 1 WLR 55, CCA and *R v Madden* [1986] Crim LR 804, CA.

[77] See also *R v Davis* [1998] Crim LR 659, CA (evidence of a solicitor's advice to the accused was admissible for the purpose of establishing the accused's reason for not answering questions in interview). See also *R v A Ltd* [2016] 4 WLR 176, CA (evidence of entries in a company director's diary was admissible for the purpose of showing the intention of the director and, as 'a controlling mind' of the company, proving the company's guilt).

[78] (1825) M'Cle&Yo 286.

[79] [1967] 1 AC 454.

At the trial the prosecution relied on the fact that each of them had in his statement to the police sought to set up a joint alibi, many of the details of which were demonstrated to be false by other evidence. The Privy Council held that the trial judge was entitled to direct the jury that although a statement made by one of the accused in the absence of another was not evidence against the other, they were entitled to compare the statements of the two accused and, if they concluded that they were false, to draw the inference that the accused had cooperated after the alleged crime and jointly concocted the story out of a sense of guilt.[80]

The statement as evidence of the fact that an offer was made

In *Woodhouse v Hall*[81] the manageress of a sauna and massage parlour was charged with acting in the management of a brothel. Plain-clothes police officers, who had entered the premises as customers, alleged that they had been offered masturbation by the manageress and other women employed there. At the trial, the justices held that the police officers' evidence of the offers made to them was inadmissible hearsay and the case was dismissed. On the prosecutor's appeal by way of case stated, Donaldson LJ held that the evidence had been wrongly excluded: 'There is no question of the hearsay rule arising at all. The relevant issue was did these ladies make these offers?'[82] The very fact that such offers had been made was relevant to the central fact in issue, namely whether the premises were being used as a sauna and massage parlour or a brothel. As Lord Ackner pointed out in *R v Kearley*,[83] 'in order to establish that the premises are being used as a brothel it is sufficient to prove that at the premises more than one woman *offers* herself as a participant in physical acts of indecency for the sexual gratification of men'.[84]

The statement as evidence of an association between the accused and a document

A statement may be capable of establishing an association between the accused and a document which contains the statement. From the association, inferences may be drawn, for example in *Lydon*,[85] that the accused may have been present where the document was found and in *Rice*,[86] that the accused may have used the document. In *R v Lydon*, the appellant, whose first name was Sean, was convicted of robbery. His defence was alibi, but near the scene of the robbery two pieces of rolled paper and a gun were found. On the pieces of paper someone had written 'Sean rules' and 'Sean rules 85', and ink of similar appearance and composition to that on the paper was found on the gun barrel. The Court of Appeal held that evidence of the pieces of paper had been properly admitted as circumstantial evidence: if the jury were satisfied that the gun was used in the robbery and that the pieces of paper were linked to the gun, the references to Sean could be a fact which would fit in with the appellant

---

[80] See also *R v Binham* [1991] Crim LR 774, CA, where evidence of B's previous statements in support of his alibi defence, together with evidence as to their falsity, was admissible as original evidence.

[81] (1981) 72 Cr App R 39, DC.

[82] *Woodhouse v Hall* (1981) 72 Cr App R 39, DC at 42. Cf, *sed quaere*, *R v Lawal* [1994] Crim LR 746, CA.

[83] [1992] 2 AC 228, HL at 257.

[84] See *Kelly v Purvis* [1983] QB 663, DC.

[85] (1987) 85 Cr App R 221, CA.

[86] [1963] 1 QB 857, CCA.

having committed the offence.[87] In addition, the references were not hearsay because they were not being admitted as evidence of matters stated; they were not being admitted to show that Sean ruled. In *R v Rice* the accused were convicted of conspiracy. Part of the prosecution case involved proving that two accused, R and H, had taken a certain flight to Manchester. A used airline ticket, bearing the name of R and of another accused, M, was admitted in evidence against R. It was held that although the ticket was inadmissible hearsay if tendered for the truth of its contents, that is, as evidence that the booking was made by R or a man of that name, it had been properly admitted. Winn J said:[88]

> The relevance of that ticket in logic and its legal admissibility as a piece of real evidence both stem from the same root, viz., the balance of probability recognized by common sense and common knowledge that an air ticket which has been used on a flight and which has a name upon it has more likely than not been used by a man of that name or by one of two men whose names are upon it.

A statement as evidence of the use to which it can be put

A statement will not be hearsay where admitted to show the use to which it can be put. In *R v Amjad*,[89] the accused was convicted of being in possession of a document containing information likely to be useful to a person committing or preparing an act of terrorism. The police had conducted a search of the accused's home and found a notebook containing a handwritten list of fitness exercises for a *Mujahaddin* fighter, which may have been copied from open source material available on the internet. The Court of Appeal held that no issue of hearsay arose: the notebook was not being admitted as evidence of matters stated, but to enable the prosecution to prove its likely usefulness to a terrorist.

'Statements' and 'matters stated'

As we have seen from s 114(1), hearsay is 'a statement not made in oral evidence in the proceedings . . . admissible as evidence of any matter stated'. This formulation covers not only 'out-of-court' statements as such, but also statements made in previous criminal or civil proceedings. 'Oral evidence', for the purposes of s 114(1) and other provisions relating to hearsay in the 2003 Act, includes evidence which, by reason of any disability, disorder, or other impairment, a person called as a witness gives in writing or by signs or by way of any device.[90]

---

[87] See also *R v McIntosh* [1992] Crim LR 651, CA (calculations concerning the purchase and sale prices of 12 oz of an unnamed commodity, not in M's handwriting but found concealed in the chimney of a house where he had been living, admissible as circumstantial evidence tending to connect him with drug-related offences); *Roberts v DPP* [1994] Crim LR 926, DC (documents found at R's offices and home, including repair and gas bills and other accounts relating to certain premises, admissible as circumstantial evidence linking R with those premises, on charges of assisting in the management of a brothel and running a massage parlour without a licence); *R v Horne* [1992] Crim LR 304, CA; and cf *R v Chrysostomou* [2010] EWCA Crim 1403 (text messages requesting drugs showed a relationship of drugs supply between the accused and the sender).

[88] [1963] 1 QB 857 at 871.

[89] [2017] 1 Cr App R 331 (22), CA.

[90] The 2003 Act, s 134(1).

'A statement'

Under s 115(2), 'a statement' is 'any representation of fact or opinion made by a person by whatever means; and it includes a representation made in a sketch, photofit, or other pictorial form'. This is a very wide definition. It covers a statement of opinion, provided that it is admissible opinion of course,[91] as well as a statement of fact.[92] The statement may have been made unsworn or on oath by any person, whether or not a person called as a witness in the proceedings in question. The representation, however, must have been made by a person—statements in computer-generated documents are not covered. The admissibility of computer-generated documents is considered separately.[93]

The phrase 'any representation . . . by whatever means' clearly covers statements made orally as well as statements made in writing, whether by hand, or by means of a typewriter, word processor, computer, or other similar device. A good common law example of oral hearsay, which continues to be hearsay under the 2003 Act, is *R v Rothwell*,[94] a case of supplying heroin. The prosecution sought to rely on evidence that the accused was seen on several occasions passing small packages to various people, together with the evidence of a drugs squad officer that the recipients were known to him as heroin users. It was held that, insofar as the officer's evidence was based on statements made to him by others, for example the alleged recipients, then the evidence would be inadmissible hearsay; but that it would not be hearsay insofar as it was based on the recipients' convictions for possession of heroin[95] or, for example, the officer's personal observation of needle marks on the recipients' forearms or his personal knowledge of the recipients being in possession of heroin or receiving treatment for heroin addiction. An example of written hearsay is provided by *R v Horsnell*.[96] The appellant was convicted of one count of conspiracy to produce cannabis and two counts of possession of criminal property. Evidence was admitted of extracts from the personal diary of the appellant's wife concerning his habit of storing large sums of cash in the family home. The diary was prepared by the wife on the advice of her solicitor because, in circumstances where her marriage to the appellant was in a poor state, the diary entries might assist in any divorce proceedings. The evidence was clearly hearsay under the 2003 Act,[97] but was admitted in the interests of justice under the exception in s 114(1)(d). The phrase 'any representation . . . by whatever means' is also wide enough to embrace statements made by conduct or signs and gestures, and statements made partly orally and partly by conduct or signs and gestures. An example of the latter is *R v Gibson*,[98] a trial for malicious wounding in which

---

[91] See the 2003 Act, s 114(3), in this chapter, under **Overview of the statutory scheme**, p 352.

[92] See also the Criminal Justice Act 1988, s 30, considered, in this chapter, under **Expert reports**, p 408.

[93] In this chapter, under **Statements produced by computers and mechanical and other devices**, p 371.

[94] (1994) 99 Cr App R 388, CA.

[95] Admissible under the Police and Criminal Evidence Act 1984, s 74 (see Ch 23, **Section 74(1) and (2): convictions of persons other than the accused**, p 767).

[96] [2012] EWCA Crim 227. See also useful examples which pre-date the 2003 Act: *R v Brown* [1991] Crim LR 835, CA (evidence of a name on an appliance, written hearsay and inadmissible to establish its ownership); and *Patel v Comptroller of Customs* [1966] AC 365, PC (evidence of a bag of seeds bearing the words, 'Produce of Morocco'). See also *R v Sealby* [1965] 1 All ER 701 (Crown Court); cf *R v Rice* [1963] 1 QB 857, CA.

[97] See s 115(3)(a). One purpose in making the diary entries was to cause another person to believe they were true. See also *R v N* (2007) 171 JPN 382, CA: a diary intended to be read by another would have been hearsay but admissible under s 119 as an inconsistent statement; if it was not intended to be read by another it would not have been hearsay, but would have been admissible as original evidence.

[98] (1887) LR 18 QBD 537, CCR.

the prosecutor gave evidence that after being hit by a stone, a woman, pointing to the door of a house, had said, 'The person who threw the stone went in there'. The Court of Appeal held that the woman's statement, which included her pointing, was hearsay. An example of a hearsay statement made solely by signs or gestures is provided by *Chandrasekera v R*.[99] The appellant was charged with murder and evidence was admitted that the victim, whose throat had been cut, had made certain signs, the effect of which was to indicate the accused. Then asked whether it was the accused who had cut her throat, she replied by nodding her head. In Lord Roche's opinion, an analogy could be drawn with a dumb person conversing by means of finger alphabet and held that the woman had effectively made a statement that the accused had cut her neck.

The inclusion, within the definition of 'a statement', of 'a representation made in a sketch, photofit or other pictorial form' reflects a principled approach which was lacking in some of the common law authorities.[100] Photographs and films are excluded from the definition and continue to be admissible, at common law, as a variety of real evidence, if relevant to the issues, including the important issues of whether an offence was committed and who committed it.[101]

Matters stated in statements: the purpose or one of the purposes of the person making the statement

Under the statutory formulation of hearsay, as we have seen, s 114(1) refers to a statement not made in oral evidence in the proceedings which is admissible as evidence of any 'matter stated'. Under s 115(3):

(3) A matter stated is one to which this Chapter applies if (and only if) the purpose, or one of the purposes, of the person making the statement appears to the court to have been—
   (a) to cause another person to believe the matter, or
   (b) to cause another person to act or a machine to operate on the basis that the matter is as stated.

The effect of s 115(3) is to narrow the ambit of s 114 so that it renders hearsay admissible as evidence of any matter stated under one of the heads set out in s 114(1) if and only if the purpose, or one of the purposes, of the person making the statement, was of the kind described in either s 115(3)(a) or s 115(3)(b). Under s 115(3)(a), the purpose, or one of the purposes, in making the statement is to cause another to believe the matter, that is, to accept that matter as true, whereas under s 115(3)(b) the purpose, or one of the purposes, in making the statement, is simply to cause another to act on the basis that the matter is as stated, that is, to act on the basis that the matter is true (or to cause a machine to operate on the basis that the matter is as stated). There appears to be considerable overlap between the two subsections, in that if the purpose is to cause another to act on the basis that a certain matter is as it has been stated, then whether or not that is the truth of the matter, the purpose, in many situations, will also be to cause the other to believe the matter. Section 115(3)(b) will apply, but not s 115(3)(a), where the purpose is to cause another to do no more than to act on the basis

---

[99] [1937] AC 220, PC.

[100] See *R v Cook* [1987] QB 417, CA, *R v Constantinou* (1989) 91 Cr App R 74, CA, and *R v Percy Smith* [1976] Crim LR 511, CA.

[101] See, eg, *R v Dodson and R v Williams* (1984) 79 Cr App R 220, (photographs), considered in Ch 9, **Visual Identification by the jury, p 288**. See also *R v Roberts* [1998] Crim LR 682, CA.

that the matter is as stated, and not to cause the other to believe the matter, perhaps because, for example, the maker of the statement is aware that the matter is not as stated or is unsure as to the truth of the matter.

Implied assertions and the interpretation of 'statements' and 'matters stated'

The Explanatory Notes to the 2003 Act state that the aim of s 115(3) is 'to overturn the ruling in *R v Kearley*[102] that "implied assertions" are covered by the hearsay rule and therefore prima facie inadmissible'. Implied assertions, which were treated as hearsay at common law, are assertions, whether made orally or in writing or by conduct, from which it is possible to infer a particular matter.[103] In *Kearley*, the police found drugs in K's flat, but not in sufficient quantities to raise the inference that he was a dealer. The police remained for several hours, intercepting ten telephone calls in which callers asked to speak to K and asked for drugs. Seven other people arrived at the flat, some with money, also asking for K and to be supplied with drugs, when K was either absent or not within earshot. At K's trial for possession with intent to supply, the officers who had intercepted the calls or received the visitors gave evidence of the conversations and K was convicted. Quashing the conviction, the House of Lords held by a majority of three to two: (i) that evidence of requests made by the callers and visitors was irrelevant because it could only be evidence of the state of mind or belief of those making the requests, when the issue at trial was whether K intended to supply drugs; and (ii) that insofar as the evidence was relevant to the issue of K's intent to supply, that is, as an implied assertion that K was a supplier, it was inadmissible hearsay, and it made no difference that there were a large number of such requests all made at the same place on the same day. The decision is open to criticism on the basis that the evidence could have been admitted as circumstantial evidence, that is, evidence from which K's intent to supply could be inferred.[104] Nonetheless, the effect of the decision was to classify implied assertions as hearsay and render them prima facie inadmissible.

The stated purpose of s 115(3)—to overturn the ruling in *Kearley*—is misleading because s 115(3) will operate to exclude from the ambit of s 114 some express as well as implied assertions. For example, if an express assertion is made by a person who is talking to himself and unaware that he is being overheard, or is contained in a memorandum or diary which is kept for purely personal purposes,[105] then plainly it is not among the purposes of the maker of the statement to cause another to believe the matter stated. Such statements are therefore not covered by, or subject to, s 114 of the 2003 Act. They would now be admissible, provided that they are relevant, and, if tendered by the prosecution, subject to the discretionary powers of exclusion. At first blush, it might be thought that s 115(3) might exclude from the ambit of s 114 an express assertion made with the purpose of causing another to *disbelieve* the matter

---

[102] [1992] 2 AC 228, HL.

[103] See, eg, *R v Van Vreden* (1973) 57 Cr App R 818 (written); *Teper v R* [1952] AC 480 (oral); *Chandrasekara v R* [1937] AC 220, PC (conduct); *Manchester Brewery Co Ltd v Coombs* (1901) 82 LT 347, Ch D at 34 (conduct); and *Wright v Doe d Tatham* (1837) 7 Ad&El 313, Ex Ch (written).

[104] See *R v Singh* [2006] 1 WLR 1564, CA per Rose LJ at [14]. See also *R v K* (2008) 172 JP 538, CA (an inquiry about the availability and price of specific drugs made by a person during a telephone call to the defendant was held to have been correctly admitted as evidence from which it could properly be inferred that the defendant was a person concerned in the supply of drugs).

[105] See, eg, *R v N* (2007) 171 JPN 382, CA; and cf *R v Horsnell* [2012] EWCA Crim 227 (a diary was hearsay because it was kept for the purpose of assisting in possible future divorce proceedings).

stated, as when the maker says, for example, 'Of course X was present . . . and pigs were flying!' However, such a statement would surely be treated as a statement made with the purpose of causing another to believe that X was absent. There may also be another sense in which the stated purpose of s 115(3) is misleading, if the narrow view of relevance expressed in *Kearley* still applies, namely that the relevance of the evidence was to the belief of the callers that K was a drugs dealer and not to K's intent to supply.[106] If the belief of the callers was not a relevant issue at trial then the evidence remains inadmissible regardless of whether the callers intended another to believe what they were saying.

In *R v Singh*,[107] it was baldly stated that 'when sections 114 and 118 are read together they . . . create . . . a new rule against hearsay which does not extend to implied assertions'.[108] *R v Singh* was approved in *R v Twist*.[109] In *R v Twist*, it was held that, by virtue of the 2003 Act, it was no longer necessary to examine statements to see whether they contained implied assertions. Hughes LJ stated:[110]

What is undoubted is that the Act abolishes the common law of hearsay except where it is expressly preserved; this court so held in *Singh* . . .

His Lordship went on to observe:[111]

The Act does not use the expression 'assertion'. Instead it speaks of a 'statement' and the 'matter stated' in it. This seems likely to have been because its framers wished to avoid the complex philosophical arguments which beset the common law, as explained in *DPP v Kearley* [1992] 2 AC 28, as to when an utterance contains an implied assertion . . .

. . .

It is therefore helpful, as it seems to us, that the Act avoids the use of the expression 'assertion' altogether, and with it the difficult concept of the 'implied assertion'.

The approach in R v Twist

In *R v Twist*, the Court of Appeal considered four appeals concerning the admissibility of text messages and laid down an approach to be taken when analysing whether a statement is hearsay under the 2003 Act.[112] It is instructive to first cite the approach and then consider how the approach was applied to the facts in each of the four appeals.

Generally . . . it is likely to be helpful to approach the question whether the hearsay rules apply in this way:

   i)   identify what relevant fact (matter) it is sought to prove;
   ii) ask whether there is a statement of that matter in the communication. If no, then no question of hearsay arises (whatever other matters may be contained in the communication);
   iii) if yes, ask whether it was one of the purposes (not necessarily the only or dominant purpose) of the maker of the communication that the recipient, or any other person, should believe that matter or act upon it as true? If yes, it is hearsay. If no, it is not

---

[106] See *R v Twist* [2011] 2 Cr App R 189 (17), CA at [20].
[107] [2006] 1 WLR 1564, CA.
[108] At [14].
[109] [2011] 2 Cr App R 189 (17) 17, CA.
[110] Ibid, at [3].
[111] At [8]–[9].
[112] At [17].

. . . As we have sought to explain, it no longer matters whether a statement is analysed as containing an implicit (or 'implied') assertion if the speaker's purpose does not include getting anyone else to accept it as true.[113]

In the first appeal, *Twist*, T had been convicted of possession of heroin with intent to supply. At his trial, evidence was admitted of 24 text messages received on two mobile phones over five days, which were mostly requests for drugs. For the prosecution, the messages were relevant to the issue of whether T was involved in the supply of drugs. Following its stated approach, the first step for the court to take was to identify the matter sought to be proved. This was obviously that the accused supplied drugs. Taking the second step, the court held that because the messages did not contain any statement that the accused supplied drugs (they were simply requests for drugs) they were not caught by the hearsay provisions. They were therefore admissible as relevant to show a relationship of 'buyer and seller' between the accused and the senders.

In the second appeal, *Boothman*, B had been convicted of possession of cannabis and cocaine with intent to supply and at his trial evidence was adduced of over 100 text messages sent to and by him. Many were orders for drugs, with some expressly referring to the number of 'lines' obtained from a recent supply. As with *Twist*, the messages were relevant to the issue whether B was involved in the supply of drugs. B had objected to their admissibility on the grounds that they were hearsay because the references to 'lines' were, according to the appellant, express representations of cocaine dealing relied on for their truth by the prosecution. It was held that the messages were not hearsay because, as in the first appeal, there was no statement in the messages of the matter which the prosecution sought to prove, namely that B was a supplier of drugs.

In the third appeal, *Tomlinson and Kelly*, T and K had been convicted of robbing two girls at gunpoint. Evidence was admitted of a text message sent to K on the morning of the robbery requesting a gun, which read, 'Need dat gun today so can sell it and give you lot da tenner back. Does faws still want it?' This was relevant to show that K was in possession of a gun and was involved in the gunpoint robbery. It was held that although the text message may have contained a statement that the appellants were in possession of a gun (the second step in the approach), the message was not hearsay. Applying s 115(3) and taking the third step, the purpose of the sender was not to cause the recipient to believe that he was in possession of a gun: this knowledge was assumed on the part of the sender. Hughes LJ stated, '. . . it was not one of the purposes of the sender to cause Tomlinson, or anyone else, to believe that Tomlinson had a gun in his possession. That was simply the common understanding of sender and recipient underlying the communication. Therefore the message was not within the Act's concept of hearsay.'[114]

---

[113] At [19].

[114] At [37]. See also *R v Noble* [2016] EWCA Crim 2219 at [60]–[71]: even if there had been statements in text messages of a 'conversational' nature, taking the third step in the *Twist* formula, there was no intention to cause the recipient to believe or act on them. Cf *R v Doyle* [2018] EWCA Crim 2198, where there was a statement in a text message and the intention was to cause the accused to believe it and react. See also *R v Elliot* (2011) 175 JP 39, CA: letters containing gang symbols and references to gang membership sent to the accused in prison were not hearsay since the authors did not have the purpose of causing the accused to believe that he himself was a member of the gang or to act on the basis that this was true; gang membership was assumed and symbols and references simply expressed gang solidarity.

In the final appeal, *L*, the appellant had been convicted of the rape of his girlfriend when they were both 15. During his trial, evidence was admitted of text messages sent by him to his girlfriend, which had included confessions and apologies for the rape. The relevance of the messages was that they were obvious admissions by L that he had raped his girlfriend. Although the messages contained statements of the matter the prosecution sought to prove (the first and second steps in the approach), they were not hearsay because, at the third step, the purpose of the accused in sending them was to admit to what he had done and apologize, not to cause the complainant to believe she had been raped, something which they both already knew had happened.

Twist received strong approval in *R v Mateza*,[115] where the Court of Appeal stated that it could not in any way improve upon the analysis it provided.[116] However, the analysis is problematic. Notwithstanding some ambiguity in the third appeal, the analysis seems to suggest that a statement requires an express representation before the hearsay provisions apply. This, it is submitted, would run counter to what was intended by the framers of the Act, namely that s 115(3) should allow for some statements to be classified as hearsay even if the statement contained no express representation. It would surely be correct to treat as hearsay a statement with an implied representation where the purpose of the maker was to cause someone else to believe that what was implied was true, or to act on it as if it were true.[117] The risks associated with such a statement are no less real because the representation is implied. That implied representations can be statements for the purposes of s 115(2) has been acknowledged in *R v Midmore*.[118] This was an 'acid attack' case. A 'WhatsApp' message comprising an image of a box of 'One Shot' sulphuric acid drain cleaner and the caption, 'This is the one face melter', was recovered from the accused's mobile phone and admitted to rebut the accused's defence that the acid had been bought for innocent purposes. The message was deemed to be a statement capable of showing the intention of the accused in purchasing the acid. In relation to the question whether the message was a statement for the purposes of s 115(2), Thomas CJ said:

> This is a short point on which views can differ. On balance, we think the better view is that [the message] was an implied representation of the intention, not simply a comment from which the intention could be inferred. It therefore fell within the definition of s 115(2) as it was a statement of the matter intended to be proved.[119]

Risks of implied assertion evidence

There can be little doubt that s 115(3) will operate to render admissible much evidence that was previously excluded as hearsay. Underlying this development of the law was the opinion that 'as a class, implied assertions are more reliable than assertions made for the purpose

---

[115] [2011] EWCA Crim 2587.

[116] Ibid at [21]–[22].

[117] As in *Teper v R* [1952] AC 480, PC, eg. For further analysis of *Twist*, see Ormerod, 'Commentary' [2011] Crim LR 793.

[118] [2017] EWCA Crim 533.

[119] At [39]. However, the message was held not be hearsay because it was not the sender's intention to cause another to believe the representation (at [40]). This reasoning is difficult to follow. What else could have been the intention of the sender? The decision is also open to criticism on the basis that the message, which was sent by a co-accused who pleaded guilty, was not relevant in showing the intention of the accused.

of communicating information'.[120] There are two compelling reasons, however, why such evidence may need to be treated with caution. The first stems from the fact that it is often possible to draw different inferences from the same conduct and, depending on the precise circumstances, this will reduce the weight to be attached to the evidence. For example, in the case of *Manchester Brewery Co Ltd v Coombs*,[121] where evidence of the conduct of customers in rejecting beer was an implied assertion giving rise to the inference that the beer provided by a brewery was bad, the weight of the assertion would surely be reduced if the customers were tourists unfamiliar with the taste of English beer. Second, there will be the risk, in some cases, of error or malicious concoction, the degree of risk varying according to the precise circumstances. For example, in *R v Kearley*, it was most unlikely, without more, that 17 callers were all mistaken or all set out with the deliberate intention of deceiving the police into believing that the accused was a dealer. However, if there had been only one or two callers, there would have been at least some risk of mistake or malice.[122]

Negative hearsay

Under the 2003 Act, as at common law, an oral out-of-court statement will amount to hearsay whether it is tendered as evidence of the existence or non-existence of a fact. Thus if the presence of A at a certain place on a certain date is in issue, evidence by B as to what he heard C say on the matter is hearsay, whether C said that he saw or did not see A on the occasion in question. However, under the Act, whether the statement is hearsay will be governed by s 115(3). According to the Explanatory Notes to the 2003 Act,[123] the situation is governed by s 115(3):[124]

> where the assertion relates to a failure to record an event, sometimes known as negative hearsay, it will not be covered by Chapter 2 [Hearsay evidence] if it was not the purpose of the person who failed to record the event to cause anyone to believe that the event did not occur.

In *DPP v Leigh*,[125] constabulary records admitted to prove the failure of the registered keeper of a vehicle to respond to a request to name a driver were not 'statements' within the meaning of s 115(2). Nor, according to the Divisional Court, were the records caught by s 115(3) because it was not the intention of the administrative staff who made the records to cause another to believe that the keeper of the vehicle had not responded to the request.[126] However, even if records which fail to record an event are deemed hearsay under s 115(3), they might still be admissible as business documents under s 117 of the Act or by exercise of the court's inclusionary discretion, that is, on the basis that it is in the interests of justice for them to be admitted.

---

[120] See Law Com No 245, *Evidence in Criminal Proceedings: Hearsay and Related Topics*, Cm 3670 (1997).

[121] (1901) 82 LT 347, ChD 347.

[122] [1992] 2 AC 228, HL, see per Lord Griffiths, one of the minority, at 349 and 353.

[123] Para 401.

[124] See, in this chapter, under 'Statements' and 'matters stated', p 363.

[125] [2010] EWHC 345, DC at [12].

[126] At [12] and [14]. For common law examples, see *R v Patel* [1981] 3 All ER 94, CA, and *R v Shone* (1982) 76 Cr App R 72, CA.

Statements produced by computers and mechanical and other devices

As we have seen, a 'statement', according to s 115(2), is any representation of fact or opinion 'made by a person' by whatever means. Thus, as the Explanatory Notes to the Act make clear:

> Subsection (2) preserves the present position whereby statements which are not based on human input fall outside the ambit of the hearsay rule. Tapes, films or photographs which directly record the commission of an offence and documents produced by machines which automatically record a process or event or perform calculations will not therefore be covered by Chapter 2 [Hearsay evidence].[127]

However, in *R v Cochrane*,[128] it was held that before the judge can decide whether computer printouts are admissible, whether as real evidence or as hearsay, it is necessary to call appropriate authoritative evidence to describe the function and operation of the computer. Even though *R v Cochrane* pre-dates the 2003 Act, it is submitted that this principle remains valid.

Where a statement generated by a computer or other machine is based on information supplied by a person, for example a printout which is a copy of a letter or a record of other information supplied by a person, then under s 129 of the 2003 Act it will not be admissible as evidence of any fact stated unless it is proved that the information was accurate. Section 129 provides as follows:

(1) Where a representation of any fact—
    (a) is made otherwise than by a person, but
    (b) depends for its accuracy on information supplied (directly or indirectly) by a person, the representation is not admissible in criminal proceedings as evidence of the fact unless it is proved that the information was accurate.
(2) Subsection (1) does not affect the operation of the presumption that a mechanical device has been properly set or calibrated.[129]

The common law principle in effect preserved by s 115(2) was described by Lord Lane CJ in *R v Wood*[130] in the following terms.

> Witnesses, and especially expert witnesses, frequently and properly give factual evidence of the results of a physical exercise which involves the use of some equipment, device or machine. Take a weighing machine; the witness steps on the machine and reads a weight off the dial, receives a ticket printed with the weight, or even hears a recorded voice saying it. None of this involves hearsay evidence. The witness may have to be cross-examined as to whether he kept one foot on the ground; the accuracy of the machine may have to be investigated. But this does not alter the character of the evidence which has been given.

Other examples may be readily imagined: a witness gives evidence that a certain event occurred at a certain time because at that time he had consulted his wristwatch; a motorist gives evidence that, according to the speedometer of his car, he was travelling at a certain speed; a forensic scientist testifies that certain of his findings involved the use of a calculator.

---

[127] Para 402.

[128] [1993] Crim LR 48, CA.

[129] The common law presumption is normally cast in wider terms, namely that mechanical instruments that are usually in working order, were in working order at the time when they were used: see **Ch 4** under **Presumptions without basic facts**, p 103.

[130] (1982) 76 Cr App R 23, CA at 26.

In *R v Wood*[131] the appellant was convicted of handling stolen metal. In order to prove that metal in his possession and metal from the stolen consignment had the same chemical composition, samples were subjected to an X-ray spectrometer and a neutron transmission monitor. The figures thus produced were then subjected to a mathematical process in order that the percentage of the various metals in the samples could be stated as figures, using a computer operated by chemists. At the trial, detailed evidence was given as to how the computer had been programmed and used. The Court of Appeal held that the trial judge had properly allowed evidence of the computer results to be admitted. The computer was used as a calculator, a tool which did not contribute its own knowledge but merely did a sophisticated calculation which could have been done manually. Lord Lane CJ said that the computer printout was not hearsay but more properly to be treated as a piece of real evidence, the actual proof and relevance of which depended upon the evidence of the chemists, computer programmer, and other experts involved.[132]

Where information is collected by the device itself
The above principle applies not only where the device in question processes information supplied, but also where the device itself collects information. Thus in *R v Spiby*[133] a printout from a computerized machine used to monitor telephone calls and automatically record such information as the numbers from and to which the calls were made and the duration of the calls, was admitted as real evidence. It was held that where information is recorded by mechanical means without the intervention of a human mind, the record made by the machine is admissible.[134] In *R v Governor of Brixton Prison, ex p Levin*[135] the issue was whether L had used a computer terminal to gain unauthorized access to the computerized fund transfer service of a bank and to make fraudulent transfers of funds from clients' bank accounts to accounts which he controlled. Each transfer request was processed automatically and a record of the transaction was copied to the computer's historical records. The House of Lords held that the printouts of screen displays of these records were admissible to prove the transfers of funds they recorded. Lord Hoffmann said: 'They do not assert that such transfers took place. They record the transfers . . . The evidential status of the printouts is no different from that of a photocopy of a forged cheque.'[136] *Taylor v Chief Constable of Cheshire*[137] may be regarded as an example of the same principle. Where a video recording from a security camera had been deleted, police officers were properly allowed to give evidence that they had watched the video recording and identified the accused shoplifting. It was held that evidence of what the officers saw on the recording was no different from evidence of a bystander who actually witnessed the incident by direct vision.[138]

---

[131] Ibid. See also *The Statue of Liberty* [1968] 1 WLR 739.

[132] See also *Castle v Cross* [1984] 1 WLR 1372, DC (an Intoximeter 3000 breath-test machine was a tool, albeit a sophisticated one, and in the absence of any evidence that it was defective, the printout, the product of a mechanical device, fell into the category of real evidence).

[133] (1990) 91 Cr App R 186, CA.

[134] Cf *R v Shephard* (1991) 93 Cr App R 139, CA (till rolls not treated as real evidence because much of the information recorded on them was supplied by cashiers).

[135] [1997] AC 741, HL.

[136] See also *R (on the application of O'Shea) v Coventry Magistrates Court* [2004] ACD 50, DC.

[137] [1986] 1 WLR 1479.

[138] The weight and reliability of the evidence would have to be assessed carefully, and, because identification was in issue, by reference to the guidelines in *R v Turnbull* [1977] QB 224, CA: see **Ch 9, Visual identification, p 278.**

Under s 16(1)(a) of the Road Traffic Offenders Act 1988, in proceedings for an offence of driving when unfit through drink or driving after consuming excess alcohol, evidence of the proportion of alcohol in a breath specimen may be given by a statement automatically produced by the device used to measure such proportion, together with a certificate, signed by a constable, that the statement relates to a specimen provided by the accused. In *Garner v DPP*[139] it was held that the purpose of this provision is to enable the facts to be established without the need to call anybody and therefore, if the certificate is defective, the printout remains admissible as real evidence[140] and can be linked to the accused by oral evidence. However, oral evidence of the reading, in the absence of the automatically produced statement, does not come up to the required standard of proof.[141]

Evasion of the rule

Given that the hearsay rule, at common law, could operate to exclude highly cogent evidence, it is perhaps not surprising that both advocates and judges employed various tactics to evade the rule. One, for example, involved asking what a conversation or document was about rather than what was actually said or written. Another involved asking about acts done which were only relevant to the extent that they raised an inference about the contents of an out of court statement: 'Did you have a conversation with X?' 'As a result of that conversation what did you do?' Both of these tactics were held to be objectionable[142] and are equally objectionable in the case of hearsay which is inadmissible under the 2003 Act.

Judicial evasion of the rule was apparent in a number of cases, especially those in which the rule would otherwise operate to exclude apparently reliable identification evidence[143] or evidence which assisted in proving a negative.[144] It is submitted that now that judges have the discretionary power under s 114(1)(d) to admit otherwise inadmissible hearsay if satisfied that it is in the interests of justice to do so, they no longer need to evade the rules.

Cases where a witness is unavailable

General

Under s 116 of the 2003 Act, first-hand hearsay statements, whether made orally or in a document, are admissible, on behalf of the prosecution or defence, subject to three conditions: first, that oral evidence given in the proceedings by the maker of the statement would be admissible as evidence of the matter stated; second, that the maker of the statement is identified; and third, that the maker of the statement does not give oral evidence for one of a number of specified reasons, which include, for example, his unfitness to be a witness or through fear. There is a fourth condition, the leave of the court, but this is imposed only where the maker of the statement does not give oral evidence through fear. This reflects the Law Commission's

---

[139] (1990) 90 Cr App R 178, DC.

[140] See also *R v Cochrane* [1993] Crim LR 48, CA.

[141] *Owen v Chesters* [1985] RTR 191, DC.

[142] See per Lord Devlin in *Glinski v McIver* [1962] AC 726, HL at 780–1 and *R v Turner* [1975] QB 834, CA at 840. See also *R v Saunders* [1899] 1 QB 490, CCR.

[143] See, eg, *R v Osborne, R v Virtue* [1973] QB 678, CA.

[144] See, eg, *R v Muir* (1983) 79 Cr App R 153, CA.

view that whereas a general leave requirement would result in inconsistent and arbitrary decision-making, always allowing judges opposed to hearsay to find reasons to exclude it, a requirement of leave in the case of the statements of witnesses not giving oral evidence through fear was necessary to avoid the danger of witnesses making statements in the knowledge that they could later claim to be frightened and thereby avoid cross-examination.[145]

A statement admissible under s 116 may be excluded by the court in the exercise of its discretionary powers of exclusion, including the power to exclude prosecution evidence under s 78 of the 1984 Act. Section 78 has particular importance, in the case of evidence admissible under s 116 without the leave of the court, as the only means of excluding evidence to ensure that the accused receives a fair trial in accordance with Art 6 of the European Convention on Human Rights. Section 78 and other statutory provisions relating to discretionary exclusion (and also those provisions which relate to the question of proof and to the capability and credibility of the maker of the statement) apply to hearsay admissible not only under s 116 but also under other sections of the Act, and for this reason, are considered separately.[146]

Section 116(1), (2), (3), and (5) provide as follows:

(1) In criminal proceedings a statement not made in oral evidence in the proceedings is admissible as evidence of any matter stated if—
  (a) oral evidence given in the proceedings by the person who made the statement would be admissible as evidence of that matter,
  (b) the person who made the statement (the relevant person) is identified to the court's satisfaction, and
  (c) any of the five conditions mentioned in subsection (2) is satisfied.

(2) The conditions are—
  (a) that the relevant person is dead;
  (b) that the relevant person is unfit to be a witness because of his bodily or mental condition;
  (c) that the relevant person is outside the United Kingdom and it is not reasonably practicable to secure his attendance;
  (d) that the relevant person cannot be found although such steps as it is reasonably practicable to take to find him have been taken;
  (e) that through fear the relevant person does not give (or does not continue to give) oral evidence in the proceedings, either at all or in connection with the subject matter of the statement, and the court gives leave for the statement to be given in evidence.

(3) For the purposes of subsection (2)(e) 'fear' is to be widely construed and (for example) includes fear of the death or injury of another person or of financial loss.

. . .

(5) A condition set out in any paragraph of subsection (2) which is in fact satisfied is to be treated as not satisfied if it is shown that the circumstances described in that paragraph are caused—
  (a) by the person in support of whose case it is sought to give the statement in evidence, or
  (b) by a person acting on his behalf,
  in order to prevent the relevant person giving oral evidence in the proceedings (whether at all or in connection with the subject matter of the statement).

Concerning the opening words of s 116(1), 'criminal proceedings', 'statement', and 'matter stated' bear the same meaning as in s 114 of the Act and call for no additional comment here.

---

[145] See Law Com No 245 (1997), paras 4.28 ff and para 8.58.
[146] See, in this chapter, under **Discretion to exclude**, p 401.

The purpose of s 116(1)(a) is to prevent s 116 from being used to admit evidence which, if the maker of the statement were called as a witness, would be inadmissible because, for example, he has no personal knowledge of the facts,[147] or the evidence constitutes expert opinion evidence which the maker is not qualified to give, or the evidence is simply irrelevant to facts in issue. Section 116(1)(a) will also operate to prevent s 116 being used where there is an overwhelming probability that the witness would rely on the privilege against self-incrimination and would decline to give evidence in the terms of the statement.[148]

The 'relevant person'

Section 116 applies to both oral and written statements. Having regard to the requirements of s 116(1)(a), (b), and (c), it is crucial, in the case of statements made in writing, to identify correctly the 'relevant person', ie the person who made the statement. Valuable guidance is provided by decisions which predate the 2003 Act. If, for example, A makes an oral statement within the hearing of B, who writes down what A says, and A reads and signs the document, then clearly A is the relevant person. Similarly, if A dictates the statement to B and checks that what B has written down is an accurate record of what he said (by reading it or having it read back to him) then, even without his signature, A is the relevant person.[149] However, if B made a written record of A's oral statement not agreed to or approved or accepted by A, A would not be the relevant person: in these circumstances he has made an oral statement, not a statement in a document.[150] B has made a statement in a document, but his statement would not be admissible under s 116 because the condition in s 116(1)(a) cannot be met— oral evidence by B would not be admissible of the matter stated because B has no direct or personal knowledge of those matters. The 'relevant person' is broad enough to include the accused who might rely on s 116 to put his account before the jury by way of hearsay where he is genuinely unable to give oral testimony, for example, where he is involuntarily absent and the trial proceeds in his absence.[151] However, it might be only in rare and exceptional circumstances that an accused's application to admit his statement would succeed.

Section 116(1)(b) reflects the view that the risk of unreliability in the case of hearsay statements made by unidentified individuals is high and ensures that where a statement is admitted, the opposing party is in a position to impugn the credibility of its maker.[152]

The effect of s 116(5)

The effect of s 116(5) is that a party cannot rely on s 116 where he, or someone acting on his behalf, has, in order to prevent the maker of the statement giving oral evidence, brought about one of the conditions set out in s 116(2). This would be the case, for example, if the party in question had murdered the maker of the statement (s 116(2)(a)) or falsely imprisoned the witness at a secret location (s 116(2)(d)) or threatened the witness so that he had fled abroad.[153] Presumably, it is for the party resisting admissibility of the statement to establish such conduct. In s 116(5), the 'relevant person' is (as s 116(1)(b) makes clear) the person who made the statement.[154]

---

[147] See *R v JP* [1999] Crim LR 401, CA, a decision under the Criminal Justice Act 1988, s 23.

[148] See *R v Hayes* [2018] 1 Cr App R 134 (10), CA at [58]–[59].

[149] *R v McGillivray* (1992) 97 Cr App R 232, CA.

[150] Cf *Re D (a minor)* [1986] 2 FLR 189 Fam D.

[151] *R v Hemberger* [2017] EWCA Crim 273.

[152] See, in this chapter, under **Credibility**, p 398.

[153] See *R v Rowley* [2013] 1 WLR 89, CA.

[154] See *R v C* [2019] Cr App R 88 (10), CA at [26]–[27].

The reasons for not calling the maker of the statement to give evidence

Section 116(2)(a) to (e) of the 2003 Act have been cast in words similar, but not identical, to words in s 23(2)(a), (b), and (c) of the Criminal Justice Act 1988 and, subject to significant changes to some of the wording, the decisions interpreting the earlier provisions provide very useful guidance as to the way in which the provisions of the 2003 Act are likely to be construed.

Relevant person unfit to be a witness because of his bodily or mental condition

Unlike its statutory precursor, which referred to a person who was 'unfit to attend as a witness', s 116(2)(b) refers to a person who is 'unfit to be a witness'. However, it is submitted that subs (2)(b) is likely to cover a person physically unable to get to court 'to be a witness' as well as a person able to attend court but unfit to give evidence, such as a witness who, by reason of his mental condition, is unable to recall the events in question.[155] In determining whether a person is unfit to be a witness, it may be appropriate for the judge to consider the availability of special measures.[156] Ordinarily, a witness who is not competent to give evidence because of lack of mental capacity will also be 'unfit to be a witness because of his . . . mental condition' for the purposes of s 116(2)(b).[157]

Relevant person outside the United Kingdom and it is not reasonably practicable to secure his attendance

The requirement in s 116(2)(c) is likely to be treated, as before, as a requirement of a strictly territorial nature and therefore will not be satisfied if the person who made the statement is a consul or embassy official in the UK.[158] The word 'attendance' was treated as capable of including the giving of evidence through live television link from outside the United Kingdom under s 32 of the 1988 Act, but not examination of a witness on commission by a court in his country of residence.[159]

The question whether it is reasonably practicable to secure the attendance of the maker of the statement should be examined not at the time when the trial opens, but against the whole background to the case. Thus in *R v Bray*[160] an argument that it was not reasonably practicable to secure the attendance of a person, because it was only when the trial started that it was realized he was overseas, was rejected by the Court of Appeal. The person had been overseas for seven months before the trial began and it had not been shown that it was not reasonably practicable to secure his attendance at the trial. In *R v C*[161] it was held that what is 'reasonably practicable' under s 116(2)(c) should be judged on the basis of steps taken or not taken by the party seeking to ensure the attendance of the witness. This accords with *R v Maloney*,[162] a decision under a prior statute with a similar provision,[163] that the word

---

[155] See *R v Setz-Dempsey* (1994) 98 Cr App R 23, CA.

[156] See *R v Ferdinand* [2014] EWCA Crim 1243. Special measures are considered in Ch 5, under **Witnesses in criminal cases**, p 152.

[157] *DPP v R* [2007] All ER 176, [2007] EWHC 1842. However, see also s 123(1), considered, in this chapter under **Capability**, p 398.

[158] *R v Jiminez-Paez* (1994) 98 Cr App R 239, CA.

[159] *R v Radak* [1999] 1 Cr App R 187, CA.

[160] (1988) 88 Cr App R 354.

[161] [2006] 1 WLR 2994, CA.

[162] [1994] Crim LR 525, CA.

[163] The Police and Criminal Evidence Act 1984, s 68(2)(a)(ii), the identical statutory precursor to the Criminal Justice Act 1988, s 23(2)(b).

'practicable' is not equivalent to physically possible and must be construed in the light of the normal steps which would be taken to arrange the attendance of a witness; and that the word 'reasonably' involved a further qualification of the duty, to secure attendance by taking the reasonable steps which a party would normally take to secure a witness's attendance having regard to the means and resources available to the parties. Thus relevant factors include such matters as the cost of travel,[164] whether an offer was made to pay the fare, the reason for any refusal to attend, and whether an approach was made to the person's employer or the British Embassy.[165] The fact that it is *possible* for a witness to attend does not on its own settle whether his attendance is reasonably practicable.[166] The test may be satisfied notwithstanding that (i) practicable arrangements have been made for the witness to attend and he states an intention to attend (because circumstances may occur at short notice which render it impracticable to secure his attendance on the day in question);[167] (ii) the witness chooses not to attend court (because the test is not whether it is reasonably practicable for the witness to attend);[168] or (iii) if there were to be an adjournment, the witness might attend at some future date (because there is no necessity to look to the future).[169]

Relevant person cannot be found even though such steps as are reasonably practicable to take to find him have been taken

Whether steps taken to find a witness are 'reasonably practicable' will depend on the facts. It would appear from *R v Adams*[170] that where a witness has agreed to attend to give evidence, there is an obligation to keep in touch with him and be alive to his needs and commitments. Further, where there has been no contact following the witness's initial agreement to attend trial, unsuccessful attempts to find the witness close to the start of the trial may well fall short of what the courts expect.[171] In *R v Adams*, the key witness in the accused's trial for possession of drugs with intent to supply, a nightclub security guard, had been contacted three months before the fixed date of the trial and confirmed he would be able to attend. He was not contacted again until the Friday before the trial was due to start on Monday, when a message was left on his mobile phone. There was no response to the message and no further action taken. It was held that the judge had been wrong to admit the statement under s 116(2)(d) as such steps as were reasonably practicable had not been taken,[172] but the statement was admissible under s 114(1)(d), in the interests of justice. However, where the judge concludes that the requirements of s 116(2)(d) are met, the statement is admissible and it is an error of approach to then consider as the 'next step', admissibility under s 114(1)(d). The next step is to consider the question of fairness and the application of s 78 of the Police and Criminal Evidence Act 1984.[173]

---

[164] *R v Case* [1991] Crim LR 192, CA. See also *R v Castillo* [1996] 1 Cr App R 438.

[165] *R v Gonzales de Arango* (1991) 96 Cr App R 399, a decision under the Police and Criminal Evidence Act 1984, s 68(2).

[166] *R v Castillo* [1996] 1 Cr App R 438,CA, followed in *R v Yu* [2006] Crim LR 643, CA.

[167] *R v Hurst* [1995] 1 Cr App R 82, CA.

[168] *R v French* (1993) 97 Cr App R 421, CA.

[169] Ibid. But in the case of a *pre-trial* application, the court will obviously need to look to the future to see whether it would be practicable for the witness's attendance to be secured at the date of the trial: *R v Hurst* [1995] 1 Cr App R 82 at 92, CA.

[170] [2008] 1 Cr App R 430 (35), CA at [13].

[171] See also *R v DT* [2009] EWCA Crim 1213, where steps taken very shortly before the hearing were insufficient.

[172] See also *R v CT* (2011) 175 JP 462, CA. Cf *R v M* [2014] Crim LR 823, CA.

[173] See *R v Kiziltan* [2018] 4 WLR 43, CA at [16].

Relevant person does not give oral evidence through fear

Section 116(2)(e) has been cast in wide terms, to permit the admission of a statement where the maker of the statement is absent through fear.[174] The section covers not only cases in which, through fear, the maker of the statement does not give (or continue to give) evidence in connection with the subject matter of the hearsay statement in question, but also cases in which, through fear, the maker of the statement does not give oral evidence at all or, having started to give oral evidence, 'dries up'. It covers, therefore, not only the potential witness who has been intimidated,[175] but also those who are scared of the process—in some cases the ordeal—of going to court and giving evidence.[176] The question of fear or otherwise has to be judged at the time when the witness would be expected to give evidence orally, but there has to be a degree of sensible give and take. Sometimes, for example, the appropriate ruling will be sought before the trial to enable prosecution counsel to decide how the case should be opened to the jury. Equally, it may suffice to show continuing fear and that the witness has disappeared.[177] Where a witness attends, goes into the witness box, but refuses to give evidence and behaves in a resentful, rude, and aggressive way, the courts should be alert to the possibility that the reason for this may be fear. Where fear is suspected, it is appropriate to give the witness the opportunity to speak quietly with someone whom the witness might regard as neutral and who is charged with the task of finding out the reason for the witness's attitude.[178]

Under subsection (3), 'fear' is to be widely construed, and it is clear from the examples given in the subsection that it is not confined to fear arising out of threats or intimidation directed at the maker of the statement himself. Nonetheless, the subsection begs the question as to just *how* widely 'fear' should be construed. Does it extend, for example, to the witness whose testimony is such that it will expose him to public humiliation or disgrace? If authorities which predate the 2003 Act are anything to go by, 'fear' falls to be construed very widely. For example, in *R v Martin*,[179] the witness said he was fearful for his family, having been approached by a silent stranger he had previously seen outside his door, and it was held that 'fear' covered not only genuine witness intimidation, but also cases of fear based on mistake or misunderstanding.[180] In *R v Horncastle*,[181] the Court of Appeal noted that, under s 116(2)(e), fear includes the fear of being seen to give evidence and fear to which a police officer has contributed, although it should not extend to fear based upon inappropriate assurances by police officers given to a witness regarding the likelihood that his evidence will be

---

[174] See also, in this chapter, under **The statutory scheme and Art 6 of the European Convention on Human Rights**, p 353.

[175] This includes a witness intimidated in a trial of more than one accused, even though not all the accused or their associates are responsible for the intimidation. In such a case, a judge need not hold a *voir dire* to establish whether the intimidation is restricted to one accused and whether the trial of the accused responsible should be severed: an accused should not be able to secure a separate trial by intimidating a witness. See *R v Harvey* [2014] EWCA Crim 54 at [54].

[176] See generally Law Com No 245, Cm 3670 (1997), paras 8.63–8.66.

[177] *R v H* [2001] Crim LR 815, CA.

[178] *R v Nelson* [2009] EWCA Crim 1600.

[179] [1996] Crim LR 589, CA.

[180] See also *R v Arnold* [2004] EWCA Crim 1293 and *R v Fairfax* [1995] Crim LR 949, CA (all that needs to be proved is that the witness does not give evidence through fear). See also *R v Acton Justices, ex p McMullen; R v Tower Bridge Magistrates' Court, ex p Lawlor* (1990) 92 Cr App R 98 at 105, DC (fear of what, and whether that is relevant, is a matter for the court's consideration in the given circumstances).

[181] [2009] 2 Cr App R 230 (15), CA.

read at trial.[182] Fear of the consequences for the accused also falls outwith the ambit of the statutory wording.[183] However, it is incumbent on the judge to rigorously test evidence of fear and investigate all possibilities of the witness giving oral evidence, and every effort has to be made to get the witness to court.[184] Further, it is not open to the trial judge to assume the witness would be in fear and to admit statements by the witness under s 114(1)(d), where no evidence of fear has been adduced by the prosecution in its application to admit the same statements under s 116(2)(d).[185]

Section 116(2)(e) may only be relied on where a witness is genuinely in fear and it is not a route to admitting the evidence of a witness who is merely reluctant.[186]

The requirement of leave where the maker of the statement does not give oral evidence through fear

Leave may only be given under s 116(2)(e) if the court considers that the statement ought to be admitted in the interests of justice, having regard to the factors set out in s 116(4). Section 116(4) provides as follows:

> (4) Leave may be given under subsection (2)(e) only if the court considers that the statement ought to be admitted in the interests of justice, having regard—
> (a) to the statement's contents,
> (b) to any risk that its admission or exclusion will result in unfairness to any party to the proceedings (and in particular to how difficult it will be to challenge the statement if the relevant person does not give oral evidence),
> (c) in appropriate cases, to the fact that a direction under s 19 of the Youth Justice and Criminal Evidence Act 1999 (special measures for the giving of evidence by fearful witnesses etc) could be made in relation to the relevant person, and
> (d) to any other relevant circumstances.

It is submitted that it is for the party seeking to admit the evidence to show that it should be admitted in the interests of justice, a test which involves considerations of fairness both to the defence and to the prosecution.[187] A 'complex balancing exercise' may be involved: 'the weight to be attached to the inability to cross-examine and the magnitude of any consequential risk that admission of the statement will result in unfairness to the accused, will depend in part on the court's assessment of the quality of the evidence shown by the contents of the statement'.[188]

The statement's contents and the risk that its admission or exclusion will result in unfairness
In the light of cases from both the domestic courts and the European Court of Human Rights, it is convenient to consider subsections 4(a) and (b) together. It is submitted that the following

---

[182] [2009] 2 Cr App R 15 at [84], [86]–[88].

[183] See *R v L* [2009] 1 WLR 626, CA, where the trial judge refused to admit the complainant's statement on this basis, a point not considered on appeal.

[184] *R v Riat* [2013] 1 WLR 2592, CA at [54(ii)]. See also *Al Khawaja and Tahery v UK* 54 (2012) EHHR 23 at [120]–[124].

[185] *R v CT* (2011) 175 JP 462, CA.

[186] *R v Freeman* [2010] EWCA Crim 1997 at [33] (Cf *Seton v UK* [2016] ECHR 318 and *R v Seton* [2010] EWCA Crim 450). However, where a reluctant witness has disappeared and cannot be found despite reasonably practicable steps to find him, s 116(2)(d) may be relied on: see *R v Lyons* [2010] EWCA Crim 2029.

[187] *R v Patel* (1992) 97 Cr App R 294, CA.

[188] See *R v Cole* [1990] 1 WLR 866 at 877, CA. See also *R v Thompson* [1999] Crim LR 747, CA, where a statement was admitted notwithstanding that its maker suffered from long-term alcohol-related problems and depression.

principles provide useful guidance as to the way in which the courts should approach their task in relation to these subsections.

1. As to the contents of a statement sought to be relied on by the prosecution, the court should consider the quality of the evidence and extent to which the accused is able to challenge it.[189]

2. The importance or otherwise of the contents of the statement to the issues in the case is a matter to be taken into account.[190] The fact that a statement goes to the crucial issues in the case may make it all the more important to admit it.[191] However, having regard to Strasbourg jurisprudence, the more important the evidence is, the more weight should be attached to the need for counterbalancing measures when deciding whether it is in the interests of justice to admit the evidence.[192]

3. Also having regard to Strasbourg jurisprudence,[193] the court should take into account not only the rights of the defence, but also the interests of the public and the victim, who can expect crimes to be fully prosecuted, and the interests of witnesses.[194] If the court is sure that a prosecution witness has been kept away by the accused, it is not a violation of Art 6 (and correspondingly, it is submitted, not contrary to the interests of justice) to admit the statement provided that (a) the quality of the evidence is compelling; (b) firm steps are taken to draw the jury's attention to aspects of the witness's credibility; and (c) a clear direction is given to the jury to exercise caution. In this situation, the accused has, by his own actions, denied himself the opportunity of examining the witness.[195]

4. In considering the risk of unfairness, it may also be relevant to consider whether the party against whom the statement is tendered has had any opportunity to interview or make inquiries of the maker of the statement;[196] but in any event this would fall within 'any other relevant circumstance' for the purposes of s 116(4)(d) (considered below).

5. The court should consider how far potential unfairness arising from the inability to cross-examine on the statement can be effectively counterbalanced by a warning to the jury about the limitations of reading out a statement, that is, the absence of opportunity to judge the maker's reliability and credibility in examination and cross-examination.[197]

---

[189] See under The statutory scheme and Art 6 of the European Convention on Human Rights, p 353. See *Price v UK* [2016] ECHR 15602/07, *Schatschaschwili v Germany* (2016) 63 EHRR 14 and *Al Khawaja and Tahery v UK* (2012) 54 EHRR 23. See also *R v Fairfax* [1995] Crim LR 949, CA, applying *R v Cole* [1990] 1 WLR 866, CA.

[190] See *Schatschaschwili v Germany* (2016) 63 EHRR 14 at [116]. See also *R v French* (1993) 97 Cr App R 421, CA at 428.

[191] *R v Patel* (1992) 97 Cr App R 294, CA. See also *R v Batt and Batt* [1995] Crim LR 240, CA.

[192] See *Schatschaschwili v Germany* (2016) 63 EHRR 14 at [116], explaining *Al Khawaja and Tahery v UK* (2012) 54 EHRR 23 at [146]–[147]. See also *Seton v UK* [2016] ECHR 318 and *Price v UK* [2016] ECHR 15602/67.

[193] See, in this chapter, under Article 6 and statements of witnesses which are 'sole or decisive', p 355.

[194] *Al Khawaja and Tahery v UK* (2012) 54 EHRR 23 at [118].

[195] See *R v Sellick* [2005] 1 WLR 3257, CA. See also *R v M(KJ)* [2003] 2 Cr App R 322. Nor is there any question of a breach of Art 6(1) and 3(d) where the evidence is sole or decisive. See *Al Khawaja and Tahery v UK* (2012) 54 EHRR 23 at [122]–[124].

[196] *R v Patel* (1992) 97 Cr App R 294, CA.

[197] See the Crown Court Compendium (July 2019), Part 1, 14–4, Example. However, there is no fixed rule as to the terms in which a warning should be given: *R v Batt and Batt* [1995] Crim LR 240, CA. Nevertheless, it is inappropriate to direct the jury that the statement is of less worth than the evidence of the witnesses in the case: *R v Greer* [1998] Crim LR 572, CA.

The court should also consider whether, having regard to other evidence available to the party seeking to admit the statement, the interests of justice will be properly served by excluding it.[198]

6. In deciding whether the accused is properly able to challenge the evidence, the judge should not embark on a detailed comparison between what might have happened if the maker of the statement had given oral evidence and had been cross-examined, and what might happen if his statement is admitted without him attending.[199] Nor is the judge required to assess the possibility of challenging the statement on the basis that the accused will not give evidence or call witnesses,[200] or that the admission of the statement will make it more difficult for the accused to exercise his right to silence because to challenge the statement effectively, he may need to give evidence.[201]

7. Where a statement of a witness in fear is admitted in the interests of justice, and the judge directs the jury on the disadvantages of not having the witness before them, it is not proper to direct them to pay less attention to the evidence in the statement than to that of the live witnesses: it is for the jury alone to decide what weight they place on the evidence.[202]

8. Where identification is in issue, neither the fact that the statement contains identification evidence, nor the fact that it is the only evidence against the accused, nor the inability to cross-examine will of itself be sufficient to justify exclusion—the quality of the evidence in the statement is the crucial factor.[203] However, the inability to probe evidence of identification by cross-examination is of utmost significance and therefore the court should be cautious about admitting such evidence, especially where there are grounds for believing that, if the evidence had been given in person, it might have been significantly undermined by cross-examination.[204] It is submitted that the court should be astute to examine all the circumstances in which the observation was made, such as the duration of the observation, the distance from which it was made, whether it was impeded in any way, the length of time between the observation and the time at which the statement was made, and so on.

9. Where hearsay evidence is sought to be admitted by an accused, its *exclusion* could result in unfairness to the accused but its *admission* could result in unfairness to a co-accused. In such a case, it seems that the court should conduct a balancing exercise which may result in the exclusion of the evidence on the basis that the damage done to the co-accused outweighs the benefit to the accused.[205] However, it is submitted that such an

---

[198] *R v Cole* [1990] 1 WLR 866 at 877, CA.

[199] *R v Radak* [1999] 1 Cr App R 187, CA.

[200] See *R v Cole* [1990] 1 WLR 866, CA. See also *R v Price* [1991] Crim LR 707, CA (notes of a conversation between the accused and another were properly admitted even though the only way in which the accused could challenge the statement was by giving evidence himself, which he could not be required to do). See also *R v Samuel* [1992] Crim LR 189, CA and *R v Moore* [1992] Crim LR 882, CA.

[201] *R v Gokal* [1997] 2 Cr App R 266, CA.

[202] Cf *R v Kennedy* [1994] Crim LR 50, CA.

[203] See *R v Setz-Dempsey* (1994) 98 Cr App R 23 at 30, CA, applying the principles enunciated by Lord Griffiths in *Scott v R* [1989] AC 1242, PC. See also *R v Dragic* [1996] 2 Cr App R 232, CA: evidence of recognition challenged on the basis that the maker of the statement was either unreliable, possibly because of drink, or had lied.

[204] *R v Setz-Dempsey* (1994) 98 Cr App R 23.

[205] As in *R v Gregory and Mott* [1995] Crim LR 507, CA, a decision under the Criminal Justice Act 1988, s 25(2)(d).

outcome would hardly be 'in the interests of justice' in a case in which, had the accused been tried separately, the evidence would have been of such benefit to him that it would have been admitted.[206]

Whether a special measures direction could be made
Subsection (4)(c) in effect requires the court to consider whether the statement ought not to be admitted in the interests of justice because a special measures direction can be given under s 19 of the Youth Justice and Criminal Evidence Act 1999.[207]

Any other relevant circumstances
'Other relevant circumstances', for the purposes of s 116(4)(d), are likely to include the circumstances in which the statement was made, including any attempts made to get the maker to make the statement in the way most favourable to the party seeking to rely upon it, the fact that the maker of the statement made prior inconsistent statements, whether oral or written,[208] any animosity by the maker of the statement toward any party,[209] and other facts or matters affecting his capability or credibility.[210] As to the last, although it may be in the interests of justice to admit the statement of a person even if he is of bad character, particularly when that bad character can readily be demonstrated, it should be excluded where he is so dishonest that the absence of an opportunity for the jury to assess him as a witness, to observe his demeanour and the manner in which he gives his evidence, would result in potential unfairness.[211]

Business and other documents

Section 117 of the 2003 Act, which provides for the admissibility of hearsay statements contained in business and other documents, is modelled on s 24 of the 1988 Act, which it replaces, but there are a number of significant differences. Under s 117, statements contained in documents are admissible as evidence of any matter stated on five conditions. The first is that oral evidence would be admissible as evidence of the matter stated. The second is that the document was created or received by a person in the course of a trade, business, profession, or other occupation or as the holder of a paid or unpaid office. The third is that the person who supplied the information, who may be the same person as the creator or receiver of the document, had or may reasonably be supposed to have had personal knowledge of the matters dealt with. The fourth, imposed only if the information was supplied indirectly, is that each person through whom it was supplied, received it in the course of a trade, business, profession, or other occupation or as the holder of a paid or unpaid office. The fifth

---

[206] *R v Duffy* [1999] QB 919, CA.

[207] See Ch 5. For example, such a direction may be made to admit a video recording of an interview of the witness as his evidence-in-chief.

[208] See *R v Tahery* [2013] EWCA Crim 1053. See also *R v Sweeting and Thomas* [1999] Crim LR 75, CA, in which it was also held that if the statement is admitted, the logical course is to admit the inconsistent statement. See now under the 2003 Act, s 124(2)(c), considered, in this chapter, under **Credibility, p 398**.

[209] See *R v Tahery* [2013] EWCA Crim 1053.

[210] See ss 123 and 124 of the 2003 Act.

[211] See *R v Lockley* [1995] 2 Cr App R 554, CA, a decision under the Criminal Justice Act 1988, s 25, where the maker of the statement had demonstrated and indeed boasted about his remarkable ability to deceive.

condition, imposed only where the statement was prepared for the purpose of pending or contemplated criminal proceedings, or for a criminal investigation, is that the supplier of the information does not give oral evidence for one of the reasons set out in s 116(2)[212] or because he cannot reasonably be expected to have any recollection of the matters dealt with in the statement. A statement admissible under s 117 may be excluded by the court in the exercise of its discretionary powers of exclusion.[213]

Section 117

Section 117 provides as follows:

(1) In criminal proceedings a statement contained in a document is admissible of any matter stated if—
   (a) oral evidence given in the proceedings would be admissible as evidence of that matter,
   (b) the requirements of subsection (2) are satisfied, and
   (c) the requirements of subsection (5) are satisfied, in a case where subsection (4) requires them to be.
(2) The requirements of this subsection are satisfied if—
   (a) the document or the part containing the statement was created or received by a person in the course of a trade, business, profession or other occupation, or as the holder of a paid or unpaid office,
   (b) the person who supplied the information contained in the statement (the relevant person) had or may reasonably be supposed to have had personal knowledge of the matters dealt with, and
   (c) each person (if any) through whom the information was supplied from the relevant person to the person mentioned in paragraph (a) received the information in the course of a trade, business, profession or other occupation, or as the holder of a paid or unpaid office.
(3) The persons mentioned in paragraphs (a) and (b) of subsection (2) may be the same person.
(4) The additional requirements of subsection (5) must be satisfied if the statement—
   (a) was prepared for the purposes of pending or contemplated criminal proceedings, or for a criminal investigation, but
   (b) was not obtained pursuant to a request under section 7 of the Crime (International Co-operation) Act 2003 or an order under paragraph 6 of Schedule 13 to the Criminal Justice Act 1988 (which relate to overseas evidence).[214]
(5) The requirements of this subsection are satisfied if—
   (a) any of the five conditions mentioned in section 116(2) is satisfied (absence of relevant person etc), or
   (b) the relevant person cannot reasonably be expected to have any recollection of the matters dealt with in the statement (having regard to the length of time since he supplied the information and all other circumstances).
(6) A statement is not admissible under this section if the court makes a direction to that effect under subsection (7).
(7) The court may make a direction under this subsection if satisfied that the statement's reliability as evidence for the purpose for which it is tendered is doubtful in view of—
   (a) its contents,
   (b) the source of the information contained in it,

---

[212] See, in this chapter, under **Cases where a witness is unavailable**, p 373.
[213] See, in this chapter, under **Discretion to exclude**, p 401.
[214] These provisions relate to the issue of letters of request.

(c) the way in which or the circumstances in which the information was supplied or received, or

(d) the way in which or the circumstances in which the document concerned was created or received.

As to the opening words of s 117(1), 'criminal proceedings', 'statement', and 'matter stated' bear the same meaning as in s 114 of the Act and call for no additional comment here. The words of s 117(1)(a) bear the same meaning as in s 116(1)(a) of the Act but whereas under s 116(a) the test is whether 'oral evidence given . . . by the person who made the statement' would be admissible as evidence of the matter stated, under s 117(1)(a) the test is simply whether *oral evidence* would be admissible as evidence of the matter stated, that is, oral evidence given by anyone. Where a statement contained in a document is an opinion, it does not meet the test for admissibility under s 117(1)(a), since oral evidence of opinion is inadmissible[215] (unless it is an expert opinion). A 'document' is defined by s 134(1) as 'anything in which information of any description is recorded', which is wide enough to include, inter alia, maps, plans, graphs, drawings, photographs, discs, audio-tapes, videotapes, films, microfilms, negatives, and computer-generated printouts.

Document created or received in the course of a trade (or business, etc)

Under s 117(2)(a), the document (or part) containing the statement must be 'created or received' by a person in the course of a trade (or business, etc). A document, given its wide definition, may be created in a number of different ways: by writing or typing (a document in writing); by drawing (a map or plan); by development (a photograph); or by recording (discs, tapes, soundtracks, etc). A document may be received by hand, by post, by fax machine, by e-mail, or by linked computers. Whatever the means by which the document is created or received, the act of creation or receipt must be in the course of a trade (or business, etc).[216] Under s 117(2)(b), the information contained in the document must have been supplied by a person who had, 'or may reasonably be supposed to have had', personal knowledge of the matters dealt with,[217] wording which allows the court, in appropriate circumstances, to infer personal knowledge on the part of the supplier.[218] Section 117(3) makes clear that the creator of the document and the supplier of the information may be one and the same person; judged in terms of potential reliability, it would be odd if a hearsay statement contained in a trade, business, or related document were to be admissible *only* if at least second-hand.

Under s 117(2)(c), if the information contained in the document was supplied indirectly, each intermediary through whom it was supplied must have received it in the course of a trade (or business, etc). It is the act of *receiving*, as opposed to the act of supplying, which

---

[215] See *R v Hayes* [2018] 1 Cr App R 134 (10), CA.

[216] This condition may be satisfied notwithstanding that the document was produced for fraudulent purposes (see *R v Gray* [2007] EWCA Crim 2658) or effected a corrupt payment (see *R v Foxley* [1995] 2 Cr App R 523, CA at 538).

[217] See *R v Humphris* (2005) 169 JP 441, CA, followed in *R v Ainscough* [2006] Crim LR 635, CA (officers lacking knowledge of the details of offences in police records of convictions); and contrast *R v Minchin* [2013] EWCA Crim 2412 (a solicitor could reasonably be supposed to have recollection of matters dealt with in an Attendance Note).

[218] See also *R v O'Connor* [2010] EWCA Crim 2287: concerning the admissibility of mobile phone records under s 117, there was nothing in the section that required a statement from an employee of the provider of the particular mobile phone to which the records relate; the judge was entitled to draw an inference simply by looking at records (whose authenticity was not disputed) that the conditions of s 117 were met. See also *R v Foxley* [1995] 2 Cr App R 523 at 536, decided under the Criminal Evidence Act 1988, and *R v Schreiber and Schreiber* [1988] Crim LR 112, CA, decided under the Criminal Evidence Act 1965, s 1.

must have been performed in the course of a trade (or business, etc). Thus, if A, a businessman and an intermediary (under s 117(2)(c)), supplies information to B, another businessman and intermediary, then provided that both A and B receive the information in the course of their respective businesses, it matters not that A is not acting in the course of his business when he supplies the information to B. The trade (or business, etc) of one intermediary need not be the same trade (or business, etc) as that of either another intermediary or the creator or receiver of the document.

Document prepared for criminal proceedings

Under s 117(4) and (5), unlike s 116, the requirement that the person who supplied the information be unable to give oral evidence for one of the specified reasons (s 116(2)(a)–(e)), is imposed only in the case of 'a statement . . . prepared for the purposes of pending or contemplated criminal proceedings, or for a criminal investigation'. This phrase is wide enough to include a witness statement taken by a police officer, a statement from a potential witness recorded by a police officer in his notebook, a statement of a potential witness, an attendance note of an interview with a potential witness made by an accused's solicitor,[219] and a custody record.[220] The phrase 'statement prepared for the purposes of contemplated criminal proceedings' has been construed to include a statement made in the course of criminal proceedings, so that a transcript of the evidence of a witness at a previous trial is admissible provided that the maker of the statement is unable to give evidence for one of the reasons specified.[221] Another difference from s 116 is the additional reason set out in s 117(5)(b), namely that the supplier of the information cannot reasonably be expected to have any recollection of the matters dealt with in the statement.[222] The word 'statement' in s 117(5)(b) bears the same meaning as in s 114 and other sections of Chapter 2 of Pt 11 of the 2003 Act[223] and does not mean the entire contents of the document. Thus if the supplier cannot reasonably be expected to have any recollection of matters dealt with in only some of the statements contained in a document, those statements may be admitted notwithstanding that he can recollect matters dealt with in other statements contained in the document.[224]

Documents of doubtful reliability

Where the requirements of s 117(1), (2), and (5) are met, the court may use s 117(6) and (7) to direct that the statement in question is nonetheless inadmissible, if satisfied that it is of doubtful reliability. It may reach this conclusion having regard to (a) its contents, which, for example, may be internally inconsistent, or inconsistent with a prior statement from the same source; (b) the source of the information, who, for example, may be shown to be dishonest or unreliable; (c) the mode and circumstances of the supply or receipt of the information; and (d) the mode and circumstances of the creation or receipt of the document, either of which may demonstrate the likelihood of inaccuracy in the contents of the statement.

---

[219] Per Kennedy J, obiter, in *R v Cunningham* [1989] Crim LR 435, CA, a decision under the Police and Criminal Evidence Act 1984, s 68.

[220] *R v Hogan* [1997] Crim LR 349, CA.

[221] *R v Lockley* [1995] 2 Cr App R 554, CA. However, the expression does not extend to a licence issued to a serving prisoner on his release from imprisonment: *West Midlands Probation Board v French* [2009] 1 WLR 1715, DC.

[222] This reason cannot be established if the supplier has some other document from which he can refresh his memory in court: per Buxton LJ in *R v Derodra* [2000] 1 Cr App R 41, CA at 44.

[223] See, in this chapter, under **'Statements'** and **'matters stated'**, p 363.

[224] *R v Carrington* (1993) 99 Cr App R 376, CA.

Admissibility in the interests of justice

The Law Commission was of the view that, in order to prevent injustice, there should be an inclusionary discretion to render admissible reliable hearsay which would not otherwise be admitted. It recognized that such a discretion, or 'safety valve', would introduce the risks of inconsistency and unpredictability, but believed that without such a discretion its proposed reforms would be too rigid. Some 'limited flexibility' needed to be incorporated. It therefore proposed that a hearsay statement should be admitted if 'despite the difficulties there may be in challenging the statement, its probative value is such that the interests of justice require it to be admissible'.[225] The inclusionary discretion in the 2003 Act has been cast more broadly and therefore relaxes the hearsay rule to a greater degree.

Section 114(1)(d): inclusionary discretion

Under s 114(1)(d) of the 2003 Act, it will be recalled, a statement not made in oral evidence in the proceedings is admissible as evidence of any matter stated if 'the court is satisfied that it is in the interests of justice for it to be admissible'. The discretion involves an evaluative exercise of judgement, weighing the significance of relevant factors including those listed in s 114(2), and it cannot be analysed in terms of a standard of proof, with specific factors needing to be proved to the criminal standard as a condition for admissibility.[226]

Section 114(1)(d) applies to both oral and written statements and can be used to admit first-hand, second-hand, or multiple hearsay, and is open to use by both the prosecution and defence.[227] However, the interests of justice will not necessarily point in the same direction for both the prosecution and the defence. Moreover, since the burden of proving the case is on the prosecution, considerable care will need to be taken in any case in which a hearsay statement would provide the prosecution with a case, when otherwise it would have none.[228] The test to be applied to an accused on a serious criminal charge will often be less exacting than that which would apply to the prosecution, but the interests of justice are synonymous not with the interests of the accused but with the public interest in arriving at the right conclusion in the case.[229]

Although the section is likely to be used as a last resort, in the sense that it will only be relied upon if the statement is not admissible under another provision of the 2003 Act, some other statutory provision, or one of the preserved common law rules, there is nothing in the section which suggests that s 114(1)(d) is a limited inclusionary discretion to be used only exceptionally. Thus the Divisional Court has observed that it is inappropriate to describe s 114(1)(d) as a 'safety valve'.[230] It follows that the provision cannot be read so as to subordinate

---

[225] Law Com No 245 (1997), Cl 9, draft bill.

[226] See *Misick v The Queen* [2015] 1 WLR 3215, PC, at [39]–[40]. See also *R v Hinds* [2017] EWCA Crim 464, where the Court of Appeal did not criticize the judge's decision not to exercise discretion in favour of the accused, which was 'finely balanced'.

[227] See *R v Freeman* [2010] EWCA Crim 1997 at [26]. The provision does not apply to confiscation proceedings under the Proceeds of Crime Act 2002, although the safeguards in s 114(2) may be adapted for use: see *R v Clipston* [2011] 2 Cr App R (S) 569 (101), CA. Nor does the provision apply in relation to evidence-in-chief by video recording admissible under the special measures provisions of the Youth Justice and Criminal Evidence Act 1999: see *DPP v R* [2007] EWHC 1842, DC.

[228] *R v Y* [2008] 1 WLR 1683, CA at [59].

[229] *R v Marsh* [2008] EWCA Crim 1816.

[230] *Sak v CPS* (2008) 172 JP 89 at [26].

it to the other exceptions.[231] Nevertheless, the section must not be lightly applied and the Court of Appeal has emphasized that the greatest care must be taken before admitting an out-of-court statement under s 114(1)(d).[232] Moreover, the inclusionary discretion should not be applied so as to render s 116 nugatory; the Court of Appeal has consistently shown reluctance to admit statements by witnesses who are not 'unavailable' for one of the statutory reasons contained in s 116(2).[233] However, the admission of evidence relating to an *uncontentious* matter has been held to be 'plainly in the interests of justice' even where the party calling the witness had taken such inadequate steps to find him that it was unable to satisfy the provisions of s 116(2)(d).[234] Furthermore, the evidence of a 'reluctant' witness which was not sole or decisive was held to be admissible to rebut the *contentious* issue of the accused's defence that it was the witness who committed the crime.[235] It is clear from the authorities that s 114(1)(d) cannot be used to admit anonymous hearsay evidence either from a known witness whose identity the prosecution seeks to withhold from the accused,[236] or the accused seeks to withhold from the prosecution,[237] or from a witness whose identity is not known at all,[238] unless the witness is untraceable and in the circumstances in which the statement was made, there is no realistic scope for questioning the credibility of the witness.[239] It has also been held that s 114(1)(d) should be the provision least capable of covering a situation where a witness refuses to give evidence in a retrial ordered by the Court of Appeal.[240] More generally, s 114(1)(d) should obviously not be used if, having regard to Art 6 of the European Convention on Human Rights, this would result in an unfair trial.[241]

[231] See *R v Y* [2008] 1 WLR 1683, CA at [47]. However, it does not take priority over common law exceptions as a route to admissibility. See *Barnaby v DPP* [2015] 2 Cr App R 53 (4): evidence being properly admissible under the common law *res gestae* principle preserved by s 118(1)4(a), there was no obligation to rely instead on s 114(1)(d).

[232] *R v Y* [2008] 1 WLR 1683, CA at [62]. See also *R v C* [2010] Crim LR 858, CA and *R v Riat* [2013] 1 WLR 2592 at [20].

[233] See *R v O'Hare* [2006] EWCA Crim 2512 at [30]; *R v Y* [2008] 1 WLR 1683, CA at [60]; *R v Marsh* [2008] EWCA Crim 1816; *R v Sadiq* (2009) 173 JP 471, CA at [24]; *R v Z* [2009] 1 Cr App R 500 (34) at [20] and [24]; *R v ED* [2010] EWCA Crim 1213 at [14]–[21]; *R v CT* (2011) 175 JP 462, CA; *R v Riat* [2013] 1 WLR 2592, CA at [20]; and *R v Warnick* [2013] EWCA Crim 2320 at [11]. See also, in this chapter, under **Article 6 and the reasons for non-attendance**, **pp 358–9** and nn **66–69**.

[234] *R v T (D)* (2009) 173 JP 425, CA. Similarly, see *R v Burton* (2011) 175 JP 385, CA, an exceptional case where the Court of Appeal held that the trial judge was justified in admitting under s 114(1)(d) statements made by a reluctant but available child witness with whom the adult accused was alleged to have had sexual activity.

[235] See *Seton v UK* [2016] ECHR 318 and *R v Seton* [2010] EWCA Crim 450.

[236] *R v Horncastle* [2010] 2 AC 373, SC at [48]; and *R v Fox* [2010] EWCA Crim 1280 at [12]; *R v Mayers* [2009] 1 WLR 195, CA at [109] and [113]; and *R v Davies* [2008] 1 AC 1128, HL at [20].

[237] See *R v Sardar* [2017] 1 WLR 917, CA, concerning anonymous statements of defence witnesses who were not prepared to disclose their identities to the prosecution other than within a tightly constrained 'confidentiality ring' (to which the prosecution would not agree).

[238] *R v Ford* [2010] EWCA Crim 2250; [2011] Crim LR 475. See also *R v Twist* [2011] 2 Cr App R 189 (17), CA at [22]; [2011] Crim LR 793, CA.

[239] In such a situation, there is no principled reason to treat the question of admissibility any differently from a case where the witness is known but after making his statement, cannot be found: *R v Brown* [2019] EWCA Crim 1143 at [34].

[240] See *R v Lawrence* [2014] 1 Cr App R 5, *R v M* [2014] Crim LR 300. Section 131(1)(a)–(c) of the 2003 Act permits hearsay evidence to be admitted in a retrial (a) by agreement; (b) under s 116; or (c) under s 114(1)(d).

[241] As regards the fairness of the trial under Art 6, see the three stage test in *Al Khawaja and Tahery v UK* (2012) 54 EHRR 23 as clarified by *Schatschaschwili v Germany* (2016) 63 EHRR 14. See, in this chapter, under **The statutory scheme and Art 6 of the European Convention on Human Rights**, p 353. See also under **Art 6 and the reasons for non-attendance**, p 358, *Seton v UK* [2016] ECHR 318.

The Court of Appeal will only interfere with a decision of a trial judge under s 114(1)(d) if it was outwith the range of reasonable decisions, because the trial judge is best placed to assess accurately the fairness of admitting evidence in the context of the trial as a whole.[242] However, the Court of Appeal will be more willing to interfere with a judge's decision under s 114(1)(d) where the judge fails to take into account, or fails to show that he has taken into account, the factors set out in s 114(2).[243]

Section 114(2): factors which must be considered

In deciding whether to exercise the power contained in s 114(1)(d), the trial judge must have regard to the non-exhaustive list of factors set out in s 114(2). Section 114(2) provides as follows:

(2) In deciding whether a statement not made in oral evidence should be admitted under subsection (1)(d), the court must have regard to the following factors (and to any others it considers relevant)—

   (a) how much probative value the statement has (assuming it to be true) in relation to a matter in issue in the proceedings, or how valuable it is for the understanding of other evidence in the case;

   (b) what other evidence has been, or can be, given on the matter or evidence mentioned in paragraph (a);

   (c) how important the matter or evidence mentioned in paragraph (a) is in the context of the case as a whole;

   (d) the circumstances in which the statement was made;

   (e) how reliable the maker of the statement appears to be;

   (f) how reliable the evidence of the making of the statement appears to be;

   (g) whether oral evidence of the matter stated can be given and, if not, why it cannot;

   (h) the amount of difficulty involved in challenging the statement;

   (i) the extent to which that difficulty would be likely to prejudice the party facing it.

Although the factors listed in s 114(2)(a)–(g) apply directly to s 114(1)(d), in *R v Riat*[244] the Court of Appeal commended them as useful aides-memoire when considering the admissibility of hearsay evidence under any other hearsay provision or its exclusion under s 78 of the Police and Criminal Evidence Act 1984.[245]

In respect of s 114(2)(a), evidence of considerable importance that would undermine the defence and point powerfully to a conviction makes the other factors, particularly s 114(2) (g), even more significant.[246] The Court of Appeal has stressed that s 114(2)(g) refers to the *inability* of a witness to give evidence rather than reluctance and it will be rare that potentially prejudicial evidence will be admitted under s 114(1)(d) where a witness is available

---

[242] *R v Musone* [2007] 1 WLR 2467, CA at [20]. See also *R v Finch* [2007] 1 WLR 1645, CA at [23] and *R v Freeman* [2010] EWCA Crim 1997 at [25].

[243] See *R v Z* [2009] 1 Cr App R 500 (34), CA. See also *R v CT* (2011) 175 JP 462, CA—the judge failed, in particular, to take account of the factors in s 114(2)(c) and (g). Cf *R v Hengari-Ajufo* [2016] EWCA Crim 1913 at [20]–[21] (all the factors addressed in a careful ruling) and *R v Seton* (2010) 174 JP 241, CA, at [19]–[24] (all the factors considered in turn).

[244] [2013] 1 WLR 2592, CA.

[245] Ibid at [22]. Although '. . . they are not a questionnaire to be answered': *R v C* [2019] 2 Cr App R 88 (11), CA at [31].

[246] *R v Z* [2009] 1 Cr App R 500 (34), CA at [24].

but reluctant, and the reluctance is not due to fear.[247] In respect of s 114(2)(d), (e), and (f), it is for the judge to make the assessment of the reliability of the maker of the statement and the circumstances in which it was made, and he should not abrogate that responsibility by saying reliability is a matter for the jury.[248] It would render nugatory s 114(2)(e), if the judge could always say the assessment of the evidence was for the jury.[249] At the very least, the judge himself must be satisfied that the evidence is properly capable of being considered reliable by the jury.[250] The correct approach to s 114(2)(h) is to focus on the difficulty in assessing the veracity of the declarant's statement and not the difficulties of challenging the witness who reports the statement,[251] which ought to be taken into account under s 114(2)(f).

In *R v Taylor*[252] two prosecution witnesses named T as a participant in an attack, having been told his name by someone else. The judge admitted this evidence under s 114(1)(d), although was unable to reach a conclusion on a number of the factors set out in s 114(2), such as the circumstances in which the informant's statement was made, his reliability, and whether he could give oral evidence. The Court of Appeal held that s 114(2) requires an exercise of judgement in the light of the factors identified and does not require an investigation, resulting in some cases in the hearing of evidence, in order to reach a conclusion by reference to each or any of the factors. On that basis, it was held that the judge's approach could not be challenged. However, the decision is surprising. As one commentator submits:[253]

> the judge should engage in some degree of investigation and, in cases where the evidence is of great importance, this might involve receiving evidence. . .[254]

Section 114(1)(d) and third party confessions

One example given by the Law Commission as to how s 114(1)(d) might be used as a 'safety valve' was based on the facts of *R v Cooper*.[255] The accused was charged with assault and a third party of similar appearance made a statement to the accused's friend, admitting that he had carried out the assault. The accused was not permitted to introduce the third party's confession. Subsequent authorities confirmed that an out-of-court confession, by a third party, to the offence with which the accused is charged, is inadmissible,[256] a stance justified on the ground that it is for the legislature, not the judiciary, to create new exceptions to the hearsay

---

[247] Ibid. See also *R v Y* [2008] 1 WLR 1683, CA at [60] and *R v Khan* [2009] EWCA Crim 86 at [15]. See also *R v Freeman* [2010] EWCA Crim 1997 at [31] and [33]; *R v ED* [2010] EWCA Crim 1213; and *R v CT* (2011) 175 JP 462, CA. See also *R v Burton* (2011) 175 JP 385, CA, where the statement of a reluctant child witness was properly admitted under s 114(1)(d). Her statement was not decisive evidence and it had been open to the accused to call her if he truly believed she would support his defence that he had not engaged in sexual activity with her.

[248] *R v Sliogeris* [2015] EWCA Crim 22 at [41], (2015) 179 JP 156, CA. See also *R v Amin* [2014] EWCA Crim 1924 at [34], an example of the application of factors (a)–(i) to evidence of incriminating conversations recorded covertly during visits received by the accused while he was on remand in prison.

[249] See *R v Musone* [2007] 1 WLR 2467, per Moses LJ at [25]–[26].

[250] *R v Sliogeris* [2015] EWCA Crim 22 at [41].

[251] *R v Marsh* [2008] EWCA Crim 816, at [19].

[252] [2006] 2 Cr App R 222 (14), CA.

[253] Ormerod, '*R v Taylor*' (case comment) [2006] Crim LR 640.

[254] See also *Maher v DPP* (2006) 170 JP 441, DC, considered later in the context of multiple hearsay.

[255] [1969] 1 QB 267, CA.

[256] *R v Turner* (1975) 61 Cr App R 67, CA. See also *R v Callan* (1994) 98 Cr App R 467, CA. As to the admissibility, for an accused, of a confession made by a *co-accused*, see the Police and Criminal Evidence Act 1984, s 76A (see Ch 15).

rule,[257] and to hold otherwise 'would be to create a very significant and, many might think, a dangerous new exception'.[258] The obvious danger is the ease with which a third party confession may be fabricated coupled with the fact that such a confession, by itself, could leave the jury 'unsure'. However, each case will now involve the court in a complex balancing exercise, having regard to the factors set out in s 114(2) in the context of the particular facts of the case. It is not without significance, for instance, that in the example given by the Law Commission, the third party was of similar appearance to the accused. *R v Finch*[259] concerned a confession by D2, who pleaded guilty, exonerating D1, but D2 was 'reluctant' to give evidence for reasons that were not compelling. The trial judge concluded that the interests of justice did not call for the evidence to be admitted by D1. Although it was plainly of substantial probative value and without it there was only the evidence of D1 himself, and therefore it was of considerable importance in the context of the case as a whole, oral evidence could be given by D2. D2's reliability was open to question if he was not prepared to support in the witness box what he had said to the police, and there would be difficulties for the prosecution in challenging his statement in his absence. The principal factor was that D2 was compellable, and therefore could have been called and subjected to cross-examination.[260] The Court of Appeal upheld the decision, observing that s 114(2) calls for the exercise of judgement by the trial judge with which it should only interfere if exercised on wrong principles or if the conclusion reached was outside the band of legitimate decisions available.[261]

Examples of appropriate use of s 114(1)(d)

While each case turns upon its own facts, the following are illustrative of circumstances in which the Court of Appeal has approved the use of s 114(1)(d) to admit otherwise inadmissible hearsay evidence. A wife made a witness statement undermining her husband's defence to a charge of raping his daughter, then retracted it and, not being compellable by virtue of s 80 of the Police and Criminal Evidence Act 1984, refused to testify; the prosecution were permitted to adduce the statement.[262] The victim of an attempted murder, a crucial witness for the prosecution, sustained horrific injuries during the offence, leaving him incapable of giving evidence other than through an intermediary: the transcript of his evidence at the first trial was admissible at a retrial.[263] An accused charged with murder made admissions to his girlfriend; the prosecution were permitted to adduce the confession at the trial of the accomplice as evidence of his involvement in the offence.[264] An accused refused to agree the

---

[257] See *Myers v DPP* [1965] AC 1001, HL.

[258] Per Lord Bridge in *R v Blastland* [1986] AC 41, HL, at 53. Contrast *Chambers v Mississippi* 410 US 295 (1973) (US Sup Court): excluding confessions of a third party deprives the accused of a fair trial.

[259] [2007] 1 WLR 1645, CA.

[260] See also *R v Marsh* [2008] EWCA Crim 1816 per Hughes LJ at [25].

[261] See also *R v Hinds* [2017] EWCA Crim 464 at [27]; *R v Seton* (2010) 174 JP 241, CA at [24]; and *R v Z* [2009] 1 Cr App R 500 (34), CA at [25].

[262] *R v L* [2009] 1 WLR 626, CA. See also *R v Horsnell* [2012] EWCA Crim 277: the fact that a witness is not compellable and, further, may have been advised that (s)he was not compellable at the time of making the statement are very important factors to be borne in mind when making a decision as to the statement's admissibility under s 114(1)(d).

[263] *R v Sadiq* (2009) 173 JP 471, CA.

[264] *R v Y* [2008] 1 WLR 1683, CA. See also *R v McLean* [2008] 1 Cr App R 156; *R v Ibrahim* [2009] 1 WLR 578, CA; and *R v B* [2008] All ER 108, [2008] EWCA Crim 365.

circumstances of a conviction admissible under the bad character provisions of the 2003 Act; the prosecution were permitted to adduce a summary of the content of his police interviews and evidence he gave at the trial for that offence.[265] A serving prisoner made telephone calls to his family from prison in which he denied involvement in a murder for which the accused sought to blame him, and expressed outrage; recordings of the calls made by prison authorities were admissible where the prisoner made it clear that he would not give evidence or make a statement to the police and where there was other overwhelming evidence against the accused.[266] The mother of the accused charged with murder recorded a conversation with a witness in which the witness purportedly admitted to having been the person who stabbed the victim; the recording would have been admissible had it been introduced during the defence case as part of the mother's testimony.[267] In a murder case, a witness was compelled to attend court but would not give evidence beyond what he had previously said in a deposition (despite being treated as hostile and being subject to cross-examination); evidence could be given by two other witnesses about what he had told them he knew and had witnessed.[268] A witness to a stabbing saw the assailant get into a car and then made a 999 call and read a number from the screen of a mobile phone of another witness present at the time who said it was the car's registration number, but that witness was untraceable and unknown; the witness who made the 999 call could give evidence of the registration number.[269]

Previous inconsistent statements of witnesses

Under s 3 of the Criminal Procedure Act 1865 (the 1865 Act), a party calling a witness who proves to be hostile may, by leave of the judge, prove that he has made at other times a statement inconsistent with his testimony.[270] Under s 4 of the 1865 Act, if a witness, upon cross-examination as to a previous inconsistent statement, does not distinctly admit that he made such a statement, proof may be given by the cross-examining party that he did in fact make it. Proof of the statement is governed by both s 4 and s 5 of the 1865 Act, s 4 applying to both oral and written statements, and s 5 applying to written statements only.[271] If the hostile witness (s 3), or the witness under cross-examination (ss 4 and 5), adopts the contents of the previous statement, then they become part of his evidence and will be evidence of the matter stated. However, as the law stood prior to the coming into force of s 119(1) of the 2003 Act, if, in criminal cases,

---

[265] *R v Steen* [2008] 2 Cr App R 380 (26).

[266] *R v Seton* (2010) 174 JP 241, CA. See also *Seton v UK* [2016] ECHR 318: admission of the evidence was compatible with Art 6(1) and 3(d). However, it has been commented that the evidence may have been admitted too readily: see *Blackstone's Criminal Practice 2019*, F17.39. In *R v Freeman* [2010] EWCA 1997, it was held that as a matter of principle reluctance is not a ground for not making a witness attend. It may be that the court in *R v Seton* was influenced by the late stage at which the accused sought to blame the witness.

[267] *R v Williams* [2014] EWCA Crim 1862.

[268] *R v Hengari-Ajufo* [2016] EWCA Crim 1913.

[269] *R v Brown* [2019] EWCA Crim 1143. Cf *R v Sardar* [2017] 1 WLR 917, CA, see n 239. See also *R v Randall* [2018] EWHC 1048 (Admin), an example of *inappropriate* use of s 114(1)(d). Where the complaint was present at court and willing to give evidence, the justices were wrong to admit her contentious statement on the basis that the accused had not identified which parts of her statement he disputed and had not otherwise engaged with the pre-trial process. Cf *R v Adams* [2008] 1 Cr App R 430 (35), CA, which provides some authority for using s 114(1)(d) where the accused has not engaged with the pre-trial process and the statement is *uncontentious*.

[270] See Ch 6, Unfavourable and hostile witnesses, p 206.

[271] See Ch 7, Cross-examination, Previous inconsistent statements, p 222.

the witness did not admit to making the statement and it was proved that he did in fact make it, the statement was not introduced as evidence of the matter stated, but went merely to his credit. Under s 119(1), the statement is admitted as evidence of any matter stated of which oral evidence by the witness would be admissible. The reasoning of the Law Commission was that if the tribunal of fact is trusted to decide that the witness lacks credibility and his testimony should be disregarded, they should also be free to accept the previous statement as reliable.[272]

Section 119(1)

Section 119(1) provides as follows:

> (1) If in criminal proceedings, a person gives oral evidence and—
>   (a) he admits making a previous inconsistent statement, or
>   (b) a previous inconsistent statement made by him is proved by virtue of section 3, 4 or 5 of the Criminal Procedure Act 1865,
>   the statement is admissible as evidence of any matter stated of which oral evidence by him would be admissible.

Section 119(1) has the merit of removing from the tribunal of fact, in this particular context, the difficult concept of a previous statement being admitted not as evidence of the matters stated but as evidence to undermine the credibility of its maker as a witness in the case. It is a radical change in the law and is a powerful tool in relation to hostile witnesses.[273] Section 119(1) is subject to the discretionary powers to exclude evidence on which the prosecution propose to rely; and, in jury trials in which the case against the accused is based wholly or partly on such a statement, the court has the power under s 125 of the Act to direct the jury to acquit if the evidence provided by the statement is so unconvincing that the conviction of the accused would be unsafe.[274] In cases where the statement is left before the jury, and the witness maintains that it is untrue, a careful direction is called for.[275]

Other previous statements of witnesses

At common law, the general rule against previous consistent statements prevents a witness from being asked in examination-in-chief about a previous out-of-court statement made by him and consistent with his testimony. Under the rule, such a statement is excluded as evidence of consistency and is also inadmissible hearsay, except to the extent that it is admissible under the 2003 Act.[276] There is the usual danger of manufactured evidence, and to allow a witness to give evidence of a previous statement which is consistent with his testimony is to encourage reception of superfluous evidence. On the other hand, one of the main justifications of the hearsay rule, the impossibility of cross-examining the maker of the statement, does not apply. Furthermore, an out-of-court statement made shortly after the events to which it relates, while those events are fresh in the memory, is likely to be more reliable than testimony at a trial some months or years later.

---

[272] Law Com No 245 (1997), para 10.89.

[273] See Ch 6, **Unfavourable and hostile witnesses, p 206.**

[274] See, in this chapter, under **Stopping the case where the evidence is unconvincing, p 400.**

[275] See *R v Joyce* [2005] EWCA Crim 1785; and *R v Billingham* [2009] 2 Cr App R 341 (20), CA at [63]. See also the Crown Court Compendium (July 2019), Part 1, 14–7.

[276] See **Ch 6.**

Section 120

Under s 120 of the 2003 Act, a provision of compromise, the previous statements of a witness only become admissible as evidence of the matters stated in five situations, four of which are plainly based upon, and in some cases expanded versions of, the rather technical common law exceptions to the rule against previous consistent or self-serving statements. Section 120 provides as follows.

(1) This section applies where a person (the witness) is called to give evidence in criminal proceedings.

(2) If a previous statement by the witness is admitted as evidence to rebut a suggestion that his oral evidence has been fabricated, that statement is admissible as evidence of any matter stated of which oral evidence by the witness would be admissible.

(3) A statement made by the witness in a document—

    (a) which is used by him to refresh his memory while giving evidence,

    (b) on which he is cross-examined, and

    (c) which as a consequence is received in evidence in the proceedings,

    is admissible as evidence of any matter stated of which oral evidence by him would be admissible.

(4) A previous statement by the witness is admissible as evidence of any matter stated of which oral evidence by him would be admissible, if

    (a) any of the following three conditions is satisfied, and

    (b) while giving evidence the witness indicates that to the best of his belief he made the statement, and that to the best of his belief it states the truth.

(5) The first condition is that the statement identifies or describes a person, object or place.

(6) The second condition is that the statement was made by the witness when the matters stated were fresh in his memory but he does not remember them, and cannot reasonably be expected to remember them, well enough to give oral evidence of them in the proceedings.

(7) The third condition is that—

    (a) the witness claims to be a person against whom an offence has been committed,

    (b) the offence is one to which the proceedings relate,

    (c) the statement consists of a complaint made by the witness (whether to a person in authority or not) about conduct which would, if proved, constitute the offence or part of the offence,

    (d) . . . [277]

    (e) the complaint was not made as a result of a threat or promise, and

    (f) before the statement is adduced the witness gives oral evidence in connection with its subject matter.

(8) For the purposes of subsection (7) the fact that the complaint was elicited (for example, by a leading question) is irrelevant unless a threat or a promise was involved.

Statements in rebuttal of allegations of fabrication

Under s 120(2), a witness's previous oral or written statement is admissible as evidence of any matter stated of which oral evidence by him would be admissible 'if . . . admitted as evidence to rebut a suggestion that his oral evidence has been fabricated', that is, if admitted under the exception to the rule against previous consistent statements. That exception arises when, in cross-examination of the witness, it is suggested to him that the account given by him in his testimony is a recent invention or fabrication.[278]

---

[277] Repealed by the Coroners and Justice Act 2009, s 112.

[278] See further Ch 6, **Previous consistent or self-serving statements**, p 193.

Although such a statement may assist the jury in their assessment of the witness's reliability, it is not independent evidence. In *R v A*[279] it was held that where such a statement is admitted under s 120, the following direction recommended by Laws LJ in *R v AA*[280] should be routinely given.

> ... juries should be directed that such a previous consistent statement or recent complaint is, if the jury accepts it was given or made and the conditions specified in section 120 are fulfilled, evidence of the truth of what was stated: but in deciding what weight such a statement should bear, the jury should have in mind the fact it comes from the same person who now makes the complaint in the witness box and not from some independent source.[281]

Statements in documents used to refresh the memory

Section 120(3), which mirrors a common law exception to the rule against previous consistent statements, applies where the witness is cross-examined on a memory-refreshing document and, as a consequence, the whole document is received in evidence. This happens when a party, or his advocate, in cross-examining the witness on the memory-refreshing document, asks questions about matters derived from parts of the document not used by the witness to refresh his memory.[282]

Statements identifying or describing a person, object, or place

Under s 120(5), read in conjunction with s 120(4), a previous oral or written statement of a witness identifying or describing a person, object, or place, will be admissible as evidence of any matter stated of which oral evidence by him would be admissible if, in evidence, he indicates that to the best of his belief he made the statement and it states the truth. Section 120(5) is based on the exception to the rule against previous consistent statements in the case of previous identification of *the accused* but, in accordance with the recommendation of the Law Commission, extends the principle to the identification, or description, of any person, object, or place.[283] In *R v Chinn*[284] it was observed that while the precise scope of s 120(5) was unclear, 'a description of a person, object or place that is made in a vacuum is of no use in criminal proceedings' and accordingly, evidence of a description or identification under s 120(5) can extend to evidence which puts the description or identification in its relevant context.[285]

Statements made when the matters were fresh in the memory

Section 120(6) operates to abolish the common law fiction that when a witness does not remember certain matters, or does not remember them well enough to give evidence about them, and therefore 'refreshes his memory' by reference to a statement made by him when the matters stated were fresh in his memory, it is the oral testimony of the witness which constitutes the evidence in the case. Commentators over many years have submitted that it

---

[279] (2011) 175 JP 437, CA.

[280] [2007] EWCA Crim 1779 at [17].

[281] See also the Crown Court Compendium (July 2019), Part 1, 14–9.

[282] See further Ch 6, **Refreshing the memory**, p 183. See also *DPP v R* [2007] EWHC 1842, DC, at [30]: the provision also covers memory refreshing from a video interview where evidence-in-chief by video recording is admitted under the provisions of the Youth Justice and Criminal Evidence Act 1999.

[283] See further Ch 6, **Previous consistent or self-serving statements**, p 193.

[284] [2012] 1 WLR 3401, CA.

[285] Ibid at [55]–[56].

would be more principled to regard the statement as a variety of admissible hearsay. This is achieved by s 120(6), which applies to previous statements made orally or in a document, provided that the witness gives the indications required by s 120(4)(b).[286]

Statements consisting of a complaint about the alleged offence

Section 120(7) is based on the exception to the rule against previous consistent statements in the case of recent complaints in sexual cases.[287] However, the statutory provisions do not codify the law, but are freestanding and provide their own criteria.[288] As stated in the fifth edition of this book,[289] what is curious is not that the common law exception had survived, but that for no good reason it was confined to sexual cases. Section 120(7), in accordance with the recommendations of the Law Commission[290] and, long before that, the Criminal Law Revision Committee,[291] extends the principle to a previous statement, oral or written, made by a person against whom *any* offence has been committed, provided that it is an offence to which the proceedings relate, and that the statement consists of a complaint about conduct which would, if proved, constitute the offence or part of the offence to which the proceedings relate.[292]

There are a number of other conditions, in addition to the requirement that the witness give the indications required by s 120(4)(b). Section 120(7)(e) requires that the complaint was not made as a result of a threat or promise, and under s 120(8), which does not follow the approach taken in the common law authorities relating to a recent complaint in a sexual case, the fact that the complaint was elicited, for example, by a leading question, is irrelevant unless a threat or promise was made. Thus it is not only irrelevant to admissibility if the complaint was made in answer to a non-leading question such as 'What is the matter?', but also if it was made in answer to a leading question such as 'Did X (naming the accused) assault you?' Although a complaint elicited by way of a leading question is bound to affect the weight to be attached to it, so far as admissibility is concerned the issue is whether it was made voluntarily in the sense that it was not obtained by a threat or promise.

Finally, s 120(7)(f) requires that before the statement is introduced in evidence, the witness 'gives oral evidence in connection with its subject matter', words which suggest that this requirement will be met provided only that the complainant gives some evidence in relation to the conduct referred to in her complaint, even if the evidence does not replicate the complaint or is not wholly consistent with it.

Where a witness's previous statement is admitted under s 120(7), it is submitted that a direction should be given to the jury similar to the direction recommended by Laws LJ in *R v AA*.[293]

---

[286] See further Ch 6, Refreshing the memory, p 183.

[287] See Ch 6, Previous consistent or self-serving statements, p 193.

[288] *R v O* [2006] 2 Cr App R 405 (27), CA.

[289] At 153.

[290] Law Com No 245 (1997), paras 10.53–10.61.

[291] 11th report, *Evidence (General)*, Cm 4991 (1972), para 232.

[292] *R v T* [2008] EWCA Crim 484: s 120(7) is restricted to complaints about offences on the indictment and does not include complaints about other offences, eg offences admitted as evidence of the defendant's bad character.

[293] *R v AA* [2007] EWCA Crim 1779 at [17]. See, in this chapter, under, **Statements in rebuttal of allegations of fabrication**, p 393. See also the Crown Court Compendium (July 2019), Part 1, 14–9.

Multiple hearsay

Multiple hearsay, as when X testifies as to what Y told him Z had said, gives rise to problems of both reliability and proof. As to reliability, although business and other written records which have passed through many hands may be no less reliable than first-hand hearsay, there are obvious risks in the case of multiple oral hearsay: in addition to the fact that the maker of the original statement may be unavailable for cross-examination, and the usual risk of manufactured or fabricated evidence, there is scope for error or distortion in the transmission or repeated transmission of information.[294] As to proof, s 121 of the 2003 Act provides as follows:

(1) A hearsay statement is not admissible to prove the fact that an earlier hearsay statement was made unless—

(a) either of the statements is admissible under section 117, 119 or 120,

(b) all parties to the proceedings so agree, or

(c) the court is satisfied that the value of the evidence in question, taking into account how reliable the statements appear to be, is so high that the interests of justice require the later statement to be admissible for that purpose.

(2) In this section 'hearsay statement' means a statement, not made in oral evidence, that is relied on as evidence of a matter stated in it.

One of the statements admissible as business document, inconsistent statement, or other previous statement

The purpose of s 121(1)(a) appears to be to allow a party to prove the fact that the 'earlier statement' was made by a 'hearsay statement' provided that either (i) the earlier statement is admissible under one of ss 117, 119, or 120; or (ii) the hearsay statement is admissible under one of those sections. As to (i), *R v Xhabri*[295] provides an example. The victim's complaint of false imprisonment was relayed by two unidentified informants to a police constable. It was held that the constable could give evidence of the informant's hearsay statement to prove the victim's earlier statement, because that earlier statement was admissible under s 120(4) and (7). The court held that the complaint was also admissible under s 121(1)(c).[296] As to (ii), suppose that D is charged with assaulting E; that H, who witnessed the assault, made an out-of-court statement to his wife, W, that D assaulted E; that H is now dead, and therefore the statement is admissible under s 116. Let us now consider three alternative developments.

1. By the time of the trial, W is also dead, and cannot prove what H said. However, before her death, W made a written statement to the police, recording the fact that H had told her that D had assaulted E. H's statement is now admissible as evidence of the matters he stated, because in this situation W's statement is admissible under s 117 to prove the fact that H's hearsay statement was made.

2. W told X that H had told her that D had assaulted E. W is called by the prosecution to prove what H said. In giving her evidence, she shows no desire to tell the truth, is

---

[294] See Law Com No 245, Cm 3670 (1997), paras 8.16 ff.

[295] [2006] 1 Cr App R 413 (26), CA.

[296] In respect of an earlier statement being admissible under s 117, see the scenario posited in *R v Usayi* [2017] EWCA Crim 1394 at [35].

treated as a hostile witness, and flatly denies that H made any statement to her that D had assaulted E. W's statement to X is then proved, by calling X to give evidence of it, by virtue of s 3 of the Criminal Procedure Act 1865. H's statement is again admissible as evidence of the matters he stated, in this situation because evidence of W's previous inconsistent statement is admissible under s 119(1)(b) of the 2003 Act to prove the fact that H's hearsay statement was made.

3. Shortly after H made his statement to W, and while the fact that he had made the statement was fresh in W's memory, she wrote a letter to Y in which she recorded that H had told her that D had assaulted E. W is called by the prosecution to prove what H said but does not remember the fact that H made his statement, and in all the circumstances, including the state of her memory and the time that has elapsed, she cannot reasonably be expected to remember the matter well enough to give oral evidence of it. However, when she is shown a copy of her letter to Y, she indicates that to the best of her belief she made the statement in the letter and to the best of her belief it states the truth. H's statement is again admissible as evidence of the matters he stated, in this situation because evidence of W's previous statement is admissible under s 120(4) and (6) to prove the fact that H's hearsay statement was made.

Admissibility by agreement

Section 121(1)(b) is self-explanatory.

Admissibility in the interests of justice

Section 121(1)(c) permits the court to admit a hearsay statement to prove that another hearsay statement was made, even if the later statement is not otherwise admissible hearsay and the parties to the proceedings do not agree to its admission. The test is whether the court is satisfied that the value of the evidence in question, taking into account how reliable the statements appear to be, is so high that the interests of justice require the later statement to be admissible for the purpose of proving that the earlier statement was made. Section 121(1)(c) is plainly designed to be a stringent test and should not be invoked where, having regard to Art 6 of the European Convention on Human Rights, it would result in an unfair trial. However, the Court of Appeal will only interfere with a trial judge's decision under s 121(1)(c) if it falls outside the range of reasonable decisions.[297] An example of the application of s 121(1)(c) is provided by *Maher v DPP*.[298] The issue was whether M had carelessly driven her car into another parked car. A witness, D, wrote the number of M's car on a piece of paper and put it under the wiperblade of the parked car. The girlfriend of the owner of the parked car, McD, phoned the police and read the number from the piece of paper—later lost or destroyed—to a police clerk, who recorded it in a log. M admitted to the police that she had driven in the car park at the material time, but denied any collision. It was held that although the log could not be used under s 121(1)(a) to prove D's 'earlier statement', because it was not admissible under ss 117, 119, or 120, it was admissible under s 121(1)(c), or ss 114(1)(d) and 114(2) (admissibility in the interests of justice), having regard to the likely reliability of the identification of the number of the car and of its transmission via McD to the police log, given the magnitude

---

[297] *R v Musone* [2007] 1 WLR 2467, CA at [20].

[298] (2006) 170 JP 441, DC. See also *R v Thakrar* [2010] EWCA Crim 1505 and *R v Friel* [2012] EWCA Crim 2871.

of the precise coincidence with the number of D's car being in the car park at the relevant time.[299] However, in *R v Walker*[300] it was held that, although s 121(1)(c) imposes a higher threshold than ss 114(1)(d) and 114(2), it is not an alternative to admissibility under those sections. Thus where a witness's statement involves both an element of first-hand hearsay and multiple hearsay, s 121(1)(c) should not be used to admit the whole of the witness's statement. It will be necessary to identify which parts of the statement are first-hand hearsay admissible under ss 114(1)(d) and 114(2), and which parts are multiple hearsay admissible under s 121(1)(c) (which is an additional test to be met).[301]

Other safeguards

Capability

Under s 123(1) of the 2003 Act, a hearsay statement cannot be admitted under s 116 (a witness is unavailable), s 119 (inconsistent statements), or s 120 (other previous statements of witnesses) if its maker did not have the 'required capability' at the time he made the statement. 'Required capability', for these purposes, means the capability of understanding questions put to him about matters stated and giving answers to such questions which can be understood,[302] a test reflecting the test for competence in criminal cases set out in s 53 of the Youth Justice and Criminal Evidence Act 1999. Under s 123(2) of the 2003 Act, a hearsay statement cannot be admitted under s 117 (business and other documents) if any person who supplied or received the information, or created or received the document or part concerned, did not have the 'required capability' at the time of supply or receipt, etc or, if any such person cannot be identified, 'cannot reasonably be assumed to have had the required capability at that time'. The procedure to be followed where there is a dispute as to whether any person had the 'required capability' is governed by s 123(4): the issue must be decided in the absence of the jury; the court may receive expert evidence and evidence from any person to whom the statement in question was made; the burden of proof is on the party seeking to adduce the statement; and the standard of proof is the balance of probabilities.

Credibility

The general purpose of s 124 of the 2003 Act is to enable the parties to attack or support the credibility of the maker of a hearsay statement who is not called as a witness as if he had been so called. In the case of a statement in a document admitted under s 117 (business and other documents), the person who supplied or received the information contained in the statement, or who created or received the document, if not called as a witness, is also to be treated as 'the maker of the statement' for the purposes of the section. Section 124 provides as follows:

---

[299] In *R v Williams* [2014] EWCA Crim 1826, a phone recording by the accused's mother of possible admissions by a witness was admissible under s 114(1)(d) provided the mother gave evidence of it, but was not admissible under s 121(1)(c) by a police officer giving evidence of it since the interests of justice required evidence of the circumstances and the context of the conversation, to enable a proper assessment of its reliability.

[300] [2007] EWCA Crim 1698.

[301] Ibid at [30].

[302] Section 123(3).

(1) This section applies if in criminal proceedings—
   (a) a statement not made in oral evidence in the proceedings is admitted as evidence of a matter stated, and
   (b) the maker of the statement does not give oral evidence in connection with the subject matter of the statement.
(2) In such a case—
   (a) any evidence which (if he had given such evidence) would have been admissible as relevant to his credibility as a witness is so admissible in the proceedings;
   (b) evidence may with the court's leave be given of any matter which (if he had given such evidence) could have been put to him in cross-examination as relevant to his credibility as a witness but of which evidence could not have been adduced by the cross-examining party;
   (c) evidence tending to prove that he made (at whatever time) any other statement inconsistent with the statement admitted as evidence is admissible for the purpose of showing that he contradicted himself.
(3) If as a result of evidence admitted under this section an allegation is made against the maker of a statement, the court may permit a party to lead additional evidence of such description as the court may specify for the purposes of denying or answering the allegation.
(4) In the case of a statement in a document which is admitted as evidence under section 117 each person who, in order for the statement to be admissible, must have supplied or received the information concerned or created or received the document or part concerned is to be treated as the maker of the statement for the purposes of subsections (1) to (3) above.

Section 124(2)(a), (b), and (c) are largely concerned with situations which, if the maker had been called as a witness, would have been governed by the rule of finality of answers on collateral issues, by the exceptions to that rule,[303] or by s 100 of the 2003 Act (non-defendant's bad character).[304] Under the rule of finality, the answers given by a witness under cross-examination to questions concerning collateral matters, including questions which go merely to the credit of the witness, must be treated as final in the sense that the cross-examining party is not permitted to call further evidence with a view to contradicting the witness. Section 124(2)(a) allows evidence attacking the credibility of the maker to be given where such evidence, had he been called as a witness, would have been admissible either under an *exception* to the rule of finality or, with the leave of the court, under s 100 of the 2003 Act. For example, evidence admissible under sub-paragraph (a) may include evidence that the maker is unfit to be believed because of some physical or mental disability,[305] one of the exceptions to the rule against finality, or, with the leave of the court under s 100 of the 2003 Act, evidence that he has been convicted of an offence or been guilty of misconduct other than misconduct resulting in conviction or caution.[306] Concerning the admissibility under s

---

[303] See Ch 7, Finality of answers to collateral questions, p 242.

[304] See Ch 19, Section 100 of the Criminal Justice Act 2003, p 562.

[305] *Toohey v Metropolitan Police Comr* [1965] AC 595, HL.

[306] See also s 6 of the Criminal Procedure Act 1865 (see Ch 7). See also *R v Riat* [2013] 1 WLR 2592, CA at [18]: concerning evidence affecting the credibility of an absent witness for the prosecution, very full enquiries should be made (more than simply checking for convictions on the Police National Computer) and all relevant material should be disclosed. In respect of an absent defence witness, the defence should supply sufficient information to enable proper checks to be made. Further, both counsel and the judge must keep the necessity for disclosure of material affecting credibility in mind throughout the trial. See also *R v Harvey* [2014] EWCA Crim 54.

100 of evidence of misconduct other than convictions or cautions, evidence which can only provide a basis for speculation and is incapable of leading to reliable conclusions does not materially contribute to the jury's deliberations and is inadmissible.[307]

The sub-paragraph may also be used to admit evidence to support the credibility of the maker. At common law a witness's previous consistent statement is exceptionally admissible to rebut a suggestion that his evidence has been fabricated.[308] Thus if the party against whom the hearsay statement is admitted suggests that it was fabricated by the maker, evidence to show that before making the statement in question he made a statement, whether written or oral, consistent with it, would be admissible to support his credibility under sub-paragraph (a).

Section 124(2)(b) applies to situations which, if the maker had been called as a witness, would have been governed by the *rule* of finality of answers on collateral issues, that is, situations in which, if the maker had been cross-examined about a matter in order to attack his credibility as a witness but had denied the matter put, evidence in rebuttal would *not* have been admissible. Under sub-paragraph (b), evidence of the matter which could have been put to the maker in cross-examination, had he been called as a witness, for example the fact that whereas he is giving his evidence through an interpreter he is able to speak English,[309] may be adduced with the leave of the court. The reasoning underlying this provision, and the statutory precursors to it on which it is closely modelled, is that since, if the maker of the statement had given evidence, he might have admitted the matter put, or his denial might not have been believed, the party against whom the hearsay statement is given in evidence might be put at an unfair disadvantage because they are unable to cross-examine the maker of the statement. In deciding whether to grant leave, it would seem that the judge should balance the risk of such unfairness against the fact that to allow evidence to the discredit of the absent maker to be given without restriction, might be unfair to him and might lead to an undue prolongation of the trial.[310]

Section 124(2)(c) allows evidence tending to prove that the maker of the hearsay statement made another statement inconsistent with it to be admitted for to show that he contradicted himself. The inconsistent statement may have been made orally or in writing and either before or after the hearsay statement. Under s 119(2) of the Act, if evidence of an inconsistent statement by any person is given under s 124(2)(c), the statement is admissible as evidence of any matter stated in it of which oral evidence by that person would be admissible.

Under s 124(3), where as a result of evidence admitted under s 124(2), an allegation is made against the maker of the statement, the court may permit additional specified evidence to be adduced in rebuttal.

Stopping the case where the evidence is unconvincing

In *R v Galbraith*[311] it was held that a submission of no case to answer should fail where the Crown's case is such that its strength or weakness depends on the view to be taken of a witness's reliability, or other matters which are, generally speaking, within the jury's province,

---

[307] See *R v Harvey* [2014] EWCA Crim 54 at [69]–[73]. See also Ch 19, Evidence of substantial probative value, p 564.

[308] See Ch 6, Statements admissible to rebut allegations of recent fabrication, p 197.

[309] See *R v Burke* (1858) 8 Cox CC 44 (see Ch 7).

[310] See generally Criminal Law Revision Committee, 11th Report, *Evidence*, Cmnd 4991 (1972), para 263.

[311] [1981] 1 WLR 1039, CA (see Ch 2).

and where on one view of the facts there is evidence on which a jury could properly conclude that the accused is guilty. The Law Commission's view was that a derogation from *R v Galbraith* could be justified in the case of hearsay evidence on the same basis as in identification cases. In identification cases, 'the case is withdrawn from the jury not because the judge considers that the witness is lying, but because the evidence even if taken to be honest has a base which is so slender that it is unreliable and therefore not sufficient to found a conviction'.[312] Similarly, in the case of hearsay, 'even though the (absent) declarant may be honest, his or her evidence, being hearsay, may be so poor that a conviction would be unsafe'.[313] Section 125 of the 2003 Act, based on cl 14 of the Law Commission's draft bill, provides as follows:

(1) If on a defendant's trial before a judge and jury for an offence the court is satisfied at any time after the close of the case for the prosecution that—
   (a) the case against the defendant is based wholly or partly on a statement not made in oral evidence in the proceedings, and
   (b) the evidence provided by the statement is so unconvincing that, considering its importance to the case against the defendant, his conviction of the offence would be unsafe,
   the court must either direct the jury to acquit the defendant of the offence or, if it considers that there ought to be a retrial, discharge the jury.

(2) Where—
   (a) a jury is directed under subsection (1) to acquit a defendant of an offence, and
   (b) the circumstances are such that, apart from this subsection, the defendant could if acquitted of that offence be found guilty of another offence,
   the defendant may not be found guilty of that other offence if the court is satisfied as mentioned in subsection (1) in respect of it.

In *R v Riat*[314] it was said that the test in s 125 is different from that in *R v Galbraith* and will involve, 'looking at . . . [the] strengths and weaknesses [of the hearsay evidence], at the tools available to the jury for testing it, and at its importance to the case as a whole'. While the judge may exercise the power under s 125 at 'any time after the close of the case for the prosecution' he ordinarily ought not do so until the close of all the evidence.[315] The same duty to direct an acquittal or discharge the jury also applies in cases in which a jury is required to determine under the Criminal Procedure (Insanity) Act 1964 whether the accused did the act or made the omission charged.[316] Section 125 is without prejudice to any other power a court may have to direct an acquittal or discharge a jury.[317]

Discretion to exclude

Section 126 of the Act provides as follows:

(1) In criminal proceedings the court may refuse to admit a statement as evidence of a matter stated if—
   (a) the statement was made otherwise than in oral evidence in the proceedings, and

---

[312] See per Lord Mustill in *Daley v R* [1994] 1 AC 117, PC at 129 (see Ch 9).
[313] Law Com No 245, Cm 3670 (1997).
[314] [2013] 1 WLR 2592, CA at [28].
[315] *R v Horncastle* [2009] 2 Cr App R 230 (15), CA at [74]. See also *R v Riat* [2013] 1 WLR 2592, CA at [29].
[316] Section 125(3).
[317] Section 125(4).

    (b) the court is satisfied that the case for excluding the statement, taking account of the
danger that to admit it would result in undue waste of time, substantially outweighs the
case for admitting it, taking account of the value of the evidence.

(2) Nothing in this Chapter prejudices—

    (a) any power of a court to exclude evidence under section 78 of the Police and Criminal
Evidence Act 1984 (exclusion of unfair evidence), or

    (b) any other power of a court to exclude evidence at its discretion (whether from prevent-
ing questions from being put or otherwise).

General

As we have seen, there is a discretion to admit hearsay under s 114(1)(d) if it is 'in the interests of justice'. The same phrase is used in two other provisions: under s 116(4), leave may be
given to admit the hearsay statement of someone who does not give oral evidence through
fear only if the court considers that the statement ought to be admitted in the interests of
justice; and under s 121(1)(c), which relates to multiple hearsay, a hearsay statement is not
admissible to prove the fact that an earlier hearsay statement was made unless the interests
of justice require it to be admissible for that purpose. Although strictly speaking, where a
court has admitted a hearsay statement under s 114(1)(d), s 116(4), or s 121(1)(c), it may proceed to consider use of one of its three discretionary powers of exclusion, this is likely to be
a pointless exercise given that it is of the opinion that it is in the interests of justice to admit
the evidence. Furthermore, in the case of s 114(1)(d) and s 116(4), the court, in considering
whether it is in the interests of justice, shall have regard, in addition to the matters listed in
s 114(2)(a)–(i) and s 116(4)(a)–(c) respectively, to any other relevant factors or circumstances,
which could, of course, include any of the factors or circumstances relevant to the exercise of
any of the discretionary powers to exclude.[318] It is for reasons of this kind, presumably, that it
has been observed that the test for excluding evidence under s 78 of the Police and Criminal
Evidence Act 1984 is unlikely to produce a different result from that of 'the interests of justice' in ss 114(1)(d) and 116(4).[319] It has also been said that the interests of justice test might
be applied, albeit cautiously, to the judgement of prejudice under s 78.[320]

    In *R v Riat* it was stated that whatever section is applied when considering the admissibility
of hearsay evidence, a careful assessment will be involved of (i) the importance of the evidence to the case; (ii) the risks of unreliability; and (iii) whether the reliability of the absent
witness can safely be tested. In relation to (ii) and (iii), a court is not required to look for independent, complete confirmation of the reliability of the evidence.[321] What is required is that
the evidence is shown to be *potentially* safely reliable.[322] *R v Tahery*[323] provides an example of
evidence that was not safely reliable. T was convicted of wounding with intent during a fight
involving some members of the Iranian and Kurdish communities. At the trial, the prosecution relied on the statement of a witness, who was absent through fear, that T had stabbed
a member of the Iranian community of which T was a member. The statement was the sole

---

[318] See *R v Riat* [2013] 1 WLR 2592, CA at [22].

[319] See, in the case of s 114(1)(d), *R v Cole* [2008] 1 Cr App R 81 (5), CA; and, in the case of s 116(4), *R v D* [2003]
QB 90, CA. Cf *R v Kiziltan* [2018] 4 WLR 43, CA, concerning a statement admissible under s 116(2)(d).

[320] *R v Ferdinand* [2014] EWCA Crim 1243.

[321] *R v Riat* [2013] 1 WLR 2592, CA at [25]. See also *R v Pedersen* [2013] EWCA Crim 464.

[322] *R v Ibrahim* [2012] Cr App R 420 (32), CA at [107]. See also *R v Riat* [2013] 1 WLR 2592, CA at [33].

[323] [2013] EWCA Crim 1053.

evidence against T and following a ruling of the Grand Chamber of the European Court of Human Rights in *Al Khawaja and Tahery v UK* that there had been a breach of Art 6(1) and (3) (d),[324] and on a reference from the Criminal Cases Review Commission, the Court of Appeal quashed the conviction. The court concluded that objective factors pointed to the unreliability of the statement, including: the witness's animosity toward T; a contradictory initial statement to the police; a lack of evidence to support the account that T had used a knife; and the inability to call evidence to rebut the statement because the Iranian community was close-knit.

The test under s 126(1)

Section 126(1), described as a 'general' discretion to exclude,[325] creates a discretionary power to exclude otherwise admissible hearsay, whether tendered by the prosecution or defence.[326] Under the balancing exercise described in s 126(1)(b), regard must be had to the case for exclusion, taking account not of the danger of waste of time—the risk of *some* waste of time is plainly acceptable—but of the danger of *undue* waste of time. This has to be weighed against the case for admission of the evidence, taking account of its 'value', a word which appears to embrace not only its probative value, or its value in understanding other evidence in the case, but also its value in the sense of its reliability or weight. It is only if the court is satisfied that the case for exclusion *substantially* outweighs the case for admission, that the discretion should be exercised. This is likely to occur, for example, where the hearsay statement is of minimal probative value and wholly or to a very large extent superfluous, because other evidence has been or will be given on the matters stated.[327]

Preservation of other exclusionary powers

Section 126(2) preserves the two pre-existing powers of the court to exclude otherwise admissible hearsay. The first is the power in s 78 of the Police and Criminal Evidence Act 1984 under which evidence on which the prosecution proposes to rely may be excluded where in all the circumstances, including those in which the evidence was obtained, it would have such an adverse effect on the fairness of the proceedings that the court ought not to admit it. The second is the common law power to exclude prosecution evidence on the basis that its prejudicial effect outweighs its probative value.[328] An example of the use of s 78 in relation to hearsay evidence is provided by *R v Andrade*.[329] The accused was convicted of raping the complainant at the house of a third party. At the trial, evidence was admitted of two text messages sent to the complainant from the third party, which said, 'Sorry about that' and 'R U mad at me'. Quashing the conviction, the court held that the evidence of the text messages should not have been admitted unless the third party was present to give evidence. Although the court regarded it as unnecessary in the circumstances of the case to classify the text messages as hearsay, it held that absent the third party, the evidence should have been excluded

---

[324] (2012) 54 EHRR 23.

[325] *R v C* [2006] 1 WLR 2994, CA.

[326] See *R v Riat* [2013] 1 WLR 2592, CA at [23].

[327] There is nothing in the language of s 126 to suggest that, when applying the test, a different approach should be taken depending on whether it is the prosecution or the defence seeking to admit the evidence, nor is there any principled justification for taking a different approach: *R v Drinkwater* [2016] 4 WLR 42, CA at [50].

[328] Both are considered in Ch 1, Truth and the fact-finding process, p 2 and Ch 11, Discretion, p 325.

[329] [2015] EWCA Crim 1722. See also *R v Kiziltan* [2018] 4 WLR 43, CA, where there was evidence of collusion between complainants.

under s 78. This was because the accused had no effective way of challenging the interpretation of the messages advanced by the prosecution, namely, that they amounted to an apology by the third party for colluding in the rape committed by the accused.

Rules of court

Under s 132 of the Act, rules of court may be made providing for the procedural conditions to be followed by a party seeking to admit a hearsay statement. The rules may require the party to serve on the other party or parties notice and particulars of the evidence[330] and may provide that the evidence is admissible if a notice has been served but there has been no service of a counter-notice objecting to the admission of the evidence.[331] Rules applicable in magistrates' courts and Crown Courts are set out in Pt 20 of the Criminal Procedure Rules 2015.[332] If a party proposing to tender evidence fails to comply with a prescribed requirement, the evidence is not admissible except with the court's leave.[333] Where the defendant seeks to adduce hearsay evidence but fails to comply, leave should be granted where any unfairness to the prosecution or co-accused may be cured, for example by an adjournment, and where the interests of justice otherwise require the evidence to be admitted, but not where to admit the evidence would cause incurable unfairness.[334] Where leave is given the court or jury may draw such inferences from a failure to comply with a prescribed requirement as appear proper.[335] However, a person is not to be convicted of an offence solely on the basis of such an inference.[336] In respect of the judge's ruling on admissibility, it is good practice for the judge to give a short ruling immediately after argument, and a more detailed ruling later in the trial. However, the detailed ruling should be given before speeches so that advocates can tailor their speeches to the ruling and, if appropriate make submissions on the proposed direction to the jury.[337]

The direction to the jury

The direction to the jury on the dangers of relying on hearsay evidence has been described as 'one of the principal safeguards designed to protect a defendant against unfair prejudice'.[338] In *R v Daley*,[339] it was held that an initial direction should be given before the hearsay evidence is heard, warning the jury of three limitations: (i) the lack of opportunity to observe the demeanour of the witness; (ii) that the statement is not made on oath; and (iii) the lack of opportunity to see the witness's statement tested on oath. The initial direction should be repeated in summing-up, where the judge should explain why the evidence was material to

---

[330] Section 132(3).

[331] Section 132(4).

[332] SI 2015/1490.

[333] Section 132(5).

[334] *R v Musone* [2007] 1 WLR 2467, CA at [37]. See also *Marine Fisheries Agency v Inter Fish Limited* [2009] EWHC 753, DC, where no unfairness was caused to the defence.

[335] Section 132(5).

[336] Section 132(7).

[337] See *R v Kiziltan* [2018] 4 WLR 43, CA at [24].

[338] Per Lord Phillips in *R v Horncastle* [2010] 2 AC 373, SC at [38], cited in *R v Daley* [2017] EWCA Crim 1971 at [50].

[339] [2017] EWCA Crim 1971.

the issues they had to resolve.[340] Where the hearsay evidence also involves evidence of bad character, the direction needs to be tailored appropriately.[341] *R v Daley* draws on guidance given by the Privy Council in *Grant v The State*,[342] where it was also stated that it is proper to direct the jury to give the statement such weight as they think fit and desirable to direct them to consider the statement in the context of the other evidence, drawing attention to any discrepancies between the statement and the oral evidence of other witnesses. Detailed guidance is provided in the Crown Court Compendium.[343]

Questions of proof

Proof of conditions of admissibility

Where it is sought to admit a hearsay statement under s 116 (or to comply with the requirement of s 117(5)(a)), because the maker of the statement is unable to give oral evidence for one of the reasons set out in s 116(2), the court should make a finding of fact, based on admissible evidence, that such a reason exists.[344] It is submitted that many of the principles established in authorities concerning proof of the conditions of admissibility contained in ss 23 and 24 of the Criminal Justice Act 1988 (and other repealed statutory precursors to the hearsay provisions of the 2003 Act) remain valid. Thus if necessary, the matter should be decided on a *voir dire*,[345] at which the party against whom the evidence is tendered is entitled to cross-examine witnesses relied on to establish the necessary facts.[346] The *voir dire* is of particular importance in cases where the maker of the statement does not give oral evidence through fear: it is highly desirable that any investigation of his reasons should be conducted in the absence of the jury and that some innocuous form of words should be used to explain his absence to the jury[347] and prevent the jury from speculating that the accused may be responsible for the absence.[348] However, there is no requirement that the judge should test statements of fear through video link or tape recording, particularly as to the reasons for the fear; courts should not test the basis of fear by calling witnesses before them, since that may create the very situation which s 116(2)(e) was designed to avoid.[349] As to the standard of proof, the prosecution must satisfy the court beyond reasonable doubt,[350] the defence on

---

[340] At [52]–[53]. See also the Crown Court Compendium (July 2019), Part 1, 14–1, para 2. See *R v Doyle* [2018] EWCA Crim 2198: the direction should have been given but failure to give it did not render the conviction unsafe.

[341] At [53]. See *R v Doyle* [2018] EWCA Crim 2198: where a conventional, although modified, direction should have been given, but the conviction was not unsafe. Cf *R v Kiziltan* [2018] 4 WLR 43, CA, where the direction on inadequate and the conviction *was* rendered unsafe.

[342] [2006] 2 WLR 835, PC. Cf *R v Stoutt* [2014] UKPC at [17].

[343] The Crown Court Compendium (July 2019), Part 1, 14–1. See, in particular, para 5(1)–(9).

[344] See *R v T (D)* (2009) 173 JP 425, CA, a decision under s 116(2)(d), in which the court stated that given the importance of the right to confrontation, it is impermissible to proceed with an application under s 116(2)(d) informally; if the facts cannot be agreed, evidence must be called and the judge must make findings of fact.

[345] See *R v Minors; R v Harper* [1989] 1 WLR 441, CA.

[346] See *R v Wood and Fitzsimmons* [1998] Crim LR 213, CA.

[347] See *R v Jennings* [1995] Crim LR 810, CA.

[348] See *R v Wood and Fitzsimmons* [1998] Crim LR 213, CA. If the jury ask why the maker has not been called to give evidence, the judge should simply say that he cannot answer the question: *R v Churchill* [1993] Crim LR 285, CA.

[349] *R v Davies* [2007] 2 All ER 1070, CA.

[350] See *R (Meredith) v Harwich Magistrates' Court* (2007) 171 JP 249, DC, a decision under s 116(2)(b) of the 2003 Act (unfit because of bodily or mental condition). See also, *R v Lyons* [2010] EWCA Crim 2029 at [9].

a balance of probabilities.[351] Evidence to establish one of the reasons may take the form of either direct testimony or admissible hearsay (including a statement itself admissible under the statutory provisions)[352] but cannot be furnished by the contents of the very statement sought to be introduced, because prima facie they are inadmissible hearsay.[353] In order to establish that the maker of a statement does not give oral evidence through fear, reliance may be placed on medical evidence.[354] Alternatively, use may be made of his out-of-court written statement of fear,[355] whether or not contained in the very statement sought to be admitted, on the basis that it constitutes original evidence admissible to prove state of mind[356] or, if it is treated as hearsay, is admissible under the *res gestae* principle which covers statements concerning the maker's contemporaneous state of mind.[357] This principle is among the common law categories of admissibility preserved by s 118 of the 2003 Act.

According to *R v Foxley*[358] evidence of the requirements contained in s 24(1) of the 1988 Act, which were broadly similar to the requirements set out in s 117(2)(a) and (b) of the 2003 Act, was often desirable, but not always essential. In that case the judge was entitled to infer from the documents themselves and from the method or route by which they had been produced before the court that the requirements were satisfied. The purpose of s 24 was to enable the document to speak for itself, a purpose that would be defeated if oral evidence were to be required in every case from the creator or keeper of the document or the supplier of the information it contained.[359]

Proof of a statement contained in a document

Section 133 of the 2003 Act provides that:

> Where a statement in a document is admissible as evidence in criminal proceedings, the statement may be proved by producing either—
>
> (a) the document, or
> (b) (whether or not the document exists) a copy of the document or of the material part of it, authenticated in whatever way the court may approve.

The word 'document' means anything in which information of any description is recorded,[360] a definition wide enough to include, for example, audio tapes, films, and videotapes. 'Copy', in relation to a document, means anything on to which information recorded in the document has been copied, by whatever means, and whether directly or indirectly,[361] a definition

---

[351] See *R v Mattey, R v Queeley* [1995] 2 Cr App R 409.

[352] See *R v Castillo* [1996] 1 Cr App R 438, CA.

[353] See *R v Case* [1991] Crim LR 192, CA and *R v Mattey, R v Queeley* [1995] 2 Cr App R 409.

[354] See *R v Waters* [1997] Crim LR 823, CA.

[355] See *R v Rutherford* [1998] Crim LR 490, CA.

[356] See *R v Fairfax* [1995] Crim LR 949, CA, relying on *R v Blastland* [1986] AC 41, HL.

[357] See *R v Fairfax* [1995] Crim LR 949 (citing *Neill v North Antrim Magistrates' Court* [1992] 1 WLR 1220, HL: see per Lord Mustill, obiter at 1228) and *R v Wood and Fitzsimmons* [1998] Crim LR 213, CA. But see also *R v Belmarsh Magistrates' Court, ex p Gilligan* [1998] 1 Cr App R 14, DC: neither possible means of admissibility was even mentioned, and Astill J pointed out that in *R v Fairfax* there had been a great deal of oral evidence of fear.

[358] [1995] 2 Cr App R 523, CA.

[359] See also, applying *R v Foxley, R v Ilyas and Knight* [1996] Crim LR 810, CA.

[360] Section 134(1).

[361] Ibid.

which would cover, among other things, a transcript of an audio tape as well as reproductions or still reproductions of the images embodied in films and videotapes, whether enlarged or not. 'Producing' would seem to refer not to counsel handing the document to the court but to a witness who is qualified to do so in accordance with the rules of evidence producing the document and saying what it is.[362] The reference to authentication appears to relate to the authentication of a copy of a document as a true copy of the original, and not to proof of the original.[363] Section 133 is considered further in **Chapter 10, Documentary evidence**.

Evidence by video recording

In the case of offences triable only on indictment and prescribed offences triable either way, where a person, other than the accused, is called as a witness, having witnessed the events constituting the offence or part of it, or events closely connected with it, and having previously given a video-recorded account of those events at a time when they were fresh in his memory, s 137 of the 2003 Act permits the court to direct that the recording be admitted as his evidence-in-chief. Section 137 is considered in **Chapter 5**.[364]

Expert evidence

Preparatory work

In many cases, a witness giving expert opinion evidence will have no personal or first-hand knowledge of the facts, or all of the facts, upon which his opinion is based. For example, a surgeon may express his expert opinion as to whether the wounds of a deceased person were self-inflicted, basing his opinion on someone else's description of the wounds. Similarly, an expert may give his expert opinion on the basis of preparatory work, such as scientific tests carried out by assistants. The facts upon which the expert opinion is based, sometimes referred to as 'primary facts', must be proved by the person with personal or first-hand knowledge of them.[365] Section 127 of the 2003 Act permits such facts to be proved by the hearsay statement of such a person unless, on an application by a party to the proceedings, that is not in the interests of justice. Section 127 provides as follows:

(1) This section applies if—
   (a) a statement has been prepared for the purposes of criminal proceedings,
   (b) the person who prepared the statement had or may reasonably be supposed to have had personal knowledge of the matters stated,
   (c) notice is given under the appropriate rules that another person (the expert) will in evidence given in the proceedings orally or under s 9 of the Criminal Justice Act 1967[366] base an opinion or inference on the statement, and
   (d) the notice gives the name of the person who prepared the statement and the nature of the matters stated.

---

[362] As under the Civil Evidence Act 1968, s 6(1) (see now the Civil Evidence Act 1995, s 8): per Staughton LJ in *Ventouris v Mountain (No 2)* [1992] 1 WLR 887, CA (see Ch 13).

[363] Cf *Ventouris v Mountain (No 2)* [1992] 1 WLR 887, CA (see Ch 13).

[364] See Ch 5, **Evidence-in-chief by video recording**, p 155.

[365] See Ch 20.

[366] See, in this chapter, under **Written statements under s 9 of the Criminal Justice Act 1967**, p 409.

(2) In evidence given in the proceedings the expert may base an opinion or inference on the statement.

(3) If evidence based on the statement is given under subsection (2) the statement is to be treated as evidence of what it says.

(4) This section does not apply if the court, on an application by a party to the proceedings, orders that it is not in the interests of justice that it should apply.

(5) The matters to be considered by the court in deciding whether to make an order under subsection (4) include—

    (a) the expense of calling as a witness the person who prepared the statement;

    (b) whether relevant evidence could be given by that person which could not be given by the expert;

    (c) whether that person can reasonably be expected to remember the matters stated well enough to give oral evidence of them.

(6) Subsections (1) to (5) apply to a statement prepared for the purposes of a criminal investigation as they apply to a statement prepared for the purposes of criminal proceedings, and in such a case references to the proceedings are to criminal proceedings arising from the investigation.

Under s 127(4), it appears that the court may only disapply the section on the application of a party and not of its own motion. Subsection (5) provides a short non-exhaustive list of the factors to be considered by the court in deciding whether to disapply the section. Absent from the list are, it is submitted, the most important factors: the extent to which the matters stated are in dispute—if they are not in dispute, then there should be no application under subsection (4)—and the risk, having regard to how difficult it will be to challenge the statement if its maker is not called as a witness, that its admission or exclusion will result in unfairness.

Nothing in s 127 affects the common law rule under which an expert witness may draw on the body of expertise relevant to his field.[367] That rule is among the common law categories of admissibility preserved by s 118 of the Act.

Expert reports

Section 30(1) of the 1988 Act provides that an expert report, that is a written report by a person dealing wholly or mainly with matters on which he is (or would if living be) qualified to give expert evidence,[368] shall be admissible as evidence in criminal proceedings whether or not the person making it attends to give oral evidence in those proceedings. The report, when admitted, shall be evidence of any fact or opinion of which the person making it could have given oral evidence.[369] However, if it is proposed that the person making the report shall not give oral evidence, the report shall only be admissible with the leave of the court.[370] In deciding whether to give leave, the court shall have regard to (i) the contents of the report; (ii)

---

[367] See *R v Abadom* [1983] 1 WLR 126, CA (see Ch 20). See also *Myers v The Queen* [2016] AC 314, PC at [63]–[67]: there is a distinction between expert evidence which is an opinion and may be based on hearsay and evidence given by an expert which is actually evidence of observable fact, and falls to be proved according to the ordinary rules of evidence.

[368] Section 30(5).

[369] Section 30(4).

[370] Section 30(2).

the reasons why it is proposed that the person making the report shall not give oral evidence; (iii) any risk, having regard in particular to whether it is likely to be possible to controvert statements in the report if the person making it does not attend to give oral evidence, that its admission or exclusion will result in unfairness to the accused or, if there is more than one, to any of them; and (iv) any other circumstances that appear to the court to be relevant.[371]

If any party to a criminal trial proposes, pursuant to s 30(1), to put an expert report in evidence at the trial, then whether or not the person making the report attends to give oral evidence in the proceedings, that party, in accordance with r 19.3 of the Criminal Procedure Rules 2015,[372] shall as soon as practicable serve the report on an officer of the court and the other party or parties. Rule 19.3 and certain related rules are set out and considered in **Chapter 20**, which concerns experts and opinion evidence generally.[373]

Written statements under s 9 of the Criminal Justice Act 1967

Under s 9 of the 1967 Act, in summary trials and trials on indictment, a written statement (with or without exhibits) by any person shall be admissible as evidence 'to the like extent as oral evidence to the like effect by that person'. The principal conditions of admissibility are that (i) the statement is signed by its maker; (ii) it contains a declaration that it is true; (iii) before the hearing a copy of it is served by the party proposing to tender it on each of the other parties; and (iv) none of the other parties or their solicitors, within seven days from the service of the copy, serves a notice objecting to the statement being tendered in evidence.[374] The last two conditions do not apply if the parties agree before or during the hearing that the statement shall be so tendered.[375] Under s 9(4), notwithstanding that a statement may be admissible by virtue of s 9, the party who served a copy of it may call its maker to give evidence and the court may, either of its own motion or on the application of any party to the proceedings, require its maker to attend court and give oral evidence. An application under s 9(4) would be appropriate, for example, where a party disputes the evidence contained in the statement but failed to serve a notice of objection in accordance with the section. Such an application may be made before the hearing.[376] Where a s 9 statement is admitted in evidence, it should normally be read out aloud.[377]

Where the prosecution tenders written statements under s 9, it is frequently not only proper, but also necessary for the orderly presentation of the evidence, for the statements to be edited. This may be either because a witness has made more than one statement whose contents should conveniently be reduced into a single comprehensive statement or because a statement contains inadmissible, prejudicial, or irrelevant material. Such editing should be carried out by a Crown Prosecutor, and not by a police officer, in accordance with the

---

[371] Section 30(3).

[372] See also Criminal Practice Direction 19A.

[373] See Ch 20, **Restrictions on, and disclosure of, expert evidence in criminal cases**, p 668.

[374] There must be strict compliance with the terms of s 9: see *Paterson v DPP* [1990] Crim LR 651, DC.

[375] Section 9(2).

[376] Section 9(5).

[377] Section 9(6). Reading aloud the statement, or a summary of the relevant parts, is obligatory in a magistrates' court: Criminal Procedure Rules 2015, r 24.5.

Criminal Practice Directions, V, Part 16A.[378] Where a witness statement is tendered by the prosecution under s 9 of the Criminal Justice Act 1967 without objection, but the accused then gives contradictory evidence, an application to call the witness who provided the statement to give oral evidence (to deal with contradictory evidence) should not be refused if the refusal might lead to a substantial injustice.[379]

Depositions of vulnerable children and young persons under s 43 of the Children and Young Persons Act 1933

Under s 42 of the 1933 Act, where a magistrate is satisfied by the evidence of a qualified medical practitioner that the attendance before a court of any child or young person in respect of whom any of certain specified offences is alleged to have been committed would involve serious danger to his life or health, the magistrate may take a deposition from him out of court. The offences specified include offences under the Offences Against the Person Act 1861, the 1933 Act itself, the Protection of Children Act 1978, and the Sexual Offences Act 2003, and any other offences involving bodily injury to a child or young person. Under s 43, a deposition taken under s 42 shall be admissible in evidence in any proceedings either for or against the accused provided, in the latter case, that it is proved that reasonable notice of the intention to take the deposition was served upon the accused and he or his legal representative had an opportunity of cross-examining the deponent.

ADDITIONAL READING

Birch and Hirst, 'Interpreting the New Concept of Hearsay' (2010) 69 (1) CLJ 72.
   A critical examination of problems with definitions in the hearsay provisions of the 2003 Act and consequences of the problems, including problems and consequences relating to the 'redrawn concept of hearsay'. A conclusion is reached that the statutory regime is undermined by the failure to provide a clear and precise definition of the basic concept of hearsay and to properly integrate the concept with existing concepts of narrative and confessions.

Dennis, 'The Right to Confront Witnesses: Meanings, Myths and Human Rights' [2010] Crim LR 255.
   An article which focuses on the principle that an accused has the right to be confronted by the witnesses against him. The different meanings of 'confrontation' are considered including the right to public trial, face-to-face confrontation, cross-examination, and to know the identity of the accuser. Some consideration is given to the decisions in *Al Khawaja and Tahery v UK* (2009) 49 EHHR 1 and *R v Horncastle* [2010] AC 373. The article concludes with a scenario to demonstrate problems with the 'sole or decisive' rule.

Heffernan, 'Calibrating the right to confrontation' (2016) 20 (2) E&P 103.
   An article which explores the challenges faced by common law courts in applying ECHR Art 6(1) and (3)(d) (the right of confrontation), with a focus on the need to evaluate the potential significance of the hearsay evidence to the prosecution's case at trial. The article draws on Redmayne's chapter, 'Confronting Confrontation', in Roberts and Hunter, *Criminal Evidence and Human Rights: Reimagining Common Law Procedural Traditions* (Oxford, 2012).

---

[378] The principles set out do not apply to documents which are exhibited (including statements under caution and signed contemporaneous notes). Nor, as a general rule, do they apply to oral statements of an accused recorded in the witness statements of interviewing police officers. Such material should remain in its original state and any editing left to prosecuting counsel at the Crown Court: see para 24.6.

[379] *London Borough of Newham v Osmar* [2015] EWHC 3800, DC.

Hoyano, 'What is Balanced on the Scales of Justice? In Search of the Right to a Fair Trial' [2014] Crim LR 4.
    An article which seeks to identify a theoretical foundation or 'bottom line' for the bedrock of a fair trial. The
    infiltration of the right to a fair trial by the idea of 'balancing' is criticized. In particular, the Grand Chamber's
    decision in *Al Khawaja and Tahery v UK* (2012) 54 EHRR 23 is criticized for losing sight of the premise that a fair
    trial is an absolute right that cannot be qualified. A framework for a fair trial is advanced: this includes, among
    other things, the reinstatement of the 'sole or decisive' rule as a 'bottom line, bedrock principle', so that no
    conviction should be based solely or decisively on hearsay evidence which violates any Convention right. The
    question is posed whether the Grand Chamber in *Al Khawaja* 'sacrificed principle to juridical, and possibly
    political, expediency, under the guise of judicial comity'.

Law Commission, *Evidence in Criminal Proceedings: Hearsay and Related Topics*, Cm 3670 (Law Com No 245, London,
    1997).
    The Law Commission's report proposing changes to the law relating to hearsay in England and Wales.

Requa, 'Absent Witnesses and the UK Supreme Court: judicial deference as judicial dialogue?' (2010) 14 E&P 208.
    Analysis of the position of absent witness hearsay evidence in the criminal law of the United Kingdom, following
    the Supreme Court's decision in *R v Horncastle* [2010] 2 AC 373. It is argued that the flexibility of the hearsay
    provisions of the 2003 Act and a permissive approach by appellate courts has increased the potential for fair trial
    violations.

Spencer, *Hearsay Evidence in Criminal Proceedings* (Hart, 2014).
    A leading text on the law relating to hearsay in criminal proceedings in England and Wales.

QUESTIONS

1. Tom and Farook are members of rival gangs in North London. Tom has been charged with the murder of Ed
   and will plead not guilty. The prosecution allege that Tom stabbed Ed in a dark alley outside a pub in Islington.
   The police questioned a number of witnesses who were smoking cigarettes outside the pub at the relevant
   time and who saw the incident, but none of them saw enough to be able to identify the person who stabbed
   Ed. Two days later, however, Farook made a written statement to the police that the person who stabbed Ed
   was Tom, but that he, Farook, was too frightened to attend trial and give oral evidence. According to Tom,
   Farook's identification is either mistaken or deliberately false. At the trial, may the prosecution give evidence of
   Farook's written statement? Give reasons for your answer.

2. Critically evaluate the decision of the Supreme Court in *R v Horncastle* [2010] 2 AC 373 in so far as it relates to
   'sole or decisive' hearsay.

 For a note-form answer see the online resources, accessible at
   www.oup.com/he/keane-mckeown13e.

Hearsay admissible by statute in civil proceedings

13

Key issues

- When and why should a statement made out of court and tendered as evidence of the facts asserted (hearsay) be admissible in civil proceedings?

- If admissible, should the party tendering the evidence be required to apply for leave to adduce it? If so, when should leave be granted?

- Should the party be required to give notice of intention to adduce the evidence? If so, what should the notice requirements be?

- Should the other party be permitted to call the maker of the statement with a view to cross-examining him? If the maker is not called for cross-examination, what opportunities should the other party have to impeach his credibility?

- How much weight should be given to hearsay evidence in civil proceedings?

- If a hearsay statement is contained in a document, how may it be proved?

The background

The Civil Evidence Act 1968

As we have seen in **Chapter 12**, under the common law rule against hearsay, any assertion, other than one made by a person while giving oral evidence in the proceedings, was inadmissible if tendered as evidence of the facts asserted. The Civil Evidence Act 1968 (the 1968 Act) constituted a major assault upon the common law rule in civil proceedings. Although it did not abolish the rule, it made provision for the admissibility of both oral and written hearsay (including statements contained in documents which were or formed part of a record) subject to certain conditions, principally (i) notification of the other parties to the litigation; and (ii) either calling the maker of the statement as a witness (in which case the statement could not be given in evidence without the leave of the court) or establishing one of a number of reasons for not calling the maker of the statement as a witness. The 1968 Act also provided for the admissibility of statements contained in computer-produced documents and gave express statutory force to a number of the common law exceptions, including informal admissions and facts contained in public documents.

The Law Commission's recommendations

In June 1988 the Civil Justice Review recommended an inquiry by a law reform agency into the usefulness of the hearsay rule in civil proceedings and the machinery for rendering it admissible. The matter was referred to the Law Commission. The response to its Consultation Paper[1] identified three major reasons for change.

1. The regime under the Civil Evidence Act 1968 was unwieldy and the law outmoded and unnecessarily difficult to understand. In particular, the rules as to notification were too complicated so that in practice compliance was the exception.

2. The statutory regime lagged behind developments in the law and practice of civil litigation which pointed to a new approach in which (a) the main emphasis is upon ensuring that, so far as possible, and subject to considerations of reliability and weight, all relevant evidence is adduced;[2] and (b) litigation is conducted in a more open climate, with more emphasis on identifying and refining the issues in advance of the trial.

3. Intelligent witnesses and litigants were confused by, and dissatisfied with, rules which sometimes operated to prevent them from giving evidence of matters which they rightly perceived as relevant and cogent.[3]

Guided by two major principles, that the law should be simplified to the greatest degree consistent with the proper functioning of the law of evidence, and that, as a general rule, all evidence should be admissible unless there is good reason for it to be treated as inadmissible,[4] the Commission recommended abolition of the hearsay rule in civil proceedings subject to safeguards such as a new simplified notice provision and statutory guidelines to assist courts

---

[1] *The Hearsay Rule in Civil Proceedings*, Consultation Paper No 117 (1991).
[2] See per Balcombe LJ in *Ventouris v Mountain (No 2)* [1992] 1 WLR 887, CA at 899.
[3] See *The Hearsay Rule in Civil Proceedings*, Law Com No 216, Cm 2321 (1993), paras 1.4–1.6.
[4] Law Com No 216, Cm 2321 (1993), para 4.2.

to assess the weight to be attached to hearsay evidence. The main recommendations of the Commission, in summary, were as follows:

1. In civil proceedings the hearsay rule should be abolished.

2. A party calling a person as a witness should not adduce evidence of a previous statement made by that person except with the leave of the court.

3. A party intending to rely on hearsay should be under a duty to give notice of that fact where this is reasonable and appropriate, according to the particular circumstances of the case. Although failure to give notice should not render the evidence inadmissible, it may detract from the weight that will be placed on it or lead to the imposition of costs sanctions.

4. There should be power for a party to call a witness for cross-examination on his hearsay statement.

5. Courts should be given guidelines to assist them in assessing the weight of hearsay evidence.

6. For business and other records there should be no additional safeguards, beyond those applicable to all other hearsay statements, and the procedure for proving such records should be simplified.

All of these recommendations were put into effect by the Civil Evidence Act 1995 (the 1995 Act).

Computer-produced documents

Before considering the detail of the Act, it is important to note that it contains no special conditions of admissibility or other specific safeguards in the case of statements in computer-produced documents. The 1968 Act contained elaborate precautions in this regard, including requirements to prove that the document was produced in the normal course of business and in an uninterrupted course of activity. Requirements of this kind reflected a fundamental mistrust and fear of the potential for error and mechanical failure. However, as the Law Commission observed, since 1968 technology has developed to an extent where computers and computer-generated documents are relied on in every area of business. It also thought that it was at least questionable whether the requirements of the Civil Evidence Act 1968 provided any real safeguard in relation to the reliability of the hardware or software concerned, and noted that in any event they provided no protection against the inaccurate inputting of data. The Commission recognized that, as confidence in the inherent reliability of computers had grown, so had concern over the potential for misuse, through the capacity to hack, corrupt, or alter information in a manner which is undetectable, but could see no reason for maintaining a different regime for the admission of computer-generated documents. It considered that the potential for misuse was best dealt with by concentrating upon the weight to be attached to such evidence, rather than by the reformulation of complex and inflexible rules of admissibility.[5]

---

[5] See generally Law Com No 216, Cm 2321 (1993), paras 3.14–3.21 and 4.43.

Admissibility of hearsay under the Civil Evidence Act 1995

Abolition of the rule against hearsay

Section 1 of the 1995 Act provides as follows:

(1) In civil proceedings evidence shall not be excluded on the ground that it is hearsay.

(2) In this Act—

    (a) 'hearsay' means a statement made otherwise than by a person while giving oral evidence[6] in the proceedings which is tendered as evidence of the matters stated; and

    (b) references to hearsay include hearsay of whatever degree.

'In civil proceedings'

The phrase 'civil proceedings' is defined by s 11 as 'civil proceedings, before any tribunal, in relation to which the strict rules of evidence apply, whether as a matter of law or by agreement of the parties'. Thus the Act applies to civil proceedings in any of the ordinary courts of law and in both tribunals and arbitrations in which the strict rules of evidence are applied, but not to the wardship jurisdiction of the High Court[7] or Coroners' Courts. The strict rules of evidence do not apply to all civil proceedings in magistrates' courts. For example, the Act does not apply to magistrates when considering whether there is reasonable cause to suspend a private hire vehicle licence under the Local Government (Miscellaneous Provisions) Act 1976.[8] In *Savings and Investment Bank Ltd v Gasco Investments (Netherlands) BV (No 2)*,[9] a decision under the equivalent provision of the Civil Evidence Act 1968, it was held that an application to commit for contempt founded on the breach of an order made in civil proceedings was itself a civil proceeding, notwithstanding the criminal standard of proof appropriate to such an application[10] and its possible penal consequences.

'Shall not be excluded'

Under s 1(1) of the 1995 Act, 'evidence shall not be excluded on the ground that it is hearsay'. The subsection needs to be considered alongside s 14(1) of the Act, which provides that:

Nothing in this Act affects the exclusion of evidence on grounds other than that it is hearsay.

    This applies whether the evidence falls to be excluded in pursuance of any enactment or rule of law, for failure to comply with rules of court or an order of the court, or otherwise.

Thus hearsay cannot be excluded because it is hearsay but will only be admissible if it does not fall to be excluded on some ground other than that it is hearsay. For example, hearsay opinion evidence which is inadmissible under the Civil Evidence Act 1972[11] falls to be excluded in pursuance of an enactment; hearsay which is irrelevant or inadmissible on grounds of

---

[6] 'Oral evidence' includes evidence which, by reason of a defect of speech or hearing, a person called as a witness gives in writing or by signs: s 13.

[7] See *Official Solicitor to the Supreme Court v K* [1965] AC 201, HL. Proceedings in the Court of Protection fall within the definition of 'civil proceedings' under the 1995 Act, s 11: *Enfield London Borough Council v SA* [2010] 1 FLR 1836. However, confiscation proceedings under the Proceeds of Crime Act 2002 do not: *R v Clipston* [2011] 2 Cr App R (S) 569 (101), CA at [46]–[50].

[8] *Westminster City Council v Zestfair Ltd* (1989) 88 LGR 288, DC; *Leeds City Council v Hussain* [2003] RTR 13, DC.

[9] [1988] 2 WLR 1212, CA.

[10] See Ch 3.

[11] See Ch 20.

public policy or privilege falls to be excluded in pursuance of a rule of law; and the hearsay opinion of an expert may fall to be excluded if a party fails to comply with r 35.13 of the Civil Procedure Rules (CPR), that is, if he fails to disclose the expert's report.

'Hearsay'

The purpose of the statutory definition of hearsay in s 1(2) is to identify the type of evidence which would have formerly been excluded by virtue of the common law rule against hearsay, that is, first-hand, second-hand, or multiple hearsay, and to which the safeguards and supplementary provisions of the Act apply. However, there is likely to continue to be reference to the common law authorities in cases in which the boundary of the definition is unclear.[12] Section 13 provides that 'statement' means 'any representation of fact or opinion, however made'. Thus the Act covers a statement of opinion, provided that it is admissible under the 1972 Act, as well as a statement of fact, whether the statement was made orally, in writing (whether hand-written, type-written, or produced by computer), or by conduct. It may be doubted, however, whether a written statement in an affidavit is covered by the Act.[13]

Original evidence

Under s 1(2)(a), hearsay is defined as a statement made otherwise than by a person while giving oral evidence in the proceedings which is 'tendered as evidence of the matter stated' and falls to be distinguished from original evidence, that is, a statement made otherwise than by a person while giving oral evidence in the proceedings which is tendered for any relevant purpose other than that of establishing any matter stated. The distinction between hearsay and original evidence is important because whereas hearsay is only admissible subject to the conditions and safeguards set out in the 1995 Act, original evidence, if sufficiently relevant, is admissible without more. In some cases, original evidence is introduced simply to show that the statement in question was made, because that is among the facts in issue in the case. Thus in defamation proceedings in which it is in issue whether the allegedly defamatory statement was made, a witness may give evidence of the making of the statement, including its terms. So-called 'operative words' provide a further illustration. The utterance of such words binds the speaker under the substantive law because a reasonable person, on hearing them, would believe that the speaker intended to be bound. Thus if the parties dispute whether a contract was entered into, evidence of the terms of the contractual offer are admissible because under the law of contract the words spoken are of legal effect if a reasonable person in the position of the offeree would have believed that the offeror intended to be bound. Likewise, words of gift accompanying a transfer of property may be admitted as original evidence. In other types of case, original evidence is introduced because the statement in question is relevant to a fact in issue, typically the state of mind of the person who heard or read it, to show what he knew, thought, or believed. Thus P may tender evidence of a certain alleged misrepresentation made to him by Q for the purpose of showing that he was thereby misled. If X brings an action against Y for malicious prosecution, then Y, in order to show the reasonableness of his conduct in the prosecution of X, may

---

[12] Law Com No 216, Cm 2321 (1993), para 4.6.

[13] In *Rover International Ltd v Cannon Film Sales Ltd (No 2)* [1987] 1 WLR 1597, Ch D at 1603 Harman J doubted whether affidavits were 'documents' for the purposes of the 1968 Act.

tender evidence of a statement made to him by Z that X had committed a criminal offence.[14] Almost all of the reported examples of original evidence have arisen in criminal cases and the topic is considered more fully in **Chapter 12**.[15]

Implied assertions

An implied assertion is an assertion, whether made orally, in writing, or by conduct, from which it is possible to infer a particular matter. For example, in *Wright v Doe d Tatham*,[16] one of the issues being the mental competence of a testator, it was held that the trial judge had properly excluded a number of letters written to the testator by certain of his acquaintances in terms from which it could legitimately be inferred that they regarded him as sane. As evidence of the truth of the implied assertion that the testator was sane, they constituted inadmissible hearsay. As to implied assertions by conduct, Parke B was of the obiter opinion that on the question of the seaworthiness of a vessel, evidence of the conduct of a deceased captain in examining every part of the vessel and then embarking on it with his family would also amount to hearsay. On the other hand, in *Manchester Brewery Co Ltd v Coombs*,[17] which concerned an alleged breach by a brewer to supply good beer, it was held, obiter, that evidence could be given that customers ordered the beer, tasted it, did not finish it, and then either left it or threw it away. Further examples are considered in **Chapter 12**.[18] In *criminal* proceedings, the courts avoid analysing hearsay by reference to the concept of implied assertions, focusing instead on whether there has been a statement of the matter sought to be proved and whether one of the purposes of the maker of the statement was to cause another to believe what was stated or act upon it as true.[19] There have been no equivalent developments in civil proceedings and it is unclear whether, for the purposes of the 1995 Act, a 'statement' covers an implied assertion. In the case of conduct, the Law Commission took the view that the question whether assertive or non-assertive conduct should come within the statutory definition of hearsay was 'a matter for judicial consideration and development'.[20] However, it seems that such consideration and development is also called for in the case of implied assertions made orally or in writing.

Evidence admissible apart from s 1

Section 1(3) and (4) of the 1995 Act provide as follows:

(3) Nothing in this Act affects the admissibility of evidence admissible apart from this section.

(4) The provisions of sections 2 to 6 (safeguards and supplementary provisions relating to hearsay evidence) do not apply in relation to hearsay evidence admissible apart from this section, notwithstanding that it may also be admissible by virtue of this section.

Various statutory provisions, apart from s 1 of the 1995 Act, provide for the admissibility of particular types of hearsay and the purpose of s 1(3) is to preserve their effect. An example is the Births and Deaths Registration Act 1953, s 34 of which provides for the admissibility of

---

[14] See *Perkins v Vaughan* (1842) 4 Man&G 988.

[15] See in Ch 12, 'Statements' and 'matters stated', p 363.

[16] (1837) 7 Ad&El 313, Ex Ch.

[17] (1901) 82 LT 347, Ch D at 349.

[18] See in Ch 12, 'Statements' and 'matters stated', p 363.

[19] Ibid. See the Criminal Justice Act 2003, s 115(3) and *R v Twist* [2011] 2 Cr App R 189 (17), CA.

[20] Law Com No 216, Cm 2321 (1993), para 4.35.

a certified copy of an entry in the register of births as evidence of the facts contained in it. Similarly, the same section provides for the proof of death, where there is evidence identifying the person named in the certificate with the person in question, by reliance on a death certificate.[21] Other important statutory provisions include the orders made under s 96 of the Children Act 1989,[22] whereby in civil proceedings[23] before the High Court or a county court, in family proceedings in a magistrates' court,[24] and in proceedings under the Child Support Act 1991, evidence given in connection with the upbringing, maintenance, or welfare of a child shall be admissible notwithstanding any rule of law relating to hearsay.[25]

Article 6(1) of the European Convention on Human Rights

In *Clingham v Kensington and Chelsea London Borough Council*[26] the Divisional Court held that there was nothing in the Human Rights Act 1998, nor in the jurisprudence of the European Court of Human Rights, which led to the automatic exclusion of hearsay evidence in civil proceedings, and that there was no requirement to give the 1995 Act any meaning which it did not naturally bear. The court also held that the admission of hearsay evidence, without the possibility of cross-examination, does not automatically result in an unfair trial under Art 6(1) of the Convention.[27]

Conditions of admissibility

Competence

Two questions arise concerning competence. First, may hearsay be admitted if the maker of the statement would not have been competent to give evidence at the time he made it? Second, if his statement is admissible, may it be proved by the statement of another who, at the time when he made his statement, would not have been competent as a witness? For example, if A makes an oral statement within the hearing of B, and A would have been competent to give evidence at that time, may A's statement be proved by B's written record as to what he said, the record having been made at a time when B would not have been competent? Section 5(1) of the Act renders explicit the competence requirements. It provides as follows:

> Hearsay evidence shall not be admitted in civil proceedings if or to the extent that it is shown to consist of, or to be proved by means of, a statement made by a person who at the time he made the statement was not competent as a witness.

---

[21] See also the Bankers' Books Evidence Act 1879 (see Ch 10) and the Marriage Act 1949, s 65(3) (see Ch 14). See also the Solicitors Act 1974, s 18.

[22] See The Children (Admissibility of Hearsay Evidence) Order 1993, SI 1993/621.

[23] 'Civil proceedings' has the same meaning as it has under the 1995 Act (by virtue of s 11): see the 1989 Act, s 96(7).

[24] The order extends not only to all the proceedings defined as 'family proceedings' by the 1989 Act, s 8(2), but also to other proceedings which are part of the magistrates' courts' family proceedings jurisdiction by virtue of the 1989 Act, s 92(2): *R v Oxfordshire County Council* [1992] 3 WLR 88, Fam D.

[25] The party seeking to adduce the evidence must show that it has a substantial connection with the upbringing, etc of the child.

[26] (2001) 165 JP 322, DC.

[27] See also *R (McCann) v Crown Court at Manchester* [2003] 1 AC 787, HL at [35]. Equally, it does not automatically follow that it would be unfair to admit hearsay evidence in civil proceedings which would not be admissible in criminal proceedings, under the Criminal Justice Act 2003, s 114(1)(d) or s 116: *R (Bonhoeffer) v General Medical Council* [2011] EWHC 1585, DC at [39].

For this purpose 'not competent as a witness' means suffering from such mental or physical infirmity, or lack of understanding, as would render a person incompetent as a witness in civil proceedings; but a child shall be treated as competent as a witness if he satisfies the requirements of section 96(2)(a) and (b) of the Children Act 1989 (conditions for reception of unsworn evidence of child).[28]

The burden of proof, under s 5(1), is borne by the party seeking to exclude the evidence.[29]

The requirement of leave

Section 1 of the 1995 Act, if unqualified, would permit a party to adduce, as evidence of the matters stated, the previous out-of-court statement of a person called as a witness. The Law Commission took the view that, in the case of previous consistent statements, a leave requirement was necessary in order to prevent the pointless proliferation of superfluous evidence, which would needlessly prolong trials and increase costs.[30] Section 6 of the Act provides as follows:

(1) Subject as follows, the provisions of this Act as to hearsay evidence in civil proceedings apply equally (but with any necessary modifications) in relation to a previous statement made by a person called as a witness in the proceedings.

(2) A party who has called or intends to call a person as a witness in civil proceedings may not in those proceedings adduce evidence of a previous statement made by that person, except—
   (a) with the leave of the court, or
   (b) for the purpose of rebutting a suggestion that his evidence has been fabricated.[31]
   This shall not be construed as preventing a witness statement (that is, a written statement of oral evidence which a party to the proceedings intends to lead) from being adopted by a witness in giving evidence or treated as his evidence.[32]

Leave is required under s 6(2)(a) whether the previous statement is a previous *consistent* statement or relates to matters other than those dealt with in the testimony of the witness, but the concluding words of s 6(2) make it clear that it is not intended that a witness statement which stands as a witness's evidence-in-chief under CPR r 32.5(2) should be regarded as a 'previous statement' for the purposes of the provision.

---

[28] See **Ch 5**. However, r 95(d) and (e) of the Court of Protection Rules 2007 (as amended by the Court of Protection (Amendment) Rules 2015) give the Court of Protection the power to admit hearsay evidence which would otherwise be inadmissible under s 5(1) of the Civil Evidence Act 1995. Under r 95(d), the Court of Protection may admit such evidence as it thinks fit and, under r 95(e), it may admit, accept, and act upon such information, whether oral or written, from a person who lacks the capacity to make a decision or any protected party or any party who lacks competence to give evidence, as the court considers sufficient although not given under oath and whether or not it would be admissible in a court of law apart from the rule. See also *Enfield London Borough Council v SA* [2010] 1 FLR 1836, COP, at [34]–[36], where it was held that r 95(d) gives the Court of Protection the power to admit hearsay which originates from a person who is not competent.

[29] *JC v CC* [2001] EWCA Civ 1625.

[30] See Law Com No 216, Cm 2321 (1993), para 4.30.

[31] Section 6(2)(b) is considered in **Ch 6, Previous consistent or self-serving statements, p 193**.

[32] Under s 6(3), the Act does not authorize the adducing of evidence of previous *inconsistent* statements otherwise than in accordance with the Criminal Procedure Act 1865, ss 3, 4, and 5; and, under s 6(4), the Act does not affect the common law rules whereby a memory-refreshing document may be rendered admissible as a result of cross-examination. Section 6(3) is considered in **Ch 6, Hostile witnesses, p 207** and **Ch 7, Admissibility as evidence of the matter stated, p 224**; and s 6(4) is considered in **Ch 6, Cross-examination on the document, p 189**.

At common law, previous statements of a witness were generally excluded both as evidence of the truth of the facts they contained and as evidence of consistency.[33] The questions naturally arise as to what considerations the court should take into account in deciding whether to grant leave, and whether leave should be granted only exceptionally. As to the former, it is submitted that, in deciding whether to grant leave, the judge should consider the importance of the previous statement in relation to the facts in issue, the reliability and weight of the statement, including all the circumstances in which it was made, and whether admission would be unjust to the other parties to the proceedings. As to the latter, it is submitted that leave should be granted not only where the witness is incapable of giving direct evidence on the matter in question because, for example, he has no recollection of the matter (in which case, the statement would not be a previous *consistent* statement), but also where, although he is capable of giving direct evidence of the matter, it is of questionable reliability or unintelligible by reason of partial loss of memory, lapse of time, age, or illness. Such an approach would accord with the spirit of *Morris v Stratford-on-Avon RDC*,[34] a decision under the equivalent leave requirement in the Civil Evidence Act 1968.[35] That was an action against the council for damages for the alleged negligence of one of their employees. The trial began some five years after the cause of action arose and the employee gave confused and inconsistent evidence. After his examination-in-chief, counsel for the defendants was granted leave to admit in chief a written statement made by the employee and given to the defendants' insurers some nine months after the accident. The Court of Appeal held that the trial judge had not erred in allowing the evidence to be admitted.

Where leave is given, there is no restriction in s 6 as to when the previous statement may be given in evidence. Thus according to the circumstances, the statement may be given in evidence before or during the witness's examination-in-chief (which would seem appropriate if likely to improve the intelligibility of his evidence), rather than at the conclusion of his examination-in-chief. Equally, there is no restriction as to *who* may prove the statement: the court may allow evidence of the making of the previous statement to be given by someone other than its maker.

Safeguards

The requirement to give advance notice

The notice provisions of the 1995 Act are simpler and more flexible than those in operation under the Civil Evidence Act 1968. The objectives of the earlier provisions were that all issues arising out of the adduction of hearsay evidence should be dealt with pre-trial and that there should be no surprises at trial. The Law Commission endorsed these objectives but believed that they could be met by a notice provision which (i) requires a party to give notice of the fact that he or she proposes to adduce hearsay; and (ii) puts the onus on

---

[33] The exceptions, in effect preserved by the 1995 Act, s 6(2)(b) and (4), relate to statements admissible to rebut allegations of recent fabrication (see **n 31** in this chapter) and memory-refreshing documents rendered admissible as a result of cross-examination (see **n 32** in this chapter).

[34] [1973] 1 WLR 1059, CA.

[35] Section 2(2).

the receiving party to demand such particulars as he requires in order to be able to make a proper assessment of the weight and cogency of the hearsay in question and to be in a position to respond adequately to it. The Commission also appreciated that circumstances can arise in litigation rendering compliance with a notice requirement impracticable. For example, some hearings need to be arranged urgently and in other cases advance notification may carry a real risk of danger to the witness or some other person. For reasons of this kind, it recommended that allowance should be made for the possibility that, in some circumstances, it would be unreasonable and impracticable to give any notice at all. With a view to further maximizing flexibility, it also recommended that the notice provisions should be subject to rules of court to allow them to be disapplied in respect of certain classes of proceedings if, as experience is gained, that is felt to be appropriate; and that the parties should also be free to agree to exclude the notice provisions.[36] Section 2 of the Act reflects these recommendations. It provides as follows:[37]

(1) A party proposing to adduce hearsay evidence in civil proceedings shall, subject to the following provisions of this section, give to the other party or parties to the proceedings—
   (a) such notice (if any) of that fact, and
   (b) on request, such particulars of or relating to the evidence, as is reasonable and practicable in the circumstances for the purpose of enabling him or them to deal with any matters arising from its being hearsay.
(2) Provision may be made by rules of court—
   (a) specifying classes of proceedings or evidence in relation to which subsection (1) does not apply, and
   (b) as to the manner in which (including the time within which) the duties imposed by that subsection are to be complied with in the cases where it does apply.
(3) Subsection (1) may also be excluded by agreement of the parties; and compliance with the duty to give notice may in any case be waived by the person to whom notice is required to be given.

The relevant rules of court are CPR r 33.2 and 33.3.[38]

33.2 Notice of intention to rely on hearsay evidence

(1) Where a party intends to rely on hearsay evidence at trial and either—
   (a) that evidence is to be given by a witness giving oral evidence; or
   (b) that evidence is contained in a witness statement of a person who is not being called to give oral evidence;
   that party complies with section 2(1)(a) of the Civil Evidence Act 1995 by serving a witness statement on the other parties in accordance with the court's order.[39]
(2) Where paragraph (1)(b) applies, the party intending to rely on the hearsay evidence must, when he serves the witness statement—
   (a) inform the other parties that the witness is not being called to give oral evidence; and
   (b) give the reason why the witness will not be called.

---

[36] See generally Law Com No 216, Cm 2321 (1993), paras 4.9 and 4.10.

[37] By virtue of r 33.39 of the Criminal Procedure Rules 2015, SI 2015/1490, the Civil Evidence Act 1995, s 2(1), does not apply to evidence in restraint of trade proceedings and receivership proceedings.

[38] CPR r 33 does not apply to claims which have been allocated to the small claims track: CPR r 27.2.

[39] See Ch 5.

(3) In all other cases where a party intends to rely on hearsay evidence at trial, that party complies with section 2(1)(a) of the Civil Evidence Act 1995 by serving a notice on the other parties which—

    (a)   identifies the hearsay evidence;

    (b)   states that the party serving the notice proposes to rely on the hearsay evidence at trial; and

    (c)   gives the reason why the witness will not be called.

(4) The party proposing to rely on the hearsay evidence must—

    (a)   serve the notice no later than the latest date for serving witness statements; and

    (b)   if the hearsay evidence is to be in a document, supply a copy to any party who requests him to do so.

33.3 Circumstances in which notice of intention to rely on hearsay evidence is not required

Section 2.1 of the Civil Evidence Act 1995 (duty to give notice of intention to rely on hearsay evidence) does not apply—

    (a)   to evidence at hearings other than trials;

    (aa) to an affidavit or witness statement which is to be used at trial but which does not contain hearsay evidence;

    (b)   to a statement which a party to a probate action wishes to put in evidence and which is alleged to have been made by the person whose estate is the subject of the proceedings; or

    (c)   where the requirement is excluded by a practice direction.

Section 2(4) of the 1995 Act provides as follows:

(4) A failure to comply with subsection (1), or with rules under subsection (2)(b), does not affect the admissibility of the evidence but may be taken into account by the court—

    (a)   in considering the exercise of its powers with respect to the course of proceedings and costs, and

    (b)   as a matter adversely affecting the weight to be given to the evidence in accordance with section 4.

This subsection reflects the view of the Law Commission that if a party does not give notice, where it would have been reasonable and practicable in all the circumstances for him to have done so, the court should *not* be allowed to refuse to admit evidence.[40] Instead, under s 2(4)(a) of the 1995 Act, the court, in exercise of its inherent powers to control the conduct of the proceedings, may grant an adjournment (to compel a party to perfect an inadequate notice or to allow the recipient time to deal with the effect of late notification) and/or may impose a costs sanction; and under s 2(4)(b), the court may take the non-compliance as a matter reducing the weight to be attached to the evidence.[41]

---

[40] The Commission was of the view that such a sanction could have the effect of simply reintroducing the rule against hearsay.

[41] See *TSB (Scotland) plc v James Mills (Montrose) Ltd (in receivership)* 1992 SLT 519, a decision of the Outer House of the Court of Session under the Civil Evidence (Scotland) Act 1988: in certain circumstances the courts may declare the evidence wholly unreliable, in effect according it no weight.

The power to call witnesses for cross-examination

Where a party adduces hearsay evidence of a statement but does not call the maker of the statement as a witness, and the other party to the proceedings wishes to challenge the statement, it is an obvious safeguard to allow the other party to call the maker with a view to cross-examining him as to both the accuracy of the statement and his credibility as a witness. The other party is allowed to do so under s 3 of the 1995 Act, but only with the leave of the court. Section 3 provides that:

> Rules of court may provide that where a party to civil proceedings adduces hearsay evidence of a statement made by a person and does not call that person as a witness, any other party to the proceedings may, with the leave of the court, call that person as a witness and cross-examine him on the statement as if he had been called by the first-mentioned party and as if the hearsay statement were his evidence in chief.

The relevant rule is CPR r 33.4, which provides as follows:

(1) Where a party—
    (a) proposes to rely on hearsay evidence; and
    (b) does not propose to call the person who made the original statement to give oral evidence, the court may, on the application of any other party, permit that party to call the maker of the statement to be cross-examined on the contents of the statement.
(2) An application for permission to cross-examine under this rule must be made not more than 14 days after the day on which a notice of intention to rely on the hearsay evidence was served on the applicant.

If the court considers that the maker of the statement, even if overseas, should attend and be cross-examined at court in person, but the party proposing to rely on the evidence refuses to obey the order of the court, then the consequence will ordinarily be that the party will not be entitled to rely upon the evidence. In such a case, the court has ample powers to exclude the statement under CPR r 32.1.[42]

Rule 33.4 normally applies when a party, having served a witness statement, proposes to rely upon it as hearsay and does not propose to call its maker as a witness. It also applies when, in the event, such a party does not put the statement in as hearsay evidence or call the witness to give evidence at the trial, and the other party, in reliance upon CPR r 32.5(5)(b),[43] then puts the statement in as hearsay evidence. In these circumstances, the first party may apply to the court for permission to call the maker of the statement to be cross-examined on its contents.[44]

Weighing hearsay evidence

The statutory guidelines on weighing hearsay evidence do not impose any new obligation on the courts but simply indicate the more important factors which a court should bear in mind when it performs its usual function of weighing the evidence before it. The Law Commission recommended such guidelines for two reasons. First, having abolished the exclusionary rule, it wished to place extra emphasis on the need for courts to be vigilant in testing the reliability of such evidence. Secondly, it thought that it was important to deter the parties from abusing

---

[42] *Polanski v Condé Nast Publications Ltd* [2004] 1 WLR 387, CA at [22]–[23] and [62]. As to CPR r 32.1, see Ch 2.

[43] See **Ch 5, Witness statements, p 150.**

[44] *Douglas v Hello! Ltd* [2003] CP Rep 42, CA.

abolition of the rule, for example by deliberately failing to give notice or by giving late and inadequate notice,[45] by relying on hearsay evidence in preference to calling a dubious witness to give direct evidence of a fact,[46] or by attempting to conceal an essential witness in a case by amassing hearsay statements on a point.[47] Section 4 of the 1995 Act provides that:

(1) In estimating the weight (if any) to be given to hearsay evidence in civil proceedings the court shall have regard to any circumstances from which any inference can reasonably be drawn as to the reliability or otherwise of the evidence.

(2) Regard may be had, in particular, to the following—
   (a) whether it would have been reasonable and practicable for the party by whom the evidence was adduced to have produced the maker of the original statement as a witness;
   (b) whether the original statement was made contemporaneously with the occurrence or existence of the matters stated;
   (c) whether the evidence involves multiple hearsay;
   (d) whether any person involved had any motive to conceal or misrepresent matters;
   (e) whether the original statement was an edited account, or was made in collaboration with another or for a particular purpose;
   (f) whether the circumstances in which the evidence is adduced as hearsay are such as to suggest an attempt to prevent proper evaluation of its weight.

The phrase 'the original statement', which is used in s 4(2)(a), (b), and (e), is defined as 'the underlying statement (if any) by—(a) in the case of evidence of fact, a person having personal knowledge of that fact, or (b) in the case of evidence of opinion, the person whose opinion it is'.[48]

Section 4(2) will be of particular importance in cases in which hearsay carries inherent dangers, making it difficult for the judge to assess the truth in the absence of the original maker of the statement, as when a defendant to a claim for a possession or anti-social behaviour order is faced in court with serious complaints made by anonymous or absent witnesses about matters that took place, if at all, many months earlier.[49]

Concerning s 4(2)(a), it seems that if it would have been reasonable and practicable for the party by whom the evidence was adduced to have produced the maker of the original statement as a witness, an inference as to unreliability may be drawn, a very strong inference indeed if, had the maker been called as a witness, the court would not have granted leave under s 6(2) to adduce evidence of the statement. It also seems that such inferences may be drawn whether or not the maker is called for cross-examination by any other party to the proceedings under s 3, although it may be that such inferences are less likely to be drawn where the other party or parties have *not* applied for leave to call and cross-examine the maker under that section.

As to s 4(2)(d), the obscure phrase 'any person involved' may be taken to include (i) the maker of the 'original statement'; (ii) the 'receiver' of the statement, that is, the person who claims to have heard or otherwise perceived the statement and/or to have recorded it in a document; and (iii) in the case of multiple hearsay, that is, in cases in which the information

---

[45] See the 1995 Act, s 4(2)(f).
[46] Ibid, s 4(2)(a).
[47] See Law Com No 216, Cm 2321 (1993), para 4.19.
[48] Section 13.
[49] *Moat Housing Group South Ltd v Harris* [2006] QB 606, CA, applied in *R (Cleary) v Highbury Corner Magistrates' Court* [2007] 1 WLR 1272, DC.

contained in the original statement is not supplied to the 'receiver' directly, any intermediaries through whom it was supplied indirectly.

Under s 4(2)(e), whether the 'original statement' was made 'for a particular purpose' (and more importantly, if it was, what that purpose was) has an obvious bearing on its likely reliability. To take an extreme example, the express purpose of the 'original statement' may have been to mislead or deceive. On the other hand, the fact that the 'original statement' was made under an important statutory or other duty may well give rise to a strong inference as to the truth of its contents.

Impeaching credibility

Section 5(2) of the 1995 Act provides that:

> Where in civil proceedings hearsay evidence is adduced and the maker of the original statement, or of any statement relied upon to prove another statement, is not called as a witness—
>
> (a) evidence which if he had been so called would be admissible for the purpose of attacking or supporting his credibility as a witness is admissible for that purpose in the proceedings; and
>
> (b) evidence tending to prove that, whether before or after he made the statement, he made any other statement inconsistent with it is admissible for the purpose of showing that he had contradicted himself.
>
> Provided that evidence may not be given of any matter of which, if he had been called as a witness and had denied that matter in cross-examination, evidence could not have been adduced by the cross-examining party.

The general purpose of s 5(2) is to ensure that evidence relating to the credibility of certain persons not called as witnesses is as admissible as if those persons had been called as witnesses. The persons in question are (i) 'the maker of the original statement' and (ii) 'the maker ... of any statement relied upon to prove another statement'. As to the former, it seems that where the maker of the 'original statement', although not called, is available as a witness, evidence is admissible for the purpose of attacking credibility notwithstanding that the party adducing it has elected not to call and cross-examine him (with the leave of the court) under s 3. As to the latter, the meaning of 'another statement' is not clear, but presumably will be taken to mean not 'a statement other than the original statement' but 'either the original statement or any other statement'. Let us suppose that A makes an oral statement (the 'original statement') within the hearing of B; B tells C what A said; C makes a written record of his conversation with B; A, B, and C are all unavailable to give evidence; and C's written record is used to prove A's oral statement. In these circumstances, evidence relating to the credibility of A and C is clearly admissible and, it is submitted, evidence relating to the credibility of B should also be admissible.

Concerning s 5(2)(a), evidence admissible for the purpose of attacking credibility would include evidence of bias or previous convictions. Concerning s 5(2)(b), it seems that whereas in civil proceedings a prior inconsistent statement of a *witness* is not only admissible to attack his credibility but, by virtue of s 6(3) and (5) of the 1995 Act, is also admissible as evidence of any matter stated therein, a prior inconsistent statement introduced under s 5(2)(b) goes to consistency only.[50] The proviso to s 5(2) ensures that the rule on finality of answers on

---

[50] Although the Law Commission thought it important to preserve the position under the 1968 Act in this regard, cf the 1968 Act, s 7(5).

collateral issues[51] operates to restrict the evidence admissible under s 5(2) in the same way as it applies in relation to *witnesses*.

Where a party, in reliance on s 5(2), intends to attack the credibility of the maker of the original statement, he must give notice of his intention to do so, to the party who proposes to give the hearsay statement in evidence, not more than 14 days after the day on which a notice of intention to rely on the hearsay evidence was served on him.[52]

Proof of statements contained in documents

The provisions of the 1995 Act governing the proof of statements contained in documents draw a distinction between (i) documents generally; and (ii) documents which are shown to form part of the records of a business or public authority.[53]

Documents generally

Section 8 of the 1995 Act provides that:

(1) Where a statement contained in a document is admissible as evidence in civil proceedings, it may be proved—
  (a) by the production of that document, or
  (b) whether or not that document is still in existence, by the production of a copy of that document or of the material part of it, authenticated in such manner as the court may approve.
(2) It is immaterial for this purpose how many removes there are between a copy and the original.

A 'document' for these purposes means 'anything in which information of any description is recorded',[54] a definition covering documents in any form and therefore wide enough to include maps, plans, graphs, drawings, photographs, discs, audio tapes, videotapes, films, microfilms, negatives, and computer-generated printouts. A 'copy', in relation to a document, means 'anything onto which information recorded in the document has been copied, by whatever means and whether directly or indirectly',[55] a definition wide enough to cover, inter alia, a transcript of an audio tape as well as reproductions or still reproductions of the images embodied in films and videotapes, etc, whether enlarged or not.

Concerning s 8(1)(a), 'production' refers not to counsel handing the document to the court, but to a witness who is qualified to do so in accordance with the rules of evidence producing the document and saying what it is.[56] However, although such direct oral evidence is preferable and will carry greater weight, it would seem that the document may also be proved by another hearsay statement admissible under the 1995 Act. Thus, where a statement has been deliberately tape-recorded but its maker is unavailable to produce the tape and give direct evidence that it is the tape he made, it seems that his out-of-court statements to the same effect could be used to prove the tape.[57]

---

[51] See Ch 7.
[52] CPR r 33.5.
[53] See also Ch 10, **Documentary evidence**, p 302.
[54] The 1995 Act, s 13.
[55] Ibid.
[56] Per Staughton LJ in *Ventouris v Mountain (No 2)* [1992] 1 WLR 887, CA at 901, a decision under the 1968 Act, s 6(1).
[57] *Ventouris v Mountain (No 2)* [1992] 1 WLR 887, CA.

The reference to 'authentication' at the end of s 8(1) appears to relate to the authentication of copies of a document as true copies of the original, and not to proof of the original.[58] Section 8(2) makes clear that copies of copies may be received in evidence (subject to authentication in such manner as the court may approve).

Records of a business or public authority

Although at one time records of a business or public authority were kept manually and responsibility could often be attributed to an individual record keeper, nowadays record keeping within an organization has been largely taken over by technology and there is often unlikely to be a witness who can give direct evidence of all or any aspects of the compilation of the records kept. For these reasons, the Law Commission recommended that documents certified as forming part of the records of a business or public authority should be capable of being received in evidence without further proof.[59] Section 9 of the 1995 Act provides that:

(1) A document which is shown to form part of the records of a business or public authority may be received in evidence in civil proceedings without further proof.

(2) A document shall be taken to form part of the records of a business or public authority if there is produced to the court a certificate to that effect signed by an officer of the business or authority to which the records belong.

For this purpose—

(a) a document purporting to be a certificate signed by an officer of a business or public authority shall be deemed to have been duly given by such an officer and signed by him; and

(b) a certificate shall be treated as signed by a person if it purports to bear a facsimile of his signature.

The precise scope of s 9(1) is unclear because the word 'records', said to mean 'records in whatever form',[60] is not otherwise defined. Hopefully, the word will not be construed as narrowly as it was under the Civil Evidence Act 1968, where it was taken to mean 'records which a historian would regard as original or primary sources, that is documents which either give effect to a transaction itself or which contain a contemporaneous register of information supplied by those with direct knowledge of the facts'. Thus copies of documents consisting of summaries of the results of research into a drug and articles and letters about the drug published in medical journals were held not to be records, but merely a digest or analysis of records;[61] and a bill of lading or cargo manifest,[62] a tithe map,[63] or a transcript of criminal proceedings[64] would rank as a record, but not a file of correspondence[65] or an anonymous

---

[58] Ibid.

[59] See Law Com No 216, Cm 2321 (1993), paras 3.12 and 4.39.

[60] Section 9(4).

[61] *H v Schering Chemicals Ltd* [1983] 1 WLR 143, QBD.

[62] See *R v Jones; R v Sullivan* [1978] 1 WLR 195, CA, a decision under the Criminal Evidence Act 1965 (see Ch 12, Background and rationale, p 350, n 4).

[63] See *Knight v David* [1971] 1 WLR 1671, Ch D.

[64] See *Taylor v Taylor* [1970] 1 WLR 1148, CA.

[65] See *R v Tirado* (1974) 59 Cr App R 80, CA, a decision under the Criminal Evidence Act 1965. Cf *R v Olisa* [1990] Crim LR 721, CA: for the purposes of the Police and Criminal Evidence Act 1984, s 68, three application forms completed by a customer of a bank did 'form part of a record' compiled by the bank officials.

document setting out a summary of legal proceedings taken or contemplated against a company.[66] In *Savings and Investment Bank Ltd v Gasco Investments (Netherlands) BV*[67] it was held that a report of inspectors appointed by the Secretary of State for Trade on the affairs and ownership of a company was not a record: it fell short of a compilation of the information supplied because it contained only a selection of that information, and went beyond such a compilation because it also contained the opinions of the inspectors.[68]

Under s 9(4), 'business' includes 'any activity regularly carried on over a period of time, whether for profit or not, by any body (whether corporate or not) or by an individual'; and 'public authority' includes 'any public or statutory undertaking, any government department and any person holding office under Her Majesty'. The wide definition of 'business' reflects the Law Commission's view that it is the quality of regularity that lends a business record its reliability, not the existence of a profit motive or the judicial nature of the person carrying on the activity. A business defined in this way may not have 'officers' in the strict sense of that word and, accordingly, under s 9(4), 'officer' includes 'any person occupying a responsible position in relation to the relevant activities of the business or public authority or in relation to its records'.

Unless the court orders otherwise, a document which may be received in evidence under s 9(1) shall not be receivable at trial unless the party intending to put it in evidence has given notice of his intention to the other parties; and where he intends to use the evidence as evidence of any fact, then he must give notice not later than the latest date for serving witness statements.[69] Where a party has given such notice, he must also give every other party an opportunity to inspect the document and to agree to its admission without further proof.[70]

The Law Commission considered that the absence of an entry in a record should be capable of being formally proved, despite the fact that proving a negative (and drawing inferences from it) is rarely possible by reference to any human source.[71] The most appropriate method of doing this was thought to be by way of affidavit. Section 9(3) provides that:

> The absence of an entry in the records of a business or public authority may be proved in civil proceedings by affidavit of an officer of the business or authority to which the records belong.

The Law Commission recognized that, although business and other records have long been treated as belonging to a class of evidence which can be regarded as likely to be reliable, there are bound to be exceptions, and it therefore recommended a specific discretion, allowing courts to disapply the certification provisions.[72] Section 9(5) provides that:

> The court may, having regard to the circumstances of the case, direct that all or any of the above provisions of this section do not apply in relation to a particular document or record, or description of documents or records.

---

[66] See *Re Koscot Interplanetary (UK) Ltd, Re Koscot AG* [1972] 3 All ER 829.

[67] [1984] 1 WLR 271, Ch D.

[68] See also *Re D (a minor)* [1986] 2 FLR 189, Fam D: notes of an interview between a solicitor and his client fell short of being a complete record of what was said. They were treated as a selective and necessarily subjective aide memoire.

[69] CPR r 33.6(2), (3), and (4).

[70] CPR r 33.6(8).

[71] See *R v Patel* (1981) 73 Cr App R 117, CA; *R v Shone* (1983) 76 Cr App R 72, CA; and generally Ch 12, **Negative hearsay, p 370**.

[72] Law Com No 216, Cm 2321 (1993), para 4.42.

Evidence formerly admissible at common law

General

Section 9 of the Civil Evidence Act 1968 preserved and gave statutory force to a number of common law exceptions to the hearsay rule (informal admissions, published works dealing with matters of a public nature, and public documents and records) without purporting to amend the law in relation to those exceptions. Subject to one important difference, this state of affairs is perpetuated by the 1995 Act. The important difference relates to informal admissions. The Law Commission considered that there was no longer any need to preserve this common law exception and recommended that the general provisions of the Act, including the notice and weight provisions, should apply to informal admissions as they apply to other hearsay statements.[73] Section 7(1) of the 1995 Act gives statutory effect to this recommendation and is considered further below, under **Evidence formerly admissible at common law, Informal admissions.** Concerning published works dealing with matters of a public nature, and public documents and records, however, the Commission recommended preserving the relevant common law rules because: (a) some of the statutory provisions which it believed should not be affected by its proposals presuppose the existence of the common law rules about public registers;[74] (b) it was not the policy of the Commission to add the procedural burden of the notice procedure where no such burden already existed; and (c) it would be rare for the weight to be attached to such evidence to be a matter for debate.[75] Section 7(2) gives statutory effect to this recommendation. The common law rules effectively preserved by the 1995 Act are considered in **Chapter 14.**

Informal admissions

Under s 7(1) of the 1995 Act, 'the common law rule effectively preserved by section 9(1) and (2)(a) of the Civil Evidence Act 1968 (admissibility of admissions adverse to a party) is superseded by the provisions of this Act'. As already noted,[76] the purpose of the subsection is to give effect to the Law Commission's recommendation that the general provisions of the Act should apply to informal admissions.[77]

The application of s 1 of the 1995 Act (admissibility)

At common law an informal admission was a statement by a party to the proceedings (or someone in privity with him) made other than while testifying in those proceedings and adverse to his case. Any such statement is now covered by s 1(1) of the Act and, by reason of the wide statutory definition of statement ('any representation of fact or opinion, however made'), an admission may be admitted whether made orally, in writing, or by conduct, demeanour, or even silence. Thus, as at common law, a person may make an oral admission when talking either to another[78] or to himself.[79] Similarly, in the case of written admissions,

---

[73] Ibid, paras 4.32 and 4.33.

[74] Evidence (Foreign, Dominion and Colonial Documents) Act 1933, s 1 (see Chs 2 and 14) and the Oaths and Evidence (Overseas Authorities and Countries) Act 1963, s 5.

[75] Law Com No 216, Cm 2321 (1993), para 4.33.

[76] See immediately above, under **General.**

[77] Section 3, however, could hardly apply to an informal admission made by a party to legal proceedings (as opposed to someone in privity with him): it would involve that party calling and cross-examining himself!

[78] See *Rumping v DPP* [1964] AC 814, HL (the maker's wife).

[79] See per Alderson B in *R v Simons* (1834) 6 C&P 540.

the admission may be contained in a communication, such as a letter, or in a diary or other private memorandum.[80] A common law example of an admission by conduct is *Moriarty v London, Chatham and Dover Rly Co*,[81] where evidence of the plaintiff's conduct in suborning witnesses was admitted as an admission by him of the weakness and falsity of his claim. Where an out-of-court accusation is made against a party, his answer, whether given by words or conduct, may constitute an admission insofar as it amounts to an acknowledgment of the truth of the whole or part of the accusation made. Presumably, even silence, by way of reply, will amount to a 'statement' where the accusation is made in circumstances such that it would be reasonable to expect some explanation or denial. At common law, in *Wiedemann v Walpole*[82] Lord Esher MR said that, in the case of a letter written upon a matter of business, the court could take notice of the ordinary course adopted by men of business to answer letters the contents of which they do not intend to admit, so that a failure to reply to such a letter could be taken as some evidence of the truth of the statements contained in it, but that a man could not reasonably be expected to reply to a letter charging him with some offence or impropriety because 'it is the ordinary and wise practice of mankind not to answer such letters'.[83]

The application of section 4 of the Act (weight)

Section 4 of the 1995 Act applies to informal admissions as it applies to other hearsay statements. However, there are a number of special considerations which are relevant to the weighing of admissions. Some of these are of a general character, but there are also two specific considerations: whether the admission relates to facts of which its maker had no personal knowledge, and whether the admission was vicarious, that is, made by someone in privity with a party to legal proceedings.

General considerations

The weight to be attached to an informal admission depends upon its precise contents, the circumstances in which it was made (eg whether it was made as a result of some threat or inducement), and any contradictory or other evidence adduced by its maker at the trial with a view to explaining it away. In some cases, the tribunal of fact will need to consider carefully whether the statement is, in fact, adverse to the case of its maker, and for this purpose regard should be had to the whole statement, including any passages favourable to its maker which qualify, explain, or even nullify so much of the statement as is relied upon as an admission. Although it may be that less weight may be attached to the favourable or self-serving parts of the statement,[84] it is clear that under the 1995 Act they are as much evidence of the facts they state as the passages relied upon as constituting an admission.[85]

Personal knowledge

An informal admission may be admitted under the 1995 Act notwithstanding that it relates to facts of which its maker has no personal knowledge[86] or amounts to no more than an

---

[80] See *Bruce v Garden* (1869) 18 WR 384.

[81] (1870) LR 5 QB 314. See also *Alderson v Clay* (1816) 1 Stark 405.

[82] [1891] 2 QB 534, CA.

[83] Cf *Bessela v Stern* (1877) 2 CPD 265, CA.

[84] See *Smith v Blandy* (1825) Ry&M 257.

[85] See *Harrison v Turner* (1847) 10 QB 482.

[86] Under s 1(2)(b), 'references to hearsay include hearsay of whatever degree'.

expression of opinion or belief.[87] The weight to be attached to such evidence will vary according to the circumstances. For example, an admission by a party as to his age, although obviously based on hearsay, concerns a matter as to which it is reasonable to expect that he has been accurately informed.[88] On the other hand, in *Comptroller of Customs v Western Electric Co Ltd*,[89] the Privy Council was of the view that an admission concerning the countries of origin of certain imported goods, made in reliance on the fact that the goods bore marks and labels indicating that they came from those countries, was evidentially worthless.[90]

Vicarious admissions

The rationale of the common law exception was the presumed unlikelihood of a person speaking falsely against his own interest, a rationale reflected in the rule that an informal admission could only be received in evidence if it was made directly (ie by a party to the legal proceedings) or vicariously (ie by someone in privity with a party). 'Privity' in this context usually denoted some common or successive interest in the subject matter of the litigation or some other relationship between the party and the privy, for example that of principal and agent, whereby the latter had actual or imputed authority to speak on behalf of the former. Under the 1995 Act, an out-of-court statement adverse to the case of a party may be received in evidence whether made by that party or by *anyone else*. However, the weight to be attached to an admission made by someone who, at common law, would have been in privity with a party is generally likely to be greater than an admission made by anyone else.

Those in privity included: (i) a predecessor in title of a party to proceedings (provided that the admission concerned title to the property in question and was made at a time when he had an interest in the property);[91] (ii) a partner (an admission or representation made by any partner concerning the partnership affairs and in the ordinary course of its business being evidence against the firm);[92] (iii) referees;[93] and (iv) agents. At common law, an admission by an agent could only be received against his principal if (a) it was made at a time when the agency existed (a matter which, apparently, could be inferred from the statements and conduct of the alleged agent himself);[94] (b) the communication in which it was made was authorized, whether expressly or by implication, by the principal;[95] and (c) it was made in the course of a communication with some third party as opposed to the principal himself.[96] Under the 1995 Act, failure to establish these three matters will not affect admissibility, but is likely to affect adversely the weight to be attached to the 'admission'.

---

[87] Under s 13, a 'statement' is defined to include 'any representation of opinion'.

[88] See, at common law, *R v Turner* [1910] 1 KB 346, CCA and *Lustre Hosiery Ltd v York* (1936) 54 CLR 134, High Court of Australia.

[89] [1966] AC 367.

[90] Ibid per Lord Hodson at 371.

[91] *Woolway v Rowe* (1834) 1 Ad&El 114. See also *Smith v Smith* (1836) 3 Bing NC 29.

[92] See the Partnership Act 1890, s 15, giving statutory force to a common law principle to the same effect. See also *Jaggers v Binnings* (1815) 1 Stark 64 and *Wood v Braddick* (1808) 1 Taunt 104.

[93] *Williams v Innes* (1808) 1 Camp 364, KB, where Lord Ellenborough CJ said (at 365): 'If a man refers another upon any particular business to a third person, he is bound by what this third person says or does concerning it, as much as if that had been said or done by himself.'

[94] See, *sed quaere, Edwards v Brookes (Milk) Ltd* [1963] 1 WLR 795, QBD.

[95] *Wagstaff v Wilson* (1832) 4 B&Ad 339; *G (A) v G (T)* [1970] 2 QB 643, CA; and *Johnson v Lindsay* (1889) 53 JP 599, DC. See also *Burr v Ware RDC* [1939] 2 All ER 688, CA and cf *Beer v W H Clench (1930) Ltd* [1936] 1 All ER 449, DC.

[96] See *Re Devala Provident Gold Mining Co* (1883) 22 Ch D 593, and cf *The Solway* (1885) 10 PD 137, P, D and Admlty.

The weight to be attached to an 'admission' made by someone who at common law would not have been in privity with a party is generally likely to be less than an admission made by that party himself or someone who would have been in privity with him. At common law there was no privity between (i) spouses, merely by virtue of their relationship of husband and wife; (ii) a parent and a child, merely by virtue of that relationship;[97] (iii) co-parties, that is, co-plaintiffs or co-defendants (or, in divorce proceedings, a respondent and a co-respondent);[98] or (iv) a witness and the party calling him.[99]

Ogden tables

Section 10 of the 1995 Act provides that:

> The actuarial tables (together with explanatory notes) for use in personal injury and fatal accident cases issued from time to time by the Government Actuary's Department are admissible in evidence for the purpose of assessing, in an action for personal injury, the sum to be awarded as general damages for future pecuniary loss.

ADDITIONAL READING

Law Commission, *The Hearsay Rule in Civil Proceedings*, Cm 2321 (Law Com No 216, London, 1993).
The Law Commission's report into the usefulness of the hearsay rule in civil proceedings and its recommendations for reform of the machinery for rendering hearsay admissible. The recommendations were put into effect by the Civil Evidence Act 1995.

---

[97] *G (A) v G (T)* [1970] 2 QB 643, CA.

[98] *Morton v Morton, Daly and McNaught* [1937] P 151, P, D and Admlty and *Myatt v Myatt and Parker* [1962] 1 WLR 570, P, D and Admlty.

[99] See *British Thomson-Houston Co Ltd v British Insulated and Helsby Cables Ltd* [1924] 2 Ch 160, CA and cf *Richards v Morgan* (1863) 4 B&S 641.

Hearsay admissible at common law

14

Key issues

- If a statement is made out of court and tendered as evidence of the facts asserted (hearsay), why should it be admissible when:

  — it was made in a public document, for example a public register;

  — it was made in a work of reference dealing with a matter of a public nature, for example a history or a map;

  — it was made by a person who, at the time when he made it, was emotionally overpowered by an event, for example a victim of a serious assault; or

  — it relates to the contemporaneous physical sensation or mental state of its maker?

Under the common law rule against hearsay, any assertion, other than one made by a person while giving oral evidence in the proceedings, was inadmissible if tendered as evidence of the facts asserted. As we have seen in **Chapters 12** and **13**, the circumstances in which hearsay is admissible in criminal proceedings are now governed by **Chapter 2** of Pt 11 of the Criminal Justice Act 2003 (the 2003 Act), and in civil proceedings hearsay is admissible subject to compliance with the conditions of admissibility set out in the Civil Evidence Act 1995 (the 1995 Act). The categories of hearsay considered in this chapter—statements in public documents, works of reference, evidence of age, evidence of reputation, and statements forming part of the *res gestae*—share two common features: all of them were established at common law as exceptions to the rule against hearsay and all of them have been preserved by statute. All of the cases considered, apart from evidence of age and *res gestae* statements, have been expressly preserved and given statutory force in both criminal proceedings (by s 118(1) of the 2003 Act) and civil proceedings (by s 7(2) and (3) of the 1995 Act). The categories relating to evidence of age and statements forming part of the *res gestae* have been preserved in criminal but not civil proceedings. However, evidence formerly admissible in these cases at common law will now be admissible in civil proceedings under the general provisions of the 1995 Act.

It is convenient to consider the common law rules separately, here, under the rubric of hearsay admissible at common law, because neither s 118 of the 2003 Act nor s 7 of the 1995 Act purports to amend the rules to which they have given statutory force. Section 7(4) of the 1995 Act provides that the words in which a rule of law mentioned in the section is described 'are intended only to identify the rule and shall not be construed as altering it in any way'; and although there is no express equivalent in s 118 of the 2003 Act, it is plain that it too is designed to identify rules of law rather than alter them. Furthermore, where evidence is admissible under one of the preserved rules, it is not subject to other statutory conditions of admissibility and safeguards. However, the common law exceptions have been narrowly construed, and much evidence failing to meet all of the common law conditions of admissibility may well be admissible in civil proceedings under the general provisions of the 1995 Act (subject to compliance with the statutory conditions) and in criminal proceedings under statutory provisions of a general nature such as ss 116 and 117 of the 2003 Act (cases where a witness is unavailable and business and other documents).[1]

Statements in public documents

Section 7(2)(b) and (c) of the 1995 Act preserve any rule of law whereby in civil proceedings—

(b) public documents (for example, public registers, and returns made under public authority with respect to matters of public interest) are admissible as evidence of the facts stated in them, or

(c) records (for example, the records of certain courts, treaties, Crown grants, pardons and commissions) are admissible as evidence of facts stated in them.

Section 118(1)1(b) and (c) of the 2003 Act preserve the same rules in criminal proceedings.

---

[1] Concerning the notice requirement for the introduction of hearsay in civil proceedings, see rr 33.2 and 33.3 of the Civil Procedure Rules 1998, SI 1998/3132. In criminal proceedings, the notice requirements of the Criminal Procedure Rules do not apply to hearsay statements admissible under a common law exception: see *Barnaby v DPP* [2015] 2 Cr App R 53 (4), DC at [20] and also r 20.2(1) of the Criminal Procedure Rules 2015, SI 2015/1490. See also *Valiati v DPP, KM v DPP* [2019] 1 WLR 1221 at [11] and **n 134**.

General

At common law, statements made in most public documents are admissible in both civil and criminal cases as evidence of the matters stated.[2] The admissibility of such evidence may be justified on the grounds of reliability and convenience. Where a record has been compiled by a person acting under a public duty to inquire into the truth of some matter and to record his findings so that the public may refer to them, the contents of that document may be presumed to be true.[3] Proof of the facts stated in the document by direct evidence would clearly be preferable, but in many cases the public official in question will be dead, otherwise unavailable, or unable to remember the facts recorded because of the time which has elapsed. The common law principles relating to public documents, though not unimportant, are of comparatively minor significance, mainly because of the existence of a wide variety of statutory provisions which cater for the admissibility of particular classes of public document in both criminal and civil proceedings. Under s 34 of the Births and Deaths Registration Act 1953, for example, a certified copy of an entry purporting to be sealed or stamped with the seal of the General Register Office, shall be received as evidence of the birth or death to which it relates.[4]

Examples

The terms of s 7(2)(b) and (c) of the 1995 Act give some idea of the different classes of public document admissible under this head. The exception applies to a variety of public papers, official registers, surveys, assessments, inquisitions, returns, and other documents made under public authority in relation to matters of public concern. Examples include: recitals in public Acts of Parliament and royal proclamations;[5] entries relating to acts of state and public matters in parliamentary journals and governmental Gazettes;[6] entries in parish registers of baptisms, marriages, and burials;[7] extracts from foreign registers kept under the sanction of public authority as to matters properly and regularly recorded in them;[8] entries in the public books of a corporation relating to matters of public interest;[9] the contents of a file from the Companies Register containing the statutory returns made by a company in compliance with the Companies Act 1948;[10] the conditions of the licence on which a prisoner

---

[2] Concerning proof of the contents of a public document upon which a party seeks to rely, see **Ch 10**.

[3] See per Parke B in *Irish Society v Bishop of Derry* (1846) 12 Cl&Fin 641, HL.

[4] See also the Marriage Act 1949, s 65(3) (proof of the celebration of a marriage by the production of a certified copy of an entry kept at the General Register Office).

[5] *R v Sutton* (1816) 4 M&S 532.

[6] *A-G v Theakston* (1820) 8 Price 89; *R v Holt* (1793) 5 Term Rep 436.

[7] Entries of the particulars of birth and death would appear to be inadmissible because outside the actual knowledge of the person making the entries: see per Geoffrey Lane LJ in *R v Halpin* [1975] QB 907 CA, at 914; cf per Lord Blackburn in *Sturla v Freccia* (1880) 5 App Cas 623, HL at 644.

[8] For example, foreign registers of baptisms and marriages: see per Lord Selborne in *Lyell v Kennedy* (1889) 14 App Cas 437, HL at 448–9. See also the Evidence (Foreign, Dominion and Colonial Documents) Act 1933, whereby an Order in Council may provide that registers of a foreign country are documents of such a public nature as to be admissible as evidence of matters regularly recorded therein.

[9] *Shrewsbury v Hart* (1823) 1 C&P 113.

[10] *R v Halpin* [1975] QB 907, CA, see, in this chapter, under **A public officer acting under a duty to inquire and record, p 436**. See now the Companies Act 2006. Other documentary records relating to companies, such as the certificate of incorporation, the register of members, and minutes of proceedings of meetings, are rendered admissible by the Act itself.

serving a term of imprisonment is released from custody;[11] statements in coastguards' books on weather conditions;[12] entries in university records relating to degrees conferred;[13] entries in Domesday Book;[14] records of assessment by commissioners of land tax;[15] inquisitions and surveys of Crown lands;[16] inquisitions in lunacy;[17] and findings of professional misconduct by the General Medical Council.[18]

Conditions of admissibility

Given the multiplicity of public documents to which the exception applies, it is perhaps not surprising that the conditions of admissibility vary, to some extent, according to the particular type of document in question. Generally speaking, however, it seems that a public document is only admissible as evidence of the truth of its contents if (a) it concerns a public matter, (b) it was made by a public officer acting under a duty to inquire and record the results of such inquiry, and (c) it was intended to be retained for public reference or inspection.[19]

A public matter

In *Sturla v Freccia*[20] Lord Blackburn expressed the opinion that 'public', in this context, should not be taken to mean the whole world: the matter in question may concern either the public at large or a section of the public. Thus an entry in the books of a manor may be public as concerning all the people interested in the manor[21] and an entry in a corporation book concerning a corporate matter or something in which all the corporation is concerned may be public in the same sense.[22]

A public officer acting under a duty to inquire and record

A statement in a public document is only admissible if it was made by a public officer, as opposed to some private individual,[23] acting in discharge of a strict duty to inquire into and satisfy himself of the truth of the facts recorded.[24] Thus whereas a certificate of the registrar of births, deaths, and marriages is admissible as prima facie—but not conclusive—evidence

---

[11] *West Midlands Probation Board v French* [2009] 1 WLR 1715, DC. However, it has been doubted whether the conditions of such a licence are hearsay evidence at all: see Ormerod, '*West Midlands Probation Board v French*' (case comment) [2009] Crim LR 283.

[12] *The Catherina Maria* (1866) LR 1 A&E 53.

[13] *Collins v Carnegie* (1834) 1 Ad&El 695.

[14] *Duke of Beaufort v John Aird & Co* (1904) 20 TLR 602.

[15] *Doe d Strode v Seaton* (1834) 2 Ad&El 171.

[16] *Duke of Beaufort v Smith* (1849) 4 Exch 450.

[17] *Faulder v Silk* (1811) 3 Camp 126; *Harvey v R* [1901] AC 601, PC.

[18] *Hill v Clifford* [1907] 2 Ch 236, CA.

[19] See generally per Lord Blackburn in *Sturla v Freccia* (1880) 5 App Cas 623, HL at 643–4.

[20] (1880) 5 App Cas 623, HL.

[21] See, eg, *Heath v Deane* [1905] 2 Ch 86, Ch D (manorial rolls).

[22] But see *Hill v Manchester and Salford Waterworks Co* (1833) 5 B&Ad 866. See also *R v Sealby* [1965] 1 All ER 701 (Crown Court).

[23] *Daniel v Wilkin* (1852) 7 Exch 429 (a survey undertaken by a private individual).

[24] *Doe d France v Andrews* (1850) 15 QB 756; *Thrasyvoulos Ioannou v Papa Christoforos Demetriou* [1952] AC 84, PC; *White v Taylor* [1969] 1 Ch 150, Ch D.

of the fact and date of a birth, death, or marriage,[25] it would appear, according to the obiter view of Swinfen Eady MR in *Bird v Keep*,[26] that information concerning the cause of death contained in a death certificate and based on information supplied by a coroner is inadmissible as evidence of the cause of death. This conclusion has been justified on the grounds that the registrar is *bound* to record the verdict of the coroner's jury and is under no duty to state the results of his own personal inquiry according to his own judgment.[27] Under the modern law, however, it seems that strict compliance with the requirement of personal knowledge on the part of a public official of the matters which he puts on file or records is no longer necessary. In *R v Halpin*,[28] in order to prove that the appellant was a director of a company at a particular point in time, the prosecution adduced in evidence a file from the Companies Register containing the annual returns made by the company under the Companies Act 1948. On appeal, it was argued that the file was inadmissible as a public document because the relevant official at the Companies Registry has no duty to inquire and satisfy himself as to the truth of the recorded facts. The Court of Appeal was satisfied that under the common law authorities it was a condition of admissibility that the official making the record either should have had personal knowledge of the matters recorded or should have inquired into the accuracy of the facts. It was also satisfied that on the facts the official in the Companies Registry had no personal knowledge of the matters which he had put on file or recorded. However, Lane LJ said:[29]

> The common law as expressed in the earlier cases which have been cited were plainly designed to apply to an uncomplicated community where those charged with keeping registers would, more often than not, be personally acquainted with the people whose affairs they were recording and the vicar, as already indicated, would probably himself have officiated at the baptism, marriage or burial which he later recorded in the presence of the churchwardens on the register before putting it back in the coffers. But the common law should move with the times and should recognize the fact that the official charged with recording matters of public import can no longer in this highly complicated world, as like as not, have personal knowledge of their accuracy.
>
> What has happened now is that the function originally performed by one man has had to be shared between two: the first having the knowledge and the statutory duty to record that knowledge and forward it to the Registrar of Companies, the second having the duty to preserve that document and to show it to members of the public under proper conditions as required.

Accordingly, it was held that where a duty is cast upon a company by statute to make accurate returns of company matters to the Registrar of Companies so that those returns can be filed and inspected by members of the public, all statements on the return are prima facie proof of the truth of their contents.

---

[25] See *Wilton & Co v Phillips* (1903) 19 TLR 390, KBD; *Brierley v Brierley and Williams* [1918] P 257, P, D and Admlty; cf *R v Clapham* (1829) 4 C&P 29: a statement in a parish register of baptisms that the person baptized was born on a particular day is not admissible as evidence of the date of birth, the record being admissible on the question of baptism not birth.

[26] [1918] 2 KB 692, CA at 697, 698 and 701.

[27] See per Scrutton LJ in *Re Stollery, Weir v Treasury Solicitor* [1926] Ch 284, CA at 322. But see also per Sargent LJ at 327: since the verdict of the coroner's jury is itself inadmissible as evidence of the truth of the facts on which it is based, it follows that the short note made of that verdict in the death certificate is also inadmissible.

[28] [1975] QB 907. See also *R v Sealby* [1965] 1 All ER 701 (Crown Court) at 703–4; cf *White v Taylor* [1969] 1 Ch 150, Ch D.

[29] [1975] QB 907 at 915.

The statement in the public document must have been made by the official whose duty it was to inquire and record. Thus an entry in a register of baptisms made by the minister of the parish is admissible, but not a private memorandum made by the parish clerk.[30] At one time it appears that an entry in a register was only admissible if made promptly.[31] However, in *R v Halpin*, where the entries in the files from the Companies Register were acknowledged to be very much out of time, Lane LJ said that this was a matter which might go to their weight, but not to their admissibility.[32] Likewise, the fact that an entry was made by an interested party may affect its weight but will not, of itself, render it inadmissible.[33]

Retention for public reference

A public document, to be admissible as such, must have been brought into existence as a document of record to be retained indefinitely: a document intended to be of temporary effect[34] or designed to serve only temporary purposes[35] is inadmissible. Additionally, the document should have been prepared for the purposes of the public making use of it and must be available for public inspection.[36] In *Lilley v Pettit*[37] it was held that the regimental records of a serving soldier were not admissible as public documents, since they were kept for the information of the Crown and executive as opposed to members of the public, who had no right of access to them. Similarly, in *R v Sealby*,[38] a car registration book was ruled to be inadmissible as evidence of its contents, for example the chassis and engine numbers, on the grounds that it is a private document issued to a car owner who is under no obligation to produce it for inspection by anyone except a police officer or a local taxation officer.

Works of reference

Section 7(2)(a) of the 1995 Act preserves any rule of law whereby in civil proceedings—

(a) published works dealing with matters of a public nature (for example, histories, scientific works, dictionaries and maps) are admissible as evidence of facts of a public nature stated in them . . .

Section 118(1)1(a) of the 2003 Act preserves the same rule in criminal proceedings.

Under the common law rule, authoritative published works of reference dealing with matters of a public nature are admissible to prove, or to assist the court in deciding whether to take judicial notice of, facts of a public nature stated in them.[39] Examples include: historical works concerning ancient public facts;[40] standard medical texts concerning the nature of a

---

[30] *Doe d Warren v Bray* (1828) 8 B&C 813.

[31] Ibid.

[32] [1975] QB 907, CA at 916.

[33] See *Irish Society v Bishop of Derry* (1846) 12 Cl&Fin 641, HL.

[34] *White v Taylor* [1969] 1 Ch 150, Ch D (a draft document).

[35] *Mercer v Denne* [1905] 2 Ch 538, CA.

[36] Per Lord Blackburn in *Sturla v Freccia* (1880) 5 App Cas 623, HL at 648; *Thrasyvoulos Ioannou v Papa Christoforos Demetriou* [1952] AC 84, PC.

[37] [1946] KB 401, DC.

[38] [1965] 1 All ER 701 (Crown Court).

[39] On judicial notice generally, see Ch 4.

[40] *Read v Bishop of Lincoln* [1892] AC 644, PC. But not facts of a private or local nature: *Stainer v Droitwich (Burgesses)* (1695) 1 Salk 281. See also *Evans v Getting* (1834) 6 C&P 586 and *Fowke v Berington* [1914] 2 Ch 308, Ch D.

disease;[41] engineers' reports within the common knowledge of engineers and accepted by them as accurate on the nature of certain soil;[42] Carlisle Tables, which set out the average life expectancy of persons;[43] dictionaries, on the meaning of English words;[44] and published maps and plans generally offered for sale to the public, even if not prepared by someone acting under a public duty, concerning facts of geographical notoriety.[45]

Evidence of age

Section 118(1)1(d) of the 2003 Act preserves the following rule of law in criminal proceedings:

(d) evidence relating to a person's age or date or place of birth may be given by a person without personal knowledge of the matter.

Since the date of a person's birth is contained in his or her birth certificate, the normal way of proving a person's age is to produce a certified copy of an entry in the register of births, which is admissible under s 34 of the Births and Deaths Registration Act 1953 as evidence of the matters stated, accompanied by some evidence to identify the person whose age is in question with the person named in the certificate. At common law, accompanying evidence of identification may be given by a person without personal knowledge of the matter, such as the evidence of a grandmother who, although present at the birth of her grandchild, was not present at the registration.[46] Similarly, the courts have acted on evidence as to age given by the person whose age is in question[47] or by another who has made enquiries as to his or her age.[48]

Evidence of reputation

Section 7(3)(a) and (b) of the 1995 Act provide as follows:

The common law rules . . . whereby in civil proceedings
(a) evidence of a person's reputation is admissible for the purpose of establishing his good or bad character, or
(b) evidence of reputation or family tradition is admissible—
(i) for the purpose of proving or disproving pedigree or the existence of a marriage,[49] or
(ii) for the purpose of proving or disproving the existence of any public or general right or of identifying any person or thing,
shall continue to have effect in so far as they authorise the court to treat such evidence as proving or disproving that matter.

---

[41] *McCarthy v The Melita (Owners)* (1923) 16 BWCC 222, CA.

[42] *East London Rly Co v Thames Conservators* (1904) 90 LT 347, Ch D.

[43] *Rowley v London and North Western Rly Co* (1873) LR 8 Exch 221, Ex Ch.

[44] *Marchioness of Blandford v Dowager Duchess of Marlborough* (1743) 2 Atk 542 (a law dictionary); *R v Agricultural Land Tribunal, ex p Benney* [1955] 2 QB 140, CA (Fowler's *Modern English Usage*).

[45] See *R v Orton* (1873) and *R v Jameson* (1896) *Stephen's Digest of the Law of Evidence* (10th edn) 48.

[46] *R v Weaver* (1873) LR 2 CCR 85. See also *Wilton & Co v Phillips* (1903) 19 TLR 390, KBD.

[47] *Re Bulley's Settlement* [1886] WN 80, Ch D.

[48] *R v Bellis* (1911) 6 Cr App R 283, CCA; *R (Y) v The London Borough of Hillingdon* [2011] EWHC 1477 (Admin).

[49] The rule preserved by s 7(3)(b)(i) for the purpose of proof or disproof of the existence of a marriage applies in an equivalent way for the purpose of proof or disproof of the existence of a civil partnership: see the Civil Partnership Act 2004, s 84(5).

> Where any such rule applies, reputation or family tradition shall be treated for the purposes of this Act as a fact and not as a statement or multiplicity of statements about the matter in question.

As to the concluding part of s 7(3), it is born of a recognition that evidence of reputation or family tradition, if tendered to establish the facts reputed or the facts according to family tradition, is necessarily composed of a multiplicity of hearsay statements and therefore, if treated as such in civil proceedings, would render impossible application of the notice and weight provisions of the 1995 Act.[50] The effect of treating such evidence as evidence of fact, in contrast, is that the party proposing to adduce the evidence will not be expected to give to the other party to the proceedings particulars of the person who had personal knowledge of the matter in question and of all the intermediaries through whom the information was conveyed to the declarant;[51] and the court, in assessing the weight of the evidence, will not be expected to have regard to a factor such as whether the person with personal knowledge made the 'original statement' contemporaneously with the occurrence or existence of the matters stated.[52]

Section 118(1)2 and 3 of the 2003 Act preserve, in criminal proceedings, the same rules as those identified in s 7(3)(a) and (b) of the 1995 Act. They also make clear that the rules are preserved in criminal proceedings only insofar as they allow the court to treat such evidence as proving the matter concerned. Thus if the matter concerned should not be open to proof of any kind, because that would be to introduce, for example, inadmissible evidence of bad character, then plainly the matter cannot be proved under any of the preserved common law rules.

Evidence of reputation for the purpose of establishing good or bad character requires no further explanation. The other preserved common law rules are technical and complex and are, perhaps, best considered under two headings, declarations as to pedigree and declarations as to public and general rights.

Declarations as to pedigree

At common law, a declaration concerning pedigree is admissible, after its maker's death, as evidence of the truth of its contents. This exception to the hearsay rule has been justified on the grounds that such declarations are often the only evidence that can be obtained concerning facts which may have occurred many years before the trial.[53] Matters of pedigree concern the relationship by blood or marriage between persons and therefore include, for example, the fact and date of births, marriages, and deaths, legitimacy, celibacy, failure of issue, and intestacy. Pedigree declarations may be oral, for example, declarations by deceased parents that one of their children, whose legitimacy is in issue, was born before their marriage; in writing, for example an entry in a family Bible, an inscription on a tombstone or a pedigree hung up in the family home; or by conduct, as when parents always treat one child as illegitimate and introduce and treat another child as the heir of the family.[54] There are three

---

[50] Law Commission, *The Hearsay Rule in Civil Proceedings*, Report No 216, Cm 2321 (1993), para 4.34.

[51] See the 1995 Act, s 2 (see Ch 13).

[52] See the 1995 Act, s 4 (see Ch 13).

[53] See per Best CJ in *Johnston v Lawson* (1824) 2 Bing 86 at 89 and generally per Lord Mansfield CJ in the *Berkeley Peerage Case* (1811) 4 Camp 401, HL.

[54] Per Lord Mansfield CJ in *Goodright d Stevens v Moss* (1777) 2 Cowp 591. See also *Vowles v Young* (1806) 13 Ves 140 (engravings upon rings).

conditions of admissibility. First, the declaration is only admissible in proceedings in which a question of pedigree is directly in issue.[55] Second, the declaration must have been made by a blood relation or the spouse of a blood relation as opposed to, for example, relations in law,[56] domestic servants, or intimate acquaintances.[57] There is no requirement, however, of personal knowledge on the part of the declarant as to the facts stated, which may amount to no more than family tradition or reputation handed down from one generation to another.[58] Third, the declaration must have been made *ante litem motam*, that is before any controversy arose upon the matter in question.[59] The controversy may create bias in the minds of members of the family rendering their declarations unreliable. However, provided that the declaration was made *ante litem motam*, the fact that the declarant had an interest in establishing the relationship in question would appear to go only to weight and not admissibility.[60]

Declarations as to public and general rights

At common law, an oral or written statement concerning the reputed existence of a public or general right is admissible, after its maker's death, as evidence of the existence of that right. The primary justification for the admissibility of such evidence is the fact that other evidence, especially in the case of ancient rights, is usually unavailable. The declaration must concern a public or general and not a private right,[61] unless the private right coincides with a public right. Thus when a question arises as to the boundary of a private estate that is conterminous with a hamlet, evidence of reputation concerning the boundary of the latter is admissible to prove the boundary of the former.[62] Public rights are those common to the public at large, such as rights to use paths,[63] highways,[64] ferries,[65] or landing-places on the banks of a river.[66] General rights are those common to a section of the public or a considerable class of persons, such as the inhabitants of a parish or the tenants of a manor.[67] In the case of a public right, it seems that any person is competent to make a declaration as to its reputed existence, because it concerns everyone, and the fact that the declarant has no knowledge of the subject goes only to weight, not admissibility. A declaration as to general rights, however, is only admissible if it was made by a person with some connection with or knowledge of the matter in question.[68] There are two further conditions of admissibility and

---

[55] *Haines v Guthrie* (1884) 13 QBD 818, CA.

[56] *Shrewsbury Peerage Case* (1858) 7 HL Cas 1.

[57] *Johnson v Lawson* (1824) 2 Bing 86.

[58] *Davies v Lowndes* (1843) 6 Man&G 471; *Doe d Banning v Griffin* (1812) 15 East 293.

[59] *Berkeley Peerage Case* (1811) 4 Camp 401, HL; *Shedden v A-G* (1860) 2 Sw&Tr 170; and *Butler v Mountgarret* (1859) 7 HL Cas 633.

[60] *Doe d Tilman v Tarver* (1824) Ry&M 141; *Doe d Jenkins v Davies* (1847) 10 QB 314. But see *Plant v Taylor* (1861) 7 H&N 211.

[61] *Lonsdale v Heaton* (1830) 1 You 58.

[62] *Thomas v Jenkins* (1837) 6 Ad&El 525. See also *Stoney v Eastbourne RDC* [1927] 1 Ch 367, CA.

[63] See *Radcliffe v Marsden UDC* (1908) 72 JP 475 Ch D.

[64] See *R v Bliss* (1837) 7 Ad&El 550. See now Highways Act 1980, s 32.

[65] *Pim v Curell* (1840) 6 M&W 234.

[66] *Drinkwater v Porter* (1835) 7 C&P 181.

[67] *Nicholls v Parker* (1805) 14 East 331. However, numerous private rights of common of the several tenants of a manor do not amount to one public right: see *Earl of Dunraven v Llewellyn* (1850) 15 QB 791. See also *White v Taylor* [1969] 1 Ch 150, Ch D (individual rights of pasturage for sheep).

[68] See *Berkeley Peerage Case* (1811) 4 Camp 401, HL; *Rogers v Wood* (1831) 2 B&Ad 245; and *Crease v Barrett* (1835) 1 Cr M&R 919.

these apply whether the declaration concerns public or general rights. First, as in the case of declarations as to pedigree, the declaration must have been made *ante litem motam*.[69] Second, the declaration must concern the reputed existence of the right in question and not particular facts tending to support or negative the existence of that right.[70]

Statements forming part of the *res gestae*

'*Res gestae*', it has been said, is 'a phrase adopted to provide a respectable legal cloak for a variety of cases to which no formula of precision can be applied'.[71] The words themselves simply mean a transaction. Under the inclusionary common law doctrine of *res gestae*, a fact or a statement of fact or opinion which is so closely associated in time, place, and circumstances with some act, event, or state of affairs which is in issue that it can be said to form a part of the same transaction as the act or event in issue, is itself admissible in evidence. The justification given for the reception of such evidence is the light that it sheds upon the act or event in issue: in its absence, the transaction in question may not be fully or truly understood and may even appear to be meaningless, inexplicable, or unintelligible. Despite judicial dicta to the contrary,[72] it is clear from the authorities that such statements have been received by way of exception to the common law rule against hearsay as evidence of the matters asserted. The multiplicity of cases in which hearsay statements have been received under the doctrine were usefully subdivided by Sir Rupert Cross into the following categories: (i) statements by participants in or observers of events or, as they would more accurately be described in the light of subsequent developments, statements by persons emotionally overpowered by an event; (ii) statements accompanying the maker's performance of an act; (iii) statements relating to a physical sensation; and (iv) statements relating to a mental state. The same categorization has been used in the 2003 Act to identify the common law rules preserved and put on a statutory footing.

In *R v Callender*[73] the Court of Appeal said that *res gestae* is a single principle and that a statement can only be admitted under the *res gestae* exception to the hearsay rule if the trial judge is satisfied that there is no real possibility of concoction or distortion. This dictum, it is submitted, has been made *per incuriam*. The requirement referred to only applies to *res gestae* statements in the first of the categories set out above.

Statements by persons emotionally overpowered by an event

Section 118(1)4(a) of the 2003 Act preserves the following rule of law in criminal proceedings:

> Any rule of law under which in criminal proceedings a statement is admissible as evidence of any matter stated if—
> (a) the statement was made by a person so emotionally overpowered by an event that the possibility of concoction or distortion can be disregarded.

---

[69] *Berkeley Peerage Case* (1811) 4 Camp 401, HL. See also *Moseley v Davies* (1822) 11 Price 162.

[70] *Mercer v Denne* [1905] 2 Ch 538, CA. See also *R v Bliss* (1837) 7 Ad&El 550.

[71] Per Lord Tomlin in *Homes v Newman* [1931] 2 Ch 112, Ch D at 120.

[72] See, eg, per Lord Atkinson in *R v Christie* [1914] AC 545, HL at 553 and per Dixon J in *Adelaide Chemical and Fertilizer Co Ltd v Carlyle* (1940) 64 CLR 514 (High Court of Australia) at 531.

[73] [1998] Crim LR 337, CA.

One of the earliest illustrations of the principle is to be found in *Thompson v Trevanion*,[74] where 'what the wife said immediate upon the hurt received and before that she had time to devise or contrive anything for her own advantage' was held to be admissible in evidence. In *R v Foster*,[75] on a charge of manslaughter by reckless driving, a statement made by the deceased immediately after he had been run down was admitted to show the cause of the accident.[76]

To the extent that some earlier cases were decided without regard to the likelihood of concoction, distortion, or error, but merely on the basis of whether the statement was spontaneous in the sense that it could be regarded as part of the event in question, they must be treated with caution. Thus it has been said that *R v Bedingfield*,[77] one of the most famous cases on the subject, 'is more useful as a focus for discussion than for the decision on the facts'.[78] Bedingfield was charged with the murder of a woman. The deceased, her throat cut, came out of a room where she had been with the accused and immediately exclaimed, 'Oh dear, Aunt, see what Bedingfield has done to me!' Cockburn CJ held that although statements made while the act is being done, such as 'Don't, Harry!' are admissible, the victim's statement could not be received in evidence because 'it was something stated by her after it was all over, whatever it was, and after the act was completed'. Commenting upon this decision in *Ratten v R*,[79] Lord Wilberforce said: 'though in a historical sense the emergence of the victim could be described as a different "*res*" from the cutting of the throat, there could hardly be a case where the words uttered carried more clearly the mark of spontaneity and intense involvement'. Of course, *R v Bedingfield* would be decided differently today.[80]

In *Ratten v R*, Ratten was convicted of the murder of his wife by shooting her, the jury having rejected his defence that a gun went off accidentally while he was cleaning it. An appeal to the Privy Council concerned the admissibility of the evidence of a telephonist that around the time of the shooting she had received a call from Ratten's house made by a sobbing woman who in a hysterical voice had said, 'Get me the police please'. It was held that the evidence was not hearsay and was properly admitted because of its relevance to the issues.[81] However, it was also held that had the statement contained an element of hearsay (ie if the words used by the wife amounted to an implied assertion of truth that she was being attacked by her husband) it would have been admissible as part of the *res gestae*. Not only was there a close association in place and time between the statement and the shooting, but also the way in which the statement came to be made, in a call for the police, and the tone of voice used, showed intrinsically that the statement was being forced from the wife by an overwhelming pressure of contemporary events.[82]

---

[74] (1693) Skin 402.

[75] (1834) 6 C&P 325 (Central Criminal Court).

[76] See also *Davies v Fortior Ltd* [1952] 1 All ER 1359, QBD where the statement in question would now be admissible under the Civil Evidence Act 1995.

[77] (1879) 14 Cox CC 341, Assizes; cf *R v Fowkes* (1856) The Times, 8 Mar (see Ch 6).

[78] Per Lord Wilberforce in *Ratten v R* [1972] AC 378, PC at 390.

[79] [1972] AC 378, PC.

[80] Per Lord Ackner in *R v Andrews* [1987] AC 281, HL.

[81] See Ch 12.

[82] By contrast, see *R v Newport* [1998] Crim LR 581, CA: evidence of the contents of a telephone call made by the victim of a murder to her friend 20 minutes before she was stabbed had been improperly admitted because the call was not a spontaneous and unconsidered reaction to an immediately impending emergency.

In *Ratten v R*, Lord Wilberforce, delivering the reasons of the Board, said:[83]

The test should be not the uncertain one whether the making of the statement was in some sense part of the event or transaction. This may often be difficult to establish: such external matters as the time which elapses between the events and the speaking of the words (or vice versa), and differences in location being relevant factors but not, taken by themselves, decisive criteria. As regards statements made after the event it must be for the judge, by preliminary ruling, to satisfy himself that the statement was so clearly made in circumstances of spontaneity or involvement in the event that the possibility of concoction can be disregarded. Conversely, if he considers that the statement was made by way of narrative of a detached prior event so that the speaker was so disengaged from it as to be able to construct or adapt his account, he should exclude it. And the same must in principle be true of statements made before the event. The test should be not the uncertain one, whether the making of the statement should be regarded as part of the event or transaction. This may often be difficult to show. But if the drama, leading up to the climax, has commenced and assumed such intensity and pressure that the utterance can safely be regarded as a true reflection of what was unrolling or actually happening, it ought to be received.

This test was applied by the Court of Appeal in *R v Nye, R v Loan*[84] and affirmed by the House of Lords, in *R v Andrews*.[85] *R v Nye, R v Loan*, was a case of 'road rage' assault following a collision between two cars. Loan, the passenger from one of the cars, assaulted Lucas, the driver of the other, by punching him in the face. Shaken, Lucas sat in his car waiting for the effect of the assault to wear off. The police arrived shortly afterwards and Lucas made a statement in the police station only a few yards away in which he identified Loan, as opposed to the driver of the other car, as his assailant. The Court of Appeal added what was described as a gloss to the test in *Ratten*, namely 'was there any real possibility of error?'[86] The court was satisfied that there had been no opportunity for concoction and no chance of error and held that Lucas' statement had been properly admitted under the *res gestae* principle as a spontaneous identification. Lawton LJ said:[87]

Was there an opportunity for concoction? The interval of time was very short indeed. During part of that interval Mr Lucas was sitting down in his car trying to overcome the effects of the blows which had been struck. Commonsense and experience of life tells us that in that interval he would not be thinking of concocting a case against anybody.

The principles in *R v Andrews*

In *R v Andrews*, the House of Lords held that the statement of the victim purporting to identify the person who had stabbed him was properly admitted under the *res gestae* doctrine. The statement was made to police officers who had arrived within minutes and was admissible even though a police officer inaccurately recorded the name spoken ('Donovan' instead of 'Donald'), the victim had been drinking to excess and he had a motive to fabricate because

---

[83] [1972] AC 378, PC at 389.

[84] (1977) 66 Cr App R 252, CA. See also *R v Turnbull* (1984) 80 Cr App R 104, CA and *R v Saunders* [2012] EWCA Crim 1185.

[85] [1987] AC 281, HL.

[86] But see further, *R v Andrews* [1987] AC 281, HL at text accompanying n 89.

[87] (1977) 66 Cr App R 252 at 256.

he bore malice against the accused. Lord Ackner summarized the relevant principles as follows:[88]

(1) The primary question which the judge must ask himself is: can the possibility of concoction or distortion be disregarded?

(2) To answer that question the judge must first consider the circumstances in which the particular statement was made, in order to satisfy himself that the event was so unusual or startling or dramatic as to dominate the thoughts of the victim, so that his utterance was an instinctive reaction to that event, thus giving no real opportunity for reasoned reflection. In such a situation the judge would be entitled to conclude that the involvement or pressure of the event would exclude the possibility of concoction or distortion, providing that the statement was made in conditions of approximate but not exact contemporaneity.

(3) In order for the statement to be sufficiently 'spontaneous' it must be so closely associated with the event which has excited the statement that it can fairly be stated that the mind of the declarant was still dominated by the event. Thus the judge must be satisfied that the event which provided the trigger mechanism for the statement was still operative. The fact that the statement was made in answer to a question is but one factor to consider under this heading.

(4) Quite apart from the time factor, there may be special features in the case, which relate to the possibility of concoction or distortion. In the instant appeal the defence relied on evidence to support the contention that the deceased had a motive of his own to fabricate or concoct, namely a malice . . . The judge must be satisfied that the circumstances were such that, having regard to the special feature of malice, there was no possibility of any concoction or distortion to the advantage of the maker or the disadvantage of the accused.

(5) As to the possibility of error in the facts narrated in the statement, if only the ordinary fallibility of human recollection is relied on, this goes to the weight to be attached to and not to the admissibility of the statement and is therefore a matter for the jury. However, here again there may be special features that may give rise to the possibility of error. In the instant case there was evidence that the deceased had drunk to excess . . . Another example would be where the identification was made in circumstances of particular difficulty or where the declarant suffered from defective eyesight. In such circumstances the trial judge must consider whether he can exclude the possibility of error.[89]

The time factor and other factors

In *Morgan v DPP*[90] it was stated that, 'The mere fact of delay is plainly a relevant factor for consideration but it is not necessarily determinative of the issue before us.'[91] *Morgan v DPP* was a domestic violence case in which evidence of a 999 call made by the complainant after a delay of about one hour was held to have been properly admitted under the *res gestae* principle. Other evidence included a recording on a police officer's bodycam of the complainant's demeanour and injuries and damage at the scene. The court affirmed that 'the primary question in a *res gestae* case, identified by Lord Ackner in *R v Andrews*, is whether the possibility of concoction can be disregarded . . .'[92] Considering all the circumstances, the district judge had been entitled to reach the conclusion that when the complainant made the 999 call and

[88] [1987] AC 281 at 300–1.
[89] See also *R v Carnall* [1995] Crim LR 944, CA.
[90] [2016] EWHC 3414, DC.
[91] At [26].
[92] At [24].

also when the police arrived, her mind was still dominated by events and the possibility of concoction could be ruled out. In another domestic violence case, *Ibrahim v CPS*,[93] the complainant had made a 999 call one hour and twenty-five minutes after her husband had left the property. It was held that the evidence was admissible under the principle because other factors could be considered alongside the time factor as to whether the possibility of concoction could be negated: the recent and developing injuries to the wife noted by police when they arrived twenty minutes after the call; the recent disturbance in the property noted by the police; the distress of the wife who was shaking and crying when the police arrived; the hysterical tone of the wife's voice during the 999 call; and subsequently, the husband's aggression toward the police leading to his arrest.

Where initial statements are made shortly after the event, they might not be admissible under the principles if a later statement is made which contains significant differences. In *Wills v DPP*,[94] the complainant, in distress, made statements to a neighbour and the police that she had just been assaulted by her father and sister-in-law. Next day she made a written statement to the police in which her account of what happened was different in a number of important respects. Quashing the conviction, the court held that the differences went to whether there had been distortion at the time she made the original statements.[95]

Res gestae statements by an available witness

In *R v Andrews* Lord Ackner said that while he accepted that the doctrine admits hearsay statements not only where the declarant is dead or otherwise not available but also when he is called as a witness, he would strongly deprecate any attempt in criminal prosecutions to use the principle as a device to avoid calling the maker of the statement, when available.[96] However, Lord Ackner's dictum does not prevent the admission of a statement under the *res gestae* principles where a witness has been served with a witness summons but fails to attend trial.[97] Nevertheless, where a witness does not attend, it is incumbent on the prosecution to make proper enquiries and efforts to secure attendance and it would be entirely wrong and inappropriate to go straight into considering whether the *res gestae* principle can be applied to admit the witness's statement.[98]

Lord Ackner's dictum does not make the non-availability of the declarant a condition of admissibility. In *Attorney General's Reference (No 1 of 2003)*[99] W was charged with a serious assault on his mother. The prosecution proposed to call witnesses to give evidence that they found Mrs W lying by the steps of her house greatly distressed and that she had made statements implicating her son, saying, among other things, 'He's gone bonkers. He threw me downstairs and set me on fire. Phone the police and the ambulance.' The prosecution did not intend to call the mother because they believed that she would give untruthful evidence and exculpate her son (she had declined to make a witness statement but had made a deposition

---

[93] [2016] EWHC 1750, DC.

[94] [2016] EWHC 3779, DC.

[95] At [16]. However, the actual test is whether the differences meant that the possibility of concoction could not be ruled out.

[96] [1987] AC 281, HL at 302. This dictum was applied in *Tobi v Nicholas* [1987] Crim LR 774, DC. See also *Barnaby v DPP* [2015] 2 Cr App 53 (4) at [32].

[97] *Edwards and Osakwe v DPP* [1992] Crim LR 576, DC.

[98] *Wills v Crown Prosecution Service* [2016] EWHC 3779, DC at [8]–[9]. See also *R v Brown* [2019] EWCA 1143, Ch 5, p 175, n 321.

[99] [2003] 2 Cr App R 453 (29), CA.

in which she said that she was not prepared to attend court to give evidence against her son). The judge ruled that the evidence of the witnesses was inadmissible and as a result the prosecution offered no evidence and not guilty verdicts were entered. The Court of Appeal held that once evidence is within the *res gestae* exception it is admissible and there is no rider, in law, that it is not to be admitted if better evidence is available or because the maker of the statement is available to give evidence. However, in such circumstances, the judge should entertain an application to exclude the evidence under s 78 of the Police and Criminal Evidence Act 1984. If the purpose of the prosecution was to adduce *res gestae* evidence without any opportunity for the defence to cross-examine the maker of the statement, the court might well conclude that the evidence would have such an adverse effect on the fairness of the proceedings that it ought to be excluded. As a general principle, the prosecution should not be permitted to rely on such part of a victim's evidence as they considered reliable, without being prepared to tender the victim to the defence, so that the defence can challenge that part of the victim's evidence on which the prosecution seeks to rely and elicit that part of her evidence on which the defence might seek to rely. Applying these principles to the facts, the Court of Appeal concluded that it had effectively come to the same conclusion as the judge, the difference being that whereas the judge had erroneously added an extra legal bar to admissibility, their Lordships would have excluded the evidence under s 78 of the 1984 Act.

Res gestae statements by an accused

The *res gestae* doctrine applies whether the statement was made by the victim of the offence, a bystander, or even, in appropriate circumstances, the accused himself. In *R v Glover*[100] a man assaulted J and was forcibly restrained. In anger, he then uttered the words, 'I am David Glover . . .', followed by a threat to shoot J and his family. Despite the possibility that the assailant was not Glover but pretending to be him, the words were held to be admissible because the opportunity for concoction or distortion was so unlikely that it could be disregarded.

Proof

Concerning the nature of the proof required to establish that a statement was made in such conditions of involvement or pressure that the possibility of concoction or error can be ruled out, it would appear that the trial judge may refer to the contents of the statement itself. However, the necessary connection between the statement and the event cannot be shown *solely* by reference to those contents because 'otherwise the statement would be lifting itself into the area of admissibility'.[101]

Directions to the jury

Concerning the summing-up, in *R v Andrews* it was held that the judge should make it clear to the jury that it is for them to decide what was said and that they should be sure that the witnesses were not mistaken in what they believed to have been said. The jury should also be satisfied that the declarant did not concoct or distort and, if there is material to raise the issue, that he was not activated by malice or ill-will. Further, the jury's attention should be drawn to any special features that bear on the possibility of mistake. In some cases judges may think it appropriate to alert the jury to the need for extra caution because the evidence

---

[100] [1991] Crim LR 48, CA.
[101] Per Lord Wilberforce in *Ratten v R* [1972] AC 378, PC at 391. See also *R v Taylor* 1961 (3) SA 614.

cannot be tested by cross-examination, but failure to do so, by itself, will not amount to a misdirection.[102] These principles are encapsulated in the guidance to judges contained in the Crown Court Compendium, Part 1.[103]

Statements accompanying the maker's performance of an act

Section 118(1)4(b) of the 2003 Act preserves the following rule of law in criminal proceedings:

> Any rule of law under which in criminal proceedings a statement is admissible as evidence of any matter stated if—
>> (b) . . . the statement accompanied an act which can properly be evaluated as evidence only if considered in conjunction with the statement.

Statements explaining an act in issue or relevant to an issue made by a person contemporaneously with his performance of that act are admissible as evidence of the truth of their contents. The best person to explain the significance of an act is often the person who performed it and the requirement of contemporaneity affords some guarantee of reliability. Typical examples are a bankrupt's statement as to his intention in going or remaining abroad[104] and, on a question of domicile, a statement of a person who has lived abroad as to whether he intends to live there permanently or only temporarily.[105] There are three conditions of admissibility. First, the statement must explain or otherwise relate to the act in question.[106] Second, the statement must be more or less contemporaneous with the act performed. In the case of continuing acts, it suffices if the statement was made during their continuance, albeit some considerable time after their commencement. Thus in *Rawson v Haigh*,[107] where the question was whether a debtor had gone overseas with the intention of avoiding his creditors, letters indicating such an intention written subsequent to the act of departure were held to be admissible on the grounds that departing the realm is a continuing act and the letters were written during its continuance. Third, the statement must be made by the person performing the act and not, for example, by someone witnessing it. In *Howe v Malkin*,[108] an action for trespass, evidence of a statement concerning the position of a boundary made by the plaintiff's father while certain work was being carried out on the land by builders was excluded.

Under this head of *res gestae*, the statement is usually admissible to explain the declarant's reasons for, or intention in, performing some independent physical act. However, in *R v McCay*,[109] in which a witness was unable to remember the number of the man he had picked out at an identification parade carried out from behind a two-way mirror, an officer who had been present was allowed to give evidence that the witness had said 'It is number eight'. The physical activity of looking at the suspect, and the intellectual activity of recognizing him, were together sufficient to amount to a relevant act in respect of which the

---

[102] *R v Carnall* [1995] Crim LR 944, CA.

[103] See the Crown Court Compendium (July 2019), Part 1, 14–13.

[104] *Rawson v Haigh* (1824) 2 Bing 99; *Rouch v Great Western Rly Co* (1841) 1 QB 51.

[105] *Bryce v Bryce* [1933] P 83. See also *Scappaticci v A-G* [1955] P 47, P, D and Admlty (declarations concerning domicile of choice).

[106] *Walters v Lewis* (1836) 7 C&P 344.

[107] (1824) 2 Bing 99. See also *Homes v Newman* [1931] 2 Ch 112, Ch D.

[108] (1878) 40 LT 196, DC.

[109] [1990] 1 WLR 645, CA.

accompanying words were admissible. In *R v Lynch*[110] the Court of Appeal confirmed that, despite earlier authority which assumed that words of identification were not covered by the *res gestae* exception,[111] the interpretation of the doctrine in *R v McCay* accurately reflected the exception. However, the court noted that the concept of words spoken being part and parcel of an act implies a very limited scope and so a description of the role played by a suspect during an alleged offence is not admissible under the exception.

Statements relating to a physical sensation or a mental state

Section 118(1)4(c) of the 2003 Act preserves the following rule of law in criminal proceedings:

> Any rule of law under which in criminal proceedings a statement is admissible as evidence of any matter stated if—
>
> (c) . . . the statement relates to a physical sensation or a mental state (such as intention or emotion).

Statements relating to a physical sensation

Statements of contemporaneous physical sensation experienced by a person are admissible as evidence of the existence of that sensation, if it is in issue or is relevant to an issue, but not as evidence of its possible causes. Thus a statement made by an ill workman to the effect that his illness was caused by an accident during employment and is causing him certain bodily or mental pain is admissible to prove the sensation of pain but not the cause of the illness.[112] *Aveson v Lord Kinnaird*[113] is an early example concerning the truth or falsity of a statement, made when a policy of life insurance was taken out by a husband in respect of his wife, that she was in a good state of health. It was held that statements of bodily symptoms made by her when lying in bed, apparently ill, were admissible to show her bad state of health at the time when the policy was effected. The authorities indicate that the exception is not confined to statements of sensation experienced at the actual moment when the maker is speaking, the requirement of contemporaneity being a question of degree.[114]

Statements relating to a mental state

Statements made by a person concerning his contemporaneous state of mind or emotion are admissible as evidence of the existence of his state of mind or emotion at that time, if it is in issue or is relevant to an issue, but not as evidence of any other fact or matter stated. Thus where a bankrupt makes a payment which is alleged to be a fraudulent preference, evidence of a statement by him that he knew he was insolvent is admissible to prove his knowledge of that fact at the time when the payment was made, but not to prove the insolvency.[115] Statements may be admitted under this head to prove such diverse matters as

---

[110] [2008] 1 Cr App R 338, CA.

[111] Even if there had been pointing or touching of the suspect: see, eg, *R v Christie* [1914] AC 545, HL, in which a child touched the sleeve of the accused and said, 'That is the man'; and *R v Gibson* (1887) 18 QBD 537, in which a woman pointed to the door of a house and said 'The person who threw the stone went in there'.

[112] *Gilbey v Great Western Rly Co* (1910) 102 LT 202, CA. See also *R v Johnson* (1847) 2 Car&Kir 354; *R v Conde* (1867) 10 Cox CC 547; *R v Gloster* (1888) 16 Cox CC 471; and cf *R v Black* (1922) 16 Cr App R 118, CCA.

[113] (1805) 6 East 188.

[114] See per Salter J, *arguendo*, in *R v Black* (1922) 16 Cr App R 118, CCA at 119; *Aveson v Lord Kinnaird* (1805) 6 East 188; and cf per Charles J in *R v Gloster* (1888) 16 Cox CC 471 (Central Criminal Court).

[115] *Thomas v Connell* (1838) 4 M&W 267.

political opinion,[116] marital affection,[117] fear,[118] and dislike.[119] It seems reasonably clear that a statement made by a person as to his intention is also admissible under this exception as evidence of the existence of such intention at the time when the statement was made.[120] The admissibility of such a statement, however, gives rise to two further questions: first, whether it can support an inference that the intention also existed at a date prior or subsequent to the date on which the statement was made and, second, in the case of a statement of intention to do a certain act, whether it is admissible to prove that such an act was done. Concerning the first question, the authorities support an affirmative answer[121] except in the case of a party's self-serving statements of intention, because 'otherwise it would be easy for a man to lay grounds for escaping the consequences of his wrongful acts by making such declarations'.[122] Concerning the second question, the authorities conflict.[123] In *R v Moghal*,[124] M was charged with aiding and abetting his mistress, S, to commit murder. S had already been tried separately and acquitted and M's defence was that S had committed the offence and that he was no more than a terrified spectator. The Court of Appeal expressed the opinion that a tape-recorded statement by S made some six months before the murder to the effect that she intended to kill the victim would have been admissible on the accused's behalf.[125] By contrast, in *R v Wainwright*,[126] Cockburn CJ ruled that evidence of a statement made by the victim of a murder on leaving her lodgings that she was going to the accused's premises was inadmissible because 'it was only a statement of intention which might or might not have been carried out'.

Admissions by agents

Section 118(1)6(a) of the 2003 Act preserves the following rule of law in criminal proceedings:

> Any rule of law under which in criminal proceedings—

> an admission made by an agent of a defendant is admissible against the defendant as evidence of any matter stated . . .

---

[116] *R v Tooke* (1794) 25 State Tr 344.

[117] *Trelawney v Coleman* (1817) 1 B&Ald 90; *Willis v Bernard* (1832) 8 Bing 376.

[118] *R v Vincent, Frost and Edwards* (1840) 9 C&P 275; *R v Gandfield* (1846) 2 Cox CC 43; and *Neill v North Antrim Magistrates' Court* [1992] 1 WLR 1220 HL at 1228–9.

[119] *R v Hagan* (1873) 12 Cox CC 357 (dislike of a child). See also per Mahon J in *Customglass Boats Ltd v Salthouse Bros Ltd* [1976] 1 NZLR 36 (New Zealand Supreme Court).

[120] See per Mellish LJ in *Sugden v Lord St Leonards* (1876) 1 PD 154 CA at 251.

[121] See per Cozens-Hardy MR in *Re Fletcher, Reading v Fletcher* [1917] 1 Ch 339, CA at 342 (proof of earlier intention) and per Lord Ellenborough in *Robson v Kemp* (1802) 4 Esp 233 (proof of subsequent intention).

[122] Per Crampton J in *R v Petcherini* (1855) 7 Cox CC 79. See also *R v Callender* [1998] Crim LR 337, CA.

[123] For a consideration of this aspect of the doctrine of *res gestae* (and what it means to 'preserve' a disputed rule of common law), see Munday, 'Legislation That Would "Preserve" the Common Law: The Case of the Declaration of Intention' [2008] LQR 46.

[124] (1977) 65 Cr App R 56, CA. See also *R v Buckley* (1873) 13 Cox CC 293, Assizes.

[125] It has been doubted, however, whether the evidence was of any relevance to the issue, namely whether M was a willing accomplice or an unwilling spectator: per Lord Bridge in *R v Blastland* [1986] AC 41, HL at 59–60.

[126] (1875) 13 Cox CC 171 (Central Criminal Court). See also *R v Pook* (1871) 13 Cox CC 172, *R v Thomson* [1912] 3 KB, CCA, and the much discussed decision of the United States Supreme Court in *Mutual Life Insurance Co v Hillman* 145 US 285 (1892).

Concerning this rule, in *R v Turner*,[127] Lawton LJ set out three principles:[128] (i) an authorized agent may make an admission on behalf of his principal; (ii) a party seeking to rely on an admission must prove the agent was so authorized; and (iii) a court is entitled to assume that what is said in court by a barrister on his client's behalf is said with his client's authority. As to the third principle, it extends to written admissions made by an advocate on his client's behalf at pre-trial proceedings. Such admissions may be information and statements entered in case management forms used in conjunction with the Criminal Procedure Rules.[129] However, in *R v Newell*,[130] it was held that the purpose of information or statements recorded in plea and case management forms (now replaced by plea and trial preparation hearing forms) in the Crown Court is to assist the court, and normally such information or statements should be excluded in the exercise of discretion under s 78 of the Police and Criminal Evidence Act 1984.[131] The court said there could be circumstances where information and statements in forms were admissible, for example, where no defence statement has been submitted and there is an ambush defence which is inconsistent with what is recorded on a form. However, '. . . provided the parties adhere to the letter and the spirit of the Criminal Procedure Rules and follow the practices . . . outlined, such cases should be very, very rare.'[132] Under the Criminal Practice Directions, the principle in *R v Newell* applies to case management forms in general. The Directions state that the identification of issues in forms at the case management stage occurs '. . .without the risk that they will be used as statements admissible in evidence against the defendant, provided the advocate follows the letter and spirit of the Criminal Procedure Rules.'[133] In *Valiati V DPP, KM v DPP*,[134] which concerned the use of statements in 'preparation for effective trial forms' in the magistrates' court, the court emphasized the importance of the practice directions and the need to follow them.[135] However, the court also made it clear that statements in case management forms are not inadmissible as a matter of law and it might still be open to the prosecution to admit them to prevent 'game playing'.[136] An example could be where the accused indicates that he will 'put the prosecution to proof', that is, that his defence does not involve presenting a positive case, but he later goes on to present such a case.[137] A formal application will be required to admit the statement contained in the form under s 118(1) and would need to be considered alongside any

---

[127] (1975) 61 Cr App R 67, CA.

[128] Ibid at [82].

[129] See *R (Firth) v Epping Magistrates' Court* [2011] 1 WLR 1818, DC. See also the Criminal Procedure Rules 2015, r 3.11(a) and r 24.13(2).

[130] [2012] 1 WLR 3142, CA.

[131] At [36].

[132] At [36].

[133] The Criminal Practice Directions, VI, 24B.4.

[134] [2019] 1 WLR 1221, DC.

[135] At [15]–[16] and [24]. See also 'Commentary' [2019] Crim LR 238.

[136] At [40], Sir Brian Leveson P, citing Irwin LJ in *R (Hassani) v West London Magistrates' Court* [2017] EWHC 1270, (Admin) at [10].

[137] At [16]. Cf *R v Newell* [2012] 1 WLR 3142, CA at [36].

application to exclude it under s 78.[138] Strict notice requirements cannot and should not apply in this type of situation.[139]

ADDITIONAL READING

Munday, 'Legislation that Would "Preserve" the Common Law: The Case of the Declaration of Intention' [2008] LQR 46. An examination of the *res gestae* exception to the hearsay rule. The position of 'declarations of intention' at common law and under s 118(1)4 is considered. Also considered is the broader question of what is meant when a statute 'preserves' a common law rule.

---

[138] At [11].

[139] The court stated that this is the type of situation envisaged by r 20.5(1)(c) of the Criminal Procedure Rules, SI 2015/1490, which gives the court power to dispense with the requirement of notice in respect of hearsay. However, it would appear that there is no such requirement in this situation: see the *'Note'* pursuant to r 20.2. See also n 1.

Confessions

15

Key issues

- Why should a confession made by an accused be admissible in evidence to prove what he admitted?

- Having regard to the ways in which a confession made by an accused may be obtained, when should the prosecution be prevented from relying upon a confession?

- When should a confession made by an accused be admissible for a co-accused?

- Should the trial judge have discretion to exclude a confession, even if it is admissible in law, and if so, on what basis (a) where the prosecution rely on the confession; (b) where a co-accused relies upon the confession?

- When a confession is given in evidence by the prosecution and implicates both its maker and a co-accused, when, if at all, should it be used against the co-accused?

- In what circumstances may a statement made in the presence of the accused be treated as a confession made by him?

- If a confession is inadmissible, should it prevent the admissibility in evidence of incriminating facts discovered in consequence of the confession (as when, eg, a confession to theft includes a statement that the stolen goods are in the accused's home, where they are subsequently found)?

Admissibility

The background

The Police and Criminal Evidence Act 1984 (the 1984 Act) brought about major changes in the law relating to the admissibility of confessions. It will be useful, however, before examining the statutory provisions, to summarize briefly the position at common law. At common law a confession (ie an out-of-court statement made by an accused against his interest), was admissible by way of exception to the hearsay rule, as evidence of the truth of its contents, on the basis that what a person says against himself is likely to be true. A confession could not be given in evidence by the prosecution unless shown by them to be a voluntary statement in the sense that it was not obtained from the accused by fear of prejudice or hope of advantage exercised or held out by a person in authority[1] or by oppression.[2] If the admissibility of the confession was in dispute, the issue fell to be determined by the trial judge on a *voir dire* in the absence of the jury. The prosecution bore the legal burden of proving beyond reasonable doubt that the confession was voluntary.[3]

Confessions defined

Confessions are now admissible, on behalf of the prosecution, under s 76(1) of the 1984 Act and, on behalf of a co-accused, under s 76A(1) of the 1984 Act. As to the meaning of 'confession' under the Act, section 82(1) adopts the inclusive definition of the word recommended by the Criminal Law Revision Committee.[4] It provides that:

In this . . . Act—
'confession' includes any statement wholly or partly adverse to the person who made it, whether made to a person in authority or not and whether made in words or otherwise;

Section 82(1) is wide enough to cover a plea of guilty. Thus if an accused pleads guilty but is subsequently granted leave to vacate the plea, the guilty plea, together with the basis of the plea, may be admitted in evidence at his trial as a confession statement.[5] In suitable cases, for example where the evidence is admissible on behalf of the prosecution under s 76(1) of the 1984 Act and the accused, at the time of entering the guilty plea was unrepresented or misunderstood the nature of the charge, it seems that the judge, as at common law, can exclude the evidence in the exercise of his discretion;[6] but if the evidence is admissible on behalf of a co-accused under s 76A(1) of the Act, there is no residual discretion to exclude it in the interests of a fair trial.[7]

---

[1] Per Lord Sumner in *Ibrahim v R* [1914] AC 599, PC at 609. In *DPP v Ping Lin* [1976] AC 574 at 597, Lord Hailsham said that he thought Lord Sumner had really said, not 'exercised', but 'excited'.

[2] Per Lord Parker CJ in *Callis v Gunn* [1964] 1 QB 495, DC at 501 and per Edmund Davies LJ in *R v Prager* [1972] 1 WLR 260, CA at 266.

[3] *R v Thompson* [1893] 2 QB 12, CCR.

[4] *Evidence (General)*, 11th Report, Cmnd 4991 (1972), paras 58 and 66.

[5] *R v Johnson* [2007] EWCA Crim 1651.

[6] *R v Rimmer* [1972] 1 WLR 268, CA. See also *R v Hetherington* [1972] Crim LR 703, CA and, generally, in this chapter, under **The discretion to exclude, p 468**.

[7] *R v Johnson* [2007] EWCA Crim 1651.

Section 82(1) covers 'mixed' statements, that is statements which are both inculpatory and exculpatory in nature.[8] However, in *R v Hasan*,[9] the House of Lords, approving *R v Sat-Bhambra*,[10] held that the subsection does not cover a statement intended by its maker to be wholly exculpatory or neutral, and which appears to be so on its face, but which becomes damaging to him at the trial because, for example, its contents can then be shown to be evasive or false or inconsistent with the maker's evidence on oath. It was further held, distinguishing *Saunders v United Kingdom*[11] that s 76(1) (and s 82(1)) were compatible with Art 6 of the European Convention on Human Rights given the unrestricted capability of s 78 to avoid injustice by excluding any evidence obtained by unfairness, including wholly exculpatory or neutral statements obtained by oppression. However, the effect is that it will be for the accused to convince the judge that the evidence was so obtained and not for the prosecution, on a *voir dire*, to disprove the matter beyond reasonable doubt. This approach is in contrast to that adopted in the United States[12] and Canada.[13]

Section 82(1) abolishes the rule at common law that a threat or inducement only operates to exclude a resulting confession if it was made or held out by 'a person in authority', typically the police officer investigating the case or interrogating the accused. A confession, for the purposes of the Act, can be made to anyone. The assumption is that the risk of an inducement resulting in an untrue confession is similar whether or not the inducement comes from a person in authority.[14]

The phrase 'whether made in words or otherwise' means that a confession can be made orally, in writing or by conduct. The Criminal Law Revision Committee gave as an example of conduct, the accused nodding his head in reply to an accusation.[15] Presumably, as at common law, the accused may also accept the accusation of another, so as to make all or part of it a confession statement of his own, by other conduct, by his demeanour, or even by his silence at the time when the accusation was made. It will be convenient to consider this topic and the common law authorities in that regard separately.[16] A confession can also be made otherwise than in words by a re-enactment by the accused of the crime committed. In *Li Shu-ling v R*[17] the accused, two days after he had confessed to murder by strangulation, agreed to re-enact the crime. He was reminded that he was still under caution and told that he was not obliged to re-enact the crime. The Privy Council held that a video recording made of the re-enactment, accompanied by a running commentary by the accused explaining his movements, had properly been admitted in evidence as a confession. By way of safeguard, it was held that: the video film should be made reasonably soon after the oral confession; the accused should be warned that he need not take part and, if he agrees to take part, should do

---

[8] See per Lord Steyn in *R v Aziz* [1995] 3 All ER 149, HL at 155; *R v Sharp* [1988] 1 All ER 65, HL (see Ch 6, **Exculpatory statements**, p 199).

[9] [2005] 2 AC 467, HL.

[10] (1989) 88 Cr App R 55, CA.

[11] (1997) 2 BHRC 358.

[12] See per Chief Justice Warren in *Miranda v Arizona* (1975) 384 US 436, US Supreme Court, at 477.

[13] See *Piché v R* (1970) 11 DLR (3d) 709, Supreme Court of Canada. See further Munday, 'Adverse Denial and Purposive Confession' [2003] Crim LR 850.

[14] See per Viscount Dilhorne in *Deokinanan v R* [1969] 1 AC 20, PC at 33. See also Criminal Law Revision Committee, 11th Report, Cmnd 4991 (1972), para 58.

[15] Ibid Annex 2 at 214.

[16] See, in this chapter, under **Statements made in the presence of the accused**, p 490.

[17] [1988] 3 All ER 138, PC.

so voluntarily; and the video recording should be shown to the accused as soon as practicable after it has been completed so that he has an opportunity to make and have recorded any comments he wishes to make about the film. It was also acknowledged that there are some crimes which it would be wholly inappropriate to attempt to re-enact on video, such as a killing committed in the course of an affray involving many people.

The conditions of admissibility

Section 76 of the 1984 Act provides that:

(1) In any proceedings[18] a confession made by an accused person may be given in evidence against him in so far as it is relevant to any matter in issue in the proceedings and is not excluded by the court in pursuance of this section.

(2) If, in any proceedings where the prosecution proposes to give in evidence a confession made by an accused person, it is represented to the court that the confession was or may have been obtained—

(a) by oppression of the person who made it; or

(b) in consequence of anything said or done which was likely, in the circumstances existing at the time, to render unreliable any confession which might be made by him in consequence thereof,

the court shall not allow the confession to be given in evidence against him except in so far as the prosecution proves to the court beyond reasonable doubt that the confession (notwithstanding that it may be true) was not obtained as aforesaid.

(3) In any proceedings where the prosecution proposes to give in evidence a confession made by an accused person, the court may of its own motion require the prosecution, as a condition of allowing it to do so, to prove that the confession was not obtained as mentioned in subsection (2) above.

Section 76(1) only applies to a confession 'made by an accused'. Thus where there is no dispute that a confession was made, but the identity of the maker is disputed, the prosecution must prove that the maker was the accused, although it seems that this may be inferred if the confession contains information about the accused which, even if known by others, is best known by the accused himself.[19]

A confession can only be given in evidence, pursuant to s 76(1), by the prosecution.[20] Under s 76A of the 1984 Act, confessions may be given in evidence for a co-accused, and the conditions of admissibility are the same as those which apply in the case of confessions adduced on behalf of the prosecution, except that the co-accused need only prove that the confession was not obtained by oppression or 'in consequence of anything said or done' on the balance of probabilities. Section 76A provides as follows:

(1) In any proceedings a confession made by an accused person may be given in evidence for another person charged in the same proceedings (a co-accused) in so far as it is relevant to any matter in issue in the proceedings and is not excluded by the court in pursuance of this section.

---

[18] 'Proceedings' means criminal proceedings, including proceedings in the UK or elsewhere before a court-martial or the Courts-Martial Appeal Court, and proceedings before a Standing Civilian Court: s 82(1).

[19] Such as his date of birth and address: see *R v Ward* [2001] Crim LR 316, CA. See also *Mawdesley v Chief Constable of the Cheshire Constabulary* [2004] 1 WLR 1035, Admin Court (an unsigned form containing information as to the identity of the driver of a car).

[20] *R v Beckford; R v Daley* [1991] Crim LR 833, CA.

(2) If, in any proceedings where a co-accused proposes to give in evidence a confession made by an accused person, it is represented to the court that the confession was or may have been obtained—

    (a) by oppression of the person who made it; or

    (b) in consequence of anything said or done which was likely, in the circumstances existing at the time, to render unreliable any confession which might be made by him in consequence thereof,

    the court shall not allow the confession to be given in evidence for the co-accused except in so far as it is proved to the court on the balance of probabilities that the confession (notwithstanding that it may be true) was not so obtained.

(3) Before allowing a confession made by an accused person to be given in evidence for a co-accused in any proceedings, the court may of its own motion require the fact that the confession was not obtained as mentioned in subsection (2) above to be proved in the proceedings on the balance of probabilities.

The purpose of s 76A is to ensure that where a co-accused proposes to rely upon a confession made by an accused, the accused has a protection against unfairness similar to that which he has when the prosecution propose to rely upon a confession. If a confession is admissible against the accused and undermines the defence of a co-accused, but in law is inadmissible against the co-accused, the prejudice to the co-accused is thought to be cured by a clear direction to the jury that the confession is no evidence against him and s 76A cannot be used to challenge its admissibility.[21]

Section 76A only operates in the case of co-accused. Thus a confession made by D1 cannot be given in evidence under s 76A for D2 if D1 pleads guilty, because D1 will then cease to be an accused and D2 will then no longer be 'charged in the same proceedings' as D1.[22] On the same reasoning, it is submitted, s 76A has no application where D1 is acquitted (either because no evidence is offered against him or he makes a successful submission of no case to answer) or he makes a successful application to sever the indictment. In such circumstances, however, D1's confession may be admissible, depending on the circumstances, under s 114(1)(d) of the Criminal Justice Act 2003.[23]

More controversial is the question whether the s 82(1) definition of a confession will be applied strictly in the context of s 76A so as to cover only that part of a statement adverse to its maker or will extend to those parts of the statement going beyond the confession and serving the interests of a co-accused.[24] Plainly, not everything said at the same time as a confession will fall within the definition. Thus if, in a case of murder, D1 denies being at the scene of the crime and D2 and D3 run cut-throat defences, each blaming the other, D1's confession that he was present at the scene may be admitted, but not an additional statement by him that D2 committed the offence, which is an exculpatory statement.[25] However, it is submitted that it would be artificial, misleading, and unfair to adopt a strict approach to statements such as 'I did it *alone*' or 'I did it, *not D2*' and that there is a strong case for going

---

[21] *R v Ibrahim* [2009] 1 WLR 578, CA.

[22] *R v Finch* [2007] 1 WLR 1645, CA.

[23] See **Ch 12**.

[24] The question was raised, but not answered, in *R v Finch* [2007] 1 WLR 1645, CA.

[25] *R v McLean* [2007] EWCA Crim 219, followed in *R v Sliogeris* [2015] EWCA Crim 22. Both statements may be admissible under s 114(1)(d) of the Criminal Justice Act 2003 (see **Ch 12**).

beyond this and using s 76A to admit anything that could fairly be said to be inextricably linked to D1's confession and which is relevant to D2's defence or undermines the prosecution case against him.

Where evidence of a confession by an accused is properly admitted in evidence in favour of a co-accused under s 76A, there is a cogent case for saying that it should not be treated as evidence in the case generally and therefore if it amounts to evidence *against* another co-accused, the judge should direct the jury that it can only be used for the first co-accused and not against the other co-accused.[26]

A confession admitted in evidence under s 76 or s 76A is admitted as evidence of the matters stated. At common law, an admissible confession was sufficient to warrant a conviction even in the absence of other evidence implicating the accused.[27] However, where a conviction was based on a confession which was equivocal or otherwise of poor quality, it could be quashed on appeal.[28] Similar principles should operate, it is submitted, in the case of confessions admitted under s 76 or s 76A.[29] In *Beeres v CPS West Midlands*,[30] a decision under s 76, it was said that where the confession is the sole evidence relied upon by the Crown, the court should be especially vigilant to ensure that it is reliable and that its admission would not be unfair for the purposes of s 78 of the 1984 Act.[31]

Under s 76(2) (or s 76A(2)), an accused may raise the question of admissibility merely by representing to the court, without adducing any evidence in support of such a representation, that the confession was or may have been obtained by the methods described in that subsection.[32] However, even if the accused has not raised the question, the court of its own motion may require the prosecution (co-accused) to prove that the confession was not obtained by the methods described, in exercise of the power conferred on it by s 76(3) (s 76A(3)). In either event, the question will then be determined in the absence of the jury on a *voir dire* at which the prosecution (co-accused) will bear the burden of proving beyond reasonable doubt (on a balance of probabilities) that the conditions of admissibility have been satisfied. If this burden is not discharged, the court has no *inclusionary* discretion, but *shall not* allow the confession to be given in evidence, even if satisfied that its contents are true.

Although the 1984 Act and the Codes of Practice issued thereunder contain a wide variety of provisions regulating, inter alia, the arrest, detention, treatment, and questioning of suspects, the fact that a confession was obtained in breach of the Act or Codes will not necessarily mean that it was obtained by the methods described in s 76(2) (and s 76A(2)).[33] However, evidence of non-compliance with the Act or Codes, either alone or together with

---

[26] See per Elias LJ, obiter, in *R v Sliogeris* [2015] EWCA Crim 22 at [37].

[27] See *R v Sullivan* (1887) 16 Cox CC 347 and *R v Mallinson* [1977] Crim LR 161, CA and contrast per Cave J in *R v Thompson* [1893] 2 QB 12.

[28] See *R v Barker* (1916) 11 Cr App R 191, CCA; *R v Schofield* (1917) 12 Cr App R 191, CCA; and *R v Pattinson* (1973) 58 Cr App R 417, CA.

[29] See also, in the case of confessions by mentally handicapped persons, s 77 (see **Ch 8**).

[30] 2 Cr App R 101 (8), (Admin) at [10].

[31] See, in this chapter, under **The discretion to exclude, p 468**.

[32] However, a representation by an advocate would normally be based on a proof of evidence or other document, such as a record of interview: see *R v Dhorajiwala* [2010] 2 Cr App R 161 (21), CA at [23].

[33] Some of the more important provisions of the Act and Codes are considered in this chapter, under **The discretion to exclude, p 468**.

other evidence, may show that the confession was obtained by such methods or, failing that, in a case in which the *prosecution* propose to adduce evidence of the confession, that is, under s 76, may nonetheless result in the confession being excluded by the court in the exercise of its discretion. Under s 67(11) of the Act, the Codes are admissible in evidence and if any provision of the Codes appears to the court to be relevant to any question arising in the proceedings, it shall be taken into account in determining that question.

Oppression

General

Under s 76(2)(a) (and s 76A(2)), a confession, in order to be admissible, must not have been obtained by oppression. Broadly speaking, this reflects the views of both the Criminal Law Revision Committee[34] and the Royal Commission on Criminal Procedure[35] that a confession obtained by oppression of a suspect should be automatically excluded in view of society's abhorrence of the use of such methods during interrogation. Before considering the meaning of 'oppression', three matters of a general nature may be noted. First, a confession obtained by oppression will be excluded whether or not it is unreliable and notwithstanding that it may be true. Second, the confession must not have been 'obtained by' oppression. Thus a confession will not be excluded where the accused confessed *before* he was subjected to some form of oppression. Equally, there will be no causal link between an interview not complying with the 1984 Act and a subsequent confession freely and voluntarily made.[36] Third, although the statute refers to oppression 'of the person who made' the confession, that is, the accused, in appropriate circumstances the oppression of another could also amount to oppression of the accused (or constitute conduct likely to render unreliable any confession which might be made by him).

The meaning of oppression

Concerning the meaning of oppression, it is convenient to examine first the way in which the word was defined at common law. Prior to the 1984 Act, oppression was taken to mean 'something which tends to sap and has sapped that free will which must exist before a confession is voluntary'[37] or, in the context of interrogation, 'questioning which by its nature, duration or other attendant circumstances (including the fact of custody) excites hopes (such as the hope of release) or fears, or so affects the mind of the suspect that his will crumbles and he speaks when otherwise he would have stayed silent'.[38] Whether or not there was oppression in any particular case involved a consideration of a wide variety of factors, including the length of time of any period of questioning, whether the accused had been given proper refreshment, and the characteristics of the accused in question.

Section 76(8) (and s 76A(7)) defines 'oppression' as including 'torture, inhuman or degrading treatment, and the use or threat of violence (whether or not amounting to torture)'. The phrase 'torture or inhuman or degrading treatment' derives from Art 3 of the European

---

[34] 11th Report, Cmnd 4991 (1972), para 60.

[35] Cmnd 8092 (1981), para 4.132. The Commission proposed exclusion on this ground only if the confession was obtained from the suspect by torture, violence, the threat of violence, or inhuman or degrading treatment.

[36] *R v Parker* [1995] Crim LR 233, CA.

[37] Per Sachs J in *R v Priestley* (1965) 51 Cr App R 1n at 1–2; applied in *R v Prager* [1972] 1 WLR 260, CA.

[38] Lord MacDermott in an address to the Bentham Club (1968) 21 CLP 10.

Convention on Human Rights and it is submitted that the English courts should be guided by the decisions of the European Court of Human Rights and the European Commission of Human Rights. In the *Greek Case*,[39] for example, the Commission defined 'degrading treatment' as that which grossly humiliates a person before others or drives a person to act against his will or conscience. Concerning the meaning of 'torture', assistance may also be derived from the way in which the offence of torture is defined in s 134 of the Criminal Justice Act 1988.[40] The inclusive nature of the definition in s 76(8) plainly indicates that the varieties of oppression it contains do not constitute a comprehensive list.

There was no reference to s 76(8) in *R v Fulling*,[41] the first case to come before the Court of Appeal on the meaning of oppression under the 1984 Act. F was convicted of obtaining property by deception. After her arrest she was taken into custody and interviewed twice on that day and once on the following day. Despite persistent questioning, she exercised her right to remain silent, but after a break in the interview on the second day, she made a confession. According to her evidence on the *voir dire*, she made the confession because during the break in that interview one of the officers told her that for the last three years her lover had been having an affair with another woman who was presently in the cell next to hers. F said that these revelations so distressed her that she could not stand being in the cells any longer and thought that by making a statement she would be released. The police denied making these revelations. The defence submitted that the confession was or may have been obtained by oppression. The judge ruled that, even on the assumption that F's version of events was the true one, there was no oppression because oppression meant something above and beyond that which is inherently oppressive in police custody and must import some oppression actively applied in an improper manner by the police.

The Court of Appeal upheld this ruling and dismissed the appeal. It was held, applying the principles set out in *Bank of England v Vagliano Bros*,[42] that since the 1984 Act was a codifying Act, rather than a consolidating Act or an Act declaratory of the common law, the court should give to the words used in it their natural meaning, uninfluenced by any considerations derived from the previous state of the law. Accordingly, the word 'oppression' was given its ordinary dictionary definition, namely, 'exercise of authority or power in a burdensome, harsh, or wrongful manner;[43] unjust or cruel treatment of subjects, inferiors, etc; the imposition of unreasonable or unjust burdens'. Lord Lane CJ pointed out that, according to one of the quotations given in the *Oxford English Dictionary*, 'There is not a word in our language which expresses more detestable wickedness than *oppression*.' His Lordship found it hard to envisage any circumstances in which oppression thus defined would not entail some impropriety on the part of the interrogator. It was held that although s 76(2)(b) is wide enough to

---

[39] (1969) 12 Yearbook 1, EComHR at 186. See also *Ireland v United Kingdom* (1978) 2 EHRR 25, para 167 (torture and inhuman treatment) and *Campbell and Cosans v United Kingdom* (1982) 4 EHRR 293. Assistance may also be derived from the decisions under the Northern Ireland (Emergency Provisions) Act 1978, s 8(2). See also the definition of 'torture' contained in Art 1 of the Draft United Nations Convention against Torture and Other Cruel, Inhuman or Degrading Treatment or Punishment.

[40] The intentional infliction by act or omission of severe physical or mental pain or suffering.

[41] [1987] 2 All ER 65, CA.

[42] [1891] AC 107, HL at 144–5.

[43] The word 'wrongful' should be understood in the context of the rest of the definition, particularly the words which precede and follow it, otherwise any breach of the Code, which might be said to be 'wrongful', could be said to amount to oppression, which clearly is not so: *R v Parker* [1995] Crim LR 233, CA.

cover some of the circumstances which were embraced by the 'artificially wide' definition of oppression at common law, and although a confession may be excluded, under s 76(2)(b), where there is no suspicion of impropriety, the remarks alleged to have been made by the officer were not likely to have made unreliable any confession which the appellant might have made.

The decision in *R v Fulling*[44] calls for comment in a number of respects. First, the first two parts of the definition of oppression given would appear to apply only in the case of someone vested with some authority, power, or control over the accused, someone akin to a person who, at common law, would have been regarded as a 'person in authority'. Second, concerning impropriety, the decision, although not explicit on the point, suggests strongly that it must be deliberate or intentional. This would accord with the former decision at common law in *R v Miller*,[45] in which it was held that, although it could amount to oppression if questions, addressed to a suspect suffering from paranoid schizophrenia, were skilfully and deliberately asked with the intention of triggering off hallucinations and flights of fancy, the mere fact that questions put to such a suspect did produce such a disordered state of mind would not, by itself, be indicative of oppression. Third, however, although oppression normally requires deliberate impropriety, not all deliberate impropriety amounts to oppression. Sometimes it will be a question of degree. Thus if an interrogator is rude and discourteous, raising his voice and using bad language, this does not constitute oppression;[46] but bullying and hectoring by officers adopting a highly hostile and intimidatory approach will amount to oppression,[47] as will a deliberate mis-statement of the evidence in order to pressurize the suspect.[48] Trickery, per se, will not necessarily constitute oppression. Thus it does not amount to oppression to make a covert tape recording of an incriminating conversation between two suspects sharing a police cell.[49]

Fourth, it seems clear that, as at common law, regard should be had to the personal characteristics of the accused, which may be of critical relevance in deciding not only whether the confession was *obtained* by oppression, but also whether particular conduct was 'burdensome', 'harsh', or 'cruel'. Thus account may be taken of the fact that the suspect is, for example, intelligent, sophisticated, and an experienced professional person,[50] or a person of below normal intelligence on the borderline of mental handicap.[51] The will of a particular suspect may be so affected by oppression in an interview that a confession made in a subsequent but properly conducted interview should be excluded.[52]

---

[44] [1987] 2 All ER 65, CA.

[45] [1986] 3 All ER 119, CA.

[46] *R v Emmerson* (1990) 92 Cr App R 284, CA. See also *R v Heaton* [1993] Crim LR 593, CA.

[47] *R v Paris* (1993) 97 Cr App R 99, CA, where the accused, who was of limited intelligence, had denied his involvement over 300 times! But see also *R v L* [1994] Crim LR 839, CA, a decision under s 76(2)(b), in which although similar methods were employed, *R v Paris* was distinguished on the grounds, inter alia, that L was of normal intelligence and the length of the interviews not excessive.

[48] *R v Beales* [1991] Crim LR 118, CC.

[49] *R v Parker* [1995] Crim LR 233, CA.

[50] *R v Seelig* [1991] 4 All ER 429, CA at 439, where it was held not to be oppressive for Department of Trade and Industry inspectors conducting an investigation of a company's affairs, to question such a person, notwithstanding that (a) in conformity with normal practice, no caution was given; and (b) refusal to answer such questions could have resulted in committal for contempt under the Companies Act 1985, s 436. It was also held that the confession made did not fall to be excluded under s 76(2)(b) or s 78.

[51] *R v Paris* (1993) 97 Cr App R 99, CA.

[52] See *R v Ismail* [1990] Crim LR 109, CA and cf *Y v DPP* [1991] Crim LR 917, DC.

A final matter concerns the relevance of the common law authorities to s 76(2)(b). Paragraph (b) is considered wide enough to cover only *some* of the circumstances embraced by the common law definition of oppression. The facts of *R v Fulling*[53] itself are instructive in this regard because, although at common law a strong argument could have been advanced to the effect that in all the circumstances of the case what the officer said, assuming that he did in fact say it, had sapped the free will of the accused or so affected her mind that her will crumbled and she spoke when otherwise she would have remained silent, the court was satisfied that, for the purposes of s 76(2)(b), what was said was not likely, in the circumstances, to have rendered unreliable any confession which she might have made in consequence.

Unreliability

The background

Section 76(2)(b) in large measure reflects the recommendations of the Criminal Law Revision Committee.[54] In order to appreciate the significance of the reliability test, it is useful to summarize the Committee's reasons for changing the rules at common law. At common law, as we have seen, the fundamental condition of the admissibility of a confession was that it should have been made voluntarily. Two reasons have been given for that rule: the first, the reliability principle, is that an involuntary confession may not be reliable because an accused subjected to threats, inducements, or oppression may make a false confession; the second, the disciplinary principle, is that the police must be discouraged from using improper methods to obtain a confession by being prevented from using the confession for the purposes of obtaining a conviction. A majority of the Committee were in favour of accepting the mixture of these two principles as the basis of the law. However, although they were also in favour of preserving the law in general, they proposed a relaxation of the strict rule that any threat or inducement, however mild or slight, should render inadmissible any resulting confession.[55] Accordingly, cases of oppression apart, they recommended that a confession should only be rendered inadmissible if made as a result of a threat or inducement of a kind likely to produce an unreliable confession.

The test

Unreliability

The word 'unreliable' is the keynote to s 76(2)(b) (and s 76A(2)(b)). It is not defined in the Act, but means 'cannot be relied upon as being the truth'.[56] Section 76(2)(b), by its express incorporation of the reliability principle, offers less scope for exclusion than existed at common law. However, it offers greater scope for exclusion than would have been the case under cl 2(2)(b) of the draft bill annexed to the 11th Report of the Criminal Law Revision Committee because, although it closely resembles the clause, it is different in one significant respect: the phrase 'anything said or done' has been substituted for 'any threat or inducement'.[57]

In reaching a decision under s 76(2)(b), a trial judge must examine all the relevant circumstances of the interrogation, both before and after what was 'said' or 'done', and take

---

[53] [1987] 2 All ER 65, CA.

[54] 11th Report, Cmnd 4991 (1972), paras 53–69. The Government rejected the proposals relating to confessions made by The Royal Commission on Criminal Procedure, Cmnd 8092 (1981).

[55] See *R v Northam* (1968) 52 Cr App R 97, CA, and *R v Zaveckas* (1970) 54 Cr App R 202, CA.

[56] Per Stuart-Smith LJ in *R v Crampton* (1991) 92 Cr App R 369, CA at 372.

[57] See *R v Harvey* [1988] Crim LR 241, CC in this chapter, under **The characteristics of the accused**, p 465.

into account the nature and effect of what was said or done, the seriousness of the offence in question and, if necessary, the terms of the confession, which may throw light on the facts concerning the interrogation.[58] The test of reliability is hypothetical: it applies not to the confession made by the accused, but to 'any confession which might be made by him'.[59] However, as Mance LJ said in *Re Proulx*, the test cannot be satisfied by postulating some entirely different confession:[60]

> The word 'any' must . . . be understood as indicating 'any such', or 'such a', confession as the applicant made. The abstract element involved also reflects the fact that the test is not whether the actual confession was untruthful or inaccurate. It is whether whatever was said or done was, in the circumstances existing as at the time of the confession, *likely* to have rendered such a confession unreliable, whether or not it may be seen subsequently (with hindsight and in the light of all the material available at trial) that it did or did not actually do so.

'Anything said or done'

The phrase 'anything said or done' has been given a wide interpretation. It includes omissions to say, or do, certain things.[61] It is not restricted to things said or done by persons in authority. However, advice properly given to the accused by his solicitor will not normally provide a basis for excluding a subsequent confession, even when, as it sometimes ought to be, it is robust and, for example, points to the advantages which may derive from an acceptance of guilt or the corresponding disadvantages of a 'no comment' interview. Nonetheless, it may do so in the case of a particularly vulnerable accused.[62] In *R v Roberts*,[63] a confession made after a shop manager's statement that, if R confessed, the police would not be called, was held to be inadmissible under s 76(2)(b), and the fact that, when the police were then called, R did not retract his confession, could not render it reliable.[64]

The phrase 'anything said or done' requires something external to the accused which was likely to have some influence on him. Thus a confession cannot be excluded on the basis that it may have been obtained in consequence of anything said or done by the accused himself which was likely to render unreliable any confession which he might have made in consequence thereof. An example is *R v Wahab*,[65] where W instructed his solicitor to approach the police to see if members of his family might be released from custody if he admitted his guilt. In *R v Goldenberg*[66] the suspect, a heroin addict, requested an interview while in police custody. The admissions he made in the interview were alleged by the defence to be an attempt

---

[58] 11th Report, Cmnd 4991 (1972) para 65.

[59] *R v Barry* (1992) 95 Cr App R 384, CA. The test is objective, but all the circumstances should be taken into account, including those affecting the accused, including his desires etc: 11th Report, Cmnd 4991 (1972) para 65.

[60] [2001] 1 All ER 57, DC at [46]. But see also *R v Cox* [1991] Crim LR 276, CA, *R v Crampton* (1991) 92 Cr App R 369, CA at 372, and *R v Kenny* [1994] Crim LR 284, CA.

[61] See, eg, *R v Doolan* [1988] Crim LR 747, CA: failure to caution, to keep a proper record of the interview, and to show that record to the suspect.

[62] *R v Wahab* [2003] 1 Cr App R 232(15), CA at [42].

[63] [2011] EWCA Crim 2974.

[64] Cf *R v Sherif* [2008] EWCA Crim 2653 where, notwithstanding a deliberate and improper decision not to arrest and caution a suspect, his confession was admitted on the basis of subsequent and properly conducted interviews in which he adopted what he had said in his first interview.

[65] [2003] 1 Cr App R 232(15), CA at [42].

[66] (1989) 88 Cr App R 285, CA.

by him to obtain bail and to be released in order to feed his addiction. It was held that the case fell outside s 76(2)(b). In *R v Crampton*[67] a heroin addict made admissions during interviews in the police station after he had been undergoing withdrawal symptoms. It was sought to distinguish *R v Goldenberg* on the grounds that the interviews held were not at the request of the accused, but conducted by the police at their own convenience. The Court of Appeal, however, doubted whether the mere holding of an interview, at a time when the suspect is undergoing withdrawal symptoms, is something 'done' under s 76(2), the wording of which seemed to postulate some 'words spoken' or 'acts done'.

Causation

Section 76(2)(b) imposes on the prosecution the burden of proving that the confession was not obtained 'in consequence' of anything said or done. This reflects the position at common law. In *DPP v Ping Lin*[68] the accused, suspected of a drugs offence, attempted to make a deal with the police whereby they would release him and in return he would disclose the name of his supplier. When told that this could not be done, he admitted that he had been dealing in heroin but made two more attempts to get some sort of bargain. An officer then said: 'If you show the judge that you have helped the police to trace bigger drug people, I am sure he will bear it in mind when he sentences you.' Subsequently, the accused made statements disclosing the name of his supplier. The House of Lords held that the statements were voluntary because there was no question of any threat or inducement being held out to him *before* he confessed. The accused may have hoped to obtain immunity or lenience, but that hope was entirely self-generated. In *R v Weeks*,[69] a decision under s 76(2)(b), the trial judge was satisfied that a confession was not obtained in consequence of what was said or done on the basis of the evidence and demeanour of the accused on the *voir dire*—he came across as a very astute young man who had previous experience of being interviewed at a police station.[70]

In *R v Rennie*,[71] a common law authority, the accused was convicted of conspiracy to obtain a pecuniary advantage by deception. The co-accused, his sister, had pleaded guilty to obtaining a pecuniary advantage by deception and a charge of conspiring with her brother was allowed to lie on the file. After his arrest, the accused at first denied any part in the offence but when a detective sergeant revealed the strength of the evidence known to him and asked, 'This was a joint operation by your family to defraud the bank, wasn't it?', the accused replied, 'No, don't bring the rest of the family into this, I admit it was my fault'. On the *voir dire*, the detective sergeant denied that he had told the accused that he would involve other members of his family but admitted that the accused was frightened of this happening. He said, 'I think he made the confession in the hope that I would terminate my inquiries into members of his family'. The judge ruled that the evidence was admissible. The Court of Appeal observed that the evidence as to the motives of the accused should not have been admitted, because the drawing of inferences was a matter for the judge and not witnesses. Nonetheless, the court acted on the assumption that the accused confessed because he hoped that inquiries would cease into the part played by his family, and posed the following question:[72]

---

[67] (1991) 92 Cr App R 369, CA.
[68] [1976] AC 574, HL.
[69] [1995] Crim LR 52, CA.
[70] See also *R v Tyrer* (1990) 90 Cr App R 446, CA at 449.
[71] [1982] 1 WLR 64, CA.
[72] Ibid at 70.

How is this principle[73] to be applied where a prisoner, when deciding to confess, not only realizes the strength of the evidence known to the police and the hopelessness of escaping conviction but is conscious at the same time of the fact that it may well be advantageous to him or . . . to someone close to him, if he confesses? How, in particular, is the judge to approach the question when these different thoughts may all, to some extent at least, have been prompted by something said by the police officer questioning him?

The answer, it was held, was not to be found from any refined analysis of the concept of causation. The judge should approach the question much as would jurors if it were for them, understanding the principle and the spirit behind it and applying common sense. Dismissing the appeal, Lord Lane CJ said:[74]

> Very few confessions are inspired solely by remorse. Often the motives of an accused are mixed and include a hope that an early admission may lead to an earlier release or a lighter sentence. If it were the law that the mere presence of such a motive, even if prompted by something said or done by a person in authority, led inexorably to the exclusion of a confession, nearly every confession would be rendered inadmissible. This is not the law. In some cases the hope may be self-generated. If so, it is irrelevant, even if it provides the dominant motive for making the confession. In such a case the confession will not have been obtained by anything said or done by a person in authority. More commonly the presence of such a hope will, in part at least, owe its origin to something said or done by such a person. There can be few prisoners who are being firmly but fairly questioned in a police station to whom it does not occur that they might be able to bring both their interrogation and their detention to an earlier end by confession.

This dictum was approved and applied in *R v Crampton*,[75] a decision under s 76(2)(b): the mere fact that the accused had been undergoing withdrawal symptoms and may have had a motive for making a confession did not mean that the confession was necessarily unreliable.

The question of causation poses particular problems when a confession made at an improperly conducted interview is repeated at a subsequent but properly conducted interview. In *R v McGovern*[76] it was held that a confession made in an interview in consequence of an improper denial of access to a solicitor was likely to be unreliable and should have been excluded. It was also held that a confession made in a properly conducted second interview on the following day was also inadmissible because the first interview tainted the second and the very fact that the suspect had already made a confession was likely to have had an effect on her in the second interview.[77]

The characteristics of the accused

The physical condition and mental characteristics of the accused are a part of the 'circumstances existing at the time' for the purposes of s 76(2)(b). Thus, in *R v Everett*[78] it was held that these circumstances obviously included the mental condition of a 42-year-old with a mental age of 8, and the material consideration was not what the police thought about his mental condition, but the nature of that condition itself. Similarly, in *R v McGovern*[79] it was

---

[73] Ie the common law principle of voluntariness.

[74] [1982] 1 WLR 64 at 69.

[75] (1991) 92 Cr App R 369, CA. See also *R v Wahab* [2003] 1 Cr App R 232(15), CA at [44]–[45].

[76] (1991) 92 Cr App R 228, CA.

[77] See also *R v Blake* [1991] Crim LR 119, CC and cf *R v Ismail* [1990] Crim LR 109, CA.

[78] [1988] Crim LR 826, CA.

[79] (1991) 92 Cr App R 228, CA.

held that the particular vulnerability and physical condition of the suspect at the time of her interview—she was borderline mentally subnormal, six months pregnant, and in a highly emotional state—formed the background for the submission that her confession should be excluded. However, the mental characteristics which may have a bearing on the question of reliability are not confined to cases of 'mental impairment' or 'impairment of intelligence or social functioning': any mental or personality abnormalities may be of relevance.[80]

The judge must consider the likely effect of what was 'said or done' on the mind of the particular accused. In some cases the things said or done may be unjustified, improper, illegal, or in breach of the 1984 Act or Codes of Practice yet not of a kind likely to render unreliable any confession which might be made by an accused who, for the sake of argument, is an experienced professional criminal with a tough character or who is otherwise capable of coping with even a vigorous interrogation.[81] In *R v Alladice*,[82] for example, it was held that although the accused, who was charged with robbery of £29,000 in cash, had been refused access to a solicitor in contravention of s 58 of the 1984 Act,[83] which was relevant to the question of whether to exclude his confession under s 76(2)(b), it was not only doubtful whether the confession had been obtained as a result of the refusal of access, but in all the circumstances there was no reason to believe that that refusal was likely to render unreliable any confession which the accused might have made. The circumstances showed that the police had acted with propriety, apart from the breach of s 58, and that the accused was well able to cope with the interviews, understood the cautions that he had been given, at times exercising his right to silence, and was aware of his rights so that, had the solicitor been present, his advice would have added nothing to the knowledge of his rights which the accused already had.[84] On the other hand, it is easy to imagine cases where, although it would be impossible to criticize the propriety of what was 'said or done', any confession which might be made by the accused would be likely to be unreliable in all the circumstances because the accused is, for example, of previous good character and highly suggestible, easily intimidated, of very low intelligence, or mentally handicapped.[85] In *R v Harvey*[86] the accused, a woman of low intelligence suffering from a psychopathic disorder, was charged with murder. Her confession was excluded under s 76(2)(b) on the grounds that it may have been obtained as a result of hearing a confession made by her lover. There was psychiatric evidence that her state of mind at the relevant time could have been such that, on hearing her lover's confession, she confessed to protect the lover in a child-like attempt to try to take the blame. There was no threat or inducement; there was no impropriety or illegality; what was said (done) was not said (done) by a person in authority; the crucial factor, in deciding whether what was said was likely to render unreliable any confession which she might have made, was her own state of mind.[87]

---

[80] *R v Walker* [1998] Crim LR 211, CA.

[81] In *R v Gowan* [1982] Crim LR 821, CA, O'Connor LJ, although not sanctioning improper or unfair questioning on the part of the police, said: 'serious and experienced professional criminals . . . must, and do, expect that their interrogation by trained and experienced police officers will be vigorous'.

[82] (1988) 87 Cr App R 380, CA.

[83] See, in this chapter, under **The right to have someone informed and the right of access to a lawyer**, p 473.

[84] For these reasons it was also held that the confession should not be excluded under s 78 (see Ch 11).

[85] See generally Gudjohnsson, *The Psychology of Interrogations, Confessions and Testimony* (London, 1992). In the case of confessions by mentally handicapped persons, see also the 1984 Act, s 77 (see Ch 8).

[86] [1988] Crim LR 241, CC.

[87] See also *R v Sat-Bhambra* (1989) 88 Cr App R 55, CA, where evidence of a confession was excluded on the basis that the accused may have been affected at the time by valium given to him by the police doctor to calm his nerves.

In some cases, of course, the confession will be excluded on the basis of *both* unjusti-fied police behaviour *and* the personal nature and characteristics of the accused, as in *R v Delaney*,[88] where the police failed to make a contemporaneous note of a one-and-a-half-hour interview with the accused, who was educationally subnormal, of low IQ, and poorly equipped to cope with sustained interrogation.[89]

Breach of provisions governing procedural fairness

It is clear from cases such as *R v Fulling*[90] and *R v Harvey*[91] that a confession may be excluded under s 76(2)(b) if there is not even a suspicion of impropriety. Equally, as we have seen, confessions obtained as a result of even serious breaches of the provisions of the 1984 Act and the Codes of Practice will not necessarily result in exclusion. Nonetheless, exclusion in many of the reported cases has been based wholly or mainly on such breaches, includ-ing the following: failure to caution, to keep a proper record of the interview or to show it to the suspect;[92] an offer of bail and numerous breaches of Code C, including a failure to keep a proper record of the interviews held;[93] questioning before allowing access to a solicitor, failure to record the admissions immediately and failure to show the note of the interview to the suspect;[94] asking a question after the suspect has been charged which is not for the purpose of clearing up an ambiguity;[95] and conducting an interview with a juvenile without an 'appropriate adult',[96] the adult present having a low IQ, being virtually illiterate, and probably incapable of appreciating the gravity of the juvenile's situation[97] or being a person with whom the juvenile has no empathy (her estranged father whom she did not wish to attend),[98] or where there has been no attempt to explain to the adult his role.[99]

Section 105 of the Taxes Management Act 1970

Concerning the admissibility of confessions in any criminal proceedings against a person for any form of fraudulent conduct in relation to tax, s 76 of the 1984 Act must be read in conjunction with s 105 of the Taxes Management Act 1970, which operates in such pro-ceedings to prevent the exclusion of statements made or documents produced in so-called 'Hansard interviews', that is, interviews at which the accused is informed of the practice of

---

[88] (1989) 88 Cr App R 338, CA.

[89] See also *R v Waters* [1989] Crim LR 62, CA and *R v Moss* (1990) 91 Cr App R 371, CA.

[90] [1987] 2 All ER 65, CA in this chapter, at n 44.

[91] [1988] Crim LR 241, CC in this chapter, at n 86.

[92] See paras 10, 11.7, and 11.11, Code C and *R v Doolan* [1988] Crim LR 747, CA. See *R v McPhee* [2016] 1 WLR 166, PC, an appeal from the Court of Appeal of the Bahamas: the accused, a youth, was removed from his cell for several hours on three occasions without any reason given in the custody record, suggesting that he had been subject to unrecorded interviews before his confession.

[93] *R v Barry* (1992) 95 Cr App R 384, CA.

[94] See the 1984 Act, s 58(4), paras 11.7 and 11.11, Code C, and *R v Chung* (1991) 92 Cr App R 314, CA.

[95] See para 16.5, Code C and *R v Waters* [1989] Crim LR 62, CA.

[96] See para 11.15, Code C. See, also *McPhee v The Queen* [2016] 4 WLR 166, PC.

[97] See *R v Morse* [1991] Crim LR 195.

[98] See *DPP v Blake* [1989] 1 WLR 432, DC, now reflected in Note 1B to Code C; and cf *R v Jefferson* [1994] 1 All ER 270, CA. See generally Hodgson, 'Vulnerable Suspects and the Appropriate Adult' [1997] Crim LR 785.

[99] *McPhee v The Queen* [2016] 4 WLR 166, PC.

HM Revenue & Customs to take into account the cooperation of the taxpayer in deciding whether to bring any prosecution for fraud.[100] Section 105(1) is in the following terms:

> Statements made or documents produced by or on behalf of a person shall not be inadmissible . . . by reason only that it has been drawn to his attention—
> (a) that where serious tax fraud has been committed the Board may accept a money settlement and that the Board will accept such a settlement, and will not pursue a criminal prosecution, if he makes a full confession of all tax irregularities, or
> (b) that the extent to which he is helpful and volunteers information is a factor that will be taken into account in determining the amount of any penalty
> and that he was or may have been induced thereby to make the statements or produce the documents.

Section 105 does not prevent reliance upon s 78 of the 1984 Act where the interview has been conducted in breach of Code C, but it is relevant to exercise of the discretion under s 78 that Parliament expected statements made at Hansard interviews to be admissible in evidence.[101]

The discretion to exclude

If the prosecution fails to discharge the burden of proving that a confession was not obtained by the methods described in s 76(2), the court, as we have seen, shall not allow the confession to be given in evidence and has no discretion to admit it, even if satisfied that it is true. It does not follow from this, however, that the confession *must* be admitted if the prosecution succeeds in proving that the confession was not obtained by those methods: s 76(1) provides that a confession *may* be given in evidence if not excluded under the section. In such cases the trial judge may exclude the confession in the exercise of her common law discretion or under s 78(1). Although these two discretionary powers overlap to a considerable extent, s 78(1) has in very large measure superseded the common law power.

Section 82(3) of the Police and Criminal Evidence Act 1984

Section 82(3) provides that:

> Nothing in this Part of this Act (ss 73–82) shall prejudice any power of a court to exclude evidence (whether by preventing questions from being put or otherwise) at its discretion.

The effect of this subsection is, in the present context, to preserve any discretion to exclude an otherwise admissible confession that the court possessed at common law prior to the 1984 Act. At common law, a trial judge, even if satisfied that a confession was made voluntarily, could exclude it as a matter of discretion on a number of different albeit overlapping grounds. Two of the grounds were made clear by the House of Lords in *R v Sang*.[102] First, as a part of his function at a criminal trial to ensure that the accused receives a fair trial, the judge has a discretion to refuse to admit evidence where, in his opinion, its prejudicial effect outweighs

---

[100] Section 105 also applies to any proceedings for the recovery of any tax due from him and any proceedings for a penalty: s 105(2).

[101] *R v Gill* [2004] 1 WLR 49, CA at [45].

[102] [1980] AC 402.

its probative value. Second, the judge has a discretion to exclude an otherwise admissible confession obtained by improper or unfair means. A third ground was that the confession was obtained in contravention of the Judges' Rules[103] or the statutory provisions governing the detention and treatment of suspects.

The discretion, in so far as it may be exercised on the first ground, was of particular use in the case of confessions made by accused suffering from mental disability.[104] Thus it was held that the discretion could be exercised in the case of a confession that came from an irrational mind or was the product of delusions and hallucinations,[105] or was made by an accused with the mental age and comprehension level of a young child.[106] However, confessions in cases of this kind and in analogous cases in which a confession was obtained when the accused was under the influence of drugs,[107] would now be likely to be excluded as a matter of law under s 76(2)(b).

Most of the reported cases in which the common law discretion was exercised on either the second or the third ground were cases involving some breach of the Judges' Rules. However, a voluntary confession could be admitted notwithstanding a breach of the rules.[108] In the exercise of the discretion (which was rarely reversed on appeal) the trial judge could examine, in addition to the breaches alleged, all the circumstances of the case, including in particular the probative value of the confession and the nature and seriousness of the offence charged.

The Judges' Rules, and many of the old statutory provisions governing the detention and treatment of suspects, have now been replaced by a wide variety of provisions contained in the 1984 Act and the Codes of Practice which have been issued pursuant to the Act. Before turning to consider the exclusion of confessions under s 78(1) of the 1984 Act, it will be convenient, therefore, to examine some general and particular provisions of the Codes of Practice and the 1984 Act.

The Codes of Practice

The matters covered

Codes A to H relate to the following matters—A: the exercise by police officers of statutory powers of stop and search; B: the searching of premises by police officers and the seizure of property found by police officers on persons or premises; C: the detention, treatment, and questioning of persons by police officers;[109] D: the identification of persons by police officers;

---

[103] The Judges' Rules were rules of practice, not law, originally drawn up by the judges of the King's Bench Division in 1912 for the guidance of the police, and designed to regulate the interrogation and treatment of suspects.

[104] On confessions by mentally handicapped persons, see also the 1984 Act, s 77 (see Ch 8).

[105] *R v Miller* [1986] 3 All ER 119, CA.

[106] *R v Stewart* (1972) 56 Cr App R 272, CCC. See also per Lord Widgery CJ in *R v Isequilla* [1975] 1 WLR 716, CA.

[107] *R v Davis* [1979] Crim LR 167, CC.

[108] *R v Prager* [1972] 1 WLR 260.

[109] In the case of an investigation by the Director of the Serious Fraud Office into a suspected offence involving serious or complex fraud, the general provisions of Code C yield to the inquisitorial regime established by the Criminal Justice Act 1987: see *R v Director of Serious Fraud Office, ex p Smith* [1992] 3 All ER 456, HL.

E: the audio recording of interviews with suspects;[110] F: the visual recording with sound of interviews with suspects; G: the statutory powers of arrest by police officers; and H: the questioning of suspects under the Terrorism Act 2000.

Persons governed by the Codes

The Codes do not apply only to police officers: under s 67(9) of the 1984 Act they also apply to other persons 'charged with the duty of investigating offences or charging offenders'.[111] This phrase covers those charged with a legal duty of the kind in question, whether imposed by statute or by the common law or by contract.[112] It covers Customs and Excise officers,[113] but is not restricted to government officials and others acting under statutory powers.[114] Whether a person satisfies the test is a question of fact in each case[115] or, more accurately, a question of mixed law and fact, involving an examination of the statute, contract, or other authority under which a person carries out his functions, as well as a consideration of his actual work.[116] Thus the test will not necessarily be satisfied by line managers conducting disciplinary interviews,[117] Department of Trade inspectors investigating a company's affairs,[118] or by those supervising a bank on behalf of the Bank of England under the Banking Act 1987,[119] but may be satisfied by commercial investigators such as company investigators,[120] store detectives,[121] and investigators employed by the Federation against Copyright Theft.[122] The test is met by officers of the Special Compliance Office, HM Revenue & Customs' investigation branch charged with investigating serious tax fraud, because such fraud inevitably involves the commission of an offence or offences.[123]

---

[110] See also *Criminal Practice Directions* V, Part 16C, which deals with such matters as the practice to be followed for: (a) amending a transcript of an interview (or editing a recording by agreement); (b) notification of intention to play a recording in court; (c) notification of objection to production of a recording; and (d) proof of a recording. Concerning video-recorded interviews with children (see **Ch 5**), departure from the 'Achieving Best Evidence' guidance on interviewing may be treated as the equivalent of a breach of one of the Codes of Practice. Account has also been taken of a failure to conform to the recommendations contained in the report of Butler Sloss LJ, the *Inquiry into Child Abuse in Cleveland*, Cm 412 (1987): see *R v H* [1992] Crim LR 516, CA. See also *R v Dunphy* (1994) 98 Cr App R 393, CA.

[111] The principles of fairness enshrined in Code C may have an even wider application: see *R v Smith* [1994] 1 WLR 1396, CA (see **Ch 11**). However, they do not appear to apply in circumstances where a police officer is present and making notes at an accused's assessment by a mental health team, during the course of which the accused makes admissions: see *R v Higgins* [2017] EWCA Crim 224.

[112] *Joy v Federation against Copyright Theft Ltd* [1993] Crim LR 588, DC.

[113] *R v Sanusi* [1992] Crim LR 43, CA.

[114] *R v Bayliss* (1994) 98 Cr App R 235, CA at 237–8.

[115] Per Watkins LJ in *R v Seelig* [1991] 4 All ER 429, CA at 439.

[116] Per Neill LJ in *R v Bayliss* (1993) 98 Cr App R 235 at 238–9 and in *R v Smith* (1993) 99 Cr App R 233, CA.

[117] *R v Welcher* [2007] Crim LR 804, CA.

[118] See *R v Seelig* [1991] 4 All ER 429, CA.

[119] See *R v Smith* [1994] 1 WLR 1396, CA.

[120] *R v Twaites; R v Brown* (1991) 92 Cr App R 106, CA.

[121] *R v Bayliss* (1994) 98 Cr App R 235, CA.

[122] *Joy v Federation against Copyright Theft Ltd* [1993] Crim LR 588, DC.

[123] *R v Gill* [2004] 1 WLR 49, CA.

The right to a caution

Paragraphs 10 and 16 of Code C, the Code of Practice for the Detention, Treatment and Questioning of Persons by Police Officers, provide as follows:

10.1 A person whom there are grounds to suspect of an offence must be cautioned before any questions about an offence, or further questions if the answers provide the grounds for suspicion, are put to them if either the accused's answers or silence (ie failure or refusal to answer or answer satisfactorily) may be given in evidence to a court in a prosecution. A person need not be cautioned if questions are for other necessary purposes, e.g.:

(a) solely to establish their identity or ownership of any vehicle;

(b) to obtain information in accordance with any relevant statutory requirement[124] . . .;

(c) in furtherance of the proper and effective conduct of a search, e.g. to determine the need to search in the exercise of powers of stop and search or to seek cooperation while carrying out a search; or

(d) to seek verification of a written record as in paragraph 11.13.[125]

. . .

10.4. As required by Code G, section 3, a person who is arrested, or further arrested, must also be cautioned unless:

(a) it is impracticable to do so by reason of their condition or behaviour at the time;

(b) they have already been cautioned immediately prior to arrest as in paragraph 10.1.

10.5. The caution which must be given on:

(a) arrest;

(b) all other occasions before a person is charged or informed that they may be prosecuted, (see section 16),

should, unless the restriction on drawing adverse inferences from silence applies, (see Annex C), be in the following terms:

'You do not have to say anything. But it may harm your defence if you do not mention when questioned something which you later rely on in Court. Anything you do say may be given in evidence.'

. . .

10.7. Minor deviations from the words of any caution given in accordance with this Code do not constitute a breach of this Code, provided the sense of the relevant caution is preserved . . .

10.8. After any break in questioning under caution, the person being questioned must be made aware they remain under caution. If there is any doubt the relevant caution should be given again in full when the interview resumes . . .

. . .

16.1. When the officer in charge of the investigation reasonably believes that there is sufficient evidence to provide a realistic prospect of conviction for the offence . . . they shall without delay, and subject to the following qualification, inform the custody officer who will be responsible for considering whether the detainee should be charged . . . When a person is detained in respect of more than one offence it is permissible to delay informing the custody officer until the above conditions are satisfied in respect of all the offences . . .

. . .

---

[124] eg, under the Road Traffic Act 1988.

[125] Para 11.13 relates to records of comments made by a suspect outside the context of an interview.

16.2. When a detainee is charged with or informed they may be prosecuted for an offence, see Note 16B, they shall, unless the restriction on drawing adverse inferences from silence applies, see Annex C, be cautioned as follows:

'You do not have to say anything. But it may harm your defence if you do not mention now something which you later rely on in court. Anything you do say may be given in evidence.'[126]

Although para 10.1 does not include a requirement that the grounds to suspect be reasonable, this is implicit, because the grounds must be assessed objectively.[127]

In *R v Shah*[128] it was held that a mere hunch or 'sixth sense', or the simple fact that the questioner is suspicious, will not suffice to bring para 10.1 into play; para 10.1 sets out an objective test in that there must be grounds for suspicion before the need to caution arises and although they may well fall short of evidence supportive of a prima facie case of guilt, they must exist and be such as to lead both to a suspicion that an offence has been committed and that the person being questioned has committed it.[129] In *R v Hunt*,[130] where officers saw H in someone else's garden putting a flick-knife in his pocket, searched him, and found the knife, it was held that at that stage the officers had ample evidence on which to suspect the commission of an offence and should have cautioned him. The answers to the questions then put, without a caution, should have been excluded under s 78. However, if a person is cautioned in respect of one offence and minutes later the police have grounds to suspect another offence, it seems that there is no requirement to caution again, under either para 10.1 or para 10.8, before putting questions about the other offence.[131]

A caution is not required under para 10.1, in respect of a person whom there are grounds to suspect of an offence, if questions are not put to him regarding his involvement or suspected involvement in that offence, but for other purposes. However, if the questions are put for two purposes, partly regarding his involvement or suspected involvement in an offence, and partly for other purposes, then a caution should be given.[132]

Paragraph 10.1 and other requirements of the Code were not intended to apply to a conversation between a suspect and officers who adopt an undercover pose or disguise, because there can be no question of pressure or intimidation by the officers as persons actually in authority or believed to be so. However, it is wrong for officers to adopt a pose or disguise to ask questions about an offence uninhibited by the provisions of the Code and with the effect of circumventing it, and if they do so, the questions and answers may be excluded under s 78.[133]

Paragraph 16.2 of the Code is designed to apply to that stage in the course of an interrogation when there is sufficient evidence to prosecute and for the prosecution to succeed. At that time,

---

[126] Where a person wishes to make a written statement under caution, he shall first be asked to write out and sign: 'I make this statement of my own free will. I understand that I do not have to say anything but that it may harm my defence if I do not mention when questioned something which I later rely on in court. This statement may be given in evidence': see para 2, Annex D, Code C. See also *R v Pall* (1991) 156 JP 424, CA and cf *R v Hoyte* [1994] Crim LR 215, CA.

[127] *R v James* [1996] Crim LR 650, CA. *R v James* and other authorities in the ensuing text and footnotes in this chapter are decisions on an earlier version of Code C.

[128] [1994] Crim LR 125, CA.

[129] See also, and cf *R v Nelson and Rose* [1998] 2 Cr App R 399, CA.

[130] [1992] Crim LR 582, CA. Cf *R v Purcell* [1992] Crim LR 806, CA.

[131] *R v Oni* [1992] Crim LR 183, CA.

[132] *R v Nelson and Rose* [1998] 2 Cr App R 399, CA.

[133] See *R v Christou* [1992] QB 979, CA (see **Ch 11**).

and subject to exceptions, questioning should cease.[134] Some of the words and phrases used in para 16.2 are the same as those used in its precursor, r III of the Judges' Rules and are likely to be interpreted in the same way. For the purposes of r III, it was held that the word 'charged' means formally charged;[135] that when a person is told 'you will be charged' it is the same as saying that a charge has in fact already been preferred;[136] and that the phrase 'informed that he may be prosecuted' covers a case where, during interrogation of a suspect who has not been arrested, the time comes when the police contemplate that a summons may be issued against him.[137]

The right to have someone informed and the right of access to a lawyer

A detailed analysis of the relevant provisions of the 1984 Act and the various Codes of Practice is well beyond the scope of this work. However, two provisions of particular significance in the present context, ss 56 and 58, do merit close consideration. They relate to the right to have someone informed when arrested and what has been called 'one of the most important and fundamental rights of a citizen',[138] namely the right of access to legal advice.[139] Section 56(1) provides that:

> Where a person has been arrested and is being held in custody in a police station or other premises, he shall be entitled, if he so requests, to have one friend or relative or other person who is known to him or who is likely to take an interest in his welfare told, as soon as is practicable except to the extent that delay is permitted by this section, that he has been arrested and is being detained there.[140]

Section 58 provides that:

(1) A person arrested and held in custody in a police station or other premises shall be entitled, if he so requests, to consult a solicitor privately at any time.

(2) Subject to subsection (3) below, a request under subsection (1) above and the time at which it was made shall be recorded in the custody record.

(3) Such a request need not be recorded in the custody record of a person who makes it at a time while he is at a court after being charged with an offence.

(4) If a person makes such a request, he must be permitted to consult a solicitor as soon as is practicable except to the extent that delay is permitted by this section.[141]

---

[134] See para 16.5, Code C and *R v Bailey* [1993] 3 All ER 513, CA. Where a suspect is charged by the police and then required by the Serious Fraud Office to attend for an interview, the Director is not required to caution him, because the Criminal Justice Act 1987 showed a parliamentary intention to establish an inquisitorial regime in relation to serious or complex fraud in which the Director could obtain by compulsion answers which might be self-incriminating. Under s 2(13), a person who without reasonable excuse fails to answer questions or provide relevant information is liable to imprisonment, a fine, or both. But see also s 2(8): subject to minor exceptions, statements made by the suspect cannot be used in evidence against him.

[135] *R v Brackenbury* [1965] 1 WLR 1475n.

[136] *Conway v Hotten* [1976] 2 All ER 213, DC.

[137] *R v Collier; R v Stenning* [1965] 1 WLR 1470, CCA.

[138] Per Hodgson J in *R v Samuel* [1988] QB 615, CA at 630. See also *R v McPhee* [2016] 4 WLR 166, PC.

[139] See also paras 5 and 6, Code C.

[140] The rights conferred are exercisable whenever the person detained is transferred from one place to another: s 56(8).

[141] Section 58 does not entitle a person, suspected of committing an offence of driving when unfit through drink or drugs or driving after consuming excess alcohol, to consult a solicitor *before* supplying a specimen for analysis: *DPP v Billington* [1988] 1 All ER 435, DC. Procedures undertaken under the Road Traffic Act 1988, s 7 (ie questions and answers leading to the giving of a specimen) do not constitute interviewing for the purposes of Code C: see *DPP v D; DPP v Rous* (1992) 94 Cr App R 185, DC and para 11.1A, Code C.

The intention behind the opening words of both s 56(1) and s 58(1) is to limit the application of the sections to a person whose detention in custody has been authorized, that is, an arrested person taken to a police station in respect of whom the custody officer is satisfied that the statutory conditions for detention are made out. Thus a person arrested while committing burglary is *in custody* on premises, but is not *held* in custody, and is therefore outside the terms of ss 56 and 58.[142] However, in *Ambrose v Harris*,[143] the Supreme Court held that under Art 6(1) and (3)(c) of the European Convention on Human Rights, the right to legal advice may arise when, even if a suspect has not been formally arrested or taken into custody, there has been a significant curtailment of his freedom of action, as in one of the cases before the court, where a suspect was detained, handcuffed, and questioned during a police search.[144] The right also arises where a person is interviewed as a witness without legal advice and during the course of questioning begins to make damaging admissions.[145]

A 'solicitor', for the purposes of s 58, means a solicitor who holds a current practising certificate and an accredited or probationary representative included on the register of representatives maintained by the Legal Aid Agency.[146]

Many of the subsections of ss 56 and 58 are cast in identical or very similar terms. In any case the person in custody must be permitted to exercise the rights conferred within 36 hours from the 'relevant time',[147] which is usually either the time at which the person arrives at the police station or the time 24 hours after the time of arrest, whichever is the earlier.[148] Delay is only permitted if four conditions are met. The first is that the person detained is in police detention for an indictable offence. The second is that the delay is authorized by an officer of at least the rank of inspector or superintendent.[149] The third condition is that the person in detention has not yet been charged with an offence, that is any offence, whether or not the one in respect of which he was originally arrested.[150] The fourth condition, contained in ss 56(5) and 58(8), is that the officer must have:

> reasonable grounds for believing that telling the named person of the arrest (exercise of the right . . . [to consult a solicitor] at the time when the person detained desires to exercise it) (a) will lead to interference with or harm to evidence connected with an indictable offence or interference with or physical injury to other persons or (b) will lead to the alerting of other persons

---

[142] *R v Kerawalla* [1991] Crim LR 451, CA.

[143] [2011] 1 WLR 2435, SC.

[144] Although s 58(1) does not apply to a person in custody after being remanded by a magistrates' court, such a person has a common law right to be permitted on request to consult a solicitor as soon as is reasonably practicable: *R v Chief Constable of South Wales, ex p Merrick* [1994] Crim LR 852, DC.

[145] See *Ibrahim v UK* [2016] ECHR 750. See also Ch 11, **The rights-based principle**, p 334.

[146] Para 6.12, Code C. Concerning non-accredited or probationary representatives, see paras 6.12A and 6.13, Code C and *R (Thompson) v Chief Constable of the Northumberland Constabulary* [2001] 1 WLR 1342, CA.

[147] Sections 56(3) and 58(5).

[148] Section 41(2).

[149] Sections 56(2)(b) and 58(6)(b) respectively. The authorization may be oral, in which case it shall be confirmed in writing as soon as possible: ss 56(4) and 58(7). The authorization under s 58(6)(b) may also be given by an officer of the rank of chief inspector if he has been authorized to do so by an officer of at least the rank of chief superintendent: s 107(1). The holder of an acting rank may be treated for the purpose of these provisions as the holder of the substantive rank: *R v Alladice* (1988) 87 Cr App R 380, CA.

[150] Para A1, Annex B, Code C and *R v Samuel* [1988] QB 615, CA.

of para 10.1 of Code C. The accused can then give proper weight to the nature of the investigation when deciding whether or not to exercise his right to obtain free legal advice under the Code and when deciding how to respond to the questions which the police propose to ask. The Act and the Codes, it was held, proceed on the assumption that a suspect in custody will know why he is there and, when being interviewed, will know at least in general terms the level of offence in respect of which he is suspected; and if he does not know, and as a result does not seek legal advice and gives critical answers which he might not otherwise have given, the evidence should normally be excluded under s 78, because its admission will have a seriously adverse effect on the fairness of the proceedings.

Breach of the 'verballing' provisions

In *R v Keenan*[179] it was held that if there have been serious and substantial breaches of the 'verballing' provisions of the Code (whereby, eg, an accurate contemporaneous record of an interview[180] should be made), evidence so obtained should be excluded. Thus confessions have been excluded on the basis of the following breaches: interviewing a juvenile in the absence of an 'appropriate adult';[181] interviewing a suspect before he has arrived at the police station and been informed of his right to free legal advice;[182] failure to tell a suspect that he is not under arrest coupled with failure to make a contemporaneous record of an interview;[183] failure to caution and to make such a record;[184] failure to give the suspect the opportunity to read and sign it as correct or to indicate the respects in which he considers it inaccurate;[185] failure to record a statement made other than in English in the language used and failure to give the opportunity to read a record and check its accuracy;[186] in a case in which the accused

---

[179] [1990] 2 QB 54, CA (see Ch 11).

[180] Under Code C, para 11.1A, an interview is the questioning of a person regarding his involvement or suspected involvement in a criminal offence or offences which, under para 10.1, Code C, must be carried out under caution. Whether there is an interview primarily turns on the nature of the questioning, rather than the number of questions or their length. Thus if an officer asks a single question directly relating to the crime, his motive being to clarify an ambiguity in a comment made by the suspect on arrest, that question and the answer to it may constitute an interview, although the officer's motive may be very relevant to the question of exclusion under s 78: *R v Ward* (1994) 98 Cr App R 337, CA. If an accused, under arrest, voluntarily offers to provide information and officers, without asking any questions, accede to that request and make a record of that information, that is not an interview, but nothing said at such a meeting can be produced in evidence at any subsequent trial: *R v Menard* [1995] 1 Cr App R 306, CA.

[181] *R v Weekes* (1993) 97 Cr App R 222, CA (para 11.15, Code C).

[182] *R v Cox* (1993) 96 Cr App R 464, CA (para 11.1; also paras 3.1, 3.2, and 10.1).

[183] *R v Joseph* [1993] Crim LR 206, CA (paras 10.2 and 11.7, Code C). Cf *Watson v DPP* [2003] All ER (D) 132 (Jun), DC.

[184] See *R v Sparks* [1991] Crim LR 128, CA (paras 10.1 and 11.7, Code C) and *R v Bryce* [1992] 4 All ER 567, CA (paras 10.8 and 11.7, Code C). See also *R v Okafor* [1994] 3 All ER 741, CA, where there was *also* a failure to remind of the right to legal advice (para 11.2, Code C).

[185] See *R v Foster* [1987] Crim LR 821, CC (para 11.11, Code C) and *R v Weerdesteyn* [1995] 1 Cr App R 405, CA, where there was also a failure to caution. Cf *R v Courtney* [1995] Crim LR 63, CA, where failure to give the suspect an opportunity to read and sign a record of comments outside the context of an interview (in breach of para 11.13, Code C) was treated as 'insubstantial'. See also *R v Park* (1993) 99 Cr App R 270, CA: if answers to exploratory questions give rise in due course to a well-founded suspicion that an offence has been committed, what has started out as an inquiry may have become an interview and if it does, the requirements of the Code must be followed in relation to both the earlier and later questioning. Thus, although a contemporaneous note is no longer possible, a record should be made as soon as practicable of the earlier questions and answers, the reason for the absence of a contemporaneous note should be recorded, and the suspect should be given the opportunity to check the record.

[186] *R v Coelho* [2008] EWCA Crim 627 (paras 13.4 and 11.13, Code C).

denied making a confession allegedly made *after* a taped interview with him, failure to give the suspect such an opportunity;[187] and undue pressure, by threatening a number of charges, instead of only two, if the suspect continued to deny the charge.[188] However, relatively trivial breaches, such as a failure to record the reason why an interview record was not completed in the course of an interview,[189] or such a breach coupled with a failure to record the time when an interview record was made,[190] have not resulted in exclusion. Moreover, even serious breaches of the 'verballing' provisions may be 'cured' by the presence of a solicitor or his clerk. In *R v Dunn*[191] D denied making a confession, allegedly made *after* his interview, during the signing of the interview notes, and in the presence of his solicitor's clerk. The 'conversation' in which the confession was made was not recorded contemporaneously and no note of it was shown to D. It was held that, despite these serious breaches, the evidence was admissible because the clerk was present to protect D's interests: she could have intervened to prevent the accused from answering, her presence would have inhibited the police from fabricating the conversation, and, if they were to fabricate, it would not simply be a question of their evidence against that of D, because she would also be able to give evidence for the accused.

The effect of breaches of Code C on subsequent interviews

If a confession is excluded under s 78 by reason of a breach of the Code, a confession made in a subsequent, but properly conducted interview *may* be tainted by the earlier breach and therefore also fall to be excluded under s 78. The question of exclusion is a matter of fact and degree which is likely to depend on whether the breaches leading to the exclusion of the first interview were of a fundamental and continuing nature and, if so, if the arrangements for the subsequent interview gave the accused a sufficient opportunity to exercise an informed and independent choice as to whether he should repeat or retract what he said in the first interview or say nothing.[192] In *R v Canale*,[193] where the first two interviews were not contemporaneously recorded and no record was shown to the accused for verification, it was held that these breaches had affected subsequent admissions which therefore should have been excluded under s 78. However, in *R v Gillard and Barrett*[194] it was held that breaches of the Code similar to those in *R v Canale* had not tainted confessions made in subsequent but properly conducted interviews. *R v Canale* was distinguished on the basis that in that case there was a nexus between the earlier and later interviews: the accused claimed that he had been induced by promises to make the admissions in the first interview and these promises may have continued to affect answers in the later interviews. The length of time separating

---

[187] *R v Scott* [1991] Crim LR 56, CA, where it was held that by admitting the confession, the judge effectively compelled the accused to give evidence. Cf *R v Matthews, R v Dennison,* and *R v Voss* (1990) 91 Cr App R 43, CA.

[188] *R v Howden-Simpson* [1991] Crim LR 49, CA (para 11.5, Code C). See also *R v De Silva* [2003] 2 Cr App R 74 (5), CA, where the confessions were made, after being cautioned, in telephone calls to other suspects which the police had induced the accused to make by the promise of a reduced sentence, if convicted.

[189] See *R v White* [1991] Crim LR 779, CA and para 11.10, Code C.

[190] See *R v Findlay; R v Francis* [1992] Crim LR 372, CA and para 11.9, Code C.

[191] (1991) 91 Cr App R 237, CA. See also Roberts, 'Questioning the Suspect' [1993] Crim LR 368 and Baldwin, 'Legal Advice at the Police Station' [1993] Crim LR 371.

[192] *R v Neil* [1994] Crim LR 441, CA, applied in *R v Nelson and Rose* [1998] 2 Cr App R 399, CA.

[193] [1990] 2 All ER 187, CA (see **Ch 11**). See also *R v Blake* [1991] Crim LR 119, CC.

[194] (1990) 92 Cr App R 61, CA.

the interviews is clearly relevant,[195] but the critical factor, it seems, is whether there is any suggestion of oppression, inducement, stress, or pressure in the earlier interview which might continue to exert a malign influence during the later interview.[196]

Interviews with persons not governed by the Codes

As already noted in this chapter, the Codes only apply to police officers and others charged with the duty of investigating offences or charging offenders.[197] However, where a confession has been made in the course of an interview with some other person, for example a doctor or psychiatrist, the court, in deciding whether to exercise the s 78 discretion, is entitled to take into account the fact that the accused did not have the benefit of the safeguards provided by the Codes. In *R v Elleray*[198] it was held that, given the need for frankness in the exchanges between a probation officer and an offender, the prosecution should only rely upon a confession made to a probation officer if it is in the public interest to do so, but where they do rely on such a confession, the court, in deciding whether to exclude it under s 78, is entitled to take into account not only the need for frankness, but also the reliability of the record of what was said, that the offender was not cautioned, and that he did not have the benefit of legal representation. On the facts of the case, the confessions were held to have been properly admitted.[199]

The *voir dire*

When a *voir dire* is necessary

If either (i) the prosecution rely on oral statements and the defence case is simply that the interview never took place or that the incriminating statements were never made or (ii) the prosecution rely on written statements and the defence case is that they are forgeries, no question of admissibility falls for the judge's decision. The issue of fact whether or not the statement was made by the accused is for the jury. However, if the accused denies authorship of a written statement and claims that he signed it involuntarily, or claims that his signature to what in fact was a confession statement was obtained by the fraudulent misrepresentation that he was signing a document of an entirely different character, he puts in issue the admissibility of the statement on which the judge must rule and, if the judge admits the statement, all issues of fact as to the circumstances of the making and signing of the statement should then be left for the jury to consider and evaluate.[200]

Subject to the foregoing, if the prosecution propose to admit evidence of a confession, the defence have two options. They may represent to the court that the confession was or may have been obtained by the methods set out in s 76(2)[201] (or in any event should be excluded

---

[195] See *R v Conway* [1994] Crim LR 838, CA, where account was taken of the fact that only 20 minutes separated the interviews.

[196] See per Taylor LJ in *Y v DPP* [1991] Crim LR 917, DC. See also *R v Glaves* [1993] Crim LR 685, CA; *R v Wood* [1994] Crim LR 222, CA; and generally Mirfield, 'Successive Confessions and the Poisonous Tree' [1996] Crim LR 554.

[197] See, under **Persons governed by the Codes**, p 470.

[198] [2003] 2 Cr App R 165 (11), CA.

[199] See also *R v McDonald* [1991] Crim LR 122, CA (see **Ch 11**).

[200] Per Lord Bridge in *Ajodha v The State* [1981] 2 All ER 193, PC at 201–2, applied in *R v Flemming* (1987) 86 Cr App R 32, CA.

[201] A suggestion, in cross-examination, that a confession was obtained improperly does not amount to a representation for the purposes of s 76(2): per Russell LJ, expressly confining his rulings to summary trials, in *R v Liverpool Juvenile Court, ex p R* [1987] 2 All ER 668, DC at 673.

by the judge in the exercise of his discretion) and the question of admissibility must then be determined on the *voir dire*.[202] Alternatively, the defence may choose not to dispute the admissibility of the confession, in which case, assuming that the court does not exercise its own powers under s 76(3) to require the prosecution to prove that the confession was not obtained by the methods set out in s 76(2), the confession may be given in evidence.[203] At common law, prior to the 1984 Act, there was a third option, namely to allow the jury to hear the evidence of the confession and subsequently, when all the evidence had been heard, to submit to the judge that, if she doubted the admissibility of the statement, she should direct the jury to disregard it.[204] However, this option has not survived the 1984 Act: on its wording, s 76 only permits the question of legal admissibility to be raised where the prosecution 'propose . . .' to give a confession in evidence. Similarly, s 78 refers to evidence on which the prosecution 'propose . . .' to rely. Accordingly, it has been said that if an accused wishes to exclude a confession under s 76, the time to make such a submission is before the confession is put in evidence and not afterwards.[205] This would also appear to be the time at which a submission based on s 78 should be made.[206]

The procedure

In cases in which an advocate for the defence intends to make a submission that a confession should be excluded, his intention will be conveyed to the advocate for the prosecution at the Plea and Trial Preparation Hearing or immediately before the trial commences, so that the confession is not referred to in the presence of the jury, whether in the prosecution opening speech or otherwise.[207] The prosecution will adduce their evidence in the normal way but at that point in time when the confession would otherwise be admitted, it will be intimated to the court that a point of law has arisen which falls to be determined in the absence of the jury.[208] The defence have no right to insist on the presence of the jury at the *voir dire*: the judge, after listening to the views of the defence, has the final word on whether the jury should remain in court.[209] At the *voir dire*, the prosecution will bear the burden of proving beyond reasonable doubt that the confession was not obtained by the methods described in s 76(2). Witnesses, in the usual case police officers, will be called to give evidence of the

---

[202] Concerning summary trials, see Ch 2, **The *voir dire*, or trial within a trial, p 37**.

[203] However, any resulting conviction may be quashed if the prosecution failed to disclose material which would have provided the defence with an informed opportunity to seek a *voir dire*: *R v Langley* [2001] Crim LR 651, CA.

[204] See per Lord Bridge in *Ajodha v The State* [1981] 2 All ER 193 at 202–3.

[205] See *R v Sat-Bhambra* (1989) 88 Cr App R 55, CA at **n 229**. See also *R v Davis* [1990] Crim LR 860, CA and *Alagaratnam v R* [2011] Crim LR 232, CA. For the position in summary trials, see *R v Liverpool Juvenile Court, ex p R* [1987] 2 All ER 668, DC (see **Ch 2**).

[206] But see, in the case of summary trials, per Russell LJ in *R v Liverpool Juvenile Court, ex p R* [1987] 2 All ER 668, DC (see **Ch 2**).

[207] *R v Cole* (1941) 165 LT 125. In the trial of an unrepresented accused, it may be prudent, if the judge has any reason to suppose that the admissibility of a statement proposed to be put in evidence by the prosecution is likely to be in issue, to explain to the accused his rights in the matter before the trial begins: per Lord Bridge in *Ajodha v The State* [1981] 2 All ER 193, PC at 203.

[208] Occasionally it is convenient to determine admissibility immediately after the jury have been empanelled, as when the evidence of the confession is so important to the prosecution case that without reference to it they cannot even open their case: see *R v Hammond* [1941] 3 All ER 318, CCA.

[209] *R v Hendry* (1988) 153 JP 166, CA, applied in *R v Davis* [1990] Crim LR 860, CA.

confession and the circumstances in which it was made and will be open to cross-examination by the advocate for the defence. The accused may then give evidence and call any witnesses who can support his version of events. The defence witnesses will also be open to cross-examination. The judge may also take into account any relevant evidence already given in the main trial, because the issue of admissibility cannot be tried in total isolation from the whole background of the case.[210] After speeches from the advocates, the judge gives his ruling. If the confession is excluded, then nothing more should be heard of it.[211] If the confession is admitted, it may be put in evidence before the jury. Either way, however, in modern English practice the judge's decision is never revealed to the jury.[212]

Wong Kam-Ming v R

The case of *Wong Kam-Ming v R*[213] gave rise to three important questions concerning the *voir dire*. They were: (i) during cross-examination of an accused on the *voir dire*, whether questions may be put as to the truth of the confession; (ii) whether the prosecution are permitted, on the resumption of the trial proper, to adduce evidence of what the accused said on the *voir dire*; and (iii) whether the prosecution are permitted, in the trial proper, to cross-examine the accused about what he said on the *voir dire*. The accused was charged with murder at a massage parlour. The only evidence against him was a signed confession in which he admitted that he was present at the parlour at the relevant time, had a knife in his hand, and 'chopped' someone. The admissibility of the confession was challenged on the ground that it was not made voluntarily. Under cross-examination on the *voir dire*, the accused was asked questions about the contents of the confession statement which were directed at establishing their truth. In answer, the accused admitted that he was present at the parlour and involved in the incident in question. The trial judge ruled that the signed confession was inadmissible. Before the jury, the judge allowed the prosecution to establish the accused's presence at the parlour by calling the shorthand writers to produce extracts from the transcript of the cross-examination on the *voir dire*. After the accused had given his evidence-in-chief before the jury, the prosecution were also permitted to cross-examine him on inconsistencies between that evidence and his evidence on the *voir dire* as recorded in the shorthand transcript. The accused was convicted and the Court of Appeal of Hong Kong dismissed his appeal. The Privy Council allowed the appeal on three grounds. First, it was held by a majority that the accused had been improperly cross-examined on the *voir dire* as to the truth of his confession statement because the sole issue on the *voir dire* was whether the statement had been made involuntarily, an issue to which its truth or falsity was irrelevant. Second, it was held that the prosecution had been improperly permitted to adduce before the jury evidence of the answers given by the accused on the *voir dire*. In the opinion of their Lordships, such evidence should not be adduced, regardless of whether the confession is excluded or admitted, because a clear distinction should be maintained between the issue of voluntariness, which is alone relevant to the *voir dire*, and the issue of guilt, which falls to be decided in the main trial.[214] Third, it was held that the prosecution had been improperly permitted to

---

[210] *R v Tyrer* (1990) 90 Cr App R 446, CA.

[211] *R v Treacy* [1944] 2 All ER 229, CCA. But see also *R v Rowson* [1986] QB 174, CA (see Ch 7); and s 76A, in this chapter, under **The conditions of admissibility, p 456.**

[212] Per Lord Steyn in *Mitchell v R* [1998] 2 Cr App R 35, PC at 42.

[213] [1980] AC 247.

[214] See also *R v Brophy* [1982] AC 476, HL, discussed in text at **pp 484–5.**

cross-examine the accused on inconsistencies between his evidence before the jury and his statements on the *voir dire* because such a course is only permitted where the *voir dire* results in the admission of the confession and the accused gives evidence before the jury on some matter other than the voluntariness of the confession, which is no longer in issue, and in so doing gives answers which are inconsistent with his testimony on the *voir dire*.

What is the status of the decision in *Wong Kam-Ming v R* in the light of the Police and Criminal Evidence Act 1984? Concerning the first part of the decision, the law remains the same under the Act. The truth of the confession is as irrelevant to the issue of 'oppression' or 'unreliability' as it was to the issue of 'voluntariness'. Section 76(2), it will be recalled, requires the prosecution to prove that the confession, 'notwithstanding that it may be true', was not obtained by the methods it describes.[215] The second and third parts of the decision, insofar as they prohibit the prosecution from leading evidence on or cross-examining the accused about what he said on the *voir dire*, continue to represent the law under the Act but only, it would appear, in relation to statements made by the accused on the *voir dire* which are not 'adverse' to him. Section 82(1) defines a confession to include *any* statement wholly or partly adverse to the person who made it. Thus if, on the *voir dire*, the accused makes an inculpatory statement relevant to his guilt on the offence charged, which can hardly be said to have been obtained by oppression or in circumstances such as to render unreliable any confession which he might have made, then regardless of whether the extrajudicial confession is excluded or admitted, the statement may be given in evidence by the prosecution under s 76(1) and the accused may be cross-examined on any inconsistencies between that statement and the evidence he gives before the jury.[216] If this is correct, it presents the accused with an unenviable choice. An accused seeking to challenge the admissibility of a confession may be obliged to testify on the *voir dire* if his challenge is to have any chance of succeeding. If he elects to contest admissibility, then to the extent that evidence given by him on the *voir dire* is admissible in evidence at the trial, he is in effect deprived of the right to choose not to give evidence before the jury. If he elects to preserve that right, however, he deprives himself of the right to challenge the admissibility of the confession.[217] An accused deprived of his rights in this manner, it has been said, would not receive a fair trial.[218] The solution, it is submitted, is for the judge to exercise his discretion under s 78 of the 1984 Act to exclude the statements made by the accused on the *voir dire* on the grounds that they would have such an adverse effect on the fairness of the proceedings that the court ought not to admit them. The issue of discretion, in this context, arose in *R v Brophy*.[219]

R v Brophy

In *R v* Brophy, the accused was tried by a judge sitting without a jury under the Northern Ireland (Emergency Provisions) Act 1978 on an indictment containing 49 counts including counts of murder, causing explosions, and belonging to a proscribed organization, namely

---

[215] *Wong Kam-Ming v R* is strong persuasive authority that the accused should not be cross-examined as to the truth of his confession on the *voir dire*: *R v Davis* [1990] Crim LR 860, CA.

[216] See Mirfield, 'The Future of the Law of Confessions' [1984] Crim LR 63 at 74.

[217] See generally per Lord Hailsham in *Wong Kam-Ming v R* [1980] AC 247 at 261 and per Lord Fraser in *R v Brophy* [1982] AC 476 at 481. For views different to those expressed, see Murphy [1979] Crim LR 364 and Pattenden (1983) 32 ICLQ 812.

[218] Per Lord Fraser in *R v Brophy* [1982] AC 476 at 482, HL.

[219] [1982] AC 476, HL.

the IRA (count 49). The only evidence connecting him with the crimes was a number of oral and written statements made to the police. The accused challenged the admissibility of the statements on the grounds that they had been obtained by torture and inhuman or degrading treatment. The trial judge, after a *voir dire*, excluded evidence of the statements. The accused, in his evidence-in-chief on the *voir dire*, said that he had been a member of the IRA during most of the period charged in count 49. When the trial resumed, the prosecution called the shorthand writer to prove the statements of the accused as to his membership of the IRA. The accused was acquitted of the first 48 counts, which were unsupported by any evidence, but convicted on count 49. The Court of Appeal in Northern Ireland allowed the appeal and the appeal to the House of Lords was dismissed. It was held that the accused's membership of the IRA was relevant to the issue on the *voir dire* because the police would probably have known this and therefore would not only have been more hostile to him but also would have expected him to have received instruction on how to avoid succumbing to the normal techniques of interrogation not involving physical ill-treatment. It was further held that, in any event, the evidence-in-chief given by an accused on the *voir dire* should be treated as relevant, unless clearly and obviously irrelevant, with the accused being given the benefit of any reasonable doubt.[220] The House concluded that the relevance of the evidence in question to the issue at the *voir dire* having been established, the consequence was that it was inadmissible in the substantive trial. In answer to a submission by the prosecution that if the evidence on the *voir dire* were admissible in the trial proper, the accused would be adequately safeguarded if the judge had a discretion to exclude any such evidence which would prejudice him unfairly, Lord Fraser said:[221]

> The right of the accused to give evidence at the *voir dire* without affecting his right to remain silent at the substantive trial is in my opinion absolute and is not to be made conditional on an exercise of judicial discretion.

Now that the actual decision in this case would appear to have been reversed by the 1984 Act, it is submitted that evidence given on the *voir dire* should be excluded from the trial proper by exercise of the discretion under s 78.[222]

The trial

Once the trial judge has ruled that a confession is admissible, the weight to be attached to it, which depends upon its content and all the circumstances in which it was obtained, is entirely a question of fact for the jury.[223] On the resumption of the trial proper, therefore, the defence is fully entitled to adduce evidence and cross-examine prosecution witnesses with a view to impeaching the credibility of the person to whom the confession was allegedly made and showing, for example, that the confession was fabricated, in whole or in part, or made

---

[220] However, if the accused goes out of his way to boast of having committed the crimes charged or uses the witness box as a platform for a political speech, such evidence will almost certainly be irrelevant to the issue at the *voir dire*: per Lord Fraser [1982] AC 476 at 481, HL.

[221] [1982] AC 476 at 483, HL.

[222] However, concerning Lord Fraser's reference to the 'right to remain silent at the substantive trial', see now the Criminal Justice and Public Order Act 1994, s 35 (**Ch 16**) and generally Mirfield, 'Two Side-Effects of Sections 34 to 37 of the Criminal Justice and Public Order Act 1994' [1995] Crim LR 612.

[223] Per Lord Parker CJ in *R v Burgess* [1968] 2 QB 112, CA at 117–18. But see the 1984 Act, s 77 (**Ch 8**).

in circumstances different from those alleged by the prosecution. Although, as we have seen, the truth of the confession is irrelevant on the *voir dire*, it is a crucial issue for the jury to consider.[224] The judge, pursuant to s 67(11) of the 1984 Act, may refer the jury to any relevant breaches of the Codes.[225] Moreover, the House of Lords in *R v Mushtaq*,[226] disapproving *Chan Wei Keung v R*,[227] held by a majority that where the judge has ruled that a confession was not obtained by oppression nor in consequence of anything said or done which was likely to render unreliable any confession, but there is some evidence before the jury that the confession may have been so obtained, and they conclude that the alleged confession was or may have been so obtained, they must disregard it. If the jury reach such a conclusion, to permit them to rely upon the confession would be to fly in the face of the policy considerations said to underlie s 76(2), namely that the rejection of an improperly obtained confession is dependent not only upon possible unreliability, but also upon the principle that a man cannot be compelled to incriminate himself and upon the importance that attaches in a civilized society to proper behaviour by the police towards those in their custody. The judge should therefore direct the jury that unless they are satisfied beyond reasonable doubt that the confession was not obtained by the means set out in s 76(2)(a) and (b), they should disregard it.[228]

The trial judge, once he has determined that a confession is admissible under s 76 of the 1984 Act, has no power, at some later stage in the trial, to reconsider its admissibility as a matter of *law*. In *R v Sat-Bhambra*[229] a confession was ruled to be admissible after a trial within a trial in which a doctor had given expert evidence to the effect that the accused, who suffered from a mild form of diabetes, could have been affected by hypoglycaemia at the time of his interrogation. When the doctor was called in the trial proper, his evidence on the issue came out more in favour of the accused. The trial judge, however, declined to reconsider his decision on admissibility on the grounds that he was precluded from so doing by the terms of s 76. The Court of Appeal held that the trial judge had acted properly. Section 76 refers to a confession which the prosecution 'proposes to give in evidence' and which the court 'shall not allow . . . to be given in evidence' and therefore, once the judge has ruled that a confession is admissible, section 76 ceases to have effect. Section 78, which, similarly, refers to evidence on which the prosecution 'proposes to rely', also ceases to have effect.[230] The judge, however, is not powerless: if, in the light of the evidence given in the trial proper, he concludes that his previous decision on admissibility has been invalidated, he may, in the exercise of his discretion to exclude under s 82(3), direct the jury to disregard the confession.[231] Alternatively, and depending on the circumstances of the case, he may either point out to the jury the evidence which affects the weight of the confession and leave the matter in their hands or, if he thinks that the matter is not capable of remedy by any form of direction, discharge the jury from giving a verdict. The same options, presumably, would be open

[224] *R v Murray* (1950) 34 Cr App R 203 at 207.

[225] See *R v Kenny* [1992] Crim LR 800, CA.

[226] [2005] 1 WLR 1513, HL.

[227] [1967] 2 AC 160, PC.

[228] *R v Pham* [2008] EWCA Crim 3182.

[229] (1989) 88 Cr App R 55, CA.

[230] Cf per Russell LJ in *R v Liverpool Juvenile Court, ex p R* [1987] 2 All ER 668 at 672–3, dealing with similar issues in relation to summary trials (see **Ch 2**).

[231] Section 82(3) is the source of the power, but the judge is likely to re-apply the s 78 criteria in the light of the new evidence: see *R v Hassan* [1995] Crim LR 404, CA.

to a judge when a confession is put in evidence and the accused *then* gives evidence to the effect that it was obtained by one of the methods described in section 76(2).[232]

Confessions implicating co-accused

If an accused goes into the witness box and gives evidence implicating a co-accused, then what he says becomes evidence for all purposes of the case and accordingly may be used by the jury as evidence against the co-accused.[233] However, subject to three exceptions, considered later in this section, where a confession is given in evidence by the prosecution and implicates both its maker and a co-accused, it is no evidence against the co-accused because a confession is admissible as evidence of the truth of its contents only as against its maker. In these circumstances, therefore, the judge is duty bound to impress upon the jury that the confession cannot be used against the co-accused.[234] It may be doubted, however, whether such a direction, even if clear and emphatic, can ever fully remove the prejudice likely to be caused to the co-accused.[235] In one case it was said that it would require mental gymnastics of Olympic standards for the jury to approach their task without prejudice.[236] One obvious solution is to order separate trials for the accused, but although the Court of Appeal in *R v Lake*[237] recognized that exceptionally this can be done, it nevertheless upheld a trial judge's refusal to order a separate trial. Another solution is to edit the confession, for example by replacing the names of any co-accused with letters of the alphabet or expressions such as 'another person' or 'someone'.[238] Alternatively, the prosecution advocate may agree not to read those parts of a confession statement which implicate a co-accused but have no real bearing on the case against its author. However, if the reference to the co-accused is exculpatory of the maker of the statement, he is entitled to have the statement read out in its entirety. As Lord Goddard CJ observed in *R v Gunewardene*,[239] in a passage approved by the Privy Council in *Lobban v R*:[240]

> It not infrequently happens that a prisoner, in making a statement, though admitting his guilt up to a certain extent, puts greater blame upon the co-prisoner, or is asserting that certain of his actions were really innocent and it was the conduct of the co-prisoner that gave them a sinister appearance or led to the belief that the prisoner making the statement was implicated in the crime. In such a case that prisoner would have a right to have the whole statement read and could complain if the prosecution picked out certain passages and left out others . . .

[232] It may also be assumed that the judge has a discretion, in this situation, to require the relevant prosecution witnesses to be recalled for further cross-examination: see per Lord Bridge in *Ajodha v The State* [1981] 2 All ER 193, PC at 202–3.

[233] See per Humphreys J in *R v Rudd* (1948) 32 Cr App R 138.

[234] *R v Gunewardene* [1951] 2 KB 600, CCA. See also *R v Blake* [1993] Crim LR 133, CA and per Lord Steyn in *Lobban v R* [1995] 1 WLR 877, PC at 889. See also the Crown Court Compendium (July 2019), Part 1, 14–15, para 7 and Example 1.

[235] See, eg, *R v Williams; R v Davis* (1992) 95 Cr App R 1, CA. See also Thornton, 'The Prejudiced Defendant: Unfairness Suffered by a Defendant in a Joint Trial' [2003] Crim LR 433.

[236] *R v Silcott* [1987] Crim LR 765, CC.

[237] (1976) 64 Cr App R 172.

[238] As suggested in *R v Silcott* [1987] Crim LR 765, CC. See also *R v Rogers and Tarran* [1971] Crim LR 413 and *R v Mathias* [1989] Crim LR 64, CC. However, insofar as *R v Silcott* and *R v Mathias* suggest that a judge has a discretionary power at the request of one accused to exclude evidence tending to support the defence of another, they do not correctly reflect the law: per Lord Steyn in *Lobban v R* [1995] 1 WLR 877, PC at 888–9 (see Ch 2).

[239] [1951] 2 KB 600, CCA at 610–11.

[240] [1995] 1 WLR 877, PC at 888 (see Ch 2).

In three exceptional situations, a confession may be admitted not only as evidence against its maker but also as evidence against a co-accused. The first exception was established in *R v Hayter*,[241] where the House of Lords held, by a majority, that in a joint trial of two or more accused for a joint offence, a jury are entitled to consider first the case in respect of accused A which is solely based on his own out-of-court admissions, and then to use their findings of A's guilt as a fact to be used evidentially in respect of co-accused B, and further that where proof of A's guilt is necessary for there to be a case to answer against B, there will be a case to answer against him notwithstanding that the only evidence of A's guilt is his own out-of-court admissions. A's confession, however, can only be admitted against B on two conditions: first, that the jury are sufficiently sure of its truthfulness to decide that on that basis alone they can safely convict A; and second, that the jury are expressly directed that when deciding the case against B they must disregard entirely anything said out of court by A which might otherwise be thought to incriminate B. In reaching this conclusion, the majority were heavily influenced by the policy considerations underlying s 74 of the 1984 Act, whereby the fact that someone other than the accused has been convicted of an offence is admissible to prove, where to do so is relevant to an issue in the proceedings, that that person committed the offence.[242] If there had been separate trials and A had been convicted, evidence of the conviction would have been admissible under s 74 of the 1984 Act in a subsequent trial of B. *R v Hayter* was distinguished in *Persad v State of Trinidad and Tobago*[243] where (i) the co-accused was *not* jointly liable for the offence; and (ii) it *was* sought to rely on A's statement insofar as it incriminated B.

The second exception is where the co-accused by his words or conduct accepts the truth of the statement so as to make all or part of it a confession statement of his own.[244]

The third exception, which is perhaps best understood in terms of implied agency, applies in the case of conspiracy: statements (or acts) of one conspirator which the jury are satisfied were said (or done) in the execution or furtherance of the common design are admissible in evidence against another conspirator, even though he was not present at the time, to prove the nature and scope of the conspiracy, provided that there is some independent evidence to show the existence of the conspiracy and that the other conspirator was a party to it.[245] Thus in *R v Blake and Tye*,[246] where the accused were charged with conspiracy to pass goods through the Custom House without paying duty, it was held that whereas a false entry by T in a counterfoil of a cheque, by which he received his share of the proceeds of the crime, was not admissible against B because it was not made in pursuance of the conspiracy, but simply as a matter of record and convenience, another false entry by T in a day book could be used in evidence against B since it was made in the execution or furtherance of their common

---

[241] [2005] 1 WLR 605, HL.

[242] See Ch 4.

[243] [2008] 1 Cr App R 140 (9), PC.

[244] See generally, in this chapter, under **Statements made in the presence of the accused, p 490**.

[245] *R v Shellard* (1840) 9 C&P 277, *R v Meany* (1867) 10 Cox CC 506, *R v Walters, R v Tovey* (1979) 69 Cr App R 115, CA, and *R v Jenkins* [2003] Crim LR 107, CA. However, if there are two conspiracies, what A does in pursuance of the first is not admissible against B in respect of his involvement in the second: *R v Gray* [1995] 2 Cr App R 100, CA at 131. For a comparative examination of this exception to the hearsay rule, including an evaluation of its possible rationale, see Spencer, 'The common enterprise exception to the hearsay rule' (2007) 11 E&P 106.

[246] (1844) 6 QB 126.

design. *R v Blake and Tye* was applied in *R v Devonport*,[247] in which the prosecution were allowed to rely on a document, dictated by one accused, which showed the proposed division of the proceeds of the conspiracy among all five accused.[248]

It does not matter in what order the evidence of the statements (or acts) of the conspirator and the 'independent evidence' is adduced.[249] Evidence of the statements (or acts) may be admitted conditionally, that is, conditional upon some other evidence of the common design being adduced; if it transpires that there is no other evidence of common design, then the statements (or acts) should be excluded.[250] The decision whether there is sufficient 'independent evidence' is for the judge alone,[251] but any consequential risk that the jury may see the 'independent evidence' as unconvincing and yet act upon the statement or act of the one conspirator in the absence of the other, may be avoided by directing the jury about any shortcomings in the evidence of the statement or act, including, if it be the case, the absence of any opportunity to cross-examine the maker of the statement or act and the absence of corroborative evidence.[252]

The following elaborations on the principle derive from *R v Platten*.[253] (1) The exception does not cover narrative, after the conclusion of the conspiracy, describing past events. (2) It covers statements made during a conspiracy and as part of the natural process of making the arrangements to carry it out, which are admissible not just as to the nature and extent of the conspiracy, but also as to the participation in it of persons absent when the statements were made. (3) Such statements can be admitted against all the conspirators even if made by one conspirator to a non-conspirator. (4) Statements about a conspirator having 'second thoughts' would be made in furtherance of the common design, because it is typical of a conspiracy for one conspirator to have doubts and to be persuaded by his co-conspirators to forget them. (5) Statements made before a conspirator was alleged to have joined the agreement can only be evidence of the origin of the conspiracy, not evidence of his part in it.

The principle does apply when, although a conspiracy is not charged, two or more people are engaged in a common enterprise: the acts and declarations of one in pursuance of the common purpose are admissible against another.[254] This extension of the principle applies to the commission of a substantive offence or series of offences by two or more people acting in concert, but is limited to evidence which shows the involvement of each accused in the commission of the offence or offences.[255] However, it does not apply to cases where individual defendants are charged with a number of separate substantive offences and the terms of a common enterprise are not proved or are ill-defined.[256] The rule is that the acts and declarations of one, in furtherance of a sufficiently defined common design, are admissible to prove a substantive offence committed by another alone, but in pursuance of the same common design.[257]

---

[247] [1996] 1 Cr App R 221, CA.

[248] See also *R v Ilyas and Knight* [1996] Crim LR 810, CA; and *R v A Ltd* [2016] 4 WLR 176, CA: where a company (a separate legal personality) is one of the accused in a conspiracy, evidence of the intention of a 'controlling mind' (eg, a director) may be relevant and admissible to prove the guilt of the company.

[249] *R v Governor of Pentonville Prison, ex p Osman* [1990] 1 WLR 277, QBD at 316.

[250] *R v Donat* (1985) 82 Cr App R 173, CA.

[251] *R v Barham* [1997] 2 Cr App R 119, CA and *R v King* [2012] EWCA Crim 805, where it was said that it is also for the judge alone to decide whether the statement (or act) was said (done) in furtherance of the conspiracy.

[252] *R v King* [2012] EWCA Crim 805, citing *Ahern v R* [1988] ALR 162, High Court of Australia.

[253] [2006] EWCA Crim 140.

[254] See, eg, *R v Jones* [1997] 2 Cr App R 119, CA.

[255] *R v Gray* [1995] 2 Cr App R 100, CA. See also *Tripodi v R* (1961) 104 CLR 1, High Court of Australia.

[256] *R v Murray* [1997] 2 Cr App R 136, CA, per Otton LJ at 148.

[257] *R v Williams* [2002] EWCA Crim 2208, approving *R v Murray* [1997] 2 Cr App R 136, CA, per Otton LJ at 148.

The foregoing common law exceptions have been preserved by statute. Section 118(1) of the Criminal Justice Act 2003 preserves: '5 Any rule of law relating to the admissibility of confessions . . . in criminal proceedings' and '7 Any rule of law under which in criminal proceedings a statement made by a party to a common enterprise is admissible against another party to the enterprise as evidence of any matter stated'.

Editing

Where a confession is given in evidence, the whole statement, including qualifications, explanations, or other exculpatory parts of it should be admitted so that the jury can fairly decide whether the statement, viewed as a whole, incriminates the accused.[258] However, where a confession statement contains inadmissible matter prejudicial to the accused, such as a reference to his previous convictions or bad character, it should be edited so as to eliminate the offending material.[259] The advocates may confer on the matter and, if necessary, the judge can take his part in ensuring that the statement is edited properly and to the right degree.[260] Although the rule is one of practice rather than law, a failure to edit may result in a conviction on indictment being quashed.[261] If the confession and the offending material are so interwoven as to be inseparable, or the removal of the latter would seriously alter the sense and meaning of the former so that they stand or fall together, the judge may, in the exercise of his discretion, exclude the entire statement on the grounds that its prejudicial effect outweighs its probative value.[262]

Statements made in the presence of the accused

Under s 82(1) of the 1984 Act, a confession, as we have seen, includes any statement adverse to the person who made it 'whether made in words or otherwise'. It would seem, therefore, that under the Act, as at common law, the accused may accept the accusation of another so as to make it wholly or in part a confession statement of his own, not only by his words but also, in appropriate circumstances, by his conduct, demeanour, or even silence. An alternative basis for the same conclusion is the inclusive nature of the statutory definition. Either way, if this construction is correct, it would enable the accused, in appropriate circumstances, to make a representation under s 76(2) (or s 76A(2)) and thereby oblige the prosecution (or co-accused) to prove that such a confession was not obtained by the methods described in s 76(2) (or s 76A(2)). If such a confession is admitted under s 76 (or s 76A), the common law authorities will provide guidance to the judge as to how she should direct the

---

[258] *R v Pearce* (1979) 69 Cr App R 365, CA at 369–70. How the judge should properly direct the jury in relation to a statement containing both inculpatory and exculpatory parts is considered in Ch 6, **Previous consistent or self-serving statements, p 193.**

[259] When a suspect is interviewed about more offences than are eventually made the subject of charges, a fresh statement should be prepared and signed omitting all questions and answers about the uncharged offences unless either they might appropriately be taken into consideration or evidence about them is admissible on the charges preferred (eg as similar fact evidence). It may, however, be desirable to replace the omitted questions and answers with a phrase such as: 'After referring to some other matters, I then said . . .', so as to make it clear that part of the interview has been omitted: see *Criminal Practice Directions* V, para 16A.4(b).

[260] *R v Weaver* [1968] 1 QB 353, CA.

[261] *R v Knight; R v Thompson* (1946) 31 Cr App R 52, CCA and *Turner v Underwood* [1948] 2 KB 284, DC.

[262] See discussion of s 82(3), in this chapter, under **Section 82(3) of the Police and Criminal Evidence Act 1984, p 468.**

jury; and the common law principle of conditional admissibility will still apply (so that, in appropriate circumstances, the judge may direct the jury to disregard the evidence). The common law rules relating to statements made in the presence of the accused, which now fall to be considered in more detail, have been preserved by s 118 of the Criminal Justice Act 2003. Section 118 preserves '5 Any rule of law relating to the admissibility of confessions . . . in criminal proceedings'.[263]

In *R v Norton*[264] the accused was convicted of having sexual intercourse with a girl under 13. Evidence was admitted of a statement made by the girl and directed at the accused, in which she identified him as the offender, and of his replies. The conviction was quashed on the grounds that there was no evidence that the accused had accepted the truth of the statement. Pickford J, giving the judgment of the Court of Criminal Appeal, made a number of important observations which may be summarized in terms of four propositions:

1. Statements made in the presence of the accused upon an occasion on which he might reasonably be expected to make some observation, explanation, or denial are admissible in evidence if the judge is satisfied that there is evidence fit to be submitted to the jury that the accused by his answer to the statements, whether given by word or conduct, including silence, acknowledged the truth of the whole or part of them.

2. If there is no such evidence fit to be left to the jury, the contents of the statements should be excluded, but they may be given in evidence even when they were denied by the accused as it is possible that a denial may be given under such circumstances and in such a manner as to constitute evidence from which an acknowledgment may be inferred.[265]

3. If the statements are admitted, the question whether the accused's answer, by words or conduct, did or did not in fact amount to an acknowledgment of them should be left to the jury.

4. The judge should direct the jury that if they conclude that the accused acknowledged the truth of the whole or any part of the statement, they may take the statement or part of it into consideration as evidence, but that without such an acknowledgment they should disregard the statement altogether.[266]

In *R v Christie*[267] the accused was convicted of indecent assault on a boy, who gave unsworn evidence. The boy's mother and a constable gave evidence to the effect that shortly after the alleged act, the boy approached the accused, identified him by saying, 'That is the man', and described the assault. They also gave evidence that the accused then said, 'I am innocent'. The Court of Criminal Appeal quashed the conviction on the grounds that, the accused having denied the truth of the boy's statement, the evidence of the mother and

---

[263] As to inferences that may be drawn pursuant to *statute* from an accused's silence on being questioned under caution by a constable or on being charged, see the Criminal Justice and Public Order Act 1994, ss 34, 36, 37, and 38 (see Ch 16).

[264] [1910] 2 KB 496, CCA.

[265] The denial may also give rise to such an inference if inconsistent with statements subsequently made by him or inconsistent with his defence at the trial, as when he denies an assault but at his trial pleads self-defence: see per Lord Moulton in *R v Christie* [1914] AC 545, HL at 560. See further *R v Z* [2003] 1 WLR 1489, CA.

[266] Cf *R v Black* (1922) 16 Cr App R 118, CCA.

[267] [1914] AC 545, HL.

constable had been improperly admitted. The House of Lords quashed the conviction on a different ground. However, it approved the approach taken in *R v Norton*, although it regarded the principles enunciated by Pickford J as valuable rules of guidance rather than strict rules of law.

When a person is accused of a crime in circumstances such that it would be reasonable to expect some explanation or denial from him, whether the accused's silence can give rise to an inference that he accepted the truth of the charge would appear to depend upon whether it was made by a police officer or some other person in authority or charged with the investigation of the crime as opposed to some other person with whom the accused can be said to have been 'on even terms'. In *Hall v R*[268] the question arose whether the silence of the accused *before* being cautioned could give rise to an inference that he accepted the truth of an accusation made by or through a police officer. The accused was convicted of unlawful possession of drugs which were found in premises occupied by him and two co-accused. A police officer told the accused that one of the co-accused had said that the drugs belonged to him, that is, the accused. The accused, who at that stage had not been cautioned, remained silent. All of the accused were convicted. The Privy Council advised that the accused's conviction be quashed. Lord Diplock, delivering the judgment of the Board, said:[269]

> It is a clear and widely known principle of the common law in Jamaica, as in England, that a person is entitled to refrain from answering a question put to him for the purpose of discovering whether he has committed a criminal offence. *A fortiori* he is under no obligation to comment when he is informed that someone else has accused him of an offence. It may be that in very exceptional circumstances an inference may be drawn from a failure to give an explanation or a disclaimer, but in their Lordships' view silence alone on being informed by a police officer that someone else has made an accusation against him cannot give rise to an inference that the person to whom this information is communicated accepts the truth of the accusation . . .
>
> The caution merely serves to remind the accused of a right which he already possesses at common law. The fact that in a particular case he has not been reminded of it is no ground for inferring that his silence was not in exercise of that right, but was an acknowledgment of the truth of the accusation.

The reasoning in *Hall v R* must now be read subject to ss 34, 36, and 37 of the Criminal Justice and Public Order Act 1994 and the corresponding caution which has replaced the caution in use at the time of the decision.[270] However, the decision in *Hall v R* may still be good law, being a case concerned with the accused's silence before caution.

Where there are two suspects and one of them answers a question put by an officer to both of them by telling a lie, similar principles apply to the issue whether the other of them, by his silence, adopted the answer of the first.[271]

In *Parkes v R*[272] the appellant was convicted of murder. At the trial, the victim's mother gave evidence that, having found her daughter injured, she went to the appellant and accused him twice of stabbing her daughter. The appellant said nothing and, when the mother threatened

---

[268] [1971] 1 WLR 298, PC.

[269] Ibid at 301.

[270] See Ch 16.

[271] *R v Collins* [2004] 1 WLR 1705, CA.

[272] [1976] 1 WLR 1251, PC.

to detain him while the police were sent for, drew a knife and attempted to stab her. On these facts the Privy Council applied the following dictum of Cave J in *R v Mitchell*:[273]

> Undoubtedly, when persons are speaking on even terms, and a charge is made, and the person charged says nothing, and expresses no indignation, and does nothing to repel the charge, that is some evidence to show that he admits the charge to be true.

Accordingly, it was held that the trial judge had not erred in instructing the jury that the appellant's reactions to the accusations, including his silence, were matters from which they could, if they saw fit, infer that he had accepted the truth of the accusation.[274] *Hall v R* was distinguished on the grounds that, in that case, the person by whom the accusation was communicated was a police officer and there was no evidence of the accused's reaction other than his silence.

It seems that the accuser and the accused may be regarded as being on even terms notwithstanding that the police have brought them together and are present when the accusation is made. In *R v Horne*,[275] shortly after an assault, the police took the accused to the scene of the crime and sat him down opposite the victim. It was held that the accused's silent reaction to an accusation then made by the victim, but unprompted by the officers present, was capable of amounting to an acceptance of the accusation made.

The dictum of Cave J in *R v Mitchell* was also applied in *R v Chandler*.[276] The accused was convicted of conspiracy to defraud, the only evidence against him being an interview with a detective sergeant in the presence of his solicitor when, both *before* and *after* being cautioned, he answered some questions and remained silent or refused to answer others. The jury were directed that it was for them to decide whether the accused had remained silent before the caution in exercise of his common law right or because he thought that had he answered he might have incriminated himself. The Court of Appeal, satisfied that the accused and the detective sergeant were speaking on equal terms, since the former had his solicitor present to advise him and, if needed, subsequently to testify as to what had been said, held that some comment on the accused's lack of frankness before he was cautioned was justified. The conviction was quashed, however, on the grounds that the trial judge had short-circuited the proper intellectual process, which involved directing the jury to determine, first, whether the accused's silence amounted to an acceptance by him of what was said and, second, if satisfied that he did accept what was said, whether guilt could reasonably be inferred from what he had accepted. The importance of the decision lies in the reservations expressed about the dicta of Lord Diplock in *R v Hall*. Lawton LJ was of the opinion that they seemed to conflict with *R v Christie* and the earlier authorities and said:[277]

> The law has long accepted that an accused person is not bound to incriminate himself; but it does not follow that a failure to answer an accusation or question when an answer could reasonably be expected may not provide some evidence in support of an accusation. Whether it does will depend on the circumstances.

---

[273] (1892) 17 Cox CC 503 at 508.
[274] For a further example, see *R v Coll* [2005] EWCA Crim 3675.
[275] [1990] Crim LR 188, CA.
[276] [1976] 1 WLR 585, CA.
[277] Ibid at 589.

In a later passage, his Lordship said:[278]

> We do not accept that a police officer always has an advantage over someone he is questioning
> . . . A young detective questioning a local dignitary in the course of an inquiry into alleged local
> government corruption may be very much at a disadvantage. This kind of situation is to be con-
> trasted with that of a tearful housewife accused of shoplifting or of a parent being questioned
> about the suspected wrongdoing of his son.

However, it seems most unlikely that reasoning of this kind could now be allowed, in effect,
to extend the circumstances in which an adverse inference can be properly drawn under ss
34, 36, and 37 of the Criminal Justice and Public Order Act 1994.[279]

Facts discovered in consequence of inadmissible confessions

At common law, the fact that a confession was inadmissible did not affect the admissibility
of any incriminating facts discovered in consequence of that confession. In *R v Warickshall*[280]
a woman was charged with receiving stolen property. In consequence of a confession made
by her, the property was found concealed in her bed at her lodgings. The confession was
excluded on the grounds that it had been obtained by promises of favour. The advocate for
the defence argued that evidence of the fact of finding the stolen property in her custody
should also be excluded since it was obtained in consequence of the inadmissible evidence.
Rejecting this argument, it was said:

> Confessions are received in evidence, or rejected as inadmissible, under a consideration whether
> they are or are not entitled to credit . . . This principle respecting confessions has no application
> whatever as to the admission or rejection of facts, whether the knowledge of them be obtained
> in consequence of an extorted confession, or whether it arises from any other source; for a fact,
> if it exists at all, must exist invariably in the same manner, whether the confession from which
> it is derived be in other respects true or false.[281]

The Criminal Law Revision Committee was in no doubt that this rule should be preserved
on the grounds that to prevent the police from using any 'leads' obtained from an inadmissible confession would interfere unduly with justice and the detection of crime.[282] The rule is
preserved by s 76(4) and by s 76A(4) of the 1984 Act, both of which provide that:

> The fact that a confession is wholly or partly excluded in pursuance of this section shall not
> affect the admissibility in evidence—
> (a) of any facts discovered as a result of the confession; . . .

These subsections appear to be compatible with the rights guaranteed by Art 6 of the European
Convention on Human Rights, especially given the court's discretionary power to exclude
facts discovered as a result of inadmissible confessions under s 78(1) of the 1984 Act.[283]

---

[278] Ibid at 590.

[279] Ch 16.

[280] (1783) 1 Leach 263.

[281] See also, in relation to evidence of facts discovered as a result of an illegal search, *Kuruma v R* [1955] AC 197
at 203–5 and *King v R* [1969] 1 AC 304.

[282] 11th Report, Cmnd 4991 (1972), para 68.

[283] See *Her Majesty's Advocate v P (Scotland)* [2011] UKSC 44.

Where incriminating facts discovered in consequence of an inadmissible confession are admitted in evidence, the question arises whether, notwithstanding that the confession itself must be excluded, evidence is admissible to show that the discovery of the facts in question was made as a result of the confession statement. For example, if an inadmissible confession of theft includes a statement that the stolen goods are hidden in a particular place, and they are found there, can the prosecution give evidence not only that they found the goods at that place but also that they found them as a result of something which the accused said? The importance of this question lies in the fact that proof that the stolen goods were hidden in a particular place, without reference to the confession, will do little or nothing to advance the prosecution case unless, as it happens, there is some link between the accused and the goods because, for example, they were found in a place frequented by him, such as his house or place of work, or bore his fingerprints. The cases at common law were in conflict. The Criminal Law Revision Committee was opposed to the admissibility of any part of the confession on the grounds that this would involve a decision on the part of the judge as to whether, in his opinion, the confession or part of it was likely to be true, an opinion which, although not binding on the jury, would be difficult for them not to be impressed by. The majority were in favour of allowing evidence to be given that the discovery of the incriminating facts was made 'as a result of a statement made by the accused'. The minority dissented on the grounds that the jury should not be informed indirectly of something of which the interests of justice require that they should not be informed directly.[284] Subject to cases in which the *defence* choose to give evidence as to how the incriminating facts were discovered, the minority view is reflected in s 76(5) and (6) and in s 76A(5) and (6) of the 1984 Act, which provide that:

(5) Evidence that a fact to which this subsection applies was discovered as a result of a statement made by an accused person shall not be admissible unless evidence of how it was discovered is given by him or on his behalf.

(6) Subsection (5) above applies—
  (a) to any fact discovered as a result of a confession which is wholly excluded in pursuance of this section; and
  (b) to any fact discovered as a result of a confession which is partly so excluded, if the fact is discovered as a result of the excluded part of the confession.

Thus where part of a confession to murder, the entirety of which is excluded because extracted by police brutality, indicates the location of the murder weapon, that part remains inadmissible even if later shown to be reliable by the discovery of the weapon in the place indicated.[285]

The Committee was also of the opinion that where something in a confession statement shows that the accused speaks, writes, or expresses himself in a particular manner and this serves to identify him with the offender, so much of the confession as is necessary to show such characteristics should be admissible for that purpose.[286] The point was illustrated by reference to *R v Voisin*.[287] The accused was convicted of murdering a woman whose body was found in a parcel together with a piece of paper bearing the handwritten words 'Bladie Belgiam'. The accused, without being cautioned, was asked by the police to write down 'Bloody Belgian'. He wrote down 'Bladie Belgiam' and this writing was admitted in evidence at his trial.

---

[284] 11th Report, Cmnd 4991 (1972), para 69.

[285] See *Lam Chi-ming v R* [1991] 3 All ER 172, PC.

[286] 11th Report, Cmnd 4991 (1972), para 69.

[287] [1918] 1 KB 531, CCA.

The accused appealed on the grounds, inter alia, that he should have been cautioned before being asked to write the words in question. The appeal failed. Although the case did not concern an inadmissible confession, the Committee was of the view that, had the words been written in an inadmissible confession, that part of it should have been admissible, not as evidence of the truth of its contents, but for the purpose of identifying the accused with the offender. Section 76(4) and s 76A(4) of the 1984 Act both provide that:

> The fact that a confession is wholly or partly excluded in pursuance of this section shall not affect the admissibility in evidence—
> (b) where the confession is relevant as showing that the accused speaks, writes or expresses himself in a particular way, of so much of the confession as is necessary to show that he does so.

ADDITIONAL READING

Gudjohnsson, *The Psychology of Interrogations and Confessions* (Chichester, 2003).
An integration of scientific knowledge of the psychological processes and research relating to interrogation with the practical, investigative, and legal issues that bear upon obtaining and using in court evidence from the interrogation of suspects. There is a particular focus upon aspects of vulnerability, confabulation, and false confessions.

Mirfield, *Silence, Confessions and Improperly Obtained Evidence* (Oxford, 1997).
An examination of the law, and the principles underlying the law, relating to confessions, improperly obtained evidence, and the 'right to silence'. Consideration is given to the position in England and the alternative approaches taken in Scotland, Ireland, Australia, Canada, and the USA.

Mirfield, 'Two Side-Effects of Sections 34 to 37 of the Criminal Justice and Public Order Act 1994' [1995] Crim LR 612.
An article suggesting that the changes effected by ss 34–37 of the Criminal Justice and Public Order Act 1994 (inferences from failure to mention facts when questioned or charged and from failure to testify and inferences from failure or refusal to account for objects, substances, etc) may have changed common law doctrine in two ways: (i) it may now be permissible to draw an inference that a suspect who remains silent in the face of police accusations accepts them as true; and (ii) restrictions on prosecution use of statements made by an accused on the *voir dire* while challenging the admission in evidence of a confession may have been attenuated.

Spencer, 'The common enterprise exception to the hearsay rule' (2007) 11 E&P 106.
A comparative examination of the common enterprise exception to the hearsay rule designed to clarify the requirements and functioning of the rule in England and Wales.

QUESTION

Dodi is arrested on suspicion of possession of illegal drugs with intent to supply. At the police station, the police for no good reason refuse Dodi access to his solicitor. They conduct a lawful strip search of Dodi, but find nothing. While Dodi is still naked, the interrogation begins. Dodi says that he knows his rights and refuses to answer questions, but 20 minutes later asks the police whether they will let him get dressed and see his solicitor if he admits his guilt. The police agree, but only if Dodi also tells them where they can find further evidence to implicate him. Dodi then admits his guilt and tells the police that they can find further evidence against him at his house. He is then allowed to get dressed and to contact his solicitor. When the solicitor arrives, Dodi tells her that his admission of guilt was false and only made because of his humiliation at being naked and because, being a drug user, he was undergoing withdrawal symptoms. The police conduct a lawful search of Dodi's house and find cannabis and weights and scales on which there are traces of cannabis resin.

At Dodi's trial, will the following be admissible?

(a) Evidence of Dodi's admissions to the police.

(b) Evidence of what the police found in Dodi's house.

 For a note-form answer see the online resources, accessible at
www.oup.com/he/keane-mckeown13e.

Adverse inferences from an accused's silence or conduct

16

Key issues

- What adverse inferences, if any, should be drawn against an accused, and why, from:

  - his failure to testify;

  - his failure, when questioned or charged, to mention facts which he could reasonably have been expected to have mentioned at that time and which he later relies on in his defence at trial;

  - his failure, on arrest, to account for any object, substance, or mark that the police reasonably believe may be attributable to his participation in the commission of an offence;

  - his refusal to consent to the police taking an intimate sample, such as a sample of blood, semen, or urine; and

  - his failure to provide advance disclosure of the defence case, the nature of his defence or the facts on which he takes issue with the prosecution?

- In the case of the second set of circumstances set out above (failure, when questioned or charged, to mention facts, etc), if the accused remained silent on legal advice, should the answer be the same?

Inferences from silence

Background—The 'right to silence'

The 'right to silence' formerly comprised two 'rights', the privilege against self-incrimination, that is, the freedom of an accused from being compelled to incriminate himself, and the 'right' not to have adverse inferences drawn from his silence. More narrowly examined, the 'right to silence' encompassed a number of specific 'rights', more accurately rules, including the following.

1. A suspect is under no legal obligation to assist the police with their inquiries.[1]

2. An accused is not obliged to give advance notice of the evidence in support of his defence; and it is wrong to make adverse comments about the fact that an accused, having been cautioned by the police, (a) remained silent;[2] (b) declined to answer some questions;[3] or (c) failed to reveal his defence.[4]

3. An accused is not a compellable witness.[5]

4. Although in appropriate circumstances a judge may invite a jury to draw adverse inferences from failure to testify, they should be directed not to assume guilt from such a failure.[6]

Prior to the Criminal Justice and Public Order Act 1994 (the 1994 Act), few provisions operated to curtail the 'right to silence' to any significant degree. Two important examples may be given. First, under the Criminal Procedure Rules, an accused who wants to introduce expert evidence must serve it on the court officer and each other party and, if he does not, may not introduce the evidence unless every other party agrees or the court gives permission.[7] Second, under the Criminal Justice Act 1987, in cases of serious or complex fraud, although an accused may depart from the case which he disclosed in pursuance of a requirement imposed by the court at a preparatory hearing, if he does so depart, or if he fails to comply with such a requirement, the judge or, with the leave of the judge, any other party, may make such comment as appears to the judge to be appropriate, and the jury or, in the case of a trial without jury, the judge, may draw such inferences as appear proper.[8]

Compared to these two provisions, ss 34–38 of the 1994 Act constitute a major curtailment of the 'right to silence'. Thus although the accused retains his 'right' to remain silent both at the trial and under interrogation, 'proper' inferences may be drawn from (i) his failure to give evidence or his refusal, without good cause, to answer any question at the trial (s 35); (ii) his failure to mention certain facts when questioned under caution or on being charged

---

[1] *Rice v Connolly* [1966] 2 QB 414.

[2] *R v Leckey* [1944] KB 80.

[3] *R v Gilbert* (1977) 66 Cr App R 237, CA; *R v Raviraj* (1986) 85 Cr App R 93, CA; and *R v Henry* [1990] Crim LR 574.

[4] *R v Lewis* (1973) 57 Cr App R 860, CA; *R v Foster* [1974] Crim LR 544, CA; and *R v Gilbert* (1977) 66 Cr App R 237. As to inferences from silence where an accused and his accuser are on 'even terms', see Ch 15, **Statements made in the presence of the accused, p 490.**

[5] The Criminal Evidence Act 1898, s 1 and the Youth Justice and Criminal Evidence Act 1999, s 53 (see Ch 5).

[6] *R v Bathurst* [1968] 2 QB 99, CA and *R v Taylor* [1993] Crim LR 223, CA.

[7] See r 19.3, SI 2015/1490 (see Ch 20).

[8] See ss 7, 9, and 10.

(s 34); and (iii) his failure or refusal to account for objects, substances, or marks (s 36) or his presence at a particular place (s 37).[9] Adverse inferences may also be drawn, by virtue of other statutory provisions, from refusal to consent to the taking of samples[10] and from failure to provide advance disclosure of the defence case.[11]

Failure to testify

Section 35 of the Criminal Justice and Public Order Act 1994
Section 35 of the 1994 Act provides as follows:

(1) At the trial of any person for an offence, subsections (2) and (3) below apply unless—
    (a) the accused's guilt is not in issue; or
    (b) it appears to the court that the physical or mental condition of the accused makes it undesirable for him to give evidence;
    but subsection (2) below does not apply if, at the conclusion of the evidence for the prosecution, his legal representative informs the court that the accused will give evidence or, where he is unrepresented, the court ascertains from him that he will give evidence.

(2) Where this subsection applies, the court shall, at the conclusion of the evidence for the prosecution, satisfy itself (in the case of proceedings on indictment with a jury, in the presence of the jury) that the accused is aware that the stage has been reached at which evidence can be given for the defence and that he can, if he wishes, give evidence and that, if he chooses not to give evidence, or having been sworn, without good cause refuses to answer any question, it will be permissible for the court or jury to draw such inferences as appear proper from his failure to give evidence or his refusal, without good cause, to answer any question.

(3) Where this subsection applies, the court or jury, in determining whether the accused is guilty of the offence charged,[12] may draw such inferences as appear proper from the failure of the accused to give evidence or his refusal, without good cause, to answer any question.

(4) This section does not render the accused compellable to give evidence on his own behalf, and he shall accordingly not be guilty of contempt of court by reason of a failure to do so.

(5) For the purposes of this section a person who, having been sworn, refuses to answer any question shall be taken to do so without good cause unless—
    (a) he is entitled to refuse to answer the question by virtue of any enactment, whenever passed or made, or on the ground of privilege; or
    (b) the court in the exercise of its general discretion excuses him from answering it.

Although s 35 preserves the accused's right not to testify on his own behalf (s 35(4)), under s 35(3) the court or jury may draw 'proper' inferences from his failure to testify or his refusal, without good cause, to answer any question. Section 35(5) creates a conclusive presumption: an accused who has been sworn and refuses to answer any question will be deemed to have

---

[9] See generally Buckle, Street, and Brown, *The Right of Silence: The Impact of the Criminal Justice and Public Order Act 1994* (Home Office Research Study No 199, 2000) and Jackson, Wolfe, and Quinn, *Legislating Against Silence: The Northern Ireland Experience* (Northern Ireland Office, 2000). See also Jackson, 'Silence and Proof: extending the boundaries of criminal proceedings in the United Kingdom' (2001) 5 E&P 145.

[10] See for example, The Police and Criminal Evidence Act 1984, ss 62–3.

[11] The Criminal Procedure and Investigations Act 1996, s 11.

[12] Or any other offence of which the accused could lawfully be convicted on that charge: s 38(2).

so refused without good cause unless either (a) he is entitled to refuse by reason of an enact-ment[13] or on the ground of privilege (eg legal professional privilege);[14] or (b) the court excuses him from answering in the exercise of its general discretion.

Under s 38(3):

A person shall not . . . be convicted of an offence solely on an inference drawn from such a fail-ure as is mentioned in section . . . 35(3) . . .

However, as we shall see, in *Condron v United Kingdom*[15] the European Court of Human Rights has held that it is incompatible with the right to silence to base a conviction solely *or mainly* on the accused's silence or refusal to answer questions or give evidence.

The 'physical or mental condition' exception

Concerning s 35(1)(b), where an accused charged with murder relies upon the defence of diminished responsibility, he will not necessarily fall within the 'mental condition' excep-tion, but whether there is scope for the drawing of an inference from his silence will turn upon the circumstances of the case.[16] There must be an evidential basis for a defence applica-tion that s 35(1)(b) applies. If there is, the judge should decide the matter in a *voir dire*, but if there is not, it is not incumbent on him to order a *voir dire* of his own volition.[17] There must also be an evidential basis for the finding of the court under s 35(1)(b). 'Extreme difficulty in giving evidence', which is quite common among accused and other witnesses who give evidence in criminal trials, does not, in itself, make it 'undesirable' for the accused to give evidence.[18] In some cases, it may be 'undesirable' for the accused to give evidence because it would have a significantly adverse effect on his physical or mental state.[19] However, s 35(1)(b) is not confined to such cases;[20] 'undesirability' may stem from other matters, such as an accused's intellectual and cognitive deficits[21] or his inability to control himself or remem-ber his evidence.[22] In deciding, the judge may take account of such additional factors as the accused's behaviour after the event, the significance of his evidence, and the extent to which any problems of communication or comprehension can be overcome by the use of an intermediary.[23] A finding of undesirability does not always need to be based on expert

---

[13] See, eg, the restrictions on adducing evidence of the accused's bad character in s 101, Criminal Justice Act 2003 (see Ch 19).

[14] See Ch 22.

[15] (2001) 31 EHRR 1.

[16] *R v Barry* [2011] 1 Cr App R 466, CA.

[17] *R v A* [1997] Crim LR 883, CA. See also *R v Anwoir* [2008] 4 All ER 582, CA.

[18] *R v Ensor* [2010] 1 Cr App R 255 (18), CA at [27] and [35]. See also *O'Donnell v UK* [2015] ECHR 16667/10, a decision on the equivalent provision in Art 4 of the Criminal Evidence (NI) Order 1988, SI 1988/1987 (NI 120) (applicant with an IQ within the bottom 1 per cent of the general population and an understanding of English equivalent to that of a 6-year-old child).

[19] *R v Ensor* [2010] 1 Cr App R 255 (18), CA.

[20] *R v Dixon* [2014] 1 WLR 525, CA.

[21] *R v Friend (No 2)* [2004] EWCA Crim 2661.

[22] *R v Tabbakh* [2009] EWCA Crim 464.

[23] *R v Dixon* [2014] 1 WLR 525, CA. See also *R v Burnett* [2016] EWCA Crim 1941 at [25], where the court said it would be unjust to draw an adverse inference where the accused, without an intermediary may not be able to do himself justice when giving evidence. But see also *R v Biddle* [2019] 2 Cr App R 209 (20), CA at [33] and [42]: it is necessary to provide some material suggesting a causative link between the absence of an intermediary and the defendant's decision not to give evidence.

medical evidence, but such evidence will be necessary in some cases, as when it is said that the accused's depression makes it undesirable for him to give evidence.[24] However, expert evidence will not necessarily be determinative.[25] In *R v Friend*[26] it was said that the language of s 35(1)(b) was such as to give a wide discretion to the trial judge, whose decision can only be impugned if *Wednesbury* unreasonable.[27]

Warning the accused

Section 35(2) places a mandatory requirement on the court to satisfy itself of the matters set out therein and the court can only do this by asking either the accused or his advocate.[28] By inference, the advocate has to be asked in a situation where it is possible to take instructions from the accused, which will not be possible where the accused has absconded.[29] Thus an adverse inference may be drawn in the case of an accused who attends court but fails to give evidence notwithstanding that no such inference may be drawn in respect of a co-accused who has absconded.[30]

Under s 35(1) the court is not required to satisfy itself of the matters specified in s 35(2) if, at the end of the prosecution case, the accused's representative informs the court that the accused will give evidence. Paragraphs 26P.2 to 26P.5 of the Criminal Practice Directions VI provide as follows:

If the defendant is legally represented

26P.2   After the close of the prosecution case, if the defendant's representative requests a brief adjournment to advise his client on the issue the request should, ordinarily, be granted. When appropriate, the judge should, in the presence of the jury, inquire of the representative in these terms:

   'Have you advised your client that the stage has now been reached at which he may give evidence and, if he chooses not to do so or, having been sworn, without good cause refuses to answer any question, the jury may draw such inferences as appear proper from his failure to do so?'

26P.3   If the representative replies to the judge that the defendant has been so advised, then the case shall proceed. If counsel replies that the defendant has not been so advised, then the judge shall direct the representative to advise his client of the consequences and should adjourn briefly for this purpose, before proceeding further.

If the defendant is not legally represented

26P.4   If the defendant is not represented, the judge shall, at the conclusion of the evidence for the prosecution, in the absence of the jury, indicate what he will say to him in the presence of the jury and ask if he understands and whether he would like a brief adjournment to consider his position.

---

[24]   *R (DPP) v Kavanagh* [2005] EWHC 820 (Admin), approved in *R v Tabbakh* [2009] EWCA Crim 464.

[25]   See *R v Ullah* [2007] EWCA Crim 798 (psychiatric evidence of 'severe social phobia') and *R v Ensor* [2010] 1 Cr App R 255 (18), CA.

[26]   [1997] 1 WLR 1433, CA.

[27]   *Associated Provincial Picture Houses Ltd v Wednesbury Corpn* [1948] 1 KB 223, CA. See also *R v Biddle* [2019] 2 Cr App R 209 (20), CA at [34], [41], and [44], citing *R v Burnett* [2016] EWCA Crim 1941 at [28] and *R v Dixon* [2014] 1 WLR 525.

[28]   *R v Cowan* [1996] 1 Cr App R 1, CA at 9.

[29]   *R v Gough* [2002] Cr App R 121 (8), CA.

[30]   *R v Hamidi* [2010] EWCA Crim 66, CA.

26P.5   When appropriate, and in the presence of the jury, the judge should say to the defendant:
'You have heard the evidence against you. Now is the time for you to make your defence. You may give evidence on oath, and be cross-examined like any other witness. If you do not give evidence or, having been sworn, without good cause refuse to answer any question the jury may draw such inferences as appear proper. That means they may hold it against you. You may also call any witness or witnesses whom you have arranged to attend court or lead any agreed evidence. Afterwards you may also, if you wish, address the jury. But you cannot at that stage give evidence. Do you now intend to give evidence?'[31]

The s 35(2) procedure is not a mere formality and it is the responsibility of both counsel and the judge to ensure that it is carried out. However, failure to follow the procedure, although an irregularity, will be immaterial to the safety of a conviction if it is clear that counsel did give the required advice to the accused.[32]

R v Cowan

Scope of section 35

In *R v Cowan*[33] the Court of Appeal rejected as contrary to the plain words of s 35, a submission that the operation of s 35(3) should be confined to exceptional cases. Three arguments were advanced in support of this submission, all of which were rejected. The first argument was that the section constituted an infringement of the accused's right to silence, but as the court stressed, the 'right of silence' had not been abolished by the section, but expressly preserved by s 35(4).

The second argument was that s 35 watered down the burden of proof and in effect put a burden on the accused to testify in order to avoid conviction. Lord Taylor CJ held that this argument was misconceived because (i) the prosecution have to establish a prima facie case before any question of the accused testifying is raised;[34] (ii) the court or jury are prohibited from convicting solely because of an inference drawn from silence (s 38(3)); and (iii) the burden of proving guilt beyond reasonable doubt remains on the prosecution throughout. Thus although the effect of s 35 is that the court or jury may regard the inference drawn from silence as, in effect, a further evidential factor in support of the prosecution case, it cannot be the only factor to justify a conviction: the totality of the evidence must prove guilt to the criminal standard.

The third argument was that an inference should only be drawn where there is no reasonable possibility of an innocent explanation for the accused's silence; that an inference should not be drawn where there are 'good reasons' for silence consistent with innocence, for example (a) where there is other defence evidence to contradict the prosecution case; (b) where an accused is nervous, inarticulate, or unlikely to perform well in the witness box; (c) where an accused is under duress or fear for his or another's safety; or (d) where—as in two of the cases before the court—an accused has attacked prosecution witnesses and decided not to give evidence because it would expose him to cross-examination on his previous convictions; and that the advocate for the defence may properly advance such reasons without the need for evidence.

---

[31] See also the Crown Court Compendium (July 2019), Part 1, 17–5, para 21.

[32] *Wright v The Queen* [2016] UKPC 181, a decision under statutory provisions in the Cayman Islands identical, in all material respects, to s 35 of the 1994 Act.

[33] [1996] QB 373, CA.

[34] For exceptions, see the Domestic Violence, Crime and Victims Act 2004, ss 6 and 6A.

In respect of this argument, the court accepted that, apart from the mandatory exceptions in s 35(1), it is open to the court to decline to draw an adverse inference and for a judge to direct or advise a jury against drawing such an inference if the circumstances of the case justify such a course. However, the court held that there needs to be either some evidential basis for declining to draw an adverse inference[35] or some exceptional factors in the case making that a fair course to take.[36] It is improper for the advocate for the defence to give to the jury reasons for his client's silence at trial in the absence of evidence to support such reasons.[37] The court stressed that the inferences permitted are only such 'as appear proper', a phrase intended to leave a broad discretion to a trial judge to decide in all the circumstances whether any proper inference is capable of being drawn by the jury. If not, he should tell them so; otherwise, it is for the jury to decide whether in fact an inference should properly be drawn.

Avoiding cross-examination on criminal record

The court also rejected the specific submission that an inference should not be drawn where an accused does not testify in order to avoid cross-examination on his record. It was pointed out that to hold otherwise would lead to the bizarre result of an accused with previous convictions being in a more privileged position than an accused with a clean record. *R v Cowan* was endorsed, in this respect, in *R v Becouarn*,[38] where the House of Lords gave two reasons for rejecting a submission that in these circumstances the judge should at least give a direction along the lines that there may be various possible other reasons why the accused did not give evidence: first, that such a direction would either signal to the jurors that the accused *does* have previous convictions, or set them off on a trail of speculation about the existence of other imaginary reasons; and second, that although fear of allowing in his convictions may be an element in a decision not to testify, reluctance to face cross-examination may be another and much more predominant element.

The direction to the jury

In *R v Cowan* the Court of Appeal considered the following matters to be essential to a proper direction to the jury on inferences from failure to testify.[39]

1. The judge must direct the jury that the burden remains on the prosecution throughout and must direct them as to the required standard of proof.

2. The judge should make clear that the accused is entitled to remain silent: it is his right and his choice.

3. The jury must be told that an inference from failure to give evidence cannot on its own prove guilt (s 38(3)).[40]

---

[35] Presumably it is open to the judge to hear such evidence on a *voir dire*, a course that would seem to be particularly important in cases in which the reasons for silence can only be established, in effect, by the accused himself.

[36] In *R v Napper* [1996] Crim LR 591, CA, it was held that the fact that the police failed to interview the accused while the alleged frauds were reasonably fresh in his mind did not warrant the conclusion that an adverse inference should not be drawn.

[37] Applied in *R v Phillips* [2015] EWCA Crim 836.

[38] [2005] 1 WLR 2589, HL. See also *R v Taylor* [1999] Crim LR 77, CA.

[39] See also the Crown Court Compendium (July 2019), Part 1, 17–5, para 17.

[40] Cowan's appeal was allowed on the basis that the jury had not been directed in accordance with point (3) (and (5)).

4. The jury must be satisfied that the prosecution have established a case to answer before drawing any inferences from silence.[41] Although the judge must have thought that there was a case to answer, the jury may not believe the witnesses whose evidence the judge considered sufficient to raise a prima facie case. It must therefore be made clear that they must find that there is a case to answer on the prosecution evidence before drawing an adverse inference from silence.[42]

5. The jury should also be directed that if, despite any evidence relied upon to explain the accused's silence, or in the absence of such evidence, they conclude that the silence can only sensibly be attributed to his having no answer, or none that would stand up to cross-examination, they may draw an adverse inference.[43]

The court further held that it is not possible to anticipate all the circumstances in which a judge might think it right to direct or advise a jury against drawing an adverse inference. Noting that it would not be wise even to give examples, as each case must turn on its own facts, the court cited with approval the following dictum of Kelly LJ in *R v McLernon*:[44]

the court has then a complete discretion as to whether inferences should be drawn or not. In these circumstances it is a matter for the court in any criminal case (1) to decide whether to draw inferences or not; and (2) if it decides to draw inferences what their nature, extent and degree of adversity, if any, may be. It would be improper and indeed quite unwise for any court to set out the bounds of either steps (1) or (2). Their application will depend on factors peculiar to the individual case . . .

Finally, the court in *R v Cowan* stressed that the Court of Appeal will not lightly interfere with a judge's exercise of discretion to direct or advise the jury as to the drawing of inferences from silence and as to the nature, extent, and degree of such inferences. As long as the judge gives the jury adequate directions of law of the kind indicated,[45] and leaves the decision to them, the Court of Appeal will be slow to substitute its own view.

The circumstances in which inferences may be drawn
In some cases, failure to go into the witness box is unlikely to have any real bearing on the issues in the case, as when the facts are not in dispute and the only issue is whether they fall within the offence charged[46] and as when an accused charged with murder admits the assault

---

[41] 'Inescapable logic' and fairness demand that this fourth 'essential' direction be given: see *R v Birchall* [1999] Crim LR 311, CA. See also *R v El-Hannachi* [1998] 2 Cr App R 226, CA. In both cases, failure to give the direction resulted in a successful appeal against conviction. However, failure to give the direction will not necessarily amount to a breach of Art 6 of the European Convention on Human Rights: see *O'Donnell v UK* [2015] ECHR 1667/10, a Northern Ireland case decided at a time when the trial judge had a discretion whether or not to give the direction according to the weight of the prosecution evidence and, on the facts, there was strong circumstantial evidence against the applicant.

[42] See further per Lord Slynn in *Murray v DPP* (1994) 99 Cr App R 396, HL, at **p 505 n 52**. Presumably, the jury will need specific guidance on the concept of 'a case to answer'. The task of deciding that matter, at the end of the trial, but on the basis of the prosecution evidence alone, would seem to be particularly onerous.

[43] Where there is no evidence to explain the accused's silence, it is not incumbent on a judge to embark on, or to invite the jury to embark on, possible speculative reasons consistent with innocence which might theoretically prompt an accused to remain silent: per Lord Taylor CJ, [1996] QB 373, CA at 386.

[44] [1992] NIJB 41, a decision on the equivalent provision in Art 4 of the Criminal Evidence (NI) Order 1988, SI 1988/1987 (NI 120).

[45] See also the Crown Court Compendium (July 2019), Part 1, 17–5.

[46] *R v McManus* [2001] EWCA Crim 2455.

on the victim but denies causation, an issue which is then resolved on the basis of the expert witnesses called.[47] It seems equally clear, however, that in other cases it may be perfectly proper to draw a strong adverse inference. Typically, such an inference is likely to be drawn where the uncontested or clearly established facts point so strongly to the guilt of the accused as to call for an explanation,[48] or where the defence case involves alleged facts which are at variance with the prosecution evidence or additional to it and exculpatory and must, if true, be within the accused's knowledge.[49]

The inferences that may be drawn

It does not follow from the last sentence that inferences may only be drawn in respect of specific facts: in appropriate circumstances, it may be proper to draw a general inference that by reason of his silence, the accused is guilty of the offence charged. In *Murray v DPP*,[50] a decision under the equivalent provision in the Criminal Evidence (NI) Order 1988,[51] M was convicted of attempted murder and possession of a firearm with intent to endanger life. There was evidence to link the accused with the attack, but he gave no evidence at trial. The trial judge said that it seemed remarkable that the accused had not given evidence and it was only common sense to infer 'that he is not prepared to assert his innocence on oath because that is not the case'. The House of Lords, upholding the conviction, held that having regard to the cumulative effect of all the circumstantial evidence against the accused, the trial judge was entitled as a matter of common sense to infer that there was no innocent explanation to the prima facie case that he was guilty. Lord Slynn said:[52]

> The accused cannot be compelled to give evidence but he must risk the consequences if he does not do so. Those consequences are not simply . . . that specific inferences may be drawn from specific facts. They include in a proper case the drawing of an inference that the accused is guilty . . .
>
> This does not mean that the court can conclude simply because the accused does not give evidence that he is guilty. In the first place the prosecutor must establish a prima facie case—a case for him to answer. In the second place in determining whether the accused is guilty the judge or jury can draw only 'such inferences from the refusal as appear proper'. As Lord Diplock said in *Haw Tua Tau v Public Prosecutor*:[53]
>
> 'What inferences are proper to be drawn from an accused's refusal to give evidence depend upon the circumstances of the particular case, and is a question to be decided by applying ordinary common sense.'
>
> There must thus be some basis derived from the circumstances which justify the inference.
>
> If there is no prima facie case shown by the prosecution there is no case to answer. Equally, if parts of the prosecution case had so little evidential value that they called for no answer, a failure to deal with those specific matters cannot justify an inference of guilt.

---

[47] See Wasik and Taylor, *Blackstone's Guide to the Criminal Justice and Public Order Act 1994* (London, 1995) 65.

[48] See, at common law, *R v Mutch* [1973] 1 All ER 178, CA. See also *R v Corrie* (1904) 20 TLR 365. See also *AB v Crown Prosecution Service* [2017] EWHC 2693.

[49] See, at common law, *R v Martinez-Tobon* [1994] 2 All ER 90, CA; and in cases where the accused bears the burden of proof, *R v Bathurst* [1968] 2 QB 99 at 107, CA.

[50] [1994] 1 WLR 1, HL.

[51] Art 4, SI 1988/1987 (NI 120).

[52] [1994] 1 WLR 1 at 11. See also the Crown Court Compendium (July 2019), Part 1, 17–5, para 16.

[53] [1982] AC 136 at 153.

On the other hand, if aspects of the evidence taken alone or in combination with other facts clearly call for an explanation which the accused ought to be in a position to give, if an explanation exists, then a failure to give any explanation may as a matter of common sense allow the drawing of an inference that there is no explanation and that the accused is guilty.[54]

Prosecution comment

Under proviso (b) to s 1 of the Criminal Evidence Act 1898, the failure of any person charged with an offence to give evidence was not to be made the subject of any comment by the prosecution. Section 1(b) was repealed by the 1994 Act. Comment is permissible. However, if the trial judge decides to direct or advise a jury against drawing an adverse inference', it is submitted that it would be good practice for him to inform the prosecuting advocate of this before closing speeches, so that the advocate refrains from comment. Conversely, if the judge decides to direct the jury that they may draw proper inferences, it is submitted that the prosecuting advocate should adhere to the kind of comment suggested (for the judge) in *R v Cowan*.

Failure to mention facts when questioned or charged

Background

The Criminal Law Revision Committee Report

In its 11th Report, the Criminal Law Revision Committee proposed that where an accused fails to mention any fact relied on in his defence which he could reasonably have been expected to mention either (i) before he was charged on being questioned by the police; or (ii) on being charged, the court should be entitled to draw such inferences as appear proper, and the caution should be replaced by a notice explaining the potentially adverse effect of silence.[55] These proposals attracted widespread criticism at the time, but in 1976 were adopted in Singapore[56] and in 1988 were adopted in Northern Ireland.[57] There was also strong judicial comment in favour of their adoption in England and Wales. In *R v Alladice*[58] Lord Lane CJ, observed that the effect of s 58 of the Police and Criminal Evidence Act 1984 (the 1984 Act)[59] was that in many cases a detainee who would otherwise have answered the questions of the police would be advised by his solicitor to remain silent and weeks later, at the trial, would often produce an explanation of, or a defence to, the charge, the truthfulness of which the police would have had no chance to check. Thus despite the fact that the explanation or defence, if true, could have been disclosed at the outset, and despite the advantage which the accused gained by those tactics, no comment could be made to the jury. The effect of s 58, it was said, was such that the balance of fairness between prosecution and defence could not be maintained unless proper comment was permitted on silence in such circumstances.

---

[54] The drawing of adverse inferences from silence in *Murray v DPP* did not violate the European Convention on Human Rights: *Murray v United Kingdom* (1996) 22 EHRR 29, ECHR; but see also Munday, 'Inferences from Silence and European Human Rights Law' [1996] Crim LR 370.

[55] Paras 28–52 and cl 11 of the draft bill: 11th Report, Cmnd 4991 (1972).

[56] See Meng Heong Yeo, 'Diminishing the Right of Silence: The Singapore Experience' [1983] Crim LR 89 and Tan, 'Adverse Inferences and the Right to Silence: Re-examining the Singapore Experience' [1997] Crim LR 471.

[57] See SI 1988/1987 (NI 120) and Jackson, 'Curtailing the Right of Silence: Lessons from Northern Ireland' [1991] Crim LR 404.

[58] (1988) 87 Cr App R 380.

[59] Section 58 gives the right of access to a lawyer (see Ch 15).

The Working Group and Royal Commission on Criminal Justice

The report of the Working Group set up by the Home Secretary in 1988 expressed the view that failure to answer police questions, even before the accused is brought to the police station, should be admissible evidence against him to show that his defence is untrue and to undermine his credibility, and he should be warned of the possibility at the outset.[60] The majority recommendation of the Royal Commission on Criminal Justice, in contrast, was that no inferences should be drawn from silence at the police station, but that when the prosecution case has been disclosed, an accused should be required to disclose his case, at the risk of adverse comment by the judge on any new defence then disclosed or any departure from the defence previously disclosed.

Section 34 of the Criminal Justice and Public Order Act 1994

Section 34 of the 1994 Act reflects the recommendations of the Criminal Law Revision Committee, and not those of the Royal Commission on Criminal Justice.[61] In *R v Hoare*[62] Auld LJ said: 'The whole basis of section 34, in its qualification of the otherwise general right of an accused to remain silent and require the prosecution to prove its case, is an assumption that an innocent defendant—as distinct from one who is entitled to require the prosecution to prove its case—would give an early explanation to demonstrate his innocence.'

Section 34 provides that:

(1) Where, in any proceedings against a person for an offence, evidence is given that the accused—
   (a) at any time before he was charged with the offence, on being questioned under caution by a constable trying to discover whether or by whom the offence had been committed, failed to mention any fact relied on in his defence in those proceedings; or
   (b) on being charged with the offence or officially informed that he might be prosecuted for it, failed to mention any such fact; or
   (c) at any time after being charged with the offence, on being questioned under section 22 of the Counter-Terrorism Act 2008 (post-charge questioning) failed to mention any such fact,

   being a fact which in the circumstances existing at the time the accused could reasonably have been expected to mention when so questioned, charged or informed, as the case may be, subsection (2) below applies.

(2) Where this subsection applies—
   (a) [repealed];
   (b) a judge, in deciding whether to grant an application made by the accused under paragraph 2 of Schedule 3 to the Crime and Disorder Act 1998;[63]
   (c) the court, in determining whether there is a case to answer; and
   (d) the court or jury, in determining whether the accused is guilty of the offence charged,[64] may draw such inferences from the failure as appear proper.

---

[60] See Zuckerman, 'Trial by Unfair Means—The Report of the Working Group on the Right of Silence' [1989] Crim LR 855. See also Greer, 'The Right of Silence: A Review of the Current Debate' (1990) 53 MLR 709.

[61] See generally Birch, 'Suffering in Silence: A Cost–Benefit Analysis of Section 34' [1999] Crim LR 769 and Leng, 'Silence pre-trial, reasonable expectations and the normative distortion of fact-finding' (2001) 5 E&P 240.

[62] [2005] 1 WLR 1804, CA at [53].

[63] Ie an application by an accused to dismiss the charge or any of the charges in respect of which he has been sent to the Crown Court (as an adult charged with an offence triable only on indictment) under the Crime and Disorder Act 1998, s 51.

[64] Or any other offence of which the accused could lawfully be convicted on that charge: s 38(2).

(2A) Where the accused was at an authorised place of detention[65] at the time of the failure, sub-sections (1) and (2) above do not apply if he had not been allowed an opportunity to consult a solicitor prior to being questioned, charged or informed as mentioned in subsection (1) above.

'On being questioned under caution . . . or on being charged'

Section 34(1)(a) only applies in the case of an accused 'on being questioned under caution'. Thus it has no application in the case of an accused who simply refuses to leave the police cell in which he is being detained in order to be interviewed by the police, but s 34(1)(b) will apply if such an accused, on being subsequently charged, fails to mention any fact relied on in his defence.[66]

The Caution

Paragraph 10.5 of Code C (the Code of Practice for the Detention, Treatment and Questioning of Persons by Police Officers) provides that the caution given before a person is charged or informed he may be prosecuted should be in the following terms:

> You do not have to say anything. But it may harm your defence if you do not mention when questioned something which you later rely on in court. Anything you do say may be given in evidence.

Paragraph 10.7 provides that:

> Minor deviations from the words of any caution given in accordance with this Code do not con-stitute a breach of this Code, provided the sense of the relevant caution is preserved.

Under Note 10D of the Code:

> If it appears a person does not understand the caution, the person giving it should explain it in their own words.

Under para 11.4 of the Code, where a 'significant silence' (a silence which might give rise to an inference under the 1994 Act) has occurred before the start of the interview at the police station, then at the start of the interview, the interviewer, after cautioning the suspect, shall put the earlier 'significant silence' to the suspect and ask him whether he confirms or denies it and if he wants to add anything.

Questioning

Section 34 applies in relation to questioning not only by constables, but also 'by persons (other than constables) charged with the duty of investigating offences or charging offend-ers'; and in s 34(1)(b), 'officially informed' means informed by a constable or any such person.[67] Under s 67(9) of the 1984 Act, which also refers to 'persons charged with the duty of investigating offences or charging offenders', it has been held, somewhat unsatisfactorily, that whether a person satisfies the test is a question of fact in each case.[68]

---

[65] 'Authorised place of detention' means a police station or other place prescribed by order made by the Secretary of State: s 38(2A).

[66] *R v Johnson* [2005] EWCA Crim 971.

[67] Section 34(4).

[68] See *R v Seelig* [1991] 4 All ER 429, CA etc (see Ch 15).

Section 34(1)(a) applies to questioning under caution by a constable 'trying to discover whether or by whom the offence had been committed'. Where there is sufficient evidence for a suspect to be charged and the interview should be brought to an end,[69] but questioning continues and is met with silence from which adverse inferences may be drawn, evidence of the silence may be excluded.[70] However, it has also been held that the sufficiency of evidence can normally only be judged after the suspect has been given an opportunity to volunteer an explanation, and that further questioning will not be in breach of the Code if the officer is still open-minded about the possibility of an explanation which might prevent the suspect from being charged,[71] in which case the officer will still be 'trying to discover whether or by whom the offence has been committed'.[72] Questioning does not have to be 'specific' in nature, ie comprise specific questions relating to identifiable facts. It is enough if the accused appreciates that he is being questioned under caution and is being invited to give his account by necessary implication.[73]

Section 34(1)(b) applies when the accused is 'charged with the offence or officially informed that he might be prosecuted for it', at which stage para 16.2 of Code C requires that the caution should be in the following terms:

> You do not have to say anything. But it may harm your defence if you do not mention now something which you later rely on in court. Anything you do say may be given in evidence.

Given this wording, there is no requirement—in order to rely on s 34(1)(b)—that an officer should go further and, for example, invite the detainee to give any explanation he may have for his conduct.[74]

An inference may be drawn from silence on being questioned under s 34(1)(a), or from silence on being charged under s 34(1)(b), or from both. Thus although in most cases it will add nothing to invite the jury to consider drawing an additional inference at the later stage, in some cases it may be possible to draw a stronger inference then, as when a suspect, after interview, is bailed to come back to the police station a week later, when he is charged, having had a long time to think back over the events. These principles derive from *R v Dervish*,[75] where it was held that if no inference can be drawn under s 34(1)(a)—the interviews in that case were inadmissible by reason of breaches of the Codes of Practice—then subject to any issue of unfairness, the trial judge may leave to the jury the possibility of drawing an inference under s 34(1)(b). However, the court added that the trial judge should not permit the jury to draw such an inference if to do so would nullify the safeguards of the 1984 Act and Codes, or if there was bad faith by the police deliberately breaching the safeguards with a view to falling back on s 34(1)(b).

---

[69] See paras 11.6 and 16.1 of Code C.

[70] See *R v Pointer* [1997] Crim LR 676, CA and *R v Gayle* [1999] Crim LR 502, CA.

[71] *R v McGuinness* [1999] Crim LR 318, CA and *R v Ioannou* [1999] Crim LR 586, CA.

[72] *R v Odeyemi* [1999] Crim LR 828, CA. But see also s 37(7) of the 1984 Act and generally Cape, 'Detention Without Charge; What Does "Sufficient Evidence to Charge" Mean?' [1999] Crim LR 874.

[73] *R v Green* [2019] EWCA Crim 411 at [20].

[74] *R v Goodsir* [2006] EWCA Crim 852.

[75] [2002] 2 Cr App R 105 (6), CA.

'Failed to mention any fact relied on in his defence'

Prepared statements

Where an accused, in interview after arrest, gives to the police a prepared statement and thereafter refuses to answer questions, he has not 'failed to mention' the facts set out in his statement. Thus in *R v Knight*,[76] where the prepared statement was wholly consistent with the defence evidence at trial, an adverse inference could not be drawn.[77] The court held that the purpose of s 34(1)(a) was early disclosure of a suspect's account and not, separately and distinctly, the subjection of that account to the test of police cross-examination. However, as the court went on to stress, giving a prepared statement is not of itself an inevitable antidote to later adverse inferences because the statement may be incomplete in comparison with the accused's later account at trial. As was pointed out in *R v Turner*,[78] the submission of a prepared statement is a dangerous course for an innocent person, who may subsequently discover at trial that something significant was omitted. In that case, it was held that the judge must identify any fact not mentioned in the prepared statement, which should be the subject of a specific direction. The court also noted that inconsistencies between the prepared statement and the accused's evidence do not necessarily amount to reliance on a fact not previously mentioned; and that where there are differences between the statement and the evidence given at trial, then depending on the precise circumstances, it may be better to direct the jury to consider the difference as constituting a previous lie,[79] rather than the foundation for a s 34 inference.

Speculative possibilities

Inferences can only be drawn under s 34 where the accused has failed to mention 'any fact', as opposed to some speculative possibility, relied on in his defence. In *R v Nickolson*[80] N, charged with sexual offences against the complainant in his house, denied in interview that anything indecent had ever occurred, but said that he was in the habit of masturbating in the bathroom. Subsequently, seminal stains were found on the complainant's nightdress and, at the trial, when asked if he could provide an explanation, N suggested that the complainant could have entered the bathroom after he had masturbated there. It was held that s 34 did not apply because N had not asserted as a fact that the complainant had visited the bathroom, but had proffered it as an explanation, something more in the nature of a theory, a possibility, or speculation. Section 34 will apply, however, if such speculation is based on a fact and the accused could reasonably have been expected to mention both the speculation and the factual basis for it.[81]

Facts disclosed before the trial

It seems clear that an inference may be drawn under s 34 from an accused's failure to mention a fact not only when the fact is first disclosed at trial, but also when the accused, having

---

[76] [2004] 1 WLR 340, CA. See also *T v DPP* [2007] EWHC 7193 (Admin).

[77] See also *R v Johnson* [2017] EWCA Crim 191. Although there was no prepared statement, the accused had set up a line of reasoning in interview which was *broadly* consistent with his evidence and some missing details were not significant.

[78] [2004] 1 All ER 1025, CA.

[79] See *R v Lucas* [1981] QB 720, CA, see **Ch 2, Lies, p 19**.

[80] [1999] Crim LR 61, CA.

[81] *R v B (MT)* [2000] Crim LR 181, CA. See, for example, *R v Lewis* [2018] EWCA Crim 1101.

initially failed to mention a fact on being questioned under caution, disclosed it at a later stage of police questioning or in a written statement to the police.[82]

Reliance on facts

The fact that the accused failed to mention must be relied on in his defence. In *R v Moshaid*,[83] in which the accused did not give or call any evidence, it was held that s 34 did not bite. It does not follow, however, that the relevant fact may be established only by the accused or a defence witness: it may also be established by a prosecution witness, either in cross-examination or examination-in-chief.[84] Thus s 34 does apply where the advocate for the defence puts or suggests the fact to a prosecution witness in cross-examination and the witness accepts it.[85] It can also apply even if the witness under cross-examination does not accept the fact put or suggested. In *R v Webber*[86] the House of Lords held that an accused relies on a fact in his defence when his advocate, acting on his instructions, puts a specific and positive case to a prosecution witness, as opposed to asking questions intended to probe or test the prosecution case,[87] even if the witness rejects the case being put. Two reasons were given. First, although questions only become evidence if accepted by the witness, where specific positive suggestions have been made, the jury may for whatever reason distrust the witness's evidence and ask themselves whether the version put for the accused may not be true. Second, since s 34(2)(c) permits the court to draw proper inferences when determining whether there is a case to answer, that is, at a stage when the accused has had no opportunity to give or adduce evidence, it would be surprising if s 34(2)(c) were intended to apply only when, unusually, specific suggestions put to a prosecution witness are *accepted* by him. It was further held that where a defence advocate adopts on behalf of his client in closing submissions evidence given by a co-accused, this may also amount to reliance on facts for the purposes of s 34.

In *R v Betts*[88] it was held that the bare admission at trial of a fact asserted by the prosecution cannot amount to reliance on a fact, but where explanation for the admitted fact is advanced by reliance on other facts, those facts may give rise to an inference if they were not mentioned on being questioned or charged. The court gave an example: if an accused admits for the first time at trial that a fingerprint was his and offers no explanation for it being found where it was, he relies on no fact, but it will be different if he also puts forward an explanation for the finding of the fingerprint. The most compelling reason for the conclusion of the court in relation to a bare admission was given by Lord Bingham in *R v Webber*:[89] rarely if ever can a s 34 direction be appropriate on failure to mention at interview an admittedly true fact, because the adverse inference to be drawn under the section is that the fact not mentioned by the accused at interview but relied on in his defence is likely to be *untrue*.

---

[82] See *R v McLernon* (1990) Belfast CC, 20 Dec, a decision under Art 3 of the Criminal Evidence (NI) Order 1988, SI 1988/1987 (NI 120).

[83] [1998] Crim LR 420, CA.

[84] *R v Bowers* [1998] Crim LR 817, CA.

[85] See *R v McLernon* [1992] NIJB 41, CA.

[86] [2004] 1 WLR 404, HL.

[87] If the judge is in doubt whether the advocate is testing the prosecution evidence or advancing a positive case, he should ask the advocate in the absence of the jury: *R v Webber* [2004] 1 WLR 404, HL at [36].

[88] [2001] 2 Cr App R 257 (16), CA.

[89] [2004] 1 WLR 404, HL at [28].

'A fact which . . . the accused could reasonably have been expected to mention'

The fact relied on must be 'a fact which in the circumstances existing at the time the accused could reasonably have been expected to mention when . . . questioned, charged, or informed, as the case may be'. If the accused gives evidence, his reason for not putting forward any fact relied on should be explored.[90] In deciding the matter, the jury will be very much concerned with the truth or otherwise of any explanation given by the accused for not mentioning the fact, because if they accept an exculpatory explanation as true, or possibly so, it will be obviously unfair to draw any adverse inference.[91]

In *R v Argent*[92] it was held that the expression 'in the circumstances' is not to be construed restrictively: account may be taken of such matters as time of day, the accused's age, experience, mental capacity, state of health, sobriety, tiredness, knowledge, personality, and legal advice. 'The accused', it was said, refers not to some hypothetical reasonable accused of ordinary phlegm and fortitude, but to the actual accused, with such qualities, apprehensions, knowledge, and advice as he is shown to have had at the time. Sometimes, therefore, the jury may conclude that it was reasonable for the accused not to have mentioned a fact because, for example, he was tired, ill, frightened, drunk, drugged, unable to understand what was going on, suspicious of the police, afraid that his answer would not be fairly recorded, worried at committing himself without legal advice, or acting on legal advice. In other cases, the jury may conclude that the accused could reasonably have been expected to mention the fact. In *R v Howell*[93] Laws LJ said:

> we do not consider the absence of a written statement from the complainant to be good reason for silence (if adequate oral disclosure of the complaint has been given), and it does not become good reason merely because a solicitor has so advised. Nor is the possibility that the complainant may not pursue his complaint good reason, nor a belief by the solicitor that the suspect will be charged in any event whatever he says. The kind of circumstance which may most likely justify silence will be such matters as the suspect's condition (ill-health, in particular mental disability; confusion; intoxication; shock, and so forth—of course we are not laying down an authoritative list), or his inability genuinely to recollect events without reference to documents which are not to hand, or communication with other persons who may be able to assist his recollection.

In deciding whether a fact is one that the accused could reasonably have been expected to mention, another relevant factor, it is submitted, is the importance of the fact to the defence in question, whether central to that defence or of only peripheral importance, because an accused cannot reasonably be expected to mention every fact, for example every last detail of an alibi as opposed to the key facts relating to where he was, when, and with whom (if

---

[90] *T v DPP* [2007] EWHC 1793 (Admin) at [26]. There is a three-stage test to be applied: (i) has the defendant relied in his defence on a fact which he could reasonably have been expected to mention; (ii) what is his explanation for not mentioning it; and (iii) if the explanation is not reasonable, is the proper inference to be drawn that he is guilty? It is unclear how s 34 affects the common law doctrine of recent possession, but see *AB v Crown Prosecution Service* [2017] EWHC 2963 at [27]–[28] in which it was said that the 3 stage test in *T v DPP* applies *mutatis mutandis* whether the potential inference arises under s 34 or at common law. See also *R v Ahmed* [2019] EWCA Crim 1085: it may not be necessary for the prosecution to assert 'late invention' if the accused has had an opportunity in his oral evidence to explain why he did not put forward the fact.

[91] Per Lord Bingham in *R v Webber* [2004] 1 WLR 404, HL at [29].

[92] [1997] 2 Cr App R 27, CA.

[93] [2005] 1 Cr App R 1 (1), CA at [24].

anybody). The nature of the fact itself may also be highly relevant, especially if of a kind likely to embarrass the accused or compromise his personal or professional life, for example the fact, in support of an alibi, that at the time of the alleged offence he was not at the scene of the crime but elsewhere, in bed with a prostitute. It would be equally relevant, to take another example, if the fact in question were of a kind likely to create a danger of reprisals against the accused, his family, or friends. Account also needs to be taken of the accused's knowledge of the case against him, and his understanding of (a) the nature of the offence in question; and (b) the facts which might go to show his innocence of that offence. Account should also be taken of any important respect in which the accused may have been misled. In *R v M(I)*[94] when officers interviewed M about an offence, they incorrectly alleged that he had committed it on a date some three months after the date alleged by the complainant. M made no comment other than to deny having committed the offence on the date put to him. At the trial, M, in his defence, relied on a fact relating to the earlier date. It was held that this was not a fact which he could reasonably have been expected to mention when interviewed about an offence on the later date.

Establishing the failure to mention a fact

Section 34(3) of the 1994 Act provides that:

> Subject to any directions by the court, evidence tending to establish the failure may be given before or after evidence tending to establish the fact which the accused is alleged to have failed to mention.

In *R v Condron and Condron* the Court of Appeal, while stressing that no hard and fast procedure should be laid down, gave the following guidance:

> In the ordinary way . . . it would seem appropriate for prosecuting counsel to adduce evidence limited to the fact that after the appropriate caution the accused did not answer questions or made no comment. Unless the relevance of a particular point has been revealed in cross-examination, it would not seem appropriate to spend time at this stage going through the questions asked at interview.
>
> If and when the accused gives evidence and mentions facts which, in the view of prosecuting counsel, he can reasonably have been expected to mention in interview, he can be asked why he did not mention them. The accused's attention will then no doubt be drawn to any relevant and pertinent questions asked at interview. The accused's explanation for his failure can then be tested in cross-examination. It will not generally be necessary to call evidence in rebuttal, unless there is a dispute as to the relevant contents of the interview.

Silence on legal advice
Whether an inference can be drawn

In *R v Condron and Condron*[95] the question arose whether an adverse inference can be drawn if the accused remained silent on legal advice. The accused, both heroin addicts, were convicted of offences relating to the supply of heroin. On their arrest, although a police doctor considered that they were fit for interview, a view of which they were aware, their solicitor considered that they were unfit to be interviewed because of their drug withdrawal

---

[94] [2012] 1 Cr App R 26 (3), CA.
[95] [1997] 1 WLR 827, CA.

symptoms. The solicitor therefore advised them not to answer questions, also advising them of the potential consequences, and making it plain that it was entirely their choice. At their trial, they gave detailed innocent explanations in relation to the prosecution evidence, which could have been given in answer to specific questions by the police in their interview. The Court of Appeal held that the trial judge had properly directed the jury that it was for them to decide whether any adverse inference should be drawn, but that it would have been *desirable* if he had given an additional direction to the effect that an adverse inference may be drawn if, despite any evidence relied on to explain the silence at interview, or in the absence of such evidence, they conclude that the silence can only sensibly be attributed to the accused having fabricated the evidence subsequently.

When the case came before the European Court of Human Rights, it held that a direction along these lines is mandatory.[96] The Court held as follows: (1) The right to silence could not be considered as an absolute right and the fact that the issue was left to the jury could not of itself be considered incompatible with Art 6. (2) The right was at the heart of the notion of a fair procedure under Art 6 and particular caution was required before a domestic court could invoke an accused's silence against him. It was incompatible with the right to base a conviction solely or mainly on the accused's silence or refusal to answer questions, or give evidence, but where a situation called for an explanation from an accused, then his silence could be taken into account in assessing the persuasiveness of the evidence against him. (3) The judge had not reflected the balance between the right to silence and the circumstances in which an adverse inference could be drawn. The judge's direction was such that the jury may have drawn an adverse inference even if satisfied with the accused's explanation of the silence. As a matter of fairness, the jury should have been directed that if they were satisfied that the accused's silence at interview could not sensibly be attributed to their having no answer or none that would stand up to cross-examination, then they should not draw an adverse inference.

The direction of the kind suggested by the Court of Appeal in *R v Condron and Condron* does not have to be geared only to the inference of subsequent fabrication, but may deal with the different inference that the accused, by the time of the interview, had already invented a false story, in whole or in part, but did not want to reveal it, because of the risk that the police might then be able to expose its falsity.[97]

Whether to give reasons for the advice

In *R v Condron and Condron* it was also held that the bare assertion, by an accused, that he did not answer questions because he was advised by his solicitor not to do so, is unlikely to prevent an adverse inference from being drawn:[98] it is necessary, if the accused wishes to invite the court not to draw an adverse inference, to go further and give the basis or reason for the advice. However, as the court pointed out, whereas a 'bare assertion' will not amount to a waiver of the legal professional privilege that attaches to communications between an accused and his solicitor prior to a police interview,[99] once the basis or reason for the advice is stated, this will amount to a waiver. The prosecution is then entitled to ask the accused or, if

---

[96] *Condron v United Kingdom* (2001) 31 EHRR 1.

[97] See, eg, *R v Taylor* [1999] Crim LR 77, CA, where T, who had given the 'bare bones' of his alibi to his solicitor, failed to mention it in interview, only furnishing the details of it in his alibi notice. See the Crown Court Compendium (July 2019), Part 1, 17–1, para 8.

[98] See, eg, *R v Roble* [1997] Crim LR 449, CA.

[99] See Ch 22.

the solicitor is also called, the solicitor, whether there were any other reasons for the advice, and the nature of the advice given, so as to explore whether the advice may also have been given for tactical reasons. It is desirable, therefore, that the judge warns the defence advocate or the accused that the privilege may be lost.[100]

In *R v Bowden*[101] it was held that if the defence reveal the basis or reason for the solicitor's advice to the accused not to answer questions, this amounts to a waiver of privilege, whether the revelation is made by the accused or by the solicitor acting as his authorized agent, and whether it is made during pre-trial questioning, in evidence before the jury, or in evidence in a *voir dire* which is not repeated before the jury. If the defence do not reveal the basis or reason for the solicitor's advice, the judge should not, in the summing-up, comment as to what a competent solicitor would have advised, which would be speculation and, if incorrect, might in effect force the accused to waive his privilege and call the solicitor to give evidence.[102]

Reasonable and genuine reliance

The courts have stressed that the jury are not concerned with the correctness of the solicitor's advice, nor with whether it complies with Law Society guidelines, but with the reasonableness of the accused's conduct in all the circumstances, including the giving of the advice.[103] Such conduct is likely to be regarded as reasonable where there is evidence that the interviewing officer disclosed to the solicitor little or nothing of the nature of the case against the accused, so that the solicitor could not usefully advise the client, or where the nature of the offence or the material in the hands of the police is so complex, or relates to matters so long ago, that no sensible immediate response is feasible.[104] However, if an accused has stayed silent on legal advice and his silence is objectively unreasonable, it will not become reasonable merely because the solicitor's advice was ill-judged or bad,[105] which has led one commentator to observe that, if that is the law, then it punishes the accused for the failings of his solicitor.[106]

In *R v Betts*,[107] applied in *R v Chenia*,[108] it was said that it is not the *quality* of the decision not to answer questions that matters, but the genuineness of the decision, whereas in *R v Howell*,[109] approved, obiter, in *R v Knight*,[110] the Court of Appeal rejected the notion that once

---

[100] It was also said that an accused (or his solicitor) who gives evidence of what was said to the solicitor in response to a prosecution allegation of recent fabrication does not thereby waive privilege. The reason is that there is no way of dealing with the allegation other than by revealing what was said, whereas when an accused volunteers information about what was said, which may enable an allegation of fabrication to be made, that is the consequence of the voluntary provision: per Hooper LJ in *R v Loizou* [2006] EWCA Crim 1719 at [84].

[101] [1999] 4 All ER 43, CA.

[102] *R v Turner* [2013] 1 Cr App R 327 (25), CA.

[103] See per Lord Bingham CJ in *R v Argent* [1997] 2 Cr App R 27, CA at 35–6 and per Rose LJ in *R v Roble* [1997] Crim LR 449, CA. Therefore a judge is entitled to 'correct' an analogy, drawn by a defence advocate when addressing the jury, with acceptance of the professional advice of a doctor or accountant: see *R v Sakyi* [2014] EWCA Crim 1784 at [16].

[104] Per Rose LJ in *R v Roble* [1997] Crim LR 449, CA.

[105] *R v Connolly and McCartney* (1992) Belfast CC, 5 June.

[106] See Pattenden, 'Inferences from Silence' [1995] Crim LR 602. See also *R v Kinsella* (1993) Belfast CC, Dec.

[107] [2001] 2 Cr App R 257 (16), CA at 270.

[108] [2004] 1 All ER 543, CA. See also *R v Compton* [2002] EWCA Crim 2835.

[109] [2005] 1 Cr App R 1 (1).

[110] [2004] 1 WLR 340, CA.

it is shown that the advice, of whatever quality, has genuinely been relied on as the reason for silence, adverse comment is thereby disallowed. However, as was pointed out in *R v Hoare*,[111] there is no real inconsistency in the authorities, because it is plain from the judgment in *R v Betts* that even where an accused has genuinely relied on legal advice to remain silent, an adverse inference may still be drawn if the jury are sure that the true reason for silence is that he had no or no satisfactory explanation consistent with innocence to give. In other words, the jury must consider whether the accused relied on the legal advice to remain silent both genuinely and reasonably. In *R v Beckles*,[112] Lord Woolf CJ said:

> in a case where a solicitor's advice is relied upon by the defendant, the ultimate question for the jury remains under s 34 whether the facts relied on at trial were facts which the defendant could reasonably have been expected to mention at interview. If they were not, that is the end of the matter. If the jury consider that the defendant genuinely relied on the advice, that is not the end of the matter. It may still not have been reasonable of him to rely on the advice, or the advice may not have been the true explanation for his silence.
>
> In *R v Betts* . . . at [54] Kay LJ . . . says:
> 'A person, who is anxious not to answer questions because he has no or no adequate explanation to offer, gains no protection from his lawyer's advice because that advice is no more than a convenient way of disguising his true motivation for not mentioning facts.'
>
> If, in the last situation, it is possible to say that the defendant genuinely acted upon the advice, the fact that he did so because it suited his purpose may mean he was not acting reasonably in not mentioning the facts. His reasonableness in not mentioning the facts remains to be determined by the jury. If they conclude that he was acting unreasonably they can draw an adverse inference from the failure to mention the facts.

The legal test, therefore, now requires both genuine and reasonable reliance. However, it is submitted that to direct the jury in such terms is both potentially misleading and needlessly complex. Ultimately, what matters is the reasonableness of the accused in relying on the advice. A lack of genuine reliance is no more than an example—and there are many examples—of unreasonableness: if an accused has relied on the advice, but not genuinely, the reliance is a sham or pretence, and the accused will not have acted reasonably in following it.[113] It is submitted that it would be better to make no reference to genuineness.[114]

Circumstances in which a section 34 direction is not appropriate

Facts accepted as true

As we have seen, a s 34 direction is not appropriate where an accused fails to mention facts on which the prosecution rely and which he accepts as true, because the adverse inference to be drawn under the section is that a matter not mentioned is untrue.[115]

---

[111] [2005] 1 WLR 1804, CA at [51].

[112] [2005] 1 All ER 705, CA at [46].

[113] See, to similar effect, Fitzpatrick, 'Commentary' [2005] Crim LR 562 and Cooper, 'Legal advice and pre-trial silence—unreasonable developments' (2006) 10 E&P 60. See also Malik, 'Silence on legal advice: Clarity but not justice?: *R v Beckles*' (2005) 9 E&P 211.

[114] A reference to genuineness appears in the 'Example' in the Crown Court Compendium (July 2019), Part 1, 17–1.

[115] *R v Webber* [2004] 1 WLR 404, HL, per Lord Bingham at [28], applied in *R v Hackett* [2011] 2 Cr App R 35, CA.

Where a Lucas direction is more appropriate

Where a lie told by the accused is relied on by the prosecution, it is usually unhelpful to give the jury, in that regard, both a s 34 and a *Lucas* direction;[116] the judge should avoid giving both directions out of an over-abundance of caution and select and adapt the direction more appropriate to the facts and issues in the case.[117] If an accused gives an explanation for his failure to mention a fact and it is that explanation which is alleged to be the lie, it suffices to give a s 34 direction which incorporates the explanation.[118] It is unnecessary, confusing, and unduly favourable to the defence to include, in the direction to the jury, the examples of innocent reasons for lying required by the *Lucas* direction.[119]

Where a similar direction would be given anyway

Even if the conditions for drawing an inference set out in s 34 are satisfied, it does not necessarily follow that the section should be invoked. In *Brizzalari v R*[120] the Court of Appeal noted that the mischief at which s 34 was primarily aimed was the positive defence following a 'no comment' interview and/or the ambush defence. The court counselled against 'the further complicating of trials and summings-up by invoking this statute, unless the merits of the individual case require that it should be done'. Thus there may be no point in invoking the section, even if it applies, if the direction of the judge will be substantially the same whether or not the section is invoked, as in *R v Maguire*,[121] where M gave one account in interview and another, different, account at trial so that in any event the Crown case was that the evidence was untruthful and the judge would have directed the jury that it was for them to decide whether to draw an adverse inference.[122]

The question in R v Mountford

Should an inference be drawn by the jury under s 34 if it can only logically be drawn by first concluding that the accused is guilty? In *R v Mountford*[123] the police entered W's flat and saw M drop from a window a package later found to contain heroin. In interview, M made no comment. Subsequently, W pleaded guilty to permitting his premises to be used for the purposes of supplying heroin and, at M's trial on a charge of possession of heroin with intent to supply, gave evidence against him. M's evidence was that he was at the flat to buy heroin from W, the dealer, and when the police had arrived, W had thrown him the heroin which he had dropped from the window. His reason for not mentioning this in interview was that he did not know what W had said and did not want to get him into trouble. It was held that inferences could not be drawn under s 34 because the jury could only be sure that this

---

[116] See *R v Rana* [2007] EWCA Crim 2261 at [11], echoed in *R v Spottiswood* [2019] EWCA Crim 949 at [46]. See also Ch 2, Lies, p 19.

[117] *R v Rana* [2007] EWCA Crim 2261, CA at [10] and [11] and *R v Hackett* [2011] 2 Cr App R 35 (3), CA at 40–41.

[118] See *R v Spottiswood* [2019] EWCA Crim 949 at [44]–[45]: where differing accounts are given by the accused at different stages of proceedings in respect of which distinct different legal principles apply, separate directions may be justified; but even in this situation, the approach endorsed is to combine the directions in accordance with Example 3 in the Crown Court Compendium, Part 1, 16–3.

[119] *R v Hackett* [2011] 2 Cr App R 35 (3), CA at 44.

[120] [2004] EWCA Crim 310.

[121] [2008] EWCA Crim 1028.

[122] See also *R v Harris* [2016] 1 Cr App R 69 (4), CA: a s 34 direction is unnecessary where the prosecution use previous inconsistent statements as matters going to credit and do not seek any other inference to be drawn.

[123] [1999] Crim LR 575, CA.

explanation was true if they were to conclude that W was the dealer, not M, and conversely could only be sure that this explanation was false if they were to conclude that M was the dealer, and not W. This element of circularity, it was held, could only be resolved by a verdict founded in no way upon an inference under s 34, but on the other evidence in the case. The same conclusion was reached in *R v Gill*,[124] but it has since been held that *R v Mountford* was concerned with its own set of specific facts and was not intended to have a general application[125] and that it will only be in rare cases of the simplest and most straightforward kind that the *Mountford* approach is appropriate.[126]

In *R v Daly*[127] however, the Court of Appeal cast doubt on the decision in *R v Mountford* on the basis that although it accepted that the fact not mentioned was closely related to the issue in the case, it could find nothing in the statutory wording which requires that the s 34 issue be capable of resolution as a separate issue in the case. In *R v Gowland-Wynn*[128] the Court of Appeal went further, Lord Woolf CJ being of the view that although it may be that *R v Mountford* and *R v Gill* can be confined to their special facts, they had the effect of emasculating and defeating the very purpose of s 34, and should be consigned to oblivion and should not be followed. Similarly in *R v Webber*[129] the House of Lords, while not expressly overruling *R v Mountford*, expressed the view that s 34 did apply to the case.

The direction to the jury

Elements of the direction

In cases where a direction under s 34 is called for, then subject to the facts of the particular case, juries should be directed in accordance with the Judicial Studies Board specimen direction,[130] which was approved by the European Court of Human Rights in *Beckles v UK*[131] in the context of the accused's silence on legal advice. The direction now to be found in the Crown Court Compendium (July 2019), Part 1, 17–1 is, speaking generally, to the same effect. The trial judge must remind the jury of the words of the caution given to the accused.[132] The judge must also direct the jury to the effect that an adverse inference can only be drawn if, despite any evidence relied upon by the accused, they conclude that the silence can only sensibly be attributed to the accused having no answer or no answer that would stand up to questioning and investigation.[133] The latter ('no answer that would stand up' etc) is worth stressing. Section 34 is not limited to cases of recent invention, that is, where the jury may conclude that the facts were invented after the interview. It also covers cases where they may conclude that the accused had the facts in mind at the time of the interview but did not believe that they would stand up to scrutiny at that time.[134] The judge must clearly identify for the

---

[124] [2001] 1 Cr App R 160 (11), CA.

[125] *R v Hearne*, 4 May 2000, unreported, CA, followed in *R v Milford* [2001] Crim LR 330, CA.

[126] *R v Chenia* [2004] 1 All ER 543, CA at [34]–[35].

[127] [2002] 2 Cr App R 201 (14), CA.

[128] [2002] 1 Cr App R 569 (41), CA.

[129] [2004] 1 WLR 404, HL.

[130] *R v Chenia* [2004] 1 All ER 543, CA at [47].

[131] [2001] 31 EHRR 1.

[132] *R v Chenia* [2004] 1 All ER 543, CA at [49]–[51].

[133] See *Condron v UK* [2001] 31 EHRR 1 at para 61; *R v Betts* [2001] 2 Cr App R 257 (16), CA; *R v Daly* [2002] 2 Cr App R 201 (14), CA; *R v Petkar* [2004] 1 Cr App R 270 (22), CA; and *R v Green* [2019] EWCA Crim 411.

[134] *R v Milford* [2001] Crim LR 330, CA. See also *R v Daniel* (1998) 2 Cr App R 373, CA at 382–3 and *R v Argent* [1997] 2 Cr App R 27, CA at 34 and 36.

jury the inferences which they may properly draw.[135] Contrary to the ruling of the Court of Appeal in *R v Doldur*,[136] the trial judge must also make clear to the jury that they must be satisfied that the prosecution have established a case to answer before drawing any inference.[137] The jury should be told that, if an inference is drawn, they should not convict 'wholly or mainly on the strength of it'. The first of those alternatives, 'wholly', is a clear way of putting the need for the prosecution to be able to prove a case to answer, otherwise than by means of an inference drawn. The second alternative, 'mainly', buttresses that need,[138] and is required because the accused's '. . . failure to mention facts could be the main influence on the jury's verdict, even though not the only one.'[139] It is also usual to direct the jury that they should only draw an inference if they consider it fair and proper to do so:[140] even if the strict requirements for drawing an inference are met, whether it is actually right to do so remains a matter for the jury's good sense and fair-mindedness.[141] It is also desirable that any proposed direction is discussed with the advocates before closing speeches and the discussion should start by a consideration whether any direction under s 34 should be given.[142] In both respects, the direction has been strongly endorsed by the Court of Appeal.[143]

Failure to give a proper direction

It does not necessarily follow from a failure to give a proper direction that there has been a breach of Art 6 of the Convention or that a conviction is unsafe. The Court of Appeal will have regard to the particular facts of the case. Factors which may count against the accused, depending on the precise nature of the misdirection or non-direction, may include the strength of the case to answer, the strength of the prosecution evidence, the fact that the accused declined to answer questions himself, rather than on legal advice, and the fact that a clear and accurate direction was given under s 35 of the 1994 Act.[144] Thus in a case involving legal advice to remain silent, failure to say anything about having to be sure that the accused remained silent not because of the legal advice, but because he had no answer to give, is likely to be fatal;[145] but failure to direct the jury to consider whether there was a case to answer will not render the trial unfair or the conviction unsafe where, on the facts, no jury could have concluded that there was no case to answer.[146] In *Adetoro v UK*[147] it was held that failure to direct the jury that adverse inferences could only be drawn if they specifically rejected the accused's explanation for silence did not render the trial unfair or the conviction unsafe, because the circumstantial evidence against the accused

---

[135] *R v Petkar* [2004] 1 Cr App R 270 (22), CA at [51].

[136] [2000] Crim LR 178, CA.

[137] See *R v Milford* [2001] Crim LR 330, CA; *Beckles v UK* [2001] 31 EHRR 1; and *R v Chenia* [2004] 1 All ER 543, CA.

[138] *R v Petkar* [2004] 1 Cr App R 270 (22), CA at [51], citing *Murray v UK* (1996) 22 EHRR 29 at 60, para 47.

[139] *R v Green* [2019] EWCA Crim 411 at [25].

[140] See also the Crown Court Compendium (July 2019), Part 1, 17–8, Example, point 4.

[141] *R v Green* [2019] EWCA Crim 411 at [24].

[142] See also the Crown Court Compendium (July 2019), Part 1, 17–1, para 14.

[143] See *R v Chenia* [2004] 1 All ER 543 at [36] and *R v Beckles* [2005] 1 All ER 705, CA at [34]. See also, *R v Green* [2019] EWCA Crim 411 at [27]–[28], where the court emphasized the value of a discussion and drew attention to the usefulness of written legal directions.

[144] See *R v Chenia* [2004] 1 All ER 543 at [59]–[65].

[145] See *R v Bresa* [2006] Crim LR 179, CA.

[146] *R v Chenia* [2004] 1 All ER 543 at [53]–[55].

[147] [2010] ECHR 609.

was overwhelming and the defence to the charge and the explanation for the silence were essentially the same, so that it was implausible that the jury would draw an adverse inference because satisfied with the explanation for silence and use that inference to reject the defence.

Functions of judge and jury

The trial judge, in directing the jury, must take care to identify the specific facts relied on at trial which were not mentioned on being questioned or charged:[148] s 34 does not apply simply because the accused made no comments at interview.[149] In *R v Argent*[150] it was made clear that under s 34 the following matters are all questions of fact for the jury: (i) whether there is some fact which the accused has relied on in his defence; (ii) whether the accused failed to mention it on being questioned or charged; and (iii) whether it is a fact which in the circumstances existing at the time he could reasonably have been expected to mention when questioned or charged.[151] It was also held that the 'proper' inferences that the jurors are permitted to draw means such inferences as appear proper to them. However, although (i) and (ii) are questions of fact for the jury, in *R v McGarry*[152] it was held that there will plainly be cases in which it is appropriate for the judge to decide as a matter of law whether there is any evidence on which a reasonable jury properly directed could conclude that either or both of those requirements has been satisfied. Thus if the prosecution accept that those requirements have not been satisfied, and the judge considers that this is a proper view, no question of inviting the jury to draw inferences from the failure of the accused to answer some of the questions put to him can arise. In *R v Argent* it was held that although the question whether the fact was one which the accused could reasonably have been expected to mention is an issue on which the judge should give appropriate directions, ordinarily the issue should be left to the jury to decide, and that only rarely should the judge direct that they should, or should not draw the appropriate inference. As to the latter direction, in *R v McGarry* it was held that where the jury are aware that the accused failed to answer questions and the judge rules that there is no evidence on which they can properly conclude that he failed to mention any fact relied on in his defence, then there should be a specific direction not to draw any adverse inference.[153] However, such a specific direction is plainly not called for where the accused gives a 'no comment' interview and gives no evidence at trial, thereby attracting a direction under s 35 of the 1994 Act, because in such a case it would be fanciful to suggest that an inference of the kind permitted by s 34 might be drawn by the jury in the absence of a direction not to do so.[154]

---

[148] *R v Webber* [2004] 1 WLR 404, HL at [27] and *R v Chenia* [2004] 1 All ER 543 at [29] and [87]. A failure to do so, however, will not necessarily render a conviction unsafe: see *R v Chivers* [2011] EWCA Crim 1212.

[149] *R v Argent* [1997] 2 Cr App R 27, CA and *T v DPP* [2007] EWHC 1793 (Admin).

[150] [1997] 2 Cr App R 27, CA at 32.

[151] The jury may need guidance as to what level of detail the accused might be expected to go into in circumstances where he has not been asked specific questions but has simply been asked to give his account: see *R v Green* [2019] EWCA Crim 411 at [23].

[152] [1999] 1 Cr App R 377, CA at 382–3.

[153] But failure to give such a direction will not necessarily render a conviction unsafe: *R v Bowers* [1998] Crim LR 817, CA. See also *R v Bansal* [1999] Crim LR 484, CA.

[154] *R v La Rose* [2003] EWCA Crim 1471.

The inferences that may be drawn

Under s 34(2) the inferences that may be drawn are 'such inferences from the failure as appear proper'. The breadth of this phrase is such that it could be construed to permit a general inference that the accused is guilty of the offence charged, a construction supported, arguably, by s 38(3) of the Act. In fact, the logical inference to be drawn is narrower and more precise, that the facts relied on in the accused's defence are not true, on the basis that, if they were true, the accused could reasonably have been expected to have mentioned them in interview or on being charged, but did not do so because of the risk that the police might then have been able to expose their falsity or because he had yet to invent them, or all of them.

The extent to which an inference drawn under s 34 will assist the prosecution in establishing a case to answer, or in proving the guilt of the accused, will obviously turn on the nature of the fact relied on in the defence and its importance to that defence. However, s 38(3) and (4) of the 1994 Act provide that:

(3) A person shall not have the proceedings against him transferred to the Crown Court for trial, have a case to answer or be convicted of an offence solely on an inference drawn from such a failure or refusal as is mentioned in section 34(2), 35(3), 36(2) or 37(2).

(4) A judge shall not refuse to grant such an application as is mentioned in section 34(2)(b), 36(2) (b) and 37(2)(b) solely on an inference drawn from such a failure as is mentioned in section 34(2), 36(2) or 37(2).

These provisions, in relation to s 34(2), seem otiose. It is true that in cases of confession and avoidance, as when the accused admits an assault but raises a defence of self-defence, rejection of that defence may result in a finding of guilt. However, since the worst possible inference that can be drawn is that the fact relied upon in the defence is untrue, then, as the example given illustrates, such an inference could not *by itself* justify a conviction (or a decision that there is a case to answer). The purpose of s 38(3) in the present context seems to be twofold. First, it requires the judge to remind himself that he is not entitled to decide that there is a case to answer solely on the basis that the relevant facts relied on by the accused in his defence are untrue. Second, it requires him to direct the jury that they are not entitled to convict solely— or, in the light of *Condron v United Kingdom*, mainly—on the basis that such facts are untrue.

Acceptance of the accusation of another by silence

Section 34(5) of the 1994 Act provides that:

This section does not—
(a) prejudice the admissibility in evidence of the silence or other reaction of the accused in the face of anything said in his presence relating to the conduct in respect of which he is charged, in so far as evidence thereof would be admissible apart from this section; or
(b) preclude the drawing of any inference from any such silence or other reaction of the accused which could properly be drawn apart from this section.

The effect of this subsection is to preserve the common law authorities whereby, in appropriate circumstances, the accused, by his conduct, demeanour, or silence, may be treated as having accepted the accusation of another so as to make it a confession statement of his own.[155]

---

[155] See Ch 15, **Statements made in the presence of the accused**, p 490. See further Mirfield, 'Two Side-Effects of Sections 34 to 37 of the Criminal Justice and Public Order Act 1994' [1995] Crim LR 612, who argues that it may now be permissible to draw an inference that a suspect who has been cautioned but remains silent in the face of police accusations accepts the truth of the accusations.

Failure or refusal to account for objects, substances, marks, etc

Sections 36 and 37 of the Criminal Justice and Public Order Act 1994

Sections 36 and 37 of the 1994 Act, which are based on ss 18 and 19 of the Irish Criminal Justice Act 1984, fall to be considered together.

Section 36 of the 1994 Act provides that:

(1)   Where—
 (a) a person is arrested by a constable, and there is—
  (i)   on his person; or
  (ii) in or on his clothing or footwear; or
  (iii) otherwise in his possession; or
  (iv) in any place[156] in which he is at the time of his arrest,
  any object, substance or mark, or there is any mark on any such object; and
 (b) that or another constable investigating the case reasonably believes that the presence of the object, substance or mark may be attributable to the participation of the person arrested in the commission of an offence specified by the constable;[157] and
 (c) the constable informs the person arrested that he so believes, and requests him to account for the presence of the object, substance or mark; and
 (d) the person fails or refuses to do so,
 then if, in any proceedings against the person for the offence so specified, evidence of those matters is given, subsection (2) below applies.
(2)   Where this subsection applies—
 (a) [repealed];
 (b) a judge, in deciding whether to grant an application made by the accused under paragraph 2 of Schedule 3 to the Crime and Disorder Act 1998;[158]
 (c) the court, in determining whether there is a case to answer; and
 (d) the court or jury, in determining whether the accused is guilty of the offence charged,[159] may draw such inferences from the failure or refusal as appear proper.
(3)   Subsections (1) and (2) above apply to the condition of clothing or footwear as they apply to a substance or mark thereon.
(4)   Subsections (1) and (2) above do not apply unless the accused was told in ordinary language by the constable when making the request mentioned in subsection (1)(c) above what the effect of this section would be if he failed or refused to comply with that request.
(4A) Where the accused was at an authorised place of detention[160] at the time of the failure or refusal, subsections (1) and (2) above do not apply if he had not been allowed an opportunity to consult a solicitor prior to the request being made.
(5)   This section applies in relation to officers of customs and excise as it applies in relation to constables.[161]
(6)   This section does not preclude the drawing of any inference from a failure or refusal of the accused to account for the presence of an object, substance or mark or from the condition of clothing or footwear which could properly be drawn apart from this section.

---

[156] For the purposes of both s 36 and s 37 'place' includes any building or part of a building, any vehicle, vessel, aircraft or hovercraft, and any other place whatsoever: s 38(1).

[157] Ie not necessarily the offence for which arrested. Cf s 37(1)(b).

[158] See n 63.

[159] Or any other offence of which the accused could lawfully be convicted on that charge: s 38(2).

[160] See n 65.

[161] Arrest by others charged with the duty of investigating offences and charging offenders will not suffice.

Section 37 of the 1994 Act provides that:

(1) Where—
    (a) a person arrested by a constable was found by him at a place at or about the time the offence for which he was arrested is alleged to have been committed; and
    (b) that or another constable investigating the offence reasonably believes that the presence of the person at that place and at that time may be attributable to his participation in the commission of the offence; and
    (c) the constable informs the person that he so believes, and requests him to account for that presence; and
    (d) the person fails or refuses to do so,
    then if, in any proceedings against the person for the offence, evidence of those matters is given, subsection (2) below applies.
(2) [Identical, in its terms, to s 36(2).]
(3) [Identical, in its terms, to s 36(4).]
(3A) Where the accused was at an authorised place of detention[162] at the time of the failure or refusal, subsections (1) and (2) do not apply if he had not been allowed an opportunity to consult a solicitor prior to the request being made.
    . . .
(4) [Identical, in its terms, to s 36(5).]
(5) This section does not preclude the drawing of any inference from a failure or refusal of the accused to account for his presence at a place which could properly be drawn apart from this section.

It has been held that, under s 36, the jury must be satisfied that the accused failed (or refused) to account for the object, substance, or mark; that an unsatisfactory explanation may amount to a failure to account;[163] and that s 36(1)(b) does not require the constable to specify in precise terms the offence in question.[164]

The direction to the jury

According to the Crown Court Compendium[165] in the case of both s 36 and s 37 the jury must be directed that they may only draw an inference if they are sure that there is no sensible explanation for the accused's failure other than that he had no answer at the trial or none that would stand up to scrutiny; and in this regard the jury must consider any explanation given for the failure and must be told that unless they are sure that that was not the genuine reason for the failure they should not draw any adverse inference.[166] If evidence is given that the accused's reason for the failure was that he had been advised by his solicitor to remain silent, the jury should be directed in the same way as when the issue arises under s 34.[167]

---

[162] See n 65.

[163] See also paras 10.10 and 10.11, Code C, issued under the Police and Criminal Evidence Act 1984, setting out the warnings to be given to a suspect under s 36 and s 37, which use the words 'fails or refuses to answer . . . or *to answer satisfactorily*' (emphasis added).

[164] *R v Compton* [2002] EWCA Crim 2835.

[165] The Crown Court Compendium (July 2019), Part 1, 17–2.

[166] Para 13.

[167] Para 14. See, in this chapter, under, Silence on legal advice, p 513.

Sections 36 and 37 contain no proviso, analogous to that contained in s 34(1), whereby an inference may only be drawn if the accused could reasonably have been expected to account for the object, substance, etc at the time when questioned about it. Notwithstanding this omission, it is submitted that the trial judge should give a clear direction to the jury that they may only draw such inferences as appear proper and that, in deciding whether to draw an inference, and if so the strength of the inference to be drawn, they should take into account the nature and personal characteristics of the accused, including, as appropriate, his age, intelligence, language, and literacy, his physical, mental, and emotional state at the time when he was questioned, and whether he has the knowledge or expertise that may be necessary to account for the presence of the particular object etc in question.[168]

The nature and strength of the inference

The nature and strength of any inference drawn under s 36 will also depend on the nature of the object, substance, etc, the extent to which evidence of its presence supports the prosecution case and the other circumstances of the case. For example, if the accused, on arrest for murder by stabbing, is found with a blood-stained knife in his pocket, his failure or refusal to account for its presence is likely to result in a highly damaging adverse inference. However, if the stabbing takes place in a very crowded pub and the blood-stained knife is found on the floor,[169] the accused's failure to account for its presence is unlikely, without more, to result in any adverse inference. Similar considerations apply to s 37.

Scope of sections 36 and 37

The scope of both s 36 and s 37 has been fixed somewhat arbitrarily. For example, if a person, suspected of murder by stabbing, fails to explain why the jacket he is wearing on arrest is blood-stained, an adverse inference may be drawn under s 36. But if such a suspect, having abandoned his blood-stained jacket at the scene of the crime, where it is found by the police, is then arrested by them on his way home and fails to explain why his jacket is blood-stained (or even why he abandoned it), no statutory adverse inference may be drawn.

The purpose of s 38(3)

Inferences under s 36 and s 37 can only be drawn where evidence is given of the presence of the object, substance, etc, or of the presence of the accused, at a place at or about the time of the offence. In some cases, that evidence, either taken alone or together with the adverse inference that can be drawn under the statutory provisions, will be sufficient to establish a case to answer or, indeed, to convict, as when a drug courier is arrested carrying a large package of heroin. Presumably, as in the case of s 34, the purpose of s 38(3)[170] in relation to s 36(2) and s 37(2), is simply to require the judge to direct the jury (or himself) that they are not entitled to convict (he is not entitled to decide that there is a case to answer) solely or, in the light of *Condron v United Kingdom*, mainly, on the basis of the inference drawn.

---

[168] As to this last factor, see Marks, 'Expert Evidence of Drug Traces: Relevance, Reliability and the right to Silence' [2013] Crim LR 810.

[169] See s 36(1)(a)(iv).

[170] See, in this chapter, under **The inferences that may be drawn**, p 521.

The discretion to exclude evidence of failure to mention facts

Section 38(6) provides that:

> Nothing in sections 34, 35, 36 or 37 prejudices any power of a court, in any proceedings, to exclude evidence (whether by preventing questions being put or otherwise) at its discretion.

In appropriate circumstances, therefore, the court could exclude evidence of the accused's failure to mention any fact under either s 78 of the 1984 Act or common law.[171] This might be appropriate, in relation to s 34, for example, in cases where it would be unfair to make use of the accused's silence by reason of breach of the provisions of the 1984 Act or the Codes, especially those relating to the caution, interrogation, and access to a solicitor (eg, failure to caution) or because the accused's silence was brought about by some other improper or unfair means (eg, threatening to beat up the accused unless he remains silent). Equally, in relation to s 36, there is obvious potential for discretionary exclusion where the evidence of the object, substance, etc was obtained illegally, improperly, or unfairly.

In *R v Condron and Condron* it was held that if the defence objection is simply that the jury should not be invited to draw any adverse inference, it will seldom be appropriate to invite the judge to rule on this before the conclusion of all the evidence, because it will not be apparent until then what are the material facts that were not disclosed or the reason for non-disclosure. It was said that only in the most exceptional case could it be appropriate to make such a submission before the introduction of the evidence by the Crown, for example where the accused is of very low intelligence and understanding and has been advised by his solicitor to say nothing.

Inferences from refusal to consent to the taking of samples

In appropriate circumstances, an adverse inference may be drawn from a suspect's refusal, without good cause, to consent to the taking of 'intimate samples' from his body. Under s 65 of the 1984 Act, an intimate sample is defined as (a) a sample of blood, semen, or any other tissue fluid, urine, or pubic hair; (b) a dental impression; and (c) a swab taken from any part of a person's genitals (including pubic hair) or from a person's body orifice other than the mouth. Section 62 of the 1984 Act, detailed consideration of which is outside the scope of this work, sets out the various conditions to be met before an intimate sample can be taken from a person. One of the conditions is that appropriate consent is given.[172] Section 62(10) provides that:

> Where the appropriate consent to the taking of an intimate sample from a person was refused without good cause, in any proceedings against that person for an offence—
> (a) the court, in determining . . .
>   (ii) whether there is a case to answer; and
> (aa) a judge, in deciding whether to grant an application made by the accused under paragraph 2 of Schedule 3 to the Crime and Disorder Act 1998 . . .;[173]
> (b) the court or jury, in determining whether that person is guilty of the offence charged,
>   may draw such inferences from the refusal as appear proper.

---

[171] See Ch 2.

[172] See s 62(1)(b), (1A)(b), and (2A)(c). 'Appropriate consent' means, in relation to a person aged 17 or over, the consent of that person; in relation to a person aged 14 or over but under 17, the consent of that person and his parent or guardian; and in relation to a person aged under 14, the consent of his parent or guardian: s 65. The consent must be given in writing: s 62(4).

[173] See n 63.

Before a person is asked to provide an intimate sample, he must be warned that if he refuses without good cause, his refusal may harm his case if it comes to trial.[174] Whether consent was refused 'without good cause' is a question of fact. In appropriate circumstances, a person's bodily or mental condition may amount to good cause. However, whether a refusal out of embarrassment or on the grounds of some deeply held personal conviction is capable of constituting good cause is less clear.

There is no equivalent to s 62(10) in the case of 'non-intimate samples' because such samples may be taken without consent, subject to compliance with the conditions that have to be met set out in s 63 of the 1984 Act.[175] Under s 65 of the 1984 Act, a non-intimate sample means: (a) a sample of hair other than pubic hair; (b) a sample taken from a nail or from under a nail; (c) a swab taken from any part of a person's body other than a part from which a swab taken would be an intimate sample; (d) saliva; and (e) a skin impression (which means any record (other than a fingerprint) which is a record (in any form and produced by any method) of the skin pattern and other physical characteristics or features of the whole or any part of a foot or any other part of a body).

Inferences from failure to provide advance disclosure of the defence case

Trials on indictment

The disclosure required

Under the rules of primary prosecution disclosure in s 3 of the Criminal Procedure and Investigations Act 1996 (the 1996 Act), the prosecutor must disclose to the accused previously undisclosed material which might reasonably be considered capable of undermining the case for the prosecution against the accused or of assisting the case for the accused, or give the accused a written statement that there is no such material. Section 5(5) of the 1996 Act is to the effect that where a person is charged with an offence for which he is sent for trial to a Crown Court and the prosecutor complies or purports to comply with s 3, the accused must give a defence statement to the court and the prosecutor.[176] The defence statement must be served during a prescribed 'relevant period' (within 28 days of primary prosecution disclosure).[177] The contents of the defence statement are prescribed by s 6A, which provides as follows:

> (1) ... a defence statement is a written statement—
>
> (a) setting out the nature of the accused's defence, including any particular defences on which he intends to rely,
>
> (b) indicating the matters of fact on which he takes issue with the prosecution,
>
> (c) setting out, in the case of each such matter, why he takes issue with the prosecution,
>
> (ca) setting out particulars of the matters of fact on which he intends to rely for the purposes of his defence, and

---

[174] Para 6.3 and Note 6D, Code D.

[175] The 1984 Act, s 61, makes similar provision for fingerprints of a person to be taken without his consent.

[176] Although there is no obligation on an accused to give a defence statement to a co-accused, if the prosecutor forms the view that a defence statement of one co-accused might reasonably be expected to assist the defence of another, it should be disclosed to the other on secondary prosecution disclosure: *R v Cairns* [2003] 1 WLR 796, CA.

[177] See s 5(C), s 12, and the Criminal Procedure and Investigations Act 1996 (Defence Disclosure Time Limits) Regulations 2011, SI 2011/209, reg 2.

(d) indicating any point of law (including any point as to the admissibility of evidence or an abuse of process) which he wishes to take, and any authority on which he intends to rely for that purpose.

(2) A defence statement that discloses an alibi must give particulars of it, including—

(a) the name, address and date of birth of any witness the accused believes is able to give evidence in support of the alibi, or as many of those details as are known to the accused when the statement is given;

(b) any information in the accused's possession which might be of material assistance in identifying or finding any such witness in whose case any of the details mentioned in paragraph (a) are not known to the accused when the statement is given.[178]

(3) For the purposes of this section evidence in support of an alibi is evidence tending to show that by reason of the presence of the accused at a particular place or in a particular area at a particular time he was not, or was unlikely to have been, at the place where the offence is alleged to have been committed at the time of its alleged commission.

R v Rochford[179] established three important matters in respect of defence statements. First, it is not open to a lawyer to advise his client not to file a defence statement, because to file such a statement is a statutory obligation. Second, s 6A does not take away the fundamental rights of legal professional privilege and the privilege against self-incrimination; the accused is required to disclose what is going to happen at the trial, not his confidential discussions with his lawyer and he is not obliged to incriminate himself, if he does not want to.[180] Third, if an accused has no positive case to advance at trial, but pleads not guilty, the defence statement should say that the accused does not admit the offence, has no positive case to advance, and calls for the Crown to prove its case.[181]

As a matter of good practice a defence statement should be signed by the accused as an acknowledgment of its accuracy to obviate error and dispute that can arise, for example, where part of the defence statement is contrary to the original instructions given by the accused to his solicitors.[182]

As to the obligation under s 6A(1), account should be taken of what can reasonably be expected of the accused having regard to how clearly the prosecution case has been put, including, for example, whether they have spelled out inferences that they will be asking the jury to draw from the evidence.[183]

The obligation under s 6A(2)(a) to give the name and address of an alibi witness is triggered by the accused's belief that the witness is able to give evidence in support of the alibi; it is not necessary that the witness can give such evidence and is willing to do so. Nor is the accused's belief in the witness's ability to give evidence dependent upon the witness giving a proof of evidence.[184]

---

[178] Failure to give notice of alibi witnesses does not render their evidence inadmissible: see *R (Tinnion) v Reading Crown Court* [2009] EWHC 2930 (Admin).

[179] [2011] 1 WLR 534, CA.

[180] [2011] 1 WLR 534, CA at [21].

[181] Ibid at [24].

[182] *R v Wheeler* [2001] Crim LR 745, CA.

[183] The Crown Court Compendium, (July 2019), Part 1, 17–4, para 6. See also *R v Duarte* [2019] EWCA Crim 1466.

[184] *Joseph Hill & Co, In re* [2013] 2 Cr App R 218, CA.

Under s 6C, there is an obligation on the defence, during a prescribed 'relevant period', to give notification of intention to call defence witnesses. Section 6C(1) provides as follows:

(1) The accused must give to the court and the prosecutor a notice indicating whether he intends to call any persons (other than himself) as witnesses at his trial and, if so—
   (a) giving the name, address and date of birth of each such proposed witness, or as many of those details as are known to the accused when the notice is given;
   (b) providing any information in the accused's possession which might be of material assistance in identifying or finding any such proposed witness in whose case any of the details mentioned in paragraph (a) are not known to the accused when the notice is given.[185]

Failure to comply

Under s 11(5) of the 1996 Act, where an accused fails to comply with the disclosure requirements of ss 5, 6A, or 6C, the court or any other party may make appropriate adverse comment and the court or jury, in deciding the question of guilt, may draw proper adverse inferences.[186] It is not open to the court to order compliance and then vest itself with the extra-statutory power to punish as a contempt of court disobedience to the order.[187] If it appears to the court at a pre-trial hearing that an accused has failed to comply fully with s 5 or s 6C, so that there is a possibility of comment being made or inferences being drawn under s 11(5), he shall warn the accused accordingly.[188] Section 11 provides as follows:

(1) This section applies in the cases set out in subsections (2), (3), and (4).
(2) The first case is where section 5 applies and the accused—
   (a) fails to give an initial defence statement,
   (b) gives an initial defence statement but does so after the end of the . . . relevant period for section 5,

   . . .

   (e) sets out inconsistent defences in his defence statement, or
   (f) at his trial—
       (i) puts forward a defence which was not mentioned in his defence statement or is different from any defence set out in the statement,
       (ii) relies on a matter which, in breach of the requirements imposed by or under section 6A, was not mentioned in his defence statement,
       (iii) adduces evidence in support of an alibi[189] without having given particulars of the alibi in his defence statement, or
       (iv) calls a witness to give evidence in support of an alibi without having complied with section 6A(2)(a) or (b) as regards the witness in his defence statement.
(3) The second case is . . .[190]

---

[185] For the guidance that police officers must follow if they interview proposed witnesses whose details are disclosed, see the Code of Practice for Arranging and Conducting Interviews of Witnesses notified by the Accused.

[186] Inferences may also be drawn where an accused departs from a case disclosed pursuant to a requirement imposed at a preparatory hearing or fails to comply with such a requirement: see ss 29, 31(4), 31(6), and 34 of the 1996 Act.

[187] *R v Rochford* [2011] 1 WLR 534, CA.

[188] Section 6E(2).

[189] A reference to 'evidence in support of an alibi' shall be construed in accordance with s 6A(3): s 11(12)(d).

[190] The second case relates to failure to disclose prior to summary trial: see, in this chapter, under **Summary trials, p 531.**

(4) The third case is where the accused—
   (a) gives a witness notice but does so after the end of . . . the relevant period for section 6C, or
   (b) at his trial calls a witness (other than himself) not included, or not adequately identified, in a witness notice.

(5) Where this section applies—
   (a) the court or any other party may make such comment as appears appropriate;
   (b) the court or jury may draw such inferences as appear proper in deciding whether the accused is guilty of the offence concerned.

(6) Where—
   (a) this section applies by virtue of subsection (2)(f)(ii) . . ., and
   (b) the matter which was not mentioned is a point of law (including any point as to the admissibility of evidence or an abuse of process) or an authority, comment by another party under subsection 5(a) may be made only with the leave of the court.

(7) Where this section applies by virtue of subsection (4), comment by another party under subsection (5)(a) may be made only with the leave of the court.

(8) Where the accused puts forward a defence which is different from any defence set out in his defence statement, in doing anything under subsection (5) or in deciding whether to do anything under it the court shall have regard—
   (a) to the extent of the difference in the defences, and
   (b) to whether there is any justification for it.

(9) Where the accused calls a witness whom he has failed to include, or to identify adequately, in a witness notice,[191] in doing anything under subsection (5) or in deciding to do anything under it the court shall have regard to whether there is any justification for the failure.

(10) A person shall not be convicted of an offence solely on an inference drawn under subsection (5).

Section 11(2) commonly applies where the accused has given oral evidence of a defence which differs from the defence set out in his defence statement.[192] However, s 11(2) may also apply where the accused has not given oral evidence.[193] Where the section does apply, the prosecution may make an application to admit the defence statement and/or provide the jury with a copy of it.[194] Where it is unclear whether the accused will be giving evidence, the prosecution should not delay too long before making the application. In *R v Duarte*,[195] the Court of Appeal held that at the stage when it is the accused's turn to give evidence and he formally indicates that he will not give evidence, it will generally be too late for the prosecution to make the application, absent a prior agreement with the defence which has been approved by the judge.[196] Such an agreement may be to the effect that the prosecution

---

[191] 'Witness notice' means a notice given under s 6C: s 11(12)(e).

[192] See s 11(2)(f)(i). See also *R v Duarte* [2019] EWCA Crim 1466.

[193] *R v Duarte* [2019] EWCA Crim 1466.

[194] See s 6E(5)(b) of the 1996 Act which states that the judge may direct that the jury be given a copy of the defence statement only if he is 'of the opinion that seeing a copy of the defence statement would help the jury to understand the case or to resolve any issue in the case'. See also *R v Duarte* [2019] EWCA Crim 1466, where the judge was wrong to allow copies of the defence statement to go to the jury. It was not clear that the defence set out in the defence statement was inconsistent with the defence advanced at trial and therefore it was not capable of helping the jury with whether he had initially put forward a 'lying defence' (see [27]–[28]).

[195] [2019] EWCA Crim 1466.

[196] See *R v Duarte* [2019] EWCA Crim 1466 at [23]. See also, s 35 of the Criminal Justice and Public Order Act 1994 covered earlier in this chapter under **Failure to testify, p 499**.

advocate will delay formally closing her case until after the accused has made a final decision about whether to give evidence, or that she will re-open her case for the sole purpose of admitting the defence statement.[197]

Under section 11(5)(b), proper inferences may be drawn only in deciding whether the accused is guilty of the offence charged, and not in deciding whether there is a case to answer.[198]

Three important matters were established in *R v Tibbs* in respect of adverse comment and inferences.[199] First, s 11 does not disallow or require leave for cross-examination of an accused on differences between his defence at trial and his defence statement—it precludes comment or invitation to the jury to draw an inference from the differences unless the court gives leave. Second, the word 'defence' in s 11 is not restricted to its general legal description (eg 'self-defence' or 'mistaken identification'), but includes the facts and matters to be relied on in the defence, otherwise there would be little, if any, scope for comparing the extent of the difference in the defences under s 11(8)(a)—on the restrictive interpretation, the defence put forward would either be the same as or different from the defence in the defence statement. Third, failure to warn the jury in accordance with s 11(10) that they cannot convict solely from drawing an adverse inference will not necessarily result in a successful appeal against conviction. The issue will turn on the particular circumstances, including the strength of the prosecution case.

The inferences that may be drawn

The proper inference to be drawn from breach of the accused's disclosure obligations is likely to be that a fact on which he relies at trial is false.[200] The jury should be directed that: (i) the drawing of an inference depends on whether they find that the reasons given by the accused for the breach are or may be good reasons;[201] if so, they should ignore the breach;[202] if they are satisfied that there was no good reason and that the breach can only be explained by the fact that the accused did not have any defence, or any defence which would stand up to scrutiny, they may bear this in mind when deciding whether his account is true and whether the prosecution have proved their case against him; but (iv) they may only do so if they conclude that it is fair and proper to do so; and (v) they must not convict the accused solely or mainly because of the breach.[203]

In some cases, the defence statement may be relied on by the Crown, or may be used by the jury, as a lie by the accused indicative of a consciousness of his guilt, in which case the jury will need to be directed in accordance with *R v Goodway*.[204]

---

[197] Ibid.

[198] Cf the 1994 Act, ss 34(2), 36(2), and 37(2).

[199] [2000] 2 Cr App R 309, CA.

[200] The Crown Court Compendium (July 2019), Part 1, 17–4, para 16. Where the prosecution invite the jury to draw this inference on the basis that the accused has changed his defence, the question whether he has in fact changed his defence must be left to the jury: *R v Duarte* [2019] EWCA Crim 1466 at [29].

[201] Ibid, para 23.

[202] Ibid, para 24.

[203] Ibid, para 25.

[204] [1993] 4 All ER 894, CA (see Ch 2).

Summary trials

Section 6 of the 1996 Act is to the effect that where a person is charged with an offence in respect of which the court proceeds to summary trial and the prosecutor complies or purports to comply with its duty to disclose unused material, then the accused *may* give a defence statement to the prosecutor, and, if he does so, must also give such a statement to the court, and must give the statement during a prescribed 'relevant period'. The magistrates' court may permit appropriate comment and draw proper inferences in the same circumstances as such comment may be permitted and such inferences may be drawn in a trial on indictment, that is, late disclosure, inconsistent defences, etc, but with the obvious exception of failure to give a defence statement.[205] As in trials on indictment, in summary cases a person shall not be convicted of an offence solely on an inference drawn under s 11(5).[206]

ADDITIONAL READING

Birch, 'Suffering in Silence: A Cost–Benefit Analysis of Section 34' [1999] Crim LR 769.
   An argument that the evidence yielded by s 34 of the Criminal Justice and Public Order Act 1994 is of insufficient importance to justify the problems it causes.

Buckle et al, *The Right of Silence: The Impact of the Criminal Justice and Public Order Act 1994* (Home Office Research Study No 199, 2000).
   A study of the effect of the provisions of the Criminal Justice and Public Order Act 1994 relating to adverse inferences from silence. The main focus is on the processing of suspects in a number of police stations but the study also looks at the effect of the legislation in court through interviews with criminal justice practitioners.

Jackson, 'Silence and Proof: Extending the boundaries of criminal proceedings in the United Kingdom' (2001) 5 E&P 145.
   An argument that relevant studies raise doubts about the fairness and effectiveness of drawing inferences from silence under the interview regime for both terrorist and ordinary suspects in Northern Ireland and England.

Leng, 'Silence pre-trial, reasonable expectations and the normative distortion of fact-finding' (2001) 5 E&P 240.
   An argument that s 34 of the Criminal Justice and Public Order Act 1994 has an implicit function to establish and enforce a norm that suspects generally should answer questions in police interview, and that the effect of the section, far from facilitating the exercise of common sense, has been to introduce unnecessary complexity and to distort the process of fact-finding.

Munday, 'Inferences from Silence and European Human Rights Law' [1996] Crim LR 370.
   A review of *Murray v UK* (1996) 22 EHRR 29, arguing that the European Court of Human Rights was far from endorsing the relevant Northern Ireland legislation on inferences from silence during interrogation, and consideration of the longer-term implications of the decision in relation to the corresponding English legislation.

Owusu-Bempah, 'Silence in suspicious circumstances' [2014] Crim LR 126.
   An article that seeks to clarify the significance of sections 36 and 37 of the Criminal Justice and Public Order Act 1994, with a particular focus on four aspects: the requirement to 'account' for suspicious circumstances; the relevance of the defence case put forward at trial; the absence of a reasonableness requirement; and the relevance of legal advice.

Quirk, *The Rise and Fall of the Right to Silence: Principle, Politics and Policy* (Abingdon, 2016).
   A comprehensive empirically-based analysis of the effects of curtailing the right to silence, with a focus on the effects of the Criminal Justice and Public Order Act 1994 within a comparative context that examines how different types of legal system regard the right and the effects of constitutional protection.

---

[205] Section 11(3).
[206] Section 11(10).

QUESTION

The police receive a call from Bob, a builder, that a tall white youth wearing a black tee-shirt has just tried to burgle his yard, which is next to a public playing field. He says that the youth tried but failed to climb over the 10 foot high wire fencing, topped by barbed wire, by which the yard is enclosed.

The call is passed on to PC King. Within three minutes of the call, he approaches the scene. Some 500 metres away from the yard, he sees Lennie, a tall white youth wearing a torn black tee-shirt, and limping. PC King arrests him for attempted burglary, saying that he has grounds to believe that he has just attempted to break into a builder's yard and giving him the usual caution. He then asks, 'How did your shirt get torn? And why are you limping? You know that if you don't answer these questions, that can be used against you at your trial. Inferences can be drawn.' Lennie says nothing.

At the police station, after consulting his solicitor, Lennie is interviewed under caution. When he is asked to account for his presence at the place where he was arrested, the solicitor advises him not to answer. Lennie does not answer the question.

At the trial, Lennie gives evidence that just before his arrest he had been playing football with his mates in the playing field next to the builder's yard but had to go home because he was badly tackled, getting a kick to his ankle and a tear to his shirt.

Lennie has a very low IQ and a limited vocabulary, which means that he only understands what is said to him if it is expressed in very basic English.

What adverse inferences, if any, may be drawn against Lennie?

 For a note-form answer see the online resources, accessible at
www.oup.com/he/keane-mckeown13e.

Evidence of character: evidence of character in civil cases

17

Key issues

- Should evidence be admitted in civil proceedings to show the disposition of the claimant or defendant towards good conduct?

- When and why should evidence be admitted in civil proceedings to show the disposition of the defendant towards misconduct?

- Why might it be more acceptable in a civil case than in a criminal case to admit evidence of the disposition of a party towards misconduct?

This chapter, together with **Chapters 18** and **19**, considers the admissibility of evidence of character. The admissibility of character evidence is governed by a number of factors which it will be useful to summarize before considering the law in detail. Two obvious considerations are whether the proceedings are civil or criminal and whether the evidence relates to the character of a party or non-party. Additionally, it is necessary to consider the nature of the character evidence in question. It may relate to either good or bad character and, in either event, may constitute evidence of a person's actual disposition, that is his propensity to act, think, or feel in a given way, or evidence of his reputation, that is his *reputed* disposition or propensity to act, think, or feel in a given way. Thus the character of a person may be proved by evidence of general disposition, by evidence of specific examples of his conduct on other occasions (including, in the case of bad conduct, evidence of his previous convictions), or by evidence of his reputation among those to whom he is known. The final important consideration is the purpose for which the character evidence in question is sought to be adduced. There are three possibilities. First, it may be adduced because the character of a person is itself in issue in the proceedings. Second, it may be adduced because of its relevance to a fact in issue, that is because of its tendency to prove that a person did a certain act, whether he did that act being in issue in the proceedings. Third, evidence of the character of a party or witness may be adduced because of its relevance to his credibility.

Character in issue or relevant to a fact in issue

In civil proceedings, evidence of the character of a party or non-party is admissible if it is in issue or of relevance to a fact in issue. The law of defamation provides a number of examples. Thus on the question of liability in an action for defamation in which justification is pleaded, the claimant's character will obviously be in issue. If, for example, the defendant has alleged that the claimant is a thief, evidence of the claimant's convictions for theft may be admitted to justify the allegation.[1] Similarly, the claimant, in order to rebut a defence of fair comment, may adduce evidence of his good reputation at the time of publication of the allegedly defamatory material.[2] The character of a claimant in an action for defamation is also of direct relevance, if he succeeds, to the quantum of recoverable damages, the damage sustained being dependent on the estimation in which he was previously held.[3]

Evidence of the disposition of the parties towards good conduct

It is submitted that evidence of the disposition of the parties to civil proceedings towards good conduct on other occasions should be admitted if it meets the ordinary requirement of relevance. However, according to the few reported decisions on the topic, such evidence has been treated as irrelevant to the facts in issue and accordingly excluded.

---

[1] Section 13 of the Civil Evidence Act 1968 provides that in libel or slander actions in which the question whether a person committed a criminal offence is relevant to an issue in the action, proof of his conviction shall be conclusive evidence that he committed the offence: see **Ch 4**.

[2] See *Cornwell v Myskow* [1987] 2 All ER 504, CA.

[3] See *Gatley on Libel and Slander* (12th edn, London, 2017), paras 33.30–33.42.

As to good conduct on the part of the defendant, in *A-G v Bowman*,[4] at the trial of an information for keeping false weights, a civil suit, Eyre CB held that the evidence of a witness to character called by the defendant was inadmissible because the proceedings were not criminal. Similarly in *A-G v Radloff*[5] the rule was justified on the basis that whereas there is a fair and just presumption that a person of good character would not commit a crime, no presumption fairly arises in most civil cases, from the good character of the defendant, that he did not commit the breach of contract or civil duty alleged against him.

As to the claimant, in *Hatton v Cooper*,[6] a case involving a collision between two cars in which there was an unusual dearth of relevant evidence, it was held that the trial judge, on the question of liability, had improperly relied on evidence from the claimant's employer that the claimant was an excellent driver, calm, assured, and composed, who never took risks. Jonathan Parker LJ said that in the context of this collision, the opinion of a third party as to the driving ability of either party was 'completely worthless'.

Evidence of the disposition of the parties towards bad conduct

In civil proceedings, evidence of the disposition of the defendant towards wrongdoing or the commission of a particular kind of civil wrong may be admissible if it is of sufficient relevance or probative value in relation to the facts in issue. Such evidence, which relates to particular acts of misconduct on other occasions, whether occurring before or after the occurrence of the facts in issue,[7] is designated 'similar fact evidence'.

Whereas in criminal proceedings the rules relating to the admissibility of similar fact evidence have reflected a paramount concern to safeguard the accused from the admission of unduly prejudicial evidence,[8] in civil proceedings, where trial is seldom by jury, the emphasis has been on probative value rather than prejudicial effect. To this extent, in civil cases, the principle of admissibility has tended to approximate to the ordinary test of relevance and accordingly similar fact evidence has been admitted more readily. In *Hales v Kerr*,[9] a negligence action in which the plaintiff alleged that he had contracted ringworm from a dirty razor used by the defendant, a hairdresser, evidence was admitted that two other customers shaved by the defendant had also contracted ringworm. In *Joy v Phillips, Mills & Co Ltd*[10] a claim was made for workmen's compensation by the father of a deceased stable boy. The boy was kicked by a horse and found nearby holding a halter. Evidence that the boy had previously teased horses with a halter was held to be admissible in rebuttal of the applicant's allegation that the accident had occurred in the course of the boy's employment. More recently, in *Jones v Greater Manchester Police Authority*,[11] civil proceedings for a sex offender order under s 2 of the Crime and Disorder Act 1998, it was held that evidence of propensity to commit

---

[4] (1791) 2 Bos&P 532n.

[5] (1854) 10 Exch 84 at 97.

[6] [2001] RTR 544, CA.

[7] *Desmond v Bower* [2010] EMLR 5, CA.

[8] See the Criminal Justice Act 2003, s 101(3), and the Police and Criminal Evidence Act 1984 s 78.

[9] [1908] 2 KB 601.

[10] [1916] 1 KB 849. See also *Barrett v Long* (1851) 3 HL Cas 395; *Osborne v Chocqueel* [1896] 2 QB 109; and *Sattin v National Union Bank* (1978) 122 Sol Jo 367, CA.

[11] [2002] ACD 4, DC.

sexual offences against young males was relevant and admissible because the purpose of the proceedings was to seek to predict the extent to which past events gave rise to reasonable cause for believing that an order was necessary to protect the public from serious harm; and that the admission of such evidence did not breach either Art 6 or Art 8 of the European Convention on Human Rights or render the proceedings unfair.

In *Mood Music Publishing Co Ltd v De Wolfe Publishing Ltd*,[12] similar fact evidence was admitted in an action for infringement of copyright. The defendants admitted the similarity between the musical work in which the plaintiffs owned the copyright and the work which they had produced, but alleged that the similarity was coincidental. Evidence was admitted to show that on other occasions the defendants had produced musical works bearing a close resemblance to musical works which were the subject of copyright. The Court of Appeal held that the evidence had been properly admitted to rebut the allegation of coincidence.

The leading authority is *O'Brien v Chief Constable of South Wales Police*.[13] The claimant had been convicted of murder. After serving 11 years in prison, his case had been referred to the Criminal Cases Review Commission and his appeal had been allowed. He then brought proceedings against the Chief Constable for misfeasance in public office and malicious prosecution, alleging that he had been 'framed' by a Detective Inspector L and a Detective Chief Superintendent C, who was said to have approved some aspects of the misconduct alleged against L. The House of Lords held that evidence had properly been admitted to show that L had behaved with similar impropriety on two other occasions and that C had done so on one other occasion. The House of Lords held that the test of admissibility in civil cases was different from that which applied in criminal cases. The test in criminal cases, propounded in *R v P*[14] and the Criminal Justice Act, required an enhanced relevance or substantial probative value because, if the evidence was not cogent, the prejudice that it would cause to the accused might render the proceedings unfair. That test led to the exclusion of evidence which was relevant on the grounds that it was not sufficiently probative. (The test, as described, is as propounded in *R v P*, but is *not* as now set out in the Criminal Justice Act 2003.[15]) There was no warrant for the automatic application of such a test in a civil suit. To do so would be to introduce an inflexibility which was inappropriate and undesirable. Lord Phillips said:[16]

> I would simply apply the test of relevance as the test of admissibility of similar fact evidence in a civil suit. Such evidence is admissible if it is potentially probative of an issue in the action. That is not to say that the policy considerations that have given rise to the complex rules . . . in sections 100 to 106 of the 2003 Act have no part to play in the conduct of civil litigation. They are policy considerations which the judge who has the management of the civil litigation will wish to keep well in mind. CPR r 1.2 requires the court to give effect to the overriding objective of dealing with cases justly. This includes dealing with the case in a way which is proportionate to what is involved in the case, and in a manner which is expeditious and fair. CPR r 1.4 requires the court actively to manage the case in order to further the overriding objective. CPR r 32.1 gives the court the power to control the evidence. This power expressly enables the court to exclude evidence that would otherwise be admissible and to limit cross-examination.

---

[12] [1976] Ch 119; cf *EG Music v SF (Film) Distributors* [1978] FSR 121. See also *Berger v Raymond & Son Ltd* [1984] 1 WLR 625.

[13] [2005] 2 AC 534, HL.

[14] [1991] 2 AC 447, HL.

[15] See the Criminal Justice Act 2003, s 101(1)(d): the test is the simple test of relevance. See **Ch 19**.

[16] At [53]–[56].

Similar fact evidence will not necessarily risk causing any unfair prejudice to the party against whom it is directed . . . It may, however, carry such a risk. Evidence of impropriety which reflects adversely on the character of a party may risk causing prejudice that is disproportionate to its relevance, particularly where the trial is taking place before a jury. In such a case the judge will be astute to see that the probative cogency of the evidence justifies this risk of prejudice in the interests of a fair trial.[17]

Equally, when considering whether to admit evidence, or permit cross-examination, on matters that are collateral to the central issues, the judge will have regard to the need for proportionality and expedition. She will consider whether the evidence in question is likely to be relatively uncontroversial, or whether its admission is likely to create side issues which will unbalance the trial and make it harder to see the wood from the trees.

Character relevant to credit

In civil proceedings, any person who gives evidence, whether or not a party to the proceedings, is liable to cross-examination as to his credibility as a witness.[18] However, as a general rule, the cross-examining party is not allowed to adduce evidence to contradict a witness's answer to a question concerning credit. The rule, and the exceptions to it, are considered in detail in **Chapter 7**.

ADDITIONAL READING

Munday, 'Case management, similar fact evidence in civil cases, and a divided law of evidence' (2006) 10 E&P 81.
An article written in the wake of the House of Lords' decision in *O'Brien v Chief Constable of South Wales Police* [2005] 2 WLR 2038, a decision which concerned the admissibility of similar fact evidence in civil cases. The article reviews experimental data which challenges the assumption that, by virtue of professional skills and experience, judges are better than jurors at performing complex adjudicative tasks and less susceptible to cognitive distortions when dealing with evidence which is emotive or potentially prejudicial. The data suggests that judges are no better at these tasks and no less susceptible to cognitive distortions than jurors.

---

[17] Experimental data suggest that judges are no better than jurors at excluding from their calculations prejudicial and inadmissible evidence. For a review, prompted by Lord Phillips' dicta, see Munday, 'Case management, similar fact evidence in civil cases, and a divided law of evidence' (2006) 10 E&P 81.

[18] See Ch 7, Cross-examination as to credit, p 219.

Evidence of character: **18**
evidence of the good
character of the accused

Key issues

- Why, and to what extent should an accused be allowed to call evidence of his previous good character?

- Where an accused has previous convictions, in what circumstances might it be acceptable for a judge to tell a jury that they should treat the accused as a person of good character?

- Where an accused has no previous convictions, in what circumstances might it be acceptable for a judge to refuse to tell a jury that they should treat the accused as a person of good character?

Introduction

This chapter concerns the circumstances in which, in criminal proceedings, evidence of the good character of the accused may be adduced because of its relevance either to a fact in issue or to credibility.[1] It also covers how the jury should be directed as to the accused's good character. In respect of good character, the position of the accused is very different to that of a witness. Historically, a person accused of having committed a crime has been entitled to rely on his good character because he is placed in jeopardy by criminal proceedings and because prejudice before the jury flows simply from the fact of being the accused in the dock. By contrast, a witness is not in jeopardy and, before the jury, is not subject to the prejudice that comes from being in the dock. The courts take the view that unless the jury hear differently, they will assume there is nothing to speak of against the credibility of the witness who gives evidence which, at the outset, he formally swears or affirms to be true.[2] To allow a witness to rely on good character is also thought to be 'oath-helping', that is, to unfairly enhance the credibility of a witness before the jury. However, if a witness's character is put in issue by the accused, the prosecution (or co-accused) will be able to adduce evidence of the witness's good character in rebuttal.[3]

The evidence admissible

In criminal proceedings, the accused is allowed to adduce evidence of his good character. It may be proved either in chief, by the evidence of the accused himself or other defence witnesses, or in cross-examination of witnesses called for the prosecution. In *R v Rowton*[4] the accused, charged with indecent assault on a boy, called witnesses to his character. It was held that evidence from the witnesses should be confined to evidence of the reputation of the accused amongst those to whom he is known and should not include evidence of the accused's specific creditable acts nor evidence of the witness's opinion of his disposition.[5] Although *R v Rowton* was decided prior to the Criminal Evidence Act 1898, s 1 of which made the accused a competent witness for the defence in all criminal cases,[6] the rule laid down would appear to apply even when the evidence of good character is given by the accused himself. Thus while the accused would normally be much better qualified to give evidence of his disposition as revealed by specific acts of creditable conduct, as opposed to evidence of his reputation, strictly speaking he must confine himself to the latter. In *R v Redgrave*,[7] a case of importuning for immoral purposes, the Court of Appeal held that the accused was not

---

[1] In criminal cases, the character of a person who is neither a party nor a witness is only rarely relevant to a fact in issue. For an example, see *R v Murray* [1994] Crim LR 927, CA.

[2] *R v Green* [2018] 4 WLR 39, CA, at [25].

[3] See *R v Mader* [2018] EWCA Crim 2454. See later in this chapter under, The good character of prosecution witnesses, p 551.

[4] (1865) Le&Ca 520, CCR.

[5] Under the principle, the witness's evidence must be based on his own personal knowledge of the accused's general reputation in the relevant community and he must share the community's view: *R v Del-Valle* [2004] EWCA Crim 1013 at [11]. The right to call witnesses under the principle is not lost because the accused will receive a good character direction: see the decision of the Northern Ireland Court of Appeal in *R v Grimes* [2017] NICA 19 at [34].

[6] See now the Youth Justice and Criminal Evidence Act 1999, s 53(1): see Ch 5.

[7] (1981) 74 Cr App R 10.

entitled to produce letters and photographs to show that he had had relationships of a heterosexual nature, because this amounted to calling evidence of particular facts to show that he was of a disposition which made it unlikely that he would have committed the offence charged. The court conceded that had the accused '. . . been a married man, or . . . confined his relationship to one girl, it might not have been all that objectionable for him to have given evidence in general terms that his relationship with his wife or the girl was satisfactory.' However, the court made it clear that this '. . . would have been an indulgence on the part of the court . . . [it] would not have been his right to have it said.'[8] The rule in *R v Rowton* has never been expressly overruled, but in modern practice it has been all but abandoned. In *R v Del-Valle*,[9] the Court of Appeal stated:

> In many respects the law has moved well beyond *Rowton* and evidence of particular opinions and acts are routinely admitted, as is evidence of good character based on the absence of convictions. Indeed it is rare for evidence of general character founded on general reputation to be adduced in a modern criminal trial.[10]

The direction to the jury

The principles in *R v Vye*

R v Vye,[11] clarified the law on how the judge should direct the jury about evidence of the good character of the accused. Lord Chief Justice Taylor laid down the following three principles.

1. If the accused testifies, the judge should direct the jury that the evidence is relevant to credibility (a first limb direction). If the accused does not give evidence at trial but relies on pre-trial answers or statements, that is, exculpatory statements made to the police or others, the judge, who is entitled to make observations about the way the jury should approach such evidence in contrast to evidence given on oath, should give a first limb direction by directing the jury to have regard to the accused's good character when considering the credibility of those statements.[12] If the accused does not give evidence and has given no pre-trial answers or statements, no issue as to his credibility arises and a first limb direction is not required.

2. The judge should direct the jury that the evidence has a probative value in relation to the issue of guilt, in that a person of good character is less likely to have committed the offence (a second limb direction). A second limb direction should be given whether or not the accused has testified or made pre-trial answers or statements.[13] It is for the judge in each case to decide how he tailors the direction to the particular circumstances. He

---

[8] Ibid at 15.

[9] [2004] EWCA Crim 1013 at [11].

[10] See also *R v Grimes* [2017] NICA 19 at [35]. The common law rule under which evidence of a person's reputation is admissible in criminal proceedings for the purpose of proving his good (or bad) character has been preserved and put on a statutory basis by s 118(1) of the Criminal Justice Act 2003. See **Ch 14**.

[11] [1993] 1 WLR 471, CA.

[12] See the Crown Court Compendium (July 2019), Part 1, 11, Example 5. See also *R v Chapman* [1989] Crim LR 60, CA.

[13] Improper disclosure that the accused had previously been arrested for an offence of the same type as the offence charged will undermine a second limb direction and effectively deprive the accused of the good character direction: *Arthurton v R* [2005] 1 WLR 949, PC.

would probably wish to indicate, as is commonly done, that good character cannot amount to a defence.

3. Where an accused of good character is jointly tried with an accused of bad character, principles 1 and 2 still apply: the accused of good character is entitled to a full direction.[14] As to any direction concerning the accused of bad character, in some cases the judge may think it best to tell the jury that there has been no evidence about his character and they must not speculate or take the absence of such information as any evidence against him. In other cases, the judge may think it best to say nothing about the absence of such information. The course to be taken depends on the circumstances of the individual case, including how great an issue was made of character during the evidence and speeches.[15]

In *R v Aziz*[16] it was held that an accused who is entitled to a good character direction in accordance with *R v Vye* will not lose that entitlement by mounting an attack on a co-accused, for example by running a cut-throat defence.[17]

The terms of the direction

The Crown Court Compendium suggests the following standard direction, in accordance with the principles stated in *R v Vye*:[18]

> Good character is not a defence to the charges but it is relevant to your consideration of the case in two ways. First, the defendant has given evidence. His good character is a positive feature of the defendant which you should take into account when considering whether you accept what he told you. Secondly, the fact that the defendant has not offended in the past may make it less likely that he acted as is now alleged against him.

In *R v JVG*,[19] referring to an earlier version of the standard direction, the Court of Appeal held that it was not a mantra to be repeated word for word and the question was whether the direction in question, taken as a whole, impresses on the jury the need to take good character into account in the accused's favour. However, judges are wise to avoid saying that the jury are 'entitled' to take evidence of good character into account, which suggests that the jury have a choice whether or not to take it into account for the purposes in question.[20] Similarly, judges

---

[14] It was held that the suggestion in *R v Gibson* (1991) 93 Cr App R 9, CA, that the judge may decide to say little if anything about the good character of the one accused, was not satisfactory and ought not to be followed. *R v Vye*, in this respect, was applied in *R v Houlden* (1993) 99 Cr App R 244, CA.

[15] See the Crown Court Compendium (July 2019), Part 1, 11, Example 7.

[16] [1996] AC 41, HL.

[17] Ibid at 52–3.

[18] The Crown Court Compendium (July 2019), Part 1, 11. See also *R v JVG* [2015] EWCA Crim 1630.

[19] [2015] EWCA Crim 1630.

[20] *R v Miah* [1997] 2 Cr App R 12, CA. See also *R v Moustakim* [2008] EWCA Crim 3096: the use of the word 'perhaps' is a significant dilution of the direction required. See also *R v M* [2009] 2 Cr App R 54 (3), CA at [11]: in telling the jury that the accused's good character was something they should *take into account*, the judge failed to make it clear that it was a factor *in his favour*. See also *R v Ahmed* [2015] 1 Cr App R 275 (21), CA: where the judge has decided to give a direction, it should not be worded in such a way as to give the jury the option of disagreeing that the accused's good character is a factor in his favour. Cf *R v JVG* [2015] EWCA Crim 1630: the judge's use of the words, 'you may think he is entitled to ask you to give weight to his previous good character' was unfortunate, but overall none of the vices identified in *R v Moustakim* [2008] EWCA Crim 3096 were present and the jury were left in doubt that the accused's good character was something that they should take into account in his favour.

should avoid saying, 'the defence ask you to consider the evidence' because this may leave the jury with the impression that the direction was no more than a reminder of a defence submission.[21] Further, it is a serious misdirection to tell the jury that they can put good character into the scales[22] or, in the case of the first limb, that good character 'might assist' them on the question of credibility.[23] Equally, good character directions should not be given in the form of a question or rhetorical question, for example 'Is it more likely that he is telling you the truth because he is a man of good character?', but in the form of an affirmative statement.[24] In *R v Vye* it was held that if the judge gives both limbs of the direction, the Court of Appeal will be slow to criticize any qualifying remarks based on the facts of the individual case.[25] Such remarks, however, must be justified.[26]

The meaning of 'pre-trial answers or statements'

In *R v Aziz*[27] the House of Lords has made clear that the phrase 'pre-trial answers or statements', as used in the first principle in *R v Vye*, refers not to wholly exculpatory statements, but only to 'mixed' statements, that is, statements containing inculpatory as well as exculpatory material which are, for that reason, tendered as evidence of the truth of the facts they contain.[28] Thus an accused who does not give evidence but relies on wholly exculpatory statements is not entitled to a first limb direction.

The accused of bad character jointly tried with the accused of good character

As to the third principle in *R v Vye*, relating to directions about the accused of 'bad character' with whom the accused of good character is jointly tried, that phrase appears to cover both an accused in respect of whom there is no evidence of character, one way or the other, and an accused of bad character whose bad character is not revealed in evidence, but not an accused whose bad character is revealed in evidence.[29] Where the jury hear no evidence of character

---

[21] *R v Gbajabiamila* [2011] EWCA Crim 734 at [18]. See also *R v Moustakim* [2008] EWCA Crim 3096, *R v MW* [2008] EWCA Crim 3091 and *R v Dillon* [2013] EWCA Crim 122.

[22] *R v Boyson* [1991] Crim LR 274, CA.

[23] *R v Gray* [2004] 2 Cr App R 498 (30), CA. See also *R v Dillon* [2013] EWCA Crim 122 at [23]: what is required is a clear statement that the jury should take the accused's good character into account when deciding whether they believe his evidence and an oblique reference to 'assessing' the accused is insufficient. See also, in the case of a Crown Court judge directing himself in an appeal from a magistrates' court, *R (Arthur) v Crown Court at Blackfriars* [2017] EWHC 3416 (Admin).

[24] *R v Lloyd* [2000] 2 Cr App R 355 and *R v Scranage* [2001] EWCA Crim 1171.

[25] *R v Vye* [1993] 1 WLR 471, CA at 477.

[26] See *R v Fitton* [2001] EWCA Crim 215: judge misdirected the jury in a qualification to the standard directions by effectively saying that an accused's good character was of less relevance and weight because the offence he was alleged to have committed was spontaneous. See also *R v Handbridge* [1993] Crim LR 287, CA: judge was wrong to have directed the jury to ignore good character unless the rest of the evidence left them in doubt about guilt. See also *R v Dillon* [2013] EWCA Crim 122: judge, in relation to propensity, should not have made remarks that the accused had 'not been caught out in the past knocking a woman about' because the remarks implied that the accused might have committed offences but had not been caught.

[27] [1996] AC 41, HL.

[28] See *R v Duncan* (1981) 73 Cr App R 359, CA and *R v Sharp* [1988] 1 All ER 65, HL, Ch 6, 'Mixed' statements, p 200. See also *R v Patel* [2010] EWCA Crim 976. See also Birch, 'The Sharp End of the Wedge: Use of Mixed Statements by the Defence' [1997] Crim LR 416.

[29] See *R v Cain* [1994] 2 All ER 398, CA, where the evidence relating to the character of three co-accused was different: there was evidence of positive good character of A, no evidence in relation to the character of B, and evidence of the previous convictions of C. Only A was entitled to a full direction.

in respect of an accused jointly tried with an accused of bad character, the guidance in the Crown Court Compendium is that in most cases it is appropriate to direct the jury not to speculate.[30]

The meaning of 'good character' and the entitlement to the direction

Difficulties have arisen in relation to what 'good character' means for the purposes of the principles established in *R v Vye* and, consequently, when an accused is entitled to the direction.[31] For example, previous convictions will not necessarily prevent an accused from being treated as a person of good character, particularly if they are spent or convictions for minor offences which have no relevance to credibility and took place a long time ago.[32] Conversely, the absence of convictions will not necessarily permit an accused to be treated as a person of good character when he has been guilty of misconduct but not convicted of any offence in respect of it. As we shall see in **Chapter 19**, 'misconduct' or 'a disposition towards misconduct' is 'bad character' for the purposes of s 98 of the Criminal Justice Act 2003. This means that an accused without previous convictions but who has been guilty of misconduct may be treated as a person of 'bad character' and evidence of his misconduct may be relied on by the prosecution.

The principles in *R v Aziz*

R v Aziz[33] was decided before the Criminal Justice Act 2003, but laid down important principles in relation to good character directions where an accused does not have previous convictions, but is guilty of dishonesty or other criminal behaviour. Two of the accused, charged with conspiracy to cheat the public revenue of VAT, pleaded not guilty and relied on the fact that they had no previous convictions, but also gave evidence of previous dishonesty, including evidence of making false mortgage applications, telling lies during interview, and not declaring full earnings for Inland Revenue purposes. Giving judgment in the House of Lords, Lord Steyn acknowledged that this was an area in which generalizations are hazardous and that a wide spectrum of cases must be kept in mind, but stated the following principles:

1. A trial judge has a residual discretion to decline to give *Vye* directions in the case of an accused without previous convictions if he considers it an insult to common sense to give such directions. A judge should never be compelled to give meaningless or absurd directions. Cases occur where an accused with no previous convictions is shown beyond

---

[30] The Crown Court Compendium (July 2019), Part 1, 11, para 9(1) and (2) and Example 8.

[31] See generally Munday, 'What Constitutes a Good Character?' [1997] Crim LR 247. See also Roberts, 'Commentary' [2010] Crim LR 232.

[32] See, eg, *R v Goss* [2005] Crim LR 61, CA (on a charge of possessing a firearm, a previous conviction for driving a motor vehicle without car insurance, in the absence of evidence to show that the accused had deliberately flouted road traffic law). See also *R v Bailey* [2017] EWCA Crim 35 (a bind over will not necessarily deprive the accused of his entitlement to an unqualified good character direction); and *R v Hamer* [2011] 1 WLR 528, CA (a fixed penalty notice issued for disorder (PND) has no effect on an accused's entitlement to a full good character direction as, by virtue of the PND scheme, such a notice does not involve an admission of guilt and is no proof that a crime has been committed). See further *R v Olu* [2011] 1 Cr App R 404 (33), CA.

[33] [1996] AC 41, HL.

doubt to have been guilty of serious criminal behaviour similar to the offence charged. A judge is not compelled to go through the charade of giving *Vye* directions where the accused's claim to good character is spurious.

2. This discretionary power is narrowly circumscribed.

3. Prima facie the directions must be given. The judge will often be able to place a fair and balanced picture before the jury by giving *Vye* directions and then adding words of qualification concerning the proved or possible misconduct.[34]

4. Whenever a judge proposes to give a direction not likely to be anticipated by counsel, he should invite submissions on his proposed directions.

Issues have arisen as to whether, under these principles, an accused without previous convictions but who has been guilty of misconduct may claim entitlement to a qualified direction as of right, subject to the narrowly circumscribed discretion to decline the direction if it would be meaningless or absurd. In *R v Durbin*,[35] a case heard shortly before, but not cited in *Aziz*,[36] it was held that an accused without previous convictions, but against whom there was evidence of dishonesty, had a right to a qualified character direction.[37] Following *Durbin*, the law developed in a problematic way, permitting an accused to claim entitlement to a good character direction under the principles in *Vye* and *Aziz* even if he had been guilty of misconduct. The leading authority on good character is now *R v Hunter*.[38]

R v Hunter

In *Hunter*, a five judge Court of Appeal conducted a thorough review of the authorities[39] and held that the law had taken 'a wrong turn' in the case of *Durbin*.[40] The court held that the Court of Appeal in *Durbin* had failed to appreciate the principle stated in *R v Buzalek*,[41] that the practice established in *Vye* of giving a good character direction on credibility and in an appropriate case, propensity, only applied where the accused was of previous good character 'in the proper sense' and that an accused who had been dishonest could not be regarded as being of good character. As a consequence, 'this led the Court in *Durbin* to proceed on a false basis that a man with an undoubtedly bad character as far as propensity and credibility were concerned was entitled to the benefit of a good character direction.'[42]

---

[34] On the facts, the two accused had not lost the right to *Vye* directions, but it would have been proper for the judge to have qualified them by reference to the admitted misconduct. However, the misconduct might now be admitted as evidence of bad character under s 101 of the Criminal Justice Act 2003 and, if so, would be the subject of a *bad* character direction. In such a situation, the judge, as a matter of fairness, might feel obliged to weave into his direction a modified good character direction provided it would not be meaningless or absurd: see *R v Hunter* [2015] 1 WLR 5367, CA at [84]. See also *R v Doncaster* (2008) JP 202, CA at [43].

[35] [1995] 2 Cr App R 84, CA.

[36] Noted in *Hunter* [2015] 1 WLR, CA at [21].

[37] Citing *R v Kabariti* (1990) 92 Cr App R 362, CA.

[38] [2015] 1 WLR 5367, CA.

[39] The 'very thorough review' was 'deliberate', so that the courts of the future might need only rely on the Court's judgment in *R v Hunter* and the judgments in *R v Vye* and *R v Aziz* when resolving issues of good character. See the 'Postscript' of the judgment in *R v Hunter* [2015] 1 WLR 5367, CA at [103].

[40] [1995] 2 Cr App R 84, CA.

[41] [1991] Crim LR 116, CA. See also *R v Zoppola-Barraza* [1994] Crim LR 833, CA.

[42] *R v Hunter* [2015] 1 WLR 5367, CA at [70]–[71].

The court was satisfied that reliance on *Durbin* in subsequent cases to extend the principles of good character under *Vye* and *Aziz* to an accused who did not have good character was misplaced.[43] The court also observed that the principles relating to character evidence had been changed significantly with the introduction of the Criminal Justice Act 2003,[44] so that evidence of an accused's misconduct, including evidence of misconduct other than convictions, which would not have been admissible formerly, was now admissible as evidence of bad character.

Having reviewed the authorities and determined it was not bound by *Durbin*, the Court of Appeal went on to state a number of 'conclusions' about the law relating to good character. The conclusions are wide ranging and it is convenient to summarize them under their separate headings.

The purpose of the summing-up

The purpose of the summing-up is to present the law and a summary of the evidence in such a way as is best to enable the jury to reach a just conclusion.[45] A judge's directions on good character relate to the law not the facts; but the extension of the circumstances in which advocates demand of judges a direction on good character has not helped effective trial management. It has led to lengthy discussions at trial about directions to juries, some convoluted directions, and a flood of applications for leave to appeal.[46] The principles in *Vye* and *Aziz* began life as good practice, but became a rule of practice because the court needed a pragmatic solution to a problem of inconsistency and uncertainty. However, the principles have been extended wrongly to enable an accused with bad character to claim a good character direction and judges feel required to give absurd or meaningless, or far too generous directions. Fairness does not require a judge to give a good character direction to a man whose claim to good character is spurious.[47]

The principles in Vye and Aziz which should be followed

The principles derived from *Vye* and *Aziz* by which the Court of Appeal remains bound are as follows:

1. The general rule is that a direction as to the relevance of good character to an accused's credibility is to be given where an accused has a good character and has testified or made pre-trial statements.

2. The general rule is that a direction as to the relevance of good character to the likelihood of an accused having committed the offence charged is to be given where an accused has a good character whether or not he has testified or made pre-trial answers or statements.

3. Where an accused A, of good character, is tried jointly with B who does not have a good character, 1 and 2 above still apply.

---

[43] For example, *R v Gray* [2004] 2 Cr App R 498 (30), CA; *R v Payton* [2006] EWCA Crim 1226; *R v PD* [2012] 1 Cr App R 448 (33), CA; and *R v Gai* [2012] EWCA Crim 2033.

[44] [2015] 1 WLR 5367, CA at [29]–[30].

[45] Ibid at [61].

[46] At [64].

[47] At [66].

4. There are exceptions to the general rule where an accused has no previous convictions but has admitted other reprehensible conduct and the judge considers it would be an insult to common sense to give directions in accordance with *Vye*. The judge then has a residual discretion to decline to give a good character direction.

5. A jury must not be misled.

6. A judge is not obliged to give absurd or meaningless directions.[48]

Clarification of what Vye and Aziz did not decide

In *Vye* and *Aziz* it was *not* decided that:

1. an accused with no previous convictions is always entitled to good character directions;

2. an accused with previous convictions is entitled to good character directions;

3. an accused with previous convictions is entitled to the propensity limb of the good character direction on the basis that he has no convictions similar or relevant to those charged;

4. an accused with previous convictions is entitled to a good character direction where the prosecution do not seek to rely upon the previous convictions as probative of guilt; or

5. a failure to give a good character direction will almost invariably lead to the quashing of the conviction.[49]

Entitlement to a good character direction under the principles in Vye and Aziz

Only an accused with absolute good character or who is deemed to be of effective good character is *entitled* to a good character direction. An accused with a record of previous convictions or who has bad character of some other kind is not entitled as of right to a good character direction.[50]

Categories of good character

The categories of good character are (i) absolute good character; and (ii) effective good character.

Absolute good character

Absolute good character refers to an accused who has no previous convictions or cautions recorded and no other reprehensible conduct alleged, admitted, or proven. An accused does not have to adduce evidence of positive good character to qualify as someone of absolute good character. Where an accused is of absolute good character, the law on his entitlement to a good character direction is settled. He is entitled to both limbs.[51] The judge must tailor the

---

[48] At [68].

[49] At [69].

[50] At [72]. See also *R v Benjamin* (21 July 2015, unreported), CA: the accused, charged with shoplifting, was not of good character in circumstances where he had two convictions which he disputed, namely, a conviction for being drunk and disorderly in 1993 of which there was no record due to the passage of time, and a conviction for assault in France in 2009 which was evidenced.

[51] Although his entitlement to the credibility limb will depend on him giving evidence or, if he does not, evidence being adduced of a mixed statement by him. See earlier, in this chapter, under The meaning of 'pre-trial answers or statements', p 542.

terms of the direction to the facts, but for consistency the standard direction in the Crown Court Bench Book (now contained in the Crown Court Compendium[52]) is commended as a basis.[53]

Effective good character

Effective good character refers to an accused who has previous convictions or cautions recorded which are old, minor, and have no relevance to the charge. In this situation the judge must make a judgement on whether to treat the accused as someone who is of effective good character. However, the judge is not obliged to treat an accused as someone who is of effective good character and in fairness to all, should be vigilant to ensure that an accused should not be given an effective good character direction if it is not merited.[54] The judge should first consider the circumstances of the past offending and the offender and then decide what is required in order to be fair to all. The judge should not leave it to the jury to decide whether to treat the accused as a person of good character.[55] If the judge decides to treat the accused as being of effective good character, the judge does not have a discretion— both limbs of the direction must be given, but modified as necessary to take into account other matters and ensure the jury is not misled.[56]

Previous convictions or cautions adduced under s 101 by the defence

Where an accused adduces evidence of previous convictions or cautions under s 101(1)(b) of the Criminal Justice Act 2003[57] which are not in the same category as the offence charged, with the aim of obtaining a good character direction on propensity, whether to give such a direction is a matter for the judge's discretion.[58] However, an accused with previous convictions or cautions has no entitlement to either limb of the direction and in relation to the judge's discretion in circumstances where the accused adduces his bad character under s 101(1)(b), it is not the 'narrowly circumscribed' type stated in *Aziz* in respect of an accused without convictions (ie the judge may only withhold it if it would be meaningless or absurd). Rather, the discretion is of the 'open textured variety' also referred to in Lord Steyn's judgment in *Aziz*,[59] that is, it is for the judge to decide whether to give any part of the direction and, if so, on what terms, considering what fairness requires. Where a judge declines to give a modified direction, the Court of Appeal will have proper regard to the exercise of discretion by the judge.[60] However, where the offences charged are serious and the earlier misconduct

---

[52] The Crown Court Compendium (July 2019), Part 1, 11, Example 1. See, in this chapter, under The terms of the direction, p 541.

[53] [2015] 1 WLR 5367, CA at [78].

[54] At [79]. See, eg, *R v Mittal* [2016] 4 WLR 91, CA: in the case of a doctor accused of stealing £130 from a patient's purse during a consultation, the judge would have been entitled to decline to give a good character direction where the doctor had no convictions but had been charged with shoplifting in Scotland in 2011 and had accepted a warning as an alternative to prosecution.

[55] Ibid. See also *R v M* [2009] 2 Cr App R 54 (3) and *R v Ahmed* [2015] 1 Cr App R 275 (21).

[56] [2015] 1 WLR 5367, CA at [80]. See also the Crown Court Compendium (July 2019), Part 1, 11, Examples 3 and 4.

[57] See Ch 1 9, Section 101(1)(b)—evidence admitted by the defendant himself, p 578.

[58] [2015] 1 WLR 5367, CA at [81]–[82].

[59] At [82] and *R v Aziz* [1996] AC 41 at 489. See also the Crown Court Compendium (July 2019), Part 1, 11, Examples 3 and 4.

[60] At [82].

is minor in nature and of a wholly different kind to the offences charged, it would be wrong to withhold a modified direction and indeed the accused might be entitled to be treated as being of effective good character.[61] Any direction in his favour would be expected to make reference to the wrongdoing admitted by the accused and then contrast it to the serious charges faced.[62] Additionally, where evidence is introduced by the accused to demonstrate a lack of propensity, it would be 'simply wrong' to direct the jury that the only way the evidence can be used is to provide support for the prosecution case, which would improperly suggest that it was admissible by the prosecution.[63]

Nevertheless, any decision to introduce evidence of previous convictions or cautions with a view to obtaining a good character direction will need to be taken carefully. First, such a decision comes with the risk that the judge might properly decline to give the direction within her discretion. Second, the prosecution might successfully apply to cross-examine the accused on the facts of the convictions or cautions, the impact of which might well outweigh the value of any modified good character direction.[64]

Bad character, other than cautions or convictions, adduced under s 101 by the prosecution

Where an accused has no previous convictions or cautions, but evidence has been admitted by the prosecution of other misconduct, the judge is obliged to give a *bad* character direction explaining the relevance of the misconduct, but may consider as a matter of fairness that she should weave into her remarks, a modified good character direction.[65] However, there will be occasions when this will be meaningless or absurd and should not be done.[66] Where the judge has declined to give a good character direction or has given a modified good character direction, the Court of Appeal should have proper regard to the exercise of discretion by the judge who has presided over the trial.[67] Where the prosecution have adduced and relied on previous *convictions* of an accused, it is difficult to conceive a good character direction that would not offend the absurdity principle stated by Lord Steyn in *R v Aziz*.[68]

Bad character, other than convictions or cautions, adduced by the defence under s 101 and not relied on by the Crown

Where an accused has no previous convictions or cautions, but has been guilty of misconduct which is not relied on by the prosecution as probative of guilt, he may seek to admit evidence of the misconduct as evidence of his bad character under s 101(1)(b) of the Criminal Justice Act 2003 in the hope of obtaining a good character direction.[69] As a result of changes to the legal landscape brought about by the bad character provisions of the Criminal Justice Act 2003, the judge's discretion to withhold the direction, in these circumstances, has changed from being a residual 'narrowly circumscribed discretion' to the 'open textured'

---

[61] See *R v Styles* [2015] EWCA Crim 1619 at [36]. See also *R v Gray* [2004] 2 Cr App R 498 (30), CA.

[62] *R v Styles* [2015] EWCA Crim 1619 at [36].

[63] Ibid at [35].

[64] See, eg, *R v Mittal* [2016] 4 WLR 91, CA.

[65] See *R v Doncaster* (2008) JP 202, CA.

[66] [2015] 1 WLR 5367, CA at [83].

[67] Ibid.

[68] Ibid. See above, under The meaning of 'good character' and the entitlement to the direction, p 543.

[69] *R v Hunter* [2015] 1 WLR 5367, CA at [85].

variety, whereby the judge is allowed 'the usual generous ambit of discretion'[70] and is free to decide whether to give the direction and, if so, in what form, having regard to what fairness demands. It would be wrong in principle to restrict the judge's discretion to being 'narrowly circumscribed' because she might then be obliged to give a good character direction to an accused who, by virtue of his bad character, has no such entitlement. Further, this could encourage prosecutors to apply to admit bad character evidence in order to pre-empt any application by the defence for a good character direction.[71]

Failure to give a direction and safety

Concerning the effect of a failure to give a good character direction on the safety of a conviction, the court in *R v Hunter* held as follows:[72]

1. There can be no fixed rule that a failure to give a good character direction is necessarily or usually fatal. There are two conflicting lines of authorities as to whether the failure to give a good character direction will necessarily or usually lead to a conviction being quashed and no guidance can be discerned.

2. The true guidance is to be found in *R v Singh*[73] where Lord Bingham stated: 'Provided that the judge indicates to the jury the two respects in which good character may be relevant, ie credibility and propensity, this court will be slow to criticize any qualifying remarks he may make based on the facts of the individual case'.

3. An appellate court should only interfere if, on the facts, it was not properly open to the judge to reach the conclusions he did, for example, a refusal to treat an accused as a person of effective good character or give a particular limb of the direction.

4. The Court of Appeal should in future approach the exercise of the judge's discretion in respect of good character directions in the same way as it approaches the exercise of discretion in respect of bad character directions where bad character evidence is admitted under s 101(1) of the Criminal Justice Act 2003, as expressed in the case of *R v Renda*.[74] Accordingly, 'the circumstances in which this Court would interfere with the exercise of judicial discretion or a fact specific judgment are limited. Context is all and the trial judge is likely to have a far better feel for the dynamics of a criminal trial and the interests of justice than an appellate court.'[75]

5. If defence advocates do not take a point on the character directions at trial or if they agree with the judge's proposed directions which are then given, these are good indications that nothing was amiss: the trial was considered fair by those present who understood the dynamics. In such cases the Court should be slow to grant extensions of time and leave to appeal.[76]

---

[70] Ibid. See [85]–[88].

[71] At [87].

[72] At [89]–[98].

[73] [2006] 1 WLR 146 PC at [30].

[74] [2006] 1 WLR 2948, per Igor Judge at [3]. See Ch 19, The role of the trial judge and the Court of Appeal, p 562.

[75] [2015] 1 WLR 5367, CA at [95]–[96].

[76] It is the duty of the defence advocate to ensure that a direction is obtained; if the issue is not raised by the advocate, the judge is under no duty to raise it himself: see *Thompson v The Queen* [1998] AC 811, affirmed in *Teeluck v The State* [2005] 2 Cr App R 378, PC. See also *Stewart v The Queen* [2011] UKPC 11.

Procedure

Concerning the procedure to be followed where defendants seek to admit evidence of their own bad character in order to obtain good character directions, the court made a number of observations.[77]

1. As a matter of good practice defendants should put the court on notice as early as possible that character and character directions are an issue that may need to be resolved. The judge can then decide whether a direction will be given, and if so its precise terms.[78]

2. The issue of a good character direction should be discussed before the evidence of bad character is adduced so that the defence will be better informed before making a decision whether to admit the evidence, the prosecution can conduct whatever checks are necessary and the judge will have the fullest possible information upon which to rule.

3. The judge should then ensure the direction is given precisely in accordance with the ruling.

Other issues relating to good character directions

Guilty and not guilty pleas to different counts of the indictment

When an accused pleads guilty to one or more counts on the indictment but not guilty to the other counts and is otherwise of good character, an issue arises as to whether a good character direction should be given. In *R v Teasdale*[79] it was held that if an accused pleads guilty to an offence which is an alternative to that on which he is being tried, and the facts are such that, if he is convicted on the greater offence then the guilty plea on the alternative offence will have to be vacated, a full good character direction should be given, but tailored to take into account the guilty plea. However, in *R v Challenger*,[80] distinguishing *R v Teasdale*, it was held that in all other cases in which an accused pleads guilty to another count on the indictment, he ceases to be a person of good character and the full character direction becomes inappropriate.[81] In *R v Hunter*, the Court of Appeal was persuaded that the decision in *R v Challenger* was more in keeping with the principles in *R v Vye*, presumably on the basis that

---

[77] [2015] 1 WLR 5367, CA at [99]–[102].

[78] See the Criminal Procedure Rules 2015, SI 2015 1490, r 21.4(8): defendants are required to give notice orally or in writing as soon as is reasonably practicable and in any event before the evidence is introduced and, in the Crown Court, at the same time, give notice orally or in writing of any direction sought to be given to the jury. See also r 25.14.

[79] [1994] 99 Cr App R 80.

[80] [1994] Crim LR 202, CA.

[81] It was further held that it would be misleading to tell a jury that an accused was of good character where they had not been made aware of his guilty plea. However, if an accused gives evidence of his guilty plea then the judge may remind the jury about any argument made to the effect that, by virtue of his admission of guilt on one count, greater weight should be attached to his assertions of innocence on the remaining counts. Note also *R v Shepherd* [1995] Crim LR 153, CA, where formal admissions went some way towards informing the jury that S had pleaded guilty to other counts. It was held that if the defence had 'grasped the nettle' and brought out in evidence that S, apart from the matters covered by the admissions, had no other convictions, then it might have been appropriate for the judge to have directed the jury that, apart from attaching such weight as they saw fit to the admissions, S was entitled to ask them to consider his case on the basis of previous good character.

once an accused pleads guilty he is not of good character in the 'proper sense' and is therefore not entitled as of right to the direction.[82]

The accused disputes misconduct relied on by the prosecution

It has already been noted that where evidence of misconduct other than convictions and cautions is relied on by the prosecution under s 101 of the Criminal Justice Act 2003, the jury are bound to receive a *bad* character direction and that in such cases the judge may also choose to 'weave in' a modified good character direction, provided it would not be meaningless or absurd.[83] However, a problem arises where evidence of an accused's misconduct is adduced which the accused disputes and, but for that evidence, he would be of good character.[84] In such circumstances, the judge should, in addition to a *bad* character direction, direct the jury that if they accept that the accused did not commit the disputed misconduct they should treat him as a person of good character, and further direct them to approach his good character in accordance with the principles in *R v Vye*.[85]

The accused tried for historic sexual offences

In cases involving historic sexual offences the accused's credibility will often be a central issue. Where the judge decides the accused should receive a full direction in accordance with *R v Vye*, the direction involves an additional component—sometimes referred to as a 'third limb'—which is an affirmative statement that because so much time has passed between the alleged offences and the present time without the accused committing any offence, it is less likely that he committed the offences charged. In *R v GJB*[86] it was held that this 'third limb' is in reality an adaptation of the normal second limb of a *Vye* direction, but is required in such cases because the accused's defence is frequently a straightforward denial and he may have little more than his good character to rely on.

The good character of prosecution witnesses

It is mostly the case that the good character of a prosecution witness is irrelevant. However, it may come into play in some situations. In *R v Mader*,[87] the Court of Appeal conducted a review of authorities and distilled the following well-established principles.

1. Generally speaking, the starting point is that evidence is not admissible simply to show that a prosecution witness is a generally truthful person who should be believed.[88]

2. Evidence is admissible if it is relevant to an issue in the trial (unless excluded under an exclusionary rule of evidence).[89]

---

[82] See *R v Hunter* [2015] 1 WLR 5367, CA at [72]. However, the court in *R v Hunter* did not address the question whether the court in *R v Challenger* was justified in distinguishing the decision in *R v Teasdale* on the basis that it did.

[83] *R v Doncaster* (2008) JP 202, CA and *R v Hunter* [2015] 1 WLR 5367, CA at [83].

[84] See, eg, *R v Olu* [2011] 1 Cr App R 404 (33), CA: the accused disputed admissions he had made in a caution, the caution having been adduced as evidence of bad character by the prosecution.

[85] See the Crown Court Compendium (July 2019), Part 1, 11, para 14 and Example 7.

[86] [2011] EWCA Crim 867 at [19].

[87] [2018] EWCA Crim 2454.

[88] See *R v Amado Taylor* [2001] EWCA Crim 1898 at [19] and see Ch 2; *R v RG* [2002] EWCA Crim 1056 at [30]; *R v Ali* [2006] EWCA Crim 1976 at [34]; and *Rv Lodge* [2013] EWCA Crim 987 at [18].

[89] *R v R v Amado Taylor* [2001] EWCA Crim at [21]; *R v RG* [2002] EWCA Crim 1056 at [30]; *Rv Ali* [2006] EWCA Crim at [34]; and *R v Lodge* [2013] EWCA Crim 987 at [18].

3. Issues to which evidence of disposition may be relevant are not closed. However: (a) the issue of consent in a sexual case is an issue to which evidence of character or disposition may be relevant;[90] and (b) if the accused's defence to a violent crime is that he was defending himself against an attack launched by the complainant, the non-violent character of the latter is no less relevant than that of the former as a matter of logic.[91]

4. If admitting evidence on the basis that it is 'issue-relevant', a trial judge must take care to ensure that the issue to which the evidence is relevant and its limitations are understood by the jury.[92] The judge should also ensure that the effect of admitting the evidence is not to water down the protection provided by the primary obligation upon the prosecution to prove its case and any good character direction that may be given for the defendant.[93]

ADDITIONAL READING

Munday, 'What Constitutes a Good Character?' [1997] Crim LR 247.
An examination of the development of the law relating to good character directions. The decision in *R v Durbin* [1995] Cr App R 84 (2) is criticized and the argument is made that the law took a 'wrong turning'. The article was cited in the judgment in *R v Hunter* [2015] 1 WLR 5367, CA at [20].

QUESTIONS

1. Referring to the relevant case law, critically analyse issues that arise where an accused seeks a good character direction in circumstances where, although he has no previous convictions, he has been guilty of past misconduct.

2. Adam, Malachi, Sandeep, and Wayne, all aged 35, are jointly charged with robbery, the prosecution case being that they robbed Brendan, the owner of a minimarket, of his day's takings of just over £10,000. The defence of each of them is mistaken identity.

Adam has a previous conviction for being drunk and disorderly when he was 18 years old. He has also received three fixed penalty notices for parking offences when he was 20 years old. He is otherwise of good character. At the trial he will give evidence. This will include evidence of his conviction for being drunk and disorderly because he wants to show the jury that he has no propensity to commit the different and more serious offence of robbery with which he is charged.

Malachi has no previous convictions and is of good character. At the trial he will not give evidence but will rely on what he said in police interviews, namely that he had been mistakenly identified, being at home with his girlfriend at the time of the offence.

Sandeep has two previous convictions for driving a car above the speed limit, both when he was 21 years old, and a third conviction for driving a car without insurance when he was 27 years old. He is otherwise of good character. He will give evidence at the trial.

Wayne was convicted of robbery of a shopkeeper, when he was 28, the case being that he robbed the shopkeeper of three £50 notes. The prosecution intend to introduce evidence of this conviction to show Wayne's propensity for robbery.

What, if anything, should the judge say to the jury about the good character of the accused, and why?

 For a note-form answer see the online resources, accessible at www.oup.com/he/keane-mckeown13e.

---

[90] See *R v R v Amado Taylor* [2001] EWCA Crim 1898. See also *R v Ali* [2006] EWCA Crim 1976 at [36].

[91] *R v R v Amado Taylor* [2001] EWCA Crim 1898.

[92] See *R v Lodge* [2013] EWCA Crim 987at [26].

[93] See *R v Green* [2018] 4 WLR 39, CA, at [25]–[26].

Evidence of character: evidence of bad character in criminal cases

19

Key issues

- In a criminal trial, when and why should the prosecution or defence be permitted to adduce evidence of the bad character of a witness or some other person?

- How might evidence of an accused's bad character prove (a) that he has committed the crime with which he is charged; and (b) that he should not be believed if he gives evidence that he did not commit the crime?

- Should evidence of an accused's bad character be admissible by the prosecution to show that he has a propensity to be untruthful?

- When and why should a co-accused be permitted to adduce evidence of an accused's bad character?

Introduction

The background to the Criminal Justice Act 2003

The admissibility of evidence of bad character in criminal cases is governed, almost exclusively, by Chapter 1 of Pt 11 of the Criminal Justice Act 2003 (the 2003 Act). Before the 2003 Act, there were both common law and statutory rules. These rules were complex and riddled with anomalies. The general rule was exclusionary. The prosecution were generally not allowed to admit evidence of the accused's bad character unless it related directly to the offence charged, or to cross-examine defence witnesses to elicit such evidence. This rule was subject to common law exceptions where the evidence was so-called 'similar fact' or 'background evidence', or where the accused raised an issue about his character. Additionally, there was an important statutory exception in s 1(3) of the Criminal Evidence Act 1898, which set out the circumstances in which the accused could lose his 'shield' against cross-examination on his bad character (eg, if he made imputations about the character of a prosecution witness or the deceased victim of the offence, or gave evidence against a co-accused). Witnesses could be cross-examined about their bad character in order to impugn their credibility, but under the common law rule of finality of answers to questions on collateral matters, the cross-examining party could not call further evidence to contradict the witness. Under exceptions to the rule of finality, evidence of a witness's character could be admitted to contradict a denial of bias or a reputation for lying,[1] and under s 6 of the Criminal Procedure Act 1865, which remains in force in amended form, evidence of a witness's convictions could be admitted if he denied them.[2]

Chapter 1, Pt 11 (ss 98–113) all but codifies the law governing the admissibility of evidence of bad character in criminal cases, abolishing the common law rules,[3] amending s 6 of the Criminal Procedure Act 1865[4] to ensure that cross-examination on a witness's previous convictions is governed by the new statutory rules, and repealing s 1(3) of the Criminal Evidence Act 1898.[5] In general terms, the Government's approach to reforming the law on bad character was informed by Auld LJ's Review of the Criminal Courts of England and Wales[6] and the Law Commission Report, *Evidence of Bad Character in Criminal Proceedings*.[7] There are, however, substantial differences between what was proposed in the Review and the Commission, and the provisions of the 2003 Act. In particular, whereas the Law Commission recommended in effect an exclusionary rule subject to exceptions under which bad character evidence could be admitted with the leave of the court, the 2003 Act is more inclusionary[8]—under its provisions evidence of the bad character of the accused falling within one of the categories of admissibility may be introduced without leave, subject, in some cases, to a discretion to exclude.

[1] See Ch 7, **Bias**, p 245.

[2] See Ch 7, **Previous convictions**, p 244. Section 3 of the Criminal Procedure Act 1865 also remains in force, which permits cross-examination by a party of his own witness where the witness is hostile: see Ch 6, **Hostile witnesses**, p 207.

[3] Section 99(1).

[4] Section 331 and para 79, Sch 36.

[5] Section 331 and para 80(b), Sch 36.

[6] HMSO, 2001.

[7] Law Com No 273, Cm 5257 (2001). For critiques of the Report, see Redmayne, 'The Law Commission's character convictions' (2002) 6 E&P 71 and Mirfield, 'Bad character and the Law Commission' (2002) 6 E&P 141.

[8] See Hansard HL vol 654 col 739 (4 Nov 2003) and para 365 of the Home Office Explanatory Notes to the 2003 Act.

The scheme contained in the 2003 Act, as we shall see, is not simple and is in parts unclear, with some key provisions being open to widely differing interpretations. It abolishes the common law rules (s 99); gives a definition of bad character evidence which is very broad (s 98); provides different tests of relevance for admitting bad character evidence of witnesses on the one hand (s 100(1)(b)) and the accused on the other (s 101(1)(d)); provides seven gateways through which the accused's bad character may be admitted (ss 101(1)(a)–(g)), with different tests of relevance depending on whether the evidence is sought to be admitted by the prosecution (s 101(1)(d)) or by a co-accused (s 101(1)(e)); and gives a discretionary power to exclude evidence (s 101(3)) which applies to two gateways (s 101(1)(d) and (g)), as well as a general power to stop a case where evidence is contaminated (s 107). A former Lord Chief Justice described s 1 of the now repealed 1898 Act as 'a nightmare of construction'[9] but the same might be said of some of the provisions of the 2003 Act, especially those governing admissibility of the bad character of the accused. It would not be unfair to describe them, to be colloquial, as something of a dog's breakfast.

Abolition of the common law rules

Section 99 of the 2003 Act provides as follows:

(1) The common law rules governing the admissibility of evidence of bad character in criminal proceedings are abolished.

(2) Subsection (1) is subject to section 118(1) in so far as it preserves the rule under which in criminal proceedings a person's reputation is admissible for the purposes of proving his bad character.

Although s 99(1) refers only to the rules governing the admissibility of evidence of bad character in criminal proceedings and not to the common law rules governing cross-examination of a witness other than the accused about his bad character, it is submitted that the intention is to cover both.[10] As to the questioning of witnesses on matters covered by the exceptions to the rule of finality of answers to collateral questions, the common law rules can certainly be said to 'govern' the admissibility of evidence of bad character, because the matters are put to the witness with a view to eliciting such evidence and, if the matters are denied, they can be proved. The common law rules permitting the questioning of witnesses on their bad character in relation to matters not covered by the exceptions to the rule of finality may also be said to 'govern' the admissibility of evidence of bad character in that they too are questions put with a view to eliciting such evidence and notwithstanding that if the witness denies the matters put, they cannot be proved.

In *R v Platt*,[11] it was stressed that the common law should not be used as a guide to interpreting the bad character provisions of the 2003 Act. However, this seems to encourage an unnecessarily blinkered approach to provisions expressly designed to put common law principles

---

[9] Lord Lane CJ in *R v Anderson* [1988] QB 678 at 686.

[10] As to the meaning of 'criminal proceedings', for the purposes of the bad character provisions of the 2003 Act, these are criminal proceedings in relation to which the strict rules of evidence apply: s 112(1). The provisions cover proceedings concerning an accused's fitness to plead under the Criminal Procedure (Insanity) Act 1964, s 4A: *R v Creed* [2011] EWCA Crim 144. See also *R v Wells* [2015] EWCA Crim 2.

[11] [2016] 4 WLR 51, CA at [27]. See also under **Evidence of the bad character of the defendant, Section 101(1) (e)—evidence of substantial probative value in relation to an important matter in issue between the defendant and a co-defendant, Admissibility**, p 601. See also n 306.

on a statutory footing and where issues of principle arise under the statutory provisions that are identical to those that arose at common law.

Section 99 does not appear to affect the general common law discretion to exclude prosecution evidence where its prejudicial effect outweighs its probative value.[12] It would seem that this discretion may continue to be exercised in respect of evidence of bad character. The phrase 'common law rules governing . . . admissibility', it is submitted, is not apt to cover a common law *discretion* to exclude.

'Bad character' defined

Under s 98 of the 2003 Act:

> References in this Chapter to evidence of a person's 'bad character' are to evidence of, or of a disposition towards, misconduct on his part, other than evidence which—
> (a) has to do with the alleged facts of the offence with which the defendant is charged, or
> (b) is evidence of misconduct in connection with the investigation or prosecution of that offence.

The definition of bad character in s 98 applies in the case of both the accused and non-defendants and covers misconduct occurring, or disposition towards misconduct existing, either before or after the offence with which the accused is charged. The definition covers circumstantial and direct evidence of bad character, notwithstanding that when dealing with circumstantial evidence the question is begged whether the evidence goes to show misconduct until the inference is drawn.[13] 'Bad character' has been defined broadly by s 98, a definition that generally reflects the common law concept. The broad definition is designed to prevent evidence which, under the pre-existing law would have been excluded, from falling outside the statutory scheme and thereby becoming admissible.[14] Although the definition does not include a person's reputation for misconduct, the common law rule under which a person's reputation is admissible for the purpose of proving his bad character, has been preserved by s 118(1)2.[15]

Misconduct

'Misconduct', for the purposes of the definition, means 'the commission of an offence or other reprehensible behaviour',[16] and 'offence' is defined to include a service offence.[17] Evidence of bad character under the Act therefore covers evidence of a person's misconduct whether or not unlawful; if unlawful, whether or not it resulted in a prosecution; and where it did result in a prosecution, whether within the jurisdiction or overseas, and whether it resulted in a conviction or an acquittal. The definition also covers evidence of misconduct in respect of which a trial is pending, evidence of an accused's misconduct which relates to other charges on the indictment, and allegations that have never been tried, for example because of a stay for abuse of process.[18] It does not cover arrest on suspicion followed by

---

[12] See Ch 2.

[13] *R v Wallace* [2008] 1 WLR 572, CA.

[14] See Hilary Benn MP, HC Committee, 23 Jan 2003, col 545.

[15] See Ch 13, Hearsay admissible at common law, Evidence of reputation, p 439.

[16] See Munday, 'What Constitutes "Other Reprehensible Behaviour" under the Bad Character Provisions of the Criminal Justice Act 2003?' [2005] Crim LR 24.

[17] Section 112(1).

[18] *R v Edwards* [2006] 1 WLR 1524, CA at [78] and [81].

release without charge,[19] nor, it seems, an allegation made but later withdrawn.[20] Although the definition does not cover, by itself, evidence that someone has been suspected or informally charged with misconduct, such evidence is generally irrelevant and therefore inadmissible.[21] Likewise, although the definition does not cover evidence of the bare fact that someone has been formally charged with an offence, such evidence is generally inadmissible because irrelevant, the fact that a man has been charged with an offence being no proof that he committed it and having no bearing on his credibility as a witness.[22] Nor does the definition cover the bare fact that someone has been convicted where that conviction has been quashed.[23]

Acquittals

As to acquittals, the definition of misconduct in effect preserves the decision of the House of Lords in *R v Z*[24] that where evidence of misconduct on the part of the accused is relevant and otherwise admissible prosecution evidence, it does not fall to be excluded because it shows or tends to show that the accused was guilty of an offence of which he was previously acquitted. In *R v Hajdarmataj*,[25] the Court of Appeal laid down the following important principles concerning the admissibility of such evidence.[26]

1. It is helpful to distinguish between the evidence of misconduct given at the earlier trial at which the accused was acquitted and the evidence of the acquittal itself. Where evidence of the first is admitted, the question of the admissibility of the second will often arise. Fairness to both sides is the guide on this question.[27]

2. Where a complainant's evidence was the essence of the case against the accused in the earlier trial and accuracy or credibility were critical questions, it may be appropriate to adduce the evidence of the fact of the acquittal as well as the complainant's evidence. This is because, if the jury are not told of the acquittal, they might wrongly conclude there was no acquittal which would be highly prejudicial. There is also a risk that, despite directions, they might search on the internet for the result of the trial.

3. Where evidence of the fact of the acquittal is admitted, the jury will be directed that it is not relevant to their considerations and they must assess the evidence for themselves.

4. Under the 2003 Act, there is no requirement that the evidence of misconduct from the previous trial, in order to be admissible, bears a striking similarity to what is alleged in the subsequent trial.

---

[19] *R v Weir* [2006] 1 WLR 1885, CA at [118].

[20] *R v Bovell* [2005] 2 Cr App R 401 (27) at [21], CA. Although a *number* of 'strikingly similar' allegations, made and then withdrawn, could be covered: see *R v Ladds* [2009] EWCA Crim 1249.

[21] See *Stirland v DPP* [1944] AC 315, HL, a decision under the Criminal Evidence Act 1898.

[22] See *Maxwell v DPP* [1935] AC 309, HL, a decision under the 1898 Act. See also *R v Renda* [2006] 1 WLR 2948, CA at [46], on the different and, it is submitted, unconvincing reasoning that in the circumstances there was 'a bare allegation, itself wholly unproved'.

[23] See *R v Hussain* [2008] EWCA Crim 1117: an accused's quashed conviction for manslaughter was not evidence of bad character, it being no more than an unproven charge.

[24] [2002] 2 AC 483, HL.

[25] [2019] EWCA Crim 303.

[26] Ibid at [37]–[38] and [43]–[46].

[27] See also *R v Mellars* [2019] EWCA Crim 42; *R v Preko* [2015] EWCA Crim 242; and *R v H(JR)* (1990) 90 Cr App R 440, CA.

5. It will be for the prosecution to satisfy the court that no injustice will be caused by introducing evidence from an acquittal. A principal safeguard is the disclosure of 'unused material' or records of any previous accounts given by witnesses in order to check for consistency.

6. Failures in this respect may be relevant to admissibility or discretionary exclusion when the prosecution make an application to admit evidence of the misconduct.

7. If the solicitors representing the accused at the second trial have unused material and/ or previous statements from the first trial at which the accused was acquitted because they represented the accused, then it may be their duty to produce them if requested to do so in accordance with Criminal Procedure Rule 15.4(1), depending on the content of the defence statement; but this does not relieve the prosecution from their duty as it is the prosecution who are making the application.

8. The safeguards which apply when seeking to introduce evidence of misconduct from an acquittal cannot be less than those which apply when there is a retrial. At a retrial it is essential for the prosecution to produce unused material and previous statements in interview or otherwise.

9. At a retrial, it will normally be essential for a prosecution application to be supported by evidence of what was said at the first trial by one means of another. It would be normal to obtain a record of evidence given by relevant witnesses in the first trial in the form of a transcript or a recording, which can be used to produce a note agreed by advocates covering relevant points. If an agreed note cannot be achieved by access to a recording or by cooperation, a transcript will normally be required.

10. Each case will turn on its own facts and the judge must consider safeguards required on a case-by-case basis when considering both admissibility and any application to exclude. Concerning admissibility, it would normally be relevant to consider the fact that the accused had been acquitted.

Other reprehensible behaviour

The word 'reprehensible' carries with it some element of culpability or blameworthiness,[28] but whether conduct is 'reprehensible' is not determined by an exercise in moral judgement. So, in *R v Fox*[29] where the accused was charged with sexual offences against children, the keeping of a private notebook recording what the court referred to as 'dirty sexual thoughts' was judged, although with caution, not to be evidence of a disposition towards reprehensible behaviour. Whether particular lawful behaviour involves culpability or blameworthiness will depend on the particular circumstances and is a question on which views are likely to differ. Verbal aggression is not necessarily reprehensible.[30] Possession of rap lyrics personally altered to include a vague threat could be reprehensible when combined with possession of photographs of the victims of a violent assault.[31] It is doubtful that exaggeration by a school pupil to fellow pupils about being pushed by a teacher after everyday misbehaviour

---

[28] *R v Renda* [2006] 1 WLR 2948, CA at [24]: the mere fact that the appellant was found unfit to plead some 18 months after an apparent incident of gratuitous violence did not, by itself, extinguish culpability at the time of the offence.

[29] [2009] EWCA Crim 653 at [30].

[30] *R v Osborne* [2007] Crim LR 712, CA.

[31] *R v Saleem* [2007] EWCA Crim 1923.

is reprehensible.[32] It is not reprehensible to have recently taken a drugs overdose.[33] Nor, generally, is it reprehensible to make a suicide attempt, and the same should be true of self harming.[34] However, drinking to excess and taking illegal drugs is reprehensible.[35] Possession of 'self portrait' photographs which show the subject sleeping with a large knife resting across his chest are 'bad taste rather than bad character'.[36] It is not reprehensible for a married heterosexual man to indulge the homosexual side of his nature with another consenting person above the age of consent.[37] It may well be reprehensible for an accused during his trial, in the absence of the jury, to make a remark from the dock to a pupil barrister along the lines of, 'what are you looking at?', where the remark is made in an aggressive way.[38] Appearance in video material published on 'YouTube' which shows membership of, or association with, gangs which exhibit violence or hostility to the police and/or links with firearms may be reprehensible behaviour.[39] A finding by a tribunal that an expert's evidence is 'not as objective and independent as it might have been' is not evidence of reprehensible behaviour by the expert.[40]

Evidence of lawful behaviour which is deemed not to be reprehensible and therefore falls outside the statutory definition, will be admissible if it is relevant to an issue in the case and not excluded by the exercise of discretion. In *R v Weir*[41] the appellant M was convicted of indecently assaulting A. At the time of the offences, M was 39 and A, 13. It was held that evidence was admissible of M's earlier sexual relationship with another girl B, who was 16 at the time, M being 34. There was no feature of this lawful relationship to make it reprehensible, such as evidence of grooming. Since evidence of the relationship was not 'evidence of bad character', it was admissible at common law as demonstrating M's sexual interest in early- or mid-teenage girls much younger than himself. This bore on the truth of his case that his interest in A was supportive and asexual.[42]

If evidence of bad character does fall within the statutory definition it can only be admitted in evidence if it satisfies the further conditions of admissibility in s 100 (non-defendant's bad character) or s 101 (defendant's bad character). Where evidence to be adduced is evidence of the accused's bad character and the accused disputes the facts relied on to establish his bad character, then a *voir dire* may be required.[43]

---

[32] *R v* [2006] EWCA Crim 1901.

[33] *R v Hall-Chung* (2007) 151 SJLB 1020.

[34] *R v M* [2014] EWCA Crim 1457 at [61].

[35] See *R v AJC* [2006] EWCA Crim 284.

[36] *R v Allen* [2009] EWCA Crim 2881 at [19].

[37] *R v IJ* [2011] EWCA Crim 2734.

[38] *R v Mahil* [2013] EWCA Crim 673.

[39] *R v Lewis* [2014] EWCA Crim 48, relying on *R v Smith* [2009] 1 Cr App R 521 (36), (evidence of gang membership may in some circumstances be evidence of bad character).

[40] *R v Jones* [2015] 1 Cr App R 50 (5), CA.

[41] [2006] 1 WLR 1885, CA.

[42] See also *R v P* (31 May 2012, unreported), CA. It was also held in *Weir* that a refusal, without reasons, to give a witness statement when a victim of crime, is not reprehensible behaviour. However, it is submitted that the evidential status of such behaviour could be affected by the motive of the victim, eg where the motive was to protect the criminal.

[43] See *R v Wright* [2000] Crim LR 851, CA, a decision under the Criminal Evidence Act 1898.

The admissibility of evidence of bad character 'to do with' the facts of the offence or in connection with its investigation or prosecution

Section 99(1) of the 2003 Act, as we have seen, abolishes the common law rules governing admissibility of evidence of bad character as defined by s 98. It follows that the common law rules continue to operate insofar as they permit evidence to be adduced which, under s 98(a), 'has to do with the alleged facts of the offence' or, under s 98(b), 'is evidence of misconduct in connection with the investigation or prosecution of that offence'.

Evidence 'to do with' the alleged facts of the offence

Section 98(a) covers such prosecution evidence, other than evidence of previous misconduct or evidence of disposition towards misconduct, as tends to show that the accused is guilty of the offence charged, such as evidence of witnesses to the crime and fingerprint evidence. The section also covers misconduct other than the offence charged, for example an assault or criminal damage committed by the accused in the course of the burglary with which he is charged. Similarly, it may cover misconduct that was the subject of another count originally in the indictment but subsequently severed[44] or misconduct in a count what has been improperly included.[45] Section 98(a) can also cover misconduct on the part of someone other than the accused, for example evidence in support of a defence of self-defence that the victim was the aggressor. In *R v Machado*,[46] it was held that on a charge of robbery, evidence was admissible that the victim had offered to supply drugs to the appellant and that he had said that he had taken an ecstasy tablet. However, the court appears to have overlooked the basic requirement of relevance. That the victim had taken drugs may well have been relevant because there was a suggestion that rather than being pushed to the ground, he fell over, but his alleged offer to supply drugs had no obvious relevance to any of the issues in the case.

Nexus in time?

Where the misconduct is sought to be admitted as relevant to the accused's motive, no nexus in time is required. In *R v Lunkulu*,[47] a gang murder, the judge applied s 98(a) and admitted as relevant evidence rather than evidence of bad character, the accused's convictions for two offences of attempted murder committed five days before the murder for which he was being tried, and one offence of possession of a firearm with intent to endanger life committed two months after the murder. The Court of Appeal held that the judge was entitled to admit the evidence as a relevant part of the prosecution case, namely that the murder occurred in the context of an ongoing feud between rival gangs. The court observed that s 98(a) includes no necessary temporal qualification and applies to misconduct whenever it occurs if it is to do with the facts of the offence. The evidence was inextricably linked to the facts of the murder and fell within s 98(a) and was not required to be admitted as evidence of bad character. However, although no nexus in time is required where evidence is being admitted to

---

[44] *R v Edwards* [2006] 1 WLR 1524, CA at [23]. See also *R v Mullings* [2011] 2 Cr App R 21 (2), CA.

[45] *R v Morris* [2019] EWCA Crim 147: count improperly included because the offence stated was summary only. Cf *R v Stark* [2015] EWCA Crim 1513.

[46] (2006) 170 JP 400.

[47] [2015] EWCA Crim 1350.

establish motive,[48] such a nexus may still be required where the evidence merely shows propensity[49] or identity.[50]

Different to propensity evidence and background evidence

Evidence admissible under s 98(a) may be distinguished from both propensity evidence which is bad character evidence potentially admissible under s 101(1)(d) and so-called 'background evidence', which is bad character evidence potentially admissible under s 101(1)(c). The distinction between evidence admissible under s 98(a) and evidence admissible under s 101(1)(d) may be apparent from the length of time between the misconduct and the offences charged, as well as from the nature of the misconduct itself. In *R v Sullivan*,[51] the Court of Appeal held that in the accused's trial for cannabis production, the judge was wrong to admit as evidence 'to do with the facts of the offence', incriminating text messages sent and received by the accused months before the period covered by the indictment. The messages included, 'Don't forget the meter readings', 'some are looking a bit yellow', and 'I keep watering and it's doing fine. Do you want it or not?' Quashing the conviction, the court held that the evidence of the text messages was not connected to or closely associated with the facts of the offence with which the appellant was charged. It was evidence which demonstrated the likelihood that the accused had been involved in earlier cannabis production outside the scope of the indictment and was therefore evidence of bad character whose admissibility was subject to s 101(1) (d) and s 101(3). If the evidence had been admissible, the jury would have required a careful bad character direction about how to approach it and absent such a direction, the conviction was unsafe. As regards the distinction between evidence which has to do with the facts of the offence and background evidence, this can be difficult to draw in some cases,[52] and as we shall see, it is possible for the same evidence to be admissible in principle under both s 98(a) and s 101(1)(c),[53] and indeed s 101(1)(d). However, if s 98(a) applies, then regardless of potential admissibility under other provisions, the evidence is admissible without more ado,[54] subject of course to the requirement of relevance and the discretion to exclude.[55]

---

[48] See also *R v Stewart* [2016] EWCA Crim 447 and *R v Sule* [2013] 1 Cr App R 42 (3) (evidence of three incidents of gang-related violence in the months before a murder). See also *R v H* [2018] EWCA Crim 2868.

[49] *R v Tirnaveanu* [2007] 2 Cr App R 295 (2), CA.

[50] An argument to the contrary was rejected in *R v Lunkulu* [2015] EWCA Crim 1350 at [23].

[51] [2015] EWCA Crim 1565.

[52] See in this chapter, under Section 101(1)(c)—important explanatory evidence, p 578. See also *R v Okokono* [2014] EWCA Crim 2521.

[53] See in this chapter under Admissibility as evidence relevant to important matters in issue and as evidence 'to do with the facts of the offence', p 580.

[54] *R v Edwards* [2006] 1 WLR 1524, CA at [1](i). See also *R v Kalu* [2007] EWCA Crim 22. See also *R v Leonard* (2009) 173 JP 366, CA at [11]: text messages sent to the accused's mobile phone suggestive of drug-dealing were to do with the alleged facts of the offence of possession of controlled drugs with intent to supply and were not evidence of bad character (but were inadmissible hearsay). Cf *R v Chrysostomou* [2010] Crim LR 942, CA: text messages recovered from the accused's mobile phone suggestive of small-scale drug-dealing were held to be evidence of bad character (and not hearsay). See also Ch 12.

[55] In cases of familial sexual abuse where evidence has been adduced alleging sexual abuse in relation to particular counts but the judge rules that there is no case to answer on those counts, the evidence no longer has to do with the facts of the offence with which the accused is charged and may become evidence of bad character. See *R v B* [2010] EWCA Crim 1251 at [14].

Evidence in connection with the investigation or prosecution of the offence

Section 98(b) covers, for example: evidence that during the investigation the police obtained evidence unlawfully or unfairly, for instance by fabricating a confession or planting evidence on the accused or in his premises; evidence that during interview the accused told lies; and evidence that during the investigation or proceedings the prosecution or the accused had sought to intimidate potential witnesses. In *DPP v Agyemayang*,[56] the Divisional Court held that previous convictions which resulted in the accused being disqualified from driving were plainly evidence of misconduct in connection with the investigation and prosecution of the offence of driving whilst disqualified and were also, in the court's view, to do with the alleged facts of the offence (see s 98(a)).

The role of the trial judge and the Court of Appeal

Provided that a trial judge has not erred in principle, the Court of Appeal will be loath to interfere with the judge's ruling under the 2003 Act on the admissibility of evidence of bad character, whether of the accused or of someone other than the accused. In *R v Renda*,[57] Sir Igor Judge P said:

> The circumstances in which this court would interfere with the exercise of a judicial discretion are limited. The principles need no repetition.[58] However, we emphasise that the same general approach will be adopted when the court is being invited to interfere with what in reality is a fact-specific judgment . . . the trial judge's 'feel' for the case is usually the critical ingredient of the decision at first instance which this court lacks. Context therefore is vital . . . The principles have been considered by this court on a number of occasions. The responsibility for their application is not for this court but for the trial judge.

Since *R v Renda* the Court of Appeal has continued to make it clear that it will not intervene in the finely balanced decision of a trial judge, even where a different judge might have reached a different conclusion.[59] Equally, the Court of Appeal has continued to consider and refine points of principle at a rate that can be fairly described as industrial.

Evidence of the bad character of a person other than the defendant

Section 100 of the Criminal Justice Act 2003

At common law a witness could be cross-examined about his previous misconduct with a view to impugning his credibility. He could be cross-examined, for example, about acts of dishonesty or immorality on his part, about lies he told or false allegations he made, about his drink or drug abuse, and so on. However, as mentioned earlier,[60] insofar as the questions could properly be said to be on collateral matters and the witness denied them, evidence was admissible in rebuttal only exceptionally. Exceptions covered previous convictions, bias, and general reputation for untruthfulness.

---

[56] (2009) 173 JP 487, DC.

[57] [2006] 1 WLR 2948, CA at [3].

[58] See Ch 2, Judicial discretion, p 47.

[59] See *R v Surgue* [2017] EWCA Crim 1840; *R v RJ* [2017] EWCA Crim 1943; *R v Noble* [2016] EWCA Crim 2219; and *R v Zawadzka* [2016] EWCA Crim 1712.

[60] See earlier, in this chapter, under **The background to the Criminal Justice Act 2003**, p 554.

In *R v Edwards*[61] it was held that subject to limits laid down in *Hobbs v Tinling*,[62] a witness could be cross-examined about any improper conduct of which he may have been guilty, for the purpose of testing his credit. The following three principles were established in *Hobbs v Tinling*.[63]

1. Questions as to credit in cross-examination are proper if of such a nature that the truth of the imputation conveyed by them would seriously affect the opinion of the court as to the credibility of the witness on the matters to which he testifies.

2. Such questions are *improp*er if the imputation they convey relates to matters so remote in time or of such a character that the truth of the imputation would not affect, or would affect in a slight degree, the opinion of the court as to the credibility of the witness on the matter to which he testifies.

3. Such questions are *improper* if there is a great disproportion between the importance of the imputation made against the witness's character and the importance of his evidence.

The Law Commission was of the view that further restraints were necessary. Three reasons were given: the power of evidence of bad character to distort the fact-finding process; the need to encourage witnesses to give evidence; and the need for courts 'to control gratuitous and offensive cross-examination of little or no purpose other than to intimidate or embarrass the witness or muddy the waters'.[64] Balancing these factors against the need not to prejudice a fair trial, the Commission recommended a test based on the degree of relevance of bad character evidence to the issues in the case. Evidence of only trivial relevance would be excluded. The views of the Commission are reflected in s 100 of the 2003 Act.

Section 100(1) provides as follows:

(1) In criminal proceedings evidence of the bad character of a person other than the defendant is admissible if and only if—
   (a) it is important explanatory evidence,
   (b) it has substantial probative value in relation to a matter which—
      (i) is a matter in issue in the proceedings, and
      (ii) is of substantial importance in the context of the case as a whole,
   or
   (c) all parties to the proceedings agree to the evidence being admissible.

Section 100 may be used by the prosecution, the accused, or any co-accused. The meaning of 'bad character' has already been considered. A 'person other than the defendant' may or may not be a witness in the case. Although, on its face, s 100 governs only the admissibility of evidence of bad character and does not, in terms, govern the asking of questions about bad character in cross-examination,[65] it is submitted that the intention is to cover both. This would be consistent with the interpretation of s 99(1) of the Act that it abolishes the common law rules relating not only to the admissibility of evidence of bad character but also to cross-examination of witnesses about bad character.[66]

---

[61] [1991] 1 WLR 207, CA.

[62] [1929] 2 KB 1, CA.

[63] Ibid at 51.

[64] Law Com No 273, Cm 5257 (2001), para 9.35. See also *R v Garratty* [2010] EWCA Crim 1156: the purpose of s 100 is to remove the right of a party to adduce misconduct which is old, irrelevant, or trivial in order to unfairly blacken the standing of a witness in the eyes of the jury, or permit unsubstantiated attacks on credit.

[65] Cf, in this regard, the Youth Justice and Criminal Evidence Act 1999, s 41.

[66] See, in this chapter, under **Abolition of the common law rules**, p 555.

Threshold conditions for admissibility

Important explanatory evidence

Section 100(2) provides as follows:

> (1) For the purposes of subsection (1)(a) evidence is important explanatory evidence if—
>
> (a) without it, the court or jury would find it impossible or difficult properly to understand other evidence in the case, and
>
> (b) its value for understanding the case as a whole is substantial.

Section 100(2) covers evidence of or a disposition towards misconduct on the part of someone other than the accused, without which the prosecution (or defence) account would be incomplete or incoherent.[67] Thus if the matter to which the evidence relates is largely comprehensible without the explanatory evidence, the evidence is inadmissible. The wording of s 100(2)(a) is a slightly different formulation of the common law rule permitting the use of background evidence, notwithstanding that it reveals the bad character or criminal disposition of the accused, where it is part of a continual background or history relevant to the offence charged and without the totality of which the account placed before the jury would be incomplete or incomprehensible.[68] The first option, 'incomplete', is probably best ignored: in the nature of things the account will be incomplete. The Explanatory Notes to the Act provide an example of s 100(2)(a) arising in a case which involves the abuse by one person of another over a long period of time: 'For the jury to understand properly the victim's account of the offending and why they (sic) did not seek help from, for example, a parent or other guardian, it might be necessary for evidence to be given of a wider pattern of abuse involving that other person.'[69] *R v Miller*[70] provides another example. The Court of Appeal held that bad character evidence exposing a witness's motive could constitute important explanatory evidence under s 100. However, the court also held that such evidence should not be admitted to support merely speculative suggestions as this would be the very type of exercise which s 100 is designed to prevent.[71]

Explanatory evidence, to be admissible, must also satisfy s 100(1)(b), that is, its value for understanding the case as a whole must be 'substantial', as opposed to minor or trivial.[72]

Evidence of substantial probative value

Under s 100(1)(b), evidence of the bad character of a person other than the accused is admissible if it has substantial probative value in relation to a matter which—(i) is a matter in issue in the proceedings; and (ii) is of substantial importance in the context of the case as a whole. As to (i), a 'matter in issue in the proceedings' means any matter in issue, whether an issue of disputed fact or an issue of credibility, and credibility as an issue for the purposes of s 100

---

[67] See Law Com No 273, Cm 5257 (2001), para 9.13.

[68] Per Purchase LJ in *R v Pettman*, 2 May 1985, CA, unreported.

[69] Para 360. For an exploration of the dangers of using the Explanatory Notes as an aid to construction, see Munday, 'Bad Character Rules and Riddles: "Explanatory Notes" and True Meanings of s. 103(1) of the Criminal Justice Act 2003' [2005] Crim LR 337.

[70] [2010] 2 Cr App R 138 (19), CA. See also *R v Kelly* [2015] EWCA Crim 817 at [62].

[71] [2010] 2 Cr App R 138 (19), CA at [19]–[20]. Where suggestions made by the prosecution in cross-examination are denied and otherwise unproven, the jury must be given a specific direction not to regard the suggestions as in any sense assisting the prosecution case.

[72] See Law Com No 273, Cm 5257 (2001), para 9.1.

is wider than a propensity to be untruthful.[73] As to (ii), evidence which goes only to some minor or trivial issue should not be admitted.[74]

The probative value must be 'substantial'—evidence of only minor probative force should not be admitted.[75] In *R v King*,[76] the Court of Appeal stated that the test for admissibility under s 100(1)(b) is one of enhanced relevance. In considering the nature of the test and how it applied, the court noted the decisions in *R v Phillips* and *R v Dizaei*.[77] In *R v Phillips*,[78] it was said that a strict reading of the statutory requirements was required. *R v Phillips* concerned the test for admissibility under s 101(1)(e), which, like s100(1)(b), prescribes a threshold condition of 'substantial probative value'. In *R v Dizaei*,[79] it was said that when considering whether evidence has substantial probative value for the purposes of s 100(1)(b), the court may legitimately take into account the risk that 'satellite litigation' can distract the jury from the real issues in the case.

Section 100(3) sets out a non-exhaustive list of the factors to which the court must have regard in assessing the probative value of the evidence. It provides as follows:

> (3) In assessing the probative value of evidence for the purposes of subsection (1)(b) the court must have regard to the following factors (and to any others it considers relevant)—
> (a) the nature and number of the events, or other things, to which the evidence relates;
> (b) when those events or things are alleged to have happened or existed;
> (c) where—
>   (i) the evidence is evidence of a person's misconduct, and
>   (ii) it is suggested that the evidence has probative value by reason of similarity between that misconduct and other alleged misconduct, the nature and extent of the similarities and dissimilarities between each of the alleged instances of misconduct;
> (d) where—
>   (i) the evidence is evidence of a person's misconduct,
>   (ii) it is suggested that that person is also responsible for the misconduct charged, and
>   (iii) the identity of the person responsible for the misconduct charged is disputed, the extent to which the evidence shows or tends to show that the same person was responsible each time.

As to when the assessment of the probative value by the judge should be made, it was held in *R v Hussain*[80] that it should be at the time of the application to admit the evidence and not after all the evidence had been called.

---

[73] *R v S* [2006] 2 Cr App R 437 (31) at [7] and [10]. See also *R v Weir* [2006] 1 WLR 1885, CA at [73].

[74] See, eg, *R v Muhadeen* [2016] EWCA Crim 1.

[75] See, eg, *R v Burchell* [2016] EWCA Crim 1559. Details of allegations contained in a police Incident Disclosure Print (IDP) about an assault by the complainant which contained contrary versions had no substantial probative value. Nor did details in another IDP of allegations not supported by any independent evidence. See also *R v Braithwaite* [2010] 2 Cr App R 149 (20), CA and *R v Warren* [2010] EWCA Crim 3267: unsupported hearsay allegations recorded against witnesses in police CRIS (intelligence) reports. Cf *R v Alexander* [2018] EWCA Crim 239: allegations recorded in CRIS reports that the accused had mistreated the complainant, admissible under s 101(1)(d). See also *R v Harvey* [2014] EWCA Crim 54 at [72]: the conditions for admissibility under s 100(1)(b) apply to evidence of the bad character of an absent witness which a party seeks to admit under s 124(2)(a) as relevant to the absent witness's credibility.

[76] [2015] EWCA Crim 1631.

[77] At [41].

[78] [2012] 1 Cr App R 332 (25), CA.

[79] [2013] 1 Cr App R 411 (31), CA.

[80] [2015] EWCA Crim 383.

Nature and number of the events etc

As to s 100(3)(a), if, for example, a key witness has previous convictions or has been guilty of improper conduct in the past, the nature and number of the offences committed or of the incidents of misconduct will have an obvious bearing in deciding its probative value in relation to the issue of his credibility as a witness. A conviction for perjury will have a probative force normally lacking in a conviction for, say, a minor motoring offence.[81] Similarly, evidence of previous false accusations may have a probative value not to be found in, say, evidence of cruelty to animals.[82] However, previous convictions which do not involve either the making of false statements or the giving of false evidence are also capable of having substantial probative value in relation to the credibility of a witness.[83] In *R v Brewster*[84] it was stated that each case will turn on its own facts and 'the question is whether the evidence of previous convictions, or bad behaviour, is sufficiently persuasive to be worthy of consideration by a fair minded tribunal upon the issue of the witness's creditworthiness.'

In *R v S*,[85] S, charged with indecent assault, was of good character. He claimed that the complainant, a prostitute, had agreed to sexual activities for £10 and that when, afterwards, he refused her demand for more money, she threatened to accuse him of rape and tried to grab a gold chain he was wearing. It was held that S should have been allowed to cross-examine her on her convictions for going equipped for theft, handling, and burglary, because they showed a propensity to act dishonestly and possessed substantial probative value on the issues whether, in effect, she had demanded money with menaces and had tried to take S's property. By contrast, in *R v Garnham*[86] it was held that the accused, tried for rape, was properly prevented from cross-examining the complainant about any of her 65 previous convictions for theft. The Court of Appeal held that the judge had been correct in his conclusion that a propensity to be dishonest was not the same as a propensity to be untruthful and that, in the circumstances of the case, the complainant's previous convictions were not of substantial probative value in relation to her credibility.

It is difficult, without more, to justify the conclusion in *R v Renda*[87] that a defence witness's conviction for a violent offence was of substantial probative value in relation to the issue of his credibility, being 'particularly germane' to the question whether a robbery had occurred

---

[81] However, see *R v Jukes* [2018] 2 Crim App R 114 (9), CA: a conviction for conspiracy to pervert the course of justice was not admissible under s 100 where the co-accused had pleaded guilty. His credibility was no longer in issue and the conviction did not have substantial probative value in relation to the other principle issues.

[82] See, eg, *R v Alexander* [2018] EWCA Crim 239, a case of domestic violence where a previous allegation by the complainant against the accused resulted in her receiving a caution for wasting police time. Cf *R v Moody* [2019] EWCA Crim 1222, where, on the facts, two false complaints by a child from two years previously did not have substantial probative value, one amounting to only trivial misbehaviour and the other not actually amounting to a complaint.

[83] *R v Stephenson* [2006] EWCA Crim 2325. This is also the case where an accused seeks to adduce the bad character of a co-accused under s 101(1)(e) (per Hughes LJ at [27]). Cf *R v Ul-Haq* [2010] EWCA Crim 1683, where a witness's previous dishonesty offences were unrelated to the offence charged and too historical. These are considerations under s 100(3)(b)—see, in this chapter, under **When events or things are alleged to have happened, etc, p 567.**

[84] [2011] 1 WLR 601, CA, per Pitchford LJ at [22]. See also *R v M* [2014] Crim LR 823.

[85] [2006] 2 Cr App R 437 (31).

[86] [2008] EWCA Crim 266.

[87] [2006] 1 WLR 2948, CA at [59].

or been fabricated by the complainant. One possible explanation is that it was a conviction after a not guilty plea, which can operate to impugn credibility.[88] In *R v South*[89] the question of whether a witness's convictions were based on guilty or not guilty pleas was considered to be relevant when assessing the probative value of the convictions in relation to credibility.[90] In *R v South*, the accused's alibi witness had 53 convictions recorded between 1978 and 1996, including convictions for theft, burglary, handling stolen goods, forgery, obtaining property by deception, and using false instruments. The court held that the judge had been wrong to permit the prosecution to cross-examine on all of these convictions without first distinguishing which offences involved 'untruthfulness' and, in turn, which of those 'untruthfulness offences' were the subject of guilty or not guilty pleas. A proper assessment of the probative value of the convictions to the credibility of the accused's alibi witness required such distinctions to be made.

When events or things are alleged to have happened, etc

As to s 100(3)(b), evidence of misconduct occurring many years ago is usually likely to have less probative value than more recent misconduct,[91] although plainly very serious misconduct in the past may have much greater probative value than recent but relatively minor misconduct. Misconduct capable of having substantial probative value includes misconduct after the commission of the offence charged in the proceedings. So, for example, where an accused seeks to blame another person who was previously a suspect but not charged, misconduct by that person after the offence could be probative of whether he rather than the accused committed the offence. In such a case, the more time that has elapsed since the offence, the less probative the misconduct is likely to be. This can be further affected by factors such as the person's age at the time of the offence and his age at the time of the trial. In *R v Ross*,[92] the Court of Appeal held that the trial judge was correct to exclude previous convictions of a former suspect, N, whom the accused sought to blame for the murder of an old lady in her home some 13 years previously. N's convictions included burglary, housebreaking, rape, and violence committed between two and nine years *after* the date of the murder. During the trial the jury had heard highly probative hearsay evidence implicating N and it was held that the convictions added little. Also, considering that N was 15 years old at the time of the murder, some of the convictions for violence committed as an adult could not be probative to show a propensity for using serious violence as a 15-year-old during a burglary.

Similarities between the misconduct and other alleged misconduct, etc

Section 100(3)(c) concerns evidence of a person's misconduct, the probative value of which, in relation to a matter in issue in the proceedings, derives from its similarity to other misconduct on his part. Thus if the accused alleges that the case against him has been fabricated by a police officer who has threatened a potential witness for the defence—evidence of which would be admissible under s 98(b)—and there is evidence that in other cases the

---

[88] See *R v Renda* [2006] 1 WLR 2948, CA at [59]; see by contrast, in the case of another appellant, Razaq at [73]. The credibility of an accused can also be impugned in the same way (see *R v Campbell* [2007] 1 WLR 2798, CA, considered, in this chapter, under **Bad character evidence under s 101(1)(d) relevant to the credibility of the accused**, p 597.

[89] [2011] EWCA Crim 754.

[90] Ibid at [25].

[91] See *R v Ul-Haq* [2010] EWCA Crim 1683.

[92] [2009] EWCA Crim 1165. See [24].

officer has also gone to improper lengths to secure a conviction, in assessing the probative value of the evidence the court should have regard to the nature and extent of the similarities, for example, whether in some of the cases he had also threatened potential defence witnesses.

Relevance of misconduct to identity, etc

Section 100(3)(d) relates to evidence, in cases in which the identity of the offender is in dispute, suggesting that a person other than the accused is responsible for the offence charged. Such evidence will often take the form of evidence of similar facts. For example, if the accused is charged with a sexual assault in a public park, the prosecution case being that the crime was committed by someone wearing eccentric clothes, and the defence being one of mistaken identity, and there is evidence that X, the resident of a house overlooking the park has previously committed sexual assaults in the park, then in assessing the probative value of the evidence, the court must have regard to the extent to which the evidence shows or tends to show that X was responsible for each of the offences, for example whether the evidence shows that X wore eccentric clothing or the same eccentric clothing on each occasion.

Satellite litigation

Where a person disputes evidence of misconduct sought to be adduced, the risk of 'satellite litigation' is a relevant consideration when assessing the probative value of the evidence.[93] The court should reflect on whether the disputed evidence would make it difficult for the jury to understand the remainder of the evidence in the case or diminish the jury's understanding of the case as a whole.[94]

Jury directions

Where the prosecution bear the burden of proof on the matter in issue to which the evidence of bad character has substantial probative value, the judge must be careful not to mislead the jury. In *R v Alexander*,[95] the trial judge improperly directed the jury that: 'if you are sure that it [the evidence of the bad character of the complainant] does demonstrate such a propensity [a propensity to make false allegations against the accused]. . .you may take it into account when you are considering whether her evidence. . .is credible.' He should have said: 'If you think that it may be that the. . .[bad character evidence] demonstrates a propensity. . .'[96]

Evidence admitted by agreement

Under s 100(1)(c) evidence of the bad character of a person other than the accused may be admitted by agreement of 'all parties to the proceedings', that is, the prosecution, the accused, and any co-accused. Under s 100(4), evidence may be admitted under s 100(1)(c) without the leave of the court.

---

[93] See *R v Dizaei* [2013] EWCA Crim 88. Evidence of an allegation against the witness that he had raped his girlfriend was inadmissible: the witness had bitterly contested the allegation and there was a risk that if the evidence was admitted two trials might be simultaneously in progress before the same jury. See also *R v King* [2015] EWCA Crim 1631 at [41].

[94] *R v Dizaei* [2013] EWCA Crim 88 at [31]–[38]. See also *R v M* [2014] Crim LR 823, CA.

[95] [2018] EWCA Crim 239.

[96] At [29]–[30].

The requirement of leave where evidence is not agreed

Section 100(4) of the 2003 Act provides that 'Except where subsection (1)(c) applies, evidence of the bad character of a person other than the defendant must not be given without the leave of the court.' Thus evidence admissible under s 100(1)(a) or (b) must not be adduced without leave. Unfortunately, however, the subsection gives no guidance as to what factors, if any, should be taken into account in deciding whether or not to grant leave, over and above the factors set out in s 100(2) and (3). In *R v S*,[97] the Court of Appeal expressed the view that the leave requirement did not give the court any further discretion as regards the admissibility of bad character evidence under s 100.[98]

On one view, s 100(4) also applies to evidence of bad character of complainants admissible under s 41 of the Youth Justice and Criminal Evidence Act 1999.[99] If that is so, then in this context also the purpose of the subsection is elusive, because it is unclear what factors, if any, should be taken into account in deciding whether or not to grant leave, over and above the matters that have to be taken into account in deciding whether to grant leave under s 41 itself. The further question arises as to what kinds of sexual behaviour on the part of the complainant should be treated as 'bad character' as defined in the 2003 Act. An alternative and preferable view, it is submitted, is that when evidence of bad character is admitted under s 41, there will of necessity be compliance with s 100(4) of the 2003 Act because of the leave requirement in s 41 itself.

Leave under both s 100(4) and s 41 will normally be considered at a ground rules hearing, as will restrictions on the scope of questioning where leave is granted.[100]

Where an accused seeks leave to question a complainant on previous allegations of sexual assault with a view to establishing that they are false, it is clear that s 100(4) of the 2003 Act rather than s 41 will apply. In *R v All-Hilly*,[101] the Court of Appeal provided guidance on granting leave in such cases. The guidance may be summarized as follows:

1. False complaints about sexual assaults are not evidence 'about any sexual behaviour' within the meaning of s 42(1)(c) of the Youth Justice and Criminal Evidence Act 1999, but are evidence of bad character.

2. Before giving leave under s 100(4) of the Criminal Justice Act 2003, the judge should be satisfied that there was a proper evidential basis for asserting that any such complaint was both made and untrue.

3. Concerning the meaning of a 'proper evidential basis', a strong factual foundation for concluding the complaint was false was not required, but there must be some material which allows the conclusion to be properly drawn.

4. Determining whether there was an evidential basis was a fact-sensitive exercise for the judge which would not be assisted by examining the facts of other cases.

5. The exercise was an exercise of judgement rather than discretion: it was for the judge to evaluate the matter on the basis of all the relevant material.

6. The ultimate question was whether the material was capable of leading to a conclusion that a previous complaint was false.

---

[97] [2009] EWCA Crim 2457.

[98] Ibid at [62].

[99] See Ch 7, Complainants in proceedings for sexual offences, p 230.

[100] See, eg, *R v Dinc* [2017] EWCA Crim 1206.

[101] [2014] 2 Cr App R 530 (33), CA. See also *R v Shabir*, 11 May 2016, CA.

Discretion to exclude

It is submitted that the general common law discretionary power to exclude evidence where its prejudicial effect outweighs its probative value may be exercised in respect of *prosecution* evidence of bad character admissible under s 100.[102] As to whether the general discretionary power to exclude prosecution evidence under s 78 of the Police and Criminal Evidence Act 1984[103] applies in the case of prosecution evidence of bad character otherwise admissible under the 2003 Act, the case law suggests an affirmative answer.[104] If so, then it will be open to the defence to submit that evidence admissible under s 100 of the 2003 Act upon which the prosecution propose to rely should be excluded where, having regard to all the circumstances, its admission would have such an adverse effect on the fairness of the proceedings that the court ought not to admit it. Where the bad character evidence sought be introduced, whether by the prosecution or the defence, is in the form of hearsay, the judge ought to have regard to the exclusionary discretion under s 126(1)(b) of the Act.[105] The provision states that the court may refuse to admit hearsay if satisfied '. . . that the case for excluding it, taking account of the danger that to admit it would result in an undue waste of time, substantially outweighs the case for admitting it, taking account of the value of the evidence.'[106]

Evidence of the bad character of the defendant

The background to s 101 of the Criminal Justice Act 2003

Before the coming into force of the 2003 Act, evidence of the accused's bad character was admissible only exceptionally and a sharp distinction was drawn between evidence adduced because of its relevance to the issue of guilt, and evidence elicited in cross-examination of the accused bearing upon his credibility as a witness. The approach under s 101 of the 2003 Act is radically different. It is not one of inadmissibility subject to exceptions, but of *admissibility* if certain criteria are met.[107] Section 101 sets out seven gateways through which evidence of the accused's bad character can be admitted. Collectively, these grounds for admissibility are much wider than those which they have replaced. Under the section, (a) no distinction is drawn between evidence introduced as a part of the prosecution's case and evidence elicited in cross-examination of the accused; (b) evidence is admissible irrespective of whether the accused gives evidence; and (c) there are no explicit limitations on the purpose for which the evidence is adduced.

The provisions in the 2003 Act relating to evidence of the bad character of the accused provoked much controversy during their parliamentary passage, especially in the House of Lords, where some members voiced the opinion that s 101 undermined the presumption of innocence.[108] A major criticism of the statutory scheme is that although it is based on the proposals of the Law Commission, each of the safeguards contained in the Law Commission framework and designed to protect the accused from the introduction of prejudicial evidence

---

[102] See, in this chapter, under **Abolition of the common law rules**, p 555.

[103] See Ch 2.

[104] See *R v Highton* [2005] 1 WLR 3472, CA; *R v Weir* [2006] 1 WLR 1885, CA; *R v Tirnaveanu* [2007] 1 WLR 3049, CA; and *R v O'Dowd* [2009] 2 Cr App R 280 (16), CA.

[105] See *R v Shaid* [2019] EWCA Crim 142.

[106] See also Ch 12, **Discretion to exclude**, p 401.

[107] *R v Weir* [2006] 1 WLR 1885, CA at [35].

[108] See, eg, Lord Alexander and Lord Kingsland, Hansard HL Vol 654 cols 729, 731, and 741 (4 Nov 2003).

has been either abandoned or diluted.[109] For example, under the Commission's proposals, in each of the four situations in which evidence of bad character of the accused was admissible, leave was required and in three of those situations there was a condition that the interests of justice required the evidence to be admissible, even taking account of its potentially prejudicial effect. Under s 101, however, leave is not required and instead of an 'interests of justice' condition, there is a discretionary power to exclude, but only on the application of the defence and only in respect of evidence admissible under two of the seven 'gateways'. The breadth of s 101, coupled with the absence of the much tighter restrictions on admissibility contained in the Law Commission's proposals, permit evidence of the accused's bad character to be admitted more readily than in the past. The effect, it is submitted, obliges judges to make much greater use of their discretionary powers to exclude such evidence.

It does not follow, however, that the prosecution should routinely apply to admit evidence of the accused's bad character. In *R v Hanson*,[110] the first Court of Appeal decision on the new provisions, it was held that the starting point should be for judges and practitioners to bear in mind that Parliament's purpose was to assist in the evidence-based conviction of the guilty, without putting those who are not guilty at risk of conviction by prejudice, and that it was accordingly to be hoped that prosecution applications to adduce evidence of an accused's bad character would not be made routinely, simply because an accused has previous convictions,[111] but would be based on the particular circumstances of each case. It was held in that case that if a judge has directed himself correctly, the Court of Appeal will be very slow to interfere with a ruling as to admissibility[112] and will not interfere unless the judge's judgment as to the capacity of prior events to establish propensity is plainly wrong or discretion has been exercised unreasonably in a *Wednesbury* sense.[113] It was also held that if, following a ruling that evidence of bad character is admissible, an accused pleads guilty, it is highly unlikely that an appeal against conviction will be entertained.

Section 101 of the Criminal Justice Act 2003

Section 101 provides as follows:

(1) In criminal proceedings evidence of the defendant's[114] bad character is admissible if, but only if
  (a) all parties to the proceedings agree to the evidence being admissible,
  (b) the evidence is adduced by the defendant himself or is given in answer to a question asked by him in cross-examination and intended to elicit it,

---

[109] See generally Tapper, 'Criminal Justice Act 2003 (3) Evidence of Bad Character' [2004] Crim LR 533.

[110] [2005] 1 WLR 3169, CA.

[111] See *R v Eyidah* [2010] EWCA Crim 987, 'a simple case [where] the jury should not have been deluged with a mass of prejudicial material, a great deal of which had absolutely nothing to do with the case at all' (per Hooper LJ at [13]).

[112] Or as to the consequences of non-compliance with notice requirements for introducing bad character evidence: *R v Malone* [2006] All ER 32, CA; *R v Spartley* [2007] All ER 233, CA; *R v Ramirez* [2009] EWCA Crim 1721; and *R v Ellis* [2010] EWCA Crim 1893.

[113] *Wednesbury Corpn v Ministry of Housing and Local Government* [1965] 1 WLR 261, CA. The position is the same when the Divisional Court considers an appeal against a decision of a magistrates' court: *DPP v Chard* [2007] EWHC 90, DC.

[114] 'Defendant', in relation to criminal proceedings, means a person charged with an offence in those proceedings: s 112(1).

(c) it is important explanatory evidence,

(d) it is relevant to an important matter in issue between the defendant and the prosecution,

(e) it has substantial probative value in relation to an important matter in issue between the defendant and a co-defendant,[115]

(f) it is evidence to correct a false impression given by the defendant, or

(g) the defendant has made an attack on another person's character.

(2) Sections 102 to 106 contain provision supplementing subsection (1).

(3) The court must not admit evidence under subsection (1)(d) or (g) if, on an application by the defendant to exclude it, it appears to the court that the admission of the evidence would have such an adverse effect on the fairness of the proceedings that the court ought not to admit it.

(4) On an application to exclude evidence under subsection (3) the court must have regard, in particular, to the length of time between the matters to which that evidence relates and the matters which form the subject of the offence charged.

Although s 101(1) governs only the admissibility of evidence of bad character and does not explicitly deal with the asking of questions about bad character in cross-examination, the intention is to cover both. The phrase 'prosecution evidence' is defined to include evidence which a witness is to be invited to give (or has given) in cross-examination by the prosecution;[116] the 'only evidence' admissible under s 101(1)(e) includes evidence which a witness is invited to give (or has given) in cross-examination by the co-defendant;[117] and the rules of court require a party to serve notice on the defendant where it is proposed to cross-examine a witness with a view to eliciting evidence of the accused's bad character.[118]

There are seven 'gateways' under s 101(1) through which evidence of the bad character of the accused may be admitted. Section 101(1)(a) provides for the admissibility of such evidence by consent of the parties. Under s 101(1)(b) such evidence may be admitted at the election of the accused, without the agreement of the other parties. Speaking generally, s 101(1) (c) is designed to admit evidence which would have been admissible at common law as so-called 'background evidence'. Section 101(1)(d) covers prosecution evidence relevant to an important matter, that is, a matter of substantial importance in the context of the case as a whole, which is in issue between the prosecution and the defence. Subsections (1)(e), (f), and (g) broadly correspond to and widen former grounds of admissibility. Section 101(1)(e) relates to evidence formerly admissible on behalf of a co-accused either on the basis of its relevance to the guilt of the accused or, in cases where the nature or conduct of the defence of the accused undermines the defence of the co-accused, to attack the credibility of the accused; s 101(1) (f) relates to prosecution evidence formerly admissible to rebut evidence of good character adduced by an accused; and s 101(1)(g) is designed to admit prosecution evidence in cases where the accused has cast an imputation on the character of another.

Before considering further each 'gateway', it is convenient first to consider some issues of general importance relating to admissibility, use, jury directions, leave and discretionary exclusion.

---

[115] 'Co-defendant', in relation to a defendant means a person charged with an offence in the same proceedings: s 112(1).

[116] Section 112(1).

[117] Section 104(2)(b).

[118] Section 111(2)(b). See the Criminal Procedure Rules 2015, SI 2015/1490, r 21.2 and 21.4.

Admissibility and use

Parties are well advised to reflect, at the time of the application to admit evidence of bad character, as to the use to which such evidence is likely to be put and be in a position to assist the judge in this regard.[119] Lord Woolf CJ made clear in *R v Highton*[120] that the use to which the evidence may be put depends upon the matters to which it is relevant rather than the gateway through which it was admitted.[121] The reasoning that leads to the admission of evidence under s 101(1)(d) may also determine the matter to which the evidence is relevant or primarily relevant once admitted. This is because, as we shall see, that provision deals separately with the accused's propensity to commit offences of the kind with which he is charged (s 103(1)(a)) and his propensity to be untruthful (s 103(1)(b)). However, under other gateways, which make no reference to the use to which the bad character evidence may be put, for example under s 101(1)(g), where admissibility depends on the accused having made an attack on another person's character, the evidence may, depending on the particular facts, be relevant not only to credibility but also to propensity to commit offences of the kind charged.

The full implications of Lord Woolf's reasoning became explicit in *R v Campbell*.[122] In that case it was submitted that in directing the jury as to the relevance of bad character evidence, the judge should have regard only to the gateway through which the evidence was introduced, unless the evidence could have been introduced through an additional gateway, in which case the jury could be directed as to its additional relevance under that gateway. Lord Phillips CJ rejected the submission on the basis that to direct the jury to have regard to bad character evidence for some purposes and disregard its relevance in other respects 'would be to revert to the unsatisfactory practices that prevailed under the old law'. This was an explicit reference to the fact that under s 1(f) of the Criminal Evidence Act 1898 it was often the case that the judge was required to direct the jury that the previous conviction was relevant only to the accused's credibility, not guilt. As Lord Phillips CJ says, this was contrary to common sense where the previous convictions showed propensity to commit the type of offence with which the accused was charged. However, it is no justification for his rejection of the submission because in such a case, under the 2003 Act, if the evidence is relevant to propensity to commit the offence charged, it is admissible under s 101(1)(d), provided it meets the requirements of that gateway, in addition to any other gateway through which it is admissible and relevant to credit. The consequence of the view adopted by Lord Phillips is that, for example, evidence of propensity to commit offences of the kind charged might be admitted under s 101(1)(g) (making an attack on another person's character) even if it is not relevant to an important matter in issue between the prosecution and the defence (a requirement under s 101(1)(d), but not under s 101(1)(g)) or does not have substantial probative value in relation to an important matter in issue between the accused and a co-accused (a requirement under s 101(1)(e), but not under s 101(1)(g)). It seems most unlikely that this is what Parliament intended.[123]

---

[119] *R v Edwards* [2006] 1 WLR 1524, CA at [1](ii). See also *R v RJ* [2017] EWCA Crim 1943.

[120] [2005] 1 WLR 3472, CA.

[121] See also *R v Abdullah* [2019] EWCA Crim 1137 at [28], where, citing *R v Highton* [2005] 1 WLR 3472, CA, the Court of Appeal stated, 'It is a long established principle that previous bad character evidence once admitted can be relied on as evidence in support of any inference or conclusion which may be properly drawn from it.' The court observed that given the way the case had developed, it was 'a classic example' of why the principle was correct (at [29]).

[122] [2007] 1 WLR 2798, CA.

[123] For further implications and a powerful critique of *R v Highton* [2005] 1 WLR 3472, CA, see Munday, 'The Purposes of Gateway (g): Yet Another Problematic of the Criminal Justice Act 2003' [2006] Crim LR 300.

Jury directions

It will be clear, from the foregoing, that the judge must exercise care when summing up. She will need to warn the jury against placing undue reliance on previous convictions, which cannot by themselves prove guilt, and also explain why they have heard the evidence and the ways in which it is relevant to and may help their decision.[124] The jury should also be told of any purposes for which the evidence may not be used.[125] Where bad character evidence is admitted and thereafter 'the ground shifts', the judge may need to direct the jury that, given the course taken by the trial, the evidence is of little weight.[126] In appropriate circumstances, which may arise when evidence of previous convictions is adduced by the accused himself under s 101(1)(b), the judge may even be required to direct the jury that the evidence does not assist on either propensity or untruthfulness.[127]

In *R v Campbell*, Lord Phillips CJ set out the following general principles governing the way in which juries should be directed about evidence admitted under s 101.[128]

1. The changes introduced by the 2003 Act should be the occasion for simplifying the directions to juries in relation to evidence of the accused's bad character.[129]

2. Decisions in this field before the 2003 Act came into force are unhelpful and should not be cited.

3. The jury should be given assistance as to the relevance of bad character evidence that is tailored to the facts of the individual case.

4. Relevance can normally be deduced by the application of common sense. The summing-up that assists the jury with the relevance of bad character evidence will accord with common sense and assist them to avoid prejudice that is at odds with this.

5. Once evidence has been admitted through a gateway it is open to the jury to attach significance to it in any respect in which it is relevant. There is no rule to the effect that in directing the jury as to relevance, the judge shall have regard only to the gateway through which the evidence was introduced or any other gateway through which it could have been introduced.

6. The extent of the significance to be attached to previous convictions is likely to depend upon a number of variables, including their number, their similarity to the offence charged, how recently they were incurred, and the nature of the defence.

7. In considering the inference to be drawn from bad character the courts have in the past distinguished propensity to offend and credibility. This distinction is usually unrealistic. If the jury learn that an accused has shown a propensity to commit criminal acts they may well also conclude that it is more likely that he is guilty and that he is less likely to be telling the truth when he says that he is not. It will be

---

[124] See per Rose LJ in *R v Edwards* [2006] 1 WLR 1524, CA at [3].

[125] See the Crown Court Compendium (July 2019), Part 1, 12–2, para 5.

[126] *R v Edwards* [2006] 1 WLR 1524, CA at [1](iv).

[127] Ibid at [87]–[104]. See generally, the Crown Court Compendium (July 2019), Part 1, 12–1–12–2.

[128] The approach laid down in *R v Campbell* [2007] 1 WLR 2798, CA, was approved by the Court of Appeal in *R v Awoyemi* [2017] 2 Cr App R 303 (22), CA.

[129] See the Crown Court Compendium (July 2019), Part 1, 12–5–12–9, for the guidance to judges on directing the jury in respect of bad character evidence admitted under gateways s 101(1)(c)–(g).

comparatively rare for the case of an accused who has pleaded not guilty not to involve some element that the prosecution suggest is untruthful.

8. Reciting the statutory wording of the gateway by which the evidence was admitted is unlikely to be helpful. The jury should be told in simple language and with reference, where appropriate, to the particular facts of the case, why the bad character may be relevant.

9. Where evidence of a crime or other blameworthy act on the part of the accused is adduced because it bears on a particular issue of fact and the evidence has no bearing on the accused's propensity to commit the offence charged,[130] this should be made plain to the jury.

10. It is highly desirable that the jury should be warned against attaching too much weight to bad character evidence, let alone concluding that he is guilty simply because of his bad character.[131]

No requirement of leave

As we have seen, s 100(4) of the 2003 Act expressly states that evidence of the bad character of a *non-defendant* 'must not be given without the leave of the court'. There is no equivalent in relation to evidence of the bad character of a *defendant* admissible under s 101(1)(c) to (g). However, whether any of the requirements for admissibility in those sub-paragraphs has been met is a question of law for the judge to decide, in appropriate cases only after holding a *voir dire*, and it is submitted that given the potentially irremediable harm of the jury hearing evidence later ruled inadmissible, counsel for the prosecution or, as appropriate, the co-accused, before introducing the evidence, will need to satisfy the judge that the statutory requirements are met.

Discretion to exclude
Section 101(3)

As to discretionary exclusion, in the case of evidence meeting the requirements of s 101(1)(d) or (g), the court has discretionary power to exclude it under s 101(3) on the basis of its adverse effect on the fairness of the proceedings. Provided that the judge, in exercising the discretion, has in mind the time factor in s 101(4), the Court of Appeal will not ordinarily interfere with his decision unless there has been some error in principle.[132] The fact that the evidence is not 'essential' to the prosecution case does not mean it should be excluded.[133] If the evidence is inherently incredible, that is likely to be a strong factor against admitting it, but whilst the judge will have regard to the potential weight of the evidence, he should not usurp the jury's function of deciding what evidence is accepted and what rejected.[134] If the evidence

---

[130] See, in this chapter, under **Important matters in issue**, p 583.

[131] As to the further principles enunciated and relating to the 2003 Act, s 103(1)(b), see in this chapter, under **Bad character evidence under s 101(1)(d) relevant to the credibility of the accused**, p 597.

[132] *R v Edwards* [2006] 1 WLR 1524, CA at [75]. See also *R v Malone* [2006] All ER 32, CA and *R v Spartley* [2007] All ER 233, CA. In *R v Lewis* [2014] EWCA Crim 48, Sir Brian Leveson P said at [128], '. . . it is important to remember that an assessment of fairness in proceedings should not only embrace consideration of fairness to the defence but also fairness to the prosecution. The second aspect of that balancing exercise is sometimes insufficiently considered.' See also, and to similar effect, *R v Witty* [2014] EWCA Crim 2333, per Spencer J at [24].

[133] *R v Lewis* [2014] EWCA Crim 48 at [104].

[134] *R v Edwards* [2006] 1 WLR 1524, CA at [82].

is based on information received by a witness from unidentified third parties, by its nature it will be difficult for the accused to challenge and therefore should be excluded.[135] It is not an error in principle to admit allegations of misconduct in respect of which the accused was told that he would not be prosecuted.[136] If the evidence is a conviction in a member State of the European Union, it is open to the court to exclude it where there is evidence that it was the result of a trial which did not meet appropriate standards of fairness.[137]

Section 101(3) is brought into play 'on an application by the accused to exclude' the evidence, wording which seems to preclude the court from exercising the power under the subsection of its own motion. However, bearing in mind Art 6 of the European Convention on Human Rights, a judge should if necessary encourage an application to exclude if it appears that admission of the evidence may have such an adverse effect on the fairness of the proceedings that it ought not to admit it.[138] Where the trial judge has used s 101(3) to exclude evidence potentially admissible under s 101(1)(d), that will not prevent him later in the trial from admitting the evidence under s 101(1)(g), because the fairness of the proceedings and the impact on it of admitting the evidence has to be gauged at the time at which the application is made and by reference to the gateway under which admissibility is sought.[139]

The fact that s 101(3) does not apply to s 101(1)(a), (b), and (e) makes perfect sense. In the case of s 101(1)(a) and (b), there is no need for a discretion to exclude—the accused already has control over whether the evidence is admitted or not. As to s 101(1)(e), which relates to evidence admissible on behalf of a co-accused, the good reason for the absence of a discretionary power to exclude is that a co-accused should be free to adduce any evidence relevant to his case whether or not it prejudices any other accused. The principle was the same, before the coming into force of s 101, in the case of both 'similar fact evidence' tendered by a co-accused and cross-examination of an accused by a co-accused under the 1898 Act.[140]

Common law and s 78 of the Police and Criminal Evidence Act 1984

The fact that s 101(3) does not apply to s 101(1)(c) and (f) is difficult to justify and raises the question whether evidence otherwise admissible under those sub-paragraphs can be excluded using common law discretionary power or s 78 of the Police and Criminal Evidence Act 1984.[141] As to the former, it is submitted that the general common law discretionary power to exclude prosecution evidence where its prejudicial effect outweighs its probative value may be exercised in respect of evidence of bad character admissible under s 101(1)(c) (if it is to be adduced by the prosecution) and s 101(1)(f) (under which only prosecution evidence is admissible).[142] As noted when considering s 100 of the 2003 Act, it is unclear whether s 78 of the 1984 Act applies in the case of prosecution evidence of bad character otherwise

---

[135] *R v Weir* [2006] 1 WLR 1885, CA at [40].

[136] *R v Edwards* [2006] 1 WLR 1524, CA at [76]. See also *R v Nguyen* [2008] 2 Cr App R 99 (9), CA, where it was held that it was not unfair to admit evidence of previous assaults which the Crown Prosecution Service had decided not to prosecute.

[137] *R v EM* [2014] EWCA Crim 1523.

[138] *R v Weir* [2006] 1 WLR 1885, CA.

[139] *R v Edwards* [2006] 1 WLR 1524, CA at [14].

[140] See *Lobban v R* [1995] 1 WLR 877, PC approving the description of this principle appearing in the 3rd edition of this book. However, in rare cases the evidence may now be excluded for failure to comply with the requirement to give notice: see *R v Musone* [2007] 1 WLR 2467, CA 517 in this chapter, under **Rules of court, p 625**.

[141] See Ch 2.

[142] See, in this chapter, under **Abolition of the common law rules, p 555**.

admissible under the 2003 Act. Two strong arguments support the view that Parliament's intention was to exclude the operation of s 78. First, there is express provision in Chapter 2 of Pt 11 of the 2003 Act, concerning hearsay evidence, that nothing in that chapter prejudices any power of a court to exclude evidence under s 78.[143] Second, if s 78 does apply, s 101(3), the critical words of which mirror those to be found in s 78, is otiose.[144] On the other hand, s 78 is plainly a provision of general application, applying to any evidence on which the prosecution propose to rely, and, arguably, should not be taken to cease to apply to particular types of prosecution evidence without express provision to that effect. The balance of case law falls firmly in favour of this position. In *R v Highton*[145] Lord Woolf CJ expressed a preliminary view that reliance can be placed on s 78 and that judges might apply s 78, as appropriate, which would avoid any risk of injustice to the accused, and that to do so would be consistent with the result to which the court would come if it complied with obligations under s 3 of the Human Rights Act 1998 to construe ss 101 and 103 of the 2003 Act in accordance with the European Convention on Human Rights. Although it was observed in *R v D*[146] that the operation of s 78 to exclude evidence of an accused's bad character was 'possibly controversial', in *R v O'Dowd*[147] it was held that s 78 should be considered where s 101(3) was not available. This is consistent with a number of other authorities.[148]

Section 101(1)(a)—evidence admitted by agreement of all the parties

Evidence of the accused's bad character may be admitted under s 101(1)(a) with the consent of all the parties, that is, the prosecution, accused, and any co-accused, and without the leave of the court.[149] However, where advocates have agreed to admit evidence of the accused's bad character, it is important that the judge is supplied with details of the evidence prior to its admission. According to the Court of Appeal in *R v DJ*:[150]

it is essential, where hearsay or bad character evidence will be put before the jury by agreement and the order of the court is not required . . . that the court is informed at the outset of the trial what has been agreed and how the advocates propose that the agreed evidence is to be placed before the jury. If an agreement is made during the trial, then the judge should be told immediately after the agreement. This is in the interests of good trial management, so that the judge can

---

[143] Section 126(2).

[144] Although it has been said that a 'significant difference' is to be found in the mandatory opening words of s 101(3) and s 78 (per Kennedy LJ in *R v Weir* [2006] 1 WLR 1885, CA at [46]), this is a distinction without a difference, as under s 78 a court has no discretion once the condition is, in its view, satisfied (per Thomas LJ in *R v Tirnaveanu* [2007] 1 WLR 3049, CA at [28]).

[145] [2005] 1 WLR 3472, CA.

[146] [2009] 2 Cr App R 306 (17), CA at [36].

[147] [2009] 2 Cr App R 280 (16), CA.

[148] *R v Weir* [2006] 1 WLR 1885, CA; *R v Tirnaveanu* [2007] 1 WLR 3049, CA. See also *R v B* [2008] EWCA Crim 1850 and *R v Fox* [2009] EWCA Crim 653. Where s 101(3) *is* available, the focus must be on that section and not s 78: see *R v Chrysostomou* [2010] EWCA Crim 1403 at [38]–[39], concerning admissibility under s 101(1)(g).

[149] See *R v Hussain* [2008] EWCA Crim 1117: both an accused and a co-accused, running cut-throat defences, had convictions for dishonesty admitted by agreement because, realistically, absent agreement, they were bound to have been admitted. See also *R v Kalu* [2007] EWCA Crim 22: evidence of a caution for excessive chastisement was admitted by agreement in a child cruelty case, presumably for the same reason. However, the court observed that a more correct analysis was that the caution may well have been to do with the facts of the offences charged. If so, it was admissible on that basis (see [12]).

[150] [2010] 2 Cr App R 8 (2), CA, per Thomas LJ at [21].

consider the advocates' proposals as to the timing and manner of putting the evidence before the jury and the directions of law that are needed in the summing-up.

Section 101(1)(b)—evidence admitted by the defendant himself

Section 101(1)(b) permits evidence of the accused's bad character to be admitted by the accused himself without the leave of the court. This option is of limited if any value in cases in which the prosecution have already adduced the evidence by virtue of one of the other sub-paragraphs of s 101(1). However, where the evidence is not admissible as a part of the prosecution case, there are two situations in which the accused may sensibly elect to admit it himself. First, if it is evidence of comparatively minor misconduct, he may adduce it on the basis that otherwise the jurors, especially if they have experience by serving in other cases, might speculate that his character is worse than it is. Second, where he adduces evidence attacking another person's character, therefore bringing into play s 101(1)(g), it may be tactically wiser for him to be frank with the jury and give evidence of his bad character himself, rather than allow the prosecution to elicit it in cross-examination. This may be a sensible course of action where the previous convictions were all based on guilty pleas because however the judge directs the jury about the bad character evidence, there is obvious scope for the defence to say to the jury, in closing submissions, that the fact that the accused has for the first time pleaded not guilty indicates that his denial on oath ought to be believed. However, where the accused adduces his convictions under s 101(1)(b) and there is a direct conflict between his evidence and the evidence of a prosecution witness, the accused cannot expect the judge, in a fair summing-up, to 'gloss over' the problem that his convictions raise in terms of his credibility.[151]

Under s 101(1)(b), the evidence may be either adduced by the accused himself or given in answer to a question asked by the defence in cross-examination,[152] provided that the question was intended to elicit it. Thus if the witness under cross-examination volunteers the evidence of bad character, it is inadmissible and the judge will need to direct the jury to ignore it or, if no direction is capable of neutralizing the prejudice to the accused and there is therefore a real risk of injustice occurring, exercise his discretion to discharge the jury and order a re-trial.[153]

Section 101(1)(c)—important explanatory evidence

Under s 101(1)(c), which may be used by either the prosecution or a co-accused, evidence of the accused's bad character is admissible if it is 'important explanatory evidence'. Section 102 provides that:

> For the purposes of section 101(1)(c) evidence is important explanatory evidence if—
> (a) without it, the court or jury would find it impossible or difficult properly to understand other evidence in the case, and
> (b) its value for understanding the case as a whole is substantial.

---

[151] *R v Speed* [2013] EWCA Crim 1650.
[152] See, eg, *R v Tollady* [2010] EWCA Crim 2614.
[153] See, in this chapter, under **Evidence admitted through inadvertence**, p 627.

Section 101(1)(c) is closely based on the recommendation of the Law Commission except that it lacks the safeguard contained in the Commission's draft clause that the court be satisfied either that the evidence carries no risk of prejudice to the accused or that the value of the evidence for understanding the case as a whole is such that, taking account of the risk of prejudice, the interests of justice nevertheless require it to be admissible.

This definition in s 102 is the same as that contained in s 100(2)(a), which applies in relation to evidence of a non-defendant's bad character. If the matter to which the proposed explanatory evidence relates is largely comprehensible without the evidence, the evidence will be inadmissible.[154] Explanatory evidence, to be admissible, must also satisfy s 102(b), that is, its value for understanding the case as a whole must be 'substantial', as opposed to minor or trivial. In *R v Edwards*,[155] a case of robbery and possession of an imitation firearm, the statement of an identification witness that she was able to recognize the accused because she had bought heroin from him every other day for a year or so, was held to have been properly admitted as important explanatory evidence in relation to the basis of her identification. However, no convincing reason was given for rejecting the submission that, given the prejudice arising from the allegation of heroin dealing, the statement should have been edited so as to disclose the frequency of the encounters, but not the reason for them.

It is submitted that when dealing with an application to admit evidence under s 101(1) (c), the court will need to identify precisely what matters are 'explained' by the evidence, whether there is other evidence which satisfactorily explains those matters, and whether the value of the evidence is such that its admission is truly called for. In *Myers v The Queen*,[156] it was stated that in relation to prosecution applications to admit bad character evidence as background evidence under the principle in *R v Pettman*:[157]

> The *Pettman* proposition, valid as it is, needs careful handling if it is not to become a token excuse for admitting the inadmissible. Claims by prosecutors that the evidence is necessary to the understanding of the case, or as is sometimes asserted, to discourage the jury from wondering about the context in which events occurred, need to be scrutinised with great care . . .[158]

It is submitted that the same may be said in relation to applications made under s 101(1)(c).

Overlap with propensity

A difficult borderline exists between explanatory evidence and evidence of propensity. In some cases, depending on the particular facts, the same evidence of misconduct may be admissible both as explanatory evidence and evidence of propensity.[159] In *R v D*[160] it was

---

[154] See *R v L* (2012) 176 JP 231, CA and also *R v Sheikh* [2013] EWCA Crim 907.

[155] [2006] 1 WLR 1524, CA. See also *R v B*, 25 February 2016, CA: evidence of allegations of sexual violence in the context of an abusive relationship were properly admitted as important explanatory evidence which enabled the jury to have a full picture of the relationship, and it was not unfair to admit the evidence in circumstances where the accused had made a strong attack on the complainant's character.

[156] [2016] AC 314, PC.

[157] Unreported, 2 May 1985. See, in this chapter under, **Important explanatory evidence**, p 564.

[158] [2016] AC 314, PC, at [52]. See also at [55]. See also *Phillip v The Diretor of Public Prosecutions (St Christopher and Nevis)* [2017] UKPC 14 at [12]: 'The admission of evidence of this kind must be justified. It is not enough that it is "part of the background". That is too easy a generalization and fails to distinguish the admissible from the inadmissible.'

[159] See, eg, *R v Okokono* [2014] EWCA Crim 2521.

[160] [2009] 2 Cr App R 306 (17), CA.

emphasized that where evidence is sought to be admitted under s 101(1)(c), the test for admissibility should be applied cautiously where it is also possible to argue that the evidence shows a propensity to commit offences. In *D*, the accused was charged with murdering his wife whom he had accused of having an affair. Using s 101(1)(c), the prosecution adduced the evidence of a former girlfriend that some 20 years previously he had acted towards her with jealous aggression and made threats to kill. The Court of Appeal held that the evidence did not have a substantial value for understanding the case, and indeed could have undermined the jury's understanding of the accused's relationship with his wife and the events leading up to her death. The evidence was really evidence of propensity and it should not have been allowed to 'slide in' as explanatory evidence.[161] Furthermore, where evidence is admitted under gateway (c), it should not readily be used, once admitted, for a purpose such as propensity, 'for which additional safeguards on different tests have first to be met'.[162]

In *R v Ladds*[163] evidence was properly admitted under s 101(1)(c) even though it was strongly indicative of the accused's propensity. The accused stabbed her partner, F, and was convicted of wounding with intent. Her defence was that F inflicted the wounds on himself and, in support, she adduced evidence that F had attempted suicide in the past. The Court of Appeal held that the judge had been right to allow the prosecution to admit as important explanatory evidence, evidence of previous 'strikingly similar' incidents where F had suffered injuries and reported that they had been inflicted by the accused. It would have been 'positively misleading' for the jury not to have heard about these incidents considering the evidence adduced by F.[164] The court also held that the evidence was admissible under s 101(1)(d) as relevant to an important matter in issue other than propensity, namely who had inflicted the wounds.[165]

Admissibility as evidence relevant to important matters in issue and as evidence 'to do with the facts of the offence'

In some cases, depending on the facts, evidence which is admissible as explanatory evidence under s 101(1)(c) may be admissible simultaneously under s 101(1)(d) as relevant to important matters in issue, including propensity, and may also be admissible as evidence to do with the facts of the offence under s 98(a).[166] Gang affiliation evidence provides a good example. Issues that arise in cases of gang crime may include whether there is a link between the accused and a gang, or between co-accused themselves to each other and to a gang, whether the accused had a motive to commit the crime alleged, and the accused's defence of innocent presence and association. Evidence of the accused's affiliation with a gang may be important explanatory evidence under s 101(1)(c) if it enables these issues to be properly understood; but these issues may also be regarded as important matters in issue between the prosecution and defence and the evidence may be admissible under s 101(1)(d) because of its relevance to the issues; and the evidence may be so inextricably linked to the facts of the offence that it falls outside the definition of bad character (s 98(a)) and is admissible simply on the basis

---

[161] Per Hughes LJ at [34]. See also *R v Saint* [2010] EWCA Crim 1924 and *R v L* (2012) 176 JP 231, CA.

[162] *R v D* [2009] 2 Cr App R 306 (17), CA.

[163] [2009] EWCA Crim 1249.

[164] [2009] EWCA Crim 1249 at [12]–[15].

[165] Ibid at [16].

[166] In relation to background evidence which is also evidence to do with the facts of the offence, see the old but good example of *R v Ellis* (1826) 6 B&C 145. See also *R v Rearden* (1864) 4 F & F 76.

of its relevance. In *R v Awoyemi*,[167] the appellants were convicted of gang-related offences of attempted murder and possession of a firearm with intent to endanger life. Evidence of gang affiliation was admitted, which included rap lyrics which were handwritten by one of the appellants and demonstrated affiliation to a gang; a gang themed 'You Tube' video featuring two of the appellants; letters sent by one of the appellants establishing his involvement in a gang, knowledge of other gang members and endorsement of gang culture including revenge for murdered members; an image of the victim of a gang murder; and the discovery of a bullet hole in the side of one of the cars of one of the appellants. It was held that the evidence was properly admitted at trial under both s 101(1)(c) as important explanatory evidence and under s 101(1)(d) as evidence of propensity, and the evidence might also have been admitted as relevant evidence to do with the facts of the offence, applying s 98(a).[168]

Evidence revealing motive

As we have just seen in relation to gang affiliation evidence, evidence revealing motive may be admissible as relevant to an important matter in issue under s 101(1)(d) (the motive itself being an important matter in issue), as important explanatory evidence under s 101(1)(c) (the motive explains other evidence in the case), and as evidence to do with the facts of the offence under s 98(a) provided that there is a sufficient nexus in time.[169] Such evidence often relates to other acts done or statements made by the accused revealing his desire to commit, or reason for committing, the offence charged.[170] However, although such evidence may be admitted as explanatory evidence under s 101(1)(c) to expose an accused's motive for acting in a particular way, it will not be admitted where it is being used to construct speculative suggestions about the accused's motive.[171]

Nexus in time

Although s 101(1)(c) includes no temporal requirement, it is submitted that evidence will not be admitted if it relates to events so distant in time from the alleged crime as to be of little if any probative value. *R v Phillips*,[172] was decided before the 2003 Act but applied the principle in *R v Pettman*[173] upon which s 101(1)(c) is based. P was charged with the murder of his wife. It was held that it would have been quite wrong to have admitted the evidence of a stormy relationship eight years before the crime, especially if thereafter it was a happy marriage.[174]

---

[167] [2016] 2 Cr App 303 (22), CA. For other examples, see *R v Lovell* [2018] 1 Cr App R (S) 364 (48), CA; *R v Stewart* [2016] EWCA Crim 447; *R v Lunkulu* [2015] EWCA Crim 1350; *R v Okokono* [2014] EWCA Crim 2521; and *R v Sule* [2012] EWCA Crim 1130. See also *Myers v The Queen* [2016] AC 314, PC, concerning the admissibility of gang affiliation evidence in a common law jurisdiction (Bermuda).

[168] However, it is submitted that the evidence was simply irrelevant to the case as it was put by the prosecution, namely a targeted 'hit' which was botched, with the accused then returning to finish the job: see 'Commentary', *R v Awoyemi* [2017] Crim LR 131, CA.

[169] See *R v Tirnaveanu* [2007] 1 WLR 3049, CA. A nexus in time will also be required where the evidence concerns the issue of identity. However, s 98(a) includes no *necessary* temporal qualification: see *R v Lunkulu* [2015] EWCA Crim 1350 at [99].

[170] See, eg, *Phillip v The Director of Public Prosecutions (St Christopher and Nevis)* [2017] UKPC 14. See also, *R v Bond* [1906] 2 KB 389. See also, in this chapter, under **Important explanatory evidence, p 564**.

[171] *R v Broome* [2012] EWCA Crim 2879.

[172] [2003] 2 Cr App R 528 (35), CA.

[173] 2 May 1985, CA, unreported.

[174] [2003] 2 Cr App R 528 (35), CA at 536. See also *R v Butler* [1999] Crim LR 835, CA, where the events had taken place three years before the offence charged.

Similarly in *R v Dolan*,[175] where the accused was charged with the murder of his baby son by shaking him forcefully, it was held to be irrelevant that in the past he had lost his temper and shown violence towards inanimate objects. The touchstones of the *Pettman* principle, said the court, were relevance and necessity.[176]

The judge's summing-up

Where background evidence is properly admitted, the jury will need to be directed carefully as to the use to which the evidence may and may not be put. The Crown Court Compendium contains the following guidance to judges:

> . . . it is helpful to address with advocates, as soon as the admissibility of the evidence is raised, the question of how it is proposed that the bad character evidence is to be used and how the jury is to be directed.[177]

Exclusionary discretion

The exclusionary discretion contained in s 101(3) does not apply to s 101(1)(c), but there is still obvious scope to use the common law discretionary power to exclude (where the prejudicial effect of the evidence is out of all proportion to its probative value), as well as the statutory discretionary power under s 78 of the Police and Criminal Evidence Act 1984 (where the evidence would have such an adverse effect on the fairness of the trial that it ought not to be admitted). Exclusion, it is submitted, would be justified when the evidence relates to particularly serious misconduct on the part of the accused and without the evidence the jury would find it difficult, but perhaps not especially difficult, to properly understand other evidence in the case.[178] A highly relevant consideration might be whether the accused is able to properly test the evidence. Where the evidence of misconduct involves stating bald conclusions about the accused, it is likely to result in unfairness because the accused may not be able to challenge the conclusions without dangerous lines of cross-examination which risk introducing yet more prejudicial evidence.[179]

Section 101(1)(d)—prosecution evidence relevant to an important matter in issue between the defendant and the prosecution

Under the carefully wrought proposals of the Law Commission, there were separate clauses governing admissibility of evidence of the accused's bad character going to the issue of his guilt and admissibility of evidence of his bad character going to the issue of his credibility.[180] This distinction was born of a recognition that the two issues usually arise at different stages of the trial and that the relevant factors for deciding the admissibility of each type of

---

[175] [2003] 1 Cr App R 281 (18), CA.

[176] *R v Dolan* [2003] 1 Cr App R 281 (18), CA at 285–6. Contrast *R v Okokono* [2014] EWCA Crim 2521.

[177] See the Crown Court Compendium (July 2019), Part 1, 12–5, para 6.

[178] See *Myers v The Queen* [2016] AC 314, PC. In relation to gang affiliation evidence admitted under the *Pettman* principle, the Privy Council said that it is necessary '. . . to look carefully at the overall effect . . . and to reach a judgment as to the balance between legitimate probative value and unfair prejudicial effect' (at 72]). See also, *sed quaere*, *R v Leathem* [2017] EWCA Crim 42: it is submitted that evidence held to have been properly admitted under s 101(1)(c) was in fact overwhelmingly prejudicial.

[179] See *Myers v The Queen* [2016] AC 314, PC at [72].

[180] Law Com No 273, Cm 5257 (2001), Draft Bill, cl 8 and cl 9.

evidence are different. In relation to the issue of guilt, the Commission proposed, that to be admissible, bad character evidence should be of substantial probative value in relation to a matter of substantial importance and should carry no risk of prejudice to the accused or, taking into account the risk of prejudice, its probative value justifies its admission in the interests of justice. As to credibility, bad character evidence was only admissible where an attack had been made on another's truthfulness.

Section 101(1)(d) of the 2003 Act however, which reflects a markedly different and less sophisticated approach, provides a single 'gateway' for the admissibility of prosecution evidence relevant to the guilt of the accused as well as evidence relevant to his credibility. Under s 101(1)(d), prosecution evidence of the accused's bad character is admissible if 'it is relevant to an important matter in issue between the defendant and the prosecution'.[181] The test is one of simple relevance or probative value.[182] There is no requirement of enhanced relevance or 'substantial probative value' as there is under s 101(1)(e) and, in relation to the bad character of someone other than the accused, under s 100(1)(b). The evidence, however, must be relevant to an important matter in issue between the accused and the prosecution.

Important matters in issue

The matters in issue between the accused and the prosecution are the disputed facts and issues of credit or credibility. In a sense, all such matters in issue between the accused and the prosecution are important, but 'important matter' is defined in the Act as 'a matter of substantial importance in the context of the case as a whole',[183] a definition which, it is submitted, will only operate to exclude evidence relevant to matters in issue which are of minor or marginal significance. The overall effect of s 101(1)(d), therefore, is to permit the introduction of prosecution evidence of the accused's bad character whenever it is relevant to any of the main matters in issue between the prosecution and the defence, and is not limited to propensity. In many cases the main issue on which the evidence of bad character has a bearing will be the accused's defence. Accordingly, in a case of possession with intent to supply Class A drugs, for example, where the matter in issue is the accused's knowledge of the drugs, a previous conviction for importing such drugs could be relevant to rebut his defence.[184] Similarly, in a case of child cruelty, evidence of allegations of the accused's wholesale ill treatment of his wife and children in the past showed a propensity to violence and was also relevant to rebut both his defence of reasonable chastisement and his own allegation that his wife had taken part in the physical chastisement of the children.[185] It is also well established that factual similarities in evidence of misconduct provided by different witnesses may rebut a defence of fabrication or accident because of the unlikelihood of a number of different witnesses independently making similar complaints of misconduct.[186] Another example of an

---

[181] Only prosecution evidence is admissible under s 101(1)(d): s 103(6).

[182] *R v Weir* [2006] 1 WLR 1885, CA at [36].

[183] Section 112(1).

[184] *R v Colliard* [2008] EWCA Crim 1175. See also *R v Jordan* [2009] EWCA Crim 953: the accused's convictions for robbery and possession of a firearm were relevant to the issue of whether he knew about the presence of a gun in the car in which he was travelling or was an innocent passenger. However, cf *R v Hay* [2018] Crim LR 400, CA.

[185] *R v B(E)* [2017] 1 Cr App R 457 (31), CA. See also *R v Spottiswood* [2019] EWCA Crim 949: in the accused's trial for murder, evidence that he had used offensive force in placing a prison officer in a headlock was admissible to rebut his defence that he placed the deceased in a headlock in self-defence.

[186] See *R v Chopra* [2007] 1 Cr App R 225 (16), CA, considered later in this chapter, under **Evidence of misconduct with similar facts, p 593**.

important matter in issue might be the accused's identity. So, in a case of dangerous driving, the accused's previous convictions for driving whilst disqualified could be relevant to the issue of whether a police officer correctly recognized the accused driving dangerously;[187] or in a case of an unprovoked assault on a stranger in a street, the accused's previous conviction for a similar unprovoked assault on a stranger in the same street with a similar degree of violence could, with other evidence, establish that the accused was the attacker.[188] Some cases may raise a variety of important matters in issue to which the same evidence of bad character may be relevant. Cases of gang crime, discussed earlier in this chapter,[189] provide good examples: important matters in issue to which evidence of an accused's bad character might be relevant in such cases include propensity, affiliation to a gang, links to co-accused who are alleged to be gang members, an association with firearms, a motive, and the rebuttal of a defence of innocent association or presence.[190]

The breadth of the provision means that prosecution applications to admit bad character evidence and defence applications to exclude under s 101(3) are regular features of most trials.

Section 101(1)(d) is supplemented by s 103, which states that 'matters in issue' between the accused and the prosecution can include (a) the question whether the accused has a propensity to commit offences of the kind with which he is charged and (b) the question whether he has a propensity to be untruthful. It is convenient to consider these two issues separately, albeit, in the case of the former, as part of the wider issue of bad character relevant to the guilt of the accused.

Bad character evidence under s 101(1)(d) relevant to the guilt of the accused

Evidence of propensity under s 103 of the Criminal Justice Act 2003

Section 103(1) and (2) of the 2003 Act provide as follows:

(1) For the purposes of section 101(1)(d) the matters in issue between the defendant and the prosecution include—
   (a) the question whether the defendant has a propensity to commit offences of the kind with which he is charged, except where his having such a propensity makes it no more likely that he is guilty of the offence;
   (b) the question whether the defendant has a propensity to be untruthful, except where it is not suggested that the defendant's case is untruthful in any respect.
(2) Where subsection (1)(a) applies, a defendant's propensity to commit offences of the kind with which he is charged may (without prejudice to any other way of doing so) be established by evidence that he has been convicted of—

---

[187] *R v Spittle* [2009] RTR 14, CA. See also *R v Eastlake* (2007) 151 SJLB 258, CA.

[188] *R v Richardson* [2014] EWCA Crim 1785. See also *R v N* [2015] Crim LR 439, CA. The use of evidence of bad character where identity is an important matter in issue, is considered further, in this chapter, under **Misconduct to prove identity**, p 595.

[189] See, in this chapter, under **Admissibility as evidence relevant to important matters in issue and as evidence 'to do with the facts of the offence'**, p 580.

[190] See also, where evidence of gang affiliation was admitted: *R v Lewis* [2014] EWCA Crim 48 (to rebut the defence of innocent presence at the scene of a riot which involved firearms and arson and was aimed at drawing the police into an ambush); *R v Elliot* [2010] EWCA Crim 2378 (to rebut the accused's defence that class A drugs and firearms found at his address did not belong to him, but belonged to another); and *R v Stewart* [2016] EWCA Crim 447 (to rebut the defence that he was merely the courier of a double barrelled shotgun and did not possess it with intent to endanger life, the evidence also being admissible under s 101(1)(c) and as relevant evidence applying s 98(a)).

(a) an offence of the same description as the one with which he is charged, or

(b) an offence of the same category as the one with which he is charged.

(3) Subsection (2) does not apply in the case of a particular defendant if the court is satisfied, by reason of the length of time since the conviction or for any other reason, that it would be unjust for it to apply in his case.

(4) For the purposes of subsection (2)—

(a) two offences are of the same description as each other if the statement of the offences in a written charge or indictment would, in each case, be in the same terms;

(b) two offences are of the same category as each other if they belong to the same category of offences prescribed for the purposes of this section by an order made by the Secretary of State.

(5) A category prescribed by an order under subsection 4(b) must consist of offences of the same type.

(6) Only prosecution evidence is admissible under s 101(1)(d) . . .

The inclusionary nature of s 103(1) indicates that the matters in issue to which evidence of bad character may be relevant are not confined to those specified in the subsection.

Propensity to commit offences of the kind charged

As to s 103(1)(a), it is conceptually confusing because propensity of the kind to which it refers was never previously treated as a matter in issue. In the past, admissible evidence of propensity was the means of establishing the matters in issue. Under the subsection, in any case in which the prosecution seek to rely upon s 101(1) (d) in relation to the issue of guilt, propensity will always be deemed to be a matter in issue, provided that it is of the kind referred to in the subsection. However, the prosecution will still need to establish that the propensity in question is an 'important' matter in issue, that is, 'a matter of substantial importance in the context of the case as a whole'[191] because s 103 is not free-standing but operates 'for the purposes of s 101(1)(d)'. If the prosecution can establish such importance, then subject to s 101(3) and, it is submitted, the common law discretion to exclude on the basis of prejudicial effect outweighing probative value, the propensity may be established under s 103(2) by evidence of a relevant conviction or in 'any other way'. Insofar as s 103(2) permits proof by evidence of a conviction, it is submitted that it too is a deeming provision, in the sense that evidence of the conviction is to be treated as, in the words of s 101(1)(d), 'evidence of the defendant's bad character' that 'is relevant to an important matter in issue', that is, the propensity.

The meaning of the exception within s 103(1)(a)—'except where his having such a propensity makes it no more likely that he is guilty of the offence'—is obscure, given that all too often evidence of propensity to commit offences of the kind charged will make it more probable that the accused committed the offence charged, albeit that in many cases it will have only limited or very limited probative force. The Explanatory Notes to the Act furnish only one illustration: where facts are undisputed and the question is whether the facts constitute the offence, 'for example, in a homicide case, whether the defendant's actions caused death'.[192]

Questions of proof

Section 103(2) provides that where the matter in issue is whether the accused has a propensity to commit offences of the kind with which he is charged, the propensity can be proved by evidence that he has been convicted of an offence of the kind referred to in either

---

[191] Section 112(1).
[192] Para 371.

s 103(2) (a) or (b). This is subject to s 103(3), whereby evidence of the conviction should not be given if the court is satisfied that it would be unjust to do so 'by reason of the length of time since the conviction or for any other reason'. Bearing in mind that s 103 exists 'for the purposes of section 101(1)(d)', that any evidence admissible under s 101(1)(d) is subject to the discretionary power to exclude contained in s 101(3) and (4), and that those subsections contain a test for exclusion similar to, but cast in different language from, the test in s 103(3), there appears to be a large degree of unnecessary overlap between those subsections and s 103(3).

The wording of s 103(2) indicates that in at least some cases proof of the mere fact of the conviction or convictions may be used to establish propensity. In other cases, however, the propensity will be established not simply by the fact of the conviction, but by evidence of the conduct which resulted in the conviction. In the latter type of case, the prosecution will doubtless use s 103(2) in conjunction with ss 74(3) and 75 of the Police and Criminal Evidence Act 1984.[193] Under s 74(3), where evidence of the fact that the accused has committed an offence is admissible and proof is given that he has been convicted of the offence, there is a rebuttable presumption that he committed the offence.[194] Under s 75, where evidence of a conviction is admissible by virtue of s 74, then without prejudice to the admissibility of any other evidence for the purpose of identifying the facts on which the conviction was based, the contents of, inter alia, the information or indictment shall be admissible for that purpose. Where reliance is placed on specific facts relating to modus operandi beyond those contained in the information or indictment, and they are disputed, then they need to be established by calling a witness to give first-hand evidence or by adducing admissible hearsay evidence in that regard.[195] However, this runs the risk of 'satellite litigation' during a trial, which could distract from the real issues and unnecessarily lengthen proceedings.[196]

Section 103(2) permits propensity to be proved by evidence of a conviction of an offence falling within either s 103(2)(a) or (b). Subsection (2)(a) refers to an offence of the same description as the one with which the accused is charged. Section 103(4)(a) makes clear that an offence will only be 'of the same description' if the statement of the offence in a written charge or indictment would, in each case, be the same. Thus, as it says in the Explanatory Notes,[197] the test relates to the law broken rather than the circumstances of the offence. Section 103(2)(b) refers to an offence of the same category as the one with which the accused is charged. By reason of s 103(4)(b) and s 103(5), an offence will be 'of the same category' if it falls within a category consisting of offences of the same type drawn up by the Secretary of State in secondary legislation. Two categories have been drawn up, a 'Theft Category' and a 'Sexual Offences (persons under the age of 16) Category'.[198] The first includes offences of theft, robbery, burglary, handling stolen goods, etc. The second includes offences of rape of a person under the age of 16, assault by penetration of a person under the age of 16, sexual

---

[193] See Ch 4. See, in the case of s 74(3), *R v O'Dowd* [2009] 2 Cr App R 280 (16), CA at [71].

[194] See, in this chapter, under **The right of an accused to challenge evidence of a conviction**, p 626. See also *R v M(E)* [2014] 2 Cr App R 484 (29), CA: where the convictions are by courts in a member State of the European Union, the jury must have the tools necessary to reach a judgment whether they could rely on the convictions as presumptive proof that the accused committed the offences to which the convictions relate.

[195] *R v Humphris* (2005) 169 J PN 718 CA and *R v Ainscough* [2006] Crim LR 635, CA.

[196] *R v O'Dowd* [2009] 2 Cr App R 280 (16), CA at [71]. See *R v McKenzie* [2008] RTR 277, CA, where the Court of Appeal deprecated the admission of evidence relating to collateral matters which could add to the length and cost of a trial and complicate the issues the jury had to decide. See also *R v McAllister* [2009] 1 Cr App R 129 (10), CA.

[197] Para 373.

[198] See Criminal Justice Act 2003 (Categories of Offences) Order 2004, SI 2004/3346.

assault on a person under the age of 16, etc.[199] Under s 103(7)–(11) offences committed outside England and Wales may be admissible as offences of the same description or category if they would constitute offences of the same description and category had they been committed in England and Wales. No new categories have been introduced. This may be because the principles in *R v Hanson*[200] (considered shortly) provide the courts with sufficient means to determine whether a previous offence is capable of establishing propensity.

Since the definition of 'bad character' provided in s 98 is broader than convictions—it is 'misconduct', which includes 'reprehensible behaviour'[201]—propensity may be proved by so-called 'non-conviction' evidence, which may take the form of evidence of a number of allegations with similar facts.[202] A risk of satellite litigation obviously arises where such evidence is disputed.[203]

The admissibility of evidence showing a propensity to offend

According to *R v Chopra*,[204] whereas at common law evidence of the accused's propensity to offend in the manner charged was prima facie inadmissible, under the 2003 Act it is prima facie *admissible*. In *R v Hanson*[205] the Court of Appeal laid down the following important principles relating to the admissibility of evidence of propensity under s 103.

1. Where propensity to commit the offence is relied upon by reference to s 101(1)(d) and s 103(1)(a), there are three questions to be considered: (i) whether the history of conviction(s) establishes a propensity to commit offences of the kind charged; (ii) whether that propensity makes it more likely that the accused committed the offence charged; and (iii) whether it is unjust to rely on the conviction(s) of the same description or category and, in any event, whether the proceedings will be unfair if they are admitted.

2. In referring to offences of the same description or category, s 103(2) is not exhaustive of the types of misconduct which may be relied upon to show evidence of propensity to commit offences of the kind charged.[206] Nor, however, is it necessarily sufficient in order to show such propensity that a conviction is of the same description or type as that charged.

3. There is no minimum number of events necessary to demonstrate such a propensity. The fewer the number of convictions, the weaker the evidence of propensity is likely to be. A single previous conviction for an offence of the same description or category will often not show propensity,[207] but may do so where, for example, it shows a tendency to

---

[199] Both categories also include an offence of (a) aiding, abetting, counselling, procuring, or inciting the commission of an offence specified; or (b) attempting to commit an offence specified.

[200] [2005] 1 WLR 3169, CA.

[201] See s 112.

[202] See *R v Mitchell* [2017] AC 571, SC. See further, in this chapter, under **Misconduct which is disputed**, p 592.

[203] *R v Mitchell* [2017] AC 571, SC.

[204] [2007] 1 Cr App R 225 (16), CA.

[205] [2005] 1 WLR 3169, CA.

[206] See *R v Johnson* [2009] 2 Cr App R 101 (7), CA: conspiracy to burgle is not an offence of the same description or category as the substantive offence of burglary, but may be admissible as evidence of propensity.

[207] See *R v Bagot* [2010] EWCA Crim 1983.

unusual behaviour, or where its circumstances demonstrate probative force in relation to the offence charged.[208]

4. Circumstances demonstrating probative force are not confined to those sharing striking similarity, but if the modus operandi has significant features shared by the offence charged, it may show propensity. When considering what is just under s 103(3), and the fairness of the proceedings under s 101(3), the judge may take into consideration, along with other factors, the degree of similarity between the previous conviction and the offence charged (albeit that they are both within the same description or prescribed category). This does not mean, however, that what used to be referred to as striking similarity must be shown before convictions become admissible.[209]

5. The judge may also take into consideration the respective gravity of the past and present offences.[210]

6. The judge must also consider the strength of the prosecution case. If there is no, or very little, other evidence against an accused, it is unlikely to be just to admit his previous convictions, whatever they are.

7. In principle, if there is a substantial gap between the dates of the commission of, and conviction for, earlier offence(s), the date of commission is generally to be regarded as being of more significance than the date of conviction when assessing admissibility. Old convictions with no special features shared with the offence charged are likely seriously to affect the fairness of proceedings adversely unless, despite their age, it can properly be said that they show a continuing propensity.[211]

8. It will often be necessary, before determining admissibility, and even when considering offences of the same description or category, to examine each individual conviction rather than merely to look at the nature of the offence or at the accused's record as a whole.

9. The sentence passed will not normally be probative or admissible at the behest of the Crown.

10. Where past events are disputed, the judge must take care not to permit the trial unreasonably to be diverted into an investigation of matters not charged on the indictment.

---

[208] In *R v Turner* [2010] EWCA Crim 2300, a case of ruthless murder, a single 15-year-old conviction for an offence contrary to the Offences Against the Person Act 1861, s 18, was properly admitted because it revealed violence of greater than normal gravity and demonstrated a propensity to commit acts of ruthless violence on strangers. See also, *R v D(M)* [2015] EWCA Crim 818, a case of two offences of rape of girls under 16 by an accused who was 17. A single previous conviction for a sexual assault on a teacher was properly admitted because it involved audacity, persistence after initial rebuffs, and carelessness as to consent, which were features of the offences charged.

[209] See *R v M* [2010] EWCA Crim 1578, applying the principles set out in paras (3) and (4). See also *R v Bowman* [2014] EWCA Crim 716 (probative force of firearms offences dating from 1990 derived from distinctive circumstances).

[210] Sometimes, therefore, a ruling on admissibility should be deferred until all of the prosecution evidence has been adduced: *R v Gyima* [2007] EWCA Crim 429. See also *R v Hewlett* [2008] EWCA Crim 270.

[211] See *R v Royston Jackson* [2011] EWCA Crim 1870: in a case of murder by strangulation the accused's previous conviction for murder was admitted, unsurprisingly, because although it was 20 years old, it was also a murder by strangulation. Other common features included both victims being male, both murders beginning with a social meeting, both involving the use of a vehicle, and the victim's bodies being left in a remote location. Cf *R v DS* [2010] EWCA Crim 1016 (extremely stale allegation of indecent assault inadmissible), and *R v Bagot* [2010] EWCA Crim 1983 (single offence of vehicle taking when the accused was 14 did not show propensity to steal cars at 18).

11. The Crown needs to have decided, at the time of giving notice of the application, whether it proposes to rely simply on the fact of conviction or also upon the circumstances of it. It is to be expected that the relevant circumstances of previous convictions will, generally, be capable of agreement, and that, subject to the trial judge's ruling as to admissibility, they will be put before the jury by way of admission. Even where the circumstances are genuinely in dispute, it is to be expected that the minimum indisputable facts will thus be admitted. It will be very rare indeed for it to be necessary for the judge to hear evidence before ruling on admissibility under the Act.

12. In any case in which evidence of bad character is admitted to show propensity the judge in summing up should warn the jury clearly against placing undue reliance on previous convictions. Evidence of bad character cannot be used simply to bolster a weak case or to prejudice the minds of the jury against the defendant.[212] A jury should be directed: (i) that they should not conclude that an accused is guilty or untruthful merely because he has previous convictions; (ii) that, although the convictions may show a propensity, this does not mean that he committed the offence charged or has been untruthful in the case; (iii) that whether they in fact show a propensity is for them to decide; (iv) that they must take into account what an accused has said about his previous convictions; and (v) that, although they are entitled, if they find propensity is shown, to take this into account when determining guilt, propensity is only one relevant factor and they must assess its significance in the light of all the other evidence in the case.[213]

The number and age of convictions

The principles in paragraphs (3) and (7) were refined and developed in *R v M*.[214] At the appellant's trial for possession of a firearm with intent to cause fear of violence the prosecution were permitted to adduce, under s 101(1)(d), evidence of a previous conviction for possession of a firearm without a certificate, which dated from some 20 years before. The Court of Appeal held that the evidence had been improperly admitted. Whilst there could be cases where the factual circumstances of a single previous conviction, even as long ago as 20 years, might be relevant to show an accused's propensity, the court observed that such cases would be rare and would involve the previous conviction exhibiting some very special and distinctive feature, such as a predilection for a highly unusual form of sexual activity,[215] or some arcane or highly specialized knowledge relevant to the offence charged. Where there were less distinctive features in common, some evidence of the propensity manifesting itself in the intervening period would be necessary in order to render the previous conviction admissible as evidence of a continuing propensity.[216]

---

[212] A case is not necessarily weak just because the ultimate issue is the credibility of the complainant and where inconsistencies in the complainant's account do not significantly undermine her credibility: *R v Steltner* [2018] EWCA Crim 1479 at [27]. Nor is a case necessarily weak where an identifying witness has given a partial identification, but there is a jigsaw of strong circumstantial evidence: *R v Howe* [2017] EWCA Crim 2400. See also *R v Spottiswood* [2019] EWCA Crim 949, where there was a clear case for the accused to meet.

[213] For examples of directions, see the Crown Court Compendium (July 2019), Part 1, 12–6, Examples 1–4.

[214] [2006] EWCA Crim 3408 at [16]; [2007] Crim LR 637, CA. See also *R v McKenzie* [2008] RTR 277, CA.

[215] A general sexual interest in children will suffice: see *R v B* [2011] EWCA Crim 1403. See also *R v Wells* [2015] EWCA Crim 2 (sexual offences with children); *R v Cornwell* [2013] EWCA Crim 2414 (a single conviction for indecency with a child in a trial for historic sexual offences); and *R v Wynes* [2014] EWCA Crim 2585 (a single previous conviction for possessing an indecent image of a child).

[216] See also, approving *R v M, R v G* [2017] 1 Cr App R 413 (27), CA at [17].

Misconduct after the offence charged

For the purposes of ss 101 and 103, evidence of propensity to offend may relate to events that occurred after the offence charged. In some cases the events may occur a long time after the offence charged. In *R v B*,[217] for example, the accused's guilty pleas in 2010 to charges of making, possessing and distributing child pornography between 2001 and 2007, were admissible as evidence of propensity in relation to offences of indecent assault against his stepdaughters between 1979 and 1982. The evidence showed sexual inclinations toward young girls of ages similar to the ages of his stepdaughters at the time of the assaults and as a matter of common sense it was unlikely that his interest in child pornography had sprung up in his later years and was wholly different from his inclinations between 1979 and 1982.[218] Similarly, in *R v Nix*,[219] where the accused was tried for sexual offences against his two daughters when they were aged between 4 and 11, it was not improper to admit evidence of his subsequent conviction for sexual assault against a stepdaughter when she was aged 24. Although the stepdaughter was an adult, the evidence of the assault when she was 24 showed a propensity to commit offences of indecency against family members. The evidence may have been rendered less powerful by the fact that the complainant was an adult and not a child, but it was nonetheless admissible and its weight was a matter for the jury. The court noted that the evidence would also have been admissible under s 101(1)(c) because it explained to the jury what made the complainants come forward as late as they did, namely learning of the accused's conviction for sexual assault against his stepdaughter.

Misconduct other than convictions

Section 103(2) states that it is without prejudice to other ways of establishing an accused's propensity to commit offences of the kind with which he is charged. Thus propensity may be established by evidence of an offence other than an offence 'of the same description' or 'of the same category' within s 103(2); the purpose of that subsection is simply to make it easier to admit evidence of convictions of the kind to which it refers.[220] It may also be established by evidence of misconduct or disposition towards misconduct that did not result in a conviction, in which case it may be proved, subject to the rules of evidence generally, in the same way as any other relevant facts.[221] Concerning evidence of a disposition towards misconduct, such evidence may be capable of demonstrating propensity since a person may be more likely to behave in a particular way if he has a disposition to do so.[222] An example might be the accused expressing, in text messages, a readiness to use random aggression if his relationships break up, even in the absence of evidence of actual aggression when his relationships have broken up.[223] Concerning evidence of misconduct, there are three types of case. The first is where the misconduct did not result in prosecution, including cases in which the

---

[217] [2011] EWCA Crim 1630. See also *R v Adenusi* [2006] Crim LR 929, CA and *R v Norris* [2013] EWCA Crim 712.

[218] See also *R v D (N)* [2013] 1 WLR 676 at [45]: a sexual interest in children is a characteristic which is unlikely to change over the years. See also *R v A* [2009] EWCA Crim 513 as to timing of child pornography and abuse.

[219] 15 March 2016, CA.

[220] *R v Weir* [2006] 1 WLR 1885, CA at [7].

[221] See *R v McKenzie* [2008] RTR 277, CA, a dangerous driving case where the accused's girlfriend had been properly permitted to give evidence of an incident when she was the accused's passenger and he had driven aggressively and taken dangerous risks.

[222] *R v Cooper* [2018] EWCA Crim 1454.

[223] Ibid.

accused was formally cautioned or previously asked to have offences taken into consideration.[224] The second is where the misconduct did result in prosecution, but the outcome was an acquittal.[225] The third arises out of s 112(2) of the 2003 Act, which provides that:

> (2) Where a defendant is charged with two or more offences in the same criminal proceedings, this Chapter (except section 101(3)) has effect as if each offence were charged in separate proceedings; and references to the offence with which the defendant is charged are to be read accordingly.

In *R v Chopra*[226] it was held that this subsection means that where an accused faces two or more counts on an indictment, evidence which suggests that he committed count 2 is, so far as count 1 is concerned, bad character evidence and can be admitted in relation to count 1, that is, it is 'cross-admissible',[227] if, but only if, it passes through one of the s 101 gateways; and that the same applies vice versa and however many counts there may be. A similar principle applies where no single piece of evidence is enough to convict the accused of any of the offences charged, and the important matter in issue is not whether the accused had a propensity to commit offences or to be untruthful, but whether the circumstantial evidence linking him to the offences, when viewed as a whole, points to his guilt of each offence.[228] Where evidence in one count is properly cross-admissible, it is difficult to argue that a defendant will be 'prejudiced or embarrassed in his. . .defence' within the meaning of the Criminal Procedure Rules 2015, r 3.21(4), justifying severance and separate trials, unless there is some other factor making this desirable (such as the need to avoid overloading an indictment or overburdening the jury).[229] Where evidence is cross-admissible between counts on an indictment which state different types of offence with different elements, directions to the jury will need to be carefully tailored and qualified.[230]

It remains to stress that even in cases where the misconduct did result in a conviction, in some such cases, as already indicated, propensity can only be established by going beyond the fact of the conviction and introducing evidence of the misconduct which resulted in the conviction. Where, in such a case, the conviction was based on a guilty plea, it is submitted that under the Act, as at common law, it would not be unfair for the prosecution to prove the plea, together with confessions made by the accused in police interviews. Although this denies the accused the opportunity to cross-examine the victim or other witnesses to the offence of which he stands convicted, it is fairer to the accused to adduce only what he admitted rather than to call the victim or other witnesses, who may give additional prejudicial evidence.[231]

---

[224] *R v Weir* [2006] 1 WLR 1885, CA at [7].

[225] See *R v Z* [2002] 2 AC 483, HL, considered, in this chapter, under **Misconduct**, p 556.

[226] [2007] 1 Cr App R 225 (16), CA.

[227] The term 'cross-admissibility' is to be used only when describing whether evidence supporting one count in the indictment could support another count in the same indictment and is not apt in relation to the admissibility of evidence of bad character which is not the subject of a count in the indictment. See *R v Suleman* [2012] 2 Cr App R 30, CA at [47]. See also *R v O'Leary* [2013] EWCA Crim 1371.

[228] *R v Wallace* [2008] 1 WLR 572, CA. See also *R v Freeman* [2009] 1 Cr App R 137 (11), CA, where evidence relating to two or more counts in the same indictment was 'cross-admissible'.

[229] See *R v Toner* [2019] EWCA Crim 447: historical offences for possession of indecent photographs of children were properly cross-admissible in respect of recent similar offences and vice versa, all offences having been the subject of counts on the same indictment and severance not being justified.

[230] *R v Cooper* [2017] EWCA Crim 43.

[231] See *R v Bedford* (1990) 93 Cr App R 113, CA.

Misconduct which is disputed

If evidence of the accused's misconduct is admissible on the issue of his guilt, it is no bar to its admissibility that it is disputed and that the jury may, in the event, reject it.[232] Thus, as has been stated earlier in this chapter, although bad character evidence may take the form of conclusive or indisputable evidence, it may also take the form of unproved allegations, as when, as we have seen, propensity is advanced by way of multiple counts none of which has been proved, their proof being a question for the jury.[233] In *R v Brima*[234] it was made clear that the task of the judge is not to determine whether misconduct does establish propensity, an issue for the jury, but whether it has the capacity to do so. That question, together with the issue whether the propensity makes it more likely that the accused committed the offence charged, will involve applying the principles laid down in *R v Hanson*,[235] and is highly fact-sensitive.

Where evidence of similar incidents of disputed misconduct is admitted, it will be for the jury to determine whether the evidence establishes propensity. In *R v Mitchell*,[236] the Supreme Court held that it is the issue of propensity which needs to be proved to the criminal standard and not the facts of individual instances of disputed misconduct advanced to support propensity.[237] According to the court, the jury are not required to consider each incident of misconduct in an 'hermetically sealed compartment' and are entitled to look at incidents 'in the round' when deciding whether propensity is proved.[238] The justification provided by the court was (i) the jury's decision-making on propensity may be properly informed by the improbability of a number of similar incidents being false; and (ii) obvious similarities in the various incidents may be mutually supportive.[239] However, it is submitted that an approach whereby disputed incidents do not need to be individually proved to the criminal standard increases the risk that a jury might act on dubious evidence, and judges will have to be particularly alert to the possibility of contamination and the need to use the power under s 107 to stop the case. Additionally, where the prosecution seek to admit a large volume of disputed incidents of misconduct, there is a real risk of unfair prejudice and satellite litigation. As the Supreme Court itself pointed out in *R v Mitchell*:[240]

> Reliance on cumulative past incidents in support of a case of propensity may indeed illuminate the truth of the currently indicted allegations, but excessive recourse to such history may skew the trial in a way which distracts attention from the central issue. Article 6(3) of the European Convention on Human Rights requires judges to actively consider whether the effect of admitting the bad character evidence will have such an adverse effect on the fairness of the trial that it ought to be excluded. That species of adverse effect can arise through the sheer weight of disputed evidence on other uncharged allegations. And that can happen even though the jury will . . . be directed to

---

[232] This was the position at common law: see *R v Rance and Herron* (1975) 62 Cr App R 118, CA.

[233] *R v Chopra* [2007] 1 Cr App R 225 (16), CA at [15].

[234] [2007] 1 Cr App R 316 (24), CA.

[235] [2005] 2 Cr App R 299 (21), CA. See, in this chapter, under **The admissibility of evidence showing a propensity to offend, p 587.**

[236] [2017] AC 571, SC.

[237] The court disagreed with a number of authorities to the extent that they suggested otherwise: *R v Lafayette* [2008] EWCA Crim 3238; *R v Ngyuen* [2008] 2 Cr App R 99 (9), CA; *R v O'Dowd* [2009] 2 Cr App R 280 (16), CA; and *R v McAllister* [2009] 1 Cr App R 129 (10), CA. *R v Nyguen* involved only one incident of misconduct, so the facts of that incident necessarily had to be proved to the criminal standard in order to prove propensity.

[238] See [39] and [49].

[239] At [43]. See also *R v Alexander* [2018] EWCA Crim 239.

[240] Per Lord Kerr at [53].

consider propensity cumulatively, if the volume of evidence received is sufficiently strong to support a conviction. It is a truism that satellite litigation is often inimical to efficient trial.

Whether misconduct establishes propensity

In some cases, it will be obvious that evidence of the accused's misconduct is capable of establishing propensity, for example, where it involves convictions for a number of recent offences of the same description as the offence charged and with factual similarities. In other cases, the question whether the misconduct is capable of establishing propensity may not be so straightforward, for example where the misconduct involves offences which are of a different description to the one charged. In such cases, the courts will need to consider very carefully the nature of the misconduct and its probative force in showing propensity. Whether the evidence is capable of showing propensity will be highly 'fact sensitive' and it is useful to consider examples which fall on either side of the line. In *R v Brima*,[241] a case of murder by stabbing, it was held that evidence of B's two previous convictions, one for assault occasioning actual bodily harm involving a stabbing, another for robbery involving the holding of a knife to the throat of the victim, were capable of establishing propensity to commit offences of the kind charged and did make it more likely that B had committed the offence charged. In *R v Highton*,[242] it was held that the previous convictions of one appellant, including convictions for offences of violence and the possession of offensive weapons, provided evidence of propensity to commit offences of the kind charged, which included kidnapping and robbery; but in the case of another appellant,[243] evidence of heroin use was not admissible under s 101(1)(d) on a charge of cultivating a controlled drug. In *R v Beverley*,[244] a case of conspiracy to import cocaine where the issue was whether B, in driving the car in which the drugs were found, was a knowing participant, it was doubted whether B's two previous convictions, assuming that they established propensity, made it more likely that B committed the offence charged. One was for simple possession of cannabis. The other was for possession of cannabis with intent to supply, a crime committed a long time earlier and which concerned a form of dealing different in nature and scale from the conspiracy charged. In *R v Lawson*,[245] a previous conviction for wounding was incapable of establishing a propensity to commit manslaughter because, on the facts, the manslaughter was a different kind of misconduct and was recklessly dangerous rather than aggressive.[246]

Misconduct with similar facts

Evidence of misconduct may derive probative force on the basis that the similarities in the evidence of the prosecution witnesses are such that, in the absence of collusion or contamination, they must be telling the truth, such is the unlikelihood of them telling the same untruth. *R v Chopra*[247] provides a good example. The indictment alleged that C, a dentist,

---

[241] [2007] 1 Cr App R 316 (24), CA.

[242] [2005] 1 WLR 3472, CA.

[243] Ibid at [25].

[244] [2006] Crim LR 1064, CA.

[245] [2007] 1 Cr App R 178 (11), CA.

[246] See also *R v Khan* [2015] EWCA Crim 1755, a case of gang-related joint-enterprise murder in which the victim was stabbed. The accused's convictions for robbery and possession of a bladed article in a gang context were admissible under s 101(1)(d) to show a propensity to offend using a knife. See also *R v Swellings* [2009] 2 Cr App R (S) 30, CA and *R v Bullen* [2008] Cr App R 364 (25), CA.

[247] [2007] 1 Cr App R 225 (16), CA.

had indecently touched three teenage patients. In each case the complainant alleged that C had deliberately placed his hand on her breast and squeezed it and in each case C denied such misconduct. The Court of Appeal upheld the judge's ruling that the evidence of each complainant could be used by the jury to support that of another, providing that the possibility of collusion or contamination between them was excluded.[248] The evidence was cross-admissible under s 101(1)(d), being relevant, in the case of each count, to the important matter in issue whether there was an offence committed by C or no offence at all. The critical question in such a case is whether the evidence of each complainant is capable of establishing propensity to commit offences of the kind charged.[249] Not all evidence of other misbehaviour will do so; there has to be a sufficient similarity or connection between the facts of the several allegations to make it more likely that each allegation is true; and, as at common law, the likelihood or unlikelihood of innocent coincidence will be a relevant and sometimes critical test. For example, one kind of assault may be capable of establishing a propensity to commit a different kind of assault. In *R v Chopra* itself, the court held that there was sufficient connection and similarity between the allegations to make them capable of establishing a propensity occasionally to molest young female patients in the course of examination and to make it more likely that each allegation was true.[250] In response to C's contention that in the case of a dentist it is interference with the breasts which is likely to be alleged if false accusations of indecency are made, since that is the area to which his hands are nearest, the Court of Appeal made two points. First, that when considering admissibility, the judge is required to assume that the evidence is truthful unless no jury could reasonably believe it.[251] Second, propensity to commit an offence remains so even in the case of a common offence or one which can readily be imagined by someone bent on making a false allegation. In this regard, the court observed that even before the 2003 Act, the suggestion that so-called 'similar fact evidence' had to go beyond the so-called stock in trade of the sexual offender had been discredited.[252]

[248] In cases where no collusion is suggested, it may still be important to direct the jury about the dangers of innocent contamination of the evidence of the complainants, as when, eg, they have talked together about their encounters with the accused: *R v Lamb* [2007] EWCA Crim 1766. Where evidence is not treated as cross-admissible, the need to direct the jury on the risk of collusion and innocent contamination will depend on the circumstances of the case: *R v N* [2011] EWCA Crim 730. See also the Crown Court Compendium (July 2019), Part 1, 13, para 14 and Example 1.

[249] In respect of proof of propensity by similar incidents of misconduct which are disputed, see *R v Mitchell* [2017] AC 571, SC. The Supreme Court stated that similar incidents do not need to be proved individually and that propensity can be proved by looking at the incidents in the round. *R v Mitchell* did not consider the question of 'cross-admissibility' as the evidence admitted was not the subject of counts on the indictment. However, the question arises whether the principle in *R v Mitchell* should apply with equal force to proof of propensity in the context of cross-admissibility. The guidance on the 'propensity approach' to cross-admissibility is provided in the Crown Court Compendium Part 1 (July 2019), 13. paras 8–10 and 15, which refers judges to the direction at 12–6, Example 1. The guidance does not appear to adopt the principle in *R v Mitchell*. However, it is not easy to see why there should be a different approach. The principle would also seem to apply to cross-admissibility in order to prove identification: see *R v Wallace* [2008] 1 WLR 572, CA. (see shortly in this chapter under **Misconduct to prove identity, p 595**).

[250] See also, at common law, *R v Sims* [1946] KB 531, CCA; *R v Bedford* (1990) 93 Cr App R 113, CA at 116; and *R v Venn* [2003] All ER (D) 207 (Feb) at [35].

[251] See, in this chapter, s 109 under **Assumption of truth in the assessment of relevance or probative value, p 621**.

[252] See *R v P* [1991] 2 AC 447, HL. The court in *R v Chopra* observed (at [12]) that the right way to deal with the new law was not first to ask what would have been the position under the old. However, it went on to say that it had no doubt that some, perhaps many, of the considerations of relevance and fairness which arose at common law in the 'similar fact' cases would continue to arise and that some of the answers might be the same.

Misconduct to prove identity

Where the accused's defence is that he has been wrongly identified as the person who committed the offence, evidence of misconduct may be relevant to prove that he was that person. A personal hallmark, 'signature behaviour' or other very striking similarity in different incidents of misconduct may prove that they have been committed by the same person.[253] In the absence of this, evidence of misconduct tending to show that a defendant has committed an offence charged in count A may be used to reach a verdict on count B and vice versa, if the circumstances of both offences (as the jury would be entitled to find them) are such as to provide sufficient probative support for the conclusion that the defendant committed both offences, and it would not be unfair to allow the jury to use the evidence in this way. However, much care is needed before admitting evidence of misconduct in order to prove the identity of the accused as the offender, not least because in many cases the evidence, without more, will usually only show that the same person committed both offences and not that that person is the accused.[254]

In *R v Wallace*,[255] the accused was convicted of three counts of robbery and one of attempted robbery in respect of four separate armed robberies of small retail businesses, involving between three and four masked robbers. In the first robbery, a stolen car was used, from which the accused's DNA and fingerprint were recovered. In the second robbery, a robber wielding a gun shown on CCTV matched the accused's description. That robber also had a mobile phone strap and trainers which were similar to those owned by the accused. In the third robbery, the robbers left behind plastic bags which had the accused's palm and fingerprints on them. In the fourth robbery, the accused admitted being at the premises where the robbery took place earlier in the morning. He also appeared and was arrested shortly after the getaway car used in that robbery had crashed. The court held that evidence from each count was circumstantial evidence which fell to be considered as bad character evidence,[256] and evidence from each count could be used collectively to show that the accused participated in all four robberies.[257]

It is submitted that *Wallace* is an example of a 'cumulative approach' to proving identity, an approach established at common law. The 'cumulative approach' may apply where there is evidence, other than the evidence of visual identification, which may enable the jury to conclude that offences A and B were committed by the same man, but that evidence by itself falls short of proving that that man was the accused in either case. In this situation, once the jury are satisfied that the evidence shows both offences to have been committed by the same man, the identification evidence of the victims can be used cumulatively in deciding whether that man was the accused.[258] Another approach established at common law which

---

[253] See *R v P* [1991] 2 AC 447 at 462; *R v W (John)* [1998] 2 Cr App R 289, CA; and *R v Mullen* [1992] Crim LR 735, CA.

[254] See the Crown Court Compendium (July 2019), Part 1, 12–6, para 12 and Example 4, and the cases referred to: *R v Holmes* [2014] EWCA Crim 420; *R v Ngando* [2014] EWCA Crim 506; *R v Dossett* [2013] EWCA Crim 710; and *R v Eastlake* [2007] EWCA Crim 603.

[255] [2008] 1 WLR 572, CA.

[256] At [30]. The court also held that had the accused been charged with conspiracy to rob rather than with four separate substantive counts, the evidence would have been admissible under s 98(a) as circumstantial evidence which was to do with the facts of the offence (at [27]).

[257] At [39].

[258] See *R v Barnes* [1995] 2 Cr App R 491, CA and *R v Grant* [1996] 2 Cr App R 272, CA.

might also be followed is 'the sequential approach'. The sequential approach is where, when deciding whether the accused committed offence A, the jury can have regard to evidence that he also committed offence B. This approach involves proof not only of similarity, but also that the accused did in fact commit offence B. Because the facts only go to show that the same man committed both offences, there must be some evidence to make the jury sure that the accused committed at least one offence.[259]

Sexual disposition to prove guilt

In the case of evidence of sexual disposition, the threshold issue under the Act is whether it amounts to evidence of a disposition towards, 'misconduct'[260] which, it will be recalled, means 'the commission of an offence or other reprehensible behaviour'.[261] If there is evidence of the commission of a sexual offence of the kind with which the accused is charged, then the prosecution will rely upon s 103(1)(a) and, if it resulted in a conviction, s 103(2).[262] However, in the case of sexual disposition which has not involved the commission of any offence, a disposition towards, say, paedophilia, incest, or bestiality will be regarded as evidence of disposition towards 'reprehensible behaviour', but not a homosexual disposition, any more than a heterosexual disposition.[263]

The admissibility of evidence of homosexual or heterosexual disposition, therefore, is not governed by the Act and will turn simply on whether it is relevant and, if so, whether it should be excluded under the common law discretion to exclude (its prejudicial effect outweighs its probative value) or under s 78 of the Police and Criminal Evidence Act 1984. Evidence of sexual disposition, it is submitted, will very often be irrelevant or unduly prejudicial, but each case will turn on its own facts. Thus if the accused, charged with a sexual offence against a man, were to assert his heterosexual disposition, then evidence of his homosexual disposition would be plainly relevant to that issue, but it would not be evidence of misconduct.[264] Evidence of homosexual disposition may also be admitted if it has a particular relevance in disproving innocent association, but only in exceptional circumstances. In *R v IL*[265] for example, it was held that evidence of homosexual disposition was sufficiently unusual in the circumstances of the case to be relevant to whether the accused had an innocent or sexual association with his male children.[266] Although in *IL*, the court acknowledged that the value to the case of the evidence of disposition was modest, it had not been unduly prejudicial to admit it in order to rebut the accused's defence that his son and stepson had made up allegations that he had committed sexual offences against them. Evidence that he had embarked on a year-long homosexual affair while married was relevant to the true nature of his family

---

[259] Per Glidewell LJ in *R v McGranaghan* [1995] 1 Cr App R 559 at 572, CA. See also *R v Rubin* [1995] Crim LR 332, CA. The principle is confined to cases in which identification is in issue: see *R v S* [1993] Crim LR 293, CA. It is probably also confined to cases in which the indictment contains two or more counts and it is the evidence on each which is potentially admissible, in relation to the other or others, as similar fact evidence. See also *R v Mullen* [1992] Crim LR 735, CA.

[260] Section 98: see, in this chapter, under 'Bad character' defined, p 556.

[261] Section 112(1).

[262] See, in this chapter, under Questions of proof, p 585.

[263] See the Crown Court Compendium (July 2019), Part 1, 20–1, Example 14.

[264] Since such evidence is not evidence of bad character, it would not be required to be admitted under s 101(1)(f) as 'prosecution evidence to correct a false impression given by the defendant': see *R v IJ* [2011] EWCA Crim 2734.

[265] [2011] EWCA Crim 2734.

[266] Ibid. See also *R v Weir* [2006] 1 WLR 1885.

life and whether he was the victim of malicious allegation by his son and stepson, and the judge had given an explicit warning to the jury not to conclude the evidence showed a propensity to commit the offences alleged.[267]

Bad character evidence under s 101(1)(d) relevant to the credibility of the accused

Under s 101(1)(d), as we have seen, prosecution evidence of the accused's bad character is admissible if 'it is relevant to an important matter in issue between the defendant and the prosecution' and although the test is one of simple rather than enhanced relevance, the requirement of relevance to an 'important matter' is a requirement of relevance to a matter in issue 'of substantial importance in the context of the case as a whole'.[268] Insofar as s 101(1)(d) may be used to attack the credibility of the accused, it is supplemented by s 103(1)(b), which provides as follows:

(1) For the purposes of section 101(1)(d) the matters in issue between the defendant and the prosecution include—

. . .

(a) the question whether the defendant has a propensity to be untruthful, except where it is not suggested that the defendant's case is untruthful in any respect.

The effect of s 103(1)(b) is that in any case in which the prosecution seek to rely upon s 101(1)(d) to attack the credibility of the accused, his propensity to be untruthful will always be deemed to be a matter in issue, except in the very rare cases in which it is not suggested that his case is untruthful in any respect. The exception would apply, for example, when the defence do not dispute the facts established by the prosecution and the only question is whether the judge should stop the case on the basis that the prosecution evidence, taken at its highest, is such that the jury, properly directed, could not convict on it.[269] The meaning of the undefined phrase 'defendant's case' is unclear, but appears to refer to the defendant's case at trial, rather than what he said during police questioning or in his disclosed defence statement but which he does not rely on at trial, notwithstanding that in many cases the prosecution case will be that the accused is not telling the truth about a particular matter at trial having regard to what he did or did not say to the police or in his defence statement. It is submitted that a plea of not guilty, by itself, cannot lead to the conclusion that the accused's case will be untruthful in some respect, because the plea simply puts the prosecution to proof.

Use of s 103(1)(b)

In *R v Campbell*,[270] Lord Phillips LCJ expressed the view that the scope for use of s 103(1)(b) was very limited:

It will be comparatively rare for the case of a defendant who has pleaded not guilty not to involve some element that the prosecution suggest is untruthful. It does not, however, follow that, whenever there is an issue as to whether the defendant's case is truthful evidence can be admitted to show that he has a propensity to be untruthful.

---

[267] See also, at common law, *R v Horwood* [1970] 1 QB 133, CA.

[268] Section 112(1).

[269] See *R v Galbraith* [1981] 1 WLR 1039, CA; see **Ch 2**.

[270] [2007] 1 WLR 2798, CA at [29]–[31].

The question whether a defendant has a propensity for being untruthful will not normally be described as an important matter in issue between the defendant and the prosecution. A propensity for untruthfulness will not, of itself, go very far to establishing the commission of a criminal offence. To suggest that a propensity for untruthfulness makes it more likely that a defendant has lied to the jury is not likely to help them. If they apply common sense they will conclude that a defendant who has committed a criminal offence may well be prepared to lie about it, even if he has not shown a propensity for lying whereas a defendant who has not committed the offence charged will be likely to tell the truth, even if he has shown a propensity for telling lies. In short, whether or not a defendant is telling the truth to the jury is likely to depend simply on whether or not he committed the offence charged. The jury should focus on the latter question rather than on whether or not he has a propensity for telling lies.

For these reasons, the only circumstances in which there is likely to be an important issue as to whether a defendant has a propensity to tell lies is where telling lies is an element of the offence charged. Even then, the propensity to tell lies is only likely to be significant if the lying is in the context of committing criminal offences, in which case the evidence is likely to be admissible under section 103(1)(a).

It is submitted that the reasoning in this pronouncement is flawed. It may well be that whether or not an accused is telling the truth is likely to depend on whether or not he committed the offence, but it simply does not follow that a propensity for untruthfulness is (i) unlikely to be an important matter in issue and (ii) that evidence of such propensity is unlikely to assist the jury. As to (i), in many cases there is a direct conflict between the evidence of the accused and that of the prosecution witnesses and the question is which side is lying as opposed to mistaken, which will be a matter of importance, if not the most important matter, in the context of the case as a whole, and its importance is not dependent on whether telling lies is an element of the offence charged. As to (ii), in such a case it will plainly assist the jury to know that the accused has a propensity for untruthfulness, especially if the prosecution witnesses do not, and this is so whether or not telling lies is an element of the offence charged.[271]

The reasoning is also difficult to reconcile with the fact that under s 101(1)(e) (the gateway that permits an accused's bad character to be admitted by a co-accused), it is recognized that evidence of propensity to untruthfulness is capable of having substantial probative value in relation to the *credibility* of the accused.[272] Further, if the reasoning were to be adopted, it would narrow the ambit of s 101(1)(d) to such an extent that it could rarely be used other than to admit evidence of propensity to commit offences of the kind charged.

In *R v N*,[273] the Court of Appeal recognized that in relation to s 103(1)(b) the approach taken by Lord Phillips in *Campbell* was more restrictive than the language of the statute required. It also noted[274] that a different and less restrictive approach, and one more in accordance with the actual statutory language, has since been advanced by another constitution of the Court of Appeal in *R v Jarvis*,[275] a decision under s 101(1)(e). The court therefore declined to follow *R v Campbell* and held that evidence of propensity to untruthfulness had been properly admitted as relevant to credibility. In *R v N*, N had been charged with historic sexual offences

---

[271] Similarly, where the sole issue in a case is whether an accused's defence of duress is truthful, evidence that he has made untruthful statements in the past to get himself out of trouble with the courts will plainly be of assistance to the jury: see *R v Belogun* [2008] EWCA Crim 2006.

[272] See *R v Lawson* [2007] 1 WLR 1191, CA and *R v Jarvis* [2007] Crim LR 232.

[273] [2014] EWCA Crim 419.

[274] Ibid at [29]. See also *R v LH* [2017] NICA 67 at [19] and [20](i).

[275] [2008] EWCA Crim 488; [2008] Crim LR 632, CA.

against the complainant when she was a child and there was a direct conflict between his evidence and hers. The complainant's evidence was that N had committed the offences when he was her babysitter and his evidence was that he had no involvement in the offences, that he was not the babysitter who abused her, and she was mistaken. The court held that the credibility and reliability of both N and the complainant were of central importance in the case and evidence showing N's propensity to be untruthful was relevant and properly admitted under s 101(1)(d).[276] The evidence was that he had been previously tried for sexual offences against a girl under the age of 16 and his evidence had been rejected as untrue by the jury who convicted him, and that, at the sentencing for those offences, he had given deliberately false instructions to his own barrister for the purposes of mitigation, namely that he had been a soldier who served in Northern Ireland and during the Falklands War, when in fact he had been in the army for less than a month before being discharged.

The evidence admissible

According to the Explanatory Notes, s 103(1)(b) 'is intended to enable the admission of a limited range of evidence such as convictions for perjury or other offences involving deception as opposed to the wider range of evidence that will be admissible where the defendant puts his character in issue by, for example, attacking the character of another person', that is, under s 101(1)(g).[277] However, the range of evidence admissible is neither as clear or limited as the Notes suggest and questions arise as to which offences other than 'perjury or other offences involving deception' might be admissible as offences showing a propensity to be untruthful. In *R v Hanson*,[278] it was held that propensity to untruthfulness is not the same as propensity to dishonesty, so that offences of benefit fraud may show a propensity to be untruthful but offences of theft by shoplifting may show no more than propensity to dishonesty.[279]

As to the limits on the range of evidence admissible, it is not confined to evidence of convictions, but may relate to instances of untruthfulness which did not amount to criminal behaviour, or which did amount to criminal behaviour, but did not result, or by the time of the trial in question had not resulted, in a conviction. Equally, propensity to be untruthful may be established by reference to convictions for offences other than, and not necessarily similar to, 'perjury or other offences involving deception', where it is clear that the jury rejected the accused's version of events. An example would be previous convictions for sexual offences, the accused having run an unsuccessful defence of alibi. In *R v Hanson*[280] it was held that previous convictions, whether for offences of dishonesty or otherwise, are only likely to be capable of showing a propensity to be untruthful where truthfulness is in issue and, in the earlier case, either there was a plea of not guilty and the accused gave an account (on arrest, in interview, or in evidence) which the jury must have disbelieved,[281] or the way in which the

---

[276] [2014] EWCA Crim 419 at [22] and [31].

[277] Explanatory Notes to the 2003 Act, para 374.

[278] [2005] 1 WLR 3169, CA.

[279] *R v Edwards* [2006] 1 WLR 1524, CA at [33]. See also *R v Garnham* [2008] EWCA Crim 266. See also *R v Foster* [2009] EWCA Crim 353 at [17] (judge wrongly directed the jury that they could take previous robbery convictions into account in deciding the accused's truthfulness).

[280] [2005] 1 WLR 3169, CA.

[281] However, in *R v LH* [2017] NICA 67 at [22], the Northern Ireland Court of Appeal doubted that a single incident of the accused having given an account which the jury must have disbelieved would necessarily establish a propensity to be untruthful.

offence was committed shows a propensity for untruthfulness, for example by the making of false representations.[282] It was also made clear that dicta as to the nature and number of previous convictions in relation to s 103(1)(a)[283] apply equally in relation to s 103(1)(b). This means that there is no minimum number of convictions necessary to show propensity to untruthfulness and a very small number of convictions or even a single conviction may show propensity where the circumstances demonstrate probative force.[284]

Exclusion

Where evidence is admissible under s 101(1)(d) by virtue of s 103(1)(b), the court has a discretionary power to exclude it under s 101(3).[285] In cases where evidence is admissible only to go to truthfulness or credit, there is a danger that the jury may even subconsciously and despite careful direction be influenced by the evidence on the question of propensity and thus guilt, and for this reason it has been said that 'a cautious test of admissibility' should be applied, whether on examination of the test of relevance under s 101(1)(d) or, which seems more apposite, on application of the discretion under s 101(3).[286]

Section 101(1)(e)—evidence of substantial probative value in relation to an important issue between the defendant and a co-defendant

Section 101(1)(e), like section 101(1)(d), is a single gateway for the admissibility of evidence going to the guilt of the defendant as well as evidence going to his credit or propensity to be untruthful. It can only be used by a co-defendant. However, simply because an application to admit evidence of bad character is made by a co-defendant, the judge is not bound to admit it; the gateway in s 101(1)(e) must be gone through.[287] Under s 101(1)(e), evidence of the defendant's bad character is admissible if 'it has substantial probative value in relation to an important matter in issue between the defendant and a co-defendant'.[288] In *R v Lawson*[289] it was said that 'the feel' of the trial judge will often be critical on the question whether evidence is capable of having substantial probative value under s 101(1)(e) and that the Court of Appeal is unlikely to interfere unless the judge was plainly wrong or *Wednesbury* unreasonable.[290]

---

[282] See also *R v Gumbrell* [2009] EWCA Crim 550 (evidence of past false representations by the accused as to his competence and qualifications as a builder admitted to show a propensity to make false representations) and *R v Ellis* [2010] EWCA Crim 163 (evidence of offences of obtaining services by deception, the use of false instruments and lies in police interview admitted in relation to the truthfulness of the accused's explanation for having an offensive weapon in a public place).

[283] See, in this chapter, under **The admissibility of evidence showing a propensity to offend**, p 587.

[284] See, eg, *R v N* [2014] EWCA Crim 419.

[285] Or, it is submitted, under the common law discretion. See, in this chapter, under **Section 101 of the Criminal Justice Act 2003, Discretion to exclude**, p 575.

[286] See per Hughes LJ in *R v Lawson* [2007] 1 WLR 1191, CA at [33].

[287] *R v Edwards* [2006] 1 WLR 1524, CA at [1](v). Where a defendant pleads guilty, the gateway that must be gone through by the co-defendant is s 100: *R v Jukes* [2018] 2 Cr App R 114 (9), CA.

[288] Cf Explanatory Notes, para 375. For example, unproven and unsupported allegations against a co-accused recorded on a police computer lack substantial probative value for the purposes of s 101(1)(e): see *R v Turner* [2011] EWCA Crim 450.

[289] [2007] 1 Cr App R 178.

[290] *Associated Provincial Picture Houses Ltd v Wednesbury Corpn* [1948] 1 KB 223, CA.

Admissibility

Important principles concerning the admissibility of evidence under s 101(1)(e) were laid down in *R v Phillips*.[291] This was a case of construction industry fraud whereby subcontractors were paid through a fraudulent company structure and invoicing scheme. The scheme enabled the retention of £14 million which should have been paid in tax, national insurance, and VAT. Two co-accused, P and S, contended they were not personally responsible for the fraud and by implication blamed each other. P sought to admit evidence of S's fraudulent behaviour which pre-dated the conspiracy charged, as well as unproven evidence of fraudulent behaviour due to be the subject of future trials. P contended that the evidence showed that S had a propensity to commit fraud and to untruthfulness and this was substantially probative of his guilt and, correspondingly, P's innocence. The trial judge agreed and held that the evidence satisfied the test under s 101(1)(e), but refused to admit it on the basis that it would generate undesirable 'satellite litigation'. The Court of Appeal held that the trial judge was wrong not to have admitted the evidence once the test for admissibility was satisfied. The principles laid down by the court can be summarized as follows:

1. When considering the admissibility of an accused's bad character under s 101(1)(e), the section, together with s 112(1), requires separate consideration of two questions. First, does the evidence that the co-accused wishes to adduce have substantial probative value? Second, is the matter in respect of which the evidence is substantially probative, a matter of substantial importance in the context of the case as a whole?

2. Although there is an element of overlap in the two questions, it is necessary to address them in turn, especially where the character evidence is not the bare fact of a conviction, but is comprised of detailed allegations and where a number of factual issues arise between the accused and co-accused.

3. The second question requires the judge to make a fact-sensitive assessment of the importance of the issue between the accused and co-accused in the context of the case as a whole. This means that where there is already evidence before the jury that is probative of the same issue, the judge is entitled to consider whether further evidence (the character evidence) is of substantial probative value to the same issue.

4. 'Substantial probative value' means enhanced capability to prove or disprove a fact in issue and the threshold is not to be understated. The purpose of the enhancement is to ensure that the probative strength of the evidence removes the risk of unfair prejudice and it is important that when considering admissibility under s 101(1)(e), regard is had for the rigour of the statutory test of *substantial* probative value to a matter in issue between the accused and co-accused which is of *substantial* importance in the context of the case as a whole.[292]

5. Once the test for admissibility is satisfied, there is no discretion to exclude under any statutory provision, or on grounds of unfair prejudice or some other unfairness. This is because there is an underlying assumption that if the statutory test of enhanced probative value upon a matter of substantial importance is met, the scope for unfairness is removed.[293]

[291] [2012] 1 Cr App R 332 (25), CA.
[292] See also *R v Apabhai* [2011] EWCA Crim 917.
[293] See [53].

The test for admissibility under s 101(1)(e) was given further consideration by the Court of Appeal in *R v Platt*.[294] In *R v Platt*, two accused, M and the appellant P were jointly tried for a murder committed in a hostel housing ex-offenders, many of whom had drug or alcohol related problems. The victim of the murder was a sex offender who had often been bullied in the hostel. His body was found with multiple injuries to his face and had been set on fire using accelerant. At the trial, M and P ran 'cut throat' defences and on an application by M, the judge admitted P's previous conviction for arson committed 23 years previously when P was 15, and two convictions for causing grievous bodily harm. The first conviction for grievous bodily harm arose out of an assault at a football match in 1993, and the second arose out of an assault in 2003 when the appellant had punched and broken the jaw of a man who, it was accepted, had jumped on him. The trial judge admitted the convictions under s 101(1) (e) on the grounds that they had substantial probative value in relation to P's credibility, which was an important matter in issue between him and M because, while not advancing a positive case that M committed the murder, P did in effect say that M was amongst those who might have done and so was likely to have killed the deceased. The judge relied on the principle laid down in the leading common law authority of *R v Randall*,[295] namely that a co-accused is entitled to disprove his guilt and may do so by admitting evidence showing an accused's propensity where this will show that his version of the facts is more probable than the accused's. Applying the principle, the judge ruled that P's convictions were admissible by M. The conviction for arson was sufficiently unusual as to have substantial probative value because it involved the use of accelerant and his convictions for grievous bodily harm had substantial probative value in showing that M's version of events was more probable than P's.

The Court of Appeal held that the evidence of the three convictions had been wrongly admitted. If the judge had solely followed the approach set out in *R v Phillips*, the court was clear that she would have concluded that none of the convictions had a substantial probative value in relation to the issue of propensity. The conclusions of the court, contained in the judgment of Thomas LCJ, may be summarized as follows.

1. The judge is bound to determine the admissibility of a defendant's bad character by a co-defendant, entirely by reference to the bad character provisions of the CJA 2003 and not by reference to the common law principles set out in the House of Lords decision in *R v Randall*.[296]

2. It is particularly important that the test set out in the Criminal Justice Act 2003 is the test solely applied for admissibility because the court has no discretion to exclude evidence admissible under s 101(1)(e) where the statutory conditions for admissibility are met, unlike the position between the prosecution and the defendant. The test of 'substantial probative value' to an important matter in issue between a defendant and a co-defendant under s 101(1)(e) is higher than that applicable under s 101(1)(d), which is the test of 'relevance' to an important matter in issue between the defendant and the prosecution.[297]

3. When applying the test in s 101(1)(e), the judge, as is explained in *R v Phillips*[298] has to answer two questions in relation to propensity: (1) whether the evidence has substantial

---

[294] [2016] 4 WLR 51, CA.
[295] [2004] 1 WLR 1413, HL.
[296] [2004] 1 WLR 56, HL at [23].
[297] At [24].
[298] [2012] 1 Cr App R 332 (25), CA.

probable value and (2) whether the matter in respect of which the evidence is substantially probative, is a matter of substantial importance in the context of the case as a whole.[299]

4. The word 'substantial' is an ordinary word and needs no gloss, because, as is pointed out in *R v Phillips*,[300] attempts to add the gloss of 'more than merely trivial' are potentially misleading. Accordingly, the word 'substantial' should not be paraphrased or the subject of exegesis, but should be given its ordinary unelaborated meaning.[301]

5. Where statute has abolished the common law applicable to a subject and provided a clear statutory code, it is neither necessary nor desirable to refer to the old law, and this is particularly so in relation to the Criminal Justice Act 2003, given the length of time that has elapsed since its coming into force.[302]

6. The Court of Appeal has emphasized the significant change brought about by the Criminal Justice Act 2003 in a number of decisions, including *R v Chopra*[303] (there has been a sea change in the law and it is not necessary to ask what the position would be under the old law); *R v Bullen*[304] (the old law is not to be brought back by a restrictive interpretation); and *R v Zafan Akhtar Saleem*[305] (different approaches are to be applied as a result of the coming into force of the 2003 Act and there is a need to concentrate on the statutory language). As a result of all the new authority on the bad character provisions of the 2003 Act, there should be no need to refer to the old law on the admissibility of character evidence.[306]

7. As to when applications to admit evidence of bad character should be made, it is usually better to postpone such applications until after some of the evidence has been heard. This approach enables the parties and the court to form a clear judgement as to the significance and value of the bad character evidence.[307]

Evidence admissible only on behalf of the co-accused

Evidence is only admissible under s 101(1)(e) on behalf of the co-defendant. The prosecution cannot rely upon s 101(1)(e), nor can another co-defendant, unless the evidence is also of substantial probative value in relation to an important matter in issue between the defendant and that other co-defendant. Section 104(2) provides that:

(2) only evidence—
  (a) which is to be (or has been) adduced by the co-defendant, or
  (b) which a witness is to be invited to give (or has given) in cross-examination by the co-defendant,
  is admissible under section 101(1)(e).

---

[299] At [26].

[300] At 348–9.

[301] At [26]. Cf the Explanatory Notes, para 375.

[302] At [27].

[303] [2007] 1 Cr App R 225 (16), CA.

[304] [2008] 2 Cr App R 364 (25), CA.

[305] [2007] EWCA Crim 1923 at [22] and [23].

[306] At [28]–[29]. Concerning this approach, see comments earlier in the chapter under **Abolition of the common law rules**, p 555.

[307] See [31].

No exclusionary discretion

Because evidence admissible under s 101(1)(e) is only admissible on behalf of a co-defendant, there is no discretionary power to exclude it.[308] As noted previously, in *R v Phillips* it was stated that there is an assumption that the requirement that evidence must have enhanced probative value before it is admitted under s101(1)(e) means the risk of unfair prejudice is removed. There is also an assumption that a co-defendant should be free to adduce any evidence relevant to his case, whether or not it prejudices the defendant, a principle established at common law and which applied in relation both to evidence going to the guilt of the defendant and to cross-examination of the defendant in order to impugn his credibility. The exclusionary discretions under s 101(3) or under s 78 of the Police and Criminal Evidence Act 1984 therefore do not apply and 'it remains good law that there is no general discretion to refuse to allow one defendant to adduce admissible evidence against another on the broad ground that its prejudicial effect exceeds its probative value.'[309] Additionally, it would appear that there is no scope for relying on Art 6 of the European Convention on Human Rights as a basis for exclusion once a judge has established that the evidence meets the requirements of the statutory test.[310] However, in rare cases where there has been a deliberate manipulation of the Criminal Procedure Rules the only way to ensure fairness might well be to exclude the evidence, even if it has the quality required by s 101(1)(e).[311]

It will be convenient to consider separately, evidence admissible under s 101(1)(e) which is relevant to the guilt of the accused and evidence which is relevant to his credibility.

Bad character evidence under s 101(1)(e) relevant to the guilt of the accused
Evidence of propensity

For the purposes of s 101(1)(e), bad character evidence will be admissible only if it has substantial probative value in relation to an important matter in issue. In *R v Phillips* the Court of Appeal said that '"substantial probative value" means enhanced capability to prove or disprove a fact in issue and the threshold is not to be understated.'[312] The second appeal in the case of *R v Edwards*[313] (*R v McLean*) considered the admissibility of evidence of the accused ML's propensity, on behalf of co-accused S, to show that ML was more likely to be the perpetrator. The complainant OT was invited to come to a flat to collect some money he was owed. When he arrived with his brother, other men were present, a fight broke out, and he was attacked and wounded. ML and S were jointly charged with wounding with intent to cause grievous bodily harm and each told an entirely different story as to what had occurred. ML said that he was not present at the time of the attack and had no involvement in it, and OT had been attacked by two others, one of whom must have been S. S said that he was present, but not a party to the attack and that ML had attacked OT and OT's brother with a knife. The Court of Appeal held that the judge was correct in allowing S to adduce, under s 101(1)(e), evidence of ML's previous convictions for violence, which were for wounding using a knife (1998), two offences of battery (2001), and an offence of affray (2004). The evidence had

---

[308] *R v Assani* [2008] EWCA Crim 2563 at [10]. See also *R v Platt* [2016] 4 WLR 51, CA at [24].
[309] See *R v Jarvis* [2008] EWCA Crim 488 at [33], citing *R v Miller* [1952] Cr App R 169.
[310] See *R v Musone* [2007] 1 WLR 2467, CA at [52].
[311] Ibid at [59]–[60].
[312] [2012] 1 Cr App R 332 (25) at 347.
[313] [2006] 1 WLR 1524, CA at [51]–[52].

substantial probative value in relation to the issue of who was more likely to be the assailant, which was an important matter in issue between S and ML within the meaning of s 112.[314]

In *R v Platt*, by contrast, evidence of the accused's propensity did not have substantial probative value and could not be introduced under s 101(1)(e). *R v Platt* is considered earlier in this chapter.[315] It will be recalled that the accused and co-accused were jointly tried for a brutal murder and that the victim's body had been set on fire using accelerant. The character evidence of the accused which was wrongly admitted under s 101(1)(e) was a 23-year-old conviction for arson and two convictions for grievous bodily harm, one 19 years old and the other 11 years old. It was held that: 'the conviction of arson was a conviction when the appellant was 15 and, although accelerant was used, it was a completely different type of offence from the offence in the present case, where accelerant was used to start a fire to attempt to destroy evidence. The grievous bodily harm offences were of some age and in a completely different context. None were of substantial probative value and they should not have been admitted.[316]

Propensity where the accused has put his own character in issue

Where an accused puts his own character in issue, this is capable of being an important matter in issue and the co-accused may adduce evidence of substantial probative value to show that the accused has a propensity and is not the kind of person he says he is. It is instructive to consider two common law illustrations of the principle, notwithstanding the injunction in *R v Platt* against using the common law as a guide to interpretation of the 2003 Act.[317] In *Lowery v R*[318] either the accused L or K, or both, must have murdered a little girl in a cruel and sadistic way. In his defence, L emphasized his good character, stressed that he was unlikely to behave in such a manner, and said that his fear of K meant that he was unable to prevent K murdering the girl. K's defence was that he was under the influence of drugs and was powerless to prevent L from killing. The Privy Council held that because L had put his character in issue by stating that he was not the sort of man to have committed the offence, K was properly allowed to call evidence of a psychologist to the effect that L had a strong aggressive drive, lacked self-control, appeared to take sadistic pleasure from observing the suffering of others, and was more likely to have committed the offence than K. In the second example, *R v Douglass*,[319] it was held that where a cut-throat defence is being run by two accused jointly charged with an offence and evidence of the bad character of one of them is relevant to the guilt or innocence of the other, the evidence is admissible whether they are alleged to have committed the offence by way of joint enterprise or by separate but contributory means. D and P were charged with causing death by reckless driving. The prosecution alleged that D had been drinking and was trying to prevent P from overtaking and that P, vying for position, had collided with an oncoming car. P did not testify, but his counsel cross-examined P's girlfriend to elicit from her that P had never drunk alcohol in the two years that she had known him. The clear purpose was to suggest that P, unlike D, was unlikely to have been affected by alcohol so as to have driven badly. Applying *Lowery v R*,[320] it was held that where

---

[314] Ie a matter of substantial importance in the context of the case as a whole.

[315] See under **Admissibility**, p 601.

[316] At [30].

[317] [2016] 4 WLR 51, CA at [24]–[29].

[318] [1974] AC 85, PC.

[319] (1989) 89 Cr App R 264, CA. Cf *R v Kennedy* [1992] Crim LR 37, CA.

[320] [1974] AC 85, PC. The court also applied the authorities, *R v Bracewell* (1978) 68 Cr App R 44, CA and *R v Miller* [1952] 2 All ER 667 (Winchester Assizes).

one accused adduces evidence of his own lack of propensity and this goes to the issue of a co-accused's guilt, the co-accused may call contradictory evidence. Accordingly, D should have been allowed to adduce evidence of P's previous convictions for motoring offences, including two drink-driving offences.

Bad character evidence under s 101(1)(e) relevant to the credibility of the accused

Insofar as s 101(1)(e) permits a co-accused to introduce evidence of the bad character of the accused relevant to his credibility, it is qualified by s 104(1), which provides as follows:

(1) Evidence which is relevant to the question whether the defendant has a propensity to be untruthful is admissible on that basis under section 101(1)(e) only if the nature or conduct of his defence is such as to undermine the co-defendant's defence.

The meaning of 'propensity to be untruthful' under s 104(1)

One might have supposed that the phrase 'propensity to be untruthful' would bear the same meaning in s 104(1) as it is said to bear in s 103(1)(b), namely that it is not the same as dishonesty and that only misconduct involving false statements or the giving of false evidence would be likely to establish it.[321] In *R v Lawson*[322] however, the court, while accepting that an offence of dishonesty will not necessarily be capable of establishing a propensity for untruthfulness, held that it did not follow that previous convictions not involving the making of false statements or the giving of false evidence are incapable of having substantial probative value in relation to the credibility of an accused. The court was also of the view that 'unreliability'—and it is possible that the court fell into error here by departing from the statutory wording of 'propensity to be untruthful'—was capable of being shown by conduct which did not involve an offence of untruthfulness, ranging from large-scale drug- or people-trafficking via housebreaking to criminal violence; but that whether in a particular case conduct is in fact capable of having the requisite probative value is for the trial judge to decide on all the facts. On the facts of the case before it, the court held that the trial judge was entitled to conclude that a previous conviction for wounding did have the requisite probative value in relation to the credibility of the accused who was charged with manslaughter. Unfortunately, however, no reasons are given—it was felt to be sufficient to defer to 'the feel of the trial judge'.[323] In *R v Jarvis*,[324] it was also held that under s 101(1)(e), evidence of propensity to untruthfulness is not restricted to the making of false statements in the witness box.[325]

The meaning of, 'if the nature or conduct of his defence is such as to undermine the co-defendant's defence'

The words 'nature or conduct of his defence' in s 104(1) make clear that the co-accused's defence may be undermined not only by the evidence of the accused or witnesses called on his behalf, but also in cross-examination of witnesses called by the prosecution or co-accused.

---

[321] See *R v Hanson* [2005] 1 WLR 3169, CA.

[322] [2007] 1 WLR 1191, CA.

[323] Cf *R v Miah* [2011] Crim LR 662, CA, a case of murder by arson, where the Court of Appeal stated obiter that it was very difficult to see how one accused's previous conviction for robbery had substantial probative value in relation to his credibility, given his guilty plea. For an exploration of the difficulties of construction posed by s 104, see Munday, 'Cut-throat Defences and the "Propensity to be Untruthful" under s 104 of the Criminal Justice Act 2003' [2005] Crim LR 624.

[324] [2008] EWCA Crim 488; [2008] Crim LR 266, CA.

[325] [2008] EWCA Crim 488, per Hughes LJ at [30].

In relation to such cross-examination it is submitted that many of the principles laid down in authorities decided under the old law remain valid in relation to s 104(1). Accordingly, as a matter of principle, answers given by an accused under cross-examination are generally to be treated as part of the cross-examiner's case and therefore the accused's bad character should not be admitted where he has been trapped into making an imputation by the form of the question put.[326] However, this would not be the case where the imputation was not necessary in answer to the question put[327] or was voluntary and gratuitous.[328] Nevertheless, the accused's answers under cross-examination do not need to be motivated by hostile intent. It is the effect of the evidence upon the minds of the jury which is material and not the state of mind of the person who gives it, and the test to be applied is therefore objective and not subjective.[329]

Section 104 requires that the nature and conduct of the defence *undermines* the co-defendant's defence and so the section will not be triggered by evidence which does no more than support the prosecution case. Principles laid down in authorities decided before the 2003 Act provide valuable guidance. Thus although in many cases evidence which supports the prosecution case will also undermine the co-accused's defence, if the evidence supports the prosecution case but does not undermine the co-accused's defence, because for example the accused has not raised a defence, it is submitted that evidence of his bad character will not be admissible to attack his credibility under s 101(1)(e).[330] Such evidence will also be inadmissible, it is submitted, where the accused gives evidence to the same effect as the prosecution on a factual matter on which there is no issue between the Crown and the co-accused, because such evidence will not undermine the co-accused's defence.[331] However, it would seem that if a co-accused has only a scintilla or iota of a defence, as when his defence is almost completely undermined by his own testimony which, although he declines to change his plea, amounts to an admission of guilt, there is still the possibility of the accused undermining it.[332] According to *R v Whitnell*,[333] decided under the 2003 Act, where the evidence is evidence of statements by the accused in interview, it does not form part of the prosecution case against the co-accused and if it is not adopted by the accused in the trial, it will not undermine the defence of the co-accused. In this situation, the honesty or reliability of the statements will not be in issue between the accused and co-accused, and, in addition, fairness to the co-accused will be protected by the judge's direction to ignore the statements when considering the case against him.[334]

Evidence which merely contradicts the co-accused or denies participation
The meaning of undermining the defence of the co-accused gave rise to difficulty in cases decided before the 2003 Act where the accused appeared merely to have contradicted the evidence given by a co-accused or to have denied participation in a joint venture. In *R v Bruce*[335]

---

[326] See *R v Jones* (1909) 3 Cr App R 67, CCA. See also *R v Britzman; R v Hall* [1983] 1 WLR 350, CA.
[327] *R v Jones* (1909) 3 Cr App R 67, CCA.
[328] *R v Courtney* [1995] Crim LR 63, CA.
[329] See *Murdoch v Taylor* [1965] AC 574, HL.
[330] Cf *R v Adair* [1990] Crim LR 571, CA.
[331] Cf *R v Crawford* [1998] 1 Cr App R 338, CA.
[332] *R v Mir* [1989] Crim LR 894, CA.
[333] [2014] 1 Cr App R 109 (9), CA.
[334] See also *R v Miah* [2011] Crim LR 662, CA: the accused did not give evidence and statements implicating the co-accused which were made by him in police interview and to medical experts (who interviewed him in relation to a defence of diminished responsibility) were deemed not to have undermined the co-accused's defence.
[335] [1975] 1 WLR 1252, CA at 1259.

for example, it was held that evidence which undermined a co-accused's defence was evidence which made his acquittal less likely,[336] and evidence which provided a different and possibly better defence would not be 'undermining' evidence.[337] It is unclear whether s 104(1) of the 2003 Act falls to be interpreted in the same way. However, it is clear that under s 104(1) evidence which on its face amounts to no more than a denial of participation in a crime or which appears to merely contradict the co-accused, may in appropriate circumstances undermine a co-accused's defence. In *R v Edwards*,[338] the Court of Appeal made the general observation that whether an accused's stance amounts to no more than a denial of participation or gives rise to an important matter in issue between a defendant and a co-defendant under s 101(1)(e) will inevitably turn on the facts of the individual case, and in making this observation, referred to the decision in *R v Varley*.[339] *R v Varley* pre-dates the 2003 Act, but provides a useful illustration of how an accused's denial of participation may undermine a co-accused's defence. V and D were jointly charged with robbery. D's defence was that he did take part but was forced to do so by threats on his life by V. V gave evidence that he had not taken part in the robbery and that D's evidence was untrue. D's counsel was given leave to cross-examine V as to his previous convictions and V was convicted. The Court of Appeal held that a mere denial of participation was not sufficient to justify the admission of the accused's character and that such a denial must lead to the conclusion that if one accused did not participate then it must have been the other who did it (although according to *R v Crawford*[340] 'must' went too far and 'may' was more appropriate). The court also held that where one accused asserts a view of the joint venture which is directly contradicted by the other, such contradiction may be evidence against the co-accused. Applying these principles, it was held that D could properly admit evidence of V's convictions[341] because V's evidence amounted to saying not only that D was telling lies, but also that D was a participant on his own and not acting under duress.

Section 101(1)(f)—prosecution evidence to correct a false impression given by the defendant

Under s 101(1)(f), prosecution evidence of the defendant's bad character is admissible if 'it is evidence to correct a false impression given by the defendant'.[342] Section 101(1)(f), together with s 105, which supplements it, are based upon the recommendations of the Law Commission, but lack the Commission's important safeguards. These included a requirement of enhanced relevance, that is, *substantial* probative value in correcting the false impression, a requirement to consider a number of detailed factors and, in the case of evidence of prejudicial effect,

---

[336] Cf *R v Hatton* (1976) 64 Cr App R 88, CA. A denied there was a plan to steal scrap metal. H gave evidence that both he and A had been parties to a plan but denied that either of them had acted dishonestly. It was held that H had given evidence against A.

Per Stephenson LJ [1975] 1 WLR 1252, CA at 1259.

[337] See also *R v Kirkpatrick* [1998] Crim LR 63, CA.

[338] [2006] 1 WLR 1524, CA.

[339] [1982] 75 Cr App R 242, CA.

[340] See *R v Crawford* [1998] 1 Cr App R 338, CA. See also *R v Kirkpatrick* [1998] Crim LR 63, CA.

[341] The evidence need not be confined to the fact of the conviction but may extend to the details of the offence: *R v Reid* [1989] Crim LR 719, CA. Cf *R v McLeod* [1994] 1 WLR 1500, CA.

[342] See *R v Assani* [2008] EWCA Crim 2563: the gateways under s 101(1)(f) and (g) are restricted to prosecution evidence and are not available to a co-accused.

a requirement that admissibility be in the interests of justice.[343] Furthermore, although it is submitted that evidence admissible under s 101(1)(f) is subject to the common law discretion to exclude and s 78 of the Police and Criminal Evidence Act 1984, it is not subject to the exclusionary discretion in s 101(3).

Section 105 of the 2003 Act provides as follows:

(1) For the purposes of section 101(1)(f)—
    (a) the defendant gives a false impression if he is responsible for the making of an express or implied assertion which is apt to give the court or jury a false or misleading impression about the defendant;
    (b) evidence to correct such an impression is evidence which has probative value in correcting it.
(2) A defendant is treated as being responsible for the making of an assertion if—
    (a) the assertion is made by the defendant in the proceedings (whether or not in evidence given by him),
    (b) the assertion was made by the defendant—
        (i) on being questioned under caution, before charge, about the offence with which he is charged, or
        (ii) on being charged with the offence or officially informed that he might be prosecuted for it, and evidence of the assertion is given in the proceedings,
    (c) the assertion is made by a witness called by the defendant,
    (d) the assertion is made by any witness in cross-examination in response to a question asked by the defendant that is intended to elicit it, or is likely to do so,
    or
    (e) the assertion was made by any person out of court, and the defendant adduces evidence of it in the proceedings.
(3) A defendant who would otherwise be treated as responsible for the making of an assertion shall not be so treated if, or to the extent that, he withdraws it or disassociates himself from it.
(4) Where it appears to the court that a defendant, by means of his conduct (other than the giving of evidence) in the proceedings, is seeking to give the court or jury an impression about himself that is false or misleading, the court may if it appears just to do so treat the defendant as being responsible for the making of an assertion which is apt to give that impression.
(5) In subsection (4) 'conduct' includes appearance or dress.
(6) Evidence is admissible under section 101(1)(f) only if it goes no further than is necessary to correct the false impression.
(7) Only prosecution evidence is admissible under section 101(1)(f).

Whether the accused has given a false impression is obviously a question for the judge. That question and the question whether there is evidence which may properly serve to correct the false impression, are fact-specific.[344] It is submitted that the risk of prejudice, where corrective evidence is admitted only to be subsequently ruled inadmissible, is such that in many cases the question of admissibility will need to be the subject of a ruling by the judge in the absence of the jury. As to the timing of applications under s 101(1)(f), they can be expected to be made when the accused is giving evidence rather than after he has finished.[345]

---

[343] Law Com No 273, Cm 5257 (2001), Draft Bill, cl 10.

[344] *R v Renda* [2006] 1 WLR 2948, CA at [19]. In an appeal, the court will often be able to determine whether the accused has given a false impression by looking at the transcript of the trial: *R v Omotoso* [2018] EWCA Crim 1394 at [45].

[345] *R v Omotoso* [2018] EWCA Crim 1394 at [51].

False impression by express or implied assertions, or assertions by conduct

A simple denial of the offence cannot be treated as either an express or implied false impression for the purposes of s 101(1)(f).[346] 'Express' false assertions, for the purposes of s 105(1) (a), would cover, for example, false assertions that the accused is of good character or a religious man or a man who earns an honest living or who would never use violence. 'Implied' false assertions would cover false assertions relating to the accused's conduct or behaviour from which it can be implied that he is of good character or honest. *R v Samuel*,[347] a decision which pre-dates the 2003 Act, provides a good example. The accused, charged with larceny, gave evidence of previous occasions on which he had restored lost property to its owner and so was held to have been properly cross-examined about his previous convictions for theft. Section 105(1)(a) is also apt to cover false assertions by the accused about his bad character. If, for example, the accused, charged with a sexual offence, falsely asserts that he has only one previous conviction, also for a sexual offence, then corrective evidence would be admissible that in fact he also has previous convictions for offences of dishonesty.

However, assertions that are too unspecific and insubstantial will not justify the introduction of bad character evidence. In *R v Ovba*,[348] for example, the accused was charged with a 'road rage' assault on a bailiff who had used his car to block in her parked car, intending to clamp it. The accused had a previous conviction for robbery and a caution for battery which were introduced in evidence when, under cross-examination, she said she was a 'friendly person' and had witnessed the effect of domestic violence when growing up. The Court of Appeal held that she had not given a false impression because what she said was too unspecific and did not amount to a factual statement that she was not the sort of person who would commit the offences charged. Equally, however, where the accused's assertions are specific, judges should take care not to 'over interpret' what the accused has said and to conclude that he has given a false impression when he has not. In *R v Omotoso*,[349] the accused was asked towards the end of his examination-in-chief, what he did for a living. He replied, 'I was actually an auditor for a company . . . and I was in the process of getting my heavy goods vehicle [HGV] licence.' The judge ruled that he had given the false impression of acting as a professional auditor when his work apparently involved stock-taking. However, in view of the fact that he had made reference to getting his HGV licence, the Court of Appeal was 'very doubtful whether the words [used]. . . could have conveyed the impression that he was acting in some professional capacity or carrying out a professional task.'[350]

An example of a false or misleading impression conveyed by conduct, for the purposes of s 105(4) and (5), would be an accused who, not being a priest, appears in the proceedings wearing a clerical dog collar. However, an accused with many previous convictions for dishonesty does not make a false assertion as to his good character by simply taking the oath or reminding the jury of the oath that he has sworn on the Bible and, on that reasoning, nor will he do so by his conduct in holding and gesticulating with a Bible while in the witness box.[351]

Under s 105(4), the court will only treat the accused as being responsible for the making of an assertion by means of his conduct 'if it appears just to do so', a hurdle presumably

---

[346] *R v Weir* [2006] 1 WLR 1885, CA at [43].
[347] (1956) 40 Cr App R 8, CCA.
[348] [2015] EWCA Crim 725.
[349] [2019] Crim LR 156, CA.
[350] Ibid at [50]–[51]. See also *R v Stokes* [2015] EWCA Crim 1911.
[351] See *R v Robinson* [2001] Crim LR 478, CA, decided under the 1898 Act, s 1(3)(ii).

designed to prevent overuse or abuse of the subsection. For example, many accused will dress up for their court appearance, wearing outfits which they would normally wear only on very special occasions. Section 105 should not cover, it is submitted, the case of the plumber or plasterer who appears in court in his best suit. It would be otherwise, however, if he were to sport a regimental tie or blazer, never having served in the army.

The evidence to correct a false impression

Evidence to correct a false impression must have probative value in correcting it,[352] but must go no further than is necessary to correct it.[353] Thus if the accused expressly asserts that he 'earns an honest living', the corrective evidence may include evidence of his previous convictions for crimes of dishonesty, but not evidence of his previous convictions for, say, assault or driving with excess alcohol. Where it is questionable whether the accused has given a false impression, but the judge has justifiable concerns that the jury could be misled, the concerns may be dealt with by a corrective admission rather than by introducing evidence of bad character. In *R v Omotoso*,[354] for example, if there had been justifiable concerns that the accused's use of the word 'auditor' might have misled the jury as to the true nature of his work (apparently, stock-taking), the problem could have been addressed by a simple admission clarifying what his work actually involved.[355]

In some cases, problems are likely to be encountered in identifying precisely what the false or misleading impression is. For example, if an accused is charged with inflicting grievous bodily harm in an 'off the ball' incident during the course of a rugby match, and gives evidence that he has no previous convictions, is evidence admissible to show his disciplinary record of violent play on the rugby field?[356] The same problem exists in the case of implied assertions or assertions by conduct. The accused wearing a clerical collar presumably conveys the impression not only that he is a priest, but also that he behaves as a priest should, and therefore the corrective evidence should not be confined to evidence which goes to show that he is not a priest, or has been defrocked, but should extend to general evidence of his misconduct or disposition to misconduct.

Withdrawal or disassociation from an assertion

Under s 105(2)(d), an accused is treated as being responsible for an assertion made by a witness cross-examined by (or, presumably, on behalf of) him, but only if the assertion was in response to a question intended to elicit it or which was likely to elicit it. If the witness volunteers a false impression about the accused, the accused will not be treated as being responsible for the making of the volunteered assertion and evidence will not be admissible to correct it.

---

[352] Section 105(1)(b).

[353] Section 105(6). *R v Omotoso* [2018] EWCA Crim 1394 is an example of a case where the evidence went 'far further than was "necessary to correct" any false impression within the meaning of s 105(6).' On the other hand, the admissibility of an item of evidence is not conditional upon it being capable, in and of itself, of amounting to a complete answer to the false impression: *R v Fender* [2018] EWCA Crim 2898 at [25].

[354] [2018] EWCA Crim 1395.

[355] At [51].

[356] Applying the 1898 Act, s 1(3)(ii), the answer in *R v Marsh* [1994] Crim LR 52, CA was, 'yes'. See also *R v Spartley* [2007] EWCA Crim 1789, where the accused charged with conspiracy to import drugs and supply them, said in his police interview that he had never been involved in the supply of drugs. Evidence of an interview with Dutch Police seven years before in which he had admitted being a cannabis courier between Spain and Holland was properly admitted.

In contrast, under s 105(2)(c) an accused is treated as being responsible for an assertion made by a witness called by him, and corrective evidence will be admissible in this situation where the witness volunteers a false impression as much as when he asserts it in answer to a question intended to elicit it or which was likely to elicit it. However, in this situation it seems that the accused can prevent the introduction of corrective evidence by disassociating himself from the assertion made by the witness, in reliance upon s 105(3). An accused who no longer stands by a false assertion made by him and introduced in evidence under s 105(2)(b) by the prosecution, would also be well advised to withdraw it.

In cases in which the accused himself makes, or adduces evidence of, a false assertion, s 105(3) also provides him with the opportunity to embark upon a damage limitation exercise. For example, if the accused makes, or adduces evidence of, a false assertion to the effect that he is of good character, but then withdraws or disassociates himself from the assertion, he will thereby prevent the admission of corrective evidence of, say, his previous convictions, but the jury will by then be aware that he is not of good character and also, in cases in which the assertion was made by him in giving his evidence, that he is not always a reliable witness. However, an accused must take the initiative if he wishes to rely on s 105(3); a concession extracted in cross-examination will not normally amount to a withdrawal or disassociation for the purposes of s 105(3).[357]

Corrective evidence as to guilt or credibility of the accused

Given the breadth of provision for the admissibility of evidence of disposition under s 101(1)(d), presumably such evidence will only rarely be admitted as corrective evidence under s 101(1)(f). Where such evidence is admitted under s 101(1)(f), however, it seems clear that it will go not only to the credibility of the accused but also to the likelihood of his guilt, and that the jury should be directed accordingly. It remains to be seen whether the position will be the same in the case of corrective evidence which involves misconduct, that is, the commission of an offence or other reprehensible behaviour. However, it is submitted that there is much force in the argument that where an accused makes, or adduces evidence of, a false assertion as to his good character, he generally does so for the purpose of showing that it is unlikely that he committed the offence charged, and the corrective evidence is introduced to show the contrary, and not merely to attack his credibility.[358]

Discretionary exclusion

If, as has been submitted, prosecution evidence admissible under s 101 may be excluded in reliance upon the common law discretionary power to exclude prosecution evidence the prejudicial effect of which outweighs its probative value, there may well be only limited scope for the exercise of the discretion in relation to evidence admissible under s 101(1)(f) since the exclusion of such evidence may seriously mislead the jury.[359]

Section 101(1)(g)—prosecution evidence where the defendant has made an attack on another person's character

Under s 101(1)(g) of the 2003 Act, prosecution evidence of the accused's bad character is admissible if 'the defendant has made an attack on another person's character'. Where s 101(1)(g) is triggered, evidence of the accused's bad character is admissible even if he elects

---

[357] *R v Renda* [2006] 1 WLR 2948, CA at [21].

[358] For dicta to this effect in relation to the 1898 Act, s 1(3)(ii), see Viscount Sankey in *Maxwell v DPP* [1935] AC 309, HL at 319 and per Lord Goddard CJ in *R v Samuel* (1956) 40 Cr App R 8, CCA at 12.

[359] See *R v Marsh* [1994] Crim LR 52, CA. See also *R v D* [2012] EWCA Crim 2163.

not to testify. The purpose of the gateway, in the case of an attack on a prosecution witness, was explained by Underhill J in *R v Lamaletie*:[360]

> The conception underlying [the] gateway . . . is that where a defendant has impugned the character of a prosecution witness the jury will be assisted in deciding who to believe by knowing the defendant's character.

Section 101(1)(g), as supplemented by s 106, is in some measure based on the recommendations of the Law Commission but, as in the case of s 101(1)(f), lacks the Commission's important safeguards, including the requirement of enhanced relevance, the requirement to consider a number of detailed factors and, in the case of evidence of prejudicial effect, the requirement that admissibility be in the interests of justice.[361] The provisions also depart from the recommendation that evidence should not be admissible under the gateway where the attack has to do with the alleged facts of the offence or is in connection with the investigation or prosecution of the offence, as when the accused blames another for the offence or asserts that another has invented the allegation against him.[362]

The evidence admissible

In terms of the evidence admissible under the gateway, the courts take a 'broad brush' approach.[363] Accordingly, convictions will be admitted which differ significantly from the offence charged, but which nonetheless enable the jury to know from what sort of person allegations against the witness came.[364] In *R v C*,[365] the Court of Appeal observed that where credibility is in issue, the authorities demonstrated that all the convictions of an accused could be potentially relevant under s 101(1)(g) to help the jury assess his character, although the factual details and circumstances of the convictions would not be required unless the issue was propensity to be untruthful.[366] In *R v C*, the accused was charged with sexual offences against his stepdaughters and gave evidence that they had colluded to make false allegations against him. Noting the fundamental nature of the accused's attack, the court held that the judge was justified in admitting convictions for vehicle theft and possession of an offensive weapon, robbery, and firearms, some of which dated from 20 years previously.

An attack on another person's character

Section 106 of the 2003 Act provides as follows:

(1) For the purposes of section 101(1)(g) a defendant makes an attack on another person's character if—

    (a) he adduces evidence attacking the other person's character,

    (b) he (or any legal representative appointed under section 38(4) of the Youth Justice and Criminal Evidence Act 1999 to cross-examine a witness in his interests) asks questions in cross-examination that are intended to elicit such evidence, or are likely to do so, or

---

[360] [2008] EWCA Crim 314 at [15]. Lord Devlin's explanation in *R v Cook* [1959] 2 QB 340 at 347 of the same principle underlying the old law was cited with approval.

[361] Law Com No 273, Cm 5257 (2001), Draft Bill, cl 9.

[362] Ibid, cl 9(2).

[363] Spencer, *Evidence of Bad Character* (Oxford, 2009) para 4.138. See also *R v Cox* [2014] EWCA Crim 804.

[364] See *R v Singh* [2007] EWCA Crim 2140 at [10]. On a charge of robbery and assault, evidence of bad character relevant to credibility properly included the accused's convictions for violent disorder, assault on police officers, harassment, criminal damage, and driving with excess alcohol.

[365] [2011] EWCA Crim 939.

[366] Ibid. See *R v Jenkins* (1945) 31 Cr App R1, CA, and *Selvey v DPP* [1970] AC 304, HL, both cited by the court in *R v C*.

(c) evidence is given of an imputation about the other person made by the defendant—

    (i) on being questioned under caution, before charge, about the offence with which he is charged, or

    (ii) on being charged with the offence or officially informed that he might be prosecuted for it.

(2) In subsection (1) 'evidence attacking the other person's character' means evidence to the effect that the other person—

    (a) has committed an offence (whether a different offence from the one with which the defendant is charged or the same one), or

    (b) has behaved, or is disposed to behave, in a reprehensible way; and 'imputation about the other person' means an assertion to that effect.

(3) Only prosecution evidence is admissible under section 101(1)(g).

Under s 106, the circumstances in which a defendant makes an attack on another person's character are different from the circumstances under s 105 in which the accused is treated as being responsible for the making of a false assertion. Thus s 106 appears not to apply where an attack on another person's character is made by the accused while being cross-examined at the hands of either the prosecution or any co-accused. However, although matters are not spelt out in the way that they are in s 105, it seems reasonably clear that s 106(1)(a) covers an attack on another person's character when either made by a witness called by the accused or contained in a hearsay statement adduced by the accused. Evidence 'given' under s 106(1)(c) may be 'given' by the prosecution, provided that it is relevant to the issues in the case and otherwise admissible, as opposed to merely providing a basis for satisfying gateway (g);[367] and because s 106 contains no equivalent of s 105(3), this will trigger s 101(1)(g) even if the accused wishes to withdraw the out-of-court statement on which the prosecution rely or to disassociate himself from it.

An 'attack on another person's character' means an attack in front of the jury and what is said in the absence of the jury in a *voir dire* should not form part of the judge's decision as to whether s 101(1)(g) is triggered (although it may provide a focus for the judge in respect of what is said in front of the jury).[368] As to the timing of an application under s 101(1)(g), where the parties have agreed that the accused's defence will involve an attack on another's character it would be usual for the application to be made before the accused gives evidence.[369] Where the judge considers that s 101(1)(g) is triggered but the prosecution makes no application, the judge must take great care if he decides to prompt one. Judges must be scrupulous not to take on the function of the prosecutor or give that appearance, and any suggestion to the prosecution must be expressed carefully.[370] Judges must also take into account the possibility that advocates may have already agreed an approach or that the prosecution advocate has reached an independent decision for good reasons.[371]

---

[367] *R v Nelson* [2006] EWCA Crim 3412. See also *R v Renda* [2006] 1 WLR 2948, CA at [29]–[38].

[368] *R v Omotoso* [2018] EWCA Crim 1394 at [53] and [58]. The judge should not have taken into consideration what was put to a police officer during an abuse of process application.

[369] Ibid at [54].

[370] Ibid at [47].

[371] Ibid at [54].

The admissibility of the attacking evidence

The definition of 'evidence attacking the other person's character' in s 106(2) must be read together with s 100 of the Act since the attacking evidence will be evidence of bad character of a person other than the accused. Under s 100, it will be recalled, except where all parties agree to the admissibility of evidence of the bad character of a person other than the accused, such evidence is only admissible with the leave of the court and such leave can only be granted if the evidence is either (a) important explanatory evidence; or (b) has substantial probative value in relation to a matter which is in issue in the proceedings and is of substantial importance in the context of the case as a whole. Thus evidence to attack another person's character which does not meet the requirements of s 100 will be inadmissible.

The person whose character has been attacked

It is clear from s 106 that 'another person' may or may not be a witness in the case. Thus an attack may be made on a victim who dies by reason of the crime, for example a victim of murder, manslaughter, or causing death by dangerous driving, a victim of an offence of violence who, by reason of the injuries sustained, is unable to be called as a witness, a victim who does not give evidence by reason of threats, interference, or intimidation, a person whose hearsay statement is in evidence in the proceedings, etc. However, it is also reasonably clear that 'another person' must be an identified individual. The definition of 'evidence attacking the other person's character' in s 106(2) clearly envisages that the identity of that person is known.

Evidence which amounts to an attack

Section 106(2)(a) covers cases in which the evidence is to the effect that the person has committed either the very offence with which the accused is charged or some other offence. Section 106(2)(b), which refers to evidence to the effect that the other person has behaved or is disposed to behave in a reprehensible way, will typically cover evidence of misconduct on the part of the police or prosecution witnesses. However, where part of the accused's defence involves cross-examining a police officer about flaws in a police investigation, this is not of itself objectionable and s 101(1)(g) should not be invoked too quickly, which might unfairly shut down a legitimate line of cross-examination.[372] Nor is it objectionable in itself for the accused to call a witness to undermine the evidence of a police officer.[373] In some situations where it appears that a legitimate line of questioning by the accused's advocate might risk going too far and triggering s 101(1)(g), a gentle hint from the judge might be sufficient.[374]

The question whether the evidence amounts to an attack on another person's character is a matter for the trial judge to assess and determine, and the Court of Appeal will not intervene unless the judge's decision is outside the range of reasonable decisions open to her.[375] In *R v Noble*,[376] the Court of Appeal held that the trial judge was entitled to consider there had been an attack on prosecution witnesses P and B in circumstances where B was challenged about having seen the accused carrying a mask and was then asked if he had spoken to P. The judge had seen and heard the evidence and could assess the tone and import of the

---

[372] *R v Omotoso* [2019] Crim LR 156, CA.

[373] Ibid.

[374] Ibid. See also *R v Noble* [2017] Crim LR 473.

[375] See *R v Noble* [2016] EWCA Crim 2219 at [81] and [82].

[376] Ibid.

cross-examination, and it was not unreasonable for her to conclude that the line of questioning followed amounted to an imputation that B and P had put their heads together. However, it is submitted that this is a decision on the borderline.[377] Other more clear-cut examples of the kind of evidence which could amount to an attack can be found in cases decided before the 2003 Act: allegations that the prosecutor or a witness for the prosecution invented the crime alleged,[378] obtained a confession by bribes,[379] deliberately held the accused on remand in order to concoct evidence,[380] manufactured a confession statement,[381] completely fabricated part of his evidence,[382] or asked a relative to have a quiet word with the accused to get him to talk and admit the offence.[383] Looking at s 106(2) as a whole, there is no doubt that, subject to discretionary exclusion, evidence of the bad character of the accused is admissible under s 101(1)(g) notwithstanding that the attack on another person's character is a necessary or justifiable part of his defence.

In *R v Hanson*[384] it was held that pre-2003 Act authorities will continue to apply when assessing whether an attack has been made on another person's character under s 101(1)(g), to the extent that they are compatible with s 106.

The distinction between an attack and assertions of innocence or denials of guilt
Under authorities which pre-date the 2003 Act, mere assertions of innocence by the accused, or emphatic denials of guilt, did not result in him losing his shield and were to be distinguished from attacks on the veracity of the prosecutor or a prosecution witness, which did have that result.[385] It is submitted that such a distinction remains valid for the purposes of s 101(1)(g). The distinction, however, is difficult and narrow, as is apparent in an early and classic example of a disputed confession, given by Lord Hewart CJ in *R v Jones*:[386]

> It was one thing for the appellant to deny that he had made the confession; but it is another thing to say that the whole thing was an elaborate and deliberate concoction on the part of the inspector.

The difficulty and narrowness of the distinction lies in the fact that in some cases, to deny that the confession was made necessarily means, by implication, that the police have fabricated evidence, and although s 106, unlike s 105, does not refer to implied as well as express assertions, it is submitted that an accused will trigger s 101(1)(g) where an attack on another person's character is made by necessary implication, rather than in terms. In *R v Britzman; R v Hall*,[387] decided before the 2003 Act, the Court of Appeal set out guidelines, some of which, it is submitted, remain valid for the purposes of s 101(1)(g). The facts were that police officers

---

[377] The court recognized that a different judge might have come to a different conclusion: ibid at [82]. See 'Commentary', [2017] Crim LR 473, CA.

[378] *Selvey v DPP* [1970] AC 304, HL. See *R v Singh* [2007] EWCA Crim 2140.

[379] *R v Wright* (1910) 5 Cr App R 131, CCA.

[380] *R v Jones* (1923) 17 Cr App R 117, CCA.

[381] *R v Clark* [1955] 2 QB 469, CCA.

[382] *R v Levy* (1966) 50 Cr App R 238, CA. See also *R v Dunkley* [1927] 1 KB 323, CCA.

[383] *R v Courtney* [1995] Crim LR 63, CA.

[384] [2005] 1 WLR 3169, CA at [14].

[385] See per Lord Goddard CJ in *R v Clark* [1955] 2 QB 469, CCA at 478, applied in *R v St Louis and Fitzroy Case* (1984) 79 Cr App R 53, CA.

[386] (1923) 17 Cr App R 117, CCA at 120.

[387] [1983] 1 WLR 350, CA.

had given evidence of admissions made by the appellant both during lengthy interviews recorded in writing and in the course of a shouting match between Britzman and Hall in the cells. The appellant denied the interviews and the shouting match had ever taken place and this was put to the officers in cross-examination. The Court of Appeal, noting that it was not a case of a denial of a single answer and that there was no suggestion of mistake or misunderstanding, held that the nature and conduct of the defence did involve imputations on the character of the prosecution witnesses. To deny that the conversations took place necessarily meant by implication that the police officers had given false evidence which they had made up to get a conviction. It was held that a distinction could not be drawn between a defence so conducted as to make specific allegations of fabrication and one in which such allegations arose by way of necessary and reasonable implication.[388] Lawton LJ stated:

> the exercise of discretion in favour of defendants . . . should be used if there is nothing more than a denial, however emphatic or offensively made, of an act or even a short series of acts amounting to one incident or in what was said to have been a short interview . . . The position would be different however if there were a denial of evidence of a long period of detailed observation extending over hours and . . . where there were denials of long conversations . . . cross-examination should only be allowed if the judge is sure that there is no possibility of mistake, misunderstanding or confusion and that the jury will inevitably have to decide whether the prosecution witnesses have fabricated evidence. Defendants sometimes make wild allegations when giving evidence. Allowance should be made for the strain of being in the witness box and the exaggerated use of language which sometimes results from such strain or lack of education or mental stability.[389]

Discretionary exclusion

Evidence admissible under s 101(1)(g) is open to discretionary exclusion under s 101(3) if it appears to the court that the admission of the evidence would have such an adverse effect on the fairness of the proceedings that the court ought not to admit it.[390] It is incumbent on the judge to consider the exclusionary discretion.[391] Evidence open to exclusion under s 101(3) is also open to exclusion, it is submitted, in reliance upon the common law discretion to exclude prosecution evidence the prejudicial effect of which outweighs its probative value.[392]

The possible grounds for discretionary exclusion now fall to be considered.

An attack on the character of a person who is not a witness or victim

To admit evidence of the accused's bad character under s 101(1)(g) by reason of an attack on the character of someone who is neither a witness nor a victim of the offence, will *normally* have such an adverse effect on the fairness of the proceedings that the court ought not to admit it. An exception would be, for example, where there is an attack on a witness or victim to the effect that he conspired with the person who is neither a witness nor a victim to fabricate the allegation. An attack on that person may influence the jury in their view of the evidence of the witness or victim.[393]

---

[388] See also *R v Owen* (1985) 83 Cr App R 100, CA.

[389] [1983] 1 WLR 350 at 355.

[390] See *R v Chrysostomou* [2010] Crim LR 942, CA.

[391] *R v Omotoso* [2019] Crim LR 156, CA.

[392] See, in this chapter, under **Discretion to exclude**, p 575.

[393] *R v Nelson* [2006] EWCA Crim 3412.

Evidence of bad character irrelevant or disproportionate to the bad character in the attack

As noted earlier, evidence admissible under s 101(1)(g) may be relevant not only to credibility but also to propensity to commit offences of the kind charged.[394]

However, it is submitted that bad character evidence that has little or no bearing on the credibility of the accused or his defence and does not show his propensity to commit offences of the kind charged, even if admissible in law, should be excluded by the exercise of discretion. For example, in a case of fraud, a previous conviction for fraud may be relevant to both credibility and propensity, but evidence of the accused's disposition towards sexual misconduct or cruelty to animals could serve no purpose but prejudice.[395] Equally, it is submitted, there is scope for exercise of the discretion where the bad character of the accused is disproportionate to the bad character of the person whose character has been attacked. In *R v Burke*,[396] Ackner LJ, rehearsing the principles from *Selvey v DPP*[397] upon which the discretion to exclude was exercised under the old law,[398] said that in the ordinary and normal case the trial judge may feel that if the credit of the prosecutor or his witnesses has been attacked, it is only fair that the jury should have before them material on which they can form their judgment whether the accused is any more worthy of belief than those he has attacked. However, he also said:

> The trial judge must weigh the prejudicial effect of the questions against the damage done by the attack on the prosecution's witnesses, and must generally exercise his discretion so as to secure a trial that is fair both to the prosecution and the defence . . .
>
> Cases must occur in which it would be unjust to admit evidence of a character gravely prejudicial to the accused, even though there may be some tenuous grounds for holding it technically admissible . . .

Attacks which are a necessary or justifiable part of the defence

It is clear that under s 101(3), impact on the fairness of the proceedings must be assessed by reference to matters other than what the motive or intention of the accused was in making an attack on another's character.[399] However, in some cases it will be obvious that the attack was necessary to enable him to establish his defence and although, as we have seen, this will not prevent the admissibility in law of his bad character, and although the discretion to exclude should not invariably or even generally be exercised in these circumstances, because that would amount to a qualification to s 101(1)(g) under the guise of discretion, it is submitted that the discretion should be exercised, as necessary, to prevent too severe an application of s 101(1)(g). However, where the accused deliberately departs to a significant extent from the ambit of his defence as the judge understood it to be and launches a wholesale attack, applying s 101(1)(g) is unlikely to affect the fairness of a trial.[400]

---

[394] See, in this chapter, under **Admissibility and use**, p 573.

[395] But see *R v Highton* [2005] 1 WLR 3472, CA, a case of common assault in which the Court of Appeal could see no grounds to challenge the judge's refusal to exclude, under s 101(3), two drink-related driving offences, failure to provide a specimen and driving with excess alcohol.

[396] (1985) 82 Cr App R 156, CA.

[397] [1970] AC 304, HL.

[398] Section 1 (3)(ii) of the Criminal Evidence Act 1989.

[399] *R v Bovell* [2005] 2 Cr App R 401(27), CA at [32]. See also *R v Singh* [2007] EWCA Crim 2140 where it was argued unsuccessfully that the accused's attack was not gratuitous.

[400] See *R v M(E)* [2014] 2 Cr App R 484 (29), CA.

Similarities between the facts of previous offences and the offence charged

As previously noted, evidence of the accused's bad character is admissible under s 101(1)(g) because of the bearing it has on the credibility of the defence case and, it is submitted, a judge should direct the jury accordingly and, in cases in which the bad character is not also admissible as propensity evidence, should further direct the jury that the evidence does not show propensity to commit the offence charged. It does not follow from this that the exclusionary discretion should always be exercised to prevent cross-examination which would lead the jury to infer that the accused is guilty of the offence charged, as when the accused is cross-examined on previous offences of a type similar to that charged, but the nature of that offence and the extent to which it resembles the offence charged, are certainly relevant matters for the judge to take into account. In deciding whether and how to exercise the discretion in respect of evidence admissible under s 101(1)(g), valuable guidance may be derived from the decisions reached in relation to exercise of the discretion to prevent cross-examination before the 2003 Act. In *R v McLeod*,[401] M was convicted of an armed robbery which involved the use of a number of stolen cars. At interview he made a confession, but in evidence he said he had nothing to do with the robbery and the police had created a false case against him and fabricated his confession. M was then cross-examined about his previous convictions, namely, (i) a robbery, following a not guilty plea and a defence of alibi; (ii) another robbery in which the victim had been locked in an understairs cupboard; (iii) theft of a car involving a change of the plates to a false registration; and (iv) handling of a car with false registration plates. Concluding that he had been properly cross-examined about these convictions, the Court of Appeal set out the following principles:

1. The primary purpose of cross-examination as to previous convictions and bad character of the accused is to show that he is not worthy of belief, not to show that he has a disposition to commit the type of offence with which he is charged.[402] But the mere fact that the offences are of a similar type to that charged or because of their number and type have the incidental effect of suggesting a tendency or disposition to commit the offence charged will not make them improper.[403]

2. It is undesirable that there should be prolonged or extensive cross-examination in relation to previous offences, because it will divert the jury from the principal issue in the case, the guilt of the accused on the instant offence, and not the details of earlier ones. Unless the earlier ones are admissible as similar fact evidence, prosecuting counsel should not seek to probe or emphasize similarities between the underlying facts of previous offences and the instant offence.[404]

3. Similarities of defences which have been rejected by juries on previous occasions, for example false alibis or the defence that the incriminating substance has been planted and whether or not the accused pleaded guilty or was disbelieved having given evidence on oath, may be a legitimate matter for questions. These matters do not show a propensity to commit the offence in question but are clearly relevant to credibility.

---

[401] [1994] 1 WLR 1500, CA.

[402] *R v Vickers* [1972] Crim LR 101, CA.

[403] See *R v Powell* [1986] 1 All ER 193, CA; *Selvey v DPP* [1970] AC 304, HL; and *R v Wheeler* [1995] Crim LR 312, CA. See also *R v Davison-Jenkins* [1997] Crim LR 816, CA.

[404] See, eg, the subsequent decision in *R v Davison-Jenkins* [1997] Crim LR 816, CA.

4. Underlying facts that show particularly bad character over and above the bare facts of the case are not necessarily to be excluded. However, the judge should be careful to balance the gravity of the attack on the prosecution with the degree of prejudice to the defence which will result from the disclosure of the facts in question. Details of sexual offences against children are likely to be regarded by the jury as particularly prejudicial to an accused and may well be the reason why in *R v Watts*[405] the court thought the questions impermissible.

Discretionary exclusion of evidence described in s 106(1)(c)

In cases in which the prosecution seek to rely on evidence falling within s 106(2), that is, evidence of an imputation made by the accused on being questioned under caution or on being charged with the offence,[406] and in which the accused can show that the evidence was obtained illegally, improperly, or unfairly, whether by virtue of breaches of the Codes of Practice or otherwise, there will be obvious scope for discretionary exclusion of the evidence, which in turn could prevent s 101(1)(g) from being triggered.[407] There may also be scope for discretionary exclusion of evidence of an imputation made by the accused on being questioned or charged where the accused wishes to withdraw or disassociate himself from the imputation at the trial. This may require more from the accused than simply not repeating it in evidence.[408]

Offences committed by defendant when a child

Section 108(2) and (3) of the 2003 Act provide as follows:

(2) In proceedings for an offence committed or alleged to have been committed by the defendant when aged 21 or over, evidence of his conviction for an offence when under the age of 14 is not admissible unless—
    (a) both of the offences are triable only on indictment, and
    (b) the court is satisfied that the interests of justice require the evidence to be admissible.
(3) Subsection (2) applies in addition to section 101.

Under s 108(2A) and (2B) offences committed by the defendant when a child include convictions for offences committed in any country outside England and Wales which would constitute offences triable only on indictment if committed in England and Wales.

Where the prosecution introduce evidence of historic misconduct by the defendant when a child between the ages of 10 and 14 and the misconduct is alleged to have happened before s 34 of the Crime and Disorder Act 1998 abolished the rebuttable presumption of *doli incapax* (the presumption of incapacity to form the intent to commit a crime by reason of age), it is incumbent on the judge to direct the jury that the presumption can only be rebutted by clear positive evidence that the defendant knew his acts were seriously wrong as distinct from mere naughtiness or childish mischief.[409] The judge must also direct the jury that, in order

---

[405] (1983) 77 Cr App R 126.

[406] See, eg, *R v Ball*, the conjoined appeal in *R v Renda* [2006] 1 WLR 2948, CA, where the attack was made in a police interview. See also *R v Lamaletie* [2008] EWCA Crim 3412.

[407] See Ch 11.

[408] See *R v Ball* [1911] AC 47, HL.

[409] See *R v MD* [2016] 2 Cr App R 289 (20), CA. See also *R v H* [2010] EWCA Crim 312 and *C (a minor) v The Director of Public Prosecutions* [1996] AC 1, HL.

to rebut the presumption, there has to be clear and positive evidence that the act occurred, which is distinct from the doing of the act itself.[410]

General

Assumption of truth in the assessment of relevance or probative value

Section 109 of the 2003 Act, provides that a court, when considering the relevance or probative value of evidence of bad character under s 100 (non-defendant) or s 101 (defendant) in order to decide whether it is admissible, should operate on the assumption that the evidence is true,[411] but need not do so if no reasonable court or jury could reasonably find it to be true. Section 109 provides as follows:

(1) Subject to subsection (2), a reference in this Chapter to the relevance or probative value of evidence is a reference to its relevance or probative value on the assumption that it is true.

(2) In assessing the relevance or probative value of an item of evidence for any purpose of this Chapter, a court need not assume that the evidence is true if it appears, on the basis of any material before the court (including any evidence it decides to hear on the matter), that no court or jury could reasonably find it to be true.

Section 109 applies to s 101(1)(e) (the admission of evidence of a defendant's bad character by a co-defendant) and to s 101(1)(f) (evidence to correct a false impression given by the defendant). Its chief importance, however, is likely to be in relation to the assessment of the probative value of 'similar fact evidence' properly so called under s 101(1)(d) (evidence of the defendant's bad character relevant to an important matter in issue between the defendant and the prosecution) and under s 100(3)(c) and (d) (evidence of a non-defendant's bad character of substantial probative value). The probative value of similar fact evidence often arises out of the nexus between the spontaneous and independent accounts of two or more witnesses. That probative value disappears, therefore, if there is also evidence to suggest that the witnesses have deliberately concocted false evidence by conspiracy or collaboration or, which is more common, the evidence of each of them has been innocently contaminated by knowledge of the account of the other, whether acquired directly, that is, in discussion with the other,[412] or indirectly, from a third person,[413] or as a result of media publicity.[414] In *R v H*[415] the House of Lords considered whether evidence carrying a real risk of collusion or contamination should be excluded by the judge or should be left to the jury with an appropriate warning. *R v H* was a case of sexual offences against a daughter and a stepdaughter between whom, the parties agreed, there existed a risk of collusion. It was held that save in very rare cases, the question of collusion goes not to the admissibility of similar fact evidence, but to its credibility, an issue for the jury, and that it would be wrong for the judge to decide whether there is a risk of collusion

---

[410] *R v PF* [2017] EWCA Crim 983, where the conviction was quashed because this part of the direction had not been given.

[411] Section 109 does not bind the jury, but they cannot use evidence of bad character unless they are sure that it is true: see *R v Dizaei* [2013] EWCA Crim 88.

[412] See *R v W* [1994] 1 WLR 800, CA.

[413] See *R v Ananthanarayanan* [1994] 1 WLR 788, CA.

[414] See per Lord Wilberforce in *DPP v Boardman* [1975] AC 421, HL at 444 and per Stuart-Smith LJ in *R v Bedford* (1990) 93 Cr App R 113, CA at 116.

[415] [1995] 2 AC 596, HL.

because he would inevitably be drawn into considering whether the evidence is untrue and hence whether there is a real possibility that the accused is innocent, the very question which the jury have to decide. The following principles derive from the judgments given.

1. Normally, where there is an application to exclude similar fact evidence carrying a risk of collusion or contamination, the judge should approach the question of admissibility on the basis that the similar facts alleged are true.

2. In very exceptional cases, evidence of collusion or contamination may be taken into account and in such cases the judge would be compelled to hold a *voir dire*.

3. If the evidence is admitted and it becomes apparent that no reasonable jury could accept it as free from collusion, the judge should direct the jury that it cannot be used for any purpose adverse to the defence.

4. Where this is not so, but the question of collusion has been raised, the judge must draw the importance of collusion to the attention of the jury and direct them that if they are not satisfied that the evidence can be relied upon as free from collusion, they cannot rely upon it for any purpose adverse to the defence.

Although s 109 is clearly based on the common law rules it replaces, there are two significant differences. First, as we have seen, it is much wider in its ambit in that it applies for the purpose of assessing the relevance or probative value of the bad character of the non-defendant as well as the defendant. Second, there is nothing to suggest that s 109(2) should be invoked only exceptionally. However, s 109(2), as drafted, is a curious provision in that where it appears to the court on the basis of the material before it, including any evidence given in a *voir dire*, that no court or jury could find the facts in question to be true, then the court 'need not assume' that those facts are true. It is submitted that the unstated but more obvious action that the court needs to take, once it has concluded that no court or jury could find the facts in question to be true, is to exclude the evidence. Whether or not the courts adopt such a robust approach, and also different approaches depending upon whether the evidence is relied upon by the defence or the prosecution, it is submitted that the third and fourth principles derived from *R v H* as set out in this section remain good law.

Stopping the case where evidence is contaminated

Under s 107 of the 2003 Act, which applies only to trials before a judge and jury, if evidence of the bad character of the accused has been admitted under any of paragraphs (c) to (g) of s 101(1), and the court is satisfied, at any time after the close of the prosecution case, that the evidence is so contaminated that the accused's conviction of the offence would be unsafe, the court must either direct the jury to acquit or, if there ought to be a retrial, discharge the jury. Section 107 of the 2003 Act provides as follows:

(1) If on a defendant's trial before a judge and jury for an offence—
    (a) evidence of his bad character has been admitted under any of paragraphs (c) to (g) of section 101(1), and
    (b) the court is satisfied at any time after the close of the case for the prosecution that—
        (i) the evidence is contaminated, and
        (ii) the contamination is such that, considering the importance of the evidence to the case against the defendant, his conviction of the offence would be unsafe, the court must either direct the jury to acquit the defendant of the offence or, if it considers that there ought to be a retrial, discharge the jury.

(2) Where—
   (a) a jury is directed under subsection (1) to acquit a defendant of an offence, and
   (b) the circumstances are such that, apart from this subsection, the defendant could if acquitted of that offence be found guilty of another offence,
the defendant may not be found guilty of that other offence if the court is satisfied as mentioned in subsection (1)(b) in respect of it.

(3) . . .[416]

(4) This section does not prejudice any other power a court may have to direct a jury to acquit a person of an offence or to discharge a jury.

(5) For the purposes of this section a person's evidence is contaminated where—
   (a) as a result of an agreement or understanding between the person and one or more others, or
   (b) as a result of the person being aware of anything alleged by one or more others whose evidence may be, or has been, given in the proceedings,
the evidence is false or misleading in any respect, or is different from what it would otherwise have been.

Section 107(5)(a) covers cases of conspiracy and collaboration, whereas s 107(5)(b) seems designed to cover cases of innocent contamination and has been cast in sufficiently wide terms, it is submitted, to cover cases in which a person became aware of the allegation of another not only directly, but also indirectly, through some third person or as a result of media coverage.

It appears that s 107 may be brought into play either on an application by the accused or by the court of its own motion. However, according to the Explanatory Notes to the Act, the test in s 107(1)(b)(ii) is designed to be a high test so that if the judge were to consider that a jury direction along the lines described in *R v H*[417] would be sufficient to deal with any potential difficulties, then the question of the safety of the conviction would not arise and the case should not be withdrawn.[418]

The following propositions relating to s 107 derive from *R v C*:[419]

1. Contamination may result from deliberate collusion, or the exercise of improper pressure, but equally may arise innocently or through inadvertence.

2. Contamination issues extend to evidence of bad character in the broad sense, as well as to unequivocal evidence of bad character arising from unchallenged evidence of previous convictions.

3. Whether the evidence of a witness is false or misleading or different from what it would have been if it had not been contaminated, requires the judge to form his own assessment, or judgment, of matters traditionally regarded as questions of fact for the jury.

---

[416] Section 107(3) is cast in terms similar to s 107(1) and is to the same effect, but applies not to a trial but to a jury determination under the Criminal Procedure (Insanity) Act 1964, s 4A(2) whether a person charged on indictment did the act or made the omission charged.

[417] [1995] 2 AC 596, HL. See, in this chapter, principles (3) and (4), under Assumption of truth in the assessment of relevance or probative value, p 622. See also, the Crown Court Compendium (July 2019), Part 1, 13, para 14 and Example 1.

[418] Explanatory Notes, paras 384 and 385.

[419] [2006] Crim LR 1058, CA.

4. The effect of s 107 is to reduce the risk of a conviction based on over-reliance on evidence of previous misconduct: the dangers inherent in contamination may be obscured by the evidence of bad character.

5. If the judge is satisfied of the matters in s 107(1)(b), then what follows is not a matter of discretion.

6. An order for retrial would not normally be susceptible to a subsequent application based on an asserted abuse of process.

In *R v C* there was a two-count indictment, the first alleging sexual assault on one child, V1, and the second alleging sexual assault on another child, V2, and the prosecution evidence on count 1 was admissible evidence of bad character relevant to the issue of guilt on count 2. In such circumstances, it is submitted, if the court is satisfied that by reason of the contamination of V1's evidence, there should be an acquittal on count 2, then the court may also be compelled, depending on the circumstances, to direct an acquittal on count 1.[420] However, the question of whether evidence has been contaminated is highly fact sensitive. Unless there is a clear misdirection or a clear failure to consider material evidence, appellate courts will not overturn a decision of the trial judge, who is considered to be in the best position to make the assessment required by s 107.[421]

Court's duty to give reasons for rulings

Section 110 of the 2003 Act gives effect to the Law Commission's proposal that there should be a duty on the court to give reasons for its rulings. The section applies not only to rulings on whether an item of evidence is evidence of bad character, but also to rulings on admissibility under s 100 (non-defendant's bad character), s 101 (defendant's bad character), and s 107 (stopping the case where the evidence is 'contaminated'). Section 110 provides as follows:

(1) Where the court makes a relevant ruling—
   (a) it must state in open court (but in the absence of the jury, if there is one) its reasons for the ruling;
   (b) if it is a magistrates' court, it must cause the ruling and the reasons for it to be entered in the register of the court's proceedings.
(2) In this section 'relevant ruling' means—
   (a) a ruling on whether an item of evidence is evidence of a person's bad character;
   (b) a ruling on whether an item of such evidence is admissible under section 100 or 101 (including a ruling on an application under section 101(3));[422]
   (c) a ruling under section 107.

Despite the mandatory nature of s 110(1), it seems likely that a failure to give reasons for a relevant ruling is, by itself, unlikely to render a conviction unsafe: the appellate court is likely to concentrate on whether the ruling itself was wrong.

---

[420] See Richardson, 'Commentary' [2006] Crim LR 1060.

[421] *R v K* [2008] EWCA Crim 3177. See also *R v Lamb* [2007] EWCA Crim 1766.

[422] Under s 101(3), the court has a discretionary power to exclude evidence otherwise admissible under either s 101(1)(d) or s 101(1)(g).

Concerning s 110(2)(b), a judge should provide a ruling in which the applicable gateway or gateways for admissibility are identified and this should happen even where there has been no written notice to admit the evidence.[423] Concerning s 110 generally, a judge is not necessarily required to give a ruling on whether an item of evidence is evidence of a person's bad character in circumstances where the prosecution do not seek to admit it and the accused does not seek to bring it before the jury with the aim of obtaining an effective good character direction or a modified good character direction.[424] In *R v Mittal*[425] the judge did not rule on the question of whether the accused's fiscal warning in Scotland was evidence of bad character in circumstances where the prosecution did not seek to admit it and the defence did not ask for anything to be said about character. However, the Court of Appeal observed that it was unfortunate that the status of the warning had not been ascertained at an earlier stage and that the position was not clearly understood by the advocates and the court at the outset of the trial. Therefore, where the status of an item of evidence relating to a person's character *might* have to be considered in a trial, the prosecution should supply full information on the subject in the pre-trial process.

An issue arises in relation to the duty to give rulings in a trial which is heard partly or wholly in private by virtue of an order issued under Part 6.6 of the Criminal Procedure Rules 2015. Where reasons for rulings are given in proceedings heard in private under such an order, the judge must be careful to avoid saying anything in open court by way of explanation which might potentially undermine or frustrate the order.[426]

Rules of court

Under s 111(1) of the 2003 Act, rules of court may make such provision as appear to be necessary or expedient for the purposes of the Act. Under s 111(2) of the 2003 Act:

(2) The rules may, and, where the party in question is the prosecution, must, contain provisions requiring a party who—
(a) proposes to adduce evidence of a defendant's bad character, or
(b) proposes to cross-examine a witness with a view to eliciting such evidence, to serve on the defendant such notice, and such particulars of or relating to the evidence, as may be prescribed.

The rules applicable in magistrates' courts and Crown Courts are set out in rule 21 of the Criminal Procedure Rules 2015. Under rule 21, where a party wants to introduce evidence of an accused's bad character, there is a requirement to give notice, whether that party is the prosecution or a co-accused.[427] Where notice has not been given, the judge has a discretion to permit notice to be given orally or in a different form to that prescribed and has power to shorten the time limit or to extend it after it has expired.[428] The time limits must be observed, but there is no requirement that an extension should only be granted

---

[423] See *R v PB* [2016] EWCA Crim 1462 at [43].

[424] See **Ch 18, Effective good character, p 547**.

[425] [2016] 4 WLR 91, CA.

[426] See *Re Times Newspapers Ltd; R v Abdulaziz* [2016] 2 Cr App R 367 (28), CA.

[427] Rule 21.4. Where the basis of an application to admit evidence of bad character changes from the basis stated in the notice, it is submitted that the application should be carefully re-thought and amended notice given. For an example of how things can go wrong when this is not done, see *R v Bullen* [2008] 2 Cr App R 364 (25), CA. See also *R v AG* [2018] 1 WLR 5876: an application to admit bad character should be made in writing, not informally, and the judge must give a ruling, however briefly the circumstances may require.

[428] Rule 21.6.

in exceptional circumstances. The court should take account of the overriding objective, the reason for failure to comply, when relevant inquiries were initiated, why they were not completed in time, and whether the accused's position has been prejudiced.[429] The judge can shorten the time limit to any degree and thus dispense with the notice requirement altogether.[430] When dealing with late applications to admit evidence of bad character, key considerations include whether the target of the application would simply be unable to deal with it and whether there is a risk of 'satellite litigation'.[431] Where a co-accused proposes to adduce bad character evidence, he should always alert counsel for the other accused to his intentions, even in a case where notice has not or could not be given.[432]

Failure to give notice

There is no provision in r 21 of the Criminal Procedure Rules 2015 to the effect that where a party fails to give notice, evidence is only admissible with leave, but in *R v Musone*[433] the Court of Appeal, relying on the overriding objective in r 1.1, including its recognition of the right to a fair trial under Art 6 of the European Convention on Human Rights, held that the court does have power to exclude the evidence. The court emphasized that it would be rare to exclude evidence of substantial probative value on this basis, and acknowledged that the judge should also consider the possibility of discharging the jury, but held that in some cases exclusion will be the only way of ensuring fairness, as in the case before it, where an accused, relying on s 101(1)(e), had deliberately sought to ambush a co-accused by giving him no opportunity of dealing properly with the allegation made. In *R v Mahil*[434] the Court of Appeal stated that a very high degree of necessity is required before a jury is discharged, but if such a necessity arises then the jury will be discharged regardless of the stage the trial has reached.[435]

The right of an accused to challenge evidence of a conviction

Where an accused seeks to challenge evidence of his bad character, the risk of 'satellite litigation' arises. In this situation, the courts will have regard for the overriding objective in determining whether and to what extent the accused may challenge the evidence. However, where the evidence is in the form of a conviction adduced by the prosecution under s 74(3) of the Police and Criminal Evidence Act 1984,[436] the overriding objective does not nullify the accused's right to attempt to rebut the presumption in the section that he committed the offence to which the conviction relates. Regardless of the risk of satellite litigation, to deny an accused the opportunity to adduce admissible evidence showing that he did not commit the offence would be likely to render a trial unfair.[437]

---

[429] *R (Robinson) v Sutton Coldfield Magistrates' Court* [2006] 2 Cr App R 208 (13), DC.

[430] *R v Lawson* [2007] 1 Cr App R 178 (11), CA at [18].

[431] *R v Jarvis* [2008] EWCA Crim 488.

[432] Ibid at [41].

[433] [2007] 1 WLR 2467, CA. See also *R v Ramirez* [2009] EWCA Crim 1721.

[434] [2013] EWCA Crim 673 at [113]–[125].

[435] Ibid at [120].

[436] See also Ch 23.

[437] *R v C* [2011] 1 WLR 1942, CA. The right extends to challenging admissions made in cautions: *R v Olu* [2011] 1 Cr App R 404 (33), CA.

Inaccurate evidence of convictions

A trial may be rendered unfair if the jury are presented with inaccurate evidence of an accused's convictions. First, such evidence may project the accused's past offending in such a way as to make it appear worse than it is. Second, where the accused denies its accuracy before the jury, the jury might reasonably conclude that the evidence is correct and by denying it, the accused's evidence is not creditworthy. It is imperative then that the judge is supplied with meticulously accurate information when considering the admissibility of the accused's convictions and that during the trial the jury are not misinformed in any way which could suggest that the convictions are worse and more serious than they in fact are.[438]

Evidence admitted through inadvertence

At common law, where the bad character of the accused was inadvertently revealed to the jury, whether by a witness or advocate, the judge could exercise his discretion to discharge the whole jury from giving a verdict and order a retrial.[439] It is submitted that common law principles developed to address the problem of inadvertent disclosure of the accused's bad character continue to provide valuable guidance. Thus much may depend on how explicit the reference to bad character was, the extent to which, if at all, the defence was to blame, and whether a direction to the jury is capable of neutralizing the prejudice to the accused.[440] Another factor may be whether the bad character revealed would have been admissible had the prosecution or a co-accused made an application to admit it.[441] The question for the judge is likely to remain whether there is a real danger of injustice occurring because the jury, having heard the prejudicial matter, may be biased.[442] Thus in appropriate circumstances, as when the effect on the jury appears to be minimal, the trial may properly continue.[443] The starting point is not that the jury should be discharged; nor is there a sliding scale whereby the burden on an accused seeking a discharge increases according to the weight or length of the case or the stage it has reached when the point arises for determination.[444]

---

[438] *R v M* [2012] EWCA Crim 1588 at [15].

[439] See, eg, *R v Tyrer* (1988) The Times, 13 Oct, CA. See generally Munday, 'Irregular Disclosure of Evidence of Bad Character' [1990] Crim LR 92.

[440] *R v Weaver* [1968] 1 QB 353, CA. See also *R v Mihal* [2013] EWCA Crim 673 at [113]–[125]. The prosecution advocate made a misjudgment choosing to adduce, without notice, evidence of an allegedly aggressive remark by the accused in order to suggest that the accused falsely portrayed himself as a mild-mannered person. Prejudice to the accused was neutralized by an emphatic direction to the jury to ignore the remark and what had been said about it, and by a generous full good character direction. See also *R v C* [2019] EWCA Crim 88 (11). A remark by a witness during cross-examination could have invited highly prejudicial speculation about the accused's good character (an important issue in the case), but the effect was not in fact to introduce bad character.

[441] See *R v Rabheru* [2013] EWCA Crim 137.

[442] *R v Docherty* [1999] 1 Cr App R 274, CA.

[443] See *R v Wilson* [2008] 2 Cr App R 39 (3), CA, where there was minimal prejudice from the risk of the jury having seen the accused's name on a Crown Court list for another unspecified matter pending. See also *R v Coughlan* and *R v Young* (1976) 63 Cr App R 33, CA and *R v Sutton* (1969) 53 Cr App R 504, CA.

[444] *R v Lawson* [2007] 1 Cr App R 277 (20), CA at [65]. However, procedural and evidential problems may arise in summary proceedings where magistrates perform the combined role of tribunal of law and fact. See Wasik, 'Magistrates: Knowledge of Previous Convictions' [1996] Crim LR 851, where the cases are reviewed.

Other provisions governing the admissibility of evidence of bad character

In addition to the provisions of the 2003 Act, various other provisions have a bearing on the admissibility or exclusion of evidence of bad character. Thus, as to admissibility, there are a number of statutory provisions whereby the conviction of, or sentence for, one offence is an essential ingredient of another. For example, under s 103 of the Road Traffic Act 1988, it is an offence to obtain a licence or drive a vehicle on a road 'while disqualified for holding or obtaining a licence'. Similarly under s 21 of the Firearms Act 1968, 'a person who has been sentenced to imprisonment for a term of three years or more' shall not at any time have a firearm or ammunition in his possession.[445] Evidence of conviction or sentence for the purposes of such statutes is probably best categorized as evidence 'which has to do with the alleged facts of the offence with which the defendant is charged' within s 98(b) of the 2003 Act.[446] As to the exclusion of evidence of bad character, nothing in the scheme under the 2003 Act affects the exclusion of evidence under either (a) the rule in s 3 of the Criminal Procedure Act 1865,[447] which prevents a party from impeaching the credit of his own witness by general evidence of bad character; or (b) s 41 of the Youth Justice and Criminal Evidence Act 1999,[448] which restricts evidence or questions about the complainant's sexual history in proceedings for sexual offences.[449]

There are three other provisions. The first two, s 27(3) of the Theft Act 1968 and s 1(2) of the Official Secrets Act 1911, provide for the admissibility of the accused's disposition towards certain kinds of wrongdoing. The Criminal Practice Directions provide for the exclusion of spent convictions.[450]

Section 27(3) of the Theft Act 1968

It will be seen in **Chapter 4** that where an accused is found in possession of recently stolen goods, an explanation is called for which, if not forthcoming, will entitle the jury to presume guilty knowledge or belief on a charge of receiving stolen goods. The task of the prosecution in proving guilty knowledge or belief is further assisted by s 27(3), which provides that:

> Where a person is being proceeded against for handling stolen goods (but not for any offence other than handling stolen goods), then at any stage of the proceedings, if evidence has been given of his having or arranging to have in his possession the goods the subject of the charge, or of his undertaking or assisting in, or arranging to undertake or assist in, their retention, removal, disposal or realisation, the following evidence shall be admissible for the purpose of proving that he knew or believed the goods to be stolen goods:

---

[445] Previous convictions may also be admitted after a verdict of guilty, if directly relevant to the question of sentence and, unless the accused denies them, formal proof is not required. Evidence of a conviction, if disputed, is also admissible where the accused pleads *autrefois convict* to prevent the prosecution proceeding against him in respect of an offence of which he has already been convicted.

[446] See, in this chapter, under **Introduction, p 554**.

[447] See Ch 6.

[448] See Ch 7.

[449] The 2003 Act, s 112(3).

[450] Criminal Practice Directions V, para 21A.

(a)   evidence that he has had in his possession, or has undertaken or assisted in the retention, removal, disposal or realisation of, stolen goods from any theft taking place not earlier than twelve months before the offence charged;

and

(b)   (provided that seven days' notice in writing has been given to him of the intention to prove the conviction) evidence that he has within the five years preceding the date of the offence charged been convicted of theft or of handling stolen goods.

Where evidence is introduced under s 27(3)(a), strict regard must be had to its terms: it was not designed to allow evidence to be given of what is in effect another offence of handling committed before the offence charged and does not permit the introduction of details of the transaction as a result of which the earlier property came into the possession of the accused.[451] However, under s 27(3)(a), providing a description of the stolen goods appears to be unavoidable.[452] Subsection 3(b) has to be read with s 73 of the Police and Criminal Evidence Act 1984, whereby the fact of a conviction may be proved by producing a certificate of conviction giving 'the substance and effect (omitting the formal parts) of the indictment and of the conviction',[453] wording which renders admissible not only the fact, date, and place of the conviction, but also a description of the stolen goods.[454] In cases in which there are a number of counts of handling on some of which the accused denies possession, the judge should warn the jury that evidence admitted under s 27(3) is relevant only to those counts in which guilty knowledge is involved and not those in which possession is the only or primary issue.[455]

It is no answer to an application to admit evidence under s 27(3)(b) to say that the previous convictions are for theft or handling of a different kind or have no bearing on a specific prosecution argument based on a system or modus operandi, because the very purpose of the subsection is to admit evidence of the general disposition of the accused to be dishonest.[456] Nevertheless, it is well established that the judge does have a discretion to exclude evidence admissible under s 27(3) where it would only be of minimal assistance to the jury or its prejudicial effect would outweigh its probative value.[457] In R v Hacker,[458] a trial for handling the bodyshell of an Escort RS Turbo motor car, in which the accused denied that the goods had been stolen and also denied guilty knowledge or belief, it was held that the judge was entitled, in his discretion, to admit evidence of a previous conviction of receiving a Ford RS Turbo motor car, evidence said to be highly relevant to the issue of knowledge.

---

[451] R v Bradley (1979) 70 Cr App R 200, CA, applied in R v Wood [1987] 1 WLR 779, CA. Possession of the earlier property may be proved by evidence of an admission by the accused under caution, in a written statement to the police, provided that the statement is edited so as to disclose only the bare fact of such possession.

[452] R v Fowler (1987) 86 Cr App R 219, CA at 226.

[453] See Ch 2.

[454] R v Hacker [1995] 1 All ER 45, HL.

[455] R v Wilkins [1975] 2 All ER 734, CA.

[456] R v Perry [1984] Crim LR 680, CA.

[457] See R v List [1966] 1 WLR 9 (Assizes); R v Herron [1967] 1 QB 107, CCA (decided under the Larceny Act 1916, s 43(1), re-enacted, with some modification, in s 27(3)); R v Knott [1973] Crim LR 36, CA; and R v Perry [1984] Crim LR 680, CA. See also R v Rasini (1986) The Times, 20 Mar, CA.

[458] [1995] 1 All ER 45, HL.

Section 1(2) of the Official Secrets Act 1911

Under s 1(1) of the Official Secrets Act 1911, it is an offence to commit various acts of espionage 'for any purpose prejudicial to the safety or interests of the State'. Evidence of disposition to commit such acts is admissible under s 1(2), which provides that:

> (2) On a prosecution under this section, it shall not be necessary to show that the accused person was guilty of any particular act tending to show a purpose prejudicial to the safety or interests of the State, and notwithstanding that no such act is proved against him, he may be convicted if, from the circumstances of the case, or his conduct, or his known character as proved, it appears that his purpose was a purpose prejudicial to the safety or interests of the State . . .

Criminal Practice Directions V, para 21A

The Rehabilitation of Offenders Act 1974 provides that in civil proceedings no evidence shall be admissible to prove that a 'rehabilitated' person has committed, been charged with, prosecuted for, convicted of, or sentenced for any offence which was the subject of a 'spent' conviction[459] unless the judge is satisfied that in the circumstances justice cannot be done in the case except by admitting such evidence.[460] The Act does not apply to criminal proceedings[461] but under para 21A.2, when considering bad character applications under the Criminal Justice Act 2003, regard should always be had to the general principles of the Rehabilitation of Offenders Act 1974. A conviction becomes 'spent' on the expiry of a 'rehabilitation period', which runs from the date of conviction, varies according to the sentence imposed, and is reduced by half for persons under 18 years old at the date of conviction.[462] Certain sentences are excluded from rehabilitation under the Act and these include imprisonment for life or for a term exceeding 30 months, a sentence of preventative detention, a sentence of detention during Her Majesty's pleasure, and a sentence of custody for life.[463]

ADDITIONAL READING

Fortson and Ormrod, 'Bad Character Evidence and Cross-Admissibility' [2009] Crim LR 313.
 An article which considers the circumstances in which evidence from one count on an indictment may be used to support another count charged in the same indictment. Issues considered include the relationship between s 98(a) and s 101 in cross-admissibility cases and the probative value of evidence cross-admitted.

Goudkamp, 'Bad character evidence and reprehensible behaviour' (2008) 12 E&P 116.
 An examination of the meaning of 'bad character' and 'reprehensible behaviour' under ss 98 and 112(1) of the Criminal Justice Act 2003. A number of useful examples are provided of behaviour that has been held not to be reprehensible. However, it is observed that the meaning of 'reprehensible behaviour' is unclear and no principle can be discerned from the authorities.

---

[459] Section 4(1)(a).
[460] Section 7(3). See also *Thomas v Metropolitan Police Comr* [1997] QB 813, CA.
[461] Section 7(2)(a).
[462] See Tables A and B under s 5(2).
[463] Section 5(1). As to how a jury should be directed on the character of an accused with previous but spent convictions, see Ch 18.

Hunter, 'Character evidence in the criminal trial' (2016) 20(2) E&P 162.
   A review of Redmayne's monograph, 'Character in the Criminal Trial' (Oxford, 2015). The review critically analyses Redmayne's approach, including the general approach, based on Bayesian modelling, that 'prior offending is among the most significant predictors of future offending' (see p 31 of Redmayne's monograph).

Lloyd-Bostock, 'The Effects on Juries of Hearing that the Defendant has a Previous Conviction' [2000] Crim LR 734.
   A study which examines the effect that evidence of previous convictions has on how jurors regard an accused. As part of the study, mock jurors were shown videos of simulated criminal trials for different offences and evidence of different types of convictions was introduced. Jurors were then asked to give a score for the effect that the evidence of the convictions had on how they regarded the accused.

Mirfield, 'Bad character and the Law Commission' (2002) 6 E&P 141.
   An assessment of the Law Commission's proposals to reform the law on bad character. The proposals are broadly welcomed insofar as they help to clarify problems in the common law concerning background evidence, similar fact, and where an accused attacks another as a necessary part of his defence. Criticism is made of some of the terminology used by the Law Commission and some of the conclusions the Commission reached.

Mirfield, 'Character and Credibility' [2009] Crim LR 135.
   An examination of the principles governing the admissibility of character evidence relevant to credibility under the Criminal Justice Act 2003, s 100(1)(b), s 101(1)(d), s 101(1)(f), and s 101(1)(g). The article concludes that case law has given rise to three and possibly four different views of what credibility means under the bad character provisions and highlights difficulties with each view.

Munday, 'Cut-throat Defences and the "Propensity to be Untruthful" under s.104 of the Criminal Justice Act 2003' [2005] Crim LR 624.
   An article which considers the approach taken to the admissibility of evidence of an accused's propensity to be untruthful at the instance of the co-accused, under ss 101(1)(e) and 104 of the Criminal Justice Act. The approach is compared with the approach taken to admissibility at the instance of the prosecution under ss 101(1)(d) and 103. The Explanatory Notes to ss 103 and 104 are referred to. Legal uncertainty created by s 104 is highlighted.

Munday, 'The Purposes of Gateway (g): Yet Another Problematic of the Criminal Justice Act 2003' [2006] Crim LR 300.
   A discussion of the content and function of s 101(1)(g) of the Criminal Justice Act 2003. The article considers, in particular, the case of R v Highton [2005] 1 WLR 3472. General comments are offered on the approach taken by the Court of Appeal to appeals based on bad character.

Redmayne, Character in the Criminal Trial (Oxford, 2015).
   A monograph which provides a comprehensive analysis of the bad character provisions of the Criminal Justice Act 2003; explores conceptual, doctrinal, and theoretical issues underlying character evidence, and examines fundamental questions about character evidence in criminal trials; and considers the use of character evidence in sentencing.

Redmayne, 'Recognising Propensity' [2011] Crim LR 117.
   An examination of how propensity to commit offences is understood under the Criminal Justice Act 2003. The article considers the distinction between propensity and 'coincidence' cases. There is a discussion of relevant case law and a number of different scenarios. It is suggested that misunderstandings about the extent to which bad character evidence proves propensity could lead to miscarriages of justice.

Redmayne, 'The Law Commission's character convictions' (2002) 6 E&P 71.
   An article which questions the basic assumptions underlying the Law Commission's recommendations for reform of the law of bad character. Assumptions in three areas are questioned: (i) exclusion; (ii) using convictions as evidence of an accused's lack of credibility; and (iii) the similar fact rule. The argument is made that the Commission does not offer a good argument for presuming that bad character evidence is prejudicial. The study by Sally Lloyd-Bostock (featured in this reading list) is challenged as a basis for presuming prejudice and criminological studies on recidivism are referred to. The argument is also made that the Commission offers no good reason for the credibility exception to the general exclusionary rule. It is cautiously suggested that the problems concerning similar fact evidence have been 'misdiagnosed' by the Commission.

QUESTIONS

1. Magda, a hospital physiotherapist, is charged with indecently touching three teenage boys, touching each of them on separate occasions. She pleads not guilty to the charges. The boys, who had broken legs, each give evidence that during their appointments with Magda, she instructed them as to how they should exercise their legs to assist a full recovery, but as she did so, she placed her hand over their genitals. Magda denies touching any of the boys in this area of their body. Is the evidence of each boy admissible against Magda to support the evidence of the other two boys? Give reasons for your answer, referring to statute and case law.

2. John and Imran are jointly charged with murdering Hari in a fight outside a nightclub, during which Hari was stabbed. John's evidence will be that he was present when the fight took place between Imran and Hari, but he did not participate in any way. Imran's evidence will be that Hari attacked John and he (Imran) tried to separate them. As he did so, John, without any warning, produced a knife and stabbed Hari. John has two recent convictions for credit card fraud. Imran has a conviction from five years previously, for inflicting grievous bodily harm with intent. Discuss the admissibility at the forthcoming trial, of the following evidence:

   (a) John's convictions;

   (b) Imran's conviction.

3. By reference to statute and case law, critically discuss the tests for the admissibility of evidence showing a propensity to untruthfulness.

 For a note-form answer see the online resources, accessible at
www.oup.com/he/keane-mckeown13e.

Experts and opinion evidence 20

- When and why should experts be allowed to give evidence of fact or opinion on facts in issue, based on their expertise?

- When and why should non-experts be allowed to give non-expert opinion evidence on facts in issue?

- What are the dangers of allowing experts to give expert evidence?

- What safeguards can be used against such dangers?

- What duties to the court should an expert witness have?

- If two or more parties to litigation wish to submit expert evidence on an issue, when should the court direct that the evidence on the issue be given by a single joint expert?

- Why should the parties disclose their expert evidence before the trial?

The general rule and the two exceptions

Any witness, including an expert, may give evidence of facts in issue or relevant to the facts in issue. An example, in the case of an expert, would be, in a murder trial, a surgeon's description of the victim's wounds, being a description not calling for or based on expertise. There are no special rules for the admissibility of such *factual* evidence from an expert.[1] However, as a general rule, no witness may give *opinion* evidence: a witness may only speak of facts he personally perceived, not of inferences drawn from those facts. To this general rule there are two exceptions. First, an appropriately qualified expert may state his opinion on a matter calling for the expertise which he possesses. Second, a non-expert witness may state his opinion on a matter not calling for any particular expertise as a way of conveying the facts which he personally perceived. There are two main reasons for the general rule. First, it has been said that, whereas any fact that a witness can prove is relevant, his opinion is not.[2] The opinion of a non-expert has no probative value in relation to a subject calling for expertise and is usually insufficiently relevant to a subject not calling for any particular expertise. Second, the general rule prevents witnesses from usurping the role of the tribunal of fact.[3] The tribunal of fact, although free to reject any opinions proffered, might be tempted simply to accept those opinions rather than draw its own inferences from the facts of the case.

The first exception is not confined to expert *opinion* but also covers expert evidence of fact, that is, evidence of fact based on the witness' expertise, as when an expert describes how a machine is configured and works[4] or gives evidence on the practices and associations of gangs.[5] This first exception stems from an acknowledgment that in some cases the tribunal of fact, in the absence of expert evidence, may be unable properly to reach a conclusion. Expert evidence is admitted because expertise is needed which the tribunal of fact simply does not possess.[6] This rationale is essentially flawed: if the tribunal of fact lacks the relevant expertise, it will often be unlikely to be able to evaluate the cogency or reliability of the expert evidence.[7] There is also a danger that the tribunal of fact may blindly defer to the expert. Furthermore, expert evidence on subjects in respect of which scientific knowledge is limited or incomplete can occasion miscarriages of justice. For example, following the successful appeal in the 'cot death' case of *R v Cannings*,[8] the Attorney General announced a review of 258 convictions relating to homicide or infanticide of a baby under 2 years old by a parent, and a similar review in civil cases was ordered by the Children's Minister. The risks of miscarriage of justice are increased by the current absence of any scheme of compulsory

---

[1] *Kennedy v Cordia (Services) LLP* [2016] UKSC 6.

[2] Per Goddard LJ in *Hollington v Hewthorn & Co Ltd* [1943] KB 587 at 595, CA.

[3] See, eg, *R v Allad* [2014] EWCA Crim 421 (non-expert entitled to explain how VAT carousel frauds operate but not to give an opinion on the issue before the jury whether the accused would have known that they had participated in a fraud). See also *R(DPP) v Stratford Magistrates' Court* [2018] 4 WLR 47 (expert entitled to explain conduct of participants at an arms fair and to invite the court to consider it was likely to be repeated at the present arms fair, but not to give an opinion that it constituted a crime).

[4] *Kennedy v Cordia (Services) LLP* [2016] UKSC 6 at [41].

[5] *Myers v R* [2016] AC 314, PC.

[6] Expert evidence will be required only rarely in judicial review proceedings, as when the decision in question is irrational because based on an error not obvious to a non-expert but which an expert can show to be incontrovertible: *R (The Law Society) v Lord Chancellor* [2018] EWHC 2094 (Admin).

[7] See Roberts and Zuckerman, *Criminal Evidence* (Oxford, 2004) 294–5.

[8] [2004] 1 WLR 2607, CA (see Ch 8).

accreditation or registration for expert witnesses and any scheme of mandatory practical training for judges and practitioners in understanding expert evidence and in assessing its likely reliability.[9]

If objection is taken to the admissibility of expert evidence, it is for the party tendering it to establish its admissibility under the first exception above.[10]

The second exception, for non-experts, stems from a recognition that the fundamental assumption upon which the general rule is based, that it is possible to distinguish between fact and opinion, is false.[11] The words of a witness testifying as to perceived facts are always coloured, to some extent, by his opinion as to what he perceived. The separation of an inference or value judgement from the facts on which it is based is often extremely difficult, sometimes impossible. In criminal proceedings, for example, a witness may identify the accused as the culprit, saying, 'He is the man I saw'. This is evidence of opinion, not fact if the witness means: 'He so resembles the man I saw that I am prepared to say that they are one and the same.' He could confine himself to a description of the man he saw and leave it to the jury to decide whether the description fits the accused. In such cases, the opinion expressed conveys the facts perceived. The witness is allowed to give his evidence in his own way which is often, although not invariably, the most natural and comprehensible way of conveying to the tribunal of fact the facts as he perceived them.

Expert evidence

Matters calling for expertise

Examples

The evidence of an expert is only admissible on a matter calling for expertise.[12] The field of expertise is large and ever-expanding. It embraces subjects as diverse as accident investigation and driver behaviour,[13] the age of a person,[14] ballistics, battered women's syndrome,[15] blood tests, breath tests, blood-alcohol levels and back-calculations thereof,[16] coercive

---

[9] For an analysis of the need for forensic science training and specific recommendations, see the House of Commons Science and Technology Committee, *Forensic Science on Trial*, HC 96–I 2005. Guides or 'Primers for courts' have now been produced by the Royal Society in respect of forensic gait analysis, accessible at https://royalsociety.org/-/media/about-us/programmes/science-and-law/royal-society-forensic-gait-analysis-primer-for-courts.pdf, and DNA analysis, accessible at https://royalsociety.org/-/media/about-us/programmes/science-and-law/royal-society-forensic-dna-analysis-primer-for-courts.pdf. Concerning the need for a better understanding by lawyers of commonly used scientific terms, see Likwornik, Chin and Bielinski, 'The diverging dictionaries of science and law' (2018) IJEP 30.

[10] *R v Atkins* [2010] 1 Cr App R 117 (8), CA at [9], approved in *R v Reed* [2010] 1 Cr App R 310 (23), CA at [113].

[11] 'In a sense all testimony to matter of fact is opinion evidence; ie it is a conclusion formed from phenomena and mental impressions': Thayer, *A Preliminary Treatise on Evidence at the Common Law* (Boston, 1898) 524.

[12] This section of the chapter concerns expert *evidence*. Civil actions without a jury in the High Court may be tried by a judge sitting with assessors. The function of assessors, principally used in the Admiralty Court in cases concerning collisions between vessels, is to assist the judge on matters of fact calling for specialized knowledge: see the Senior Courts Act 1981, s 70, the County Courts Act 1984, s 63, and the Civil Procedure Rules r 35.15.

[13] See *R v Dudley* [2004] EWCA Crim 3336.

[14] *R (I) v Secretary of State for the Home Department* [2005] EWHC 1025 (Admin) and *N (a child) (residence order), Re* [2006] EWHC 1189 (Fam).

[15] See *R v Hobson* [1998] 1 Cr App R 31, CA and *R v Goldie* [2013] EWCA Crim 1472.

[16] Ie calculation of the amount of alcohol eliminated in the period between driving and providing a specimen in order to show that a person's alcohol level was above the prescribed limit at the time of driving. See *Gumbley v Cunningham* [1989] 1 All ER 5, HL.

control,[17] drug traces,[18] earprint identification,[19] facial mapping[20] or facial identification by video superimposition,[21] fingerprint identification,[22] gait identification,[23] firearms discharge residue,[24] the practices, mores, and associations of gangs,[25] voice identification,[26] DNA or genetic fingerprinting,[27] indented impressions left on one document as a result of writing on another,[28] insanity, lip-reading,[29] physical signs of child sexual abuse,[30] 'shaken baby syndrome',[31] Sudden Infant Death Syndrome (SIDS),[32] terrorism,[33] the genuineness of works of art, and the state of public opinion.[34] Frequently recurring examples of matters upon which expert evidence is admissible include medical, scientific, architectural, engineering, and technological issues and questions relating to standards of professional competence, market values, customary terms of contracts, and the existence of professional and trade practices. Handwriting may be proved either by a non-expert familiar with the handwriting in question[35] or by a qualified expert, but an expert should be called

[17] *R v Challen* [2019] EWCA Crim 916.

[18] For cases and critical commentary, see Marks, 'Expert evidence of drug traces: relevance, reliability and the right to silence' [2013] Crim LR 810.

[19] *R v Dallagher* [2003] 1 Cr App R 195 (12), CA; *R v Kempster* (*No 2*) [2008] 2 Cr App R 256 (19), CA.

[20] *R v Stockwell* (1993) 97 Cr App R 260, CA; *R v Mitchell* [2005] EWCA Crim 731.

[21] *R v Clarke* [1995] 2 Cr App R 425, CA.

[22] See generally *R v Smith* [2011] 2 Cr App R 174 (16), CA and Cole and Roberts, 'Certainty, Individualisation and the Subjective Nature of Expert Fingerprint Evidence' [2012] Crim LR 824.

[23] *R v Ferdinand* [2014] EWCA Crim 1243.

[24] *R v George (Barry)* [2007] EWCA Crim 2722; *R v Joseph* [2010] EWCA Crim 2580; and *R v George* [2015] 1 Cr App R 183 (15).

[25] *Myers v R* [2016] AC 314, PC.

[26] *R v Robb* (1991) 93 Cr App R 161, CA.

[27] For a basic description of the method by which DNA profiling is carried out, see *R v Gordon* [1995] 1 Cr App R 290, CA at 293–4. It may be used to identify criminal suspects, by showing their presence at a particular place at a particular time, to show their possession of an article (see, eg, *R v Sampson* [2014] EWCA Crim 1968), and to decide questions of pedigree. In evaluating DNA evidence, use should not be made of Bayes Theorem, or any similar statistical method of analysis, because it plunges the jury into inappropriate and unnecessary realms of theory and complexity: *R v Adams* [1996] 2 Cr App R 467, CA. As to the procedure to be adopted when DNA evidence is introduced, see *R v Doheny and Adams* [1997] 1 Cr App R 369, CA. See also Redmayne, 'The DNA Database: Civil Liberty and Evidentiary Issues' [1995] Crim LR 437, 'Sittin' in the Dock with the Bayes' (2001) NLJ 201, and The Forensic Science Regulator, *The Interpretation of DNA Evidence (including low-template DNA)* (2012). For controversy about the use of Low Copy Number DNA, following the concerns expressed in *R v Hoey* [2007] NICC 49, see *R v Reed* [2010] 1 Cr App R 310, CA; *R v Broughton* [2010] EWCA Crim 549, CA; *R v C* [2011] 3 All ER 509, CA; Jamieson, 'LCN DNA analysis and opinion on transfer: *R v Reed and Reed*' (2011) 15 E&P 161; and Naughton and Tan, 'The need for caution in the use of DNA evidence to avoid convicting the innocent' (2011) 15 E&P 245.

[28] Impressions may be detected using Electrostatic Detection Apparatus (ESDA). ESDA has been useful not only in dating documents and determining the origin of anonymous communications, but also in showing whether pages were written in sequence and whether there were subsequent additions to the contents: see *R v Wellington* [1991] Crim LR 543, CA and generally Giles, 'Good Impressions' (1991) NLJ 605.

[29] *R v Luttrell* [2004] 2 Cr App R 520 (31), CA.

[30] *R v S* [2012] EWCA Crim 1433.

[31] *R v Henderson* [2010] 2 Cr App R 185 (24), CA.

[32] See *R v Cannings* [2004] 1 WLR 2607, CA (see **Ch 8 at p 273**, and, in this chapter, under **Sudden Infant Death Syndrome, p 651**).

[33] *R v Ahmed* [2011] EWCA Crim 184.

[34] eg concerning reputation in passing-off actions. See *Sodastream Ltd v Thorn Cascade Co Ltd* [1982] RPC 459 and *Lego Systems A/S v Lego M Lemelstrich Ltd* [1983] FSR 155. Cf *Reckitt & Colman Products v Borden Inc (No 2)* [1987] FSR 407.

[35] *Doe d Mudd v Suckermore* (1837) 5 Ad&El 703.

in criminal cases tried by jury when, pursuant to s 8 of the Criminal Procedure Act 1865, disputed handwriting is compared with a specimen sample of handwriting proved to the satisfaction of the court to be genuine.[36] Expert opinion is admissible on questions of a literary or artistic nature, for example in relation to the defence of 'public good' under s 4 of the Obscene Publications Act 1959.

Points of foreign law

A point of foreign law is a question of fact to be decided on the evidence by the judge (see **Chapter 2**). Foreign law is usually proved by the evidence, including opinion evidence, of an expert[37] who may refer to foreign statutes, decisions, and textbooks.[38] If the evidence of the experts conflicts, the judge is bound to look at the sources of knowledge from which the experts have drawn, in order to decide between the conflicting testimony.[39] However, the judge is not at liberty to conduct his own research into those sources and to rely on material not adduced in evidence in order to reject the expert evidence.[40]

At common law, the consequence of treating foreign law as a question of fact is that where there has been an English decision on a particular point of foreign law and the same point subsequently arises again, it must be decided afresh on new expert evidence.[41] This remains the position where a point of foreign law arises in English criminal proceedings. The position in civil proceedings, however, was altered by s 4 of the Civil Evidence Act 1972. Section 4(2)(a) provides that a previous determination by an English court of superior status, whether civil or criminal, on a point of foreign law shall, if reported in citable form,[42] be admissible in evidence in civil proceedings. Section 4(2)(b) provides that except where there are two or

---

[36] *R v Harden* [1963] 1 QB 8, CCA: see generally Ch 10, **Proof of Handwriting, p 311**.

[37] An exception exists in the case of the construction of provisions of foreign legislation admitted in evidence under the Evidence (Colonial Statutes) Act 1907: see the authorities cited in *Jasiewicz v Jasiewicz* [1962] 1 WLR 1426. Under the 1907 Act, s 1, copies of Acts, ordinances, and statutes passed by the legislature of any part of Her Majesty's dominions exclusive of the UK and of orders, regulations, and other instruments issued or made under the authority of any such Act, ordinance, or statute, if purporting to be printed by the government printer of the possession shall be received in evidence by all courts in the UK without proof that copies were so printed. See also the Colonial Laws Validity Act 1865, s 6. The British Law Ascertainment Act 1859 permits English courts to state a case on a point of foreign law for the opinion of a superior court in another part of Her Majesty's dominions. The opinion pronounced is admissible in evidence on the point of foreign law in question. Under s 25(3) of the Immigration Act 1971, breach of the immigration law of a member State of the European Union, for the purposes of assisting unlawful immigration contrary to s 25 of the 1971 Act, may be proved conclusively by a certificate of the member State. Section 25(3) is permissive—the breach may be proved by an expert or by admission: *R v Bina* [2014] 2 Cr App R 496 (30).

[38] It may also be proved by the witness statement of an expert (if admissible) or by a statement of agreed facts pursuant to the Criminal Justice Act 1967, s 10: *R v Ofori (No 2)* (1993) 99 Cr App R 223, CA.

[39] Per Lord Langdale MR in *Nelson (Earl) v Lord Bridport* (1845) 8 Beav 527 at 537 and per Scarman J in *Re Fuld's Estate (No 3), Hartley v Fuld* [1968] P 675 at 700–3.

[40] Per Lord Chelmsford in *Duchess Di Sora v Phillipps* (1863) 10 HL Cas 624 at 640 and per Purchas LJ in *Bumper Development Corpn Ltd v Metropolitan Police Comr* [1991] 4 All ER 638, CA at 643–6. See also *Harley v Smith* [2010] EWCA Civ 78.

[41] *M'Cormick v Garnett* (1854) 23 LJ Ch 777.

[42] ie where the report, if the question had been as to the law of England and Wales, could have been 'cited as an authority' in legal proceedings in England and Wales: s 4(5).The words 'cited as an authority' include findings or decisions on foreign law whether or not they were necessary to the ultimate decision: *Joint Stock Co 'Aeroflot-Russian Airlines' v Leeds* [2017] 1 WLR 4537 (Ch). Obiter findings and decisions may not be cited as binding precedent, but may be persuasive, their persuasiveness depending on the cogency of the reasoning upon which they are based (at [22]).

more previous determinations which conflict, the foreign law on the point in question shall be taken to be as previously determined unless the contrary is proved. Section 4(2)(b) raises a presumption that the earlier decision is correct. However, the court which has to consider the question for a second time decides for itself what weight to attach to the previous decision and, although it is desirable to reach consistent conclusions, the subsection is not to be construed as laying down a general rule that the presumption can only be displaced by particularly cogent evidence.[43]

Matters within or outwith the experience and knowledge of the tribunal of fact

In *R v Turner*[44] it was held that where the triers of fact can form their own opinion without the assistance of an expert, the matter in question being within their own experience and knowledge, the opinion evidence of an expert is inadmissible because unnecessary. This test has been applied repeatedly in the authorities which now fall to be considered. However, in these authorities there is scant recognition that views may legitimately differ as to whether a particular matter is within the experience and knowledge of jurors and that, even if it is not, expert evidence may be unnecessary because the matter could be dealt with better by an educative judicial direction, as in, for example, cases of allegedly mistaken identification.[45] It is submitted that a test of necessity is also too strict; a better formula, which could apply to both expert opinion evidence and evidence of fact based upon an expert's expertise would be that set out in r 702 of the US Federal Rules, namely whether the evidence 'will assist the trier of fact to understand the evidence or to determine a fact in issue'.[46]

Leave should not be granted to call a professor of psychology or other medical evidence to demonstrate the likely deterioration of the memory of an ordinary witness.[47] On the other hand, although a witness's ability to remember events will ordinarily be well within the experience of jurors, in rare cases in which a witness gives evidence of an event said to have occurred during 'the period of childhood amnesia', which extends to the age of about 7, and the evidence is very detailed and contains a number of details that are extraneous to the central feature of the event, an appropriately qualified expert may give evidence that it should be treated with caution and may be unreliable because recall of events during that period will be fragmented, disjointed, and idiosyncratic rather than a detailed narrative account.[48] Similarly, although expert opinion evidence is likely to be inadmissible in relation to the dangers of visual identification evidence,[49] it is submitted that it may properly be admitted on such matters as the accuracy of estimates of age and the relative accuracy

---

[43] *Phoenix Marine Inc v China Ocean Shipping Co* [1999] 1 All ER 138.

[44] [1975] QB 834, per Lawton LJ at 841.

[45] See Ch 10.

[46] See *Kennedy v Cordia (Services) LLP* [2016] UKSC 6 at [46]–[48].

[47] *R v Browning* [1995] Crim LR 227, CA.

[48] *R v H (JR) (childhood amnesia)* [2006] 1 Cr App R 195 (10), CA. However, this decision has been doubted, having regard to criticisms of the methodology of the expert: *R v Anderson* [2012] EWCA Crim 1785. In any event, the ambit of the decision should not be widened and care should be taken in the case of a narrative which has become 'polished' simply as a part of the process of the police questioning a witness and then drafting his statement: *R v S; R v W* [2007] 2 All ER 974, CA.

[49] See *Gage v HM Advocate* [2011] HCAJC 40 and Roberts, 'Expert evidence on the reliability of eyewitness identification—some observations on the justifications for exclusion: *Gage v HM Advocate*' (2012) 16 E&P 93.

of sequential and simultaneous identification procedures.[50] An expert may give evidence of false memory syndrome or recovered memory syndrome, being subjects outside the knowledge and experience of jurors, but only where a sound factual foundation for it has been established, for example by medical evidence that memories were recovered during counselling or psychotherapy.[51] Expert evidence may be admitted as to the dangers of evidence produced by hypnotherapy, not to express an opinion on the witness's truthfulness, but to criticize the techniques of the hypnotherapist and express an opinion about the danger that *if* the witness's recollection was falsely engendered, the witness would regard it as genuine memory.[52]

Expert evidence is inadmissible on the question whether an unidentified person shown in a photograph is under the age of 16.[53] It is also inadmissible on a trial for posting packets containing indecent articles, on the ordinary meaning of the words 'indecent or obscene'.[54] Similarly, in the ordinary case, the issue of obscenity in prosecutions under the Obscene Publications Act 1959 falls to be tried without the assistance of expert evidence.[55] *DPP v A & B C Chewing Gum Ltd*[56] was not an 'ordinary case', but 'a very special case'[57] which should be regarded as 'highly exceptional and confined to its own circumstances'.[58] The accused was charged with publishing for gain obscene battle cards which were sold together with packets of bubble gum. The Divisional Court held that the magistrates had improperly refused to admit the evidence of experts in child psychiatry concerning the likely effect of the cards on children. In a prosecution under s 5 of the Public Order Act 1986, arising out of naked rambling, expert evidence as to public attitudes, and the likely reaction of children, to nudity, will not be allowed.[59]

---

[50] See *R v Forbes* [2009] ACTSC 1, considered by Roberts, 'Eyewitness identification and expert insight: *R v Forbes*' (2010) 14 E&P 57. A jury may also be assisted by a non-expert if 'sufficiently expert *ad hoc*' (see *R v Howe* [1982] 1 NZLR 618 at 627) as in *R v Clare and Peach* [1995] 2 Cr App R 333, CA, where an officer who had viewed a video about 40 times, examining it in slow motion, gave evidence as to whether those shown were the accused. Ironically, research suggests that the accuracy of identification is not significantly enhanced by repeated replay: Bruce et al, 'Face Recognition in Poor Quality Video Evidence from Security Surveillance' (1999) 10 *Psychological Science* 243. See also Munday, 'Videotape Evidence and the Advent of the Expert Ad Hoc' (1995) 159 JP 547. See also, in the case of police transcripts of poor quality covert recordings, Fraser and Stevenson, 'The power and persistence of contextual priming: more risks in using police transcripts to aid jurors' perception of poor quality covert recordings' (2014) 18 E&P 205.

[51] *R v H* [2014] EWCA Crim 1555.

[52] *R v Clark* [2006] EWCA Crim 231. As to the dangers of admitting evidence of recovered memory, see Ring, 'Due process and the admission of expert evidence on recovered memory in historic child sexual abuse cases: lessons from America' (2012) 16 E&P 66.

[53] *R v Land* [1998] 1 Cr App R 301, CA.

[54] *R v Stamford* [1972] 2 QB 391.

[55] *R v Anderson* [1972] 1 QB 304 per Lord Widgery CJ at 313. Cf *R v Skirving; R v Grossman* [1985] 2 All ER 705, where the jury needed expert evidence on the characteristics of cocaine and the different effects of various methods of ingesting the drug on the user and abuser in order to decide whether a book had a tendency to deprave and corrupt.

[56] [1968] 1 QB 159.

[57] Per Ashworth J in *R v Stamford* [1972] 2 QB 391, CA at 397.

[58] Per Lord Widgery CJ in *R v Anderson* [1972] 1 QB 304 at 313. See also the doubts expressed about the case by Lord Dilhorne in *DPP v Jordan* [1977] AC 699, HL at 722.

[59] *Gough v DPP* [2013] EWHC 3267 (Admin).

Mental states

The distinction between matters calling for expertise and matters within the experience and knowledge of the jury is also illustrated by cases concerning a person's mental state. As we shall see, many of the decisions reflect the view that expertise is only called for in the case of a person suffering from a mental illness, a view which, it is submitted, is unnecessarily inflexible. Farquharson LJ observed in *R v Strudwick*:[60]

> The law is in a state of development in this area. There may well be other mental conditions about which a jury might require expert assistance in order to understand and evaluate their effect on the issues in a case.

Expert psychiatric evidence is a practical necessity in order to establish insanity,[61] diminished responsibility,[62] or automatism while asleep.[63] Concerning the defence of duress by threats, expert medical evidence is admissible for the purposes of the subjective (but not the objective) test, provided that the mental condition or abnormality in question is relevant and its effects are outside the knowledge and experience of laymen.[64] According to *R v Walker*[65] psychiatric evidence may be admissible to show that an accused was suffering from some mental illness, mental impairment, or recognized psychiatric condition, provided persons generally suffering from such a condition might be more susceptible to pressure and threats. The evidence could assist the jury in deciding whether a reasonable person suffering from such a condition might have been impelled to act as the accused did. However, where an accused was not suffering from such an illness, impairment, or condition, evidence is not admissible that he was especially timid, suggestible, or vulnerable to pressure and threats.[66] Concerning the defence of loss of self-control under s 54 of the Coroners and Justice Act 2009, it is submitted that psychiatric evidence will generally be inadmissible but, by analogy with the authorities relating to duress, may be admitted to show that an accused was suffering from some disorder or disability of the mind affecting his degree of tolerance and self-restraint.[67]

Except where the accused comes into the class of mental defective or is afflicted by some medical condition affecting his mental state, expert medical or psychiatric evidence is not admissible on the question of *mens rea*.[68] In *R v Masih*,[69] the Court of Appeal held that, generally speaking, if an accused comes into the class of mental defective, with an IQ of 69

---

[60] (1993) 99 Cr App R 326, CA at 332.

[61] See the Criminal Procedure (Insanity and Unfitness to Plead) Act 1991, s 1(1), in this chapter, under Expertise, p 643.

[62] See *R v Bunch* [2013] EWCA Crim 2498: medical evidence is relevant to all of the ingredients of the defence and is critical to the issue in s 2(1)(a) of the Homicide Act 1957. See also *R v Chan-Fook* [1994] 2 All ER 552, CA, applied in *R v Morris* [1998] 1 Cr App R 386, CA: where psychiatric injury is relied on to support a charge of assault occasioning actual bodily harm and is not admitted by the defence, the Crown should call expert evidence.

[63] *R v Smith* [1979] 1 WLR 1445, CA.

[64] *R v Hegarty* [1994] Crim LR 353, CA. See also *R v Horne* [1994] Crim LR 584, CA; and cf *R v Hurst* [1995] 1 Cr App R 82, CA.

[65] [2003] All ER (D) 64 (Jun).

[66] See also *R v Jackson-Mason* [2014] EWCA Crim 1993 (expert evidence of suggestibility not relevant where the issue was not duress but what the accused thought or believed).

[67] See also *R v Challen* [2019] EWCA Crim 916 (expert evidence concerning the effect of coercive control admitted in an appeal against a conviction for murder on grounds of diminished responsibility and provocation).

[68] *R v Chard* (1971) 56 Cr App R 268, CA. See also *R v Reynolds* [1989] Crim LR 220, CA; *R v Wood* [1990] Crim LR 264, CA; and, in the case of adolescents, *R v Coles* [1995] 1 Cr App R 157, CA.

[69] [1986] Crim LR 395, CA.

or below, then insofar as that defectiveness is relevant to an issue, expert evidence may be admitted, provided that it is confined to an assessment of the accused's IQ and an explanation of any relevant abnormal characteristics, to enlighten the jury on a matter that is abnormal and *ex hypothesi* outside their experience; but where an accused is within the scale of normality, albeit at the lower end, expert evidence should generally be excluded.[70]

In *R v Toner*,[71] a case of attempted murder in which a doctor gave evidence that T may have been suffering from a minor hypoglycaemic state, it was held that the defence should have been permitted to cross-examine him as to whether the effect of such an attack could have negatived T's special intent to kill and to cause serious bodily harm. The Court of Appeal saw no distinction between such medical evidence and medical evidence as to the effect of a drug on intent: both matters were outside the ordinary experience of jurors. Similarly in *R v Huckerby*[72] it was held that evidence that the accused was suffering from post-traumatic stress disorder, a recognized mental condition with which the jury would not be expected to be familiar, was admissible because relevant to an essential issue bearing upon his guilt or innocence, namely whether it caused him to panic and cooperate with criminals in circumstances where he would otherwise not have done so.

Credibility

Expert evidence is generally inadmissible on the issue of a witness's credibility,[73] but is obviously called for in relation to matters affecting credibility of which the jury may be unaware.[74] In *Re S (a child) (Adoption: Psychological Evidence)*,[75] an appeal against a care order, the judge at first instance had relied on the results of a personality questionnaire, including a 'Lie-Scale' measuring the mother's willingness to distort her responses in order to create a good impression. Allowing the appeal, it was held that the results of personality or psychometric tests should only rarely have any place in such cases because it is for the tribunal of fact to decide questions of credibility.

---

[70] However, as Hodgson J stated in *R v Silcott* [1987] Crim LR 765 (see [1988] Crim LR 293): 'To draw a strict line at 69/70 does seem somewhat artificial.' For a critical analysis of the notion that there is a clear line dividing normality and subnormality, see Mackay, 'Excluding Expert Evidence: A Tale of Ordinary Folk and Common Experience' [1991] Crim LR 800. See also *R v Hall* (1987) 86 Cr App R 159, CA and *R v Henry* [2006] 1 Cr App R 118 (6), CA; contrast *Schultz v R* [1982] WAR 171 (Supreme Court of Western Australia). See also *R v Lupien* (1970) 9 DLR (3d) 1 (Supreme Court of Canada): psychiatric evidence is admissible to show a person's lack of capacity to form intent.

[71] (1991) 93 Cr App R 382, CA.

[72] [2004] EWCA Crim 3251.

[73] See *R v Henry* [2006] 1 Cr App R 118 (6), CA (the accused); *R v C* [2012] EWCA Crim 1478 (a complainant in a sexual case); and *R v Joyce* [2005] NTS 21 (a prosecution witness).

[74] See *R v S* [2006] EWCA Crim 2389; *R v Mulindwa* [2017] 2 Cr App R 94 (10); and *R v Robinson* [1994] 3 All ER 346, CA (all considered in Ch 7). See also, in this chapter, *R v H* [2014] EWCA Crim 1555 and *R v Clark* [2006] EWCA Crim 231, under **Matters within or outwith the experience and knowledge of the tribunal of fact**, p 638, and *Re M and R (minors)* [1996] 4 All ER 239, CA, under **Evidence on ultimate issues**, p 657. Cf *R v Hayes* [2018] 1 Cr App R 134 (10), CA: medical evidence of the accused's mental distress was not admissible as to the credibility of his reasons for entering into an agreement under the Serious Organised Crime and Police Act 2005—the jury would have readily understood the pressure and distress the accused was under.

[75] [2004] EWCA Civ 1029.

Impact of sexual offences on victims

In its consultation paper *Convicting Rapists and Protecting Victims—Justice for Victims of Rape* (2006), the Government proposed that prosecutors should be able to present general expert evidence about the psychological impact of sexual offences upon victims. This impact is not necessarily within the understanding of the average juror and expert evidence is capable of dispelling popular myths and misconceptions and explaining behaviour which might otherwise be thought to be puzzling, including, for example, delay in making a complaint.[76] In the light of the responses to the consultation paper, the Government's proposal was replaced by a proposal to provide information packs or videos for jurors or to give them special warnings.[77] The original proposal, however, reflected an assumption that expert evidence concerning the behavioural symptoms typical of victims of sexual abuse is currently not admissible because it relates to their credibility. The assumption is erroneous, it is submitted, because such evidence, if general in nature and if it does not include an opinion on the credibility of the victim, simply provides the tribunal of fact with relevant information by which it may better evaluate the witness's evidence.[78]

Propensity of a co-accused

In *Lowery v R*,[79] the Privy Council held that the trial judge had properly permitted K to call a psychologist to give evidence that L, his co-accused, was aggressive, lacking in self-control, and more likely to have committed the offence than K. *Lowery v R* was relied upon in *R v Randall*[80] where the House of Lords expressly declined to explore any doubts about the admissibility of *expert* evidence on propensity.[81] However, in *R v Turner*[82] Lawton LJ said:

> We adjudge *Lowery v R* to have been decided on its special facts. We do not consider that it is an authority for the proposition that in all cases psychologists and psychiatrists can be called to prove the probability of the accused's veracity.[83]

Reliability or truth of a confession

Expert evidence of a psychiatrist or psychologist is admissible on the issue of the reliability or truth of a confession.[84] It has been said that such evidence is inadmissible before the jury on the issue of the truth of a confession made by an accused who, although he may have

---

[76] For a comparative review of the admissibility of expert evidence to explain delay, see Lewis, 'Expert evidence of delay in complaint in childhood sexual abuse prosecutions' (2006) 10 E&P 157.

[77] For guidance on directions that should be given in relation to unwarranted assumptions in sexual cases, see the Crown Court Compendium (July 2019), Part 1, 20–1.

[78] See also Ellison, 'Closing the credibility gap: The prosecutorial use of expert witness testimony in sexual assault cases' (2005) 9 E&P 239; Dempsey, *The Use of Expert Testimony in the Prosecution of Domestic Violence* (London, 2004); and Cossins, 'Expert witness evidence in sexual assault trials: questions, answers and law reform in Australia and England' (2013) 17 E&P 74.

[79] [1974] AC 85.

[80] [2004] 1 WLR 56, HL.

[81] See Per Lord Steyn at [30].

[82] [1975] QB 834, CA at 842.

[83] See also *Toohey v Metropolitan Police Comr* [1965] AC 595, HL; *R v MacKenney* [2004] 2 Cr App R 32, CA; and *R v Robinson* [1994] 3 All ER 346 (all in Ch 7); *R v Bracewell* (1978) 68 Cr App R 44; and *R v Rimmer and Beech* [1983] Crim LR 250, CA.

[84] See *R v Walker* [1998] Crim LR 211, CA and *R v Ward* [1993] 1 WLR 619, CA.

an abnormal personality, does not suffer from mental illness and is not below normal intelligence.[85] This is misleading because the evidence admissible is not confined to evidence of personality disorders so severe as properly to be categorized as mental disorders. The test is not whether the abnormality fits into a recognized category such as anti-social personality disorder. That is neither necessary nor sufficient. There are two requirements. First, the abnormal disorder must be of the type which might render the confession unreliable, and in this respect there must be a very significant deviation from the norm. Second, there should be a history pre-dating the making of the confession, based not solely on what the accused says, which points to or explains the abnormality. When such evidence is admitted, the jury should be directed that they are not obliged to accept it, but may consider it as throwing light on the personality of the accused, bringing to their attention aspects of it of which they might otherwise have been unaware.[86] The evidence of a psychologist is also admissible to show the likely unreliability of a confession made by someone not suffering from any abnormal disorder if it is a 'coerced compliant confession', that is a confession brought about by fatigue and inability to control what is happening, which may induce a vulnerable individual to experience a growing desire to give up resisting the suggestions put to him so that eventually he is overwhelmed by the need to achieve the immediate goal of ending the interrogation.[87]

Expert witnesses

Expertise

A witness is competent to give expert evidence only if, in the opinion of the judge, he is properly qualified in the subject calling for expertise[88] and courts need to be scrupulous to ensure that 'expert' evidence is indeed based upon specialized experience, knowledge, or study—mere self-certification is insufficient.[89] The requirement applies in the case of evidence of fact based upon an expert's expertise as well as expert opinion evidence.[90] In rare cases, it will be necessary to hold a *voir dire* to decide whether a purported expert should be allowed to give evidence, but in the vast majority of cases the judge will be able to make the decision on the basis of written material. If the defence want to contest the competence of an expert in a *voir dire*, the burden is on them to make an application to the judge.[91] However, if a witness can give relevant evidence, is not an expert, and will give no expert opinion, the application is bound to fail.[92] The judge, during the trial, also has the power, should the need arise, to remove a witness's 'expert' status and limit his evidence to factual matters.[93]

---

[85] *R v Weightman* (1990) 92 Cr App R 291, CA.

[86] *R v O'Brien* [2000] Crim LR 676, CA, applied in *R v Smith* [2003] EWCA Crim 927. See also *R v Childs* [2014] EWCA Crim 1884.

[87] *R v Blackburn* [2005] 2 Cr App R 440 (30), CA.

[88] But see the Criminal Procedure (Insanity and Unfitness to Plead) Act 1991, s 1(1): a jury shall not acquit on the ground of insanity except on the evidence of two or more registered doctors, at least one of whom is approved by the Secretary of State as having appropriate expertise.

[89] *R v Atkins* [2010] 1 Cr App R 117 (8), CA at [27].

[90] *Kennedy v Cordia (Services) LLP* [2016] UKSC 6 at [50]. Those instructing expert witnesses must also satisfy themselves as to the witness's expertise: *R v Pabon* [2018] EWCA Crim 420 at [77].

[91] *R v Francis* [2013] EWCA Crim 123.

[92] *R v Foulger* [2012] EWCA Crim 1516.

[93] *R v G* [2004] 2 Cr App R 638 (38), CA.

An expert may have acquired his expertise through study, training, or experience. An engineer who understands the construction of harbours, the causes of their destruction, and how remedied, may express his opinion on whether an embankment caused the decay of a harbour.[94] A police officer with qualifications and experience in accident investigation may give expert opinion evidence on how a road accident occurred.[95] A police officer may give expert evidence of the practices, mores, and associations of gangs (unless it is inadmissible evidence of bad character) if he has made a sufficient study, by formal training or practical experience, to acquire a balanced body of specialized knowledge not available to the jury, as opposed to simple and not necessarily balanced anecdotal evidence.[96] A doctor experienced in emergency medicine and who would have dealt with many thousands of cases of lacerations and cuts may express an opinion that certain injuries were not caused by a pin but were likely to have been caused by a blade.[97] Someone with no medical qualifications but with experience and knowledge of drug abuse through charitable work, drug projects, and personal research may give expert opinion evidence as to what quantities of ecstasy are consistent with personal use and how users acquire an increasing tolerance of the drug.[98] On the other hand, a medical orderly experienced in the treatment of cuts is not sufficiently qualified to express an opinion on whether a cut to the forehead was caused by a blunt instrument or a head-butt;[99] and an osteoarticular pathologist may give his opinion on whether fractured ribs could have caused a person's death, but not on the other possible causes of death.[100]

There is no requirement that the witness should have acquired his expertise professionally or in the course of his business. Thus in *R v Silverlock*[101] it was held that a solicitor who had studied handwriting for 10 years, mostly as an amateur, had properly been allowed to give his opinion as to whether certain disputed handwriting was that of the accused.

Many authorities concern the competence of a witness to give expert opinion evidence on a point of foreign law. A person has been held to be suitably qualified for these purposes if he is a practitioner in the foreign jurisdiction in question,[102] a former practitioner,[103] a person who has not practised in the jurisdiction but is qualified to do so,[104] or a person who has acquired the appropriate expertise other than by practice, whether by academic study,[105] as an embassy official,[106] or in the course of some non-legal profession or business such as

[94] *Folkes v Chadd* (1782) 3 Doug KB 157.

[95] *R v Oakley* (1979) 70 Cr App R 7, CA; *R v Murphy* [1980] QB 434, CA. Cf *Hinds v London Transport Executive* [1979] RTR 103, CA. See also, in this chapter, *R v Hodges* [2003] 2 Cr App R 247 (15), CA, under **Evidence of facts upon which an opinion is based**, p 654. See also, *sed quaere, R v Somers* [1963] 1 WLR 1306, CCA.

[96] *Myers v R* [2016] AC 314, PC at [58]. See also *R v Fender* [2018] EWCA Crim 2829.

[97] *R v Francis* [2013] EWCA Crim 123.

[98] *R v Ibrahima* [2005] Crim LR 887, CA. Cf, in this chapter, *R v Edwards* [2001] EWCA Crim 2185 under **Evidence of facts upon which an opinion is based**, p 654.

[99] *R v Inch* (1989) 91 Cr App R 51, C-MAC.

[100] *R v Clarke* [2013] EWCA Crim 162.

[101] [1894] 2 QB 766, CCR.

[102] *Baron de Bode's Case* (1845) 8 QB 208.

[103] *Re Duke of Wellington, Glentanar v Wellington* [1947] Ch 506.

[104] *Barford v Barford and McLeod* [1918] P 140.

[105] *Brailey v Rhodesia Consolidated Ltd* [1910] 2 Ch 95.

[106] *Dost Aly Khan's Goods* (1880) 6 PD 6.

banking[107] or trading.[108] Although at common law there is authority that a practitioner in the jurisdiction in question should *always* be called,[109] in civil proceedings s 4(1) of the Civil Evidence Act 1972 now declares that:

> a person who is suitably qualified to do so on account of his knowledge or experience is competent to give expert evidence as to the law of any country or territory outside the United Kingdom, or of any part of the United Kingdom other than England and Wales, irrespective of whether he has acted or is entitled to act as a legal practitioner there.

Independence

As we shall see, the role of an expert witness is special because he owes a duty to the court which he must discharge notwithstanding the interest of the party calling him.[110] A conflict of interest does not automatically disqualify an expert, because the key question is whether his evidence is independent, but if the conflict is material or significant, which is a question for the court and not the parties, the evidence should be excluded or ignored, and therefore a party who wishes to call an expert with a potential conflict of interests of any kind should disclose the details to the other party and to the court at the earliest possible opportunity.[111] Only rarely will the court admit the evidence of an expert who has a financial interest in the outcome of the litigation.[112] Whether a conflicting duty will disqualify an expert from giving evidence will depend on the circumstances of the case.[113] If an expert has a personal or other connection with a party which might consciously or subconsciously influence or bias his evidence, this will not normally disqualify him, but will go to the weight to be attached to his evidence.[114] An employee of a party can be an independent expert, provided that the party can demonstrate that the employee has not only the relevant experience but also an awareness of his overriding duty, as an expert witness, to the court.[115] Similarly, in the case of an expert who is an employee of a third party, it has been held that an acknowledged risk of a subliminal but not conscious bias or lack of objectivity goes to weight and not admissibility.[116] In *R v Smith*[117] the Court of Appeal, noting that a person outside a police Fingerprint Bureau cannot become fully qualified as a fingerprint expert in England and Wales, observed that it is essential for the proper administration of justice that there are independent persons expert in fingerprint examination.

---

[107] *de Beéche v South American Stores* [1935] AC 148, HL; *Ajami v Comptroller of Customs* [1954] 1 WLR 1405, PC.

[108] *Vander Donckt v Thellusson* (1849) 8 CB 812.

[109] *Bristow v Sequeville* (1850) 5 Exch 275.

[110] See per Cresswell J in *National Justice Cia Naviera SA v Prudential Assurance Co Ltd, The Ikarian Reefer* [1993] 2 Lloyd's Rep 68.

[111] *Toth v Jarman* [2006] EWCA Civ 1028. The requirement of independence applies to an expert in respect of both expert evidence of opinion and evidence of fact based on his expertise: *Kennedy v Cordia (Services) LLP* [2016] UKSC 6 at [44].

[112] *R (Factortame Ltd) v Secretary of State for Transport, Local Government and the Regions* [2002] EWCA Civ 932 at [72]–[73].

[113] *Toth v Jarman* [2006] EWCA Civ 1028 at [99]–[110].

[114] *Field v Leeds City Council* [2001] CPLR 129; and generally *Rowley v Dunlop* [2014] EWHC 1995 (Ch) at [21].

[115] *Field v Leeds City Council* [2001] CPLR 129. See also *Meat Corporation of Namibia Ltd v Dawn Meats (UK) Ltd* [2011] EWHC 474 (Ch) (a consultant to a party).

[116] *R v Stubbs* [2006] EWCA Crim 2312, CA at [59].

[117] [2011] 2 Cr App R 174 (16), CA.

Reliability

No need for certainty

A jury are entitled to rely on an expert opinion notwithstanding that it falls short of scientific certainty. Thus in a murder trial a judge should not withdraw a case from the jury merely by reason of the fact that an expert giving evidence for the prosecution as to the cause of death agrees as a theoretical possibility that the victim could have died from another cause consistent with innocence.[118] Nor should expert evidence be excluded or withdrawn from the jury where prosecution and defence experts disagree, but each is of the view that the opinion of the other is valid and tenable.[119]

The requirement of sufficient reliability

On a number of occasions, English judges have cited with approval the test for the admissibility of expert opinion evidence propounded in *R v Bonython*[120] a test which also applies where an expert gives evidence of fact based on his expertise.[121] Under the test, in addition to the issues of whether the subject matter of the opinion calls for expertise and whether the witness has requisite expertise, reference is also made to 'whether the subject matter of the opinion forms part of a body of knowledge or experience which is sufficiently organized or recognized to be accepted as a reliable body of knowledge or experience, a special acquaintance with which by the witness would render his opinion of assistance to the court'.[122] However, English common law, with notable exceptions, has been generally reluctant to impose a requirement of reliability, which is curious given the obvious dangers, especially in criminal trials, of allowing the tribunal of fact to rely on 'expert' testimony of questionable reliability.[123] In *R v I*,[124] for example, it was held that expert opinion evidence should have been admitted notwithstanding that it rested on a hypothesis that could have been tested to ensure its reliability, but was not.

R v Gilfoyle,[125] one of the exceptions, was a murder trial in which the only other possible explanation for the death was suicide. The Court of Appeal refused to hear the fresh evidence of a psychologist who had carried out a 'psychological autopsy' of the deceased. One of the reasons given for this conclusion was that the expert had identified no criteria by reference to which the court could test the quality of his opinions: there was no database comparing real and questionable suicides and there was no substantial body of academic writing approving his methodology.[126]

---

[118] *R v Gian* [2009] EWCA Crim 2553, CA.

[119] *R v Hookway* [2011] EWCA Crim 1989.

[120] (1984) 38 SASR 45.

[121] *Kennedy v Cordia (Services) LLP* [2016] UKSC 6 at [44] and [54].

[122] Extraneous information may also affect the reliability of an expert's opinion, as when expert fingerprint examiners are told, eg, that the suspect has an alibi or has confessed: see Dror and Cole, 'The vision in "blind justice": Expert perception, judgment and visual cognition in forensic pattern recognition' (2012) 17(2) *Psychonomic Bulletin & Review* 161 and Dror and Rosenthal, 'Meta-analytically Quantifying the Reliability and Biasability of Forensic Experts' (2008) 53(4) *J Forensic Sci* 900.

[123] See generally Redmayne, *Expert Evidence and Criminal Justice* (Oxford, 2001) ch 5, O'Brian Jr, 'Court scrutiny of expert evidence: Recent decisions highlight the tensions' (2003) 7 E&P 172 and the report of the House of Commons Science and Technology Committee, *Forensic Science on Trial*, HC 96–1 2005, which recommends the establishment of a Forensic Science Advisory Council to develop a gate-keeping test for expert evidence.

[124] [2012] EWCA Crim 1288.

[125] [2001] 2 Cr App R 57 (5), CA.

[126] *R v Kwaik* [2013] EWCA Crim 2397 appears to be another example. A computerized accident reconstruction technique was held to be insufficiently robust to undermine significantly the Crown's case because it only covered some simulations, a large number of variables relating to braking, steering, etc not having been explored.

Determining whether evidence is sufficiently reliable

The Law Commission, in its 2011 Report on Expert Evidence in Criminal Proceedings,[127] proposed that there should be an explicit 'gate-keeping' role for the trial judge involving a determination whether the proffered evidence is sufficiently reliable to be admitted. It recommended that it should be for the party wishing to rely on the expert evidence, whether the prosecution or the accused, to show that it is sufficiently reliable to be admitted, having regard to a number of specified factors.[128] The Government declined to follow this recommendation and did not introduce a statutory reliability test. Instead, it invited the Criminal Procedure Rules Committee to consider amendments to its rules to ensure that judges are provided with more information about the expert evidence that it is proposed to adduce in order to increase the likelihood of challenges to its admissibility. Rule 19.4(h) now requires that an expert's report must include such information as the court may need to decide whether the evidence is sufficiently reliable to be admissible in evidence; and the Criminal Practice Directions now incorporate the reliability factors recommended by the Law Commission. Paragraphs 19A.4–19A.6 of the Criminal Practice Directions V provide as follows.

19A.4 In its judgment in *R v Dlugosz and Others* [2013] EWCA Crim 2, the Court of Appeal observed (at paragraph 11): 'It is essential to recall the principle which is applicable, namely in determining the issue of admissibility, the court must be satisfied that there is a sufficiently reliable scientific basis for the evidence to be admitted. If there is then the court leaves the opposing views to be tested before the jury.' Nothing at common law precludes assessment by the court of the reliability of an expert opinion by reference to substantially similar factors to those the Law Commission recommended as conditions of admissibility, and courts are encouraged actively to enquire into such factors.

19A.5 Therefore factors which the court may take into account in determining the reliability of expert opinion, and especially of expert scientific opinion, include:

(a) the extent and quality of the data on which the expert's opinion is based, and the validity of the methods by which they were obtained;

(b) if the expert's opinion relies on an inference from any findings, whether the opinion properly explains how safe or unsafe the inference is (whether by reference to statistical significance or in other appropriate terms);

(c) if the expert's opinion relies on the results of the use of any method (for instance, a test, measurement or survey), whether the opinion takes proper account of those matters, such as the degree of precision or margin of uncertainty, affecting the accuracy or reliability of those results;

---

[127] Law Com No 325 (2011).

[128] For critical commentary of the consultation paper on which the Report is based (see Consultation Paper No 190 (2009)), see Roberts, 'Rejecting General Acceptance, Confounding the Gate-keeper: the Law Commission and Expert Evidence' [2009] Crim LR 551 and Hartshorne and Miola, 'Expert evidence: difficulties and solutions in prosecutions for infant harm' (2010) 30(2) *Legal Studies* 279. For critical commentary on the Report, see Edmond and Roberts, 'The Law Commission's Report on Expert Evidence in Criminal Proceedings' [2011] Crim LR 844 and Edmond, 'Is reliability sufficient? The Law Commission and expert evidence in international and interdisciplinary perspective' (2012) 16 E&P 30. See also Ward, 'Expert Evidence and the Law Commission; Implementation without Legislation?' [2013] Crim LR 561 and Danaher, 'Blind expertise and the problem of scientific evidence' (2011) 15 E&P 207.

(d) the extent to which any material upon which the expert's opinion is based has been reviewed by others with relevant expertise (for instance, in peer-reviewed publications), and the views of those others on that material;

(e) the extent to which the expert's opinion is based on material falling outside the expert's own field of expertise;

(f) the completeness of the information which was available to the expert, and whether the expert took account of all relevant information in arriving at the opinion (including information as to the context of any facts to which the opinion relates);

(g) if there is a range of expert opinion on the matter in question, where in the range the expert's own opinion lies and whether the expert's preference has been properly explained; and

(h) whether the expert's methods followed established practice in the field and, if they did not, whether the reason for the divergence has been properly explained.

19A.6 In addition, in considering reliability, and especially the reliability of expert scientific opinion, the court should be astute to identify potential flaws in such opinion which detract from its reliability, such as:

(a) being based on a hypothesis which has not been subjected to sufficient scrutiny (including, where appropriate, experimental or other testing), or which has failed to stand up to scrutiny;

(b) being based on an unjustifiable assumption;

(c) being based on flawed data;

(d) relying on an examination, technique, method or process which was not properly carried out or applied, or was not appropriate for use in the particular case; or

(e) relying on an inference or conclusion which has not been properly reached.

As to paragraph 19A.4, the Practice Direction does not include a definition of 'sufficient reliability' of the kind proposed by the Law Commission and therefore gives no indication of the weight required of the evidence to be admitted.[129] As to paragraph 19A.5, reliability factors of the kind detailed, including those set out in *Frye v United States*[130] and *Daubert v Merrell Dow Pharmaceuticals*,[131] may be desirable in principle, but raise additional and complex questions and issues: whether particular scientific techniques have been generally accepted; identification of the scientific community by which there may have been such general acceptance, which could be a community reflecting a broad or narrow field of expertise; whether scientific techniques may be reliable even if not, or not yet, accepted by a scientific community;[132] and whether reliance on general acceptance by a scientific community amounts to a usurpation of the role of the trial judge.[133]

In *R v H*[134] Sir Brian Leveson said that the foregoing changes called for the adoption of 'a new and more rigorous approach on the part of advocates and the courts to the handling of expert evidence.' The examples of expert evidence which now fall to be considered

---

[129] Ward, 'A new and more rigorous approach to expert evidence in England and Wales?' (2016) 19(4) E&P 228.

[130] 293 F 1013 (DC Cir, 1923).

[131] 509 US 579 (1993).

[132] See, eg, the concern expressed in *R v Hoey* [2007] NICC 49 about the absence of validation guidelines for LCN DNA tests compared to the 'normal' SGM+ DNA tests.

[133] Roberts, 'Drawing on Expertise: Legal Decision-making and the Reception of Expert Evidence' [2008] Crim LR 443 at 455–7.

[134] [2014] EWCA Crim 1555.

involve authorities decided prior to the coming into force of these changes. It is submitted that these authorities should be treated with caution, especially in the light of the dictum from *R v H* and notwithstanding that, as has been observed,[135] the 'active encouragement' to which paragraph 19A.4 refers falls short of an *obligation* to enquire into the relevant factors.

Earprints

In *R v Dallagher*,[136] where identity was in issue, evidence was received from two experts who had examined earprints. The expertise of earprint comparison was in its relative infancy, and after the trial it emerged that other forensic scientists had misgivings about the extent to which earprint evidence alone could, in the state of knowledge at that time, safely be used to identify a suspect. It was held that the expert evidence had been properly admitted, but the appeal was allowed and a retrial ordered on the basis that the fresh evidence, if given at trial, might reasonably have affected the approach of the jury to the identification evidence of the experts and thus affected their decision to convict.[137]

Lip-reading

In *R v Luttrell*[138] the court, while accepting that the reliability of expert evidence can be relevant to the issue of admissibility, rejected the argument that lip-reading evidence as to what was said by someone talking on a CCTV recording should not be admitted unless it could be seen to be reliable because the methods used were sufficiently explained to be tested in cross-examination and so to be verifiable or falsifiable.

DNA transference

In *R v Reed*[139] expert evidence as to the possible ways in which DNA may have been transferred was held to be admissible: the underlying scientific knowledge on such transferability was thought to be sufficiently reliable but 'plainly incomplete'.

Facial mapping

In *R v Atkins*[140] it was held that an expert in facial mapping could express a view as to the extent to which his findings supported identification of the accused notwithstanding the absence of a statistical database by which such a view could be given a numerical value, provided that it was made crystal clear to the jury that such a view was an expression of subjective opinion.

Low-template DNA

R v Atkins was followed in *R v Dlugosz*,[141] where experts were permitted to give evaluative evidence on low-template DNA derived from mixed samples in the absence of statistical evidence of the relevant DNA match probability.

---

[135] See Dennis, 'Tightening the Law on Expert Evidence' [2015] Crim LR 1.
[136] [2003] 1 Cr App R 195 (12), CA.
[137] See also *R v Kempster (No 2)* [2008] 2 Cr App R 256 (19), CA.
[138] [2004] 2 Cr App R 520 (41), CA.
[139] [2010] 1 Cr App R 310 (23), CA at [111] and [119].
[140] [2010] 1 Cr App R 117 (8), CA.
[141] [2013] 1 Cr App R 425 (32), CA.

Footwear marks

In *R v T*,[142] where it was held, in relation to footwear mark comparison evidence, that there are no sufficiently reliable data for an expert to express an opinion based on the use of a mathematical probability formula, the court was nonetheless of the view that an expert may give an evaluative opinion that a shoe could have made a mark based on class characteristics resulting from manufacture and identifying characteristics such as damage to the sole.[143]

Gait

Similarly in *R v Ferdinand*[144] a consultant podiatric surgeon was allowed to give evidence of the similarity of gait of the suspect and the accused in the absence of a database to support his assessment of the frequency of the common features he identified, an assessment founded mainly on his clinical experience, as opposed to the population at large.

Voice identification

The dangers of the relaxed approach taken to gait evidence in *R v Ferdinand* are highlighted by the decisions in *R v Robb*[145] and *R v O'Doherty*[146] in respect of voice identification evidence. In *R v Robb* a lecturer in phonetics was held to be well qualified by his academic training and practical experience to express an opinion as to the identity of a voice, notwithstanding that his auditory technique, which was to pay close attention to voice quality, pitch, and pronunciation, was not generally respected by other experts in the field because it was not supplemented and verified by acoustic analysis based on physical measurements of resonance, frequency, etc. In *R v O'Doherty* the prosecution expert at the trial gave evidence based on the same technique as the expert in *R v Robb*. On appeal, the Court of Appeal for Northern Ireland received fresh expert evidence to the effect that auditory techniques, unless supplemented and verified by acoustic analysis, were an unreliable basis of speaker identification and that, based on an acoustic analysis, the voice on the tape was not that of the accused. Allowing the appeal, the court observed that since *R v Robb*, 'time has moved on'. It was held that in the present state of scientific knowledge, no prosecution should be brought in Northern Ireland in which one of the planks is voice identification given by an expert which is solely confined to auditory analysis; there should also be expert evidence of acoustic analysis.[147] However, in *R v Flynn*[148] it has since been stated, but without any specific amplification, that it is 'neither possible nor desirable' to go as far as the Northern Ireland Court of Appeal in this respect.[149]

---

[142] [2011] 1 Cr App R 85 (9), CA.

[143] For critical analysis, see Redmayne et al, 'Forensic Science Evidence in Question' [2011] Crim LR 347 and Morrison, 'The likelihood-ratio framework and forensic evidence in court: a response to *R v T*' (2012) 16 E&P 1.

[144] [2014] EWCA Crim 1243.

[145] (1991) 93 Cr App R 161, CA.

[146] [2003] 1 Cr App R 77 (5), CA (NI).

[147] The court made three exceptions to its general statement: where the voices of a known group are being listened to and the issue is which voice has spoken which words; where there are rare characteristics rendering a speaker identifiable; and where the issue relates to the accent or dialect of the speaker.

[148] [2008] 2 Cr App R 266, CA at 281. See also Ch 9, **Voice identification**, p 298.

[149] For a critical review of the authorities on voice comparison evidence, see Morrison, 'Admissibility of forensic voice comparison testimony in England and Wales' [2018] Crim LR 20.

Sudden Infant Death Syndrome

In the context of medical expert evidence on the cause of injury or death, particular caution is needed where the scientific knowledge is or may be incomplete and also where the expert opinion evidence is not relied upon as additional material in support of a prosecution, but is fundamental to it.[150] In *R v Cannings*[151] Judge LJ, delivering the judgment of the Court of Appeal, said:

> Experts in many fields will acknowledge the possibility that later research may undermine the accepted wisdom of today. 'Never say never' is a phrase which we have heard in many different contexts from expert witnesses. That does not normally provide a basis for rejecting the expert evidence, or indeed for conjuring up fanciful doubts about the possible impact of later research.

However, the court went on to say that in the case of two or more sudden unexplained infant deaths in the same family, in many important respects we are still at the frontiers of knowledge. It was held that, for the time being, where a full investigation is followed by a serious disagreement between reputable experts about the cause of death and a body of such expert opinion concludes that natural causes cannot be excluded as a reasonable and not a fanciful possibility, the prosecution of a parent or parents for murder should not be started or continued in the absence of additional cogent evidence extraneous to the expert evidence and tending to support the conclusion of deliberate harm.[152]

R v Cannings was distinguished in *R v Kai-Whitewind*.[153] K-W was convicted of the murder of her infant son. She had had difficulty bonding with the child and there was evidence that shortly after he was born she had felt like killing the child. The child died while in her sole care. On the day he died, she had sought medical advice after he had developed a spontaneous nosebleed, an extremely rare occurrence in the case of an infant. Post-mortem examinations revealed new and old blood in the lungs. According to the prosecution experts, this was consistent with two distinct episodes of upper airway obstruction, but the views of the defence experts were that death by natural causes was more probable than unnatural death or that the cause of death was unascertained. The appeal against conviction was dismissed. It was held that *R v Cannings* concerned inferences based upon coincidence, or the unlikelihood of two or more infant deaths in the same family, or one death where another child or other children in the family had suffered from unexplained 'Apparent Life Threatening Events'. There was essentially no evidence beyond the inferences based upon coincidence which the prosecution experts were prepared to draw but as to which other reputable experts in the same specialist field took a different view. Hence the need for additional cogent evidence. It did not follow from this that whenever there was a conflict between expert witnesses, the case for the prosecution had to fail unless the conviction was justified by evidence independent of the expert witnesses. In the instant case there was a single death, it was not suggested that any inference should be drawn against the accused from any previous incident involving any of her children, and the evidence about the child's condition found on the post-mortem examination was evidence of fact and precisely the kind of material which was sought and could not be found in *R v Cannings*. The dispute between experts about the

---

[150] *R v Holdsworth* [2009] Crim LR 195, CA.
[151] [2004] 1 WLR 2607, CA at [178].
[152] See also **Ch 8 at p 273**.
[153] [2005] 2 Cr App R 457 (31), CA.

interpretation of the findings at the post-mortem did not extinguish the findings themselves, and the jury had been entitled to evaluate the expert evidence, taking account of facts found at the post-mortem and bearing in mind in addition, for example, that they related to an infant whose mother had spoken about killing him, had made a comment about smothering another child, who might have delayed reporting his death, and who had elected not to give evidence.[154]

DNA profiles and fingerprint data

In respect of the reliability of DNA profiles and fingerprint data which the prosecution may seek to rely on, additional safeguards are provided by the Accreditation of Forensic Science Providers Regulations.[155] The Regulations provide that competent law enforcement authorities may only use a forensic science provider to perform laboratory activity that (a) results in a DNA profile or dactyloscopic (fingerprint) data and (b) is requested in relation to the prevention, detection, or investigation of a crime, if that provider is accredited to EU standards of accreditation on general requirements for the competence of testing and calibration laboratories.[156]

The duty of the lawyer

Lawyers who propose to adduce expert evidence are under a duty to assess whether the expert has the necessary expertise. They should also disclose to the expert all of the relevant factual material which they intend should contribute to the expert's evidence, including not only material which supports their client's case but also material they are aware of, which points in the other direction.[157]

The duty of the expert

In civil proceedings, under r 35.3 of the Civil Procedure Rules, the expert has a duty to help the court on the matters within his expertise, a duty that overrides any obligation to the person who has instructed him or by whom he is paid. In similar vein, under r 19.2 of the Criminal Procedure Rules 2015[158] in criminal proceedings an expert has a duty to the court to help it to achieve the overriding objective by giving objective unbiased opinion on matters within his expertise, a duty that overrides any obligation to the person by whom he is instructed or paid[159] and that includes obligations: (a) to define his area or areas of expertise in his report and when giving evidence; (b) when giving evidence in person, to draw to the court's attention any question the answer to which would be outside his area or areas of expertise; and (c) to inform all parties and the court if his opinion changes from that contained in a report served as evidence or given in a statement. The duty of the expert as described in these rules builds on and, to an extent, overlaps with, the descriptions

---

[154] For critical commentary, see [2006] Crim LR 348, CA. *R v Cannings* was also distinguished in *R v Hookway* [2011] EWCA Crim 1989 where prosecution did not depend exclusively or almost exclusively on disputed expert evidence about mixed DNA profiles and the disagreement between the experts was not about whether DNA implicated H, but about its strength.

[155] SI 2018/1276.

[156] Ibid, Regulations 3 and 4, and the Explanatory Note to Regulation 4.

[157] *Kennedy v Cordia (Services) LLP* [2016] UKSC 6 at [57].

[158] SI 2015/1490.

[159] An expert called by the prosecution in breach of the duty may be personally responsible for the accused's costs: see s 19 of the Prosecution of Offences Act 1985 and *R (DPP) v Aylesbury Crown Court* [2018] 4 WLR 30.

of the obligations of an expert set out by Cresswell J in *National Justice Cia Naviera SA v Prudential Assurance Co Ltd, The Ikarian Reefer*[160] and the guidance for experts giving evidence involving children provided by Wall J in *In re AB (child abuse: expert witnesses)*.[161] In *R v Harris*[162] it was held that these descriptions were also very relevant in criminal proceedings. Some of the factors set out by Cresswell J in *The Ikarian Reefer* were summarized in *R v Harris*[163] as follows:

1. Expert evidence presented to the court should be and be seen to be the independent product of the expert uninfluenced as to form or content by the exigencies of litigation.

2. An expert witness should provide independent assistance to the court by way of objective unbiased opinion in relation to matters within his expertise. An expert witness in the High Court should never assume the role of advocate.[164]

3. An expert witness should state the facts or assumptions on which his opinion is based. He should not omit to consider material facts which detract from his concluded opinion.

4. An expert should make it clear when a particular question or issue falls outside his expertise.

5. If an expert's opinion is not properly researched because he considers that insufficient data are available then this must be stated with an indication that the opinion is no more than a provisional one.

6. If, after exchange of reports, an expert witness changes his view on material matters, such changes of view should be communicated to the other side without delay and when appropriate to the court.

In *In re AB (child abuse: expert witnesses)* Wall J, referring to cases in which there is a genuine disagreement on a scientific or medical issue or where it is necessary for a party to advance a particular hypothesis to explain a given set of facts, said:[165]

> Where that occurs, the judge [in a criminal case, the jury] will have to resolve the issue which is raised. Two points must be made. In my view, the expert who advances such a hypothesis owes a very heavy duty to explain to the court that what he is advancing is a hypothesis, that it is controversial (if it is) and to place before the court all material which contradicts the hypothesis. Secondly, he must make all his material available to the other experts in the case. It is the common experience of the courts that the better the experts the more limited their areas of disagreement, and in the forensic context of a contested case relating to children, the objective of the lawyers and the experts should always be to limit the ambit of disagreement on medical issues to the minimum.[166]

---

[160] [1993] 2 Lloyd's Rep 68 at 81.

[161] [1995] 1 FLR 181.

[162] [2006] 1 Cr App R 55 (5), CA.

[163] Ibid at [271].

[164] See also *R v Oliver* [2016] EWCA Crim 1053 (expert improperly commenting on the legal merits of the case against the accused, including the relevance of some of the prosecution evidence).

[165] [1995] 1 FLR 181 at 192.

[166] See also CPR r 35.12 and r 19.6 of the Criminal Procedure Rules, both considered, in this chapter, under respectively: **Discussions between experts, p 666** and **Pre-hearing discussions, p 669**.

In *R v Harris* the court emphasized[167] that developments in scientific thinking should not be kept from the court simply because they remain at the stage of a hypothesis, but that it is of the first importance that the true status of the expert's evidence is frankly indicated to the court. In cases involving allegations of child abuse, it was said that the judge should be prepared to give directions in respect of expert evidence, taking into account the guidance to which the court had referred.

R v Puaca[168] illustrates the importance of compliance with the obligations on an expert. In that case, a murder conviction was quashed because the conclusions of the Crown's pathologist could not safely be relied on. It was held that it was wholly wrong for a pathologist carrying out the first post-mortem at the request of the police or the coroner to have left it to the defence to instruct a pathologist to prepare a report setting out contrary arguments.

In *Myers v R*[169] it was held that a police officer giving evidence as an expert is under the duties set out in *R v Harris* and must fully understand that he is not simply a part of the prosecution team.[170] It was also held that such an officer must give detailed information about how he reached his conclusions and any sources relied upon.[171]

Evidence of facts upon which an opinion is based

In many—probably most—cases, the expert will have no personal or first-hand knowledge of the facts upon which his opinion is based. For example, in *Beckwith v Sydebotham*[172] shipwrights expressed their opinion on the seaworthiness of a ship which they had not examined. In such a case, the expert should state the *assumed* facts upon which his opinion is based and examination-in-chief and cross-examination should take the form of *hypothetical* questions. The facts upon which the expert's opinion is based, sometimes referred to as 'primary facts', must be proved by admissible evidence,[173] and if they are not proved, expert evidence on them will be irrelevant.[174] The primary facts may be proved by calling the person with personal or first-hand knowledge of them to give direct evidence of them. Thus in *R v Mason*,[175] a murder trial in which a witness who had seen the deceased's body was called to describe the wounds, a surgeon, who had not seen the body, was asked whether the deceased had died from natural causes or in consequence of his wounds and whether the wounds could have been self-inflicted.[176] Alternatively, under s 127 of the Criminal Justice Act 2003, the primary facts may be proved by the hearsay statement of the person with personal or first-hand knowledge of them, unless, on an application by a party to the proceedings, that is not in the interests of justice.[177] In some cases, the

---

[167] [2006] 1 Cr App R 55, CA at [270].

[168] [2005] EWCA Crim 3001.

[169] [2016] AC 314, PC.

[170] Ibid at [59] and [60].

[171] Ibid at [68].

[172] (1807) 1 Camp 116.

[173] Per Lawton LJ in *R v Turner* [1975] QB 834, CA at 840.

[174] *R v Berberi* [2015] 2 Cr App R 11 (2).

[175] (1911) 7 Cr App R 67, CCA.

[176] See also *R v Bradshaw* (1985) 82 Cr App R 79: concerning diminished responsibility, although doctors called by the defence cannot state what the accused told them about past symptoms to prove those symptoms, which would be inadmissible hearsay, they can give evidence of what the accused said to explain their opinions; but if their opinions are based entirely on what the accused said and there is no direct evidence of the symptoms, the defence case would be based upon a flimsy or non-existent foundation.

[177] See Ch 12, Expert evidence, p 407.

expert will have personal or first-hand knowledge of the facts in question, as when he examines an exhibit or visits the *locus in quo*, and in such a case he may testify as to both fact and opinion. In any event the expert should be asked in examination-in-chief to state the facts or assumed facts upon which his evidence is based so that the court can assess the value of his opinion.[178] 'If the expert has been misinformed about the facts or has taken irrelevant facts into consideration or has omitted to consider relevant ones, the opinion is likely to be valueless.'[179]

Although an expert cannot prove primary facts upon which his opinion is based but of which he has no personal or first-hand knowledge, because that would be a breach of the rule against hearsay,[180] he is entitled to rely upon facts forming part of the body of expertise relevant to his field as a part of the process of forming an opinion and, in this sense, is not subject to the rule against hearsay in the same way as a non-expert or witness of fact. *English Exporters (London) Ltd v Eldonwall Ltd*,[181] which must now be read subject to the Civil Evidence Act 1995, provides an instructive example. In that case, landlords applied for the determination of a reasonable interim rent under the Landlord and Tenant Act 1954. Megarry J held that a professional valuer, called as an expert witness to give his opinion as to the value of the property, could not give evidence of comparable rents of which he had no personal knowledge in order to establish those rents as matters of fact, because that would amount to inadmissible hearsay. However, he was entitled to express opinions that he had formed as to values even though those opinions had been formed by reference to matters of which he had no first-hand knowledge but had learned about from sources such as journals, reports of auctions and other dealings, and information, relating to both particular and more general transactions, obtained from professional colleagues and others. Under the same doctrine, although an expert is not entitled to confirm his opinion by reference to the evidence of another expert, not to be called, on the same issue,[182] he may fortify his opinion by referring not only to any relevant research, tests, or experiments which he has personally carried out, whether or not expressly for the purposes of the case, but also to works of authority, learned articles, research papers, letters, and other similar material written by others and comprising part of the general body of knowledge falling within the field of expertise of the expert in question.[183] Similarly an expert giving evidence of fact based on his expertise may draw on

---

[178] But it seems that where an expert expresses an opinion based on primary facts derived from his use of a computer, eg the printout of a machine used by him to analyse the chemical constituents of a substance believed to be a particular drug, there is no *obligation* to produce the printout: see *R v Golizadeh* [1995] Crim LR 232, CA.

[179] Per Lawton LJ in *R v Turner* [1975] QB 834 at 840. For an example, see *R v Moore* [2017] EWCA Crim 1304. Cf *R v Metcalfe* [2016] 2 Cr App R 297 (21), considered in Ch 2. The High Court has power to order that all the factual evidence be given by both sides before any expert evidence is received: *Bayer v Clarkson Puckle Overseas Ltd* [1989] NLJR 256, QBD.

[180] See, eg, *R v Jackson* [1996] 2 Cr App R 420, CA.

[181] [1973] Ch 415. See also *Ramsay v Watson* (1961) 108 CLR 642.

[182] *Hong Kong Special Administrative region v Kissel* [2014] HKCFA 39, where the issue was diminished responsibility.

[183] *Davie v Edinburgh Magistrates* 1953 SC 34, Court of Session; *Seyfang v GD Searle & Co* [1973] QB 148 at 151; and *R v Ahmed* [2011] EWCA Crim 184. See also per Bingham J in *H v Schering Chemicals Ltd* [1983] 1 WLR 143, QBD at 148 ('the results of research published by a reputable authority in a reputable journal'). However, the court is only entitled to use those parts of the material which have been relied upon by the expert or upon which he has been cross-examined: see *Collier v Simpson* (1831) 5 C&P 73. The suggestion in *Myers v R* [2016] AC 314, PC at [66] that the test as to whether an expert may rely upon hearsay should simply be whether his opinion is 'grounded on a body of learning or study' seems unduly restrictive and would not accommodate decisions such as *R v Hodges* [2003] 2 Cr App R 247, CA (see text at n 186).

the general body of knowledge and understanding in which he is skilled, including the work and literature of others.[184]

In *R v Abadom*[185] the accused was convicted of robbery. The prosecution case rested on evidence that he had broken a window during the robbery and fragments of glass embedded in his shoes had come from the window. An expert gave evidence that, as a result of a personal analysis of the samples, he found that the glass from the window and the glass in the shoes bore an identical refractive index. He also gave evidence that he had consulted unpublished statistics compiled by the Home Office Central Research Establishment which showed that the refractive index in question occurred in only 4 per cent of all glass samples investigated. He then expressed the opinion that there was a very strong likelihood that the glass in the shoes came from the window. On appeal it was argued that the evidence of the Home Office statistics was inadmissible hearsay because the expert had no knowledge of the analysis on which the statistics had been based. The appeal was dismissed on the grounds that once the 'primary facts' on which an opinion is based have been proved by admissible evidence, the expert is entitled to draw on the work of others as part of the process of arriving at his conclusion. The primary facts in the instant case, that is the refractive indices of the glass from the window and the glass in the shoes, had been proved by the expert himself on the basis of his own analysis. Accordingly he was entitled to refer to the Home Office statistics and this involved no infringement of the hearsay rule. Experts, it was said, should not limit themselves to drawing on material which has been published in some form: part of their experience and expertise lies in their knowledge and evaluation of unpublished material. The only proviso is that they should refer to such material in their evidence so that the cogency and probative value of their conclusions can be tested and evaluated by reference to it.

R v Abadom was applied in *R v Hodges*,[186] a case of conspiracy to supply heroin, in which a very experienced drugs officer gave evidence partially derived from what he had been told by others, including other officers, informants, and drug users, as to the usual method of supplying heroin, its purchase price in a particular place at the time, and what weight was more than would have been for personal use alone. The relevant primary facts were the observations of the activities of the accused, the finding of 14 grams of heroin in the possession of one of them, and the finding of other drugs paraphernalia in his house. The court distinguished *R v Edwards*,[187] where the issue was whether the accused intended to supply the ecstasy tablets found in his possession or whether they were for personal consumption. Witnesses for both the prosecution and defence, neither of whom had any medical or toxicological qualification, were not allowed to give evidence, based on what they had been told by drugs users, rather than any academic materials, as to the personal consumption rates of ecstasy tablet users, and the impact of use in terms of developing tolerance or suffering serious harm. The evidence was held to have been properly excluded on the basis that the witnesses lacked the appropriate expertise to exempt their opinions from the rule against hearsay.[188]

---

[184] *Kennedy v Cordia (Services) LLP* [2016] UKSC 6 at [41] and [42] and *Myers v R* [2016] AC 314, PC at [63].

[185] [1983] 1 All ER 364, CA.

[186] [2003] 2 Cr App R 247 (15), CA.

[187] [2001] EWCA Crim 2185.

[188] Cf *R v Ibrahima* [2005] Crim LR 887, CA at n 98.

The common law doctrine under discussion has been preserved, in criminal proceedings, by statute. Section 118(1)8 of the Criminal Justice Act 2003 preserves 'Any rule of law under which in criminal proceedings an expert witness may draw on the body of expertise relevant to his field'.

Evidence on ultimate issues

Historically, the courts have striven to prevent any witness from expressing his opinion on an ultimate issue, that is one of the very issues which the court has to determine.[189] The justification is that insofar as such evidence might unduly influence the tribunal of fact, it prevents witnesses from usurping the function of the court: witnesses are called to testify, not to decide the case. The justification is open to criticism on a number of levels.[190] The objection of undue influence makes no allowance for cases in which the tribunal of fact is a professional judge rather than a jury, overlooks the frequency of conflicts in expert testimony, and is largely incompatible with the very justification for admitting expert evidence, that the drawing of inferences from the facts in question calls for an expertise which the tribunal of fact does not possess.

In both civil and criminal proceedings an expert may now give his opinion on an ultimate issue. Under s 3(1) of the Civil Evidence Act 1972, 'where a person is called as a witness in any civil proceedings, his opinion on any relevant matter on which he is qualified to give expert evidence shall be admissible in evidence'; and under s 3(3), 'relevant matter' includes an issue in the proceedings in question'. In family law cases involving suspected child abuse, expert evidence may relate to the presence and interpretation of physical, mental, behavioural, and emotional signs, but often necessarily includes a view as to the likely veracity of the child. In *Re M and R (minors)*,[191] it was held that it is 'plainly right' that 'issue' in s 3(3) *can* include an issue of credibility and that when dealing with children the court needs 'all the help it can get'.[192] In the normal case, as we have seen, expert evidence of credibility will be inadmissible because unnecessary, being a matter on which the tribunal of fact can form its own opinion unaided.

In criminal cases, an expert may be called to give an opinion on an ultimate issue, although according to *Pora v R*[193] only where 'necessary in order that his evidence provide substantial help to the trier of fact'.[194] Examples include expert evidence on the following issues: 'facial mapping' to establish identity;[195] whether a person died in consequence of his wounds and whether they could have been self-inflicted;[196] in a murder trial, whether the accused's conduct after the offence indicated that he knew the nature of the act and that it was contrary to the law, both issues being central to the defence of insanity within the M'Naghten rules;[197] and diminished responsibility, in a case where the expert has properly expressed a view on

---

[189] See *Haynes v Doman* [1899] 2 Ch 13, CA.

[190] See generally the 17th Report of the Law Reform Committee, *Evidence of Opinion and Expert Evidence*, Cmnd 4889 (1970), paras 266–71; 11th Report, Criminal Law Revision Committee, Cmnd 4991 (1972); and Jackson, 'The Ultimate Issue Rule: One Rule Too Many' [1984] Crim LR 75.

[191] [1996] 4 All ER 239, CA.

[192] Ibid at 249.

[193] [2015] UKPC 9.

[194] See, for example, *R(DPP) v Stratford Magistrates' Court* [2018] 4 WLR 47, (Admin), considered at n 3.

[195] *R v Hookway* [1999] Crim LR 750, CA.

[196] *R v Mason* (1911) 7 Cr App R 67, CCA. See also *R v Smith* [1979] 1 WLR 1445, CA (automatism while asleep).

[197] *R v Holmes* [1953] 1 WLR 686, CA.

all four of the relevant matters set out in s 2 of the Homicide Act 1957 as amended.[198] Two principles which apply in the case of any expert evidence take on a particular importance where the evidence relates to an ultimate issue. First, the judge must make it clear that the jury are not bound by the expert's opinion.[199] Second, an expert must provide material on which the jury can form its own conclusions; mere assertions are likely to supplant the jury's role as ultimate decision maker.[200]

Weight

Where expert opinion evidence is properly adduced, the weight to be attached to it is a matter entirely for the tribunal of fact. An expert must explain the basis of his evidence; without such an explanation, his evidence is worthless.[201] The duty of experts, it has been said, 'is to furnish the judge or jury with the necessary scientific criteria for testing the accuracy of their conclusions, so as to enable the judge or jury to form their own independent judgment by the application of these criteria to the facts proved in evidence'.[202] Similarly, it is incumbent on magistrates to approach expert evidence critically, even if no expert is called on the other side, and to be willing to reject it if it leaves questions unanswered.[203]

In criminal cases in the Crown Court, the judge should make clear to the jury that they are not bound by expert opinion evidence on an issue; the issue is for them to decide.[204] In the civil context, although lay evidence should not be preferred to expert evidence without good reason,[205] there is no principle of law preventing a judge from preferring the evidence of lay claimants whom he finds to be honest over the evidence of a jointly instructed expert with whose evidence he can find no fault.[206] Similarly, on the question whether or not a will was forged, a court may prefer the evidence of non-expert attesting witnesses to that of a handwriting expert.[207]

A question that has given rise to conflicting views is whether expert evidence should be accepted if uncontradicted. The leading authority is *R v Brennan*[208] where it was held[209] that if there is no rational or proper basis for departing from uncontradicted and unchallenged expert evidence, juries may not do so: such evidence may only be rejected for a reason. The

---

[198] *R v Brennan* [2014] EWCA Crim 2387 at [51]. See also *R v Udenze* [2011] EWCA Crim 1381 (in a rape case, expert evidence as to the effects of alcohol on the complainant's ability to give informed consent); and *R v Hodges* [2003] 2 Cr App R 247 (15), CA (in a case of supplying drugs, expert evidence that the amount found was more than would have been for personal use alone).

[199] *R v Stockwell* (1993) 97 Cr App R 260 at 265–6, approved in *R v Sellu* [2016] EWCA Crim 1716.

[200] See *Pora v R* [2015] UKPC 9 at [24] and *R v Sellu* [2016] EWCA Crim 1716 at [141] and [142].

[201] *Kennedy v Cordia (Services) LLP* [2016] UKSC 6 at [48].

[202] Per Lord President Cooper in *Davie v Edinburgh Magistrates* 1953 SC 34 Court of Session at 40. Thus concerning voice identification, the jury, in forming their own judgement on the opinions of the experts, are entitled to know the features of the voice to which they paid attention (*R v Robb* (1991) 93 Cr App R 161 at 166) and to hear the tapes which they analysed (*R v Bentum* (1989) 153 JP 538, CA).

[203] *DPP v Wynne* [2001] EWHC 21 (Admin).

[204] *R v Fitzpatrick* [1999] Crim LR 832, CA and, where the evidence is given on an ultimate issue, per Lord Taylor CJ in *R v Stockwell* (1993) 97 Cr App R 260. As to the time when the judge should give directions on expert evidence, see the Crown Court Compendium (July 2019), Part 1, 10–3, para 13.

[205] See *Re B (a minor)* [2000] 1 WLR 790, CA.

[206] *Armstrong v First York Ltd* [2005] EWCA Civ 277. See also *Stevens v Simons* [1988] CLY 1161, CA.

[207] *Fuller v Strum* [2002] 1 WLR 525. See also, to the same effect in respect of signatures on conveyancing documents, *Kingley Developments v Brudenell & Ors* [2016] EWCA Civ 980.

[208] [2015] 1 WLR 2060, CA.

[209] At [44].

court approved the following direction, after the usual directions and appropriate stress on the need to consider all the evidence: 'Where, as here, there is no dispute about findings made by an expert you would no doubt wish to give effect to them, although you are not bound to do so if you see good reason to reject them.'[210] In *R v Sanders*,[211] a case concerning the defence of diminished responsibility, it was held that if there are no other circumstances to consider, unequivocal, uncontradicted medical evidence favourable to an accused should be accepted by a jury and they should be so directed; but where there are other circumstances to consider, then the medical evidence, though unequivocal and uncontradicted, must be assessed in the light of those circumstances. In *R v Brennan*[212] it was held that where, at the close of evidence, expert evidence of diminished responsibility is uncontradicted and an application is made to withdraw the case of murder, the trial judge must evaluate all the circumstances of the case, looking at both the expert evidence and any other evidence; and if, applying the ordinary principles of *R v Galbraith*,[213] his considered view is that on the evidence taken as a whole no properly directed jury could properly convict of murder, that charge should not be left to the jury;[214] but where there are facts or circumstances which might cast a different light on otherwise uncontradicted expert evidence and the charge of murder is left to the jury, those facts and circumstances should be raised by the prosecuting advocate in discussion with the judge prior to closing speeches and should be specifically identified in the judge's summing up as capable of providing a rational basis for rejecting the expert evidence.

On a trial of fitness to plead, unless the unfitness is clear, the court should rigorously examine the psychiatric evidence before reaching its conclusion.[215]

If there is conflicting expert evidence, the tribunal of fact is obviously forced to make a choice. For these purposes, no less than when deciding whether to accept the evidence of even a single expert witness, the tribunal of fact may take into account an expert's qualifications and how they were acquired, his credibility, the degree of reliability of his opinion, and the extent to which, if at all, his evidence-in-chief was based on assumed facts which do not accord with those ultimately established.

An opinion will not necessarily be more persuasive simply because it is shared by two experts.[216]

In *R v Henderson*[217] it was held that in cases concerning 'shaken baby syndrome' in which the prosecution is able by calling experts to identify a non-accidental injury and the defence can

[210] Endorsing *R v Brennan* in this respect, the Supreme Court in *R v Golds* [2016] UKSC stated (at [51]) that '. . . it will also ordinarily be wise to advise the jury against attempting to make themselves amateur psychiatrists, and that if there is undisputed expert evidence the jury will probably wish to accept it, unless there is some identified reason for not doing so.' However, in *R v Sargeant* [2019] EWCA Crim 1088 at [50], the Court of Appeal deprecated any suggestion that *R v Golds* laid down a requirement for specific legal directions in respect of diminished responsibility and that the failure to give the 'amateur psychiatrists' warning might render a conviction unsafe. See also, the Crown Court Compendium (July 2019), Part 1, 10–3, paras 4 and 14(3)(b), and Note 3.

[211] (1991) 93 Cr App R 245, CA.

[212] [2014] EWCA Crim 2387.

[213] [1981] 1 WLR 1039, CA: see Ch 2, **Submission of no case to answer in the Crown Court, p 41.**

[214] However, a court should be cautious about doing this because a murder trial is a particularly sensitive event, the accused bears the burden of proving diminished responsibility, and a finding of diminished responsibility requires the accused to address all matters set out in the Homicide Act 1957, s 2: *R v Golds* [2016] UKSC 61.

[215] *R v Walls* [2011] 2 Cr App R 61 (6), CA.

[216] *R v Meachen* [2009] EWCA Crim 1701.

[217] [2010] 2 Cr App R 185 (24), CA.

identify no alternative cause, it does not automatically follow that the prosecution has proved its case, because the evidence may be insufficient to exclude, beyond reasonable doubt, an unknown cause. The jury should be reminded of any realistic possibility of an unknown cause and directed that, unless the evidence leads them to exclude it, they cannot convict; and they should also be reminded that special caution is needed where expert evidence is fundamental to the prosecution.[218] The court also gave the following general guidance on the content of the summing-up in cases in which the evidence to prove guilt consists only of expert evidence. There must be a logically justifiable basis for accepting or rejecting the evidence. The issues should be identified and, one by one, the evidence which goes to the resolution of each should be identified. The guidance given in *R v Harris*[219] is of assistance not only to judges, practitioners, and experts, but also juries. The jury should be asked to judge, if the issue arises, whether the expert has assumed the role of an advocate, influenced by the side calling him, or whether he has gone outside his area of expertise. The jury should examine the basis of the opinion. Can the expert point to a recognized, peer-reviewed source of the opinion? Is his clinical experience up to date and equal to the experience of others whose evidence he seeks to contradict? Finally, the judge should identify those reasons which would justify accepting or rejecting any conflicting expert opinion.

The capacity of jurors to apply the *Henderson* directions and accept or reject expert evidence, especially in complex cases, is open to debate. As commentators have observed, there is an urgent need for empirical research to gauge jury comprehension of expert evidence and for consideration of reforms aimed at increasing juror engagement and understanding, such as guidance on note-taking and greater use of technological aids.[220]

Restrictions on, and disclosure of, expert evidence in civil cases

In *Access to Justice, Final Report*,[221] Lord Woolf regarded expert evidence as one of the major generators of unnecessary cost in civil litigation, operating against the principles of proportionality and access to justice. He also reiterated concerns about the lack of impartiality of experts, or what has been called the 'hired gun syndrome': 'it is often quite surprising to see with what facility and to what extent, their views can be made to correspond with the wishes or the interests of the parties who call them'.[222] Lord Woolf's Final Report made a number of recommendations which formed the basis of the rules to be found in Pt 35 of the Civil Procedure Rules and its accompanying Practice Direction.[223] In the case of testifying experts, the rules, in addition to imposing an overriding duty to the court,[224] create a duty to restrict the amount of expert evidence, and introduce new requirements as to the form in which

---

[218] What matters is the essence of the direction, not its precise terms: *R v Arshad* [2012] EWCA Crim 18.

[219] [2006] 1 Cr App R 55 (5), CA, considered at **nn 162–3**.

[220] Cohen and Heffernan, 'Juror Comprehension of Expert Evidence: A Reform Agenda' [2010] Crim LR 195. See also Freckelton et al, *Expert Evidence and Criminal Jury Trials* (Oxford 2016), which draws on a study carried out in three Australian jurisdictions to explore the presentation and comprehension of expert evidence in criminal jury trials.

[221] HMSO (1996).

[222] Taylor, *Treatise on the Law of Evidence* (12th edn, London, 1931) 59.

[223] Excepting rr 35.1, 35.3, 35.7, and 35.8, Pt 35 does not apply to claims allocated to the small claims track: CPR r 27.2(1)e. See also the Civil Justice Council Guidance for the Instruction of Experts in Civil Claims, accessible at https://www.judiciary.gov.uk/related-offices-and-bodies/advisory-bodies/cjc/cjc-publications/guidance-for-the-instruction-of-experts-in-civil-claims/.

[224] See, in this chapter, under **The duty of the expert, p 652**.

expert evidence shall be given and as to advance disclosure. They do not apply, however, to an 'advising expert', ie an expert retained by a party for the purpose of advising that party, who owes no duty to the court and whose advice, if given in contemplation of legal proceedings, will be privileged against disclosure. This is because an expert, for the purposes of Pt 35 of the rules, is 'a person who has been instructed to give or prepare expert evidence for the purposes of proceedings'.[225] It also follows, from this definition, that Pt 35 does not control the admission of any other type of expert evidence, for example the report of an expert not instructed by, and wholly independent of, any of the parties,[226] including articles of a scientific nature published in the academic literature, although a party intending to rely on such hearsay material will be required to comply with the notice provisions of the Civil Evidence Act 1995.[227]

The duty and power to restrict expert evidence

The duty to restrict expert evidence is governed by r 35.1.

> 35.1 Expert evidence shall be restricted to that which is reasonably required to resolve the proceedings.

The court's power to restrict expert evidence is governed by r 35.4, which provides as follows:

(1) No party may call an expert or put in evidence an expert's report without the court's permission.

(2) When parties apply for permission they must provide an estimate of the costs of the proposed expert evidence and identify—

(a) the field in which expert evidence is required and the issues which the expert will address; and

(b) where practicable, the name of the proposed expert.

(3) If permission is granted it shall be in relation only to the expert named or the field identified under paragraph (2). The order granting permission may specify the issues which the expert evidence should address.

(3A) Where a claim has been allocated to the small claims track or the fast track, if permission is given for expert evidence, it will normally be given for evidence from only one expert on a particular issue.

(3B) In a soft tissue injury claim, permission—

(a) may normally only be given for one expert medical report;

(b) may not be given initially unless the medical report is a fixed cost medical report.

. . .

(4) The court may limit the amount of a party's expert's fees and expenses that may be recovered from any other party.

Where, for no good reason, an application for permission to call an expert under r 35.4 is not made in good time, it is unlikely to be granted if made so shortly before the trial that it would work a significant injustice to the other side.[228]

---

[225] CPR r 35.2(1).

[226] *Rogers v Hoyle* [2014] EWCA Civ 257 at [62] and [63] (a report by the Department of Transport's Air Accident Investigation Branch).

[227] *Interflora Inc v Marks and Spencer plc* [2013] EWHC 936 (Ch).

[228] *Calenti v North Middlesex NHS Trust* (2001) LTL 10 Apr 2001, QBD. See also *Eli Lilley v Genetech, Inc* [2018] EWHC 3522 (Pat), where the claimants proceeded with 'brazen disregard of the Court's orders and the well-established practice for the admission of experimental evidence' (at [15]).

Written reports

Under the rules, there is a presumption—in the case of claims on the fast track, a strong pre-sumption—that if expert evidence is permitted, it should be given by means of an expert's written report, rather than by calling the expert as a witness. Rule 35.5 provides as follows:

(1) Expert evidence is to be given in a written report unless the court directs otherwise.

(2) If a claim is on the small claims track or the fast track, the court will not direct an expert to attend a hearing unless it is necessary to do so in the interests of justice.

The single joint expert

Rule 35.7 challenges the notion that where both parties wish to adduce expert evidence, there is a need for two experts: it permits the court to direct that the evidence should be given by a single joint expert. The parties themselves may agree to such a direction, which the court may then approve. Of course, there is nothing in the Civil Procedure Rules to pre-vent a party from instructing his own expert, and this may well be thought to be appropriate in a case in which a claimant needs expert assistance in order to decide whether he has a valid claim at all. However, where a party obtains an expert's report without the approval of the court, there is a real risk that he will not recover his costs in this respect: under rule 35.4, the court may refuse permission to admit the report or call the expert, and under rule 35.7 may direct the use of a jointly instructed expert.

Rule 35.7 does not create a presumption in favour of a direction that there should be one expert only, but in many cases, such a direction will give effect to the 'overriding objective', especially in saving expense and putting the parties on an equal footing. However, much may turn on the value and complexity of the litigation: single joint experts are not com-monly appointed in Commercial Court cases, and there is a greater willingness to permit two experts in multi-track cases, which are typically more complex than fast track claims. It can be wrong to appoint a single joint expert on a medical issue on which there are different schools of thought.[229] In *Peet v Mid Kent Healthcare Trust*,[230] a claim of medical negligence, it was said that whereas in the great majority of cases non-medical evidence dealing with quantum should be given by a single expert rather than by experts called by each party, it is sometimes difficult to restrict the medical evidence because of the difficult issues as to the appropriate form and standard of treatment required.

Rule 35.7 provides as follows:

(1) Where two or more parties wish to submit expert evidence on a particular issue, the court may direct that the evidence on that issue is to be given by a single joint expert.

(2) Where the parties who wish to submit the evidence ('the relevant parties') cannot agree who should be the single joint expert, the court may—

(a) select the expert from a list prepared or identified by the relevant parties; or

(b) direct that the expert be selected in such other manner as the court may direct.

In most cases, it is likely that the court will expect the parties to be able to agree who the expert should be. Given the overriding duty of the expert to the court, it may be difficult for a party to object to a particular expert, even if it is known that he has previously been

---

[229] *Oxley v Penwarden* [2001] Lloyds Rep Med 347, CA. See also *Casey v Cartwright* [2007] 2 All ER 78, CA.

[230] [2002] 1 WLR 210, CA at [6]–[7].

instructed extensively or exclusively by the firm of solicitors representing the other party, or has previously acted only on behalf of, say, defendant employers or insurance companies.

Rule 35.8 deals with the instructions to be given to a single joint expert:

(1) Where the court gives a direction under rule 35.7 for a single joint expert to be used, any relevant party may give instructions to the expert.

(2) When a party gives instructions to the expert that party must, at the same time, send a copy to the other relevant parties.

(3) The court may give directions about—
   (a) the payment of the expert's fees and expenses; and
   (b) any inspection, examination or experiments which the expert wishes to carry out.

(4) The court may, before an expert is instructed—
   (a) limit the amount that can be paid by way of fees and expenses to the expert; and
   (b) direct that some or all of the relevant parties pay that amount into court.

(5) Unless the court otherwise directs, the relevant parties are jointly and severally liable for the payment of the expert's fees and expenses.

In cases in which one party has exclusive access to information about the basic facts on which expert opinion will need to be based, it will be difficult if not impossible for the other party to properly instruct an expert without access to that information. Rule 35.9 therefore empowers the court to direct the one party to provide such information to the other.

Where the court makes such a direction, the document served must include sufficient details of all the facts, tests, experiments, and assumptions which underlie any part of the information to enable the other party to make or obtain a proper interpretation of the information and an assessment of its significance.[231]

Where the parties have instructed a single joint expert, it is not permissible for one party to have a conference with the expert in the absence of the other, without the latter's prior written consent. A conclusion to the contrary would be inconsistent with the concept of a jointly instructed expert owing an equal duty of openness and confidentiality to both parties.[232]

Where a court has directed that evidence on an issue be given by a single joint expert and the parties agree who the expert should be, a party who is unhappy with the expert's report will be refused permission to call a further expert unless such refusal would be unjust having regard to the 'overriding objective'.[233] The discretion may be exercised against the party if there is only a modest amount at stake and therefore it would be disproportionate to adduce further expert evidence.[234] Other relevant factors to be taken into account include the nature and importance of the issues, their number, the reasons for requiring another expert, the effect of adducing the additional evidence, and any delay likely to be caused.[235]

Under para 7.3 of the Pre-Action Protocol for Personal Injury Claims, before any party instructs an expert, he should give the other party the name(s) of one or more experts whom he considers suitable to instruct. Under para 7.6, the other party may object to one or more of the named experts and the first party should then instruct a mutually acceptable expert. Such an expert needs to be distinguished from a single joint expert. The latter is instructed

[231] PD 35, para 4.
[232] *Peet v Mid Kent Healthcare Trust* [2002] 1 WLR 210, CA.
[233] *Daniels v Walker* [2001] 1 WLR 1382, CA.
[234] Ibid.
[235] *Cosgrave v Pattison* [2001] CPLR 177, Ch D.

by both parties, both are liable for his fees, and both have an equal right to see his report. A mutually acceptable expert is instructed on behalf of one party, who is usually liable to pay his fees, and his report is protected by litigation privilege, unless the instructing party chooses to waive it. Thus although the Protocol encourages and promotes voluntary disclosure of medical reports, it does not require it.[236]

Written questions to experts

In cases in which expert evidence takes the form of a written report, whether prepared by a single joint expert or an expert instructed by a party, there will obviously be no opportunity to question him on oath in order either to clarify any part of his report or to challenge him on such matters as his methodology, the reasons for his opinion, any expert literature upon which he has relied, opposing expert opinion, and so on. For reasons of this kind, provision has been made to allow written questions to be put to the expert before the trial. Rule 35.6 provides as follows:

(1) A party may put written questions about an expert's report (which must be proportionate) to—
    (a) an expert instructed by another party; or
    (b) a single joint expert appointed under rule 35.7.
(2) Written questions under paragraph (1)—
    (a) may be put once only;
    (b) must be put within 28 days of service of the expert's report; and
    (c) must be for the purpose only of clarification of the report; unless in any case,
        (i) the court gives permission; or
        (ii) the other party agrees.
(3) An expert's answers to questions put in accordance with paragraph (1) shall be treated as part of the expert's report.
(4) Where—
    (a) a party has put a written question to an expert instructed by another party; and
    (b) the expert does not answer that question, the court may make one or both of the following orders in relation to the party who instructed the expert—
        (i) that the party may not rely on the evidence of that expert; or
        (ii) that the party may not recover the fees and expenses of that expert from any other party.

Rule 35.6(2)(c) allows a party, with the permission of the court or other party, to ask about matters not covered in the expert's report, provided that they are within his expertise, and thereby renders the expert akin to a court expert.[237] The fact that experts can be required to answer written questions normally means that there is no need for a single joint expert's evidence to be amplified or tested by cross-examination of the expert. The court has a discretion to permit such amplification or cross-examination, but this should be restricted as far as possible.[238] If, exceptionally, the expert is to be subject to cross-examination, then he should know in advance what topics are to be covered, and where fresh material is to be adduced for his consideration, this should be done in advance of the hearing.[239]

---

[236] *Carlson v Townsend* [2001] 3 All ER 663, CA. But see also *Edwards-Tubb v JD Wetherspoon plc* [2011] 1 WLR 1373, CA considered at **n 253**.

[237] *Mutch v Allen* [2001] CPLR 200, CA.

[238] *Peet v Mid Kent Healthcare Trust* [2002] 1 WLR 210, CA at [28].

[239] *Popek v National Westminster Bank plc* [2002] EWCA Civ 42.

The contents of the expert's report

An expert's report must comply with the requirements set out in Practice Direction 35,[240] which provides that a report must give details of the expert's qualifications; give details of any literature or other material relied on; set out the substance of all facts and instructions given to him which are material to the opinions expressed or upon which those opinions are based;[241] make clear which facts in the report are within his own knowledge; say who carried out any examination, measurement, test, or experiment which he has used for the report, give the qualifications of that person, and say whether or not it was carried out under his supervision; where there is a range of opinion on the matters dealt with in the report, summarize it and give reasons for his own opinion; contain a summary of his conclusions; if he is not able to give his opinion without qualification, state the qualification; and state that he understands his duty to the court and has complied with that duty.[242] His report must also be verified by a statement of truth.[243] Under r 35.10(2), at the end of the expert's report there must be a statement that he understands his duty to the court and has complied with it. Rule 35.10(3) and (4) provide as follows:

(3) The expert's report must state the substance of all material instructions, whether written or oral, on the basis of which the report was written.

(4) The instructions referred to in paragraph (3) shall not be privileged against disclosure but the court will not, in relation to those instructions—

(a) order disclosure of any specific document; or

(b) permit any questioning in court, other than by the party who instructed the expert, unless it is satisfied that there are reasonable grounds to consider the statement of instructions given under paragraph (3) to be inaccurate or incomplete.

Paragraph 5 of PD 35 states that cross-examination of the expert on the contents of his instructions will not be allowed unless the court permits it (or unless the party who gave the instructions consents to it). Paragraph 5 also states that if the court is satisfied that there are 'reasonable grounds' under r 35.10(4)(b), then it will allow the cross-examination where it appears to be in the interests of justice to do so.

The intention behind r 35.10(4) is to encourage the setting out fully of material instructions and facts, including, for example, witness statements provided to the experts and the previous report of another expert. However, the obligation under r 35.10(3) is not to set out all the information and material supplied to the expert, but to disclose the 'substance of all material instructions'. Ordinarily the expert is to be trusted to comply with r 35.10(3), and under r 35.10(4) the party on the other side may not as a matter of course call for disclosure: there must be some concrete fact giving rise to the 'reasonable grounds' to which r 35.10(4) refers.[244]

The requirements of PD 35 are intended to focus the mind of the expert on his responsibilities in order that litigation may progress in accordance with the overriding principles in CPR Pt 1. If an expert demonstrates that he has no conception of those requirements, as when he

---

[240] CPR r 35.10(1).

[241] It is a significant failing for an expert not to make it clear that she has sought advice or an opinion from someone else: *Pinkus v Direct Line* [2018] PIQR 20, QB.

[242] PD 35, para 3.2.

[243] Ibid, para 3.3.

[244] *Lucas v Barking, Havering and Redbridge Hospitals NHS Trust* [2004] 1 WLR 220, CA.

fails to include in his report statements that he understands his duty to the court and has complied with it, and statements setting out the substance of all material instructions, then he may properly be debarred from acting as an expert witness in the case.[245] Moreover, in appropriate circumstances, the court may make a costs order against an expert who, by his evidence, has caused significant expense to be incurred, and has done so in flagrant and reckless disregard of his duties to the court.[246]

Discussions between experts

Rule 35.12 is another provision designed to save court time and reduce costs. It allows the court, at any stage, in cases in which the parties have been permitted to use competing experts, to direct a 'without prejudice'[247] discussion between the experts for the purpose of requiring them to identify the issues in the proceedings and, where possible, to reach agreement on an issue. The court may specify the issues which the experts must discuss. It may also direct that following the discussion the experts must prepare a statement for the court showing the issues on which they agreed and the issues on which they disagreed with a summary of their reasons for disagreeing. Such a statement is not an admission and does not bind the parties, but is not privileged, even if made with an eye to assisting a mediation which, in the event, is unsuccessful.[248] However, the content of the *discussion* between the experts shall not be referred to at the trial unless the parties agree; and where the experts do agree on an issue, their agreement will not bind the parties unless they expressly agree to be bound by it.

If a party is dissatisfied with the revised opinion of his own expert following a discussion between experts, permission to call a further expert should only be granted where there is good reason to suppose that the expert modified his opinion or agreed with the expert instructed by the other side for reasons which cannot properly or fairly support his revised opinion, such as stepping outside his expertise or otherwise showing himself to be incompetent.[249]

Disclosure, non-disclosure, and inspection

Rules 35.11 and 35.13 provide as follows:

35.11   Where a party has disclosed an expert's report, any party may use that expert's report as evidence at the trial.

. . .

35.13   A party who fails to disclose an expert's report may not use the report at the trial or call the expert to give evidence orally unless the court gives permission.

Where an expert has been asked to prepare a report, the dominant purpose being to use it in relation to anticipated or pending litigation, the report will be the subject of litigation privilege.[250] Neither the Civil Evidence Act 1972 nor the Civil Procedure Rules compel the disclosure of privileged documents. However, under r 35.13 a party will normally only be allowed to introduce an expert report in evidence, or call its maker, if he has disclosed the

[245] *Stevens v Gullis* [2000] 1 All ER 527, CA.
[246] *Phillips v Symes (No 2)* [2005] 1 WLR 2043, Ch D.
[247] See Ch 22, **Without prejudice negotiations**, p 749.
[248] *Aird v Prime Meridian Ltd* [2007] BLR 105, CA.
[249] *Stallwood v David* [2007] 1 All ER 206, QBD.
[250] See Ch 22, **Communications with third parties—litigation privilege**, p 732.

report. Although the court may give permission for the evidence to be adduced notwithstanding failure to disclose the report, it is submitted that the cards-on-the-table approach to civil litigation, which the courts will generally expect of the parties, is such that permission will rarely be granted, and then only in very exceptional circumstances.

Rule 35.13 does not provide a power to order disclosure of drafts of experts' reports, prepared for the purpose of discussion with a party's advisers prior to the completion of the expert's final report, and protected by litigation privilege. The specific and limited exemption from privilege of the material instructions pursuant to r 35.10(4)[251] shows that there was no intention to abrogate the privilege attaching to draft expert reports.[252] However, in *Edwards-Tubb v JD Wetherspoon plc*[253] it was held that if a claimant has obtained a report from an expert, A, but chooses not to rely on it and seeks permission under r 35.4(1) to rely on the evidence of expert B, the court has the power to give permission on condition that A's report is disclosed to the other party. Such a condition should usually be imposed because 'expert shopping' is undesirable; but it would seem that the condition is not mandatory and need not be imposed if on the facts there is no sound basis for concern about undesirable expert shopping or suspicion of abuse of process.[254] To impose a condition (as is usual) is not to abrogate legal professional privilege, but to require a waiver of privilege as a condition of being permitted to rely on the substitute expert. These principles apply whether expert A was consulted before or after the issue of proceedings, provided that he is an expert as defined in r 35.2, that is, a person who has been instructed to give or prepare expert evidence for the purpose of proceedings, but have no application where a party has elected to take private advice, before embarking on the personal injuries pre-action protocol procedure, from an expert not instructed to write a report for the court.

The effect of r 35.11 is that where a party has been given permission to use an expert and has disclosed his expert's report, then the opposing party may use it as evidence at the trial, and this remains the case even if the first party has changed his mind and no longer intends to rely upon it.

Directions and agreed directions

When a court allocates a case to the fast track, directions it gives for the management of the case will include directions on expert evidence. If the parties have filed agreed directions, the court may approve them. Agreed directions may include a direction that no expert evidence is required; or directions for a single joint expert, or the exchange and agreement of expert evidence and without prejudice discussions between experts.[255] There are similar provisions for cases allocated to the multi-track.[256]

Under r 35.14, an expert may file a written request for directions to assist him in carrying out his function as an expert. Rule 35.14 provides a useful safeguard for the expert in need of further guidance as to what is being asked of him, especially in cases where to take further instructions from a party may be regarded as a breach of his overriding duty to help the court.

---

[251] See, in this chapter, under The contents of the expert's report, p 668.

[252] *Jackson v Marley Davenport Ltd* [2004] 1 WLR 2926, CA.

[253] [2011] 1 WLR 1373, CA. See also *Beck v Ministry of Defence* [2005] 1 WLR 2206, CA and per Dyson LJ, obiter, in *Vasiliou v Hajigeorgiou* [2005] 1 WLR 2195, CA.

[254] See *Daniel Alfredo Condori Vilca v Xstrata Limited, Compania Minera Antapaccay SA* [2017] EWHC 1582, QB.

[255] See r 28.2 and 28.3 and PD 28 paras 3.5–3.9.

[256] See r 29.2 and 29.4 and PD 29 paras 4.6–4.13.

Restrictions on, and disclosure of, expert evidence in criminal cases

Streamlined Forensic Reporting

Streamlined Forensic Reporting (SFR) is a case management procedure for the staged producing of expert evidence introduced across the criminal justice system in 2013. It is used
for fingerprint identification, DNA, drugs, footwear, toxicology, marks and traces, firearms/
ballistics, and digital analysis results. The object is to reduce costs and delays and to ensure
compliance with case management requirements through early identification of the real
issues. For example, the initial police forensic findings are disclosable in a SFR Stage 1 report
to the defence who are required to either formally admit or contest the result. Detailed consideration of the SFR procedure is outside the scope of this work.[257]

The contents of the expert's report

In criminal proceedings, the required contents of an expert's report are set out in r 19.4 of
the Criminal Procedure Rules 2015,[258] are based on the guidance given in *R v B (T)*,[259] and
mirror those required in civil proceedings under PD 35, which have been considered earlier
in this chapter.[260] The only material differences from the civil rules are that: there is no
requirement to set out any instructions given to the expert; the report must include such
information as the court may need to decide whether the expert evidence is sufficiently
reliable to be admissible as evidence;[261] and the report must be verified not by a statement
of truth but by the same declaration of truth as for a witness statement.[262] Concerning a
declaration by the expert to the effect that he understands his duty to the court under r
19.2, best practice is to set out, even if only in summary, an express acknowledgment of the
duty and the important obligation to provide objective and unbiased advice.[263] Where the
expert has based an opinion on an inference or representation of fact or opinion made by
another, the report must identify the person, give his or her qualifications, relevant experience and any accreditation, and certify that the person had personal knowledge of matters
stated in the representation.[264] Under r 19.5, a party who serves on another party or on the
court an expert report must at once inform the expert of that fact. An expert report must
be transparent and include material such as formulae and statistics on which the expert has
relied in reaching his opinion, without which the court cannot properly evaluate reliability
and admissibility.[265]

---

[257] See Guidance issued by the CPS, accessible at https://www.cps.gov.uk/legal-guidance/streamlined-forensic-
reporting-guidance-and-toolkit. For critical analysis, see Sallavaci, 'Streamlined reporting of forensic evidence in
England and Wales: Is it the way forward?' (2016) 20(3) E&P 235.

[258] SI 2015/1490.

[259] [2006] 2 Cr App R 22, CA.

[260] Under **Restrictions on, and disclosure of, expert evidence in civil cases**, p 660.

[261] Rule 19.4(h).

[262] Rule 19.4(k).

[263] See *R (DPP) v Stratford Magistrates' Court* [2018] 4 WLR 47 at [34]. Failure to do so offers a line of
cross-examination.

[264] Rule 19.4(e). For an example where an expert failed to do this in a civil context, see *Pinkus v Direct Line* [2018]
PIQR 20, QB.

[265] *R v T* [2011] 1 Cr App R 85, CA.

Pre-hearing discussions

Under r 19.6 of the Criminal Procedure Rules, where more than one party wants to introduce expert evidence, the court may direct the experts to discuss the expert issues and prepare a statement for the court of the matters on which they agree and disagree, giving their reasons. The contents of the discussion must not otherwise be referred to without the court's permission.[266]

Single joint experts

Under r 19.7 of the Criminal Procedure Rules, where more than one accused wants to introduce expert evidence on an issue, the court may direct that the evidence on that issue be given by one expert only. If the co-accused cannot agree who the expert should be, the court may select the expert from a list prepared or identified by them or direct that the expert be selected in another way. Where the court gives a direction under r 19.7 for a single joint expert to be used, each of the co-accused may give instructions to the expert and, if so, must at the same time, send a copy of his instructions to the other co-accused.[267] The court may also give directions about any examination, measurement, test, or experiment which the expert wishes to carry out.[268] The court may also determine an application by a party to withhold information which otherwise would be included, but which the party thinks ought not to be revealed to another party in the public interest.[269]

Disclosure

At common law, the prosecution at a trial on indictment are not permitted to take the defence by surprise by adducing any evidence of which they have not given advance notice to the defence; and where such notice has not been given, the accused may apply for an adjournment.[270] The Royal Commission on Criminal Procedure proposed the introduction of an additional requirement of pre-trial disclosure in the case of defences depending on medical or expert scientific evidence, where the element of surprise involves some risk of the trial being adjourned, so that the prosecution may evaluate the evidence, undertake further inquiries and, if necessary, call their own experts in rebuttal.[271] The recommendation was adopted. Rule 19 of the Criminal Procedure Rules 2015 provides as follows:

19.3 (1) A party who wants another party to admit as fact a summary of an expert's conclusions must serve that summary—

    (a) on the court officer and on each party from whom that admission is sought;

    (b) as soon as practicable after the defendant whom it affects pleads not guilty.

(2) A party on whom such a summary is served must—

    (a) serve a response stating—

        (i) which, if any, of the expert's conclusions are admitted as fact, and

        (ii) where a conclusion is not admitted, what are the disputed issues concerning that conclusion; and

---

[266] Rule 19.6(3).
[267] Rule 19.8(1) and (2).
[268] Rule 19.8(3).
[269] Rule 19.9(1).
[270] *R v Wright* (1934) 25 Cr App R 35, CCA.
[271] Cmnd 8092 (1981), para 8.22.

    (b) serve the response—
        (i)   on the court officer and on the party who served the summary,
        (ii) as soon as practicable, and in any event not more than 14 days after service of the summary.

(3) A party who wants to introduce expert evidence otherwise than as admitted fact must—
    (a) serve a report by the expert which complies with rule 19.4 (Content of expert's report) on—
        (i)   the court officer, and
        (ii) each other party;
    (b) serve the report as soon as practicable, and in any event with any application in support of which that party relies on that evidence;
    (c) serve with the report notice of anything of which the party serving it is aware which might reasonably be thought capable of—
        (i)   undermining the reliability of the expert's opinion, or
        (ii) detracting from the credibility or impartiality of the expert;
    (d) if another party so requires, give that party a copy of, or a reasonable opportunity to inspect—
        (i)   a record of any examination, measurement, test or experiment on which the expert's findings and opinion are based, or that were carried out in the course of reaching those findings and opinion, and
        (ii) anything on which any such examination, measurement, test or experiment was carried out.

(4) Unless the parties otherwise agree or the court directs, a party may not—
    (a) introduce expert evidence if that party has not complied with paragraph (3);
    (b) introduce in evidence an expert report if the expert does not give evidence in person.

To assist with the assessment described in Rule 19.3(c) above, the Criminal Practice Directions 2015 provide examples of matters that should be disclosed.[272] The list is not comprehensive, but includes such matters as: adverse judicial comment; where an appeal has been allowed because of a deficiency in the expert's evidence; lack of accreditation or other commitment to prescribed standards; and history of poor performance in quality or proficiency assessments, of lax or inadequate scientific methods, of failure to observe recognized standards in the expert's area of expertise or of failure to adhere to the standards expected of an expert witness in the criminal justice system. The Directions also provide that where an expert, or corporation or body with which the expert works, has been criticized without full investigation, for example by adverse judicial comment, it is reasonable to expect those criticized to provide information about the conduct and conclusions of any independent investigation into the incident and explain remedial action taken, if any.[273] In this respect, the Criminal Procedure Rules require disclosure of matters which the expert or party introducing the expert's evidence is aware, but do not require persistent or disproportionate enquiry, because the courts will know that there may be occasions where neither the expert nor the party will be aware of criticism.[274] Under the Criminal Procedure Rules, it is incumbent on both the prosecution and the defence to alert the court and the other side at the earliest practicable

---

[272] Para 19A.7.
[273] Para 19A.8
[274] Para 19A.9.

moment if they intend, or may intend, to adduce expert evidence. If a party fails totally to comply with either the spirit or the letter of the Criminal Procedure Rules, a judge will be entitled to refuse to admit the evidence.[275]

In *R v Ward*[276] the Court of Appeal held that the rules (strictly, the original version of the rules) are helpful, but not exhaustive: they do not in any way supplant or detract from the prosecution's general duty of disclosure in respect of scientific evidence, a duty which exists irrespective of any request by the defence. That duty is not limited to documentation on which the opinion or finding of an expert is based, but extends to anything which may argu-ably assist the defence. It is a positive duty which, in the case of scientific evidence, obliges the prosecution to make full and proper inquiries from forensic scientists to ascertain whether there is discoverable material. Moreover, an expert witness who has carried out or knows of experiments or tests which tend to cast doubt on the opinion he is expressing is under a clear obligation to bring the records of such experiments or tests to the attention of the solicitor instructing him (so that they may be disclosed to the defence)[277] or the expert advising the defence. The importance of these principles was starkly illustrated in *R v Clark*,[278] where, on a reference back to the Court of Appeal by the Criminal Cases Review Commission, Sally Clark's convictions for the murder of her two infant sons were quashed, a forensic pathologist having failed to disclose that in the case of one of the infants, a form of potentially lethal bacteria, which could not be excluded as the possible cause of death, had been isolated.

Case management where the evidence of guilt consists of only expert evidence

In *R v Henderson*[279] the Court of Appeal gave the following general guidance on case manage-ment in cases in which the evidence to prove guilt consists of only expert evidence. Justice depends upon proper advanced preparation and control of the evidence from the stage of investigation onwards. A jury can only approach conflicting expert evidence if it is properly marshalled and controlled before it is presented to them. The judge who is to hear a case should also deal with the pre-trial hearing and it is desirable that he has experience of the complex issues and understanding of the learning. Proper and robust pre-trial management is essential in order to identify the real issues and avoid unnecessary detail. Before the trial the judge should be in a position to identify whether the expert evidence is admissible. Generally, the court should direct a meeting of experts under r 19.6 of the Criminal Procedure Rules.[280] The meeting should take place well in advance of the trial and be attended by all significant experts, including the defence experts. A careful detailed minute should be prepared and signed by all participants. Usually others, particularly legal representatives, should not attend. Defence experts are not obliged to reveal a previous report they have made in the case, nor to reveal adverse criticism by judges in the past, but a judge may be able to use his powers under the Criminal Procedure Rules to ensure advance disclosure of any such reports or criticism. Failure to do so would expose the expert to cross-examination on those matters. The repre-sentatives of the accused should satisfy themselves that any such report or criticism is dis-closed. Failure to do so by either side will only cast suspicion upon the cogency of the opinion.

---

[275] *R v Ensor* [2010] 1 Cr App R 255 (18), CA.

[276] [1993] 1WLR 619, CA.

[277] See also per Stuart-Smith LJ in *R v Maguire* [1992] 2 All ER 433, CA at 447.

[278] [2003] EWCA Crim 1020.

[279] [2010] 2 Cr App R 185 (24), CA.

[280] See, in this chapter, under **Pre-hearing discussions**, p 669.

Non-expert opinion evidence

A non-expert witness may give opinion evidence on matters in relation to which it is impossible or virtually impossible to separate his inferences from the perceived facts on which those inferences are based. In these circumstances, the witness is permitted to express his opinion as a short-hand means of conveying to the court the facts he perceived. The admissibility of non-expert opinion evidence is largely a question of degree and the matters open to proof by such evidence defy comprehensive classification. Examples include the identification of persons,[281] voices,[282] objects[283] and handwriting,[284] speed,[285] temperature, weather, and the passing of time. A non-expert may describe the condition of objects, using adjectives such as 'good', 'new', 'worn', and 'old'. Similarly, non-expert opinion evidence is admissible as to the value of objects. In *R v Beckett*,[286] a non-expert expressed the opinion that a plate-glass window was worth more than five pounds. However, although the point was not canvassed in the case, it seems clear that non-expert opinion evidence of value is only admissible in respect of commonplace objects, of which a plate-glass window is perhaps best regarded as a borderline example, as opposed to works of art, antiques, and other objects the valuation of which obviously calls for specialized skill or knowledge. A non-expert may also give opinion evidence of a person's age,[287] health, bodily or emotional state, or reaction to an event or set of circumstances. Although a person's sanity is a matter calling for expertise, it would appear that a close acquaintance may express his opinion as a convenient way of conveying the results of his observations of that person's behaviour.[288] A similar distinction was drawn in *R v Davies*.[289] It was held that on a charge of driving when unfit through drink, whereas the fitness of the accused to drive is a matter calling for expert evidence, a non-expert may properly give his general impression as to whether the accused had 'taken drink', provided that he describes the facts upon which his impression is based. Similarly, and subject to the same proviso, a non-expert may give his opinion as to whether an accused was 'drunk'.[290] In *R v Hill*[291] it was held that scientific evidence is not always required to identify a prohibited drug, but police officers' descriptions of a drug must be sufficient to justify the inference that it is the drug alleged.

---

[281] *R v Tolson* (1864) 4 F&F 103.

[282] *R v Robb* (1991) 93 Cr App R 161, CA; *R v Deenik* [1992] Crim LR 578, CA. See also *R v Flynn* [2008] 2 Cr App R 266 (20).

[283] *Lucas v Williams & Sons* [1892] 2 QB 113 (a picture); *Fryer v Gathercole* (1849) 13 Jur 542 (a pamphlet).

[284] *Doe d Mudd v Suckermore* (1837) 5 Ad&El 703: see **Ch 10**.

[285] The Road Traffic Regulation Act 1984, s 89(2): see **Ch 8**.

[286] (1913) 8 Cr App R 204.

[287] *R v Cox* [1898] 1 QB 179.

[288] Per Parke B in *Wright v Doe d Tatham* (1838) 4 Bing NC 489 at 543–4. See also *Pinkus v Direct Line* [2018] PIQR 20, QB at [79]–[81]: evidence of a former friend of the claimant about his resilience, including his opinion that he saw no sign of the claimant having any psychological condition, in particular PTSD, of which the friend had had personal experience following military service in Northern Ireland. However, in criminal cases, expert psychiatric evidence is necessary in order to establish insanity: the Criminal Procedure (Insanity and Unfitness to Plead) Act 1991, s 1(1), considered at **n 88**.

[289] [1962] 1 WLR 1111, C-MAC.

[290] *R v Tagg* [2002] 1 Cr App R 22 (2), CA.

[291] (1992) 96 Cr App R 456, CA.

At common law, as we have seen, the courts were opposed to any witness expressing his opinion on an ultimate issue, that is one of the very issues which the judge or jury have to decide. In civil proceedings the rule has been abolished. Section 3(2) of the Civil Evidence Act 1972 declares that:

> where a person is called as a witness in any civil proceedings, a statement of opinion by him on any relevant matter on which he is not qualified to give expert evidence, if made as a way of conveying relevant facts personally perceived by him, is admissible as evidence of what he perceived.

Under s 3(3) '"relevant matter" includes an issue in the proceedings in question'.

Concerning non-expert opinion evidence in criminal proceedings, the rule may subsist.[292] In *R v Davies*[293] Lord Parker CJ held that although a witness could properly state the impression he formed as to whether the accused driver had taken drink, his opinion as to whether as a result of that drink he was fit or unfit to drive a car was inadmissible, being 'the very matter which the court itself has to determine'.[294] However, the rule is easily evaded by a careful choice of words, and sometimes it is simply ignored. In *R v Beckett*,[295] it will be recalled, a witness valued a window at more than five pounds, yet that was exactly the issue to be determined by the court.

ADDITIONAL READING

Cossins, 'Expert witness evidence in sexual assault trials: questions, answers and law reform in Australia and England' (2013) 17 E&P 74.
An article that investigates whether educative information should be admitted in sex assault trials via an expert witness or a judicial direction to counter jury reliance on misconceptions based on victim and gender stereotypes when assessing the credibility of complainants. It also investigates the type of expert evidence that would be admissible and the legislative models for doing so, based on Australian reforms.

Edmond, 'Legal versus non-legal approaches to forensic science evidence' (2016) 20(1) E&P 3.
An article that contrasts conventional English approaches to the admission and evaluation of expert evidence with the criteria being promoted by peak scientific organizations. It suggests that admissibility jurisprudence and legal practice might be misguided and that courts have privileged the wrong kind of heuristics in their attempts to engage with scientific and technical forms of knowledge. It also questions whether conventional admission standards, even in conjunction with trial safeguards, provide jurors and judges with the kinds of information required to rationally assess much of the incriminating expert evidence routinely presented.

Edmond and Roberts, 'The Law Commission's Report on Expert Evidence in Criminal Proceedings' [2011] Crim LR 844.
A critical analysis of the proposal of the Law Commission for reliability-based admission of expert evidence in criminal cases.

Ellison, 'Closing the credibility gap: The prosecutorial use of expert witness testimony in sexual assault cases' (2005) 9 E&P 239.
An examination of some of the credibility barriers confronting complainants in sex cases, a critical assessment of US developments in the use of experts to educate jurors and restore credibility to the complainants' accounts, and an exploration of the potential admissibility of 'educational' expert witness evidence in England and Wales.

---

[292] But see 11th Report, Criminal Law Revision Committee, Cmnd 4991 (1972), para 270. The Committee, recommending the enactment for criminal proceedings of provisions similar to those contained in the 1972 Act, s 3, said: 'we have no doubt that this is the present law, but it seems desirable for the statute to be explicit'.

[293] [1962] 1 WLR 1111, C-MAC. See also *Sherrard v Jacob* [1965] NI 151, NICA.

[294] In Eire, the witness has been allowed to express an opinion on both matters: see *A-G (Rudely) v James Kenny* (1960) 94 ILTR 185.

[295] (1913) 8 Cr App R 204, CCA.

Hartshorne and Miola, 'Expert evidence: difficulties and solutions in prosecutions for infant harm' (2010) 30(2) Legal Studies 279.

A consideration of the problems with the provision of expert evidence in prosecutions for infant harm, an evaluation of the solutions to these problems, including the proposals of the Law Commission, and a suggestion for the use of a gate-keeping panel of senior judges.

Jackson, 'The Ultimate Issue Rule: One Rule Too Many' [1984] Crim LR 75.

A critical analysis of the ultimate issue rule, arguing for its abolition.

Lewis, 'Expert evidence of delay in complaint in childhood sexual abuse prosecutions' (2006) 10 E&P 157.

A comparative review of the use of expert evidence to explain delay in complaint, and to dispel jury myths, misconceptions, and misunderstanding, in prosecutions for childhood sexual abuse.

Redmayne, *Expert Evidence and Criminal Justice* (Oxford, 2001).

A monograph on expert evidence in criminal cases in the UK, using comparative material, drawing on material from disciplines including forensic science, psychology and probability theory, and examining in detail particular issues such as battered women's syndrome and fingerprinting.

Roberts, 'Drawing on Expertise: Legal Decision-making and the Reception of Expert Evidence' [2008] Crim LR 443.

Discussion of reliability as a condition of the admission of expert evidence, a critique of the English liberal approach to admissibility, and consideration of the development of a judicial gate-keeping function, suggesting the need to adopt pre-trial procedures providing for the direct involvement of experts in the gate-keeping process.

Ward et al, 'Forensic Science, Scientific Validity and Reliability: Advice from America' [2017] Crim LR 357.

An article that explores various criticisms and recommendations of the report produced by the US President's Council of Advisors on Science and Technology, *Forensic Science in Criminal Courts: Ensuring Scientific Validity of Feature-Comparison Methods.*

QUESTION

Critically evaluate the law relating to the admissibility of expert evidence in criminal trials in England and Wales.

 For a note-form answer see the online resources, accessible at www.oup.com/he/keane-mckeown13e.

Public policy

21

Key issues

- What types of relevant and otherwise admissible evidence should be excluded on the basis of public interest immunity (PII), that is, on the basis that disclosure would not be in the public interest?

- Should ultimate decisions on PII be taken by the courts or the executive?

- How can the interests of the accused be safeguarded when the prosecution apply to the court for immunity from disclosure in the public interest?

- Should evidence be withheld from disclosure solely on the basis that it was given in confidence, for example information given by a patient to a doctor?

- Should courts have power to require a journalist to disclose the source of information contained in a publication and, if so, in what circumstances?

- Where evidence is protected by PII, in what circumstances, if any, should it be possible to waive such immunity?

- In civil proceedings in which there is evidence disclosure of which would be damaging to the interests of national security, when, if at all, should such evidence be relied upon by one party and by the court, but not be revealed to the other party?

A party to litigation has an obvious interest in the admission of any item of evidence which supports his own case or undermines that of his opponent. Such an interest coincides with a public interest that justice should be done between litigants by the reception of all relevant evidence. The public interest in efficient and fair trials may also be seen as underlying the rules of disclosure in civil litigation, that is, the rules requiring a party to state that a document exists or has existed. Under those rules, a litigant is obliged to make pre-trial disclosure of, inter alia, the documents on which he relies and the documents which adversely affect his own case or adversely affect, or support, another party's case, even though such documents may not be admissible evidence at the trial.[1] There is also a public interest, however, in enabling material to be withheld where its production would harm the nation or the public service. Where these two kinds of public interest clash and the latter prevails over the former, relevant and otherwise admissible evidence is excluded at trial. Such material is said to be withheld by reason of 'public interest immunity'(PII).[2]

The development of the modern law

Civil cases

Decisions on PII for the courts, not the executive

In *Duncan v Cammell Laird & Co Ltd*,[3] material which might have affected national security, by assisting a foreign power, at a time when the country was at war, to understand the structure and design of a submarine, was understandably withheld. Lord Simon held that where a minister decides against disclosure of a document on the grounds that it would be injurious to national defence or good diplomatic relations or because it belongs to a class of documents which it is necessary to keep secret for the proper functioning of the public service, his decision is binding upon the courts. This statement of law gave rise to considerable judicial criticism because it enabled executive claims to PII to succeed notwithstanding that disclosure involved only the smallest probability of injury to the public service and non-disclosure involved the gravest risk of injustice to a litigant.[4] By 1956, the tide began to turn. In that year, the Lord Chancellor announced that PII would not be claimed in respect of certain classes of document including, for example, medical reports of prison doctors in negligence actions against doctors or the Crown and documents relevant to the defence in criminal proceedings.[5] In *Conway v Rimmer*[6] the House of Lords, while in no doubt that the outcome in *Duncan v Cammell Laird & Co Ltd* was correct, was also of the unanimous opinion that whether relevant evidence should be withheld in the public interest is ultimately a question for the decision of the courts and not the executive. It was held that a minister's affidavit or certificate is not final: although an objection to production by the Crown was entitled to the greatest weight, the court could ask for a clarification or amplification of the objection

---

[1] See generally CPR Pt 31.

[2] The expression 'Crown privilege' has been judicially disapproved on the ground that there is no question of any privilege in the ordinary sense of the word: see per Lord Reid in *Rogers v Home Secretary* [1973] AC 388 HL at 400; but cf per Lord Scarman in *Science Research Council v Nassé* [1980] AC 1028 at 1087.

[3] [1942] AC 624, HL.

[4] See, eg, *Ellis v Home Office* [1953] 2 QB 135, CA and *Broome v Broome* [1955] P 190.

[5] See 197 HL Deb (1956) col 741. Further concessions were made in 1962: 237 HL Deb (1962) col 1191.

[6] [1968] AC 910.

and had the power to inspect the documents privately and order their production notwithstanding the minister's objection. Concerning the test to be applied in deciding whether the objection should be upheld, their Lordships held that the court should balance two public interests, that of the state or public service in non-disclosure and that of the proper administration of justice in the production of the documents.

Contents claims and class claims

In *Conway v Rimmer*, a distinction was drawn between a 'contents' claim, that is a claim that it would be against the public interest to disclose the contents of a particular document, and a 'class' claim, that is a claim that a document, whether or not it contains anything the disclosure of which would be against the public interest, belongs to a class of documents which ought to be withheld. In the case of 'contents' claims, Lord Reid said:[7]

> However wide the power of the court may be held to be, cases would be very rare in which it could be proper to question the view of the responsible Minister that it would be contrary to the public interest to make public the contents of a particular document.

In the case of 'class' claims, however, although certain classes of document of a high level of public importance, such as Cabinet minutes and documents concerned with policy-making within government departments, should hardly ever be disclosed, whatever their contents might be, because such disclosure 'would create or fan ill-informed or captious public or political criticism' or 'would be quite wrong and entirely inimical to the proper functioning of the public service',[8] there was a wide difference between such documents and routine reports. 'There may be special reasons for withholding some kinds of routine reports, but the proper test to be applied is to ask . . . whether the withholding of a document because it belongs to a particular class is really "necessary for the proper functioning of the public service".'[9] The House was especially critical of the argument that whole classes of documents should be withheld on the grounds of candour and uninhibited freedom of expression with and within the public service.

In *Conway v Rimmer* the plaintiff, a former probationary police constable who had been charged with but acquitted of stealing a torch, brought an action against his former superintendent claiming damages for malicious prosecution. The Home Secretary objected to the production of five reports, four relating to the plaintiff's conduct as a probationer and the fifth leading to his prosecution for theft, on the grounds that they belonged to classes of documents, namely police reports to senior officers and reports on criminal investigations, the production of which would be injurious to the public interest. The House of Lords held that whereas the reports might be of vital importance to the litigation in question, they were of a routine nature and it was most improbable that their disclosure would prejudice the public interest. The documents were ordered to be produced for inspection. Subsequently, the House itself read the documents and, having done so, ordered that they be made available to the plaintiff.

---

[7] Ibid at 943. See also per Lord Upjohn at 993.

[8] Ibid per Lords Reid and Upjohn at 952 and 993 respectively.

[9] [1968] AC 910 per Lord Reid at 952, citing Lord Simon in *Duncan v Cammell Laird & Co Ltd* [1942] AC 624 at 642. See also per Lord Reid in *Rogers v Secretary of State for the Home Department* [1973] AC 388, HL at 400–1.

In *Conway v Rimmer* Lord Reid said:[10] 'I do not doubt that there are certain classes of documents which ought not to be disclosed whatever their contents may be.'[11] However, a contrary view was taken in *Burmah Oil Co Ltd v Bank of England*,[12] where Lord Keith said:[13]

> The courts are . . . concerned with the consideration that it is in the public interest that justice should be done and should be publicly recognized as having been done. This may demand, . . . in a very limited number of cases, that the inner workings of government should be exposed to public gaze, and there may be some who would regard this as likely to lead, not to captious or ill-informed criticism, but to criticism calculated to improve the nature of that working as affecting the individual citizen.

That the court should be prepared, where appropriate, to require the disclosure of even high-level government papers was reasserted, in principle, in *Air Canada v Secretary of State for Trade (No 2)*,[14] where Lord Fraser said:[15]

> I do not think that even Cabinet minutes are completely immune from disclosure in a case where, for example, the issue in a litigation involves serious misconduct by a Cabinet minister. Such cases have occurred in Australia (see *Sankey v Whitlam*)[16] and in the United States (see *Nixon v United States*)[17] but fortunately not in the United Kingdom: see also the New Zealand case of *Environmental Defence Society Inc v South Pacific Aluminium Ltd (No 2)*.[18] But, while Cabinet documents do not have complete immunity, they are entitled to a high degree of protection against disclosure.

In 1996 the Lord Chancellor announced that the division between class and content claims would be brought to an end and that in future ministers would focus on the damage that disclosure would cause, only claiming immunity when they believed that disclosure would cause real damage or harm to the public interest. It was said that damage will normally have to take the form of direct or immediate threat to the safety of an individual or the nation's economic interests or relations with a foreign state, although in some cases, such as damage to a regulatory process, the anticipated damage might be indirect or longer term. In any event the nature of the harm will need to be clearly explained and ministers will no longer be able to claim immunity for internal advice or national security by reference to the general nature of the document. Non-governmental bodies claiming immunity are not bound by the statement, but it is obviously desirable for the same approach to be taken across the board.

---

[10] [1968] AC 910 at 952.

[11] See also per Lords Hodson, Pearce and Upjohn at 973, 987, and 993 respectively.

[12] [1980] AC 1090.

[13] At 1134.

[14] [1983] 2 AC 394, HL. See also *Williams v Home Office* [1981] 1 All ER 1151, QBD and *Re HIV Haemophiliac Litigation* [1996] PIQR P220.

[15] At 432. The quotation makes clear that the weight of the public interest in the administration of justice (which is weighed against the public interest in non-disclosure) depends not only on the importance of the material to the litigation in hand but also on the public importance of the litigation itself. See also per Ackner LJ in *Campbell v Tameside Metropolitan Borough Council* [1982] QB 1065 at 1076; and generally Allan (1985) 101 LQR 200.

[16] (1978) 21 ALR 505.

[17] 418 US 683 (1974).

[18] [1981] 1 NZLR 153.

Material disclosing serious criminal misconduct

There is no absolute bar to a claim for PII where the claim, if successful, would prevent the disclosure of evidence of serious criminal misconduct by officials of the state, even in the case of torture, cruel, inhuman, or degrading treatment or other war crimes.[19]

Criminal cases

In criminal proceedings, as we shall see, the rule against the disclosure of sources of police information was established some 200 years ago. In remarkable contrast, it is only relatively recently that the English courts have given any consideration to the applicability to criminal proceedings of the general doctrine of PII. The question appears to have arisen for the first time in *R v Governor of Brixton Prison, ex p Osman*.[20] Noting that the seminal cases make no reference to criminal proceedings, Mann LJ held that the civil principles do apply in criminal cases, but involve a different balancing exercise: although the judge should balance the public interest in non-disclosure against the interests of justice in the particular case, the weight to be attached to the interests of justice in a criminal case touching and concerning liberty, and very occasionally life, is plainly very great indeed.[21] In *R v Keane*[22] Lord Taylor CJ held that when the court is seised of the material, the judge should balance the weight of the public interest in non-disclosure against the importance of the documents to the issues of interest to the defence, present and potential, so far as they have been disclosed to him or he can foresee them. However, as we shall see, the House of Lords has since made clear in *R v H*[23] that the golden rule is full prosecution disclosure and that although some derogation from the golden rule can be justified, it should always be to the minimum necessary to protect the public interest and it should never imperil the overall fairness of the trial. It was also held that if it does imperil the overall fairness of the trial, then fuller disclosure should be ordered even if this leads or may lead the prosecution to discontinue the proceedings so as to avoid having to make disclosure. Furthermore, the judge's initial ruling is not necessarily final. He is under a continuous duty to keep his initial decision under review—issues may emerge at a later stage so that the public interest in non-disclosure may be eclipsed by the defendant's need for access.[24] In deciding whether or not to order disclosure, the judge is not confined to admissible evidence but may take into account hearsay material.[25]

In *R v Ward*[26] it was held that the decision as to what should be withheld from disclosure is for the court, not the prosecution, the police, the DPP, or advocates.[27] A prosecution decision to withhold relevant evidence without notifying the judge would be a violation of Art 6 of the European Convention on Human Rights.[28] The prosecution cannot be judge in their

---

[19] *R (Mohamed) v Secretary of State for Foreign and Commonwealth Affairs* [2009] EWHC 152.

[20] [1991] 1 WLR 281, QBD.

[21] Approved in *R v Keane* [1994] 1 WLR 746, CA.

[22] [1994] 1 WLR 746, CA.

[23] [2004] 2 AC 134, HL.

[24] *R v H* [2004] 2 AC 134, HL at [36]. See also *R v Bower* [1994] Crim LR 281, CA; *R v Brown (Winston)* [1994] 1 WLR 1599, CA; and ss 14 and 15 of the Criminal Procedure and Investigations Act 1996.

[25] *R v Law* (1996) The Times, 15 Aug.

[26] [1993] 1 WLR 619, CA.

[27] See also, in the case of a co-accused, *R v Adams* [1997] Crim LR 292, CA.

[28] *Rowe and Davis v UK* (2000) 30 EHRR 1. See also *Dowsett v UK* [2003] Crim LR 890.

own cause and if they are not prepared to let the court decide, the prosecution will have to be abandoned. However, in exceptional cases, the Crown Prosecution Service may voluntarily disclose to the defence documents in a class covered by PII without referring the matter to the court for a ruling, subject to the safeguard of first seeking the written approval of the Treasury Solicitor.[29]

The rule in *R v Ward*[30] that it is for the *court* to decide what material should be withheld is now reflected in the statutory rules relating to pre-trial disclosure in Pt 1 of the Criminal Procedure and Investigations Act 1996. Section 21(2) preserves the common law rules as to whether disclosure is in the public interest.

The scope of exclusion on grounds of public policy

General

Conway v Rimmer paved the way for a generalization of the principles of public policy, which has led to a widening of the heads of public interest which the courts will recognize. Thus it is now clear that documents, to be protected, need not relate to the workings of central government at all: the public also has an interest in the effective working of non-governmental bodies and agencies performing public functions such as local authorities,[31] the Gaming Board (replaced by the Gambling Commission in 2007),[32] the National Society for the Prevention of Cruelty to Children (NSPCC),[33] and the Law Society.[34] It is tempting to generalize the principles completely and to say that evidence will be excluded whenever a public interest in its non-disclosure is asserted which outweighs the importance of receiving the evidence in the particular case. This was an argument put forward in *D v NSPCC*[35] in answer to the proposition that PII is restricted to the effective functioning of departments or organs of central government. Both propositions were rejected by the House of Lords in favour of the middle view that although 'the categories of the public interest are not closed and must alter from time to time whether by restriction or extension as social conditions and social legislation develop',[36] nevertheless the court can proceed only by analogy with interests which have previously been recognized by the authorities.[37]

In that case, the NSPCC, a body established by royal charter and given statutory power, along with the police and local authorities, to bring care proceedings, sought to honour a promise given to an informant that his identity would not be revealed. The plaintiff claimed damages for the injury to her health caused by the negligence of the NSPCC in pursuing the allegations of the informant that she had maltreated her child, allegations which proved

---

[29] See *R v Horseferry Road Magistrates, ex p Bennett (No 2)* [1994] 1 All ER 289, DC.

[30] [1993] 1 WLR 619, CA.

[31] See, eg, *Re D (infants)* [1970] 1 WLR 599, CA and *Gaskin v Liverpool City Council* [1980] 1 WLR 1549, CA (child-care records).

[32] *R v Lewes Justices, ex p Home Secretary* [1973] AC 388, HL, considered, in this chapter, under **The proper functioning of the public service, Examples, p 687**.

[33] *D v NSPCC* [1978] AC 171, HL (name of informant who prompted NSPCC inquiry).

[34] *Buckley v Law Society (No 2)* [1984] 1 WLR 1101, Ch D (names of informants whose complaints led to the Law Society's inquiry into a solicitor's conduct). See also *Medway v Doublelock Ltd* [1978] 1 WLR 710: an affidavit of means supplied in divorce proceedings can be withheld in subsequent litigation on grounds of public policy.

[35] [1978] AC 171, HL. See per Lord Diplock at 219–20 where the arguments are summarized.

[36] Per Lord Hailsham at 230.

[37] Per Lord Simon at 240, Lord Diplock at 219, and Lord Hailsham (with whom Lord Kilbrandon agreed) at 226.

groundless. The House of Lords upheld the NSPCC's application to withhold from discovery documents disclosing the identity of the informant. Their Lordships held that the value of the NSPCC's work was indicated by statutory recognition of its function, by evidence that informants were more willing to approach the NSPCC than the police or local authorities, and by other statutory and common law authority acknowledging the importance of providing for the welfare of children. Relying on the analogy of judicial refusal to compel disclosure of sources of police information, they held that in both situations the public interest in the uninhibited flow of information justified the refusal to order disclosure since otherwise the sources of information would be expected to dry up.[38] Although the actual result of the case was no doubt desirable, the reasoning by which that result was achieved is open to criticism. In particular, reliance on the constraint of precedent seems an unsatisfactory means of containing the undesirable effect of an over-generalized principle. If the constraint is applied, it must result in arbitrary distinctions. The relevance of statutory recognition must also be questioned: activities conducted without statutory provision or regulation can also be of great public importance.

It is convenient to consider the cases in which a claim to PII has been made under the heads of 'National security, diplomatic relations and international comity', 'Information for the detection of crime', 'Judges and jurors', 'The proper functioning of the public service', and 'Confidential relationships'. In considering these cases, it needs to be remembered that there are always four variables capable of affecting the outcome, namely: (i) the importance of the public function in question; (ii) the extent to which disclosure would prejudice the effective exercise of that function; (iii) the importance of the material in question to the just determination of the litigation; and (iv) the public importance of that litigation.

National security, diplomatic relations, and international comity

Evidence will almost certainly be excluded in the interests of national security, good diplomatic relations, and international comity. *Duncan v Cammell Laird & Co Ltd*, as we have seen, furnishes an example in relation to national security. In *Asiatic Petroleum Co Ltd v Anglo-Persian Oil Co Ltd*[39] the Court of Appeal upheld a decision not to produce a letter containing information concerning the Government's plans in respect of its campaign in Persia during the First World War. Other examples under this head include communications between the governor of a colony and the colonial secretary,[40] and communications between the commander-in-chief of forces overseas and the Government[41] and diplomatic despatches.[42]

Concerning national security, it seems that a ministerial certificate will be conclusive. In *Balfour v Foreign and Commonwealth Office*[43] B, dismissed from his post as Vice-Consul in Dubai, complained to an industrial tribunal of unfair dismissal and sought disclosure of documents in the possession of the Foreign Office. Immunity was claimed on the grounds

---

[38] Cf *R v Bournemouth Justices, ex p Grey* [1987] 1 FLR 36, DC: it was difficult to envisage a father being dissuaded from admitting parentage to an adoption society on the basis of his knowledge that a later denial of such parentage might result in the earlier admission being used against him.

[39] [1916] 1 KB 822, CA.

[40] *Hennessy v Wright* (1888) 21 QBD 509.

[41] *Chatterton v Secretary of State for India in Council* [1895] 2 QB 189, CA.

[42] *M Isaacs & Sons Ltd v Cook* [1925] 2 KB 391.

[43] [1994] 1 WLR 681, CA.

that disclosure of material in the documents relating to the security and intelligence services would be contrary to the public interest. Both the Foreign Secretary and Home Secretary signed certificates particularizing the nature and content of the material attracting immunity and the reasons for the claim. The Court of Appeal upheld the decision to refuse disclosure. It was held that although there must always be vigilance by the courts to ensure that PII of whatever kind is raised only in appropriate circumstances and with appropriate particularity, once there is an actual or potential risk to national security demonstrated by an appropriate certificate, the court should not exercise its right to inspect. In reaching its decision, the court approved and applied the dictum of Lord Diplock in *Council of Civil Service Unions v Minister for the Civil Service*[44] (when dealing with the question of national security in a completely different context):

> National security is the responsibility of the executive government; what action is needed to protect its interests is . . . a matter on which those on whom the responsibility rests, and not the courts of justice, must have the last word. It is par excellence a non-justiciable question. The judicial process is totally inept to deal with the sort of problems which it involves.

It is also in the public interest of the United Kingdom that the contents of confidential documents addressed to, or emanating from, foreign sovereign states, or concerning the interests of such states in relation to international territorial disputes between them, should not be ordered by the courts of this country to be disclosed by a private litigant without the consent of the states in question, because to order disclosure in such cases may be against the public interest in the maintenance of international comity and an English court should not be seen to be forcing the disclosure of such documents for the ostensible purpose of pronouncing, albeit indirectly, on the merits of such a dispute, the resolution of which is a question of politics.[45] The comity of nations also justifies an English court, in the exercise of its discretion, in refusing to authorize the issue of letters of request inviting the courts of a friendly foreign state to use their powers to assist in the obtaining of evidence, from witnesses resident in that or another friendly state, in order to show that the motives of the government of the friendly foreign state, in promulgating a particular law, were such that the law is unenforceable in the United Kingdom.[46]

Information for the detection of crime

Police informers

If a witness called at trial is a police informer in relation to the crime charged, the court should be told and, unless there is a very strong countervailing interest not to do so, his status should be revealed.[47] However, it is in the public interest to protect the identity of informers, not only for their own safety, but also to ensure that the supply of information about criminal activities does not dry up. Accordingly, there is a rule, established since at least the

---

[44] [1985] AC 374, HL at 412.

[45] See per Brightman and Donaldson LJJ in *Buttes Gas & Oil Co v Hammer (No 3)* [1981] QB 223, CA.

[46] *Settebello Ltd v Banco Totta and Acores* [1985] 1 WLR 1050, CA. See also *Fayed v Al-Tajir* [1988] QB 712, CA per Mustill and Kerr LJJ, CA at 480 and 410 respectively: international comity requires that an inter-departmental memorandum prepared and circulated in the London embassy of a friendly foreign state should not be admitted as the foundation of an action for libel.

[47] *R v Patel* [2001] EWCA Crim 2505.

late eighteenth century, that a witness in civil or criminal proceedings may not be asked to disclose the name of a police informer.[48] Likewise, no order for disclosure will be made which will have that effect. Even if the party entitled to object does not invoke the rule, the judge is nonetheless obliged to apply it.[49] However, the rule will be overridden where, in a criminal trial, strict enforcement would be likely to cause a miscarriage of justice, that is, where the accused can show good reason to expect that disclosure of the name of the informant will assist him in establishing his innocence.[50] The decision on disclosure is for the judge and therefore if the prosecution are of the view that there should be disclosure, they should refer the matter to the court, which must reach its own decision.[51]

In *Marks v Beyfus*[52] the plaintiff claimed damages for malicious prosecution. In the course of the trial, he asked the Director of Public Prosecutions to name his informants, but the judge disallowed the question. This ruling was upheld by the Court of Appeal on the ground 'that this was a public prosecution, ordered by the Government (or by an official equivalent to the Government) for what was considered to be a public object, and that therefore the information ought not, on grounds of public policy, to be disclosed'.[53] Lord Esher said:[54]

> I do not say it is a rule which can never be departed from; if upon the trial of a prisoner the judge should be of opinion that the disclosure of the name of the informant is necessary or right in order to show the prisoner's innocence, then one public policy is in conflict with another public policy, and that which says that an innocent man is not to be condemned when his innocence can be proved is the policy that must prevail. But, except in that case, this rule of public policy is not a matter of discretion; it is a rule of law . . .

Although it has been suggested that the possibility of a miscarriage of justice *dictates* disclosure,[55] it seems that a balancing exercise should be performed, even though, if the disputed material may prove the accused's innocence or avoid a miscarriage of justice, the balance will come down resoundingly in favour of disclosure.[56] Nonetheless, it has been held that judges need to scrutinize applications for disclosure of details about informants with very great care. They should be astute to see that assertions of a need to know such details (because essential to the running of a defence) are justified. In some cases, the informant is an informant and no more; in others he may have participated in the events constituting, surrounding, or following the crime. Even when the informant has participated, the judge will need to consider whether his role so impinges on an issue of interest to the defence, present or potential, as to make disclosure necessary.[57]

---

[48] *R v Hardy* (1794) 24 State Tr 199. In principle, the rule should prevent disclosure of not only the name of the informer but also any information that will enable him to be identified: see *R v Omar* 2007 ONCA 117.

[49] See per Lord Esher MR in *Marks v Beyfus* (1890) 25 QBD 494, CA at 500 and per Mann J in *R v Rankine* [1986] 2 All ER 566, CA at 569.

[50] Per Lawton LJ in *R v Hennessey* (1978) 68 Cr App R 419, CA at 426. See also *R v Hallett* [1986] Crim LR 462, CA.

[51] *R (WV) v Crown Prosecution Service* [2011] EWHC 2480 (Admin).

[52] (1890) 25 QBD 494, CA.

[53] Per Lord Esher MR at 496–7. It would seem that bodies authorized by statute to bring prosecutions may claim the immunity, but not an individual prosecuting in a private capacity.

[54] (1890) 25 QBD 494, CA at 498.

[55] Per Mann LJ in *R v Governor of Brixton Prison, ex p Osman* [1991] 1 WLR 281, QBD at 290.

[56] Per Lord Taylor CJ in *R v Keane* [1994] 1 WLR 746, CA at 751–2.

[57] Per Lord Taylor CJ in *R v Turner* [1995] 1 WLR 264, CA.

In *R v Agar*[58] the prosecution case was that A, on arrival at the house of X, found police officers present and, when he ran off, threw away a packet containing drugs. A alleged that the police had entered into an arrangement with X, an informer, to ask him to go to X's house and that the drugs allegedly found had been planted by the police. It was held that although an accused cannot discover the identity of an informer by pretending that something is part of his case when in truth it adds nothing to it, and although it *may* be that a defence which is manifestly frivolous and doomed to failure must be sacrificed to the general rule protecting informers, on the facts the defence should have been permitted to elicit that X had told the police that A would be coming to his house, which would have identified him as an informer. Such evidence was necessary to enable A to put forward his defence that he had been set up by X and the police acting in concert.[59]

Owners or occupiers of premises used for police surveillance

In *R v Rankine*[60] it was held that the rule is not confined to the identification of police informers but also prevents the identification of premises used for police surveillance and the owners and occupiers of such premises. However, if the accused alleges that disclosure of the identification of such premises is necessary in order to establish his innocence, the prosecution must provide a sufficient evidential base to enable the trial judge properly to determine whether to afford the protection sought. In *R v Johnson*[61] the Court of Appeal held that there are two minimal evidential requirements for these purposes. First, the officer in charge of the observations, who normally should be of at least the rank of sergeant, should give evidence that he visited the premises to be used and ascertained the attitude of the occupiers to the use to be made of the premises and the possible disclosure thereafter of the use made and of facts which could lead to the identification of both premises and occupiers. He may additionally inform the court of any difficulties encountered in the particular locality in obtaining assistance from the public. Second, an officer of at least the rank of chief inspector should give evidence that immediately before the trial he visited the premises and ascertained whether the occupiers were still the same and, whether they were or not, what their attitude was to the possible disclosure of the use made of the premises and of facts which could lead to the identification of both premises and occupiers.[62]

Johnson was convicted of supplying drugs. The police alleged that he had been seen selling the drugs in a particular street by officers situated in buildings in the locality. The prosecution argued that the evidence which their witnesses should be compelled to give should not go further than revealing that all the observation points were within a given maximum distance from the scene of the offence. The advocate for the defence submitted that this would enable officers to cover up inconsistencies in their evidence and gravely embarrass him in his efforts to test in cross-examination precisely what they could see from their various locations having regard to the layout of the street and the objects in it, including trees.

---

[58] [1990] 2 All ER 442, CA.

[59] See also *R v Vaillencourt* [1993] Crim LR 311, CA and *R v Reilly* [1994] Crim LR 279, CA. Cf *R v Slowcombe* [1991] Crim LR 198, CA, where the identity of the informer would have contributed little or nothing to the defence being run, and *R v Menza and Marshalleck* [1998] Crim LR 58, CA.

[60] [1986] QB 861, CA.

[61] [1988] 1 WLR 1377, CA.

[62] There is no requirement of a threat of violence before protection can be afforded to the occupier—it suffices if he is in fear of harassment: *Blake v DPP* (1992) 97 Cr App R 169, DC.

In the jury's absence, the police gave evidence as to the difficulty of obtaining assistance from the public for observation purposes and revealed that the occupiers, all of whom were also occupiers at the material time, did not wish their names and addresses to be disclosed because they feared for their safety. The judge ruled that the officers should not reveal the location of the premises used. The appeal was dismissed: although the conduct of the defence was to some extent affected by this restraint, it had led to no injustice.[63]

In *R v Brown, R v Daley*[64] the Court of Appeal emphasized that the extension of the exclusionary rule established in *R v Rankine* was based on the protection of the owner or occupier of the premises and not on the identity, *simpliciter*, of the observation post. The accused were convicted of theft from a parked car. The chief prosecution witnesses were two officers who gave evidence that they had witnessed the commission of the offence as part of a surveillance operation conducted from an unmarked police vehicle. The defence was that their evidence had been fabricated. The judge allowed the prosecution to withhold information relating to the surveillance and the colour, make, and model of the police vehicle. The appeal was allowed. It was held that evidence of police methods and techniques, if relevant, was admissible. Even if PII could be successfully invoked to exclude evidence of sophisticated methods of criminal investigation, a possibility which the court was not prepared to rule out, the prosecution, in applying to exclude evidence on such a basis, would have to identify with precision the evidence to be excluded, give reasons for exclusion, and support the application by the independent evidence of senior officers. On the facts, this had not been done.

Application of the principle in civil cases

Disclosure to show that an accused is innocent of a criminal offence is not, as was once intimated,[65] the sole exception to a general rule against disclosure. In *Chief Constable of Greater Manchester Police v McNally*,[66] civil proceedings for, inter alia, malicious prosecution, the trial judge had ordered the Chief Constable to disclose whether an individual, X, who had allegedly threatened a prosecution witness at the criminal trial, was a police informer. The Court of Appeal held that judges in civil cases are entitled to balance the public interest in the protection of an informer against the public interest in a fair trial but are required to give very considerable weight to the former interest and to reduce the weight of the latter, given that it is a civil trial at which liberty is not at stake. However, there were no grounds for interfering with the ruling of the judge who had properly given significant weight to three factors: that the evidence could have been decisive of the outcome of the case; that although the claimant's liberty was not at stake, he was seeking redress for wrongful deprivation of liberty for over 10 months while in custody awaiting trial; and that although X had not consented to disclosure of information that he was an informer, the scope for protecting him was limited by the fact that both sides knew who he was.[67]

---

[63] *R v Johnson* was applied in *R v Hewitt; R v Davis* (1991) 95 Cr App R 81, CA. See also *R v Grimes* [1994] Crim LR 213, CA.

[64] (1987) 87 Cr App R 52, CA.

[65] See per Lord Diplock in *D v NSPCC* [1978] AC 171 at 218.

[66] [2002] 2 Cr App R 617 (37), CA.

[67] Cf *Re W (children) (care proceedings: disclosure)* [2003] EWHC 1624 (Fam), which concerned information received by a local authority from the police, the disclosure of which in care proceedings, in the form in which it was provided, would have prejudiced covert police operations and enabled an informant to be identified.

Informers wishing to reveal their identity

In *Savage v Chief Constable of Hampshire*[68] it was held that if a police informer wishes to sacrifice his own anonymity, he may do so, because in such circumstances the primary justification for non-disclosure, that disclosure would endanger his safety, disappears. In appropriate circumstances, however, it may be that notwithstanding the wishes of the informer, there remains a significant public interest which would be damaged by disclosure, as when disclosure might assist others involved in crime, reveal police methods of operation, or hamper police operations.

Judges and jurors

There are restrictions on the extent to which those involved in the conduct of a trial can be called to give evidence of the proceedings. They differ from the other heads of public policy in that although they prevent certain people being called to prove certain facts, for the most part they do not prevent proof of those facts by other means. These rules, which might equally well be considered under the heading of competence and compellability, or privilege, have played little, if any, part in the general development of PII.

A litigant may wish to prove what was said in earlier litigation. The court record and a properly proved transcript, where available, will usually be the best means, but in principle anyone who witnessed the proceedings may be called. However, a judge, including a Queen's Bench or Chancery Master, cannot be compelled to give evidence of those matters of which she became aware relating to and as a result of the performance of her judicial functions, as opposed to some collateral matter, for example a crime committed in the face of the court. Nonetheless the judge is competent to give evidence, and if a situation arises where her evidence is vital, she should be able to be relied on not to assert her non-compellability.[69]

A jury's verdict cannot be impeached by the evidence of a juror about deliberations in the jury room.[70] Accordingly, the Court of Appeal in *R v Thompson*[71] refused to hear evidence to the effect that a juror had read a list of the accused's previous convictions, which had not been revealed in evidence. However, during the course of a trial an irregularity relating to the jury should be drawn to the attention of the trial judge in the absence of the jury; the judge's investigation of the facts may involve questioning individual jurors involved; and the inquiries should be directed towards ascertaining whether the individual jurors can remain faithful to their oath.[72]

The proper functioning of the public service

Examples

PII has been successfully claimed in respect of a variety of state interests on the grounds that protection is necessary for the proper functioning of the public service.[73] It is quite clear, for

---

[68] [1997] 1 WLR 1061, CA.

[69] *Warren v Warren* [1997] QB 488, CA.

[70] See, eg, *R v Roads* [1967] 2 QB 108, in which a juror was not allowed to prove that she disagreed with the verdict.

[71] [1962] 1 All ER 65. See also per Lord Atkin in *Ras Behari Lal v R* (1933) 102 LJPC 144; *R v Bean* [1991] Crim LR 843, CA (an allegation of undue judicial pressure to reach a verdict); and *R v Lucas* [1991] Crim LR 844, CA (an allegation of undue pressure on one juror by the others). Cf *R v Newton* (1912) 7 Cr App R 214.

[72] See *Criminal Practice Directions* VI, Part 26M; *R v Mirza* [2004] 1 AC 118; and *R v Smith and Mercieca* [2005] 2 All ER 29.

[73] At one time 'class' claims succeeded on this ground even in the case of documents of a relatively routine nature. See, eg, *Re Joseph Hargreaves* [1900] 1 Ch 347 and *Anthony v Anthony* (1919) 35 TLR 559. Decisions of this kind pre-date *Conway v Rimmer* [1968] AC 910, and it is most unlikely that they would be followed today.

example, that subject to the court's assessment of the strength of the claim for immunity in each case and the importance of the material to the litigation, immunity may be claimed for communications to and from ministers and high-level government officials regarding the formulation of government policy.[74] In *Conway v Rimmer* itself it was recognized that internal communications of the police force (quite apart from those relating to the investigation of crime) would in appropriate cases qualify for immunity on the ground that the public have an interest in the proper functioning of the police force which, though not a government department, 'carries out essential functions of government'. Concerning communications which do relate to the investigation of crime, it has been held that PII attaches to documents and information upon the strength of which search warrants have been obtained[75] and also to reports sent by the police to the DPP, even if the prosecution has been completed, whether successfully or not.[76] In the latter case, it was held that it is important for the proper functioning of the criminal process of prosecution that there should be freedom of communication between police forces and the DPP in seeking his legal advice, without fear that the documents will be subject to inspection, analysis, and investigation in subsequent civil proceedings. There is also a clear public interest in the non-disclosure of international communications between police forces or prosecuting authorities, essentially so as not to divulge information useful to criminals and not to inhibit the fullest cooperation between such authorities in different jurisdictions.[77]

In *R v Lewes Justices, ex p Home Secretary*[78] an unsuccessful applicant for a gaming licence sought disclosure, in libel proceedings against the police, of a letter sent by the police to the Gaming Board, which had requested information in the course of its statutory duty to investigate the applicant's suitability for a licence. The House of Lords refused the application, being clearly impressed by the importance of the Board's function in controlling the social evils which might otherwise have been expected to follow in the wake of the newly legalized activity of gaming. An analogy was drawn with the principle relating to police informers: although the risk of disclosure might not inhibit the police, it would affect the wells of voluntary information. The plaintiff was thus, in effect, deprived of his cause of action.[79]

In *Lonrho plc v Fayed (No 4)*[80] the question arose whether, in the absence of consent to disclosure by a taxpayer, PII attaches to documents relating to his tax affairs in the hands of the Inland Revenue. A majority of the Court of Appeal, noting Parliament's clear intention (subject to specified exceptions) to prohibit disclosure by the Revenue of a taxpayer's affairs,

---

[74] See, eg, *Burmah Oil Co Ltd v Bank of England* [1980] AC 1090, and *Air Canada v Secretary of State for Trade (No 2)* [1983] 2 AC 394, in this chapter, under **Contents claims and class claims**, p 678; cf *Williams v Home Office* [1981] 1 All ER 1151, CA.

[75] *Taylor v Anderton* (1986) The Times, 21 Oct, Ch D.

[76] *Evans v Chief Constable of Surrey* [1988] QB 588, QBD.

[77] *R v Horseferry Road Magistrates, ex p Bennett (No 2)* [1994] 1 All ER 289, DC, although in that case the balance favoured disclosure, the documents being relevant to the issue whether B had been unlawfully returned to the jurisdiction.

[78] [1973] AC 388, also referred to as *Rogers v Secretary of State*.

[79] See also *Lonrho Ltd v Shell Petroleum* [1980] 1 WLR 627, HL where immunity was granted, in subsequent litigation, for evidence given to the Bingham inquiry into the operation of sanctions against Rhodesia: although the inquiry had powers to compel evidence to be given, its effectiveness depended on a voluntary supply of information which in turn required a valid guarantee of confidentiality. Cf *Hamilton v Naviede* [1995] 2 AC 75, HL.

[80] [1994] QB 755, CA.

answered the question in the affirmative on the grounds that as a matter of public policy, the state should not by compulsory powers obtain information from a citizen for one purpose and then use it for another. Thus the confidentiality of such documents will only be over-ridden if the party seeking disclosure shows very strong grounds for concluding that on the facts of the particular case the public interest in the administration of justice outweighs the public interest in preserving the confidentiality. The court also held, unanimously, that no PII attaches to documents relating to tax affairs held by the taxpayer himself (or his agents).

The statutory functions of keeping import records for the purposes of Customs and Excise legislation (see *Norwich Pharmacal Co v Customs and Excise Comrs*)[81] and inquiring into the true nature of a person's trade in order to make a proper assessment to tax (see *Alfred Crompton Amusement Machines Ltd v Customs and Excise Comrs (No 2)*)[82] are both in principle capable of attracting PII. In the *Norwich Pharmacal* case, however, it was held that there was no seri-ous risk that importers would be less likely to comply with their statutory duty to give the necessary information simply because of the possibility of that information being disclosed in civil proceedings, whereas in the *Alfred Crompton* case the information to be supplied by third parties about a trader's activities, even though supplied under statutory compulsion, was sufficiently sensitive to justify the fear that the Commissioners' functions would be hampered unless they were able to give an effective guarantee. Disclosure was thus required in the former case but denied in the latter.[83]

In *Science Research Council v Nassé*[84] the House of Lords firmly rejected a claim to immunity in relation to routine confidential employers' reports on employees seeking promotion.[85] *D v NSPCC*[86] was applied: PII can be extended only by analogy with previous authority. Lord Edmund-Davies[87] noted that PII had thus far been limited to bodies exercising statutory functions or duties in respect of which an analogy could be drawn with the principle relating to police informers.

Statements obtained for investigation of complaints against the police
In the case of statements obtained for the purposes of an investigation of a complaint against the police under the statutory complaints procedures, a class claim to immunity would tend to be largely self-defeating. Thus although it would be possible to justify immunity on the

---

[81] [1974] AC 133, HL.

[82] [1974] AC 405, HL.

[83] Immunity can attach to evidence taken in a statutory Department of Trade investigation of a company (per Lord Widgery CJ, obiter, in *R v Cheltenham Justices, ex p Secretary of State for Trade* [1977] 1 WLR 95) and also to a report to the Secretary of State following a DTI inquiry into the activities of a company (see *Day v Grant* [1987] 3 All ER 678, CA at 680). The former case was distinguished in *London and County Securities v Nicholson* [1980] 1 WLR 948, on the grounds that the importance of the evidence tipped the scales the other way. See also, in this chapter, *Multi Guarantee Co Ltd v Cavalier Insurance Co Ltd* (1986) The Times, 24 June, Ch D, under **Waiver and secondary evidence, pp 698–9**: the immunity attaching to notes recording information given in confidence to officials of the DTI is capable of 'evaporating'. Concerning statutes requiring the disclosure of information and governing the extent to which it can be used in other proceedings, see generally Eagles, 'Public interest immunity and statutory privilege' (1983) 42 CLJ 118.

[84] [1980] AC 1028, HL.

[85] But also held that if discovery was not necessary for fairly disposing of the proceedings, it could be refused on the grounds of breach of confidence. See, in this chapter, under **Confidential relationships, p 689**.

[86] [1978] AC 171, HL.

[87] [1980] AC 1028 at 1073–4, approving the dicta of Browne LJ in the Court of Appeal.

basis of (i) a candour argument (witnesses might be inhibited by the possibility of disclosure in subsequent litigation); and (ii) the underlying public interest in the maintenance of a law-abiding and uncorrupt police force, the consequences of immunity would prevent the complainant from seeing the relevant documents in any subsequent proceedings brought against the police. For reasons of this kind, in *R v Chief Constable of the West Midlands Police, ex p Wiley*[88] the House of Lords held that there is no PII for such documents on the basis of a class claim.[89] It also held, however, that a claim to immunity may succeed on the basis of the contents of a particular document. Thus a claim could succeed in the case of a document containing, for example, police material on policy or operational matters or the identity of an informant. It was held that any contents claim should be decided in the proceedings in which the documents are relevant, such as a subsequent civil action in respect of the alleged misconduct (rather than in any collateral proceedings), because the conflicting public interests for and against disclosure will vary from case to case and the relationship between the conflicting interests may vary as the case proceeds to trial and even during the trial.[90]

The House of Lords in *ex p Wiley* left open the question whether reports prepared by the investigating officers form a class which is entitled to immunity. Subsequently, the Court of Appeal in *Taylor v Anderton*[91] answered the question in the affirmative, as to working papers as well as such reports, holding that production of such material should only be ordered, therefore, where the public interest in disclosure of their contents outweighs the public interest in preserving their confidentiality. In reaching this decision, Sir Thomas Bingham MR was particularly influenced by (i) the fundamental public interest in ensuring that those responsible for maintaining law and order are themselves law-abiding and honest; and (ii) the need for investigating officers to feel free to report on professional colleagues or members of the public without the undesirably inhibiting apprehension that their opinions may become known to such persons.

PII does not attach to statements made in a police grievance procedure, initiated by an officer, alleging racial or sexual discrimination.[92]

Confidential relationships

There are many important relationships which depend on the assumption that confidences will be respected. Examples include the relationship between doctor and patient, journalist and source, and priest and penitent. In *Alfred Crompton Amusement Machines Ltd v Customs and Excise Comrs (No 2)*[93] it was emphasized that confidentiality is never a sufficient ground of immunity, even though it is often a necessary condition. Thus at common law, in the absence of some additional consideration, as when the person claiming immunity is exercising a statutory function the effective performance of which would be impeded by disclosure,

---

[88] [1995] 1 AC 274, HL.

[89] There is no immunity for written complaints prompting investigations against the police: *Conerney v Jacklin* [1985] Crim LR 234, CA.

[90] See also *Peach v Metropolitan Police Comr* [1986] QB 1064, CA and *Ex p Coventry Newspapers Ltd* [1993] QB 278, CA.

[91] [1995] 1 WLR 447, CA.

[92] *Metropolitan Police Comr v Locker* [1993] 3 All ER 584, EAT.

[93] [1974] AC 405, HL.

a claim to PII will not succeed. An example of such an additional consideration is provided by *Re Barlow Clowes Gilt Managers Ltd*.[94] It was held that the liquidators of a company are under no duty to assist its directors, in defending criminal charges, by providing them with information obtained by the liquidators from third parties in circumstances of confidentiality and by assurances, express or implied, that it would be used only for the purpose of the liquidation, because if there comes to be a generally perceived risk of such disclosure, there is an obvious danger that professional men will no longer cooperate with liquidators on a voluntary basis, which would jeopardize the proper and efficient functioning of the process of compulsory liquidation.[95]

The question will often arise on disclosure, which under the Rules of the Supreme Court was known as discovery. RSC Ord 24, r 8 provided that the court should refuse to order discovery 'if and so far as it is of opinion that discovery is not necessary either for disposing fairly of the cause or matter or for saving costs'. In *Science Research Council v Nassé*[96] it was held that this provision provided the test to be used by an industrial tribunal, in discrimination proceedings, in deciding whether to order the discovery of confidential reports on employees and applicants for employment. The following propositions derive from the judgment of Lord Wilberforce:

1. There is no principle in English law by which documents are protected from discovery by reason of confidentiality alone, but, in the exercise of its discretion to order discovery, a tribunal may have regard to the fact that disclosure will involve a breach of confidence.

2. Relevance, though necessary, is not automatically a sufficient ground for ordering discovery.

3. The ultimate test is whether discovery is necessary for disposing fairly of the proceedings: if it is, then discovery must be ordered notwithstanding confidentiality, but where the court is impressed with the need to preserve confidentiality, it will consider carefully whether the necessary information can be obtained by other means not involving a breach of confidence.

---

[94] [1992] Ch 208, Ch D. See also *Lonrho Ltd v Shell Petroleum* [1980] 1 WLR 627, HL and *Lonrho plc v Fayed (No 4)* [1994] QB 775, CA, above, under **The proper functioning of the public service, Examples, pp 686–8**; *R v Umoh* (1986) 84 Cr App R 138, CA (immunity for discussions between a prisoner and a legal aid officer); *R v H* [2019] 1 Cr App R 331 (25) (immunity for discussions between those convicted and those charged with their supervision or rehabilitation, unless disclosure necessary for very good reason, eg, to avoid imminent future criminality); *R v K* (1993) 97 Cr App R 342, CA (immunity for an interview with a child victim of a sexual offence conducted for therapeutic purposes, unless disclosure necessary in the interests of justice, eg, to assist an accused whose liberty is at stake); and *Morrow v DPP* [1994] Crim LR 58, DC (immunity for confidential documents relating to abortions carried out under the Abortion Act 1968). The matrimonial reconciliation cases considered in Ch 22 may also be regarded as a limb of PII—see, eg, per Lords Hailsham and Simon in *D v NSPCC* [1978] AC 171 at 226 and 236–7 respectively. Private privilege is available to protect certain types of communication between a lawyer and his client: see Ch 22.

[95] However, if the information is 'material evidence' for the purposes of a witness summons in the criminal proceedings, then the criminal court must balance the competing interests for and against disclosure and in the case of very serious criminal charges at least, this may well result in disclosure: see *R v Clowes* [1992] 3 All ER 440, CCC.

[96] [1980] AC 1028, HL.

4. In order to decide whether discovery is necessary notwithstanding confidentiality, a tribunal should inspect the documents; it will also consider whether justice can be done by 'covering up', substituting anonymous references for specific names or, in rare cases, a hearing in camera.

Science Research Council v Nassé remains the leading authority when courts are faced with an application for disclosure of confidential documents, but in deciding on such applications under the Civil Procedure Rules, account must be taken of the overriding objective. In particular, it is necessary to deal with cases justly, which includes saving expenses and dealing with cases with proportionality, and it is not proportionate to make an order for the supply of documents that will result in duplication.[97]

In *British Steel Corpn (BSC) v Granada Television Ltd*[98] Granada had received from a BSC employee copies of secret documents from BSC's files. Some of the documents were then used in a programme on the national steel strike. Granada had promised the informant that his identity would not be disclosed. BSC applied for an order that Granada disclose the identity of the informant. They relied upon the principle in *Norwich Pharmacal Co v Customs and Excise Comrs*,[99] namely that a person who becomes involved in the tortious acts of another, even if innocently, is under a duty to assist a person injured by those acts by disclosing the identity of the tortfeasor. The House of Lords ordered Granada to disclose the identity of the informant. It was accepted, however, that where possible, judges will respect the confidence:[100]

> Courts have an inherent wish to respect this confidence, whether it arises between doctor and patient, priest and penitent, bankers and customer, between persons giving testimonials to employees, or in other relationships . . . But in all these cases the court may have to decide, in particular circumstances, that the interest in preserving this confidence is outweighed by other interests to which the law attaches importance.

On the facts, Lord Wilberforce concluded that 'to confine BSC to its remedy against Granada and to deny it the opportunity of a remedy against the source would be a significant denial of justice'.[101] His Lordship approved the dictum of Lord Denning MR in *A-G v Mulholland*,[102] applying similar principles in relation to cross-examination at trial:

> The judge will respect the confidences which each member of these honourable professions receives in the course of it, and will not direct him to answer unless not only it is relevant but also it is a proper and, indeed, necessary question in the course of justice to be put and answered. A judge is the person entrusted, on behalf of the community, to weigh these conflicting interests—to weigh on the one hand the respect due to confidence in the profession and on the other hand the ultimate interest of the community in justice being done. . . . If the judge determines that the journalist must answer, then no privilege will avail him to refuse.

Disclosure of the source of information contained in a publication is now governed by statute.

---

[97] *Simba-Tola v Elizabeth Fry Hospital* [2001] EWCA Civ 1371.

[98] [1981] AC 1096, HL.

[99] [1974] AC 133.

[100] Per Lord Wilberforce [1981] AC 1096 at 1168.

[101] [1981] AC 1096 at 1175.

[102] [1963] 2 QB 477 at 489–90. See also *A-G v Lundin* (1982) 75 Cr App R 90, DC: there is no liability for contempt for refusal to answer unless the question is both relevant and necessary.

Disclosure of sources of information in a publication

The general prohibition on disclosure

Section 10 of the Contempt of Court Act 1981 was enacted to bring domestic law in this respect into line with Art 10 of the European Convention on Human Rights, which provides:

1. Everyone has the right to freedom of expression . . .
2. The exercise of these freedoms, since it carries with it duties and responsibilities, may be subject to such formalities, conditions, restrictions or penalties as are prescribed by law and are necessary in a democratic society, in the interests of national security, territorial integrity or public safety, for the prevention of disorder or crime, for the protection of health or morals, for the protection of the reputation or rights of others, for preventing the disclosure of information received in confidence, or for maintaining the authority and impartiality of the judiciary.

Section 10 of the Contempt of Court Act 1981 provides:

No court may require a person to disclose, nor is any person guilty of contempt of court for refusing to disclose, the source of information contained in a publication[103] for which he is responsible, unless it be established to the satisfaction of the court that disclosure is necessary in the interests of justice or national security or for the prevention of disorder or crime.[104]

In *Ashworth Hospital Authority v MGN Ltd*[105] the House of Lords held that s 10 gives effect to the general requirements of Art 10 in the narrow context of the protection of the sources of information of the press; that Art 10 permits the right of freedom of expression to be circumscribed where necessary in a democratic society to achieve a number of specified 'legitimate aims'; and that the approach to the interpretation of s 10 should, insofar as possible (i) equate the specific purposes for which disclosure of sources is permitted under s 10 with the 'legitimate aims' under Art 10; and (ii) apply the same test of necessity to that applied by the European Court of Justice when considering Art 10. The House also accepted the approach of the European Court in *Goodwin v UK*[106] that as a matter of general principle the 'necessity' for any restriction of freedom of expression must be convincingly established and that limitations on the confidentiality of journalistic sources call for the most careful scrutiny by the court. It was held that any restriction on the right to freedom of expression must meet two further requirements: (i) the exercise of the disclosure jurisdiction, because of Art 10(2), should meet a 'pressing social need' and (ii) the restriction should be proportionate to the 'legitimate aim' which is being pursued.

The construction of s 10 was considered by the House of Lords for the first time in *Secretary of State for Defence v Guardian Newspapers Ltd.*[107] The House was of the firm view that s 10 substitutes for the discretionary protection which existed at common law a rule of wide and general application subject only to the four exceptions specified:[108] the prohibition does

---

[103] Section 10 applies to the publication of photographs as well as written information: *Handmade Films (Productions) Ltd v Express Newspapers* [1986] FSR 463, Ch D at 468.

[104] For the power to issue warrants to obtain information in confidential journalistic material in the interests of national security or for the purposes of preventing or deterring serious crime, see ss 20 and 28, Investigatory Powers Act 2016.

[105] [2002] 1 WLR 2033, HL. The text derives from the judgment of Lord Phillips MR in the Court of Appeal ([2001] 1 WLR 515), which was expressly endorsed by the House of Lords.

[106] (1996) 22 EHRR 123, ECHR.

[107] [1985] AC 339, HL.

[108] Per Lord Scarman at 361.

not differentiate between disclosure in interim proceedings for discovery prior to trial and disclosure at the trial itself and is not qualified by the nature of the proceedings or of the claim in respect of which the proceedings are brought.[109] Accordingly, it is sufficient to attract the protection of the section that an order of a court *may*, but not necessarily *will*, have the effect of disclosing a source of information.[110] Moreover, where a person seeks delivery up of a document which is his property in order to identify the informant from it, a judge, in exercising his discretion to order up delivery of goods under s 3 of the Torts (Interference with Goods) Act 1977, should have regard, when appropriate, to s 10, and should not make such an order unless the case falls within one of the four exceptions. It was also held that it is a question of fact, not discretion, whether a particular case falls within one of the exceptions, the burden being on the party seeking disclosure to prove on a balance of probabilities that disclosure is 'necessary'.[111] However, if a party seeks disclosure on an interim application, the court should be careful not to order disclosure unless the evidence before it establishes that the inference of necessity is unlikely to be displaced when all the evidence is produced and tested at trial.[112] Section 10 requires actual necessity to be established: expediency, however great, is not enough.[113]

Disclosure necessary in the interests of justice

The leading domestic authority on whether disclosure is necessary in the interests of justice is *X Ltd v Morgan-Grampian Ltd*.[114] The plaintiffs, X Ltd, two private companies, prepared a business plan in order to negotiate a bank loan to raise additional working capital. A copy of the plan was stolen. The next day, an unidentified source gave G, a journalist, information about the planned loan. G decided to write an article about X Ltd. X Ltd obtained an injunction against the defendant publishers, M-G Ltd, restraining publication of information derived from the plan, and applied under s 10 for an order disclosing the name of the source, their intention being to bring proceedings against him for recovery of the plan, an injunction to prevent further publication, and damages. The House of Lords held that, by reason of the *Norwich Pharmacal* principles, the court had jurisdiction to order M-G Ltd to disclose G's notes and that although the information obtained from the source had not been 'contained in a publication', the information having been received for the purposes of publication, it should be subject to s 10, since the purpose underlying the statutory protection of sources is as much applicable before as after publication.

The following propositions derive from the judgment of Lord Bridge.

1. Where a judge asks himself the question, 'Can I be satisfied that disclosure of the source of *this* information is necessary to serve *this* interest?' he has to engage in a balancing exercise.

---

[109] Per Lord Diplock at 344–5 and 349.

[110] See, eg, per Lord Bridge at 372.

[111] Per Lords Diplock and Scarman at 350 and 364 respectively.

[112] Per Lord Scarman at 364. See also *Handmade Films (Productions) Ltd v Express Newspapers* [1986] FSR 463, Ch D.

[113] Per Lord Diplock at 359, applied in *Handmade Films (Productions) Ltd v Express Newspapers* [1986] FSR 463, Ch D. Cf per Lord Griffiths in *Re an Inquiry Under the Company Securities (Insider Dealing) Act 1985* [1988] AC 660, HL at 704: 'I doubt if it is possible to go further than to say that "necessary" has a meaning that lies somewhere between "indispensable" on the one hand and "useful" or "expedient" on the other, and to leave it to the judge to decide towards which end of the scale of meaning he will place it on the facts of any particular case.'

[114] [1991] 1 AC 1, HL.

2. He starts with three assumptions: that the protection of sources is itself a matter of high public importance; that nothing less than necessity will suffice to override it; and that the necessity can only arise out of concern for another matter of high public importance, one of the four interests listed in s 10.

3. The question whether disclosure is necessary 'in the interests of justice' gives rise to a difficult problem of weighing one public interest against another. Lord Diplock, in *Secretary of State for Defence v Guardian Newspapers Ltd*, said that the word 'justice' is used in the sense of the administration of justice in the course of legal proceedings in a court of law or tribunal.[115] This definition of justice was too narrow: it is 'in the interests of justice' that persons should be enabled to exercise important legal rights and to protect themselves from serious legal wrongs, whether or not resort to legal proceedings in a court of law is necessary to obtain those objectives. Thus if an employer is suffering grave damage from the activities of an unidentified disloyal employee, it is in the interests of justice that he should be able to identify him to end his contract of employment, notwithstanding that no legal proceedings may be necessary to do so.

4. It is only if the judge is satisfied that disclosure in the interests of justice is of such preponderating importance as to override the statutory privilege that the threshold of necessity will be reached.

5. This is a question of fact, but calls for the exercise of discriminating and sometimes difficult value judgements, to which many factors will be relevant on both sides of the scale. In favour of disclosure there will be a wide spectrum within which the particular case must be located. For example, if the party seeking disclosure shows that his very livelihood depends on it, the case will be near one end of the spectrum, but if what he seeks to protect is a minor interest in property, the case will be at or near the other end. On the other side, there is also a wide spectrum. One important factor is the nature of the information: the greater the legitimate public interest in it, the greater the importance of protecting the source. Another significant factor is the manner in which the information was obtained by the source: the importance of protecting the source will be enhanced if the information was obtained legitimately, but will be diminished if obtained illegally, unless counterbalanced by a clear public interest in publication, as when the source acts in order to expose iniquity.

Applying those principles to the facts, it was held that disclosure of G's notes was necessary in the interests of justice. The publication of X Ltd's plan during their refinancing negotiations would involve a threat of severe damage to their business, and consequently to the livelihood of their employees, which could only be defused by identification of the source, either as the thief or as the means of identifying the thief, which would then allow X Ltd to bring proceedings to recover the plan. Furthermore, the source was involved in a gross breach of confidentiality which was not counterbalanced by any legitimate interest in publication of the information.

---

[115] [1985] AC 339, HL at 350. See also *Maxwell v Pressdram Ltd* [1987] 1 WLR 298, CA at 300 and 308–9 (essential to identify and define the issue in the legal proceedings); and *Handmade Films (Productions) Ltd v Express Newspapers* [1986] FSR 463, Ch D (a claim for discovery based on the *Norwich Pharmacal* principle (see text at n 99) may come within 'the interests of justice', but the claimant must show that he needs the name of the unknown wrongdoer because he intends to sue him—it is insufficient that an action *may* be brought).

In *Ashworth Hospital Authority v MGN Ltd*[116] it was said that the wider interpretation of the 'interests of justice' in *X Ltd v Morgan-Grampian Ltd* accords more happily with the scheme of Art 10 than the interpretation of Lord Diplock in *Secretary of State for Defence v Guardian Newspapers Ltd*. Confirming that 'interests of justice' in s 10 means interests that are justiciable, it was also observed that it is difficult to envisage any such interest that would not fall within one or more of the Art 10 'legitimate aims'.

The leading case in the European Court of Human Rights is *Goodwin v UK*,[117] which dealt with the same facts as those which had been the subject of the House of Lords decision in *X Ltd v Morgan-Grampian Ltd*, but under Art 10 of the European Convention on Human Rights. The tests which the European Court and the House of Lords applied were substantially the same,[118] but the European Court came to the opposite conclusion. This, however, is not as surprising as it might initially seem. As Thorpe LJ pointed out in *Camelot Group plc v Centaur Communications Ltd*,[119] the making of a value judgement on competing facts is very close to the exercise of a discretion based on those facts, and there was a lapse of six years between the decisions in London and Strasbourg, a period in which standards fundamental to the performance of the balancing exercise may change materially. In the *Camelot Group* case, the plaintiff company, which was authorized to run the National Lottery, intended to publish its 1997 final accounts. An unidentified employee of the company leaked a copy of the draft accounts to a journalist, who published an article disclosing their contents. The company sought an order which would effectively result in the disclosure of the identity of the source of the leaked information. The Court of Appeal held that a court, in assessing whether it is necessary to order disclosure in the interests of justice, may take account of an employer's wish to identify a disloyal employee so as to end his employment, and that in certain cases this factor alone may be strong enough to outweigh the public interest in the protection of the anonymity of press sources. On the facts, it held that the necessity for an order for disclosure of the source had been established: there was unease and suspicion among the company's employees which inhibited good working relationships, and there was a continuing threat of disclosure of further information, a risk that the employee might prove untrustworthy in some new respect in the future, by revealing, for example, the name of a public figure who had won a large prize. Moreover, it did not significantly further the public interest to secure the publication of the accounts a week earlier than planned.

In *Saunders v Punch Ltd*[120] the court refused to make an order to disclose the identity of a source of information the nature of which suggested that he had seen records of meetings between the plaintiff and his lawyers which were protected by legal professional privilege. It was held that although the privilege is of massive importance in the administration of justice, it will not inevitably and always preponderate in the balancing exercise which the court must carry out in deciding whether disclosure is in the interests of justice. The question in each case is, 'Are the interests of justice so pressing as to require the ban on disclosure to be overridden?', a question which on the facts of the case was answered in the negative.

---

[116] [2002] 1 WLR 2033, HL. The text derives from the judgment of Lord Phillips in the Court of Appeal ([2001] 1 WLR 515), which was expressly endorsed by the House of Lords.

[117] (1996) 22 EHRR 123, ECHR.

[118] See *Camelot Group v Centaur Communications Ltd* [1999] QB 124, CA at 135 and 138.

[119] [1999] QB 124, CA at 138–9.

[120] [1998] 1 WLR 986, Ch D.

Disclosure necessary in the interests of national security

In *X Ltd v Morgan-Grampian Ltd*, Lord Bridge held that once it is shown that disclosure will serve the interests of national security, the necessity of disclosure follows almost automatically, because those interests are of such overriding importance. *Secretary of State for Defence v Guardian Newspapers Ltd* turned on the quality of evidence relied on by the claimant. A copy of a secret Ministry of Defence memorandum, concerning the handling of publicity relating to the installation of nuclear weapons, had been 'leaked' to the *Guardian* newspaper. The Crown sought its return in order to identify the informant from markings made on the document. The House of Lords was unanimous in its view that where the Crown seeks an interim order for disclosure under this exception, the supporting affidavits should spell out, with the utmost particularity, all relevant material as to why disclosure is necessary. The House divided, however, on whether the evidence on which the Crown relied was sufficient to discharge the onus of proving necessity. A majority were satisfied that it was. The risk to national security lay not in the publication of the particular document but in the possibility that the person who had leaked it might in future leak other classified documents relating to the deployment of nuclear weapons, the disclosure of which would have much more serious consequences on national security.

Disclosure necessary for the prevention of crime

In *X Ltd v Morgan-Grampian Ltd*, Lord Bridge held that once it is shown that disclosure will serve the interests of the prevention of crime, the necessity of disclosure follows almost automatically, because those interests are of such overriding importance, although a judge might properly refuse disclosure if the crime is of a trivial nature. Disclosure may be ordered if necessary for the prevention of crime generally rather than a particular identifiable future crime or crimes. Accordingly, in *Re an Inquiry Under the Company Securities (Insider Dealing) Act 1985*[121] the House of Lords held that a journalist who had made use of confidential price-sensitive information about takeover bids, leaked to him by a source inside one of the relevant government departments, was not entitled to the protection of s 10. Although inspectors appointed by the Secretary of State to investigate suspected leaks of this kind, and who had requested the journalist to reveal his source, were unable to show that they would take steps to prevent the commission of a particular future crime, nonetheless they needed the information for the purpose of exposing the leaking of official information and criminal insider trading and preventing such behaviour in the future. However, as in the case of the other exceptions, a claim will only succeed on the basis of the prevention of crime if there is clear and specific evidence to prove 'necessity'. In *X v Y*[122] employees of the plaintiffs, a health authority, had supplied a national newspaper with information obtained from hospital records identifying two doctors who were carrying on general practice despite having contracted AIDS. The defendants had paid for the information. The plaintiffs sought disclosure by the defendants of their sources on the grounds that this was necessary for the prevention of crime.[123] The claim failed through lack of proof: although appropriate deterrent action could take a variety of forms—such as warning the culprits, dismissal, or criminal investigation—the plaintiffs had adduced no evidence as to what security procedures existed, what inquiries had been made to identify the sources, whether they had referred the matter to the police, and whether criminal investigation was the intended or likely consequence.

[121] [1988] AC 660, HL.

[122] [1988] 2 All ER 648, QBD.

[123] Under the Public Bodies Corrupt Practices Act 1889 and the Prevention of Corruption Act 1906.

Procedural issues

Civil cases

Taking the objection

In civil litigation, a claim to PII usually arises at the disclosure stage. Under CPR r 31.19, a party to litigation (or someone who has received an application for non-party disclosure) may apply, without notice, for an order permitting him to withhold disclosure of a document on the grounds that disclosure would damage the public interest. Under r 31.19(6) the court, for the purposes of deciding such an application, may require the person seeking to withhold disclosure to produce the document to the court and may invite any person, whether or not a party, to make representations. Where a government department is a party to the litigation, it will make the application.[124] In other cases, the application may be made by the party possessing the documents on its own initiative or at the request of the relevant department, as in *Burmah Oil Co Ltd v Bank of England*.[125] If necessary, the head of the department or the Attorney General may intervene to prevent documents being disclosed. The claim must usually be supported by affidavit evidence from the relevant minister or head of department, identifying the documents and the grounds for withholding them in as much detail as possible. In the case of a ministerial objection, a certificate signed by the minister may suffice. Concerning information or documents to be disclosed by a witness, the issue will often be raised before the judge at trial. In any case, the judge himself should take the point if necessary for if there is a public interest to be protected it must be protected regardless of party advantage.[126]

If a party to civil litigation holds documents in a class prima facie immune, he should (save perhaps in a very exceptional case) assert that the documents are immune and decline to disclose them, since the ultimate judge of where the balance of public interest lies is not him but the court.[127]

Waiver and secondary evidence

Whether PII can be waived appears to turn on a variety of factors, including: the time (whether before or after a ruling by the court); whether or not immunity is claimed at all; whether the decision on waiver is being made by a relevant Secretary of State on behalf of his department, an ordinary litigant, or the maker and recipient of the document in question; the nature of the document; and the extent to which 'the cat is already out of the bag'.

It is often said that PII cannot be waived. This was asserted by Lord Simon in *R v Lewes Justices, ex p Home Secretary*,[128] where it led to disapproval of the term 'Crown Privilege'—it is the duty of a party to assert the immunity, even if it is to his disadvantage in the litigation. The principle was forcefully reasserted by Bingham LJ in *Makanjuola v Metropolitan Police Comr*:[129] a party claiming immunity is not claiming a right but observing a duty and therefore the immunity cannot be waived—although one can waive rights, one cannot waive duties. Neither of these two dicta, however, is of general application. As Lord Woolf pointed out in

---

[124] See s 28 of the Crown Proceedings Act 1947.

[125] [1980] AC 1090, HL.

[126] See, eg, Viscount Simon LC in *Duncan v Cammell Laird & Co Ltd* [1942] AC 624 at 642, citing *Chatterton v Secretary of State for India* [1895] 2 QB 189 at 195.

[127] Per Bingham LJ in *Makanjuola v Metropolitan Police Comr* [1992] 3 All ER 617 at 623.

[128] [1973] AC 388 at 407.

[129] [1992] 3 All ER 617 at 623.

R v Chief Constable of the West Midlands Police, ex p Wiley,[130] Lord Simon was referring to the situation *after* the court has determined that the public interest against disclosure outweighs that of disclosure, and the *Makanjuola* case was not one involving a department of state. As far as the contents of documents are concerned, Lord Woolf thought it most unlikely that the principle of PII can be used to prevent a department of state from disclosing documents which it considers it appropriate to disclose. Equally, as to class claims, it was doubted whether the courts would ever interfere, after the event, with governmental decisions in favour of disclosure. It is not clear, however, whether a Secretary of State is under a *duty*, before objecting to disclosure of any particular documents of a class prima facie entitled to PII, to consider whether the public interest in non-disclosure of those particular documents is outweighed, on the facts of the particular case, by the public interest in those documents being available in the administration of justice. The proposition, it has been said, is 'at least arguable'.[131]

Concerning waiver by ordinary litigants, where a party other than a government department is in possession of documents in respect of which the courts have already established that class immunity applies, the court may intervene to prevent disclosure, but if the party in question has consulted the Attorney General or other appropriate minister, who has endorsed the party's decision to disclose, the court, if the matter comes before it, will act on their views. In a situation of doubt, however, the question of disclosure should normally be left to the court.[132]

Concerning waiver by the maker and recipient of confidential documents, the authorities are not clear. In *Science Research Council v Nassé*[133] inability to waive the immunity was among the reasons given for resisting its extension: if the immunity applied, it could not be waived either by the employer or by the employer with the consent of the subject of a report and its author.[134] However, a different approach was taken in *Campbell v Tameside Metropolitan Borough Council.*[135] Lord Denning reasserted, obiter, a distinction he had drawn in *Neilson v Laugharne*:[136] in the case of documents in a higher category, including all those which must be kept top secret because their disclosure would be injurious to national defence, diplomatic relations, or the detection of crime, the immunity cannot be waived; but in the case of documents within a lower category, including documents which are kept confidential in order that subordinates should be frank and candid in their reports, or for any other good reason, immunity can be waived by the maker and recipients of the confidential document.[137] A similar approach was also taken in *Multi Guarantee Co Ltd v Cavalier Insurance Co Ltd*[138]

---

[130] [1995] 1 AC 274, HL at 298.

[131] Per Rattee J in *Bennett v Metropolitan Police Comr* [1995] 2 All ER 1, Ch D at 13.

[132] Per Lord Woolf [1995] 1 AC 274, HL at 297–8. See also per Lawton LJ in *Hehir v Metropolitan Police Comr* [1982] 1 WLR 715 at 722: if the reason for the immunity is the need to protect the public interest, individuals should be unable to waive it for their own purposes.

[133] [1980] AC 1028, per Lords Wilberforce and Fraser at 1066–7 and 1082 respectively.

[134] See also per Lord Donaldson MR in *Makanjuola v Metropolitan Police Comr* [1992] 3 All ER 617, CA at 621.

[135] [1982] QB 1065, CA.

[136] [1981] QB 736, CA.

[137] See also per Lord Cross in *Alfred Crompton Amusement Machines Ltd v Customs and Excise Comrs (No 2)* [1974] AC 405 at 434 and per Brightman LJ in *Hehir v Metropolitan Police Comr* [1982] 1 WLR 715 at 723, whose approach was endorsed by Lord Woolf in *R v Chief Constable of the West Midlands Police, ex p Wiley* [1995] 1 AC 274, HL at 299: 'If the purpose of the immunity is to obtain the co-operation of an individual to the giving of a statement, I find it difficult to see how that purpose will be undermined if the maker of the statement consents to it being disclosed.'

[138] (1986) The Times, 24 June, Ch D.

where it was held that although PII cannot be waived, it is capable of evaporating if those involved in the giving and receiving of the information consent to its disclosure. The fact that the partial disclosure had already significantly eroded the immunity was a relevant consideration in balancing the public interest in non-disclosure against the interest of the proper administration of justice in disclosure. Knox J, while acknowledging that it was a matter of degree in any particular case, said that if the cat had got all four legs out of the bag, there was little point in holding on to its tail.

In *R v Governor of Brixton Prison, ex p Osman*[139] certain documents protected by PII had been disclosed in a previous application for habeas corpus, although they had not been read in open court. It was held that prior disclosure of a document is a matter to be taken into account in the balance: if there has been publication to the whole world, then the public interest in non-disclosure must collapse. On the facts, however, the small degree of publication that had occurred could not upset the balance, which came down heavily in favour of immunity.

Similar considerations presumably apply in relation to secondary evidence. Obviously, the submarine plans in *Duncan v Cammell Laird & Co Ltd*[140] could not be proved by any means; in *R v Lewes Justices, ex p Home Secretary*[141] a copy of the allegedly libellous letter had somehow been obtained by the person to whom it referred, but because PII applied he was not able to prove that letter by any means. However, if information is freely available to the public, the fact that that information also forms the subject matter of a protected communication will surely not prevent proof of the information from the public sources. In each case, it is submitted, the question should be whether, on the particular facts, the public interest really does require non-disclosure; if there has been limited disclosure, immunity may still be justified, especially if the disclosure was wrongful.

Disclosure, production, and inspection

Before any question of PII can be raised, the document has to be one which should be disclosed within the rules normally applicable in civil litigation.[142] Under CPR r 31.6, standard disclosure requires a party to disclose only (a) the documents on which he relies; (b) the documents which adversely affect his own case, adversely affect another party's case, or support another party's case; and (c) the documents he is required to disclose by a relevant practice direction. If the party seeking disclosure falls at this hurdle, the question of PII will simply not arise.[143] Moreover, the court, in deciding whether to dispense with or limit standard disclosure, or whether to make an order for specific disclosure or specific inspection under r 31.12, must seek to give effect to the 'overriding objective' of enabling it to deal with the case justly, which includes saving expense and ensuring that it is dealt with expeditiously

---

[139] [1991] 1 WLR 281, QBD at 290–1.

[140] [1942] AC 624, HL.

[141] [1973] AC 388, HL.

[142] Per Wood J in *Evans v Chief Constable of Surrey* [1988] QB 588, QBD at 592–3, citing Lord Scarman in *Burmah Oil Co Ltd v Bank of England* [1980] AC 1090 at 1141 and Lord Edmund-Davies in *Air Canada v Secretary of State for Trade (No 2)* [1983] 2 AC 394 at 441.

[143] See *Evans v Chief Constable of Surrey* [1989] 2 All ER 594, a decision under the Rules of the Supreme Court, now replaced by the Civil Procedure Rules.

and fairly, etc.[144] If the party seeking disclosure falls at these hurdles, again the question of immunity will simply not arise.[145]

If these hurdles are surmounted, but PII is claimed, the judge will have to ask first whether the head of public interest on which reliance is placed is at least 'analogous' to those which have already been recognized by authority. He will also have to assess the strength of the objector's reasons for saying that disclosure will prejudice that public interest. If a prima facie claim to immunity is thus made out, the person seeking disclosure must establish that the public interest in the administration of justice in the case 'tips the scales decisively in his favour'.[146] In some cases, it will be obvious from the description of the documents and the nature of the litigation that the claim to immunity is either groundless or unanswerable. In other cases a more detailed assessment of the content of the documents is needed. In *Conway v Rimmer*[147] Lord Reid said:

> If [the judge] decides that on balance the documents probably ought to be produced, I think that it would generally be best that he should see them before ordering production and if he thinks that the Minister's reasons are not clearly expressed he will have to see the documents before ordering inspection.

Various objections to judicial inspection have been put forward. In *Duncan v Cammell Laird & Co Ltd*[148] the House of Lords regarded it as a wrongful communication between the judge and one party to the exclusion of the other. This reasoning was firmly rejected in *Conway v Rimmer*, but it remains true that a party may be aggrieved that the judge has seen material to which he has been denied access.[149] Other considerations were put forward by Lord Wilberforce in *Burmah Oil Co v Bank of England*,[150] namely (i) that judges should not lightly undertake to question a responsible minister's assessment of the weight of the public interest in non-disclosure; and (ii) that inspection can be a very time-consuming activity which has to be conducted without the assistance of fully informed argument. Such considerations led Lord Wilberforce to uphold the claim to immunity without inspecting the documents. However, the other members of the House of Lords held that inspection was justified once it was shown that it was likely that the documents would contain material substantially useful to the party seeking discovery. On the facts, this test was satisfied, but after inspection disclosure was refused because it was not found to be 'necessary either for disposing fairly of the cause or matter or for saving costs'.

In *Air Canada v Secretary of State for Trade*[151] it was accepted that the ministerial documents probably did contain material which was relevant to the issues in the case, but without inspection it was impossible to know which side that material would favour. Lord Fraser

---

[144] See Ch 2, Exclusionary discretion, Civil cases, p 48.

[145] See per Lord Woolf in *R v Chief Constable of the West Midlands Police, ex p Wiley* [1995] 1 AC 274, HL at 288,430 and per Sir Thomas Bingham MR in *Taylor v Anderton* [1995] 2 All ER 420, CA at 432–5, all decisions under the Rules of the Supreme Court.

[146] Per Lord Edmund-Davies in *Burmah Oil Co Ltd v Bank of England* [1980] AC 1090 at 1127, citing Lord Cross in *Alfred Crompton Amusement Machines Ltd v Customs and Excise Comrs (No 2)* [1974] AC 405 at 434.

[147] [1968] AC 910 at 953.

[148] [1942] AC 624 per Viscount Simon LC at 640–1.

[149] Per Lord Denning MR in *Neilson v Laugharne* [1981] QB 736 at 748–9.

[150] [1980] AC 1090 at 1117.

[151] [1983] 2 AC 394.

was of the opinion that a court should not embark upon a private inspection of documents unless persuaded that such an inspection is likely to satisfy it that it ought to take the further step of ordering the documents to be produced publicly. On this basis, Lord Fraser, together with Lords Wilberforce and Edmund-Davies, held that the court should only inspect if the party seeking disclosure has shown 'that the documents are very likely to contain material which would give substantial support to his contention on an issue which arises in the case and that, without them, he might be deprived of the means of . . . proper presentation of his case'.[152] In the words of Lord Wilberforce,[153] there must be 'some concrete ground for belief which takes the case beyond a mere "fishing expedition"'. The judge should only inspect where he has definite grounds for expecting to find material of real importance to the party seeking disclosure; he is not entitled to 'take a peep' on the off-chance of finding something useful, for his function is to see fair play between the parties and he has neither power nor duty to go beyond that to ascertain the truth independently for himself. The reasoning of the majority was based partly on the ordinary principles of discovery and partly on the adversarial nature of the English trial system. Lords Templeman and Scarman argued that discovery is an exception to the adversarial principle; its function is not only to supply evidence to the other side but also to give some indication of the strength of one's own hand and thus to encourage settlement and save costs. They therefore disputed the need for the party seeking disclosure to show that the material would support his case, and held that the court should inspect documents if they are very likely to be necessary for the just determination of the issues in the case or, in other words, if their disclosure may materially assist *any* of the parties to the proceedings. However, they agreed that the documents should be withheld without inspection because it had not been shown that the documents were likely to contain sufficiently relevant material which was not already available from other sources. Where a prima facie claim to PII is properly made out, the court is no doubt justified in refusing even to inspect unless a case in favour of disclosure has been made out, in order to prevent litigants from embarking on 'fishing expeditions'. However, it is submitted that the reasoning of Lords Templeman and Scarman adequately achieves this end. Their reasoning appears to have prevailed: ordinarily the modern practice, in a case in which a party satisfies the general threshold test for disclosure but his opponent makes out a prima facie claim to immunity, is for the court to proceed to inspect in order to undertake the balancing exercise.[154] However, it seems that if there is a ministerial certificate demonstrating an actual or potential risk to national security, the court should not exercise its right to inspect.[155]

In order to ensure, as far as possible, that a claim to PII is not wrongly overridden, Lord Reid in *Conway v Rimmer*[156] said that the party objecting to disclosure should always be able to appeal against the judge's ruling before the documents are produced. The importance of this possibility of appeal, even before the judge inspects the documents, was emphasized in *Burmah Oil Co Ltd v Bank of England*.[157] In *Air Canada v Secretary of State for Trade*[158] Bingham J,

---

[152] Per Lord Edmund-Davies at 435.

[153] At 439.

[154] See, eg, *Goodridge v Chief Constable of Hampshire Constabulary* [1999] 1 WLR 1558, QBD.

[155] See *Balfour v Foreign and Commonwealth Office* [1994] 1 WLR 681, CA, in this chapter, under **National security, diplomatic relations, and international comity**, pp 681–2.

[156] [1968] AC 910 at 953.

[157] [1980] AC 1090 at 1136 per Lord Keith and at 1147 per Lord Scarman.

[158] [1983] 2 AC 394.

the trial judge, was provisionally inclined to order production of the documents but decided to inspect them first. He therefore ordered inspection, but stayed the order pending an appeal.[159]

Partial disclosure

Proper objections to disclosure may sometimes be overcome by allowing names and sensitive or irrelevant material to be covered up. This course has been sanctioned in relation to material protected by PII[160] as well as material protected on the grounds of confidentiality alone.[161] In *Science Research Council v Nassé* Lord Edmund-Davies seems to have approved Lord Denning's suggestion in the Court of Appeal that disclosure can be limited to the other side's lawyers.[162]

In *R v Chief Constable of the West Midlands Police, ex p Wiley*[163] Lord Woolf was of the opinion that, in general, PII is provided against disclosure of documents or their contents and is not, in the absence of exceptional circumstances, an immunity against the use of knowledge obtained from the documents. If the legal advisers of a party in possession of material which is the subject of immunity from disclosure are aware of the contents of that material, they should consider it their duty to assist the court and the other party to mitigate any disadvantage resulting from the non-disclosure. Thus it may be possible to provide any necessary information without producing the actual document or it may be possible to disclose a part of the document or to disclose on a restricted basis. In many cases, cooperation between the legal advisers of the parties should avoid the risk of injustice.

Closed material procedures

Common law

In *Al Rawi v Security Service*[164] the claimants alleged that the Security Service had been complicit in their detention and ill-treatment by foreign authorities at various locations, including Guantanamo Bay. The defendants filed an open defence but said that they were in possession of material which they wished the court to consider but which should in the public interest be withheld from disclosure. This material was in a closed defence and the defendants sought parallel open and closed proceedings and parallel open and closed judgments. At trial, therefore, a preliminary issue arose: whether it was lawful and proper for the court to order a closed material procedure (CMP), that is, a procedure in which (a) the defendants would comply with their obligations for disclosure of documents and rely on pleadings and written and oral evidence, but without disclosure of such material to the claimants if such disclosure would be contrary to the public interest (the withheld material being described as closed material); (b) disclosure of the closed material would be made to special advocates (ie advocates appointed to represent the interests of the claimants, but not permitted to take instructions from them) and, where appropriate, the court; and (c) the court would ensure

---

[159] The approach to inspection laid down in *Air Canada v Secretary of State for Trade* is inappropriate in criminal cases. See, in this chapter, under **The development of the modern law, Criminal cases**, p 679. See also per Phillips J in *R v Clowes* [1992] 3 All ER 440 at 455, CA and per Mann LJ in *R v Governor of Brixton Prison, ex p Osman* [1991] 1 WLR 281, QBD at 290.

[160] See, eg, per Lord Pearce in *Conway v Rimmer* [1968] AC 910 at 988.

[161] *Science Research Council v Nassé* [1980] AC 1028, in this chapter, under **Confidential relationships**, pp 690–1.

[162] [1980] AC 1028, HL at 1077, citing [1979] QB 144 at 173.

[163] [1995] 1 AC 274, HL at 306–7.

[164] [2011] UKSC 34.

that the closed material would not be disclosed to the claimants or any other person, unless satisfied that such disclosure would not be contrary to the public interest. The claimants argued that in relation to the closed material a conventional *ex parte* PII exercise should be conducted. The trial judge answered the question raised by the preliminary issue in the affirmative. The Court of Appeal answered the question in the negative. The defendants appealed and, although the claims were then settled on confidential terms, the appeal to the Supreme Court was allowed to continue.

The Supreme Court, by majority, upheld the decision of the Court of Appeal. It was held that the court had no power at common law to order a CMP in ordinary civil litigation. The issues of principle raised by such a procedure were so fundamental that it could only be introduced by Parliament. It was not for the courts to extend the use of the procedure beyond the use thus far sanctioned by Parliament, for example under the Prevention of Terrorism Act 2005 and the Counter-Terrorism Act 2008.[165] It was acknowledged that in certain circumstances a CMP is also necessary in order to achieve real justice and a fair trial, for example in cases involving children, where disclosure would defeat the object of protecting and promoting the best interests of the child[166] and intellectual property proceedings, where disclosure of confidential material beyond 'confidentiality rings' (ie the lawyers only) would defeat the object of the proceedings brought to protect a commercial interest.[167] However, in general the court should not exercise its power to regulate its own procedures in such a way as to sanction departure from the fundamental principles of open justice and natural justice: under the CMP a party is excluded from the closed part of the trial and therefore would not see the witnesses or see or read the closed documents, the submissions, or the judgment. Nor could these flaws be cured by a special advocate, who would be hampered by not being able to take instructions from his client. In contrast, there could be no objection to the use of special advocates as part of the PII process.[168] That process respects the common law principles in that if the documents are disclosed as a result of the process, they are available to both parties and the court, and if they are not disclosed they are available neither to the other parties nor to the court. There is nothing objectionable about excluding a party from the PII process and there can be no objection to improving the position of that party in the process by the use of a special advocate.

Competition and Markets Authority v Concordia International RX (UK)[169] establishes an exception to the general ban on the use of the CMP. Applying *R (Haralambous v St Albans Crown Court)*,[170] it was held that the High Court, on an application under ss 28 and 28A of the Competition Act 1998 to enter premises for the purposes of an investigation under the Act,

---

[165] Parliament has now extended use of the procedure—see, in this chapter, under **The Justice and Security Act 2013**, p 704.

[166] See *Secretary of State for the Home Department v MB* [2008] AC 440 at [58]. See also *Re A (a child) (disclosure)* [2012] UKSC 60 per Lady Hale SCJ at [34]: 'It is arguable that a greater latitude may be allowed in children's cases where the child's welfare is the court's paramount concern. But the arguments against making such an inroad into the normal principles of a fair trial remain very powerful'.

[167] Material protected by PII cannot be disclosed in confidentiality rings, the use of which is limited to the protection of commercially sensitive information: *Competition and Markets Authority v Concordia International RX (UK)* [2018] EWCA Civ 1881.

[168] See per Lord Bingham in *R v H* [2004] 2 AC 134, HL, considered, in this chapter, under 'Special counsel', p 709.

[169] [2018] EWCA Civ 1881.

[170] [2018] 2 WLR 357, SC, considered under **Closed material procedures**, p 708.

may have regard to material which should not be disclosed to the subject of the warrant by reason of PII and that if that person applies to vary or set aside the warrant, the court can consider such material by way of a CMP.[171]

The Justice and Security Act 2013

The parliamentary response to *Al Rawi v Security Service* is to be found in Pt 2 of the Justice and Security Act 2013 (the 2013 Act), which enables civil courts to order a CMP in the case of material the disclosure of which would damage the interests of national security. The principal justification that was put forward for the provisions in Pt 2 of the Act was the need to allow the security services to argue the merits of their case by referring the court to highly sensitive but relevant evidence which would otherwise be withheld under the PII process, which, in turn, would lead, in some cases at any rate, to the expensive settlement of what were considered to be speculative compensation claims. A court will not order a CMP unless it is necessary to do so, and it will not be necessary if there are satisfactory alternatives, which include an application for PII.[172] A CMP is an exceptional procedure and will be used only rarely, but there is no reason to give the statutory provisions a narrow or restrictive construction, subject to compliance with Art 5 of the European Convention on Human Rights (right to liberty and security).[173] The provisions should be given their natural meaning. Appropriate safeguards against inappropriate or excessive use of a CMP are built into the provisions themselves.[174]

Section 6(1) and (2) of the 2013 Act provide as follows:

(1) The court seised of relevant civil proceedings may make a declaration that the proceedings are proceedings in which a closed material application may be made to the court.
(2) The court may make such a declaration—
    (a) on the application of—
        (i) the Secretary of State (whether or not the Secretary of State is a party to the proceedings), or
        (ii) any party to the proceedings, or
    (b) of its own motion.

'Relevant civil proceedings' are any proceedings, other than 'proceedings in a criminal cause or matter', before the High Court, the Court of Appeal, the Court of Session, or the Supreme Court.[175] 'Proceedings in a criminal cause or matter' covers proceedings by way of High Court judicial review of decisions made in criminal causes, including for example decisions by the Director of Public Prosecutions to prosecute or not to prosecute.[176] A 'closed material application' is an application made to the court by the party or parties to the proceedings who would be required to disclose 'sensitive material',[177] that is, 'material the disclosure of which

---

[171] There is no additional exception in the case of extradition proceedings: *VB v Westminster Magistrates' Court* [2014] UKSC 59. See also *R (British Sky Broadcasting Ltd) v Commissioner of Police of the Metropolis* [2014] UKSC 17.

[172] *R (Sarkandi) v Secretary of State for Foreign and Commonwealth Affairs* [2015] EWCA Civ 687 at [61] and [62].

[173] See s 14(2)(c).

[174] *R (Sarkandi) v Secretary of State for Foreign and Commonwealth Affairs* [2015] EWCA Civ 687 at [58] and [59] and *McGartland v Secretary of State for the Home Department* [2015] EWCA Civ 686 at [35].

[175] Section 6(11).

[176] *Belhaj v Director of Public Prosecutions* [2018] 3 WLR 435, SC.

[177] Section 6(8).

would be damaging to the interests of national security',[178] for permission not to disclose the material otherwise than to (i) the court; (ii) any person appointed as a special advocate; and (iii) the Secretary of State, if a party to the proceedings and not the applicant.[179] 'National security' has been deliberately not defined, but it seems clear that it will cover UK intelligence material which, if disclosed, would reveal the identity of UK intelligence officers, their sources, and their capability, as well as foreign intelligence material provided by another country on a promise of confidentiality (so-called 'control principle' material), and will not cover documents the disclosure of which would be damaging to international relations, such as diplomatic exchanges.[180] A 'special advocate' is someone appointed by the Attorney General (in relation to proceedings in England and Wales)[181] to represent the interests of a party in proceedings in which there is a declaration under s 6 from which the party (and any legal representative of the party) is excluded,[182] but who is not responsible to that party.[183]

The circumstances in which a declaration may be made under s 6(1) are governed by s 6(3)–(6).

(3) The court may make such a declaration if it considers that the following two conditions are met.

(4) The first condition is that—
  (a) a party to the proceedings would be required to disclose sensitive material in the course of the proceedings to another person (whether or not another party to the proceedings), or
  (b) a party to the proceedings would be required to make such a disclosure were it not for one or more of the following—
    (i) the possibility of a claim for public interest immunity in relation to the material,[184]
    (ii) the fact that there would be no requirement to disclose if the party chose not to rely on the material,
    (iii) section 56(1) of the Investigatory Powers Act 2016 (exclusion for intercept material),
    (iv) any other enactment that would prevent the party from disclosing the material but would not do so if the proceedings were proceedings in relation to which there was a declaration under this section.

(5) The second condition is that it is in the interests of the fair and effective administration of justice in the proceedings to make a declaration.

(6) The two conditions are met if the court considers that they are met in relation to any material that would be required to be disclosed in the course of the proceedings (and an application under subsection (2)(a) need not be based on all of the material that might meet the conditions or on material that the applicant would be required to disclose).

---

[178] Section 6(11). The phrase 'would be damaging' does not require the party to show actual damage—the test is a prediction of damage, the same test as that used in respect of PII: *Khaled v The Security Service* [2016] EWHC 1727 (QB) at [43]–[46].

[179] Section 6(11) and s 8(1)(a).

[180] See para 29, Joint Committee on Human Rights, *Legislative Scrutiny: Justice and Security Bill*, HL Paper 59, HC 370 (2012); and *HM Government Response to the Joint Committee on Human Rights Fourth Report of Session 2012–13: Legislative Scrutiny: Justice and Security Bill*, Cm 8533 (2013).

[181] Section 9(2) and (3).

[182] Section 9(1) and s 8(1).

[183] Section 9(4).

[184] This condition requires the court to consider not what the outcome of a PII claim might be but simply whether a party would be required to make disclosure were it not for the *possibility* of a PII claim: *R (Sarkandi) v Secretary of State for Foreign and Commonwealth Affairs* [2015] EWCA Civ 687 at [50].

In the case of an application by the Secretary of State, there is an additional hurdle set out in s 6(7).

> (7) The court must not consider an application by the Secretary of State under subsection 2(a) unless it is satisfied that the Secretary of State has, before making the application, considered whether to make, or advise another person to make, a claim for public interest immunity in relation to the material on which the application is based.

Under s 7 of the Act, where a court has made a declaration under s 6, it must keep the declaration under review and may at any time, including the stage at which it has examined the relevant material, revoke it if it considers that 'the declaration is no longer in the interests of the fair and effective administration of justice in the proceedings'.

It is clear, from the deliberate use of the word 'may' in both s 6(3) and s 7, that whether a declaration is made and, if so, whether it should be revoked, are matters for the judge to decide in the exercise of his discretion. However, Parliament has also deliberately not required the court, in deciding these matters, to conduct a balancing exercise under which the public interest in the fair and open administration of justice should be weighed against the public interest in favour of a CMP.

In *CF v The Security Service*,[185] the first case in which the statutory provisions were considered, the court flatly rejected the argument that because the PII process is necessarily fairer than the process following a declaration under s 6, the former process should always be concluded before a declaration is made. The wording of s 6(7) makes quite clear that the pre-condition is that the Secretary of State should have considered making a PII application and, by necessary implication, decided against proceeding in that way. It was also held that whether a declaration 'is in the interests of the fair and effective administration of justice in the proceedings' turns on the specific circumstances of each case and cannot properly turn on objections which would arise in every case and which would, therefore, if successful, subvert the intention of Parliament. The specific circumstances to which the court had regard included: the fact that no court could fairly try the case without the material, because in the absence of disclosure one side would win and the other side lose by default; the likelihood that a PII application, if made, would succeed; and the fact that the allegations in question were made by the claimants and not the state. The court went on to note that Parliament, in restricting the ambit of the statutory provisions to material affecting national security, has created problematic anomalies. First, if a claim to PII succeeds on the basis of potential damage to the international relations of the UK, that material cannot be introduced into a CMP, yet material of potential damage to national security will be seen and assessed by the court in the CMP. In such a situation, if the PII material favours the claimant, counsel for the government would have a clear duty not to take a point which conflicted with material of which he was aware but which could not be deployed. Second, where the claim for PII based on damage to international relations fails, the choice that the Secretary of State then has, to abandon the case or issue in question in order to avoid disclosure, ceases to be a practical choice where there has been a declaration under s 6, unless the issues to which the PII material relates are quite discrete from the case to be addressed within the CMP.

---

[185] [2013] EWHC 3402 (QB).

Criminal cases

General

Under para 65 of the *Attorney General's Guidelines on Disclosure for Investigators, Prosecutors and Defence Practitioners*, a prosecutor, before making an application to the court to withhold material in the public interest, should aim to disclose as much material as he properly can, by giving the defence redacted or edited copies or summaries. Under para 66 of the *Guidelines*, prior to or at the hearing the court must be provided with full and accurate information about the material. The Court of Appeal has stressed that where an *ex parte* hearing is held, it is imperative in all cases that the Crown is scrupulously accurate in the information provided.[186] Where a trial judge or the Court of Appeal learns that prosecution witnesses, in the course of a PII hearing, lied in their evidence, the prosecution are likely to be tainted beyond redemption, however strong the evidence against the accused otherwise was.[187] Paragraph 66 of the *Guidelines* also provides that the prosecution advocate must examine all material which is the subject matter of the application and make any necessary enquiries of the investigator.[188]

The procedure to be adopted where the prosecution apply for immunity from disclosure is set out in Pt 15 of the Criminal Procedure Rules[189] which, generally speaking, reflect the following principles laid down by Lord Taylor CJ in *R v Davis*.[190] Whenever possible, which will be in most cases, the prosecution must notify the defence of the application, indicating the category of material in question, so that the defence have the opportunity of making representations to the court. If to disclose even the category would be to reveal too much, the prosecution should notify the defence that an *ex parte* application will be made. In highly exceptional circumstances where to reveal even the fact of an *ex parte* application would be to reveal too much, an *ex parte* application may be made without notice. However if, in any case, the judge takes the view that the defence should be aware of the category of material and should have the opportunity of making representations, or at any rate should have notice of the application, he may so order.

The *ex parte* procedure is contrary to the general principles of open justice in criminal trials and should only be adopted on the application of the Crown for the specific purpose of enabling the court to test a claim that immunity or sensitivity justifies non-disclosure.[191] Thus, a *defence* application, such as an application for details of an informer to be disclosed, should not be heard *ex parte*.[192] An *ex parte* application on the part of the prosecution will not necessarily amount to a violation of Art 6 of the European Convention on Human Rights, whether the application is made at the trial[193] or in the Court of Appeal,[194] but unfairness caused at the trial by an improper failure to disclose material to the judge will not necessarily be remedied by an *ex parte* examination of the material by the Court of Appeal.[195]

---

[186] *R v Jackson* [2000] Crim LR 377, CA.

[187] *R v Early* [2003] 1 Cr App R 288, CA.

[188] See also *R v Menga* [1998] Crim LR 58, CA.

[189] SI 2015/1490.

[190] [1993] 1 WLR 613, CA.

[191] *R v Keane* [1994] 1 WLR 746, CA at 750. See also *R v Smith* [1998] 2 Cr App R 1, CA.

[192] *R v Turner* [1995] 1 WLR 264, CA; *R v Tattenhove* [1996] 1 Cr App R 408, CA.

[193] *Jasper v UK* (2000) 30 EHRR 441. See also *Atlan v UK* [2002] 34 EHRR 833 and *R v Lawrence* [2002] Crim LR 584, CA.

[194] *R v Botmeh* [2002] 1 WLR 531, CA.

[195] *Rowe and Davis v UK* (2000) 30 EHRR 1. See also *Atlan v UK* [2002] 34 EHRR 833.

Judicial use of information immune from disclosure

It is wrong and contrary to Art 6(1) for a judge to make use of information immune from disclosure to the defence in reaching a decision on the admissibility of evidence. In *Edwards v UK*[196] the applicant was charged with a drugs offence following an undercover operation. On an *ex parte* application to withhold material, the judge ruled against disclosure. On a subsequent unsuccessful defence application under s 78 of the Police and Criminal Evidence Act 1984 to exclude the evidence of the only undercover officer to be called by the prosecution, on the basis of entrapment, the judge ruled that he had seen nothing in the course of the *ex parte* application that would have assisted the defence in their application under s 78. The European Court, finding a violation of Art 6(1), held that since the PII evidence may have related to facts connected with the s 78 application, the defence were not able fully to argue the case on entrapment. However certain the trial judge was that the evidence did not assist the defence, this overlooked the possibility that the defence could have countered the evidence or shown it to be mistaken or otherwise unreliable.[197]

Edwards v UK was distinguished in *R v May*[198] where the judge, in confiscation proceedings under the Criminal Justice Act 1988, stated that he had ignored anything attracting immunity that had been revealed to him in earlier *ex parte* PII proceedings. The Court of Appeal rejected a submission, made in reliance on *Edwards v UK*, that since the judge may have been influenced by the material he had seen, however much he had tried to put it out of his mind, he should have recused himself or at least appointed 'special counsel'.[199] *Edwards v UK* was distinguished on the grounds that the Strasbourg court had proceeded on the basis that the trial judge *had* taken into account the material that the accused had been denied an opportunity to counter. It was held that if a judge is of the view that despite his best efforts he is unlikely to be able to ignore the undisclosed material, to the detriment of the accused, then he should consider the appointment of 'special counsel', but that in many cases the judge can be relied upon to put such material out of his mind.

Closed material procedures

The nature of a closed material procedure has already been considered in the context of civil proceedings.[200] There is no power to order a CMP in a criminal trial, where any claim to PII will be decided in the usual way,[201] but exceptionally may be used in other criminal contexts. Thus in *R (Haralambous) v St Alban's Crown Court*[202] it was held that: a magistrates' court, on an *ex parte* application for the issue of a search and seizure warrant under s 89 of the Police and Criminal Evidence Act 1984, may have regard to material protected by PII without disclosing it to a person affected by the warrant; a Crown Court, on an application made *inter partes* under s 59 of the Criminal Justice and Police Act 2001 for an order authorizing retention of unlawfully seized material, can operate a CMP to have regard to information which should not be disclosed by reason of PII; and where such decisions are challenged by judicial review, the High Court can also conduct a CMP.

---

[196] (2003) 15 BHRC 189.

[197] See also *R v H* [2004] 2 AC 134, HL, overruling *R v Smith* [2001] 1 WLR 1031; and *R v Ali* [2008] EWCA Crim 146.

[198] [2005] 1 WLR 2902, CA.

[199] See, in this chapter, under 'Special counsel', p 709.

[200] See, in this chapter, under Closed material procedures, p 702.

[201] See, in this chapter, under General, p 707.

[202] [2018] 2 WLR 357, SC.

'Special counsel'

'Special counsel' are independent advocates appointed to represent the interests of the accused, to whom material may be disclosed that must not be disclosed to the accused and who have been approved to act as 'special counsel' by the Attorney General. In *Edwards v UK*, the court referred to the recommendation, in Sir Robin Auld's *Review of the Criminal Courts of England and Wales*,[203] that 'special counsel' be introduced in those cases at first instance and on appeal where the court considers prosecution applications for immunity from disclosure in the absence of the defence.[204] In *R v H*[205] it was argued that it is a violation of Art 6 for a trial judge to rule on a claim to immunity, in the absence of adversarial argument on behalf of the accused, where the material in question is or may be relevant to a disputed issue of fact which the judge has to decide in order to rule on an application which will effectively determine the outcome of the proceedings. It was also argued that the *Edwards v UK* principle applies whenever the defence relies on entrapment as a basis for staying the case as an abuse of process or excluding prosecution evidence. The House of Lords held that to adopt such an approach would be to put the judge in a straitjacket. Lord Bingham laid down the following governing principles. The golden rule is full disclosure to the defence of any material held by the prosecution which weakens its case or strengthens that of the defence. In circumstances where such material cannot be disclosed, fully or at all, without the risk of serious prejudice to an important public interest, some derogation from the rule can be justified, but should always be to the minimum necessary to protect the public interest, and should never imperil the overall fairness of the trial. If prosecution claims for PII were operated with scrupulous attention to these principles, and with continuing regard to the proper interests of the accused, there should be no violation of Art 6. The appointment of 'special counsel' raises ethical problems, since the lawyer cannot disclose to his client the material which is the basis of the application and cannot take full instructions from him, as well as practical problems of delay, expense, and continuing review.[206] None of these problems should deter the court from appointing an approved advocate as 'special counsel' where it is necessary, in the interests of justice, to secure protection of an accused's right to a fair trial. However, such appointments would be exceptional and should not be ordered unless and until the trial judge is satisfied that no other course will adequately meet the overriding requirement of fairness to the accused.

In *R v Austin*,[207] the Court of Appeal stressed that the dicta in *R v H* about the use of 'special counsel' related to the issues of disclosure and admissibility and expressly declined to reach a conclusion on the separate question whether 'special counsel' can be appointed at first instance to assist a judge, on the substantive issue of abuse of process, in reaching his decision by reference to material not seen by the defence. A distinction was also drawn between use of 'special counsel' at first instance and on appeal. It is essential that the Court of Appeal can view material which is undisclosed to an appellant, the prime consideration of the court

---

[203] HMSO, 2001, paras 193–7.
[204] See also *Jasper v UK* (2000) 30 EHRR 441.
[205] [2004] 2 AC 134, HL.
[206] Ibid per Lord Bingham at [22].
[207] [2013] EWCA Crim 1028.

being the safety of the conviction, and although in many cases the Court of Appeal will be able to reach a view without the need for 'special counsel', in some cases it may be in the interests of justice for 'special counsel' to be appointed.[208]

Magistrates' courts

Where a magistrates' court, whether made up of a district judge or lay justices, hears an application for non-disclosure on the grounds of PII and rules that the material in question is inadmissible, ordinarily it should proceed to hear the case itself, because of the court's duty of continuing review, and should exercise its discretion to order the case to be tried by a different bench only in exceptional circumstances, as when material was introduced at the non-disclosure hearing which was prejudicial and irrelevant to the question of admissibility.[209] Magistrates, in deciding an application for non-disclosure, should apply the same principles that apply in proceedings on indictment, but where it is known that a contested issue as to the disclosure of sensitive material is likely to arise, and the magistrates have discretion to send the case to the Crown Court for trial, they would be well advised to commit.[210] For this reason, the occasions on which it will be appropriate to appoint 'special counsel' in the magistrates' court will be even rarer than in the Crown Court.[211]

ADDITIONAL READING

Jackson, 'The role of special advocates: Advocacy, due process and the adversarial tradition' (2016) 20(4) E&P 343.
An examination of the claim that special advocates may be justified on human rights grounds of fairness in bringing a measure of procedural fairness to closed material proceedings; and a consideration of the extent to which they pose a threat to the adversarial tradition.

---

[208] Ibid, citing *R v Chisholm* [2010] EWCA Crim 258 at [46].

[209] *R v Stipendiary Magistrate for Norfolk, ex p Taylor* [1998] Crim LR 276, DC. See also *R v Bromley Magistrates' Court, ex p Smith* [1995] 1 WLR 944, DC (and cf *R v South Worcestershire Magistrates, ex p Lilley* [1995] 1 WLR 1595, DC); *R (DPP) v Acton Youth Court* [2001] 1 WLR 1828; *R v H* [2004] 2 AC 134, HL at [43]–[44]; and s 14 of the Criminal Procedure and Investigations Act 1996. See also Bisgrove, 'Judges as Tribunal of Fact: To What Extent do the Provisions for a Defendant to be Tried on Indictment by a Judge sitting without a Jury Conflict With the Defendant's Right to a Fair Trial Where Issues of PII are Present?' [2010] Crim LR 702.

[210] See generally *R v Bromley Magistrates' Court, ex p Smith* [1995] 1 WLR 944, DC, distinguishing *R v DPP, ex p Warby* [1994] Crim LR 281, DC on the basis that it concerned committal proceedings.

[211] *R v H* [2004] 2 AC 134, HL.

Privilege

22

Key issues

- What is the justification for the rule that no one should be compelled to answer any question if the answer would have a tendency to expose him to a criminal charge ('the privilege against self-incrimination')?

- In what circumstances should the privilege be abrogated by statute?

- What is the justification for legal professional privilege, ie the rules that a client should be able to maintain the confidentiality of (a) communications between him and his lawyer made for the purposes of obtaining and giving legal advice ('legal advice privilege'); and (b) communications between him or his lawyer and third parties, such as potential witnesses, the dominant purpose of which was preparation for contemplated or pending litigation ('litigation privilege')?

- What exceptions should there be to legal professional privilege?

- If material is protected by legal professional privilege, for how long should the protection last?

- If someone other than the client, lawyer, or relevant third party obtains material protected by legal professional privilege, may she be compelled to produce it or give evidence about it?

- What is the justification for the rule that a party to civil proceedings should not be compelled to answer questions about what was said in the course of negotiations held with the other party to the proceedings and designed to settle their dispute ('without prejudice' privilege)?

- What exceptions should there be to 'without prejudice' privilege?

The nature of privilege

General

This chapter concerns several well-established principles whereby relevant evidence is excluded not because it is unreliable or irrelevant to the facts in issue, but because of extrinsic considerations which are held to outweigh the value that the evidence would have at trial. Three types of privilege fall to be considered: (i) the privilege against self-incrimination (protecting a person from being compelled to answer a question if the answer would tend to expose him to a criminal charge); (ii) legal professional privilege (protecting the confidentiality of the lawyer-client relationship); and (iii) 'without prejudice' negotiations (enabling settlement negotiations to be conducted without fear of proposed concessions being used in evidence at trial as admissions). These heads of privilege entitle certain people, whether parties to litigation or witnesses, to refuse to disclose material relating to particular matters, and in some cases to prevent others, such as their lawyers, from doing so. Questions of privilege arise most frequently in connection with oral or documentary evidence to be given at trial, whether criminal or civil, and documents to be produced by a party for inspection at the disclosure stage of civil litigation.[1] The drawing of inferences adverse to a witness or party claiming privilege is not permitted.[2]

The differences between privilege and public interest immunity

There are important differences between privilege and public interest immunity. First, where a person satisfies the conditions for claiming privilege, he is entitled to refuse to answer the question or disclose the document in issue—there is no question of the judge balancing the particular weight of the claim to privilege against the value of the evidence at trial. Second, the heads of privilege are upheld for the benefit of clearly identified people. If those people choose to waive their privilege, or fail to claim it, nobody else can claim it. If a judge improperly rejects a *non-party* witness's claim to privilege, there can be no appeal for there has been no infringement of either party's rights.[3] If, however, the judge improperly rejects a party's claim to privilege, for example by requiring disclosure of privileged documents on discovery or by compelling a party who is giving evidence to answer questions as to privileged matters, then that party can appeal since he will have suffered a wrong. Similarly, if a judge improperly accepts a claim to privilege, whether made by a party or non-party witness, then the party who would otherwise have been entitled to call for the documents or tender the evidence will have suffered a wrong on the basis of which he ought to be able to appeal. A third difference from public interest

---

[1] Privilege is often relevant at other stages of litigation, eg in relation to: (i) the special procedures established in *Norwich Pharmacal Co v Customs and Excise Comrs* [1974] AC 133 and ss 33 and 34 of the Senior Courts Act 1981, whereby a non-party or intended party can sometimes be compelled to produce documents for information for use in civil litigation; (ii) the execution of a search order (formerly known as an Anton Piller order), under which the person to whom it is addressed is required to allow an intending claimant to search premises and remove material which may be relevant in subsequent civil litigation; and (iii) requests or orders for further information under CPR r 18.1.

[2] *Wentworth v Lloyd* (1864) 10 HL Cas 589.

[3] See, eg, in relation to the privilege against self-incrimination, *R v Kinglake* (1870) 22 LT 335.

immunity concerns secondary evidence. A successful claim to privilege prevents certain people from being compelled to give evidence of particular matters, but there will be no objection to those matters being proved by other evidence, if available. However, if a claim to public interest immunity succeeds, it will not be possible to prove the excluded facts by any other means.

The difference between privilege and non-compellability

A witness who is competent but not compellable can choose whether to give evidence at all.[4] Having chosen to give evidence, such a witness, like a compellable witness, must answer all questions properly put to him (and is liable to be committed for contempt if he refuses) except those in respect of which he is entitled to claim privilege. Privilege entitles witnesses to refuse to give evidence on particular matters.

The privilege against self-incrimination

' . . . an archaic and unjustifiable survival from the past . . .'

The privilege against self-incrimination is deep-rooted in English law and history. It became a part of the common law after the abolition of the Court of Star Chamber,[5] and it is based on a traditional reluctance to compel anyone, on pain of punishment, to give incriminating evidence against himself.[6] Today, the privilege is at a crossroads. Although it is theoretically intact, Parliament and the courts have recognized the unsatisfactory results of the privilege. Parliament has, in prescribed circumstances, abrogated or modified it. The courts, doubtless frustrated by the piecemeal, inconsistent, and somewhat illogical nature of parliamentary reform, have started to substitute a different protection, thereby rendering invocation of the privilege in some civil proceedings superfluous. However, there is a need for a more comprehensive approach to the major problem so powerfully presented by Lord Templeman in *AT & T Istel v Tully*:[7]

> the privilege can only be justified on two grounds, first that it discourages the ill-treatment of a suspect and secondly that it discourages the production of dubious confessions. Neither of these considerations applies to the present appeal. It is difficult to see any reason why in civil proceedings the privilege . . . should be exercisable so as to enable a litigant to refuse relevant and even vital documents which are in his possession or power and which speak for themselves. And it is fanciful to suggest that an order on [the first defendant] to say whether he has received [the second plaintiff's] money and if so what has happened to that money could result in his ill-treatment or in a dubious confession. I regard the privilege . . . exercisable in civil proceedings as an archaic and unjustifiable survival from the past when the court directs the production of relevant documents and requires the defendant to specify his dealings with the plaintiff's property or money.

---

[4] See **Ch 5**.

[5] *Holdsworth's History of English Law* vol 9 (London, 1944) 200.

[6] The privilege cannot be asserted in the absence of compulsion: see *R v McGeough* [2015] UKSC 62 (statements made in an application for asylum).

[7] [1993] AC 45, HL at 53.

The nature and scope of the privilege

The classic formulation of this privilege is that of Goddard LJ in *Blunt v Park Lane Hotel*:[8]

> The rule is that no-one is bound to answer any question if the answer thereto would, in the opinion of the judge, have a tendency to expose [him] to any criminal charge, penalty or forfeiture which the judge regards as reasonably likely to be preferred or sued for.[9]

This rule applies in both civil and criminal proceedings. However, in civil proceedings a witness can no longer refuse to answer on the ground that to do so would tend to expose him to forfeiture;[10] and in criminal proceedings the position of an accused who elects to testify is governed by s 1(2) of the Criminal Evidence Act 1898, which provides that: 'A person charged in criminal proceedings who is called as a witness in the proceedings may be asked any question in cross-examination notwithstanding that it would tend to criminate him as to any offence with which he is charged in the proceedings.' In *Jones v DPP*[11] a majority of the House of Lords was of the opinion that s 1(2) permits only such questions as tend directly to criminate the accused as to the offence charged and does not permit questions which tend to do so indirectly, such as questions concerning the misconduct of the accused on other occasions.[12]

The privilege against self-incrimination enables a witness to refuse to answer questions in court and also to refuse to produce documents or things. As to pre-trial proceedings, the privilege may arise only if a party seeks to compel disclosure and the production of a document, or to compel an answer to a request for further information in order to assist his case: the privilege does not enable a party to refuse to enter a defence to a civil claim, because there is no *compulsion* to file a defence or to plead anything which provides information to the claimant.[13]

The privilege applies to search orders,[14] covering not only the parts of the order which require the defendant to produce and verify information and documents, but also the parts requiring him to permit the plaintiff to enter, search, and seize documents.[15] It also applies to disclosure ancillary to a freezing injunction, if production of the documents or information sought would tend to expose the defendant to a prosecution in the United Kingdom.[16] It does not follow, however, that a search order which would expose a defendant to a real risk of criminal prosecution can never be made or executed. Such an order may properly be made

---

[8] [1942] 2 KB 253, CA at 257.

[9] 'Answer' should be qualified by the word 'truthful'. See *Dushkar Kanchan Singh v The Queen* [2010] NZSC 161: a claim of privilege cannot be based on a prospective risk of prosecution for perjury.

[10] Civil Evidence Act 1968, s 16(1)(a).

[11] [1962] AC 635, HL.

[12] Cf *R v Anderson* [1988] QB 678, CA in which the Court of Appeal was inclined to think that questioning about the fact that the accused was 'wanted' by the police, which tended to destroy her innocent explanations of prima facie damning circumstances, might have been permissible under s 1(2).

[13] *Versailles Trade Finance Ltd v Clough* [2001] All ER (D) 209, (2001) The Times, 1 Nov, CA.

[14] *Rank Film Distributors Ltd v Video Information Centre* [1982] AC 380, HL. But see now s 72 of the Senior Courts Act 1981, in this chapter, under **Section 72 of the Senior Courts Act 1981**, p 723.

[15] *Tate Access Floors Inc v Boswell* [1991] Ch 512, Ch D.

[16] *Sociedade Nacional de Combustiveis de Angola UEE v Lundqvist* [1991] 2 QB 310, CA. The privilege is also available in respect of the risk of contempt proceedings either in the action in which the privilege is invoked or in some other action: *Memory Corpn plc v Sidhu* [2000] Ch 645, Ch D. An alleged contemnor cannot be compelled to answer questions at an interim stage the answers to which might expose him to an application to commit for contempt and cannot be compelled to answer a request for further information as regards such an application: *Great Future International Ltd v Sealand Housing Corporation* [2004] EWHC 124 (Ch).

if it contains a proviso to the effect that (i) the defendant should be advised of his right to obtain immediate legal advice before execution of the order, including advice that he may be entitled to claim the privilege against self-incrimination; and (ii) the order will have effect only insofar as the defendant does not claim the privilege. If such advice is given in everyday language and the defendant properly understands it but declines to claim the privilege, the order may then be executed.[17]

At common law, there is no exception to the privilege preventing an agent, trustee, or other fiduciary from claiming the privilege, as against a principal, in an action brought against him by the principal to recover money or property, or an account of such money or property, for which the agent, trustee, or fiduciary is accountable.[18]

'Criminal charge, penalty, or forfeiture'

The term 'criminal charge' is self-explanatory, but under s 14(1)(a) of the Civil Evidence Act 1968 (the 1968 Act), if the claim to privilege is made in civil proceedings, 'the right of a person . . . to refuse to answer any question or produce any document or thing if to do so would tend to expose that person to proceedings for an offence . . . shall apply only as regards criminal offences under the law of any part of the United Kingdom'.[19] Although there is no *absolute* privilege against self-incrimination under foreign law, the possibility of self-incrimination, or the incrimination of others, under foreign law is a factor which can be taken into account in deciding whether, and on what terms, a disclosure order should be made.[20] However, the scope for restricting disclosure of otherwise clearly relevant facts on this basis is limited and likely to be confined to cases where disclosure might have serious consequences for persons still resident in the foreign state in question.[21] Concerning a 'penalty', s 14(1)(a) provides that if the claim to privilege is made in civil proceedings, the penalty must be provided for by the law of any part of the United Kingdom. Penalties now arise mainly under statutes such as those relating to the Revenue. It does not matter that liability to the penalty may arise without court proceedings, provided that it can ultimately be enforced in English courts. EU regulations, incorporated into English law by virtue of the European Communities Act 1972, are an abundant source of penalties.[22] It seems that proceedings for civil contempt are proceedings for the 'recovery of a penalty' within s 14(1) in respect of which there is a privilege against self-incrimination.[23] Exposure to forfeiture refers to the risk of forfeiting property. This part of the rule has become obsolete because courts now have wide powers to grant relief against such a risk.

---

[17] *IBM United Kingdom Ltd v Prima Data International Ltd* [1994] 4 All ER 748, Ch D.

[18] *Bishopsgate Investment Management Ltd (In Provisional Liquidation) v Maxwell* [1992] 2 All ER 856, CA and *Tate Access Floors Inc v Boswell* [1991] Ch 512, Ch D.

[19] There is no clear authority on the point in relation to criminal proceedings.

[20] *Arab Monetary Fund v Hashim* [1989] 1 WLR 565, Ch D.

[21] *Arab Monetary Fund v Hashim (No 2)* [1990] 1 All ER 673, Ch D.

[22] See, eg, *Rio Tinto Zinc Corpn v Westinghouse Electric Corpn* [1978] AC 547, HL. 'Additional damages' which may be awarded under statutes for breach of copyright are not a penalty: *Rank Film Distributors Ltd v Video Information Centre* [1982] AC 380, CA at 425; *Overseas Programming Co Ltd v Cinematographische Commerz-Anstalt and Iduna Film GmbH* (1984) The Times, 16 May, QBD.

[23] See *Cobra Golf Ltd v Rata* [1998] Ch 109, Ch D and *Bhimji v Chatwani (No 2)* [1992] 1 WLR 1158, Ch D, not following *Garvin v Domus Publishing Ltd* [1988] 3 WLR 344, Ch D. Cf *Crest Homes plc v Marks* [1987] AC 529, HL.

'A tendency to expose'

In *R v Boyes*[24] the court, while acknowledging that, if it appears that the witness is in danger, he should be allowed great latitude in judging for himself the effect of any particular question, held:

> To entitle a party called as a witness to the privilege of silence, the court must see, from the circumstances of the case and the nature of the evidence which the witness is called to give, that there is reasonable ground to apprehend danger to the witness from his being called to answer
> . . . The danger to be apprehended must be real and appreciable with reference to the ordinary operation of law in the ordinary course of things; not a danger of an imaginary and unsubstantial character . . .[25]

A claim to privilege cannot succeed merely on the basis that it was made on legal advice; the duty of the court is non-delegable and therefore it cannot simply adopt the conclusion of a lawyer advising the witness, whose advice may or may not be correct.[26] If necessary, the judge may hear the witness's explanation in camera. He must make due allowance for the possibility that apparently innocuous questions may, when combined with other material, give rise to damaging inferences.[27] It is sufficient to support a claim that the answers sought might lead to a line of inquiry which would or might form a significant step in the chain of evidence required for a prosecution.[28] On the other hand, a claim to privilege will not succeed if the evidence against the witness is already so strong that if proceedings are to be taken at all they will be taken whether or not the witness answers. This is a question of fact for the judge, who should not ignore the possibility that although some evidence is already available to the authorities, additional evidence from the witness may increase the risk of proceedings being taken.[29] The triviality or staleness of the offence may lead the court to treat the likelihood of prosecution as too remote.[30] A person's claim to privilege will not succeed where the Crown has given an assurance to her that she will not be prosecuted and therefore any prosecution based on evidence obtained from her would be halted as an abuse of process.[31]

[24] (1861) 1 B&S 311, QB.

[25] Per Cockburn CJ at 330, approved in *Den Norske Bank ASA v Antonatos* [1999] QB 271, CA. See also *Dushkar Kanchan Singh v The Queen* [2010] NZSC 161. Cf *Triplex Safety Glass Co Ltd v Lancegaye Safety Glass (1934) Ltd* [1939] 2 KB 395: privilege may be claimed on the ground of exposure to criminal libel proceedings even though such proceedings are rare.

[26] *R (Crown Prosecution Service) v Bolton Magistrates' Court* [2004] 1 WLR 835, DC.

[27] Per Cockburn CJ in *R v Boyes* (1861) 1 B&S 311, QB at 330; see also *British Steel Corpn v Granada Television Ltd* [1981] AC 1096, HL, especially per Megarry V-C in the Chancery Division (at 1108).

[28] Per Beldam LJ in *Sociedade Nacional de Combustiveis de Angola UEE v Lundqvist* [1991] 2 QB 310, CA at 332, citing Lord Wilberforce in *Rank Film Distributors Ltd v Video Information Centre* [1982] AC 380 at 443.

[29] *Rio Tinto Zinc Corpn v Westinghouse Electric Corpn* [1978] AC 547. In *Khan v Khan* [1982] 1 WLR 513, CA a witness was required to answer questions about his use of the proceeds of a cheque. His conduct 'reeked of dishonesty' and evidence as to his use of the proceeds did not materially increase the risk of prosecution for theft of the cheque.

[30] See per Lord Fraser in *Rank Film Distributors Ltd v Video Information Centre* [1982] AC 380 at 445: the risk of prosecution for trivial offences under s 21 of the Copyright Act 1956 was not enough to establish the privilege, partly because the likelihood of prosecution was too remote, but also because it would be 'unreasonable to allow the possibility of incrimination of such offences to obstruct disclosure of information which would be of much more value to the owners of the infringed copyright than any protection they might obtain from s 21'.

[31] See *R (DPP) v Leicester Magistrates' Court* [2016] 1 Cr App R 74 (5), DC.

Spouses, civil partners, strangers, and companies

In most cases the witness claiming privilege will do so because he fears prosecution himself. If he chooses not to claim the privilege or, in ignorance, fails to claim it—the judge may, but is not obliged to, remind him of his rights—no one else can claim it on his behalf.

A witness in either civil or criminal proceedings cannot claim privilege in respect of questions the answers to which would tend to incriminate strangers.[32] In civil proceedings, under s 14(1)(b) of the 1968 Act, the right of a person to assert the privilege 'shall include a like right to refuse any question or produce any document or thing if to do so would tend to expose the spouse or civil partner of that person to proceedings for any such criminal offence or for the recovery of any such penalty'. However, the privilege remains that of the witness and, if he chooses to answer, the spouse or civil partner cannot complain. In criminal proceedings, however, it seems that a witness cannot claim privilege in respect of questions the answers to which would tend to incriminate his spouse.[33]

Because the privilege is a privilege against *self*-incrimination, office-holders, employees, or agents of a company may claim the privilege themselves, but cannot refuse to answer questions which would tend to incriminate the company or render it liable to a penalty under, for example, an EU regulation.[34] Equally, the company cannot refuse to answer questions which would tend to incriminate the office-holders.[35]

Statutory provisions

Statutory withdrawal of privilege

Pursuant to a variety of statutes and statutory instruments, specified persons in specified circumstances must answer questions for specified purposes notwithstanding that their answers may incriminate them. Some of the provisions abrogate the privilege expressly; others do so impliedly. However, clear language (express or by necessary implication) is required to show that Parliament intended to abrogate such a fundamental principle of the common law.[36] Sometimes, as we shall see, the statute may additionally prevent any answer from being used in a subsequent criminal prosecution. However, where there is a statutory revocation of the privilege without restricting the use that may be made of the answer, its use in subsequent criminal proceedings would amount to a violation of the Art 6 right to a fair hearing.[37] For example, in *R (Bright) v Central Criminal Court*[38] the majority view was that s 9(1) of the Police and Criminal Evidence Act 1984, whereby a judge may order production of certain types of material for the purposes of a criminal investigation, has excluded the privilege against self-incrimination.[39] However, if the subject of the order is prosecuted, the judge may consider

---

[32] See *Ex p Reynolds* (1882) 20 Ch D 294, cited by Megarry V-C in *British Steel Corpn v Granada Television Ltd* [1981] AC 1096 at 1106, Ch D.

[33] Per Lord Diplock in *Rio Tinto Zinc Corpn v Westinghouse Electric Corpn* [1978] AC 547 at 637 and, but only by inference, *R v Pitt* [1983] QB 25, CA. Contrast *R v All Saints, Worcester* (1817) 6 M&S 194.

[34] Per Lord Diplock in *Rio Tinto Zinc Corpn v Westinghouse Electric Corpn* [1978] AC 547 at 637–8.

[35] Per Beldam LJ in *Sociedade Nacional de Combustiveis de Angola UEE v Lundqvist* [1991] 2 QB 310, CA at 336.

[36] *R (Malik) v Crown Court at Manchester* [2008] 4 All ER 403, DC at [73].

[37] *Saunders v UK* (1997) 23 EHRR 313 at para 68.

[38] [2001] 1 WLR 662.

[39] Contrast *R (Malik) v Manchester Crown Court* [2008] 4 All ER 403. In *R (River East Supplies Ltd) v Crown Court at Nottingham* [2017] 2 Cr App R 384 (27), the court described as 'powerful' the argument that prevailed with the majority in *R (Bright) v Central Criminal Court*.

Art 6 of the European Convention on Human Rights and whether to exclude the material under s 78 of the Police and Criminal Evidence Act 1984. *Beghal v DPP*,[40] a majority decision of the Supreme Court, concerned para 2 of Schedule 7 to the Terrorism Act 2000, whereby a person questioned at a port for the purposes set out is required to answer on pain of prosecution for failure to do so. This statutory power was construed by the majority to abrogate the privilege by necessary implication on the basis that it would be rendered largely nugatory if the privilege did apply.

Compatibility with Art 6 of the European Convention on Human Rights

The implied rights within Art 6 are not of an absolute character, but can be qualified or restricted, and a statute which does qualify or restrict those rights will be compatible with Art 6 if there is an identifiable social or economic problem that the statute is intended to deal with and the qualification or restriction is proportionate to that problem. *Brown v Stott*,[41] a Scottish case, concerned the introduction of evidence of an admission obtained from the accused under s 172(2)(a) of the Road Traffic Act 1988, under which, where the driver of a vehicle is alleged to be guilty of one of a number of road traffic offences, including driving with excess alcohol and speeding, 'the person keeping the vehicle shall give such information as to the identity of the driver as he may be required to give by or on behalf of a chief officer of police'. Under s 172(3), if he fails to comply with such a requirement he shall be guilty of an offence (punishable by a fine, mandatory endorsement, and discretionary disqualification from driving). It was held that evidence of an admission obtained from the accused under s 172(2)(a) did not infringe the right to a fair hearing. There was a clear public interest in the enforcement of road traffic legislation and s 172 was not a disproportionate response to the serious social problem of the high incidence of death and injury on the roads caused by the misuse of motor vehicles. The section permitted a single, simple question to be put, the answer to which cannot by itself incriminate the suspect, and the penalty for non-compliance is moderate and non-custodial. Furthermore, all who own or drive motor cars know that by doing so they subject themselves to a regulatory regime which is imposed because the possession and use of cars are recognized to have the potential to cause grave injury. A virtually identical approach to s 172 has since been taken in *O'Halloran and Francis v UK*.[42]

Subsequent attempts to distinguish *Brown v Stott* on the grounds that, under Scottish law, the driver's admission must be corroborated, have failed; and it was applied in *Mawdesley v Chief Constable of the Cheshire Constabulary*,[43] a case of driving in excess of the speed limit. The reasoning of the Privy Council in *Brown v Stott* falls to be compared with that of the European Court of Human Rights in *Heaney and McGuinness v Ireland*.[44] H and M were arrested on suspicion of involvement in a terrorist bombing. They were required to account for their movements under s 52 of the Offences Against the State Act 1939, which makes it a criminal offence, punishable by six months' imprisonment, for a person detained on suspicion of a defined terrorist offence to fail to account for his movements. They refused to do so and were prosecuted under

---

[40] [2015] UKSC 49.

[41] [2001] 2 WLR 817, PC.

[42] [2007] ECHR 15809/02. The principles and outcome were the same in *Lückhof and Spanner v Austria* (2008) Application Nos 58452/00 and 61920/00, where the penalties for non-compliance were fines and also, in default, imprisonment.

[43] [2004] 1 WLR 1035, QBD.

[44] [2001] 33 ECHR 264.

s 52. They were also charged with membership of the IRA under s 21 of the Act. They were convicted of the charge under s 52, but acquitted of the charge under s 21. The European Court of Human Rights found a violation of Art 6 on the basis that the degree of compulsion created by the threat of a prison sentence under s 52 'with a view to compelling them to provide information relating to charges against them under that Act', in effect destroyed the very essence of the right to silence and the privilege against self-incrimination. As Aikens J observed in *R v Kearns*[45] the court attached importance to the fact that the purpose of obtaining information under s 52 was to provide evidence for other charges under s 21 of the 1939 Act.[46]

In *R v Allen (No 2)*,[47] A was convicted of cheating the public revenue of tax by concealing or failing to disclose profits. He had provided a schedule of assets, in compliance with a notice given by the inspector under s 20 of the Taxes Management Act 1970, but had omitted to list his beneficial interest in shares issued by offshore companies. Under s 98(1) of the Act, a person who fails to comply with a s 20 notice is liable to a penalty. The House of Lords held that the s 20 notice could not constitute a violation of the right against self-incrimination, denying the right to a fair trial, because the state, for the purpose of collecting tax, is entitled to require a citizen to inform it of his income and to enforce penalties for failure to do so. A's further application to the European Court of Human Rights failed. It was held that the requirement to declare assets disclosed no issue under Art 6(1), even though there was a penalty for failure to comply. The case was one of making a false declaration of assets, not one of forced self-incrimination in relation to some previously committed offence, nor one of being prosecuted for failing to provide information which might incriminate him in pending or anticipated criminal proceedings.[48]

Compulsory production of pre-existing documents and materials

An important distinction is to be drawn between statements made by the accused under compulsion, which, depending on the circumstances, may involve infringement of the right to silence or the right not to incriminate oneself, and the compulsory production of pre-existing documents and materials, sometimes referred to as 'independent' material, which involves no infringement of those rights. According to the majority of the European Court in *Saunders v UK*:[49]

> The right not to incriminate oneself is primarily concerned . . . with respecting the will of an accused person to remain silent. As commonly understood in the legal systems of the Contracting Parties to the Convention and elsewhere, it does not extend to the use in criminal proceedings of material which may be obtained from the accused through compulsory powers but which have an existence independent of the will of the suspect, such as, inter alia, documents acquired pursuant to a warrant, breath, blood and urine samples and bodily tissue for the purposes of DNA testing.[50]

---

[45] [2003] 1 Cr App R 111, CA at [41].

[46] See also *R v K(A)* [2010] 1 Cr App R 44, CA.

[47] [2002] 1 AC 509, HL.

[48] *Allen v UK* [2003] Crim LR 280. Cf *JB v Switzerland* [2001] Crim LR 748, ECHR.

[49] (1997) 23 EHRR 313 at para 69.

[50] However, there are exceptions to the exception, as when the evidence is obtained by forced medical intervention constituting inhuman or degrading treatment involving a high degree of force in defiance of the will of the accused: *Jalloh v Germany* [2007] Crim LR 717, ECHR. See also *Gäfgen v Germany*, Application No 22978/05, 1 June 2010, ECHR, Ch 3.

This principle was applied in *Attorney General's Reference (No 7 of 2000)*[51] where the accused, a bankrupt, completed a preliminary questionnaire and admitted having lost money by gambling. He was then required to produce documents to the Official Receiver under the Insolvency Act 1986; if he had failed to do so he would have been in contempt of court. He was charged with the offence of materially contributing to or increasing the extent of his insolvency by gambling and the documents which he had produced formed the basis of the prosecution case against him. The Court of Appeal held that use of the documents relating to his gambling would not violate his rights under Art 6. The court adopted the reasoning of La Forest J in *Thompson Newspapers Ltd v Director of Investigation & Research*[52] that, whereas a compelled statement is evidence that would not have existed independently of exercise of the power of compulsion, evidence which exists independently of the compelled statement could have been found by other means and its quality does not depend on its past connection with the compelled statement. The principle was also applied in *R v Hundal*,[53] on charges of belonging to a proscribed organization, in relation to items seized following a search under the Terrorism Act 2000. *C plc v P*[54] concerned intellectual property proceedings in which indecent images of children were found on a computer which was the subject of a search order. The Court of Appeal held that the offending material was not privileged from disclosure to the police. A majority of the court reached this conclusion applying the principle from *Saunders v UK*.[55] In *R (River East Supplies Ltd) v Crown Court at Nottingham*[56] the Divisional Court rejected a submission that it should follow three decisions of the House of Lords[57] insofar as they had operated on the assumption that the privilege *does* extend to 'independent' material.

In *R (Malik) v Crown Court at Manchester*,[58] it was said that in deciding whether to exercise the *discretion* to order production of 'independent' documents, the privilege against self-incrimination is an important relevant factor to be taken into account, but as the court observed in *R (River East Supplies Ltd) v Crown Court at Nottingham*,[59] on the best view of existing authority the privilege against self-incrimination does not apply to 'independent' documents and therefore no question of the exercise of judicial discretion can arise.

Production of information for extra-judicial purposes

A further important distinction has been drawn between the production of information for extra-judicial purposes rather than for use in judicial proceedings. In *R v Kearns*[60] Aikens J, after reviewing the Strasbourg and UK cases, said:

> A law will not be likely to infringe the right to silence or not to incriminate oneself if it demands
> the production of information for an administrative purpose or in the course of an extra-judicial

---

[51] [2001] 1 WLR 1879, CA.

[52] (1990) 54 CCC 417 (Supreme Court of Canada).

[53] [2004] 2 Cr App R 307 (19), CA.

[54] [2007] 3 All ER 1034, CA.

[55] See also, applying the ratio of the majority in *C plc v P*, *R v S* [2009] 1 All ER 716, CA (a key to data in encrypted files) and *R (River East Supplies Ltd) v Crown Court at Nottingham* [2017] 2 Cr App R 384 (27). In *C plc v P* the majority advanced other grounds for reaching its conclusion, but these were doubted in *R (River East Supplies Ltd) v Crown Court at Nottingham*, ibid at [72]–[80].

[56] [2017] 2 Cr App R 384 (27).

[57] *Rio Tinto Zinc Corporation v Westinghouse Electric Corporation* [1978] AC 547, *Rank Film Distributors Ltd v Video Information Centre* [1982] AC 380, and *AT & T Istel v Tully* [1993] AC 45.

[58] [2008] 4 All ER 403, DC at [78].

[59] [2017] 2 Cr App R 384 (27) at [102].

[60] [2003] 1 Cr App R 111 (7), CA at [53].

enquiry. However if the information so produced is or could be used in subsequent judicial proceedings, whether criminal or civil, then the use of the information in such proceedings could breach those rights and so make that trial unfair.

In *R v Hertfordshire County Council, ex p Green Environmental Industries Ltd*[61] a summons was issued against the company, the local authority having served a notice under s 71 of the Environmental Protection Act 1990 requesting certain information and the company having refused to provide that information. It was held that the s 71 notice did not constitute any form of adjudication and therefore Art 6 was not infringed by its service. In *R v Kearns*, K, a bankrupt, was charged with an offence contrary to s 354(3) of the Insolvency Act 1986 of failing without reasonable excuse to account for the loss of part of his property, having been required to do so by the Official Receiver. It was held that s 354 does not breach an accused's right to remain silent or not to incriminate himself and does not contravene the right of a person to have a fair trial under Art 6. First, the demand for information was made in the course of an extra-judicial procedure and not in order to provide evidence to prove a case against K. Second, at the time of the demand, there was no other charge against K.[62] Third, there was no possibility that any information obtained could be used in subsequent criminal proceedings. Fourth, even if s 354 did infringe the 'absolute' right to silence and/or the right not to incriminate oneself, the s 354 regime was a proportionate legislative response to the problem of administering and investigating bankrupt estates.[63]

Provisions preventing use of answers in subsequent criminal proceedings
Typically, statutory provisions do not simply abrogate the privilege against self-incrimination, but also prevent the answers from being used in evidence in any subsequent criminal proceedings in which the person who answered the question is charged with a specified offence. These provisions, individually different, collectively resemble a patchwork quilt to which new additions can always be made. Some important examples are now set out.

Section 98 of the Children Act 1989
Section 98(1) provides that in any proceedings in which a court is hearing an application relating to the care, supervision, or protection of a child, no person shall be excused from giving evidence on any matter or answering any question put to him in the course of his giving evidence on the ground that doing so might incriminate him or his spouse or civil partner of an offence. Under s 98(2), a statement or admission made in such proceedings shall not be admissible in evidence against the person making it or his spouse or civil partner in proceedings for an offence other than perjury.[64] It has been held, in decisions since doubted,[65] that the phrase 'statement or admission made in such proceedings' is to be construed widely to include not only the written and filed statements of the evidence which a party intends to

---

[61] [2000] 2 AC 412, HL.

[62] Cf *Heaney and McGuinness v Ireland* (2001) 33 EHRR 264, ECHR, in this chapter, under **Compatibility with Art 6 of the European Convention on Human Rights, pp 718–19.**

[63] See also *R v Brady* [2004] 3 All ER 520, CA, where it was held that statements obtained on pain of penalty by the Official Receiver under s 235 of the Insolvency Act 1986 could be disclosed to the Inland Revenue for the purpose of investigating possible offences of cheating the public revenue and laying information to obtain search warrants.

[64] However, a family court may direct disclosure of such material to the police for the purposes of a criminal investigation: *In re C (a minor) (care proceedings: disclosure)* [1997] 2 WLR 322, CA.

[65] Per Butler-Sloss LJ and Sir Roger Parker in *Re G (a minor)* [1996] 1 WLR 1407, CA.

adduce and oral admissions made by a parent to a guardian *ad litem*,[66] but also, at least once the proceedings have begun, oral statements made to social workers charged with carrying out the local authority's duties of investigation.[67] The purpose of s 98(2) is to protect a witness who is required to give evidence in relation to a child when such evidence would incriminate him or his spouse or civil partner. Thus it will not prevent the advocate for the accused from putting a 'statement or admission' to his spouse as a previous inconsistent statement in order to challenge her evidence or to attack her credibility.[68]

Section 2 of the Criminal Justice Act 1987

Under s 2, the Director of the Serious Fraud Office may require any person under investigation for a suspected offence involving serious or complex fraud, or any other person, to answer questions, furnish information, and produce documents. Under s 2(8), a statement in response to such a requirement may only be used in evidence against its maker (a) on a prosecution for an offence of knowingly or recklessly making a false or misleading statement (in purported compliance with a requirement under s 2); or (b) on a prosecution for some other offence where in giving evidence he makes a statement inconsistent with it. However, under s 2(8AA), the statement may not be used against its maker by virtue of (b) unless evidence relating to it is adduced or a question relating to it is asked, by him or on his behalf, in the proceedings arising out of the prosecution.

Section 434 of the Companies Act 1985

Under Pt XIV of the 1985 Act, officers and agents of a company and others possessing relevant information are obliged to answer questions put by inspectors appointed to investigate suspected fraud in the conduct or management of a company. Under s 434(5A) and (5B) of the Act, in criminal proceedings in which the person who answered such a question is charged with an offence, other than an offence under s 2 or s 5 of the Perjury Act 1911 (false statements made on oath otherwise than in judicial proceedings or made otherwise than on oath), (a) no evidence relating to the answer may be adduced; and (b) no question relating to it may be asked, by or on behalf of the prosecution, unless evidence relating to it is adduced or a question relating to it is asked in the proceedings by or on behalf of the person charged.

Section 31(1) of the Theft Act 1968

Section 31(1) requires questions to be answered and orders to be complied with 'in proceedings for the recovery or administration of any property, for the execution of any trust or for an account of any property or dealings with property' notwithstanding that compliance may expose the witness or his spouse or civil partner to a charge for an offence under the Theft Act. The section goes on to provide that the answers may not be used in proceedings for any such offence.[69] However, neither the revocation of the privilege nor the restriction on the use of the answers applies to any other offences, a limitation which prompted Sir Nicolas Browne-Wilkinson V-C to express the hope that Parliament would urgently extend s 31 so as to remove the privilege in relation to all civil claims relating to property, including claims for damages, but on terms that the statements made in documents disclosed should not be admissible in *any* criminal proceedings.[70]

---

[66] See *Oxfordshire County Council v P* [1995] 2 WLR 543, Fam Div.
[67] See *Cleveland County Council v F* [1995] 1 WLR 785, Fam Div.
[68] See *Re K (minors)* [1994] 3 All ER 230, Fam Div.
[69] See also s 9 of the Criminal Damage Act 1971.
[70] *Sociedade Nacional de Combustiveis de Angola UEE v Lundqvist* [1991] 2 QB 310, CA at 338.

In cases where there is a claim to privilege in respect of both a Theft Act offence and a non-Theft Act offence, the test, in each case, is whether to answer the question would create or increase the risk of proceedings for that offence. If the test is satisfied in the case of the Theft Act offence, s 31 will apply and prima facie the question must be answered. For the non-Theft Act offence, the test is whether to answer would create or increase the risk of proceedings for that offence, separate and distinct from its connection with the Theft Act offence. If the answer is in the negative, there is no privilege; but if in the affirmative, the privilege will subsist.[71]

Section 13 of the Fraud Act 2006

Section 13 is modelled on s 31(1) of the Theft Act 1968. It requires questions to be answered and orders to be complied with in 'proceedings relating to property' (that is, proceedings for the recovery or administration of any property, etc), notwithstanding that compliance may result in incrimination of an offence under the 2006 Act or a 'related offence', but prevents the answers from being used in evidence in proceedings for any such offence. 'Related offence' means conspiracy to defraud or 'any other offence involving any other form of fraudulent conduct or purpose'. In *Kensington International Ltd v Republic of Congo*[72] the Court of Appeal was reluctant to construe s 13 narrowly. First, it was held that 'proceedings relating to property' covers *Norwich Pharmacal* proceedings[73] brought to compel disclosure in aid of pending substantive proceedings relating to property, because the proceedings should be viewed as a whole so as to include the substantive proceedings. Second, it was held that the phrase 'any other offence involving any other form of fraudulent conduct or purpose' includes offences of offering or giving a bribe notwithstanding that they do not require proof of dishonesty. It also includes money laundering under s 328(1) of the Proceeds of Crime Act 2002.[74]

Section 72 of the Senior Courts Act 1981

The decision in *Rank Film Distributors Ltd v Video Information Centre*[75] that the privilege against self-incrimination applied to Anton Piller orders, now known as search orders, seriously undermined the effectiveness of that remedy, particularly in relation to breach of copyright, which often involves offences of fraud. Accordingly, the decision was rapidly reversed for the purposes of proceedings concerning intellectual property and passing off by s 72 of the Senior Courts Act 1981, the effect of which may be summarized as follows.[76] In proceedings brought to prevent any apprehended infringement of rights pertaining to any intellectual property (ie patent, trade mark, copyright, design right, registered design, technical or commercial information, or other intellectual property)[77] or any apprehended passing off, questions must be answered and orders complied with even though the person complying may thereby expose himself or his spouse or civil partner to proceedings for a related offence

[71] See *Renworth Ltd v Stephansen* [1996] 3 All ER 244 per Morritt LJ at 254, CA; but see also *Khan v Khan* [1982] 1 WLR 513, CA.

[72] [2007] EWCA Civ 1128.

[73] *Norwich Pharmacal Co v Commissioners of Customs & Excise* [1974] AC 133, HL.

[74] *JSC BTA Bank v Ablyazov* [2010] 1 Cr App R 131, CA.

[75] [1982] AC 380, HL.

[76] The terms of the section are complex and should be referred to for detail. See also *Universal City Studios v Hubbard* [1984] Ch 225, CA.

[77] Section 72(5). Commercially confidential information is 'commercial information': *Phillips v News Group Newspapers Ltd* [2013] 1 AC 1, SC.

or for the recovery of a related penalty. In proceedings for an infringement (or for passing off) which, it is alleged, has already occurred, or proceedings to obtain disclosure of information relating to such an infringement (or passing off), the privilege is withdrawn only in relation to (i) any offence committed by or in the course of the infringement (or passing off); (ii) offences of dishonesty or fraud committed in connection with the infringement (or passing off); and (iii) penalties incurred in connection with the infringement (or passing off). By s 72(3), answers compelled by reason of the withdrawal of privilege cannot be used in proceedings for the offence disclosed or for the recovery of any penalty liability to which was disclosed. Section 72 affects only proceedings for infringement of intellectual property rights and passing off: the decision in *Rank Film Distributors Ltd v Video Information Centre* still applies to the use of search orders for other purposes.

Substituted protection

In *AT & T Istel Ltd v Tully*,[78] a claim was made for damages and repayment of money obtained by fraud. A major police investigation was launched. The plaintiffs were granted a wide-ranging order for Mareva injunctions and disclosure, requiring the defendants to disclose all dealings regarding the money. Paragraph 33 of the order contained a condition that no disclosure made in compliance with it would be used as evidence in the prosecution of an offence alleged to have been committed by the person required to make that disclosure or by any spouse of that person. The order was subsequently varied and the plaintiffs appealed against the variation. Before the appeal, the Crown Prosecution Service (CPS) informed the plaintiffs that it did not seek to intervene in the civil proceedings, that it already had a large amount of potential evidence, and that it would not be prevented by para 33 from using that material or any other material obtained independently of the civil proceedings. The House of Lords restored the original order. Noting that the proceedings were not covered by any of the statutory modifications of the privilege, but were similar to situations in which Parliament had intervened, the House could see no reason why the defendants should blatantly exploit the privilege to deprive the plaintiffs of their civil rights and remedies. The courts were entitled to substitute a different protection in place of the privilege, provided it was adequate. The protection would be adequate if the CPS unequivocally agreed not to make use, directly or indirectly, of the material divulged in compliance with the order. Accordingly, a majority of the House held that, given the terms of para 33 and the clear indication by the CPS that it did not seek to use any of the material to be divulged in compliance with the order, the original order should stand.[79]

On the reasoning of the House, the principle of substituted protection is capable of application in many situations other than those which arose in *AT & T Istel v Tully*. However, those who, in the future, seek to confine the principle, will doubtless rely on the views of Lord Lowry, who emphasized that the decision of the House did not represent a breakthrough in relation to the privilege, being a decision on its own facts.[80]

---

[78] [1993] AC 45, HL.

[79] See also *Re O* [1991] 2 WLR 475, CA, approved by the House of Lords in *AT & T Istel Ltd v Tully*, and *Re Thomas* [1992] 4 All ER 814, CA. An affidavit sworn by a person in compliance with such an order cannot be admitted in evidence against him in any subsequent criminal trial, but subject to proper directions from the judge may be used to show his inconsistency and impugn his credit: *R v Martin* [1998] 2 Cr App R 385, CA.

[80] [1993] AC 45, HL at 69.

Legal professional privilege

The nature of the privilege

The common law doctrine of legal professional privilege enables a client to maintain the confidentiality of (i) communications between him and his lawyer made for the purpose of obtaining and giving legal advice, the privilege in this case being known as 'legal advice privilege'; (ii) communications between him or his lawyer and third parties (such as potential witnesses and experts) the dominant purpose of which was preparation for contemplated or pending litigation, the privilege in this case being known as 'litigation privilege'; and (iii) items enclosed with or referred to in such communications and brought into existence for the purposes set out in (i) and (ii).

Section 10 of the Police and Criminal Evidence Act 1984 (the 1984 Act), which is intended to reflect the common law position,[81] provides that:

(1) Subject to subsection (2) below, in this Act 'items subject to legal privilege' means—

    (a) communications between a professional legal adviser and his client or any person representing his client made in connection with the giving of legal advice to the client;

    (b) communications between a professional legal adviser and his client or any person representing his client or between such an adviser or his client or any such representative and any other person made in connection with or in contemplation of legal proceedings and for the purposes of such proceedings; and

    (c) items enclosed with or referred to in such communications and made—

        (i) in connection with the giving of legal advice; or

        (ii) in connection with or in contemplation of legal proceedings and for the purposes of such proceedings, when they are in the possession of a person who is entitled to possession of them.

(2) Items held with the intention of furthering a criminal purpose are not items subject to legal privilege.

For the purposes of legal professional privilege, 'lawyer' includes, as well as solicitors and advocates, employed legal advisers[82] and overseas lawyers.[83] Internal communications by in-house lawyers are not protected by the privilege in relation to investigations into alleged infringements of EU competition law.[84] The privilege does not apply in relation to 'appropriate adults' required in the case of vulnerable detainees under Code of Practice C issued pursuant to the Police and Criminal Evidence Act 1984.[85] Nor does it apply, at common law, in relation to professionals other than solicitors, barristers, or appropriately qualified overseas

---

[81] See the majority view of the House of Lords in *R v Central Criminal Court, ex p Francis and Francis* [1989] AC 346, HL, in this chapter, under **Fraud, p 741**, especially per Lord Goff at 797; and *R v R* [1994] 4 All ER 260, CA, in this chapter, under **Items enclosed with or referred to in communications, p 736**.

[82] *Alfred Crompton Amusement Machines Ltd v Customs and Excise Comrs (No 2)* [1974] AC 405; *AM & S Europe Ltd v EC Commission* [1983] QB 878, ECJ per Advocate General Sir Gordon Slynn at 914. It is possible that the privilege may also attach to communications between the police and the Director of Public Prosecutions, if they are seeking legal advice in circumstances analogous to a client approaching his solicitor for advice: per Moore-Bick J, obiter, in *Goodridge v Chief Constable of Hampshire Constabulary* [1999] 1 WLR 1558, QBD at 1564.

[83] *Re Duncan* [1968] P 306. The term 'proceedings' in this context includes proceedings in other jurisdictions: see *Re Duncan*.

[84] *Akzo Nobel Chemicals Ltd v European Commission* [2010] EU ECJ C-550/07.

[85] *RE v United Kingdom* [2015] ECHR 62498/11.

lawyers, who have specialized knowledge of the law and advise on it, such as accountants who provide expert advice on tax law.[86] However, pursuant to statute a privilege parallel to legal professional privilege does apply to communications between a person and his patent agent,[87] trade mark agent,[88] or licensed conveyancer,[89] and individuals who are not solicitors or barristers but who are authorized persons for the purposes of providing advocacy, litigation, conveyancing, or probate services.[90]

The privilege survives the death of a client and vests in his personal representative or, once administration is complete, the person entitled to his estate,[91] and those persons are entitled to either claim or waive the privilege.[92]

The rationale of the privilege

The rationale of the rules of legal professional privilege is that they encourage those who know the facts to state them fully and candidly without fear of compulsory disclosure.[93] In *R v Derby Magistrates' Court, ex p B*[94] Lord Taylor CJ said:

> The principle . . . is that a man must be able to consult his lawyer in confidence, since otherwise he might hold back half the truth. The client must be sure that what he tells his lawyer in confidence will never be revealed without his consent. Legal professional privilege is thus much more than an ordinary rule of evidence . . . . It is a fundamental condition on which the administration of justice as a whole rests.

In relation to litigation privilege, it is this confidentiality which enables lawyers to encourage strong cases and discourage weak ones, which is in the interests of the state.[95] However, in the absence of contemplated litigation, it is questionable whether there is any temptation for the client to be less than candid or 'to hold back half the truth',[96] and even if this is a real likelihood, it is equally questionable whether it should override the public interest that wherever possible the courts should reach their decisions on the basis of all relevant evidence. As Lord Phillips MR forcefully observed in *Three Rivers District Council v Governor and Company of the Bank of England (No 6)*:[97]

> The justification for litigation privilege is readily understood. Where, however, litigation is not anticipated it is not easy to see why communications with a solicitor should be privileged. Legal advice privilege attaches to matters such as the conveyance of real property or the drawing up

---

[86] *R (Prudential plc) v Special Commissioner of Income Tax* [2013] 2 AC 185, SC. See also Mitchell, 'Comparative standards of legal advice privilege for tax advisers and optimal reform proposals for English law' (2015) 19(4) E&P 246.

[87] Copyright, Designs and Patents Act 1988, s 280.

[88] Trade Marks Act 1994, s 87.

[89] Administration of Justice Act 1985, s 33.

[90] Legal Services Act 2007, s 190.

[91] *Bullivant v A-G for Victoria* [1901] AC 196, HL.

[92] *R v Molloy* (Deceased) [1997] 2 Cr App R 283, CA.

[93] See *Waugh v British Railways Board* [1980] AC 521, HL at 531–2 per Lord Wilberforce, and also at 535–6 per Lord Simon. As to the court's respect for other confidential relationships, see Ch 21, **Confidential relationships**, p 689.

[94] [1996] AC 487, HL at 507–8.

[95] See per Bingham LJ in *Ventouris v Mountain* [1991] 1 WLR 607, CA at 611.

[96] See Alexander, 'The Corporate Attorney–Client Privilege: A Study of the Participants' (1989) St John's L Rev 191.

[97] [2004] QB 916, CA at [39].

of a will. It is not clear why it should. There would seem little reason to fear that, if privilege were not available in such circumstances, communications between solicitor and client would be inhibited.

Establishing the privilege

The evidential burden of establishing legal professional privilege is on the party claiming it.[98] The question of privilege is for the court, which must consider very carefully the evidence supporting the claim; an assertion of privilege or a statement of the purpose for which a document was created is not determinative. The evidence supporting the claim should show something of the deponent's analysis of the documents and the purposes for which they were created, preferably by reference to such contemporaneous material that can be referred to without disclosing the privileged matters. Usually the evidence should come from the persons whose motivation and state of mind is in issue, that is, the client or, if the client is a company, those responsible for instructing the lawyers on the company's behalf. Evidence from the lawyers will be of secondary value.[99] The court has a general discretion to inspect the document for which privilege is claimed to see whether the test has been correctly applied. Although it should be cautious about doing so, inspection is not limited to cases in which, without sight of the document, it is 'reasonably certain' that the test has been misapplied. The discretion should be exercised in accordance with the overriding objective.[100]

Communications between lawyer and client—legal advice privilege

General

A client may, and his lawyer must (subject to the client's waiver) refuse to disclose written or oral communications between them made for the purpose of giving or receiving legal advice about any matter, whether or not litigation was contemplated at the time.[101] The principle applies whether the client or lawyer is a party to the litigation in which the question arises or a mere witness; and it covers the production of documents containing or evidencing such communications as well as oral evidence about them. It also covers documents intended to be such communications, even if not in fact communicated.[102] There is no requirement to show that the purpose of giving or receiving legal advice was the dominant purpose.[103]

The communication must have been confidential and, if not actually made in the course of a relationship of lawyer and client, must at least have been made with a view to the establishment of that relationship.[104] A client care letter is not privileged if it merely sets out the terms on which the solicitor is to act for the client.[105] However, an engagement letter that sets out

---

[98] *Westminster International BV v Dornoch* [2009] EWCA Civ 1323 at [36].

[99] *Director of the Serious Fraud Office v Eurasian Natural Resources Corporation Ltd* [2017] EWHC 1017 (QB) at [39]–[41].

[100] *W H Holding Ltd v E20 Stadium LLP* [2018] EWCA Civ 2652.

[101] *Greenough v Gaskell* (1833) 1 My&K 98.

[102] See *Three Rivers District Council v Governor and Company of the Bank of England (No 5)* [2003] QB 1556, CA at [21].

[103] *Director of the Serious Fraud Office v Eurasian Natural Resources Corporation Ltd* [2019] 1 All ER 1026, CA at [131]–[132].

[104] *Minter v Priest* [1930] AC 558.

[105] *Dickinson v Rushmer* (2002) 152 NLJ 58. Confidential information passed to a solicitor but not covered by the privilege may be protected from disclosure, but the protection may be overridden by other considerations: see, in the case of contact details supplied simply for the purposes of enabling communication, *JSC BTA Bank v Solodchenko* [2013] Ch 1, Ch D and Ch 20, Confidential relationships, p 689.

what the advice will cover is privileged.[106] Legal advice privilege extends to the instructions given by the client to his solicitor, or by the solicitor to the barrister, and a barrister's opinion taken by a solicitor.[107] It does not extend to records of time spent with a client on attendance sheets, time sheets, or fee records, because they are not communications between client and legal adviser, or to records of appointments, because they are not communications made in connection with legal advice.[108] Similarly, such items as a conveyance or other legal document will not necessarily be protected by the privilege, unless made in connection with the giving of legal advice (or in connection with or in contemplation of legal proceedings and for the purposes of such proceedings).[109]

Provided that a communication was made in a professional capacity for the purposes of giving or receiving legal advice, the whole communication will be privileged, including any parts of it in which the solicitor conveyed to the client information which he had received in a professional capacity from a third party: such information cannot be hived off from the rest of what was said so as to become not privileged.[110] However, documents emanating from, or prepared by, independent third parties and then passed to the lawyer for the purposes of advice are not privileged. In *Three Rivers District Council v Governor and Company of the Bank of England (No 5)*[111] it was held that legal advice privilege only protects direct communications between the client and the lawyer, and evidence of the content of such communications, and that in the case of a corporate client the privilege will only cover (a) communications with those officers or employees expressly designated or nominated to act as 'the client' and not (b) documents prepared by other employees or ex-employees, even if prepared with the dominant purpose of obtaining legal advice, prepared at the lawyer's request, or sent to the lawyer. As to (a), the legal advice will remain privileged if sent to the Board of Directors directly, instead of via the 'designated officers or employees', because the Board is the manifestation of the corporate client.[112] If a solicitor is retained by a company to carry out investigations to provide it with legal advice and that requires him to speak to employees or others who are not 'designated officers or employees', the communications are not covered by legal advice privilege, even if the employees have been authorized by the company to speak to him.[113]

It is submitted that the 'designation' approach is too restrictive, not least because, as one commentator has pointed out, it operates in an unprincipled way to exclude other officers and employees with equivalent or greater authority to act 'as the client', such as, in the case in question, the Governor of the Bank.[114] Equally, however, the 'dominant purpose' test may be too wide and operate to prevent access to relevant facts. The answer may be to adopt the test used in the United States,[115] which limits the corporate client to those who play

---

[106] *Edward C Behague v The Commissioners for Her Majesty's Revenue & Customs* [2013] UKFTT 596 (TC).

[107] *Bristol Corpn v Cox* (1884) 26 Ch D 678.

[108] *R v Crown Court at Manchester, ex p Rogers* [1999] 1 WLR 832, DC.

[109] *R (Faisaltex Ltd) v Preston Crown Court* [2009] 1 WLR 1687, DC at [70], a decision under s 10 of the Police and Criminal Evidence Act 1984.

[110] *Re Sarah C Getty Trust* [1985] QB 956, QBD.

[111] [2003] QB 1556, CA.

[112] *Director of the Serious Fraud Office v Eurasian Natural Resources Corporation Ltd* [2017] EWHC 1017 (QB) at [84].

[113] *The RBS Rights Issue Litigation* [2016] EWHC 3161 (Ch) at [79]–[93], approved in *Director of the Serious Fraud Office v Eurasian Natural Resources Corporation Ltd* [2017] EWHC 1017 (QB) at [85]–[91].

[114] Loughrey, 'Legal advice privilege and the corporate client' (2005) 9 E&P 183. See also Passmore, 'Watch what you say' (2006) NLJ 668 April 21.

[115] See *Upjohn Co v United States* 499, US 383, 101 SCt 677 (1981) at 684.

a substantial role in deciding and directing the corporation's response to the legal advice given.[116] In *Director of the Serious Fraud Office v Eurasian Natural Resources Corporation Ltd*[117] the Court of Appeal said that it would have departed from *Three Rivers District Council v Governor of the Bank of England (No 5)*, if it had been open to it to do so. It noted that the case operates to the disadvantage of large corporations, where the information upon which the legal advice is sought is unlikely to be in the hands of the main board or 'designated officers or employees'; in the case of individuals and many small businesses, the information can normally be obtained by the individual or board members. It was also noted that the case is out of step with international common law in an area where commonality is desirable, particularly since so many multinational companies operate across borders and have subsidiaries in numerous common law countries.

Communications between opposing parties

There is generally no protection for communications between opposing parties or their advisers, unless they can be treated as 'without prejudice' settlement negotiations.[118] Thus the privilege does not cover a solicitor's attendance note recording what took place in chambers or in open court, in the course of a hostile litigation, in the presence of the parties on both sides.[119] Similarly, if a solicitor has made an attendance note of a meeting or telephone conversation between the lawyers for each side, any subsequent communication by the lawyers to their respective clients, informing them about the discussion, advising them, and seeking further instructions, will be privileged, but the attendance note itself is not privileged. This remains the case, even if the discussion was 'without prejudice', although that may prevent the note from being given in evidence until the without prejudice ban has been removed.[120]

Solicitor instructed by two clients

In *Buttes Gas and Oil Co v Hammer (No 3)*[121] it was held that where a solicitor is instructed by two clients, communications between him and one of the clients will not be privileged against the other client insofar as they concern the subject matter in which they are jointly interested but, whether or not the communication is disclosed to the other client, they will be protected as against outsiders. Thus where two parties employ the same solicitor for a conveyancing transaction, communications between either of them and the solicitor, in his joint capacity, must be disclosed in favour of the other. However, the waiver of privilege implied at the outset of a joint retainer ceases to apply in respect of communications made after the emergence of a conflict of interest between the two clients.[122] Similarly, the privilege cannot be claimed by

---

[116] For an assessment of the implications of adopting the various tests, see Loughrey, 'Legal advice privilege and the corporate client' (2005) 9 E&P 183. See also Swift and Querée, 'Practical thinking' (2015) NLJ 4 Sept 13.

[117] [2018] EWCA Civ 2006 at [123]–[130].

[118] *Grant v Southwestern and County Properties Ltd* [1975] Ch 185, Ch D: the plaintiff was obliged to produce on discovery a tape-recording of a discussion between the parties even though made for the purposes of instructing his solicitor in connection with contemplated litigation. However, if, after a meeting between opposing parties, one of them makes a record of the meeting for his solicitor, that record will be protected. 'Without prejudice' settlement negotiations are considered, in this chapter, under **Settlement negotiations**, p 749.

[119] *Ainsworth v Wilding* [1900] 2 Ch 315.

[120] *Parry v News Group Newspapers Ltd* [1990] NLJR 1719, CA.

[121] [1981] QB 223, CA (reversed on other grounds, [1982] AC 888, HL), applied in *Guinness Peat Properties Ltd v Fitzroy Robinson Partnership (a firm)* [1987] 1 WLR 1027, CA.

[122] *TSB Bank plc v Robert Irving & Burns (a firm)* [2000] 2 All ER 826, CA.

the directors of a company against its shareholders, except in the case of communications made for the purposes of litigation between the company and the shareholders.[123]

Where there has been no joint retainer, but advice has been given to directors of a company by solicitors retained by the company, then, except in cases where the directors and the company are in reality one and the same, a director, in order to succeed, when a claim of joint interest privilege is made, will need to establish that: he sought advice in an individual capacity; he made that clear to the lawyer; the lawyer knew or ought to have appreciated that he was communicating with the director on that basis; the company knew or ought to have appreciated the legal position; and the communication with the lawyer was confidential.[124]

Communications that do not specifically seek or convey legal advice

'Legal advice', for the purposes of legal advice privilege, does not mean advice given by a lawyer without more, but advice about legal rights and liabilities. However, some communications may enjoy privilege even if they do not specifically seek or convey legal advice. In *Balabel v Air-India*,[125] which concerned a conveyancing transaction, the privilege extended to communications between the appellants and their solicitors such as drafts, working papers, attendance notes, and memoranda. It was held that in most solicitor and client relationships, especially where a transaction involves protracted dealings, there will be a continuum of communications and meetings between the solicitor and client; and where information is passed between them as part of that continuum, the aim being to keep both informed so that legal advice may be sought and given as required, privilege will attach. However, in *Director of the Serious Fraud Office v Eurasian Natural Resources Corporation Ltd*[126] it was held that 'working papers' are protected only if they would betray the tenor of the legal advice given to the client; and a verbatim note of what the solicitor was told by a prospective witness is not, without more, covered by legal advice privilege just because the solicitor interviewed him with a view to using the information provided as a basis for advising his client. This was questioned on appeal, but the Court of Appeal declined to resolve the issue, having held that the interview notes in the case before it were covered by litigation privilege.[127]

In *Nederlandse Reassurantie Groep Holding NV v Bacon & Woodrow (a firm)*[128] it was held that where a solicitor's advice relates to the commercial wisdom of entering into a transaction in respect of which legal advice is also sought, all communications between the solicitor and the client relating to the transaction will be privileged, even if they do not contain advice on matters of law or construction, provided that they are directly related to the performance by the solicitor of his professional duty as legal adviser.[129] According to

---

[123] *Woodhouse & Co (Ltd) v Woodhouse* (1914) 30 TLR 559; *CAS (Nominees) Ltd v Nottingham Forest plc* [2001] 1 All ER 954, Ch D.

[124] *R (Ford) v Financial Services Authority* [2012] 1 All ER 1238, QBD.

[125] [1988] Ch 317, CA.

[126] [2017] EWHC 1017 (QB) at [95]–[97].

[127] *Director of the Serious Fraud Office v Eurasian Natural Resources Corporation Ltd* [2019] 1 All ER 1026, CA at [141]–[142].

[128] [1995] 1 All ER 976, QBD.

[129] See also *R v Crown Court at Inner London Sessions, ex p Baines and Baines* [1988] QB 579, DC: privilege does attach to advice given in conveyancing transactions on factors serving to assist towards a successful completion, including the wisdom or otherwise of proceeding with it, the arranging of a mortgage and so on, but does not attach to the records of the conveyancing transaction itself.

The Sagheera,[130] the practical emphasis should be on the dominant purpose of the retainer. If it is to obtain and give legal advice, although in theory individual documents may fall outside that purpose, in practice it is most unlikely that they will. If, however, the dominant purpose is some business purpose, the documents will not be privileged, unless exceptionally advice is requested or given, in which case the relevant documents probably are privileged.

The leading authority is *Three Rivers District Council v Governor and Company of the Bank of England (No 6)*.[131] After the collapse of the Bank of Credit and Commerce International (BCCI) in 1991, Bingham LJ was appointed to inquire into its supervision by the Bank of England, which had statutory responsibilities and duties in relation to UK banks. The Bank appointed a Bingham Inquiry Unit (BIU) to deal with all communications between the Bank and the inquiry and solicitors were retained to advise generally on all dealings with the inquiry. One of the main functions of the BIU was to prepare and communicate information and instructions to the Bank's solicitors. The solicitors gave advice as to the preparation and presentation of evidence to the inquiry and as to submissions to be made. After the publication of the inquiry report, depositors and BCCI, by its liquidators, brought proceedings against the Bank and sought the widest possible disclosure from the Bank. The Court of Appeal held that the only documents for which privilege could be claimed were communications between BIU and the solicitors seeking or giving advice as to legal rights and liabilities.

The House of Lords allowed the appeal of the Bank. Lord Scott accepted as correct the approach of Taylor LJ in *Balabel v Air India*,[132] who had said that, for the purpose of attracting the privilege, 'legal advice is not confined to telling the client the law; it must include advice as to what should prudently and sensibly be done in the relevant legal context' but that 'to extend privilege without limit to all solicitor and client communications upon matters within the ordinary business of a solicitor and referable to that relationship [would be] too wide'. Lord Scott said that if a solicitor became the client's 'man of business', responsible for advising him on matters such as investment and other business matters, the advice might lack a relevant legal context.[133] The judge would have to ask whether it related to the rights, liabilities, obligations, or remedies of the client under either private or public law, and, if so, whether the communication fell within the policy underlying the justification for the privilege, the criterion being an objective one. It was held that although there may be marginal cases where the answer is not easy, the present case was not marginal. The preparation of the evidence to be submitted, and the submissions to be made, to the inquiry had been for the purpose of enhancing the Bank's prospects of persuading the inquiry that its discharge of its public law obligations was not deserving of criticism and had been reasonable. The presentational advice given for that purpose had been advice 'as to what should prudently and sensibly be done in the relevant legal context', namely, the inquiry and whether the Bank had properly discharged its public law duties, and fell squarely within the policy reasons underlying legal advice privilege.

---

[130] [1997] 1 Lloyd's Rep 160, QBD at 168.

[131] [2005] 1 AC 610, HL.

[132] [1988] Ch 317 at 330–1.

[133] See, eg, *AAZ v BBZ* [2016] EWHC 3349 (Fam) (arranging insurance).

Communications with third parties—litigation privilege

General

In *W H Holdings Ltd v E20 Stadium LLP*[134] Sir Terence Etherton MR described the main principles governing the scope of litigation privilege in the following terms.

i)   Litigation privilege is engaged when litigation is in reasonable contemplation.

ii) Once litigation privilege is engaged it covers communications between parties or their solicitors and third parties for the purpose of obtaining information or advice in connection with the conduct of the litigation, provided it is for the sole or dominant purpose of the conduct of the litigation.

iii) Conducting the litigation involves deciding whether to litigate and also includes whether to settle the dispute giving rise to the litigation.[135]

iv) Documents in which such information or advice cannot be disentangled or which would otherwise reveal such information or advice are covered by the privilege.

v)   There is no separate head which covers internal communications falling outside the ambit of litigation privilege as described above.

The privilege, which is a basic or fundamental right, covers, for example, statements from potential witnesses and experts. It also attaches to the identity and other details of witnesses intended to be called in adversarial litigation, civil or criminal, and whether or not their identity was the fruit of legal advice.[136]

The privilege only applies in the context of proceedings that are adversarial, not investigative or inquisitorial.[137] The test is whether litigation was reasonably in prospect; it does not have to be shown that it was more likely than not that adversarial litigation would ensue but it is insufficient to show that there was only a possibility of litigation, even if a distinct possibility, or a general apprehension of future litigation.[138] On the question whether *criminal* proceedings were in reasonable contemplation, there is no general principle that privilege cannot attach until either a suspect knows the full details of what an investigation is likely to unearth or a decision to prosecute has been taken; and the fact that a formal investigation has not commenced will be relevant, but not necessarily determinative.[139]

The privilege covers documents 'brought into existence', that is created, by a party for the purpose of instructing the lawyer and obtaining his advice in the conduct of the litigation,[140] but not documents obtained by a party or his adviser for the purpose of litigation which did not come into existence for that purpose.[141] A copy or translation of an unprivileged

---

[134] [2018] EWCA Civ 2652 at [27].

[135] Thus in both civil and criminal cases the privilege can cover legal advice given to head off, avoid, or settle reasonably contemplated proceedings, including advice in a document created with the intention or understanding that it would be shown to the prospective adversary, eg, a position statement prepared for a mediation (*Director of the Serious Fraud Office v Eurasian Natural Resources Corporation Ltd* [2018] EWCA Civ 2006 at [102]).

[136] *R (Kelly) v Warley Magistrates' Court* [2008] 1 Cr App R 195.

[137] *Re L* [1997] AC 16, HL; *Three Rivers District Council v Governor and Company of the Bank of England (No 6)* [2005] 1 AC 610, HL.

[138] *USA v Philip Morris* [2003] EWHC 3028 (Comm) at 68.

[139] *Director of the Serious Fraud Office v Eurasian Natural Resources Corporation Ltd* [2018] EWCA Civ 2006 at [99]–[100], disapproving comments to the contrary approved, obiter, in *R v Jukes* [2018] 2 Cr App R 114 (9) at [23]. Such obiter approval is also to be found in *R (AL) v Serious Fraud Office* [2018] EWHC 856 (Admin) at [108].

[140] Per James LJ in *Anderson v Bank of British Columbia* (1876) 2 Ch D 644 at 656. See also *Southwark and Vauxhall Water Co v Quick* (1878) 3 QBD 315, CA.

[141] *Ventouris v Mountain, The Italia Express* [1991] 1 WLR 607, CA.

document in the control of a party does not become privileged merely because the copy or translation was made for the purpose of the litigation,[142] but privilege will attach to a copy of an unprivileged document if the copy was made for the purpose of litigation and the original is not and has not at any time been in the control of the party claiming privilege.[143] Privilege will also attach where a solicitor has copied or assembled a selection of third party documents for the purposes of litigation, if its production will betray the trend of the advice he is giving his client,[144] but this principle does not extend to a selection of own client documents, or copies or translations representing the fruits of such a selection, made for the purposes of litigation.[145]

The dominant purpose test

The leading authority is *Waugh v British Railways Board*.[146] The plaintiff's husband, an employee of the defendant, was killed in a railway accident. In proceedings for compensation, the plaintiff sought discovery of routine internal reports prepared by the defendant regarding the accident. The House of Lords held that, in order to attract privilege, the dominant purpose of preparation of the reports must have been that of submission to a legal adviser for use in relation to anticipated or pending litigation. While this was undoubtedly one of the purposes of the reports, it was not the dominant one, another equally important purpose being to inform the Board about the cause of the accident in order that steps could be taken to avoid recurrence. Accordingly, privilege could not be claimed and disclosure of the reports was ordered.

The dominant purpose test, which in each case involves a determination of fact, can give rise to difficulty.[147] However, in many cases of accident investigation it will be possible to conclude that the major purpose was the prevention of recurrence. The courts will not be deterred from reaching such a conclusion, where appropriate, even if those under whose direction the report was prepared depose that its dominant purpose was submission to solicitors in anticipation of litigation and the report itself refers only to that purpose.[148] In *Neilson v Laugharne*[149] the plaintiff's demand for compensation for alleged police misconduct prompted the police to initiate the statutory complaints procedure. Statements taken for the purpose of that procedure were clearly obtained in anticipation of litigation but it was held that the dominant purpose was that of the complaints procedure. The statements therefore did not attract legal professional privilege in subsequent litigation against the police. In *Re Highgrade Traders Ltd*,[150] by contrast, it was held that the dominant purpose of the preparation of reports procured by an insurance company from specialists in fire investigations, in a case where arson was suspected, was to assess the strength of a claim which, if persisted

---

[142] *Dubai Bank Ltd v Galadari* [1990] Ch 98, CA (copies) and *Sumitomo Corp v Credit Lyonnais Rouse Ltd* [2002] 1 WLR 479, CA.

[143] *The Palermo* (1883) 9 PD 6, CA and *Watson v Cammell Laird & Co Ltd* [1959] 1 WLR 702, CA.

[144] *Lyell v Kennedy (No 3)* (1884) 27 Ch D 1.

[145] *Sumitomo Corp v Credit Lyonnais Rouse Ltd* [2002] 1 WLR 479, CA.

[146] [1980] AC 521.

[147] Especially in the case of reports prepared by liquidators where litigation is a real possibility (see, eg, *Rawlinson and Hunter Trustees SA v Akers* [2014] EWCA Civ 136) and investigations by companies under threat of a claim by HMRC (see, eg, *Bilta (UK) Ltd (in liquidation) v Royal Bank of Scotland plc* [2017] EWHC 3535 (Ch)).

[148] See *Lask v Gloucester Health Authority* (1985) 2 PN 96, CA.

[149] [1981] QB 736, CA.

[150] [1984] BCLC 151, CA.

in, would in all likelihood have resulted in litigation. The insurance company was primarily interested in questions of liability rather than prevention or recurrence. Oliver LJ made it clear that the privilege will attach to a document, whether it was 'brought into existence' before or after a decision was made to instruct a solicitor, provided that litigation was reasonably in prospect and the document was prepared for the sole or dominant purpose of enabling a solicitor to advise whether a claim should be made or resisted.

In *Guinness Peat Properties Ltd v Fitzroy Robinson Partnership (a firm)*[151] it was held that the dominant purpose of a document should be ascertained by an objective view of the evidence as a whole, having regard not only to the intention of its author, but also to the intention of the person or authority under whose direction it was procured. The plaintiffs, building developers, had notified the defendants, engaged by them to act as architects for the construction of a building, of an alleged design fault. The defendants, in order to comply with the condition of their insurance policy, which required immediate notification of claims, thereupon wrote a letter to their insurers enclosing relevant memoranda and expressing their own views on the merits of the claim. In the course of discovery in the action which ensued, the question arose whether the letter was privileged. The defendants conceded that it was not *their* purpose, in writing the letter, to obtain legal advice or assistance. The Court of Appeal held that it could look beyond that intention to the intention of the insurers who had procured its genesis. Their intention, in requiring an immediate written notice of claim, was to enable them to submit it, together with other relevant documentation, to their lawyers for advice on whether the claim should be resisted. The letter was therefore privileged.

In *Jones v Great Central Rly Co*,[152] it was held that if a client communicates with a lawyer via a third party who is merely an agent for communication, privilege can be claimed, but that if the third party has to make a preliminary decision on the matter, the privilege is lost. Accordingly, it was held that no privilege attached to information supplied by a dismissed employee to a trade union official for the purpose of enabling the latter to decide whether to refer the claim to the union's lawyers. This case was distinguished in the *Guinness Peat Properties* case on the grounds, inter alia, that the relationship between the trade union and the member was not the equivalent of that between the insurers and the insured where the insurers were, in all but name, the effective defendants to any proceedings. It was further held that since the insurers and the insured had a common interest and a common lawyer, the principle in *Buttes Gas and Oil Co v Hammer (No 3)*[153] applied: the letter was privileged in the hands of each of them as against all outsiders.

In *Re Barings plc*[154] Sir Richard Scott V-C doubted the correctness of the decisions in both *Re Highgrade Traders Ltd* and the *Guinness Peat Properties* case on the grounds that disclosure of the documents in those cases would not have impinged upon the inviolability of lawyer/client communications. In his view, the reason for extending the privilege to documents brought into existence for the dominant purpose of litigation is to prevent the disclosure of documents which will reveal the lawyer's view of his client's case or the advice he has given, and therefore there is no general privilege for such documents independent of the need to keep inviolate communications between client and legal adviser. Thus if the documents do

---

[151] [1987] 2 All ER 716, CA.
[152] [1910] AC 4, HL.
[153] [1981] QB 223, CA; see, in this chapter, under **Solicitor instructed by two clients**, p 729.
[154] [1998] Ch 356, Ch D.

not relate in some fashion to such communications, there is no element of public interest to override the ordinary rights of litigants on discovery. In *Re Barings plc* a report on the conduct of the directors of Barings Bank was prepared on behalf of administrators in compliance with their statutory duty to report to the Department of Trade and Industry, under s 7(3) of the Company Directors Disqualification Act 1986, where it appeared to them that the conduct of directors made them unfit to be concerned in the management of a company. In subsequent disqualification proceedings, the Secretary of State resisted inspection of the report on the grounds of privilege. The Vice-Chancellor held that the report was not privileged. *Re Highgrade Traders Ltd* and the *Guinness Peat Properties* case were distinguished on the basis that, whereas in those cases the makers of the documents had a choice whether to bring them into existence and it was therefore possible to investigate their purpose in doing so, the maker of a s 7(3) report is obliged by law to make the report, which is not procured by anyone. It was accepted that the statutory purpose underlying s 7(3) was to assist the Secretary of State to decide whether to commence disqualification proceedings, and that Parliament must have expected that the Secretary of State, in reaching his decision, would put the report before his legal advisers for their advice, but it was held that the question of privilege depended not on identifying this parliamentary purpose and expectation, but on whether there was a public interest requiring protection from disclosure sufficient to override the disclosure rights given to litigants. In the absence of any such public interest, it was ruled that the report was not protected from disclosure.

The rules on disclosure in civil cases

Where a proof of evidence from a witness is privileged, CPR r 32 does not compel disclosure, but if the party who took the proof wishes to adduce evidence of fact from the witness at the trial, then he is generally required to disclose it in advance.[155] Once the statement has been disclosed, it is no longer privileged.[156] Similar principles apply in the case of a written opinion of an expert that is protected by privilege.[157]

Disclosure of evidence in criminal cases

Provision has also been made for the mutual disclosure of expert evidence in criminal cases.[158] The defence, in advance of a trial on indictment, are also entitled to know not only the evidence the prosecution intend to call, but also, as a general rule, 'unused material', that is statements from persons on whose evidence the prosecution do not intend to rely.[159]

Items enclosed with or referred to in communications

Under s 10(1)(c) of the 1984 Act, as we have seen, material subject to legal professional privilege includes items, enclosed with or referred to in communications covered by the two

---

[155] See generally Ch 5, Witness statements, p 150.

[156] Thus it may be relied upon, by the other party, in support of an application for specific disclosure of documents referred to in it: *Black & Decker Inc v Flymo Ltd* [1991] 1 WLR 753, Ch D (citing *Comfort Hotels Ltd v Wembley Stadium Ltd* [1988] 1 WLR 872, Ch D), a decision under the Rules of the Supreme Court Ord 38, r 2A, the precursor to the current rules.

[157] See generally Ch 20, The contents of the expert's report, p 665 and Disclosure, non-disclosure, and inspection, p 666.

[158] See Ch 20, Restrictions on, and disclosure of, expert evidence in criminal cases, p 668.

[159] The disclosure of unused material, a large topic outside the scope of this work, is governed by the scheme to be found in Pt 1 (ss 1–21) of the Criminal Procedure and Investigations Act 1996.

categories of protected material, which were made in connection with the giving of legal advice, etc. An 'item' could include, for example, a model made, or a bodily sample taken, for the purpose of obtaining expert advice. In *R v R*,[160] in which a scientist had carried out DNA tests at the request of the defence solicitors on a blood sample provided by the accused, it was held that the prosecution were not entitled either (i) to produce the sample in evidence; or (ii) to adduce the opinion evidence of the scientist based on the sample. Section 10(1)(c) was said to apply to both issues. The word 'made' meant 'brought into existence' for the purpose of obtaining legal advice, etc; the sample was an item 'made' for such a purpose; and therefore the accused was entitled to object both to its production and, whether or not it was produced or no longer existed, to opinion evidence based upon it.

The subject matter of privilege

Communications not facts

Under the doctrine of legal professional privilege, the client may avoid disclosure of his instructions to his lawyer and of his lawyer's advice to him: the lawyer may still be compelled to give evidence of facts directly perceived by him, if relevant to the facts in issue, even though his perception of them only occurred in the course of an interview with his client. Thus he may be required to admit the fact of having met his client and to give evidence about the physical or mental condition of his client[161] or about his handwriting.[162] Similarly, a solicitor present in court when his client was sentenced may be compelled in a subsequent prosecution to give evidence as to the identity of that person and to produce attendance notes, with anything attracting privilege blacked out.[163]

Pre-existing documents

Whereas privilege does attach to a document prepared for the purposes of obtaining legal advice, a pre-existing document given into the custody of a solicitor for the purpose of obtaining such advice or sent by a solicitor to a third party in connection with the litigation can, at common law, attract no greater protection in the hands of the solicitor or third party than it had in the hands of the client.[164] Thus in *R v Justice of the Peace for Peterborough, ex p Hicks*,[165] in which the client had sent to his solicitor, for the purposes of gaining legal advice, a forged document, a warrant was ordered to search the solicitor's premises and seize the document. The document was not privileged in the hands of the solicitor because it would have been open to seizure by warrant in the hands of the client.[166] Similarly, in *R v King*[167] the prosecution in a case of conspiracy to defraud were able to subpoena a handwriting expert, instructed by the defence, to produce documents sent to him by the accused's solicitors as sample handwriting even though the instructions to him, and his report, remained privileged. A further

---

[160] [1994] 1 WLR 758, CA.

[161] *Jones v Godrich* (1845) 5 Moo PCC 16.

[162] *Dwyer v Collins* (1852) 7 Exch 639.

[163] *R (Howe) v South Durham Magistrates' Court* [2004] EWHC 362 (Admin).

[164] Cf *Lyell v Kennedy (No 3)* (1884) 27 Ch D 1.

[165] [1977] 1 WLR 1371, DC.

[166] Dicta of Swanwick J in *Frank Truman Export Ltd v Metropolitan Police Comr* [1977] QB 952, which provide the only authority to the contrary, were doubted in *R v King* [1983] 1 WLR 411, CA.

[167] [1983] 1 WLR 411, CA.

example is furnished by *Financial Reporting Council Ltd v Sports Direct International plc*[168] where it was held that legal professional privilege cannot be claimed for a document not privileged in itself but attached to an email seeking or giving legal advice.

Under s 8 of the Police and Criminal Evidence Act 1984, warrants of entry and search may be issued if, inter alia, a justice of the peace is satisfied that the material sought does not consist of or include 'items subject to legal privilege' or 'special procedure material'. The phrase 'items subject to legal privilege', as we have seen, is defined in s 10 of the 1984 Act. In *R v Guildhall Magistrates' Court, ex p Primlaks Holdings Co*[169] Parker LJ held that s 10(1)(c) does not cover pre-existing documents which were not *made* in connection with the giving of legal advice or in connection with or in contemplation of legal proceedings and for the purposes of such proceedings, but that such documents would constitute 'special procedure material'. Under s 14(2), such material includes material, other than items subject to legal privilege, in the possession of a person who acquired or created it in the course of any trade, business, profession, etc and holds it subject to an express or implied undertaking to hold it in confidence.[170] Under s 9, the police may obtain access to 'special procedure material', for the purposes of a criminal investigation, by making an application *inter partes* to a circuit judge.[171] In the *Guildhall Magistrates' Court* case, Parker LJ held that a solicitor's correspondence with his client, and its enclosures, if not privileged, whether by reason of s 10(2) or otherwise, falls squarely within s 14(2) and that if the police are aware that what they seek includes items which are prima facie subject to legal privilege, they should not make an *ex parte* application under s 8, but should proceed under s 9 when the matter can be fully aired before a circuit judge.[172] However, it seems that a solicitor may voluntarily disclose special procedure material to the police because the object of the statutory provisions is to protect from disclosure not the suspect, but the person who has acquired or created the material, and it is for that person to decide whether he wishes to make disclosure, bearing in mind the degree of confidence reposed in him.[173]

Exceptions to the privilege

In *R v Derby Magistrates' Court, ex p B*[174] the appellant was suspected of murder. He admitted responsibility and was charged, but before his trial changed his story and alleged that his stepfather had carried out the murder and that although he, the appellant, was present and took some part, he did so under duress. At his trial, he was acquitted. The stepfather was subsequently charged with the murder and at the committal proceedings the appellant was called as a prosecution witness. The advocate for the defence sought to cross-examine him

---

[168] [2019] 2 All ER 974, Ch D.

[169] (1989) 89 Cr App R 215, DC at 225.

[170] A document forged by a solicitor or supplied by him to a fraudulent client is not special procedure material because, from its nature, it could not have been acquired or created in the course of the profession of a solicitor: *R v Leeds Magistrates' Court, ex p Dumbleton* [1993] Crim LR 866, DC.

[171] Each party should know what material the other is asking the court to take into account and should have a fair opportunity to respond to it and therefore the judge has no power to hear some of the evidence *ex parte*: *R (British Broadcasting Ltd) v Commissioner of Police of the Metropolis* [2014] UKSC 17.

[172] See also *R v Crown Court at Southampton, ex p J and P* [1993] Crim LR 962, DC.

[173] See *R v Singleton* [1995] 1 Cr App R 431, a decision relating to 'excluded material' within the meaning of s 11 of the 1984 Act.

[174] [1996] AC 487, HL.

about the factual instructions he had given to his solicitors prior to his allegation against his stepfather. The appellant declined to waive his privilege. The magistrates issued summonses directing the appellant and his solicitor to produce documentary evidence of the factual instructions, on the basis that the public interest that all relevant and admissible evidence should be made available to the defence outweighed the public interest which protected confidential communications between a solicitor and a client. An application for judicial review was refused, but the House of Lords allowed the appeal. It was held that since the client must be sure that what he tells his lawyer in confidence will never be revealed without his consent, there could be no question of a balancing exercise[175]—once any exception to the general rule is allowed, the client's confidence is necessarily lost. The solicitor would have to qualify his assurance and the purpose of the privilege would be undermined. However, Lord Nicholls, who also rejected any question of a balancing exercise, noted that in cases where the client no longer has any interest in maintaining the privilege, the privilege is spent. His Lordship preferred to reserve his final view on the point, but said:[176]

> I would not expect a law, based explicitly on considerations of the public interest, to protect the right of a client when he has no interest in asserting the right and the enforcement of the right would be seriously prejudicial to another in defending a criminal charge or in some other way.

Despite the sweeping pronouncements in the *Derby Magistrates* case as to the absolute and permanent nature of legal professional privilege, there are four exceptions: statutory provisions, fraud, reports for the purposes of care proceedings under the Children Act 1989 and cases in which instructions given or advice received are in issue in litigation.[177]

Statutory provisions

Statute may override the privilege either expressly or by necessary implication, the latter being one which necessarily follows from the express provisions of the statute construed in their context.[178] However, even if a statute does override the privilege, it may still be declared incompatible with the right of privacy under Art 8 of the European Convention on Human Rights, the European Court of Human Rights having said that the privilege is a fundamental human right which can be invaded only in exceptional circumstances.[179] A statute that allows *access* to privileged material will not necessarily override the privilege. *Avonwick Holdings Ltd v Willmont and Sayers*[180] concerned s 311(1) of the Insolvency Act 1986, whereby a trustee in bankruptcy shall take possession of certain documents belonging to the bankrupt including

---

[175] Overruling, in this respect, *R v Barton* [1973] 1 WLR 115, CC and *R v Ataou* [1988] QB 798, CA. See also *R (Morgan Grenfell) v Special Commissioner of Income Tax* [2003] 1 AC 563, HL and *B v Auckland District Law Society* [2003] 2 AC 736, PC.

[176] [1996] AC 487, HL at 513.

[177] A fifth exception was established in *R v Brown* [2015] EWCA Crim 1328 in circumstances which are likely to recur only very rarely. Communications between the accused and his lawyers took place in the presence of nurses to whom he was handcuffed in order to avoid the risk of him harming himself. There were no secure facilities at the court to remove the risk and there was no suggestion of misuse by the nurses of the privileged communications.

[178] See per Lord Hobhouse in *R (Morgan Grenfell) v Special Commissioner of Income Tax* [2003] 1 AC 563, HL at [45], applied in *B v Auckland District Law Society* [2003] 2 AC 736, PC.

[179] See per Lord Hoffmann, obiter, in *R (Morgan Grenfell) v Special Commissioner of Income Tax* [2003] 1 AC 563 at [7] and [39], citing *Foxley v UK* (2000) 8 BHRC 571 at 581.

[180] [2016] EWCA Civ 1138.

any which would be privileged from disclosure in any proceedings. It was held that the provision does not override privilege; the trustee may take possession of privileged documents and use information from them for the purpose of fulfilling his statutory function but cannot waive the bankrupt's privilege by passing the information on to third parties.[181]

Fraud

Fraud was referred to by Lord Lloyd in the *Derby Magistrates* case as 'a well-recognized exception'.[182] In *R v Cox and Railton*[183] it was held that if a client seeks legal advice intended to facilitate or guide him in the commission of a crime or fraud, the legal adviser being ignorant of the purpose for which the advice is sought, the communication between them is not privileged. The exception also applies if the solicitor *is* a party to the crime or fraud but not, it was held in *Butler v Board of Trade*,[184] if he merely volunteers a warning to the client that his conduct, if persisted in, may result in a prosecution. The exception can only be relied on if there is prima facie evidence of the client's criminal purpose.[185] Although the court may look at the communications themselves, if necessary, to determine whether they came into existence in furtherance of such a purpose,[186] as a rule it should not do so; there should be some exceptional factor of real weight before the court looks at the communications, and the mere fact that the test is not satisfied by other non-privileged material is not such a factor.[187]

The exception is not confined to cases in which solicitors advise on or set up criminal or fraudulent transactions yet to be undertaken, but also covers criminal or fraudulent conduct undertaken for the purposes of acquiring evidence in or for litigation.[188]

There are a number of limitations on the scope of this exception. First, although not limited to crimes, it does not extend to communications concerning all intended legal wrongs. In *Crescent Farm (Sidcup) Sports Ltd v Sterling Offices Ltd*[189] Goff J said:[190]

> It is clear that parties must be at liberty to take advice as to the ambit of their contractual obligations and liabilities in tort and what liability they will incur whether in contract or tort by a proposed course of action without thereby in every case losing professional privilege. I agree that fraud in this connection is not limited to the tort of deceit and includes all forms of fraud and dishonesty such as fraudulent breach of contract, fraudulent conspiracy, trickery and sham contrivances, but I cannot feel that the tort of inducing a breach of contract . . . comes within that ambit.

---

[181] See also *R v McE* [2009] AC 908, HL (covert surveillance of communications between someone in custody and his lawyer, as permitted by the Regulation of Investigatory Powers Act 2000); and *Financial Reporting Council Ltd v Sports Direct International plc* [2019] 2 All ER 974, Ch D (production to a regulator, by either the client of a regulated person or the regulated person himself, of documents privileged in the hands of the client, the production being solely for the purposes of a confidential investigation by the regulator into the conduct of the regulated person).

[182] [1996] AC 487 at 509.

[183] (1884) 14 QBD 153, CCR.

[184] [1971] Ch 680.

[185] *O'Rourke v Darbishire* [1920] AC 581. But see also *Derby & Co Ltd v Weldon (No 7)* [1990] 1 WLR 1156, Ch D: the court will be very slow to deprive a party of the privilege on an interlocutory application and will judge each case on its facts.

[186] *R v Governor of Pentonville Prison, ex p Osman* [1990] 1 WLR 277, QBD at 310.

[187] *BBGP Managing General Partner Ltd v Babcock & Brown Global Partners* [2011] Ch 296, Ch D.

[188] *Dubai Aluminium Co Ltd v Al Alawi* [1999] 1 WLR 1964, QBD.

[189] [1972] Ch 553.

[190] [1972] Ch 553 at 565.

Trespass and conversion are also outside the scope of the doctrine.[191] However, privilege will not attach to advice on a scheme, in breach of an employee's confidential duty of fidelity and involving the secret use of the employer's time and money, to take other employees (and the employer's customers) and to make profit from them in a competing business developed to receive them on leaving the employer's service.[192] Equally, if there is strong prima facie evidence that a transaction has been devised to prejudice the interests of a creditor by putting assets beyond his reach, privilege will not attach to legal advice on how to structure such a transaction.[193] The same reasoning applies to transactions intended to prevent or reduce financial relief in matrimonial proceedings.[194] Nor does privilege attach to advice on how to cloak as a dismissal for redundancy dismissal of an employee for making complaints of disability discrimination.[195]

In *Kuwait Airways Corporation v Iraqi Airways Co*[196] it was confirmed that the fraud exception can apply to litigation privilege, as well as legal advice privilege. It was also held that whereas a prima facie case of fraud may suffice where the issue of fraud is not one of the very issues in the action, where it is such an issue then a very strong prima facie case of fraud is required. In *Chandler v Church*[197] the plaintiffs alleged that the defendant had fraudulently manipulated to his own advantage various share transactions. They sought discovery of communications between him and his solicitors on the basis of prima facie evidence showing that he had obtained their assistance to enable him to mislead the court by putting forward false documents and pretending that certain transactions were genuine. Hoffmann J held that although it does not matter whether the fraud concerns an earlier transaction or the conduct of the proceedings in question, disclosure at an interlocutory stage based on prima facie evidence of fraud in the conduct of the very proceedings in which the discovery is sought carries a far greater risk of injury to the party against whom discovery is sought, should he turn out to have been innocent, than disclosure of advice concerning an earlier transaction. The risk of injustice to the defendant in being required to reveal communications with his lawyers for the purpose of his defence, together with the damage to the public interest which the violation of such confidences would cause, outweighed the risk of injustice to the plaintiffs.[198]

In a criminal case, a claim to privilege can be defeated where there is evidence of a conspiracy to pervert the course of justice, but this can only happen, in a case where an alibi has been raised and the conspiracy relates to the alleged falsity of the alibi, if there is evidence of the conspiracy that is 'freestanding and independent' in the sense that it can be looked at in isolation from the case as a whole.[199]

The exception does not extend to the correspondence between a lawyer and an assignee or victim of a fraudsman. In *Banque Keyser Ullmann SA v Skandia (UK) Insurance Co Ltd*[200]

---

[191] Per Rix J in *Dubai Aluminium Co Ltd v Al Alawi* [1999] 1 WLR 1964, QBD at 1968.

[192] *Gamlen Chemical Co (UK) Ltd v Rochem Ltd* [1980] 1 All ER 1049.

[193] *Barclays Bank plc v Eustice* [1995] 1 WLR 1238, CA.

[194] *AAZ v BBZ* [2016] EWHC 3349 (Fam) at [21] and [22].

[195] *X v Y Ltd* UKEAT/0261/17/JOJ.

[196] [2005] 1 WLR 2734, CA.

[197] [1987] NLJ Rep 451, Ch D.

[198] See also *R v Crown Court at Snaresbrook, ex p DPP* [1988] QB 532. See also per Lord Goff in *Central Criminal Court, ex p Francis & Francis (a firm) v Central Criminal Court* [1989] AC 346, HL at 397.

[199] *R (Hallinan, Blackburn-Gitting and Nott (a firm)) v Middlesex Guildhall Crown Court* [2005] 1 WLR 766, applied in *R v Minchin* [2013] EWCA Crim 2412.

[200] [1986] 1 Lloyd's Rep 336, CA.

insurance policies, issued to borrowers to cover banks against failure of the borrowers to repay, were assigned to the banks. The loans were not repaid and the banks claimed under the policies. The insurers denied liability on the grounds that the policies had been obtained by the fraud of the borrowers. The contention of the insurers that by reason of the borrowers' fraud no privilege attached to the correspondence passing between the banks and their lawyers was rejected.

Section 10(2) of the 1984 Act, as we have seen, provides that 'items held with the intention of furthering a criminal purpose are not items subject to legal privilege'. In *R v Crown Court at Snaresbrook, ex p DPP*[201] it was held, giving these words their natural meaning, that it is the person holding the items in question whose intention is relevant. This construction was rejected in *R v Central Criminal Court, ex p Francis & Francis (a firm)*.[202] A majority of the House of Lords was of the opinion that s 10(2) was intended to reflect the position at common law, and not to restrict the principle of *R v Cox and Railton* to those cases in which the legal adviser has the intention of furthering a criminal purpose; and therefore that the intention referred to in that subsection could be that of the person holding the document or that of any other person.[203] Accordingly, it was held that conveyancing documents innocently held by a solicitor in relation to the purchase of a property by a client, intended by a third party, a relative of the client, to be used to further the criminal purpose of laundering the proceeds of illegal drug trafficking, were not items subject to legal privilege.[204]

In *R v Leeds Magistrates' Court, ex p Dumbleton*[205] a warrant was issued to search for and seize documents held by a solicitor and allegedly forged by him and another. It was held that the documents were not covered by s 10(1), because the phrase 'made in connection with . . . legal proceedings' meant lawfully made and did not extend to forged documents or copies thereof; and in any event the items were held with the intention of furthering a criminal purpose, the word 'held' in s 10(2) relating to the time at which the documents came into the possession of the person holding them.

Proceedings under the Children Act 1989

Care proceedings under the Children Act 1989 are non-adversarial: the court's duty is to investigate and to undertake all necessary steps to arrive at an appropriate result in the paramount interests of the welfare of the child. If a party to such proceedings, on obtaining an unfavourable expert's report, were to be able to suppress it and maintain a case at variance with it, judges would sometimes decide cases affecting children in ignorance of material facts and in a way detrimental to their best interests. For these reasons, in *Oxfordshire County Council v M*[206] it was held that in care proceedings in which the court gives leave to a party

---

[201] [1988] QB 532, QBD.

[202] [1989] AC 346, HL.

[203] As Lord Oliver observed, however, in his powerful dissenting judgment: 'There is not, so far as I am aware, any authority in the common law dealing with the question of whether a criminal intent on the part of a stranger to the relationship of solicitor and client destroys the privilege of the client. If, therefore, the subsection does indeed bear the meaning now sought to be ascribed to it . . . it is breaking new ground and the legislative intent has to be gathered not from some supposed logical extension of the common law rule but from the words which Parliament has chosen to use' (at 388). Cf *Banque Keyser Ullmann SA v Skandia (UK) Insurance Co Ltd* [1986] 1 Lloyd's Rep 336, CA (see text at n 200), to which none of their Lordships referred.

[204] See also *R v Crown Court at Northampton, ex p DPP* (1991) 93 Cr App R 376, DC.

[205] [1993] Crim LR 866, DC.

[206] [1994] 2 WLR 393, CA.

to obtain expert reports, it has power to override litigation privilege and require the report to be filed and served on the other parties. However, the promotion of the welfare of the child does not require that communications between a client and a lawyer should also be disclosed.[207] The same distinction was made in *Re L*,[208] where a majority of the House of Lords rejected a contention that the absolute nature of the privilege attaching to the solicitor–client relationship extends to all other forms of legal professional privilege. The majority approved *Oxfordshire County Council v M*, subject to one qualification: privilege had not been *overridden* in that case because it never arose in the first place, having been excluded by necessary implication from the terms and overall purpose of the 1989 Act. It has also been held that the exception under consideration does not extend to override privilege which has properly arisen and is maintainable in proceedings other than those under the 1989 Act, such as criminal proceedings against the father of the child.[209]

Instructions or advice in issue in litigation

Sometimes the question of what instructions were given to a lawyer or what advice was received may be an issue in the litigation, and this may result in privilege being abrogated. For example, where the court is asked to exercise its power under s 33 of the Limitation Act 1980 to allow an action to be brought out of time, it will be relevant for the court to know what advice the applicant received at various times as to his chances of success.[210] Similarly, the instructions given to a solicitor will have to be disclosed if a question arises whether or not the client authorized him to write letters to his opponent stating that he would accept a certain sum in settlement of his claim.[211]

Duration of the privilege

'As a general rule, one may say once privileged always privileged.'[212] Documents prepared for one set of proceedings continue to be privileged for the purpose of subsequent litigation, even if the litigation originally anticipated never took place;[213] and documents relating to property rights which are privileged in the hands of one person continue to be privileged in the hands of successors-in-title to the property.[214] In order to claim in a subsequent action the privilege which prevailed for the first action, there must be a sufficient connection of subject matter for the privileged material to be relevant to the subsequent action (because if the material is irrelevant the question of disclosure cannot even arise) and the person originally entitled to the privilege or his successor must be a party to the subsequent action; there is no additional requirement that the subject matter of the two actions should be identical or substantially the same or that the parties to the two actions should be the same.[215]

---

[207] *Oxfordshire County Council v M* [1994] 2 WLR 393, CA, per Steyn LJ at 405.

[208] [1997] 1 AC 16, HL.

[209] *S County Council v B* [2000] 2 FLR 161.

[210] *Jones v GD Searle & Co Ltd* [1979] 1 WLR 101, CA.

[211] *Conlon v Conlons Ltd* [1952] 2 All ER 462, CA.

[212] Per Lindley MR in *Calcraft v Guest* [1898] 1 QB 759, CA at 761.

[213] *Pearce v Foster* (1885) 15 QBD 114, CA.

[214] *Minet v Morgan* (1873) 8 Ch App 361; *Crescent Farm (Sidcup) Sports Ltd v Sterling Offices Ltd* [1972] Ch 553. The principle relates to assertion of the privilege, not waiver (*Re Lemos* [2018] 1 All ER 313, Ch D).

[215] *The Aegis Blaze* [1986] 1 Lloyd's Rep 203, CA.

Legal professional privilege is that of the client or his successor in title. Accordingly, a third party from whom a statement was obtained for the dominant purpose of anticipated or pending litigation cannot claim protection in respect of the contents of that statement if he himself becomes a party to wholly independent litigation. *Schneider v Leigh*[216] was an action in libel. The plaintiff was claiming, in other proceedings, damages for personal injuries against a company whose solicitors had obtained a medical report, to which privilege attached, from a doctor whom they intended to call as a witness in those proceedings. The plaintiff regarded the document as defamatory, began the instant action against the doctor, and sought disclosure of the full report. It was held that the doctor was not entitled to rely on the company's privilege. The court, however, recognizing that the personal injuries action had yet to be disposed of, ordered that inspection of the report should take effect only on the conclusion of that action.

Where there are likely to be joint proceedings against the client and the third party, it may be that the third party will nonetheless be effectively protected by the client's privilege. In *Lee v South West Thames Regional Health Authority*[217] the health authorities of Hillingdon (H) and South West Thames (SWT) were both involved in the treatment of a patient which went badly wrong. H, for the purpose of getting legal advice about anticipated litigation against themselves, obtained from SWT a report of their involvement. On an application against SWT under s 33(2) of the Senior Courts Act 1981 for pre-action discovery of the report, it was held that although the privilege was that of H and not SWT, it was SWT's right and duty to assert H's privilege until such time as H no longer had an interest in non-disclosure. Since the proceedings against H and SWT would go together, the plaintiff would be unable to use the report against either of them.

Secondary evidence

Legal professional privilege prevents evidence from being given, or documents from being produced, by particular persons: the client, his lawyer, the relevant third parties (where applicable), and any agents for communication, such as secretaries or clerks.[218] If some other person overhears a privileged conversation or obtains a privileged document or a copy of it, he may be compelled to give evidence in that regard or to produce the document or copy. The leading case, *Calcraft v Guest*,[219] involved *copies* of privileged documents, but it is clear that under the principle, the originals, if available, can be produced.[220] The principle operates not only where the communication was disclosed by inadvertence or error on the part of the person otherwise entitled to assert the privilege, but also where the communication was obtained by improper or even unlawful means.

In *R v Tompkins*[221] an incriminating note from the accused to his advocate was found on the floor of the court and handed to the advocate for the prosecution. The Court of Appeal

[216] [1955] 2 QB 195, CA.

[217] [1985] 1 WLR 845, CA.

[218] The same restrictions apply to a clinical case manager appointed to assist a severely injured person and involved in the client's litigation by attending conferences with lawyers and experts: *Wright v Sullivan* [2006] 1 WLR 172, CA.

[219] [1898] 1 QB 759, CA.

[220] See per Lord Simon in *Waugh v British Railways Board* [1980] AC 521 at 536; *Rumping v DPP* [1964] AC 814; and *R v Governor of Pentonville Prison, ex p Osman* [1990] 1 WLR 277, QBD at 310.

[221] (1977) 67 Cr App R 181.

upheld the judge's ruling allowing the prosecution to show the note to the accused and to cross-examine him as to matters referred to in it. It is submitted that the court was correct in holding that the accused could not actually be asked to prove the note, since he was still entitled to assert his privilege in relation to it, but in principle it must have been permissible for the prosecution to tender the note in evidence themselves, subject to the possibly difficult task of proving authorship. In *R v Cottrill*,[222] applying *R v Tompkins*, it was held that a statement made by the accused to his solicitors, and sent by them to the prosecution without his knowledge or consent, could be used by the prosecution in cross-examination as a previous inconsistent statement, subject to s 78 of the 1984 Act.[223]

A litigant who has in his possession copies of documents to which legal professional privilege attaches may use them as secondary evidence in the litigation, but if he has not yet used them in that way, the mere fact that he intends to do so will not prevent a claim against him, by the person in whom the privilege is vested, for delivery up of the copies and for an injunction to restrain him from disclosing or making any use of any information contained in them.[224] In *Lord Ashburton v Pape*,[225] a party to bankruptcy proceedings, obtained by a trick copies of confidential and privileged correspondence between Lord Ashburton and his solicitors. The Court of Appeal granted an injunction preventing Pape from using the copies in the bankruptcy proceedings. In deciding whether to grant an injunction, the normal rules relating to the grant of equitable remedies apply. Thus delay is a relevant factor, as is the conduct of the party seeking the injunction, including the clean hands principle. Where, as in *ISTIL Group Inc v Zahoor*[226] the privileged documents show that evidence has been forged and that there has been an attempt to mislead the court, the public interest in supporting the privilege will be outweighed by the public interest in the proper administration of justice.

The principle in *Lord Ashburton v Pape* is not confined to cases in which the privileged material is obtained by trickery. In *Guinness Peat Properties Ltd v Fitzroy Robinson Partnership (a firm)*[227] it was held that it may also apply where the privilege is lost by inadvertence. That was a case in which one party to litigation had, on disclosure, mistakenly included in his list of documents to the production of which he did not object, a document for which privilege could properly have been claimed and which should have been included in the list of documents to the production of which he did object. The relevant principles in this situation were summarized by Slade LJ as follows:[228]

1. The court will ordinarily permit the party who made the error to amend his list.[229]

2. Once the other party has inspected the document, the general rule is that it is too late for the first party to correct the mistake by applying for injunctive relief.[230]

---

[222] [1997] Crim LR 56, CA.

[223] See also *R v Willis* [2004] EWCA Crim 3472.

[224] Per May LJ in *Goddard v Nationwide Building Society* [1987] QB 670, CA at 683.

[225] [1913] 2 Ch 469, CA.

[226] [2003] EWHC 165 (Ch).

[227] [1987] 1 WLR 1027, CA.

[228] Ibid at 1045–6.

[229] See, eg, *C H Beazer (Commercial and Industrial) Ltd v R M Smith Ltd* (1984) 3 Const LJ 196.

[230] See *Re Briamore Manufacturing Ltd* [1986] 1 WLR 1429, Ch D. However, in that case the first party conceded that secondary evidence of the documents would be admissible and the court was not reminded of the decision in *Lord Ashburton v Pape*.

3. However, if the other party or his solicitor either (a) has procured inspection of the relevant document by fraud; or (b) on inspection realized that he has been permitted to see the document only by reason of an obvious mistake, the court has power to grant an injunction. Examples include *Goddard v Nationwide Building Society*,[231] in which the plaintiff's solicitors sent the defendant a copy of an attendance note recording conversations with the plaintiff, and the defendant thereupon pleaded the substance of the contents in his defence, and *English and American Insurance Co Ltd v Herbert Smith & Co*,[232] in which a clerk to a barrister instructed by the plaintiff's solicitor mistakenly handed over to the defendant's solicitors a bundle of papers including instructions to the barrister, the barrister's notes, letters from the solicitor to the plaintiff, and statements of witnesses. In both cases an injunction and an order for delivery up was granted.

4. In such cases, the court should ordinarily grant the injunction unless it can properly be refused on general principles affecting the grant of a discretionary remedy, for example on the grounds of inordinate delay.[233]

In *Webster v James Chapman & Co*[234] Scott J held that the court should balance the interests of the one party in seeking to keep the information confidential against the interests of the other in seeking to make use of it, taking account of not only the privileged nature of the document, but also such matters as how the document was obtained and its relevance to the issues in the action. This approach was rejected in *Derby & Co Ltd v Weldon (No 8)*.[235] The Court of Appeal, without referring to *Webster v James Chapman & Co*, held that where an injunction is sought in aid of legal professional privilege, the court is not required to carry out such a balancing exercise. Dillon LJ said:[236]

> where the privilege is being restored because the inspection was obtained by fraud or by taking advantage of a known mistake, there is to my mind no logic at all in qualifying the restoration of the status quo by reference to the importance of the document. 'You have taken advantage of an obvious mistake to obtain copies of documents; we will order you to return all the ones that are unimportant to you but you can keep the ones that are important' would be a nonsensical attitude for the court to adopt.

In deciding whether disclosure has occurred as a result of an obvious mistake, the party claiming the injunction has the burden of proving, on a balance of probabilities, that the mistake would have been obvious to a reasonable solicitor, rather than to the actual recipient of the disclosed document, although the reaction of the actual recipient can be relevant. A reasonable solicitor, in deciding whether the privilege had been waived, would approach the question without bias towards his client and would take into account such factors as the extent of the claim to privilege in the list of documents, the nature of the document disclosed, the complexity of the discovery, the way it had been carried out, and the surrounding

---

[231] [1987] QB 670, CA.

[232] [1988] FSR 232, Ch D.

[233] If solicitors realize that documents have been mistakenly disclosed to them but, on the instructions of their client read them, an injunction may also be granted to restrain them from acting for the client in the proceedings in question: see *Ablitt v Mills & Reeve* (1995) The Times, 25 Oct, Ch D.

[234] [1989] 3 All ER 939, Ch D.

[235] [1991] 1 WLR 73, CA.

[236] Ibid at 99. See also per Nourse LJ in *Goddard v Nationwide Building Society* [1987] QB 670, CA at 685.

circumstances. Thus in *IBM Corpn v Phoenix International*,[237] from which these principles derive, and in which discovery involving a substantial number of documents had been carried out under a tight timetable and without due care, it was held that a reasonable solicitor would have realized that there was a risk of mistakes being made and would not have concluded, as the recipient had, that a deliberate decision had been made to disclose a document containing legal advice. In *Pizzey v Ford Motor Co Ltd*,[238] on the other hand, where discovery was slight and not complex, a reasonable solicitor would have assumed that privilege had been waived deliberately and not in error.

CPR r 31.20 provides that in civil cases in which a party inadvertently allows a privileged document to be inspected, the party who has inspected the document may use it or its contents only with the permission of the court. The decision should be made in accordance with the principles established in the foregoing cases.[239]

Public policy may also prevent a party from relying upon the principle of *Calcraft v Guest*. In *ITC Film Distributors v Video Exchange Ltd*[240] documents were obtained by a trick in court in the course of civil proceedings. By that stage in the case there were difficulties in the way of granting injunctive relief, but the judge made interesting use of *D v NSPCC*[241] to hold that the public interest that litigants should be able to bring their documents into court without fear that they may be filched by their opponents, required an exception to the rule in *Calcraft v Guest*. The decision, it is submitted, correct in itself, results in an illogical distinction between documents stolen within court and those stolen without.

No less indefensible, it is submitted, is the distinction stemming from *Butler v Board of Trade*,[242] another decision made on grounds of public policy. It was held that the principle of *Lord Ashburton v Pape* cannot be used to prevent the prosecution from tendering relevant evidence in a public prosecution.[243] There is much to be said for allowing the spirit of *Lord Ashburton v Pape* to prevail in criminal as well as civil proceedings.[244]

Waiver

A client may elect to waive the legal professional privilege that he could otherwise assert. However, whether he has in fact waived privilege depends not on his subjective intention; it is determined by an objective analysis of his conduct.[245] If he has waived the privilege, he cannot then reassert it. Thus a litigant who deliberately produces a privileged document for inspection on disclosure or serves notice of a conversation with his solicitor under the notice provisions relating to hearsay in civil cases, cannot at trial claim privilege for that communication.[246] However, if a document has been disclosed for a limited purpose only, privilege will

---

[237] [1995] 1 All ER 413, Ch D.

[238] [1994] PIQR P15, CA.

[239] *Al Fayed v Metropolitan Police Commissioner* [2002] EWCA Civ 780.

[240] [1982] Ch 431.

[241] [1978] AC 171. See Ch 21, pp 680–1.

[242] [1971] Ch 680.

[243] The same point, in the case of a *private* prosecution, was expressly left open.

[244] Per Nourse LJ in *Goddard v Nationwide Building Society* [1987] QB 670, CA at 686; and see *R v Uljee* [1982] 1 NZLR 561, NZCA.

[245] *Armia Ltd v Daejan Developments Ltd* [1979] SC 56 at 72.

[246] Merely referring to the existence of a document in pleadings or affidavits will not amount to waiver, though quoting from it may do so: see *Tate & Lyle International Ltd v Government Trading Corpn* [1984] LS Gaz R 3341, CA.

not be waived generally, and the court is precluded from conducting a balancing exercise, because a lawyer must be able to give his client an unqualified assurance not only that what passes between them shall never be revealed without his consent, but also that should he consent to disclosure within limits, those limits will be respected.[247] Thus where privileged documents prepared by a claimant for a civil action against a person are handed over to the police in accordance with the claimant's duty to assist in a criminal investigation, charges are preferred against that person and copies of the documents are disclosed to him by the prosecution, this cannot be construed as either an express or implied waiver of the claimant's privilege in relation to the civil action, because to hold otherwise would be contrary to public policy.[248] Similarly, on the assessment of costs in civil cases, disclosure of privileged material is viewed as a waiver only for the purposes of the assessment: the privilege can be reasserted subsequently.[249]

The disclosure of part of a privileged document on disclosure constitutes a waiver of privilege of the entire contents of the document unless the other part deals with a separate subject matter so that the document can be divided into two separate and distinct documents.[250] Similarly, a litigant is not entitled to edit his evidence, relying on the favourable parts of a privileged communication but refusing to say anything about the rest. Thus if part of a privileged document is put in evidence at trial, the other side can require the whole document to be disclosed, unless the remaining part concerns such a distinct subject matter as to be capable of severance.[251] The question whether 'cherry picking' is taking place, so that fairness requires the whole document to be adduced to prevent the court from being misled by seeing only part of it out of context, can only be answered by the judge after he has read the whole of it.[252] Where a party deploys privileged material in interim proceedings, such as an application for summary judgment, in order to advance his case on the merits, such deployment engages the waiver principle, and the deploying party cannot then turn the clock back, even if he has not yet made up his mind whether to use the deployed material at trial.[253] However, a distinction has to be drawn between a reference to having been given advice to a particular effect, which does not amount to waiver of the right to claim privilege in respect of the advice itself at the subsequent trial, and disclosure of the substance or content of that advice, which does amount to such a waiver.[254]

---

[247] *B v Auckland District Law Society* [2003] 2 AC 736, PC.

[248] *British Coal Corpn v Dennis Rye Ltd (No 2)* [1988] 1 WLR 1113, CA. See also *Financial Reporting Council Ltd v Sports Direct International plc* [2019] 2 All ER 974, Ch D (waiver for statutory audit purposes not extending beyond the statutory auditor to the regulator of statutory auditors).

[249] See *Goldman v Hesper* [1988] 1 WLR 1238, CA (an inter partes assessment) and *Dechert LLP v Eurasian Natural Resources Corporation Limited* [2016] EWCA Civ 375 (a solicitor-own client assessment). See also *South Coast Shipping Co Ltd v Havant Borough Council* [2003] 3 All ER 779, Ch D.

[250] *Pozzi v Eli Lilly & Co* (1986) The Times, 3 Dec, QBD.

[251] *Great Atlantic Insurance Co v Home Insurance Co* [1981] 1 WLR 529, CA. See also *George Doland Ltd v Blackburn, Robson, Coates & Co* [1972] 1 WLR 1338, QBD: if a client seeks to support his credit at trial by reference to what he said to his solicitor on one occasion, he cannot object to being cross-examined as to what he said to his solicitor about the same subject matter on other occasions.

[252] *Derby & Co Ltd v Weldon (No 10)* [1991] 1 WLR 660, Ch D.

[253] *Dunlop Slazenger International Ltd v Joe Bloggs Sports Ltd* [2003] EWCA Civ 901 and *Berezovsky v Abramovich* [2011] EWHC 1143 (Comm).

[254] *Derby & Co Ltd v Weldon (No 10)* [1991] 1 WLR 660, Ch D. See also *Hellard v Irwin Mitchell* [2012] EWHC 2656 (Ch) and *Re D (a child)* [2011] 4 All ER 434, CA.

If a cross-examining advocate puts to an opposing witness a statement taken on behalf of his own client, even only a small part of it, he waives his client's privilege in the statement and thereby entitles the advocate for the party who called the witness to re-examine him on the whole of the statement. However, the risk of permitting such lengthy re-examination can be avoided either by the advocates agreeing that part only of a statement may be put without the whole being opened up for re-examination, or by the cross-examining advocate preparing written questions to be handed to the witness either in the witness-box or several days previously.[255] If it is suggested to an accused that his evidence on specific matters is a recent invention and his solicitor is called to give evidence in rebuttal, the questioning of the solicitor will be confined to the specific matters, but if the accused discloses the solicitor's attendance notes, this amounts to a waiver of privilege of their entire contents.[256]

The principle under discussion, if taken to extremes, could lead to the disclosure of a vast array of otherwise privileged material, including proofs of evidence, memoranda prepared by solicitors, and instructions to barristers.[257] The courts have therefore been obliged to find ways of limiting the principle. In *George Doland Ltd v Blackburn, Robson, Coates & Co*[258] a distinction was drawn between legal advice and litigation privilege. It was held that oral conversations and documents relating to the subject matter in question were only liable to disclosure insofar as they were covered by the first type of privilege. A different approach, however, was adopted in *General Accident Fire and Life Assurance Co Ltd v Tanter*.[259] In that case privilege had been waived in relation to a conversation which took place at a time when litigation was anticipated and to which litigation privilege applied. Hobhouse J held that if the party entitled to the privilege puts the conversation in evidence (as opposed to being cross-examined about it) then waiver relates to 'the transaction', that is, what was said on the occasion in question, and does not extend to the subject matter of the conversation. Thus although the opposite party is entitled to call for, inspect, and cross-examine on other privileged communications relating to what was actually said in the conversation, he is not entitled to see or use such other privileged communications as may exist relating to the subject matter of the conversation.[260]

Fulham Leisure Holdings Ltd v Nicholson Graham and Jones (a firm)[261] makes clear that the decision on disclosure may involve a number of different stages. The starting point is to identify the 'transaction' or 'act' in respect of which disclosure was made. That may be identifiable simply from the nature of the disclosure; one is entitled to look at the purpose for which the material was disclosed or the point in the action to which it was said to go. However,

---

[255] *Fairfield-Mabey Ltd v Shell UK Ltd* [1989] 1 All ER 576, QBD.

[256] *R v Hall* [2015] EWCA Crim 581.

[257] Suggested in argument in *General Accident Fire and Life Assurance Co Ltd v Tanter* [1984] 1 WLR 100, though on the facts the judge was able to avoid that result.

[258] [1972] 1 WLR 1338, QBD.

[259] [1984] 1 WLR 100.

[260] Hobhouse J declined to follow *George Doland Ltd v Blackburn, Robson, Coates & Co* [1972] 1 WLR 1338 insofar as it could be treated as an authority to the contrary. It was also held that the distinction drawn in that case between the two types of privilege was not a criterion applicable in all cases and was not applicable in the instant case. See also *Derby & Co Ltd v Weldon (No 10)* [1991] 1 WLR 660, Ch D, where Vinelott J, in the case of a single conversation, different parts of which were covered by the different types of privilege, refused to sever the two types of privilege and to say that one was waived but not the other: both had been waived.

[261] [2006] 2 All ER 599, ChD.

the court should determine objectively what the real transaction is. If it is wider than at first thought and only part of the material involved in the transaction has been disclosed, further disclosure will be ordered. Finally, if it is apparent from the disclosure that the transaction is in fact part of 'some bigger picture', then further disclosure will be ordered if necessary to avoid unfairness or misunderstanding of what has previously been disclosed.

The institution of civil proceedings by a client against his solicitor constitutes an implied waiver of privilege. The waiver can only extend to matters which are relevant to an issue in the proceedings, but must go far enough not merely to enable the client to establish his cause of action but to enable the solicitor to establish a defence. Thus it may extend beyond the communications relating to the specific retainer forming the subject matter of the proceedings to communications relating to earlier retainers which are relevant to the issue between the parties.[262] However, there is no implied waiver of privilege merely because a person's state of mind or actions are in issue and his state of mind or actions may have been influenced by legal advice.[263]

Without prejudice negotiations

Settlement negotiations

General

Communications between opposing parties to a civil action, or between their solicitors, do not attract legal professional privilege. In the absence of any other protection, therefore, if one party were to make a concession on the question of liability in the course of settlement negotiations which, in the event, were to fail, the other party would be able to use it against him at the trial as a damaging admission. In order to remove this risk and thereby encourage the settlement of civil litigation, the rule is that privilege attaches to oral or written statements made 'without prejudice', that is without prejudice to the maker of the statement if the terms he proposes are not accepted.[264] The privilege is the joint privilege of both parties and extends to their solicitors.[265] It can only be waived with the consent of each of the parties.[266] The protection of admissions against interest is the most important practical effect of the rule, but to dissect out admissions and withhold protection from the rest of without prejudice communications would be to create huge practical difficulties and would be contrary to the underlying objective of giving protection to the parties to speak freely about all the issues in the litigation.

---

[262] *Lillicrap v Nalder & Son (a firm)* [1993] 1 WLR 94, CA. Cf *Nederlandse Reassurantie Groep Holding NV v Bacon & Woodrow (a firm)* [1995] 2 Lloyd's Rep 77, QBD, where NRG, having obtained advice from lawyers and other professionals, began proceedings against its *non-legal advisers*.

[263] *Farm Assist Ltd (in liquidation) v Secretary of State for Environment, Food and Rural Affairs* [2008] EWHC 3079 (TCC).

[264] See per Lindley LJ in *Walker v Wilsher* (1889) 23 QBD 335, CA at 337. See also, in the case of pre-termination negotiations between employer and employee: s 14 of the Enterprise and Regulatory Reform Act 2013. There is nothing in criminal law akin to 'without prejudice': *R v Hayes* [2005] 1 Cr App R 557, CA, where the prosecution were entitled to cross-examine H on a previous inconsistent statement in a letter sent by his solicitor to the CPS suggesting that he might plead guilty to a lesser offence.

[265] *La Roche v Armstrong* [1922] 1 KB 485.

[266] Inclusion of a without prejudice document in a party's list of documents on disclosure does not amount to waiver: *Galliford Try Construction Ltd v Mott MacDonald* [2008] EWHC 603 (TCC).

As Walker LJ observed in *Unilever plc v The Procter & Gamble Co*,[267] 'Parties cannot speak freely at a without prejudice meeting if they must constantly monitor every sentence, with lawyers . . . sitting at their shoulders as minders.'[268] Thus in *Ofulue v Bossert*[269] the House of Lords held that privilege attaches to a statement made in without prejudice negotiations if it is an 'admission' of a matter that the parties do not even dispute and therefore is not in issue. In *Muller v Linsley & Mortimer (a firm)*[270] Hoffmann LJ said that the public policy basis of the privilege is to prevent anything said from being used as an admission, that is, for the truth of the facts admitted, rather for some other relevant purpose, for example to show the falsity of the statement or simply to establish the fact that the admission was made.[271] In *Ofulue v Bossert*, however, a majority of the House held that such a distinction was too subtle to apply in practice and would often risk falling foul of the problem identified by Walker LJ (in the passage just quoted).

The basis of the rule is one of public policy, to encourage those in dispute to settle their differences without recourse to, or continuation of, litigation, and in *Barnetson v Framlington Group Ltd*[272] it was held that to give full effect to this policy, a dispute may engage the rule notwithstanding that litigation has not begun. On the question of how proximate negotiations must be to the start of the litigation, the court held that the privilege is not confined to negotiations once litigation has been threatened or shortly before it has begun, because that would be an incentive to the parties to escalate the dispute in order to gain the benefit of the rule. On the other hand, the ambit of the rule should not be extended further than necessary in the circumstances of any particular case to promote the policy underlying it. Auld LJ held that the question is highly case sensitive; that the claim to privilege cannot turn on purely temporal considerations; and that the crucial consideration will be whether, in the course of the negotiations, the parties contemplated or might reasonably have contemplated litigation if they could not agree.

Without prejudice privilege may be asserted at the trial itself, whether in relation to liability, quantum, or costs.[273] It may also be asserted in interim proceedings such as a hearing of a summons for security for costs.[274] There is no general exception to the exclusionary rule in interim proceedings.[275] The contents of without prejudice correspondence can be disclosed in an application to strike out for want of prosecution, but if it fails the privilege can be asserted at the trial itself.[276] However, where, on an interim application, one party deploys without prejudice material in support of his case on the underlying merits of the claim, the other party is entitled to use other parts of that material at the trial.[277]

---

[267] [2000] 1 WLR 2436, CA at 2449.

[268] However, there is nothing to prevent the parties from expressly agreeing that some parts of their discussions are 'without prejudice' and that others are 'on the record', ie unprotected: *R v K(A)* [2010] 1 Cr App R 44, CA. The issue whether a party's conduct amounts to waiver may occasion difficulty, especially in the case of a litigant in person: see *Sang Kook Suh v Mace (UK) Limited* [2016] EWCA Civ 4.

[269] [2009] UKHL 16.

[270] [1996] PNLR 74, CA.

[271] See also per Lord Hoffmann in *Bradford & Bingley plc v Rashid* [2006] 1 WLR 2066, HL at 2072.

[272] [2007] 1 WLR 2443, CA.

[273] *Walker v Wilsher* (1889) 23 QBD 335, CA. But see also, in this chapter, under **Offers without prejudice except as to costs**, p 754.

[274] *Simaan General Contracting Co v Pilkington Glass Ltd* [1987] 1 WLR 516, CA.

[275] *Leigh Ravenscroft v Canal & River Trust* [2016] EWHC 2282 (Ch).

[276] *Family Housing Association (Manchester) Ltd v Michael Hyde & Partners (a firm)* [1993] 1 WLR 354, CA.

[277] *Somatra Ltd v Sinclair Roche and Temperley* [2000] 1 WLR 2453. See also CPR r 31.22.

If the negotiations succeed and a settlement is concluded, the without prejudice correspondence remains privileged: such correspondence is inadmissible in any subsequent litigation connected with the same subject matter, whether between the same or different parties, and is also protected from subsequent disclosure to other parties to the litigation.[278] Similarly, in a case in which negotiations did not result in a settlement, it was held that it is 'strongly arguable' that the principles governing the admissibility, in subsequent proceedings, of a statement made in without prejudice negotiations to settle earlier proceedings, should be the same as those which would govern its admissibility in the earlier proceedings, and that it is hard to see how the contrary could even be argued where the two sets of proceedings involve the same parties and very closely connected issues.[279] However, if evidence of damaging admissions made in the course of 'without prejudice' communications falls into the hands of the prosecuting authorities, it is admissible in subsequent criminal proceedings against the party who made the admissions, subject to the discretion to exclude under s 78 of the 1984 Act, because the public interest in prosecuting crime is sufficient to outweigh the public interest in the settlement of disputes.[280]

The essential pre-condition for a claim to without prejudice privilege is the existence of a dispute. Thus in *Bradford & Bingley plc v Rashid*[281] the House of Lords held that the without prejudice rule had no application to open communications between a creditor and a debtor which dealt only with whether, when, and to what extent the debtor could meet his admitted liability. For a majority of their Lordships, since the debt was admitted, there was simply no dispute to be compromised.[282] Whether there is a dispute is sometimes a question of some nicety, as in *BNP Paribas v Mezzotero*.[283] While a grievance of M about perceived discrimination was being processed, the employer convened a without prejudice meeting, said to be independent of the grievance, at which M was advised that her job was no longer viable and an offer of a redundancy package was made. In a subsequent tribunal application claiming, inter alia, sex discrimination, it was held that M could rely on what was said at the meeting because there was no dispute at that time. Upholding this ruling, the Employment Appeal Tribunal held that there was no evidence of an employment dispute before the meeting. The grievance related to her continuing employment, not the threat of termination of employment, and therefore could not be treated as evidence of a dispute.

Conciliation and mediation schemes

The privilege attaches to any discussions that take place between actual or prospective parties with a view to avoiding litigation, including discussions within conciliation and mediation schemes.[284] The principles governing confidentiality, privilege, and without prejudice privilege in relation to mediation proceedings are as follows. The proceedings are confidential as

---

[278] *Rush & Tompkins Ltd v Greater London Council* [1989] AC 1280, HL. However, the privilege will not prevent inspection of the terms of a settlement if relevant in determining the extent of the liability of a third party against whom one of the parties to the settlement is seeking a contribution: *Gnitrow Ltd v Cape plc* [2000] 1 WLR 2327, CA.

[279] *Ofulue v Bossert* [2009] UKHL 16.

[280] *R v K(A)* [2010] QB 343, CA. Cf s 54(3) of the Evidence Act 2006 (NZ).

[281] [2006] 1 WLR 2066, HL.

[282] Equally, the privilege will not protect correspondence designed to prevent a dispute arising: *Prudential Assurance Co Ltd v Prudential Insurance Co of America* [2002] EWHC 2809, Ch D.

[283] [2004] IRLR 508, EAT.

[284] See *Smiths Group plc v Weiss* [2002] EWHC 582, Ch D.

between the parties and as between the parties and the mediator and therefore even if the parties agree that the matters can be referred to outside the mediation, the mediator can enforce the confidentiality provision. The court will generally uphold the confidentiality, but not where it is necessary in the interests of justice for evidence to be given of the confidential matters. The proceedings are also covered by without prejudice privilege, which exists as between the parties and which they can waive; it is not a privilege of the mediator. If another privilege, for example legal professional privilege, attaches to documents which are produced by a party and shown to a mediator, that party retains the privilege and it is not waived by the disclosure or by waiver of the without prejudice privilege.[285]

Use or non-use of the expression 'without prejudice'

In deciding whether negotiations are 'without prejudice', the fact that the expression 'without prejudice' is not actually used is 'not without significance',[286] but does not conclude the matter: provided that there is some dispute and an attempt is being made to settle it, the courts should be ready to infer that the attempt is without prejudice.[287] In order to decide whether or not a document was bona fide intended to be a negotiating document, the court has to look at the intention of the author and how the document would be received by a reasonable recipient. If the document is marked 'without prejudice' that is a factor that the court should take into account. It is an indication that the author intended it to be a negotiating document and, in many cases, a recipient would receive it on the understanding that the marking indicated that the author wished to attempt negotiation.[288] However, the heading 'without prejudice' does not conclusively or automatically render privileged a document so marked; if privilege is claimed for such a document but challenged, the court can look at it to determine its nature.[289] The privilege can attach to a document headed 'without prejudice' even if it is an 'opening shot', but the rule is not limited to documents which are offers; privilege attaches to all documents marked 'without prejudice' and forming part of negotiations, whether or not they contain offers, subject only to the recognized exceptions.[290]

Exceptions

There are a number of exceptions to the principle of 'without prejudice' privilege.[291] Without prejudice material is admissible if the issue is whether or not the negotiations resulted in

---

[285] *Farm Assist Ltd v Secretary of State for the Environment, Food and Rural Affairs (No 2)* [2009] EWHC 1102 (TCC). On the question whether there is a distinct privilege attaching to the mediation process, see [33] ff.

[286] *Prudential Assurance Co Ltd v Prudential Insurance Co of America* [2002] EWHC 2809, Ch D.

[287] *Chocoladefabriken Lindt & Sprungli AG v Nestlé Co Ltd* [1978] RPC 287 at 288–9. If negotiations begin on a without prejudice basis, they remain so unless the party wishing to change them to an open basis makes this clear to the other party: *Cheddar Valley Engineering Ltd v Chaddlewood Homes Ltd* [1992] 1 WLR 820. However, open letters written after the negotiations and 'without prejudice' correspondence have finished and come to nothing, are not privileged: *Dixons Stores Group Ltd v Thames Television plc* [1993] 1 All ER 349.

[288] *Schering Corpn v Cipla Ltd* (2004) The Times, 10 Nov, Ch D.

[289] *South Shropshire District Council v Amos* [1986] 1 WLR 1271, CA.

[290] *South Shropshire District Council v Amos* [1986] 1 WLR 1271, CA at 1277–8. See also *Rochester Resources Limited v Lebedev* [2014] EWHC 2185 (Comm).

[291] For a non-exhaustive, but nonetheless extensive, list of the exceptions, see per Robert Walker LJ in *Unilever plc v The Procter & Gamble Co* [2000] 1 WLR 2436, CA at 2445–6.

an agreed settlement.[292] It is also admissible to show that a settlement agreement should be rectified.[293] Facts identified during the without prejudice negotiations which lead to a settlement agreement, which form part of its factual matrix or surrounding circumstances, and which but for the without prejudice rule would be admissible as an aid to construction of a settlement agreement, will also be admissible for that purpose.[294] The rule cannot be used to exclude an act of bankruptcy (such as a letter containing an offer to settle which also states the writer's inability to pay his debts as they fall due).[295] In *Ofulue v Bossert*[296] the House of Lords left open the question whether, and if so to what extent, a statement made in without prejudice negotiations would be admissible if 'in no way connected' with the issues in the case the subject of the negotiations. The privilege cannot be claimed when an agreement concluded between the parties during the negotiations should be set aside on the grounds of fraud or undue influence.[297] Negligent misrepresentations, however, will not prevent a claim to the privilege.[298] The privilege cannot be claimed if exclusion of the evidence would act as a cloak for perjury, blackmail, or other 'unambiguous impropriety',[299] but this exception should be applied only in the clearest cases of abuse.[300] As to perjury, the exception will apply in the case of a defendant who says that unless the case is withdrawn, he will give perjured evidence and will bribe other witnesses to perjure themselves.[301] However, the test is not whether there is a serious and substantial risk of perjury.[302] The exception will not apply where an admission is alleged to have been made that demonstrates that the pleaded case must be false[303] or where an admission is made that demonstrates that perjury has been committed in the past.[304] As to blackmail, the exception will apply where a claimant says that his claim is bogus and is being brought to 'blackmail' the defendant into a settlement of their real differences;[305] and it is not necessary for threats to fall within any formal definition of blackmail for them to be regarded as unambiguously improper.[306] An example of other 'unambiguous impropriety' would be where an employer in dispute with a black employee says during discussions aimed at settlement, 'We do not want you here because you are

---

[292] *Walker v Wilsher* (1889) 23 QBD 335, CA at 337; *Tomlin v Standard Telephones and Cables Ltd* [1969] 1 WLR 1378, CA. It is also admissible on the question whether a mediation resulted in an agreed settlement: *Brown v Rice* [2007] EWHC 625 (Ch).

[293] See *Pearlman v National Life Assurance Co of Canada* (1917) 39 OLR 141; *Butler v Countrywide Finance Ltd* (1992) 5 PRNZ 447; and per Lord Clarke in *Oceanbulk Shipping and Trading SA v TMT Asia Ltd* [2011] 1 AC 662, SC at [33].

[294] *Oceanbulk Shipping and Trading SA v TMT Asia Ltd* [2011] 1 AC 662, SC. For critical commentary, see Zuckerman, 'Without prejudice interpretation—with prejudice negotiations: *Oceanbulk Shipping and Trading SA v TMT Asia Ltd*' (2011) 15 E&P 232.

[295] *Re Daintrey, ex p Holt* [1893] 2 QB 116.

[296] [2009] UKHL 16 at [92].

[297] *Underwood v Cox* (1912) 4 DLR 66.

[298] *Jefferies Group & Kvaerner International*, 19 Jan 2007, unreported.

[299] The expression used by Hoffmann LJ in *Forster v Friedland* [1992] CA Transcript 1052.

[300] *Forster v Friedland*, [1992] CA Transcript 1052 and *Fazil-Alizadeh v Nikbin* (1993) The Times, 19 Mar, CA.

[301] *Greenwood v Fitts* (1961) 29 DLR (2d) 260, BC CA.

[302] *Berry Trade Ltd v Moussavi* [2003] EWCA Civ 715.

[303] [2003] EWCA Civ 715. See also *Sang Kook Suh v Mace (UK) Limited* [2016] EWCA Civ 4: the exception does not apply where a party simply denies the admissions allegedly made.

[304] *Savings and Investment Bank Ltd v Fincken* [2004] 1 WLR 667, CA.

[305] *Hawick Jersey International Ltd v Caplan* (1988) The Times, 11 Mar, QBD.

[306] *Ferster v Ferster* [2016] EWCA Civ 717 at [24].

black': such evidence should not be excluded from consideration by a tribunal hearing a subsequent complaint of race discrimination.[307]

Offers without prejudice except as to costs

CPR Pt 36 codifies the practice at common law whereby a party could make an offer in a letter headed 'without prejudice except as to costs', thereby reserving his right to refer to the letter, should the action proceed to judgment, on the question of costs. Under Pt 36, a written offer, called a 'Part 36 offer', may be made with a view to settling the whole or part of a claim (or counterclaim or other additional claim). The offer may be made at any time, including before the commencement of the proceedings.[308] If it is an offer by a defendant to pay a sum of money in settlement of a claim, it must be an offer to pay a single sum of money.[309] If the offer is not accepted, normally the court must not be told about it until all questions of liability and quantum have been decided,[310] but if, at that stage, the judgment is no better than the offer, then normally, and unless the court considers it unjust to do so, it will order that the defendant is entitled to the costs that he has incurred since the date of expiry of the 'relevant period',[311] which is usually a period of not less than 21 days specified in the Pt 36 offer.[312]

Matrimonial reconciliation cases

A privilege, similar to that which attaches to 'without prejudice' communications, has been developed to cover communications made in the course of matrimonial conciliation, matrimonial proceedings being in contemplation. In *D v NSPCC*[313] Lord Simon said:

> With increasingly facile divorce and a vast rise in the number of broken marriages, with their concomitant penury and demoralization, it came to be realized, in the words of Buckmill LJ in *Mole v Mole*:[314] 'in matrimonial disputes the state is also an interested party: it is more interested in reconciliation than in divorce'. This was the public interest which led to the application by analogy of the privilege of 'without prejudice' communications to cover communications made in the course of matrimonial conciliation (see *McTaggart v McTaggart*;[315] *Mole v Mole*;[316] *Theodoropoulas v Theodoropoulas*[317]) so indubitably an extension of the law that the textbooks treat it as a separate category of relevant evidence which may be withheld from the court. It cannot be classed, like traditional 'without prejudice' communications, as a 'privilege in aid of litigation . . .'.

---

[307] Per Cox J in *BNP Paribas v Mezzotero* [2004] IRLR 508, EAT. See also per Smith LJ, obiter, in *Brunel University v Vaseghi* [2007] IRLR 592, CA at [32]; and cf *Brodie v Nicola Ward (t/a First Steps Nursery)* [2008] All ER (D) 115 (Feb), EAT, where, in proceedings for unfair constructive dismissal, the employee was prevented from using a without prejudice letter from the employer's solicitor which, she claimed, was the 'last straw' causing her to resign.

[308] Rule 36.7.

[309] Rule 36.6(1). Special provision is made in personal injury claims in respect of future pecuniary loss: see rr 36.5(3) and 36.18.

[310] Rule 36.16(2).

[311] Rule 36.17(3).

[312] See rr 36.3(g) and 36.5(1)(c).

[313] [1978] AC 171 at 236–7.

[314] [1951] P 21, CA.

[315] [1949] P 94, CA.

[316] [1951] P 21, CA.

[317] [1964] P 311, CA.

In *Mole v Mole* it was established that the privilege applies to communications by a spouse not only with an official conciliator such as a probation officer but also with 'other persons such as clergy, doctors or marriage guidance counsellors to whom the parties or one of them go with a view to reconciliation, there being a tacit understanding that the conversations are without prejudice'.[318] In *Theodoropoulas v Theodoropoulas* Sir Jocelyn Simon P, having held that the same rule applied where a private individual is enlisted specifically as a conciliator, said:[319]

> Privilege [also] attaches to communications between the spouses themselves when made with a view to reconciliation. It also extends to excluding the evidence of an independent witness who was fortuitously present when those communications were made and who overheard or read them.[320]

The privilege is that of the spouses and can only be waived by them jointly. The intermediary cannot object to such waiver.

In proceedings under the Children Act 1989, evidence cannot be given of statements made by one or other of the parties in the course of meetings held, or communications made, for the purpose of conciliation. It is important to preserve a cloak over all attempts at settlements of disputes over children. However, an exception exists in the very unusual case where the statement clearly indicates that the maker has in the past or is likely in the future to cause serious harm to the well-being of a child. In these exceptional cases, it is for the trial judge to decide, in the exercise of his discretion, whether or not to admit the evidence, and he should do so only if the public interest in protecting the interests of the child outweighs the public interest in preserving the confidentiality of attempted conciliation.[321]

ADDITIONAL READING

Auburn, *Legal Professional Privilege: Law and Theory* (Oxford, 2000).
  A comparative examination of the principles underlying legal professional privilege which challenges the traditional view that the privilege must be absolute in order to achieve its stated goals and asserts that in appropriate circumstances more weight should be given to the values underlying the disclosure of evidence.

Loughrey, 'An unsatisfactory stalemate: *R (on the application of Prudential Plc)* v *Special Commissioner of Income Tax*' (2014) 18 E&P 65.
  A critical analysis of the decision of the Supreme Court that legal advice privilege only applies to advice provided by a legal professional.

Loughrey, 'Legal advice privilege and the corporate client' (2005) 9 E&P 183.
  A consideration of the question of which corporate communications attract legal advice privilege, assessing the implications of adopting a narrow 'control group' test and a broad 'dominant purpose' test for determining the scope of the privilege. The English approach is compared with approaches adopted elsewhere, particularly in the US.

---

[318] [1951] P 21 at 24 per Denning LJ.

[319] [1964] P 311 at 314.

[320] See also Law Reform Committee, 16th Report, *Privilege in Civil Proceedings*, Cmnd 3472 (1967), para 36.

[321] *Re D (minors)* [1993] Fam 231, CA.

Passmore, 'Watch what you say' (2006) NLJ 668 April 21.

A critical analysis of the decision in *Three Rivers District Council v Governor and Company of the Bank of England (No 5)* [2003] QB 1556, CA, exploring the practical problems relating to pre-litigation risk management to which it gives rise.

Thanki, ed, *The Law of Privilege* (Oxford, 2011).

A comprehensive work of reference and an informed critique of legal professional privilege, without prejudice privilege, and the privilege against self-incrimination.

Vaver, '"Without Prejudice" Communications—Their Admissibility and Effect' [1974] U Br Col LR 85.

An examination of the rules concerning the admissibility and effect of communications made 'without prejudice', including a historical analysis and consideration of the conceptual rationale of the rule.

Judgments as evidence of the facts upon which they were based

23

Key issues

● When, and why, should the fact that a person has been convicted of an offence be admissible in evidence for the purpose of proving that he committed that offence in (a) subsequent civil proceedings or (b) subsequent criminal proceedings?

Introduction

This chapter considers the circumstances in which a judgment in a civil case or verdict in a criminal case is admissible in subsequent proceedings as evidence of the facts on which it was based. The problem may be illustrated by two examples. If Mr A is granted a decree of divorce from Mrs A, irretrievable breakdown being established by reason of the fact that Mrs A committed adultery with Mr B, can Mrs B, on her petition for divorce, rely on the decree as evidence of the fact that Mr B committed adultery with Mrs A?[1] If D1 is convicted of the theft of goods, can the Crown, in a prosecution of D2 for handling those goods, rely upon D1's conviction as evidence that the goods were stolen? The common law answers to questions of this kind were largely, if not entirely, governed by the decision in *Hollington v Hewthorn & Co Ltd*.[2] That case tipped the balance in favour of the view supported by most preceding case law, that previous judgments are not admissible as evidence of the facts on which they were based.

The principle of *Hollington v Hewthorn & Co Ltd*

Hollington v Hewthorn & Co Ltd concerned a collision between two cars. The plaintiff, the owner of one of the cars, brought a negligence action against both the driver of the other car, who had been convicted of careless driving (at the time and place of the accident), and his employer. The Court of Appeal held that the plaintiff was not entitled to admit the conviction of the defendant driver as evidence of his negligence. The decision was based largely on the view that the civil court would know nothing of the evidence before the criminal court (and the arguments before it) and that the opinion of the criminal court was 'irrelevant'. The word 'irrelevant' was not being used in the traditional sense; the true justification for the rule lies in the requirements of a fair trial—the responsibility of the judge to make his own independent assessment of the evidence that he receives entails that weight ought not to be attached to conclusions reached by another court.[3]

The principle of *Hollington v Hewthorn & Co Ltd also* applied to cases where the subsequent proceedings were criminal. In *R v Spinks*[4] F had stabbed someone with a knife and had been convicted of wounding with intent to do grievous bodily harm. At the trial of Spinks for assisting F by concealing the knife with intent to impede the apprehension or prosecution of a person who had committed an arrestable offence, namely F, the Court of Appeal held that the Crown could not rely on F's conviction as evidence that he had committed the arrestable offence of wounding. Since there was no other admissible evidence that F had committed such an offence, Spinks' conviction was quashed.

The rule in *Hollington v Hewthorn & Co Ltd* attracted much criticism. Its effect, in both civil and criminal proceedings, has been largely removed by the Civil Evidence Act 1968 (the 1968 Act) and the Police and Criminal Evidence Act 1984 (the 1984 Act).

---

[1] See *Sutton v Sutton* [1970] 1 WLR 183, PD.

[2] [1943] KB 587, CA.

[3] *Rogers v Hoyle* [2013] EWHC 1409 (QB) at [93]–[104] and [2014] EWCA Civ 257 at [39]–[40].

[4] [1982] 1 All ER 587. See also *R v Hassan* [1970] 1 QB 423, CA.

Civil proceedings

Narrowly stated, *Hollington v Hewthorn & Co Ltd* decided that a conviction of a criminal offence is inadmissible in civil proceedings as evidence of the fact that the person convicted committed the offence. The Law Reform Committee, observing that the onus of proof in criminal cases is higher than in civil cases, and the degree of carelessness required to convict a person of careless driving is, if anything, greater than that required to sustain a civil action for negligence, described the decision as offensive to one's sense of justice.[5] Sections 11–13 of the 1968 Act give effect to the Committee's recommendations. They overrule *Hollington v Hewthorn & Co Ltd* insofar as it applies, in civil cases, to previous criminal convictions and also findings of adultery and paternity in previous civil proceedings.

Previous convictions in civil proceedings generally—s 11 of the Civil Evidence Act 1968

Section 11 of the 1968 Act not only reverses the rule in *Hollington v Hewthorn & Co Ltd* as narrowly stated, but also creates a persuasive presumption: the person convicted, once his conviction has been proved, shall be taken to have committed the offence in question unless the contrary is proved. Section 11 provides that:

(1) In any civil proceedings the fact that a person has been convicted of an offence by or before any court in the United Kingdom or of a service offence[6] (anywhere) shall (subject to subsection (3) below) be admissible in evidence for the purpose of proving, where to do so is relevant to any issue in those proceedings, that he committed that offence, whether he was so convicted upon a plea of guilty or otherwise and whether or not he is a party to the civil proceedings; but no conviction other than a subsisting one shall be admissible in evidence by virtue of this section.

(2) In any civil proceedings in which by virtue of this section a person is proved to have been convicted of an offence by or before any court in the United Kingdom or of a service offence—

   (a) he shall be taken to have committed that offence unless the contrary is proved; and

   (b) without prejudice to the reception of any other admissible evidence for the purpose of identifying the facts on which the conviction was based, the contents of any document which is admissible as evidence of the conviction, and the contents of the information, complaint, indictment or charge-sheet on which the person in question was convicted, shall be admissible in evidence for that purpose.

Meaning of 'civil proceedings'

Concerning s 11(1), 'civil proceedings' includes, in addition to civil proceedings in any of the ordinary courts of law, (a) civil proceedings before any other tribunal in relation to which the strict rules of evidence apply and (b) an arbitration or reference, whether under an enactment or not, but does not include civil proceedings in relation to which the strict rules of evidence do not apply.[7] Subsection (3), to which s 11(1) is subject, provides that nothing in s 11 shall prejudice the operation of, inter alia, s 13, which, as we shall see, relates to proceedings

---

[5] 15th Report, Cmnd 3391 (1967), para 3.

[6] ie an offence that the Court Martial has jurisdiction to try.

[7] Section 18(1).

for defamation. A 'conviction' includes one in respect of which an absolute or conditional discharge was imposed.[8] A conviction against which an appeal is pending is 'subsisting' but not one which has been quashed on appeal.[9] The Act has no application to adjudications of guilt in police disciplinary proceedings[10] or to foreign convictions.[11]

The burden and standard of proof

There can be no dispute that s 11(2)(a) has the effect of reversing the legal burden of proof in respect of the commission of the offence. Thus if A sues B for conduct on the part of B in respect of which B stands convicted, it is for B to prove, on a balance of probabilities, that he did not commit the offence; it is not sufficient for someone in B's position to establish that the conviction is unsafe, that the judge in the criminal trial, or the Court of Appeal, made an error, or that the prosecution was an abuse of process.[12] There is a divergence of judicial opinion, however, as to what weight should be attached to the conviction in deciding whether the onus resting on B has been discharged. In *Stupple v Royal Insurance Co Ltd*[13] Buckley LJ said:[14]

> proof of conviction under this section gives rise to the statutory presumption laid down in section 11(2)(a), which, like any other presumption, will give way to evidence establishing the contrary on the balance of probability, without itself affording any evidential weight to be taken into account in determining whether that onus has been discharged.

Lord Denning MR, however, took the view that although the conviction is not conclusive, it does not merely shift the burden of proof but is a weighty piece of evidence of itself.[15] In *Hunter v Chief Constable of West Midlands*[16] Lord Denning MR went further. In answer to the question how, for the purposes of s 11(2)(a), a convicted man is to prove the contrary, his Lordship expressed the view, obiter:

> Only, I suggest, by proving that the conviction was obtained by fraud or collusion, or by adducing fresh evidence. If the fresh evidence is inconclusive, he does not prove his innocence. It must be decisive, it must be conclusive, before he can be declared innocent.

---

[8] Section 11(5). See also *R v Foster* [1984] 2 All ER 679, CA: the effect of a free pardon is to remove all pains, penalties, and punishments ensuing from the conviction but not to eliminate the conviction itself.

[9] See *Re Raphael, Raphael v D'Antin* [1973] 1 WLR 998: rather than finally dispose of civil proceedings in reliance on a conviction subsequently liable to be quashed, the proceedings may be adjourned pending the appeal. However, an application to the Criminal Cases Review Commission should not be equated with a pending appeal: *CXX v DXX* [2012] EWHC 1535 (QB).

[10] *Thorpe v Chief Constable of Greater Manchester Police* [1989] 2 All ER 827, CA.

[11] See *Union Carbide Corpn v Naturin Ltd* [1987] FSR 538, CA. However, even if the rule in *Hollington v Hewthorn & Co Ltd* covers foreign convictions, it will not apply where the issues in the criminal and civil proceedings are identical: *Director of the Assets Recovery Agency v Virtosu* [2008] EWHC 149 (QB). See also *Arab Monetary Fund v Hashim (No 2)* [1990] 1 All ER 673, Ch D.

[12] *Raja v Van Hoogstraten* [2005] EWHC 1642, Ch D.

[13] [1971] 1 QB 50.

[14] Ibid at 76.

[15] Ibid at 72. See also *Taylor v Taylor* [1970] 1 WLR 1148, CA, per Davies LJ at 1152.

[16] [1982] AC 529, HL, reported in the Court of Appeal as *McIlkenny v Chief Constable of West Midlands Police Force* [1980] QB 283, CA at 320.

When the case came before the House of Lords, however, Lord Diplock, disapproving this dictum, said:[17]

> The burden of proof of 'the contrary' that lies on a defendant under section 11 is the ordinary burden in a civil action, ie proof on a balance of probabilities, although in the face of a conviction after a full hearing that is likely to be an uphill task.

More recent authorities are to the effect that the weight to be attached to the conviction is a matter for the trial judge and in some cases, therefore, it will be a weighty piece of evidence of itself.[18] The weight will depend on the particular circumstances of the case, including, for example, whether the decision was unanimous or by a majority. Regard may also be had to a transcript of the evidence given in the criminal proceedings, a copy of the judge's summing-up,[19] the views of the Court of Appeal, in the case of an unsuccessful appeal, and any fresh evidence that has subsequently become available to the parties.

Abuse of process

A defence that challenges the correctness of a conviction cannot automatically be struck out as an abuse of process, because s 11(2) gives a defendant a right to challenge the conviction. However, it may be struck out if it amounts to an attempt at re-litigation on essentially the same evidence or is designed merely to vex the claimant.[20] Even if the defence is not struck out as an abuse, the claimant may still succeed in an application for summary judgment where there is an 'absence of realism' in the suggestion that the defendant will be able to prove that he did not commit the offence.[21]

Documents identifying facts of the conviction

Where a trial does take place, s 11(2)(b) provides for the admissibility of specific types of document for the purpose of identifying the facts on which the conviction was based. Provision is also made for the admissibility of duly certified copies of such documents, which shall be taken to be true copies unless the contrary is shown.[22] A transcript of a judge's summing-up is not admissible under s 11(2)(b) itself, but is admissible, for the purposes referred to in s 11(2)(b), under the Civil Evidence Act 1995.[23]

Procedural requirements

Under Practice Direction 16, para 8.1, a claimant who wishes to rely on evidence under s 11 must include in his particulars of claim a statement to that effect and give details of the type of conviction and its date, the court or court-martial which made it, and the issue in the claim to which it relates.

---

[17] [1982] AC 529, HL at 544.

[18] *Phoenix Marine Inc v China Ocean Shipping Co* [1999] 1 All ER 138 at [143] and *CXX v DXX* [2012] EWHC 1535 (QB) at [39]. It has been suggested that assessment of the weight of the conviction would be 'an impossibly difficult task': see *Cross on Evidence* (5th edn, London, 1979) 458. Cf Zuckerman (1971) 87 LQR 21.

[19] Such evidence is admissible pursuant to the Civil Evidence Act 1995: see Ch 13.

[20] See *Brinks Ltd v Abu-Saleh* [1995] 1 WLR 1478 and *CXX v DXX* [2012] EWHC 1535 (QB) at [34] and cf *J v Oyston* [1994] 1 WLR 694.

[21] *CXX v DXX* [2012] EWHC 1535 (QB) at [34].

[22] Section 11(4). Corresponding provisions for the admission of copies of such documents under ss 12 and 13 are contained in ss 12(4) and 13(4).

[23] See *Brinks Ltd v Abu-Saleh (No 2)* [1995] 1 WLR 1487, Ch D, a decision under the hearsay provisions of the Civil Evidence Act 1968.

Previous convictions in defamation proceedings—s 13 of the Civil Evidence Act 1968

Section 13 of the 1968 Act applies to defamation proceedings. In such proceedings, the section, giving effect to the recommendations of the Law Reform Committee, not only reverses the rule in *Hollington v Hewthorn & Co Ltd*, as narrowly stated, but also creates a conclusive presumption: the person convicted, once his conviction has been proved, shall conclusively be taken to have committed the offence in question.[24] The effect of this is twofold: (i) it prevents a convicted person from using the defamation action to reopen the issues determined at the criminal trial,[25] and (ii) it protects from civil liability a person who chooses to state that another is guilty of an offence of which he stands convicted. Accordingly, a defamation action based on the defendant's statement that the plaintiff committed an offence in respect of which he has been convicted will be struck out as an abuse of the process of the court unless the statement also contains some other legally defamatory matter.[26] Section 13 reads as follows:

(1) In an action for libel or slander in which the question whether the plaintiff did or did not commit a criminal offence is relevant to an issue arising in the action, proof that, at the time when the issue falls to be determined, he stands convicted of that offence shall be conclusive evidence that he committed that offence; and his conviction thereof shall be admissible in evidence accordingly.

(2) In any such action as aforesaid in which by virtue of this section the plaintiff is proved to have been convicted of an offence, the contents of any document which is admissible as evidence of the conviction, and the contents of the information, complaint, indictment or charge-sheet on which he was convicted, shall, without prejudice to the reception of any other admissible evidence for the purpose of identifying the facts on which the conviction was based, be admissible in evidence for the purpose of identifying those facts.

(2A) In the case of an action for libel or slander in which there is more than one plaintiff—

    (a) the references in subsection (1) and (2) above to the plaintiff shall be construed as references to any of the plaintiffs, and

    (b) proof that any of the plaintiffs stands convicted of an offence shall be conclusive evidence that he committed that offence so far as that fact is relevant to any issue arising in relation to his cause of action or that of any other plaintiff.

(3) For the purposes of this section a person shall be taken to stand convicted of an offence if but only if there subsists against him a conviction of that offence by or before a court in the United Kingdom or (in the case of a service offence) a conviction (anywhere) of that service offence.[27]

Previous findings of adultery and paternity

Section 12 of the 1968 Act not only reverses the rule in *Hollington v Hewthorn & Co Ltd* insofar as it applied to previous findings of adultery and paternity, but also creates a persuasive presumption in respect of such findings. Section 12 provides that:

(1) In any civil proceedings—

    (a) the fact that a person has been found guilty of adultery in any matrimonial proceedings; and

---

[24] 15th Report, Cmnd 3391 (1967), para 26 ff. Parliament did not accept, however, the Committee's accompanying recommendation that in defamation proceedings evidence of an acquittal should be conclusive evidence of innocence. See *Loughans v Odhams Press* [1963] 1 QB 299, CA, in this chapter, under **Previous acquittals**, pp 763–4.

[25] See, eg, *Hinds v Sparks* [1964] Crim LR 717 and *Goody v Odhams Press Ltd* [1967] 1 QB 333.

[26] *Levene v Roxhan* [1970] 1 WLR 1322, CA.

[27] As to the meaning of subsisting convictions, see, in this chapter, under **Previous convictions in civil proceedings generally—s 11 of the Civil Evidence Act 1968**, p 759.

(b) the fact that a person has been found to be the father of a child in relevant proceedings[28] before any court in England and Wales or Northern Ireland or has been adjudged to be the father of a child in affiliation proceedings before any court in the United Kingdom;

shall (subject to (3) below) be admissible in evidence for the purpose of proving, where to do so is relevant to any issue in those civil proceedings, that he committed the adultery to which the finding relates or, as the case may be, is (or was) the father of that child, whether or not he offered any defence to the allegation of adultery or paternity and whether or not he is a party to the civil proceedings; but no finding or adjudication other than a subsisting one shall be admissible in evidence by virtue of this section.

(2) In any civil proceedings in which by virtue of this section a person is proved to have been found guilty of adultery as mentioned in subsection (1)(a) above or to have been found or adjudged to be the father of a child as mentioned in subsection (1)(b) above—

(a) he shall be taken to have committed the adultery to which the finding relates or, as the case may be, to be (or have been) the father of that child, unless the contrary is proved; and

(b) without prejudice to the reception of any other admissible evidence for the purpose of identifying the facts on which the finding or adjudication was based, the contents of any document which was before the court, or which contains any pronouncement of the court, in the other proceedings in question shall be admissible in evidence for that purpose.

(3) Nothing in this section shall prejudice the operation of any enactment whereby a finding of fact in any matrimonial or affiliation proceedings is for the purposes of any other proceedings made conclusive evidence of any fact.

Modelled as it is on s 11, s 12 of the 1968 Act calls for little comment. 'Matrimonial proceedings' are defined to include, inter alia, any matrimonial cause in the High Court or family court in England and Wales and any appeal arising out of any such cause.[29] As in the case of previous convictions under s 11, the legal burden in relation to the finding of adultery or paternity admitted under s 12 is placed upon the party seeking to disprove that finding. The standard of proof required to discharge the burden is proof on a balance of probabilities.[30] A claimant who wishes to rely on evidence under s 12 of a finding or adjudication of adultery or paternity must include in his particulars of claim a statement to that effect and give details of the finding or adjudication and its date, the court which made it, and the issue in the claim to which it relates.[31]

Previous acquittals

In *Packer v Clayton*,[32] which pre-dates *Hollington v Hewthorn & Co Ltd*, Avory J was of the opinion that in affiliation proceedings, the respondent's acquittal of a sexual offence against the applicant would be admissible to show that the jury were not convinced by the latter's evidence. However, if the principle of *Hollington v Hewthorn & Co Ltd* applies to previous acquittals, they are inadmissible as evidence of innocence in subsequent civil proceedings, such as affiliation proceedings. This conclusion may be justified on the grounds that an allegation

---

[28] 'Relevant proceedings' means proceedings under the Children Act 1989 or proceedings which would have been relevant proceedings for the purposes of s 12 before the passing of the 1989 Act: see s 12(5).

[29] Section 12(5).

[30] *Sutton v Sutton* [1970] 1 WLR 183, PD.

[31] PD 16, para 8.1.

[32] (1932) 97 JP 14, DC.

not proved beyond reasonable doubt may be susceptible of proof on a balance of probabilities, as it was, for example, in *Loughans v Odhams Press*.[33] As a matter of policy, however, it is arguable that a person acquitted of an offence should be granted some measure of immunity from assertions to the contrary. Parliament has rejected the proposal that in defamation proceedings evidence of an acquittal should be conclusive evidence of innocence.[34] Whether, at common law, evidence of an acquittal is nonetheless *some*, albeit only prima facie, evidence of innocence, not only in defamation actions but also in civil proceedings generally, is, on the present state of the authorities, unclear.

Other previous findings

Subject to exceptions, the principle of *Hollington v Hewthorn & Co Ltd* would appear to apply in respect of judicial findings in previous *civil* proceedings. In *Secretary of State for Trade and Industry v Bairstow*,[35] the Secretary of State brought proceedings under the Company Directors Disqualification Act 1986, seeking a disqualification order against B. Prior to the proceedings, B had been dismissed by the company of which he had been the managing director, his claim for wrongful dismissal against the company had been dismissed, and his appeal against that decision had failed. The Court of Appeal held that the principle of *Hollington v Hewthorn & Co Ltd* was not confined to cases in which the earlier decision was that of a court exercising a criminal jurisdiction and accordingly the judge's factual findings in the wrongful dismissal proceedings were inadmissible, in the proceedings under the 1986 Act, as evidence of the facts on which they were based.

The exceptions

The exceptions are findings of adultery and paternity, which, as we have seen, are now governed by s 12 of the 1968 Act. In the light of the somewhat novel observations of Lord Denning MR in *Hunter v Chief Constable of West Midlands*,[36] there is arguably a third exception. In that case, Lord Denning MR was of the opinion that a party to civil proceedings can only challenge a previous decision *against* himself by showing that it was obtained by fraud or collusion or by adducing fresh evidence which he could not have obtained by reasonable diligence before, to show conclusively that the previous decision was wrong. On this view, if a driver runs down two pedestrians, a finding of negligence against the driver in an action brought by one of the pedestrians could only be challenged in a subsequent action brought against him by the other in the limited way indicated. Applying the principle in *Hollington v Hewthorn & Co Ltd* to the same example, however, the earlier finding of negligence would be inadmissible as evidence of the driver's negligence in the subsequent proceedings.[37]

---

[33] [1963] 1 QB 299, CA.

[34] See, in this chapter, under **Previous convictions in defamation proceedings—s 13 of the Civil Evidence Act 1968, p 762.**

[35] [2003] 3 WLR 841, CA.

[36] [1982] AC 529, HL, reported in the Court of Appeal as *McIlkenny v Chief Constable of West Midlands Police Force* [1980] QB 283, CA at 320. Although the views of Lord Denning MR in this respect were to some extent doubted when the case came before the House of Lords, Lord Diplock, giving the judgment of the House, found it unnecessary expressly to consider the topic of issue estoppel (at 540–1).

[37] In practice, problems of this kind are often avoided by virtue of the procedural provisions relating to joinder of parties and causes of action: see generally CPR Pts 19 and 20.

Non-judicial findings

The principle of *Hollington v Hewthorn & Co Ltd* has been held to apply not only to judicial findings in previous civil proceedings, but also to the previous findings set out in the reports of inspectors under the Companies Act 1967 (see now Pt XIV of the Companies Act 1985),[38] to an arbitration award,[39] and to findings in extra-statutory reports.[40] Similarly, the principle of *Hollington v Hewthorn & Co Ltd* has been held to apply to findings of the Solicitors Disciplinary Tribunal that a solicitor has been dishonest.[41] However, in the earlier case of *Hill v Clifford*,[42] the Court of Appeal held that a finding by the General Medical Council that a dentist had been guilty of professional misconduct was admissible as prima facie evidence of such misconduct in subsequent civil proceedings concerning the dissolution of his partnership, a decision which may be explicable on the basis that the Council was under a statutory duty of inquiry.[43] However, in such a case the court is still entitled to reach its own view of the facts as previously found.[44]

The rule in *Hollington v Hewthorn & Co Ltd* does not apply to the opinions of an expert as opposed to the findings of a judge. Thus in a negligence claim arising out of a plane crash, regard may be had to the contents of a report produced by the Department of Transport's Air Accident Investigation Branch, including its conclusions as to the probable causes of the crash.[45]

Criminal proceedings

Previous convictions

The application of the principle of *Hollington v Hewthorn & Co Ltd* in criminal cases meant that at the trial of a person charged with handling stolen goods, the previous conviction of the thief was inadmissible as evidence that the goods allegedly received were stolen.[46] Likewise, a woman's convictions for prostitution were inadmissible as evidence of her prostitution at the trial of a man charged with living off her immoral earnings.[47] The Criminal Law Revision Committee thought it was quite wrong, as well as being inconvenient, that in cases of this kind the prosecution should be required to prove again the guilt of the person concerned,[48] and recommended, in respect of convictions of persons other than the accused, a provision in criminal proceedings corresponding to s 11 of the 1968 Act. Section 74 of the Police and Criminal Evidence Act 1984 Act only gives effect to this recommendation but

---

[38] *Savings and Investment Bank Ltd v Gasco Investments (Netherlands BV)* [1984] 1 WLR 271, Ch D.

[39] *Land Securities plc v Westminster City Council* [1993] 1 WLR 286.

[40] *Three Rivers District Council v Bank of England (No 3)* [2003] 2 AC 1, HL (the findings of Bingham LJ in relation to the collapse of the Bank of Credit and Commerce International).

[41] *Conlon v Simms* [2007] 3 All ER 802, CA.

[42] [1907] 2 Ch 236.

[43] See also *Faulder v Silk* (1811) 3 Camp 126 and *Harvey v R* [1901] AC 601 (inquisitions in lunacy as prima facie evidence of a person's unsoundness of mind).

[44] *Clifford v Timms* [1908] AC 12.

[45] *Rogers v Hoyle* [2015] QB 265.

[46] *R v Turner* (1832) 1 Mood CC 347 at 349.

[47] *R v Hassan* [1970] 1 QB 423, CA. See also *R v Spinks* [1982] 1 All ER 587, CA, in this chapter, under The Principle of *Hollington v Hewthorn & Co Ltd*, p 758.

[48] 11th Report, Cmnd 4991 (1972), paras 217 ff.

also makes similar provision in relation to the previous convictions of *the accused*: without affecting the law governing the admissibility of the accused's past misconduct, it provides that where evidence of the accused's commission of an offence *is* admissible, if the accused is proved to have been convicted of that offence he shall be taken to have committed it unless the contrary is proved. The section is without prejudice to (i) the admissibility in evidence of any conviction which would be admissible apart from the section;[49] and (ii) the operation of any statutory provision whereby a conviction or finding of fact in criminal proceedings is made conclusive evidence of any fact for the purposes of any other criminal proceedings.[50]

Section 74 of the 1984 Act provides that:

(1) In any proceedings the fact that a person other than the accused has been convicted of an offence by or before any court in the United Kingdom or any other member State[51] or by a Service court outside the United Kingdom shall be admissible in evidence for the purpose of proving that that person committed that offence, where evidence of his having done so is admissible, whether or not any other evidence of his having committed that offence is given.

(2) In any proceedings in which by virtue of this section a person other than the accused is proved to have been convicted of an offence by or before any court in the United Kingdom or any other member State or by a Service court outside the United Kingdom, he shall be taken to have committed that offence unless the contrary is proved.

(3) In any proceedings where evidence is admissible of the fact that the accused has committed an offence, if the accused is proved to have been convicted of the offence—

(a) by or before any court in the United Kingdom or any other member State; or

(b) by a Service court outside the United Kingdom,

he shall be taken to have committed that offence unless the contrary is proved.

Section 75(1) of the 1984 Act provides that:

Where evidence that a person has been convicted of an offence is admissible by virtue of s 74 above, then without prejudice to the reception of any other admissible evidence for the purpose of identifying the facts on which the conviction was based—

(a) the contents of any document which is admissible as evidence of the conviction; and

(b) the contents of—

(i) the information, complaint, indictment or charge-sheet on which the person in question was convicted, or

(ii) in the case of a conviction of an offence by a court in a member State (other than the United Kingdom), any document produced in relation to the proceedings for that offence which fulfils a purpose similar to any document or documents specified in sub-paragraph (i),

shall be admissible in evidence for that purpose.[52]

The terminology of s 74

Concerning the terminology of s 74, 'proceedings' means criminal proceedings, including service proceedings.[53] A conviction, for the purposes of the section, includes a conviction in

---

[49] Section 74(4)(a): eg proof of a witness's conviction pursuant to s 6 of the Criminal Procedure Act 1865. See Ch 7.

[50] Section 74(4)(b). The saving appears to have been included not with any particular statute in mind but because of local and private enactments and the possibility of future public enactments: see Criminal Law Revision Committee, 11th Report, Cmnd 4991 (1972), Annex 2, 233.

[51] ie any other EU member State.

[52] Provision is also made for the admission of duly certified copies of such documents: s 75(2).

[53] Section 82(1).

respect of which a probation order or absolute or conditional discharge was imposed,[54] but not an admission of an offence in a police caution.[55] A person is 'convicted' only if the conviction is 'subsisting'.[56] A subsisting conviction means either a finding of guilt that has not been quashed on appeal or a formal plea of guilt that has not been withdrawn; whether the accused has been sentenced or not is irrelevant.[57] A 'Service court' means a court-martial or a Standing Civilian Court.[58]

Foreign convictions

Foreign convictions, apart from convictions by Service courts outside the United Kingdom and convictions in other EU member States, are clearly not covered by s 74, but may be admissible under the bad character provisions of the Criminal Justice Act 2003[59] and, if admissible, may be proved under s 7 of the Evidence Act 1851.[60] The rule in *Hollington v Hewthorn & Co Ltd* does not apply, in criminal proceedings, to foreign convictions, since it has been treated as a rule 'governing the admissibility of evidence of bad character' and thus abolished by s 99(1) of the Criminal Justice Act 2003.[61]

Section 74(1) and (2): convictions of persons other than the accused
Relevance of the convictions

Section 74(1) has an obvious application where proof of the commission of an offence by a person other than the accused is admissible to establish an essential ingredient of the offence with which the accused is charged. Thus where A is seen transferring goods to B and they are jointly charged with handling the goods, A's guilty plea is admissible at B's trial to prove that the goods were stolen.[62]

In *R v Robertson; R v Golder*,[63] a decision under the original version of s 74(1), it was held that evidence of the commission of the offence may be relevant not only to an issue which is an essential ingredient of the offence charged, but also to less fundamental evidential issues arising in the proceedings. It was also held that the subsection is not confined to the proof of convictions of offences in which the accused on trial played no part; and that where the evidence is admitted, the judge should be careful to explain to the jury its effect and limitations.[64] In the case of Robertson, who was charged with conspiracy with two others to commit burglary, evidence that the others had been convicted of a number of burglaries was admissible because it could be inferred from their commission of these offences that there was a conspiracy between them and that was the very conspiracy which the prosecution sought to prove that Robertson was a party.

[54] Section 75(3).
[55] *R v Olu* [2010] EWCA Crim 2975. Where evidence of such an admission is admitted, an accused may challenge it: *R v Olu* [2010] EWCA Crim 2975.
[56] Section 75(4).
[57] *R v Robertson; R v Golder* [1987] QB 920, CA. See also *R v Foster* [1984] 2 All ER 679, CA.
[58] Section 82(1).
[59] See Ch 19.
[60] *R v Kordasinski* [2007] 1 Cr App R 238, CA. Section 7 is considered in Ch 10, p 308.
[61] *R v Kordasinski* [2007] 1 Cr App R 238, CA. Section 99(1) is considered in Ch 19, pp 555–6.
[62] *R v Pigram* [1995] Crim LR 808, CA.
[63] [1987] QB 920, CA.
[64] See also per Staughton LJ in *R v Kempster* (1989) 90 Cr App R 14 at 22, CA and *R v Boyson* [1991] Crim LR 274, CA.

In respect of Golder, who was convicted of a robbery committed at garage X, two of his co-accused pleaded guilty to that robbery and also to another committed at garage Y. The evidence against Golder consisted primarily of a confession statement, which he alleged to have been fabricated by the police, in which he referred to both robberies. It was held that evidence of the guilty pleas of the co-accused was admissible: proof of their commission of the offence at garage X was relevant because it showed that there had in fact been a robbery at that garage; and proof of the commission of both offences was relevant because it showed that the contents of the alleged confession were in accordance with the facts as they were known and therefore more likely to be true.

R v Robertson; R v Golder was applied in *R v Castle*,[65] where C and F were charged with robbery and F pleaded guilty. At an identification parade, the victim said 'yes' in respect of C, 'possibly' in respect of F. Evidence of the guilty plea was admissible because it was relevant to the issue of the reliability of the identification of C: by confirming the correctness of the 'possible' identification of F, it also tended to confirm the correctness of the positive identification of C.[66]

Although in most cases s 74(1) has been relied on by the prosecution, in appropriate circumstances it may also be used by an accused to adduce evidence of the convictions of a co-accused which are relevant to an issue in the proceedings.[67]

Exclusion under s 78 of the Police and Criminal Evidence Act 1984

In *R v Robertson; R v Golder* it was stressed that s 74 should be used sparingly and not where, although the evidence is technically admissible, its effect is likely to be slight, particularly if there is any danger of contravening s 78 of the 1984 Act.[68] A judge, in deciding an application under s 78, should make a ruling and if she decides to admit the evidence, should, in the ruling, give a cogent reason for her decision.[69] If a conviction is admitted under s 74, an appeal against a judge's ruling not to exclude it under s 78 will only succeed if no judge could reasonably have made it or it was made on a false basis.[70] However, in *R v Denham* that a decision under s. 78, rather than a discretion, is better described as 'an exercise of judgment on which a balance is struck on the issue of fairness.'[71] This is because 'pure discretion' would unduly restrict the accused's ability to mount a challenge.[72]

In *R v Kempster*[73] it was initially unclear whether the prosecution were relying on the evidence to prove the accused's guilt or merely to prevent mystification of the jury. Although in

---

[65] [1989] Crim LR 567, CA.

[66] *R v Castle* was followed in *R v Gummerson and Steadman* [1999] Crim LR 680, CA, a case of *voice* identification. See also *R v Buckingham* (1994) 99 Cr App R 303, CA.

[67] See *R v Hendrick* [1992] Crim LR 427, CA where, on the facts, the convictions were irrelevant.

[68] See also *R v Skinner* [1995] Crim LR 805, CA.

[69] *R v Hillier* (1992) 97 Cr App R 349, CA.

[70] *R v Smith* [2007] EWCA Crim 215, *R v Abdullah* [2010] EWCA Crim 3078 and *R v O'Brien* [2016] EWCA Crim 698 (decision of trial judge to admit upheld notwithstanding that all three members of the Court of Appeal would have excluded it). But see also *R v Denham* [2017] 1 Cr App R 64 (7), CA: the decision whether to admit is a question of judgment in which a balance has to be struck on the issue of fairness, because if it were a question of pure discretion the basis of challenge to a judge's decision might be unduly confined; ultimately the decision whether to admit is either right or wrong.

[71] At [40].

[72] Ibid. 'Ultimately the decision whether to admit evidence in these circumstances is either right or wrong.'

[73] (1989) 90 Cr App R 14, CA.

the event the jury were encouraged to use the evidence to prove guilt, there was no clear or informed decision by the judge as to any adverse effect it might have had on the fairness of the proceedings. Quashing the convictions, the Court of Appeal highlighted the importance of ascertaining the purpose for which the evidence is adduced before deciding whether it should be excluded under s 78, and held that if the evidence is admitted, the judge should ensure that the advocate adducing it does not seek to use it for any other purpose. Similarly, in *R v Boyson*[74] the Court of Appeal, *per curiam*, deprecated what it saw as the growing practice of allowing irrelevant, inadmissible, prejudicial, or unfair evidence to be admitted simply on the grounds that it is convenient for the jury to have 'the whole picture'.

Examples
Whether a conviction admissible under s 74 should be excluded under s 78 depends on the particular facts. In *R v Mattison*[75] M was charged in one count with gross indecency with D, and D, in another count, was charged with gross indecency with M. D pleaded guilty, M not guilty, his defence being a complete denial. It was held that evidence of the guilty plea was relevant to M's trial but the judge, given M's defence, should have exercised his discretion under s 78 to exclude it.[76] That decision falls to be compared with *R v Turner.*[77] T and L were driving separate cars and L overtook T, hit an oncoming vehicle, and killed the passenger in his own car. The prosecution case was that the drivers were racing. L pleaded guilty to causing death by reckless driving and T, tried on the same charge, denied racing. It was held that L's guilty plea was relevant, because the prosecution case was that L had been the principal, T the aider and abettor, but that it did not establish that L and T were racing, the essential issue at T's trial. The judge having made it clear that the evidence did not amount to an admission by L that he was racing, there was nothing unfair in admitting it.[78]

Conspiracy cases
The question of exclusion under s 78 is of particular importance in conspiracy and related cases. In *R v O'Connor*[79] B and C were jointly charged in one count with conspiracy to obtain property by deception. B pleaded guilty, C not guilty. Evidence of B's guilty plea was admitted, together with the details in the count against him, as permitted by s 75. It was held that the evidence should have been excluded under s 78 because B's admission that he had conspired with C might have led the jury to infer that C, in turn, must have conspired with B.

---

[74] [1991] Crim LR 274, CA. See also *R v Hall* [1993] Crim LR 527, CA; *R v Mahmood and Manzur* [1997] 1 Cr App R 414, CA; and *R v Downer* [2009] 2 Cr App R 452, CA.

[75] [1990] Crim LR 117, CA.

[76] Where a co-accused pleads guilty but the prosecution do not seek to rely on s 74, it may be sufficient, depending on the circumstances, for the jury to be told that the guilty plea is not probative against the accused: see *R v Turpin* [1990] Crim LR 514, CA. In a case involving joint enterprise, it is insufficient for the judge to direct the jury that they must be sure that each of the accused was a party to the enterprise—they should be told that it is essential that they put the guilty plea of the co-accused out of their minds: *R v Betterley* [1994] Crim LR 764, CA. However, a warning will not suffice if the jury cannot properly consider the case of the accused in isolation from that of the co-accused, in which case the judge should discharge the jury and order a new trial: *R v Fedrick* [1990] Crim LR 403, CA. See also *R v Marlow* [1997] Crim LR 457, CA.

[77] [1991] Crim LR 57, CA.

[78] See also *R v Bennett* [1988] Crim LR 686, CA; *R v Stewart* [1999] Crim LR 746, CA; and *R v O'Brien* [2016] EWCA Crim 698.

[79] (1986) 85 Cr App R 298, CA.

The same reasoning was applied in *R v Curry*,[80] where C was convicted of conspiracy to obtain property by deception. She had been charged with two others, W and H, and H had pleaded guilty. The prosecution case was that W drove the accused to the shops where C, with H's knowledge, used H's credit card to obtain the goods, H's intention being to report the card as stolen so as to avoid liability for payment. Evidence of H's guilty plea was admitted to establish the existence of an unlawful agreement to deceive. The conviction was quashed on the basis that the evidence clearly implied as a matter of fact, albeit not law, that C had been a party to the conspiracy. The court said that s 74 should be used sparingly, especially in cases of conspiracy and affray, and should not be used where the evidence, expressly or by necessary inference, imports the complicity of the accused.

In another conspiracy case, *R v Lunnon*,[81] which was distinguished in *R v Curry*, a guilty plea was held to have been properly admitted. *R v Lunnon* also involved three accused jointly charged with conspiracy, but it was held that evidence of the guilty plea of one of them had been properly admitted to prove the existence of the conspiracy because the judge had separated for the jury two questions, whether there was a conspiracy and who was a party to it, and had made it clear that despite the evidence, they could acquit the accused.[82] In *R v Shirt*[83] the guilty pleas of co-accused were properly admitted because the judge had given a clear direction that the pleas had 'extremely limited relevance', namely they were limited to the existence of the conspiracy and did not in any way bear on the other issues which needed to be resolved in order to convict the accused.[84] Similarly in *R v Denham*,[85] on charges of conspiracy, evidence of the guilty pleas of co-accused were held to have been properly admitted on the grounds that it neither shut off the defence of the accused nor closed down the issue for the jury—their defences were not that there were no conspiracies, but that they were not party to them. The test, it was said, is unfairness to, and not difficulty for, the defence.[86]

In *R v Abdullah*[87] it was held that evidence of a guilty plea may be admitted if the count against the accused and former co-accused is amended to allege 'with others unknown', which enables the judge to direct the jury that the conviction does not help in any way on the question whether any of the co-accused on trial are guilty of conspiracy.

In deciding whether the guilty plea of a co-accused should be excluded under s 78, regard should be had not only to the interests of the accused, but to those of the prosecution and of justice as a whole.[88] On this basis, in the case of a joint enterprise, an initial decision to exclude the guilty plea may be reversed in order to avoid the jury being misled by the evidence of the accused.[89]

---

[80] [1988] Crim LR 527, CA.

[81] [1988] Crim LR 456, CA.

[82] See also *R v Chapman* [1991] Crim LR 44, CA where C and seven others were charged with conspiracy to obtain by deception. It was held that a guilty plea by one of the others to two specific counts of obtaining by deception, incidents in which he was involved with C, were relevant and admissible and did not inevitably import the complicity of C. See also *R v Hunt* [1994] Crim LR 747, CA.

[83] [2019] 1 Cr App R 199 (15).

[84] At 207.

[85] [2017] 1 Cr App R 64 (7), CA.

[86] At [39].

[87] [2010] EWCA Crim 3078.

[88] *R v Stewart* [1995] 1 Cr App R 441, CA.

[89] *R v Tee* [2011] EWCA Crim 462.

Section 78 may be invoked successfully on the basis that the prosecution, by relying on s 74, do not have to call the person convicted, thereby depriving the defence of the opportunity to challenge or test him in cross-examination.[90] The argument was rejected in *R v Robertson; R v Golder*[91] on the basis that R's name did not appear on any of the burglary counts to which the co-accused had pleaded guilty, and that even if the co-accused had given evidence in accordance with their pleas, R's advocate would have been unlikely to cross-examine them or, if he had, would have seriously prejudiced R. However, as Staughton LJ observed in *R v Kempster*,[92] although such cross-examination may be unlikely in some cases, or else turn out to be a disaster, one cannot always assume that.

An application under s 78 may succeed where a co-accused has pleaded guilty but the evidence was far from conclusive against him, on the basis that to allow the conviction to be proved might deprive the remaining accused of the opportunity to challenge that evidence.[93] An application may also succeed where, a co-accused having pleaded guilty towards or at the end of the prosecution case, it would be unfair to admit evidence of the plea because, had it been entered and put in evidence earlier, cross-examination might have been conducted differently.[94]

Burden and standard of proof

Section 74(2) has the effect of placing the legal burden in relation to the commission of the offence (by a person other than the accused) on the party seeking to disprove it. Where that burden is borne by the accused, the standard of proof required to discharge it is the standard ordinarily required where the legal burden on a particular issue is borne by the accused, namely proof on a balance of probabilities.[95] It will be necessary for the judge to give the jury a direction to this effect (a reverse burden direction).[96]

Section 74(3): convictions of the accused

The purpose of s 74(3)

It is clear from the wording of s 74(3) that its purpose is not to define or enlarge the circumstances in which evidence of the fact that the accused has committed an offence is admissible, but simply to assist, where such evidence is admissible, in proving that fact.[97] The conviction is admissible as evidence of the commission of the offence and the accused shall

---

[90] This was part of the ratio in *R v O'Connor* (1986) 85 Cr App R 298, CA, see text at n 79.

[91] [1987] QB 920, CA.

[92] (1989) 90 Cr App R 14, CA at 22.

[93] *R v Lee* [1996] Crim LR 825, CA. Cf *R v Merchant* [2018] 1 Cr App R 165 (11): it did not have an adverse effect on the fairness of the proceedings to admit guilty plea of a co-accused to prove a conspiracy to defraud when fixing the LIBOR rate for the US dollar because the plea '. . . did not prove too much' (at p 177).

[94] See *R v Chapman* [1991] Crim LR 44. The evidence may also be excluded under s 78 where it adds little to an already strong case: *R v Warner* (1992) 96 Cr App R 324, CA. See also *R v Humphreys and Tully* [1993] Crim LR 288, CA.

[95] See *R v Carr-Briant* [1943] KB 607, Ch 3.

[96] See Ch 3, **Where the accused bears the legal burden**, p 86. See also the Crown Court Compendium (July 2019), Part 1, 5–2, Example 2 and 12–2, para 2. See further, *R v Merchant* [2018] 1 Cr App R 165 (11): it was unclear whether a reverse burden direction was required where the direction had not been sought at trial and the relevant accused's defence was that he had not conspired with the party whose guilty plea had been admitted. See also *R v Shirt* [2019] 1 Cr App R 199 (15): where it comes to light during cross-examination that the co-accused whose guilty plea has been admitted suffered mental health problems, comment by advocates may be permitted regarding the reliability of the plea, subject to an overall direction to avoid speculation (at 207).

[97] *R v Harris* [2001] Crim LR 227, CA.

be taken to have committed the offence unless the contrary is proved. The subsection operates to place on the accused the legal burden of disproving the commission of the offence on a balance of probabilities.

The situations in which s 74(3) applies

Section 74(3) appears to apply in four types of situation. The first is where the accused denies that he committed some previous offence which the prosecution seek to prove as an element of the offence with which he is charged. Thus when, after an accused's conviction of causing grievous bodily harm with intent, the victim dies from his injuries, and the accused is charged with his murder, the prosecution need only prove that death resulted from the injuries. It is for the accused to prove, if he can, that he did not inflict the grievous bodily harm or had no intent to do so.[98] The second situation is where the prosecution seek to adduce evidence of, or of a disposition towards, misconduct on the part of the accused that 'has to do with' the alleged facts of the offence charged, under s 98(a) of the Criminal Justice Act 2003.[99] The third situation is where the accused's commission of an offence, other than that with which he is charged, is admissible as evidence of his bad character under s 101 of the Criminal Justice Act 2003.[100] The fourth situation is where, a conviction having been proved as part of the prosecution case pursuant to statutory provisions such as s 101 of the Criminal Justice Act 2003, s 27(3)(b) of the Theft Act 1968, or s 1(2) of the Official Secrets Act 1911, the accused denies having committed the offence in question.

It could be argued that s 74(3) also applies where, after a finding of guilt or a guilty plea, a previous conviction is proved in order to guide the court on the question of sentence, but the accused denies having committed the offence in question. However, it is submitted that in such a situation, the question whether the accused committed the offence is irrelevant: it is the *fact* of the previous conviction which is relevant to the determination of an appropriate sentence; if the accused denies the conviction, it can be proved in the ordinary way under s 73 of the 1984 Act.[101]

Evidence of a previous conviction may be excluded under s 78 of the 1984 Act, but it would be improper to exercise that discretion in order to circumvent s 74(3) on the basis of 'judicial or academic distaste for it'.[102]

Avoidance of a 'retrial'

In *R v C*[103] the following guidance was given with a view to ensuring that, where an accused seeks to rebut the presumption under s 74(3), both sides may adduce relevant evidence without, in effect, turning the trial into a retrial of the earlier offence. It is submitted that the guidance, applicable in relation to s 74(3), is no less applicable under s 74(2). The accused is entitled to adduce evidence to seek to prove, whether by cross-examination of prosecution witnesses or by calling evidence of his own, that he was not guilty. If he does so, it is open to the prosecution to call evidence in rebuttal. It is essential that the defence statement identifies all the ingredients of the case which the accused will advance, which will enable

---

[98] *R v Clift* [2013] 1 WLR 2093, CA.

[99] For an illustration, see *R v Okokono* [2014] EWCA Crim 2521. As to s 98(a), see Ch 19, pp 560–2.

[100] See Ch 19, pp 571–2.

[101] See Ch 2, Convictions and acquittals, p 54.

[102] *R v Clift* [2013] 1 WLR 2093, CA.

[103] [2011] 1 WLR 1942, CA.

the prosecution to prepare draft admissions of fact and collate the necessary prosecution evidence. The prosecution are not required, if the accused merely denies that he was guilty of the offence, to prove that he was, or to assist him to prove that he was not, or to call witnesses for either purpose.[104]

Previous acquittals

In the absence of some exceptional feature, evidence of an acquittal is generally inadmissible in a subsequent trial.[105] The reason is that in most cases it is not possible to be certain why the jury acquitted. Evidence of an acquittal will be admissible where there is a clear inference from the verdict that the jury rejected a witness's evidence because they did not believe him and his credibility is directly in issue in the subsequent trial.[106] Even if admissible, however, evidence of the acquittal is not conclusive evidence of innocence and does not mean that all relevant issues in the trial were resolved in favour of the accused.[107]

ADDITIONAL READING

Munday, 'Proof of guilt by association under section 74 of the Police and Criminal Evidence Act 1984' [1990] Crim LR 236.
An article which critically analyses the operation of s 74, covering: (i) whether Parliament intended s 74 to be applied to the kind of cases which have come before the Court of Appeal; (ii) the artificiality of the distinction made in directions to the jury, that evidence of a co-accused's guilty plea is only evidence of the fact that an offence occurred and is not evidence of the accused's guilt; (iii) the inability of an accused to properly challenge the evidence of a co-accused who is not present; and (iv) the difficulty any accused would face in proving, on the balance of probabilities, that the co-accused did not commit the offence to which the guilty plea relates.

---

[104] See also, applying *R v C, R v Lunkulu* [2015] EWCA Crim 1350.

[105] *Hui Chi-ming v R* [1991] 3 All ER 897, PC.

[106] *R v Deboussi* [2007] EWCA Crim 684, considered, with the other authorities, in Ch 2, **Irrelevance, p 25**.

[107] *R v Terry* [2005] QB 996, CA, disapproving the dictum of O'Connor LJ in *R v Hay* (1983) 77 Cr App R 70 at 75. See also *R v Colman* [2005] QB 996.

INDEX

A

Abuse of process 322–3, 761

Accomplices
background 257–9
care warnings to jury 266–7
where interest in giving
false evidence 266–7
identification of 'supporting
material' 261–2

Accused
bad character
abolition of common law
rules 555–6
admitted by agreement of
all parties 577–8
admitted by agreement of
defendant 578
attacks by accused
on character of
another 612–20
background 554–5
correcting false impressions
by accused 608–12
defined 556–9
exclusionary
discretion 575–7
facts connected with
offence 560–2
'important explanatory
evidence' 578–84
issues of
credibility 597–600
issues of guilt 584–97
judge's summing up 574–5
legislative
background 570–2
offences committed when
child 620–1
requirement of leave 575
relevant to issue
between accused and
co-accused 600–8
role of judge and Court of
Appeal 562
statutory provisions 570–2
use to which evidence
put 573
competence and
compellability
for co-accused 130
for himself 128–30
for prosecution 128
cross-examination
of witnesses
personally 216–17

good character
admissible
evidence 539–40
categories of good
character 546
directions to jury 540–50
meaning 550–2
other issues 550–2
previous convictions 765–7
right to silence
failure to account for
objects, substances
or marks, or
presence 522–5
failure to mention facts
before trial 21, 70, 262,
506–21
failure to testify 499–506
meaning and scope
498–9
statements on
accusation 190–2,
199–202
status of evidence under
special measures 168–70

Acquittals
autre fois acquit 37
previous findings as evidence
civil cases 763–4
criminal cases 773
proof 54–5

Admissibility
see also **Discretionary
powers; Relevance**
best evidence rule 31–2
conditional admissibility 31
confessions
background 407, 454
defined 454–6
fraudulent tax
conduct 467–8
oppression 459–62
required conditions 456–9
unreliability 462–70
exclusionary rules 30
function and scope of *voir
dire* 37–40
illegally or unfairly obtained
evidence
overview 320–1
principles for
exclusion 321–2
rules of law 322–5
multiple admissibility 30–1
overview 22–3

Admissions
admissibility as hearsay in
civil cases
statutory provisions 429
weight of evidence 430–2
by agents 450–2
execution of documents 313
failure to deal with facts in
issue 9
formal admissions
civil cases 124
criminal cases 125
informal admissions
distinguished 124

Adultery findings 762–3

Advance disclosure
inferences from failure
to provide summary
trials 531
trials on indictment 526–30

Affirmations *see* **Oaths and
affirmations**

Age
admissibility as hearsay in
civil cases 439
proof 54

Agents 450–2

Alibis
Lucas direction 19–22
supporting evidence 287–8

Anonymity
informers 682–3
witnesses
care warnings to jury 268
general rule 170–5

Appearance 314–15

Assertions *see* **Implied
assertions**

Attempts
need for corroboration 257

Autre fois **acquit and
convict** 37

B

Bad character
accused
abolition of common law
rules 555–6
admitted by agreement of
all parties 577–8
admitted by agreement of
defendant 578
attacks by accused
on character of
another 612–20

Bad character (*Cont.*)
background 554–5
correcting a false
impression by
accused 608–12
defined 556–9
exclusionary
discretion 575–7
facts connected with
offence 560–2
'important explanatory
evidence' 578–84
issues of credibility 597–600
issues of guilt 584–97
judge's summing up 574–5
legislative
background 570–2
matters in issue 582–4
offences committed when
child 620–1
requirement of leave 575
relevant to issue
between accused and
co-accused 600–8
role of judge and Court of
Appeal 562
statutory provisions 570–2
use to which evidence
put 573
assumption of truth 621–2
civil cases 535–7
contaminated evidence 622–4
criminal cases practice
direction 630
disposition towards bad
character
espionage 630
theft 628
evidence admitted
inadvertently 627
failure to give notice 626
persons other than defendant
exclusionary
discretion 570
requirement for
permission 569
statutory provisions 562–3
threshold
conditions 564–8
power to make rules of
court 625–6
reasons for court
rulings 624–5
right to challenge evidence of
convictions 626–7
Bankers books
competence and
compellability 142

proof of contents 309–11
Best evidence rule
documentary
evidence 304–6
general rules 31–2
Bias
bad character evidence 562
cross-examination 245–6
exception to rule of
finality 245–6
expert witnesses 645
Birth certificates 53–4
Blood tests 17
Burden of proof
see also **Reverse burden of
proof**
civil cases
evidential burden 39–40,
80–4
legal burden 78–80
evidential burden 60–1
legal burden
civil cases 78–80
criminal cases 62–77
incidence 61–2
meaning 58–9
overview 58
previous convictions 760–1,
771
right to begin 84
voir dire 94–5
Business documents
admissibility as hearsay in
civil cases 427–8
admissibility as hearsay in
criminal cases 382–6

C
Capacity
example of circumstantial
evidence 16
presumptions
marriage 105
mental capacity 103–4
testamentary capacity 114
special measures 162–3
statement of person unfit to
be a witness 376
Care warnings
accomplices
background 257–9
identification of
'supporting
material' 261–2
sexual complaints 263–4
accomplices who are
co-accused 264–5
anonymous witnesses 268

cell confessions 265–6
children 267–8
confessions by mentally
handicapped
persons 269–72
hearsay in criminal
cases 404–5
inferences which may be
drawn from silence 520
lip-reading evidence 272–3
matrimonial cases 269
special measures
evidence 167–8
succession claims 269
sudden infant death
syndrome 273–4
voice identification 295–7
witnesses tainted by
improper motive 264
Cautions
confessions
breach of 'verballing'
provisions 479–81
statutory provisions 471–3
failure to mention facts
before trial 508
CCTV
lip-reading evidence
care warnings to
jury 272–3
species of real
evidence 315
recognition of people 284
Cell confessions 265–6
Character evidence
see also **Bad character; Good
character**
civil cases
disposition towards bad
character 535–7
disposition towards good
character 534–5
relevance 534
criminal cases
bad character 554–630
good character of
accused 543–50
practice direction 630
Children
Abrogation of privilege
against self-
incrimination under
Children Act 1989, s 98
721–2
admissibility of depositions
as hearsay in criminal
cases 410
care warnings to jury 267–8

competence and
    compellability
    civil cases 140–1
    criminal cases 132–6,
        136–9
exclusion of litigation
    privilege under Children
    Act 1989 741–2
presumption of
    legitimacy 107–9
restrictions on bad character
    evidence 620–1
standard of proof in cases
    involving care of
    children 92–3
sudden infant death
    syndrome
    care warnings to
        jury 273–4
treatment in court
    cross-examination 225–30
    examination-in-chief
        174–5, 180–1
vulnerable witnesses
    aids to
        communications 162
    circumstances in which
        special measures
        given 164–5
    eligible witnesses 162–3
    evidence in private 157–8
    examination of
        witness through
        intermediary 162,
        169–70
    removal of wigs and
        gowns 158
    special measures
        directions 162–3
    video-recorded
        evidence 157–62

Circumstantial evidence
examples 15–22
meaning and
    importance 14–15

Civil cases
burden of proof
    evidential burden 80–4
    legal burden 78–80
character evidence
    credibility 537
    disposition towards bad
        character 535–7
    disposition towards good
        character 534–5
    relevance 534
competence and
    compellability

children 140–1
general rule 127–8
development of law 3–5
documentary evidence 302
exclusionary discretion 47–9
expert witnesses 652–4
    contents of report 665–6
    court directions 667
    discussion between
        experts 666
    restrictions on
        evidence 660–1
    single joint experts
        662–4
    use in evidence 666–7
    written questions 664
    written reports 662
failure to give
    evidence 17–19
failure to provide
    evidence 18–19
formal admissions 124
hearsay evidence (common
    law rules)
    declarations of
        pedigree 440–1
    public documents 434–8
    public rights 441–2
    reference works 438–9
    reputation 439–40
hearsay evidence (statutory
    rules)
    abolition of rule
        against 415
    advance notice 420–2
    background 413–14
    conditions of
        admissibility 418–20
    cross-examination of
        witnesses 423
    impeaching
        credibility 425–6
    informal
        admissions 429–32
    Ogden tables 432
    proving
        documents 426–32
    weighing the
        evidence 423–5
illegally or unfairly obtained
    evidence 325–6
judgments as evidence
    defamation 762
    previous acquittals
        763–4
    previous
        convictions 759–63
    previous findings 764–5

previous findings
    of adultery and
    paternity 762–3
legal professional
    privilege 735
no case submissions 43
privilege against
    self-incrimination 717
public interest immunity
    development of modern
        law 676–9
    informers 685
    procedural issues 697–702
right to begin 84
standard of proof
    evidential burden 93–4
    legal burden 86–93
witnesses
    discretionary powers 148
    statements 150–2
    time for adducing
        evidence 146, 146–9
    training and
        familiarisation 176–7
    video link evidence 144
    witnesses to be
        called 149–50

Civil partners
competence and
    compellability 130–6
privilege against
    self-incrimination 717

Closed material procedures
common law
    provisions 702–4
statutory provisions 704–6

Collateral facts 10–11

Comparative behaviour 22

Compellability
accused
    for co-accused 130
    for himself 128–30
bankers immunity 142
children
    civil cases 140–1
    criminal cases 132–6,
        136–9
diplomatic immunity 142
general rule 127–8
persons of unsound mind
    civil cases 141
    criminal cases 132–6,
        136–9
public interest immunity
    distinguished 713
sovereign immunity 142
spouses
    for accused 130

Compellability (*Cont.*)
  for co-accused 134–5
  former spouses 135–6
  for prosecution 130–4
Competence
  accused
    for co-accused 130
    for himself 128–30
    for prosecution 128
  admissibility as hearsay in
    civil cases 418–19
  bankers' immunity 142
  children
    civil cases 140–1
    criminal cases 132–6,
    136–9
  diplomatic immunity 142
  expert witnesses 643–5
  general rule 127–8
  persons of unsound mind
    civil cases 141
    criminal cases 132–6, 136–9
  sovereign immunity 142
  spouses
    for accused 130
    for co-accused 134–5
    former spouses 135–6
    for prosecution 130–4
Computer statements 371–3
Conclusive evidence 22
Conditional admissibility 31
Conduct
  failure to provide advance
    disclosure of defence
    summary trials 531
    trials on
      indictment 526–30
  failure to provide intimate
    samples 525–6
  right to silence 498–9
Confessions
  see also **Admissions**
  acceptance of accusations
    made in presence of
    accused 490–4
  admissibility
    background 407, 454
    fraudulent tax
      conduct 467–8
    oppression 459–62
    required conditions 456–9
    unreliability 462–70
  background 454
  care warnings to jury
    cell confessions 265–6
    mentally handicapped
      persons 269–72

defined 454–6
exclusionary discretion
  breach of verballing
    provisions 479–81
  cautions 471–3
  interviews with non-police
    professionals 481
  PACE Codes 469–70
  procedural fairness 476–9
  right to have someone
    informed 473–6
  right to legal advice 473–6
  statutory provisions 468–9
expert evidence 642–3
facts consequent upon
  inadmissible
  confessions 494–6
improperly obtained
  confessions 324
voir dire
  procedure 482–3
  when necessary 481–2
weight of evidence
  editing 490
  implicating
    co-accused 487–90
  matter for jury 485–7
Confidential
  relationships 689–91
Construction of ordinary
  words 35–6
Continuance
  example of circumstantial
    evidence 17
  presumption of continuation
    of life 103
Convictions
  autre fois convict 37
  cross-examination
    on previous
    convictions 244–5
  previous convictions as
    evidence of commission
    of offence in civil
    cases 759–63
  previous convictions as
    evidence of commission
    of offence in criminal
    cases
  convictions of
    accused 771–3
  convictions of
    persons other than
    accused 765–71
  propensity to commit
    crime 589–91
  proof 54–5

Corroboration
  care warnings to jury
    accomplices 257–66
    accomplices who are
      co-accused 264–5
    anonymous witnesses 268
    cell confessions 265–6
    children 267–8
    matrimonial cases 269
    succession claims 269
    sudden infant death
      syndrome 273–4
    witnesses tainted by
      improper motive 264
  meaning 254–5
  overview 253–4
  question of law 36
  special need for caution
    confessions by mentally
      handicapped
      persons 269–72
    lip-reading evidence 272–3
  statutory requirements
    attempts 257
    perjury 255–6
    speeding 256–7
    treason 256
Credibility
  character evidence
    bad character 597–600
    civil cases 537
  expert evidence 641
  hearsay evidence
    civil cases 425–6
    criminal cases 398–400
Criminal investigation and
  prosecution
  no protection for journalistic
    sources 696
  public interest
    immunity 682–6
Criminal cases
  burden of proof
    evidential burden 80–4
    legal burden 62–77
  character evidence
    bad character 554–630
    good character of
      accused 539–52
    practice direction 630
  competence and
    compellability
    accused 128–30
    children 136–9
    general rule 127–8
    persons of unsound
      mind 141

spouses 130–6
development of law 5–6
documentary evidence 302
evidential burden 39–40
exclusionary
    discretion 49–53
expert witnesses
    contents of report 668
    disclosure 669–70
    pre-hearing
        discussions 669
    single joint experts 669
failure to give
    evidence 19–22
failure to provide
    evidence 18–19
formal admissions 125
hearsay evidence (common
        law rules)
    admissions by
        agents 450–2
    age 439
    persons emotionally
        overpowered by
        events 442–8
    res gestae 442–52
    statements accompanying
        performance of
        act 448–9
    statements of physical
        sensations or mental
        state 449
hearsay evidence (statutory
        rules)
    admissible in interests of
        justice 386–91
    background and
        rationale 350–1
    depositions, vulnerable
        children and young
        persons 410
    documents 382–6
    expert evidence 407–9
    general
        admissibility 352–3
    meaning 360–3
    multiple hearsay 396–8
    previous statements
        392–5
    other safeguards 398–405
    previous inconsistent
        statements 391–2
    proof 405–7
    'statements' and 'matters
        stated' 363–73
    video-recorded
        evidence 407

witnesses
    unavailable 375–82
    written statements 409–10
illegally or unfairly obtained
        evidence
    background 326–8
    covert recording and
        filming 338–9
    disciplinary
        principle 332–3
    entrapment 339–45
    identity 337
    improper detention and
        questioning 335–7
    improper searches 335
    reliability principle 332
    rights-based
        principle 334–5
    statutory
        provisions 329–32
judgments as evidence
    previous acquittals 773
    previous
        convictions 765–73
memory refreshing, statutory
        provisions 184–5
no case submissions
    Crown Court 41–2
    magistrates court 42–3
privilege against
        self-incrimination
    'criminal charge, penalty or
        forfeiture' defined 715
    history and rationale 713
    scope 714–15
    'tendency to expose'
        defined 716
public interest immunity
    development of modern
        law 679–80
    procedural issues 707
rebuttable presumptions of
        law 100–1
standard of proof
    evidential burden 93–4
    legal burden 85–6
witnesses
    discretionary
        powers 152–4
    order of witnesses
        154–5
    sexual complaints 166–7
    special measures 155–75
    time for adducing
        evidence 146–9
    training and
        familiarisation 175–6

video link evidence 144–5
video-recorded
    evidence 155
    witnesses to be
        called 153–4
Cross-examination
    by accused in person 216–17
    answers to collateral
        questions
    bias 245–6
    capacity to give reliable
        evidence 246–8
    general rule 242–4
    previous
        convictions 244–5
    documents 222
    effect of failure to
        cross-examine 221–2
    hostile witnesses 207–12
    liability of witnesses to
        cross-examination
        215–16
    meaning 215
    memory refreshing 181–2,
        189–91
    permitted questions
        credit of witness 219–21
        facts in issue 218–19
        overriding
            objectives 217–18
    power to call witnesses in
        civil cases 423
    previous statements 222–5
    sexual complaints
        lifting off
            restrictions 233–42
        rationale 230–1
        statutory
            restrictions 231–3
    special measures
        directions 160–2
    young and vulnerable
        witnesses 225–30
        Criminal Practice
            Directions 225–8
        Crown Court
            Compendium
            guidelines 229
        distressed witnesses 229
        Judicial College Bench
            Checklist: Young Witness
            Cases 228–9
        witness training
            and professional
            conduct 230
**Customs and professional
        practices** 121

D

Death
care warnings to jury
succession claims 269
sudden infant death
syndrome 273–4
certificates 53–4
presumptions
basic facts 110
presumed facts 110–11
statutory provisions 111–13
proof 53–4
Defamation 762
Demeanour of witnesses 315
Demonstrations 317–19
Diminished responsibility
reverse burden of proof 63
Diplomatic immunity 142,
681–2
Direct testimony 11
Directions
Bad character of
accused 574–5
care warnings to jury
accomplices 257–66
accomplices who are
co-accused 264–5
anonymous witnesses 268
cell confessions 265–6
children 267–8
close examination of
circumstances 281–2
confessions by mentally
handicapped
persons 269–72
lip-reading evidence 272–3
matrimonial cases 269
recognition of people 282–4
succession claims 269
sudden infant death
syndrome 273–4
terms of *Turnbull*
directions 281
visual identification 278–9
voice identification 295–7
witnesses tainted by
improper motive 264
expert evidence
case management 667
disclosure 669–70
failure to account for
things 523–4
failure to mention facts
before trial 516–20
failure to testify 503–4
function of judge and jury 34
good character of accused

entitlement to a
direction 540–50
other issues 550–2
hearsay in criminal
cases 404–5
hostile witnesses 201
special measures 156–7
sexual complaints 166–7
summing up by judge 44–6
Disclosure
expert evidence
pre-hearing
discussions 669
procedure 669–70
single joint experts 669
expert evidence in civil cases
contents of report 665–6
court directions 667
discussion between
experts 666
restrictions on
evidence 660–1
single joint experts 662–4
use in evidence 666–7
written questions 664
written reports 662
expert evidence in criminal
cases
contents of report 668
failure to provide advance
disclosure of defence
summary trials 531
trials on
indictment 526–30
journalistic sources
interests of justice 693–6
national security 696
prevention of crime 696
statutory protection 692–3
legal professional privilege
civil cases 735
criminal cases 735
privilege
legal professional
privilege 725
self-incrimination 719–21
without prejudice
negotiations 749–54
public interest
immunity 699–702
Discretionary powers
bad character of accused 562
see also **Exclusionary**
discretion
cross-examination of sexual
complainants 233–42
exclusionary discretion

civil cases 47–9
criminal cases 49–53
hearsay in criminal
cases 401–4
hostile witnesses 207–12
inclusionary discretion 47
memory refreshing out of
court 182–4, 191–2
scope 47
time for adducing
evidence 146–9
video link evidence 144
witnesses
civil cases 144
criminal cases 152–4
Disposition towards bad
character
civil cases 535–7
criminal cases 556–9
espionage 630
theft 628
DNA evidence
expert evidence 636, 652
genetic fingerprint tests 16
legal professional
privilege 736
presumption of
legitimacy 108
reliability principle 332
self-incrimination 719–20
Documentary evidence
see also **Statements**
admissibility as hearsay in
civil cases
business documents 427–8
computer-produced
documents 414
proof generally 426–7
public documents 427–8
admissibility as hearsay in
criminal cases 382–6
civil cases 302
criminal cases 302
cross-examination 222
defined 302
hearsay evidence of
association with
accused 362–3
legal professional
privilege 736–7
meaning 12–13
memory refreshing
cross-examination on
document 181–2,
189–91
required conditions
179–81, 187–9

proof 406–7
  contents 303–11
  execution 311–14
  stamping
    requirements 313–14
proof of previous acquittals
    and convictions
    554–5, 761
real evidence 315
theft of privileged documents
    in court 323
Domicile 92
Dominant purpose test
    733–5

E
Entrapment
illegally or unfairly obtained
    evidence 339–45
undercover operations after
    offence 345–7
Evidence *see* **Judicial**
    evidence
Evidential burden
civil cases 80–4
criminal cases 39–40
legal professional
    privilege 727
standard of proof 93–4
Examination-in-chief
general rule 174, 180
hostile witnesses 207–12
impeachment of own
    witness 196, 205, 206
judicial interventions 182–3
jury notes 183
leading questions 181–2
memory refreshing
    in court 176–81
    out of court 182–4, 191–2
    overview 176, 183–4
statutory provisions 184–5
visually recorded
    interviews 193
previous statements
    common law
    exceptions 186–8, 195–9
  on discovery of
    incriminating
    articles 192, 202
  general rule 184–6, 193–5
  identification 192–5,
    202–5
  memory refreshing
    196, 205
  part of *res gestae*
    195–6, 205

previous inconsistent
    statements 205–6
rebuttal of recent
    fabrication 188–9,
    197–9
statements on
    accusation 190–2,
    199–202
unfavourable witnesses 196–
    7, 207
video-recorded
    evidence 157–62
young witnesses 174–5,
    180–1
Exclusionary discretion
bad character
    accused 575–7
    attacks by accused
      on character of
      others 617–20
    correcting false impressions
      by accused 612
    evidence showing
      a propensity to
      offend 587–97
    'important explanatory
      evidence' 582
    issues of credibility 600
    persons other than
      accused 570
    relevant to an issue
      between accused and
      co-accused 604
civil cases 47–9
confessions
    breach of verballing
      provisions 479–81
    cautions 471–3
    interviews with non-police
      professionals 481
    PACE Codes 469–70
    procedural fairness 476–9
    right to have someone
      informed 473–6
    right to legal advice 473–6
    statutory provisions 468–9
criminal cases 49–53
development of law 3–5
failure to account for
    things 525
hearsay in criminal
    cases 401–4
illegally or unfairly obtained
    evidence
    civil cases 325–6
    criminal cases 328–47
    key principles 321–2

overview 320–1
overview 30
previous convictions of
    persons other than
    accused 768–9
visual identification 293–4
Execution of documents
admissions and
    presumptions 313
general rule 311
proof of attestation 312–13
proof of handwriting 311–12
Expert evidence
admissibility as hearsay in
    criminal cases
    preparatory work 407–8
    reports 408–9
competence 643–5
disclosure in civil cases
    contents of report 665–6
    court directions 667
    discussion between
      experts 666
    restrictions on
      evidence 660–1
    single joint experts
      662–4
    use in evidence 666–7
    written questions 664
    written reports 662
disclosure in criminal cases
    contents of report 668
    disclosure 669–70
    pre-hearing
      discussions 669
    single joint experts 669
duty of expert 652–4
duty of lawyer 652
facts upon which evidence
    based 654–7
foreign law 637–8
independence 645
matters calling for expertise
    examples 635–6
matters within knowledge
    of court 638–43
non-expert opinion
    evidence 672–3
reliability 646–52
ultimate issues 657–8
weight of evidence 658–60

F
Facial mapping 315
Facts
    see also **Questions of fact**
    collateral facts 10–11

Facts (*Cont.*)
consequent upon
inadmissible
confessions 494–6
expert evidence
foreign law 637–8
matters within knowledge
of court 638–43
upon which evidence
based 654–7
formal admissions
civil cases 124
criminal cases 125
informal admissions
distinguished 124
investigation of truth 2–3
judgments as evidence
background 758
civil cases 759–63
criminal cases 765–73
judicial notice
after inquiry 119–24
personal knowledge 122–4
without inquiry 117–19
legal professional
privilege 736
presumptions
applicability 101
conflicting
presumptions 116–17
continuance of life 103
death 109–14
definitions and
classification 99
guilty knowledge 102
intention 102
legitimacy 107–9
marriage 104–7
*omnia praesumuntur rite esse
acta* 113–14
res ipsa loquitur 114–16
seaworthiness 103
wills 114
relevant facts 10
similar facts cases 593–4
Fair trial (Art 6)
anonymity of witnesses 173
application of exclusionary
discretion 49–50
cross-examination in sexual
cases 238
exclusion of hearsay 403
illegally or unfairly obtained
evidence 330–1
no automatic exclusion
of hearsay in civil
cases 418–20

presumption of
innocence 68–9
privilege against self-
incrimination 718–19
public interest
immunity 679–80
reverse burden of proof
incompatibility with
Art 6(2) of European
Convention on Human
Rights 68–77
regulatory offences 76–7
statutory scheme for hearsay
absent witnesses 354–5
applicable
statements 353–4
exclusionary
discretion 403
Horncastle and *Al Khawaja*
distinguished 356–7
reasons for
non-attendance 358–9
sole or decisive rule 355–8
statements not sole or
decisive 358
undercover operations after
offence 346–7
Films
illegally or unfairly obtained
evidence 338–9
real evidence 315–17
visual identification
analysis of images 289–90
pre-trial procedure 290–4
Foreign law
evidence of previous
convictions 767
expert evidence 637–8
proof 119
question of fact 36
Formal admissions
civil cases 124
criminal cases 125
informal admissions
distinguished 124
Freedom of expression (Art 10)
protection of journalistic
sources
disclosure in interests of
justice 695
statutory provisions 692

G
Good character
accused
admissible
evidence 539–40

directions to jury 540–50
meaning 550–2
other issues 550–2
civil cases 534–5
prosecution witnesses 27–8

H
Hearsay evidence
see also **Confessions**
birth certificates 53–4
civil cases (common law
rules)
declarations of
pedigree 440–1
public documents
434–8
public rights 441–2
reference works 438–9
reputation 439–40
civil cases (statutory rules)
abolition of rule
against 415
advance notice 420–2
background 413–14
conditions of
admissibility 418–20
cross-examination of
witnesses 423
impeaching
credibility 425–6
informal
admissions 429–32
Ogden tables 432
proving
documents 426–32
weighing the
evidence 423–5
criminal cases (common law
rules)
admissions by
agents 450–2
age 439
persons emotionally
overpowered by
events 442–8
res gestae 442–52
statements accompanying
performance of
act 448–9
statements of physical
sensations or mental
state 449
criminal cases (statutory rules)
admissible in interests of
justice 386–91
background and
rationale 350–1

depositions of vulnerable
    young persons 410
documents 382–6
expert evidence 407–9
general
    admissibility 352–3
    meaning 360–3
multiple hearsay 396–8
negative hearsay 370
other previous
    statements 392–5
other safeguards 398–405
previous inconsistent
    statements 391–2
proof 405–7
'statements' and 'matters
    stated' 363–73
video-recorded
    evidence 407
witnesses
    unavailable 375–82
written statements 409–10
documents admissible by
    statute 306
meaning 12
*Hollington v Hewthorn & Co
    Ltd*, rule in 758
Hostile witnesses 207–12
Human rights
denial of access to
    solicitor 478–9
fair trial (Art 6) *see* **Fair trial
    (Art 6)**
prohibition of torture (Art 3)
    evidence obtained by
        torture 324
    public interest
        immunity 679
    protection of journalistic
        sources
        disclosure in interests of
            justice 695
        statutory provisions 692

I
Identification
admissibility of previous
    statements as hearsay in
    criminal cases 394
example of circumstantial
    evidence 16–17
illegally or unfairly obtained
    evidence 337
previous statements 192–5,
    202–5
propensity to commit
    crime 595–6

visual identification
    analysis of images 289–90
    close examination of
        circumstances 281–2
    description and
        identification
        distinguished 280–1
    false alibis 287–8
    good quality evidence 285
    by jury 288–9
    persons with the
        accused 280
    poor quality
        evidence 285–6
    pre-trial procedure 290–4
    recognition of
        people 282–4
    special need for
        caution 279–80
    supporting evidence 286–7
    terms of *Turnbull*
        direction 281
    Turnbull guidelines 278–81
    underlying risks 277–8
    where issue not identity
        but what accused
        did 280
voice identification
    pre-trial procedure 297–8
    risks 295
    warning 297
**Illegally or unfairly obtained
    evidence**
civil cases 325–6
criminal cases
    background 326–8
    covert recording and
        filming 338–9
    disciplinary
        principle 332–3
    entrapment 339–45
    identity 337
    improper detention and
        questioning 335–7
    improper searches 335
    reliability principle 332
    rights-based
        principle 334–5
    statutory
        provisions 329–32
    overview 320–1
    principles for
        exclusion 321–2
    rules of law
        abuse of process 322–3
        evidence obtained by
            torture 324

improperly obtained
    confessions 324
    intercepted evidence 325
    theft of privileged
        documents in court 323
Implied assertions
civil cases 417
criminal cases
    approach in *R v
        Twist* 367–9
    meaning and scope 366–7
    oral assertions 316–17
    risks 369–70
    'statements' and 'matters
        stated' 364–6
Inclusionary discretion
best evidence rule 31–2
no discretionary power 47
Incriminating articles 202
inferences from failure
    or refusal to account
    for 522–4
statements made on
    discovery of 202
Inferences
failure to give evidence
    examples of circumstantial
        evidence 17–19
failure to provide advance
    disclosure of defence
    summary trials 531
    trials on
        indictment 526–30
failure to provide intimate
    samples 525–6
right to silence
    examples of circumstantial
        evidence 17–19
    failure to account for
        things 522–5
    failure to mention facts
        before trial 506–21
    failure to testify 499–506
Insanity 63
Intercepted evidence 325
International comity
    681–2
Intimate samples
failure to provide 17
inferences which may be
    drawn 525–6
Intimidated witnesses
special measures
    aids to
        communications 162
    circumstances in which
        given 163–6

Intimidated witnesses (*Cont.*)
  directions 156–7
  eligible witnesses 162–3
  evidence in private 157–8
  examination of
    witness through
    intermediary 162, 169–70
  meaning and scope 155–7
  removal of wigs and
    gowns 158
  screens 157
  status of evidence 167–70

J
Journalistic sources
  see **Public interest**
  immunity
Judges
  see also **Directions**
  care warnings to jury
    accomplices 257–66
    accomplices who are
    co-accused 264–5
    anonymous witnesses 268
    cell confessions 265–6
    children 267–8
    lip-reading evidence
    272–3
    matrimonial cases 269
    recognition of
    people 282–4
    succession claims 269
    sudden infant death
    syndrome 273–4
    terms of *Turnbull*
    directions 281
    visual identification 278–9
    voice identification 295–7
    witnesses tainted by
    improper motive 264
  discretionary powers
    exclusionary
    discretion 47–53
    inclusionary discretion 47
    scope 47
  examination-in-chief
    jury notes 183
    questioning of
    witnesses 182–3
  judicial notice
    after inquiry 119–24
    personal knowledge 122–4
    without inquiry 117–19
  public interest immunity
    issues 686
  questions of law 34
  summing up to jury

bad character
  evidence 574–5, 582
  evidential burden 44–6
  use of information immune
  from disclosure 708
  warnings to jury
    hearsay in criminal
    cases 404–5
    inferences which may be
    drawn from silence 520
    special measures
    evidence 167–8
Judgments as evidence of facts
  background 758
  civil cases
    defamation 762
    previous acquittals 763–4
    previous
    convictions 759–63
    previous findings 764–5
    previous findings
    of adultery and
    paternity 762–3
  criminal cases
    previous acquittals 773
    previous
    convictions 765–73
Judicial evidence
  circumstantial evidence
    examples 15–22
    meaning and
    importance 14–15
  conclusive evidence 22
  documentary
    evidence 12–13
  hearsay evidence 12
  meaning and scope 11
  real evidence 13
  testimony 11
Judicial notice
  after enquiry 119–24
  custom and professional
    practices 121
  political facts 120–1
  readily demonstrable
    facts 121–2
  without inquiry 117–19
Juries
  assessment of
    confessions 485–7
  care warnings to jury
    accomplices 257–66
    accomplices who are
    co-accused 264–5
    anonymous witnesses 268
    cell confessions 265–6
    children 267–8

lip-reading evidence 272–3
matrimonial cases 269
recognition of
  people 282–4
succession claims 269
sudden infant death
  syndrome 273–4
terms of *Turnbull*
  directions 281
visual identification 278–9
voice identification 295–7
witnesses tainted by
  improper motive 264
notes to judge during
  examination-in-chief 183
personal knowledge 119
public interest immunity
  issues 686
questions of fact 34
summing up by judge
  bad character
    evidence 574–5, 582
    evidential burden 44–6
visual identification 288–9
warnings from judges
  hearsay in criminal
    cases 404–5
    inferences which may be
    drawn from silence 520
    special measures
    evidence 167–8

L
Leading questions 181–2
Legal advice
  confessions
    denial of access to
    solicitor 478–9
    procedural fairness 476–9
    statutory provisions 473–6
  professional privilege
    communications between
    lawyer and client 727–9
    instructions or advice in
    issue 742
    non-advisory
    communications 730–2
  right to silence 513–16
  special counsel 709–10
Legal professional privilege
  communications between
    lawyer and client 727–9
  communications between
    opposing parties 729
  communications not
    facts 736
  duration 742–3

evidential burden 727
exceptions
  children 741–2
  fraud 739–41
  instructions or advice in
    issue 742
  overview 737–8
  statutory provisions 738–9
nature 725–6
non-advisory
  communications 730–2
pre-existing
  documents 736–7
protected material
  communications between
    lawyer and client 727–9
  'items' 735–6
  third party
    communications 732–6
rationale 726–7
secondary evidence 743–6
solicitor instructed by two
  clients 729–30
waiver 746–9
Legitimacy 107–9
Lies
  see also Credibility
  as original evidence 393–4
  bad character evidence
    correcting false impressions
      by accused 608–12
    issues of
      credibility 597–600
  by accused 19–22
  hearsay evidence of the fact
    that it is false 361–2
  Lucas direction 19–22
  need for corroboration of
    perjury 255–6
  perjury 37
  rebuttal of recent
    fabrication 188–9, 197–9
  unreliable confessions
    background 462
    statutory test 462–70
Lip-reading evidence
  care warnings to jury 272–3
  species of real evidence 315
Lost documents 307
Lucas direction 19–22

M
Marriage
  presumptions
    cohabitation 107
    conflicting
      presumptions 117

essential validity 105–7
formal validity 104–5
statutory provisions 113
proof 92
Memory refreshing
  admissibility of previous
    statements as hearsay in
    criminal cases 394–5
  in court
    common law rules 176–7,
      184
    cross-examination on
      document 181–2,
      189–91
    present and past recorded
      recollections 177–8,
      185–7
    required conditions 179–
      81, 187–9
    out of court 182–4, 191–2
    overview 176, 183–4
    previous statements 196, 205
    visually recorded
      interviews 193
Mental health
  burden of proof for
    insanity 63
  competence and
    compellability of
    witnesses
    civil cases 141
    criminal cases 132–6,
      136–9
  corroboration of
    confessions 269–72
  cross-examination on
    capacity to give reliable
    evidence 246–8
  expert evidence 640–1
  presumed testamentary
    capacity 114
  standard of proof 93
  vulnerable witnesses
    aids to
      communications 162
    eligible witnesses 162–3
    evidence in private 157–8
    examination of
      witness through
      intermediary 162,
      169–70
    removal of wigs and
      gowns 158
    special measures
      directions 162–3
    video-recorded
      evidence 157–62

Motive
  bad character evidence 581
  example of circumstantial
    evidence 15–16
Multiple admissibility 30–1
Multiple hearsay 396–8

N
National security
  no protection for journalistic
    sources 696
  public interest
    immunity 681–2
Negative hearsay 370
No case submissions
  unconvincing hearsay
    evidence 400–1
  civil cases 43
  Crown Court 41–2
  magistrates court 42–3
  poor quality visual
    identification 285–6
Non-expert opinion
  evidence 672–3
Not guilty pleas 10

O
Oaths and affirmations
  142–3, 248
Ogden tables 432
Omnia praesumuntur rite esse
  acta 113–14
Opinion evidence
  expert witnesses
    competence 643–5
    disclosure in civil
      cases 660–1
    disclosure in criminal
      cases 669–70
    duty in civil cases 652–4
    facts upon which evidence
      based 654–7
    independence 645
    matters calling for
      expertise 635–43
    reliability 646–52
    ultimate issues 657–8
    weight of evidence 658–60
  non-expert witnesses 672–3
  overview 634–5
Opportunity 16
Oppression 459–62
Original evidence
  hearsay distinguished
    civil cases 415–17
    criminal cases 360
  meaning 12

P

Particulars of claim 9

Paternity
failure to provide blood test 17
previous findings 762–3
standard of proof 92

Pedigree 440–1

Perjury
need for corroboration 255–6
question of law 37

Photographs
real evidence 315–17
visual identification
analysis of images 289–90
pre-trial procedure 290–4

Political facts 120–1

Preparatory acts 16

Presumptions
conflicting
presumptions 116–17
death 54
basic facts 109–10
presumed facts 110–11
statutory
provisions 111–13
definitions and classification
irrebuttable presumptions
of law 101
overview 99
presumptions of
continuation of life 103
presumptions of
fact 101–17
presumption of guilty
knowledge 102
presumption of
intention 102
presumptions without
basic facts 758
rebuttable presumptions of
law 100–1
seaworthiness 103
without basic facts 103–4
execution of documents 313
innocence 68–9
marriage 92
cohabitation 107
conflicting
presumptions 117
essential validity 105–7
formal validity 104–5
statutory provisions 113
*omnia praesumuntur rite esse
acta* 113–14
previous findings of adultery
and paternity 762–3
res ipsa loquitur 114–16
wills 114

Previous convictions
see also **Bad character** and
Judgments as evidence
cross-examination 244–5
as evidence in civil
cases 759–63
propensity to commit
crime 589–91

Previous statements
admissibility as hearsay in
criminal cases
previous inconsistent
statements 391–2
previous statements
392–5
res gestae 442–52
cross-examination 222–5
examination-in-chief
common law
exceptions 186–8, 195–9
on discovery of
incriminating
articles 187, 202
general rule 184–6, 193–5
identification 192–5,
202–5
memory refreshing 196,
205
part of *res gestae* 195–6,
205
rebuttal of recent
fabrication 188–9, 197–9
statements on
accusation 190–2,
199–202
hostile witnesses 207–12
memory refreshing out of
court 184, 192, 192–3

Privilege
legal professional privilege
communications between
lawyer and client 727–9
communications between
opposing parties 729
communications not
facts 736
duration 742–3
evidential burden 727
exceptions 737–42
nature 725–6
non-advisory
communications 730–2
pre-existing
documents 736–7
rationale 726–7
secondary evidence 743–6
solicitor instructed by two
clients 729–30

waiver 746–9
non-compellability
distinguished 713
public interest immunity
distinguished 712–13
self-incrimination
civil cases 717
'criminal charge, penalty or
forfeiture' defined 715
denial of access to
solicitor 478–9
history and rationale 713
scope 714–15
statutory
exclusions 717–24
substituted protection 724
'tendency to expose'
defined 716
without prejudice
negotiations
matrimonial
reconciliations 754–5
offers except as to costs 700
settlement
negotiations 749–54

Proceeds of crime 93

Proof
acquittals 54–5
age 54
birth certificates 53–4
burden of proof
civil cases 78–80
criminal cases 62–77
evidential burden 60–1,
80–4
legal burden 58–9
overview 58
previous convictions
760–1, 771
right to begin 84
voir dire 94–5
convictions 54–5
death 53–4
documentary evidence
contents 303–11
execution 311–14
stamping
requirements 313–14
documents in civil cases
business and public
documents 427–8
generally 426–7
evidential burden
civil cases 80–4
criminal cases 39–40
formal admissions
civil cases 124
criminal cases 125

informal admissions
distinguished 124
hearsay in criminal cases
conditions of
admissibility 405–6
statements contained in
documents 406–7
judicial notice
after inquiry 119–24
personal knowledge 122–4
without inquiry 117–19
presumptions
conflicting
presumptions 116–17
death 109–14
definitions and
classification 99
legitimacy 107–9
marriage 104–7
*omnia praesumuntur rite esse
acta* 113–14
res ipsa loquitur 114–16
wills 114
standard of proof
evidential burden 93–4
legal burden 85–6
voir dire 94–5
Propensity to commit crime
bad character
evidence 579–80
evidence showing
a propensity to
offend 587–97
expert evidence 642
previous convictions 589–91
statutory provisions 584–5
Public documents
admissibility 308–9
common law rules 434–8
hearsay in civil cases 427–8
**Public interest
immunity** 688–9
development of modern law
civil cases 676–9
criminal cases 679–80
privilege
distinguished 712–13
procedural issues
Attorney General's
Guidelines 707
closed material
procedures 702–6
disclosure, production and
inspection 699–702
judicial use of information
immune from
disclosure 708
magistrates' court 710

partial disclosure 702
special counsel 709–10
taking objections 697
waiver and secondary
evidence 697–9
scope of exclusion
confidential
relationships 689–91
general principles
680–1
information for crime
detection 682–6
international
comity 681–2
judges and juries 686
national security 681–2
public service
functions 686–9
Public rights
declarations 441–2

Q
Questions of fact
construction of ordinary
words 35–6
foreign law 36
function of jury 34
reasonableness 37
Questions of law
autre fois acquit and
convict 37
construction of ordinary
words 35–6
corroboration 36
facts prior to
admissibility 37–40
function of judge 34
irrebuttable
presumptions 101
perjury 37
rebuttable
presumptions 100–1
standard of proof 85–6

R
Re-examination
general principles 249
special measures
directions 160–2
Real evidence
appearance of persons and
animals 314–15
demeanor of witnesses 315
demonstrations 317–19
documents 315
facial mapping 315
lip-reading evidence 315
material objects 314

meaning 13
recordings, films and
photographs 315–17
views 317–19
Reasonableness
as question of fact or law 37
Recognition of people
by police officers 284
reliability 282–4
Recordings
illegally or unfairly obtained
evidence 338–9
real evidence 315–17
Rectification 92
Reference works 438–9
**Rehabilitation of
offenders** 244–5, 630
Relevance
bad character evidence
statutory
provisions 597–600
untruthfulness 597–600
character evidence in civil
cases 534
exclusionary rules 30
facts 10
meaning and scope 23–30
previous convictions of
persons other than
accused 767–8
Reliability
expert evidence 646–52
visual identification
pre-trial procedure 290
recognition of
people 282–4
Reputation 439–40
Res gestae
admissibility as hearsay in
criminal cases
admissions by
agents 450–2
meaning 442
statements accompanying
performance of act
448–9
statements by persons
emotionally
overpowered 442–8
statements relating to
physical or mental
state 449–50
previous statements 195–6,
205
Res ipsa loquitur 114–16
Reverse burden of proof
challenges based on
incompatibility 77

Reverse burden of proof (*Cont.*)
express statutory
    exceptions 63
implied statutory exceptions
    examples 64–5
    Magistrates' Courts Act
        1980 63–4
    provisions giving rise to
        difficulty 65–6
    trials on indictment 66–8
incompatibility with Art 6(2)
    of European Convention
    on Human Rights 68–77
insanity 63
regulatory offences 76–7
Right to silence
see also **Self-incrimination**
inferences which may be
    drawn
    examples of circumstantial
        evidence 17–19
    failure to account for
        things 522–5
    failure to mention facts
        before trial 506–21
    failure to testify 499–506
meaning and scope 498–9

S
Screens 157
Seaworthiness 103
Self-incrimination
    see **Privilege**
Settlement negotiations
conciliation and mediation
    schemes 751–2
exceptions to general
    rule 752–4
general rule 749–51
offers without prejudice
    except as to costs 754
use or non-use of the
    expression 'without
    prejudice' 752
Sexual complaints
admissibility of previous
    statements as hearsay in
    criminal cases 395
bad character
    evidence 596–7
care warnings to jury 263–4
cross-examination
    lifting of
        restrictions 233–42
    rationale 230–1
    statutory
        restrictions 231–3

expert evidence of impact on
    victims 642
previous statements 186–7,
    195–7
special measures
    directions 166–7
Silence *see* **Right to silence**
Similar facts cases 593–4
Sole or decisive hearsay
exclusion 355–8
'reluctant' witnesses' 387
Sovereign immunity 142
Special counsel 709–10
Special measures
aids to communications 162
circumstances in which
    given 163–6
directions 156–7
    sexual complaints 166–7
eligible witnesses 162–3
    age or incapacity 162–3
    fear or distress 163
evidence in private 157–8
examination of witness
    through intermediary
    general provisions 162
    status of evidence 169–70
meaning and scope 155–7
removal of wigs and
    gowns 158
screens 157
status of evidence 167–70
video link evidence
    cross-examination or
        re-examination 160–2
    evidence-in-chief 158–60
    live television link 157
Speeding 256–7
Spouses
see also **Civil partners**
care warnings to jury in
    matrimonial cases 269
competence and
    compellability
    for accused 130
    for co-accused 134–5
    former spouses 135–6
    for prosecution 130–4
presumption of marriage
    cohabitation 107
    essential validity 105–7
    formal validity 104–5
    statutory provisions 113
privilege against
    self-incrimination 717
without prejudice
    negotiations 754–5

Stamping of
    documents 313–14
Standard of proof
evidential burden 93–4
legal burden
    civil cases 86–93
    criminal cases 85–6
    overview 84–5
voir dire 94–5
Standards of comparison 22
Statements
    see also **Confessions;**
        Documentary evidence
acceptance of accusations
    made in presence of
    accused 490–4
admissibility as hearsay in
    civil cases
    advance notice 420–2
    conditions of
        admissibility 418–20
    cross-examination of
        witnesses 423
    defined 415–17
    impeaching
        credibility 425–6
admissibility as hearsay in
    criminal cases
    association between
        the accused and a
        document 362–3
    computers and
        other mechanical
        devices 371–3
    depositions of vulnerable
        young persons 410
    documents 382–6
    evasion of rules 373
    fact that an offer was
        made 362
    implied assertions
        366–70
    meaning 360–3
    original evidence
        distinguished 360–2
    previous inconsistent
        statements 391–2
    previous statements 392–5
    res gestae 442–52
    statement as evidence of
        use 363
    'statements' and 'matters
        stated' 363–73
    witnesses
        unavailable 375–82
    written statements 409–10
previous statements

cross-examination 222–5
hostile witnesses 207–12
Submissions of no case *see* **No case submissions**
Sudden infant death syndrome
care warnings to jury 273–4
expert evidence 651–2
Sufficiency of evidence
general requirements 40–1
no case submissions
civil cases 43
Crown Court 41–2
magistrates court 42–3
Summing up by judge *see* **Directions**

T
Testimony 11
Torture
evidence obtained by torture 324
public interest immunity 679
Treason
need for corroboration 256
Trial within a trial *see* *Voire dire*
Turnbull **directions**
close examination of circumstances 281–2
terms of direction 281
visual identification 278–9, 279–80

U
Ultimate issues rule 657–8
Undercover police operations
after offence 345–7
entrapment 339–45
Unfavourable witnesses 196–7, 207
Unreliable confessions
background 462
exclusionary rule 462–70

V
Video link evidence
general rules 144–5
special measures directions
cross-examination or re-examination 160–2
evidence-in-chief 158–60
live television link 157
Video-recorded evidence
admissibility as hearsay in criminal cases 407

confessions 455–6
general rule 155
lip-reading evidence
care warnings to jury 272–3
species of real evidence 315
special measures directions
status of evidence 168–9
Views 317–19
Visual identification
analysis of images 289–90
description and identification distinguished 280–1
false alibis 287–8
good quality evidence 285
by jury 288–9
persons with the accused 280
poor quality evidence 285–6
pre-trial procedure
duty to make and keep records 290–1
exclusion of evidence for breaches of Code D 293–4
informal viewings 292
recognition from images 291
test of reliability 290
recognition of people
by police officers 284
reliability 282–4
special need for caution 279–80
supporting evidence 286–7
Turnbull direction
close examination of circumstances 281–2
general requirements 278–9
terms of direction 281
underlying risks 277–8
what accused did 280
Voice identification
pre-trial procedure 297–8
risks 295
warning to jury 295–7
Voir dire
burden and standard of proof 94–5
confessions
procedure 482–3
R v Brophy - right of accused to give evidence 484–5
when necessary 481–2
facts prior to admissibility 37–40

hostile witnesses 197–8, 208
Vulnerable witnesses
admissibility of depositions by children 410
special measures
aids to communications 162
circumstances in which given 163–6
directions 156–7
eligible witnesses 162–3
evidence in private 157–8
examination of witness through intermediary 162, 169–70
meaning and scope 155–7
removal of wigs and gowns 158
screens 157
status of evidence 167–70
treatment in court
cross-examination 225–30
examination-in-chief 174–5, 180–1
video-recorded evidence 157–62

W
Warnings to jury *see* **Care warnings**
Weight of evidence
admissibility distinguished 33
confessions
editing 490
implicating co-accused 487–90
matter for jury 485–7
expert evidence 658–60
hearsay in civil cases 423–5
hostile witnesses 211–12
informal admissions in civil cases 430–2
meaning and scope 33
memory refreshing out of court 184, 192–3
personal knowledge of judge and jury 122–4
previous statements 200–1
Without prejudice negotiations
matrimonial reconciliations 754–5
settlement negotiations

Without prejudice
   negotiations (*Cont.*)
   conciliation and mediation
      schemes 751–2
   exceptions to general
      rule 752–4
   general rule 749–51
   offers without prejudice
      except as to costs 754
   use or non-use of the
      expression 'without
      prejudice' 752
Witnesses
   absent witnesses
      exclusion of hearsay
         354–5
      reasons for
         non-attendance 358–9
   admissibility of hearsay in
      criminal cases when
      unavailable
      acceptable reasons for not
         calling witness 376–82
   capability 398
   credibility 398–400

   generally 373–5
   submissions of no
      case 400–1
civil cases
   court control of
      evidence 149–50
   discretionary powers 148
   statements 150–2
   training and
      familiarisation 176–7
competence and
   compellability
   accused 128–30
   bankers' immunity 142
   children 136–41
   diplomatic immunity 142
   general rule 127–8
   persons of unsound
      mind 141
   sovereign immunity 142
   spouses 130–6
criminal cases
   discretionary
      powers 152–4
   order of witnesses 154–5

   sexual complaints 166–7
   special measures 155–75
   training and
      familiarisation 175–6
   video-recorded
      evidence 155
demeanor 315
oaths and affirmations 142–3
privilege against
      self-incrimination
   civil cases 717
   'criminal charge, penalty or
      forfeiture' defined 715
   history and rationale 713
   scope 714–15
   statutory
      exclusions 717–24
   substituted protection
      724
   'tendency to expose'
      defined 716
time for adducing
      evidence 146–9
video link evidence
      144–5